CITIES OF THE UNITED STATES

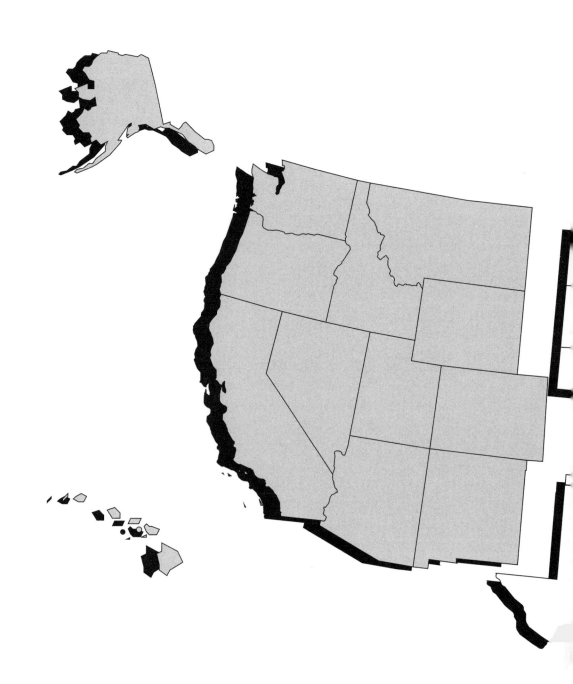

ISSN 0899-6075

CITIES OF THE UNITED STATES

FIFTH EDITION

A Compilation of Current Information on
Economic, Cultural, Geographic, and Social Conditions

In Four Volumes
Volume 2:
The West

Alaska
Arizona
California
Colorado
Hawaii
Idaho
Montana
Nevada
New Mexico
Oregon
Utah
Washington
Wyoming

THOMSON

GALE

Detroit • New York • San Francisco • San Diego • New Haven, Conn. • Waterville, Maine • London • Munich

Cities of the United States, Fifth Edition

Project Editors
Lisa C. DeShantz-Cook, Jacqueline K. Mueckenheim, Kristy Swartout

Editorial Support Services
Luann Brennan, Grant Eldridge, Wayne D. Fong

Imaging and Multimedia
Leitha Etheridge-Sims, Lezlie Light, Jillean McCommons, Dan Newell, Christine O'Bryan

Rights and Acquisitions
Edna M. Hedblad, Shalice Shah-Caldwell, Kim Smilay

Product Design
Jennifer Wahi

Composition and Electronic Prepress
Evi Seoud

Manufacturing
Rita Wimberley

LIBRARY OF CONGRESS CATALOGING-IN-PUBLICATION DATA

ISBN 0-7876-7369-2 (set)
ISBN 0-7876-7370-6 (v.1)
ISBN 0-7876-7371-4 (v.2)
ISBN 0-7876-7372-2 (v.3)
ISBN 0-7876-7373-0 (v.4)
ISSN 0899-6075

This title is also available as an e-book.
ISBN 1-4144-0600-2 (set)
Contact your Thomson Gale sales representative for ordering information.

Printed in the United States of America
10 9 8 7 6 5 4 3 2 1

Volume 2—The West

Contents

Volume 1—The South

Contents

Volume 3—The Midwest

Contents

Volume 4—The Northeast

Contents

INTRODUCTION

Cities of the United States (CUS) provides a one-stop source for all the vital information you need on 189 of America's top cities—those fastest-growing, as well as those with a particular historical, political, industrial, and/or commercial significance. Spanning the entire country, from Anaheim to Virginia Beach, each geographically-arranged volume of *CUS* brings together a wide range of comprehensive data. The volumes include: *The South; The West; The Midwest;* and *The Northeast.*

Within each volume, the city-specific profiles organize pertinent facts, data, and figures related to demographic, economic, cultural, geographic, social, and recreational conditions. Assembling a myriad of sources, *CUS* offers researchers, travelers, students, and media professionals a convenient resource for discovering each city's past, present, and future.

For this completely updated fifth edition, eleven new cities have been added, providing even greater access to the country's growing urban centers. The new city profiles include:

- Akron, OH

- Aurora, IL

- Casper, WY

- El Paso, TX

- Fort Smith, AR

- Henderson, NV

- Huntington, WV

- Mesa, AZ

- Nampa, ID

- Overland Park, KS

- Warwick, RI

Key Features Unlock Vital Information

Cities of the United States offers a range of key features, allowing easy access to targeted information. Features include:

- Section headings—Comprehensive categories, which include **History, Geography and Climate, Population Profile, Municipal Government, Economy, Education, Research, Health Care, Recreation, Convention Facilities, Transportation,** and **Communications** (including city web sites), make it easy for you to locate answers to your specific questions.

- Combined facts and analysis—Fact-packed charts and detailed descriptions bring you the statistics and the rest of the story.

- "In Brief" fact sheets—One-page "at a glance" overviews provide the essential facts for each state and each city profiled.

- Economic information—Detailed updates about such topics as incentive programs, development projects, and largest employers help you rate the business climate using criteria that matter to you.

- Directory information—Contact information at the end of many entry sections provides addresses, phone numbers, and email addresses for organizations, agencies, and institutions you may need to contact.

- Detailed maps—City landmarks, mileage scales, and regional insets allow you to locate many of the points of interest described in main city entries, as well as provide a greater perspective on the city in which you are interested.

- Selected bibliography listings—Historical accounts, biographical works, and other print resources suggest titles to read if you wish to learn more about a particular city.

- Web sites for vital city resources—Access points to URLs for information-rich sources, such as city government, visitors and convention bureaus, economic development agencies, libraries, schools, and newspapers provide researchers an opportunity to explore cities in more detail.

- Enlightening illustrations—Numerous photographs highlight points of interest to you.

- Handy indexing—A referencing guide not only to main city entries, but also to the hundreds of people and place names that fall within those main entries, leading you directly to the information you seek.

Designed For a Variety of Users

Whether you are a researcher, traveler, or executive on the move, *CUS* serves your needs. This is the reference long sought by a variety of users:

- Business people, market researchers, and other decision-makers will find the current data that helps them stay informed.

- People vacationing, conventioneering, or relocating will consult this source for questions they have about what's new, unique, or significant about where they are going.

- Students, media professionals, and researchers will discover their background work already completed.

Hurricanes of 2005 and Their Impact on the United States

The powerful hurricanes of 2005—Hurricane Katrina on August 29 followed by Hurricane Rita on September 24—devastated the Gulf Coast region of the United States. From Alabama to the shores of Texas, these two hurricanes had profound impact—from the loss of lives to the loss of infrastructure (utilities, roads, commerce), industry, and manufacturing. Cities directly hit by these hurricanes, such as New Orleans, Louisiana and Biloxi, Mississippi, will undergo recovery efforts for years to come, and it is unknown at the time of publication of *Cities of the United States,* 5th edition just how long and how far-reaching that recovery will be.

It is also important to note that not only are the cities hit directly by these hurricanes affected; cities that have offered refuge to evacuees and contributed greatly to the relief efforts will continue to be affected as they work to aid the recovery efforts, putting their own development initiatives on hold. Cities such as Mobile, Alabama; Baton Rouge, Louisiana; and Jackson, Mississippi will also continue to experience the effects of these unprecedented natural disasters.

The essays profiled herein for the states of Alabama, Louisiana, Mississippi, and Texas were updated prior to August 2005 and reflect information that was then current.

Definitions of Key Statistical Resources

Following are explanations of key resources used for statistical data:

ACCRA (The Council for Community Economic Research; formerly the American Chamber of Commerce Researchers Association): The Cost of Living Index, produced quarterly, provides a useful and reasonably accurate measure of living cost differences among urban areas. Items on which the Index is based have been carefully chosen to reflect the different categories of consumer expenditures, such as groceries, housing, utilities, transportation, health care, and miscellaneous goods and services; taxes are excluded. Weights assigned to relative costs are based on government survey data on expenditure patterns for midmanagement households (typically the average professional worker's home, new construction with 2,400 square feet of living space). All items are priced in each place at a specified time and according to standardized specifications. Information regarding ACCRA and the Cost of Living Index can be found at www.accra.org. Please note that the ACCRA Cost of Living Index and ACCRA housing price information are reprinted by permission of ACCRA.

Metropolitan Statistical Area (MSA): The U.S. Office of Management and Budget (OMB) provides that each Metropolitan Statistical Area must include (a) at least one city with 50,000 or more inhabitants, or (b) a U.S. Census Bureau-defined urbanized area (of at least 50,000 inhabitants) and a total metropolitan population of at least 100,000 (75,000 in New England). The term was adopted in 1983. The term "metropolitan area" (MA) became effective in 1990. During the 2000 Census, the MSA standards were revised, establishing Core Based Statistical Areas (CBSAs). CBSAs may be either Metropolitan Statistical Areas or Micropolitan Statistical Areas. It is important to note that standards, and therefore content of 1990 Census MSAs, are not identical to 2000 Census MSA standards. Additional information regarding MSAs can be found at http://census.state.nc.us/glossary/msa.html.

FBI Crime Index Total: The total number of index offenses reported to the FBI during the year through its Uniform Crime Reporting Program. The FBI receives monthly and annual reports from law enforcement agencies throughout the country. City police, sheriffs, and state police file reports on the number of index offenses that become known to them. The FBI Crime Index offenses are: murder and non-negligent manslaughter; forcible rape; robbery; aggravated assault; burglary; larceny; motor vehicle theft; and arson.

Estimates of population: Between decennial censuses, the U.S. Bureau of the Census publishes estimates of the population using the decennial census data as benchmarks and data available from various agencies, both state and federal, including births and deaths, and school statistics, among other data.

Method of Compilation

The editors of *Cities of the United States* consulted numerous sources to secure the kinds of data most valuable to you. Each entry gathers together economic information culled in part from the U.S. Department of Labor/Bureau of Labor Statistics and state departments of labor and commerce, population figures derived from the U.S. Department of Commerce/Bureau of the Census and from city and state agencies, educational and municipal government data supplied by local authorities and historical narrative based on a variety of accounts. Along with material supplied by chambers of commerce, convention and visitors bureaus, and other local sources, background information was drawn from periodicals and books chosen for their timeliness and accuracy. Through print resources, web sites, email contact, and/or phone calls with agency representatives, the information reflects current conditions.

Acknowledgments

The editors are grateful for the assistance provided by dozens of helpful chambers of commerce and convention and visitors bureau professionals, as well as municipal, library, and school employees for their invaluable generosity and expertise.

Comments and Suggestions Welcome

If you have questions, concerns, or comments about *Cities of the United States*, please contact the Project Editors:

Cities of the United States
Thomson Gale
27500 Drake Road
Farmington Hills, MI 48331
Phone: (248)699-4253
Toll-free: (800)347-GALE
Fax: (248)699-8075
URL: http://www.gale.com

Map Credits

Regional and city maps for *Cities of the United States,* 5th edition, were created by Teresa San Clementi and XNR Productions Inc.

* * * *

Photo Credits—Volume 2

Photographs appearing in *Cities of the United States,* 5th edition, Volume 2—*The West* were received from the following sources:

ALASKA:
Anchorage—photograph. Courtesy of the Anchorage Convention and Visitors Bureau. Reproduced by permission: p. 5; photograph. Courtesy of the Anchorage Convention and Visitors Bureau. Reproduced by permission: p. 14
Fairbanks—skyline, photograph. © Alaska Division of Tourism. Reproduced by permission: p. 19; showing Trans-Alaska oil pipeline, photograph. Courtesy of the Fairbanks Convention and Visitors Bureau. Reproduced by permission: p. 24
Juneau—showing shopping and business district, photograph by Susan D. Rock. Reproduced by permission: p. 31

ARIZONA:
Flagstaff—photograph by Peter L. Bloomer, Horizons West. Reproduced by permission: p. 43; showing Riordan Mansion, photograph. Riordan Mansion State Historic Park. Reproduced by permission: p. 50
Mesa—photograph. Mesa Convention and Visitors Bureau. Reproduced by permission: p. 55
Phoenix—photograph. Copyright © 1999 Jessen Associates, Inc. Reproduced by permission: p. 69; showing Yavapai County Fair, photograph. Copyright © 1999 Jessen Associates, Inc. Reproduced by permission: p. 77
Scottsdale—photograph. © Buddy Mays/Corbis: p. 81; showing Taliesin West, architecture by Frank Lloyd Wright, photograph. G. E. Kidder Smith/Corbis: p. 88
Tucson—photograph. © David Bean, 1991. Metropolitan Tucson Convention & Visitors Bureau. Reproduced by permission: p. 91; showing dancers in folklorico dress, photograph by Gill Kenny. © Metropolitan Tucson Convention & Visitors Bureau. Reproduced by permission: p. 98

CALIFORNIA:
Anaheim—skyline and waterfront, photograph. Courtesy of the Anaheim/Orange County Convention and Visitors Bureau: p. 105; Disneyland, Anaheim, California, July 17, 1955, photograph. AP/Wide World Photos. Reproduced by permission: p. 112
Fresno—photograph by James Blank. © James Blank. Reproduced by permission: p. 117; photograph by James Blank. © James Blank. Reproduced by permission: p. 124
Los Angeles—photograph by James Blank. © James Blank. Reproduced by permission: p. 127; showing Capitol Records, photograph by James Blank. © James Blank. Reproduced by permission: p. 136
Monterey—photograph. Courtesy Monterey Peninsula Visitor and Convention Bureau. Reproduced by permission: p. 141; showing Steinbeck Plaza, Cannery Row, photograph. © Grant Huntington. Courtesy of Monterey Peninsula Visitor and Convention Bureau. Reproduced by permission: p. 150
Oakland—photograph. Oakland Convention & Visitors Authority. Reproduced by permission: p. 155; showing Jack London Square, photograph by James Blank. © James Blank. Reproduced by permission: p. 164
Riverside—photograph by Michael Elderman. Courtesy of the City of Riverside. Reproduced by permission: p. 167; showing Mission Inn, photograph by James Blank. © James Blank. Reproduced by permission: p. 175
Sacramento—photograph. Sacramento Convention & Visitors Bureau. Reproduced by permission of Tom Myers Photography: p. 179
San Diego—showing skyline from Harbor Island, photograph by James Blank. © James Blank. Reproduced by permission: p. 191; showing Old Point Loma Lighthouse at Cabrillo National Monument, photograph by James Blank. © James Blank. Reproduced by permission: p. 199
San Francisco—photograph. Ets-Hokin Studios. Reproduced by permission: p. 205; showing Golden Gate Bridge, photograph by James Blank. © James Blank. Reproduced by permission: p. 214

San Jose—photograph. © Craig Lovell/Corbis: p. 219
Santa Ana—showing Santa Ana Courthouse Building, photograph. © Vince Streano/Corbis: p. 229; showing Bowers Museum, photograph. Bowers Museum. Reproduced by permission: p. 236

COLORADO:
Boulder—photograph. © 2005 Robert Castellino and the Boulder Convention & Visitors Bureau. Reproduced by permission: p. 243; showing Rocky Mountains, photograph. © 2005 Robert Castellino and the Boulder Convention & Visitors Bureau. Reproduced by permission: p. 251
Colorado Springs—photograph. Colorado Springs Convention & Visitors Bureau. Reproduced by permission: p. 255; showing Pikes Peak and Garden of the Gods, photograph by James Blank. © James Blank. Reproduced by permission: p. 262
Denver—photograph by James Blank. © James Blank. Reproduced by permission: p. 267; showing The Navarre Building/Museum of Western Art, photograph. Courtesy of Denver Metro Convention & Visitors Bureau. Reproduced by permission: p. 274
Fort Collins—photograph. Landscape Imagery. Reproduced by permission: p. 279

HAWAII:
Hilo—showing pond at Liliuokalani Gardens, photograph by Greg Vaughn. Hawaii Visitors Bureau. Reproduced by permission: p. 291; showing rainbow waterfall, photograph. Hawaii Visitors Bureau. Reproduced by permission: p. 299
Honolulu—showing State Capitol, photograph by James Blank. © James Blank. Reproduced by permission: p. 303; showing Iolani Palace, photograph. Hawaii Visitors Bureau. Reproduced by permission: p. 310

IDAHO:
Boise—photograph. Boise Convention & Visitors Bureau. Reproduced by permission: p. 317; showing State Capitol, photograph. © Kevin R. Morris/Corbis: p. 324
Nampa—photograph. © Dean Conger/Corbis: p. 327

MONTANA:
Billings—photograph by Phil Bell. Reproduced by permission: p. 339
Butte—photograph by Walter J. Hinick. Reproduced by permission: p. 349; showing U.S. High Altitude Sports Center, photograph. Reproduced by permission: p. 356
Helena—photograph: p. 361

NEVADA:
Carson City—showing State Capitol, photograph by James Blank. © James Blank. Reproduced by permission: p. 375; showing facade of the Nevada State Library, photograph. © Dave G. Houser/Corbis: p. 383
Henderson—photograph. Courtesy of City of Henderson, Nevada. Reproduced by permission: p. 387
Las Vegas—photograph by James Blank. © James Blank. Reproduced by permission: p. 397; showing Statue of Liberty, photograph. © Richard Cummins/Corbis: p. 404
Reno—photograph. Courtesy of the Reno Sparks Convention & Visitors Authority. Reproduced by permission: p. 409; photograph by James Blank. © James Blank. Reproduced by permission: p. 416

NEW MEXICO:
Albuquerque—photograph by James Blank. © James Blank. Reproduced by permission: p. 423; showing dancers outside the Indian Pueblo Cultural Center, photograph by Ron Behrmann. Albuquerque Convention and Visitors Bureau. Reproduced by permission: p. 431
Las Cruces—photograph by Mike Groves. Las Cruces Convention and Visitors Bureau. Reproduced by permission: p. 435; showing folklorico dancer, photograph by Jack Hauptmann. Las Cruces Convention and Visitors Bureau. Reproduced by permission: p. 443
Santa Fe—photograph. Courtesy of Santa Fe Convention and Visitors Bureau. Reproduced by permission: p. 447; Palace of the Governors, photograph. AP/Wide World Photos. Reproduced by permission: p. 454

OREGON:
Eugene—showing skyline from the top of Skinners Butte, photograph by Len Stolfo/Upshotz.com. Reproduced by permission: p. 461; showing King Estate Winery Complex, photograph. © Charles O'Rear/Corbis: p. 468

Portland—photograph by James Blank. © James Blank. Reproduced by permission: p. 471; photograph by James Blank. © James Blank. Reproduced by permission: p. 479

Salem—showing State Capitol, photograph. Salem Convention & Visitors Association. Reproduced by permission: p. 483; showing Bush House, photograph. Salem Convention & Visitors Association. Reproduced by permission: p. 490

UTAH:

Provo—photograph by Ron H. MacDonald. Provo City Corporation, Economic Development Office. Reproduced by permission: p. 497; showing America's Freedom Festival, photograph by Ron H. MacDonald. Provo City Corporation, Economic Development Office. Reproduced by permission: p. 504

Salt Lake City—photograph. © Joseph Sohm; ChromoSohm Inc./Corbis: p. 509; showing skyline along Temple Square, photograph by James Blank. © James Blank. Reproduced by permission: p. 517

WASHINGTON:

Bellingham—photograph. Reproduced by permission: p. 523; showing Whatcom Museum of History & Art, photograph. Bellingham/Whatcom County Convention & Visitors Bureau. Reproduced by permission: p. 531

Olympia—showing State Capitol, photograph by James Blank. © James Blank. Reproduced by permission: p. 535; showing Washington State War Monument, photograph. © Philip James Corwin/Corbis: p. 544

Seattle—photograph by Michael Schweitzer. Reproduced by permission: p. 549; showing Seattle Art Museum, photograph by Miroslawa Bossowska. Reproduced by permission: p. 556

Spokane—photograph by Alan Bisson. © Spokane Area Convention and Visitors Bureau. Reproduced by permission: p. 561; showing clock tower, photograph. Alan Bisson. © Spokane Area Convention and Visitors Bureau. Reproduced by permission: p. 568

Tacoma—photograph. Courtesy Tacoma-Pierce County Convention and Visitors Bureau. Reproduced by permission: p. 571

WYOMING:

Casper—photograph. Casper Area Convention and Visitors Bureau. Reproduced by permission: p. 585

Cheyenne—photograph by James Blank. © James Blank. Reproduced by permission: p. 597; showing cattle ranch, photograph. Cheyenne Area Convention & Visitors Bureau. Reproduced by permission: p. 604

CITIES OF THE UNITED STATES

ALASKA

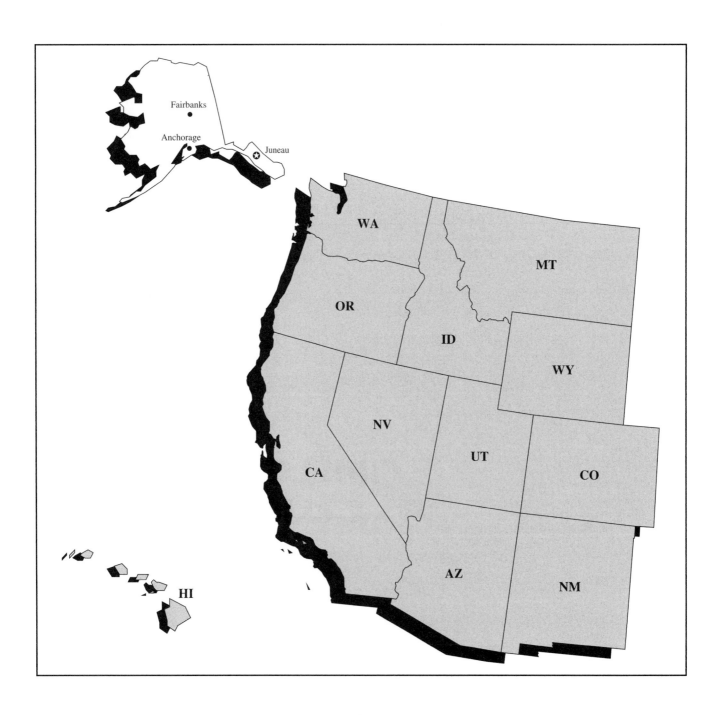

The State in Brief

Nickname: Land of the Midnight Sun
Motto: North to the future

Flower: Forget-me-not
Bird: Willow ptarmigan

Area: 663,267 square miles (2000; U.S. rank: 1st)
Elevation: Ranges from sea level to 20,320 feet above sea level
Climate: Summers are short and hot, winters long and intensely cold

Admitted to Union: January 3, 1959
Capital: Juneau
Head Official: Governor Frank H. Murkowski (R) (until 2006)

Population
    1980: 402,000
    1990: 570,000
    2000: 626,932
    2004 estimate: 655,435
    Percent change, 1990–2000: 14.0%
    U.S. rank in 2004: 47th
    Percent of residents born in state: 38.1% (2000)
    Density: 1.1 people per square mile (2000)
    2002 FBI Crime Index Total: 27,745

Racial and Ethnic Characteristics (2000)
    White: 434,534
    Black or African American: 21,787
    American Indian and Alaska Native: 98,043
    Asian: 25,116
    Native Hawaiian and Pacific Islander: 3,309
    Hispanic or Latino (may be of any race): 25,852
    Other: 9,997

Age Characteristics (2000)
    Population under 5 years old: 47,591
    Population 5 to 19 years old: 160,526
    Percent of population 65 years and over: 5.7%
    Median age: 32.4 years (2000)

Vital Statistics
    Total number of births (2003): 10,071
    Total number of deaths (2003): 3,158 (infant deaths, 67)
    AIDS cases reported through 2003: 271

Economy
    Major industries: Oil, government, commercial fishing, food processing, lumber, mining
    Unemployment rate: 7.4% (January 2004)
    Per capita income: $33,254 (2003; U.S. rank: 14th)
    Median household income: $55,143 (3-year average, 2001-2003)
    Percentage of persons below poverty level: 9.0% (3-year average, 2001-2003)
    Income tax rate: None
    Sales tax rate: None

Anchorage

The City in Brief

Founded: 1915 (incorporated, 1920)

Head Official: Mayor Mark Begich (since July 2003)

City Population (Anchorage municipality)
1980: 174,431
1990: 226,338
2000: 260,283
2003 estimate: 270,951
Percent change, 1990–2000: 15.0%
U.S. rank in 1980: 78th
U.S. rank in 1990: 69th (State rank: 1st)
U.S. rank in 2000: 75th (State rank: 1st)

Metropolitan Area Population
1980: 174,431
1990: 226,338
2000: 260,283

2003 estimate: 270,951
Percent change, 1990–2000: 15.0%
U.S. rank in 1980: 78th
U.S. rank in 1990: 69th
U.S. rank in 2000: 75th

Area: 1,955 square miles (2000)
Elevation: 132 feet above sea level
Average Annual Temperature: 35.8° F
Average Annual Precipitation: 15.71 inches of rain; 70.6 inches of snow

Major Economic Sectors: Government, trade, services, transportation (air)
Unemployment Rate: 5.1% (December 2004)
Per Capita Income: $25,287 (1999)

2002 FBI Crime Index Total: 13,670

Major Colleges and Universities: University of Alaska Anchorage, Alaska Pacific University

Daily Newspaper: *Anchorage Daily News*

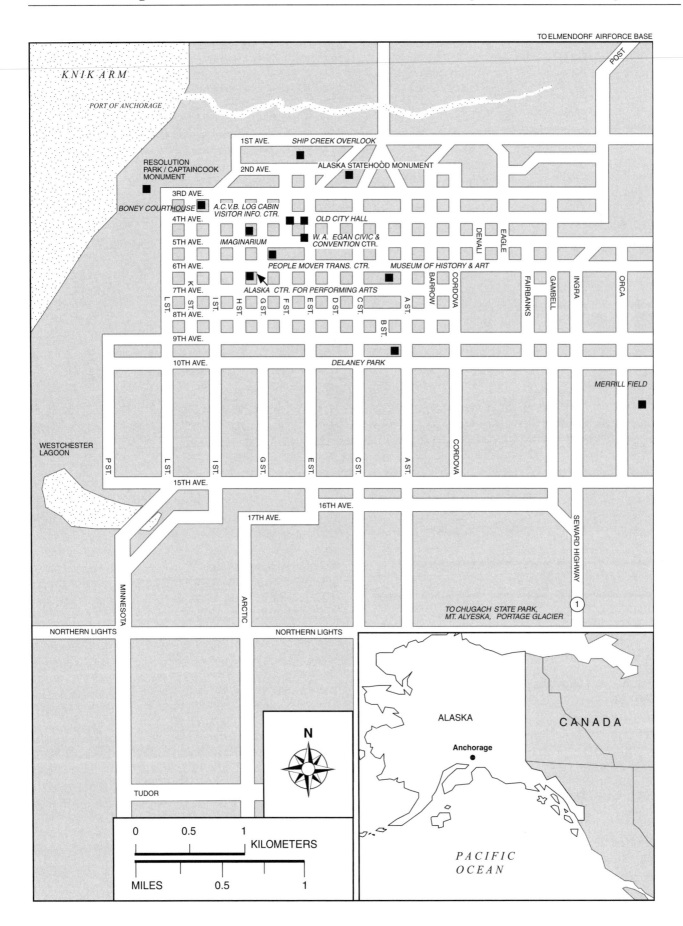

Introduction

Anchorage is the home of 42 percent of the state's residents and is the commercial heart of south-central and western Alaska. When its brief modern history is considered—the town of Anchorage was founded in 1915 as a railroad construction headquarters—the fact that Anchorage stands as a sophisticated metropolis in the midst of rugged wilderness can be appreciated as a phenomenon. A visit to the city will dispel myths about its long, dark winters: Anchorage's climate is relatively mild with distinct seasons, winters similar to Denver's, and short-daylight periods confined to late December. A high per capita income, low taxes, and a low crime rate are among the positive qualities that have earned Anchorage a place among the country's most livable cities.

Geography and Climate

Located in south-central Alaska in a wide valley, Anchorage is bordered on the west, north, and south by Knik Arm and Turnagain Arm of Cook Inlet. The Chugach Mountains to the east have a general elevation of 4,000 to 5,000 feet, with peaks from 8,000 to 10,000 feet. These mountains block warm air from the Gulf of Mexico, keeping precipitation relatively low. The Alaska Range to the north protects the city from cold air from the state's interior; thus temperatures in Anchorage are usually 25 to 30 degrees warmer than temperatures in the rest of the state. While the area has four seasons, their length and characteristics differ from those of the middle latitudes; snows arrive in October and leave in mid-April, while annual average snowfall is seventy inches. Daylight hours vary from 19 in late June to 6 in late December.

Area: 1,955 square miles (2000)

Elevation: 132 feet above sea level

Average Temperatures: January, 20° F; July, 65° F; annual average, 35.8° F

Average Annual Precipitation: 15.71 inches of rain; 70.6 inches of snow

History

Native American Trade Center Transformed by Discovery of Gold

The Anchorage area was settled more than 6,000 years ago as a summer fishing camp for the Tanaina tribe. Until the seventeenth century it was under the dominance of the Pacific Eskimos; then in 1650 the Eskimos were defeated in battle by the Tanaina where Point Woronzof is now located on the shore of Knik Arm. By 1700 the area had become a major trade center for Native Americans, Eskimos, and Aleuts.

The first European to explore the territory around the inlet was the British explorer Captain James Cook, who claimed the land for England in 1778 and after whom Cook Inlet was named. Russian settlers moved onto Upper Cook Inlet in the late 1890s, establishing settlements inhabited by traders and missionaries. With the sale of Alaska to the United States in 1867, Russia turned over its holdings on Cook Inlet to the Alaska Commercial Company of San Francisco. In 1882 gold was discovered in streams along Turnagain Arm, causing a population explosion as steamships from Seattle brought prospectors who settled in the Matanuska and Sustina Valleys to pan for gold.

City Becomes Major Railroad, Aviation, Military Center

Another growth spurt occurred in 1915 when Ship Creek was chosen as the mid-point construction headquarters for the government-owned Alaska Railroad that was to be built from Seward to Fairbanks. A town site was soon established at Ship Creek, land was auctioned off, and the new town was called Anchorage. By 1920, the year of its incorporation, Anchorage had developed into a major city. The Alaska Railroad was completed in 1923; that same year Anchorage's first airfield was built, initiating the aviation industry that within a decade became a vital part of the city's economy. Anchorage established its own airline in 1926 and in 1935 Merrill Field was opened. In 1935 the city also experienced another population boom with the migration of dust bowl farmers from the Midwest into the Matanuska Valley.

The foundation of another important element of Anchorage's economy, the military defense complex, was formed with the military buildup in Alaska during the late 1930s. Fort Richardson and Elmendorf Field Air Force Base were established near the city; the Alaska Highway, the American military supply line to northern defense headquarters and a link between Anchorage and other parts of the country, was completed in 1942. Through World War II and into the early 1950s the city expanded, the population increasing to 43,314 in 1950 at a rate of more than 600 percent in a decade. In 1951 International Airport opened, making Anchorage a primary connection for transpolar air traffic between Europe and Asia.

City Devastated by Earthquake; Oil Discovered

Anchorage suffered a severe setback in 1964 when it was struck by a devastating earthquake, one of the most serious ever recorded in North America. Damage was extensive, but within two years the city had recovered and was moving into another phase of prosperity resulting from the discovery of oil on Cook Inlet. The city and borough governments merged in 1975 to form the municipality of Anchorage, and in 1978 "Project 80s" was initiated. A development plan of major proportions, Project 80s involved the construction of the George M. Sullivan Arena, the William A. Egan Convention and Civic Center, and the Anchorage Center for the Performing Arts; the final stage of the project, the Center for the Performing Arts, was completed in 1988. A collapse in world crude oil prices brought statewide recession in 1986, causing high unemployment rates and a population decrease in Anchorage.

Oil Spilled in Prince William Sound

Anchorage made international headlines on Good Friday, March 24, 1989, when the grounded oil tanker *Exxon Valdez* spilled nearly 11 million gallons of crude oil into nearby Prince William Sound, forming a slick that eventually reached into the Gulf of Alaska and beyond. Anchorage served as the command post for cleanup efforts costing more than $2.5 billion. Only a small amount of oil remained by the mid-1990s, and seals, whales, and bald eagles had returned to the region. U.S. government biologists and scientists for the Exxon Corporation continued to disagree over the issue of damage to animals, with Exxon contending that the damage was less than what government scientists claimed. In 1994 an Anchorage jury ordered Exxon Corp. to pay more than $5 billion to fishermen and others who could show that they had been financially hurt by the oil spill.

A Time of Growth

In the 1990s Anchorage began to experience record economic growth that continues today. The Anchorage Economic Development Corporation predicts an increase of 2,100 jobs in Anchorage for 2005, an increase of 1.5 percent over 2004. If that prediction holds true, the year will mark Anchorage's 17th straight year of job growth.

Alaska has become increasingly attractive as a tourist destination. Seventeen of the nation's twenty highest peaks reside in the state; six mountain ranges can be seen from Anchorage alone. In 2002, Anchorage was one of ten cities to receive the 2002 All-America City Award, an award designated by the National Civic League. The city's favorable business climate, commitment to education, thriving cultural life, and stunning natural beauty combine to make today's Anchorage a strong and growing city.

Historical Information: Anchorage Museum of History and Art Archives, 121 West Seventh Avenue, Anchorage, AK 99501; telephone (907)343-6189

Population Profile

Metropolitan Area Residents
1980: 174,431
1990: 226,338
2000: 260,283
Percent change, 1990–2000: 15.0%
U.S. rank in 1980: 78th
U.S. rank in 1990: 69th
U.S. rank in 2000: 75th

City Residents
1980: 174,431
1990: 226,338
2000: 260,283
2003 estimate: 270,951
Percent change, 1990–2000: 15.0%
U.S. rank in 1980: 78th
U.S. rank in 1990: 69th (State rank: 1st)
U.S. rank in 2000: 75th (State rank: 1st)

Density: 153.4 people per square mile (2000)

Racial and ethnic characteristics (2000)
   White: 188,009
   Black or African American: 15,199
   American Indian and Alaska Native: 18,941
   Asian: 14,433
   Native Hawaiian and Pacific Islander: 2,423
   Hispanic or Latino (may be of any race): 14,799
   Other: 5,703

Percent of residents born in state: 32.1% (2000)

Age characteristics (2000)
   Population under 5 years old: 20,033
   Population 5 to 9 years old: 21,867
   Population 10 to 14 years old: 21,501
   Population 15 to 19 years old: 19,662
   Population 20 to 24 years old: 17,694
   Population 25 to 34 years old: 40,113
   Population 35 to 44 years old: 48,210
   Population 45 to 54 years old: 38,803

Population 55 to 59 years old: 11,240
Population 60 to 64 years old: 6,918
Population 65 to 74 years old: 8,895
Population 75 to 84 years old: 4,284
Population 85 years and older: 1,063
Median age: 32.4 years

Births (2003)
Total number: 4,284

Deaths (2003)
Total number: 1,222 (of which, 19 were infants under the age of 1 year)

Money Income (1999)
Per capita income: $25,287
Median household income: $55,546
Total households: 95,080

Number of households with income of . . .
less than $10,000: 3,948
$10,000 to $14,999: 3,774
$15,000 to $24,999: 8,936
$25,000 to $34,999: 10,251
$35,000 to $49,999: 15,199
$50,000 to $74,999: 21,506
$75,000 to $99,999: 13,597
$100,000 to $149,999: 12,266
$150,000 to $199,999: 3,203
$200,000 or more: 2,400

Percent of families below poverty level: 5.1% (32.4% of which were female householder families with related children under 5)

2002 FBI Crime Index Total: 13,670

Municipal Government

The municipality of Anchorage is administered by a mayor-assembly form of government, with the mayor and eleven assembly members elected to three-year terms.

Head Official: Mayor Mark Begich (since July 2003; current term expires June 30, 2006)

Total Number of City Employees: 4,300 (2003)

City Information: Municipality of Anchorage, PO Box 196650, Anchorage, AK 99519; telephone (907)343-4431 (mayor's office)

Economy

Major Industries and Commercial Activity

While the U.S. economy has shown declines in recent years, Alaska's economy has shown a relatively stable growth of two percent annually. The United States government and the oil industry have been integral to the Anchorage economy. The federally funded Alaska Railroad gave Anchorage its start; later the military defense system supported an essentially undiversified economic base. This base expanded in the 1970s when the Trans-Alaska Pipeline, one of the largest construction projects in history, brought thousands of workers and increased service industries.

Although Juneau is the state capital, Anchorage is the state's government center. In 2003, Anchorage employed 4,300 state government employees, and 10,000 federal government employees.

Anchorage is the state's primary transportation, communications, trade, service, and finance center. Anchorage makes up 42 percent of the state's population but accounts for 47 percent of the employment. Today, the four major sectors that drive Anchorage's local economy are oil and gas, the military (three military posts are located at the airport), transportation, and the convention and tourism industry.

Alaska's oil production accounts for more than 22 percent of the nation's oil reserves. Anchorage may not be the hub of production, but the city acts as the administrative center for the industry. While the sector only accounts for two percent of the local employment, the importance to Anchorage's economy is greater, accounting for about eight percent of local salaries and wages.

The military in Anchorage is a constant presence. Elmendorf Air Force Base, Fort Richardson Army Post, and Kulis Air National Guard base are all located at the Ted Stevens Anchorage International Airport. The three military posts employ 8,500; military personnel and their family members boost local economy by patronizing businesses. In addition, nearly 10 percent of Anchorage's population is comprised of military personnel and family members.

The transportation industry in Anchorage is the busiest in the state. The Ted Stevens Anchorage International Airport (ANC) accounts for another 10 percent of Anchorage's employed, either directly or indirectly. The ANC flies more than 560 transcontinental cargo flights each week; the airport's economic impact is felt as far away as the North Pole, where jet fuel is refined and loaded onto the more than 100 rail cars that then travel by Alaska Railroad to service ANC daily. The Alaska Railroad transports freight and passengers; in summer months the Railroad transports passengers to popular destinations throughout the state. The Port of Anchorage accounts for delivery of more than 90 percent of the consumer goods arriving in Alaska.

The tourism and convention industry, along with the service businesses that sprout up around the industry, are a major driving force in Anchorage economy. Mainly due to its central location, Anchorage acts as the gateway to the state of Alaska, thereby funneling tourists, conventioneers and other visitors through the area. Alaska's tourism industry accounts for more than 30,000 statewide jobs and an estimated (2003) economic impact of nearly $80 million in Anchorage alone. The market for trade shows and conventions in the city is growing; the 2003 economic impact of meetings sold during that year equaled more than $71 million.

Items and goods produced: fisheries' products, wood and wood products, petroleum products, coal, minerals

Incentive Programs—New and Existing Companies

The most widely used local incentives include customized job training programs, low interest loans, municipal revenue bonds, and property tax abatement. Anchorage Economic Development Corporation, a public-private partnership, assists new and existing businesses with information on taxes and utilities and on available sites and buildings, which are said to be plentiful.

Local programs—The Municipality of Anchorage offers a program that exempts some types of economic development properties from taxation. Inventory that is held for shipment outside of Alaska may also be exempt from local inventory taxes.

State programs—The Governor's Office of International Trade provides assistance and information to firms interested in foreign trade and investment, organizes trade missions and promotions, and sponsors trade shows and seminars. Several areas in the city are located in Anchorage's Foreign Trade Zone, the two most notable being the Ted Stevens Anchorage International Airport and the Port of Anchorage. The World Trade Center assists businesses seeking to enter or expand their role in international trade. The Alaska Export Assistance Center helps local businesses expand into foreign markets.

Job training programs—The University of Alaska Anchorage offers classes and degree programs to businesses and individuals on logistics and on doing business in Pacific Asia and the former Soviet Union. The university also partners with the Alaska Economic Development Corporation to provide a Mentor Program that connects students with business leaders. Lunchtime forums highlight a different business industry each time.

Development Projects

In April 2005 residents will be asked to approve $46.9 million in bonds for projects involving road improvements, public transportation, and public safety. Residents will be asked to approve more funds to build a new $93 million civic center and to help fund the $100 million planned expansion at the Anchorage Museum of Art and History. Other projects in the works or in planning stages include developing ski terrain at the Winner Creek-Glacier Valley north of the Alyeska Resort in Girdwood. Development of this area is expected to bring thousands more skiers each winter, with another 320,000 visitors expected each summer; this could mean a generation of $74 million annually in gross revenues and the creation of about 900 new jobs. Other projects involve revitalizing neighborhoods, such as the Eagle River Downtown Revitalization and the Mountain View Arts and Cultural District.

In transportation, a $250 million expansion is underway at the Port of Anchorage in 2005. The expanded facility is expected to generate more than 2,300 jobs once completed and will accommodate the area's cruise and military business. Merrill Field has constructed two new taxiways, and an apron expansion in 2005 will add more space and accommodations for ski-equipped aircraft in winter and aircraft with tundra tires in summer. In late 2004, Congress approved funding for several intermodal facilities to be built throughout the city at museums, medical centers, and other destinations. The 2004 summer road construction season completed 41 road and safety projects with a total cost of about $45 million.

Anchorage has a strong commitment to preserving land for recreation. Part of this commitment involves the Foster-A-Flower program; in 2004 downtown businesses bought more than 200 hanging flower baskets, each at $75, to beautify the area. Five new dog parks were created in Anchorage in 2004.

Economic Development Information: Anchorage Economic Development Corporation, 900 West Fifth Avenue, Suite 300, Anchorage, AK 99501; telephone (907)258-3000; toll-free (800)462-7275; fax (907)258-6646; email aedc@aedcweb.com. Municipality of Anchorage, 632 W. Sixth Avenue, Anchorage, AK 99501

Commercial Shipping

Anchorage's sea and air ports combine with its railroad to make the area the primary cargo distributor in the state. The Port of Anchorage, the largest seaport in Alaska, is a year-round shipping point with five terminals served by three major carriers, which bring four to five ships from the Pacific Northwest and Asia each week. More than four million tons of iron and steel products, containerized freight, bulk petroleum, cement, wood products, and various other commodities crossed the Port's docks in 2003. More than 50 air carriers and 9 freight forwarders connect Anchorage to the rest of the country and the world beyond. The airport is said to be one of the busiest cargo airports in North America; in 2002, Anchorage was second to Memphis in having the most cargo landed weight in the country, and third ranked in the world for most cargo landed weight. Municipal Merrill Field airport serves the intrastate needs of business, banking, and commerce. The Alaska Railroad provides rail freight service; in 2003 the railroad moved more than eight million tons of freight across 525 miles of track. More than 30 motor freight carriers link Anchorage with major market areas.

Labor Force and Employment Outlook

Anchorage boasts an abundant and well-educated labor pool with a relatively low median age. Ninety percent of residents are high school graduates, and approximately 65 percent of Anchorage's adult residents have completed at least one year of college. In addition, wage rates in Anchorage tend to be higher than wages in other areas of the country due to an abundance of higher-level positions available. Anchorage employment levels rose 28 percent between 1995 and 2003, due mainly to a 40 percent increase in the private support sector. In that same period, the services industry increased 114 percent, reflecting the area's attractiveness as a tourist destination.

Expansion and diversification have given Anchorage's economy the ability to absorb fluctuations in the business cycle or unexpected economic events. Anchorage now has a steady year-round employment base, with a summer boost from tourism and construction activities. The international cargo business in Anchorage continues to grow; Anchorage is equidistant to both Asia and Europe, and is 9 hours flying time to nearly the entire industrialized world, making it a good location for warehousing and distribution. About 10 percent of the city's employment can be attributed either directly or indirectly to the airport.

According to the Anchorage Economic Development Corporation, job growth in Anchorage is expected to be in the service sector, which would include jobs in health and social services, hospitality, trade, and finance and real estate. Contributing to Anchorage's economy will be the addition of 2,000 Stryker Brigade soldiers to Fort Richardson as part of a nationwide reorganization.

The following is a summary of data regarding the Anchorage metropolitan area labor force, 2003 annual averages.

Size of non-agricultural labor force: 142,600

Number of workers employed in . . .
  natural resources and mining: 2,200
  construction: 8,500
  manufacturing: 1,800

  trade, transportation and utilities: 33,000
  information: 4,600
  financial activities: 8,800
  professional and business services: 16,000
  educational and health services: 17,300
  leisure and hospitality: 14,600
  other services: 5,700
  government: 30,000

Average hourly earnings of production workers employed in manufacturing: $12.01 (statewide average)

Unemployment rate: 5.1% (December 2004)

Largest employers (2003)	*Number of employees*
Providence Health System Alaska	3,566
Safeway Stores, Inc. (retail-grocery)	3,135
Wal-Mart/Sam's Club	2,443
Fred Meyer (retail-grocery)	2,341
Alaska Airlines	1,726
BP Exploration, Inc. (oil and gas production)	1,417
Banner Health System	1,243
NANA Management Services	1,227
Yukon-Kuskokwim Health Corporation	1,217
ASRC Energy Services	1,171
Federal Express	1,094
VECO Inc. (oil field services)	1,018

Cost of Living

The personal tax burden in Alaska is extremely low, while the cost of living is significantly higher than much of the rest of the nation. Residents benefit from distributions from the Permanent Fund, a savings account established in 1976 by voters allowing residents to receive 25 percent of the state's royalty oil revenue. Senior citizens enjoy a $150,000 property tax exemption or a renter's rebate.

The following is a summary of data regarding several key cost of living factors for the Anchorage area.

2004 (3rd Quarter) ACCRA Average House Price: $349,640

2004 (3rd Quarter) ACCRA Cost of Living Index: 122.5 (U.S. average = 100.0)

State income tax rate: None

State sales tax rate: None

Local income tax rate: None

Local sales tax rate: 8% on rental cars, fuel, alcohol, tobacco

Property tax rate: Graduated from 7.91 mills to 18.15 mills levied on full assessed value

Economic Information: Alaska Department of Labor, Research & Analysis Section, 3301 Eagle Street, Suite 202, PO Box 107018, Anchorage, AK 99510-7018; telephone (907)269-4863; fax (907)269-4870

Education and Research

Elementary and Secondary Schools

The Anchorage School District prides itself on test scores that are better than state and national averages. The district's 50,000 students represent a diverse array of ethnic backgrounds. In the 1990s Anchorage voters approved more than $500 million in school construction that continues today. Two middle schools and nine elementary schools were built, and the new South Anchorage High School, serving 1,600 students, opened for the 2004-2005 school year. The new Eagle River High School will open in fall 2005 and will educate 800 students, relieving crowding at Chugiak High School. Many of the other Anchorage schools have undergone expansions or upgrades since 1990.

The school system is administered by a nonpartisan, seven-member school board that appoints a superintendent on the recommendation of a selection task force. The system faced budget hardships, making cuts to supplies and services in the 2004-2005 school year. A 2005-2006 budget was announced with hopes for increased funds, pending approval from state legislature.

The following is a summary of data regarding the Anchorage School District as of the 2004–2005 school year.

Total enrollment: 50,000

Number of facilities
  elementary schools: 59
  middle schools: 9
  senior high schools: 7
  other: 1 middle/high school, 1 K-12 school, 1 vocational
    school, 10 specialized schools, 5 charter schools

Student/teacher ratio: 25:1

Teacher salaries
  minimum: $35,284
  maximum: $66,286

Funding per pupil: $8,764 (2001-2002)

A small percentage of students attend private and parochial schools in the Anchorage area.

Public Schools Information: Anchorage School District, 4600 DeBarr Road, Anchorage, AK 99508-3126; telephone (907)742-4000

Colleges and Universities

Anchorage boasts one of the highest percentages of residents with postsecondary degrees in the country. Two fully accredited universities are located there: the University of Alaska Anchorage (UAA), which enrolls more than 17,000 students, and Alaska Pacific University, a private institution affiliated with the United Methodist church with about 700 enrolled students. Both institutions offer undergraduate degrees in a wide range of disciplines and master's degrees in such fields as biological sciences, business and management, logistics, and engineering. Also located in the Anchorage area are several vocational, specialty, and technical schools.

Libraries and Research Centers

In addition to its main branch downtown, the Anchorage Municipal Libraries system operates five branches throughout the city. Holdings consist of more than 452,000 books, nearly 1,700 periodical subscriptions, and films, records, tapes, art reproductions, and sheet music. Special collections at the system's main Loussac Library include the Alaska Collection, featuring more than 25,000 books and documents on Alaska and the North, and the Loussac Children's Collection, with materials for parents and people who work with children. Nearly 50 special libraries and research centers are located in Anchorage, most of them affiliated with the University of Alaska Anchorage and specializing in the fields of environment, natural resources, art, history, law, and education. ARLIS, or Alaska Resources Library and Information Services, features a collection of more than 200,000 books, 700 journals, and a variety of other sources of information about Alaska. Housed on the University of Alaska campus, ARLIS contains the collection of The Oil Spill Public Information Center, featuring scientific data from the *Exxon Valdez* oil spill damage. The National Center for Infectious Diseases Arctic Investigations Program seeks to improve the quality of life of arctic and subarctic people.

Public Library Information: Anchorage Municipal Libraries, 3600 Denali St., Anchorage, AK 99503; telephone (907)343-2975

Health Care

Anchorage is a primary medical treatment center for the state of Alaska and is home to the two largest hospitals in the state, Providence Alaska Medical Center and Alaska Regional Hospital. The new $157 million 100-bed hospital on

Elmendorf Air Force Base opened in 2001. The new Elmendorf Hospital replaces the existing 50-bed hospital, which suffered structural damage during the 1964 earthquake, and serves the state's military population.

Providence Alaska Medical Center, with 341 beds and more than 600 staff physicians, is the main medical referral center in the state, offering such specialized treatment as open heart surgery and neonatal care. In 2001, the hospital added a new state-of-the-art emergency department as part of a 100,000 square foot expansion. Alaska Regional Hospital provides neurosurgery and spinal and orthopedic surgery; a maternity center, critical care units, and emergency services, including an air ambulance, are maintained. A $7 million renovation at Alaska Regional Hospital included a new trauma and open-heart surgery room. Anchorage Neighborhood Health Center offers three family practice clinics featuring medical, dental, pharmaceutical, and mental health services. The North Star Behavioral Health System provides mental health and substance abuse treatment programs through several facilities.

Recreation

Sightseeing

An ideal way to see the points of interest in downtown Anchorage is to take a walking tour. A circular route—beginning at Old City Hall, original seat of the municipal government, and ending two blocks away at the Pioneer Schoolhouse, the first school in Anchorage—provides a leisurely stroll through the city's history. Principal attractions along the way include the Ship Creek Viewpoint with a view of the site of Tanaina summer fish camps. Nearby are the David Leopold House, built in 1917 for the city's first mayor; and Boney Memorial Courthouse, housing fine examples of nineteenth-century art motifs of Alaskan natives and animals. The Oscar Anderson House Museum in Elderberry Park is Anchorage's only historic house museum, and gives visitors a glimpse into the life of the family that occupied the home as well as Anchorage history.

Resolution Park, featuring the Captain Cook Monument, commemorates the two-hundredth anniversary of Cook's exploration of the area. Adjacent to the park are historic Anchorage homes, including the first permanent frame residence in the city. Located on the southern edge of downtown is Delaney Park, known as "The Park Strip," once a firebreak for the original town site and later the city's first airfield.

The Alaska Zoo features hundreds of animals; special attractions are the natural land habitat for brown bears and an aquarium for seals and otters. Points of interest in north Anchorage include St. Nicholas Russian Church. The oldest

building in the municipality, the church is located at Eklutna, the site of the first Tanaina settlement east of Knik Arm; the cemetery's "spirit" houses are reminders of the blend of native tradition and missionary influence.

In south Anchorage are the Potter Section House and Crow Creek Mine, the first non-native settlement. An example of a nineteenth-century placer mine, Crow Creek is still in operation, and rental equipment is available for those wishing to pan for any gold that remains. Local fur factories provide regularly scheduled tours of their facilities. Sightseeing and "flightseeing" tours of the Anchorage area and day trips to attractions such as Mt. McKinley and Portage Glacier can be arranged through bus and air services.

Arts and Culture

Dating back to Territory days when opera was staged regularly and when the city had an orchestra before it had paved streets, the performing arts have been an integral part of life in Anchorage. The city's arts community, with more than 75 organizations offering cultural experiences ranging from classical music to native dance, provides a striking contrast to the surrounding wilderness. The Anchorage Concert Association, founded in 1950 to bring international performers to local audiences, is still active, sponsoring about 22 music, dance, and theatre productions each year.

Many of these performances are presented in the downtown Alaska Center for the Performing Arts, a modern complex housing four theaters, including the new Elvera Voth Hall, an 1,800 square foot performance and rehearsal space opened in 2003. A significant contribution to the Anchorage arts community, the center offers a year-round schedule of more than 600 events and furnishes a showcase for local performers. The center's resident companies include Alaska Dance Theatre, Alaska Junior Theater, Anchorage Concert Association, Anchorage Concert Chorus, the Anchorage Symphony Orchestra, Anchorage Opera, and Whistling Swan Productions.

Dance thrives in Anchorage with the Alaska Dance Theater, as well as Native American, Eskimo, and Russian folk troupes.

The Anchorage Symphony Orchestra, formed in 1946 and today featuring 80 musicians, hosts a September-to-May season with performances of classics and young people's concerts. The Anchorage Opera offers three full-scale opera productions per season. The Alaska Chamber Singers, a chorale ensemble of 40 voices, offer performances at various venues throughout the city.

Interest and participation in the visual arts has been encouraged in Anchorage by "1% for Art in Public Places," a 1978 law setting aside for the purchase of commissioned

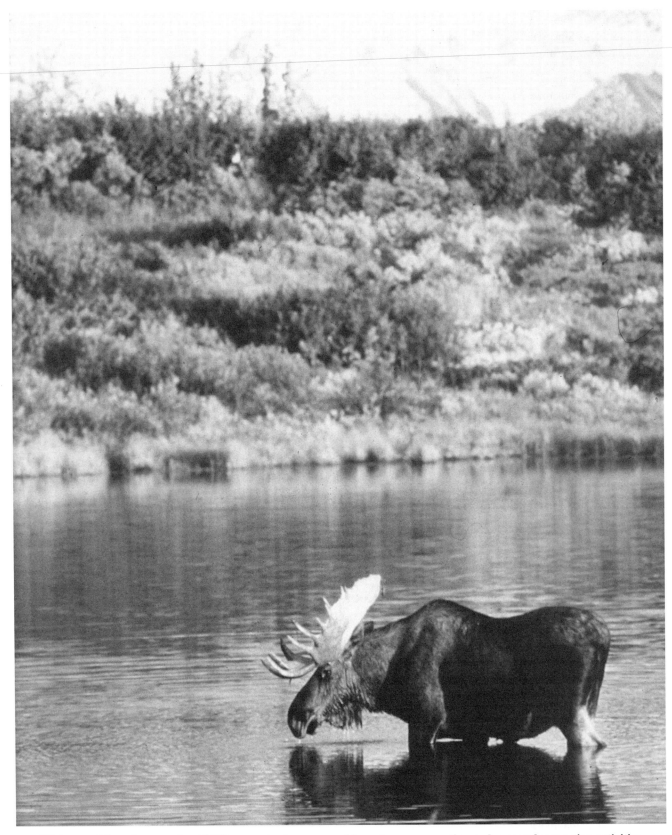

With over 162 parks spanning 13,200 acres, Anchorage provides nature preservation and seasonal recreation activities.

artwork at least one percent of construction costs of all public buildings. Since 1978, $5.8 million has been spent on 267 works of art in more than 100 buildings.

Museums and galleries in Anchorage specialize in science, history, and arts and crafts. Imaginarium is a science discovery center with a variety of hands-on experience exhibits, a 10-foot tall Tyrannosaurus Rex, a planetarium, and a preschool learning area. The Alaska Aviation Heritage Museum traces the history of state aviation and prominent aviators, with a theater, observation deck, and historic planes. The Anchorage Museum of History and Art features a permanent collection of 17,500 objects and 2,000 artifacts; the museum is also responsible for a $5.8 million collection of 276 works of art viewable in public buildings around the city. In early 2005 the museum was in the planning stages of a 70,000 square foot expansion, funded by a private donor endowment to the tune of $50 million, with matching federal and state funds. The 15,000 square foot Alaska Gallery in the museum displays a collection of more than 1,000 objects of traditional and modern native art with demonstration exhibits. At the Alaska Native Heritage Center the visitor can explore five distinct Alaska Native cultures through interpretive displays, films, and daily performances by traditional storytellers. A trail from the Welcome House leads to Native Tradition Bearers—artists and performers at five traditional village exhibits surrounding a lake on the 26-acre grounds.

Festivals and Holidays

The year kicks off in Anchorage with the Annual Anchorage Folk Festival, offering more than 120 musical performances by local and guest acts, and the Great Alaska Beer and Barleywine Festival. February offers the Fur Rendezvous, known as the ''Fur Rondy'' (dating back to 1936 and one of the 10 largest festivals in the nation), a popular 10-day celebration of the annual fur-auctioning and social gathering of trappers and miners. The world-famous cross country Iditarod Trail Sled Dog Race starts in downtown Anchorage the first Saturday in March. Also in March and coinciding with the Iditarod is the Tour of Anchorage, a cross-country ski event with varying race lengths.

April follows up with the Alyeska Spring Carnival & Slush Cup, and May brings the Alaska Native Youth Olympics. June events include the Three Barons Renaissance Faire and the Mayor's Midnight Sun Marathon.

Live music can be heard all summer long on Wednesday and Friday afternoons from the park at Fourth Avenue and E Street. Other summer fare includes the annual July 4th Celebration and the Bear Paw Festival at Eagle River in July; August offerings include the Alyeska Blueberry & Mountain Arts Festival and the Arctic Thunder Elmendorf Air Force Base Open House and Air Show.

Among the fall highlights are the Alaska State Fair in late August and early September, followed in October by the Nye Frontier Hockey Classic. The year closes out with Thanksgiving weekend events that include an annual production of *The Nutcracker* by the Cincinnati Ballet and the Town Square Tree Lighting Ceremony, and in December the Anchorage International Film Festival.

Sports for the Spectator

The Wells Fargo Sports Complex at the University of Alaska Anchorage hosts Seawolves National Collegiate Athletic Association (NCAA) hockey, basketball, and volleyball competition. The Alaska Aces of the East Coast Hockey League are based in Anchorage and play at Sullivan Arena. The Carrs Great Alaska Shootout collegiate basketball tournament is a major event that draws fans from throughout the state and nation.

Sled dog racing is the official state sport and Anchorage hosts several main sledding events. The world famous Iditarod Trial Sled Dog Race originates in Anchorage and runs more than 1,000 miles to Nome, the course taking from 10 days to a month to complete. The World Championship Sled Dog Races, the most famous sprint race, is held during the Fur Rendezvous and draws racers from all over the world.

Sports for the Participant

With more than 162 parks covering 14,000 acres, residents have a multitude of choices for year-round and seasonal outdoor activities. Park facilities include shelters, pools, camping, more than 40 ball fields, 59 tennis courts, winter ice skating, and programming for recreational events. Mountain climbing can be pursued at the 500,000-acre Chugach State Park, situated within the city limits; hiking and horseback-riding trails are located in several other municipal parks. Salmon and trout fishing facilities are maintained on rivers, creeks, and lakes, and licensed hunting is regulated by the Alaska Department of Fish and Game.

During summer the midnight sun provides additional time for recreation. Popular activities include boating, kayaking, and river rafting on the flowing waters within the municipality limits. Free loaner bicycles are available for use on downtown bike trails; among other public facilities are 4 golf courses, 5 indoor pools, several lakes, and 49 tennis courts. With 120 miles of paved trails and 300 miles of unpaved and wilderness trail, Anchorage's extensive trail system attracts both residents and visitors. One of the most popular routes is the Tony Knowles Coastal Trail, an 11-mile asphalt trail that runs from downtown to Kincaid Park (which has its own system of 43 miles of wooded trail). Flattop Mountain is a popular hike; both beginner and expert hikers can summit the 3,510 foot mountain (3 miles round trip) as a day hike. Cyclists and runners enjoy the multitude of trails in and around Anchorage.

Runners have been traveling to Anchorage to participate in the Mayor's Midnight Sun Marathon since its inception in 1974. *Bicycling* magazine called Anchorage's trail system one of the best in the United States.

Winter sports enthusiasts can find a wide range of choices, including dog sledding, ice skating, skiing, sledding, snowshoeing, snowmobiling, and skating on several rinks, including two Olympic-sized hockey rinks. Dog sled rides and tours are available through local vendors. The municipality maintains more than 200 miles of cross-country ski trails, including 40 kilometers lit for night skiing, plus sledding hills and snowmobile trails. Alaska's largest ski resort is 40 minutes from downtown Anchorage. Alyeska Resort boasts an annual average of 742 inches of snowfall and a lift capacity of more than 10,000 skiers per hour on its 9 lifts.

Shopping and Dining

More than a dozen shopping centers, including five major malls, are located in Anchorage. Downtown's Fifth Avenue Mall houses major national retail chains such as Eddie Bauer, The Gap, Body Shop, and Banana Republic, but products native to Alaska are the major shopping attractions, with foods, ivory, jewelry, gold, furs, seal oil candles, and Eskimo and Aleut basketry among the most popular items. Shoppers can visit workshops to see fur styling, jewelry crafting, and wool making demonstrations. The Anchorage Saturday Market operates both Saturday and Sunday throughout the summer at Third Avenue and E Street. Shoppers will find fresh baked goods and vegetables, handmade jewelry and crafts, and unique Native art.

More than 350 restaurants in Anchorage offer a variety of ethnic cuisines. The local specialty is fresh seafood, particularly salmon, served at most restaurants in settings that offer views of mountain ranges and oceangoing vessels departing the Port of Anchorage.

Visitor Information: Anchorage Convention and Visitors Bureau, 524 W. Fourth Avenue, Anchorage, AK 99501; telephone (907)276-4118

Convention Facilities

Anchorage is rapidly gaining distinction as a convention and meeting site. The city's downtown convention center is within walking distance of fine restaurants, unique shops, and world-class cultural events. The extraordinary experience of enjoying first-class amenities in close proximity to untouched wilderness attracts an increasing number of groups to Anchorage yearly.

The principal meeting place in Anchorage is the William A. Egan Civic and Convention Center. The complex contains 45,000 square feet of meeting and exhibit space accommodating groups of 20 to 2,776 people; other features include 189 custom exhibit areas, simultaneous interpreting facilities, and complete catering service. Across the street from Egan Center and adjoined by a skybridge is the Alaska Center for the Performing Arts, which provides theater-style meeting halls seating 350 to 2,100 people.

In April 2005 voters will be asked to approve a 4 percent increase in hotel and motel taxes to help fund the new Anchorage Civic & Convention Center. Proponents of the new center say that the city's needs have outgrown the current Egan Civic and Convention Center. At a proposed cost of $93 million, the new center plans include a 50,000 square foot exhibit hall, a second 25,000 square foot multiuse exhibit hall, and several breakout rooms totaling 12,000 square feet. The proposal includes a covered walkway attaching the new center to the Egan Center.

Located 2 miles from downtown is the George M. Sullivan Arena, which accommodates trade shows with 32,000 square feet of usable space and parking for 1,800 vehicles. The Anchorage Museum of History and Art is available to host special events in its atrium. Other meeting facilities are available at the University of Alaska–Anchorage, Alaska Pacific University, and major hotels in the metropolitan area. In total, Anchorage features more than 8,000 hotel and motel rooms, and more than 850 beds in bed and breakfast and hostel accommodations.

Convention Information: Anchorage Convention and Visitors Bureau, 524 W. Fourth Ave., Anchorage, AK 99501; telephone (907)276-4118

Transportation

Approaching the City

The majority of travelers come to Anchorage by plane, arriving at Anchorage International Airport, located ten minutes west of downtown. A major stop for transpolar flights, the airport is one of the busiest in the country and is served by more than 50 freight and passenger air carriers.

For those heading to Anchorage by car, the major route into the city is Alaska 1, which is Glenn Highway as it enters from the northeast and Seward Highway (scenic S.R. 1/9) as it enters from the south. The Alaska Railroad, headquartered in Anchorage, provides passenger rail service within Alaska.

Traveling in the City

Downtown Anchorage is laid out in a series of square blocks, a pattern typical of early western railroad towns. All lettered streets run north-south and numbered streets run east-west, with Northern Lights Boulevard dividing north from south and A Street dividing east from west.

Anchorage's bus-based public transit system is the People Mover, which provides a convenient way to see the city, as buses stop at major points of interest and extend to all suburbs. The Share-A-Ride service connects people living in the same area for car or vanpooling, and in some cases municipally-owned vans are provided. AnchorRides offers paratransit services to residents with disabilities. Four major taxi companies and several private shuttle companies offer transportations services throughout Anchorage.

Communications

Newspapers and Magazines

The major daily newspaper in Anchorage is the morning *Anchorage Daily News.* Several other newspapers are published in Anchorage, including *Petroleum News,* a paper covering the petroleum industry in Alaska and Canada; and the *Sourdough Sentinel,* a weekly covering happenings at Elmendorf Air Force Base. Also published in Anchorage are *Northern Pilot Magazine, Alaska Business Monthly,* which focuses on state business developments, and *Senior Voice.*

Television and Radio

Anchorage has four commercial television stations. The city is also served by cable television and by fourteen AM and FM radio stations broadcasting a variety of formats such as adult contemporary, country, and broadcasts from National Public Radio and American Public Radio.

Media Information: *Anchorage Daily News,* 1001 Northway Drive, PO Box 149001, Anchorage, AK 99514-9001; telephone (907)257-4200.

Anchorage Online

Alaska Department of Education and Early Development. Available www.educ.state.ak.us/home.html

Anchorage Convention and Visitors Bureau. Available www.anchorage.net

Anchorage Daily News. Available www.adn.com

Anchorage Economic Development Corporation. Available www.aedcweb.com

Anchorage Municipal Libraries. Available www.lexicon.ci .anchorage.ak.us

Anchorage School District. Available www.asd.k12.ak.us

Municipality of Anchorage Home Page. Available www.ci .anchorage.ak.us

State of Alaska. Available www.state.ak.us

Selected Bibliography

Muir, John, *Travels in Alaska* (Boston, New York: Houghton Mifflin, 1915)

Rich, Kim, *Johnny's Girl: A Daughter's Memoir of Growing Up in Alaska's Underworld* (New York: Morrow, 1993)

Woodward, Kesler E., *Painting in the North: Alaskan Art in the Anchorage Museum of History and Art.* (Seattle: University of Washington Press, 1993)

Fairbanks

The City in Brief

Founded: 1901 (incorporated 1903)

Head Official: Mayor Steve M. Thompson (since 2001)

City Population
   1980: 22,645
   1990: 30,843
   2000: 30,224
   2003 estimate: 30,970
   Percent change, 1990–2000: − 2.4%
   U.S. rank in 1990: 878th
   U.S. rank in 2000: Not reported (State rank: 3rd)

Metropolitan Area Population (Fairbanks North Star Borough)
   1980: 53,983
   1990: 77,720

   2000: 82,840
   Percent change, 1990–2000: 6.6%
   U.S. rank in 1980: Not reported
   U.S. rank in 1990: Not reported
   U.S. rank in 2000: Not reported

Area: 32.67 square miles (2000)
Elevation: 432 feet above sea level
Average Annual Temperature: 30.4° F
Average Annual Precipitation: 11.5 inches with 67.8 inches of snowfall

Major Economic Sectors: Government, services
Unemployment Rate: 7.6% (January 2005)
Per Capita Income: $19,814 (1999)

2002 FBI Crime Index Total: Not reported

Major Colleges and Universities: University of Alaska Fairbanks

Daily Newspaper: *Fairbanks Daily News-Miner*

Introduction

Fairbanks is the second-largest city in Alaska, the northernmost city in the United States, and one of only a few communities in the entire world where a concentration of people is living at such an extreme northern latitude. Despite being the trade, transportation, and cultural center of the Alaskan Interior, Fairbanks has maintained much of its frontier character. Mining camps, swinging-door saloons, and unpaved roads mingle with modern hotels and restaurants, a symphony orchestra, and an internationally known research university. Fairbanks has almost continuous daylight from the middle of May through the end of July; on June 21st, the longest day of the year, Fairbanks has more than 20 hours of sunlight. The most distinctive feature of the city, however, is its weather: with long winter nights, snow covering the ground six months of the year, Fairbanks is quintessentially Alaska.

Geography and Climate

Fairbanks is located in the Tanana Valley in the Interior of Alaska, 358 miles north of Anchorage and 125 miles south of the Arctic Circle. Significant changes in solar heat during the year produce a wide variation of temperatures from winter to summer. During the summer months (June and July) the sun is above the horizon 18 to nearly 21 hours per day and temperatures are often in the high 80s. From November to March, daylight ranges from 10 to less than 4 hours daily, and temperatures can drop to −60 degrees Fahrenheit. During the winter, ice fog can occur if the temperature drops below −20 degrees Fahrenheit. Fairbanks rarely experiences windy conditions.

Area: 32.67 square miles (2000)

Elevation: 432 feet above sea level

Average Temperatures: January, −10.2° F; August, 55.4° F; annual average, 30.4° F

Annual Average Precipitation: 11.5 inches with 67.8 inches of snowfall

History

Discovery of Gold Brings Prospectors, Settlers

Fairbanks was founded accidentally in 1901 by Captain E. T. Barnette. On his way to set up a trading post on the Tanana River, Barnette was instead stranded on the Chena River when the riverboat in which he was traveling was forced to turn back. As he was making plans to move his supplies to a more profitable location, gold was discovered about 12 miles away, near Fox. An Italian prospector, Felix Pedro, is credited with having made the discovery on July 22, 1902. Every year on that date, Fairbanks commemorates the gold strike with the Golden Days celebration.

During the ensuing gold rush, Barnette's trading post became the center of activity for prospectors who swarmed into the area. A settlement grew up and was named for Senator Charles Fairbanks of Indiana who served as vice president under Theodore Roosevelt from 1905-1909; the town was incorporated in 1903. Barnette was elected the first mayor of Fairbanks. He is credited with establishing telephone service, fire protection, sanitation ordinances, electricity and steam heat, but he soon fell into disfavor as a result of his involvement in a bank failure that caused many citizens to lose their savings.

Oil and Military Buildup Replace Gold as Economic Pillars

By 1910 the population of Fairbanks grew to 3,541 people, although more than 6,000 miners lived and worked their claims north of town. During World War I, however, gold activity declined and the population of the town decreased. The start of the construction of the Alaska Railroad brought another boom period, so that by 1930 the population was restored to about half of its previous level.

In 1922 the Alaska Territorial legislature accepted lands granted by the United States Congress, creating the Alaska Agricultural College and School of Mines, which grew into the University of Alaska Fairbanks. During World War II the Alaska Highway was constructed as part of the military buildup, and Fairbanks experienced yet another boom period when thousands of military personnel were located at nearby Eielson Air Force Base and Ladd Field (now Fort Wainwright). Military personnel in the area grew from 10 in 1940 to 5,419 in 1950. Following the war, the Fairbanks population again declined, but during the following decade the community experienced gradual growth.

The Fairbanks North Star Borough was established on January 1, 1964, by an act of the Alaska State Legislature. The Borough includes the cities of Fairbanks and North Pole and encompasses 7,361 square miles (4.7 million acres), making it the fourth largest borough in the state.

In August 1967, just weeks before the expected winter freeze-up, the city was swept by a flood that inundated 95 percent of its residences and left the city under eight feet of water. Fairbanks recovered from the extensive damage, and with the discovery in 1968 of oil on the north slope of the Brooks Mountain Range, the city entered a new era of expansion.

Construction of the Trans-Alaska oil pipeline triggered one of the city's largest booms, and the population is estimated to have reached 70,000 persons in 1977. With the completion of the pipeline construction, the community's economy went into a serious decline, but it soon recovered with the injection of state revenues in the early 1980s. By the mid-1980s, however, crude oil prices had dropped and Alaska slipped into a severe recession, with Fairbanks experiencing the most abrupt decline in the state. Since then the local economy has recovered somewhat, but high unemployment rates continued into the new millennium.

Today, Fairbanks is a popular tourist destination; visitors are attracted to its boundless opportunities for outdoor adventure and its pioneer spirit still reflected in its gold mines, saloons and frontier towns.

Historical Information: Fairbanks Historic Preservation Foundation, telephone (907)456-8848; Tanana Yukon Historical Society, telephone (907)455-8947

Population Profile

Metropolitan Area Residents (Fairbanks North Star Borough)
1980: 53,983
1990: 77,720
2000: 82,840
2003 estimate: 85,978
Percent change, 1990–2000: 6.6%
U.S. rank in 1980: Not reported
U.S. rank in 1990: Not reported
U.S. rank in 2000: Not reported

City Residents
1980: 22,645
1990: 30,843
2000: 30,224
2003 estimate: 30,970
Percent change, 1990–2000: − 2.4%
U.S. rank in 1990: 878th
U.S. rank in 2000: Not reported (State rank: 3rd)

Density: 948.7 people per square mile (2000)

Racial and ethnic characteristics (2000)
White: 20,150
Black or African American: 3,370
American Indian and Alaska Native: 2,994
Asian: 821
Native Hawaiian and other Pacific Islander: 164
Hispanic or Latino (may be of any race): 1,854
Other: 740

Percent of residents born in state: 30.4% (2000)

Age characteristics (2000)
Population under 5 years old: 2,908
Population 5 to 9 years old: 2,503
Population 10 to 14 years old: 2,233
Population 15 to 19 years old: 2,283
Population 20 to 24 years old: 3,423
Population 25 to 34 years old: 5,588
Population 35 to 44 years old: 4,340
Population 45 to 54 years old: 3,262
Population 55 to 59 years old: 989
Population 60 to 64 years old: 709
Population 65 to 74 years old: 1,086
Population 75 to 84 years old: 700
Population 85 years and older: 200
Median age: 27.6 years

Births (2003, Fairbanks North Star Borough)
Total number: 1,565

Deaths (2002, Fairbanks North Star Borough)
Total number: 283

Money Income (1999)
Per capita income: $19,814
Median household income: $40,577
Total number of households: 11,075

Number of households with income of . . .
less than $10,000: 822
$10,000 to $14,999: 820
$15,000 to $24,999: 1,468
$25,000 to $34,999: 1,615
$35,000 to $49,999: 2,052
$50,000 to $74,999: 2,167
$75,000 to $99,999: 1,086
$100,000 to $149,999: 802
$150,000 to $199,999: 206
$200,000 or more: 94

Percent of families below poverty level: 7.4% (41.8% of which were female householder families with related children under 5)

2002 FBI Crime Index Total: Not reported

Municipal Government

Fairbanks North Star Borough (FNSB), similar to a county, is governed by an 11-member assembly and an elected mayor who is the chief executive officer. The mayor serves for three years as the executive and administrative officer of the city; elected council members serve for staggered three-year terms. Administration for the public school system is the responsibility of the FNSB.

Head Official: Mayor Steve M. Thompson (since 2001; current term expires 2007)

Total Number of City Employees: 468 (2005)

City Information: City of Fairbanks, 800 Cushman, Fairbanks, AK 99701; telephone (907)459-6793; fax (907) 459-6787

Economy

Major Industries and Commercial Activity

As Alaska's second largest city, Fairbanks is an important trading, transportation, military, regional service and supply center. City, borough, state and federal government services are located here. The government services sector, including the military, employs more than one-third of the region's workers. The city's international airport serves villages in the region, is a supply point for North Slope oil fields, and is a center for the transport of cargo by international carriers.

Military activity is a significant contributor to the local economy. The combined payrolls at Fort Wainwright and Eielson Air Force Base are in excess of $354 million. According to the Fairbanks Economic Development Corporation, the total economic impact of the two military bases to the Greater Fairbanks community is $390.9 million annually. A total of almost 17,000 military active duty personnel lived in Fairbanks North Star Borough in 2004, comprising more than 20 percent of the total borough population. This figure is an increase of 1.6 percent from the previous year. In 2003, the United States Army Alaska began the transformation of the 172nd Brigade from a Light Infantry Brigade to a Stryker Brigade. One-third of the more than 1000 soldiers, plus dependents and support personnel, is already posted at Fort Wainwright, with the balance to be transferred to the Fort possibly as early as 2006 when housing and related infrastructure are in place. The Fairbanks North Star Borough's economy will benefit from the housing construction, rental and utility income, wages, and additional visitors these soldiers bring to the area.

Tourism and mining also comprise a large percentage of the commercial activity in the region. Each summer, approximately 325,000 visitors travel to Fairbanks. However, visitor numbers have declined from a high in the summer of 2001. The Fort Knox gold mine is the largest producing gold mine in the state. It produces 1,200 ounces of gold daily and

employs 360 permanent year-round workers. Despite gold prices tumbling below $300 per ounce, the mine is still acquiring prospects in the region in order to expand its operation. To date, more than $200 million in gold has been extracted from the mining district. The mine is expected to remain in operation through 2010.

Incentive Programs—New and Existing Companies

State programs—The Governor's Office of International Trade provides assistance and information to firms interested in foreign trade and investment, organizes trade missions and promotions, and sponsors trade shows and seminars.

Local programs—The Small Business Development Center (SBDC) offers seminars, counseling, and workshops for new and established businesses to support their existence and help them grow. The Procurement Technical Assistance Center (PTAC) assists businesses who contract with local, state, or federal government.

Job training programs—A variety of training programs exist to help meet the business needs of Fairbanks employers; many are organized through the local educational institutions. Tanana Chiefs' Conference offers a wide array of programs for tribal populations through its Employment and Training Department. The Chamber of Commerce offers the School Business Partnership, which allows businesses and schools to work together.

Development Projects

Fairbanks and other Alaska officials are working toward the development of an 800-mile natural gas pipeline, which would run from the North Slope to a liquefied natural gas (LNG) plant to be developed at Valdez for export to the rest of North America. The All-Alaska Gas Pipeline will run parallel to the existing Trans-Alaska Oil Pipeline. In 2005, the Alaska Gasline Port Authority (AGPA) had reached a development agreement with Sempra LNG to assist in the development of the All-Alaska Pipeline Project and market the related LNG. Work was underway to acquire permits and the rights of way from Yukon Pacific for building the pipeline. The first LNG tanker is projected to leave the terminal at Valdez sometime around 2011. A 40 percent portion of project revenues will be shared among the Alaskan municipalities. The cost of the pipeline could approach $9 billion.

A major plan to redevelop the land surrounding the river bend in the Chena River for recreational, commercial and residential use is on the drawing board. Plans include the creation of a public riverwalk to provide direct access to the river and its recreational opportunities, along with the improvement of Pioneer Park and Carlson Center. Along the river, the construction of a fish hatchery and indoor/outdoor tennis courts, as well as the demolition of a sewer treatment

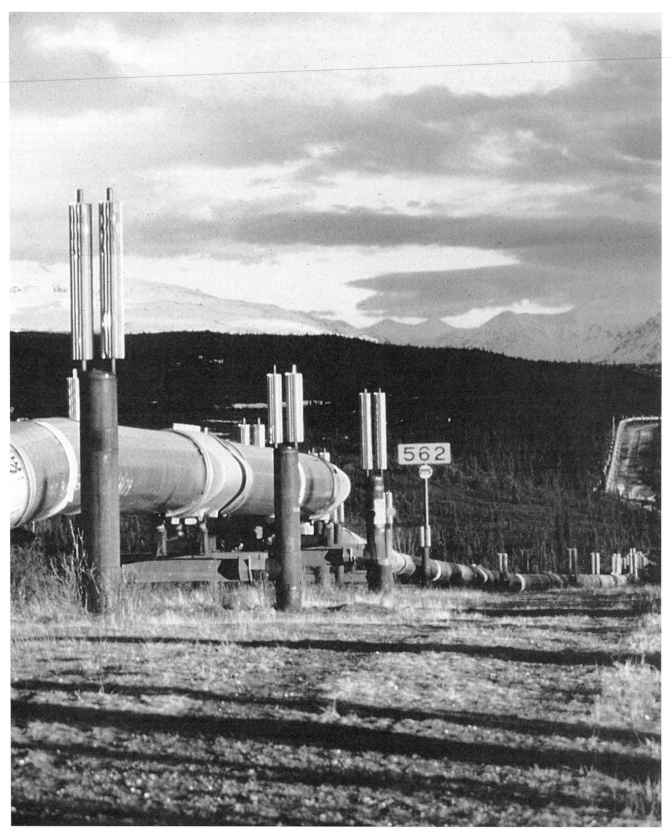

Construction of the Alaskan oil pipeline triggered one of the city's largest periods of growth.

facility are scheduled for 2005 and 2006. The Chena Riverbend Project is slated for completion in 2010.

Construction of a new $25 million fish hatchery is also planned for Fairbanks. A feasibility study was completed in 2004, with design, site selection, environmental assessment, and site preparation scheduled for 2005-2006. The actual construction of the hatchery is planned for 2007-2008, with operation to begin the following year. Not only is the hatchery expected to increase the number of stocked catchable fish to provide a better fishing experience for tourists, it will also be an important tourist destination itself. It could also be the source of research dollars for the University of Alaska Fairbanks' fish biology program.

Fairbanks' extreme climate has become a real asset for the area as the city was chosen as the site for the construction of a Research Test Facility (RTF) for the Cold Climate Housing Research Center (CCHRC). It will be built on land adjacent to the University of Alaska Fairbanks campus. Plans call for it to be the first of several test facilities in a future research test park. RTF construction alone is expected to have a $4.5 million impact on the area's economy, with an additional annual direct economic impact of between $800,000 in 2005 to $1.4 million in 2009.

Commercial Shipping

As the only large city and main business center in interior Alaska, Fairbanks is a major transportation hub. Goods are shipped via truck, air and the Alaska Railroad. Fairbanks International Airport functions as the air freight distribution and supply center for the region. In 2003, the airport handled almost 200 million tons of air transit freight. Fourteen motor freight carriers transport goods through facilities in the city.

Labor Force and Employment Outlook

Continued slow population growth is projected in Fairbanks, especially among the working-age population. However, the Fairbanks North Star Borough has seen its population steadily increase over the past four decades. The senior population is projected to nearly triple by 2020, while the school-age population will grow about 10 percent by 2005 then hold steady for the next 15 years. Fairbanks-area businesses that cater to the needs of seniors will prosper, but there will be more competition by employers to find workers. The construction of the All-Alaska Pipeline is expected to bring new jobs to the area with a total of 7,600 total new jobs to the State of Alaska. The transfer of military personnel to Fort Wainwright will also augment the area's labor force. The projection for growth in the construction industry through 2012 is 15.5 percent statewide.

The following is an annual summary of data regarding the Fairbanks labor force, 2004 annual averages.

Size of non-agricultural labor force: 36,900

Number of workers employed in . . .
  natural resources and mining: 900
  construction: 2,700
  manufacturing: 500
  trade, transportation and utilities: 7,300
  information: 600
  financial activities: 1,400
  professional and business services: 2,100
  education and health services: 4,100
  leisure and hospitality: 4,100
  other services: 1,300
  government: 11,500

Average hourly earnings of production workers employed in manufacturing: $12.16

Unemployment rate: 7.6% (January 2005)

Largest private employers	Number of employees
Banner Health System	1,204
Alyeska Pipeline Service Co.	1,007
Tanana Chiefs Conference	669
Fairbanks Gold Mining Co.	376
Petro Star	308

Cost of Living

Despite Alaska's reputation for its high cost of living, prices in Fairbanks compare favorably with those in many other North American cities. In 2002, Fairbanks's cost of living index was lower than New York or Boston, for example. In addition, the personal tax burden for Fairbanks residents is extremely low. Residents benefit from distributions from the Permanent Fund, a savings account established in 1976 by voters allowing residents to receive 25 percent of the state's royalty oil revenue. Senior citizens enjoy a $150,000 property tax exemption or a renter's rebate. The availability of vast natural resources insures utility costs somewhat lower than the national average.

The following is a summary of data regarding key cost of living factors for the Fairbanks area.

2004 (3rd Quarter) ACCRA Average House Price: $349,615

2004 (3rd Quarter) ACCRA Cost of Living Index: 128.4 (U.S. average = 100.0)

State income tax rate: None

State sales tax rate: None

Local income tax rate: None

Local sales tax rate: None

Property tax rate: 20.777 mills for city of Fairbanks; (7.171 City and 13.606 Borough areawide)

Special taxes: 5% alcohol tax (city only); 16% tobacco tax (8% city/8% borough); 8% accommodations tax (city only)

Economic Information: Alaska Department of Labor, Research and Analysis, PO Box 25501, Juneau, AK 99802-5501.

Education and Research

Elementary and Secondary Schools

Public elementary and secondary schools in Fairbanks are part of the Fairbanks North Star Borough School District (FNSBSD), the second largest in the state. The district is administered by a nonpartisan, seven-member school board with three non-voting advisory members, which appoints a superintendent. Students in the district come from 50 different language backgrounds. The district opened a new Fairbanks Magnet School for grades K-8 at Barnette Elementary School in fall 2005. The Yukon-Koyukuk School District, headquartered in Fairbanks, covers the Western interior of Alaska. Serving an area of 65,000 square miles, the district is larger than the state of Washington. The District's 11 schools serve 10 villages with 500 school-aged children in grades K-12. More than 90 percent of the students are Tanana or Koyukon Athabaskan Indians.

The following is a summary of data regarding public schools in the FNSBSD as of the 2003–2004 school year.

Total enrollment: 15,412

Number of facilities
   elementary schools: 19
   middle schools: 4
   junior/senior high: 1
   senior high schools: 3
   other: 1 vocational education center, 1 correspondence
      school, 2 charter schools, 1 magnet school

Student/teacher ratio: 17.5:1

Teacher salaries (2004-2005)
   minimum: $35,605
   maximum: $69,073

Funding per pupil: $6,691

Private schools, including seven religious schools, with an enrollment of about 1,800 students, provide alternative forms of education in the Fairbanks area.

Public Schools Information: Fairbanks North Star Borough School District, 520 Fifth Avenue, Fairbanks, AK 99701-4756; telephone (907)452-2000

Colleges and Universities

Fairbanks is home to the University of Alaska Fairbanks (UAF), which offers 162 degrees in more than 112 disciplines to its 10,400 students. Programs of study include developmental programs and certificate, associate, baccalaureate, and graduate/professional programs in the arts, sciences, career fields, and professions. It is Alaska's only doctoral-granting institution. UAF possesses unique strengths in both the physical and natural sciences and offers a broad array of engineering programs with particular emphasis on the northern environment. UAF is the state's center for the study of Alaska native cultures and languages, and also offers a northern studies program.

Libraries and Research Centers

The Fairbanks North Star Borough Public Library operates a main facility in the city, the Noel Wien Public Library, and a branch in the city of North Pole, which is a community of 1,600 residents 11 miles from Fairbanks. Mail library service is available. The library houses about 269,000 volumes, periodicals, tapes, and films. The Elmer E. Rasmuson Library at the University of Alaska Fairbanks houses more than 1.75 million items, making it the largest library in the State. Its holdings include books, periodicals, photography, manuscripts, films, oral histories, rare books, maps, microfiches, tapes, records, and prints. Its Alaska and Polar Regions collection is one of the world's finest.

The University of Alaska Fairbanks (UAF) ranks among the top 100 universities in the nation for its research and development activities. It also ranks 55th out of 200 universities in the amount of research money awarded by the National Science Foundation. In 2003-2004, UAF received $175 million for research activities, more than triple the amount received just six years earlier. Among UAF's many outstanding research schools and institutes are the School of Fisheries and Ocean Science, the Geophysical Institute, the Institute of Arctic Biology, the Polar Ice Coring Office, the Institute of Northern Engineering, and the Agriculture and Forestry Experiment Station. The Arctic Region Supercomputing Center, a collaboration between the UAF and the Department of Defense, supports computational research in science and engineering with emphasis on high latitudes and the arctic. A $32 million, 100,000-square-foot International Arctic Research Center provides office and research space for scientists from around the world. Research at the Center focuses on four major spheres: arctic ocean circulation, arctic atmosphere, permafrost/frozen soil, and arctic vegetation. The most recent addition to research efforts at UAF is the Office of Electronics Miniaturization (OEM), which replaces the former Center for Nanosensor Technology. The Office boasts a Class 10,000 Clean Room, equipped with Chip-Scale Packaging and related technologies. UAF is engaged in prototyping design development and production through a cooperative agreement with the Department of Defense's Defense MicroElectronics Activity (DMEA). Finally, the Poker Flats Research Range, located 33 miles north of Fairbanks, is a scientific rocket launching facility owned by the University of Alaska under contract to NASA. Poker Flat houses many scientific instruments for the study of the arctic atmosphere and ionosphere.

The Cold Climate Housing Research Center in Fairbanks researches and develops the latest building technologies and products for cold climate regions. Alaska's full range of climatic conditions and a cold season which lasts for six months or longer provides researchers ample time to conduct experiments and evaluations of housing performance. The Agricultural Research Service projects in the area focus on aquaculture, crop protection, plant diseases, and plant, microbial and insect genetics.

Public Library Information: Fairbanks North Star Borough Public Library and Regional Center, 1215 Cowles Street, Fairbanks, AK 99701; telephone (907)459-1020

Health Care

Fairbanks Memorial Hospital, the only civilian hospital in the region, serves 98,000 people in an area covering some 250,000 square miles. Operated by the Banner Health System, Fairbanks Memorial is a modern 142-bed facility that has been expanded and remodeled several times since its opening in 1972. Recent additions to the hospital include a newly expanded laboratory, Mental Health wing and Cancer Treatment Center. Memorial Hospital's sister hospital in Denali Center is a 110-bed facility.

Bassett Army Hospital at Fort Wainwright serves military personnel and retirees. Clinics in the area are the Tanana Valley Clinic, the Fairbanks Clinic, and a public health center.

Recreation

Sightseeing

Fairbanks is rich in frontier history. One of the main attractions is Pioneer Park, a 44-acre historic theme park on the banks of the Chena River. The Park features a Gold Rush Town with authentic historic buildings, a Native Village

with Indian and Eskimo architecture and artifacts, and the riverboat Nenana in drydock. The Kitty Hensley House, home of one of Fairbanks's early citizens, has been restored and is open to the public in Gold Rush Town. A narrow gauge railroad train meanders through the park, and a mini golf course, a mining operation, three museums, and an art gallery are also part of the fun. The Alaska Centennial Center for the Arts is located at Pioneer Park.

There are 20 National Historic Register buildings within the Fairbanks area, including Creamer's Dairy Wildlife Refuge; these sites are a living testament to the area's rich cultural history. Several churches and buildings in the city are of architectural interest. Muskoxen, caribou and reindeer can be seen at the Large Animal Research Station at the University of Alaska Fairbanks which offers tours of its facility from June through September.

Hot springs, gold dredges, gold camps, and engineering projects such as the first water system in permafrost ground and the Trans-Alaska Oil Pipeline are attractions in the outlying areas. The art of extracting gold from the frozen Alaskan ground is on display at Gold Dredge No. 8, which also has a dining hall and offers an opportunity to pan for gold. The Ester Gold Camp, a popular family attraction, features a 1900s gold camp site and town, a dining hall buffet dinner, a Saloon Show and a view of the Northern Lights set to music. The El Dorado Gold Mine offers two-hour guided tours through a permafrost tunnel, a walking tour of a mining camp, and a chance to pan for gold.

A recommended day trip is a visit to Denali National Park, 120 miles south of Fairbanks. Within its boundaries is North America's tallest mountain, Mt. McKinley (also known locally as Denali). Wildlife such as moose, grizzly bear, mountain sheep, and caribou can be seen in their natural habitat. During the summer months colorful carpets of wildflowers add to the beauty of the park.

The Georgeson Botanical Garden, on the University of Alaska Fairbanks campus, offers tours in the summer months. The sternwheeler Riverboat Discovery paddles the Chena River for a three-and-a-half hour cruise and makes stops to visit Iditarod kennels, a traditional Athabascan fish camp and an Old Chena Indian Village.

Fairbanks visitors can take advantage of one or more tour packages to explore the area's beauty, wildlife, and opportunities for outdoor fun. Choices for guided tours are plentiful and varied and can include tours by horseback, canoe, raft, boat, plane, car, snowmobile, dogsled, jet boat, or even hot air balloon. Day-long and multi-day trips are available to a number of destinations for individuals and groups.

The Aurora Borealis is one natural wonder that visitors shouldn't miss when visiting the area. Recommended viewing is from September to April, with February, March, September, and October as the very best months (the midnight sun makes viewing difficult in the summer months). There are a variety of options for viewing the Northern Lights, with special guided tours of the Aurora Circle and lodges catering to Aurora viewers.

Arts and Culture

As the cultural center of the Interior, Fairbanks is home to the Fairbanks Symphony Orchestra, the Arctic Chamber Orchestra, Fairbanks Art Association, Fairbanks Shakespeare Theatre, and the Fairbanks Drama Association & Fairbanks Children's Theatre. Musical comedy revues and light opera productions are staged by the Fairbanks Light Opera Theater, the Center Stage, and the Palace Saloon.

The city has several museums relating to the natural and cultural history of the area. The University of Alaska Museum of the North is one of the most frequently visited tourist attractions in the state and is the only natural and cultural museum in Alaska. Blue Babe, the Ice Age's only restored steppe bison mummy, Alaska's largest public display of gold and Alaskan native artifacts are on exhibit. Scheduled to open in September 2005 is an addition which will display the museum's art collection, and house office space and lab space for processing animals and performing DNA testing. Fairbanks Community Museum chronicles the history of Fairbanks from its founding in 1901 to the present with a focus on the Gold Rush era and mining. In the same building is the Dog Mushing Museum which exhibits sleds, clothing, harnesses, trophies, and cold weather expedition gear. Life-size ice sculptures are on view at the Fairbanks Ice Museum which preserves year-round some of the sculptures carved during the World Ice Art Championships held annually in March.

The Alaska Public Lands Information Center provides both exhibits and recreation information on state and federal land in Alaska for those planning a trip to the ''back country.'' Information on camping grounds, hiking trails, scenic drives, and fishing spots is available. Several art galleries are also located in Fairbanks, including the Alaska House Art Gallery and Tundra Walker Studio.

Festivals and Holidays

The North American Championship Preliminary Sled Dog Races are held in December and January. In February the Yukon Quest International Dog Sled Race is a 1,000-mile run on gold rush trails. The Tesoro Iron Dog Gold Rush Classic, also in February, is the world's longest snowmobile race. In February or early March the Ice Alaska/Winter Carnival showcases the World Ice Art Championships, an 11-day international ice carving competition. Folk, celtic, bluegrass, orchestral, and gospel music are all on stage at the Fairbanks Folk Festivals held in February and June. March is the month

for the Open North American Sled Dog Championships, which attracts top sprint mushers from the U.S., Canada, Europe, and Japan, as well as the Junior North American Sled Dog Championships. Native people from all over the state gather to share their dancing, singing, storytelling, and traditional arts and crafts at the Annual Festival of Native Arts.

June is a busy month, with the Midnight Sun Baseball Game during the summer solstice when the sun never sets and the Yukon 800, a marathon riverboat race. Music, theater, story telling, creative writing, visual arts, dance, and ice skating are on display at the Fairbanks Summer Arts Festival on the campus of the University of Alaska Fairbanks during the last two weeks in July. Also in July, Golden Days celebrates the rich gold-mining history of Fairbanks; a hairy chest, legs, and beard contest is one highlight of the five-day festival. In the World Eskimo-Indian Olympics, another July event, Native people from all over the Arctic compete in games of strength and endurance; among other highlights are storytelling and Native dances.

The Tanana Valley State Fair is held in August, followed by Oktoberfest. The Athabascan Old-Time Fiddling Festival in November celebrates a musical format that is a composite of French Canadian and Scottish-Arcadian styles fused with Native tunes. Fairbanks celebrates the Winter Solstice each weekend in December with Santa, live music, and family activities downtown.

Sports for the Spectator

The Fairbanks area supports a baseball team, the Alaska Goldpanners, college players from the lower 48 who play their games at Growden Field. The University of Alaska Fairbanks Nanooks basketball and ice hockey teams host games on the University of Alaska campus and in the Carlson Center in town.

Dog mushing is the official sport of the state of Alaska, and Fairbanks is the site of mushing competitions throughout the winter. Mushing demonstrations can be seen in summer, but serious racing requires cool temperatures and snow. The Fairbanks Curling Club hosts competitions with teams from throughout Alaska, Canada, and the United States. The Greater Fairbanks Racing Association sponsors summer stock and sprint car racing nearly every weekend starting Memorial Day weekend through Labor Day at the Mitchell Raceway. The Sundawgs Rugby Football Club plays rugby during the Golden Days festival in July. Fairbank's junior ice hockey team is the Ice Dogs, a North American Hockey League team.

Sports for the Participant

Running is a popular activity in Fairbanks. The Equinox Marathon, said to be the second most challenging marathon in the U.S., is a 26-mile race to the top of Ester Dome. The Midnight Sun Run is held in conjunction with the celebration of the summer solstice, and the Chena River 5K Run is held in May.

Many city and area parks offer facilities for a variety of year-round indoor and outdoor recreational activities. Among the most popular pursuits are downhill and cross-country skiing, fishing, canoeing, goldpanning, hiking, hockey, hunting, ice skating, jogging, nature walks, tennis, swimming, volleyball, and racquetball. Smooth paved trails along the Chena River are ideal for biking and rollerblading. Fairbanks boasts three golf courses including the northernmost golf course, where during the mid-summer, golfers can play golf 24 hours a day. Winter is a favorite time for swimming in nearby hot springs. A skate board park and volleyball courts are located at Growden Park. Birch Hill Park, a few minutes north of Fairbanks, is a 460-acre park with hiking and running trails, mountain biking, and bird watching in the summer.

Shopping and Dining

Fairbanks has a number of shopping malls and neighborhood stores. Specialty shops feature Alaska native arts and crafts and jewelry fashioned from ivory, jade, and hematite, as well as handmade fur garments. Visitors can watch the manufacture of Alaskan birch bowls at the Great Alaskan Bowl Company where they are also for sale. Santa Claus House, located 13 miles from Fairbanks in the city of North Pole, has become a landmark, drawing visitors from throughout the world to shop for Alaskan gifts, jewelry, and clothing. Local farmers and craft makers display their wares at the Farmers' Market, open Wednesdays and Saturdays from May through the end of summer next to the Tanana Valley Fair Grounds. The city's main commercial district extends along Airport Way, between University Ave. and Cushman St. where most of the fast-food chains and malls can be found. Many bars, restaurants and businesses that cater to the university crowd are located along University Ave. and College Rd.

Dozens of restaurants in Fairbanks provide a wide range of cuisine in casual and elegant settings. Area restaurants specialize in fish from inland waters to more casual fare including miners's stew served in the dining halls of the local gold mines. Visitors can also enjoy Japanese, Korean, Mongolian, and Mexican specialties. Salmon, halibut and cod are the specialties at the Alaska Salmon Bake, one of the more popular venues with its Palace Theater and Saloon in Gold Rush Town. Located in Pioneer Park, it features evening entertainment in the summer with its ''Golden Heart Revue.''

Visitor Information: Fairbanks Convention and Visitors Bureau, 550 First Avenue, Fairbanks, AK 99701-4790; telephone (907)456-5774; toll-free (800)327-5774; fax (907)452-4190

Convention Facilities

More than 12 hotels and more than 65 bed-and-breakfast properties in Fairbanks offer a combined total of 2,000 guest accommodations and a wide variety of meeting space. The largest meeting and exhibition facility is the Carlson Center, which features a 35,000-square-foot arena and several meeting rooms, for a combined total of 50,000 square feet of space that can accommodate more than 1,200 meeting participants, 200 trade show exhibits, or 4,000 people for a concert or sports event. The Alaska Centennial Center for the Arts at Pioneer Park houses a 384-seat theater, art gallery, exhibit areas, meeting rooms and all-purpose hall. Also at Pioneer Park is the Birch Hill Cross Country Ski Center which has a 2,400 square foot assembly room. The Chief Peter John Tribal Hall (capacity 750 people) and Mushers Hall are downtown banquet and meeting facilities. The University of Alaska Museum of the North and the Tanana Valley State Fair also provide many options for meeting spaces for any type of function.

Hotel properties with meeting and conference facilities include the Fairbanks Princess Riverside Lodge, Westmark Fairbanks Hotel and Conference Center, Wedgewood Resort, Pike's Waterfront Lodge, Regency Fairbanks Hotel, and Sophie Station Hotel. Chena Hot Springs Resort, located 56 miles outside of Fairbanks, offers meeting space that can accommodate more than 100 people.

Convention Information: Fairbanks Convention and Visitors Bureau, 550 First Avenue, Fairbanks, AK 99701; telephone (907)457-3282; toll-free (800) 327-5774, fax (907)452-4190; email info@explorefairbanks.com

Transportation

Approaching the City

The Fairbanks International Airport is served by Alaska Airlines, Alaska Central Express, Cargolux Airlines International and Lufthansa. Alaska Airlines has regularly scheduled daily flights to Anchorage and Seattle. Direct connections to major cities and international connections are made through Anchorage International Airport. Airport shuttle service into Fairbanks is available.

Principal routes into Fairbanks are the Alaska Highway, running southeast to northwest, which connects the city with the lower 48 states through Canada, and the George Parks Highway, leading south to Anchorage. Fairbanks is also connected with Anchorage via the Richardson Highway.

The Dalton Highway connects Fairbanks to Prudhoe Bay near the Arctic Ocean.

The Alaska Railroad, which links Fairbanks to Anchorage, Denali Park, and Seward on the Kenai Peninsula, has Fairbanks for its northern terminus.

Traveling in the City

Chartered bus tours operate throughout the tourist season in Fairbanks. The Metropolitan Area Commuter System (MACS) operates four bus routes and the Van Tran paratransit services. Alaska Cab provides taxi service in Fairbanks.

Communications

Newspapers and Magazines

The major daily newspaper in Fairbanks is the *Fairbanks Daily News-Miner,* published in the morning. The *Northstar Weekly* is distributed in Fairbanks, North Pole and surrounding communities. The University of Alaska Fairbanks publishes the *Sun Star Newspaper.*

Television and Radio

Five television stations broadcast in Fairbanks; cable is available. Seventeen AM and FM radio stations broadcast in the Fairbanks metropolitan area, providing a variety of music, news, and information programming.

Media Information: *Fairbanks Daily News-Miner,* 200 North Cushman St., Fairbanks, AK 99707; telephone (907)456-6661

Fairbanks Online

City of Fairbanks website. Available www.ci.fairbanks.ak .us

Fairbanks Convention and Visitors Bureau. Available www .explorefairbanks.com

Fairbanks Daily News-Miner. Available www.newsminer .com

Fairbanks Economic Development Corporation. Available www.investfairbanks.com

Fairbanks North Star Borough Home Page. Available www .co.fairbanks.ak.us

Fairbanks North Star Borough School District. Available www.northstar.k12.ak.us

Fairbanks North Star Public Library. Available www.co .fairbanks.ak.us

Greater Fairbanks Chamber of Commerce. Available www .fairbankschamber.org

State of Alaska. Available www.state.ak.us

University of Alaska Fairbanks. Available www.uaf.edu

Selected Bibliography

Anders, Joyce J., *Anders of Two Rivers* (Fairbanks, Alaska: Jenny M. Publishers, 1997)

Blunk, R. Glendon, *Yearning Wild: Exploring the Last Frontier and the Landscape of the Heart* (Montpelier, Vermont: Invisible Cities Press, 2002)

Cole, Dermot, *Amazing Pipeline Stories* (Epicenter Press, 1997)

Cole, Dermot, *Fairbanks: A Gold Rush Town that Beat the Odds* (Epicenter Press, 1999)

Fejes, Claire, *Cold Starry Night: An Alaskan Memoir* (Fairbanks, Alaska: Epicenter Press, 1996)

Juneau

The City in Brief

Founded: 1880, incorporated, 1970

Head Official: Mayor Bruce Botelho (NP) (since 2003)

City Population
  1980: 19,528
  1990: 26,751
  2000: 30,711
  2003 estimate: 31,187
  Percent change, 1990–2000: 14.8%
  U.S. rank in 1980: Not reported
  U.S. rank in 1990: 1,013th
  U.S. rank in 2000: 989th (State rank: 2nd)

Metropolitan Area Population (City is considered a Metropolitan Area)
  1980: 19,528
  1990: 26,751
  2000: 30,711
  Percent change, 1990–2000: 14.8%
  U.S. rank in 1990: Not reported
  U.S. rank in 2000: Not reported

Area: 3,255 square miles (2000; Borough)
Elevation: Ranges from sea level to 3,800 feet above sea level
Average Annual Temperature: 41.9° F
Average Annual Precipitation: 91.32 inches

Major Economic Sectors: Government, services
Unemployment rate: 7.2% (January 2005)
Per Capita Income: $26,719 (1999)

2002 FBI Crime Index Total: Not reported

Major Colleges and Universities: University of Alaska Southeast

Daily Newspaper: *Juneau Empire*

Introduction

The city and borough of Juneau is one of Alaska's most popular tourist destinations and one of the state's most important ports. Juneau is unique in that it is accessible only by air and sea. Annually, more than 800,000 cruise-ship passengers visit the city between May and September. Many are surprised to find a vibrant community with professional theater, museums, art galleries, and historical sites in a small-town atmosphere. The area has a temperate climate with weather on par with that of Seattle. Juneau had been one of the world's major gold mining areas until the 1940s when costs outstripped the value of the gold; however, the industry has had a resurgence with a significant project having gained approval in 2005. The city's economy relies heavily on the government workers who make up the majority of the work force, along with fishermen, loggers, and miners. Nearby Glacier Bay, Admiralty Island, and the Juneau Icefield offer spectacular scenery, and sightseeing flights are available year-round.

Geography and Climate

The city of Juneau is located on the mainland of southeastern Alaska's Panhandle on the narrow southeastern strip bordering the Canadian province of British Columbia, approximately 1,000 miles northwest of Seattle, Washington. Most of the city lies on the mainland of Alaska, although Douglas Island, which is connected by a bridge, is also part of Juneau. The Gastineau Channel separates the island from the main part of the city, which is surrounded by the Tongass National Forest. The city climbs the tree-lined slopes of Mount Roberts and Mount Juneau, which rise from the water's edge to more than 3,500 feet.

The city has a mild, rainy climate with a year-round ice-free harbor. The Pacific Ocean currents temper the weather, and average summer temperatures are in the 60s with many days reaching into the high 70s or low 80s. Juneau's winters are comparable to those of Minneapolis or Chicago.

Area: 3,255 square miles (Borough, 2000)

Elevation: Ranges from sea level to 3,800 feet

Average Temperatures: January, 23.0° F; July, 56.0° F; annual average, 41.9° F

Average Annual Precipitation: 91.32 inches

History

In the late 1800s when gold prospecting began in the Gastineau Channel region, the area was a fishing ground for local Tlingit Native Americans. A mining engineer from Sitka, George Pilz, offered a reward to any local native chief who could show him the site of gold-bearing ore. After Chief Kowee of the Auk Tlingit arrived in Sitka with ore samples from the Gastineau Channel, Pilz outfitted Joseph Juneau and Richard Harris for a trip to investigate the lode.

The prospectors reached the area in 1880, and although they found gold samples, they did not follow the gold to its source. After their return to Sitka, Pilz sent them out again. On the second trip Harris and Juneau climbed Snow Slide Gulch at the head of Gold Creek and observed the mother lode of Quartz Gulch, and Silver Bow Basin. They staked a 160-acre town site on the beach. By the next year more than 100 prospectors had arrived in the settlement, which was later named in honor of Joseph Juneau.

Within a few years, Juneau grew to a center for large-scale hard-rock mining, and tunnels and shafts wound through the surrounding hills. Two great mills were developed, the Alaska-Juneau at the south end of the city and the Alaska-Gastineau at Thane.

In May 1882 John Treadwell established the Alaska Mill & Mining Company with the construction of a five-stamp mill. The Treadwell Gold Mining Company produced more than $70 million of gold before it closed. Treadwell's production peaked in 1915, but a 1917 flooding of three of its mines after a cave-in spelled its demise. The Alaska-Gastineau closed in 1921 when operations became too expensive. The final big mill, Alaska-Juneau, folded in 1944 as a result of high prices and labor shortages due to World War II.

By the beginning of the twentieth century, Juneau had become a transportation and regional trading center. It assumed the title of Alaska's capital in 1906 following its transfer from Sitka. In 1931 the Federal and Territorial Building, now the State Capitol Building, was constructed. Juneau has remained the state capital despite attempts to move the capital elsewhere. In 2005 the city announced its desire to build a modern, $100 million facility to replace the aging Capitol Building. Today, government—local, state or federal—employs one out of every two workers and tourism is the largest private-sector employer in Juneau. A federally recognized Native American tribe lives within the Juneau community.

With its vast natural wonders, temperate climate, and position as the capital city, Juneau has the foundation for a long-term prosperous community as can be seen in its population growth since 1980. The Juneau Economic Development Council has programs in place to create positive business conditions for new and existing companies.

Historical Information: Juneau-Douglas City Museum, 155 S. Seward St., Juneau, AK 99801; telephone (907)586-3572; email mary_pat_wyatt@ci.juneau.ak.us

Population Profile

Metropolitan Area Residents (City is considered a Metropolitan Area)
1980: 19,528
1990: 26,751
2000: 30,711
Percent change, 1990–2000: 14.8%
U.S. rank in 1980: Not reported
U.S. rank in 1990: Not reported
U.S. rank in 2000: Not reported

City Residents
1980: 19,528
1990: 26,751
2000: 30,711
2003 estimate: 31,187
Percent change, 1990–2000: 14.8%
U.S. rank in 1980: Not reported
U.S. rank in 1990: 1,013th
U.S. rank in 2000: 989th (State rank: 2nd)

Density: 11.3 people per square mile (2000)

Racial and ethnic characteristics (2000)
   White: 22,969
   Black or African American: 248
   American Indian and Alaska Native: 3,496
   Asian: 1,438
   Native Hawaiian and Pacific Islander: 116
   Hispanic or Latino (may be of any race): 1,040
   Other: 323

Percent of residents born in state: 38.0% (2000)

Age characteristics (2000)
   Population under 5 years old: 2,003
   Population 5 to 9 years old: 2,339
   Population 10 to 14 years old: 2,541
   Population 15 to 19 years old: 2,321
   Population 20 to 24 years old: 1,686
   Population 25 to 34 years old: 4,286
   Population 35 to 44 years old: 5,781
   Population 45 to 54 years old: 5,514

   Population 55 to 59 years old: 1,456
   Population 60 to 64 years old: 916
   Population 65 to 74 years old: 1,084
   Population 75 to 84 years old: 615
   Population 85 years and older: 169
   Median age: 35.3 years

Births (2003)
   Total number: 400

Deaths (2000–2002)
   Total number: 428 (of which, 12 were infants under the age of 1 year)

Money income (1999)
   Per capita income: $26,719
   Median household income: $62,034
   Total households: 11,534

Number of households with income of . . .
   less than $10,000: 404
   $10,000 to $14,999: 407
   $15,000 to $24,999: 974
   $25,000 to $34,999: 1,111
   $35,000 to $49,999: 1,653
   $50,000 to $74,999: 2,525
   $75,000 to $99,999: 2,183
   $100,000 to $149,999: 1,625
   $150,000 to $199,999: 390
   $200,000 or more: 262

Percent of families below poverty level: 3.7% (29.2% of which were female householder families with related children under 5)

2002 FBI Crime Index Total: Not reported

Municipal Government

Juneau, a home-rule municipality, has a council-manager type of government formed via elections held every three years. In 1970 the city merged with the city of Douglas and other areas of the Juneau Borough to become the city and borough of Juneau. The Borough Assembly is comprised of the mayor and eight assembly members.

Head Official: Mayor Bruce Botelho (NP) (since 2003; current term expires 2006)

Total Number of City Employees: 1,536 (2004)

City Information: City and Borough of Juneau, 155 S. Seward St., Juneau, AK 99801; telephone (907)586-3300

Economy

Major Industries and Commercial Activity

Nearly half of Juneau's working population is employed by the federal, state, or local government. All state departments have offices in Juneau, including the Superior and District Courts. A large federal building houses the regional headquarters of several federal agencies. Those with the largest number of workers are the U.S. Forest Service, National Park Service, National Marine Fisheries Service, Bureau of Indian Affairs, U.S. Fish and Wildlife Service, U.S. Postal Service, and the U.S. Coast Guard. It is estimated that for each government worker, one private sector job is needed to supply the services required by the government workers.

Tourism is the largest private-sector employer. The number of non-Alaskan visitors to Juneau tops 800,000 each year, accounting for about half of the total Alaska visitor market. The majority of visitors travel between May 1 and October 1, though year-round travel is growing. During that time, the harbor is filled with cruise ships bringing tourists from the ''Lower 48'' and around the world.

Commercial fishing and fish processing are another important sector of the local economy. Salmon hatcheries and a cold storage facility operate in town, the latter processing two million pounds of salmon, halibut, black cod, and crab annually.

Transportation and trading are the other important sectors of the economy. Manufacturing jobs had been almost nonexistent but that area has become a focal point for government programs resulting in a growth spurt.

Kenneccott Greens Creek Mine, on Admiralty Island near the city, produces gold, silver, lead, and zinc, and is one of the largest silver mines in North America. In December 2004 an environmental impact study was completed allowing for the Kensington Gold Mine project to proceed. It is expected to create about 200 construction jobs for two years, then roughly 250 positions for its 10 to 15 years of operation.

The $900 million Regional Corporation Alaska Native Land Claims Settlement Act (ANCSA) was enacted in 1971 to help compensate the native Alaskans for the lands taken from them when the United States purchased the Alaskan Territory from Russia in 1867. Two of Alaska's 13 regional native Alaskan corporations are located near Juneau. Sealaska, the ANCSA regional corporation for Southeast Alaska that serves 17,500 Tlingit and Haida shareholders, has its headquarters in Juneau. Goldbelt Inc., the urban native village corporation, is also located near Juneau and

handles about 3,500 shareholders of primarily Alaska Native heritage. The two corporations are in the business of money management, producing timber, and studying diversification into the area of mineral rights. Juneau is also the home of Klukwan Forest Products, Inc., which holds 23,000 acres of forested land within the area's rainforest.

Items and goods produced: processed fish, ore, forest products

Incentive Programs—New and Existing Companies

Local programs—The Southeast Alaska Revolving Loan Fund (RLF), since its formation in 1997, has developed a capital pool of about $5 billion to assist area businesses in retaining and creating jobs. Entrepreneurs can go to the Business Assistance Center (BAC) for information, workshops, and a variety of other services.

State programs—The Governor's Office of International Trade provides assistance and information to firms interested in foreign trade and investment, organizes trade missions and promotions, and sponsors trade shows and seminars. The Office of Economic Development provides business assistance to new and existing Alaskan businesses and industry. Programs include business counseling, Made in Alaska, RAPIDS: Rural Alaska Project Identification and Delivery System, and the Alaska Economic Information System.

Job training programs—Business start up services are offered by the state of Alaska on a case-by-case basis.

Economic Development Information: Alaska Department of Community and Economic Development, Research & Analysis Section; telephone: (907)465-4508; fax (907)465-4506; email raweb@labor.state.ak.us. Juneau Economic Development Council, 612 W. Willoughby Ave., Ste. A, Juneau, AK 99801-1732; telephone (907)463-3662; fax (907)463-3929; email administrator@jedc.org

Commercial Shipping

The Juneau airport includes a paved 8,456-foot runway and a seaplane landing area. Marine facilities include a seaplane landing area at Juneau Harbor, two deep draft docks, five small boat harbors, and a state ferry terminal. The Alaska Marine Highway System and cargo barges provide year-round services. Juneau's docks are used primarily for the cruise ships bringing tourists to Juneau.

Labor Force and Employment Outlook

Because so many are employed in government, Juneau's workforce is better educated than is the statewide workforce and per capita income is higher. However, dependence on one industry leaves Juneau vulnerable to severe economic distress when government falters. Ongoing efforts are being made to diversify Juneau's economy. The overall labor force demonstrated significant increases in all major categories. Manufacturing and financial industries have shown great successes, and construction and mining continues to grow with the Kensington Gold Mine starting production. Employment in the service sector should remain strong. Tourism is vibrant, and there has been a change in the characteristics of the typical visitor to Alaska. Many of the new travelers are younger, more independent, and interested in family, adventure, and environment-related activities.

The following is a summary of data regarding the Southeast Region labor force as of 2003.

Size of nonagricultural labor force: 36,250

Number of workers employed in . . .
  construction and mining: 2,050
  manufacturing: 1,850
  trade, transportation, and utilities: 7,050
  information: 500
  financial activities: 1,250
  professional and business services: 1,400
  educational and health services: 3,450
  leisure and hospitality: 3,550
  other services: 1,150
  government: 13,650

Average monthly earnings of production workers employed in manufacturing: $2,611

Unemployment rate: 7.2% (January 2005)

Largest employment sectors
and employers (2003)   *Number of employees*
  Federal, state, and local government   17,105
  Southeast Alaska Regional Health
    Corp.   705

Cost of Living

The personal tax burden in Alaska is extremely low. Residents benefit from distributions from the Permanent Fund, a savings account established in 1976 by voters allowing residents to receive 50 percent of the state's royalty oil revenue. Senior citizens enjoy a $150,000 property tax exemption or a renter's rebate. The availability of vast natural resources insures utility costs somewhat lower than the national average. However, in Juneau, the overall costs are significantly higher than the U.S. average (about 30%).

2004 (3rd Quarter) ACCRA Average House Price: $390,000

2004 (3rd Quarter) ACCRA Cost of Living Index: 134.5
  (U.S. average = 100.0)

State income tax rate: None

State sales tax rate: None

Local income tax rate: None

Local sales tax rate: 5.0%

Property tax rate: varies; the highest mill level that will be levied in 2005 is 12.00. This includes the levy for general government, schools, fire, and debt service. Levy is per $1,000 of assessed valuation; assessment ratio = 100% for residential.

Economic Information: Alaska Department of Labor & Workforce Development, Research & Analysis Section, PO Box 25501, Juneau, AK 99802-5501; telephone (907)465-4500; fax (907)465-2101; email raweb@labor.state.ak.us

Education and Research

Elementary and Secondary Schools

Juneau's schools offer special programs for secondary school students, including the Project of Assisted Learning, an alternative approach; the Entrepreneurship Program, with an emphasis on vocational education; and special education programs for children with special needs. Due to Juneau's geographic location, the schools also offer programs focusing on the sea.

The following is a summary of data regarding Juneau's public schools as of the 2003–2004 school year.

Total enrollment: 5,475

Number of facilities
  elementary schools: 6
  junior high/middle schools: 2
  senior high schools: 1

Student/teacher ratio: 17.5:1

Teacher salaries
  minimum: $34,606
  maximum: $67,305

Funding per pupil: $6,497

Public Schools Information: Juneau School District, 10014 Crazy Horse Dr., Juneau, AK 99801; telephone (907)463-1700

Colleges and Universities

Enrolling 700 full-time and 2,000 part-time students, the University of Alaska Southeast's (UAS) Juneau location on the shores of the Inside Passage serves as the main campus, with two other administrative units of the University of Alaska statewide system (in Ketchikan and Sitka), and focuses on general liberal arts education. The university proper offers certificate, associate of arts, associate of applied science, baccalaureate, professional, and master's degree programs in the applied areas of business, fisheries, liberal arts, science, public administration, and teacher education. The university's two-year and certificate program in vocational and technical education supplies employees for local business and industry.

Libraries and Research Centers

The 18,000 square foot Juneau Public Library has a unique design built upon a parking garage in a beautiful waterfront location, with holdings of about 70,000 volumes. In March 2005 it began offering the Alaska Library Network Catalog (ALNCAT) which provides access to all state libraries' collections. The Juneau Public Library and its two branches are part of the Capital City Libraries consortium, a cooperative catalog and circulation system shared with the Alaska State Library since 1989, the University of Alaska Southeast Egan Library, the Juneau-Douglas High School Library, and the Alyeska Central School Library. Holders of library cards at one of these libraries may borrow from any of the others and have access to library resources from home.

Other libraries in the city include the Alaska State Libraries, Archives & Museums, which encompass legislative information, policy issues and Alaskan history; the U.S. Bureau of Mines Library (with a collection of more than 20,000 publications); the U.S. Forest Service Library; the Alaska Historical Library; and other state level governmental libraries.

Public Library Information: Juneau Public Libraries, 292 Marine Way, Juneau, AK 99801; telephone (907)586-5249

Health Care

Juneau is served by Bartlett Memorial Hospital, a city-owned facility that began an extensive $40 million expansion project in 2005. Bartlett Memorial also operates the Juneau Recovery Hospital, a medical model facility for the detoxification and rehabilitation of persons with alcohol or other drug dependencies. Other Juneau health facilities are the Juneau Alliance for Mental Health, Inc. (JAMHI), and the Teen Health Clinic.

Recreation

Sightseeing

A good place for visitors to start exploring Juneau is at the Davis Log Cabin Visitor Center, which offers guides and maps. The Downtown Historic District of the city contains many buildings dating back to 1880 and has wider sidewalks reminiscent of the old boardwalks. The Governor's Mansion, built in 1912, is not open to the public on a regular basis but tours can be arranged by contacting the governor's office. Alaska's State Capitol Building, with columns fashioned from a quarry on Prince of Wales Island, houses both the governor's office and state legislative offices and is open for tours. From January through May visitors may watch floor sessions from the galleries. The House of Wickersham, built in 1898 and the former home of famous local judge, James Wickersham (1837–1939), contains historic memorabilia as well as a genuine Chickering grand piano circa late 1800s, and is listed on the National Register of Historic Places.

The Juneau-Douglas City Museum includes various exhibits related to the areas's rich history and provides educational and public programs while concentrating on the city's mining history. Tours are available of the St. Nicholas Orthodox Church, the oldest original Russian Orthodox church in the state, which was founded in 1893. The Shrine of St. Therese, a chapel located on an island north of Juneau that is connected to the city by a narrow path, has stations of the cross on a trail circumnavigating the chapel in the surrounding woods and can be visited year-round.

The Last Chance Basin Historic District, usually referred to as the Jualpa Mining Camp, features many old mine buildings and attractions for visitors such as gold panning and, in summer, an outdoor salmon bake. A 5,000-gallon aquarium full of local sea life is the highlight of the Macaulay Salmon Hatchery, which is located three miles from downtown. Green Angel Gardens is a botanical facility featuring a variety of local plants and a salmon stream located near a low, active volcano.

Nature is the star at Juneau, and the walk-up Mendenhall Glacier, located 13 miles from downtown, is a must-see experience. It features a visitor center, built in 1962, which describes the progression of the glacier and the icecap from which it descends; the visitor center also features a movie and self-guided walking tour map. The 1,500-square-mile Juneau Icefield, the birthplace of the Mendenhall Glacier and 37 others, is located just over the mountains behind the city and is the fifth largest in North America. Light plane charters and helicopters offer an up-close tour.

Many visitors enjoy taking walking tours of Juneau's four local harbors, where fishing boat captains are usually amenable to discussing the day's catch. Whalewatching and wildlife viewing charter boat tours are a popular visitor attraction; a variety of companies offer tours from in or around Juneau, and many guarantee sightings.

Arts and Culture

The Alaska State Museum, established in 1900 when the state was a territory, offers more than 27,000 fine historical, cultural, and artistic collections under one roof. Juneau's gold rush history is captured at the Juneau-Douglas City Museum, which also contains a "Back to the Past" hands-on room for children, and a large relief map of Juneau's topography. Juneau has a very active artists' community, and there are many works of art located in public areas throughout downtown, including sculptures and totem poles.

Alaska's only professional theater company, Perseverance Theatre of Juneau, presents a variety of classic, comedic, and dramatic plays during its fall-winter-spring season that typically draws 20,000 annually. The Naa Kahidi Theater, supported by the Sealaska Heritage Foundation, performs ancient Tlingit legends via storytelling for special events. The Gold Nugget Revue presents comedic historical adventures of Juneau's history, along with cancan dancers and other entertainment.

Festivals and Holidays

April is the time for the annual Alaska Folk Festival, which has been running since the mid-1970s. Music lovers assemble for the 10-day Juneau Jazz & Classics Festival in May. August's Golden North Salmon Derby, a tradition since 1947, offers big prizes, including scholarships, for catching big fish.

Sports for the Participant

Juneau has five mountain peaks within reasonable day-trip distances, affording many hiking and climbing opportunities. Hiking trails lead from downtown to overlooks on 3,576-foot Mt. Juneau, 3,819-foot Mt. Roberts, and 3,337-foot Mt. Bradley (also known as Mt. Jumbo). The Mt. Roberts tramway travels from Juneau's waterfront to an elevation of nearly 2,000 feet. Guided tours, a restaurant, and theater are available at the upper terminal. The Juneau visitor's center offers free guides to more than two dozen trails to glaciers and historic gold mining ruins.

Fishing, sailing, kayaking, and river rafting are available on the protected waters of the Inside Passage. In summers, operators offer gentle river rafting, salmon watching, and gold panning. Picnics, camping, fishing, and beachcombing are popular on the area's beaches.

Mendenhall is the only golf course in Southeast Alaska, a par-three, nine-hole course built on private land behind the airport and only 10 miles from downtown. Winter downhill

skiing and snowboarding are offered at Eaglecrest, 12 miles from the city's downtown, with alpine runs, Nordic trails, and a vertical drop of 1,400 feet. Helicopter ski packages are available from late November through early April.

Juneau also has a racquet club, indoor rock-climbing, several aerobic studios, yoga classes, and local Parks and Recreation Department seasonal sports programs that welcome visitors.

Shopping and Dining

Visitors will find galleries, shops, and restaurants throughout the downtown Juneau area. Specialty shops and gift shops offer hand-crafted work by local artists. Nugget Mall, the largest shopping destination, is within walking distance of the airport; its more than 35 stores feature Alaskan gifts and clothing and the mall has a visitor information center. Senate Shopping Mall houses eight eclectic shops from Native art to flyfishing supplies. Merchant's Wharf, an office and shop complex, is located at harborside. Gift shops and taverns line South Franklin Street. The Emporium Mall contains specialty shops and stores, as well as the Heritage Coffee Co., a sandwich and coffee shop on the main floor. Fantastic mountain views and a traditional steak and seafood menu are signatures of the historic Hangar on the Wharf restaurant.

The state's most famous bar, the lively Red Dog Saloon, provides local pictorial history, music, and excitement, especially when cruise ships are in port.

Visitor Information: Juneau Convention and Visitors Bureau, One Sealaska Plz., Ste. 305, Juneau, AK 99801; telephone (907)586-1737; toll-free (800)587-2201; fax (907)586-1449; email info@traveljuneau.com

Convention Facilities

Centennial Hall Convention Center, just across the street from the waterfront, is three blocks away from the heart of Juneau's downtown with its shops and restaurants. Built in 1983, Centennial Hall has 7 meeting rooms ranging from 300 square feet to an 11,275-square-foot, column-free ballroom. The ballroom can be divided into three separate rooms, each with state-of-the-art light and sound systems. Centennial Hall also has two lobbies that provide an additional 4,200 square feet for receptions, displays, and relaxation. Juneau also offers meeting spaces in majestic settings atop Mt. Roberts, on the banks of the Gastineau Channel, or overlooking Auke Lake.

Convention Information: Juneau Convention and Visitors Bureau, One Sealaska Plz., Ste. 305, Juneau, AK 99801; telephone (907)586-1737; toll-free (800)587-2201; fax (907)586-1449; email info@traveljuneau.com

Transportation

Approaching the City

Juneau International Airport covers 80,000 square feet of land and is serviced daily by Alaska Airlines. The city is about a two-hour flight north from Seattle, or approximately a 90-minute flight southeast from Anchorage. In 2005 a study was in process to determine the specific renovations needed to modernize the aging facility. Juneau has no direct road and rail links. The Alaska Marine Highway ferry system provides car and passenger connections into Juneau from other southeast communities, as well as Bellingham, Washington (a two and one-half day trip) and Prince Rupert, British Columbia (a 24-hour trip). The ferries have staterooms, observation decks, cocktail lounges, and heated solariums. A variety of regional air taxi services and chartered flights are available to nearby attractions and smaller towns. Barge lines serve Juneau from Seattle several times per week. Power boats, sailboats, and kayaks are also available to rent for trips to the Inside Passage.

Traveling in the City

Egan Drive is one of the major streets in Juneau, running from one end of town to the other and following the shoreline of the Gastineau Channel. The downtown area is divided into a grid with Main Street crossing the numbered streets and passing the Capitol building and other major sites. Bus service is provided by the Capitol Transit line with 16 buses in its fleet. Buses and vans meet every ferry from mid-April to the end of September, providing inexpensive service to downtown and the airport. Local air taxi operators fly both wheel and float planes.

Communications

Newspapers and Magazines

Juneau Empire is the city's daily newspaper and *Inside Passage,* the official newspaper of the Catholic Diocese of Juneau, is produced biweekly from September through May and monthly from June to August.

Television and Radio

ABC and PBS television stations are based in Juneau. Cable television is available, and there are five AM and FM radio stations broadcasting news, adult contemporary music, public radio, and album-oriented rock.

Media Information: Juneau Empire, Morris Communications Corp., 3100 Channel Dr., Juneau, AK 99801; telephone (907)586-3740; (907)586-9097

Juneau Online

Alaska Communications Systems. Available www.acs alaska.com

Alaska Department of Labor & Workforce Development, Research & Analysis Section. Available almis.labor.state.ak .us

Alaska State Library. Available www.library.state.ak.us

Alaska State Museum. Available www.museums.state.ak .us/asmhome.html

City of Juneau Home Page. Available www.juneau.org

Juneau Borough Schools. Available www.jsd.k12.ak.us

Juneau Chamber of Commerce. Available www.juneau chamber.com

Juneau Convention and Visitors Bureau. Available www .traveljuneau.com or www.juneau.com

Juneau Economic Development Council. Available www .jedc.org

Juneau Empire. Available www.juneauempire.com

Juneau Public Library. Available www.juneau.org/library/ index.php

State of Alaska. Available www.state.ak.us

Selected Bibliography

Alaska Natural History Association. *Juneau Trails: Guide to the Trails of Juneau, Alaska,* telephone Forest Service Information Center at (907)586-8751

Discover Southeast Alaska with Pack and Paddle, published by The Mountaineers of Seattle, telephone (800)284-8554

Raban, Jonathan. *Passage to Juneau: A Sea and Its Meanings* (New York: Pantheon Books, 1999)

ARIZONA

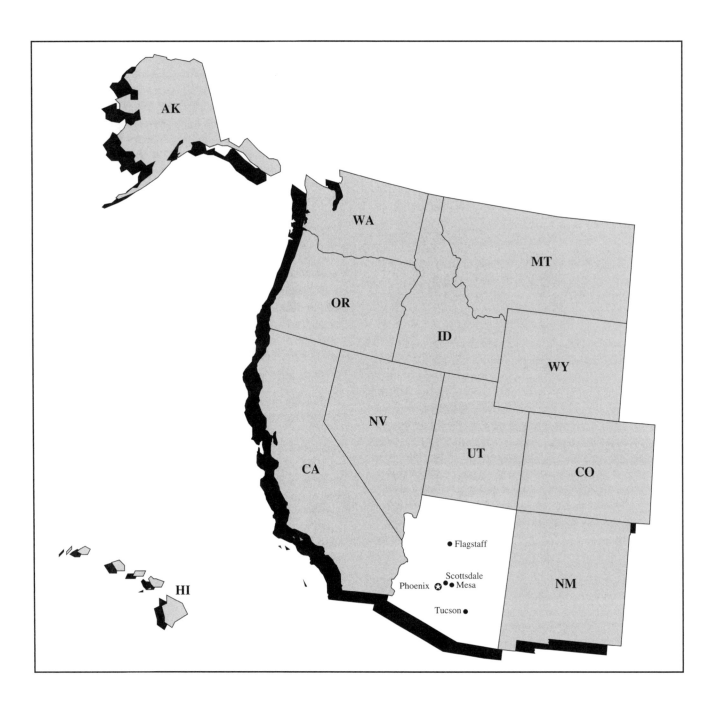

The State in Brief

Nickname: Grand Canyon State
Motto: *Ditat Deus* (God enriches)

Flower: Blossom of the saguaro cactus
Bird: Cactus wren

Area: 113,635 square miles (2000; U.S. rank: 6th)
Elevation: Ranges from 100 feet to 12,670 feet above sea level
Climate: Dry and sunny, but heavy snows in the high central area

Admitted to Union: February 14, 1912
Capital: Phoenix
Head Official: Governor Janet Napolitano (D) (until 2007)

Population
    1980: 2,718,000
    1990: 3,750,000
    2000: 5,130,632
    2004 estimate: 5,743,834
    Percent change, 1990–2000: 40.0%
    U.S. rank in 2004: 18th
    Percent of residents born in state: 34.7% (2000)
    Density: 45.2 people per square mile (2000)
    2002 FBI Crime Index Total: 348,467

Racial and Ethnic Characteristics (2000)
    White: 3,873,611
Black or African American: 158,873
American Indian and Alaska Native: 255,879
Asian: 92,236
Native Hawaiian and Pacific Islander: 6,733
Hispanic or Latino (may be of any race): 1,295,617
Other: 596,774

Age Characteristics (2000)
    Population under 5 years old: 382,386
    Population 5 to 19 years old: 1,135,802
    Percent of population 65 years and over: 13.0%
    Median age: 34.2 years (2000)

Vital Statistics
    Total number of births (2003): 90,931
    Total number of deaths (2003): 43,346 (infant deaths, 591)
    AIDS cases reported through 2003: 4,127

Economy
    Major industries: Services, trade, manufacturing, agriculture
    Unemployment rate: 4.2% (January 2005)
    Per capita income: $26,931 (2003; U.S. rank: 39th)
    Median household income: $42,062 (3-year average, 2001-2003)
    Percentage of persons below poverty level: 13.9% (3-year average, 2001-2003)
    Income tax rate: ranges from 2.87% to 5.04%
    Sales tax rate: 5.6% (food and prescription drugs are exempt)

Flagstaff

The City in Brief

Founded: 1881

Head Official: Mayor Joseph Donaldson (R) (since 2000)

City Population
   1980: 34,743
   1990: 45,857
   2000: 52,894
   2003 estimate: 61,030
   Percent change, 1990–2000: 13.3%
   U.S. rank in 1980: 676th
   U.S. rank in 1990: 543rd (State rank: 10th)
   U.S. rank in 2000: 673rd (State rank: 13th)

Metropolitan Area Population
   1990: 101,760
   2000: 122,366

Percent change, 1990–2000: 20.2%
U.S. rank in 1990: Not reported
U.S. rank in 2000: 237th

Area: 63.58 square miles (2000)
Elevation: 6,899 feet above sea level
Average Annual Temperature: 45.8° F
Average Annual Precipitation: 21.3 inches of rain
Major Economic Sectors: government, trade, manufacturing, research and development, services (especially tourism)
Unemployment Rate: 5.4% (January 2005)
Per Capita Income: $18,637 (1999)

2002 FBI Crime Index Total: 5,597

Major Colleges and Universities: Northern Arizona University, Coconino County Community College

Daily Newspaper: *Arizona Daily Sun*

Introduction

Located along the fabled American highway, Route 66, Flagstaff is the largest city and regional center in northern Arizona. Known as "the Gateway to the Grand Canyon," it is the county seat for Coconino County, the second largest in the nation, with 12 million acres. At 7,000 feet, Flagstaff is one of the highest cities in the United States. This attractive community sits at the base of the San Francisco Peaks, Arizona's highest point at 12,633 feet. There are many tales surrounding how the city got its name. A popular one holds that a group from Boston stripped a pine tree on the Fourth of July and placed a flag atop it. Flagstaff boasts a refurbished downtown and a top-rate museum, and its colony of college students make for a lively atmosphere.

Geography and Climate

Flagstaff is located 146 miles due north of Phoenix, 150 miles west of Albuquerque, and 525 miles east of Los Angeles.

Flagstaff enjoys a four-season climate. Because of its high elevation, the city has cool summers in which air conditioners are mostly unnecessary, not the desert conditions one might expect. The altitude and low humidity result in clean air and relatively mild weather year round. Occasional late-afternoon thunder showers are common from July through September, and snow usually first occurs in mid-October, and is heaviest December through March. The snow, which averages just under 100 inches per year, generally melts off rather quickly. The city experiences about 300 days of sunshine annually.

Area: 63.58 square miles (2000)

Elevation: 6,899 feet above sea level

Average Temperatures: January, 29.7° F; July, 66.1° F; annual average, 45.8° F

Annual Average Precipitation: 21.3 inches

History

Local Springs and Railroad Draw Settlers

It is said that it is the springs that first drew people to the Flagstaff area of dry, northern Arizona. The Sinagua, Anasazi, and Cohonino tribes were the first to settle there. Ruins of the pueblos and cliff dwellings belonging to the Navaho nation and Hopi tribes can still be found in the forests and lands surrounding present-day Flagstaff. A mountain man named Antoine Leroux knew the location of a source of water at the base of the San Francisco Peaks, and in 1876 a group of New Englanders left from Boston in search of the excellent farm land that they had heard about in highly exaggerated stories. They started a settlement in present-day Leroux Springs later in the year. According to legend, it was this group who placed a flag on top of a denuded pine tree, celebrating the Centennial of the Declaration of Independence, and thus gave the city the name by which it has been known ever since.

In 1882, the arrival in Flagstaff of the Atlantic and Pacific Railroad started a building boom. The site of what is today downtown Flagstaff was selected because the railroad wanted to build its new depot on flat land. The brick-fronted building that merchant P.J. Brennan erected for a new store still exists, now serving as a popular saloon and pool hall. Shortly after the arrival of the railroad, a sawmill began operations to accommodate the railroad's need for wooden ties. The new sawmill provided jobs for more than 250 people. Wood was easily attainable, as the city is near the world's largest forest of ponderosa pines.

For more than half a century, beginning in the 1880s, miles of spur rail line extended in all directions from the city. The men who engaged in the sawmill industry developed their own culture. Author Rose Houk describes "logger lingo" in which "coffee was referred to by its brand name, Arbuckle; pancakes were 'blankets;' [and] biscuits were 'doorknobs.'"

Sheep ranching got started in the mid-1880s and became big business in Flagstaff. Many of the sheep ranchers were of Basque or Spanish heritage. At the same time, cattle raising was begun by a group of Mormons at Leroux Spring.

City Becomes Observatory Site

In 1894, Andrew E. Douglass of Boston chose Flagstaff as the site for an astronomical observatory. Douglass placed the Lowell Observatory there in part because of the clear skies that good telescope viewing requires. During that same year a reform school was built, which was later to serve as the first building of what is now Northern Arizona University. In 1930 astronomer V.M. Slipher discovered the planet Pluto at the observatory. Lowell Observatory has stayed in the forefront of science, notably with its research in the area of bodies within the solar system such as satellites (moons), near-Earth asteroids, and comets.

Wildland-Urban Interface

In June and July 2002 the catastrophic Rodeo-Chediski fire grabbed national attention as the worst fire in Arizona history. Affecting Coconino County and its contiguous neighbors Navajo, Apache, and Gila Counties, the fire burned approximately 468,000 acres, the bulk of which was Ft. Apache Indian Reservation and national forest land; destroyed almost 500 homes; and cost $43 million to quell. More than $34 million in federal disaster aid was directed to the area. Flagstaff itself was not directly affected because of city leaders' and civic groups' proactive work in land use planning and response training.

In the past decade, some of Flagstaff's citizens became concerned about increasing development, mostly due to tourism, and preserving the very environment that makes the area special. Plans were developed to ensure a balance between economic opportunity and growth limits. Today, the city seems to have met and exceeded this goal. Mayor Joe Donaldson sums it up: "Flagstaff is a community raved about in many magazines as the place to invest, develop, vacation and just plain enjoy. Flagstaff prides itself in the miles of internal majestic scenic trails, multi modal transportation opportunities. . . . The community boasts of its efforts in achieving sustainable economic strength while preserving its pristine environment through community activism, emulated quality of life ordinances and resolutions driven through extensive community driven processes. Flagstaff is not just a place. It is a way of life where people become one with their environment."

Historical Information: The Historical Society, Northern Arizona University, Cline Library, PO Box 6022, Flagstaff, AZ 86011-6022; telephone (520)523-6802

Population Profile

Metropolitan Area Residents
1990: 101,760
2000: 122,366
Percent change, 1990–2000: 20.2%
U.S. rank in 1990: Not reported
U.S. rank in 2000: 237th

City Residents
1980: 34,743
1990: 45,857
2000: 52,894
2003 estimate: 61,030
Percent change, 1990–2000: 13.3
U.S. rank in 1980: 676th
U.S. rank in 1990: 543rd (State rank: 10th)
U.S. rank in 2000: 673rd (State rank: 13th)

Density: 831.9 people per square mile (2000)

Racial and ethnic characteristics (2000)
   White: 41,214
   Black or African American: 927
   American Indian and Alaska Native: 4,210
   Asian: 660
   Native Hawaiian or Pacific Islander: 65
   Hispanic or Latino (may be of any race): 8,500
   Other: 3,201

Percent of residents born in state: 41.6% (2000)

Age characteristics (2000)
   Population under 5 years old: 3,546
   Population 5 to 9 years old: 3,410
   Population 10 to 14 years old: 3,599
   Population 15 to 19 years old: 4,762
   Population 20 to 24 years old: 9,004
   Population 25 to 34 years old: 8,654
   Population 35 to 44 years old: 7,457
   Population 45 to 54 years old: 6,433
   Population 55 to 59 years old: 1,876
   Population 60 to 64 years old: 1,327
   Population 65 to 74 years old: 1,658
   Population 75 to 84 years old: 909
   Population 85 years and older: 259
   Median age: 26.8 years

Births (2000)
   Total number: 1,031

Deaths (2000)
   Total number: 253

Money income (1999)
   Per capita income: $18,637
   Median household income: $37,146
   Total households: 19,355

Number of households with income of . . .
   less than $10,000: 2,035
   $10,000 to $14,999: 1,335
   $15,000 to $24,999: 2,866
   $25,000 to $34,999: 2,789
   $35,000 to $49,999: 3,258
   $50,000 to $74,999: 3,360
   $75,000 to $99,999: 1,793
   $100,000 to $149,999: 1,279
   $150,000 to $199,999: 343
   $200,000 or more: 297

Percent of families below poverty level: 10.6% (49.0% of which were female householder families with related children under 5 years)

2002 FBI Crime Index Total: 5,597

Municipal Government

Flagstaff has a council/manager form of government with a mayor and six council members elected at large. Mayoral elections are held every two years; council members serve four years, and elections are staggered every two years.

Head Official: Mayor Joseph Donaldson (R) (since 2000; current term expires 2006)

Total Number of City Employees: 678 permanent, 271 temporary or seasonal (2005)

City Information: City of Flagstaff, 211 W. Aspen, Flagstaff, AZ 86001; telephone (520)774-5281

Economy

Major Industries and Commercial Activity

New scientific and high tech research and development industries have located to Flagstaff, broadening the economic base of tourism, government, education, and transportation, which replaced the lumber, railroad, and ranching eras.

Research activities are important to the city's economy. The most well-known facility, Lowell Observatory, is currently celebrating the 75th anniversary of the discovery of Pluto, and has done pioneering work in observations of near-Earth phenomena such as asteroids, comets, and belt systems; and in the field of interferometric studies, in which a distributed network of small telescopes together create images of celestial bodies with much higher resolutions than any other single telescope can produce.

Items and goods produced: dog and cat food; surgical/medical instruments and apparatus; wind generators; circuit boards; packaging products; recycled paper products for commercial use

Incentive Programs—New and Existing Companies

Most programs in Arizona are offered at the state level. The Greater Flagstaff Economic Council is a public/private agency that serves the city, county, Chamber of Commerce, and local businesses.

Local programs—The city offers an Infrastructure Assistance Incentive Fund with up to $100,000 available per economic development project.

State programs—Flagstaff businesses in recently expanded Enterprise Zone areas may receive direct state income tax credits based on the number of net new employees hired. Any qualified position is eligible if the position is a full-time permanent job, if the employer pays an hourly wage of above $7.55 an hour (raised from $5.77 in 1997); and if the employer provides health insurance and pays at least 50 percent of the insurance cost. If at least 35 percent of new employees live in any Enterprise Zone areas, then all new net employees qualify for eligibility. Any unused state income tax credits may be carried forward for up to five taxable years, providing the business remains in the Enterprise Zone. Other Enterprise Zone incentives include tax breaks for companies that make more than a $1 million investment and retain a new hire for more than three years. Other programs give tax credits on the cost of installing recycling equipment, exemptions for contractors and vendors of solar energy devices, for pollution control, purchase of construction materials, and research and development investment. State lottery proceeds provide fixed-asset loans to companies for expansion, relocation, and consolidation.

Job training programs—The Flagstaff Job Service Center gives aid to employers in advertising openings, evaluating applicants, and immigration certification. The state of Arizona offers matching funds of up to 75 percent to businesses for the training of workers for new jobs in the state. Through the new federal Workforce Investment Act (WIA), formerly Job Training Partnership Act, employers may receive up to 50 percent of their wages back during initial training periods. Customized training programs are also available.

The Small Business Development Center is jointly funded by the U.S. Small Business Administration and Coconino County Community College. This one-stop center offers free one-on-one counseling, training, and technical assistance in all aspects of small business management.

Development Projects

Downtown Flagstaff completed a major $7 million project upgrading its commercial area surrounding the Visitors Center in the 1990's. Flagstaff 2020 Vision Project began then, when some citizens began to question whether increasing development was compatible with preservation of what made the area special. The plan laid out a five year plan to balance economic opportunity with growth limits, and was replaced in 2002 with the Regional Growth and Transportation Plan, which governs land use, transportation, open space, and trail systems. Another development project in the works is dependant upon pending federal legislation, which will authorize the procurement of 1,100 acres surrounding the airport for business park, light industrial, residential development, runway expansion, and municipal uses.

In 2003, the Lowell Observatory and Discovery Communications announced a cooperative effort on a $30 million telescope that will bring unprecedented wide range views and deep imaging surveys of the night skies. The Discovery Channel Telescope's unique design will allow it to switch from extremely wide-field focus to much more detailed spectroscopy, infrared imaging and other applications. In addition to significantly advancing capacity for research, the telescope will also be used for real-time worldwide broadcasting and for science education programs for the public. The expected completion date for the telescope is 2009.

Commercial Shipping

Air cargo carriers flying direct from Flagstaff Pulliam Airport are Federal Express and United Parcel Service. The city has ten motor freight carriers. The one-day truck radius extends to Salt Lake City, San Francisco, Albuquerque, El Paso, Los Angeles, and parts of Mexico. Flagstaff is served by Burlington Northern and Santa Fe Railways.

Labor Force and Employment Outlook

Northern Arizona, which includes Flagstaff, Sedona, and Payson, has experienced a massive influx of tourists and retirees in recent years. After concerns were voiced by residents about the continued development and its impact on the environment, developers and environmentalists are working together to achieve a balance between economy and landscape preservation. Government is one of the largest employment sectors in Flagstaff. Tourism, and the service and construction industries in concert, create employment opportunities as well.

The following is a summary of data regarding the Coconino County labor force, 2004 annual averages:

Size of nonagricultural labor force: 60,000

Number of workers employed in . . .
  construction and mining: 3,400
  manufacturing: 3,100
  trade, transportation, and utilities: 9,200
  information: 400
  financial activities: 1,600
  professional and business services: 3,300
  educational and health services: 6,700
  leisure and hospitality: 11,800
  other services: 1,800
  government: 18,400

Average hourly earning of production workers employed in manufacturing: $16.56

Unemployment rate: 5.4% (January 2005)

Largest employers:	*Number of employees*
Northern Arizona University	3,393
Flagstaff Medical Center	1,999
Flagstaff Unified School District	1,700
W.L. Gore & Associates	1,300
Coconino County	1,075
City of Flagstaff	948
Grand Canyon Railway	400
Walgreens Distribution Center	400
Coconino Community College	400
SCA Tissue	279
Pepsi Cola Bottling Plant	250

Cost of Living

Housing costs in Flagstaff run somewhat higher than the national average. The typical rent for a two-bedroom apartment is about $850 per month. Food and health care also run a bit higher than the nation as a whole.

The following is a summary of data regarding several key cost of living factor in the Flagstaff area.

2004 (3rd Quarter) ACCRA Average House price: $336,338

2004 (3rd Quarter) ACCRA Cost of Living Index: 111.5 (U.S. average = 100.0)

State income tax rate: Ranges from 2.87% to 5.04%

State sales tax rate: 5.60%

Local income tax rate: none

Local sales tax rate: 1.51% city; .80% county

Property tax rate: $9.89 per $100 of assessed value (2003)

Economic Information: Flagstaff Chamber of Commerce, 101 W. Route 66, Flagstaff, AZ 86001-5598; telephone (520)774-4505. Greater Flagstaff Economic Council, S. Milton Road, Flagstaff, AZ 86001; telephone (520)779-7658; toll-free (800)595-7658; fax (520)556-0940

Education and Research

Elementary and Secondary Schools

The Flagstaff Unified School District is widely recognized as one of the finest in the Southwest. It offers a wide range of programs to meet the needs of students with diverse backgrounds, interests, and abilities. Through use of nontraditional approaches, Project New Start helps students on the verge of dropping out, and the Teen Parent Program assists young mothers to continue their education while pregnant and during the months following childbirth. Flagstaff was the first school system in the U.S. to implement drug-and-alcohol prevention programs in both its elementary and secondary schools. The district also participates in Communities in Schools, which provides families with access to a range of social services through the schools. Other programs include artists-in-residence, after-school classes for high school credit, Suzuki violin program, parenting programs, bilingual education, and magnet and alternative programs, among others.

The following is a summary of data regarding the Flagstaff Unified School District as of the 2003-2004 school year.

Total Enrollment: 11,433

Number of facilities
  elementary schools: 9
  middle schools: 2
  high schools: 3
  other: 2 alternative schools and 5 magnet schools

Student teacher ratio: elementary, 23:1; middle schools, 24:1; high schools, 32:1 (2005)

Teacher salaries (2003-2004)
  minimum: $28,280
  maximum: $54,000

Funding per pupil: $6,000 including capital

Colleges and Universities

Northern Arizona University (NAU) has more than 13,000 undergraduate and 5,000 graduate students and offers small classes, respected and accessible faculty and advisers, comprehensive libraries, computer labs, research opportunities, career placement, cultural programs and events, recreational facilities, and intramural and NCAA athletics. NAU students can choose from 108 baccalaureate degrees and 55 graduate studies programs. Unique programs range from Colorado Plateau-based forestry to global-ranging bioterrorism. More pedestrian fields such as physical therapy and hotel/restaurant management are available. The university's Center for Excellence in Education promotes a competency based approach to teacher education.

Coconino County Community College, a two year college educating more than 3,000 students, offers programs for students to continue their higher education or to enter the business world.

Libraries and Research Centers

The Flagstaff City-Coconino County Public Library consists of a main library, a combined school-branch library in Flagstaff, and eight affiliate branches throughout the county. The main library, built in an attractive ski-lodge style, features four fireplaces and local Native American art. The library contains more than 170,000 volumes and an extensive collection of Arizona and Southwest publications.

Other special collections include a U.S. genealogy collection, the Economic Development Information Center, a large print collection, and the City of Flagstaff Archives.

For its small population, the city is home to a large number of research collections and special libraries, including Lowell Observatory, the Museum of Northern Arizona, the U.S. Geological Survey, the Arboretum (Transition Zone Horticultural Institute), the Cross Cultural Dance Resources Institution, and Northern Arizona University's Cline Library Special Collections and Archives Division.

The many research centers and institutes at Northern Arizona University include the Colorado Plateau Research Station, the Center for Quaternary Studies, and the Institute for Native Americans. The university's Distance Learning Network provides 10 classes per day to non-campus students across the state and is used by many private corporations for special research needs. The U.S. Geological Survey Flagstaff Field Center supports such research as Space Mission support, water locating, earth geology, and image processing.

Public Library Information: Flagstaff City/Coconino County Public Library, 330 West Aspen Avenue, Flagstaff, AZ 86001; telephone (520)779-7670; fax (520)774-9573

Health Care

Flagstaff Medical Center (FMC) is Northern Arizona's regional referral medical facility and has the only Level II trauma center in the area. Prominent departments of Flagstaff Medical Center are The Heart Center, The Cancer Center, Imaging/Radiology, Sports Medicine Center of Northern Arizona, Women and Infants Center, and a Children's Health Department that recently moved into a new building. FMC has 238 inpatient beds and 178 physicians active on staff. The center's parent corporation, Northern Arizona Healthcare, also has facilities in nearby Sedona and Verde Valley.

Recreation

Sightseeing

Flagstaff, originally a railroad town, now houses its visitors center in the Tudor revival-style Santa Fe Station, where one can pick up maps for walking tours of the city. The Lowell Observatory, possibly the city's most famous structure, presents visitors with hands-on exhibits, historic displays, and a scenic campus located near downtown. Tours, sky shows, demonstrations, and lectures are offered throughout the

The Riordan Mansion in Flagstaff.

year. The observatory's oldest telescope is housed in an historic wooden dome, and night sky viewing is offered in evening hours during most of the year.

The Arboretum at Flagstaff, with the highest elevation of a botanical research garden in the nation, displays a fascinating variety of plant life native to the region, and features a Threatened and Endangered Plant Conservation Program. Its 10 gardens include an Herb Garden of 250 specimens, a Constructed Wetland wherein native plants purify water, a butterfly garden, organic vegetable garden, and other gardens spread over 200 acres with scenic trails. Visitors to Coconino National Forest may spot American bald eagles and black bear in the world's largest ponderosa pine forest, which ranges in elevation from 2,600 to 12,633 feet. The Eldon Pueblo Archaeological Project at the National Forest informs visitors about archaeological concepts, values, laws, and practices through personal experience. Programs for children are also available.

Guides escort tourists through the Riordan Mansion State Historic Park, a mansion with forty rooms and more than 13,000 square feet of living area. This 1904 duplex contains original artifacts, handcrafted furniture, and personal mementos of the Riordan family, who lived there early in the twentieth century. The park also offers a visitor center, a self-guided tour of the grounds, and picnic tables. Reservations are recommended for tours.

Three national monuments in the area draw visitors for their history and breathtaking beauty. The pristine, stream-cut gorge at Walnut Canyon National Monument offers walking trails that reveal the ancient cliff dwellings built into the steep canyon walls where the Sinagua people lived nearly a thousand years ago. The on-site museum displays artifacts that paint a picture of what life was like for these early inhabitants of the area. Located in the shadow of the San Francisco peaks, the Wupatki National Monument was once home to the farmers and traders of the Anasazi and Sinagua tribes at this monument can be seen four pueblos offering a glimpse into the past. (Wupatki is Hopi for ''big house.'')

Fifty thousand years ago an enormous iron-nickel meteorite, falling through space at about 30,000 to 40,000 miles per hour, struck a rocky plain of northern Arizona with an explosive force greater than 20 million tons of TNT. It left behind a crater, called the meteor Crater, which today is 550 feet deep and 2.4 miles in circumference. The adjacent Museum of Astrogeology offers exhibits, movies and lectures that vividly describe the impact and the awesome results.

The Grand Canyon is about 80 miles northwest of Flagstaff. There one can view one of the most spectacular examples of arid land erosion in the world. The park covers 1,904 square miles, including 277 miles of the Colorado River. South Rim facilities are open year-round, and North Rim facilities are open mid-May through mid-October. The Grand Canyon Railway lets one travel in grand style on a vintage train from Williams, Arizona to the South Rim, across 65 miles of beautiful Arizona countryside.

Arts and Culture

The Coconino Center for the Arts, a modern glass-front building, is the site of many cultural activities in Flagstaff, including symphonic, orchestral, and choral performances. It is also home to the 10-day Festival of Native American Arts in August. Visual arts and literary and educational programs edify both locals and visitors. The center's 4,000 square foot gallery presents the work of a variety of artists throughout the year. Annual exhibits of note held at the center include the Youth Art Exhibit held in March or April, which features the works of students throughout Coconino County; and the Trappings of the American West exhibit in May and June, which highlights contemporary cowboy arts and crafts by artists throughout the Southwest and Canada, and also offers cowboy poetry readings and musical performances.

The Flagstaff Symphony Orchestra (FSO) has been bringing enjoyment to local audiences since its founding in 1950. The FSO performs in the 1,500-seat Ardery Auditorium, giving eight concerts during its September through April season as well as Youth Concerts, a Lollipop concert in December for very young children, and pops series in nearby ShowLow and Sedona. The Museum of Northern Arizona also plays host to many entertainment events throughout the year. Theatrikos, a popular local theatre group, performs five mainstage productions per year; is involved in project P.E.A.C.E (Prevention, Education, and Creative Expression) which helps to prevent teen violence through theatre and peer interaction; and offers classes on acting, scene building, lighting design, voice, and the like. Theatrikos's home, the Flagstaff Playhouse, was renamed the Doris Harper-White Community Playhouse after one of its founders and longest member. It is an intimate black box theatre with 99 seats.

Flagstaff's premier museum is the Museum of Northern Arizona, which introduces museum-goers to the native peoples and natural sciences of the Colorado Plateau region. Permanent galleries and changing exhibits explore anthropology, biology, geology, and fine art. Native American art is for sale at the museum shop and there is a nature trail on the grounds.

The history of Flagstaff from the time of cowboys to the lumberjacks and railroaders to the astronomers is presented at the Arizona Historical Society Pioneer Museum. Exhibits include early medical equipment, saddles, household and livestock items, and a 1929 Baldwin locomotive.

Festivals and Holidays

Summer events in Flagstaff center around the rodeo and ethnic cuisine. Fans of the rodeo enjoy the Arizona High

School Rodeo finals, which take place the first weekend of every June at the Coconino county Fair Grounds. High school students compete in such events as barrel racing, bareback riding, saddle bronco riding, bull riding, team roping, calf roping, and goat tying. The annual Chili Cook-off held during that same weekend features live music and contests for both adults and children. On the second Saturday in June, the Great Fiesta Del Barrio & Fajita Cook-off celebrates the customs and culture of the local Hispanic community. The third weekend in June brings the Pine Country Pro Rodeo, which draws contenders to the Coconino County Fairgrounds. The Arizona Highland Celtic Festival offers music, Irish dancing, and whiskey tastings. The Festival of Native American Arts, held during July and August, includes an exhibit, outdoor market, dances, workshops and demonstrations celebrating the arts, crafts, culture, and traditions of Native Americans throughout the Southwest. August's Flagstaff Summerfest Festival in the Pines tops off the summer season with the finest in arts and crafts, food, and entertainment.

Every Labor Day Weekend the Coconino County Fair takes places at the fairgrounds in Fort Tuthill Park. Highlights of the fair include exhibits, livestock, entertainment, a demolition derby, and carnival. The Flagstaff Festival of Science, a 10-day event held annually at the end of September, promotes science awareness through hands-on exhibits, interactive displays, field trips, and world-class scientist participants.

Flagstaff kicks off the winter season as children young and old delight in the Playthings of the Past exhibit, which runs from November through January and features dolls, trains, cars, and castles from the 1880s through the 1960s. During December, Riordan Mansion offers holiday tours of its festively decorated turn-of-the-century rooms. February's Flagstaff Winterfest features nearly 100 events: sled dog races, skiing competitions, and other snow events, llama play days, sleigh rides, concerts, cultural events, and historic walking tours are all on schedule. The Arizona Special Olympics is a competition for mentally and physically challenged athletes that is held during the last weekend in February.

Sports for the Spectator

The Arizona Cardinals of the National Football league and the Phoenix Suns, affiliates of the National Basketball Association, hold preseason training camps in Flagstaff. A variety of NCAA-sanctioned events are hosted at Northern Arizona University, including football, men's and women's basketball, volleyball, track and swimming. NAU's Skydome, where many athletic events are held, is one of the largest wood-domed structures in the world; the university's Wall Aquatic Center is a high-altitude training site for U.S. and international Olympic swimmers and divers.

The Coconino County Horse Races—a tradition for more than 50 years—features thoroughbreds and quarter horses and is held annually over the Fourth of July weekend at Fort Tuthill Downs.

Sports for the Participant

Flagstaff has 29 parks with 2 swimming pools, 1 public 18-hole golf course and 5 private ones, an ice-skating rink, 16 tennis courts, 2 bowling alleys, a skeet-and-trap facility, and a ski resort. FUTS, the Flagstaff Urban Trails System, runs through the city and provides several multi-use trails varying in length from one to five miles. Northern Arizona University's Wall Aquatic Center has an Olympic size pool that is open to the public. The city's transportation network of interstate highways makes it easy to explore the national forests surrounding the city. Popular forest-based activities include hiking, mountain biking, and horseback riding. Coconino National Forest offers more than 320 miles of hiking trails. In town, trailheads access Mount Elden from the east and west. The Arizona Snowbowl atop the San Francisco Peaks, with a base elevation of 9,000 feet, is higher in elevation than most resorts in Utah, Colorado, and California. It offers skiers a vertical drop of 2,300 feet, four chairlifts and more than 30 slopes, the longest of which stretches more than a mile. Its chairlift becomes a 6,450-foot-long ''Scenic Skyride'' during the summer. Flagstaff Nordic Center, 16 miles north of the city, offers 25 miles of groomed trails for every level of skier.

Shopping and Dining

Flagstaff is the primary commercial center in northern Arizona. The city boasts many fine art galleries, antique shops and specialty shops, as well as 13 major shopping centers. Flagstaff's proximity to a number of Indian reservations provides shoppers with a variety of Native American arts and crafts. The historic downtown shopping area has nearly 200 gift shops, boutiques, and clothing stores. Import stores downtown specialize in South American and Mexican goods. The Flagstaff Mall, an enclosed shopping center with more than 60 stores, recently went through a 500,000 square foot expansion project. The Gallery Shop at Coconino Center for the Arts specializes in hand-made arts and crafts by area artists.

Flagstaff's more than 200 restaurants range from casual southwestern to European-style with food served in the historic atmosphere of turn-of-the-century buildings. Ethnic cuisine ranges from Italian, Mexican, and Asian, to Middle Eastern and Bohemian. Music fans enjoy visiting the Museum Club, a Depression-era Route 66 road house and the Southwest's largest log cabin, which continues to present popular country musicians.

Visitor Information: The Flagstaff Visitor Center, (520)774-9541

Convention Facilities

Flagstaff's largest conference hotel, with 248 guest rooms, is the Little America hotel. With 10,000 square feet of conference space, the facility can accommodate 360 people classroom style, 675 people theater style, and 460 people for banquets. The Radisson Woodlands Hotel, with 183 guest rooms, has 6,000 square feet of conference space and can accommodate 168 classroom style, 375 theater style, and can handle banquets for up to 350 people. Nearly 70 area hotels offer more than 4,900 rooms.

Transportation

Approaching the City

I-40, providing east-west coast access, runs through the center of Flagstaff. Access to the south is via I-17. U.S. routes 89 and 180 run between Flagstaff and the Grand Canyon. At Pulliam Airport, located just four miles south of downtown Flagstaff, America West Express provides hourly flights to Phoenix, where national and international connections can be made. Amtrak offers two daily trains from Flagstaff that connect with trains to Chicago and Los Angeles, and Greyhound-Trailways has interstate and intrastate bus service.

Traveling in the City

Flagstaff has developed many of the traffic congestion problems that come with rapid growth. Some estimates say that traffic has more than tripled since 1974. Two major traffic improvements are underway; one on I-40 and the other a new bridge over the railway at 4th Street and at Route 66. Shuttle and tour bus service is provided by Grayline/Nava-Hopi Tours and Mountain Line.

Communications

Newspapers and Magazines

The city's daily newspaper, the *Arizona Daily Sun*, is published weekdays in the evenings and on Saturday and Sunday mornings. The *Canyon Shopper* is published weekly, and the *Navajo-Hopi Observer* serves the Native American peoples of northern Arizona. The monthly *Mountain Living Magazine* features topics of community interest, and the *Arizona Guide* describes things to do and see in the area.

Television and Radio

Flagstaff has three television stations and cable is available throughout most of the city. Fifteen AM and FM radio stations broadcast out of the city, offering a wide range of formats.

Media Information: The *Arizona Daily Sun,* 417 W. Santa Fe Ave., PO Box 1849, Flagstaff, AZ 86002; telephone (520)774-4545

Flagstaff Online

Arizona Daily Sun. Available www.azdailysun.com

Arizona School Report Cards. Available www2.ade.state.az.us/srcs

City of Flagstaff home page. Available www.flagstaff.az.gov

Flagstaff Chamber of Commerce. Available www.flagstaff.az.us

Flagstaff Community Profile. Available www.commerce.state.az.us/comm/flagstaf.pdf

Flagstaff Convention and Visitors Bureau. Available www.flagstaffarizona.org/info.htm

Flagstaff Online. Available www.flagstaff.az.us

Flagstaff Unified School District. Available www.flagstaff.k12.az.us

Selected Bibliography

Aitchison, Stewart, *Red Rocks, Sacred Mountains: The Canyons and Peaks from Sedona to Flagstaff* (Stillwater, MN: Voyager Press, 1992)

Ashworth, Donna, *Against This Ground: Biography of a Small Mountain* (Flagstaff, Ariz., Small Mountain Books, 1994)

Cline, Platt, *Mountain Town: Flagstaff's First Century* (Flagstaff, Northland Press, 1994)

Houk, Rose, *The Peaks* (Phoenix; Arizona Highways, 1994)

Mesa

The City in Brief

Founded: 1878 (incorporated in 1883)

Head Official: Mayor Keno Hawker (since 2000)

City Population
  1980: 152,453
  1990: 288,091
  2000: 396,375
  2003 estimate: 432,376
  Percent change, 1990-2000: 37.6%
  U.S. rank in 1990: 53rd (3rd in state)
  U.S. rank in 2000: 51st (3rd in state)

Metropolitan Area Population (PMSA)
  1980: 1,508,030
  1990: 2,122,101
  2000: 3,251,876

Percent change, 1990-2000: 53.2%
U.S. rank in 2000: 14th

Area: 125.18 square miles (2000)
Elevation: 1,241 feet above sea level
Average Annual Temperature: 84.5° F
Average Annual Precipitation: 8.5 inches

Major Economic Sectors: aerospace/aviation, agri-business, automotive, business services, education services, electronics, health services, manufacturing, retail, transportation services
Unemployment Rate: 4.0% (January 2005)
Per Capita Income: $19,601

2002 FBI Crime Index Total: 33,335

Major Colleges and Universities: Arizona State University East, Mesa Community College, East Valley Institute of Technology

Daily Newspapers: *East Valley Tribune*

Introduction

Founded by Mormon agricultural pioneers, Mesa today is growing like a weed. Far enough from Phoenix to retain its small town feel yet near enough to the big city to encourage the growth of technological and manufacturing industries, Mesa has become more than a retirement community and has evolved into a tourist mecca in its own right. Layers of native, frontier, and Mexican history have combined to form a city of eclectic tastes and offerings, from the prehistoric farming canals deep in the ground to the aviation businesses that take to the skies.

Geography and Climate

Desert, mountains, water—somehow Mesa got it all. Located along a spit of the Sonoran Desert, Mesa is warm and arid every month of the year and enjoys the flora and fauna of the desert clime. Saguaro and prickly pear cacti are abundant, along with varieties of cholla, and the dry soil outside the city is wandered by rattlesnakes, jack rabbits, bobcats, hawks, and owls. While Mesa gets 320 days of sunshine annually and temperatures in the 100s during the summer, the city also has easy access to six local lakes and two nearby rivers. The Superstition Mountain range just to the east of the city provides some altitude to the mesas and valleys of the area.

Area: 125.18 square miles (2000)

Elevation: 1,241 feet above sea level

Average Temperatures: January, 54.1° F; July, 91.1° F; annual average, 84.5° F

Average Annual Precipitation: 8.5 inches

History

The First Farmers

More than 2,000 years ago, Mesa's agricultural destiny was carved out by the Hohokam Indians who settled the area. The Hohokam were peaceful farmers who developed a sophisticated and effective network of irrigation canals that turned the arid land around Mesa into arable soil. Eventually, the Hohokam people seemed to disappear from the area; it is theorized that the tribe may have morphed into the Tohono O'dham tribe or that the Hohokam were driven out of the future Mesa area by Apache Indians. Regardless, the tribe left an indelible mark on the desert that served farmers of all nationalities well for centuries.

Spanish explorers and conquistadores followed—both Francisco Vasquez de Coronado and Father Eusebio Kino passed near Mesa as they searched for treasure and sought to convert Native Americans. The Mesa-Phoenix area also lay along the route to the legendary seven cities of Cibola sought by Estevanico (or Esteban), a former Muslim slave who became an explorer after hurricanes and battles with Native Americans decimated his former crew in Florida. As quickly as the Spanish attempted to put down roots in southwestern Arizona, the Apache tribe drove them out again in a tradition that lasted through the 1700s.

The Mexican War and the U.S. Civil War largely occupied the time and resources of the United States military during the early and mid-1800s, and its forces were operating at less than full power when the government decided to intervene in the clashes between native peoples and European settlers in the Southwest after a portion of Arizona was ceded to the U.S. The Western Indian Wars in the later 1800s were spotted with massacres and relocations; in the Mesa area, the U.S. Army did battle with the Apaches until the tribe agreed to resettlement. Unfortunately, several competing Apache tribes were co-located, resulting in a resumption of hostilities until the military was able to negotiate a surrender by Apache Chief Geronimo in 1886. It was in relative peace that a group of Mormon farmers, dealing with relocation and persecution themselves, established the settlement of Fort Utah in Lehi, just north of Mesa.

Mesa Takes Root

A decade before Chief Geronimo's surrender, the 85 intrepid members of the First Mesa Company left Utah and Idaho. The group was composed of Latter-Day Saints, some of whom practiced polygamy and who had been intrigued by the descriptions of Arizona brought back to church elders by the Mormon Battalion that fought during the Mexican War and traveled through Arizona on its way back to Utah. Stopping briefly in Lehi, the First Mesa Company moved on to the mesa, where they discovered and began clearing the irrigation canals left by the Hohokam people. The Second Mesa Company set out from Idaho about a year later; with the best land in Mesa already claimed, these pioneers established a nearby community called Stringtown, which was eventually absorbed into modern Mesa.

In the late 1800s, a flood in Lehi washed away Fort Utah; it had become evident over time that the lower desert lands were prone to sudden and unexpected flooding, allowing table-top Mesa to flourish. It began to look like a city, complete with an adobe pesthouse to control smallpox outbreaks, a city hall, saloons, and *The Mesa Free Press*, which has existed continuously under a variety of names since 1892 and is currently known as *The East Valley Tribune*.

Dr. A.J. Chandler played a significant role in the foundation of Mesa. Using heavy machinery, he enlarged the Hohokam canals and made them more effective in agricultural enterprises. Dr. Chandler was the force behind the construction of the first office complex in Mesa, and he started the first electric power plant. When the municipal government purchased the utility in 1917, it became one of a handful of Arizona cities to own such a service. Earnings from utilities solely funded capital expenditures until the 1960s and also provided the financial underpinning for Works Progress Administration (WPA) projects during the Great Depression. WPA projects included the first dedicated hospital facility, a new city hall and library, sidewalks, paved streets, parks, and a recreation department for the city.

Layers of Culture

By 1940, Mesa had achieved its standing as the third largest city in Arizona, boasting 7,000 inhabitants. Joining the Tohono O'dham Indians, the Hispanics and the Mormons living in Mesa in the early 1900s were African American families (including a veterinarian) and families of Chinese and Japanese heritage who farmed and owned a variety of local businesses. This eclectic populace provided an interesting backdrop for events during the second World War, particularly considering the proximity of the internment camp at the Gila River Indian Reservation nearby.

World War II had another lasting cultural and industrial impact with the development of Falcon Field Airport and Williams Air Force Base as training sites for pilots. British pilots trained at Falcon Field, while U.S. pilots trained at Williams; many of those military families stayed in the Mesa area after the war ended. The aeronautical training and supply facilities at Falcon Field and Williams Air Force Base attracted aviation and aerospace companies to Mesa, propelling a switch from citrus and cotton farming to high-tech employment in the mid-1960s.

Twenty-First Century Mesa

Williams Air Force Base was closed in September of 1993 and was quickly reborn as Williams Gateway Airport. The aviation industry gives Mesa its wings today, with weather conditions that are near-perfect for training and testing every month of the year. Both Williams Gateway and Falcon Field are home to national and international aeronautical companies that develop aircraft and aviation systems both for the commercial aviation industry as well as for the military. The climate and geography have also made Mesa a golf destination, to the extent that local universities have developed golf-related degree programs that have been accredited by the Professional Golf Association.

Historical Information: Mesa Historical Museum, 2345 N. Horne Street, Mesa, AZ 85211; telephone (480)835-7358; email: mesamuseum@netzero.net

Population Profile

Metropolitan Area Residents (CMSA)
1980: 1,508,030
1990: 2,122,101
2000: 3,251,876
Percent change, 1990-2000: 53.2%
U.S. rank in 2000: 14th

City Residents
1980: 152,404
1990: 288,091
2000: 396,375
2003 estimate: 432,376
Percent change, 1990-2000: 37.6%
U.S. rank in 1990: 53rd (3rd in state)
U.S. rank in 2000: 51st (3rd in state)

Density: 3,171.3 people per square mile (2000)

Racial and ethnic characteristics (2000)
  White: 323,655
  Black or African American: 9,977
  American Indian and Alaskan Native: 6,572
  Asian: 5,917
  Native Hawaiian and Pacific Islander: 932
  Hispanic or Latino (may be of any race): 78,281
  Other: 38,271

Percent of residents born in state: 33%

Age characteristics
  Population under 5 years old: 32,592
  Population 5 to 9 years old: 30,259
  Population 10 to 14 years old: 28,842
  Population 15 to 19 years old: 28,774
  Population 20 to 24 years old: 32,488
  Population 25 to 34 years old: 61,551
  Population 35 to 44 years old: 56,124
  Population 45 to 54 years old: 43,807
  Population 55 to 59 years old: 15,913
  Population 60 to 64 years old: 13,149
  Population 65 to 74 years old: 26,546
  Population 75 to 84 years old: 20,320
  Population 85 years and over: 6,010
  Median age: 32.0 (2000)

Births (Maricopa County, 2004)
  Total number: 60,480

Deaths (Maricopa County, 2004)
Total number: 23,497 (of which, 395 were infants under the age of 1 year)

Money income (1999)
Per capita income: $19,601
Median household income: $42,817
Total households: 146,700

Number of households with income of . . .
less than $10,000: 8,758
$10,000 to $14,999: 8,104
$15,000 to $24,999: 19,061
$25,000 to $34,999: 21,131
$35,000 to $49,999: 28,482
$50,000 to $74,999: 31,494
$75,000 to $99,999: 15,636
$100,000 to $149,999: 10,093
$150,000 to $199,999: 2,320
$200,000 or more: 1,621

Percent of families below poverty level: 6.2% (20% of which were female householder families with related children under 5 years)

2002 FBI Crime Index Total: 33,335

Municipal Government

The city of Mesa has established a charter under which it operates, with citizens of the municipality electing a mayor and six district council members. Council members serve four-year terms; every two years, there is an election for three seats on the council. The mayor serves a four-year term in office. A vice mayor, chosen by the council, assists the mayor and council in administration of the city government.

Head Official: Mayor Keno Hawker (since 2000; current term expires 2008)

Total Number of City Employees: 4,105 (2005)

City Information: City of Mesa, 20 E. Main Street, Mesa, AZ 85201; telephone (480)644-2055

Economy

Major Industries and Commercial Activity

The arid, warm climate of Mesa has made it a top-flight locale for aeronautical industries that range from manufac-

turing to educational. Boeing maintains a facility at Falcon Field Airport where flight control panels are created, tested, and installed in freighters. The Mesa plant was the site of the development of the Apache Longbow helicopter during the 1990s and continues to research and develop military aeronautical equipment. Boeing Training Services and Systems not only equips pilots with the latest knowledge in flight but puts together training packages that can be administered to prospective pilots in other locations.

The local airports host a number of aviation training businesses, including Arizona Aviation, Eagle's Roost Aviation Services, and Professional Flight Instruction. Airplane and helicopter medical transport, maintenance, and tour operations range from Airevac Services to Eagle Rescue.

TRW Vehicle Safety Systems, Inc., is the subsidiary of a Fortune 500 company and stands at the head of Mesa manufacturers. The plant produces vehicle restraint systems and other safety equipment, which is sold to automakers from around the world. TRW has been on the leading edge of safety system integration of restraint belts, air bags, crash sensors, and steering wheel technologies. Some of those restraint and safety systems might find their way into the heavy machinery and large vehicles produced by Empire Southwest Machinery in Mesa, where buses and caterpillars are researched and refined. The Empire Regional Training Center offers classes in machinery management, maintenance and repair as well.

The technology of golf has evolved into a thriving industry in Mesa. A sophisticated golf driving range and PING Swing Analysis Lab at Arizona State University East supports not only the golf-related majors at the college but also serves the community in perfecting its game.

Items and goods produced: aeronautical equipment, military equipment, vehicles, vehicle safety systems

Incentive Programs—New and Existing Companies

Local programs—Local business development assistance is available through the Neighborhood Economic Development Corporation (NEDCO), a partnership between the public and private sectors in support of community development and community reinvestment. NEDCO oversees the Business Development Loan Program, along with Individual Development Accounts that stimulate the creation of small businesses. Funding support comes from joint ventures between NEDCO and its partner financial institutions, as well as New Markets Tax Credit and private social investment dollars. NEDCO's Mesa Grande Commercial Revitalization Program works hand in hand with low income neighborhood groups to further development of cooperative housing and microenterprises.

State programs—The State of Arizona encourages businesses to invest in areas with higher poverty and/or unemployment rates through its Enterprise Zone Program, which provides income or premium tax credits along with property tax benefits. Construction of industrial and manufacturing facilities is supported via the state Private Activity Bond program. New businesses at the Williams Gateway Airport in Mesa can take advantage of the state Military Reuse Zone program, established in 1992 to lessen the economic impact of military base closures. Businesses sited at the former Williams Air Force Base can benefit from property reclassification, tax credits and transaction privilege tax exemptions.

Williams Gateway Airport also lies within a Foreign Trade Zone, an area that is essentially treated as if it were outside of U.S. Custom Territory. This allows for imported goods to be stored in the zone duty-free and without full customs formalities. Foreign Trade Zones additionally allow businesses to realize significant real and personal property tax reductions.

Other State of Arizona business incentive programs include tax credits for research and development, pollution control, and information technology training. The state also offers a Waste Reduction Assistance Program to new and existing businesses.

Job training programs—The Neighborhood Economic Development Corporation (NEDCO) offers technical assistance and workforce training as part of its services locally. Maricopa Workforce Connections is a county branch of the state workforce development office, serving Maricopa County businesses and job seekers. Employers can access recruitment, screening, job matching, corporate restructuring, and job training services, while county residents in search of employment can tap into education and job training opportunities, career planning services, vocational counseling, specialized support services, job placement, and a national job database. The State of Arizona also operates the Arizona Job Training Program to tailor training plans to the evolving industry landscape. The Arizona Apprenticeship System maintains more than 100 registered apprenticeship opportunities that pair education with on-the-job training. The state's job workforce development programs are underscored by job training and hiring tax credits for companies providing specialized training or hiring employees in a targeted group.

Development Projects

The state of Arizona is experiencing exponential growth, as exemplified by Mesa's population and industry leaps over the past 20 years; this has spurred the state to institute "Growing Smarter" legislation in reference to municipal planning efforts. The city of Mesa's priority work plan for 2004-2005 demonstrates this careful approach as it lays out development strategies for the Williams Gateway Airport area, including recruitment of a new passenger airline, ex-

pansion of cargo services with a new 25,000 square foot cargo storage facility, and improvements to roads and utilities that make Williams Gateway a more attractive business destination. The city has been in negotiations with Cessna as a new Williams Gateway business, holding out as a carrot the great weather, skilled local workforce and business incentives available.

Looking even farther into the future, the "Mesa 2025" strategic plan has identified areas of focus for economic development for the next 20 years, including the 4,560 acres that comprise the Falcon Field Airport corridor (business park and industrial usage), the Town Center/Main Street corridor (light rail, other rapid transit, business development, historical, and cultural development), and the Santan Freeway corridor (a combination of residential, commercial, industrial and mixed use).

The city is participating in an ongoing redevelopment and historical preservation effort, with particular emphasis on the town center. Four sites in downtown are on the National Register of Historic Places: the Evergreen area, West 6th Street, Glenwood Wilbur, and Temple. In an effort to support older neighborhoods that are reporting decline, the City of Mesa has instituted a Neighborhood Opportunity Zone plan that coordinates residents, government, businesses, and non-profits in planning and implementing neighborhood improvements.

Largely funded by the 1998 "Quality of Life" sales tax, the Mesa Arts Center will open its doors in 2005 as a 212,775 square foot performing arts, visual arts and art education hub for the entire state of Arizona. The Arts Center was designed to reflect the aesthetic sensibilities of the Sonoran Desert on its exterior; inside is a complex of four theaters, exhibit space, art education classrooms, and Mesa Contemporary Arts' Galleries. The Mesa Arts Center is the largest facility of its kind in the state and is expected to drive economic development in the downtown area while it anchors the art scene locally and regionally.

In 2004 the City of Mesa developed a cutting-edge Transportation Management Center as part of its Intelligent Transportation System, using the latest technology to improve the flow of traffic through the city. Large-scale improvements on freeways, arterial streets and mass transit programs, funded by a proposition passed in 2004, will keep Mesa an accessible destination for businesses.

Commercial Shipping

Mesa is served by two local airports, a major international airport 12 miles to the west, and a network of freeways, highways, and rail. The Williams Gateway Airport can accommodate corporate, cargo, military, and general aviation craft. A 21,500 square foot storage hangar and a 25,000 square foot air cargo facility are available for shipping concerns, and the airport resides in Foreign Trade Zone #221, allowing for landing and storing import merchandise without full customs formalities.

Falcon Field Airport doubles as an industrial park, offering a variety of charter, general aviation, and cargo flights daily. Sky Harbor International Airport, located between Mesa and Phoenix, is a major aeronautical enterprise that handles 788 tons of air cargo daily and has a $72 million economic impact on the area. The amount of cargo passing through Sky Harbor is expected to increase between 10 and 11 percent per year. Sky Harbor joins Williams Gateway Airport in Foreign Trade Zone #221, easing customs requirements for imported goods and providing some tax relief for those businesses.

Several freeways, U.S. highways, and state highways pass through Mesa, including U.S. 60 (known as Superstition Freeway) and state highways 87 and 89. The Santan Freeway 202 creates a bypass around the more congested downtown area, and Interstates 10 and 17 are quickly accessible from the city. Mesa is the headquarters for several trucking companies of national scope and is located conveniently near many more in Phoenix. Driving conditions are good year-round, and Mesa is within an 8-hour drive of Albuquerque, El Paso, Las Vegas, Los Angeles, San Diego, Tucson, and several major cities in Mexico. Mesa is also served by Union Pacific Railroad, which has 32,832 miles of track in most states west of the Mississippi River.

Labor Force and Employment Outlook

Census data from the past three decades indicates that Mesa will continue to grow, and it's expected that the economy will grow apace. Despite its agrarian past, it seems likely that farming, fishing, and forestry occupations will decline within the next 10 years, while healthcare, education, construction, and sales will all likely increase their niche in the local job market.

Certain occupational areas such as architecture, transportation, and industry are expected to experience steady growth or remain stable.

The following is a summary of data regarding the Phoenix-Mesa-Scottsdale metropolitan statistical area labor force, 2004 annual averages.

Size of nonagricultural labor force: 1,674,800

Number of workers employed in . . .
   natural resources and mining: 2,000
   construction: 140,000
   manufacturing: 130,500
   trade, transportation and utilities: 339,600
   information: 35,700

   financial activities: 137,400
   professional and business services: 270,900
   educational and health services: 172,600
   leisure and hospitality: 160,500
   other services: 64,200
   government: 220,900

Average hourly earnings of production workers employed in manufacturing: $13.84

Unemployment rate: 4.0% (January 2005)

Largest employers	Number of employees
Mesa Public Schools	10,132
Banner Health System	6,100
Boeing	4,300
City of Mesa	4,105
AT&T	2,800
WalMart	1,775
TRW Safety Systems	1,450
Empire Southwest Machinery	1,000

Cost of Living

The following is a summary of data regarding key cost of living factors for the Mesa area.

2004 (3rd Quarter) ACCRA Average House Price: $254,751

2004 (3rd Quarter) ACCRA Cost of Living Index: 99.2 (U.S. average = 100.0)

State income tax rate: From 2.87% to 5.04%

State sales tax rate: 5.6%

Local income tax rate: None

Local sales tax rate: .15%

Property tax rate: 0%

Economic Information: City of Mesa, Office of Economic Development, Mesa City Plaza, 20 E. Main Street, Suite 200, PO Box 1466, Mesa, AZ 85201; telephone (480)644-2398; toll-free (800)290-MESA

Education and Research

Elementary and Secondary Schools

The Mesa Public Schools System has come a long way from its pioneer farmer roots, when classes were taught in a shack made of cottonwood. These days, the emphasis is on preparing students to function in the new technology of the information age. Classes are geared toward the development of students who can use the latest technology and can think critically in the course of their learning experiences. The school district plans for every student to graduate with a skill or trade that will lead to future employment; to that end, the district has created and implemented a Career and Technical Education (CTE) curriculum. The program is comprised of five areas of concentration, including agricultural education, business education, family and consumer sciences, industrial technology, and informational technology. Hands-on learning is stressed, with some high school students enrolled in a Cooperative Office Education program that allows them to attend classes in the morning and work at local businesses in the afternoon.

With job preparedness as a district-wide concern, it makes sense that Mesa School District would also contain a well-developed and well-supported service learning program, with community-based education suggested in art, business, computer technology, and foreign language classes.

Mesa Public Schools offers 12 alternative education programs spanning kindergarten to 12th grade and running the gamut from early education centers, to support for home-schooled students, to institutions created for drop-out prevention and retrieval.

The following is a summary of data regarding the Mesa Public Schools as of the 2004–2005 school year.

Total enrollment: 74,916

Number of facilities
  elementary schools: 57
  junior high schools: 13
  high schools: 6
  alternative: 12

Student/teacher ratio: 17:1

Teacher salaries
  Minimum: $31,641
  Maximum: $62,065

Funding per pupil: $4,787

Public Schools Information: Mesa Public Schools, 63 E. Main Street, #101, Mesa, AZ 85201-7422; telephone (480)472-0000

Colleges and Universities

Arizona State University (East Campus) in Mesa functions as a polytechnic institute, or vocational college, offering its nearly 4,000 students degrees in 29 educational concentrations including business, agribusiness, engineering technology, professional pilot training, health and wellness, and education. Baccalaureate, masters and doctoral degrees are

all available through the Mesa campus. In June 1999, the university received accreditation by the Professional Golfers Association and is one of the first state universities west of the Mississippi to offer both a Professional Golf Management program and a Golf and Facilities Management major.

Masters and doctoral degrees are available through the Arizona School of Health Sciences, which offers programs such as medical informatics, advanced physician assistant studies, sports medicine, occupational therapy, and audiology. Fieldwork experiences occur in a variety of urban and rural placements, allowing for practical application of academic concepts.

The largest of the 10 Maricopa Community Colleges, Mesa Community College (MCC) offers its student body of 27,000 the only biotechnology studies program in the state of Arizona. Well-respected Fire Science and Nursing academic programs are underscored by a service learning program that has become a blueprint for community colleges across the country. Courses within a variety of disciplines send their students out into the local community to do meaningful volunteer work that employs the theoretical concepts learned in class. Additionally, MCC provides AmeriCorps service scholarships to students who are performing volunteer work or completing unpaid internships.

East Valley Institute of Technology (EVIT) is billed as Arizona's first regional technological education district, serving high school students from 10 East Valley school districts (including Mesa Public Schools). The programs at EVIT are the result of partnerships with local industry and business in an effort to prepare students with the skills needed for future employment. High school students can attend half-days at EVIT and the rest of the school day at their own school. EVIT additionally offers adult education classes under the banner of Evenings at EVIT.

Highly specialized training is available to would-be pilots and transitioning former members of the military at Williams Gateway Airport Educational Campus, which includes tenants such as Advanced Training Systems International, Inc. and Airline Transport Professionals. Keller Graduate School of Management also maintains a Mesa branch with a range of business-related masters degrees. Adult learners can also enroll at the Mesa campus of Ottawa University and the University of Phoenix.

Libraries and Research Centers

The City of Mesa Library system is comprised of one centrally located main library facility, with two branch libraries covering the southwest and northeast portions of the city. The main library is home to the Mesa Room, an archive of local history items and special collections regarding Mesa. Besides offering general library services, the City of

Mesa Library coordinates reading programs for children, book discussion groups, special exhibits and lectures.

The Research Library at the Mesa Southwest Museum contains non-circulating materials dedicated to the natural and cultural history of the Southwest.

The East Library at Mesa's branch of Arizona State University offers access to hundreds of databases and thousands of online journals and periodicals, which can be searched remotely. The library provides a call center for help, along with live tech support. The library features the Naxos Music Library, an online compendium of classical music with a sprinkling of other musical genres.

Arizona State University (ASU) East also houses several high-tech facilities for specialized research, including the Golf Driving Range and PING Swing Analysis Lab, which refine the work of students in Professional Golf and Golf Facilities Management programs. ASU's Agribusiness Center incorporates a Consumer Behavior Research Lab with a Market/Trading Room, along with a testing theater for students in the pre-veterinary medicine program. An altitude chamber and a simulator lab provide the latest facilities for pilot training, while the College of Technology and Applied Sciences benefits from the Microelectronics Teaching Factory, a 15,000 square foot manufacturing facility available to both students and local industry partners. ASU East is in the process of constructing a 34,600 square foot research facility to house Applied Biological Research labs, the Applied Cognitive Sciences Center, the Health Lifestyles Center, and the Plant Made Pharmaceutical Research and Manufacturing Facility.

Public Library Information: City of Mesa Main Library, 64 East 1 Street, Mesa AZ 85201; telephone (480) 644-2207

Health Care

Mesa is home to four medical centers, three of which are part of the Phoenix-based Banner Health company. The Banner Mesa Medical Center (formerly Mesa Lutheran Hospital) has 258 acute care beds and 62 behavioral health and rehabilitation beds; this full-service community hospital offers acute care for adults, intensive and emergency care, pediatrics, labor and delivery, medical imaging, and surgery. Banner Desert Medical Center offers the community 600 licensed beds for adult acute care, emergency services, intensive care, oncology and cardiology specialties, orthopedics, and neurology. Banner Desert additionally operates a Children's Hospital staffed by medical specialists in pediatric emergency, and surgical, intensive, and rehabilitative care. The third Banner facility is Banner Baywood Medical Center; currently

licensed for 239 beds, the hospital is undergoing major expansion that will add 123 patient care beds and increase the size of several departments. Banner Baywood's Orthopedic Institute has been ranked in the top 100 orthopedic programs nationally, according to the Health Network. Other specialty programs and services include an ambulatory treatment unit, intensive care and emergency services, pain management programs, endoscopy and wound/ostomy care. The Banner Baywood Heart Hospital is located on the same campus, with a capacity of 111 beds after a recent expansion. BBHeart provides specialized cardiology services to the East Valley community, offering advanced cardiac diagnostics and treatment.

Mesa General Hospital has served the community for 40 years, offering 126 licensed beds for care ranging from cardiac services, intensive and critical care, imaging, rehabilitation, and wound treatment. Mesa General is also home to the Arizona Diagnostic and Surgical Center and is a designated Diabetes Care Center of Arizona.

Mesa's proximity to Phoenix allows access to hundreds of medical professionals in family practice, specialty practices, outpatient psychiatric services and alternative medicine practices.

Recreation

Sightseeing

A tour of Mesa might best be started at the very beginning, at the Park of the Canals near the intersection of McKellips Road and Horne Street north of the downtown area. Visitors can see the innovative irrigation systems established by the original Hohokam Indian residents of Mesa, with the effectiveness of the canals demonstrated by the Brinton Desert Botanical Garden at the same location. The Botanical Garden hosts special events in season, along with desert gardening workshops and concerts in what can be a surreal setting. The Salt River is just northwest from the Park of the Canals, making for a water-themed day in the desert.

On the way back to Mesa's town center, it's an easy stop at the former Lehi School, circa 1913, which now houses the Mesa Historical Museum and provides snapshots into the lives of early settlers of the communities that have blended to form modern Mesa. The historic downtown section of Mesa features attractions ranging from the Wild West era to modern arcades. The Ellis-Johnson home, the Alhambra Hotel, the Vance Auditorium and the former Southside Hospital all echo back to the beginnings of Mesa. The Mesa Southwest Museum provides scholarly, scientific, and fun background for sites visited in the city and beyond.

Immediately east of the original Mesa town site is the Temple Historic District, encompassing two residential divisions. Homes from the early 1920s line streets that were named for the Mormon pioneers who helped shape present-day Mesa and who laid the foundations for the Arizona Temple of the Church of Jesus Christ of Latter-Day Saints built in 1927. The temple is open for tours.

From Mesa, visitors and history buffs can embark on sightseeing adventures such as the Apache Trail Jeep Tour, which follows the stagecoach and freight wagon route from Mesa to Globe through the Superstition Mountains. Somewhere in those mountains, the Lost Dutchman Mine waits to be found again. The Goldfield Ghost Town resurrects its history as a thriving mining community that bit the dust when the mine petered out. At its height, there were three saloons, a boarding house, a general store, blacksmith shop, brewery, schoolhouse, and bordello. Along the finger of the Sonoran Desert that points across the East Valley, a smorgasbord of desert succulents can be encountered: saguaro, prickly pear, varieties of cholla, hedgehog cactus, and ocotillos. When the mountains and desert become too dry, visitors can head northeast to Saguaro Lake for a paddleboat excursion on the *Desert Belle* past canyon walls and Arizona wildlife.

Arts and Culture

The new Mesa Arts Center, expected to open in 2005, is the largest arts center in Arizona at 212,775 square feet of space for performing arts facilities, visual arts galleries and studios, and art education classrooms. The outside of the complex is as inviting as the inside, with a design reflective of the surrounding Sonoran Desert in hue, shape and landscaping. A 700-foot Shadow Walk serves as a cool outdoor plaza for events or relaxing during a tour. Located in the heart of downtown Mesa, the Arts Center campus contains three buildings, including a four-theater complex. The theater spaces are: the 1,588-seat Tom and Janet Ikeda Theater; the 550-seat Virginia G. Piper Repertory Theater; the 200-seat Nesbitt/Elliott Playhouse; and the 98-seat Anita Cox Farnsworth Studio Theater. The other facilities on the Arts Center campus are the Mesa Contemporary Arts Building and the Art Studios' classrooms and work areas.

Ballet Etudes will eventually be housed within the Mesa Arts Center, offering serious ballet performers an experience akin to a professional dance company. Ballet Etudes stages "The Nutcracker" annually, along with a Spring Repertory performance. The dancers have performed with the Mesa Symphony Orchestra, soon also to be located under the Arts Center roof. Besides its five scheduled orchestral performances each season, the Mesa Symphony Orchestra does outreach in the public schools and provides vouchers that allow students and their families to attend future performances at a reduced rate. The Metropolitan Youth Symphony involves 275 excellent young musicians in a minimum of three concerts each season, providing a professional-level experience for aspiring performers. The Sonoran Desert Chorale's 56 vocalists present four major concerts each season, with selections ranging from the classical to the Broadway stage.

Billed as "theatre for children by children," the East Valley Children's Theatre encourages creativity, self-confidence, and expression through community theatrical performances. The company puts on three productions each season, along with a host of workshops and classes for youth between the ages of 8 and 18. Also offering three plays per season is the Southwest Shakespeare Company, which strives to bring classical theater to the masses through dynamic live performances. The actors are able to share their appreciation for the Bard via student matinees, post-show seminars, and play introductions. For theater along with edible fare, the Broadway Palm West Dinner Theatre is recommended.

At the Arizona Museum for Youth, exhibits are tailored for young children to 12-year-olds, although adults will also enjoy the explanatory and interactive displays. Tours, opportunities to contribute to masterpieces, art classes, and workshops all happen at this fun and stimulating site located at Robson and Pepper streets.

Housed in the original 1913 Lehi Schoolhouse, the Mesa Historical Museum contains a wealth of artifacts donated by Mesa's pioneer families and linked to the city's colorful past. Also on the grounds is the Settler's Adobe House, reconstructed in the scale and manner of the first permanent homes as the new residents attempted to deal with life in the desert heat.

The natural and cultural histories of Mesa and its environs are the focus of the Mesa Southwest Museum. A $4.5 million expansion in 1996 brought the museum to its current size of 80,000 square feet, and another $4.5 million funded new exhibits for the expanded area. Collections include Spanish Colonial relics, artifacts of mining, reflections of Arizona's role in World War II (including Japanese relocation camps), Hohokam ceramics and jewelry, and evidence of Arizona's former function as ocean floor. The museum's Archaeology Team has several active excavations that are open to the public.

Arts and Culture Information: Mesa Arts Center, 1 East Main Street, PO Box 1466, Mesa, AZ 85211-1466; telephone (480)644-6501

Festivals and Holidays

The desert heat in summer dictates that festivals and outdoor events in Mesa are concentrated in winter, spring and fall months with a bit of a summer siesta in between. The year kicks off in January with the Martin Luther King, Jr., Festival, where the civil rights pioneer is feted with music, food, and carnival rides. In February, Mesa joins forces with Phoenix and other East Valley communities to put on the Blues Blast at the Mesa Amphitheatre. National and local blues artists perform a day-long concert that gets central Arizona in the groove. In mid-March, the Old World Folk Music Festival celebrates centuries-old indigenous music from a variety of cultures. From March through April, Free Community Concerts are performed, including a family series with puppetry and theater as well as the Courtyard Series on Thursday nights.

Cinco de Mayo festivities start May off, with a two-day cultural fiesta in Pioneer Park. For 45 years, Mesa has held a Fourth of July party; the Mesa Symphony Orchestra typically provides a rousing rendition of ''The Star Spangled Banner.'' The United Mesa Firefighter Charities usher in cooler weather in September with the Annual Firefighters Benefit Bash. Live music, auctions and raffles all collect proceeds that benefit firefighters and their families during difficult times. Later in September, Mesa honors its history during the Annual Constitution Celebration, featuring a parade, picnics and music.

Native American art, culture, music, dancing, and food are the focus of the Mesa Pow Wow in late October. Elaborate native dress and dance competitions attract visitors from many tribes and states. From November through April, art takes to the streets with Mesa's Sculptures in the Streets program, during which the public can stroll through temporary sculpture displays along downtown Main Street. In December, Main Street is again the destination for holiday celebrations in the downtown area. Mesa's Merry Main Street decks the halls with lights, gingerbread houses, tempting wrapped packages and a visit by Santa.

Sports for the Spectator

The Chicago Cubs get ready for baseball season at Mesa's own Hohokam Field. In 2004, baseball fans at Hohokam Field broke attendance records for Major League Baseball Spring Training. The Cactus League gets started in early March and wraps the Spring Training season up in approximately a month. Locals and visitors get the opportunity to preview not just the Cubs but also their impressive roster of opponents, including the Colorado Rockies, San Diego Padres, and the Oakland A's.

Baseball doesn't end in March, though—Mesa and Hohokam Field are also hosts to Golden League and Fall League baseball. The Golden League subsidizes professional independent teams in Arizona and California at present; the Mesa Miners play ball from May through August. In October and November, Fall League baseball picks up the slack, with the Mesa Solar Sox providing a preview of the next generation of Major League Baseball players.

Mesa Community College's Thunderbirds compete in a variety of sports at the National Junior College Athletic Association level, with teams in baseball, basketball, football, soccer, and track. Phoenix offers more professional and collegiate sports options, from the Cardinals football team to the Suns basketball program to the Diamondbacks baseball organization.

Sports for the Participant

The name of the game in Mesa is golf—local courses abound and a short drive provides access to even more holes stunningly situated in desert and mountain terrain. Local courses in Mesa include Fiesta Lakes Golf Club (public; 9 holes), Royal Palms Golf Course (public; 9 holes), Augusta Ranch Golf Club (private; 18 holes), Las Sendas Golf Club (public; 18 holes), and Superstition Springs Golf Club (9 holes), just to name a few. Toka Sticks Golf Course on the grounds of the Williams Gateway Airport offers the unique opportunity to fly in, play 18 holes and fly out again. Mountain Brook Golf Club is located outside of Mesa but is set in the desert just below the Superstition Mountains, making it a dramatic experience for the golfer.

The Gene Autry Sports Complex contains tennis courts, indoor volleyball courts and beach volleyball pits. Lessons are offered, and players can join leagues or drop in on specified days.

Mesa may be in the desert, but watersports are still available. Rafting and tubing on the Salt River are popular summertime thrills, while local lakes like Saguaro are typically good spots for anglers to try for walleye, largemouth and brown trout, bluegills, channel catfish, and crappie.

The Superstition Mountains east of Mesa offer hikes of all levels of difficulty and duration, including the 1.5 mile Massacre Grounds trail, the Peralta Trail to the Fremont Saddle, and the steep Siphon Draw trail. The Tonto National Forest to the north of Phoenix and Mesa is the fifth largest forest in the United States, providing opportunities for a range of outdoor activities such as hiking, rock climbing, and camping. For a classic hiking adventure, trekkers can head north to the Grand Canyon.

Shopping and Dining

The Mesa Market Place Swap Meet covers 55 acres with more than 1,600 booths under a canopy to give an outdoor shopping experience with shade and water misters to keep customers cool. The Swap Meet is open year-round with great bargains and unusual merchandise. Antiques and collectibles are often found among the shops in the historic downtown area of Mesa, while more recognizable stores can be encountered at the Fiesta Mall, Superstition Springs Center, and The Village Square at Dana Park. Mesa holds a

Community Farmers Market downtown all year, with vendors providing fresh produce and other goods in a street fair atmosphere.

As might be expected, Mesa's culinary specialty is Mexican-Southwestern food, with burgers and pizza coming in second and third. There's something for every taste, though, in Mesa's menu of Chinese, Japanese, sushi, Italian, Greek, steak, and homestyle eateries. Local and chain coffee shops abound, as well.

Convention Facilities

The Main Hall of the Mesa Convention Center offers 15,000 square feet of open space that can be used for trade show exhibits, banquets, dances, concerts and other events. An additional 4,000 square feet can be added by leaving the adjacent meeting rooms open to the Main Hall. The Conference Center features a 100-seat conference theatre that possesses multi-media capabilities for presentations and teleconferences. Breakout rooms and an executive conference room are also available.

The Mesa Amphitheatre hosts more than 70 events per year; festival-style seating can accommodate 4,200 for commercial shows and outdoor festivals.

The Arizona Golf Resort and Conference Center has a 12,000 square foot space for meetings and exhibitions, bolstered by an additional 5,000 square feet of general session rooms, training rooms, board rooms, outdoor courtyards, and even onsite Championship Golf. The Marriott Phoenix Mesa Hotel and Convention Center offers 52,000 square feet of meeting and function space. The 18,000 square foot Exhibit Hall is accompanied by the 9,000 square foot Arizona Ballroom and an outdoor amphitheatre that can accommodate up to 5,200 people.

Transportation

Approaching the City

Phoenix Sky Harbor Airport is located approximately 12 miles to the west of Mesa and is served by 21 airlines that connect the East Valley area to 109 cities in the United States and around the world. Sky Harbor is a major hub for Southwest and America West airlines but also has services through airlines such as United, Delta Frontier, and Sun Country. Non-stop international flights are available via Aeromexico, Air Jamaica, British Airways, Lufthansa, Air

Canada, and America West Airlines. The local airfields, Williams Gateway and Falcon Field, offer charter flights in the southwest.

Several freeways, U.S. highways and state highways pass through or near Mesa, including U.S. 60 (known as Superstition Freeway) and state highways 87 and 89. The Santan Freeway 202 creates a bypass around the more congested downtown area, and Interstates 10 and 17 are quickly accessible from the city. Greyhound Bus service maintains a branch in Mesa, with daily departures and arrivals.

Traveling in the City

Mesa is laid out on a straightforward north-south, east-west grid pattern as regards its major streets. Center Street and Main Street are perpendicular to each other and, as suits their names, intersect in the city center in a manner that provides a handy reference point and makes city navigation relatively easy.

Bus service within Mesa is provided by Valley Metro, which runs buses 6 days a week for about 16 hours per day. There are 9 local routes and 4 express routes to Phoenix. Mesa operates a Dial-A-Ride program for people with mobility or vehicle operation issues, plus the city offers RideChoice options to elderly and disabled patrons who either use the bus, cabs or are driven to their destinations by friends or family members.

Mesa has styled itself as a bicycle-friendly city, with 70 miles of bicycle routes and 40 miles of bicycle lanes. The city plans for more bicycle route and lane construction in the future, along with facilities at bike destinations.

Communications

Newspapers and Magazines

The Mesa area is served by *The East Valley Tribune,* which is delivered daily and is available online by subscription. *Get Out,* an affiliate of the daily paper, supplies dining and entertainment information for Mesa residents and tourists alike. Another online news alternative for the East Valley is offered by *Newszap.com.* Mesa Community College publishes its campus paper, *The Mesa Legend.* Spanish language speakers can check out *La Voz* and *Prensa Hispana,* while other local publications write to the interests of the Catholic, Jewish, and senior populations in Mesa.

Television and Radio

Phoenix is Mesa's source for network television broadcast stations, being home to affiliates of CBS, ABC, NBC, and

Fox. Mesa Channel 11 provides local coverage of council meetings and announcements of local events.

Mesa is within hearing distance of a wide variety of AM and FM radio stations with signals originating in Phoenix; formats run the gamut from talk radio to National Public Radio to classical music to rock and roll. KDKB 93.3 FM is based in Mesa and plays a hard rock rotation.

Mesa Online

City of Mesa home page. Available www.ci.mesa.az.us

City of Mesa Library. Available www.mesalibrary.org

Mesa Chamber of Commerce. Available www.mesachamber .org

Mesa Convention and Visitors Bureau. Available www .mesacvb.com/index.cfm

Mesa Historical Museum. Available www.mesaaz.org/index .htm

Mesa Town Center Corporation. Available www.mesatown center.com

Selected Bibliography

Our Town: The Story of Mesa, Arizona, 1878-1991 (Mesa, AZ: Mesa Public Schools, 1991.)

Phoenix

The City in Brief

Founded: 1864 (incorporated, 1881)

Head Official: Mayor Phil Gordon (since 2003)

City Population
  1980: 789,704
  1990: 983,015
  2000: 1,321,045
  2003 estimate: 1,388,416
  Percent change, 1990–2000: 34.4%
  U.S. rank in 1980: 9th
  U.S. rank in 1990: 9th
  U.S. rank in 2000: 10th (State rank: 1st)

Metropolitan Area Population
  1980: 1,509,000
  1990: 2,238,498
  2000: 3,251,876

  Percent change, 1990–2000: 45.3%
  U.S. rank in 1980: 24th
  U.S. rank in 1990: 20th
  U.S. rank in 2000: 14th

Area: 475.09 square miles (2000)
Elevation: 1,058 feet above sea level
Average Annual Temperature: 72.6° F
Average Annual Precipitation: 8.3 inches

Major Economic Sectors: Services, government, manufacturing

Unemployment Rate: 4.0% (January 2005)
Per Capita Income: $19,833 (1999)

2002 FBI Crime Index Total: 109,916

Major Colleges and Universities: University of Phoenix, Arizona State University, Maricopa Community Colleges

Daily Newspapers: *The Arizona Republic, The Phoenix Gazette*

Introduction

Phoenix, the capital of Arizona, is a study in contrasts. As the center of "the Valley of the Sun," the city has traditionally been associated with Old West myths, tourist resorts, and Sun Belt retirement communities. While it retains strong links with this image—frontier history permeates the city's culture and architecture, tourism continues to thrive, and people still spend their golden years here—Phoenix is also emerging as one of the "newest" cities in the nation. It is among the country's fastest expanding metropolitan areas, and with children under the age of 14 comprising a significant percentage of its inhabitants, Phoenix is adding a youthful contrast to its traditions as a frontier desert town and a place "where the old-timers go to retire." With a growing labor force and population, friendly business environment, affordable housing, and low cost of living, the area is ideal for businesses and residents alike. In 2004 the Milken Institute bestowed upon Phoenix a third place ranking on its annual "Best Performing Cities: Where America's Jobs are Created and Sustained" list.

Geography and Climate

Located in the Salt River Valley in the south central part of the state, Phoenix is situated on flat desert terrain, bordered by lakes and the Superstition Mountains to the east and surrounded by the Phoenix Mountain Preserve. The climate is warm, with low humidity. The most remarkable weather feature is sunshine approximately 325 days per year, making Phoenix one of the sunniest cities in the country.

Area: 475.09 square miles (2000)

Elevation: 1,058 feet above sea level

Average Temperatures: January, 67° F; July, 106.0° F; annual average, 72.6° F

Average Annual Precipitation: 8.3 inches

History

Native Americans Removed to Make Way for White Settlers

The city of Phoenix stands on the site of a prehistoric settlement built by Native Americans, the Hohokam tribe, who had established a thriving culture but who vanished without a trace around 1450 A.D. Thought to be the ancestors of the Pima—"Hohokam" means "those who have gone" in Pima—the Hohokam had constructed a sophisticated system of irrigation canals, many of which are still in use today, that remain as evidence of their existence.

Permanent resettlement of the Hohokam site did not come until the late 1860s; in the interim the area shared the history of the rest of the state. Hispanic conquistadors invaded Arizona in the 1500s in search of the Seven Cities of Cibola, bringing with them cattle, horses, and new agricultural methods. They were followed by miners, traders, and farmers whose presence was tolerated by the Native Americans until the 1850s, when it became apparent that the white settlers were encroaching on their land. Battles between the settlers and the tribes brought intervention by the U.S. military and the tribes were eventually confined to reservations.

City Thrives as Trade Center; Irrigation Aids Farms, Industry

In 1864 a U.S. Army post, a supply camp for nearby Camp McDowell, was set up on the ruins of the Hohokam settlement. Then in 1867 the Hohokam's irrigation canals were rebuilt by two settlers, one of whom called the place "Phoenix." He predicted that, like the mythical phoenix bird rising from its own ashes, a great city would emerge from the ruins. Incorporated in 1881, Phoenix rapidly developed into a major trading center with the building of the railroad in 1887 and became the capital of the Arizona territory in 1889; it was named the capital of the state of Arizona in 1912.

Phoenix gained a reputation as a rowdy frontier town because of its saloons, gambling palaces, and general outlaw atmosphere. Law and order were restored by the turn of the century, however, and Phoenix entered a new phase. The railroad, bringing settlers from throughout the country, established an immigration pattern that has continued steadily without interruption; during the three decades following World War II, for instance, the population of Phoenix increased from roughly 107,000 to nearly 790,000 people.

Major technological advances during the first half of the twentieth century—the Roosevelt Dam on the Salt River, the Southern Pacific Railroad, the advent of air conditioning, and the Central Arizona Project aqueduct system—brought about agricultural and industrial development that also fueled tremendous growth. In the 1990s Phoenix went through its third major growth boom in four decades, partly a result of a large influx of people from California. The city has begun to experience the effects of urban sprawl, including serious air pollution. Entering the twenty-first century, Phoenix's landscape consists of Hispanic colonial and Indian pueblo architecture interspersed with gleaming highrise office buildings. The economic success of the area has spurred a continuing population growth and nearly all business indicators present positive gains. The City Council has allotted $1 billion in public and private projects to enhance and maintain the community. This foresight, in conjunction with the natural appeal of the environment, prepares the city for boundless prosperity.

Historical Information: Phoenix Museum of History, 105 N. 5th St., Phoenix, AZ 85004-4404; telephone (602)253-2734; email exhibits@pmoh.org

Population Profile

Metropolitan Area Residents

1980: 1,509,000
1990: 2,238,498
2000: 3,251,876
Percent change, 1990–2000: 45.3%
U.S. rank in 1980: 24th
U.S. rank in 1990: 20th
U.S. rank in 2000: 14th

City Residents

1980: 789,704
1990: 983,015
2000: 1,321,045
2003 estimate: 1,388,416
Percent change, 1990–2000: 34.4%
U.S. rank in 1980: 9th
U.S. rank in 1990: 9th
U.S. rank in 2000: 10th (State rank: 1st)

Density: 2,781.9 people per square mile (2000)

Racial and ethnic characteristics (2000)
White: 938,853
Black or African American: 67,416
American Indian and Alaska Native: 26,696
Asian: 26,449
Native Hawaiian and Pacific Islander: 1,766
Hispanic or Latino (may be of any race): 449,972
Other: 216,589

Percent of residents born in state: 34.6% (2000)

Age characteristics (2000)
Population under 5 years old: 114,516
Population 5 to 9 years old: 111,367
Population 10 to 14 years old: 99,471
Population 15 to 19 years old: 97,425
Population 20 to 24 years old: 103,873
Population 25 to 34 years old: 227,481
Population 35 to 44 years old: 211,442

Population 45 to 54 years old: 157,615
Population 55 to 59 years old: 52,623
Population 60 to 64 years old: 38,437
Population 65 to 74 years old: 58,309
Population 75 to 84 years old: 36,879
Population 85 years and over: 11,607
Median age: 30.7 years

Births (2003)
Total number: 25,749

Deaths (2003)
Total number: 7,902 (of which, 174 were infants under the age of 1 year)

Money income (1999)
Per capita income: $19,833
Median household income: $41,207
Total households: 466,114

Number of households with income of . . .
less than $10,000: 37,689
$10,000 to $14,999: 27,862
$15,000 to $24,999: 63,160
$25,000 to $34,999: 65,783
$35,000 to $49,999: 82,180
$50,000 to $74,999: 89,831
$75,000 to $99,999: 45,918
$100,000 to $149,999: 33,461
$150,000 to $199,999: 9,674
$200,000 or more: 10,556

Percent of families below poverty level: 11.5% (41.3% of which were female householder families with related children under 5 years)

2002 FBI Crime Index Total: 109,916

Municipal Government

The capital of Arizona and the Maricopa County seat, Phoenix has a council-manager form of government. The eight council members serve staggered four-year terms, representing districts of the city, while the mayor is elected at large to a four-year term and also serves as a member of the council. Phoenix has won international recognition and many awards for the quality of management of the city.

Head Official: Mayor Phil Gordon (since 2003; current term expires 2007)

Total Number of City Employees: 13,095 (2004)

City Information: City of Phoenix, 200 W. Washington St., Phoenix, AZ 85003; telephone (602)262-6011

Economy

Major Industries and Commercial Activity

Manufacturing and tourism, traditionally the base of the city's economy, continue to be important to Phoenix. Major industrial products manufactured by companies located in the metropolitan area include aircraft parts, electronic equipment, agricultural chemicals, radios, air-conditioning equipment, leather goods, and native American crafts.

Tourism is an especially vital part of the economy. With more than 10 million visitors from the throughout the United States and Canada annually visiting for the warm weather and sunshine in the Valley of the Sun, Phoenix continues to be an important resort center. Flights from Phoenix travel to 89 locations within the United States and 17 cities internationally including destinations in Norway, Sweden, Greenland, Mexico, India, and Canada. The airport is constantly seeking to improve its facilities as is demonstrated by the nearly 80 ongoing slated projects costing an upwards of $600 million.

As the result of the population boom, the economy of Phoenix has taken on new dimensions in recent decades by moving into technology and service industries. Tourism and business services in particular now account for nearly 77 percent of the area's total employment. Another sector of growth has been financial services and banking as several significant processing and/or regional headquarters operations call Phoenix home: American Express, Chase Bank, Bank of America, Discover Card Services, and Wells Fargo Bank. High technology and aerospace firms hold a considerable share of the manufacturing jobs throughout the state (56 percent).

Population and economic growth have made Phoenix the center of the state's economy. More than a third of the state's entire labor force works in the Phoenix metropolitan area. Further, many *Fortune* 500 companies operate within the area such as Boeing, Bank of America, Time Warner Telecom, IBM, and Intel.

Items and goods produced: aircraft and aircraft parts, electronic equipment, steel castings and fabrications, flour, boxes, agricultural chemicals, aluminum products, radios, mobile homes, air conditioning machinery, creamery products, beer, liquor, saddles and leather goods, apparel, native American and Mexican novelties

Incentive Programs—New and Existing Companies

Funding and assistance for business development in Phoenix are available through the Business Development Finance Corporation, Southwestern Business Financing Corp., the Phoenix Industrial Development Authority (PIDA), the Small Business Innovation Research Program (SBIR), and the Arizona Commerce and Economic Development Commission.

Local programs—Employers locating facilities in the 100-square-mile City of Phoenix Enterprise Zone (COPEZ), as designated by the Arizona Department of Commerce, can earn state corporate income tax credit for each net new job created in the zone. Tax credits can total up to $3,000 per hire (with a maximum of 200 annually) over a three-year period. The city of Phoenix is the administrator of Foreign Trade Zone #75, which allows companies to reduce or defer payment of customs duties on imported products; companies operating in the zone can benefit from an 80 percent reduction in real and personal property tax. EXPAND (Expansion Assistance and Development Program) was formed to facilitate a growing company's need for funds to acquire capital.

State programs—Arizona has a favorable tax structure for businesses, collecting no corporate franchise tax; in addition, business inventories are exempt from property taxes. The State of Arizona has adopted a four-year accelerated depreciation schedule for certain personal property devoted to any commercial or industrial use. There are weight-distance tax exemptions and transaction privilege tax refunds for the motion picture industry, and exemptions from taxation for secured and unsecured personal property relating to construction work in progress. Qualified employers that provide technical training for their employees are eligible for the Technology Training Tax Credit.

Job training programs—The Arizona Legislature has allocated $7 million for the administration of the Arizona Work Force Development and Job Training program, targeted at new and existing businesses. Funds are available on a grant basis and range from $2,000 to $5,000 per job. In addition, Arizona State University and the Maricopa Community College district work with area employers to maintain continuing education programs for local workers.

Development Projects

A rapidly growing young city, Phoenix has required more recent construction activities than more mature cities. The first phase of a $600-million construction project for the Phoenix Civic Plaza will, once all three phases are complete, boost the plaza's national rank from 67th to the top 25 by tripling its size. One new research institute (Translational Genomics Research Institute (TGEN) was built in the downtown area for $46 million while another large facility opened in late 2004 on the campus of Arizona State University.

Economic Development Information: City of Phoenix Community and Economic Development Office, 200 W. Washington St., 20th Fl., Phoenix AZ 85003; telephone (602)262-5040; fax (602)495-5097

Commercial Shipping

Phoenix is located at the center of market areas stretching along interstate highways from southern California to western Texas, Colorado, Utah, and Mexico. More than 50 companies provide motor freight service. Rail service is available from two transcontinental rail lines. The Phoenix metropolitan area economy benefits from air cargo service through Phoenix Sky Harbor International Airport, where American Airlines and American West provide wide-body freight service.

Labor Force and Employment Outlook

The local labor force is described as young, plentiful, and well-educated. Arizona consistently ranks in the top five growth states, and workers are attracted by the quality of life to be enjoyed. A right-to-work state, Arizona has union membership of 3.6 percent in the private sector.

In March 2005 Manpower, Inc.'s employment outlook survey indicated that 36 percent of employers in the greater Phoenix area intend to expand their workforce in nearly all major categories including construction, durable goods manufacturing, transportation, trade, and finance. This exceeds the national average of 30 percent. In fact, the Arizona Department of Economic Security reported the area's labor force growth as 7.2 percent in 2003–2004 (with 1.8 million workers in 2004) while the national level was 0.6 percent. Growth is expected to top 550,000 jobs by 2012 with significant gains in the professional, service, and technical fields.

The following is a summary of data regarding the Phoenix-Mesa-Scottsdale metropolitan area non-agricultural labor force, 2004 annual averages.

Size of non-agricultural labor force: 1,674,800

Number of workers employed in . . .
   natural resources and mining: 2,000
   construction: 140,000
   manufacturing: 130,500
   trade, transportation, and utilities: 339,600
   information: 35,700
   financial activities: 137,400
   professional and business services: 270,900
   educational and health services: 172,600
   leisure and hospitality: 160,500
   other services: 64,200
   government: 220,900

Average hourly earnings of production workers employed in manufacturing: $13.84

Unemployment rate: 4.0% (January 2005)

Largest employers	Number of employees
State of Arizona	50,363
Wal-Mart	18,677
Banner Health Systems	13,756
Maricopa County	13,482
City of Phoenix	13,095
Honeywell International Inc.	12,000
U.S. Postal Service	11,406
Wells Fargo Company	11,000
Arizona State University	10,005
Albertson's-Osco	9,500

Cost of Living

The cost of living for the area is below that of the national average according to the Greater Phoenix Economic Council. Phoenix boasts affordable new and existing housing, with median-range homes at costs below the national average as reported by the Arizona State University Real Estate Center in April 2004.

The following is a summary of data regarding several key cost of living factors for the Phoenix area.

2004 (3rd Quarter) ACCRA Average House Price: $254,751

2004 (3rd Quarter) ACCRA Cost of Living Index: 99.2 (U.S. average = 100.0)

State income tax rate: Ranges from 2.87% to 5.04%

State sales tax rate: 5.6% (food and prescription drugs are exempt)

Local income tax rate: None

Local sales tax rate: 1.4% plus 0.7% county rate

Property tax rate: Varies by school district. The 2004 average was $16.95 per $100 of assessed valuation

Economic Information: Greater Phoenix Economic Council, Two N. Central Ave., Ste. 2500, Phoenix, AZ 85004; telephone (602)256-7700 or (800)421-4732; fax (602)256-7744; email info@gpec.org

Education and Research

Elementary and Secondary Schools

A total of 58 separate school districts serve the entire Maricopa County. The city of Phoenix is served by 16 separate public school districts, each with its own school board and superintendent. The Greater Phoenix area has an extensive magnet school program with an emphasis on specialized course work in career fields such as aeronautics and aerospace, agri-business, and computer studies, among others.

The following is a summary of data regarding school districts in the Phoenix area as of the 2003–2004 school year.

Total enrollment: 626,461

Number of facilities
  elementary schools: 95
  middle schools: 32
  senior high schools: 67

Student/teacher ratio: ranges from 16.4:1 to 22:1, depending on school district

Teacher salaries
  average: $44,404

Funding per pupil: ranges from $4,980 to $8,304, depending on school district

More than 80 private elementary and high schools are also located in Phoenix, providing alternative educational services.

Public Schools Information: Maricopa County Superintendent of Schools, 301 W. Jefferson St., Ste. 660, Phoenix, AZ 85003; telephone (602)506-3866

Colleges and Universities

Phoenix has 79 private technical and business colleges, including the University of Phoenix and Maricopa Community Colleges, the second-largest public community college system in the United States. The University of Phoenix has garnered the spot as the nation's top private university via its innovative online degree program and 163 campuses throughout North America. Both offer undergraduate degrees in a wide range of disciplines and graduate degrees in such fields as business and management and education. Other colleges in Phoenix include Grand Canyon University and a campus of the Arizona State University (ASU), the largest university in the Rocky Mountain area with an enrollment of about 58,000 students and 2,165 full-time faculty, based in nearby Tempe. ASU boasts a strong science orientation; the Phoenix campus (named West Campus) focuses on upper division and graduate courses.

Libraries and Research Centers

The Phoenix Public Library system consists of the main branch downtown and 13 branches located throughout the city. Located in 280,000 square feet, the central library's collection numbers nearly one million volumes as well as magazines, newspapers, tapes, films, slides, and art reproductions. Special collections include the Arizona Room that features a variety of resources related to Arizona's rich history. The Arizona State Library, Archives, and Public Records also focuses on the state's history and includes law, government, and genealogy holdings. More than 50 special libraries and research centers are located in Phoenix; most are affiliated with colleges, medical centers, and government agencies and specialize in such fields as medicine, business, and technology. Arizona State University's Engineering Center focuses on microelectronics, CAD/CAM, telecommunications, and computer science.

The Translational Genomics Research Institute (TGEN) held its grand opening in March 2005 with a 170,000 square foot facility. The first of several facilities to be constructed, the $46 million center will employ 450 people. The Arizona Biodesign Institute on the campus of Arizona State University is contributing to Phoenix's growth by luring scientists and biotechnological companies to the area. Four modules are set for completion by 2007; the first opened with 250,000 square feet in the fall of 2004.

Public Library Information: Phoenix Public Library, 1221 N. Central Ave., Phoenix, AZ 85004; telephone (602)262-4636

Health Care

Along with population growth in Phoenix has come an increased demand for health care services; meeting this need, the Phoenix medical community has become a major industry in the metropolitan area. More than 33,000 medical personnel are employed in the region. Forty-two licensed hospitals, providing in excess of 8,000 beds, serve the Phoenix metropolitan area; more than 2,000 physicians, dentists, psychiatrists, chiropractors, osteopaths, and ophthalmologists attend to health care needs.

The largest health care facilities in Phoenix are the Maricopa Integrated Health System with 621 beds; St. Joseph's Hospital and Medical Center, housing 520 beds; the 600-bed Banner Desert Medical Center; the Barrow Neurological Institute, known internationally for the treatment of neurological disorders; and Good Samaritan Regional Medical Center, with 619 beds. In 2000 a bone marrow transplant program for children was launched after Phoenix Children's Hospital Foundation supplied a grant to underwrite the salary costs for a physician who specializes in pediatric bone marrow transplants.

Recreation

Sightseeing

A visitor to the Phoenix metropolitan area will find many sights and attractions, some of them related to frontier history and the natural beauty of Salt River Valley. A principal attraction in Phoenix since 1939 is the Desert Botanical Garden on 50 acres of Papago Park, containing 10,000 desert plants that represent half of the 1,800 existing species of cactus. Also located in Papago Park is the Phoenix Zoo, a privately funded, non-profit zoo, where 1,200 animals are exhibited.

Historic Heritage Square near downtown is a city block of restored Victorian houses preserved as replicas of homes in the late 1800s and converted into museums, shops, and restaurants; a highlight is the elegant Rosson House. Also downtown is the National Native American Cooperative, which features dancers, foods and crafts, and a monthly Indian market October through May. In neighboring Scottsdale is Taliesin West, a national historic landmark built as the desert home of architect Frank Lloyd Wright.

Scottsdale is also the site of Rawhide, a replica of a 1880s western town that offers a variety of activities, including stagecoach and burro rides, a petting zoo, and stunt shows. Located in nearby Tempe is Big Surf, ''Arizona's ocean.''

Old West-style entertainment, such as stagecoach rides, covered wagon campfire circles, and simulated gunfighter shootouts, is available to groups by reservation through various commercial enterprises in the area. Scenic day trips to the Grand Canyon and other sights near metropolitan Phoenix are provided by several bus and airplane charter services. Encanto Park is the home of the Enchanted Island Amusement Park with a variety of rides geared for the younger set.

Arts and Culture

Phoenix has a vital performing arts community, which was enriched with the 1989 opening of the Herberger Theatre Center. Located downtown next to the Phoenix Civic Plaza Convention Center and Symphony Hall, the complex is designed to augment existing cultural facilities. The Herberger Theater is used primarily for music, dance, and dramatic performances and includes an art gallery.

The Phoenix Center Youth Theatre, CityJazz, Dance Phoenix, and the Phoenix Children's Chorus call the Phoenix Center for the Arts their home. A variety of theater and drama, including amateur, professional, children/family-oriented, and experimental productions, is offered by companies in the Phoenix area. Founded in 1920, the Phoenix Theatre Little Theater is one of the oldest continuously running companies in the country. The Arizona Theatre Company, based in Phoenix, is in residence at the Herberger Theater Center and offers about 25 weeks of performances. Other local troupes include Childsplay, Actors Theatre of Phoenix, and Centre Dance Ensemble.

Housed in Symphony Hall, the Phoenix Symphony Orchestra performs an extensive classical repertoire and presents pops concerts with well-known guest artists. Phoenix hosts the state's professional ballet company and other international dance companies. The Arizona Opera also gives regular performances for Phoenix area audiences. Touring artists perform at the America West Arena, Celebrity Theatre, Gammage Auditorium, and the Cricket Pavilion.

More than 40 museums and 150 art galleries in the Phoenix area offer a range of educational and cultural experiences. The Arizona Hall of Fame Museum, opened in 1902, honors people who have contributed to Arizona heritage. Featuring the history of central Arizona, the Arizona Historical Society Museum includes replications of old-time shops and stores. The family-oriented Shemer Art Center and Museum presents primarily local and state artists. The Arizona Science Center provides interactive exhibits for children and adults in such areas as energy, life science, and health. The Hall of Flame Fire Fighting Museum houses the world's most extensive collection of fire-fighting apparatus, equipment, and memorabilia. Anthropological exhibits, fine arts, and historic arts of Native American cultures of the Southwest are specialties at the Heard Museum, which boasts 18,000 works of art and artifacts. The Phoenix Art Museum contains a permanent collection of 17,000 objects focusing on European, American, Western American, Latin American, and Asian arts and costume design. Owned and operated by artisan members, the Craftsmen's Cooperative Gallery at Heritage Square features handmade arts and crafts.

Festivals and Holidays

Highlights from the Phoenix special events calendar include the Tostitos Fiesta Bowl Football Classic, which opens the year with a game between two of the country's best collegiate teams on New Year's Day at Sun Devil Stadium. Also held in January are the Arizona National Livestock Show (since 1948) and the Parada del Sol Parade and Rodeo.

The Heard Museum Guild Annual Indian Fair and Market takes place in March, featuring Native American culture. Also in March is the St. Patrick's Day Parade and Irish Family Fare. The Desert Botanical Garden's Annual Cactus and Succulent Show and Sale is offered in April. In May the Cinco de Mayo festival celebrates the 1862 Mexican victory over the French with various activities throughout the Phoenix area. The Arizona State Fair, billed as one of the most successful in the nation, takes place in October and November. The fall also brings the Way Out West Oktoberfest. The

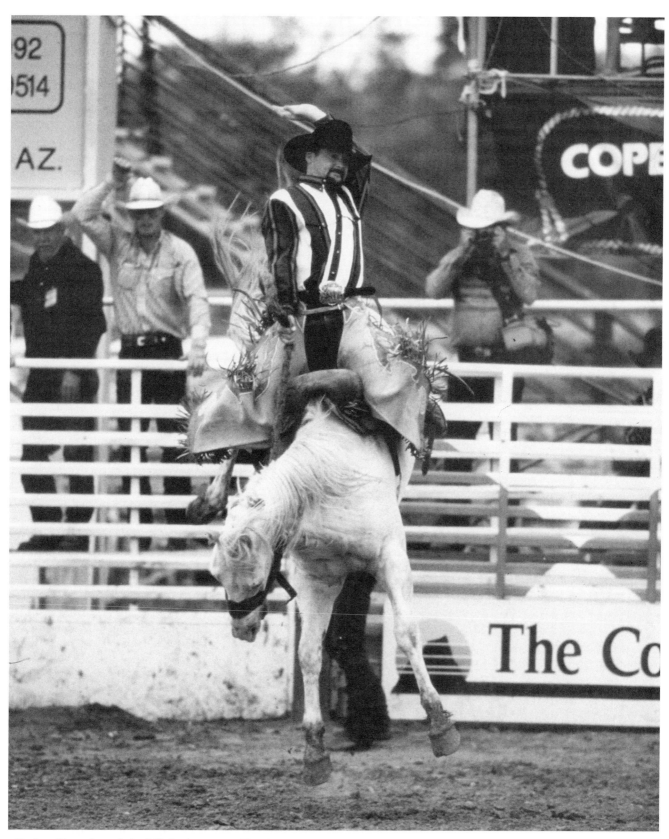

Rodeo riders show their skill during events like those held at the Parada del Sol Parade and Rodeo and the Yavapai County Fair.

year ends with the APS Fiesta of Light Parade and Victorian Holiday Celebration, two December celebrations of the holiday season in downtown Phoenix. During the final week of the month the Fiesta Bowl events precede the New Year's Day Fiesta Bowl game with the Pageant of Bands, the Fiesta Bowl Parade, and sports and cultural events.

Sports for the Spectator

Phoenix fields teams in all major league sports. The city is home to two professional basketball teams, the Phoenix Suns of the National Basketball Association, and the Phoenix Mercury of the Women's National Basketball Association, both of which play their games at the America West Arena. Professional football is represented by the National Football League's Arizona Cardinals and the Arena Football League's Rattlers while professional hockey is represented by the National Hockey League's Phoenix Coyotes and the East Coast Hockey League's Phoenix Roadrunners. In 1998 the major league baseball team, the Arizona Diamondbacks, were formed and began play at Bank One Ball Park, built especially for them. In 2001 the expansion team defeated the powerhouse New York Yankees to capture their first World Series crown.

From March through early April, exhibition baseball games are held nearly every day by the 12 major league baseball teams that hold spring training in Phoenix at the Cactus League games. Other popular sporting events are polo matches and greyhound, horse, and auto racing. The Phoenix Greyhound Park features greyhound races year round, and Turf Paradise schedules thoroughbred racing from September through May. The Phoenix International Raceway, built in 1964, boasts the world's fastest one-mile oval paved track for auto racing, and the Manzanita Speedway holds Sprint, midget, and stockcar races.

Annual sporting events in the Phoenix area include professional golf tournaments, such as the FBR Open, with about 500,000 attendees, and the LPGA Safeway International at the Superstition Mountain Golf and Country Club; the Formula One Grand Prix auto race in April; and World Championship Tennis.

Sports for the Participant

Phoenix's consistently warm climate permits such year-round outdoor activities as camping, backpacking, hiking, horseback riding, mountain climbing, swimming, boating, fishing, water skiing, skating, tennis, and golf. In metropolitan Phoenix and the surrounding valley area, there are more than 1,100 tennis and racquetball courts, more than 190 championship golf courses (many designed by golfing legends Arnold Palmer and Jack Nicklaus), and many natural and man-made lakes and waterways with facilities for a variety of water sports. Contained within the city limits is South Mountain Regional Park, said to be the largest municipal park in the world, which offers horseback riding, hiking trails, and a view of the city. Three snow skiing resorts are within traveling distance of the city.

Shopping and Dining

Retail establishments in Phoenix range from large malls and shopping centers—including several downtown—that feature nationally known department stores to small specialty shops offering products made by local artists and craftsmen. Located downtown the Arizona Center is a uniquely landscaped mall on three acres of land. Close to the center city is Biltmore Fashion Park, a collection of exclusive and stores anchored by Macy's and Saks Fifth Avenue. Nearby is Town & Country Shopping Center, considered Arizona's original open-air mall; two blocks away is Tower Plaza Mall. Located in the northeast sector of the city is Colonnade Mall, winner of the International Council of Shopping Centers ''Beauty of Design'' award. A variety of shops in metropolitan Phoenix specialize in such items as native American arts and crafts, products made from Arizona copper, leather crafts, and Western apparel.

Restaurants in Phoenix have become more sophisticated with the city's growth and prosperity. They offer a variety of cuisines, including traditional American, Italian, Continental, Oriental, and French. Specialties are Southwestern and Mexican dishes with an emphasis on regional foods such as chilies, jicama, local game, and citrus. A popular attraction is Rustler's Roost, a landmark and one of the busiest dining establishments west of the Mississippi. With a scenic mountaintop view of the surrounding area, the restaurant features a mineshaft entrance and walls decorated with the brands of local cattle ranches. Selected by *Food and Wine* magazine as Distinguished Restaurants of North America were Different Point of View, Le Orangerie, and Vincent Guerithault on Camelback.

Visitor Information: Greater Phoenix Convention & Visitors Bureau, 400 E. Van Buren St., Ste. 600, Phoenix, AZ 85004; telephone (602)254-6500; fax (602)253-4415; email visitors@visitphoenix.com

Convention Facilities

Phoenix is a popular gathering place for large and small groups that wish to conduct business in a pleasurable environment. Known for its resorts, Phoenix offers plentiful hotel space (about 10,000 rooms in the central city alone), a year-round warm climate, and a variety of leisure activities. These factors have contributed to an increase in group business in metropolitan Phoenix since 1980. Nearly 40 percent of visitors to the Valley come to attend a convention.

The Phoenix Civic Plaza and Convention Center, with 300,000 square feet of meeting and exhibit space in 43 breakout meeting rooms providing a total seating capacity for more than 29,000 people, has been the city's primary convention facility since 1972. A $600-million expansion is planned that will by 2008 increase the space to 900,000 square feet. Meeting space is also available at Veterans Memorial Coliseum, at Arizona State University, and at area hotels.

Convention Information: Phoenix Civic Plaza and Convention Center, 111 N. 3rd St., Phoenix, AZ 85004; telephone (800)AT-CIVIC

Transportation

Approaching the City

Located near downtown, the Phoenix Sky Harbor International Airport is serviced by 23 airlines with direct flights from most cities in the United States and several locations abroad. More than 108,000 passengers are served on a daily basis, which is comparable to the Miami and San Francisco airports. Its importance to the area is highlighted by an estimated $72 million daily economic impact.

Interstate routes into the city are Interstate 10 (the Papago Freeway), entering from the west, and Interstate 17 (the Black Canyon Freeway), entering from the north. These highways join at Van Buren Street and 27th Avenue, becoming the Maricopa Freeway and then forming the Pima Freeway southeast of the city. State Route 89 (Grand Avenue Expressway) enters diagonally from the northwest, joins State Route 60 at Van Buren Street downtown then intersects the city laterally to the east, becoming the Superstition Freeway. A 20-year ''Regional Transportation Plan'' was passed by voters in November 2004 to alleviate excessive traffic congestion by building new or renovating existing freeways; 2007 is the earliest projected start date.

Traveling in the City

Phoenix made the top ten list in 2003 for most improved transit systems by the trade journal, *Metro Magazine*. Travel in the city is facilitated by the simple grid layout. The Phoenix Transit System provides daily bus service in the metropolitan area.

Communications

Newspapers and Magazines

Phoenix's major daily newspaper is the morning *The Arizona Republic*. The smaller-circulation *The Phoenix Gazette* is published in the evenings on Monday through Saturday. Among the many other daily and weekly periodicals published in Phoenix are the *Arizona Business Gazette, Arizona Informant, Jewish News of Greater Phoenix,* and *New Times* (which features arts, entertainment, and restaurants). Magazines published in Phoenix include *Phoenix Magazine* and *Arizona Highways.*

Television and Radio

Phoenix is served by seven television stations and by two cable television companies. Twenty-six AM and FM radio stations, including Hispanic-language radio, also broadcast in Phoenix.

Media Information: The Arizona Republic, Phoenix Newspapers Inc., 200 E. Van Buren St., Phoenix, AZ 85004; telephone (602)444-8000; toll-free (800)331-9303

Phoenix Online

The Arizona Republic. Available www.azcentral.com/arizona republic

Arizona School Report Cards. Available www.ade.state.az.us/srcs

City of Phoenix Home Page. Available www.ci.phoenix.az.us

Greater Phoenix Convention & Visitors Bureau. Available www.phoenixcvb.com

Greater Phoenix Economic Council. Available www.gpec.org

Phoenix Museum of History. Available www.pmoh.org

Phoenix Public Library. Available www.ci.phoenix.az.us/LIBRARY/pplidx.html

Selected Bibliography

Bartlett, Michael H., and Thomas M. Kolaz, *Archaeology in the City: A Hohokam Village in Phoenix, Arizona* (Tucson: University of Arizona Press, 1986)

Hait, Pam, *Shifra Stein's Day Trips from Greater Phoenix, Tucson, and Flagstaff* (Charlotte, NC: East Woods Press, 1986)

Scottsdale

The City in Brief

Founded: 1888 (incorporated, 1951)

Head Official: Mayor Mary Manross (NP) (since 2004)

City Population
  1980: 88,622
  1990: 130,099
  2000: 202,705
  2003 estimate: 217,989
  Percent change, 1990–2000: 55.8%
  U.S. rank in 1980: 141st
  U.S. rank in 1990: 139th
  U.S. rank in 2000: 99th (State rank: 5th)

Metropolitan Area Population (CMSA)
  1980: 1,509,175
  1990: 2,238,480

  2000: 3,251,876
  Percent change, 1990–2000: 45.3%
  U.S. rank in 1980: 26th
  U.S. rank in 1990: 20th
  U.S. rank in 2000: 14th

Area: 184.5 square miles (2000)
Elevation: 1,250 feet above sea level
Average Annual Temperature: 70.3° F
Average Annual Precipitation: 7.05 inches

Major Economic Sectors: Services; trade; finance, insurance and real estate; manufacturing
Unemployment Rate: 4.0% (January 2005)

2002 FBI Crime Index Total: 10,134

Major Colleges and Universities: Scottsdale Community College

Daily Newspaper: *Scottsdale Progress Tribune*

Introduction

Scottsdale is a popular winter vacation mecca in the area of Arizona known as the "Valley of the Sun." A tiny farming community of 2,000 people covering only 1 square mile in 1951, Scottsdale has become a vibrant city of more than 200,000 residents encompassing nearly 200 square miles. Its many golf courses and resorts attract visitors from around the world. Art galleries abound amid the towering palm trees, purple shadowed mountains, and pastel landscapes. The city boasts more than 300 sunny days per year. The lively restaurants, nightclubs, and cultural and sporting events add a metropolitan touch, yet cowboy ranches and Indian reservations are a brief ride away. In addition to its booming tourism industry, Scottsdale has become a diverse high technology center and is becoming recognized as a leader in health care and medical research. It offers a vast array of recreational activities including biking, hiking, white water rafting, horseback riding, and ballooning. The arts are flourishing in the city, which has its own symphony orchestra and more art showcases per capita than almost any other world city.

Geography and Climate

Scottsdale is located in central Arizona, just northeast of Phoenix. With an area of more than 184.5 square miles, the distance between the most extreme northern and southern points in Scottsdale is 31 miles; the distance between the farthest east and west points in 11.5 miles. Scottsdale enjoys more sunshine than any other area in the United States. Low humidity year-round makes even high temperatures comfortable. Most of the yearly rainfall occurs July through September and December through March.

Area: 184.5 square miles (2000)

Elevation: 1,250 feet above sea level

Average Temperatures: January, 51.2° F; July, 91.2° F; annual average, 70.3° F

Average Annual Precipitation: 7.05 inches

History

Irrigation Leads to Thriving Agriculture Industry

Prior to its founding, the Scottsdale area was made up of barren desert lands, distinguished only by the intricate canals of the Hohokam Indians.

Scottsdale was founded in 1888 by U.S. Army Chaplain Winfield Scott, a Baptist minister from New York. That same year the construction of the Arizona Canal, which provided irrigation to a wide geographic area, was completed by Frank Murphy. Winfield Scott and his brother, George Washington Scott, who shared a dream of developing a thriving town in the desert, first grew citrus and other fruits, peanuts, and sweet potatoes on their land.

Air Quality Attracts Settlers, Manufacturers, Artists

Early settlers included people searching for better health and others who were attracted by the fresh desert air. History shows that many of these people were culturally-minded and nurtured the arts from the beginning. The city was first called Orangedale because of the orange orchards along Camelback Mountain, but the name was changed to Scottsdale in 1894 in honor of its founder.

From 1894 through the 1940s Paradise Valley ranchers drove their cattle through the city each spring and fall on their way to the stockyards or the train depot at Tempe where the cattle were shipped to market.

Modern development began after World War II when Motorola opened a plant in Scottsdale, the first of many electronics manufacturing plants to locate in the area. Artists and crafts persons also became attracted to the city, and the population grew from 2,000 people in 1950 to 10,000 people by 1960. By 1965 the city had grown to 55,000 residents. The city was incorporated in 1951 and received its city charter in 1961.

Through the 1960s the city preserved an Old West look of wood buildings and quaintly lettered signs, calling itself "the West's most Western town." As the "Old West" theme became less prominent, the city began billing itself as the "Arts Capital of the Southwest." Galleries shared the avenues with western wear stores, and the magnificent Scottsdale Center for the Arts was built, permitting year-round exhibits and concerts for residents and visitors.

Scottsdale's area was greatly increased by the annexation of territory north of the city in the 1980s. A great part of this area is made up of uninhabited desert and hilly land, much of which is maintained in its natural state. Although manufacturing remains the state's largest employer, tourism is now the city's major industry.

In recent years Scottsdale has spent almost $4 million on the renovation of the downtown area with new landscaping, entrances, signage and public art, making it a most appealing desert oasis.

Historical Information: Scottsdale Historical Society, Inc., PO Box 143, Scottsdale, AZ 85252; telephone (480)946-0394

Population Profile

Metropolitan Area Residents (CMSA)

1980: 1,509,175
1990: 2,238,480
2000: 3,251,876
Percent change, 1990–2000: 45.3%
U.S. rank in 1980: 26th
U.S. rank in 1990: 20th
U.S. rank in 2000: 14th

City Residents

1980: 88,622
1990: 130,099
2000: 202,705
2003 estimate: 217,989
Percent change, 1990–2000: 55.8%
U.S. rank in 1980: 141st
U.S. rank in 1990: 139th (State rank: 6th)
U.S. rank in 2000: 99th (State rank: 5th)

Density: 1,096 people per square mile (in 2000)

Racial and ethnic characteristics (2000)
White: 186,883
Black or African American: 2,501
American Indian and Alaska Native: 1,240
Asian: 3,964
Native Hawaiian and Pacific Islander: 167
Hispanic or Latino (may be of any race): 14,111
Other: 4,603

Percent of residents born in state: 18.3% (2000)

Age characteristics (2000)
Population under 5 years old: 10,444
Population 5 to 9 years old: 11,188
Population 10 to 14 years old: 11,256
Population 15 to 19 years old: 9,900
Population 20 to 24 years old: 9,798
Population 25 to 34 years old: 28,973
Population 35 to 44 years old: 32,677
Population 45 to 54 years old: 30,544
Population 55 to 59 years old: 13,215
Population 60 to 64 years old: 10,826
Population 65 to 74 years old: 18,581
Population 75 to 84 years old: 11,734
Population 85 years and older: 3,569
Median age: 41 years

Births (2003)
Total number: 2,795

Deaths (2003)
Total number: 2,088 (of which, 17 were infants under the age of 1 year)

Money income (1999)
Per capita income: $39,158
Median household income: $57,484
Total households: 90,602

Number of households with income of . . .
less than $10,000: 4,762
$10,000 to $14,999: 3,375
$15,000 to $24,999: 8,337
$25,000 to $34,999: 9,355
$35,000 to $49,999: 13,076
$50,000 to $74,999: 17,561
$75,000 to $99,999: 10,594
$100,000 to $149,999: 11,907
$150,000 to $199,999: 4,791
$200,000 or more: 6,844

Percent of families below poverty level: 3.4% (25.2% of which were female householder families with related children under 5 years)

2002 FBI Crime Index Total: 10,134

Municipal Government

Scottsdale's government consists of a mayor and six city council members elected at large who serve staggered four-year terms. The council appoints a city manager, city clerk, city treasurer, city attorney, and city judge.

Head Official: Mayor Mary Manross (since 2000; current term expires June 2008)

Total Number of City Employees: 1,700 (2005)

City Information: City of Scottsdale, PO Box 1000, Scottsdale, AZ 85252; telephone (480)994-2414

Economy

Major Industries and Commercial Activity

Tourism is Scottsdale's major industry and largest employer, providing jobs to 39 percent of the city's workers. Today, Scottsdale is home to more than 60 hotels and resorts with a combined total of more than 12,000 rooms. The city is also home to numerous high-technology firms such as Motorola Research and Development and Medical Operations. In addition, it is the location for a number of regional and national corporate headquarters.

Aviation is one of the fastest growing sectors of the Arizona economy. The Scottsdale Airport/Airpark was begun in the 1960s as a fully planned facility specifically designed to meet the needs of employers with air transportation requirements. By 2004, the Airpark had become one of Scottsdale's top employment centers, with nearly 50,000 people employed in retail, service, technological, and manufacturing industries. The Airpark houses some 2,200 businesses in all with a combined economic impact of nearly $3 billion annually.

Items and goods produced: electronics, wearing apparel, aerial maps

Incentive Programs—New and Existing Companies

Local programs—To encourage commercial development and facilitate the paperwork involved, the city offers developers a "One-Stop Shop" where all the necessary permits can be obtained from one office. The Scottsdale Chamber of Commerce administers The Scottsdale Partnership, which is actively involved in attracting and retaining businesses, offering incentives such as entrepreneurial start-up assistance and free, confidential business counseling. To encourage economic development, Scottsdale recently began a building permit fee waiver program which has spurred investment by hundreds of businesses.

State programs—Arizona is a pro-business state. It levies no unitary tax, no inventory tax, no franchise tax, no municipal income tax, and no sales tax on direct sales to the state or federal government. It has developed targeted incentives to encourage the recruitment of desirable new businesses and to encourage the growth of existing businesses.

Job training programs—A work force recruitment and job training program is administered by the state and provides training and retraining for specific employment opportunities with new and expanding businesses and businesses undergoing economic conversion. Scottsdale Community College offers training classes for local businesses ranging from nursing to the hospitality industry, to computer operations and other skills.

Development Projects

Groundbreaking began in 2000 on the $140 million Scottsdale Waterfront project, a retail, dining, entertainment, office, and residential complex planned on 12 acres southwest of Scottsdale and Camelback roads on the north side of the Arizona Canal. The development will also be home to the Fiesta Bowl headquarters and museum; five acres will consist of public open space that will feature an outdoor amphitheater, recreation paths along the canal, and public art.

Phase One of the project is planned for completion by late 2005. In 2004, the City of Scottsdale, Arizona State University, and the ASU Foundation entered into a partnership to develop the ASU Scottsdale Center for New Technology and Innovation on 42 acres of land that was the former site of the Los Arcos Mall. The city agreed to purchase the site from the ASU Foundation for $41.5 million with the provision that the site would be available to the ASU Foundation to develop the ASU Scottsdale Center. The Center will focus on technology commercialization, entrepreneurship, and business development. When completed in 2006, the Center is expected to provide approximately 4,000 jobs and a return of approximately $146 million in direct revenues to the city.

Economic Development Information: Scottsdale Chamber of Commerce, 4343 N Scottsdale Road, Scottsdale, AZ 85251; telephone (480)945-8481; fax (480)947-4523. Scottsdale Economic Development Department, One Civic Center, 7447 E. Indian School Road, Scottsdale, AZ; telephone (480)994-7989

Commercial Shipping

Air freight is handled at Phoenix Sky Harbor International Airport, a 20-minute drive from downtown Scottsdale. Arizona is crisscrossed by five U.S. interstate highways and by a growing system of state roadways. The interstates permit rapid motor freight delivery because of their by-pass features, no slowdown in the metro areas, and no toll roads or toll bridges. Numerous general interstate and transcontinental truck lines serve the city and state. Although there are no railroads in Scottsdale's city limits, the Southern Pacific and the Santa Fe lines connect in adjacent Tempe.

Labor Force and Employment Outlook

Scottsdale's labor force offers a complex blend of skills, abilities, and experience levels, and more than 100,000 highly educated and skilled workers. Scottsdale's economic base is primarily supported by the hospitality and tourism industries; other supports are business, professional and financial services, healthcare, retail, electronics, and corporate headquarters.

The following is a summary of data regarding the Scottsdale labor force, 2004 annual averages.

Size of non-agricultural labor force: 1,674,800

Number of workers employed in . . .
  natural resources and mining: 2,000
  construction: 140,000
  manufacturing: 130,500
  trade, transportation and utilities: 339,600
  information: 35,700
  financial activities: 137,400
  professional and business services: 270,900
  educational and health services: 172,600

leisure and hospitality: 160,500
other services: 64,200
government: 220,900

Average hourly earnings of production workers employed in manufacturing: $13.85

Unemployment rate: 4.0% (January 2005)

Largest employers	Number of employees
Scottsdale Healthcare Group	4,473
Mayo Clinic Scottsdale Systems	4,000
General Dynamics-Decision Systems #48	3,600
Scottsdale Unified School District	2,700
Advance PCS	2,700

Cost of Living

The cost of living in the Phoenix metropolitan area, of which Scottsdale is a part, is above the national average.

2004 (3rd Quarter) ACCRA Average House Price: $349,640

2004 (3rd Quarter) ACCRA Cost of Living Index: 122.5 (U.S. average = 100.0)

State income tax rate: Ranges from 2.87% to 5.04%

State sales tax rate: 5.6% (food and prescription drugs are exempt)

Local income tax rate: None

Local sales tax rate: 1.65%

Property tax rate: $9.30 per $100 of assessed value for a Scottsdale resident living within the Scottsdale Unified School District (2004)

Economic Information: Scottsdale Chamber of Commerce, 4343 N Scottsdale Road, Scottsdale, AZ 85251-4498; telephone (480)945-8481

Education and Research

Elementary and Secondary Schools

The Scottsdale Unified School District (SUSD) consistently receives outstanding support from city voters. Its high school students rate highest in the state on the SAT and ACT tests. The district offers special education services for all handicapped children, including programs for those that are moderately and severely handicapped, that are strategically located throughout the district. An English-as-a-Second Language program is available to help children who are limited in their ability to speak English. All of the district's elementary schools offer some type of on-campus after-school program. Elementary and middle school students with high academic ability are tested for participation in the district's gifted program. Desert Mountain High School offers the International Baccalaureate (IB) program to qualified students. The accelerated courses across all content areas allow students to complete pre-university work for college credit. Sierra Vista Academy, opened in 2003, is a transitional school for grades 4 through 12 that offers a non-traditional curriculum to students who have not experienced academic success in the traditional learning environment. As of 2005, the SUSD had more excelling schools than any other Arizona school district.

The following is a summary of data regarding the Scottsdale Unified School District as of the 2004–2005 school year.

Total enrollment: 26,360

Number of facilities
  elementary schools: 20
  junior high/middle schools: 7
  senior high schools: 5
  alternative schools: 1

Student/teacher ratio: between 17:1 and 20:1

Teacher salaries
  minimum: $31,160
  maximum: $60,933

Funding per pupil: $5,402

The Scottsdale/Paradise Valley area has a number of private academies, college prep, charter day, and child-care schools, including the nationally known Judson School and P.A.L.S. Play and Learn Schools.

Public Schools Information: Scottsdale Public Schools, 3811 North 44th Street, Phoenix, AZ 85018; telephone (480)952-6100

Colleges and Universities

Scottsdale Community College is part of the Maricopa Community College system, the second largest such system in the country. It offers an extensive selection of educational programs including associate's degrees and technical degrees. The college provides training classes for local businesses, continuing education courses, and community service programs. Ottawa University, based in Kansas, has one of several satellite campuses in Scottsdale; it is designed to meet the higher educational needs of adults with jobs and/or family responsibilities. Also located in Scottsdale are Phoenix Seminary, the Scottsdale Culinary Institute, Scottsdale Artists School, and the Frank Lloyd Wright School of Architecture/Taliesin West.

Students in Scottsdale also have access to nearby institutions: Arizona State University, located in adjacent Tempe; Southwest College of Naturopathic Medicine & Health Sciences; and the University of Phoenix.

Libraries and Research Centers

The Scottsdale Public Library System, established in 1960, includes one main library and three branch libraries, two of which are shared-use facilities located on the campuses of Desert Mountain Schools and Desert Mountain High School. The library has more than 800,000 items and 700 periodical subscriptions. The library system has a computer network of more than 200 terminals, 150 of which provide direct access to the Internet. The libraries within the system are the Civic Center Library, Mustang Library, Palomino Library (at Desert Mountain High School), and Arabian Library (on the campus of Desert Canyon Schools). In 2005, construction was expected to begin on the new Arabian Library, an $8.7 million stand-alone facility that will replace the current Arabian Library upon its completion in 2007.

At the Samuel C. Johnson Medical Research Building on the grounds of Mayo Clinic Scottsdale, scientists study molecular genetics, molecular immunology and chemistry, and molecular and cell biology. Construction began in 2004 for the Mayo Clinic Collaborative Research Building, a 100,000 square foot biomedical research facility.

Public Library Information: Civic Center Library (Main Library), 3839 N. Drinkwater Blvd., Scottsdale, AZ 85251-4405; telephone (480)312-2474

Health Care

Scottsdale offers the services of more than 1,000 doctors and has a full range of medical services available. The largest health care providers are Scottsdale Healthcare and Mayo Clinic Scottsdale. Since its inception in 1962 as the City Hospital of Scottsdale, Scottsdale Healthcare has grown to include three campuses, two hospitals, and outpatient centers. Scottsdale Healthcare offers one of the busiest Level 1 trauma centers in the state, as well as outpatient surgery, cardiology and oncology services, a diabetes center, and weight reduction surgery.

Mayo Clinic Scottsdale, a 332-physician group practice, providese health care in 65 medical and surgical specialties and programs. The Mayo Clinic Hospital provides inpatient care as well as emergency rooms and urgent care services.

Recreation

Sightseeing

Scottsdale celebrates the life of the West through a variety of attractions. Old Scottsdale hearkens back to pioneer days with its wooden sidewalks, blacksmith shop, mission, church, and the 1909 Little Red School House, now home to the Scottsdale Historical Society Museum. Rawhide Wild West Town is the state's largest western theme attraction, with a replica of a frontier town, stagecoach and burro rides, gunfights, petting ranch, museum, gold panning, and country music and food. Rawhide will close at the Scottsdale location at the end of 2005 and will reopen 35 miles from North Scottsdale. WestWorld of Scottsdale is a 120-acre equestrian center and special events facility. Many local companies offer trips via jeep, covered wagon, helicopter, and air balloon of the mountains, desert, and canyons surrounding Scottsdale. Day trips can be arranged to Kinishba and Tuzigoot or Canyon de Chelly, which are prehistoric pueblo villages. In Verde Valley, the five-story Montezuma Castle National Monument is a twelfth-century cliff dwelling carved into solid rock by the Sinagua Indians.

Arts and Culture

Scottsdale is a nationally recognized art mecca with more than 125 art galleries, the Scottsdale Center for the Arts, the Scottsdale Artists School, and a variety of public artworks, primarily downtown. Scottsdale has an ''ArtWalk'' every Thursday night that begins at the Scottsdale Center for the Arts; it offers an opportunity to meet artists and observe their work. The Fleischer Museum is dedicated to the American Impressionism California school of art, which flourished from the early twentieth century until the 1940s. It features landscapes, and architectural, figural, and still life paintings. Cosanti, an Arizona *istoric Site, is a unique complex of concrete structures designed and constructed by Paolo Soleri. Tours of where Soleri Windbells are made and sold are offered. Taliesin West/Frank Lloyd Wright Foundation is an architectural masterpiece and Wright's former home and studio. The world's largest art gallery, the Scottsdale Celebration of Fine Art, features 125 fine artists and crafts persons from across the country. The Scottsdale Museum of Contemporary Art, located in the city's Old Town district, houses modern and contemporary works from around the world. The House of Broadcasting, Inc. celebrates Arizona's radio and television history.

Other museums of interest in Scottsdale include the Buffalo Museum of America, with collections relating to the buffalo, and the Heard Museum North, focusing on Native American artists.

Scottsdale's showcase for the performing arts is the Scottsdale Center for the Arts, where symphonies and Broadway

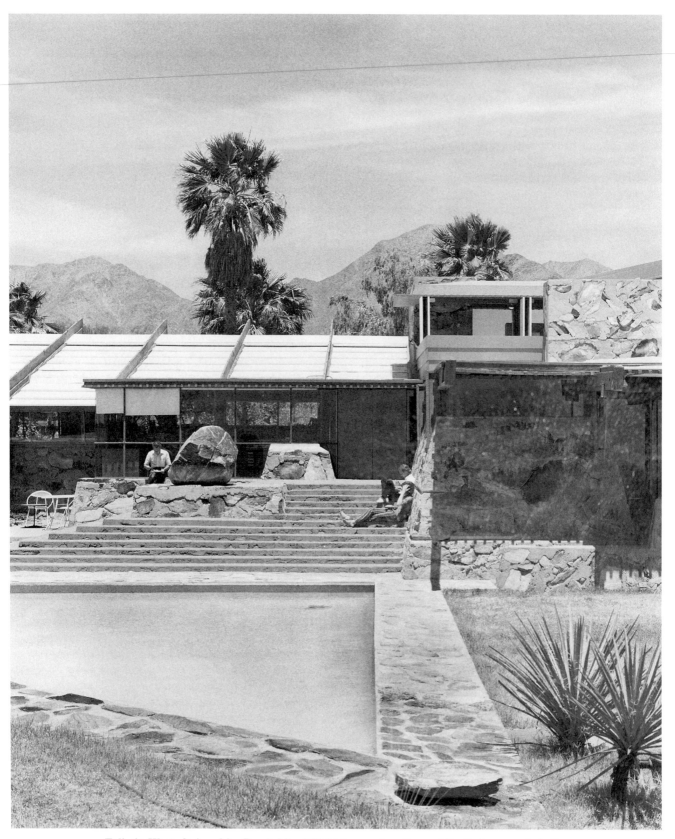

Taliesin West, designed by Frank Lloyd Wright, served as the architect's home and studio.

plays are performed. Scottsdale Desert Stages Theatre presents children's, main stage, and professional productions. The newly renovated Theatre 4301 presents live theatre in an intimate setting.

Festivals and Holidays

Scottsdale's annual Barrett-Jackson Classic Car Auction in January is one of the largest in the world. In February, the Parada del Sol includes a rodeo and ends with the world's largest "horse-drawn parade." Also in February, the Scottsdale Arabian Horse Show—the world's largest all-Arabian horse show—attracts Arabian horse breeders and buyers from around the world.

The Festival of the West, a three-day celebration of cowboy life at Rawhide each March, features western film and television stars, western antiques, western art and music, cowboy poetry, and other events. Also in March, the Scottsdale Arts Festival showcases the work of nearly 200 nationally acclaimed artists. Indian Artists of America showcases 125 of the country's premier talents. The Desert Classic Invitation Team Roping event is also in March.

The Culinary Arts Festival in April showcases local and nationally-known chefs. Scottsdale celebrates the holiday season with the Tree Lighting and Concert at the Scottsdale Mall in December, and with displays featuring more than 500,000 holiday lights at McCormick-Stillman Railroad Park.

Sports for the Spectator

Although Scottsdale fields no major league sports teams, sports fans have easy access to events in Phoenix. Scottsdale is the spring training home of the San Francisco Giants Major League Baseball team. Scottsdale Stadium is also one of the playing sites for the Arizona Fall League, where the stars of the future vie for a shot at Major League Baseball in the Arizona Fall League competition.

Professional golf has an enthusiastic following in Scottsdale. January's Phoenix Open Golf tournament is held at Scottsdale's Tournament Players Club; it attracts the Professional Golfers' Association (PGA) Tour's finest players to one of the most respected national tournaments. All the major senior golfers come to The Tradition at Desert Mountain Senior PGA Tournament at Desert Mountain Golf Club in April. One of Scottsdale's more unique golfing events is the Scottsdale Celebrity Chef Golf Invitational in May.

Sports for the Participant

Scottsdale has more than 500 acres of developed park land, 36 acres of lakes, 37 miles of bike trails, and about 200 miles of non-paved multiuse recreational trails. Many of Scottsdale's 38 parks are located within the Indian Bend Wash

Greenbelt, a 7.5-mile-long flood control project that uses a system of parks, lakes, and golf courses as an alternative to a conventional concrete channel. Pools and recreation centers also meet the needs of Scottsdale residents year-round. Residents may participate in youth and adult sports and recreation programs.

There are nearly 200 golf courses in the Scottsdale area, including 28 public golf courses. The Robb Report rated Scottsdale "America's Best Place to Live for Golf" in 2002. The course for P.F. Chang's Rock'n'Roll Marathon runs through Scottsdale and nearby cities, beginning at the Arizona State Capitol in Phoenix and ending in Tempe. Held in January, the marathon attracts thousands of distance runners due to its flat, fast course and live musical entertainment. Tennis, horseback riding, swimming, rollerblading, and fishing are among the other year-round recreational opportunities available in Scottsdale.

Shopping and Dining

Scottsdale has more than 2,500 retail shops with everything from hand-stitched leather boots to designer fashions. Upscale shopping centers such as Scottsdale Fashion Square, Biltmore Fashion Park, and Borgata of Scottsdale feature retailers such as Burberry, Gucci, Louis Vuitton and Tiffany & Company. Old Town Merchants Association, with more than 150 shops and restaurants, captures the flair of the Old West with traditional and southwestern merchandise. Scottsdale Pavilions is a shopping center that offers mass retailers such as Target, Home Depot, and Best Buy. El Pedregal Festival and Marketplace has courtyard amphitheater facilities surrounded by boutiques, galleries and restaurants. Native American arts and crafts are available at Chief Dodge Indian Jewelry & Fine Arts, Gilbert Ortega Gallery of Indian Art, and Iverson's Indian Arts.

Scottsdale has an excellent selection of first-class dining establishments among its more than 500 restaurants. Notable among them are Mary Elaine's in The Phoenician resort and the Marquesa Restaurant in the Fairmont Scottsdale Princess, both of which have earned the prestigious AAA Five Diamonds award. Ethnic offerings include Southwestern specialties, Italian, French, Japanese, Chinese, Polynesian, Greek, Thai, Indian, and Continental cuisine. Mesquite grills abound, and Western fare served in cookout or ranch settings is popular.

Visitor Information: Scottsdale Chamber of Commerce, 7343 Scottsdale Mall, Scottsdale, AZ 85251-9800; telephone (480)945-8481; toll-free (800)877-1117

Convention Facilities

El Zaribah Shrine Auditorium is a multiuse facility with a 12,000-square-foot ballroom, eight break-out rooms, and a stage that can be used for banquets, seminars, and trade shows. Many hotels and resorts provide meeting space within the city. Among them are the Phoenician Resort, offering 60,000 square feet; the Hyatt Regency Scottsdale at Gainey Ranch, offering 43,000 square feet; Marriott's Camelback Inn Resort; and Marriott's Mountain Shadows Resort. Rawhide Western Town & Desert Cookouts stages banquets. The Hilton Scottsdale Resort & Villas encompasses more than 16,000 square feet of versatile meeting and conference space. WestWorld is one of the most sought-after equestrian show facilities in the country.

Convention Information: Scottsdale Chamber of Commerce, 7343 Scottsdale Mall, Scottsdale, AZ 85251-4253; telephone (480)945-8481 or (800)877-1117

Transportation

Approaching the City

Phoenix Sky Harbor International Airport, located about 15 miles west of downtown Scottsdale, is served by 23 airlines with direct flights from most cities in the United States and several locations abroad. Scottsdale is served by Greyhound Bus Lines and by the Phoenix Transit System. Interstate-10, and I-17, U.S. 60 and 89, and AZ 87 are near the city.

Traveling in the City

Scottsdale Road is the major north-south thoroughfare through the city. Scottsdale Trolley is a free downtown shuttle for tourists and shoppers in operation from November through May. The Regional Public Transportation Authority operates public transit bus routes throughout Paradise Valley and links to Scottsdale business and residential districts via the wheelchair-accessible ''Scottsdale Connection.''

Communications

Newspapers and Magazines

The *Scottsdale Tribune* is the city's daily newspaper, published in the morning. Other newspapers published in Scottsdale are *Scottsdale Airpark News*, and the weekly *Scottsdale Views*, a community paper. *Scottsdale Times* is a free human interest community newspaper with a humorous slant. Magazines published locally are *944 Magazine, American Indian Art Magazine, Document Management, Exhibitor Times,* and *Frank Lloyd Wright Quarterly.*

Television and Radio

Although Scottsdale does not have any television or radio stations within its borders, television and radio stations do broadcast in Paradise Valley, and cable is available.

Media Information: Scottsdale Tribune, Cos Arizona Publications, 7525 E. Camelback Rd., PO Box 1150, Scottsdale, AZ 85252-1150, telephone (480)941-2300

Scottsdale Online

Arizona School Report Cards. Available www2.ade.state.az .us/srcs

City of Scottsdale Economic Vitality Department. Available www.scottsdaleaz.gov/departments/deptDetail.asp?deptID =34

City of Scottsdale Home Page. Available www.scottsdaleaz .gov

Scottsdale Chamber of Commerce. Available www .scottsdalechamber.com

Scottsdale Convention and Visitors Bureau. Available www .scottsdalecvb.com

Scottsdale Public Library. Available www.library.scotts daleaz.gov

Selected Bibliography

Frondorf, Shirley, *Death of a ''Jewish American Princess:'' The True Story of a Victim on Trial* (New York: Villard Books, 1988)

Tucson

The City in Brief

Founded: 1775 (incorporated, 1853)

Head Official: Mayor Bob Walkup (R) (since 1999)

City Population
  1980: 330,537
  1990: 415,444
  2000: 486,699
  2003 estimate: 507,658
  Percent change, 1990–2000: 16.7%
  U.S. rank in 1990: 34th
  U.S. rank in 2000: 37th (State rank: 2nd)

Metropolitan Area Population
  1980: 531,000
  1990: 667,000

  2000: 843,746
  Percent change, 1990–2000: 26.5%
  U.S. rank in 1990: 62nd
  U.S. rank in 2000: 57th

Area: 194.7 square miles (2000)
Elevation: 2,390 feet above sea level
Average Annual Temperature: 68° F
Average Annual Precipitation: 11 inches

Major Economic Sectors: High technology industry, services, tourism, government
Unemployment Rate: 4.1% (January 2005)
Per Capita Income: $16,322 (2000)

2002 FBI Crime Index Total: 50,171

Major Colleges and Universities: University of Arizona, Pima Community College, University of Phoenix

Daily Newspapers: *The Arizona Daily Star; Tucson Citizen*

Introduction

Traditionally known for its dry and sunny climate, Tucson is gaining a new reputation for high culture and high technology. With record increases in population, the city has become a Southwest center for opera, theater, ballet, symphony, and visual arts as well as the economic and industrial focal point of an area known as the "Silicon Desert." Consistently pleasant weather and a beautiful desert setting continue to make Tucson a popular tourist attraction. Proud of a multicultural heritage composed of Native American, Spanish, Mexican, and Anglo influences, residents call their hometown "Old Pueblo," a name hearkening back to rough and exciting pioneer days.

Geography and Climate

Tucson is located in southeastern Arizona, 60 miles north of the Mexican border. Established in the valley of the Sonoran Desert, the city is surrounded by the Sierrita and Santa Rita mountain ranges to the south and the Rincon Mountains rising to 7,000 feet above sea level to the east. With more than 300 days of sunshine a year Tucson's climate lends itself to a variety of outdoor activities and enjoyment.

Area: 194.7 square miles (2000)

Elevation: 2,390 feet above sea level

Average Temperatures: January, 39° F; July, 78° F; annual average, 68° F

Average Annual Precipitation: 11 inches

History

Four Governments Claim Tucson Territory

Tucson is an extremely old settlement with a rich layering of history and pre-history. Archaeological excavations have revealed adobe huts, pit houses, and irrigation systems built by the Hohokam tribe who inhabited and farmed the area nearly 2,000 years ago. The Hohokam have since vanished; in fact, their name, meaning "those who have vanished," was given to them by the Pimas, the Native Americans who occupied the site of present-day Tucson when the first white settlers arrived, and after whom Pima County is named. "Tucson" is also derived from a Pima word, "Stjukshon"

or "Chuk-son," meaning "spring at the foot of a black mountain."

Since its founding Tucson has operated under four governments: Spain, Mexico, the United States, and the Confederacy. One of the first Spanish visitors was Father Eusebio Francisco Kino, a Jesuit missionary who arrived in 1687. Tucson was officially founded as a Spanish colony less than one hundred years later, in 1775, and the Spanish settlers built the Presidio of San Augistin del Tucson as protection from the Apache. Part of this walled presidio still exists today, and its nickname, "Old Pueblo," is now extended to the city as a whole.

When Mexico won independence from Spain in 1821, Tucson became a Mexican town. In 1853 the United States acquired from Mexico the Gadsden Purchase, a strip of land that included Tucson. Before 1863, when Arizona gained territorial status, Tucson briefly belonged to the Confederacy, then became the capital of the Arizona Territory in 1867.

Tucson played an integral role in the romance of the Old West. The city was the scene of gunfights, brawls, and attacks by Native Americans; neighboring Tombstone was the site of the legendary gunfight at the O.K. Corral. Tucson also participated in the great gold rush when prospectors moved east from California into Arizona. The effects of this migration were lasting, since Tucson became the center of a mining industry that continued unabated into the 1970s.

Healthy Climate Attracts Settlers, Tourists

By the time it became the 48th state in 1912, Arizona was famous for the sunny climate and dry air that made it ideal as a healthful spot where people could visit and settle. In 1920 Tucson became the first city in the nation to have a municipal airport. At the same time, major highways were being built. Tourism became one of Tucson's strongest industries and remains so today. During World War II the city contributed to the war effort when the government established the Davis-Monthan Air Force Base nearby. Tucson has since emerged as a major cultural center and one of the most sophisticated cities in the Southwest.

Today's Tucson is the second largest city in Arizona with more than 840,000 people living in its metropolitan area. Public and private sectors continue to join forces to improve Tucson's standard of living and business environment. With an expanding economy based on high-technology industries, modern Tucson aggressively preserves its multicultural heritage and pioneer spirit.

Historical Information: Arizona Historical Society, Tucson Museum, 949 East Second Street, Tucson, AZ, 85719; telephone (520)628-5774

Population Profile

Metropolitan Area Residents

1980: 531,000
1990: 667,000
2000: 843,746
Percent change, 1990–2000: 26.5%
U.S. rank in 1990: 62nd
U.S. rank in 2000: 57th

City Residents

1980: 330,537
1990: 415,444
2000: 486,699
2003 estimate: 507,658
Percent change, 1990–2000: 16.7%
U.S. rank in 1980: 45th
U.S. rank in 1990: 34th
U.S. rank in 2000: 30th (State rank: 2nd)

Density: 2,500.1 people per square mile (2000)

Racial and ethnic characteristics (1999)
White: 341,424
Black or African American: 21,057
American Indian and Alaskan Native: 11,038
Asian: 11,959
Native Hawaiian and Pacific Islander: 796
Hispanic or Latino (may be of any race): 173,868
Other: 81,988

Percent of residents born in state: 38.2% (2000)

Age characteristics (2000)
Population under 5 years old: 35,201
Population 5 to 9 years old: 34,189
Population 10 to 14 years old: 31,939
Population 15 to 19 years old: 38,170
Population 20 to 24 years old: 47,428
Population 25 to 34 years old: 76,394
Population 35 to 44 years old: 72,289
Population 45 to 54 years old: 57,608
Population 55 to 59 years old: 19,597
Population 60 to 64 years old: 16,056
Population 65 to 74 years old: 29,117
Population 75 to 84 years old: 21,394
Population 85 years and older: 7,317
Median age: 32.1 years

Births (2003)
Total number: 12,799

Deaths (2003)
Total number: 7,719

Money income (1999)
Per capita income: $16,322
Median household income: $30,981
Total households: 209,609

Number of households with income of . . .
less than $10,000: 25,225
$10,000 to $14,999: 16,717
$15,000 to $24,999: 34,714
$25,000 to $34,999: 31,708
$35,000 to $49,999: 33,463
$50,000 to $74,999: 29,487
$75,000 to $99,999: 11,946
$100,000 to $149,999: 6,531
$150,000 to $199,999: 1,713
$200,000 or more: 1,380

Percent of families below poverty level: 13.7% (47.8% of which were female householder families with related children under 5 years)

2002 FBI Crime Index Total: 50,171

Municipal Government

Tucson, the seat of Pima County, has a council-manager form of government, with a seven-member council that includes the mayor. All are elected to a four-year term.

Head Official: Mayor Bob Walkup (R) (since 1999; current term expires December 2007)

Total Number of City Employees: 5,933 (2002)

City Information: City of Tucson, PO Box 27210, Tucson, AZ 85726-7210; telephone (520)791-4533

Economy

Major Industries and Commercial Activity

Copper mining has traditionally been a vital part of the city's economy; in 1976, for instance, one of every twenty Tucson residents was a copper miner. Seven years later, a combination of foreign competition and depressed copper prices forced a dramatic downturn in mining industries nationwide, with the result that only four-tenths of a percent of the working population was employed in mining by the mid 1980s. The early 1990s saw an upturn in the mining industry again. In Arizona the mining industry continues to contribute to the economy, although locally and globally the industry has shown signs recently indicating a slowdown.

At the time of the mining crisis, Tucson and southern Arizona looked to economic diversity. In the 1980s the area experienced economic growth from Davis-Monthan Air Force Base with more than 9,200 employees and the University of Arizona with more than 11,000 employees as well as growth in the high-tech and service industries, particularly in banking.

Today the Tucson economy is based on the arts, tourism, manufacturing and high-tech industries. Unique because of Tucson's relatively small size is the fact that a ballet, symphony, live theater, and opera call Tucson home. Tucson's dependably dry and sunny climate assures continuing growth in tourism, an industry that employs about 1 in 10 workers in the metropolitan area labor force and brings in well over 1.5 billion dollars annually. Manufacturing activity has doubled in the last 10 years and includes such companies as AlliedSignal, Weiser Lock, 3M, Burr-Brown, Environmental Air Products, Inc., Krueger Industries, Inc., and Raytheon Missile Systems Company. Marked changes have come about elsewhere in Tucson's economic base, however, with copper mining being most deeply affected.

Tucson has actively promoted expansion in the high-technology industry. The Milkin Institute ranked Tucson the seventh Best Performing City out of 200 Metropolitan Areas in large part because of job growth in the high-tech arena. More than 300 local companies are directly involved in information technology. Other growing high-technology areas are bioindustry, aerospace, environmental technology, plastics and advanced composite materials, and teleservices. It is hoped that these industries will continue to be a catalyst, drawing companies to Tucson.

Another factor in the renewed strength of Tucson's economic base is the building or relocation of major corporations in the area. Industry leaders include Raytheon Missile Systems, IBM, Honeywell, Texas Instruments, Intuit, America Online, and Bombardier Aerospace.

Tucson has become more involved in international trade and has developed close partnerships with Mexico. One development asset in Tucson is the city's proximity to the Mexican border. The city actively encourages the growth of twin-plant or ''maquiladora'' industries locating part of their operations in Tucson. Increased expansion is predicted in the manufacture of electronics, aerospace, and computer component products.

Items and goods produced: aircraft and aircraft parts, electronic equipment, steel castings and fabrications, flour, boxes, agricultural chemicals, aluminum products, radios, mobile homes, air conditioning machinery, cream-

ery products, beer, liquor, saddles and leather goods, apparel, native American and Mexican novelties

Incentive Programs—New and Existing Companies

Local programs—The Greater Tucson Economic Council's foundation is based on an industry cluster concept. The cluster concept attracts and empowers new businesses by promoting collaboration, enhancing research and production capabilities, and creating more powerful advocacy for common needs. The six business clusters include: aerospace, life sciences, environmental technology, information technology, optics, and advanced materials. The Tucson Metropolitan Chamber of Commerce works to promote a favorable business atmosphere conducive to attracting, sustaining, and expanding industrial and service sector employers. Its Economic Development Division provides information, counseling, training, and other services. The University of Arizona, one of the top research universities in the country, plays an active role in attracting businesses and encouraging the entrepreneurial spirit in Tucson.

State programs—Arizona is a pro-business state. It levies no unitary tax, no inventory tax, no franchise tax, no municipal income tax, and no sales tax on direct sales to the state or federal government. It has developed targeted incentives to encourage the recruitment of desirable new businesses and to encourage the growth of existing businesses. Innovative programs designed to encourage job growth include the Workforce Development and Job Training Progam, Enterprise Zones, Foreign Trade Zones, and Research and Development tax credits.

Job training programs—A work force recruitment and job training program is administered by the state and provides training and retraining for specific employment opportunities with new and expanding businesses and businesses undergoing economic conversion.

Development Projects

More than 900 million dollars of investment and tax dollars is funding The Downtown Rio Nuevo project which will add new attractions, shopping, restaurants, infrastructure, office space and residential housing in downtown Tucson. More than 1,100 housing projects are planned or under construction. Other new developments will include parking garages, streetscapes, and enhancements to arts districts and museums.

Economic Development Information: Tucson Metropolitan Chamber of Commerce, 465 West St. Mary's Road, PO Box 991, Tucson, AZ 85702; telephone (520)792-1212; fax (520)882-5704. Greater Tucson Economic Council, 33 N Stone, Ste 800, Tucson, AZ 85701; telephone (800)374-4769

Commercial Shipping

Tucson is linked to national and worldwide markets via Tucson International Airport, which receives service from major air cargo carriers. The Union Pacific railroad provides freight service; 39 motor freight carriers ship goods through facilities in Tucson.

Labor Force and Employment Outlook

Tucson attracts 18,000 to 20,000 new residents each year and offers a work force from which employers can draw relatively young and productive workers. Tucson has committed itself, through its educational institutions, to train and retrain potential employees. About 83 percent of residents have completed high school and 27 percent have 4 or more years of college education; 63 percent (age 16 and over) are in the labor force.

The following is a summary of data regarding the Tucson metropolitan area labor force, 2004 annual averages

Size of non-agricultural labor force: 359,100

Number of workers employed in . . .
  natural resources and mining: 1,300
  construction: 23,900
  manufacturing: 28,300
  transportation and utilities: 58,000
  information: 7,500
  financial activities: 16,600
  professional and business services: 42,200
  educational and health services: 47,700
  leisure and hospitality: 38,800
  other services: 14,700
  government: 79,500

Average hourly earnings of workers employed in manufacturing: $14.53

Unemployment rate: 4.1% (January 2005)

Largest private employers	*Number of employees*
Raytheon Missile Systems	10,200
Phelps Dodge	3,783
Carondelet Health Care	3,328
Fry's Food and Drug	3,000
TMC Health Care	2,350
Asarco	2,700

Cost of Living

According to the Metropolitan Tucson Chamber of Commerce, in 2004 the median sales price for a single family unit was $128,900. Average size for these units was 2,798 square feet. The average apartment rental rate for a two-bedroom unit was $707.00.

The following is a summary of data regarding key cost of living factors for the Tucson area.

2004 (3rd Quarter) ACCRA Average House Price: $254,751

2004 (3rd Quarter) ACCRA Cost of Living Index: 99.2 (U.S. average = 100.0)

State income tax rate: Ranges from 2.87% to 5.04%

State sales tax rate: 5.6% (food and prescription drugs are exempt)

Local income tax rate: None

Local sales tax rate: 2.0% (real estate, groceries, and prescriptions are exempt)

Average property tax rate: $17.00 per $100 of assessed valuation (2003); rate is assessed at 25% of fair market value of a home.

Economic Information: Tucson Metropolitan Chamber of Commerce, 465 West St. Mary's Road, PO Box 991, Tucson, AZ 85701; telephone (520)792-1212; fax (520)882-5704; email info@tucsonchamber.org. Pima County Treasurer, telephone (520)740-8344

Education and Research

Elementary and Secondary Schools

Pima County has 17 school districts, of which Tucson Unified School District is the largest, with an enrollment approaching 61,000 students. All districts focus on building basic skills. Gifted, honors, advance placement, English-as-a-Second-Language, computer literacy, special education, extended school year, sports, music, theater, arts, and homebound programs are among the special offerings. Vocational and business programs prepare students for entry into a job or further occupational education. Tucson's Canyon View Elementary School received Arizona's A+ Award for education in 2003.

The following is a summary of data regarding the Tucson Unified School District as of the 1999–2000 school year.

Total enrollment: approximately 61,000

Number of facilities
  elementary schools: 73
  junior high schools: 19
  senior high schools: 10
  other: 11 alternative programs

Student/teacher ratio: 29:1

Teacher salaries (2002–2003)
   minimum: $28,872
   maximum: $53,494

Funding per pupil: $3,426.00 (2002–2003)

Thirty-five self-regulating and parochial schools operate in Pima County. These range from boarding schools offering a college preparatory curriculum to schools that provide basic education with religious instruction. Tucson is also home to the Arizona School for the Deaf and Blind.

Public Schools Information: Arizona Department of Education, 1535 W. Jefferson Street, Phoenix, AZ 85007; telephone (602)542-5393; hotline (800)352-4558

Colleges and Universities

Institutions of higher learning located in Tucson include the University of Arizona, Pima Community College, Tucson College of Business, and the University of Phoenix (Tucson). The University of Arizona has 150 undergraduate, 200 master's doctoral and specialist programs in 18 colleges and 12 schools. Pima Community College consists of 5 campuses in southern Arizona offering on campus, alternative-style and online courses.

Libraries and Research Centers

The Tucson-Pima Library has 21 locations. The system's collection consists of more than 1.2 million volumes, nearly 200,000 book titles, and more than 4,000 periodical subscriptions, plus records, films, and videotapes. A special collection focuses on Southwestern literature for children. Voters approved a $12.6 million bond issue in May 2004 to upgrade the library's branch facilities.

The University of Arizona Library holds more than 5 million volumes and nearly 27,000 serials and collections that include photography, science-engineering, Japanese and Chinese studies and Southwestern Americana. Also located in the city are a number of specialized scientific libraries associated with high-technology industries.

Biosphere 2, located 30 miles northeast of Tucson, was formerly the site of research into global climate change by Columbia University's Lamont-Doherty Earth Observatory. Tours of the inside and outside of the glass-and-steel geodesic structure are available. Research activities in such fields as architecture, engineering, astronomy, geology, geochemistry, minerals and mining, agriculture, fish and wildlife, arid lands and water, biotechnology, immunology, gerontology, sleep disorders, anthropology, Southwestern culture, and international studies are conducted at centers in the Tucson area.

Public Library Information: Tucson-Pima Public Library, 101 North Stone Avenue, Tucson, AZ 85701; telephone (520)791-4391; Infoline, telephone (520)791-4010

Health Care

Tucson has long had a reputation for its healthful climate. For the past century its warm, dry air has attracted people suffering from such respiratory illnesses as asthma and tuberculosis. The city continues to attract wealthy residents from across Mexico's border who travel to Tucson for health care.

Tucson's medical community includes about 15 hospitals with 1,700 beds and more than 300 health care agencies; 1,750 physicians serve the area. The University Medical Center, the teaching hospital of the University of Arizona (with the state's only medical school), specializes in the research of respiratory illness, cancer, and heart disease. Providing health care to residents throughout southern Arizona, Tucson Medical Center houses Southern Arizona's Level One Trauma Center. The 60-bed Tucson Heart Hospital offers inpatient and outpatient cardiovascular and cardiology services. Tucson also offers internationally known health and spa retreats and alternative health care centers.

Health Care Information: Pima County Medical Society, physician referral service, 5199 Farness Drive, Tucson, AZ 85712; telephone (520)795-7985

Recreation

Sightseeing

The variety of things to do and see in Tucson extends from the heart of the city to the surrounding area. Three historic districts—El Presidio, Armory Park, and Barrio Historico—provide convenient focal points for a walking tour of downtown Tucson. Around El Presidio, the old adobe wall that was part of the original town, are clustered other historic structures, among them restored homes of the city's early settlers and political leaders, as well as an artisans' marketplace housed in an adobe.

Located in the Barrio Historico district, El Tiradito—the "Wishing Shrine"—is one of the nation's genuine folk shrines. A few blocks away, at the edge of the Armory Park district, is the site of the printing office of a Spanish-language newspaper founded in 1878. Other popular attrac-

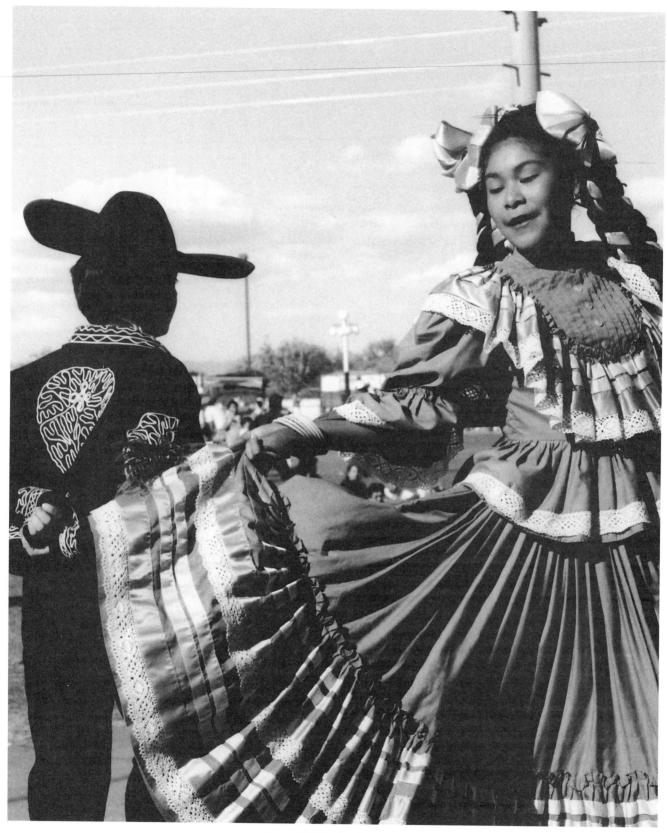

Young Folklorico dancers.

tions in the city include Tucson's world famous zoo, situated in Gene C. Reid Park, and the Tucson Botanic Gardens.

The ideal way to view the landscape surrounding Tucson is to take a leisurely driving tour that winds through miles of scenic Sonora desert, the only place where Saguaro cactus grows, ending at Mt. Lemmon. Covered with stands of aspen, Ponderosa pine, and Douglas fir, Mt. Lemmon offers vistas of the desert.

Other interesting excursions include Colossal Cave, one of the largest caves in the world, and Sabino Canyon, in nearby Colorado National Forest. Kartchner Caverns State Park, home of the world's largest living cave offers guided cave tours, hikes, and group use areas. Popular visitor attractions are Old Tucson, a western theme park and the site of a television and movie set, and Mission San Xavier del Bac, called the ''White Dove of the Desert'' because of its striking appearance from a distance.

Arts and Culture

Tucson is the ''arts mecca'' of the American Southwest, offering a wealth of cultural activities: theater, opera, ballet, and symphony, as well as galleries and museums. The Tucson Arts District Partnership lies in the heart of downtown Tucson and includes the Tucson Music Hall, the Tucson Community Center, and the Temple of Music and Art. Tucson's Arizona Theatre Company, the leading professional theater company in the state, has received national recognition, including grants and citations from the Ford Foundation, the National Endowment of the Arts, and the White House Committee on the Arts. Its productions range from the classics to recent Broadway hits during a September-to-April season at the Temple of Music and Art. Off-Broadway shows and musicals are the forte of the Invisible Theatre, while a.k.a. Theatre presents experimental and modern works.

The award-winning Tucson Symphony offers a nine-month season of classical music at the Tucson Music Hall. The Arizona Opera makes Tucson its home, performing a standard repertoire along with less-frequently performed works. Dance lovers can see performances of Ballet Arizona, which is based in Tucson. The Gaslight Theatre presents old-fashioned melodrama. The ''UApresents'' series at the University of Arizona Centennial Hall brings performances and groups like Oliver, the American Virtuosi Baroque Theater and Moscow Philharmonic Orchestra to delight audiences.

Tucson is home to several museums and galleries. The Arizona State Museum, specializing in the archaeology and ethnology of Arizona, is noted for having one of the most comprehensive southwestern archaeology collections in existence. The Arizona Historical Society houses a museum, research library, and Arizona mining exhibit; the society also administers Fort Lowell Museum and Sosa-Carrillo-Frèmont

House. Featuring military equipment, the Fort Lowell Museum is an 1865 reconstruction of the home of the fort's commanding officer. The Sosa-Carillo-Frèmont House, built around 1858, is one of the oldest adobe houses in Tucson and is furnished in original period pieces. Exhibits such as dinosaur canyon, an ocean discovery center and unique arts for kids can be found at the Tucson Children's Museum. The Pima Air and Space Museum features more than 75 acres of different kinds of military and civilian aircraft.

Arizona-Sonora Desert Museum, 14 miles west of downtown, is one of southern Arizona's most popular attractions. It exhibits hundreds of native plants and animals in their natural habitats. The Flandrau Science Center and Planetarium, on the campus of the University of Arizona, presents exhibits pertaining to optical science, astronomy, and space exploration, many of them encouraging visitor experimentation. For those interested in astronomy, the 56-mile trip to Kitt Peak National Observatory to gaze through one of the telescopes in the world's largest collection of optical solar telescopes is well worth the drive. The Tucson Museum of Art specializes in crafts, textiles, furnishings, and fine arts, including pre-Columbian and western American pieces. The University of Arizona Center for Creative Photography offers permanent and changing exhibitions of photographs and is home to 60,000 works by 2,000 photographers such as Ansel Adams, Richard Avedon, and Edward Weston. Tucson boasts an active community of artists and artisans. Local commercial galleries show their work, which includes paintings, jewelry, and pottery.

Arts and Culture Information: Tucson Museum of Art and Historic Block, telephone (520)624-2333; Tucson-Pima Arts Council, 10 E. Broadway Rd., Tucson, AZ 85701; telephone (520)624-0595; email info@tucsonpimaarts council.org

Festivals and Holidays

Tucson celebrates its history and multicultural heritage with a variety of activities throughout the year. Mid-winter's La Fiesta de los Vaqueros features riding and roping events. Beginning in March, the six-week Tucson Festival features events that showcase the city's unique culture. Also in March the Annual Wa:k Pow Wow Conference brings together southwestern tribes who present inter-tribal pow wow songs and dances. The month of April offers the Tucson International Conference featuring a full week of culture, music and dancing. In May Tucson's Mexican-American community commemorates Mexico's victory against France with the four-day Cinco de Mayo Festival. Tucson's patron saint is honored in the Fiesta de San Augustin in August, and in September the Hispanic community celebrates Mexico's independence from Spain. El Nacimiento, on the grounds of the Tucson Museum of Art, ushers in the Christmas holiday season with displays of folk art. It is followed by Fiesta Navidad, a Mexican mariachi Christmas celebration.

Tucson is the site of other events of interest to both residents and visitors. For several weeks in the winter colored stones, gems and beads are on show at various locations in the city. The Fourth Avenue Street Fair is held twice each year, usually in March and December.

Sports for the Spectator

Although Tucson does not field any teams in the major leagues, there is plenty of action for sports fans. Tucson is home to the University of Arizona Wildcats teams, which compete in Pacific Athletic Conference (PAC-10) basketball and football. The University of Arizona Icecats play hockey at Tucson Convention Center.

Fans of amateur and professional baseball can enjoy a full schedule. Hi Corbett Field is the spring training site for the Colorado Rockies of the National League, and the Tucson Sidewinders, AAA affiliate of the Arizona Diamondbacks, play a full schedule of summer baseball at Corbett Field. Tucson Electric Park is the site where the Arizona Diamondbacks and the Chicago White Sox have spring training. Greyhound races are held year-round at Tucson Greyhound Park. Stock car races are on view at Tucson Raceway Park, the only asphalt short track in Arizona.

Golf is very popular in Tucson, and major annual events include the Chrysler Classic of Tucson golf championship in February. Ranked by *Bicycling* magazine as one of the nation's top three cities for cycling, Tucson hosts the prestigious El Tour de Tucson cycling event each fall, as well as many tennis tournaments.

Sports for the Participant

Tucson's warm, sunny climate offers the outdoor sports enthusiast weather that rarely disrupts planned activities. The city of Tucson maintains 125 parks with jogging tracks, bike paths, and riding trails, 26 swimming pools, 5 municipal golf courses and 3 tennis centers. Swimming, boating, and fishing can be enjoyed in public and private pools and lakes. More than 4,500 participants run or walk in the Tucson Marathon, half marathon or 5k each December. Surrounding mountain ranges offer a variety of recreational opportunities. Mount Lemmon ski area receives an average of 175 inches and offers 3 months of skiing each year. In keeping with Tucson's western traditions, local ranches offer horseback riding; and for those who want to step back into the past, there are even opportunities to pan for gold or participate in a cattle drive.

Shopping and Dining

Shopping for necessities or for pleasure can be equally rewarding in Tucson at neighborhood retail centers, regional malls, shopping plazas, and numerous shops and boutiques conveniently located throughout the area. Downtown's Fourth Avenue historic shopping and arts district is a popular destination, with its more than 100 galleries and unusual shops. Many shops specialize in indigenous goods and crafts such as Mexican handicrafts and decorative items, Indian kachina dolls, baskets, pottery, and moccasins. Traditional western clothing, boots, and other leather goods are also available in Tucson.

The city's restaurants are famous for Southwestern cuisine. Local specialties include carne seca, beef that has been marinated in lime and cilantro then sun-dried; cinnamon chicken; black bean hummus; and prickly pear cactus. Diners can find a wide diversity of other ethnic fare, ranging from Greek to Thai, as well as traditional American food.

Visitor Information: Metropolitan Tucson Convention and Visitors Bureau, 100 S. Church Ave., Tucson, AZ 85701; telephone (520)624-1817; email info@visittucson.org

Convention Facilities

With an expanded convention center and with additional meeting facilities available in many of the more than 200 hotels and resorts, Tucson is emerging as a primary convention and meeting destination in the Southwest. Besides a consistently warm climate and a wealth of leisure activities, Tucson offers more than 16,000 hotel rooms in the metropolitan area.

To keep pace with hotel and resort developments that have gained for Tucson a reputation as an ideal setting for large and small group functions, the Tucson Convention Center offers flexible facilities for all types of meeting and convention needs. The center offers 205,000 square feet of meeting space and 3 exhibition halls as well as a music hall, arena, small auditorium and 8 meeting rooms for groups of 50 to 1,000 people. A spacious foyer and galleria are designed to accommodate pre-function activities.

Convention Information: Metropolitan Tucson Convention and Visitors Bureau, 100 South Church Ave., Tucson, AZ 85701; telephone (520)624-1817; fax (520) 884-7804; email greatmeetings@visittucson.org.

Transportation

Approaching the City

Visitors arriving in Tucson by plane are greeted by the recently expanded Tucson International Airport, located a few miles south of the city. In January 2005 the airport completed a terminal expansion project allowing TIA to handle 7 million passengers in ticketing and baggage claim. A comprehensive master plan provides for even more development over 20 years to accommodate the area's rapidly growing needs and will include a runway relocation, additional runway, expanded passenger areas and terminal complex, as well as additional cargo, corporate and support facilities. Served by 12 major airlines, Tucson International provides daily flights to cities in the United States, Mexico, and abroad.

Principal highway routes into the city are Interstate 10, which runs between Los Angeles and El Paso and passes through downtown on a northwest-southeast axis, and Interstate 19, which originates at the Mexican border and merges with Interstate 10 in Tucson. Amtrak provides train service and Greyhound Trailways provides bus service.

Traveling in the City

Tucson, located in a narrow, elliptical valley, is laid out in a grid pattern. The city is essentially serviced by surface roads, which can be congested during rush hours. Some major cross-town roads may suddenly dead end, necessitating a switch to a roundabout route. Numbered streets south of Speedway Boulevard run east-west, and numbered avenues west of Euclid Avenue run north-south. Residential and commercial pockets are scattered throughout the city, which can cause confusion. Drivers should be aware that during rush hours, the center or left-turn lane on major east-west thoroughfares becomes a one-way traffic lane.

Tucson's public mass transit system, operated by Sun Tran Transit, provides service for 60,000 riders each day to major points within the city and the surrounding area, including the airport. Arizona has deregulated the ground transportation industry so that cab fare in Tucson is negotiable. The Old Pueblo Historic Trolley runs between the Fourth Ave Business District and the University of Arizona campus. Future expansion of the trolley will bring the line downtown to the Tucson Convention Center and the Rio Nuevo Development Area.

Communications

Newspapers and Magazines

Tucson readers choose from among three daily newspapers: *The Arizona Daily Star* (every morning), the *Tucson Citizen*

(Monday through Saturday evenings), and the business paper, the *Daily Territorial. Desert Airman* is a weekly newspaper for military personnel at Davis-Monthan U.S. Air Force Base. Magazines published in Tucson include *Tucson Weekly,* which contains information about the arts and area news, *Tucson Guide Quarterly,* which publishes *Tucson Official Visitor's Guide* and *Tucson Lifestyle Monthly Magazine.* Several scholarly journals are also published in Tucson.

Television and Radio

Tucson's eight television stations include five network affiliates, two public stations, and one independent; a cable system is also available. Twenty AM and FM radio stations broadcast from Tucson, which also receives programming from neighboring communities.

Media Information: The Arizona Daily Star and *Tucson Citizen,* TNI Partners, PO Box 26767, Tucson, AZ 85726-6767; telephone (520)573-4400.

Tucson Online

The Arizona Daily Star home page. Available www .azstarnet.com

Arizona School Report Cards home page. Available www .ade.az.gov/srcs/main.asp

City of Tucson home page. Available www.ci.tucson.az.us

Greater Tucson Economic Council home page. Available www.futurewest.com

Metropolitan Tucson Convention & Visitors Bureau home page. Available at www.visittucson.org

Tucson Citizen home page. Available www.tucsoncitizen .com

Tucson Metropolitan Chamber of Commerce home page. Available at www.tucsonchamber.org

Tucson-Pima Library home page. Available www.lib.ci .tucson.az.us

Selected Bibliography

Griffith, James S., *Hecho a Mano: The Traditional Arts of Tucson's Mexican American Community* (Tucson: University of Arizona Press, 2000)

Hait, Pam, *Shifra Stein's Day Trips from Greater Phoenix, Tucson, and Flagstaff* (Charlotte, NC: East Woods Press, 1986)

CALIFORNIA

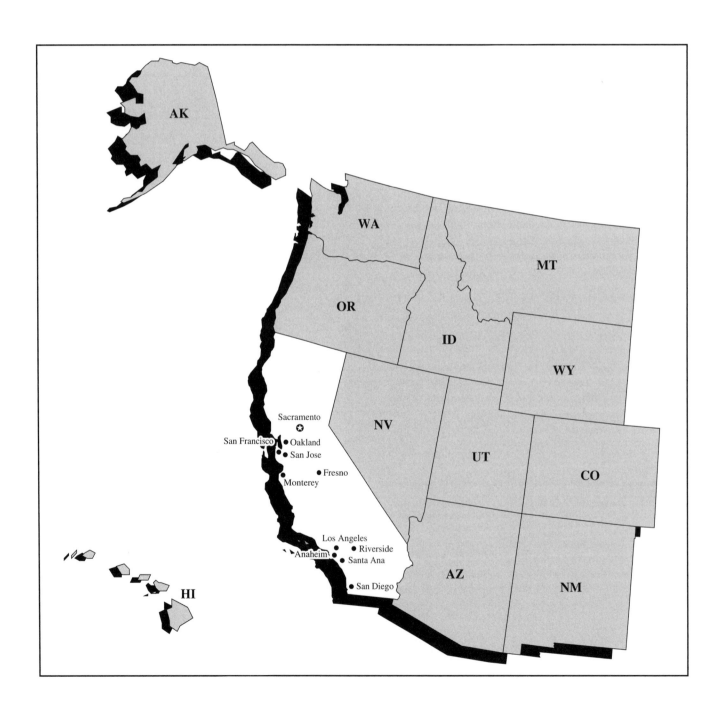

The State in Brief

Nickname: Golden State
Motto: *Eureka* (I have found it)

Flower: Golden poppy
Bird: California valley quail

Area: 163,695 square miles (2000; U.S. rank: 3rd)
Elevation: Ranges from 282 feet below sea level to 14,494 feet above sea level
Climate: Extremely varied, with zones ranging from subtropical to subarctic, but in the main two seasons—wet from October to April, dry from May to September

Admitted to Union: September 9, 1850
Capital: Sacramento
Head Official: Governor Arnold Schwarzenegger (R) (until 2007)

Population
1980: 23,668,000
1990: 30,380,000
2000: 33,871,653
2004 estimate: 35,893,799
Percent change, 1990–2000: 13.8%
U.S. rank in 2004: 1st
Percent of residents born in state: 50.2% (2000)
Density: 217.2 people per square mile (2000)
2002 FBI Crime Index Total: 1,384,872

Racial and Ethnic Characteristics (2000)
White: 20,170,059
Black or African American: 2,263,882
American Indian and Alaska Native: 333,346
Asian: 3,697,513
Native Hawaiian and Pacific Islander: 116,961
Hispanic or Latino (may be of any race): 10,966,556
Other: 5,682,241

Age Characteristics (2000)
Population under 5 years old: 2,486,981
Population 5 to 19 years old: 7,747,590
Percent of population 65 years and over: 10.6%
Median age: 33.3 years (2000)

Vital Statistics
Total number of births (2003): 541,046
Total number of deaths (2003): 219,487 (infant deaths, 2,560)
AIDS cases reported through 2003: 55,750

Economy
Major industries: Agriculture, manufacturing (transportation equipment, electronics, machinery), biotechnology, aerospace, tourism
Unemployment rate: 5.8% (January 2005)
Per capita income: $33,403 (2003; U.S. rank: 11th)
Median household income: $48,979 (3-year average, 2001-2003)
Percentage of persons below poverty level: 12.9% (3-year average, 2001-2003)
Income tax rate: ranges from 1.0% to 9.3%
Sales tax rate: 7.25% (food and prescription drugs are exempt)

Anaheim

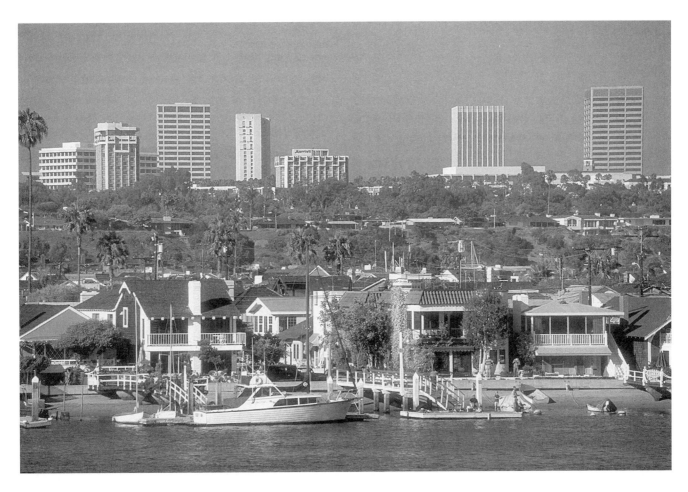

The City in Brief

Founded: 1857 (incorporated, 1876)

Head Official: Mayor Curt Pringle (since 2002)

City Population
  1980: 219,494
  1990: 266,406
  2000: 328,014
  2003 estimate: 332,361
  Percent change, 1990–2000: 23.1%
  U.S. rank in 1980: 62nd
  U.S. rank in 1990: 59th (State rank: 10th)
  U.S. rank in 2000: 64th (State rank: 10th)

Metropolitan Area Population (PMSA)
  1980: 1,933,000

  1990: 2,411,000
  2000: 2,846,289
  Percent change, 1990–2000: 18.1%
  U.S. rank in 1980: 2nd (CMSA)
  U.S. rank in 1990: 2nd (CMSA)
  U.S. rank in 2000: 2nd (CMSA)

Area: 48.9 square miles (2000)
Elevation: 137 feet above sea level
Average Annual Temperature: 70.0° F
Average Annual Precipitation: 11.0 inches

Major Economic Sectors: Services, trade, manufacturing
Unemployment Rate: 4.1% (January 2005)
Per Capita Income: $18,266 (1999)

2002 FBI Crime Index Total: 12,198

Major Colleges and Universities: None

Daily Newspaper: *Orange County Register*

Introduction

Contrary to popular notion, Anaheim is not a suburb of Los Angeles, but rather is the largest and wealthiest (with more than $1 billion in assets) of the 34 cities that comprise Orange County, and one of the fastest growing cities in California. A major entertainment mecca, Anaheim is one of the top convention sites and vacation destinations in the United States, with nearly 20,000 hotel rooms. Major attractions in or near Anaheim range from Disneyland, Knott's Berry Farm, and the Movieland Wax Museum to Medieval Times, San Juan Capistrano Mission, and the Anaheim Convention Center, the centerpiece of the city. In 2001, Anaheim completed a transformation of epic proportions, with a $5 billion renovation of its resort areas. In 2004 Orange County, which has more than 42 miles of coastline and beaches and is comprised of the well-known towns Huntington Beach, Newport Beach, and Laguna Beach, had 43.6 million visitors.

Geography and Climate

Anaheim is located approximately 27 miles south of downtown Los Angeles, 31 miles southeast of the Los Angeles International Airport, and 13 miles from the Pacific coast. The Santa Ana Mountains lie to Anaheim's east. Industrial and commercial areas along with a majority of the residential sections are relatively flat. The newer residential areas are in rolling terrain in the foothills of the Santa Ana Mountains. Anaheim's average temperature is 70 degrees. Summers are moderate to hot with cool evenings, and winters are mild with very little rain. In fact, there are only 38 days each year with even a one one-hundredth inch sprinkle.

Area: 48.9 square miles (2000)

Elevation: 137 feet above sea level

Average Temperatures: January, 57.0° F; July, 74.0° F; annual average, 70.0° F

Average Annual Precipitation: 11.0 inches

History

City Settled By German Winemakers

Anaheim was founded in 1857 by a group of German settlers who gave it the German name meaning ''home by the river.'' The settlers were part of a group who first came to the United States during the German Revolution of 1848 and settled in San Francisco. Fifty members of that German community decided to move south when they learned about an abundance of cheap land that was once part of a Spanish land grant. The German colonists purchased the 1,165 acres of coastal plains for $2 an acre. Two of the Germans had a wine-making business. Attracted by the area's moderate climate, the settlers decided to make wine production the region's economic foundation. A civil engineer named George Hansen was hired to plan a carefully thought-out community with fences to protect the planned vineyards from roaming cattle. To allow future growth, specific parcels were set aside for construction of a school and other public buildings.

With the introduction of irrigation, Anaheim remained a prosperous wine producing region until the 1880s. During the period of 1860 to 1885, Anaheim wineries produced more than 1.25 million gallons of wine annually. In the 1880s, a blight completely wiped out the vineyards, destroying a thriving business. The orange and citrus industry was then developed and prospered, as did the city of Anaheim. The Southern California Fruit Growers Exchange, which was later renamed Sunkist, was organized in 1893.

Disneyland Displaces Agriculture as Major Industry

The railroad had a positive effect on the city's development. Railroad service was provided by the Southern Pacific Railway, which established itself in the city in 1875. The Santa Fe Railroad followed soon after. The coming of the railroads permitted the city to expand to include other markets. Businesses prospered and the population grew.

Despite earlier failed attempts to become independent of the city of Los Angeles, Orange County was formed in 1889. Beginning in the late 1920s the city underwent rapid industrial development. A huge flood in 1938 caused the creation of a program to control the Santa Ana River, and the Prado Dam was built upstream to regulate the flow of the sometimes violent waterway.

Agriculture remained the principal industry of the city until the mid 1950s, when the legendary Walt Disney chose Anaheim as the site for construction of his world-famous Disneyland amusement park. Millions of people each year are drawn to the area to enjoy this wonderful fantasy world.

The growth of Anaheim as a recreational attraction increased in the 1960s with the opening of Anaheim Stadium—current home of the Los Angeles Angels of Anaheim baseball team and now called Angel Stadium of Anaheim. In 1967 the Anaheim Convention Center was opened. In December 2000, the center was expanded by 40 percent; its 815,000 square feet of exhibit space makes it the largest exhibit facility on the West Coast.

Today Anaheim/Orange County is one of the fastest growing areas in California. The city is a mix of business, residential, and resort interests.

Population Profile

Metropolitan Area Residents (Orange County PMSA)

1980: 1,933,000
1990: 2,410,668
2000: 2,846,289
Percent change, 1990–2000: 18.1%
U.S. rank in 1980: 2nd (CMSA)
U.S. rank in 1990: 2nd (CMSA)
U.S. rank in 2000: 2nd (CMSA)

City Residents

1980: 219,494
1990: 266,406
2000: 328,014
2003 estimate: 332,361
Percent change, 1990–2000: 23.1%
U.S. rank in 1980: 62nd
U.S. rank in 1990: 59th (State rank: 10th)
U.S. rank in 2000: 64th (State rank: 10th)

Density: 6,702.0 people per square mile (2000)

Racial and ethnic characteristics (2000)
   White: 179,627
   Black or African American: 8,735
   American Indian and Alaska Native: 3,041
   Asian: 39,311
   Native Hawaiian and Pacific Islander: 1,393
   Hispanic or Latino (may be of any race): 153,374
   Other: 95,907

Percent of residents born in state: 44.4% (2000)

Age characteristics (2000)
   Population under 5 years old: 30,206
   Population 5 to 9 years old: 30,282
   Population 10 to 14 years old: 24,837
   Population 15 to 19 years old: 22,959
   Population 20 to 24 years old: 25,020
   Population 25 to 34 years old: 58,417
   Population 35 to 44 years old: 51,578
   Population 45 to 54 years old: 36,063
   Population 55 to 59 years old: 12,436
   Population 60 to 64 years old: 9,443
   Population 65 to 74 years old: 14,383
   Population 75 to 84 years old: 9,177
   Population 85 years and older: 3,213
   Median age: 30.3 years

Births (Orange County; 2002)
   Total number: 44,796

Deaths (Orange County; 2002)
   Total number: 16,789 (of which, 216 were infants under the age of 1 year)

Money income (1999)
   Per capita income: $18,266
   Median household income: $47,122
   Total households: 96,902

Number of households with income of . . .
   less than $10,000: 5,769
   $10,000 to $14,999: 4,777
   $15,000 to $24,999: 10,812
   $25,000 to $34,999: 12,769
   $35,000 to $49,999: 16,954
   $50,000 to $74,999: 20,236
   $75,000 to $99,999: 11,532
   $100,000 to $149,999: 9,461
   $150,000 to $199,999: 2,486
   $200,000 or more: 2,106

Percent of families below poverty level: 10.4% (37.7 % of which were female householder families with related children under 5 years)

2002 FBI Crime Index Total: 12,198

Municipal Government

Anaheim has a council-manager form of government. The four members of the city council are elected to four-year terms in alternate slates every two years. A mayoral election is held every four years.

Head Official: Mayor Curt Pringle (since 2002)

Total Number of City Employees: approximately 2,100 (2004)

City Information: Anaheim City Hall, 200 S. Anaheim Blvd., Anaheim, CA 92805; telephone (714)765-5100

Economy

Major Industries and Commercial Activity

Tourism is the major industry in Anaheim. An ever-growing number of visitors has caused hotels, motels, restaurants, and retail centers to be built to meet their demands. At the time of Disneyland's opening in 1955, Anaheim had only 87 hotel/motel rooms; presently, those numbers have grown to nearly 20,000. The rise in tourism has encouraged the city to update and add to its facilities. Since being dedicated in 1967, the Anaheim Convention Center has undergone five major expansions, the most recent of which, completed in December 2000, enlarged the center by 40 percent to 1.6 million square feet. Tremendous infrastructure changes in the Anaheim Resort district (surrounding Disneyland and Anaheim Convention Center area) during the past few years have included 15,000 new trees, shrubs, and flowers, as well as improved signage. In 2004, visitors spent $7.3 billion in Orange County (a nearly 8 percent increase from the previous year), $3.6 billion of which was generated by Disneyland alone.

Tourism and business have built a healthy interdependence over the years. The city has become more economically diverse with the development of business and manufacturing firms; Anaheim is currently home to more than 15,000 businesses. It is a center of enterprise for multinational firms, as well as regional and local companies. Located within Anaheim are more than 100 manufacturing plants. The city of Anaheim has been successful in retaining some businesses that had considered leaving by offering loans, tax and utility rebates, subsidies, and job-training incentives.

Items and goods produced: electronic components, electrical machinery, chemicals, guidance and navigation systems, locks, plastics, processed food, aircraft parts, fabricated metal products, communications equipment

Incentive Programs—New and Existing Companies

State programs—California's Commerce & Economic Development Program offers financial solutions by helping businesses secure capital to invest in major public, private, and nonprofit ventures; providing export assistance and financing; and supporting small businesses by offering financial assistance, training, and technical assistance.

Local programs—Anaheim offers qualifying firms economic development rates, new construction incentives, and energy efficiency incentives. Anaheim's "Powerful Partnership for Business," comprised of the city's Community Development and Public Utilities departments, creates customized business programs for economic development support. These include Redevelopment Agency loans and assistance, utility loans and assistance, job training, energy efficiency strategies, environmental assistance, fast-track permitting, and financial assistance and subsidies.

Job training programs—Anaheim's Job Training Program (JTP) offers subsidies of up to 50 percent of an employee's wages for up to six months in order to assist with customized

on-the-job training programs that can help new and expanding businesses. California's Employment Training Panel (ETP) contracts with employers to provide training for new workers as well as workers likely to be displaced without retraining. The highly successful program has been responsible for a return on investment of more than $5 for every $1 in ETP funds spent on training, as measured in benefits to businesses, workers, and the state's economy.

Development Projects

In 2001 a massive $5 billion renovation of the Anaheim Resort District (the greater Anaheim Convention Center/ Disneyland area, comprised of 1,100 acres) was completed. The project began in 1994 when the city of Anaheim approved a $174 million Anaheim Resort Capital Improvement Program designed to transform the district into a more attractive, pedestrian-friendly destination. Among the results are a 55-acre themed park called Disney's California Adventure, brought about by a $1.4 billion investment in all Disney properties. California Adventure, which opened in February 2001 and is adjacent to Disneyland, pays tribute to the Golden State. The Anaheim Convention Center underwent a $177 million expansion, completed in December 2000. The expansion increased the size of the center by 40 percent; it now houses 815,000 square feet of exhibit space, making it the largest exhibit facility on the West Coast. Also completed is a $396 million "freshening" of the entire Resort District with landscaping and infrastructure improvements, including the addition of 15,000 new trees, shrubs, and flowers, and improved signage. The Anaheim Resort Transit (ART), which began operating in 2001, features 10 buses, two trams, and 25 trolleys providing access to all area resorts, attractions, hotels, restaurants, and shops. In the summer of 2005, Disneyland will begin an 18-month celebration of its 50th anniversary with several new attractions expected to draw more visitors to the park than ever before.

Economic Development Information: City of Anaheim Economic Development, City Hall East, 200 South Anaheim Boulevard, First Floor, Anaheim, CA 92805; telephone (714)765-4323

Commercial Shipping

The city's transportation access is excellent, and is in proximity to several airports, two major ports of call, interstate access, and an extensive public transit system. Freight service is provided by Southern Pacific, Santa Fe, and Union Pacific railroads, which maintain about 30 miles of railroad track in the city.

Labor Force and Employment Outlook

Economic development in Anaheim has created thousands of new jobs. As of early 2005, Orange County has the lowest unemployment rate—around 4.1 percent—among California's 52 counties.

The following is a summary of data regarding the Santa Ana/ Anaheim/Irvine area labor force, 2004 annual averages.

Size of non-agricultural labor force: 1,460,000

Number of workers employed in . . .
  natural resources and mining: 600
  construction: 91,800
  manufacturing: 183,200
  trade, transportation, and utilities: 264,300
  information: 33,500
  financial activities: 131,200
  professional and business services: 259,600
  educational and health services: 130,400
  leisure and hospitality: 164,500
  other services: 47,300
  government: 153,200

Average hourly earnings of production workers employed in manufacturing: $13.38

Unemployment rate: 4.1% (January 2005)

Largest employers
in Orange County	*Number of employees*
Disneyland	21,000
County of Orange	19,000
University of California at Irvine	15,000
CKE Restaurants, Inc.	14,000
Federal Government	11,800
Boeing Aerospace	10,080
State of California	10,000
Albertson's	8,700
St. Joseph Health Care System	8,500
Tenet Healthcare	8,300

Cost of Living

The following is a summary of data regarding key cost of living factors for the Anaheim area.

2004 (3rd Quarter) ACCRA Average House Price: $674,000

2004 (3rd Quarter) ACCRA Cost of Living Index: 151.5 (U.S. average = 100.0)

State income tax rate: Ranges from 1.0% to 9.3%

State sales tax rate: 6.0% (food and prescription drugs are exempt)

Local income tax rate: None

Local sales tax rate: 1.75%

Property tax rate: 1.0% of assessed valuation

Economic Information: Anaheim Chamber of Commerce, 201 East Center Street, Anaheim CA, 92805; telephone (714) 758-0222

Education and Research

Elementary and Secondary Schools

Anaheim is served by the Anaheim City School District, which operates the elementary schools, and the Anaheim Union High School District, which oversees the junior high and high schools. The city is noted for excellent schools offering a full array of learning programs from basic curriculum instruction to college preparation, athletics, and special education.

The following is a summary of data regarding Anaheim City and Anaheim Union High school districts, as of the 2002-2003 school year.

Total enrollment: 53,713

Number of facilities
  elementary schools: 23
  junior high/middle schools: 8
  senior high schools: 13

Student/teacher ratio: 21.5:1 (elementary school); 24.5:1 (junior high and high school)

Teacher salaries (Union High School District, 2004)
  minimum: $40,986
  maximum: $77,057

Funding per pupil, 2000-2001: $5,975 (Anaheim City); $6,681 (Anaheim Union)

Public Schools Information: Anaheim City School District, 1001 South East Street, Anaheim, CA 92805-5749; telephone (714)517-7500; Anaheim Union High School District, 501 Crescent Way, Anaheim, CA, 92803-3520; telephone (714)999-3511

Colleges and Universities

Although there are no colleges in the city of Anaheim proper, Orange County is the home of the following four-year institutions located with 30 minutes of Anaheim: California State University at Fullerton, Chapman University, and University of California at Irvine.

Libraries and Research Centers

The Anaheim Public Library holds about 460,530 volumes, and nearly 11,000 audio and video materials. The library's special collections include the Anaheim History Collection. The library is comprised of a central library, four branches—Haskett (closed for reconstruction and scheduled to reopen in 2006), Euclid, Sunkist, and Canyon Hills—and one bookmobile. Other Anaheim libraries consist of those of local hospitals and companies, including Anaheim Memorial Medical Center, Western Medical Center Hospital, and Boeing Co. The Richard Nixon Library & Birthplace is in Yorba Linda, a 15-minute drive from Anaheim.

The Anaheim Research Center, founded in 2002, conducts psychiatric and medical research.

Public Library Information: Anaheim Public Library, 500 West Broadway, Anaheim CA 92805; telephone (714)765-1880

Health Care

Anaheim has medical facilities sufficient to meet the needs of one of California's largest population centers. Area hospitals boast state-of-the-art facilities and top quality care. Several hospitals are located within the city. Anaheim Memorial Hospital offers general medical, critical care, and surgical services, as well as centers for specialized care including: The Advanced Endovascular Institute; The Birth Place; The Breast Center; Chest Pain Center; Emergency Services; The HeartCare Center; Orthopedics; Outpatient Heart Failure Clinic; Pain Management Center; and Women's Health and Wellness Center. Anaheim General Hospital's main hospital campus includes emergency room services, intensive care, an obstetrical unit, radiology, in-patient and out-patient surgery department, telemetry, and a wide range of additional services. Kaiser Foundation Hospital's key services include: general medical, surgical and intensive care; cardiac intensive care; cardiology, neurology, and orthopedics departments; pediatric medical and surgical care; and obstetrics. Western Medical Center/Anaheim offers service in the following areas: acute medicine and critical care; ambulatory care; behavioral medicine; cardiac rehabilitation; emergency care; radiology services; women's and children's health services; and sleep disorder care.

Recreation

Sightseeing

Anaheim's crown jewel attraction is Disneyland, America's most popular theme park. Visitors can stroll through the park's eight "lands", which together offer more than 60 major rides, 50 shops, and 30 restaurants: futuristic Tomorrowland provides an out-of-this-world atmosphere; Adventureland reproduces the exotic surroundings of Asia, the Middle East, and the South Seas; Frontierland is based on the Wild West; Fantasyland, with Sleeping Beauty's Castle and the It's a Small World ride, is the heart of Disneyland; Critter Country is home to cute woodland creatures; Main Street U.S.A. is based on small-town America of a century ago; New Orleans Square reproduces the atmosphere of turn-of-the-century New Orleans; and Mickey's Toontown is a cartoon playland. Special entertainment, shopping, and dining are featured at Disneyland year-round. Special attractions include Indiana Jones Adventure; Space Mountain and Star Tours, exciting flight-simulation journeys; Splash Mountain, an 87-foot-high log flume ride based on Disney's "Song of the South" characters; Big Thunder Mountain Railroad; and the Haunted Mansion. Disneyland's newest area is California Adventure. Requiring a separate admission ticket, it is based on the fun adventures offered by California, and is divided into four themed districts: Paradise Pier has classic "Golden Age" amusement park attractions along the beach; Hollywood Pictures Backlot celebrates the movie business; The Golden State is a tribute to California's natural beauty; and "a bug's land", inspired by the film *A Bug's Life* is designed from a bug's perspective. Disneyland opened in 1955, and in the summer of 2005 will be celebrating its golden anniversary with several new attractions: Buzz Lightyear Astro Blasters, in Tomorrowland, is an interactive game in which visitors join Buzz Lightyear to battle the evil Emperor Zurg; Space Mountain, also in Tomorrowland, is being re-launched with new special effects; at Disneyland's Parade of Dreams, a new Main Street U.S.A. parade, spectators can meet Disney characters and watch floats transform into shows; a new nighttime celebration will feature spectacular pyrotechnics; Disneyland: The First 50 Years will provide an exclusive look at the park's 50 years, through artwork, models and design, and film; Sleeping Beauty Castle has been renovated; larger-than-life images of Disney characters on display are massive photo collages comprised of photos taken at the park over the past 50 years.

Knott's Berry Farm in nearby Buena Park, once a small berry farm business, has grown into one of the most popular theme parks in the country. The park, now a 150-acre complex with more than 100 rides and dozens of shops and restaurants, is especially known for its thrill rides. Distinct theme areas are Ghost Town, an Old West mining town reproduction; Camp Snoopy, which features special rides and activities for small children; The Boardwalk, a colorful tribute to the Southern California beach culture that features ocean-related rides and attractions; Indian trails, which showcases the traditions and cultures of Native Americans; Fiesta Village, a celebration of Spanish California; and Wild

Disneyland's most famous landmark, Sleeping Beauty Castle, stands at the gateway to the Magic Kingdom's Fantasyland area.

Water Wilderness water park. Special attractions include Montezooma's Revenge, a roller coaster that goes from 0 to 60 miles per hour in just 3 seconds; Jaguar!, a roller coaster that twists, spirals, speeds up, and slows down, mimicking a jaguar stalking its prey; Supreme Scream ascends 214 feet and then plunges straight down at about 50 mph; and Bigfoot Rapids is a whitewater river raft ride.

Other nearby attractions include Buena Park's Movieland Wax Museum, where more than 300 lifelike figures of famous movie stars are on view in realistic costumes and posed in scenes from classic movies; and Medieval Times, an elaborate dinner tournament where eleventh-century knights in armor joust and a feast is presented. The Taco Bell Discovery Science Center, in Santa Ana, houses hands-on exhibits in themed areas: Discovery Stadium, Quake Zone, Dynamic Earth, Air and Space Exploration, and Kidstation. Hobby City is a 10-acre collection of miniature buildings; it includes a doll and toy museum inside a miniature replica of the White House. Nearby Adventure City is a two-acre theme park for children aged 2 to 12. The Mission San Juan Capistrano, 30 miles south of Anaheim, was founded in 1776 and is the birthplace of Orange County. Beautiful and romantic, it is considered the "jewel of the missions." Its Serra Chapel is believed to be California's oldest standing building.

Arts and Culture

The 3,000-seat Segerstrom Hall at the Orange County Performing Arts Center in nearby Costa Mesa hosts world-class performances of symphony, ballet, and opera, as well as Broadway shows; the 300-seat Founders Hall in the Center offers innovative jazz and cabaret programming as well as the best in chamber music. The Center is also home to the Philharmonic Society of Orange County, Pacific Symphony Orchestra, Opera Pacific, and Pacific Chorale. The Center is currently undergoing an expansion; a new 2,000-seat concert hall and 500-seat music theater are scheduled for completion by September 2006.

Numerous other theaters dot Orange County. Fullerton Civic Light Opera Company, based in nearby Fullerton, is one of the largest musical theater companies in Southern California; their productions are presented four times annually at Plummer Auditorium. The auditorium, built in 1930, seats more than 1,300 and hosts a variety of theatrical productions and community-oriented cultural programs. South Coast Repertory Theatre, in Costa Mesa, is a Tony award-winning theater that presents professional productions of contemporary and classical plays on its three stages. The Grove Theater Center, in Garden Grove, is home to the 178-seat Gem Theater and 550-seat Festival Amphitheater; the complex offers year-round plays as well as participatory events.

Arrowhead Pond of Anaheim is a 650,000 square foot arena hosting concerts and family shows; Pearson Park Amphi-

theater is an open-air facility that features family entertainment all summer long; and the Grove of Anaheim presents comedy and music artists in an intimate setting.

The Anaheim Museum highlights the history of the city's original German settlers, its establishment as a wine and citrus colony, and the early Disneyland days depicted in changing exhibits. Mother Colony House, one of the city's first buildings, showcases antiques and other historical items of Anaheim's earliest periods. Bowers Museum of Cultural Art, in nearby Santa Ana, occupies a landmark mission-style building; its exhibits reflect cultural arts from California and around the world.

Festivals and Holidays

The St. Patrick's Day Festival at the Anaheim Farmer's Market features Irish dancers, music, and food. St. Boniface Parish Fiesta in April features international foods, rides, and games. The first weekend in May brings the Cinco de Mayo Fiesta, featuring a soccer tournament, the crowning of a fiesta queen, and a Sunday bilingual Mass, as well as rides, food, and entertainment; the fiesta draws approximately 100,000 people throughout the weekend. The Greek Festival, also in May, features Greek foods, pastries, music, and folkdancers, and a marketplace with vendors selling a variety of items. The Anaheim Children's Art Festival in late May draws 7,000 visitors annually to its art-and-craft projects in staffed booths. June's Taste of Anaheim offers ethnic food, fun, and displays. Anaheim Hills 4th of July Festival & Parade includes a pancake breakfast, dog show, 5K and 10K run/walk, parade, food and game booths, and fireworks. At nearby Laguna Beach's Pageant of the Masters, famous paintings and statuary come to life through the use of live models and an orchestra each night during the months of July and August. Anaheim Fall Festival & Halloween Parade in late October features a parade, pancake breakfast, rides, games, and live entertainment. Knott's Berry Farm transforms into Knott's Scary Farm and then Knott's Merry Farm to celebrate Halloween and Christmas. The Christmas Parade at Disneyland features many popular Disney characters as well as Santa Claus. Nutcracker Holiday, held the first Saturday in December, features musicians, carolers, and a tree-lighting ceremony.

Sports for the Spectator

The Major League Los Angeles Angels of Anaheim baseball team, World Series Champion in 2002, plays its home games at Angel Stadium of Anaheim (formerly called Edison International Field), a baseball-only facility with seating for 45,050. The Mighty Ducks of Anaheim, a National Hockey League team owned by the Walt Disney Company, won the 2003 Western Conference championship; they play at the four-level, 17,174-seat Arrowhead Pond of Anaheim. Arrowhead Pond is also home of National Lacrosse League's Anaheim Storm, and the J. R. Wooden Classic, which features some of the nation's top basketball teams. Los Alamitos Race Course, fifteen minutes west of Disneyland, features the world's fastest horses in quarter horse, Arabian, thoroughbred, paint, and Appaloosa racing. Costa Mesa Speedway at Orange County Fairgrounds holds speedway races on Saturday nights, April through October.

Sports for the Participant

Anaheim has 44 parks totaling approximately 650 acres. Among them, Oak Canyon Nature Center, a 58-acre natural park in the Anaheim Hills, provides excellent opportunities for short hikes. A year-round stream meanders through the park, which consists of three adjoining canyons with four miles of hiking trails. Tennis is available at several Anaheim hotels, and the city maintains more than 50 public courts. Anaheim Hills, a public country club, offers a challenging 18-hole golf course in the natural terrain of the Santa Ana Canyons. H. G. "Dad" Miller is a well kept course surrounded by lovely old trees and a natural lake; it was Tiger Woods' home course during high school. Disney ICE Glacial Gardens, official training facility of the Mighty Ducks, offers public skating and pick up hockey.

Orange County has a 42-mile coastline filled with public and state beaches. Sailing cruises, whale watching, surfing, and swimming are available at sites along the coastline. The county has a regional trail system consisting of 220 miles of built trails. The 30-mile Santa Ana River Trail is a running/bike path that follows the Santa Ana River in the San Bernardino Mountains. Snow skiing is available at nearby Bear Mountain ski resort. Orange County is home to 39 public golf courses.

Shopping and Dining

Downtown Disney, a 120-acre shopping, restaurant, and entertainment complex adjacent to Disneyland, features one-of-a-kind Disney-themed shops and trend-setting restaurants. It is open to the public, with no admission charge. Anaheim Indoor Marketplace is an outlet mall with more than 200 variety stores. Timeless Quilts offers fabrics and quilting supplies in a 1920s Craftsman house, while Hobby City offers a collection of antique dolls and toys from around the world. South Coast Plaza Village in Costa Mesa offers an immense collection of international stores clustered around a Village Green in an open-air environment. Fashion Island Newport Center, in Newport Beach, is an upscale shopping area with open-air courtyards and covered patios overlooking the ocean; it features more than 200 shops, 40 restaurants, and two movie theaters. Westfield Shoppingtown MainPlace in Santa Ana is another large upscale center, with more than 200 specialty shops and restaurants.

Dining experiences in Anaheim run the gamut from ethnic specialties such as Armenian, Cajun, Chinese, Cuban, Ger-

man, Indian, Italian, Japanese, Mexican, Middle Eastern, Peruvian, and Thai to places with unique ambiance such as canneries, gold mines, and Victorian houses. There are more than 60 restaurants and cocktail lounges in the immediate area of the Anaheim Convention Center. In nearby Orange, Watson Drugs and Soda Fountain, established in 1899, has been the set for several movies; it offers burgers and sweets.

Visitor Information: Anaheim/Orange County Visitor and Convention Bureau, 800 West Katella Avenue, Anaheim, CA 92802; telephone (714)999-8999; fax (714)991-8963

Convention Facilities

The Anaheim Convention Center, a sparkling, glass-walled facility, completed a $177 million expansion and redesign in December 2000. The expansion enlarged the center by 40 percent to 1.6 million square feet. The center houses 815,000 square feet of exhibit space, making it the largest exhibit facility on the West Coast. Prefunction areas total 200,000 square feet, and meeting and ballroom space on the building's second and third levels total 130,000 square feet. The center hosts an average of more than 1,300 events annually, including national conventions, conferences, corporate meetings, trade shows, and a variety of public events such as concerts and home and garden shows. Situated on 53 acres in the Anaheim Resort district, the center is within walking distance of more than 12,000 hotel rooms.

Convention Information: Anaheim/Orange County Visitor and Convention Bureau, 800 West Katella Avenue, Anaheim, CA 92802; telephone (714)999-8999; fax (714)991-8963

Transportation

Approaching the City

The main artery running through Anaheim is the Santa Ana Freeway (Interstate 5), which also connects Los Angeles and San Diego. Interstate 5 links Anaheim with the Riverside Freeway, the Garden Grove Freeway, the Orange Freeway, and the Costa Mesa Freeway. Los Angeles International Airport (LAX), the third busiest airport in the world, is located 31 miles from Anaheim. LAX serves 88 airlines and handles thousands of international and domestic flights per year. Santa Ana's John Wayne Airport, 16 miles from Anaheim, serves 12 commercial air carriers and is generally used for domestic travel. Metrolink, a regional commuter rail system, links travelers to activity centers in Orange and surrounding counties; it has two stations located in Anaheim: Anaheim station and Anaheim Canyon station. Amtrak provides railway transportation with a station located at Angel Stadium. Greyhound offers daily bus service to anywhere in the United States.

Traveling in the City

The Santa Ana Freeway traverses Anaheim's downtown running northwest to southeast. The Garden Grove Freeway runs east and west through the city, and the Orange Freeway runs north and south through the city. The Orange County Transportation Authority operates buses daily throughout Orange County. Anaheim Resort Transit buses, trams, and trolleys provide connections between hotels, Anaheim attractions, the convention center, shopping, dining, and evening entertainment locations, along nine interchangeable routes.

Communications

Newspapers and Magazines

The primary daily newspapers serving Anaheim and surrounding Orange County are the *Orange County Register* published in Santa Ana, and the *Times Orange County* published in Costa Mesa. *Anaheim Hills News* and the *Anaheim Bulletin* are weekly newspapers published in Anaheim. Other weeklies published in Orange County include *OC Weekly*, published in Costa Mesa, and *Excélsior*, a Spanish-language newspaper published in Santa Ana. Magazines published in the county include *Surfing* and *Westways*.

Television and Radio

Anaheim is served by two television stations broadcasting from Orange County—a public broadcasting station and an independent station based in Irvine—as well as several stations based in Los Angeles. Cable television is also available. 30 AM and 44 FM radio station serve the Orange County/Los Angeles area.

Media Information: *Orange County Register,* Freedom Communications Inc., 625 N. Grand Ave., Santa Ana, CA 92701; telephone (877)469-7344

Anaheim Online

Anaheim City School District. Available www.acsd.k12.ca .us

Anaheim Orange County Visitor & Convention Bureau. Available www.anaheimoc.org

Anaheim Public Library. Available www.anaheim.net/ comm_svc/apl/index.html

City of Anaheim home page. Available www.anaheim.net

Greater Anaheim Chamber of Commerce. Available www .anaheimchamber.org

Orange County Department of Education. Available www .ocde.k12.ca.us

Orange County Register. Available www.ocregister.com

Selected Bibliography

Newhan, Ross, *The Anaheim Angels: A Complete History* (New York: Hyperion, 2000)

Fresno

The City in Brief

Founded: 1872 (incorporated 1885)

Head Official: Mayor Alan Autry (since 2001)

City Population
  1980: 217,491
  1990: 354,091
  2000: 427,652
  2003 estimate: 451,455
  Percent change, 1990–2000: 20.7%
  U.S. rank in 1980: 65th
  U.S. rank in 1990: 47th
  U.S. rank in 2000: 40th

Metropolitan Area Population
  1980: 515,000
  1990: 667,000
  2000: 922,516

Percent change, 1990–2000: 38.3%
U.S. rank in 1980: 67th
U.S. rank in 1990: 59th
U.S. rank in 2000: 53rd

Area: 99.1 square miles (2000)
Elevation: 328 feet above sea level
Average Annual Temperature: 62.5° F
Average Annual Precipitation: 9.86 inches

Major Economic Sectors: Agriculture, trade, services, manufacturing, government
Unemployment Rate: 13.0% (January 2005)
Per Capita Income: $15,010 (1999)

2002 FBI Crime Index Total: 33,909

Major Colleges and Universities: California State University, Fresno; Fresno City College; Fresno Pacific University

Daily Newspaper: *The Fresno Bee*

TO LOST LAKE, YOSEMITE

SIERRA VALENTINE MARKS VAN NESS WEST FRUIT WALNUT FULTON BLACKSTONE FRESNO FIRST MILLBROOK CEDAR MAPLE CHESTNUT SIERRA CLOVIS

BULLARD

5TH ST.

41

CALIFORNIA STATE UNIVERSITY AT FRESNO

BARSTOW

BARSTOW

SHAW

SHAW

99

HUGHES

GETTYSBURG

GETTYSBURG

CLOVIS

ASHLAN

ASHLAN

PEACH

ENTERPRISE CANAL

DAKOTA

SHIELDS

SHIELDS

MARKS WEST FRUIT WALNUT FULTON BLACKSTONE FRESNO FIRST MILLBROOK CEDAR MAPLE CHESTNUT

FRESNO AIR TERMINAL

CLINTON

MCKINLEY

FRESNO CITY COLLEGE

MCKINLEY

OLIVE

OLIVE

BELMONT

ROEDING PARK

BELMONT

99

NIELSEN

DIVISADERO

MEUX HOUSE

TULARE

WHITESBRIDGE

180

LIBRARY

NEW CITY HALL

KINGS CANYON

180

FRESNO-CHANDLER AIRPORT

AMTRAK

WILLOW

CONVENTION CTR.

KEARNEY

KEARNEY

VISITOR INFO. CTR.

BUTLER

FRESNO

CALIFORNIA

MARKS HUGHES WEST FRUIT WALNUT FIG ELM

CALIFORNIA

FRESNO PACIFIC UNIVERSITY

N

CHURCH

99

FAIRGROUNDS

CHURCH

JENSEN

41

JENSEN

ANNADALE

NORTH

NORTH

CENTRAL

MARKS WEST WALNUT ELM

AMERICAN

LINCOLN

0   1   2
KILOMETERS

MILES   0.5   1   1.5   2

TO KINGS CANYON, SEQUOIA

OR   ID
WY
NEVADA   UTAH   CO
Fresno
CALIFORNIA   ARIZONA   NM

MEXICO

Introduction

The seat of Fresno County, Fresno is the commercial, financial, and cultural center of the San Joaquin Valley and the central California region. The city is the business and transportation hub for four separate agricultural regions in what has been called the agribusiness center of the world. Fresno is also known as the gateway to Yosemite, Kings Canyon, and Sequoia national parks. The city is given an international flavor by a diverse citizenry representing more than 70 nationalities and the largest refugee population in the United States. Over the last two decades, Fresno has been one of the fastest growing cities in the United States. Estimated population had exceeded 450,000 by 2003 and official census numbers revealed a 20.7 percent increase in population between 1990-2000.

Geography and Climate

Fresno is located in the fertile San Joaquin Valley in the central part of California, about halfway between San Francisco and Los Angeles. The terrain in Fresno is relatively flat, with a sharp rise to the foothills of the Sierra Nevada Mountains about 15 miles eastward. The weather is usually sunny, with over 200 clear days each year. Summers are typically hot and dry, while winters are mild and rainy. Spring and fall are the most pleasant seasons.

Area: 99.1 square miles (2000)

Elevation: 328 feet above sea level

Average Temperatures: January, 39.6° F; August, 94.1° F; annual average, 62.5° F

Average Annual Precipitation: 9.86 inches

History

Settlement of Fresno Delayed Until Arrival of Railroad

Fresno means "ash tree" in Spanish, and it was the name given by early Spanish explorers to a stretch of white ash trees along the banks of the San Joaquin River. These explorers did not settle the region where Fresno is now located, however, because they considered it uninhabitable. The site was in fact to remain undeveloped until the late nineteenth century. In the early part of the century, potential settlers were discouraged from staying permanently by the presence of the native population. Unlike other California cities, Fresno did not get its start during the gold rush, for prospectors simply passed through the area on the way to the Sierras. After the gold rush the land was used for cattle grazing.

The first permanent settlement is said to have been established in the 1860s by an immigrant from Holland who was joined by a few other people; but the cluster of dwellings was not actually considered a town. In 1872 the Central Pacific Railroad was constructed through the San Joaquin Valley; the railroad builders laid out a town, calling it Fresno Station for the name of the county, which had been taken from the grove of trees along river. A station was built on the present site of downtown Fresno.

The county seat at that time was Millerton, a town 25 miles to the south. In order to gain access to rail transportation, Millerton residents voted to transfer the seat to Fresno Station and the entire population moved. The town was rough and desolate, the countryside barren. The introduction of irrigation and grape-growing in the valley brought prosperity, however; Fresno was incorporated as a city in 1885. Soon vineyards were being planted by local inhabitants as well as Italian, French, and Swiss immigrants who had bought 20-acre parcels of land.

Development of Raisin and Fig Industries

When the dry white wine produced from the area's vineyards proved less than satisfactory, the grapes were cultivated for raisins, which were naturally produced by the continuous sunlight in the valley. Following an unusually large yield of more than one million pounds of raisins that drove the price down to two cents a pound in 1894, the Raisin Growers Association was organized in 1898 to protect the raisin industry. In 1886, Frank Roeding and his son began growing figs in the area; having experimented with caprification, the cross-fertilization of the Smyrna fig by the fig wasp, they started another successful industry.

By 1900 the population of Fresno had reached 12,470 people, and the city drafted its first charter. During the following decade agriculture continued to flourish, with cotton growing and sweet wine production emerging as new industries. Fresno became the residential and commercial center of an increasingly prosperous region. With the expansion of manufacturing along with agriculture, Fresno was by the end of World War II a major metropolitan area. Today Fresno County is the nation's leading agricultural county, producing more than three billion dollars' worth of crops each year; crops now include nuts, melons, grains, rice, and vegetables. The city of Fresno has become the center of trade, commerce, finance, and transportation for the San Joaquin Valley.

Historical Information: California History & Genealogy Room, Fresno County Library, 2420 Mariposa, Fresno, CA 93721; telephone (559)488-3195

Population Profile

Metropolitan Area Residents
1980: 515,000
1990: 667,000
2000: 922,516
Percent change, 1990–2000: 38.3%
U.S. rank in 1980: 67th
U.S. rank in 1990: 59th
U.S. rank in 2000: 53rd

City Residents
1980: 217,491
1990: 354,091
2000: 427,652
2003 estimate: 451,455
Percent change, 1990–2000: 20.7%
U.S. rank in 1980: 65th
U.S. rank in 1990: 47th
U.S. rank in 2000: 40th

Density: 4,315 people per square mile (2000)

Racial and ethnic characteristics (2000)
White: 214,556
Black or African American: 35,763
American Indian and Alaska Native: 6,763
Asian: 48,028
Native Hawaiian and other Pacific Islander: 583
Hispanic or Latino (may be of any race): 170,520
Other: 99,898

Percent of residents born in state: 61.7 (2000)

Age characteristics (2000)
Population under 5 years old: 38,996
Population 5 to 9 years old: 41,584
Population 10 to 14 years old: 38,324
Population 15 to 19 years old: 37,027
Population 20 to 24 years old: 35,309
Population 25 to 34 years old: 63,085
Population 35 to 44 years old: 60,172
Population 45 to 54 years old: 46,932
Population 55 to 59 years old: 15,060
Population 60 to 64 years old: 11,589
Population 65 to 74 years old: 20,061
Population 75 to 84 years old: 14,302
Population 85 years and over: 5,211
Median age: 28.5 years

Births (Fresno County, 2002)
Total number: 14,766

Deaths (Fresno County, 2002)
Total number: 5,785 (of which, 102 were infants under the age of 1 year)

Money income (1999)
Per capita income: $15,010
Median family income: $35,892
Total households: 139,969

Number of households with income of . . .
less than $10,000: 19,827
$10,000 to $14,999: 11,862
$15,000 to $24,999: 23,114
$25,000 to $34,999: 20,110
$35,000 to $49,999: 21,767
$50,000 to $74,999: 22,646
$75,000 to $99,999: 9,998
$100,000 to $149,999: 6,993
$150,000 to $199,999: 1,704
$200,000 or more: 1,948

Percent of families below poverty level: 20.5 (59.0 % of which were female householder families with related children under 5 years)

2002 FBI Crime Index Total: 33,909

Municipal Government

Fresno has a strong-mayor form of government, with seven council members and the mayor elected at large. A city manager is hired by the council. Fresno is also the Fresno County seat.

Head Official: Mayor Alan Autry (since 2001; current term expires 2009)

Total Number of City Employees: 3,921 (2004)

City Information: City of Fresno, 2600 Fresno Street, Fresno, CA 93721; telephone (559)621-7770

Economy

Major Industries and Commercial Activity

Agriculture is the backbone of the Fresno area, employing nearly 20 percent of the workforce and providing more than

$3.5 billion for the local economy. More jobs are tied into the agricultural industry than any other industry in the Freso area; estimates are that one in three jobs in all are related to agriculture. A majority of America's produce is grown in California's Central Valley, and Fresno County is the number one agricultural county in the United States. By 2005 more than 7,500 farmers were growing 250 types of crops on 1 million acres of some of the world's most productive farmland. Major crops are grapes, cotton, cattle, tomatoes, milk, plums, turkeys, oranges, peaches, and nectarines. A large food processing industry has developed around the agricultural activity; a number of canning, curing, drying, and freezing plants are located in the area.

An Ernst and Young study also tapped Fresno as an ideal location for manufacturing and distribution, due to its proximity within one day's drive of 35 million people. Manufacturing concerns in this Port of Entry region produce farm machinery, metal products, transportation equipment, stone, clay, and glass products, lumber and wood products, furniture and fixtures, and electrical equipment. Government, services, and trade are also important economic sectors.

Incentive Programs—New and Existing Companies

Local programs—In 2002 the City of Fresno was one of just seven localities nationwide to be awarded a lucrative Federal Empowerment Zone designation. The U.S. Department of Housing and Urban Development will fund this program until December 31, 2009. Business that are located in the Empowerment Zone are eligible for significant incentives that will encourage expansion, including up to $3,000 per employee per year, tax deductions on property investment and capital gains, tax-free rollover of certain gains, and tax-exempt financing through state or local government bonds. The City of Fresno is specifically interested in attracting new businesses involved with flexible food manufacturing, irrigation and agricultural technology, agile industrial manufacturing, advanced logistics, smart commerce and customer services.

In addition to these programs, the city also has other programs such as the Community Development Block Grant (CDBG) and the Fresno Redevelopment Agency (RDA) and its finance authority, that can be useful when considering Industrial Development Bonds. The City has also developed relationships with other agencies such as the Fresno County Workforce Development Corporation and the Fresno Chamber of Commerce and Economic Development Corporation, which offer assistance to the developer and other companies considering a move to the City of Fresno.

State programs—The city of Fresno has one of the largest Enterprise Zones in California. Within the zone, the State of California provides business tax credits covering a wide range of hiring, financing, and capital investment activities. Among

the advantages of investing in Enterprise Zones in 2005 was a Net Operating Loss carry-forward of up to 100 percent for up to 15 years; $31,544 or more in state tax credits to firms for each qualified employee hired; and sales tax credits to corporations on purchases of $20 million per year of qualified machinery and machinery parts. The State Loan Guarantee Program provides working capital loans, and Small Business Administration loans are available to assist in financing fixed-capital and operational expenditures. All programs are administered through the State of California Commerce and Economic Development Program.

Development Projects

The most significant development in recent years, the Save Mart Center on the campus of Fresno State University, opened in late 2003 as a venue for national touring concert acts, as well as Fresno State home basketball games. Several downtown developments have revitalized the area, including the Tower at Convention Center Court, an 11-story complex completed in 2003, as well as several other office towers. A new federal courthouse will be the tallest building in Fresno. These and other planned developments are part of the city's Vision 2010 that aims to bring residents back to the area.

Economic Development Information: Economic Development Department, Jeffrey Reid, City Manager, 2600 Fresno St (2nd floor), Fresno, CA 93721; telephone (559)498-4591; fax (559)488-1015; email economicdev@fresno.gov

Commercial Shipping

International freight shipments to and from the entire region flow through the Fresno Yosemite International Airport, a direct port of entry. The nation's largest parcel carriers, FedEx, UPS, and DHL, operate from there. Rail freight services are provided by both the Burlington Northern-Santa Fe and Southern Pacific railroads. Nearly 200 truck firms are based within the Fresno County borders.

Labor Force and Employment Outlook

Fresno continues to diversify its economy toward non-agricultural industries. In 2002, two major manufacturers, Sinclair Systems and Rayovac Corporation, moved their headquarters to the Fresno area. Fresno's labor force is productive, motivated, flexible, and relatively young. Steady population growth has occurred faster than local business expansion or new business development. Unemployment rates fluctuate seasonally, due mainly to the high demand for agricultural labor at certain times of the year. A large number of immigrants, both regional and international, provide a continuous supply of employable people with diverse skills. Job availability is aided by a cooperative effort between business and government to attract new industry.

The following is summary of data regarding the city of Fresno labor force, 2004 annual averages.

Size of non-agricultural labor force: 285,800

Number of workers employed in . . .
 natural resources and mining: 200
 construction: 20,000
 manufacturing: 27,400
 trade, transportation and utilities: 55,800
 information: 4,400
 financial activities: 13,700
 professional and business services: 27,300
 educational and health services: 35,400
 leisure and hospitality: 24,000
 other services: 10,700
 government: 66,400

Average hourly earnings of production workers employed in manufacturing: $12.14

Unemployment rate: 13.0% (January 2005)

Largest employers	*Number of employees*
Fresno County Unified School District	10,000
Fresno County	6,492
Community Medical Centers	5,500
City of Fresno	3,131
Zacky Farms	2,500
St. Agnes Medical Center	2,400

Cost of Living

Fresno boasts a cost of living that is low compared to other California cities.

The following is a summary of data regarding several key cost of living factors for the Fresno area.

2004 (3rd Quarter) ACCRA Average House Price: $390,843

2004 (3rd Quarter) ACCRA Cost of Living Index: 119.3 (U.S. average = 100.0)

State income tax rate: Ranges from 1.0% to 9.3%

State sales tax rate: 6.0% (food and prescription drugs are exempt)

Local income tax rate: None

Local sales and use tax rate: 1.975%

Property tax rate: Limited to 1% of assessed value by state law. In some cases the local taxing body can add up to 0.15%

Economic Information: Fresno Chamber of Commerce, 2331 Fresno Street, Fresno, CA 93716; telephone (559)495-4800

Education and Research

Elementary and Secondary Schools

The Fresno Unified School District is the fourth largest in California, with a 2004 budget of $869 million. A five-member, nonpartisan board of education hires a superintendent. Overall the district has underperformed due to a wide variety of problems including financial woes, mismanagement, and a highly diverse student population with large numbers of immigrant and non-English-speaking students, many of whom are impoverished. In 2005 more than 50 percent of the district's schools were scoring in the bottom 10 percent in California and the district as a whole was at the risk of a state takeover.

The following is a summary of data regarding the Fresno Unified School District as of the 2003–2004 school year.

Total enrollment: 80,421

Number of facilities
 elementary schools: 61
 junior high schools: 19
 senior high schools: 8

Student/teacher ratio: 20.6:1

Teacher salaries
 minimum: $34,326
 maximum: $61,100

Funding per student: $8,351

Additionally there are 15 private schools serving K-12 students in Fresno, including several Catholic elementary and high schools, other Christian and religious schools, and secular private institutions.

Colleges and Universities

California State University at Fresno (commonly known as Fresno State), part of the 23 campus California State University system, is a four-year accredited university offering doctoral, graduate, and undergraduate degrees in about 100 fields to its more than 22,000 students. With 26 nationally accredited departmental programs, Fresno State is the largest post-secondary institution in the city and sits on a 327 acre campus and adjacent to a 1,083 acre University Farm in the northeast section of Fresno. Fresno City College is a 2-year community college with more than 21,000 students. California's oldest community college, Fresno City College offers Associate's degrees in more than 100 disciplines. Many are designed to transfer to four-year institutions. The University of California San Francisco School of Medicine operates a branch in Fresno that provides medical internship and residency training. Nearly two dozen other schools, including private colleges and universities, law schools, technical schools, and professional graduate schools operate in Fresno County.

Libraries and Research Centers

The Fresno County Public Library has a main library and 34 branches throughout the Fresno area. The system further links to the San Joaquin Valley Library system, a cooperative network of nine public library systems with shared information databases across six counties in the Central Valley. In addition to more than 1.1 million volumes, the Fresno County Library also offers nearly 2,000 periodical subscriptions, 1 million government publications, 47,000 video materials, and 87,000 audio materials. There are special services for the handicapped and visually impaired, as well as special collections on the Japanese and Hmong languages, Pulitzer Prize-winning author and Fresno native William Saroyan, oral history, and holdings of the Fresno Genealogical Society. Research activities in such fields as agriculture, forestry, irrigation, viticulture and enology, and information processing are conducted at centers in the Fresno area.

Public Library Information: Fresno County Public Library, 2420 Mariposa Street, Fresno, CA 93721-2285; telephone (559)488-3195

Health Care

Eight hospitals operate in the city of Fresno, the three largest being Community Medical Center Fresno, St. Agnes Medical Center, and University Medical Center. Nearby Children's Hospital Central California has more than 255 beds on a 50-acre campus in Madera.

Recreation

Sightseeing

The 67-mile Blossom Trail offers arguably the best look at what makes the Fresno area unique, with a plunge into some of the most productive agricultural land in the world. The annual Blossom Trail kickoff comes each February, and motorists and hikers through the farm country can come upon stunning displays of blossoming peach, nectarine, plum, orange, and almond trees in full bloom. The family-run Simonian Farms at the end of the trail cultivate more than one hundred varieties of fruits and vegetables and can be toured via a hay wagon.

Fresno is less than an hour away from the Sierra Nevada Mountains and three of the nation's most popular national parks. Yosemite, King's Canyon, and Sequoia National Parks offer spectacular canyons, waterfalls, and forests of 4,000-year-old bristlecone pine trees and giant sequoias, the largest trees in the world.

Downtown Fresno offers the Fulton Mall, a beautiful area of stores, restaurants, landscaped grounds, fountains, and sculpture that covers a ten-block area. It contains one of the finest collections of public art in the nation, arranged throughout the central business district. Roeding Park, two miles northwest of the downtown area, contains the Fresno Zoo, the third largest in California; Rotary Playground, a mechanical park for children; Chaffee Zoological Gardens; and Storyland, offering display and walk-through depictions of children's stories.

Arts and Culture

The William Saroyan Theater is the cultural center of Fresno. Luxurious seating for 2,300 people and near-perfect acoustics highlight the theater, home to the Fresno Philharmonic Orchestra and the Fresno Ballet and site of many cultural events throughout the year. Other venues for the performing arts are the Good Company Players Second Space Theatre, presenting comedy and drama; Roger Rocka's Dinner Theatre; historic Tower Theatre, presenting touring performers; Theatre Three, presenting eight varied performances annually in a 107-seat facility; and Warnors Theatre.

The Fresno City and County Historical Society operates the Kearney Mansion and Fort Miller Blockhouse, two historical museums, extensive archives on the history of Fresno, and tours of the city's historic buildings. Meux Home, a restored historical structure in downtown Fresno, features a number of exhibits relating to the region's history, displayed on a rotating basis. Architecture buffs might wish to contemplate the futuristic design of the City Hall, located near the historic district containing Meux Home and St. John's Cathedral.

The Discovery Center is a hands-on science museum and outdoor education center; it features Native American exhibits, a cactus garden, worm farms, ponds, and a greenhouse.

The Fresno Art Museum is the only modern art museum between San Francisco and Los Angeles and has three main galleries, an exhibition concourse, and a unique "Childspace"; it offers art classes for adults and children. The Metropolitan Museum of Art, Science, and History contains collections of European still lifes, tromp l'oeil oil paintings, and exhibits focusing on the cultural heritage of Central California, including exhibits dedicated to author and Fresno native William Saroyan.

Arts and Culture Information: City of Fresno Cultural Arts Office, telephone (559)498-1181

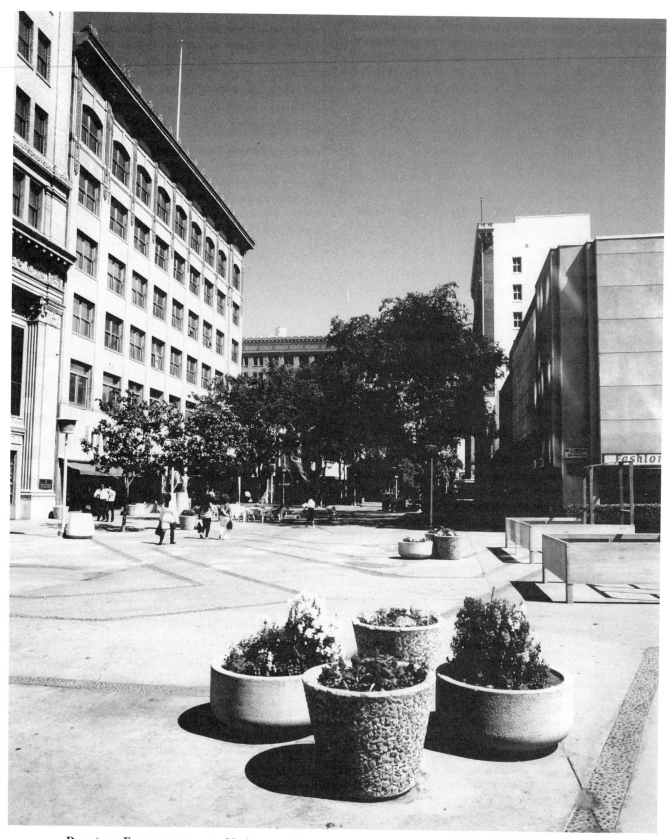

Downtown Fresno covers a ten-block area with an array of shops, restaurants, fountains, and sculptures.

Festivals and Holidays

Fresno schedules a number of special cultural and ethnic events throughout the year. A variety of activities are planned by communities along the Blossom Trail to coincide with the peak growing season, beginning in late February or early March. A Renaissance Festival is held annually in March on the campus of Fresno City College. The Bob Matthias Fresno Relays take place every spring, as they have for more than 75 years. Beginning each June there are bi-weekly free concerts in Woodward Park. July brings the Obon Odori Festival, a Japanese carnival of crafts, games, food, music, and dance. The High Sierra Regatta at Hunting-ton Lake is a prestigious yachting event held on two consec-utive weekends in July. The Big Fresno Fair happens at the Fairgrounds in October.

Sports for the Spectator

The Fresno Grizzlies, a Triple-A affiliate of the San Fran-cisco Giants, play baseball at the new downtown ballpark, Grizzlies Stadium. The Central Valley Coyotes play profes-sional Arena Football at 11,000-seat Selland Arena. Minor League hockey can be seen with the Fresno Falcons at the new Save Mart Center, and the Fresno Heatwave play ABA pro basketball at Selland Arena. The Fresno State University Bulldogs play basketball at Selland Arena and football at Bulldog Stadium. Men's baseball and women's softball teams compete at Beiden Field.

Sports for the Participant

A number of area lakes and reservoirs provide a full range of water recreation in the immediate Fresno area. But with three of America's great national parks within a 90-minute drive, Fresno offers arguably the greatest range of recrea-tional options of any large metropolitan area in the U.S. Nearby Yosemite, Sequoia/Kings Canyon, and Death Valley National Parks offer flat, scorching desert vistas to high mountain streams and skiing, and everything in between. The numerous streams and rivers in the area offer some of California's finest trout and largemouth bass fishing, as well as rafting and canoeing. The hills and nearby mountains contain many campsites and hiking trails; snow skiing is less than 90 minutes away at Sierra Summit, while Lake Tahoe is just a bit further in the Sierra Nevada range.

More than 2,000 children age 3-12 play on 175 teams in the sports of baseball, basketball, and football, and participate in karate lessons. The city of Fresno operates 3 major regional parks, including the highly popular Chaffee Zoo, as well as 27 playgrounds and community centers, 14 swim-ming pools, 3 eighteen-hole golf courses, and tennis courts. There are 5 additional public golf courses in the immediate Fresno area.

Shopping and Dining

Fulton Mall, a popular sightseeing spot, is the major shopping complex in Fresno's downtown area. Other important shop-ping centers are the Fashion Fair Mall and Manchester Mall. The Sierra Vista Mall in Clovis contains several large retail outlets and a number of smaller specialty shops. Numerous smaller centers and antique shops are spread throughout the city. Of unique interest is the international gift shop in the Mennonite Quilting Center in downtown Reedley.

More than 500 restaurants in Fresno, many housed in his-toric buildings, offer a wide selection of dining experiences for every taste and price range, including hearty regional and western dishes, Mexican specialties, and European and in-ternational cuisines.

Visitor Information: Fresno Convention and Visitors Bu-reau, 808 M Street, Fresno, CA 93721; telephone (559)233-0836; toll-free (800)788-0836; fax (559)445-0122; email TourFresno@aol.com

Convention Facilities

The Fresno Convention and Conference Center is an award-winning complex covering five city blocks in the downtown district. It contains a 168,172-square-foot exhibit hall, a theater that seats 2,300 people, an 11,000-seat arena, and a 13,120 square-foot multi-use ballroom. The William Saroyan Theatre in the convention center complex is home to the Fresno Philharmonic Orchestra and the Fresno Ballet and is also available for meetings. California State Univer-sity, Fresno, offers several large facilities, and the major hotels in the area feature extensive meeting, banquet, and ballroom accommodations. More than 7,000 hotel/motel rooms are available in Fresno.

Convention Information: Fresno Convention and Visitors Bureau, 808 M Street, Fresno, CA 93721; telephone (559)233-0836; toll-free (800)788-0836; email FCVBsales @aol.com

Transportation

Approaching the City

The Fresno Yosemite International Airport is served by 11 local and national air carriers and offers scheduled service to more than 25 of the nation's major cities.

State Highway 99 runs through the center of the city and connects with Interstate 5, the major north-south highway in the state. State Highways 41 and 168, running north and south, and State Highway 180, running east and west, connect the city with the Sierra Nevada Mountains and western California.

Amtrak provides daily passenger rail schedules through Fresno County with connections to northern and southern California. Fresno County is poised to maintain its dominant rail position in California as the state continues with plans for high speed rail service, which will connect the Central San Joaquin Valley with San Francisco and the Los Angeles basin. The proposed rail service would transport passengers at more than 200 miles per hour and move 68 million passengers annually by 2020. Transcontinental bus service is also available.

Traveling in the City

Most of Fresno is laid out in a grid of streets running east-west and north-south. West Avenue is the dividing line for east and west designations, and Whites Bridge Avenue and Kings Canyon Road divide the city north and south.

Fresno Area Express has 18 fixed-route bus service lines and Handy Ride Para transit service with a fleet of more than 100 buses.

Communications

Newspapers and Magazines

One daily newspaper serves Fresno readers: *The Fresno Bee. Fresno Business Journal* is published weekly. Four other special interest papers are published in Fresno. Of the eleven magazines published in the city, six focus on agriculture.

Television and Radio

Cable television is available throughout Fresno. In addition, major network broadcast television (CBS, NBC, ABC, Fox, and PBS) are available locally. As expected of any midsized American city, a wide variety of radio programming is available from 17 FM and AM stations.

Fresno Online

California Mission Studies Association. Available www.ca-missions.org/links.html

City of Fresno Home Page. Available www.ci.fresno.ca.us

Fresno Bee. Available www.fresnobee.com

Fresno Chamber of Commerce. Available www.fresnochamber.com

Fresno Convention & Visitors Bureau. Available www.fresnocvb.org

Fresno County Economic Development Corporation. Available www.fresnoedc.com

Fresno County Library. Available www.sjvls.lib.ca.us/fresno

Fresno Unified Public Schools. Available www.fresno.k12.ca.us

Selected Bibliography

Burnett, Brenda Preston, *Andrew Davidson Firebaugh and Susan Burgess Firebaugh: California Pioneers* (Rio Del Mar, Calif.: Rio Del Mar Press, 1995)

Los Angeles

The City in Brief

Founded: 1781 (incorporated 1850)

Head Official: Mayor James K. Hahn (D) (since 2001)

City Population
  1980: 2,966,850
  1990: 3,485,557
  2000: 3,694,820
  2003 estimate: 3,819,951
  Percent change, 1990–2000: 5.9%
  U.S. rank in 1980: 3rd
  U.S. rank in 1990: 2nd (State rank: 1st)
  U.S. rank in 2000: 2nd (State rank: 1st)

Metropolitan Area Population (PMSA)
  1980: 7,478,000
  1990: 8,863,000
  2000: 9,519,338

Percent change, 1990–2000: 9.3%
U.S. rank in 1980: 2nd (CMSA)
U.S. rank in 1990: 2nd (CMSA)
U.S. rank in 2000: 2nd (CMSA)

Area: 469.1 square miles (2000)
Elevation: 340 feet above sea level
Average Annual Temperature: 63.9° F
Average Annual Precipitation: 17 inches

Major Economic Sectors: Services; manufacturing; government; finance, insurance, and real estate
Unemployment Rate: 5.8% (January 2005)
Per Capita Income: $26,733 (1999)

2002 FBI Crime Index Total: 190,992

Major Colleges and Universities: University of California, Los Angeles (UCLA), University of Southern California (USC), California Institute of Technology

Daily Newspaper: *Los Angeles Times*

Introduction

Los Angeles is the second largest city in the United States in terms of population and one of the largest in terms of area. It is the center of a five-county metropolitan area and is considered the prototype of the future metropolis—a city on the cutting edge of all of the advantages and the problems of large urban areas. The glamour of Hollywood, Beverly Hills, the Sunset Strip, and the famous beaches have added to Los Angeles's reputation as a California paradise and have contributed to the area's phenomenal growth. Los Angeles is a city of fascinating diversity, incorporating one of the largest Hispanic populations in the United States, a major Asian community, and sizable populations of nearly every ethnic background in the world. Los Angeles is also a center of international trade and banking, manufacturing, and tourism. The city offers something for everyone in its large conglomeration of separate and very different districts: a sleek, ultra-modern downtown, miles of beautiful beaches, mansions and stunning canyon homes built with opulent luxury, and some of the world's most glamorous shopping and dining. Beneath the glitter, though, is a troubled, racially divided city, with extremely high unemployment rates for young African Americans and Latinos.

Geography and Climate

Los Angeles lies on a hilly coastal plain with the Pacific Ocean as its southern and western boundaries. The city stretches north to the foothills of the Santa Monica Mountains and is bounded by the San Gabriel Mountains to the east. Numerous canyons and valleys also characterize the region, making it an area of diverse climatic conditions. The predominant weather influence is the warm, moist Pacific air, keeping temperatures mild throughout the year. Summers are dry and sunny—the city averages 329 days of sun per year—with most of the precipitation occurring during the winter months. Smog and air pollution are common problems, gathering in the coastal basin during periods of little air movement. Other unusual weather phenomena include the Santa Ana winds, which bring hot, dusty winds of up to 50 miles per hour from the surrounding mountains, and the occasional flash floods in the canyon areas, causing mudslides.

Area: 469.1 square miles (2000)

Elevation: 340 feet above sea level

Average Temperatures: January, 57.0° F; August, 72.0° F; annual average, 63.9° F

Annual Average Precipitation: 17 inches

History

Spanish and Anglos Settle, Trade Industry Thrives

The area around present-day Los Angeles was first explored by Europeans in 1769 when Gaspar de Portola and a group of missionaries camped on what is now called the Los Angeles River. Franciscans built Mission San Gabriel about 9 miles to the north in 1771. In 1781, Felipe de Neve, governor of Alte California, founded a settlement called El Pueblo de Nuestra Senora la Reina de los Angeles, which means "the pueblo of our lady the queen of angels." In its early years, the town was a small, isolated cluster of adobe-brick houses and random streets carved out of the desert, and its main product was grain.

Although the Spanish government placed a ban on trading with foreign ships, American vessels began arriving in the early 1800s, and the first English-speaking inhabitant settled in the area in 1818. He was a carpenter named Joseph Chapman, who helped build the church facing the town's central plaza, a structure that still stands. After Mexico, including California, gained its independence from Spain in 1821, trade with the United States became more frequent. The ocean waters off the coast of California were important for whaling and seal hunting, and a number of trading ships docked at nearby San Pedro to buy cattle hides and tallow. By the 1840s, Los Angeles was the largest town in southern California.

City Becomes American Possession; Gold Discovered

During the war between the United States and Mexico in 1846, Los Angeles was occupied by an American garrison, but the citizens drove the fifty-man brigade out of town. The Treaty of Cahuenga, signed in 1847, ended the war in California, adding Los Angeles and the rest of California to American territory. The Sierra Nevada gold strike in 1848 in the mountains to the north of Los Angeles provided the town with a booming market for its beef, and many prospectors settled in the area after the gold rush. Los Angeles was incorporated in 1850 with a reputation as one of the toughest towns in the West. "A murder a day" only slightly exaggerated the town's crime problems, and suspected criminals were often hanged by vigilante groups. Lawlessness reached a peak in 1871, when, after a Chinese immigrant accidentally killed a white man, an angry mob stormed into the Chinatown district, murdering sixteen people. After that, civic leaders and concerned citizens began a successful campaign to bring law and order to the town.

The Southern Pacific Railroad reached Los Angeles in 1876, followed by the Santa Fe Railroad nine years later. The two rival companies conducted a rate war that eventually drove the price of a ticket from the eastern United States down to five dollars. This price slashing brought thousands of settlers to the area, sending real estate prices to unrealistically high levels. By 1887, lots around the central plaza sold for up to one thousand dollars a foot, but the market collapsed in that same year, making millionaires destitute overnight. People in vast numbers abandoned Los Angeles, sometimes as many as three thousand a day. This flight prompted the creation of the Chamber of Commerce, which began a worldwide advertising campaign to attract new citizens. By 1890, the population had climbed back up to fifty thousand residents.

Oil, Agriculture, Moving Pictures, Manufacturing Build City

In the 1890s, oil was discovered in the city, and soon another boom took hold. By the turn of the century almost fifteen hundred oil wells operated throughout Los Angeles. In the early 1900s, agriculture became an important part of the economy, and a massive aqueduct project was completed. The city's growth necessitated the annexation of the large San Fernando Valley, and the port at San Pedro was also added to give Los Angeles a position in the international trade market.

The motion picture industry thrived on the Los Angeles area's advantages after the first decade of the twentieth century, and by 1930 it had earned the city the nickname of "Tinseltown." Large manufacturing concerns also began opening factories during that time, and the need for housing created vast areas of suburban neighborhoods and the beginnings of the city's massive freeway system. The Depression and the midwestern drought of the 1930s brought thousands of people to California looking for jobs.

To accommodate its growing population, the city instituted a number of large engineering projects, including the construction of the Hoover Dam, which channeled water to the city from the Colorado River and provided electricity from hydroelectric power. The area's excellent weather made it an ideal location for aircraft testing and construction, and World War II brought hundreds of new industries to the area, boosting the local economy. By the 1950s, Los Angeles was a sprawling metropolis. It was considered the epitome of everything new and modern in American culture—a combination of super highways, affordable housing, and opportunity for everyone.

City Grapples with Pollution, Racial Unrest

The Los Angeles dream began to fade in the 1960s. Despite the continued construction of new freeways, traffic congestion became a major problem; industry and auto emissions created smog and pollution. Frustration over living conditions came to a head in August 1965, when riots erupted in the African American ghetto of Watts, and more unrest developed in the Hispanic communities of East Los Angeles.

Reacting to these new problems, the city adopted strict air pollution guidelines and took steps to bring minorities into the political process, culminating in the 1973 election of Mayor Tom Bradley, the city's first African American mayor. Over the next two decades, public transportation was improved, and a subway system was funded and began limited operations. The downtown area became a thriving district of impressive glass skyscrapers.

The city's reputation was severely tarnished by a rebellion that broke out in April 1992 following the acquittal of four white police officers accused of beating an African American motorist—a beating that was captured on videotape by a bystander and broadcast worldwide. The ensuing melee left more than 50 people dead and resulted in an estimated 1 billion dollars in damage.

Los Angeles Enters Twenty-First Century

Los Angeles began to emerge from the recession of the mid-1990s, but like much of the country, the city was dealt another blow after the terrorist attacks of September 11, 2001. In response to the ensuing economic downturn, the mayor created the Los Angeles Economic Impact Task Force, which brought together business leaders from across the city to develop recommendations for strengthening the local economy. The result has been an increase in tourism, retail sales, and other continuing signs of recovery.

Historical Information: History Division, Natural History Museum of Los Angeles County, 900 Exposition Boulevard, Los Angeles, CA 90007; telephone (213)744-3352

Population Profile

Metropolitan Area Residents (PMSA)
1980: 7,478,000
1990: 8,863,052
2000: 9,519,338
Percent change, 1990–2000: 9.4%
U.S. rank in 1980: 2nd (CMSA)
U.S. rank in 1990: 2nd (CMSA)
U.S. rank in 2000: 2nd (CMSA)

City Residents
1980: 2,966,850
1990: 3,485,557
2000: 3,694,820
2003 estimate: 3,819,338
Percent change, 1990–2000: 5.9%
U.S. rank in 1980: 3rd
U.S. rank in 1990: 2nd (State rank: 1st)
U.S. rank in 2000: 2nd (State rank: 1st)

Density: 7,876.8 people per square mile (in 2000, based on 1998 land area)

Racial and ethnic characteristics (2000)
White: 1,734,036
Black or African American: 415,195
American Indian and Alaska Native: 29,412
Asian: 369,254
Native Hawaiian and Other Pacific Islander: 5,915
Hispanic or Latino (may be of any race): 1,719,073
Other: 949,720

Percent of residents born in state: 50.2% (2000)

Age characteristics (2000)
Population under 5 years old: 285,976
Population 5 to 9 years old: 297,837
Population 10 to 14 years old: 255,604
Population 15 to 19 years old: 251,632
Population 20 to 24 years old: 299,906
Population 25 to 34 years old: 674,098
Population 35 to 44 years old: 584,036
Population 45 to 54 years old: 428,974
Population 55 to 59 years old: 143,965
Population 60 to 64 years old: 115,663
Population 65 to 74 years old: 187,11
Population 75 to 84 years old: 125,829
Population 85 years and over: 44,189
Median age: 31.6 years

Births (2002; Los Angeles County)
Total number: 151,167

Deaths (2002; Los Angeles County)
Total number: 59,586 (of which, 825 were infants under the age of 1 year)

Money income (1999)
Per capita income: $20,671
Median household income: $36,687
Total households: 1,276,609

Number of households with income of . . .
less than $10,000: 80,406
$10,000 to $14,999: 59,912
$15,000 to $24,999: 117,692
$25,000 to $34,999: 102,635
$35,000 to $49,999: 117,119
$50,000 to $74,999: 128,202
$75,000 to $99,999: 74,400
$100,000 to $149,999: 67,897
$150,000 to $199,999: 23,631
$200,000 or more: 35,145

Percent of families below poverty level: 18.3% (50.9% of which were female householder families with related children under 5 years)

2002 FBI Crime Index Total: 190,992

Municipal Government

The government of Los Angeles is a complex institution, with many departments operating independently of the central legislative and executive body. The fifteen-member city council and the mayor are elected to four-year terms, as are the city attorney and the controller. The county of Los Angeles is governed by a five-member board of supervisors, although many districts are separate and self-governing.

Head Official: Mayor James K. Hahn (D) (since 2001; current term expires 2005)

Total Number of City Employees: 35,895 (2002)

City Information: City Hall, 200 North Spring Street, Los Angeles, CA 90012; telephone (213)485-2121

Economy

Major Industries and Commercial Activity

California has always been known as an "incubator" of new ideas, new products and entrepreneurial spirit. Southern California has led the way in celebrating and nurturing that spirit. The people, institutions of knowledge, great climate and infrastructure have enabled the Los Angeles region to emerge as a leading business, trade and cultural center—a creative capital for the twenty-first century. The city is the largest manufacturing center in the West, one of the world's busiest ports, a major financial and banking center, and the largest retail market in the United States.

Los Angeles is the largest major manufacturing center in the United States, with 500,000 workers in manufacturing activities in 2003. The largest components are apparel (68,300 jobs), computer and electronic products (60,000 jobs), transportation products (54,600 jobs), fabricated metal products (49,900 jobs), food products (44,800 jobs), and furniture (27,400 jobs). The last few years have witnessed major economic expansion. The three-tiered, traditional economy (aerospace, entertainment, and tourism) has evolved into a well balanced, multi-tiered economic engine driven by unparalleled access to world markets.

Steel fabrication is the second largest industry in manufacturing, followed closely by fashion apparel. In the United States, only Detroit produces more automobiles than the Los Angeles area, a fitting statistic for the city with more cars per capita than any other in the world. The "big three" U.S. auto manufacturers, along with Honda, Mazda, Nissan, Toyota, Volkswagen, and Volvo, have all located design centers in Los Angeles. The manufacture of heavy machinery for the agricultural, construction, mining, and oil industries contributes significantly to the local economy. Los Angeles is also a major producer of furniture and fixtures, as well as petroleum products and chemicals, print material, rubber goods, electronic equipment, and glass, pottery, ceramics, and cement products.

Los Angeles is the nation's largest port in terms of value of goods handled and tonnage. Proximity to the major Pacific manufacturing nations—Japan, Korea, and Taiwan—and easy access to transcontinental rail and truck shipping, plus the large commercial facilities available at Los Angeles International Airport make the Los Angeles Customs District the largest in the nation. The city's prominence in international trade is evidenced by the nearly 50 U.S. headquarters of foreign companies located in the area.

The banking and finance industry in Los Angeles is one of the largest in the United States. More than 100 foreign and countless domestic banks operate branches in Los Angeles, along with many financial law firms and investment banks. Entertainment, in the form of film, television, and music production, is the best known industry in Los Angeles, focusing worldwide attention on the city and making Los Angeles a major tourist destination. Tourism employs more than 468,000 people in the entire metropolitan area.

Other prominent industries in the Los Angeles area include health services, education, high-technology research and development, professional fields such as architecture and engineering, and a large construction business, both commercial and residential.

Items and goods produced: agricultural and seafood products, aircraft and aircraft parts, furniture fixtures, ordnance missiles, electrical and electronic equipment, stone, clay, glass, apparel, textiles, toys, fabricated metals, rubber, plastic, motion pictures, petroleum, coal

Incentive Programs—New and Existing Companies

Local programs—LA's Business Team, part of the Mayor's Office of Economic Development, is a one-stop shop for business developers. Through strategic industry and government alliances, the Business Team links businesses to a network of opportunities including financing, tax incentives, real estate, low-interest loans, job training programs, permits, and more. It is also working to develop emerging industries in Los Angeles, such as the environmental technology and biomedical industries. The Team will even cross jurisdictional lines to open doors for businesses at the federal, state, and country levels. Financial incentives are available in Federal Empowerment Zones, State Enterprise Zones, and City Tax Free Zones. Businesses wishing to expand or locate in Greater Los Angeles will find assistance

through the Los Angeles County Economic Development Corporation.

Six business tax reforms were signed into law by the mayor in late 2001. These are designed to enhance the fairness of city tax laws by bringing more businesses into compliance while providing expedited and fair methods to settle tax disputes and assessments. To encourage local entrepreneurs, he has proposed exempting small start-up businesses from paying business taxes for their first two years of operation. The mayor's office also hosted a biomedical industry roundtable with more than twenty biomedical community leaders to discuss action the city can take to make Los Angeles more attractive to the industry.

Small- or medium-sized business may be eligible for technical assistance at one of the six Los Angeles Business Assistance Centers (BACs). The centers are operated by community based organizations and/or local colleges and universities and are funded by the City of Los Angeles Industrial and Commercial Development Division (ICD). Assistance is provided through a combination of in-house counselors, school faculty and private business professionals.

State programs—A variety of programs administered by state and federal sources are available to Los Angeles businesses. Those include: Manufacturers' Investment Credit, Partial Sales of Use Tax Exemption, In-Lieu Sales or Use Tax Refund, Research & Development Tax Credit, Net Operating Loss Carryover, Foreign Trade Zones, Recycling Market Development Zone, Childcare Tax Credit, Work Opportunity Tax Credit, Enterprise Zones, and others.

Job training programs—Private Industry Council (PIC) members appointed by the mayor encourage economic development through job training. The PIC works cooperatively with the Los Angeles City Council, Mayor's Office of Economic Development, Community Development Department, and California Employment Development Department to arrange for customized job hiring, recruiting, training, and retraining programs.

Development Projects

Greater Los Angeles was bustling with construction activity at the turn of the century. The Los Angeles downtown area has undergone a renaissance, with new museums, entertainment centers, sports venues, and more. Among the many projects were the Walt Disney Concert Hall, the new home of the Los Angeles Philharmonic since the 2002-2003 concert season, and the New Catholic Cathedral, a $189 million Mother Church for the Archdiocese of Los Angeles that was completed in 2002. Los Angeles Center Studios, a $105 million project described as the largest full-service independent film studio to be developed since the 1920s, began an expansion at the end of 2002 that added 900,000 square feet, including a full-service commissary, additional offices and meeting rooms, and eight additional stages.

Hollywood is being refurbished as well, with the famous Mann's Chinese Theatre having undergone a major renovation. A new shopping, dining, and entertainment center located in the heart of Hollywood is designed to mirror a 1916 classic movie set. The five-story, open-air complex, called Hollywood and Highland, includes the Renaissance Hollywood Hotel, more than 60 specialty shops, public art exhibitions, six movie screens, restaurants, nightclubs, and the Kodak Theatre.

Economic Development Information: LA's Business Team, telephone (800)472-2278; email team4biz@mayor.ci .la.ca.us. Los Angeles County Economic Development Corporation, 515 South Flower Street, 32nd Floor, Los Angeles, CA 90071; telephone (888)452-3321; fax (213)622-7100; email info@laedc.org

Commercial Shipping

International trade is a major component of the Los Angeles area economy. The Los Angeles Customs District (including the ports of Long Beach and Los Angeles, Port Hueneme, and Los Angeles International Airport) is the nation's largest, based on value of two-way trade. In 2003, this totaled $235 billion. Import and export shipping through Los Angeles International Airport (LAX) is expected to jump 140 percent by 2015. With its increasingly expanding air cargo system, LAX is set for major expansion in 2006. Several major transcontinental rail systems, used by a number of rail shipping companies, terminate in Los Angeles. The Alameda Corridor, a $2.4-billion, high-speed cargo rail system linked to the Port of Los Angeles and completed in 2002, will make it even easier to ship products across the globe. All of the major interstate truck companies maintain large facilities in the metropolitan area.

Labor Force and Employment Outlook

Los Angeles offers a diverse employment pool, with a wide range of schooling and skills. A large number of immigrants—international, national, and regional—provide a steady source of labor with strong links to important trading partners like Mexico and Asia. With Los Angeles International Airport serving as the so-called new Ellis Island for foreign immigration to this country, the metropolitan region has achieved a new ethnic and cultural diversity in its workforce.

Services, wholesale and retail trade, manufacturing, government, financial service industries, transportation, utilities, and construction contribute significantly to local employment. The County of Los Angeles is the top ranked county in manufacturing in the united States.

By the end of the 1990s biotechnology emerged as one of California's largest employers at 210,000 jobs, surpassing such traditional strongholds as aerospace and the entertainment industry. Greater Los Angeles already is home to significant biotech manufacturing. More than 2,500 companies in Southern California make pharmaceuticals and other medical products. Other major industries showing growth at the start of the twenty-first century are international trade and tourism.

The following is a summary of data regarding the Los Angeles-Long Beach metropolitan area nonagricultural labor force, 2004 annual averages.

Size of nonagricultural labor force: 3,992,100

Number of workers employed in . . .
  natural resources and mining: 3,800
  construction: 139,400
  manufacturing: 484,200
  trade, transportation, and utilities: 780,100
  information: 208,100
  financial activities: 243,200
  professional and business services: 561,000
  educational and health services: 467,600
  leisure and hospitality: 373,100
  other services: 144,800
  government: 586,500

Average hourly earnings of production workers employed in manufacturing: $18.67

Unemployment rate: 5.8% (January 2004)

Largest employers	*Number of employees*
Los Angeles County	93,354
Los Angeles Unified School District	78,085
U.S. Government	56,100
University of California	36,354
City of Los Angeles	35,895
State of California (noneducation)	32,300
Kaiser Permanente	27,635
The Boeing Company	23,468
Ralph's Grocery Co.	17,211

Cost of Living

Living costs in the metropolitan area are significantly higher than the national average.

The following is a summary of data regarding key cost of living factors for the Los Angeles area.

2004 (3rd Quarter) ACCRA Average House Price: $704,500

2004 (3rd Quarter) ACCRA Cost of Living Index: 155.8 (U.S. average = 100.0)

State income tax rate: Ranges from 1.0% to 9.3%

State sales tax rate: 6.0% (food and prescription drugs are exempt)

Local income tax rate: None

Local sales tax rate: 1.25%

Property tax rate: Varies according to location

Economic Information: Los Angeles Area Chamber of Commerce, 350 South Bixel Street, PO Box 3696, Los Angeles, CA 90051-1696; telephone (213)580-7500; fax (213)580-7511

Education and Research

Elementary and Secondary Schools

The Los Angeles Unified School District (LAUSD) is the country's second largest district, with a K–12 student enrollment of more than 746,800. Geographically, it encompasses 704 square miles, an area that includes the City of Los Angeles and all or parts of 28 other cities, as well as some unincorporated areas of Los Angeles County. Faced with unprecedented economic downswings and tremendous cuts from the State of California, LAUSD had to find ways to reduce spending in 2003 by more than 360 million dollars.

Los Angeles public schools began operating under the "90-30" system in the early 1990s. To save the costs of building new schools in a district that takes in 15,000 more students each year, students attend school for 90 days, then take 30 days off, year-round.

The following is a summary of data regarding Los Angeles public schools in Los Angeles as of the 2004–2005 school year.

Total enrollment: 904,799 (includes adult schools and childrens' centers)

Number of facilities
 elementary schools: 434
 junior high schools: 78
 senior high schools: 56
 other: 14 multilevel; 21 magnet schools; 140 centers; 20 special education; 45 continuation high schools; 7 primary centers; 11 opportunity schools; 6 opportunity high schools; 1 newcomer school; 26 community adult; 5 regional occupation centers; 4 skills centers; 110 early education centers

Student/teacher ratio: 22:1

Teacher salaries
 minimum: \$41,177
 maximum: \$72,247

Spending per pupil: \$6,719 (2001–2002)

Public Schools Information: Los Angeles Unified School District, 333 South Beaudry Avenue, Los Angeles, CA 90017

Colleges and Universities

The Los Angeles area is home to three campuses of the University of California system, seven from the California State University system, and twenty private colleges and universities. The two largest are the University of California, Los Angeles (UCLA), and the University of Southern California (USC), nationally known as major research universities. Other prominent colleges and universities in the area include the California Institute of Technology (Cal Tech), Loyola Marymount University, the Claremont colleges, Pepperdine University, and Mount St. Mary's College.

Libraries and Research Centers

The Los Angeles Public Library System operates 69 branches throughout the metropolitan area with a total of more than 6 million volumes. The main branch is the third largest public library in the country. The system also maintains holdings of maps, audio tapes, films and videos, art reproductions, mobile libraries, and special services for the visually impaired. Its special collections include California history, African American fiction, genealogy, Japanese prints, rare books, and the nation's largest collection of materials on food and drink, including several thousand menus, primarily from California restaurants.

Both UCLA and USC operate major libraries whose holdings number more than 6.2 million and 2.7 million volumes respectively. The Los Angeles County Law Library consists of 9 branches with a collection totaling more than 700,000 volumes in all areas of law and legal issues. More than 150 other specialized and private libraries serve the Los Angeles area.

Some of the most advanced research in the world is conducted at Los Angeles' three major institutions of higher learning (UCLA, USC, and the California Institute of Technology). Between 1923 and 2001, twenty Nobel prize winners came from Los Angeles institutions. Research activities are conducted in such fields as archaeology, oral history, folklore and mythology, international studies, AIDS, cystic fibrosis, schizophrenia, radiology and thalmology manufacturing automation, laser studies, marine sciences, sickle cell anemia, oncology, neonatology, astronomy, seismology, hydraulics, radiation, foreign policy, armament and disarmament, desert studies, and ocean studies. Los Angeles has become a mecca for researchers searching for ways to understand the changing character of America.

Public Library Information: Los Angeles Public Library System, 630 West Fifth Street, Los Angeles, CA 90071-2097; telephone (213)228-7000

Health Care

Los Angeles is the primary health care and treatment center for the southern California region. It is the second largest health care market in the country and is at the forefront of major changes taking place in the health care industry. In recent years, many community hospitals have closed and overcapacity threatens more closures. In the vast metro Los Angeles area, there are 822 hospitals and clinics. It has been estimated that nearly a third of the hospitals would soon close and others would consolidate so that California's health care industry will eventually be dominated by four or five huge hospital networks, but lawsuits and other problems have led the state's hospital system into uncertainty and turmoil.

With more than 600 beds, UCLA Medical Center is known worldwide as a health care innovator. Its highly experienced staff consists of more than 1,000 physicians and 3,500 nurses, therapists, technologists, and support personnel. Offering comprehensive care from the routine to the highly specialized, its physicians are some of the best in the country. Other factors contributing to the Center's top rankings include specialized intensive care units, state-of-the-art inpatient and outpatient operating suites, a Level-1 trauma center, and the latest diagnostic technology. UCLA Medical Center includes UCLA Children's Hospital; the Jules Stein Eye Institute; the Doris Stein Eye Research Center; UCLA's Jonsson Cancer Center, officially designated by the National Cancer Institute as one of the most comprehensive cancer centers in the country; and a network of health care facilities that brings UCLA-quality care to a growing number of California communities.

Recreation

Sightseeing

The immense size of Los Angeles and the innumerable activities offered by the city make its attractions seem limitless. Different sections of the city offer a wide range of sights and diversions, from the more than 40 miles of city-operated Pacific beaches in the west to the mountains in the east and the vast urban areas in between. The downtown district not only forms one of the nation's most modern skylines, but also preserves many historic buildings. Some of the original structures in the city can be found in El Pueblo de los Angeles State Historic Park. To the east is Olvera Street, a Hispanic district that recreates the atmosphere of old Mexico's open-air markets. Chinatown is just north of the downtown area, and to the south Little Tokyo is the social, cultural, religious, and economic center for southern California's more than 200,000 Japanese American residents, the largest concentration of Japanese people outside of Asia.

Hollywood and other districts devoted to the film and television industry are among the most popular attractions in Los Angeles. Universal Studios Hollywood features guided tours of some of the world's most famous imaginary places, and live tapings of television shows can be viewed at several studios. The world's first psychological thrill ride—the Revenge of the Mummy—opens there in June 2005. Nearby Beverly Hills, an independent community completely surrounded by the city, is home to many film stars, where opulent mansions enjoy proximity to some of the world's most exclusive stores and restaurants. A trip to Los Angeles is not complete without a visit to the newly refurbished Mann's Chinese Theatre and the "Walk of Fame" sidewalk featuring the handprints and footprints of movie legends.

Griffith Park, the city's largest, features the Los Angeles Zoo, with more than 2,000 animals; Griffith Observatory, which contains two refracting telescopes; and the Greek Theater, a natural outdoor amphitheater. Hancock Park contains the Rancho La Brea Tar Pits, where prehistoric fossil remains are displayed alongside life-size renditions of the species common to the area in prehistory.

Three of the nation's most popular theme parks are located in the Los Angeles area. Six Flags Magic Mountain is 25 minutes north of Hollywood in Valencia and features 260 acres of rides and family-oriented fun. Knott's Berry Farm in Buena Park offers rides, attractions, live entertainment, shops, and restaurants. World-famous Disneyland, located in Anaheim, is home to eight imaginary lands, rides, adventures, and the famous Disney characters.

The Pacific oceanfront provides a variety of attractions, including carnival-like Venice Beach and Muscle Beach, home to hundreds of bodybuilders. Marina Del Ray, known as "L.A.'s Riviera," is the world's largest man-made marina. Catalina Island features island tours and a casino.

Arts and Culture

The performing arts thrive in the city of Los Angeles. Many consider it the entertainment capital of the world, where

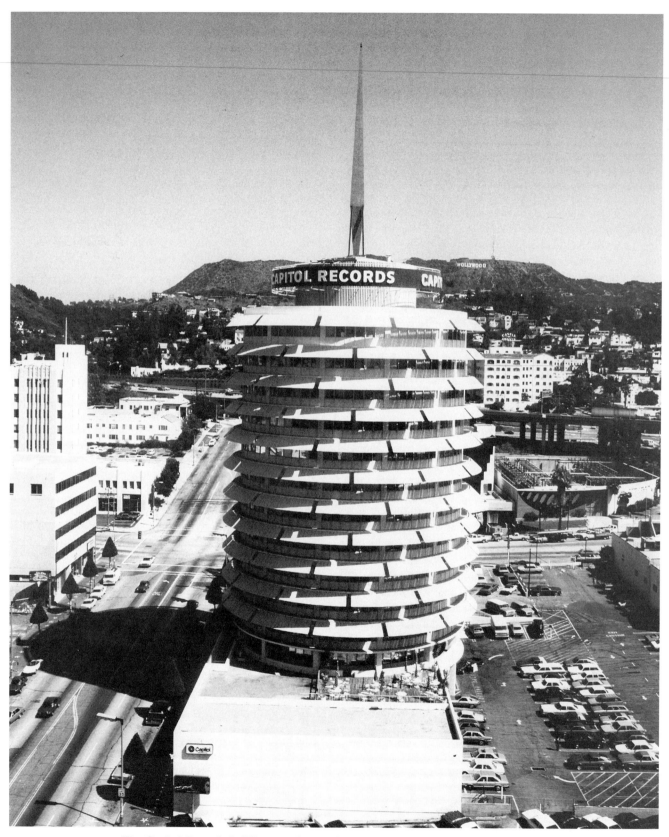

The Capitol Records building stands near Los Angeles's famous "Hollywood" sign.

major television and film projects develop daily. One of America's premier symphony orchestras, the Los Angeles Philharmonic, performs during the winter at the new Walt Disney Concert Hall; the orchestra gives summer concerts at Hollywood Bowl, an open-air amphitheater designed by Frank Lloyd Wright. The Los Angeles Opera and Master Chorale performs at the 3,197-seat Dorothy Chandler Pavillion.

Theater in Los Angeles benefits from the motion picture and television industry. Famous personalities can often be seen in area theaters, including the Henry Fonda Theatre, the Ahmanson Theatre, and the Center Theatre Group at the Mark Taper Forum. The internationally acclaimed Joffrey Ballet performs and maintains offices in Los Angeles.

The Los Angeles area is filled with museums for every taste. The Natural History Museum of Los Angeles County features displays of paleontology and history, minerals, animal habitats, and pre-Columbian culture. The Page Museum located at the Rancho La Brea Tar Pits is one of the world's most famous fossil localities, recognized for having the largest and most diverse collection of extinct Ice Age plants and animals in the world. The Hollywood Wax Museum houses more than 350 wax figures depicting famous people. The California Museum of Science and Industry, one of the most visited museums in the West, includes the Mitsubishi IMAX Theatre, the Gehry-designed Aerospace Hall, Technology Hall, the Kinsey Hall of Health, and the California Science Center. The Los Angeles Children's Museum is a hands-on museum, designed to help children learn as they experiment with a number of exhibits. The history of California comes alive at the Gene Autry Western Heritage Museum in Griffith Park, the Southwest Museum, the Hollywood History Museum, and the Wells Fargo Museum. The early Spanish colonial history of the region can be experienced by visiting one of nine mission churches located in and around the city. The Museum of Tolerance is a high-tech, hands-on experiential museum that focuses on racism and prejudice in America and the history of the Holocaust through unique interactive exhibits.

The Museum of Contemporary Art houses a large permanent collection of approximately 5,000 objects in all visual media, ranging from masterpieces of abstract expressionism and pop art to recent works by young and emerging artists. Paintings, drawings, sculpture, illuminated manuscripts, decorative arts, and European and American photographs are on display at the J. Paul Getty Museum, which is undergoing a major construction project scheduled for completion in 2006. The Los Angeles County Museum of Art features permanent installations of pre-Columbian, Far Eastern, European, and American artwork, as well as a number of traveling exhibits. Other museums in the region include the California Afro-American Museum, the Armand Ham-

mer Museum of Art at UCLA, and the many museums to be found on "Museum Row" on the city's west side.

Festivals and Holidays

Los Angeles' events calendar begins with the Tournament of Roses Parade in Pasadena on New Year's Day, an event featuring floral floats decorated by hand. Chinese New Year is celebrated each February in Chinatown with the Golden Dragon Parade and other celebrations. In March or April Olvera Street is host to a Blessing of the Animals festival on the Saturday before Easter. April features the spectacular Easter Sunrise services at the Hollywood Bowl and the annual Academy Awards event sponsored by the Academy of Motion Picture Arts and Sciences.

Cinco de Mayo, a Mexican festival in May, is celebrated in a number of places throughout the Southern California area. May also brings the Calico Spring Festival at Calico Ghost Town in Yermo and the elegant Affaire in the Gardens, a fine arts and crafts show in Beverly Hills. June features the Ojai Wine Festival in Ojai and the Playboy Jazz Festival at the Hollywood Bowl. The Fourth of July is celebrated in a variety of ways throughout the city, including fireworks on the oceanfront. July also features the Orange County Fair in Costa Mesa and the International Surf Festival on the South Bay. One of the oldest Japanese American festivals, the Nisei Week Japanese Festival occurs each August in Little Tokyo.

Los Angeles celebrates its birthday each September in the downtown Plaza, and Catalina Island hosts the Annual Art Festival, a September tradition since 1958. September also brings the L.A. County Fair in Pomona, a two-week celebration of agriculture and livestock featuring horse races and prize pies. Mexican Independence Day is also celebrated with a fiesta for three days in mid-September in El Pueblo de los Angeles State Historic Park. November features the Dia de Los Muertes, the "Day of the Dead," a traditional Mexican festival on the first of November. The holiday season begins in December with the Christmas Afloat Boat Parade and the L.A. Art Fair, offering for sale museum-quality artworks from around the world. Los Posadas, a traditional Mexican festival recreating the New Testament story of Mary and Joseph's journey to Bethlehem, takes place each year during the week before Christmas.

Sports for the Spectator

The 21,000-seat Staples Center is home to the National Basketball Association's Clippers and Lakers, and the National Hockey League's Kings. Baseball's National League Dodgers play an April- October season at a refurbished Dodger Stadium. Los Angeles is also home to the Women's National Basketball Association team, the Sparks, and Major League Soccer team, the Galaxy. The Los Angeles Angels of

Anaheim professional baseball team and the Mighty Ducks professional hockey team play in nearby Anaheim.

Collegiate sports are represented by UCLA and USC, both Division I National Collegiate Athletic Association (NCAA) institutions; they field championship caliber teams in every major sport. The annual Rose Bowl, one of the major traditional post-season college football games, is played on New Year's Day in Pasadena. Hollywood Park and Santa Anita Park are both nationally known thoroughbred racing facilities.

Sports for the Participant

The Los Angeles area offers a broad range of activities for the athletically inclined. The miles of city-operated beaches along the Pacific are popular for swimming, surfing, and all forms of boating. Winter skiing areas are less than an hour's drive away from the city. The Los Angeles Parks and Recreation Department operates several hundred parks that feature swimming pools, playing fields, golf courses, and tennis courts.

Shopping and Dining

Los Angeles is a shoppers' paradise, with more than 1,500 department stores as well as countless smaller specialty shops, a number of fashionable shopping plazas, and many large urban malls. An exclusive group of stores along Rodeo Drive is the most famous shopping district in the area, but there are a number of others, including Melrose Avenue, offering the latest and wildest trends in fashion. Westwood Village is a collection of interesting boutiques and restaurants that offers a thriving night life. The Beverly Center in West Los Angeles is one of the nation's busiest malls. Celebrity sightings there are not uncommon, and Japanese tourists come by the thousands to shop as part of planned sightseeing tours.

Ethnic specialty shops can be found in Little Tokyo, Koreatown, Chinatown, East Los Angeles, and on Olvera Street. The Farmer's Market and Shopping Village in downtown Los Angeles offers fresh produce, import shops, and elegant cafes. Westwood Village and the neighboring UCLA campus are a cultural and entertainment hub filled with shops, bistros, and architectural landmarks.

The Los Angeles area, home to some of America's finest restaurants, enjoys some 20,000 dining establishments, from fast food chains to exclusive gourmet restaurants frequented by Hollywood stars. Ethnic specialties from nearly every country in the world can be found in Los Angeles. Fresh seafood and beef, as well as produce from the nearby agricultural regions, are served in most of the city's restaurants.

Visitor Information: Los Angeles Convention & Visitors Bureau, 633 West Fifth Street, Suite 6000, Los Angeles, CA 90071; telephone (213)624-9746

Convention Facilities

The major convention and meeting facility in Los Angeles is the Los Angeles Convention Center. Situated on 63 landscaped acres, the complex is centrally located within easy access of hotels, restaurants, nightlife, shops, recreational activities, and sightseeing attractions. With 720,000 square feet of exhibition and 147,000 square feet of meeting room space, the center has become the largest convention facility on the West Coast. There are more than 14,000 hotel rooms and two major airports near the convention center.

Convention Information: Los Angeles Convention and Visitors Bureau, 633 West Fifth Street, Suite 6000, Los Angeles, CA 90071; telephone (213)624-7300; fax (213)624-9746

Transportation

Approaching the City

Los Angeles International Airport (LAX), just west of the downtown area, is the fourth largest airport in the world in terms of passengers handled, and the airport is served by dozens of major airlines with thousands of flights each year. Nearby Burbank-Glendale-Pasadena Airport is served by six major airlines. Greyhound carries passengers to a terminal in downtown Los Angeles. Amtrak has invested $100 million in new passenger trains in recent years; its *Pacific Surfliner* carries passengers from San Diego through Los Angeles to San Luis Obispo.

Three interstate highways converge in the Los Angeles area: I-5 approaching from Canada in the north, I-15 from Las Vegas to the west, and I-10 connecting Los Angeles with Arizona and the Southwest. State Highway 1, the Pacific Coastal Highway, skirts the city along the ocean.

Traveling in the City

Los Angeles is perhaps best navigated by automobile, although the city's massive, complex web of limited-access freeways, one of the most extensive in the nation, still struggles to accommodate heavy commuter traffic. The Los Angeles Department of Transportation has implemented a state-of-the-art computer system to manage the city's street traffic, but Los Angeles is still among the places with the worst traffic in the nation, according to a study by Cambridge Systematics for the American Highway Users Alliance.

The Los Angeles County Metropolitan Transit operates frequent local and express bus service throughout the city and to major area attractions. It also operates Metro Blue Line light rail service, the new Metro Red Line light rail service to Hollywood, and the Metro Red Line subway. The Metro Orange Line began with construction of a bridge across the Los Angeles River and is slated for an August 2005 completion. The $880 million Metro Gold Line, which will add 6 miles of track, is scheduled to begin running in 2009. The Mid-City/Exposition Light Rail Transit Project is the newest proposed extension of the 62 station Metro Rail System; preliminary engineering design work began in 2003. The City of Los Angeles Department of Transportation operates the DASH shuttle system; downtown DASH lines link major business, government, retail and entertainment centers within downtown. The Convention Center, the Garment and Jewelry districts, Olvera Street, the Metro Blue Line, and Union Station are easily accessible via DASH lines.

Communications

Newspapers and Magazines

Los Angeles readers are served by the morning *Los Angeles Times.* More than 100 foreign-language, special-interest, business, alternative, and neighborhood papers are published weekly in Los Angeles. *La Opinion* is the largest Spanish-language newspaper in the United States, with a daily circulation of 128,495. *Los Angeles* magazine, a monthly covering events and topics of importance to the metropolitan area, and a number of nationally distributed magazines, such as *Guns and Ammo,* and *Bon Appetit* are also published in the city.

Television and Radio

Sixteen television stations broadcast in the Los Angeles area. The 33 AM and FM radio stations broadcasting there feature a wide assortment of music, news, and information programming; stations broadcasting in surrounding communities are also received in Los Angeles.

Media Information: *Los Angeles Times,* Times Mirror Square, Los Angeles, CA 90053; telephone (213)237-5000.

Los Angeles Online

City of Los Angeles Home Page. Available www.ci.la.ca.us

La Opinion. Available www.laopinion.com

Los Angeles Area Chamber of Commerce. Available www.lachamber.org

Los Angeles Convention and Visitors Bureau. Available www.lacvb.com

Los Angeles Economic Development Corporation. Available www.laedc.org

Los Angeles Public Library. Available www.lapl.org

Los Angeles Times. Available www.latimes.com

Selected Bibliography

Allende, Isabel, *The Infinite Plan* (New York: HarperCollins, 1993)

Cameron, Robert W., *Above Los Angeles* (San Francisco: Cameron and Co., 1990)

Cole, Carolyn Kozo, and Kathy Kobayashi, *Shades of Los Angeles: Pictures from Ethnic Family Albums* (New York: Norton, 1996)

Gebhard, David, and Robert Winter, *Architecture in Los Angeles* (Gibbs M. Smith Inc., Peregrine Smith Books, Salt Lake City, UT, 1985)

Hacker, Andrew, *Two Nations: Black and White, Separate, Hostile, Unequal* (New York: Scribner, 1992)

Moore, Charles, Peter Becker, and Regula Campbell, *The City Observed: Los Angeles* (Vintage Books, 1984)

Mosley, Walter, *White Butterfly* (New York: W.W. Norton, 1992)

Monterey

The City in Brief

Founded: 1770 (incorporated, 1850)

Head Official: Mayor Dan Albert (since 1986)

City Population
  1980: 27,558
  1990: 31,954
  2000: 29,674
  2003 estimate: 29,960
  Percent change, 1990–2000: −8.9%
  U.S. rank in 1980: Not reported
  U.S. rank in 1990: Not reported
  U.S. rank in 2000: Not reported (State rank: 237th)

Metropolitan Area Population (PMSA)
  1980: 290,000
  1990: 355,660
  2000: 410,762
  2003 estimate: 415,800
  Percent change, 1990–2000: 13%
  U.S. rank in 1990: 102nd (PMSA)
  U.S. rank in 2000: 103rd (MSA)

Area: 8.44 square miles (2000)
Elevation: 10 feet above sea level
Average Annual Temperature: 57° F
Average Annual Precipitation: 19.29 inches

Major Economic Sectors: Services, trade, government
Unemployment Rate: 12.9% (December 2004)
Per Capita Income: $27,133 (1999)

2002 FBI Crime Index Total: 1,369

Major Colleges and Universities: Monterey Peninsula College, Monterey Institute of International Studies

Daily Newspaper: *The Monterey County Herald*

Introduction

Monterey, the largest city on the Monterey Peninsula, is a beautiful seaside community with a vast array of recreational and cultural activities. Bustling with fashionable restaurants, shops, and nightspots, Monterey has preserved more of its history than any other California city. Once the capital of the Spanish territory of California, Monterey has restored its historic buildings and Spanish adobes, and displays these treasures on the magnificent crescent of blue water that is Monterey Bay.

Geography and Climate

Monterey is located on the Monterey Peninsula, which is 120 miles south of San Francisco, 60 miles south of San Jose, and 345 miles north of Los Angeles. The peninsula is bordered by Monterey Bay to the north, the Pacific Ocean to the west, and Carmel Bay to the south.

Although characterized by cool, dry summers and wet winters, the regions of Monterey County exhibit considerable climatic diversity. The warmest months are July through October, and the rainiest are November and April. Summer months often can be foggy, especially early and late in the day, due to the chilly and unchanging water temperatures of the Pacific Ocean.

Area: 8.44 square miles (2000)

Elevation: 10 feet above sea level

Average Temperatures: January, 53° F; July, 60° F; annual average, 57° F

Average Annual Precipitation: 19.29 inches

History

Early Settlements

Native Americans known as the Esalen lived in the area of present-day Monterey from 500 B.C. to 500 A.D., and probably much longer. The Esalen were displaced in 500 B.C. by the Ohlone Indians, who were drawn to the area by the abundance of fish and wildlife and other natural resources. The Indians hunted quail, geese, rabbit, bear, and other wildlife, gathered plants, and caught fish, mussels, abalone, and shellfish. Several of their village sites have been identified and preserved.

Monterey was first seen by Europeans when Portuguese explorer Juan Rodriquez Cabrillo spotted La Bahia de los Pinos (Bay of Pines) in 1542 on a journey in search of riches in the New World. But high winds prevented him and his crew from landing. In 1602, Spanish explorer Don Sebastian Viscaino officially named the port in honor of Spain's Count of Monte Rey under whose order he was sailing. Viscaino's 200 men gave thanks for their safe journey in a ceremony held under a large oak tree overlooking the bay.

In 1770, an expedition by land and sea brought Gaspar de Portol and Franciscan Father Junipero Serra to Monterey. There they established the Mission and Presidio (military post) of San Carlos de Borromeo de Monterey, and the City of Monterey. Under the same oak tree where Viscaino's crew members had prayed, Father Serra said mass for his brave group. A year later, in 1771, Father Serra moved the mission to nearby Carmel, which offered a better agricultural and political environment; the Presidio Church in Monterey, however, continued in use.

Becomes Capital of Spanish California

In 1776, Spain named Monterey the capital of Baja (lower) and Alta (upper) California. This same year, Captain Juan Bautista de Anza arrived with the first settlers for Spanish California, most of them bound for San Francisco. For decades, Monterey's soldiers and their wives lived at the Presidio. In 1818, Argentinean revolutionary Hippolyte Bouchard sacked the town in an effort to destroy Spain's presence in California. Soon the residents began to expand outside the Presidio, creating homesteads throughout Monterey.

In April 1822, when Mexico gained its independence from Spain, Monterey became the Mexican capital. California soon pledged its loyalty to the Mexican government.

Spain had not allowed foreigners to trade with California, but Mexico opened up the area to international trade, and Monterey was made California's sole port of entry. Traffic with English and American vessels for the hide and tallow trade became an important part of the economy. A dried steer hide valued at about a dollar was termed a "California bank note." The hides were shipped to New England, where they were used to make saddles, harnesses, and shoes. Tallow was melted down in large rendering pots and poured into bags of hides or bladders to be delivered to the trading ships; in the end, most of the tallow was made into candles.

By 1827, foreign trade had become very important and a custom house was built in Monterey. The booming trade, especially with New England, attracted a number of Americans—called "Yanquis"—to Monterey. Many of them married into Mexican families and became Mexican citizens. In the mid-1830s, Mexican rulers redistributed much of the local land formerly run by the Catholic Church and huge cattle ranches were formed. An elite class of landed ''Californios'' grew up in the area. In 1842, the U.S. government sent Thomas Larkin to Monterey to head the first American consulate in California.

Statehood Attained

In July 1846 Commodore John Drake Sloat's flagship arrived in Monterey Bay and his troops raised the American flag, claiming the region for the United States, and gaining the territory without a fight from the Mexicans. American occupation continued until the Treaty of Guadalupe Hidalgo was signed in 1848, making all of Alta California part of the United States. This included the land now known as California, Utah, Nevada, and parts of Arizona, Colorado, New Mexico, and Wyoming.

In Monterey, U.S. Naval Chaplain Walter Colton was appointed to serve as Monterey's first American Alcalde, a position defined as mayor and judge. Colton, a well-educated and just man, was considered well qualified to hold this important position. In 1846, he and Robert Semple established California's first newspaper, *The Californian.* Colton also designed and supervised the construction of the first public structure built under the American flag, Colton Hall, which served as a public school and town meeting hall.

In 1849, delegates from throughout Alta California met in Colton Hall in Monterey to create a constitution for the people of the new U.S. territory. The new constitution was signed on October 13, 1849. In 1850, the U.S. Congress voted to adopt California as the thirty-first state of the Union. San Jose was chosen as the seat for the first legislature. (The official definition of a state capital is where the legislature sits; therefore Monterey never was the state capital.)

During the next decade Monterey lost much of its political influence. But at the same time it was becoming an important center for the whaling industry. Asian and European fishermen began arriving there, drawn by the developing fishing industry. Influences from these Japanese, Chinese, Portuguese, and Italian immigrants formed a basis for the city's culture that lives on to today.

Serves as County Seat; Sardine Trade Develops

After California gained its statehood, the legislature formed counties. Monterey served as the Monterey County seat of government until 1873, when Salinas was named to that role. Further transformation of Monterey took place in the 1870s when the first railroad was built, connecting the quiet fishing town with cosmopolitan San Francisco and cities beyond. In the 1880s, the local whaling industry disappeared and civic leaders turned to tourism to revive the local economy. By the mid-1880s, tourism flourished in the area, with thousands flocking to the seaside resort annually.

By the 1920s, the sardine market had grown greatly and the section of Monterey known as Cannery Row was established. During the next two decades, a score of canneries and reduction plants grew up in the area. Workers processed an estimated 250,000 tons of sardines each year. Monterey became known as the ''Sardine Capital of the World.'' The rough and rollicking vicinity of Cannery Row was made famous in the John Steinbeck novels *Cannery Row* and *Sweet Thursday.*

Abandoned Warehouses Revitalized; Tourism Grows

In the 1940s, for reasons still in dispute, the sardine population began a rapid decline. Theories explaining the sardines' disappearance range from water pollution to a change in currents to warmer climates or just being ''fished out.'' The once-thriving Cannery Row soon became a ghost town of empty warehouses.

In the second half of the twentieth century, tourism once again gained importance and the old abandoned warehouses were converted into shops, restaurants, and galleries. Today, tourism has become the number one industry in Monterey, growing out of the city's efforts to preserve its historic and natural resources. Monterey has gained a reputation for excellence in environmental protection and this has served to enhance its visitor industry. Visitors flock to the seaside town of Monterey to capture a glimpse of the city's past and enjoy the sounds and sights it has to offer.

Historical Information: Monterey County Historical Society, PO Box 3576, Salinas, CA 93912; telephone (831)757-8085

Population Profile

Metropolitan Area Residents
1980: 290,000
1990: 355,660
2000: 410,762
2003 estimate: 415,800
Percent change, 1990–2000: 13%
U.S. rank in 1990: 102nd (PMSA)
U.S. rank in 2000: 103rd (MSA)

City Residents
1980: 27,558
1990: 31,954
2000: 29,674
2003 estimate: 29,960
Percent change, 1990–2000: −8.9%
U.S. rank in 1980: Not reported
U.S. rank in 1990: Not reported
U.S. rank in 2000: Not reported (State rank: 237th)

Density: 3,516.9 people per square mile (2000)

Racial and ethnic characteristics (2000)
White: 23,985
Black or African American: 749
American Indian and Alaska Native: 170
Asian: 2,205
Native Hawaiian and other Pacific Islander: 86
Hispanic or Latino (may be of any race): 3,222
Other: 1,603

Percent of residents born in state: 41.6% (2000)

Age characteristics (2000)
Population under 5 years old: 1,477
Population 5 to 9 years old: 1,421
Population 10 to 14 years old: 1,263
Population 15 to 19 years old: 1,961
Population 20 to 24 years old: 2,695
Population 25 to 34 years old: 5,382
Population 35 to 44 years old: 4,638
Population 45 to 54 years old: 4,031
Population 55 to 59 years old: 1,279
Population 60 to 64 years old: 1,117
Population 65 to 74 years old: 1,974
Population 75 to 84 years old: 1,699
Population 85 years and older: 737
Median age: 36.1 years

Births (Monterey County, 2001)
Total number: 7,176

Deaths (Monterey County, 2001)
Total number: 2,470 (of which, 39 were infants under the age of 1 year)

Money income (1999)
Per capita income: $27,133
Median household income: $49,109
Total households: 12,656

Number of households with income of . . .
less than $10,000: 887
$10,000 to $14,999: 621
$15,000 to $24,999: 1,262
$25,000 to $34,999: 1,431
$35,000 to $49,999: 2,261
$50,000 to $74,999: 2,865
$75,000 to $99,999: 1,403
$100,000 to $149,999: 1,307
$150,000 to $199,999: 304
$200,000 or more: 315

Percent of families below poverty level: 4.4% (46.3% of which were female householder families with related children under 5 years)

2002 FBI Crime Index Total: 1,369

Municipal Government

Monterey operates with a council-city manager form of government. The policymaking branch of the city government, the city council, consists of five members: the mayor, elected to a two-year term, and four council members, elected to four-year terms. The city manager, appointed by the council, serves as the city's professional administrator.

Head Official: Mayor Dan Albert (since 1986; current term expires November 2006)

Total Number of City Employees: 464 (full and part-time) (2005)

City Information: Mayor's Office, City of Monterey, 340 Tyler St., Monterey, CA 93940-2487; telephone (831)646-3760

Economy

Major Industries and Commercial Activity

Once a leading fishing and whaling port, Monterey county's economic mainstays now are tourism and the military. While tourism has always been a major component in the city's economy, it has become the dominant industry in the last 30 years, supporting more than one third of Monterey jobs. Today, hotel taxes provide 29 percent of the city budget and the main source of funding for municipal services is derived from the visitor industry. The prime tourist season runs April through Thanksgiving. While the city's economy suffered greatly from the lack of travel due to the events of September 11, 2001, Monterey tourism is on the rebound. The Monterey Bay Aquarium is the prime attraction, and numerous restaurants, art galleries, gift shops, and an Antiques Mall have created a wide variety of shopping opportunities. Tourists also come to observe the special events tied to the historic Cannery Row Area, made famous by novelist John Steinbeck, local son of the nearby city of Salinas. Its reputation as a world class golfing destination brings golfers to the championship golf courses at Pebble Beach and other area courses. Independent travelers (those not with a tour group) make up the largest class of overnight visitors to the Monterey Bay Area and are primarily from elsewhere in California. It is estimated that 4 million people visit Monterey each year. The city's population increases to nearly 70,000 during tourist seasons.

Due to its strategic location, Monterey has historically been a key military outpost. Today, the city's military installations continue to provide tremendous support to the economy, particularly through its educational institutions. The Army's Defense Language Institute provides language instruction for agents of the FBI, Drug Enforcement Administration, and Border Patrol. The Naval Postgraduate School offers advance classroom training for Naval officers. The Fleet Numerical Meteorology and Oceanography Center, operated by the Navy, is one of the world's leading numerical weather prediction centers. According to the *Monterey County Herald,* these institutions contribute $1 billion to the local economy. The economic impact of spending by the School and employees of the Naval Postgraduate School alone amounts to $140.2 million channeled into the local economies of Monterey County. However, the changing needs of the military, coupled with its efforts to streamline operations, threaten the closure of many of the country's military bases and those in California are not exempt.

The government employs 18 percent of the county's workforce. Other significant sectors of Monterey's economy include trade, transportation and utilities which account for 16 percent of all employment in the county. Workers in the leisure and hospitality sector, including arts, recreation, entertainment, accommodations and food service, make up 12 percent of the workforce.

As Monterey looks to the future, the challenge will be to balance the cyclical nature of the tourist economy while finding ways to provide higher paying jobs. Monterey will increasingly see its economy based on educational and research activities. Marine biology and the environmental sciences are expected to make a very large impact on the economy of the region.

Items and goods produced: vegetables, fish and seafood, light manufactured products

Incentive Programs—New and Existing Companies

Local programs—The California Coastal Rural Development Corporation operates a variety of small business loan programs, as well as Monterey's Micro-Business Loan Program. The Central Coast Small Business Development Center (SBDC) provides no-cost, hands-on technical assistance and support to small businesses on California's Central Coast. Confidential counseling, classes, workshops, seminars, and loan programs are available through the SBDC.

State programs—With the Manufacturers' Investment Credit, companies that purchase manufacturing or R&D equipment for use anywhere in California are allowed a tax credit equal to six percent of the costs paid or incurred for acquiring the property. Other incentives include the California research and development tax credit, which allows companies to receive a credit of 8 percent for qualified research expenses (research done in-house), and 12 percent for basic research payments (payments made in cash to an outside company). The Califor-

nia Association for Local Economic Development (CALED) offers conferences, workshops, an on-site Professional Advisory Service, technical assistance and problem solving.

Job training programs—The Private Industry Council (PIC) offers specialized services designed for laid off workers who have been displaced from their jobs due to plant closures or relocation. Programs for older workers, limited English speakers, offenders, physically handicapped youth, teen parents, and other at risk youth are also available. The city of Monterey can also provide information about agencies that assist international businesses with training employees. JobLINK of Monterey County provides employment and training opportunities and services to laid off workers, long-term unemployed, displaced homemakers, and persons over 55. The California Employment Development Department offers computerized job matching and placement, job search workshops, job listings, a Job Club, information on unemployment insurance, and job training programs.

Development Projects

When a change in military needs led to the downsizing of Fort Ord in 1993, the 13,000 soldiers and family members who lived there were relocated. The city is making efforts to replace the lost revenue by redeveloping the area into an educational, residential, commercial and light industrial center. A Base Reuse Plan has been developed to guide the planning and implementation process through 2014. Plans include removing toxins from military use from the site and constructing housing at all income levels, making recreational improvements, and conserving a portion of the land for endangered species. Once the process is started, it is estimated that it will take five to seven years to complete the relocation, rehabilitation, hazard abatement, and demolition removal activities at the Fort. In 2005, the U. S. Army had finished a substantial amount of the clean-up, but more funds were needed to complete the project. The Defense Language Institute, the Naval Postgraduate School and the Coast Guard station now occupy 750 acres of the property, which has been annexed to the Presidio of Monterey. California State University at Monterey Bay and the Monterey Institute of International Studies have opened campuses there, as well as the University of California at Santa Cruz, with a new research center on the property. The remaining half of the property is being turned over to the U.S. Bureau of Land Management to manage as open spaces.

Monterey City Council approved a building permit for the construction of an IMAX theater in Cannery Row. Also on Cannery Row, plans call for a Monterey Peninsula Hotel. A new Public Service Center or City Hall project was also being considered in 2005.

Economic Development Information: California Coastal Rural Development Corp., 479 Pacific St., #5A, Monterey,

CA 93940; telephone (831)641-0722; fax (831)641-0723. Central Coast Small Business Development Center at Cabrillo College, 6500 Soquel Drive, Aptos, CA 95003; telephone (831)479-6136

Labor Force and Employment Outlook

Monterey County's civilian labor force totaled 200,000 workers in 2002. The area employs both seasonal and year-round workers since the visitor industry accounts for such a large part of the economy. Despite seasonal fluctuations, the labor force grew 2 percent over 2001 figures. According to the Monterey Peninsula Chamber of Commerce, the ratio of people in the labor force and employment roles have remained constant since 1998. One challenge to attracting new employees to the city of Monterey has been its lack of affordable housing. Since the jobs fueled by the tourist industry in Monterey tend to be lower paying jobs, affordable housing is especially needed. In recent history, between 9.4 and 10.4 percent of the population was unemployed. It reached 12.9 percent in December 2004.

The following is a summary of data regarding the Monterey area, 2003 annual averages.

Size of nonagricultural labor force: 130,000

Number of workers employed in . . .
　natural resources and mining: 200
　construction: 6,500
　manufacturing: 7,700
　trade, transportation and utilities: 25,200
　information: 2,400
　financial activities: 6,600
　professional and business services: 14,400
　educational and health services: 12,100
　leisure and hospitality: 19,400
　other services: 4,400
　government: 31,000

Average hourly earnings of production workers employed in manufacturing: $15.50

Unemployment rate: 12.9% (December 2004)

Largest employers (Salinas Valley)	*Number of employees*
Dole Fresh Vegetables	4,700
County of Monterey	4,435
Tanimura and Antle Inc.	3,000
Naval Postgraduate School	2,600
Escamilla and Sons Inc., Spreckels	2,060
Salinas Valley Memorial Healthcare System	1,900
D'Arrigo Bros. Co. of CA	1,700
Fresh Express, Fresh Food	1,650

Largest employers (Salinas Valley)	*Number of employees*
CDC Correctional Training Facility, Soledad	1,531
Household	1,526

Cost of Living

The following is a summary of data regarding several key cost of living factors for the Monterey area.

2004 (3rd Quarter) ACCRA Average House Price: $766,310 (San Jose metro)

2004 (3rd Quarter) ACCRA Cost of Living Index: 170.8 (San Jose metro) (U.S. average = 100.0)

State income tax rate: 1.0% to 9.3%

State sales tax rate: 6%

Local income tax rate: None

Local sales tax rate: 1.25% (county)

Property tax rate: 1% of assessed value

Economic Information: Monterey Peninsula Chamber of Commerce, 380 Alvarado St., Monterey, CA 93940; telephone (861)648-5360; fax (831) 649-3502; e-mail info @mpcc.com.

Education and Research

Elementary and Secondary Schools

The Monterey Peninsula Unified School District encompasses Monterey City schools as well as those of Marina, Fort Ord, Sand City, Seaside, and Del Rey Oaks. In addition to a well-rounded curriculum, the schools offer a gifted and talented program (GATE) for fourth and fifth grade students and an independent study program for motivated students who wish to study on their own.

The following is a summary of data regarding the Monterey public school system as of the 2002–2003 school year.

Total enrollment: 12,312

Number of facilities
　elementary schools: 13
　junior high/middle schools: 4
　senior high schools: 2
　other: 4

Student/teacher ratio: 20.9:1

Teacher salaries (2004-2005)
  minimum: $34,186
  maximum: $68,022

Funding per pupil: $7,994

Monterey is also home to several religious schools and to the York School associated with the Episcopal faith, Santa Catalina School (Catholic school for girls), and Possibility House, a Montessori pre-school.

Public Schools Information: Monterey Peninsula Unified School District, 700 Pacific St., Monterey CA 93940-5730; telephone (831)645-1200

Colleges and Universities

Monterey's major institution of higher learning is Monterey Peninsula College. The college offers courses to prepare students for transfer to four-year institutions, to prepare for the workplace, to update work skills or prepare for a new career, to gain a general education, and to improve basic skills in mathematics, reading, writing, and science.

The Monterey Institute of International Studies offers graduate programs in international business, a graduate school of language and educational linguistics, a graduate school of translation and interpretation, and a graduate school of international policy studies. Other Institute programs are language intensives, an intensive English as a Second Language program, and court and medical interpreting. The school also offers tailored courses for individuals requiring intensive language and cultural training for work outside their native country or with foreign nationals in the United States.

The Naval Postgraduate School is an academic institution whose emphasis is on study and research programs relevant to the U.S. Navy's interests, as well as to the interests of other arms of the Department of Defense. Its campus houses state-of-the-art laboratories, academic buildings, a library, government housing, and recreational facilities to serve its nearly 1,500 students. The student body consists of officers from the five U.S. uniformed services, officers from approximately 30 other countries, and a small number of civilian employees. The school offers master of arts degrees in national security affairs, master of science degrees in a wide variety of fields, and bachelor's and doctoral degrees in various engineering fields. Another educational institution associated with the military is the Defense Language Institute operated by the Army. Its Foreign Language Center, located on the Presidio of Monterey, is the world's largest language institute.

Golden Gate University's Monterey Bay Campus offers undergraduate and graduate degree programs in business, public administration, health care, and technology. The Orange County-based Chapman University maintains a Monterey campus which offers baccalaureate degrees in a variety of subjects. California State University's Monterey Bay campus on the grounds of Fort Ord offers 12 undergraduate programs to approximately 3,500 students.

Libraries and Research Centers

Monterey Public Library is the largest public library on the Monterey Peninsula. The library houses more than 120,000 volumes, video and audio cassettes, and CDs, subscribes to 375 magazines and newspapers, and operates one bookmobile. The California History Room contains a unique collection of books, selected magazine and newspaper articles, maps, government documents, photographs, and archival material about the city of Monterey and the Monterey Peninsula. Additional library programs and collections include the Local History Partners, which provides access to local history materials through a partnership with the Colton Hall Museum, the Monterey History and Art Association, and the Teen Zone and Youth Services collections.

Other local libraries include the Colton Hall Museum Library, the CTB McGraw-Hill Library, the Maritime Museum of Monterey Library, the Monterey Bay Aquarium Library, the Community Hospital of the Monterey Peninsula Medical Library, The Monterey County Herald Library, and the U.S. Navy Library. College libraries are housed at the Monterey Institute of International Studies, the Naval Postgraduate School, and Monterey Bay Peninsula College.

Local research institutes include the Monterey Institute of International Studies' Center for East Asian Studies, Center for Nonproliferation Studies, and Center for Russian and Eurasian Studies. The Monterey Bay Aquarium Research Institute's research program focuses on deep-sea exploration in Monterey Bay, one of the most biologically diverse bodies of water in the world. The Institute's two research vessels and remotely-operated vehicles provide access to the Monterey Canyon, an underwater canyon two miles deep. The Naval Research Laboratory is the Navy and Marine Corps' corporate research lab. The lab conducts research on the atmosphere, develops weather interpretation systems for the Department of Defense, and studies the effects of the atmosphere on Naval weapons systems.

Public Library Information: Monterey Public Library, 625 Pacific St., Monterey, CA 93940; telephone (831)646-3932; fax (831)646-5618

Health Care

Community Hospital of the Monterey Peninsula is a non-profit system serving the Monterey Peninsula and surrounding communities with 17 locations that include outpatient facilities, satellite laboratories, mental health clinics, Breast Care Center, Comprehensive Cancer Center, Family Birth Center, Sleep Disorders Center, and two hospice facilities. The 172-bed Natividad Medical Center, an acute care hospital in nearby Salinas, is owned and operated by Monterey county and is affiliated with the University of California at San Francisco School of Medicine.

Recreation

Sightseeing

Monterey's Cannery Row, popularized by the books of Nobel and Pulitzer award winner John Steinbeck, is one of America's most famous streets. Today Cannery Row features a variety of shops, restaurants, and attractions, including American Tin Cannery Premium Outlets and A Taste of Monterey Wine Tasting Room. The Blue Fin Cafe & Billiards overlooks Steinbeck Plaza and offers a panoramic view of Monterey Bay and Cannery Row. Steinbeck's Spirit of Monterey Wax Museum recreates the history of Cannery Row through life-sized characters and narration. The Edgewater Family Fun Center, across from the Cannery, has the area's largest video arcade, a snack bar, old-time photos, a magic shop, and bike and surrey rentals. Other amusements in Cannery Row include a shop which rents reproductions of old roadster convertibles, an old-fashioned portrait studio, and a ceramic painting studio.

Fisherman's Wharf and Wharf #2 stretch side-by-side into the Monterey Harbor. Fisherman's Wharf is lined with seafood restaurants, fish markets, art galleries, shops, candy stores, a theater, and fish and diving companies. Municipal Wharf #2 is a working fish pier where commercial fishing boats can be seen unloading their daily catch. On holidays, the fisherman often decorate their craft with colorful strings of lights.

Cannery Row's Monterey Bay Aquarium features marine life ranging from playful sea otters to drifting jellyfish, octopuses, giant ocean sunfish, green sea turtles, swirling yellow-fin tuna, and hundreds of other creatures. A recent addition is a white shark, the only one on exhibit in the world. Slated for a May 2005 opening is a new exhibit entitled, "Ocean's Edge: Coastal Habitats of Monterey Bay." The aquarium showcases the largest ocean sanctuary in the United States in a three-story-tall living kelp forest, the million-gallon Outer Bay exhibit, a jellyfish gallery, expanded touch pools, and dozens more recently renovated galleries and exhibits.

Monterey State Historic Park downtown marks the spot where the U.S. flag was first officially raised on July 7, 1846, heralding California's statehood. Ten buildings, including the Custom House, California's first theater, and several former 1830s residences, now museums, preserve the area's heritage.

Tours are available of Colton Hall, a local landmark from the time when Monterey was the capital of Alta California. The hall was built to serve as a public school and town meeting hall and now is a museum. California's first Constitution was drafted there 150 years ago.

Visitors to the area enjoy whale watching (best in winter) and fishing trips. Other popular tours departing from Monterey can be guided or self-guided. Wine tasting, sightseeing, and agricultural education tours are available, as well as movie tours of scenes from popular movies filmed in the area. Point Pios Lighthouse at the northernmost tip of the Monterey Peninsula is open for guided tours. The 17-mile drive along the coast through Pebble Beach affords spectacular views of rugged coastline and animals in their natural habitats.

Arts and Culture

The Monterey Museum of Art has a fine collection of early Christian, Asian, American folk, ethnic, and tribal art. It also offers photographic exhibits and rotating exhibits of major American artists. The museum is housed in two facilities, Pacific Street and La Mirada. Pacific Street, located across from Colton Hall in the historic center of Monterey, includes eight galleries as well as the Buck Education Center and Library. The Monterey Museum of Art at La Mirada is situated in one of Monterey's oldest neighborhoods and is surrounded by magnificent gardens and picturesque stone walls. It began as a two-room adobe structure and later became an elegant home where international and regional celebrities were entertained. Visitors today experience the same exquisitely furnished home and spectacular rose and rhododendron gardens. Visitors view the museum's permanent collection and changing exhibitions in four contemporary galleries, including the Dart Wing designed by renowned architect Charles Moore, that complement the original estate.

The Monterey Conference Center features impressive permanent and rotating collections. Sculptures, paintings, and tapestries from contemporary local artists adorn its walls and public spaces. Visitors are greeted by *Two Dolphins*, a nine-foot-tall sculpture composed of thousands of pieces of inlaid wood. The work, created by Big Sur artist Emile Norman, depicts two dolphins in flight as they dance across the sea. On the center's second floor, the Alvarado Gallery presents an ever-changing array of art from Peninsula artists.

Festivals and Holidays

Colorful events fill Monterey's calendar throughout the year. In January the annual migration of the gray whales is

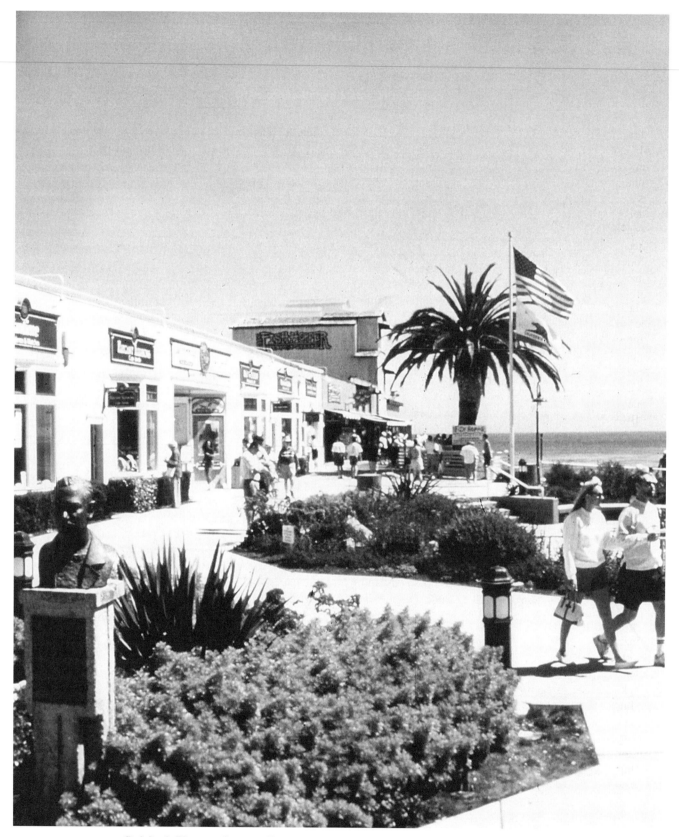

Steinbeck Plaza at Cannery Row contains many specialty shops, cafes, and galleries.

saluted through a variety of events such as art projects, story telling, whale watching, and exhibits. The sounds of Dixieland and Swing fill the March air during the three days of Dixieland Monterey, held in various venues with dance floors and special events.

The spotlight is on young, up-and-coming musicians during the three-day Next Generation Jazz Festival held annually in April. The Annual Sea Otter Classic, the largest bicycle festival in the country, features road cycling, mountain biking, downhill, and BMX events. Original hand-made arts and crafts are for sale at the Spring Arts & Crafts Fair. The Old Monterey Plein Air Painting and Art Promenade showcases artists of all ages busy at work on the streets of Monterey. The Monterey Wine Festival, held at the end of April, featuring California wines exclusively, consists of tastings, educational seminars, and cooking demonstrations.

On May 15, Cannery Row celebrates the life and times of Ed ''Doc'' Ricketts, a revolutionary marine biologist and mentor of John Steinbeck. Mountain bikers can race solo or team up to ride as many laps as possible in the 24 Hours of Adrenalin Cycle Race. ''Back to the Boatyard'' Beer Festival is a lively celebration of great beers in May. Three days of blues music on three stages is the focus of the Monterey Bay Blues Festival at the Monterey Fairgrounds in June.

July's big events include the Community Fourth of July Parade, picnic and fireworks, the commemoration of John Drake Sloat's landing in Monterey on July 8, and the Obon Festival at the Buddhist Temple. August is enlivened by the Annual Winemaster's Celebration, the Turkish Festival, the Monterey County Fair, and the Historic Automobile Races. Crowds dine and dance at September's Annual Bay ReggaeFest, Rock and Art Festival, Annual Greek Festival, Festa Italia-Santa Rosalia Festival, the Cherry's Jubilee classic car show, the Fishermen's Fiesta and the Monterey Beer Festival. The world-famous Monterey Jazz Festival offers non-stop jazz by top performers as well as food, art, and jazz clinics. Fresh seafood, music, and crafts are the focus of October's Old Monterey Seafood & Music Festival. A re-enactment of California's first Constitutional Convention takes place each October on California Constitution Day. International Day in October celebrates cultural diversity in entertainment, food and cultural demonstrations from 35 countries. A week-long focus on the history of Monterey is History Fest Monterey. The Monterey Sports Car Championships features Le Mans style racing as the main event at the Mazda Raceway Laguna Seca.

November's annual Great Wine Escape Weekend showcases the products of local vintners. Runners of all ages participate in the Big Sur Half Marathon and 5K Run, and the Cannery Row Christmas Tree Lighting welcomes the arrival of Santa Claus to the city. Christmas in the Adobes

showcases Monterey's historic buildings illuminated and decorated for the holidays. December also brings the Annual Monterey Cowboy Poetry and Music Festival. First Night Monterey draws crowds throughout the city to music, dance, and poetry events to welcome in the New Year.

Sports for the Spectator

World-class automobile racing events are held at the Laguna Seca Raceway, east of downtown Monterey. The raceway also hosts five major racing events annually including Indy car, motorcycle, and historic automobile events. The World Superbike Championships and the Honda Grand Prix are also held at the Raceway.

Sports for the Participant

The City of Monterey Sports Center is the largest family fitness facility on the Monterey Peninsula, offering a full range of fitness activities, as well as two pools and a water slide. The city has several neighborhood parks. The El Estero Park complex, a 45-acre city-wide multi-use recreation area in the center of the city, offers paddleboats, swimming, picnicking, and an exercise course. Located in the park complex are a number of recreational facilities including the Dennis The Menace Park, designed by the popular cartoon character's creator Hal Ketcham. It features a steam engine, sway bridge, a sandy hills slide, a rollerslide, sun bridge, garden maze, and a handicap play area. The Monterey Youth Center is a multi-use recreation facility for youth and adult activities. The Monterey Youth Center Dance Studio is a professional dance studio with a wooden floor, wall mirrors, ballet bars, and a public address system. Located next to Lake El Estero is the Monterey Skate Park designed for skateboarders and inline skaters. The city also boasts two ballparks.

Monterey Bay Waterfront Park/Window on the Bay offers 4.1 acres of turf and landscaped areas adjacent to the beach that feature five sand volleyball courts and picnic and grill facilities. The Monterey Tennis Club has six lighted tennis courts and a pro shop.

Private sea kayak outfitters help visitors discover Monterey by sea, by paddling through the kelp forest along Cannery Row and observing sea otters and the abundant marine life. Diving, skydiving, and sailing are all available to sports enthusiasts on Monterey Bay.

Shopping and Dining

Del Monte Center, Monterey's traditional regional shopping center, anchored by Macy's and Mervyn's, has approximately 90 businesses offering a wide variety of goods and services. Recent additions to the center include California Pizza Kitchen, Ann Taylor Loft, and a Century 13 Theatre. Monterey has a busy downtown shopping area. The Old Monterey

Market Place is one of the largest in the United States, attracting thousands of tourists and residents downtown every Tuesday afternoon. New Monterey, an emerging commercial area with an eclectic mix of new businesses, includes Lighthouse Avenue, and is located three blocks up the hill from Cannery Row. The former sardine canning factories of Cannery Row have become the center of more than 50 factory outlets. North Fremont, adjacent to the Monterey Fairgrounds, is a high traffic area and serves the many tourists who attend activities at the Monterey Fairgrounds.

Monterey's extensive marine life, along with the native American, Spanish, Mediterranean Rim, and Asian heritages of its citizens from various eras has influenced the local cuisine. Restaurant choices run the gamut from American Regional to Asian, British, California, Continental, French, Indian, Island Grill, Italian, Mexican, Swiss, and seafood cuisines. Monterey restaurant chefs are inspired by the abundance of robustly flavored signature area crops such as lettuce, artichokes, garlic, strawberries, and a variety of mushrooms.

Visitor Information: Monterey County Convention & Visitors Bureau, 150 Olivier St., PO Box 1770, Monterey, CA 93942; telephone (831)649-1770; toll-free (888)221-1010.

Convention Facilities

Convention activity in Monterey is heaviest from early April through Thanksgiving. The Monterey Conference Center, with 58,000 square feet of meeting space, a 19,600-square-foot exhibit hall, a 1200-seat ballroom, and a 494-seat theater, hosts more than 220 events annually.

The Monterey Meeting Connection, located in the heart of the city's historic district and adjoining Fisherman's Wharf, is an alliance of the Monterey Conference Center and its adjoining hotels—the Portola Plaza, the Monterey Marriott, and the Hotel Pacific. The Connection features 800 guest rooms and suites, an amphitheater, and 61,000 square feet of flexible function space. Other hotels that offer a variety of spaces for meetings are the Hyatt Regency Monterey, Hilton Monterey, Monterey Plaza Hotel and Spa, Casa Munras Garden Hotel, and the Monterey Beach Resort. A variety of other facilities also feature spaces for large functions including Adventures by the Sea, Alexander Julien Wine Estate, Culinary Center of Monterey, and the Monterey Bay Aquarium.

Convention Information: Monterey Conference Center, One Portola Plaza, Monterey, CA 93940; telephone (831)646-3370; fax (831)646-3777. Monterey County Convention & Visitors Bureau, 150 Olivier St., PO Box 1770, Monterey, CA 93942-1770; telephone (831)649-1770; toll-

free (888)221-1010. Monterey Convention Authority, 380 Alvarado St., Suite 201, Monterey, CA 93940; telephone (831)646-3388; toll-free (888)742-8091

Transportation

Approaching the City

Direct access to Monterey is provided from San Jose and San Francisco via Highway 156 off State Route 101. Access from Los Angeles is achieved via State Route 101 and Highway 68. Monterey Peninsula Airport, 3.5 miles from downtown Monterey, provides passenger service from Monterey with non-stop flights to Los Angeles, San Francisco and Phoenix, with connections to 200 domestic and foreign locations. Airlines serving Monterey include American/American Eagle, United/United Express, and America West/America Express. Five major car rental companies operate from the airport. Monterey Salinas Transit buses (Route 21) also service the airport.

The Monterey-Salinas Airbus provides 11 trips daily to the San Jose and San Francisco international airports from downtown Monterey. Pick up service is available from hotels and private homes. Greyhound Lines offers regular bus service to northern and southern California.

Traveling in the City

Five taxi companies operate in Monterey County. The Monterey-Salinas Transit (MST) operates 84 buses on 32 routes, and covers the Monterey Peninsula and Salinas Valley. MST provides rural transit service to Carmel Valley and seasonal service to Big Sur. Its Waterfront Area Visitors Express (WAVE) Shuttle Service provides low-cost transportation to the Monterey Bay Aquarium and other waterfront areas.

Communications

Newspapers and Magazines

Monterey's local daily newspaper is *The Monterey County Herald. Monterey County Weekly* covers news, art and entertainment. Journals published in the city include *Mortuary Management* and *Your World of Birds.* Also published locally is *Spudman Magazine,* which is devoted to potato growing.

Television and Radio

Monterey is home to one commercial television station, one cable service provider, and three FM stations.

Media Information: The Monterey County Herald, 8 Upper Ragsdale Drive, Monterey CA 93940-5730; telephone (831)372-3311

Monterey Online

California Coastal Rural Development Corporation. Available www.calcoastal.org

City of Monterey home page. Available www.monterey.org

Community Hospital of the Monterey Peninsula. Available www.chomp.org

Monterey Conference Center. Available www.monterey .org/mcc

Monterey Convention Authority. Available www.monterey conventionauthority.com

Monterey Convention & Visitors Bureau. Available www .monterey.com

The Monterey County Herald. Available www.monterey herald.com

Monterey County Historical Society. Available users.dedot .com/mchs

Monterey Jazz Festival. Available www.montereyjazz festival.org

Monterey Peninsula Chamber of Commerce. Available www.mpcc.com

Monterey Peninsula Unified School District. Available www.mpusd.k12.ca.us

Monterey Public Library. Available www.monterey.org/ library

Selected Bibliography

Benson, Jackson J., *True Adventures of John Steinbeck, Writer: A Biography* (New York: Penguin Books, 1990)

Fink, Augusta, *Monterey: The Presence of the Past* (San Francisco: Chronicle Books, 1972)

Fisher, Anne B., *No More a Stranger* (Stanford, CA: Stanford University Press, 1946)

Ford, Tirey Lafayette, *Dawn and the Dons: The Romance of Monterey, with Vignettes and Sketches by Jo Mora* (San Francisco: A.M. Robertson, 1926)

Hobbs, Fredric, *The Spirit of the Monterey Coast* (Palo Alto, CA: Tioga Pub., 1995)

Jeffers, Robinson, *Selected Poems* (New York: Vintage, 1965)

Reinstedt, Randall A., *Ghosts, Bandits, and Legends of Old Monterey* (Carmel, CA: Ghost Town Publications, 1974)

Steinbeck, John, *Cannery Row* (New York: Viking, 1945)

Steinbeck, John, *Tortilla Flat* (New York: Grosset and Dunlap, 1935)

Oakland

The City in Brief

Founded: 1820 (incorporated, 1854)

Head Official: Mayor Jerry Brown (since 1998)

City Population
1980: 339,337
1990: 372,242
2000: 399,484
2003 estimate: 398,844
Percent change, 1990–2000: 7.3%
U.S. rank in 1980: 43rd
U.S. rank in 1990: 39th
U.S. rank in 2000: 50th (State rank: 8th)

Metropolitan Area Population (PMSA)
1980: 1,762,000
1990: 2,108,078
2000: 2,392,557
Percent change, 1990–2000: 12.6%
U.S. rank in 1980: 5th (CMSA)
U.S. rank in 1990: 4th (CMSA)
U.S. rank in 2000: 5th (CMSA)

Area: 56 square miles (2000)
Elevation: 42 feet above sea level
Average Annual Temperature: 56.7° F
Average Annual Precipitation: 23 inches

Major Economic Sectors: Trade, services, government
Unemployment Rate: 8.44% (September 2004)
Per Capita Income: $21,936 (1999)

2002 FBI Crime Index Total: 29,875

Major Colleges and Universities: Holy Names College, Mills College, Patten College, Merritt College, California College of Arts & Crafts

Daily Newspaper: *Oakland Tribune*

Introduction

The city of Oakland is known as the heart of the East Bay section of the San Francisco Bay Area. It is a heavily populated and industrialized belt that is home to about half the residents of the San Francisco-Oakland urban area. An important seaport, Oakland is a major business and manufacturing center. Oakland's waterfront is lined with docks as befits this historical transportation and distribution hub. Oakland was among the first ports globally to specialize in the intermodal container operations whose advantages have revolutionized international trade. With its strategic Pacific Rim location, about 75 percent of Oakland's foreign trade is with Asia. Oakland has an ethnically and culturally diverse population, with a majority of African American citizens.

Geography and Climate

Oakland lies at the center of the Pacific Coast between Canada and Mexico. It is located on the east side of the San Francisco Bay, and is connected to the city of San Francisco by the San Francisco-Oakland Bay Bridge. Oakland boasts 19 miles of coastline to the west and magnificent rolling hills to the east. The flat plain of San Francisco Bay comprises about two-thirds of the city and the remainder of the city's terrain lies in the foothills and hills of the East Bay range. Residents and area visitors can take advantage of one of the most beautiful views in the world – the San Francisco Bay, the Golden Gate and Oakland Bay Bridges, and the sparkling Pacific Ocean. Cities adjacent to Oakland include Berkeley to the north; San Leandro to the south; Alameda across the estuary; Piedmont, a small city completely surrounded by Oakland; and Emeryville, a city that lies on the bay between Oakland and Berkeley. Oakland is the only city in the United States with a natural saltwater lake, 115-acre Lake Merritt, wholly contained within its border.

Oakland has earned the nickname "bright side of the Bay" because of its sunny skies and moderate year-round climate. Humidity remains high while precipitation is low. Almost all the city's rainfall occurs between October and January. The temperature usually reads about five degrees warmer than San Francisco, and the warmest months are September and October. The area's climate has been ranked number one in the country by *Places Rated Almanac*.

Area: 56 square miles (2000)

Elevation: 42 feet above sea level

Average Temperatures: January, 49.9° F; July, 62.1° F; annual average, 56.7° F

Average Annual Precipitation: 23 inches

History

Spaniards Settle Area, Followed by Hunters, Loggers

The first inhabitants of present-day Oakland were the Costanoans, peaceful tribes known for their basket making and the success of their hunting and gathering way of life.

In 1772 an expedition came from Spain, led by Lieutenant Pedro Fages and Father Crespi, who camped along Lake Merritt. In 1820 Don Luis Maria Peralta received a large land grant, which included the area that is now Oakland, from the Spanish crown in recognition of his soldiering career. Don Luis never lived on his ranch, but divided the land among four of his sons who settled and operated ranches in the area. At that time, the territory was governed by the Republic of Mexico, which had become independent of Spain in 1821.

In the 1840s hunters and loggers came to the area, followed by adventurers traveling to the gold fields. Some stayed and built squatter shacks on the Peralta land, creating several small settlements which later became part of Oakland.

In 1848, the Treaty of Guadalupe-Hidalgo officially ceded California to the U.S., and two years later California became the thirty-first state in the Union. Regulation of land deeds became the responsibility of the new state government. The Peraltas presented their claim to the Federal Land Commission in 1852.

Railroad Spurs Growth

In 1850 Edson Adams, Horace Carpentier, and Andrew Moon had settled on land near the present foot of Broadway. They planned a town, sold lots, and secretly rushed "An Act to Incorporate the Town of Oakland" to the State Legislature. The city, which was named for the groves of lovely oaks that grew along the hills, was granted a charter on May 4, 1852, about the same time that ferry service to San Francisco was initiated. It became an incorporated city with an elected mayor and council two years later. During this period the Peralta land case continued through the American legal system. By the time the land claim was finally confirmed in 1877, the Peraltas had sold most of their property to pay legal fees and taxes.

The completion of the Southern Pacific railroad line in 1869 transformed Oakland, which had been chosen as the terminus of the transcontinental railroad, into an important part of the Metropolitan Bay Area, second only to San Francisco. For the next several decades the railroad controlled the city's political and economic life. The railroad also stimulated economic development and the creation of an electric street car system which spurred rapid population and territorial growth.

Originally, the area of the city was quite small, but annexations in 1872, 1891, 1897, and finally in 1910 brought the city to its present size. Along with the 1906 earthquake in San Francisco, which resulted in a sizable number of new residents in-migrating, Oakland experienced a rapid rise in population that reached over 150,000 people by 1910 and continued its growth through World War II. By the 1920s Oakland had become the core city of the East Bay, the Alameda County seat, and a rival to San Francisco for leadership in the Bay Area as a whole.

Oakland experienced great losses from the 1989 Loma Preita earthquake, which caused the upper deck of the Nimitz freeway in West Oakland to collapse, killing 41 people. The earthquake also caused part of the San Francisco Bay Bridge to fall down on the Oakland side, and a number of buildings in the business district and residential areas suffered severe damage. In 1991 Oakland was struck by a firestorm, which burned more than 3,000 homes to the ground, killed 25 people, and accrued $1.5 billion in damage. The fire remains one of the most damaging firestorms in the history of the state.

By the end of the 1980s, Oakland was the sixth largest city in the state with a highly diverse and integrated population of more than 350,000 residents. Population growth continued into the 1990s, when Oakland began to experience an increasing vitality. In 1998 former California Governor and presidential candidate Jerry Brown was overwhelmingly elected mayor of Oakland. Brown has brought sweeping change to the city, ranging from fixing potholes to increasing the size of the police force to forcing the resignations of entrenched managers and department heads, and encouraging business development in the city. In March 2004, Oakland voters approved a measure which affirmed the ''strong mayor'' system by altering the city charter to give the mayor chief executive power rather than the city manager as had been the case.

As the city entered the new millennium, it was faced with mounting challenges of crime, and school and housing problems. In 2003 the state of California took over control of the financially strapped Oakland Unified School District and appointed a State Administrator to oversee the district's operations. While property values soared in Oakland and surrounding areas in the early part of the new millennium, the challenge became lack of affordable housing necessary

to attract new residents to the city. Mayor Jerry Brown's 10K Downtown Housing Initiative was developed to attract 10,000 new residents to downtown Oakland by encouraging the development of subsidized housing units. By 2005 more than 5,100 units towards the goal of 6,000 had been built.

Historical Information: Oakland History Room, Oakland Public Library, 125 14th Street, Oakland, CA 94612; telephone (510)238-3222

Population Profile

Metropolitan Area Residents (PMSA)
1980: 1,762,000
1990: 2,108,078
2000: 2,392,557
Percent change, 1990–2000: 12.6%
U.S. rank in 1980: 5th (CMSA)
U.S. rank in 1990: 4th (CMSA)
U.S. rank in 2000: 5th (CMSA)

City Residents
1980: 339,337
1990: 372,242
2000: 399,484
2003 estimate: 382,369
Percent change, 1990–2000: 7.3%
U.S. rank in 1980: 43rd
U.S. rank in 1990: 39th
U.S. rank in 2000: 50th (State rank: 8th)

Density: 7,126.6 people per square mile (2000)

Racial and ethnic characteristics (2000)
   White: 125,013
   Black or African American: 142,460
   American Indian and Alaska Native: 2,655
   Asian: 60,851
   Native Hawaiian and other Pacific Islander: 2,002
   Hispanic or Latino (may be of any race): 87,467
   Other: 46,592

Percent of residents born in state: 47.1% (2000)

Age characteristics (2000)
   Population under 5 years old: 28,292
   Population 5 to 9 years old: 30,134
   Population 10 to 14 years old: 26,502
   Population 15 to 19 years old: 24,664
   Population 20 to 24 years old: 28,958
   Population 25 to 34 years old: 72,315
   Population 35 to 44 years old: 63,310
   Population 45 to 54 years old: 53,865

Population 55 to 59 years old: 17,188
Population 60 to 64 years old: 12,468
Population 65 to 74 years old: 20,662
Population 75 to 84 years old: 15,145
Population 85 years and older: 5,981
Median age: 33.3 years

Births (2002, Alameda County)
Total number: 21,802

Deaths (2002, Alameda County)
Total number: 9,564 (of which, 91 were infants under the age of 1 year)

Money income (1999)
Per capita income: $21,936
Median household income: $41,055
Total households: 150,971

Number of households with income of . . .
less than $10,000: 19,896
$10,000 to $14,999: 9,891
$15,000 to $24,999: 18,541
$25,000 to $34,999: 18,380
$35,000 to $49,999: 23,009
$50,000 to $74,999: 25,333
$75,000 to $99,999: 14,056
$100,000 to $149,999: 12,955
$150,000 to $199,999: 4,437
$200,000 or more: 4,473

Percent of families below poverty level: 16.2% (43.1% of which were female householder families with related children under 5 years)

2002 FBI Crime Index Total: 29,875

Municipal Government

Oakland has a strong-mayor form of government, with the mayor and eight council members elected to four-year terms. The mayor appoints a city administrator to carry out its policies. In 2004, voters approved Measure P which altered the city charter permanently by changing the city manager position to a "city administrator" who reports to the mayor.

Head Official: Mayor Jerry Brown (since 1998; current term expires 2006)

Total Number of City Employees: 5,044 (2002)

City Information: City of Oakland, One Frank H. Ogawa Plaza, Oakland, CA 94612; telephone (510)444-CITY

Economy

Major Industries and Commercial Activity

Oakland's leading industries are business and health care services, transportation, food processing, light manufacturing, government, arts, culture, and entertainment. The Port of Oakland is one of the busiest ports in the world for container ships. Nearly 200,000 jobs are related to the movement of cargo through Oakland marine terminals. Chief exports at the port include fruits and vegetables, waste paper, red meat and poultry, resins, chemicals, animal feed, raw cotton, wood and lumber, crude fertilizers/minerals, industrial machinery, and cereal. Oakland's principal imports include auto parts, computer equipment, wearing apparel, toys, games and items made of plastic, processed fruits and vegetables, fasteners and household metal products, red meat, pottery, glassware and ceramics, iron and steel, beverages, and lumber products.

Oakland is an important commercial center. Approximately 13 percent of Oakland's work force is employed in the wholesale and retail trade. The city has hundreds of manufacturing plants employing almost 9 percent of the city's workers. Shipbuilding has flourished along the city's inner harbor. Other major industries include electrical equipment, chemicals, glass, automobiles and trucks, and pharmaceuticals. Oakland's leading industry sectors include business services, health care services, transportation, food processing, light manufacturing, government, arts, culture and entertainment.

Oakland's business community faced some major problems in the 1980s and 1990s. The Loma Prieta Earthquake in 1989 not only caused physical damage but caused many companies to consider relocation. Although Alameda County had economic growth in the 1980s, Oakland did not participate in that growth and the economy actually declined. Major plant closures in the late 1980s and 1990s included Gerber Products, General Electric, National Lead, American Can, and Oakland's largest manufacturing facility, Transamerican Delaval, which had employed 1,600 workers. The ripple effect of these closures led to the closing of many small businesses that had been suppliers to these firms. The city received a designated Urban Enterprise Zone to help alleviate the employment situation, particularly for inner city residents. By the late 1990s Oakland's economy was showing some vitality. In 2002, Oakland was ranked the 8th best city in the nation for business in the *Forbes* annual survey of the Best Places in America for Business and Careers. In the mid-2000s, Oakland benefited from a strong and diverse business environment. Among its major corporations were Clorox, Kaiser Permanente, Cost Plus, Dreyer's Grand Ice Cream, APL Limited, and Rainin Instruments. According to the Landauer Realty Group, out of the 60 largest office markets in the United States, Oakland was expected to have the strongest market for the next several years.

Items and goods produced: processed foods, transportation equipment, fabricated metal products, non-electrical machinery, electrical equipment, clay and glass products

Incentive Programs—New and Existing Companies

Local programs—The city of Oakland's Business Development Office assists businesses in getting established, finding suitable locations, and in expansion and growth. Oakland's Development Action Team works directly under the mayor and city manager to streamline all economic development, redevelopment, planning, zoning, building services, and housing development processes in support of key development projects. Incentives range from an industry-specific business tax abatement program to assistance with locating space and identifying its workforce. Oakland takes full advantage of existing state and federal programs to provide a full set of incentives and has a municipal lending unit to assist businesses looking for capital, technical assistance, and training. Oakland has been designated as an Enhanced Enterprise Community (EEC), a designation that allows businesses that hire from the EEC zone to be eligible for federal tax incentives including the Work Opportunity Tax Credit and the Welfare to Work Tax Credit. The Industrial Development Bond Program, Manufacturers's Investment Credit, and the Retail and Entertainment Catalyst Tenant Improvement Program (TIP) are among other financial incentives for bringing businesses to the city. Incentives are also provided for environmentally-friendly businesses through a Sustainable Development Initiative. Financial assistance programs for improving neighborhood commercial districts include the Business Improvement District Assistance program and the Commercial Property Façade Improvement Program. The Oakland Business Development Corporation provides loans to small businesses who may not qualify for traditional bank financing. Brownfields programs including the Cal ReUSE Environmental Site Assessment Loan Program, Oakland Brownfields Revolving Loan Fund, and the Urban Land Redevelopment (ULR) Program provide incentives for reutilizing brownfields which are underutilized sites where reuse is complicated by the threat of environmental contamination.

State programs—The Oakland Urban Enterprise Zone and Oakland Foreign Trade Zone offer state and federal tax incentives. The state of California's Recycling Market Development Zone (RMDZ) Program helps create the markets necessary to use recycled materials and helps companies retool to produce goods from the discarded materials. The Oakland/Berkeley RMDZ is one of twelve located in California. The zone encourages the retention, expansion, and attraction of recycling businesses by offering a recycling equipment state tax credit of up to $250,000; low-interest loans of up to $1 million; engineering and technical assistance; and marketing assistance for the goods produced.

Job training programs—The city of Oakland serves as the liaison between new and existing companies and all of the educational and training organizations in the East Bay, including Peralta Community College District Partnership, Oakland Higher Education Center, Eastbay Works One-Stop Career Center, Department of Adult Education, Alameda County Workforce and Resource Development, and the Private Industry Council. The Oakland Workforce Investment Board offers a multitude of assistance and training opportunities to assist small businesses in recruiting a qualified workforce.

Development Projects

In 2005, more than 60 major development projects were underway in the city of Oakland. More than $50 million has been invested to turn the Old Oakland historic district into a sophisticated turn-of-the-century retail and commercial area, while preserving each building's ornate Victorian facade. Jack London Square, a popular waterfront retail and entertainment district, was completed in 2002 and features 10 restaurants and cafes and 12 specialty retail shops. The Wood Street Development Project is a redevelopment of the former Central Station, warehouses, and signal tower into 1,570 housing units, retail shops, and non-retail commercial space. The ''Oak to Ninth'' project is a 10-year redevelopment of 62 acres of waterfront property owned by the Port of Oakland. Plans call for the construction of 3,100 residences, commercial space, structured parking, approximately 27 acres of public open space, 2 renovated marinas, and a wetlands restoration area.

The Port of Oakland's $500-$600 million Vision 2000 program will expand and improve marine terminals and develop transportation infrastructures. Two new maritime terminals will be developed, as well as a new intermodal rail facility. The Port of Oakland and the U.S. Army Corps of Engineers are working together on a harbor deepening project to accommodate the new generation of container vessels arriving in Oakland. Other slated projects include widening and deepening the harbor entrance, the outer and inner harbor channels, and two turning basins to 50 feet, as well as relocating utility lines. The Port is also deepening its berths and strengthening its wharves as part of the project. All dredged material is being reused to restore Bay Area wetlands.

Economic Development Information: City of Oakland Business Development Office, telephone (510)238-3627; toll-free (877)2OAKLAND. Oakland Metropolitan Chamber of Commerce, 475 14th Street, Oakland, CA 94612-1903; telephone (510)874-4800; fax (510)839-8817

Commercial Shipping

The Port of Oakland is the 4th largest container port in the United States and 20th in the world. The Port of Oakland occupies 19 miles on the mainland shore of San Francisco Bay, one of the finest natural harbors in the world. There are 10 container facilities, 20 deepwater berths, and 35 container cranes. On-dock storage space exceeds 600,000 square feet. Major expansion of the port was under way in 2005 to expand the port's capabilities. The port's facilities are backed by a network of local roads and interstate freeways, warehouses, and intermodal railyards. Oakland offers direct, competitive rail service to the Midwest and Atlantic and Gulf coasts for Overland Common Point, micro-bridge, and mini-landbridge service via the two railroads that serve the port. All major carriers serve the port and many maintain terminals in the harbor area.

Air freight through Oakland International Airport totals more than 1.4 billion pounds, and more than 76 million pounds of air mail pass through the airport each year.

Port Information: Port of Oakland, 530 Water St., Oakland, CA 94607, telephone (510)627-1100.

Labor Force and Employment Outlook

The Oakland labor force is described as skilled, educated, and available to employers who need managerial/executive, professional, sales, technical, and clerical staff. Nearly one-third of area residents have a college degree, and about 100,000 students attend local institutions of higher learning. Although the Oakland area benefits from a diverse economic base, it suffered a loss of 50,000 jobs from 2001 to 2004, according to the Economic Development Alliance for Business. However, a rebounding economy in 2005 was expected to add 12,500 jobs in the East Area, with further gains in 2006. Employment growth rates through 2015 will be highest in the area of manufacturing.

The following is a summary of data regarding the Oakland metropolitan area labor force, 2003 annual averages.

Size of non-agricultural labor force: 1,024,700

Number of workers employed in . . .
  natural resources and mining: 800
  construction: 67,200
  manufacturing: 97,400
  trade, transportation and utilities: 198,000
  information: 32,300
  financial activities: 67,900
  professional and business services: 143,400
  educational and health services: 117,400
  leisure and hospitality: 80,600
  other services: 37,700
  government: 182,100

Average hourly earnings of production workers employed in manufacturing: $18.33

Unemployment rate: 4.3% (December 2004)

| *Largest private employers* | |
(East Bay)	*Number of employees*
Kaiser Foundation Health Plan Inc.	22,500
SBC Communications Inc. (Pacific Bell)	10,132
Alameda County	9,638
University of California at Berkeley	9,168
Contra Costa County	8,467
U.S. Postal Service, Oakland District	8,283
Lawrence Livermore National Lab	7,837
Safeway Inc.	7,680
State of California	7,600

Cost of Living

The following is a summary of data regarding key cost of living factors for the Oakland area.

2004 (3rd Quarter) ACCRA Average House Price: $647,278

2004 (3rd Quarter) ACCRA Cost of Living Index: 152.3 (U.S. average = 100.0)

State income tax rate: Ranges from 1.0% to 9.3%

State sales tax rate: 6%

Local income tax rate: None

Local sales tax rate: 1.25%

Property tax rate: ranges from 1.22% to 1.3773% of assessed values (2005)

Economic Information: Oakland Chamber of Commerce, 475 Fourteenth Street, Oakland, CA 94612-1903; telephone (510)874-4800

Education and Research

Elementary and Secondary Schools

The Oakland Unified School District (OUSD) is the eleventh largest school district in the state. The district has a rich ethnic diversity with a little more than one-half African American students and the rest a mixture of Hispanic, white, combined Asian, and other students, including Native Americans. It has recently suffered a decline in student enrollment due to a changing job market and migration to nearby communities with lower housing costs. In 2003 the district's financial crisis led to a takeover by the State of California and the appointment of a State Administrator. OUSD has made gains in academic achievement and even surpassed the state's averages for the 2003-2004 school year. However, the district continues to face substantial academic and financial challenges. Oakland Unified is the only district in the state to allocate funds directly to each school based on enrollment and student demographics. Recently, Oakland's 20 charter schools have made significant improvements in student achievement, with nearly five times the growth of Oakland's district schools from 2003 to 2004. The district's graduation rate for 2003-2004 was 85.7 percent.

The following is a summary of data regarding Oakland's public schools as of the 2003–2004 school year.

Total enrollment: 52,501

Number of facilities
   elementary schools: 60
   junior high/middle schools: 20
   senior high schools: 12
   other: 20 charter schools

Student/teacher ratio: 18.2:1

Teacher salaries
   minimum: $37,090
   maximum: $66,680

Funding per pupil: $8,410 (2001-2002)

Oakland has about 53 private schools.

Public Schools Information: Oakland Unified School District, 1025 Second Avenue, Oakland, CA 94606; telephone (510)879-8200

Colleges and Universities

Mills College is a private liberal arts school with an enrollment of more than 1,100 students that serves female undergraduates but admits men to its graduate school. The college grants bachelor's and master's degrees, and offers courses leading to California teaching credentials. Two of the four Peralta Community College District campuses are located in Oakland; they are Merritt College, a publicly supported coeducational junior college with an enrollment of nearly 6,000 students and Laney College, which offers associate's degrees in arts and science, pre-apprenticeship programs, and job retraining to its more than 11,000 students. The school offers liberal arts, technical-vocational, and general education programs in both day and evening schools. Holy Names College is a Catholic, liberal arts college that enrolls more than 900 students, primarily women. The college provides both bachelor's and master's programs. More than 700 students are enrolled at Patten University, a private co-educational school affiliated with the Christian Evangelical Churches of America, Inc. Patten awards associate and bachelor degrees. California College of the Arts is a four-year independent college of art and design. Its Oakland campus houses undergraduate art students. Naropa University of Boulder, Colorado, maintains a branch campus in Oakland; it offers an accredited Master of Liberal Arts in Creation Spirituality.

Libraries and Research Centers

The Oakland Public Library contains more than 1.3 million items and serves more than 430,000 area residents. The library has 15 branches, 1 bookmobile, a Second Start Literacy Program, Teen Homework Assistance Program and PASS! Homework Assistance Program. Bilingual collections include Spanish, Chinese, Japanese, Korean, Tagalog, Cambodian, Thai, Laotian, and Vietnamese collections. Special collections cover African American history, business, gay/lesbian issues, Oakland history, and religion; a unique feature is a tool lending library. The main library is also a government documents repository.

Oakland has two research centers associated with the University of California: the California Agricultural Experiment Station and the Tobacco-Related Disease Research Program. Another major research center in the city is the Children's Hospital Oakland Research Institute. It is one of the top ten federally funded pediatric research facilities in the nation. Other research institutes in the city encompass the areas of art, third world development, child care, health, community economics, earthquakes, mental health, labor, Hispanic education, and disabilities.

Public Library Information: Oakland Public Library, 125 Fourteenth Street, Oakland, CA 94612; telephone (510)238-3134

Health Care

Oakland's largest private, not-for-profit medical center is the Alta Bates Summit Medical Center with three campuses and two acute care hospitals in the Oakland region. The Medical Center was formed from the January 2000 merger of Summit Medical Center, Alta Bates Medical Center, and Sutter Health. Its Summit campus specializes in cardiovascular care, orthopedics, women and infants, wellness and prevention, and seniors. The Alta Bates campus, based in Berkeley, is recognized for its care of women and infants, In Vitro Fertilization Program, and its high risk obstetrics program. Alta Bates includes the Herrick Campus, once known as Herrick Hospital and Health Center. The 205-bed Children's Hospital Oakland has the region's only pediatric trauma center, largest pediatric intensive care unit, and one of largest sickle cell treatment and research centers in the world.

Recreation

Sightseeing

Historic buildings in Oakland include the Camron-Stanford House, a beautifully restored Victorian house on Lake Merritt. The Pardee Home Museum is an historical treasure in the heart of the Preservation Park Historical District. Dunsmuir House and Gardens features 40 acres of hills and gardens that are the site of public events. The Greek Orthodox Church of the Ascension is a modern Byzantine architectural gem, with icons painted on the dome; the church is nestled in the Oakland Hills. The Morcom Amphitheater of Roses provides a stunning horticultural display of more than 8,000 rose bushes surrounded by Mediterranean architecture. The landmark Paramount Theatre is a restored 1930s movie palace that still hosts a variety of arts events.

Popular entertainment and amusement sites include Children's Fairyland, a three-dimensional theme park with more than 60 sets recreating nursery rhymes, fairy tales, and legends; and the Western Aerospace Museum, displaying aeronautical artifacts and housing an aircraft library and gift shop. The Oakland Zoo in Knowland Park is home to 440 native and exotic animals and an African Lion Exhibit; its Children's Zoo is expected to open in 2005. Curious persons of all ages are welcome at the Chabot Space and Science Center which completed its new facility in January 2000 and features a planetarium, observatory and exhibits.

Another popular spot is the Jack London Square and Village, which was once the stomping grounds of the city's most colorful literary figures. It houses many quaint shops, restaurants, and a Farmer's Market along its scenic Boardwalk. The Presidential Yacht Potomac, Franklin Delano Roosevelt's "floating white house," hosts dockside tours and history cruises from its port at Jack London Square. Several museums are part of the Jack London Square complex including the African American Museum and Library, Lightship Relief floating lighthouse, the Museum of Children's Art, and the Oakland Museum of California. The Oakland Museum of California is lauded for its displays of California art, history and natural science. The Ebony Museum of Art at Jack London Village displays and sells African American art.

Arts and Culture

The Oakland East Bay Symphony presents symphonic music during its November through May subscription concert series, which is presented at the Paramount Theatre. The Symphony also provides accompaniment to performances by the Oakland Ballet. The Malonga Casquelourd Center for the Arts (the former Alice Arts Center) is home to the Oakland Ballet, Citicentre Dance Theater, Dimensions Dance Theater, Oakland Ensemble Theater, and Bay Area Blues Society. Oakland Ensemble Theatre, the city's only professional resident theater, produces contemporary, insightful works from an African American perspective. Blues, jazz, and gospel concerts are promoted by the Bay Area Blues Society. Woodminster Summer Musicals are performed July through September in the open-air Woodminster Amphitheater in the scenic Joaquin Miller Park in the Oakland hills.

New to the Oakland civic center area are the Craft & Cultural Arts Gallery and the Oakland Art Gallery which opened in 2001. Samuel's Gallery features a large collection of cards, prints, posters, and original graphics by African American artists.

Festivals and Holidays

The African Cultural Festival, popularly known as "The Africans are Coming," features dance in its many African forms performed by five sub-Saharan repertory companies. Oakland celebrates its birthday on May 4th with its annual Celebration in the Plaza, featuring live music with guest performers, famous Oakland celebrities, living history exhibits, walking tours, food booths, and art exhibits. Oakland's rich Spanish heritage is saluted at the annual Cinco de Mayo celebration which includes a parade and many festival activities. June's Festival at the Lake is a multi-cultural festival that features entertainment, arts, children's activities, an international food fair, and community programs. August's Chinatown Streetfest with its arts, food and crafts of the cultures of China, Vietnam, Japan, Korea, the Philippines, and others, celebrates the city's Asian community.

The first week in September is the date for the Art & Soul Festival with more than 150 artisans displaying their music and crafts at multiple stages around the city. Another annual fall occurrence is the Black Cowboy Parade downtown, always held the first Saturday in October. The holiday season is greeted by a Christmas Tree Lighting Celebration, a parade of lighted yachts at Jack London Square's waterfront and a holiday parade sponsored by the *Oakland Tribune*.

Sports for the Spectator

The National Football League's Oakland Raiders play at Network Associations Coliseum, also home to the Oakland Athletics of major league baseball's American League. The National Basketball Association's Golden State Warriors play at the Oakland Arena. The Oakland Banshees play women's tackle football. Sears Point International Raceway in nearby Sonoma offers a wide variety of motorsports events year round. The excitement of thoroughbred racing is offered at Golden Gate Fields in Albany, only minutes from Oakland.

Jack London Square hosts many shops and restaurants along its Boardwalk and contains artifacts from the author's life.

Sports for the Participant

Joaquin Miller Park offers 10 trails featuring spectacular views of the entire Bay Area. Joggers enjoy the 3.18-mile jogging path that encircles the shoreline of Lake Merritt. Surrounded on three sides by Lake Merritt, 122-acre Lakeside Park offers picnic areas, putting greens, lawn bowling, boat rentals, and Japanese and herb gardens. The Redwood Regional Park and Roberts Regional Recreation Area covers more than 2,000 acres in the city of Oakland and Contra Costa County. They include an amphitheater fire circle, horse and hiking trails, picnic and play areas, volleyball court, exercise course, and heated outdoor swimming pool. The Temescal Regional Recreation Area's 48 acres including a 13-acre lake provide swimming, fishing, picnicking, and a children's play area. Willows Skate and Surf in nearby Alameda offers roller skating, skate boards, and surf boards. Ice skating is available seven days a week at the Oakland Ice Center. Oakland's three municipal golf courses, Metropolitan Golf Links, Lake Chabot Golf Course, and Montclair Golf Course, accommodate avid and beginning golfers alike. Oakland also maintains 59 outdoor tennis courts and 7 public outdoor pools located throughout the city.

Shopping and Dining

Boutiques and specialty shops offering men's and women's apparel, household goods, toys and ethnic gift items are featured at Jack London Village. Other shopping areas include the City Center downtown, Rockridge, Piedmont Avenue, Lakeshore, and Grand Avenues. City Center is a popular pedestrian plaza with a mix of shops and restaurants. The Oakland Artisan Marketplace is open Fridays in Oakland's Frank Ogawa Plaza and Saturdays and Sundays in Jack London Square. One of the oldest and most culturally diverse markets in the city is the Old Oakland Farmer's Market, open year-round on Fridays downtown where shoppers find Asian produce, fresh flowers, potted plants, herbs, bakery items, fresh fish and seafood, and wild game and poultry.

The Jack London Square is home to a variety of restaurants in a wonderful waterfront setting. Unusual fare and cuisine from around the world is offered at 12 eateries on the Square. Restaurants include specialties such as Mexican, Indonesian, Cajun, Northern Italian, Greek, Japanese, sushi, seafood, and classic American cuisine. From upscale to modest, Oakland has offerings for traditionalists as well as adventurous gourmets.

Convention Facilities

The Oakland Convention Center/Marriott Oakland City Center complex is one of the first structures in California to house both a convention center and hotel. An atrium lobby joins the two-story convention center with the 483-room hotel. Convention center meeting facilities can accommodate 6,000 people and banquet facilities seat 3,900 diners. There is a 48,000-square-foot exhibition hall that can be divided into smaller halls, 12 additional meeting rooms, and a parking garage. Approximately 7,500 square feet of additional meeting space is available on the center's second level, with 8,000 square feet inside the hotel. The Marriott offers an additional 25,000 square feet of flexible function space.

The Henry J. Kaiser Convention Center is a multifunction facility consisting of the Kaiser Arena, Calvin Simmons Theatre and two banquet/ballrooms. Kaiser Arena can accommodate up to 8,000 patrons for a variety of events and has a banquet capacity of 1,500 people. The arena's 23,000-square-foot hardwood floor accommodates up to 150 eight-foot by ten-foot trade show booths. The 1,900-seat Calvin Simmons Theatre has been restored to European splendor with a gilt-trimmed proscenium stage. The center's ballroom and goldroom host many functions of all types.

Other large facilities include the Network Associates Coliseum and Arena Complex, which features an outdoor stadium for baseball and an indoor arena; the state-of-the-art County of Alameda Conference Center; and the California Ballroom.

Transportation

Approaching the City

Oakland can be reached from San Francisco by traveling east across the Bay Bridge via Interstate 80 and continuing south to Oakland on I-580 or I-980. Oakland International Airport is located only twelve minutes from downtown. A dozen airlines serve Oakland International Airport, with 208 daily departures. The airport has major thoroughfares to Denver, Chicago, Dallas, Seattle, Portland, and Los Angeles. Bay Area Rapid Transit (BART) offers a dedicated connection to the airport and high-speed rail service between East Bay cities and San Francisco with eight stations in Oakland. Four shuttles also serve the airport. Amtrak schedules frequent arrivals through its terminal at Jack London Square. Greyhound bus service is also available.

Traveling in the City

Major routes through Oakland include Interstate 980, which runs north and south through the city, and Interstate 880, the Nimitz Freeway, which runs east and west.

A network of city buses operates throughout 600 miles of East Bay. The Bay Area Transit System (BART) provides wide-ranging subway service on four East Bay lines into San Francisco. The Alameda/Oakland Ferry cruises into Jack London Square from San Francisco's Ferry terminal and Pier 41. Three taxi companies service the city.

Communications

Newspapers and Magazines

The morning *Oakland Tribune,* published in Hayward, is the city's daily newspaper. The *Inter-City Express* is the daily legal and real estate paper. Other weekly, biweekly and monthly publications include *The Catholic Voice, El Mundo, Oakland Bay Area Observer, Oakland Post, Sing Tao Daily, East Bay Voice, Alameda Times-Star* and *The Montclarion.*

Among the magazines published in Oakland are *The Black Scholar, California Agriculture, Creation Spirituality Magazine, Song Moi, Dance Magazine Inc.* and *News Hunter.*

Television and Radio

Oakland has one commercial network television station, a cable network, and an FM station. KTVU is the local Fox affiliate television station and KTOP is the government access cable channel.

Media Information: *Oakland Tribune,* Inside Bay Area, 401 13th Street, Oakland, CA. 94612; telephone (510)208-6300.

Oakland Online

City of Oakland Home Page. Available www.oaklandnet.com

Community and Economic Development Agency. Available www.business2oakland.com/main

Economic Development Alliance for Business. Available www.edab.org

Oakland Metropolitan Chamber of Commerce. Available www.oaklandchamber.com

Oakland Public Library. Available www.oaklandlibrary.org

Oakland Tribune. Available www.insidebayarea.com/oaklandtribune

Oakland Unified School District. Available webportal.ousd.k12.ca.us/index.aspx

Visitor Information. Available www.oaklandchamber.com

Selected Bibliography

Bradford, Amory, *Oakland's Not for Burning* (New York: McKay, 1968)

Irvin, Dona L., *The Unsung Heart of Black America: A Middle-Class Church at Midcentury* (Columbia: University of Missouri Press, 1992)

Levy, Frank, *Urban Outcomes: Schools, Streets, and Libraries* (Berkeley: University of California Press, 1974)

Riverside

The City in Brief

Founded: 1870 (incorporated, 1883)

Head Official: Mayor Ronald O. Loveridge (since 1994)

City Population
    1980: 170,591
    1990: 226,546
    2000: 255,166
    2003 estimate: 281,514
    Percent change, 1990–2000: 12.6%
    U.S. rank in 1980: 83rd
    U.S. rank in 1990: 68th
    U.S. rank in 2000: 78th

Metropolitan Area Population (PMSA)
    1980: 1,558,000
    1990: 2,588,793
    2000: 3,254,821

Percent change, 1990–2000: 25.7%
U.S. rank in 1980: 2nd (CMSA)
U.S. rank in 1990: 2nd (CMSA)
U.S. rank in 2000: 2nd (CMSA)

Area: 85.6 square miles
Elevation: 847 feet above sea level
Average Annual Temperature: 66.0° F
Average Annual Precipitation: 10.2 inches

Major Economic Sectors: Light and medium manufacturing, retail trade, education, and government
Unemployment Rate: 5.5% (January 2005)
Per Capita Income: $17,882 (1999)

2002 FBI Crime Index Total: 15,161

Major Colleges and Universities: University of California, Riverside; California Baptist University, La Sierra University, Riverside Community College

Daily Newspaper: *The Press-Enterprise*

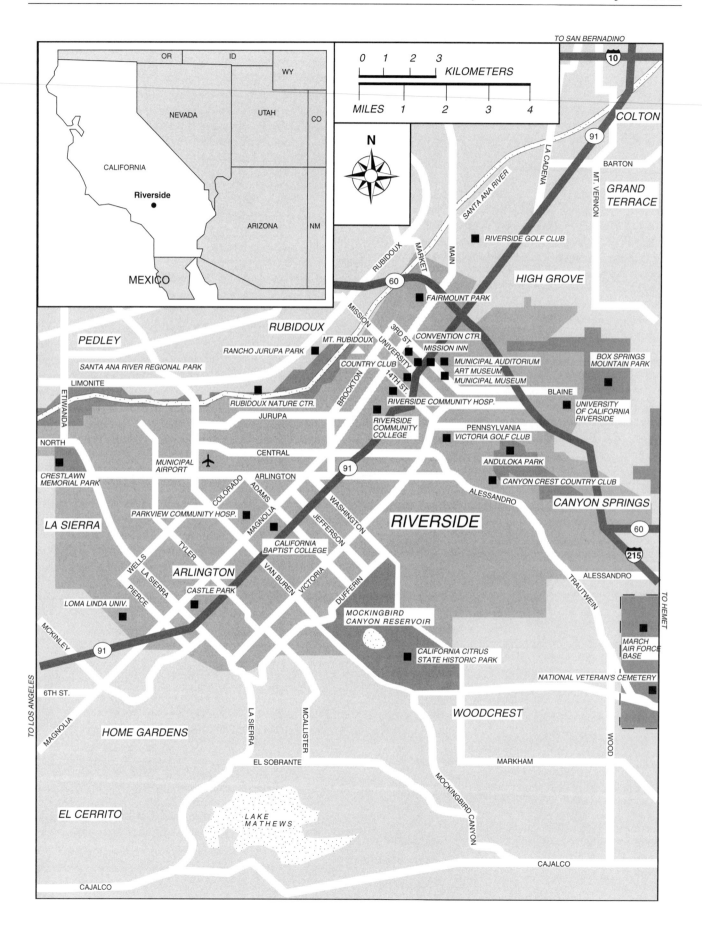

Introduction

The city of Riverside, located within one hour of the city of Los Angeles, began as the center for the navel orange-growing industry in the United States. Today the city has a large and diverse and economy, in addition to affordable housing; both qualities have made it attractive to employers and employees and have helped Riverside become the 11th largest city in California. In fact Riverside leads all the other Southern California cities that comprise the Inland Empire in total jobs and large businesses.

Recreational opportunities such as beaches, ski slopes, and desert resorts are within an hour's drive. Cultural activities run the gamut from community theater to symphonic concerts to ballet. The Mission Revival style hotel built in the city's early days has become the world-famous Mission Inn favored by presidents, royalty, and movie stars. Riverside is blessed with an abundance of space. Through coordinated city planning, Riverside has combined the best of the past with the promise of unlimited future possibilities.

Geography and Climate

Riverside is located at the center of the Inland Empire area of Southern California, which is comprised of the western parts of the two counties that comprise the Riverside-San Bernardino area. Riverside is 10 miles south southwest of San Bernardino and 53 miles east of Los Angeles. Located on the Santa Ana River, the city is near the San Bernardino Mountains. The climate is characterized as mild and semi-arid. Summer highs frequently reach over 90° F, but evening temperatures can drop as much as 30 to 49 degrees accompanied by cool breezes. Low humidity keeps even hot summer days from being oppressive. The average rainfall each year is generally 10 to 12 inches, falling mostly from September through April.

Area: 85.6 square miles (2000)

Elevation: 847 feet above sea level

Average Temperatures: January, 55.0° F; July, 79.0° F; annual average, 66.0° F

Average Annual Precipitation: 10.2 inches

History

The Rancho Era

The first European visitors to the area of present-day Riverside were Captain Juan Bautista de Anza and his thirty-four seasoned soldiers, who arrived in the area from Arizona in 1774 in search of a land route to California. At that time the Valley of Paradise was inhabited by Native Americans, who lived in the niches in the rocky hills and foraged for food. The natives lived in the area relatively undisturbed until 1821, when the lands of California became the property of Mexico.

Shortly thereafter Juan Bandini, a prominent political figure in California, was given a piece of land called El Rancho Jurupa, which he later presented to Abel Stearns, the husband of one of his daughters. The Stearns sold the land to Louis Rubidoux, who along with other ranchers, ruled the land. After Rubidoux's death part of the land was purchased by John North, who decided to build a community of ethical people devoted to establishing good schools, churches, and libraries. The new town was called Riverside and its original square, called "Mile Square," remains the heart of the city. Within a few years of its founding, railroad tracks were built connecting the city to far-off places.

Oranges and Irrigation

Around 1875 a mutant Brazilian orange tree that produced fruit with no seeds was brought to the city. In the rich soil by the Santa Ana River the fruit flourished under the abundant sunshine. By 1887 the navel orange had become the dominant crop in Riverside and other California cities.

About the same time, with the financial aid of people from England, Matthew Gage, an immigrant from Canada, began work on a canal to bring water to all of Riverside, parts of which had no water available. With the irrigation made possible by Gage's canal, Riverside's greatest growth period began. Three new subdivisions—White's Addition, Hall's Addition, and Arlington Heights—were developed.

Economic strides were made in the 1880s when a number of local fruit growers joined together to pick and sell fruit under one brand name they could all use, and to grade their oranges for quality. The plan expanded and by 1893 a group of all the growers of California was formed under the name of the Southern California Fruit Exchange, now known as Sunkist. The development of refrigerated railroad cars and innovative irrigation systems established Riverside as the state's wealthiest city per capita by 1895.

In 1873 James Roe, a druggist and teacher, moved to the city and by the late 1870s had launched the *Riverside Press* weekly newspaper that later became the current daily publication, *The Press-Enterprise.*

World Wars Establish Military Presence

During World War I, March Field, now March Air Reserve Base, was established for the training of aviators. In 1920, Ernest Louis Yeager began the E. L. Yeager Construction Company, Inc., which, with the assistance of his three sons, completed over a half century of master construction projects. In the latter half of this century the Food Machinery Corporation was formed to produce machinery for packing citrus fruits efficiently and rapidly.

During World War II March Field was expanded and another base, Camp Haan, was begun across from March Field. The site is now occupied by the new National Veteran's Cemetery. A third base was built, called Camp Anza, which later became a subdivision called Arlanza.

Riverside prides itself on its background, and there is strong community support for the historic preservation of architectural structures. Riverside has 22 properties listed on the National Register of Historic Places.

A Promising Future

In recent years Riverside has given much attention to diversifying its economy and creating a sustainable community. In 2004 Partners for Livable Communities recognized Riverside as one of America's "Most Livable Communities" in the mid-sized city category. The award—which is given out every decade—recognizes Riverside's strides in preparing itself for a global economy through strategic business plans. However, it also acknowledges Riverside's constant nurturing of its community—something the city has done since it blossomed in 1883.

Historical Information: Riverside Municipal Museum, 3580 Mission Inn Avenue, Riverside, CA 92501; telephone (909)826-5273

Population Profile

Metropolitan Area Residents (PMSA)
1980: 1,558,000
1990: 2,588,793
2000: 3,254,821
Percent change, 1990–2000: 25.7%
U.S. rank in 1980: 2nd (CMSA)
U.S. rank in 1990: 2nd (CMSA)
U.S. rank in 2000: 2nd (CMSA)

City Residents
1980: 170,591
1990: 226,546
2000: 255,166
2003 estimate: 281,514
Percent change, 1990–2000: 12.6%
U.S. rank in 1980: 83rd
U.S. rank in 1990: 68th
U.S. rank in 2000: 78th

Density: 3,104 people per square mile (2000)

Racial and ethnic characteristics (2000)
   White: 151,377
   Black or African American: 18,906
   American Indian and Alaska Native: 2,779
   Asian: 14,501
   Native Hawaiian or Pacific Islander: 991
   Hispanic or Latino (may be of any race): 97,315
   Other: 53,591

Percent of residents born in state: 56.5% (2000)

Age characteristics (2000)
   Population under 5 years old: 20,435
   Population 5 to 9 years old: 22,559
   Population 10 to 14 years old: 21,379
   Population 15 to 19 years old: 23,145
   Population 20 to 24 years old: 22,216
   Population 25 to 34 years old: 37,324
   Population 35 to 34 years old: 39,140
   Population 45 to 54 years old: 29,565
   Population 55 to 59 years old: 9,293
   Population 60 to 64 years old: 7,056
   Population 65 to 74 years old: 11,811
   Population 75 to 84 years old: 8,420
   Population 85 years and older: 2,823
   Median age: 29.8 years

Births (2002, Riverside County)
   Total number: 26,691

Deaths (2002, Riverside County)
   Total number: 12,830 (of which, 170 were infants under the age of 1 year)

Money income (1999)
   Per capita income: $17,882
   Median household income: $41,646
   Total households: 86,044

Number of households with income of . . .
   less than $10,000: 8,334
   $10,000 to $14,999: 4,927
   $15,000 to $24,999: 10,133
   $25,000 to $34,999: 10,865
   $35,000 to $49,999: 13,565

$50,000 to $74,999: 16,058
$75,000 to $99,999: 8,638
$100,000 to $149,999: 6,678
$150,000 to $199,999: 1,375
$200,000 or more: 1,555

Percent of families below poverty level: 11.7% (48.2% of which were female householder families with related children under 5 years)

2002 FBI Crime Index Total: 15,161

Municipal Government

Riverside has a council-manager form of government. The seven-member council is comprised of persons elected for four-year terms from geographically designated wards. A mayor is elected from the city at large for a four-year term and acts as the presiding officer of the council.

Head Official: Mayor Ronald O. Loveridge (since 1994; current term expires 2005)

Total Number of City Employees: 2,623 (2005)

City Information: City of Riverside, 3900 Main Street, Riverside, CA 92522; telephone (951)826-5311

Economy

Major Industries and Commercial Activity

Although Riverside's beginnings are steeped in agriculture, today the economy relies heavily on government, education, manufacturing, and retail; however, affordable land space and housing are attracting employees and skilled laborers to the city. The city's Development Department Activity Update for 2003/2004 shows that Riverside ranks number one in almost all economic measures among the 53 cities in the area, including largest number of businesses and total jobs.

In recent years Riverside has placed a major emphasis on expanding its technology areas by developing high-tech industrial business parks. For example, the city, county, and University of California at Riverside all cooperate within the 856-acre Riverside Regional Technology Park. The complex offers a high-speed fiber optic telecommunications system that supports voice, video, and data information. Bourns Engineering and I/O Software, Centrum Analytical labs, and Luminex Software, Inc. have all chosen Riverside for new headquarters operations. Riverside also has taken strides in developing its industrial and manufacturing sectors. In the last 10 years Riverside has attracted more than 125 industrial employers, according to the city's Development Department. Riverside's light manufacturing base now includes such sectors as electrical instruments; plastics; wood, glass, and metal fabrication; food processing; recreational vehicles; and imaging equipment.

Riverside also hopes to see huge economic growth with the addition of shipping company DHL to its fold. The $18.6 billion company chose the March Air Reserve Base as its West Coast hub over two other Inland Empire locations. In addition the city's retail industry continues to grow as population continues to rise.

Items and goods produced: electrical instruments; plastics; wood, glass, and metal fabrication; recreational vehicles; food processing; aircraft parts; motorcycle parts; citrus-packing; precision plastic injection molders; home furniture; and medical imaging equipment.

Incentive Programs—New and Existing Companies

Local programs—The City of Riverside Development Department offers many programs and services to help businesses grow and succeed in the Southern California marketplace. These programs and services include: industrial development bond financing, local and state designated Enterprise Zones, redevelopment incentives, accelerated processes for plan checks and building permit fees, employment hiring and training programs, mapping services, high-speed Internet bandwidth within the city limits, and very competitive electric and water utility rates.

State programs—The Agua Mansa Enterprise Zone, which is partially located in the northeast corner of Riverside, is one of the state's designated Enterprise Zones. Business incentives and tax credits are provided to those businesses that operate or invest within a designated enterprise zone. Riverside also is home to a state Recycled Market Development Zone that offers financial incentives to companies interested in promote recycling as part of their manufacturing process.

Job training programs—The federal Workforce Investment Act (WIA) provides a cooperative effort between employers and the Riverside County Workforce Development Board. An employer can receive assistance with employer-specific training and financial incentives, such as reimbursements, tax credits, and direct payments for the training of new employees. Employers can also receive reimbursement for a portion of the employee's wages during an on-the-job training period. The State Employment Development Department offers employers assistance and incentives for hiring qualified individuals. These include the Work Opportunity and Welfare-to-Work Tax Credit for employers that are hiring qualified summer youth and other eligible individuals, such as certain veteran populations or older adults on supplemental social security.

Development Projects

Riverside has seen its industrial sector grow with the addition of the 56-acre University Research Park (URP), a project with the University of California, Riverside. URP is housed within Hunter Park and is the core of the recently designated 856-acre Riverside Regional Technology Park. Future plans for the Park include a 40,000 square foot technology business incubator.

Downtown Riverside also has been the focus of a rash of new developments. In 2002 Riverside Community Hospital opened a $20 million Emergency Room and Trauma Center. The Market Street Gateway, which is the entrance to Riverside off State Highway 60, has undergone vast aesthetic changes to attract more residential and retail developments. Market Street will also be the home of a new 126,000-square foot Corporate Center, located across from Fairmount Park. The historic Fox Theater located downtown is currently undergoing restoration to become another multi-use venue in Riverside.

The Riverside Planning and Building Department has presented its General Plan for 2025. This plan outlines objectives for the future of Riverside in regards to housing, circulation, land use, economic outlook, arts and culture, and education. Some of the projects proposed in the General Plan for 2025 include improvements to the Riverside Municipal Airport, city parks, March Air Reserve Base/March Inland Port Airport, and more. The General Plan also proposes continuing support of the development of a contemporary state-of-the-art campus for the Riverside School of the Arts near White Park in downtown Riverside. The addition of shipping company DHL to the area promises to provide $65 million in new construction, according to the Riverside Chamber of Commerce.

Commercial Shipping

Riverside is adjacent to one of the major rail-freight centers in the state. Rail service to the city includes UPSP's main line and BNSF's main line and branch lines. The Riverside Municipal Airport, an excellent general aviation facility, accommodates private aircraft, charter services, and air-related businesses. More than sixty-five trucking companies are based in or have facilities in Riverside and provide a broad range of interstate, regional, and local freight services. The one-day area served from Riverside has a population of more than 30 million people, which is more than one-tenth of the U.S. population.

Labor Force and Employment Outlook

The Inland Empire used to be the bedroom community for the larger metropolitan area. A relatively high percentage of the labor force commuted to jobs outside the two counties. But from 1980 to 2000 about 1.3 million people migrated to the area because it offered large tracts of affordable residential land, more than in coastal areas. The California Employment Development Department notes that Inland Empire's affordable housing and advantageous location have helped it create more new jobs than any other area. And the future forecast is just as bright. The influx of skilled professionals has helped the Inland Empire's economy become more focused on high tech, professional, and corporate jobs. These areas grow at a compound annual rate of 3.4 percent, adding 83,605 jobs, according to the Southern California Association of Governments. Blue-collar construction, manufacturing, and logistics sectors are expected to increase at 2.6 percent per year, adding 89,787 jobs. The Southern California Association of Governments forecasted that the Inland Empire's employment base will expand by 408,946 jobs from 2000-2010.

The following is a summary of data regarding the Riverside-San Bernardino metropolitan area labor force, 2004 annual averages.

Size of nonagricultural labor force: 1,149,700

Number of workers employed in . . .
   construction and mining: 119,000
   manufacturing: 120,000
   trade, transportation and utilities: 250,400
   information: 13,700
   financial activities: 45,200
   professional and business services: 125,100
   educational and health services: 117,700
   leisure and hospitality: 115,200
   other services: 38,700
   government: 211,400

Average hourly earnings of production workers employed in manufacturing: $13.57

Unemployment rate: 5.5% (January 2005)

Largest city employers	Number of employees
University of California, Riverside	5,336
Riverside Unified School District	3,553
City of Riverside	2,642
Pacific Bell	1,800
Kaiser Permanente	1,700
The Press Enterprise Co,	1,300
Alvord Unified School District	1,200
Riverside Community Hospital	1,053

Cost of Living

Residential housing costs within Riverside are among the lowest in Southern California, a fact that has caused numerous companies and individuals to relocate to the area in recent years.

2004 (3rd Quarter) ACCRA Average House Price: $424,106

2004 (3rd Quarter) ACCRA Cost of Living Index: 119.9 (U.S. average = 100.0)

State income tax rate: Ranges from 1.0% to 9.3%

State sales and use tax rate: 6%

Local income tax rate: None

Local sales and use tax rate: 1.75%

Property tax rate: Approximately 1.25% of assessed valuation; assessment ratio = 100% for residential

Economic Information: City of Riverside Development Department, 3900 Main Street, Riverside, CA 92522; toll-free (877)RIV-SIDE (877-748-7433); email devdept @riversideca.gov. Greater Riverside Chamber of Commerce, 3985 University Avenue, Riverside, CA 92501; telephone (951)683-7100

Education and Research

Elementary and Secondary Schools

The Riverside Unified School District and the Alvord Unified School District, which accommodates the southwestern part of the city and adjacent unincorporated areas, serve the city of Riverside.

There are 42,000 students enrolled in kindergarten through grade 12 in 45 schools in the Riverside Unified School District. The following is a summary of data regarding the Alvord Unified School District as of the 2003-2004 school year.

Total enrollment: 19,200

Number of facilities
  elementary schools: 12
  junior high/middle schools: 4
  senior high chools: 3 (includes 1 continuation high school)

Student/teacher ratio: 23:1

Teacher salaries
  average: $59,867

Funding per pupil: $6,357

Public Schools Information: Alvord Unified School District, 10365 Keller Avenue, Riverside, CA 92505; telephone (951)509-5000. Riverside Unified School District, 3380 14th Street, Riverside, CA 92501; telephone (951)788-7134

Colleges and Universities

The University of California, Riverside (UCR) is one of the most diverse public universities in the nation; *U.S. News and World Report* ranked UCR third in this distinction. The university is experiencing more growth than any other University of California campuses, and as a result it launched a Long Range Development Plan in 2004 to meet the demands of an expected enrollment of 25,000 by 2010. Projects include more off-campus housing near the UCR campus in downtown Riverside. Considered a major research university and national center for the humanities, UCR offers bachelor's degrees in more than 75 disciplines, 36 doctoral programs, and 40 master's degree programs. The School of Education offers master's and doctoral programs in addition to teaching credentials in several other programs; UCR also offers a College of Engineering. La Sierra University, with more than 1,900 students, is a Seventh-Day Adventist institution that offers course work in undergraduate and graduate programs. California Baptist University is a Christian liberal arts institution with more than 2,000 students that offers degree programs in such areas as behavioral sciences, business administration, liberal arts, and Christian studies. California Southern Law School, which operates part-time evening classes, offers programs in the practice and theory of law. Riverside Community College (RCCD), a two-year school with its main campus downtown, offers a number of associate degree programs in a variety of fields. Local vocational schools feature programs in business services, contractor's licensing, medical services, and other areas of technology and trade. The Accrediting Commission for Community and Junior Colleges has recently approved RCCD's request to evolve from a three-campus system to a multi-college system by 2007.

Libraries and Research Centers

The Riverside Public Library has the third largest public library collection in the Southwest; only Los Angeles and Las Vegas public libraries have larger collections. The main library facility is located in historic downtown, and six other branches operate within the city. The Riverside Local History Research Center is a partnership between Riverside Municipal Museum and Riverside Public Library. Special collections at the Riverside Public Library include Spanish language, genealogy, local history, historical photographs, and U.S. documents. The Riverside County Library System, Moreno Valley Public Library, Murrieta Public Library, and College of the Desert are part of the Riverside County Network, an automated network that deploys approximately

350 computer/terminal workstations in library branches throughout the region.

Other local libraries include those associated with local churches, colleges, and businesses, the California School for the Deaf Library, the county historical commission library, county law library, and the University of California Riverside Library. UCR's Library has four separate libraries, including a media library, a science library, and the Tomás Rivera Library.

Public Library Information: Riverside Public Library, 3581 Mission Inn Avenue, Riverside, CA 92501; telephone (951)826-5201

Health Care

Riverside Community Hospital, a growing critical care facility, is the largest hospital in western Riverside County with a total of 369 beds. In 2002 Riverside opened a $20 million Emergency Room and Trauma Center. Kaiser Permanente Medical Care (217 beds) and Parkview Community Hospital Medical Center (193 beds) are Riverside's other main hospitals. The addition of the new Riverside County Regional Medical Center in Moreno Valley adds to the quality health care, specialty clinics, and research facilities that are easily accessible to area residents.

Recreation

Sightseeing

One of Riverside's most attractive sites, Victoria Avenue, was constructed in 1891-92. The 8.3 miles of divided street are planted with hedgerow roses, eucalyptus, palm, and crepe myrtle trees with a multipurpose trail. Thirty-nine acres of hilly tree-lined paths with more than three thousand blooming plant species from around the world are on view at the Botanical Gardens of the University of California, Riverside. The Gardens are also a wildlife sanctuary with almost two hundred bird species officially observed. The Mission Inn, a completely renovated National Historic Landmark hotel, is a unique blend of architectural styles and houses priceless pieces of art. The Teen Challenge Program is headquartered in the Spanish-style Benedict Castle, which was built in 1931. Overlooking the city of Riverside is the 1,337-foot Mt. Rubidoux, which is the site of the World Peace Tower and a large cross dedicated to Father Junipero Serra.

Heritage House, a restored two-story Victorian home completed in 1892 in the Queen Anne style, is open for tours. Visitors are also welcome at the Jensen-Alvarado Ranch, a historic ranch completely restored to portray rural life. The ranch features a variety of live animals, a duck pond, and citrus groves and fruit orchards.

Castle Park, a 25-acre family recreation park, features miniature golf, arcades, amusement rides, and a restored 1909 carousel. A model railroad at Hunter Park offers train rides when operating. Cuttings from the Parent Navel Orange Tree, planted in 1875, started the entire billion-dollar citrus industry in the United States. The tree, which can be seen at the Magnolia and Arlington area, still bears fruit.

Arts and Culture

Riverside is home to a variety of performing arts, theater, dance, and music organizations. The Children's Performing Art Center of California offers puppetry, mime, story spinning, and family entertainment every weekend through KIDSTUFF. The KIDSTUFF children's theater is housed in Riverside's Life Arts Building. The Performing Arts Program of the University of California, Riverside offers quality plays, musicals, and other acts through its University Theatre and other campus venues. The historic Riverside Municipal Auditorium—located in downtown Riverside—showcases live performances that range from popular music acts to comedy to dance throughout the year. The historic Fox Theater that is located downtown is currently undergoing restoration to become another multiuse venue in Riverside.

The Riverside Community Players, founded in 1926, is one of the oldest continuously active community theater groups in the United States and holds workshops in acting and staging techniques in addition to performing six productions annually. The Riverside Youth Theatre provides training for much younger thesbians and showcases their talents with a few reasonably priced performances per year.

The Riverside Chorale holds several concerts during the year featuring significant works of music. The Riverside Civic Light Opera, the oldest opera-in-English group in the nation, presents four or five shows per season. The Riverside County Philharmonic performs four subscription concerts each year October through May. The free public concerts of the Riverside Concert Band, Inc. provide an opportunity for young musicians to perform with more experienced players at official functions in the city. Riverside Community College's Civic Light Opera offers its Performance/Riverside season at the college's Landis Auditorium.

Dance enthusiasts will enjoy traditional Mexican dances performed by The Ballet Folklorico De Arlanza, whose members range in age from 5 to 23 years old. Annual

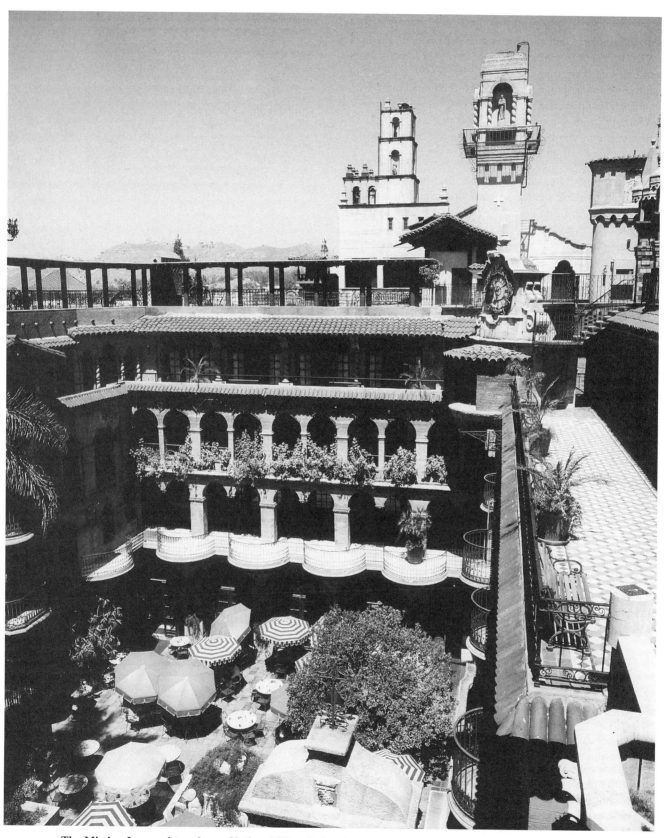

The Mission Inn, registered as a National Historic Landmark, was built in stages between 1902 and 1931.

professional productions of the *Nutcracker* plus a spring performance are offered by the Riverside Ballet Theatre, founded in 1969.

The Riverside Ballet Theater calls the historic Aurea Vista Hotel its home. It is only one of the many art groups found in the building. Another historic structure that serves as a art center in Riverside is the Life Arts Building, home to KIDSTUFF. Built as a YMCA in 1909, the Life Arts Building is home to more than 30 artists' studios and includes art galleries for the Riverside Community Arts Association and Media Sound Productions, a high-tech recording studio.

The Riverside Arts Council, a nonprofit organization staffed by volunteers, presents classes, demonstrations, shows, and sales of artworks. Members promote the cultural life of Riverside through leadership in educational, financial, and technical assistance to artists, art organizations, and community groups.

Riverside has an interesting variety of museums to be enjoyed by residents and visitors alike. The March Air Force Museum displays more than 60 aircraft and missiles, both inside and outside, on a 35-acre site adjacent to March Field. The Riverside Municipal Museum tells the story of the city's history, depicts the development of the citrus and other local manufacturing industries, and features touring exhibits. One of the largest collections of cameras and photos in the world is on display at the University of California, Riverside California Museum of Photography. Rare Indian artifacts, basketry, pottery, and handicrafts are on view at the Sherman Indian Museum. The Mission Inn Museum, located at the historic Mission Inn, presents an eclectic display of historic artifacts, paintings of the California Missions painted in the 1800s, oriental *objects d'art,* arts and crafts furniture, marble sculptures, and many photographs. The Riverside Arts Museum, which offers 20 major exhibits a year, also is located downtown near the Mission Inn Museum.

Festivals and Holidays

February brings the annual Dickens Festival, a literary festival honoring the writer Charles Dickens that encourages reading and enjoyment of the dramatic and cultural arts by the general public. Riverside also hosts the Black History Parade on the third Saturday in February. And the Riverside Ballet Theatre hosts its Sweetheart Dance in February, which is open to the public.

In March the Riverside Arts Council presents Evening for the Arts to benefit the local arts community. April brings the annual Riverside Airshow at the Riverside Municipal Airport and the annual Orange Blossom Festival. The Orange Blossom Festival is two days of entertainment, vendors, a parade, turn-of-the-century costumes and events that celebrate Riverside's citrus heritage. May's Cinco De Mayo

is a celebration with music, entertainment, and food. The Vintage Home Tour and Restoration Faire featuring historically significant homes takes place in June. June also marks the beginning of Riverside Wednesday Night in downtown Riverside; the program lasts until September and offers a certified Farmer's Market, arts and crafts, food, live entertainment, petting zoo, pony rides, and kiddie rides. In the summer months Fairmount Park offers a wide range of family programs and a peaceful setting. Independence Day features fireworks atop Mt. Rubidoux and two other city sites, which can be viewed from Riverside's Wheelock Field.

Fall ushers in a new lineup of programming in Riverside. September is the month of the Annual Mayor's Ball for the Arts, with an evening of banquets, costumes, prizes, and awards. Riverside Jazz Fest goes on for a weekend in September at Fairmount Park. October features Fiesta de la Familia in celebration of Hispanic Heritage month. Halloween weekend brings spooky tales of ghouls with Ghostwalk Riverside.

November brings the Mission Inn 5K/10K Run through notable areas of downtown. But it also kicks off the holiday season with the Christmas Tree Lighting and Mission Inn Festival of Lights. December's Christmas Open House brightens spirits with music and entertainment at the Riverside Municipal Museum, and the Riverside Ballet Theatre Company performs the annual *Nutcracker* ballet.

Sports for the Participant

Riverside has more than 45 neighborhood and community parks and 2 state parks available to sports enthusiasts. Six neighborhood parks have tennis courts and swimming pools. The city parks also have a combined total of 15 soccer fields and more than 40 ballfields—which includes the lighted baseball stadium at Riverside Sports Complex that seats 3,500.

County parks offer natural environments for hiking, horseback riding, cycling, fishing, and camping. The 180-plus acre Fairmount Park offers fishing and sailing on Lake Evans, paddleboats, wildlife and bird watching, lawn bowling, golfing, playgrounds, and evening concerts. An outdoor recreational facility on 350 acres, Rancho Jurupa Park (a county park) has 10 miles of hiking and horseback riding trails, stocked lakes, campsites with utility hookups, and the Louis Rubidoux Nature Center.

The California Citrus State Historic Park is currently being expanded for visitors. Lake Perris State Recreation Area has 8,800 lakeside acres waiting for water-skiing, boating, sailing, and windsurfing. Skiing in the nearby Big Bear area and hot air ballooning near the Temecula wineries are two popular winter activities.

Golfers can choose from 6 public and 3 private courses. Miniature golf enthusiasts can find four different 18-hole miniature courses at the Castle Amusement Park. Bicyclists can find out about a wealth of trails and events through the Riverside Bicycle Club. Even bowlers and skaters have numerous options within Riverside's city limits.

Shopping and Dining

The Inland Empire's shopping outlet is Ontario Mills, home to more than 200 specialty stores and 24 anchor stores. Riverside itself has two other major shopping malls: the 1.1-million square foot Galleria at Tyler and the recently transformed Riverside Plaza. The Riverside Plaza, housed within Riverside's Magnolia Center and historic craftsman-era "Wood Street" neighborhood, now sports a "Main Street" look and feel to its stores and shops. Downtown Riverside also offers a wide arrange of specialty stores. The Canyon Springs shopping center located on the eastern edge of Riverside has national retail stores, while Canyon Crest Towne Center has specialty shops in a residential area five minutes from downtown.

From coffeehouse fare to Cantonese favorites, Riverside has restaurants for every taste. Sandwich shops and casual eateries abound along with purveyors of ethnic delights including Mexican, French, Italian, Greek, Japanese, Thai, and British fish 'n' chips.

Visitor Information: Visitor Center, 3660 Mission Inn Avenue, Riverside, CA 92501; telephone (909)684-4636

Convention Facilities

Riverside Convention Center is located near downtown and has 45,000 square feet of multiuse space that can accommodate up to 2,000 people for special events. The Convention Center also has an outdoor, well-lit plaza available for open-air exhibits. Within walking distance from the Convention Center are 500 hotels, and another 500 are located within driving distance. The Riverside Municipal Auditorium, built in the Spanish Revival style with Moorish accents is the home of the local symphony orchestra, opera, and ballet, and is available for special events.

Convention Information: Riverside Convention and Visitors Bureau, 3750 University Ave., Suite 175, Riverside, CA 92501; telephone (951)222-4700 or (888)748-7733; fax (951)222-4712.

Transportation

Approaching the City

Ontario International Airport is located 18 miles northwest of Riverside, and serves the region with more than 11 commercial airlines. The city renovated the Riverside Airport to better serve small aircraft and business travelers. Among the renovations includes the Sky Links Airport Golf Course.

Several interstate highways passing through or near the city of Riverside include I-15/215, which runs north-south, and I-10, which runs east-west just north of the city. Other major freeways in the area are Highway 60 and Highway 91. These routes provide direct access to metropolitan areas of Los Angeles and Orange County. Nearly 3,000 miles of county-maintained roads and nearly 700 miles of roads maintained by the state provide service to business, industry, and motorists in the region. A toll lane for commuters traveling between Riverside and Orange County on Highway 91 is the newest freeway addition.

Metrolink is a regional rail system that includes commuter and other passenger services and links Riverside to employment and activity centers in Los Angeles and Orange County.

Greyhound Bus Lines offers both intrastate and interstate service. The Riverside Transit Agency provides service to Riverside County within a 2,500-square-mile area; it also maintains two commuter routes to Orange County, San Bernardino, and Los Angeles, and offers Dial-A-Ride service for outlying areas. Amtrak serves the city with connections to surrounding and far-away states.

Traveling in the City

Within the city of Riverside, State Highway 91 runs northwest and southeast through the city, and State Highway 60 runs northwest to southeast through the northern part of the city. Major thoroughfares include Magnolia Avenue, Allesandro Boulevard, University Avenue, and Arlington Avenue.

Communications

Newspapers and Magazines

The city's daily newspaper is *The Press-Enterprise.* Other newspapers are UC-Riverside's *Highlander Online,* California Baptist University's *The Banner, Black Voice News, Riverside Green Sheet,* and *La Prensa Spanish Weekly.*

Magazines, newsletters, and journals published in Riverside include *Riverside Business Journal, Nutrition News, Riverside Review, Latin American Perspectives, Inland Empire Family Magazine,*and *Cinefex.*

Television and Radio

No television stations are based in Riverside, but cable is available. Riverside has three AM radio stations featuring Hispanic and religious programming and three FM stations featuring contemporary hits, adult contemporary, and religious programming.

Media Information: The Press Enterprise, PO Box 792, Riverside, CA 92502-0792; telephone (951)684-1200

Riverside Online

Alvord Unified School District. Available www.alvord.k12 .ca.us

City of Riverside Home Page. Available www.riversideca .gov

Greater Riverside Chamber of Commerce. Available www .riverside-chamber.com

Press Enterprise. Available www.pe.com or www.press enterpriseonline.com

Riverside Community Online. Available www.smartriver side.com

Riverside Convention and Visitors Bureau. Available www .riversidecb.com

Riverside County. Available www.co.riverside.ca.us

Riverside County Library System. Available www.riverside .lib.ca.us

Riverside Unified School District. Available www.rusd.k12 .ca.us

Selected Bibliography

Patterson, Tom, *A Colony for California: Riverside's First Hundred Years* (Riverside, Calif.: The Museum Press of the Riverside Museum Associates, 1996)

Sacramento

The City in Brief

Founded: 1839 (incorporated, 1850)

Head Official: Mayor Heather Fargo (since 2000)

City Population
    1980: 275,741
    1990: 369,365
    2000: 407,018
    2003 estimate: 445,335
    Percent change, 1990–2000: 3.0%
    U.S. rank in 1980: 52nd
    U.S. rank in 1990: 41st
    U.S. rank in 2000: 49th

Metropolitan Area Population
    1980: 1,100,000
    1990: 1,481,102
    2000: 1,796,857

    Percent change, 1990–2000: 21.3%
    U.S. rank in 1980: 32nd
    U.S. rank in 1990: 26th
    U.S. rank in 2000: 25th (Sacramento/Yolo CMSA)

Area: 97.2 square miles (2000)
Elevation: 30 feet above sea level
Average Annual Temperature: 59.0° F
Average Annual Precipitation: 17.18 inches

Major Economic Sectors: Government, services, trade
Unemployment Rate: 5.4% (January 2005)
Per Capita Income: $18,721 (1999)

2002 FBI Crime Index Total: 30,780

Major Colleges and Universities: California State University; University of California at Davis; American River College; Sacramento City College; Cosumnes River College

Daily Newspapers: *The Sacramento Bee*

OR
ID
WY
NEVADA
UTAH
CO
Sacramento
CALIFORNIA
ARIZONA
NM
MEXICO

0   1   2
KILOMETERS
MILES   0.5   1   1.5   2

N

NORTHGATE
NORWOOD
RIO LINDA
EL CAMINO
ARDEN WAY
TO AUBURN
RICHARDS
DEL PASO
AUBURN
160
80

SACRAMENTO RIVER
TO SACRAMENTO METROPOLITAN AIRPORT
TO REDDING
99
5
SACRAMENTO
AMERICAN RIVER
CALIFORNIA EXPOSITION
C ST.
12TH ST.
18TH ST.
STATE RAILROAD MUSEUM
DISCOVERY MUSEUM
F ST.
OLD SACRAMENTO
H ST.
I ST.
CITY HALL
J ST.
GOVERNORS MANSION
L ST.
CAPITOL MALL
CROCKER ART MUSEUM
3RD ST.
STATE CAPITOL MUSEUM
STATE CAPITOL
N ST.
STATE LIBRARY
VIETNAM VETERANS MEMORIAL
CAPITOL
TO CALIFORNIA STATE UNIVERSITY
STATE INDIAN MUSEUM
TOWE AUTO MUSEUM
P ST.
10TH ST.
11TH ST.
13TH ST.
15TH ST.
16TH ST.
17TH ST.
SUTTERS FORT
ARCO ARENA
S ST.
T ST.
19TH ST.
21ST ST.
24TH ST.
29TH ST.
ALHAMBRA
FOLSOM
TO SAN FRANCISCO
80
5
80
16
BROADWAY
VALLEJO
99
50
TO PLACERVILLE
RIVERSIDE
13TH AVE.
LAND PARK
FREEPORT
160
STOCKTON
99
WILLIAM LAND PARK AND ZOO
TO STOCKTON
FAIRYTALE TOWN
TO SACRAMENTO EXECUTIVE AIRPORT
TO STOCKTON
BROADWAY

Introduction

Sacramento, the capital of the state of California, began its life as a Gold Rush city when thousands of prospectors descended upon Captain John Sutter's settlement, New Helvetia, in hopes of striking the mother lode. Today Sacramento is a city of gracious tree-lined streets and, famous for flowers that bloom all year, it is known as the "Camellia Capital of the World." A significant percentage of the food that America consumes is produced in Sacramento, which is at the center of the fruitful Sacramento Valley. Since the nineteenth century the city has been a major transportation hub for the West Coast.

Geography and Climate

Sacramento lies in the center of California's broad and fruitful Sacramento Valley, 72 miles northeast of San Francisco. Shielded by the Sierra Nevada Mountains to the east, the California Coast ranges to the west, and the Siskiyou Mountains to the north, the city enjoys a mild climate for most of the year. In the summer, however, "northers" blow from the Siskiyou Mountains, bearing pollens and heat. This is mitigated by Sacramento's extremely low humidity and the cool ocean breezes. The winters are rainy.

Area: 97.2 square miles (2000)

Elevation: 30 feet above sea level

Average Temperatures: January, 45.0° F; July 73.0° F; annual average, 59.0° F

Average Annual Precipitation: 17.18 inches

History

Gold Rush Begins in Sacramento

The Sacramento area was originally inhabited by the Nisenan, a branch of the Maidu, who lived in the valley for 10,000 years before white settlers arrived. Spanish soldiers from Mission San Jose, under the command of Lieutenant Gabriel Morago, discovered the Sacramento and American rivers in 1808. The area was not settled until 1839. That year, with the permission of Mexico, Captain John Sutter, a Swiss immigrant who had fled his homeland to escape debtor's prison, built a settlement on 76 acres and called it New Helvetia, after his homeland. He built a fort called

Sutter's Fort (which has been restored and can still be seen today). Sutter also constructed a landing on the Sacramento River that he called the Embarcadero and contacted a millwright, James Marshall, to help build the settlement. It was Marshall who in 1848 discovered a gold nugget, thus precipitating the great California Gold Rush of 1849. Sutter's Embarcadero became the gateway to the mines, but Sutter was financially ruined by the influx of newcomers from all over the world who trampled his settlement; even his employees left him to make their fortune.

Sacramento, Spanish for "Holy Sacrament," was originally the name of a nearby river that is now called the Feather River; in 1849 the name was taken for the town, which was incorporated in 1850. Sacramento was a rowdy place, full of successful miners who spent their money on gambling and dance halls. In its early days, the town encountered difficulties, with floods in 1849 and 1853 and a fire in 1852. But Sacramento survived to become the capital of California in 1854, paying the state $1 million for the honor.

Railroad Arrives; Agriculture Surpasses Gold Mining

In 1855 construction began on the Sacramento Valley Railroad, with the financial backing of shopkeepers known as the Big Four: Collis P. Huntington, Mark Hopkins, Charles Crocker, and Leland Stanford (after whom Stanford University is named). In 1856 Sacramento became the terminus of California's first railroad. Then came the Pony Express and, in 1861, the transcontinental telegraph. The Central Pacific Railroad joined the east and west coasts in 1869, permitting Sacramento farmers to ship their produce to the east. The railroad also transformed what had been a six-month trip between the coasts to six days; in time it also superseded the river as a means of transportation. In another important change, agriculture eventually replaced the gold mines as the primary industry.

Mather Field was established to prepare planes to fly to Europe during World War I; McClellan Air Force Base was established in 1937 and was an important base of operations during World War II. These military installations drew a large influx of people into the area, many of whom stayed after World War II and spurred the development of the private sector. The first suburban shopping mall in the United States was established in North Sacramento in 1945. Like many cities in the United States, downtown Sacramento had fallen into decay by the 1950s, since most of the moneyed population had moved to the suburbs. The city eventually experienced a resurgence, marked by the redevelopment of the downtown area, with the city's historical sections being preserved and restored. Sutter's Embarcadero, for instance, now houses shops and restaurants. Sacramento's redevelopment has been acclaimed as one of the most successful in the United States. Today's Sacramento is experiencing further growth; population within the six-county Sacramento Region increased by 20 percent between 1990 and 2000. The city's economic growth, livability, and comparatively low cost of living has made it one of California's fastest-growing metropolitan areas.

Historical Information: Sacramento Room, Sacramento Public Library, 828 I Street, Sacramento, CA 95814-3576; telephone (916)264-2700

Population Profile

Metropolitan Area Residents

1980: 1,100,000
1990: 1,481,102
2000: 1,796,857
Percent change, 1990–2000: 21.3%
U.S. rank in 1980: 32nd
U.S. rank in 1990: 26th
U.S. rank in 2000: 24th (Sacramento/Yolo CMSA)

City Residents

1980: 275,741
1990: 369,365
2000: 407,018
2003 estimate: 445,335
Percent change, 1990–2000: 3.0%
U.S. rank in 1980: 52nd
U.S. rank in 1990: 41st
U.S. rank in 2000: 49th

Density: 4,189.2 people per square mile (in 2000)

Racial and ethnic characteristics (2000)
  White: 196,549
  Black or African American: 62,968
  American Indian and Alaska Native: 5,300
  Asian: 67,635
  Native Hawaiian and Pacific Islander: 3,861
  Hispanic or Latino (may be of any race): 87,974
  Other: 70,705

Percent of residents born in state: 56.5% (2000)

Age characteristics (2000)
  Population under 5 years old: 29,066
  Population 5 to 9 years old: 32,864
  Population 10 to 14 years old: 31,465
  Population 15 to 19 years old: 29,863
  Population 20 to 24 years old: 30,195
  Population 25 to 34 years old: 63,321
  Population 35 to 44 years old: 61,483
  Population 45 to 54 years old: 52,118

  Population 55 to 59 years old: 16,783
  Population 60 to 64 years old: 13,417
  Population 65 to 74 years old: 23,052
  Population 75 to 84 years old: 17,312
  Population 85 years and older: 6,079
  Median age: 32.8 years

Births (2002, Sacramento County)
  Total number: 19,243

Deaths (2002, Sacramento County)
  Total number: 9,578 (of which, 170 were infants under the age of 1 year)

Money income (1999)
  Per capita income: $18,721
  Median household income: $37,048
  Total households: 154,893

Number of households with income of . . .
  less than $10,000: 18,437
  $10,000 to $14,999: 11,745
  $15,000 to $24,999: 21,372
  $25,000 to $34,999: 21,285
  $35,000 to $49,999: 26,118
  $50,000 to $74,999: 28,775
  $75,000 to $99,999: 12,605
  $100,000 to $149,999: 10,170
  $150,000 to $199,999: 2,374
  $200,000 or more: 2,012

Percent of families below poverty level: 15.3% (46.7% of which were female householder families with related children under 5 years)

2002 FBI Crime Index Total: 30,780

Municipal Government

Sacramento has a council-manager form of government. The council is comprised a mayor elected at large, and eight council members elected by district; all serve staggered four-year terms. A city manager is hired by the council.

Suburban growth after World War II outpaced the city's ability to annex land (county residents consistently defeated city efforts to annex). The result has been that two-thirds of Sacramento's residents live outside the borders of any incorporated city. Urbanized areas, therefore, are still governed by a system designed for rural counties.

Head Official: Mayor Heather Fargo (since 2000)

Total Number of City Employees: 4,695 (2004)

City Information: City Hall, 915 I Street, Suite 205, Sacramento, CA 95814; telephone (916)264-5407

Economy

Major Industries and Commercial Activity

Sacramento began as a city rich from gold and railroad money. Productive mines still operate in the area, and the city remains an important transportation center. Sacramento's deep-water port, connected to the San Francisco Bay via a 43-mile channel, is an important West Coast hub for the handling of cargo from ocean-going ships. As the junction of the state's major railroad, the Southern Pacific Transportation Company, Sacramento maintains its position at the top of the rail transportation industry. As state capitol of California, Sacramento's largest employment sector has historically been federal, state, and local government. As is true of California in general, the Sacramento area is rich in agriculture; products of the fertile Sacramento Valley region include fruits and vegetables, rice and other grains, meat, beet sugar, and almonds.

Today the city's economy is broadly based. Government and transportation are the largest sectors of employment in the area, and agriculture and mining—while still important in the region—have been surpassed by information, technology service, leisure and hospitality, education and health services, and construction. Technology-related companies such as Intel and Hewlett-Packard are among the Sacramento area's largest employers; proximity to research centers, and a well-educated labor pool, have drawn such companies to the area. Sacramento's fastest-growing employment areas in the early 2000s include financial activities, professional and business services, and education and health services.

Items and goods produced: high-technology items, medical equipment and other health-related products, dairy products, feeds, meat, brick and clay products, mining equipment, lumber boxes

Incentive Programs—New and Existing Companies

Local programs—A number of organizations work to attract and assist businesses in the Sacramento area. Among them are the Sacramento Metro Chamber of Commerce, the Downtown Development Group, and the Sacramento Area Commerce and Trade Organization (SACTO). Sacramento's Economic Development Department and its partners offers loan programs to assist the development of small businesses. The city of Sacramento's facade rebate programs help businesses pay for building improvements; the city also offers business incentives to businesses located

within Sacramento's three Urban Enterprise Zones and two LAMBRA areas. The Recycling Market Development Zone program offers incentives to small and medium-sized manufacturing businesses. The Sacramento Municipal Utility District, California's largest customer-owned utility, offers discounts for new and expanding businesses.

State programs—California's Commerce & Economic Development Program offers financial solutions by helping businesses secure capital to invest in major public, private, and nonprofit ventures; providing export assistance and financing; and supporting small businesses by offering financial assistance, training, and technical assistance.

Job training programs—The Sacramento Training and Response Team (START), a partnership of 11 job assistance and training programs, helps companies recruit, train, and hire employees.

Development Projects

Sacramento's healthy economy is reflected in the city's numerous recent development projects. Developments in Sacramento's downtown area include: a five-story, 200,000 square foot expansion of City Hall, to be completed in 2005; new hotels including a 32-story hotel that opened in 2001, an 8-story hotel that opened the following year, and a 239-room hotel scheduled to open in 2005; and construction of the Wells Fargo Pavilion, a 2,500-seat theater that replaces the Music Circus tent. Two of Sacramento's medical centers—University of California at Davis Medical Center and Kaiser Permanente's South Sacramento Hospital—are currently undergoing massive expansions.

Economic Development Information: Sacramento Metro Chamber of Commerce, 917 Seventh Street, Sacramento, CA 95814; telephone (916)552-6808; fax (916)443-2672

Commercial Shipping

With an international airport, rail hub, seaport, and junction of three freeways within ten miles of downtown, Sacramento is ideally situated for commercial shipping. Inland 85 miles from San Francisco, the Port of Sacramento admits international ocean-going vessels through a deep-water channel connecting it with San Francisco Bay. The port's specialty is handling dry-bulk cargos, and it utilizes the most modern equipment on the West Coast for that purpose. The city is served by three major rail lines. Union Pacific Railroad is the largest railroad in North America; its J. R. Davis Yard, in Sacramento County, is the largest rail facility on the west coast. More than 500 motor freight carriers serve the Sacramento area.

Labor Force and Employment Outlook

Employers have access to a large and well-educated labor pool. The Sacramento region's economy is among the strongest in California, and job growth has remained positive in the early 2000s. During 2003-2004, the area known as the Sacramento Region (comprised of 6 counties) gained more than 7,700 jobs; in comparison, the nearby San Francisco Bay Region lost more than 126,000 jobs in that timeframe. Government employment is the largest employment sector in the area. Among California's 471,000 government employees, nearly 25 percent are employed in the Sacramento area.

The following is a summary of data regarding the Sacramento/Arden-Arcade/Roseville area labor force, 2004 annual averages.

Size of non-agricultural labor force: 856,100

Number of workers employed in . . .
  natural resources and mining: 600
  construction: 70,300
  manufacturing: 47,000
  trade, transportation, and utilities: 146,200
  information: 20,900
  financial activities: 60,000
  professional and business services: 97,500
  educational and health services: 84,400
  leisure and hospitality: 79,400
  other services: 28,300
  government: 221,000

Average hourly earnings of production workers employed in manufacturing: $15.01

Unemployment rate: 5.4% (January 2005)

Largest employers
(non-government):   *Number of employees*
  UC Davis Medical Center   8,500
  Intel   6,500
  Sacramento City Unified School
    District   6,000
  Hewlett-Packard Co.   4,500

Cost of Living

Sacramento's housing prices relative to San Francisco and southern California have been kept low by an abundance of cheap land.

The following is a summary of data regarding several key cost of living factors for the Sacramento area.

2004 (3rd Quarter) ACCRA Average House Price: Not reported

2004 (3rd Quarter) ACCRA Cost of Living Index: Not reported (U.S. average = 100.0)

State income tax rate: Ranges from 1.0% to 9.3%

State sales tax rate: 6.0% (food and prescription drugs are exempt)

Local income tax rate: none

Local sales tax rate: 1.75%

Property tax rate: 1.0% of total assessed value

Economic Information: Sacramento Metro Chamber of Commerce, 917 Seventh Street, Sacramento, CA 95814; telephone (916)552-6808; fax (916)443-2672

Education and Research

Elementary and Secondary Schools

The Sacramento City Unified School District, among the largest in the state, is Sacramento's primary school district and has a student enrollment of 52,850 in its 80 schools as of the 2002-2003 school year. Other districts in Sacramento are: Grant Joint Union High, with 12,682 students in 14 schools; Natomas Unified, 7,653 students in 10 schools; North Sacramento Elementary, 5,552 students in 11 schools; Robla Elementary, 2,323 students in 5 schools; Del Paso Heights, 2,155 students in 5 schools; and California Education Authority, 214 students in one school.

The following is a summary of data regarding the Sacramento City Unified School District as of the 2002-2003 school year.

Total enrollment: 52,850

Number of facilities
  elementary schools: 64
  middle schools: 8
  senior high schools: 14

Student/teacher ratio: 21.2:1

Teacher salaries
  minimum: $36,408
  maximum: $67,918

Funding per pupil: $7,414 (2000-2001 school year)

Sacramento also has 84 private and parochial schools.

Public Schools Information: Sacramento City Unified School District, 5735 47th Avenue, Sacramento, CA 95824; telephone (916)643-7400

Colleges and Universities

Sacramento is home to a number of colleges and universities. Four-year institutions include California State University (CSU), with an enrollment of approximately 25,700 students. CSU has the following academic divisions: Arts and Letters; Business Administration; Education; Engineering and Computer Science; Health and Human Services; Natural Sciences and Mathematics; Social Sciences and Interdisciplinary Studies; and Continuing Education. CSU offers 60 undergraduate degree programs and 40 graduate programs. Golden Gate University, which offers undergraduate and graduate programs in business and management, information technology, taxation, and law, has a Sacramento campus (its main campus is in San Francisco). Nearby is the University of California at Davis, which boasts a highly regarded medical center—the primary teaching facility of the university's School of Medicine—located in Sacramento. A new $40 million education building for 200 first- and second-year medical students at the center that will double the number of students on campus and is scheduled for completion in 2006. Two-year colleges in Sacramento are American River, Cosumnes River, and Sacramento City colleges.

Libraries and Research Centers

The Sacramento Public Library operates a 160,000-square-foot Central Library that opened plus 25 branches and bookmobiles. Holdings include 1.8 million volumes and 3,952 periodical subscriptions, plus audio and video tapes, recordings, maps, and art reproductions. Among the special collections are Californiana, the history of printing, and city planning and urban development. One of the library branches, 38-year-old Carmichael Library, is currently closed and undergoing a $6.8 million renovation and expansion that will increase its square footage from 5,905 to 19,490; the library is scheduled to reopen in summer of 2006.

The California State University, Sacramento, Library holds 1.2 million volumes, 4,444 e-books, nearly 5,000 periodical subscriptions, 12,847 audio/visual materials, plus maps and government documents. Sacramento is also the headquarters of the California State Library with special collections of federal and state government documents; its holdings include 777,509 volumes. The Braille and Talking Book Library has 55,000 titles and 15 periodical subscriptions.

The Western Ecological Research Center (WERC), which has 14 field stations in California and one in Nevada, is headquartered in Sacramento. WERC offers its clients and partners the research and technology needed to support the management of Pacific Southwestern ecosystems. WERC's scientists are experts in such fields as herpetology, conservation biology, wetlands ecology, and ecological restoration. The research centers and institutes of the nearby University of California at Davis (UC) perform research in a wide variety of areas such as food safety and cleaner fuel technologies. UC Davis's renowned Health System, which is based in Sacramento, has more than 550 research studies—including basic science, translational, and clinical research—underway as of early 2005. The center has performed cutting edge research in such areas as autism and cancer. Other research centers in the Sacramento area conduct inquiries in such fields as natural history and grain studies.

Public Library Information: Sacramento Public Library, 828 I Street, Sacramento, CA 95814-3576; telephone (916)264-2770

Health Care

Sacramento is well served by medical care facilities. The acclaimed University of California at Davis Medical Center is located in Sacramento. Its 141-acre campus includes a 528-bed hospital. Originally founded in 1852 as Sacramento County Hospital, it was acquired by the university and renamed The University of California, Davis Medical Center in 1973. The campus's Shriner's Hospital for Children, providing pediatric care in three specialty programs—orthopaedics, spinal cord injury treatment and rehabilitation, and acute burn treatment and rehabilitation—was built in 1997. The medical center is the region's only Level I comprehensive adult and pediatric trauma center. Specialty services include a Trauma Service that utilizes Life Flight; a Burn Center; a kidney transplant service; a regional poison control center; a corneal transplant service; a regional mental health program; an extensive family practice program; a Neonatal Intensive Care Unit; a comprehensive rehabilitation center; and seven specialized intensive care units including a Neurological Surgery Intensive Care Unit. The medical center is undergoing a $6.1 million addition to its Cancer Center, scheduled for completion in 2005, and has several other development projects in the works. The expansion, at a cost of more than $400 million, is expected to be completed by 2012.

Sutter Medical Center, Sacramento, includes Sutter General Hospital, Sutter Memorial Hospital, and Sutter Center for Psychiatry. In 2003, Sutter Memorial Hospital and Sutter General Hospital became the first hospitals on the West Coast to begin utilizing electronic ICU with advanced video and electronic monitoring as a remote high-tech surveillance system of their most critically ill patients. Among the specialties of the hospitals are critical care, neuroscience, renal dialysis, respiratory rehabilitation, spinal care, and urology. Sutter Center for Psychiatry provides psychiatric and mental health services to adults, adolescents and children age five and older. Mercy General Hospital, operated by Catholic Healthcare West, offers specialty services that include a birth center, eye and heart institutes, and orthopedic, neuroscience, spine, and rehabilitation services. Kaiser Permanente has launched an expansion of its South Sacramento hospital, which will add 200,000 square feet to the hospital complex. The project includes a five-story hospital tower with 81 new hospital beds; a two-story outpatient surgery building; a four-story parking structure; a helicopter pad; and a new, single-story emergency department building. The outpatient surgery center is projected to open in mid-2008, followed by completion of the hospital addition in 2009.

Recreation

Sightseeing

Sacramento is a river town, virtually created by the California Gold Rush. Along the bank of the Sacramento River is the Old Sacramento Historic Area, a 28-acre National Historic Landmark that attracts more than 5 million visitors annually. This atmospheric area, with wooden-slat sidewalks and horse-drawn carriages on its cobblestone streets, gives the visitor a sense of the vitality and bustle generated by the thousands of hopeful prospectors who streamed through Sacramento in the mid-nineteenth century. Old Sacramento's museums, shops, and restaurants preserve its historical character. The Old Sacramento Waterfront offers a variety of activities, including touring and riding on nineteenth-century boats, visiting the depots of the Central Pacific railroad, and exploring the bustling Public Market. In midtown Sacramento, Sutter's Fort, the first Euro-American settlement in Sacramento, has been restored and preserved. The 1839 adobe fort contains relics of pioneer and goldrush days. Exhibits include living quarters, a blacksmith shop, a bakery, a prison, and livestock areas. The State Capitol building within 40-acre Capitol Park was built in 1869; it is similar in style to the U.S. Capitol building. Underneath its 120-foot high rotunda are ornate chandeliers, imposing staircases, and marble floors. Visitors can tour the offices of the Governor, Attorney General, Secretary of State, and Treasurer, and view exhibits about the history of California's state government. In Sacramento's south side, the Sacramento City Cemetery, established in 1849, contains the graves of more than 25,000 pioneers, immigrants, their families, and descendants; among its first interments were more than 600 victims of the 1850 Cholera Epidemic.

The Sacramento Zoo displays more than 400 exotic animals in their natural settings, including red pandas, snow leopards, lemurs, zebras, chimpanzees, jaguars, and many others. The zoo emphasizes protection of endangered animals, and faithful recreation of natural habitats. Adjacent to the zoo is Fairytale Town for children, a park based on themes from fairy tales and nursery rhymes. Water World USA, the only wave pool in Northern California, has the highest water slides in the West; its "Honolulu Halfpipe" Extreme Surf Slide is scheduled to open in 2005.

Sacramento is within easy driving distance of other atmospheric Gold Country towns: Coloma has Marshall Gold Discovery State Historic Park, where James Marshall's discovery of gold in 1848 started the Gold Rush; Placerville features Hangtown's Gold Bug Mine, a fully-lighted mine shaft; Sutter Creek has a charming array of Victorian homes and balconied buildings; Jackson retains a European character from its early Italian- and Serbian-American miners; Columbia has Columbia State Historic Park, where visitors can ride a stagecoach and pan for gold. Sacramento is conveniently located for day trips to Northern California's outdoor attractions. The city is only a few hours away from Yosemite National Park; from the Napa-Sonoma Valley, where most of California's finest wines are produced; and from Lake Tahoe.

Arts and Culture

Sacramento is rich in theater. California's largest nonprofit musical theatre—The California Musical Theatre, formerly known as Sacramento Light Opera Association or SLOA—is based here. It provides Music Circus productions during the summer and Broadway Series productions during the rest of the year. Since its first performance in 1951, Music Circus has staged numerous productions of some 150 musicals; classics such as *The King and I, Oklahoma!,* and *Show Boat* are well represented. Music Circus presented its music theatre under a circus-style open-air tent until its move in 2003 to the new 2,200-seat Wells Fargo Pavilion. Performances are in the round, with 360-degree seating. California Musical Theatre's Broadway Series, begun in 1989, offers Broadway hits with national stars. Productions are at the 2,452-seat Sacramento Community Center Theater, across from the Capitol building.

The 24th Street Theatre, a 296-seat auditorium at the Sierra 2 Center for the Arts and Community, is home to the Light Opera Theatre of Sacramento (LOTS), which brings light opera, such as the works of Gilbert and Sullivan, to the Sacramento area. The Sacramento Theater Company maintains its own resident company offering classical and modern plays at its 300-seat Mainstage and 85-seat Stage Two. The B Street Theatre, Sacramento's Professional New Works Theatre Company, produces contemporary theatrical works. Garbeau's Dinner Theatre, in nearby Rancho Cordova, is housed in a restored winery. In all, more than 80 groups present live theatrical performances throughout the region.

For music lovers, the all-volunteer Camellia Symphony season runs from October through mid-May, and includes six concerts (one of which, at the Sunrise Mall on Mother's Day, is free), and several special fundraising concerts. The Sacramento Opera has performed more than 40 operas; the opera season runs from September to March and includes 3 performances. The 73-member Sacramento Philharmonic presents 5 concerts annually from November through May.

The Sacramento Ballet, comprised of 22 artists, 8 apprentices, and 4 trainees, performs both classical and contemporary ballet. They present 5 performance series annually.

Sacramento is home to the oldest art museum in the West. Established in 1873, the Crocker Art Museum's permanent collection features European paintings by such masters as Rembrandt and Bruegel; a renowned collection of drawings; Indian and Persian miniature paintings; American (especially Californian) paintings; decorative arts and ceramics; photography; and contemporary art. The California State Railroad Museum displays the history of the railroads and makes special note of the fact that Sacramento was once the terminus of the transcontinental railroad. The 100,000 square-foot museum displays 21 locomotives and railroad cars, half of which may be walked through, as well as 46 exhibits. On weekends between April and September, visitors can ride the Museum's Sacramento Southern Railroad on a six-mile route along the Sacramento River. The Discovery Museum features interactive history, science, and technology exhibits examining the evolution of everyday life in Sacramento, on such topics as the gold rush and other periods of local California history, the history of the Sacramento Valley's topomorphology, and food processing technology. The Towe Auto Museum explores car culture and automotive history, and has more than 150 vintage automobiles on display. The State Indian Museum, on the grounds of Sutter's Fort, displays the jewelry, art, clothing, baskets, and other artifacts of the native Americans who lived in the area.

Festivals and Holidays

Sacramento Jazz Jubilee, the world's largest congregation of jazz bands, takes place during Memorial Day weekend; it features more than 100 bands and attracts more than 100,000 listeners. The Bridge to Bridge Waterfront Festival in July is a two-day event featuring boat races, boating exhibitors, and Coast Guard and wakeboard demonstrations. From mid-August through early September Sacramento hosts the California State Fair, one of the largest agricultural fairs in the country, at the California Exposition; the fair's features include a concert series, rides, horse racing, numerous competitions, extreme sports demonstrations, indoor and outdoor exhibits and shows, and a kids park. During the four-day Gold Rush Days festival over Labor Day weekend, the

Gold Rush era is recreated in Old Sacramento, with historic characters, covered wagons and horse-drawn carriages, street dramas, musicians, dancers, arts and crafts, and exhibits; the streets of Old Sacramento are covered with dirt and only horse-drawn vehicles are permitted. The California International Marathon in December starts in Folsom and ends at the Sacramento State Capitol building.

Sports for the Spectator

The NBA Sacramento Kings and WNBA Sacramento Monarchs bring professional basketball to Sacramento; they play at Arco Arena, a 442,000 square foot venue that seats 17,317. The Kings won Pacific Division titles in 2001-02 and 2002-03, and advanced to the 2002 Western Conference Finals. In 2000, professional minor league baseball returned to Sacramento after a 27-year absence when the Sacramento River Cats, formerly the Vancouver Canadians, moved to 11,092-seat Raley Field. The River Cats have won four Pacific Coast League South Division titles (in 2000, 2001, 2003, and 2004) and PCL Championships in 2003 and 2004. Professional tennis is represented by the Capitals of the World TeamTennis League. As of 2005, the 20-year-old team has been five-time champion of the World TeamTennis (WTT) League Championship and King Trophy. The Sacramento State Hornets are among the Sacramento area's college sports teams.

Sports for the Participant

Sacramento, the "River City," provides many forms of water recreation. The American River offers boating, swimming, and calm- and white-water rafting. Nearby Folsom Lake and Lake Natoma offer sailing and windsurfing. All the waters in the Sacramento area are stocked with fish; king salmon run in the American and Sacramento Rivers. The American River Bike Trail, stretching from Sacramento's Discovery Park to Folsom Lake, provides nearly 35 miles of scenic trail used by cyclists, walkers, joggers, and bird watchers. More than 120 city parks dot Sacramento encompassing over 2,000 acres, and Sacramento is roughly two hours from five national forests. The Sacramento area's municipal golf courses comprise 540 acres. Sacramento has several equestrian centers and many horseback riding trails. More than two dozen ski resorts, most within 120 miles, are located in the nearby Sierra-Nevada Mountains.

Shopping and Dining

Sacramento is home to several shopping malls and hundreds of boutiques and specialty shops. Old Sacramento is a popular and atmospheric shopping area; its Public Market is a European-style, open-air market featuring bakeries, fish, poultry, meat, produce, flowers, and assorted ethnic shops. Other major shopping areas in Sacramento include: Downtown Plaza, with more than 150 shops, many restaurants, and a cinema; Town and Country Village with 55 shops was built in 1946, making it Sacramento's oldest shopping center; Arden Fair has more than 150 shops, restaurants, a cinema, and foodcourt; Pavilions offers cosmopolitan shopping and fine dining; Sunrise Mall and Florin Mall each have approximately 100 shops and restaurants and a cinema; and Folsom Premium Outlets has more than 80 stores.

Restaurants are plentiful in Sacramento, featuring cuisine ranging from traditional American, to inventive Californian, to a wide variety of ethnic fare. Many eateries are concentrated in Old Sacramento, as well as along J Street and Capitol Avenue between 19th and 29th streets, and Fair Oaks Boulevard between Howe and Fulton streets.

Visitor Information: Sacramento Convention and Visitors Bureau, 1608 I Street, Sacramento, CA 95814; telephone (916)808-7777.

Convention Facilities

The principal meeting place is the Sacramento Convention Center, located downtown. The complex contains three buildings: the 134,000 square foot Exhibit Hall can be divided into 5 areas and is equipped with risers to create arena seating for 6,500 people; the elegant 25,000-square-foot Ballroom, which can be divided into 10 meeting rooms, accommodates 1,500 people banquet-style or 2,500 theater-style; and the 11,200-square-foot Activity Building features 12 meeting rooms. Nearby Memorial Auditorium, built in 1926 and registered as a historic landmark, provides convertible meeting space with a total capacity of 4,500 people; the building contains Memorial Hall, the Little Theater, and meeting rooms. The Convention Center and Memorial Hall are located within walking distance of hotels, shops, restaurants, and points of interest.

Located five miles from downtown is the California Exposition (Cal Expo), a large facility with more than 200,000 square feet of exhibit space on a 780-acre site. Designed for events such as agricultural shows and trade conventions, the center provides outdoor exhibit areas and unlimited parking.

Hotels and motels in the metropolitan area, providing more than 10,000 rooms, offer meeting facilities for large and small groups.

Convention Information: Sacramento Convention and Visitors Bureau, 1608 I Street, Sacramento, CA 95814; telephone (916)808-7777.

Transportation

Approaching the City

The Sacramento International Airport, 12 miles northwest of downtown, receives service from 13 major carriers and one commuter airline. Also in Sacramento, the Executive Airport serves private planes.

The primary north-south routes to Sacramento are I-5 (the Pan American Highway) and U.S. 99; the major east-west routes are I-80 and U.S. 50, connecting Sacramento to San Francisco to the southwest, and Lake Tahoe to the northeast.

Passenger train service is available through Amtrak. Boat/bus excursions are offered between Sacramento and San Francisco.

Traveling in the City

Most of Sacramento's downtown streets are one-way, with a synchronized traffic light system. The major thoroughfares are the freeways: Interstate 80 and Business 80, which run from the west to the northeast, and Interstate 5, which runs north and south. Other important roads are the Garden Highway, running east and west, and State Highway 99, coming from the southern part of the city to join Business 80. In downtown Sacramento, the streets running east and west are named by letter; streets running north and south are designated by number.

Sacramento Regional Transit Company (RT) operates more than 250 buses on 80 area bus routes. The RT also owns the electrically powered light rail system, which consists of 76 light rail vehicles traversing 30 miles of light rail, connecting the suburbs with downtown. The bus and rail systems are accessible to the disabled community. In 2002, the systems served 27 million passengers.

Communications

Newspapers and Magazines

Sacramento offers one major daily newspaper, the morning *The Sacramento Bee*. Sacramento's second largest newspaper is the *Sacramento News and Review*, a weekly alternative paper. There are also a number of ethnic newspapers, including Italian, Spanish, and Jewish publications. *The Sacramento Observer* is considered one of the finest African American newspapers in the country. The *Sacramento Business Journal* reports on happenings in business and industry. *Sacramento Magazine* highlights local entertainment and lifestyles. Nearly 30 magazines and journals are published in Sacramento.

Television and Radio

One public and eight commercial television stations, representing ABC, CBS, NBC, FOX, UPN, WB, Telemundo, and Univision, broadcast in Sacramento, where cable is also available. In the Sacramento area, 41 AM and FM radio stations broadcast music, news, talk, Spanish, and Christian programming.

Media Information: The Sacramento Bee, 2100 Q Street, Sacramento, CA 95852; telephone (916)321-1000

Sacramento Online

City of Sacramento Home Page. Available www.cityof sacramento.org

Metro Sacramento Chamber. Available www.metrochamber .org

Sacramento Bee. Available www.sacbee.com

Sacramento City Unified School District. Available www .scusd.edu

Sacramento Convention & Visitors Bureau. Available www .sacramentocvb.org

Sacramento Public Library. Available www.saclibrary.org

Selected Bibliography

Kelley, Robert Lloyd, *Battling the Inland Sea: American Political Culture, Public Policy, and the Sacramento Valley, 1850–1986* (Berkeley: University of California Press, 1989)

San Diego

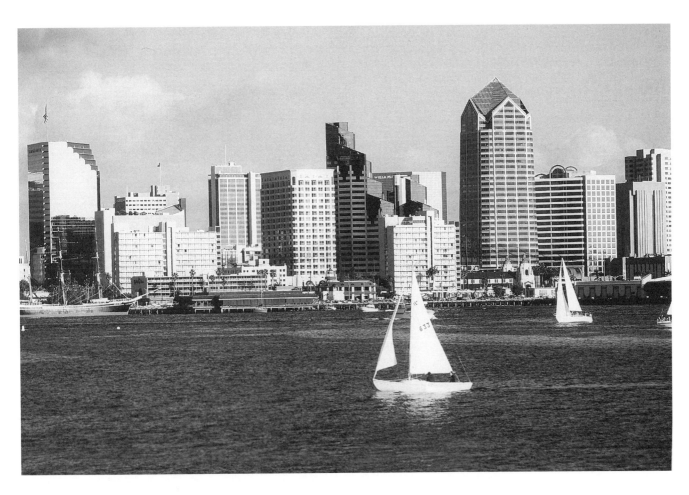

The City in Brief

Founded: 1769 (incorporated, 1850)

Head Official: Mayor Dick Murphy (R) (since 2000)

City Population
  1980: 875,538
  1990: 1,110,623
  2000: 1,223,400
  2003 estimate: 1,266,753
  Percent change, 1990–2000: 10.1%
  U.S. rank in 1980: 8th
  U.S. rank in 1990: 6th
  U.S. rank in 2000: 11th

Metropolitan Area Population
  1980: 1,862,000
  1990: 2,498,016
  2000: 2,813,833

  Percent change, 1990–2000: 12.6%
  U.S. rank in 1980: 19th
  U.S. rank in 1990: 15th
  U.S. rank in 2000: 17th

Area: 324.3 square miles (2000)
Elevation: Ranges from sea level to 1,591 feet above sea level
Average Annual Temperature: 63.2° F
Average Annual Precipitation: 9.32 inches

Major Economic Sectors: Manufacturing, government, services, agriculture
Unemployment Rate: 4.6% (January 2005)
Per Capita Income: $23,609 (1999)

2002 FBI Crime Index Total: 50,124

Major Colleges and Universities: University of California San Diego, University of San Diego, San Diego State University, Scripps Institution of Oceanography

Daily Newspapers: *The San Diego Union-Tribune*

TO DEL MAR

MINGEI INT'L MUSEUM

LA JOLLA BAY

SAN DIEGO MUSEUM OF CONTEMPORARY ART

LA JOLLA

TORREY PINES

LA JOLLA

BIRD ROCK

FALSE POINT

LORING

PACIFIC BEACH

CRYSTAL PIER

MISSION BAY

52

BALBOA

?

AERO

15

MISSION SAN DIEGO DE ALCALA

MISSION VILLAGE

PACIFIC OCEAN

FIESTA ISLAND

VACATION ISLAND

SEA WORLD

SAN DIEGO

163

805

FRIARS

QUALCOMM STADIUM

MISSION

INGRAHAM

MISSION BEACH

STADIUM

8

JUNIPER SERRA MUSEUM

JUAN

OLD TOWN

FT. STOCKTON

WASHINGTON

UNIVERSITY

4TH AVE.

5TH AVE.

ADAMS

EL CAJON

30TH ST.

BALBOA PARK

SAN DIEGO SPORTS ARENA

SUNSET CLIFFS

ROSECRANS

OCEAN BEACH

5

MUSEUM OF ART

LAUREL

SAN DIEGO ZOO

MUSEUM OF NAT. HIST.

MUSEUM OF PHOTOGRAPHIC ARTS

HALL OF CHAMPIONS

PACIFIC RELATIONS

POINT LOMA

NIMITZ

SAN DIEGO INT'L AIRPORT

HARBOR

SAN DIEGO AEROSPACE MUSEUM

BALBOA STADIUM

POINT LOMA COLLEGE

CATALINA

HARBOR ISLAND

MARITIME MUSEUM

SANTE FE TRAIN DEPOT

SAN DIEGO CITY COLLEGE

94

SHELTER ISLAND

BROADWAY

SPRECKELS THEATRE

GASLAMP DISTRICT

30TH ST.

MARKET

CONV. CTR.

SEAPORT VILLAGE

HARBOR

IMPERIAL

COMMERCIAL

POINT LOMA

MCLAIN

ALAMEDA

CORONADO

ORANGE

75

OCEAN VIEW

NATIONAL

5

N

SILVER STRAND

CABRILLO NAT'L MONUMENT

MAIN

TO TIJUANA

SAN DIEGO BAY

SILVER STRAND STATE BEACH

NATIONAL CITY

0 1 2 3

KILOMETERS

MILES 1 2 3 4

OR

ID

WY

NEVADA

UTAH

CO

CALIFORNIA

ARIZONA

NM

San Diego

MEXICO

Introduction

San Diego, "the Birthplace of California," is a city of many guises. It is not only a major naval base and an important natural harbor, but it is also a top tourist attraction and resort area, a prominent high-technology, aerospace, and aviation production community, and a fertile agricultural area. San Diego's port and its proximity to Mexico give the city an international flavor, and a revitalized downtown area adds to the exciting atmosphere. The mild climate attracts many new residents and industries each year. A nondescript town until the 1940s, San Diego now has more than 1.2 million residents and is California's second largest city. San Diego's phenomenal growth has brought it well-deserved national attention. The city keeps this growth balanced by careful preservation of history and a strong emphasis on art, culture, and recreation.

Geography and Climate

San Diego is just 20 miles north of Mexico, situated in the rolling hills and mesas that rise from the Pacific shore to join with the Laguna Mountains to the east. Its bay is one of the country's finest natural harbors. The city covers a large area of vastly different terrain: miles of ocean and bay shoreline, densely forested hills, fertile valleys, and mountains, canyons, and desert. The climate varies in a similar manner. On the coast, the temperatures are mild and constant, while in the desert areas, the temperature can fluctuate as much as 30 degrees in one day. San Diego is about 120 miles south of Los Angeles.

The climate in San Diego is tempered by the Pacific Ocean air, keeping the summers cool and the winters warm. Severe weather is rare in the area; snow is almost unknown, and the city averages only three thunderstorms a year. September and October often bring hot eastern winds from the desert, producing what are usually the hottest days of the year.

Area: 324.3 square miles (2000)

Elevation: Ranges from sea level to 1,591 feet above sea level

Average Temperatures: January, 55.4° F; August, 72.2° F; annual average, 63.2° F

Average Annual Precipitation: 9.32 inches

History

Spanish, Mexicans, Americans Lay Claim to San Diego Region

Portuguese explorer Juan Rodriguez Cabrillo, the discoverer of California, sailed into what is now San Diego Bay and claimed the surrounding region for the King of Spain in 1542. The bay was named in 1602 by another Spanish explorer, Don Sebastian Viscaino. The first European settlement there was established in 1769, when the Franciscan fathers established a mission on a hill overlooking the bay, close to a large Native American village. The mission was the first in a chain of twenty-one that the sect built throughout California. The mission was burned down by the local tribes and later almost completely destroyed by an earthquake, but the determined Franciscans rebuilt each time. Today, the restored mission still conducts Mass every Sunday.

By the 1830s, a small but thriving trading village had developed on the bay, in the district now called "Old Town." The town was an important shipping point for cattle hide and quarried stone. The famous cobblestone streets of Boston are said to have been paved with San Diego stone. San Diego became the capital of Mexican California after Mexico achieved independence from Spain in 1822. It was a much fought-over prize during the Mexican War, changing hands numerous times before the U.S. Army established permanent American rule in late 1846. The town was incorporated as a city in 1850.

City Thrives, Declines, Thrives Again

Throughout the next twenty years the town was an important whaling port. Then in 1867, San Francisco land-developer Alonzo E. Horton bought a 1,000-acre plot of what was to become downtown San Diego. Horton laid out streets, built a wharf and a hotel, and donated land for churches. A gold strike in 1870 and numerous land booms in the area increased the population rapidly. In 1885, when the Santa Fe Railroad and a number of eastern investors arrived, 40,000 people lived in the city.

By the turn of the century, however, San Diego was plunged into a slump. Failed businesses and unwise real estate speculations caused the population to dwindle to 17,000 people. The city began a period of slow, steady growth, helped by the Panama-California Exposition in celebration of the completion of the Panama Canal in 1915. The fledgling aircraft industry, which found the desert climate and terrain an ideal testing environment, also aided San Diego's recovery. An aggressive policy of attracting new people and industry contributed to growth, but the city remained relatively obscure, overshadowed by Los Angeles and San Francisco to the north.

City Becomes Naval Base; Rise of Agriculture and Industry

Japan's bombing of Honolulu's Pearl Harbor at the beginning of World War II forced the U.S. Navy to seek another suitable Pacific base. They chose San Diego, and almost overnight the city became a busy military center, home base for a large number of naval trainees, many of whom relocated to the city as civilians after the war. In the post-war era the city emerged as the headquarters of the Eleventh Naval District and the Naval Air Command; installations include major U.S. Navy and Marine training centers, the West Coast's main supply depot, a naval hospital and laboratories, and a large fleet stationed in the bay. Along with the military came related support industries and a large number of naval and aviation defense contractors.

Growth begun during World War II has continued unabated. San Diego spread to extend almost 20 miles in each direction, developing small, distinct communities in the nearby canyons and valleys; these areas retain a separate identity while being incorporated into San Diego. With this growth came diversity. To the south, San Diego connects with a rich agricultural area that produces much of California's famous fruit and vegetable produce, shipped worldwide from the easily accessible port. To the north the wealthy leisure class developed a resort community of hotels, spectacular cliff homes, and recreational amenities. Throughout the city commercial and industrial corridors began growing, and many corporations moved their headquarters to the region.

Downtown Declines, Revives

During the 1960s and early 1970s the San Diego downtown area declined when businesses and residents moved to the suburbs in large numbers. The city's growth continued despite these problems, and by the mid-1970s San Diego had surpassed San Francisco as California's second largest city. An efficient freeway system and a coordinated effort by the Centre City Development Corporation—a comprehensive group of developers, financial experts, and civic leaders—kept the downtown area alive.

Today downtown San Diego is revitalized with new energy and is experiencing a renaissance as growth continues: as of 2004, more than 100 residential, commercial, retail, and entertainment development projects in San Diego's downtown area were underway or on the drawing board. Thoughtful planning has produced an impressive skyline of mirrored office towers blended with innovative shopping and residential developments, parks, and historic districts, all designed to serve the people who use them. Atria, attractive public

gathering spaces, and overhead walkways encourage visitors and residents alike to enjoy the downtown area.

Historical Information: San Diego Historical Society, Museum of San Diego History, 1649 El Prado, Balboa Park, San Diego, CA 92101; telephone (619)232-6203

Population Profile

Metropolitan Area Residents
1980: 1,862,000
1990: 2,498,016
2000: 2,813,833
Percent change, 1990–2000: 12.6%
U.S. rank in 1980: 19th
U.S. rank in 1990: 15th
U.S. rank in 2000: 17th

City Residents
1980: 875,538
1990: 1,110,623
2000: 1,223,400
2003 estimate: 1,266,753
Percent change, 1990–2000: 10.1%
U.S. rank in 1980: 8th
U.S. rank in 1990: 6th (State rank: 2nd)
U.S. rank in 2000: 11th (State rank: 2nd)

Density: 3,771.9 people per square mile (2000)

Racial and ethnic characteristics (2000)
   White: 736,207
   Black or African American: 96,216
   American Indian and Alaska Native: 7,543
   Asian: 166,968
   Native Hawaiian and Pacific Islander: 5,853
   Hispanic or Latino (may be of any race): 310,752
   Other: 210,613

Percent of residents born in state: 40.3% (2000)

Age characteristics (2000)
   Population under 5 years old: 82,523
   Population 5 to 9 years old: 87,347
   Population 10 to 14 years old: 79,520
   Population 15 to 19 years old: 85,664
   Population 20 to 24 years old: 110,614
   Population 25 to 34 years old: 217,032
   Population 35 to 44 years old: 198,474
   Population 45 to 54 years old: 148,127
   Population 55 to 59 years old: 48,016
   Population 60 to 64 years old: 38,075
   Population 65 to 74 years old: 65,922

Population 75 to 84 years old: 47,639
Population 85 years and older: 14,447
Median age: 32.5 years

Births (2002, San Diego County)
Total number: 43,951

Deaths (2002, San Diego County)
Total number: 19,356 (of which, 197 were infants under the age of 1 year)

Money income (2000)
Per capita income: $23,609
Median household income: $45,733
Total households: 451,126

Number of households with income of . . .
less than $10,000: 37,637
$10,000 to $14,999: 25,745
$15,000 to $24,999: 54,563
$25,000 to $34,999: 54,499
$35,000 to $49,999: 70,654
$50,000 to $74,999: 87,022
$75,000 to $99,999: 50,492
$100,000 to $149,999: 43,452
$150,000 to $199,999: 13,558
$200,000 or more: 13,502

Percent of families below poverty level: 10.6% (17.9% of which were female householder families with related children under 5 years)

2002 FBI Crime Index Total: 50,124

Municipal Government

San Diego uses a council-manager form of government, which it adopted in 1931. The mayor and eight council members are elected every four years, and they appoint the city manager.

Head Official: Mayor Dick Murphy (R) (since 2000; current term expires November 2008)

Total Number of City Employees: 11,085 (2004)

City Information: City Hall, 202 C Street, San Diego, CA 92101; telephone (619)236-5555

Economy

Major Industries and Commercial Activity

San Diego's economy, once dominated by military and defense endeavors (now the city's second largest economic sector) is led by manufacturing, particularly in the areas of shipbuilding and repair, industrial machinery and computers, metals production, and the manufacture of toys and sporting goods. In 2002, manufacturing contributed $25 billion to the county's economy. International trade is an important part of San Diego's economy, accounting for 37 percent of its manufacturing dollars. In 2001, goods moving through San Diego customs totaled $33.6 billion. The border between the San Diego area and Tijuana is the busiest in the world.

Since the founding of San Diego, the city's economy has been tied to San Diego Bay, a natural harbor which today is one of California's five major ports. It is an important link in the nation's international shipping trade; the port's two marine cargo facilities are the National City Marine Terminal, which is a primary port of entry for Honda, Acura, Volkswagen, Isuzu, Mitsubishi Fuso, and Hino Motors vehicles; and Tenth Avenue Marine Terminal, which handles a wide variety of commodities. The port also has a growing cruise ship operation, with more than 180 cruise ships docking annually.

San Diego's harbor has had the most significant impact on the local economy, however, through the Eleventh Naval District Headquarters, the base for the U.S. Navy Pacific fleet, which is located on the bay. San Diego is the Navy's principal location for West Coast and Pacific Ocean operations. Increases in military and homeland defense spending during the early 2000s has contributed to economic growth in San Diego. The military/defense industry is the city's second largest economic sector, bringing more than $13 billion into the local economy annually. The Marine Corps Base Camp Joseph H. Pendleton, the Marine Corps Recruit Depot, Marine Corps Air Station at Miramar, Naval Air Station North Island, Naval Station San Diego, and Naval Submarine Base, San Diego, are among San Diego's military installations.

With the San Diego Zoo and Sea World, a variety of historical and cultural attractions, and year-round good weather, San Diego is a top destination for tourists. In 2004, *Travel and Leisure* magazine ranked it America's second favorite city (behind Honolulu). San Diego's tourism industry is the third largest segment of its economy, with more than 26 million visitors to the county bringing more than $5.6 billion in annual revenues. Service industries have seen continued growth in recent years, specifically in areas such as dining, lodging, shopping and recreation services. San Diego regularly ranks as a top-10 U.S. vacation destination for international travelers.

The fourth largest segment of the economy is agriculture. San Diego County is the 20th largest agricultural producer in the nation. It is a top producer of nursery products, flowers, foliage plants, and avocados.

San Diego is a center for high technology and biotechnology. Nearly 160,000 high-technology workers are employed at 1,400 companies throughout San Diego. High technology growth areas include the biomedical, software, telecommunications and security sectors. Among all U.S. metropolitan areas, San Diego has the third largest concentration of biotech companies, with more than 32,000 biotech jobs at 499 companies.

Items and goods produced: acoustical materials, adhesives, airplane parts, bamboo, dairy products, electronics transmission and distribution equipment, plastic, rubber products, awnings, beverages, paper, clothing, dental products, detergents, computers, televisions

Incentive Programs—New and Existing Companies

Local programs—The city of San Diego offers permit and regulatory assistance, problem solving, regulatory reform, and project troubleshooting for large companies interested in expanding in the San Diego area. Most of these companies must be creating or retaining 200 or more jobs, generating $500,000 in annual revenue to the city, or be located in one of the City's three Enterprise Zones. The city's Business Cooperation Program offers incentives that can lower operating and facility costs for a variety of businesses. San Diego has 18 business improvement districts, 15 redevelopment project areas, 3 enterprise zones, a foreign trade zone, recycling market development zones, and a renewal community.

State programs—California's Commerce & Economic Development Program offers financial solutions by helping businesses secure capital to invest in major public, private, and nonprofit ventures; providing export assistance and financing; and supporting small businesses by offering financial assistance, training, and technical assistance.

Job training programs—The city of San Diego works closely with the San Diego Workforce Partnership, a nonprofit community corporation that supports the region's workforce and employers through education, training, and employment services.

Development Projects

Recent development highlights in San Diego include the expansion of the San Diego Convention Center, completed in 2001, and the construction of PETCO Park, which opened in 2004. The new 1.7 million square foot convention facility features 615,701 square feet of exhibit space. PETCO Park, home of the San Diego Padres, is located downtown and has 42,000 seats. In 2002, a $312.3 million program to build or improve 24 San Diego libraries was approved. As of 2004,

more than 100 residential, commercial, retail, and entertainment development projects in San Diego's downtown area were underway or on the drawing board.

Economic Development Information: City of San Diego Economic Development Division, 600 B Street, Suite 400, San Diego, CA 92101; telephone (619)533-4233; fax (619)533-5250; email sdbusiness@sandiego.gov

Commercial Shipping

The Port of San Diego handles hundreds of merchant ships each year; nearby Tijuana, Mexico, is also a duty-free port. The Burlington Northern Santa Fe (BNSF) railroad connects San Diego to major market areas. More than 80 trucking companies are established in metropolitan San Diego, providing freight, hauling, or equipment services. Air cargo services are maintained at San Diego International Airport, which handles more than 70,000 tons of cargo annually.

Labor Force and Employment Outlook

A large portion of the San Diego work force is derived from in-migration, creating a diverse population. In 2002, San Diego added nearly 20,000 jobs, while the nation as a whole experienced an economic recession. Among the three occupations expected to see the most growth in San Diego in the near future, all are in the information technology field. A 2005 report by the San Diego Workforce Partnership indicates that the occupations with the highest growth rate between 2001-2008 are expected to be computer support specialists (57.9 percent growth), network and computer systems administrators (51.9 percent), and network systems and data communications analysts (50.0 percent). According to the same report, occupations forecasted to have the most opportunities for job seekers—the most job openings between 2001 and 2008—include janitors and cleaners, security guards, laborers, stock clerks, computer support specialists, bookkeepers, and elementary school teachers.

The following is a summary of data regarding the San Diego/Carlsbad/San Marcos area labor force, 2004 annual averages.

Size of non-agricultural labor force: 1,258,600

Number of workers employed in . . .
   natural resources and mining: 400
   construction: 87,300
   manufacturing: 104,200
   trade, transportation, and utilities: 214,400
   information: 36,400
   financial activities: 81,500
   professional and business services: 205,100
   educational and health services: 121,300
   leisure and hospitality: 145,200
   other services: 47,600
   government: 214,700

Average hourly earnings of production workers employed in manufacturing: $13.70

Unemployment rate: 4.6% (January 2005)

Largest employers	Number of employees
Federal Government	44,200
State of California	32,400
San Diego Unified School District	25,230
University of California at San Diego	21,444
County of San Diego	17,700
City of San Diego	11,085
Qualcomm Inc.	10,431
Sharp HealthCare	8,111

Cost of Living

The following is a summary of data regarding key cost of living factors for the San Diego area.

2004 (3rd Quarter) ACCRA Average House Price: $597,641

2004 (3rd Quarter) ACCRA Cost of Living Index: 144.8 (U.S. average = 100.0)

State income tax rate: Ranges from 1.0% to 9.3%

State sales tax rate: 6.0% (food and prescription drugs are exempt)

Local income tax rate: None

Local sales tax rate: 1.75

Property tax rate: 1.00% of assessed valuation in city proper

Education and Research

Elementary and Secondary Schools

The San Diego Unified School District is the second largest school district in the state and eighth largest urban school district in the country. Its nonpartisan five-member board is elected every four years, and the superintendent is hired by the board. The district operates 24 magnet schools offering in-depth studies in areas ranging from science and research to journalism and telecommunications.

The following is a summary of data regarding the San Diego Unified School District as of the 2004-2005 school year.

Total enrollment: approximately 136,000

Number of facilities
  elementary schools: 113
  middle level schools/junior high schools: 23

senior high school: 27
other: 39 (4 atypical, 10 alternative, and 25 charter)

Student/teacher ratio: 18.8:1 (in 2002-2003)

Teacher salaries
  minimum: $34,517
  maximum: $66,653

Funding per pupil: $7,508 (2000-2001 school year)

Public Schools Information: San Diego City Schools, Eugene Brucker Education Center, 4100 Normal Street, San Diego, CA 92103; telephone (619)725-8000

The San Diego area is also served by a number of parochial and private schools.

Colleges and Universities

Major universities in San Diego include the University of California at San Diego (UCSD), San Diego State University (SDSU), and the University of San Diego (USD), which is a Catholic university. UCSD, one of the University of California's 10 campuses, is regarded as a top institution for higher education and was recently rated seventh best public university in the nation by *U.S. News and World Report.* Campus enrollment is approximately 23,000. UCSD has six undergrad colleges all on one campus, each maintaining its own set of requirements while sharing departmental majors: Thurgood Marshall College, John Muir College, Revelle College, Roosevelt College, Sixth College, and Warren College. UCSD's graduate and professional schools include: the acclaimed Scripps Institution of Oceanography (one of the oldest and largest centers for marine science research and graduate training in the world), School of Medicine, School of International Relations and Pacific Studies, School of Pharmacy and Pharmaceutical Sciences, Jacobs School of Engineering (graduate and undergraduate), and Rady School of Management. SDSU, the oldest and largest university in San Diego and third largest in the state, has an enrollment of nearly 34,000. A readers' poll in the *San Diego Union-Tribune* in 2004 ranked SDSU "Best Local College/University." SDSU offers bachelor's degrees in 81 areas of study, 59 master's degrees, and 13 joint-doctoral degrees. USD, a private, Roman Catholic university, has an enrollment of 7,262; the university offers more than 60 bachelor's, master's and doctoral degrees, and is particularly noted for its law and nursing schools.

Libraries and Research Centers

In 2004, *Library Journal* named San Diego Mayor Dick Murphy "Politician of the Year" for his commitment to the city's public libraries. In 2002, the mayor and city council approved a $312.3 million program to build or improve 24 libraries; among the goals of the program is a new, state-of-the-art downtown library. San Diego is served by two major library systems. The San Diego Public Library operates 34 branches in addition to the main library, maintaining more than 2.8 million volumes, 310 e-books, 4,116 periodical subscriptions, 168,265 audio/visual materials, and collections such as local and state history, rare books and the history of printing, and U.S. Department of Patents documents. The San Diego County Library system consists of a main branch and 31 branches, two bookmobiles, and an adult literacy site with a combined total of more than 1.4 million volumes available. Special collections include audio and video tapes, films, art reproductions, extensive Filipino, Spanish, and Vietnamese collections, and special services for the deaf, including closed-captioned video tapes and talking books. More than 30 other public, private, and research libraries serve the metropolitan area.

A large number of specialized research centers functioning in such subject areas as oceanography, nuclear energy, astronomy, and biological sciences are scattered throughout San Diego. Among the most prominent research centers are the Salk Institute for Biological Studies, which focuses on molecular biology, genetics, neuroscience, and plant biology, and the Palomar Observatory, a center for astronomy research, located atop San Diego county's Mount Palomar.

Public Library Information: San Diego Public Library, 820 E Street, San Diego, CA 92101; telephone (619)236-5800.

Health Care

The San Diego county medical community includes 26 accredited hospitals, with a total of more than 6,600 beds. The largest networks are ScrippsHealth and Sharp Healthcare, which maintain hospitals and walk-in clinics throughout the county. Scripps Mercy Hospital, the city's longest-running and largest hospital, was established in 1890 and has 517 beds. San Diego's research and specialty institutions include the Salk Institute of Biology—established by Jonas Salk, developer of the polio vaccine—which conducts research in such areas as genetics and neuroscience; Children's Hospital and Health Center, the county's designated Pediatric Trauma Center; the Naval Medical Center, which provides care to officers, personnel, and their dependents and is among the largest and most technologically advanced military health care centers in the world; and the Scripps Research Institute, internationally recognized for its research in immunology, molecular, and cell biology.

Health Care Information: San Diego County Medical Society, 3702 Ruffin Road, Suite 206, San Diego, CA 92123; telephone (858)565-8888

Recreation

Sightseeing

San Diego and its surrounding communities offer a wide range of tourist attractions for every taste, from amusement parks to historic buildings and scenic wilderness.

Animals play a major role in San Diego's tourist trade. The world-famous San Diego Zoo, 100 acres of lush, tropical landscape filled with more than 4,000 animals representing some 800 species, contains some of the rarest species in captivity. Moving sidewalks, an aerial tramway, and open-air buses run through the exhibits. Highlights include giant pandas, Australian koalas, rare Chinese golden monkeys, a large reptile collection, a 1-acre children's zoo, and a beautiful free-flight walk-through aviary. Habitats have been crafted to replicate desert, tropical rain forest, savanna, scrubland, island, tundra, ocean and coastline, prairie and steppe, temperate forest and taiga, river, lake, and wetland ecosystems as closely as possible. Among the habitats are Ituri Forest, which simulates a four-acre African rainforest; Tiger River, an Asian rainforest; and Polar Bear Plunge, representing Arctic tundra. The zoo's newest exhibit, Absolutely Apes, features orangutans and siamangs living together as they would in the wild. Absolutely Apes is the first phase of the under-construction New Heart of the Zoo, which will be a three-acre Asian and African rainforest containing many rare and endangered animals in the center of the zoo.

The San Diego Wild Animal Park, a 2,200-acre preserve operated by the San Diego Zoo, is located 30 miles north of downtown. Designed to protect endangered species, the park features more than 3,200 animals living in natural habitats modeled after African, Asian, and Australian terrain. The park is known for its successful breeding of such species as the southern white rhino and Arabian oryx. Visitors can walk the park or use the monorail system that traverses through the heart of the park. During summer months, the rail system also operates after dark, and lamps light the active animal areas. Nairobi Village provides special exhibits, refreshments, and other services.

Sea World San Diego, home of Shamu the killer whale and Baby Shamu (the original Shamu died long ago, but his successors bear his name), is a 150-acre marine park, located along Mission Bay, that offers a number of marine exhibits, live shows, aquariums, the world's largest shark exhibit, playgrounds and rides, and the $25 million Places of Learning educational complex. Sea World's Wild Arctic area is a massive, multimillion dollar project combining motion simulation theater technology, live marine mammal viewing, and interactive educational exhibits. At Shark Encounter, visitors come face to face with sharks by walking through a 57-foot tube that

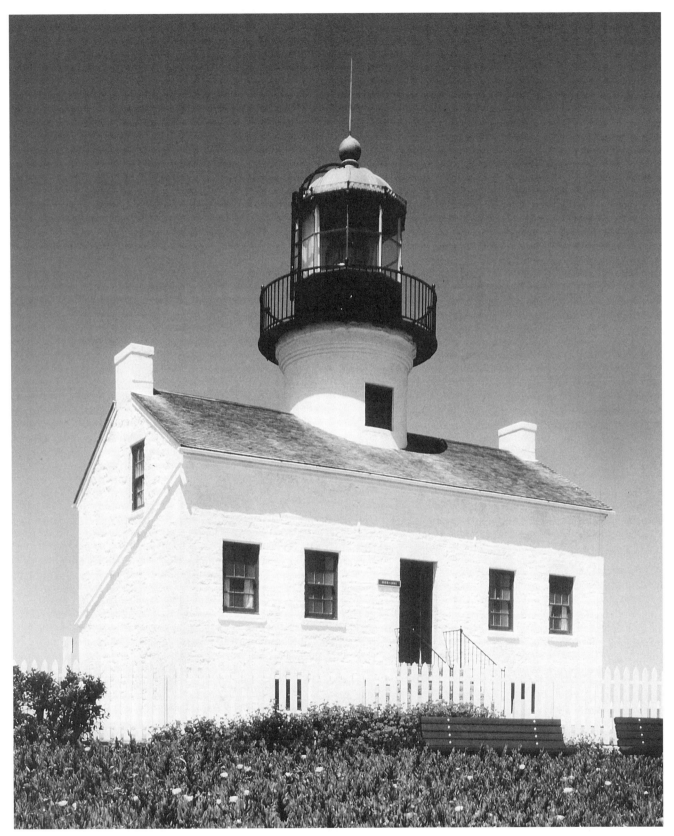

Point Loma lighthouse rests at Cabrillo National Monument, which commemorates the site where California was discovered.

passes through a 280,000-gallon habitat. Shipwreck Rapids transforms visitors into island castaways who journey on raftlike inner tubes trying to find their way back to civilization.

LEGOLAND California, located in Carlsbad, stimulates creativity and imagination through hands-on recreation. Six play areas feature attractions, rides, building opportunities, and more than 1,000 LEGO models. AQUAZONE Wave Racers, one of the park's rides, are ''Wave Activated Vehicles Equipped with Radar Antennas Capable of Evading Random Sprays'' as they hydroplane across wakes created by dual carousels. New in 2005 is Knights' Tournament, a unique robotic coaster ride that allows participants to choose their own destiny.

The center of San Diego preserves two separate historic districts representing two different periods. Old Town evokes San Diego's Spanish and Mexican heritage. Many of its nineteenth-century adobe buildings have been restored and filled with museums, shops, and restaurants. Old Town was preceded, in 1769, by the Spanish establishment of California's first mission and military fortress, on nearby Presidio Hill. Gaslamp Quarter is a 16-block restored Victorian district downtown, featuring antiques, arts and crafts, offices, shops, and restaurants. Two-hour walking tours of the district depart from William Heath Davis House, one of the area's first residences, on Saturdays.

Several of the original missions in the area, including California's first, Mission Basilica San Diego de Alcalá, which moved from Presidio Hill to its present site in 1774, still hold Mass and are open to the public for tours. San Diego Bay harbors the *Star of India,* a 100-year-old sailing vessel, and several U.S. Navy ships that are open to the public. At Point Loma the Cabrillo National Monument commemorates the spot where California was discovered and includes a restored lighthouse, a whale overlook, and a visitor's center.

The nearby 600,000-acre Anza-Borrego Desert State Park, east of San Diego, is a unique collection of geological formations, plants, and animals that has been described by *Flower and Garden* magazine as ''a perfect first desert encounter.'' The Cleveland National Forest north of the city, and other local cliffs, mesas, and canyons offer an abundance of natural scenic pleasures, as do the many flower plantations in the hills outside of San Diego. Tijuana, Mexico, the most visited border town in the world, is an exciting and exotic adventure for shoppers, sightseers, and sports enthusiasts. The Mexican border is a 20 minute ride away, accessed by restored trackless trolleys that depart from the renovated Santa Fe Railway Depot in downtown San Diego.

Arts and Culture

San Diego's citizens and business community are very supportive of the arts. Drama, music, and the visual arts are important elements of the city's personality. Theater, in all its varieties, is available year round. Musical offerings range from formal affairs, symphonies, and operas, to oceanside picnic concerts under the stars and arena-sized rock concerts. Over 90 area museums as well as a number of small art galleries cater to the historic- and artistic-minded.

A large theater community is rising to national prominence in San Diego, and the area's proximity to Hollywood attracts many stars to the more than 40 innovative local theater companies. The centerpiece of San Diego culture is the Simon Edison Centre for the Performing Arts, called ''one of the best theater complexes in the U.S.'' by *Time* magazine. It consists of the Lowell Davies Festival Theater, a large outdoor arena; the Cassius Carter Centre Stage, a 225-seat theater-in-the-round; and the Tony Award-winning 581-seat Old Globe Theater, a reproduction of Shakespeare's Globe Theater. The theatre complex stages classic and contemporary works throughout the year, with an emphasis on Shakespeare during the summer. Numerous other theater groups are located in the area, including the La Jolla Playhouse at University of San Diego at La Jolla, which stages plays and musicals from April through December at the university's 492-seat Mandell Weiss Theatre and 384-seat Mandell Weiss Forum; the San Diego Repertory Theatre, which produces progressive, culturally diverse plays at the Lyceum Theatre's 545-seat Stage Theatre and 270-seat Space Theatre; and the Lamb's Players Theater, which stages musicals, dramas, comedies, and adventurous world premieres, primarily at the company's 350-seat resident theatre in Coronado. San Diego has a thriving dinner-theater population as well.

Music and dance are also well-represented in San Diego. The San Diego Symphony performs classical masterworks, interactive performances, outdoor summer pops, family festivals, and community concerts, altogether more than 100 performances annually. The La Jolla Music Society presents visiting orchestras, soloists, and ensembles. The San Diego Chamber Orchestra presents its classical repertoire and Carnival Concerts Series (designed for families) at venues across San Diego County. The acclaimed San Diego Opera attracts star international performers; its grand productions at the San Diego Civic Theatre run from January through May. The California Ballet Company provides year-round contemporary and classical professional ballet, while historical and cultural dance exhibitions are offered by organizations such as the Traditional Chicano-Azteca Dance Circle, the Samahan Philippine Dance Company, the Pasacat Philippine Performing Arts Company, and Teye Sa Thiosanne, an African drum and dance company.

Balboa Park is the nation's largest cultural city park. Covering 1,200 acres, it is home to the San Diego Zoo, most of San Diego's museums, performing arts venues, and restaurants, as well as cultivated and wild gardens and a number of historic buildings and exhibits. In all, more than 85 cultural and recreational organizations are located here. The park was originally the site of the Panama-California International Exhibition in 1915 and 1916 (which celebrated the opening of the Panama Canal), and most of the buildings are restored exhibit halls from that period, serving as examples of Spanish Revival architecture.

There are 15 museums located in Balboa Park. Among them is the San Diego Museum of Art, established in 1922; it is the oldest and largest art museum in the region. Highlights of the museum's permanent collections include its Spanish baroque, Renaissance, and contemporary California paintings; Indian miniatures; South Asian art; and numerous works by Toulouse-Lautrec. Traditional and modern sculpture is exhibited in an outdoor garden. The Mingei International Museum emphasizes traditional and modern folkart, craft, and design from outside the United States and Europe. The Museum of Photographic Arts, devoted to collecting, conserving and exhibiting still photography and film, has a permanent collection of more than 7,000 works, as well as a state-of-the-art 226-seat movie theater, and a 20,000-volume library. The San Diego Natural History Museum features exhibits on local plants, animals, and geological specimens; in 2001, the opening of a new 90,000 square foot wing more than doubled the museum's size. The San Diego Aerospace Museum features aeronautical exhibits, from the dawn of flight through the space age. The Reuben H. Fleet Science Center houses more than 100 scientific hands-on exhibits, the nation's first Omnimax theater, a virtual reality attraction, and a motion simulation ride. The San Diego Museum of Man, devoted to anthropology, is comprised of a group of buildings documenting the history of mankind, Indians of the three Americas, and human birth, plus various temporary exhibits. The San Diego Model Railroad Museum is the world's largest operating model railroad museum, at 28,000 square feet; highlights include four massive scale model layouts and a toy train gallery. The San Diego Hall of Champions Sports Museum is the largest multi-sport museum in the country at 70,000 square feet.

Other attractions in the park include the House of Pacific Relations, a cluster of 15 cottages representing 30 nationalities, and the Spreckels Organ Pavilion, containing the largest outdoor organ in the nation, played on Sundays by a civic organist. The Spanish Village Art Center presents artists and craftspeople at work in buildings resembling a charming town square in Spain, and the San Diego Art Institute features prominent local artists.

The Junipero Serra Museum is located on the site where Father Junipero Serra and Captain Gaspar de Portola established California's first mission and military fortress, in Presidio Park overlooking Old Town. It displays exhibits

covering the history of the San Diego area from 1562 to the present. The San Diego Maritime Museum, located on the waterfront, is comprised of three historic ships—the 1863 tall ship *Star of India,* the 1898 ferry *Berkeley,* and the 1904 steam yacht *Medea*—as well as numerous nautical exhibits. The Museum of Contemporary Art San Diego (MCASD), with San Diego and La Jolla locations, presents more than 3,000 artworks, created after 1950, in its permanent collection; across the street from the San Diego location, the historic 1915 Santa Fe Depot baggage building is currently being remodeled to become part of MCASD and is scheduled to open in 2006.

Arts and Culture Information: City of San Diego Commission for Arts and Culture 1010 Second Avenue, Suite 555, San Diego, CA 92101; telephone (619)533-3050

Festivals and Holidays

San Diego's events calendar begins with the New Year's Day Race, a yacht regatta in San Diego Bay. In March, the San Diego Latino Film Festival, spanning 10 days, is the largest Latino film festival in the country. ArtWalk is a two-day April event showcasing visual and performing fine arts exhibits in San Diego's Little Italy neighborhood. May events include the Cinco de Mayo Celebration, which brings historical reenactments, folkloric music and dance, and Mexican food and fun to Old Town; Gator Bay two-day Cajun zydeco music and food festival; and the Ethnic Food Fair, featuring food from more than 25 nations.

A gala celebration on the Fourth of July features special events throughout the region, including several parades, outdoor concerts, a hot-air balloon race, and fireworks. The Harlem West Fest, also in July, is a premier African American festival held in the Gaslamp Quarter. Another July event, held at Imperial Beach, is Sand Castle Days, the world's longest-running and largest sand castle competition. America's Finest City Week is celebrated city-wide in August and features a large variety of events including concerts, sports events, carnivals, and more. The San Diego Film Festival in September celebrates American and international cinematic arts.

In late September, the city celebrates the Cabrillo Festival to commemorate the discovery of California by Spanish explorer Juan Rodríguez Cabrillo. The San Diego Bay Wine & Food Festival in November is a culinary celebration featuring more than 150 wineries and cuisine from many fine area restaurants. The San Diego Thanksgiving Dixieland Jazz Festival is a five-day classic jazz event held during Thanksgiving weekend, showcasing traditional, swing, and dixieland jazz. The Christmas season inspires some of the major celebrations of the year, sparking festivals, parades, and light displays in many locations. Other Christmas events include the Parade of Lights, a display of decorated boats in San

Diego Bay; the festive rituals of Las Posadas; and the Holiday Bowl, a college football game. December also marks the beginning of the whale migration season off Point Loma.

Sports for the Spectator

Sports are varied in San Diego. Major League Baseball's San Diego Padres play April through September at PETCO Park, which opened in 2004; PETCO, located downtown, has 42,000 seats, and its seating bowl sections are named after neighborhoods. The National Football League's San Diego Chargers, 2004 AFC West Division champions, play at 70,561-seat Quallcomm Stadium. Quallcomm is also home to San Diego State University's Aztecs. The San Diego Gulls play minor-league hockey at San Diego Sports Arena. San Diego also hosts a major bicycle Grand Prix race each year. Nearby Del Mar Thoroughbred Club, founded by entertainer Bing Crosby in 1937, offers horseracing from July through September, and Tijuana, Mexico features the excitement of jai alai, bullfighting, and greyhound racing.

Sports for the Participant

Sports Illustrated magazine calls San Diego "the sports and fitness capital of the U.S." The Pacific Ocean and numerous bays in the area provide a wide range of activities: swimming, sailing, water skiing, snorkeling, and deep sea sport fishing, among others. Mission Bay Park is the largest aquatic park in the nation; it consists of 4,235 acres, 46 percent land and 54 percent water. The park offers 44 miles of beachfront recreation area, as well as inland trails and jogging tracks. San Diego-La Jolla Underwater Park and Ecological Reserve at La Jolla Cove provides excellent snorkeling and scuba diving opportunities. San Diego's public park system maintains extensive recreation facilities, public pools, jogging paths, and playing fields. There are more than 1,300 public and private tennis courts in the county, as well as more than 90 golf courses. The most popular bike route in the area is Route S21, which extends 15 miles along the beach between La Jolla and Oceanside. Winter sports such as skiing are available in the nearby mountains.

Shopping and Dining

San Diego offers a wide variety of shopping experiences, from small shops in renovated historical districts such as Old Town, which resembles a Mexican marketplace, and the Gaslamp Quarter, where Victorian buildings house antique stores, art galleries, and boutiques, to the large suburban shopping malls, many located in the Mission Valley region. Downtown San Diego's massive Westfield Shoppingtown Horton Plaza, adjacent to the Gaslamp district, is a five-level, open-air plaza filled with department stores and nearly 200 upscale specialty shops. Seaport Village is a 14-acre shopping, dining, and entertainment complex featuring 75 shops and restaurants in a harborside setting. Nearby Ti-

juana provides a colorful variety of bazaars, open-air markets, and handcrafted goods.

Seafood and authentic Mexican cuisine are dining specialties in the San Diego area. Many distinctive restaurants, ranging from formal luxury dining to sidewalk cafes can be found in the historical districts, the modern plazas, and along the waterfront. A large number of international and ethnic restaurants add variety to the dining fare.

Visitor Information: San Diego Convention & Visitors Bureau, 401 B Street, Suite 1400, San Diego, CA 92101; telephone (619)232-1212

Convention Facilities

The San Diego Convention Center, which doubled in size upon an expansion in 2001, is located downtown along San Diego Bay. The 1.7 million square foot facility features 615,701 square feet of exhibit space; 204,114 square feet of meeting space including two 40,000 square foot ballrooms; and 284,494 square feet of pre-function, lobby, and registration space. The center is within a mile of 7,500 first-class hotel rooms, and is only 10 minutes from the airport. Meeting space is also available at the 2,975-seat Civic Theatre, a multipurpose convention and performing arts center adjacent to City Hall.

A number of downtown hotels are designed to accommodate major conventions, providing extensive meeting and banquet facilities, as well as exhibit space. Nearly 45,000 rooms are available in the San Diego area.

Convention Information: San Diego Convention & Visitors Bureau, 401 B Street, Suite 1400, San Diego, CA 92101

Transportation

Approaching the City

San Diego International Airport Lindbergh Field is located 3 miles from downtown and provides major domestic and foreign air service from 18 passenger carriers and 6 cargo carriers. In 2004, 16 million passengers used the airport. Amtrak's *Pacific Surfliner* route carries passengers from San Diego through Los Angeles, Oxnard, and Santa Barbara, to San Luis Obispo. Amtrak's San Diego station is in the historic Santa Fe Depot, north of Seaport Village. A commuter rail service, The Coaster, runs between San Diego, Solana Beach, Encinitas, Carlsbad, and Oceanside.

San Diego is located at the junction of two major north-south routes that originate in Canada. Interstate 5 from Los Angeles and I-15 from Las Vegas meet in San Diego and continue to the Mexican border. I-8 enters San Diego from the east.

Traveling in the City

The San Diego Transit Corporation, the largest of San Diego county's bus operators, has a fleet of 275 buses traveling 29 routes covering San Diego, El Cajon, La Mesa, National City, as well as portions of San Diego County's unincorporated area. The San Diego Trolley travels in the downtown area, through Mission Valley and east county communities, and to the Mexican border. Carriage rides through the downtown area are available from Embarcadero Marina Park.

Communications

Newspapers and Magazines

San Diego is served by *The San Diego Union-Tribune,* the result of the 1992 merger of the city's two dailies. Readers can choose from among a number of weekly, ethnic, and community papers as well, such as *La Prensa San Diego,* a weekly English/Spanish newspaper. *San Diego Magazine* publishes articles of regional interest; several other technical and special interest magazines, such as *San Diego Home/ Garden, Computer Edge,* and *San Diego Metropolitan* (focusing on business news), are also published in the area.

Television and Radio

Ten television stations broadcast in the San Diego area, representing ABC, CBS, NBC, FOX, WB, Univision (two stations), PBS, a local independent station focusing on news, and an Oceanside-based station focusing on local government and media. The region is also serviced by cable television. More than 30 radio stations serve the San Diego area, providing a wide variety of musical and information programming, some broadcasting in Spanish.

Media Information: *The San Diego Union-Tribune,* PO Box 120191, San Diego, CA 92112; telephone (619)299-3131. *San Diego Magazine,* 1450 Front Street, San Diego, CA 92101; telephone (619)230-9292

San Diego Online

City of San Diego Home Page. Available www.ci.san-diego.ca.us

San Diego Convention & Visitors Bureau. Available www.sandiego.org

San Diego County Library. Available www.sdcl.org

San Diego Daily Transcript. Available www.sddt.com

San Diego Public Library. Available www.sannet.gov/public-library

San Diego Regional Chamber of Commerce. Available www.sdchamber.org

San Diego Unified School District. Available www.sandi.net

The San Diego Union-Tribune. Available www.uniontrib.com

Selected Bibliography

Cameron, Robert, *Above San Diego: A New Collection of Historical and Original Aerial Photographs of San Diego* (San Francisco: Cameron and Co., 1990)

Schad, Jerry, *Afoot and Afield in San Diego* (Berkeley: Wilderness Press, 1998)

Urrea, Luis Alberto, *Across the Wire: Life and Hard Times on the Mexican Border* (New York: Anchor Books/Doubleday, 1993)

San Francisco

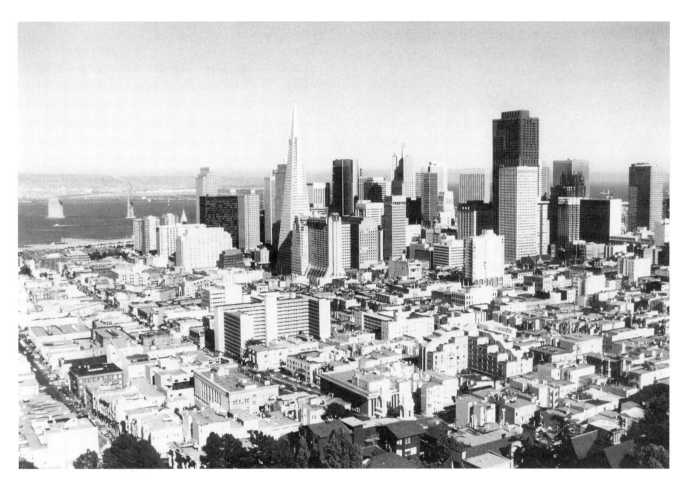

The City in Brief

Founded: 1776 (incorporated, 1850)

Head Official: Mayor Gavin Newsom (D) (since 2004)

City Population
  1980: 678,974
  1990: 723,959
  2000: 776,733
  2003 estimate: 751,682
  Percent change, 1990–2000: 7.3%
  U.S. rank in 1980: 13th
  U.S. rank in 1990: 14th
  U.S. rank in 2000: 18th

Metropolitan Area Population (PMSA)
  1980: 1,489,000
  1990: 1,603,678
  2000: 1,731,183

Percent change, 1990–2000: 7.8%
U.S. rank in 1980: 5th (CMSA)
U.S. rank in 1990: 4th (CMSA)
U.S. rank in 2000: 5th (CMSA)

Area: 47 square miles (2000)
Elevation: 155 feet above sea level
Average Annual Temperature: 58.3° F
Average Annual Precipitation: 22.1 inches

Major Economic Sectors: Services; trade; finance, insurance, and real estate; government
Unemployment Rate: 3.6% (December 2004)
Per Capita Income: $34,556 (2000)

2002 FBI Crime Index Total: 42,671

Major Colleges and Universities: San Francisco State University; University of California, San Francisco; University of San Francisco; Golden Gate University

Daily Newspapers: *San Francisco Chronicle; San Francisco Examiner*

Introduction

The term ''melting pot'' is used to describe many American cities and towns. This is indeed true for San Francisco, one of the few truly international cities in the United States. The neighborhoods are varied, yet each features a cohesiveness as unique as its inhabitants. Rows of elegant houses, the famous cable cars, clusters of ethnic neighborhoods, and the colorful waterfront all add to the distinctive international flavor of the city. Nearly half of those who live in the Bay Area were born outside of the United States or have at least one nonnative parent. The city's well-known hills offer stunning views of the Pacific Ocean and San Francisco Bay, and feature a wide array of shops, restaurants, and cosmopolitan nightlife. In addition to its diversity and charm, San Francisco is a major financial and insurance center, an international port, and the gateway to Silicon Valley, America's premier high-technology center. The consistently spring-like weather and unique atmosphere attract corporations as well as visitors, and the solid economic base keeps them there.

Geography and Climate

San Francisco occupies the tip of a peninsula halfway up the coast of northern California, surrounded on three sides by bodies of water: the Pacific Ocean, the Golden Gate strait, and the San Francisco Bay. The city is laid out in a grid over some 40 hills, reaching heights of nearly 1,000 feet; this sometimes causes wide variations in temperature and sky conditions in different areas of town. The Pacific air keeps the temperatures generally moderate, rarely ranging above 75 degrees or below 45 degrees, leading San Francisco to be called ''the air-conditioned city.'' The climate is very similar to coastal areas on the Mediterranean.

Although temperatures remain relatively constant, there are two definite seasons—wet and dry—with more than 80 percent of annual precipitation taking place between November and March. Perhaps the most distinctive feature of the local climate is the banks of fog that can roll in off the ocean, quickly covering various areas of the city, and then disappear just as quickly. The fog is most common on summer mornings, coming off the cooler ocean and backing up against the hills, but it also comes from the colder inland areas during the winter. The fog affects different elevations in varying amounts, covering the city in complex patterns of fog and sunshine.

Area: 47 square miles (2000)

Elevation: 155 feet above sea level

Average Temperatures: January, 52.3° F; August, 62.4° F; annual average, 58.6° F

Average Annual Precipitation: 22.1 inches

History

Spanish Discover City; Franciscan Friars Build Missions

Because thick fog banks usually obscure the narrow entrance to the bay, the area where San Francisco now stands and the adjacent natural harbor remained undiscovered by seafaring adventurers for more than two hundred years after the original Spanish explorers found California. It was left to an overland expedition of Spanish soldiers from Mexico to stumble upon the bay by accident in 1769 while trying to reach Monterey. In 1776 Colonel Juan Bautista de Anza founded the first European settlement in the Bay Area by establishing a military garrison, or Presidio, on the southern shore of the Golden Gate. That same year the Franciscan Order built Mission Dolores, the sixth Roman Catholic mission in what eventually became a chain of twenty-one missions along the coast of California.

Until the 1830s almost all of the inhabitants were missionaries, trying—without much success—to convert the local Costanoan tribe to Christianity; but eventually a small village was built up around the Presidio and the mission. The village, called Yerba Buena, was mapped out in 1839 by Jean Jaques Vioget, a Swiss surveyor, but it continued to be small and remote throughout most of the 1840s. The quiet town of a few hundred inhabitants was visited infrequently by whaling ships, traders from the East Coast, and frontier hunters and trappers. Farming and a small but steady market in trading cattle hides and tallow were the main sources of commerce.

America Wins California; Gold Discovered

The American flag was raised in the town's central square in 1846, marking the annexation of California by the United States after the war with Mexico; one year later the name of the town was changed to San Francisco. Soon after the annexation, the town's population was nearly doubled by the arrival of a group of 238 Mormon settlers, led by Sam Brannan. It was Brannan who ran through the muddy streets of San Francisco less than two years later shouting ''Gold!,'' thus altering the city's fate. Within a year, more than 40,000 people had journeyed through the area on their way to the gold fields around Sutter's Mill in the Sierra foothills, about 140 miles away. Some 35,000 of those people stayed on to live in San Francisco. The city was incorporated in 1850.

The gold prospectors came from all corners of the globe and tended to settle in areas according to their nationalities, one reason for the distinctive international flavor of modern San Francisco. Demand for food and shelter outstripped the supply, and many people lived in tents, cooking over campfires. Whole crews abandoned their ships in the harbor, leaving hundreds of empty hulls that were brought ashore and used as temporary warehouses, stores, and as the foundations of the town's new buildings. Gambling halls, saloons, hotels, and stores sprang up almost daily, only to be destroyed by frequent fires and then quickly rebuilt. It was a wild and reckless time; rampant lawlessness was common, so much so that in 1851 concerned citizens banded together into vigilante groups and rounded up the worst violators, eventually restoring order to the town.

Gold Boom Goes Bust; Industry, Shipping Thrive

The gold boom declined by the mid-1850s, but the town continued to grow with increases in industry and shipping. The 1859 silver boom in Nevada and the completion of the transcontinental railroad in 1869 also contributed their share to the city's prosperity. The downtown area grew full of large stone buildings and warehouses along the docks, and the surrounding hills were filled with impressive residential homes. By the turn of the century, San Francisco was home to a population of more than a third of a million people and was the ninth largest city in the country.

April 18, 1906, brought disaster to the city in the form of a major earthquake and fire that killed more than 500 people, devastated 3,000 acres in the heart of the city, and left almost 1,000 residents homeless. Among the heroes of the day were the U.S. Navy, who stretched a mile-long fire hose from Fisherman's Wharf over Telegraph Hill and down to Jackson Square, saving historic buildings. Before the ashes were cold, the townspeople set out to rebuild the city, and by 1915, when San Francisco hosted the Panama-Pacific International Exposition in honor of the opening of the Panama Canal, no traces of the fire and earthquake were visible.

Rise of Finance, Commerce, Culture

During the mid-twentieth century, San Francisco secured its position as the financial, commercial, and cultural center of northern California. The completion of the Golden Gate Bridge in 1937, after four years of exhausting work, was the major event of the period and a symbol of the city's new-found prominence. Designer Joseph Strauss tried for more than a decade to convince disbelievers that the plans for the construction of the bridge were feasible, and many people still doubted that it could stand for long even after its completion. The structure, the second-longest suspension bridge in the world, is more than three-quarters of a mile in length, supported by two 746-foot towers. It remains one of the outstanding engineering achievements of all time, drawing hundreds of thousands of tourists each year.

World War II boosted the already strong economy of the city, which became a major supply and troop shipping port for the Pacific fronts and an important area for defense industries. It was also during this time that large numbers of the area's Oriental citizens were interred in work camps in the region. After the war, the city pointed the way to peace when delegates representing almost all of the world's countries gathered in San Francisco to draw up the charter of the United Nations.

The post-war era brought continued growth and prosperity. San Francisco's downtown area began to develop a skyline of high-rise buildings while carefully preserving many of the historical structures and green spaces. A large stretch of high-technology industries eventually built up in the nearby area known as Silicon Valley. The city fought problems of urban blight encountered in the 1960s and 1970s with an extensive urban-renewal program, developing the downtown section and introducing a major Rapid Transit System in 1974 to provide access to the center city. The assassinations of Mayor George Moscone and City Supervisor Harvey Milk in November 1978 were a blow to the city's progressive image. The city elected its first woman mayor, Diane Feinstein, in 1979.

Another major earthquake occurred on October 17, 1989, ending decades of tranquility in the San Francisco Bay Area. The region has recovered strongly, showing a spirit of cooperation and determination. Today, San Francisco is considered a "gem" among cities. While other metropolitan areas build freeways to deal with urban sprawl, San Francisco remains a compact city with a flourishing downtown business and retail center, and charming neighborhoods. The city boasts many famous landmarks, including the Golden Gate Bridge, Fisherman's Wharf, Ghirardelli Square, Chinatown, and cable cars.

Historical Information: California Historical Society, 678 Mission Street, San Francisco, CA 94105; telephone (415)357-1848; fax (415)357-1850. Chinese Historical Society of America, 965 Clay Street, San Francisco, CA 94108; telephone (415)391-1188. San Francisco African American Historical and Cultural Society, Fort Mason Center, Bldg. C, Room 165, San Francisco, CA 94123; telephone (415)441-0640

Population Profile

Metropolitan Area Residents (PMSA)
1980: 1,489,000

1990: 1,603,678
2000: 1,731,183
Percent change, 1990–2000: 7.8%
U.S. rank in 1980: 5th (CMSA)
U.S. rank in 1990: 4th (CMSA)
U.S. rank in 2000: 5th (CMSA)

City Residents
1980: 678,974
1990: 723,959
2000: 776,733
2003 estimate: 745,774
Percent change, 1990–2000: 3.0%
U.S. rank in 1980: 13th
U.S. rank in 1990: 14th
U.S. rank in 2000: 18th (State rank: 4th)

Density: 16,634.4 people per square mile (2000)

Racial and ethnic characteristics (2000)
White: 385,728
Black or African American: 60,515
American Indian and Alaska Native: 3,458
Asian: 239,565
Native Hawaiian and Pacific Islander: 3,844
Hispanic or Latino (may be of any race): 109,504
Other: 50,368

Percent of residents born in state: 51.2% (2000)

Age characteristics (2000)
Population under 5 years old: 31,633
Population 5 to 9 years old: 31,564
Population 10 to 14 years old: 30,813
Population 15 to 19 years old: 33,334
Population 20 to 24 years old: 56,054
Population 25 to 34 years old: 180,418
Population 35 to 44 years old: 133,804
Population 45 to 54 years old: 107,718
Population 55 to 59 years old: 35,026
Population 60 to 64 years old: 30,258
Population 65 to 74 years old: 53,955
Population 75 to 84 years old: 37,929
Population 85 years and over: 14,227
Median age: 36.5 years

Births (2001)
Total number: 8,210

Deaths (2001)
Total number: 8,138 (of which, 57 were infants under the age of 1 year)

Money income (1999)
Per capita income: $34,556 (2000)
Median household income: $55,221
Total households: 328,850

Number of households with income of . . .
less than $10,000: 32,261
$10,000 to $14,999: 16,394
$15,000 to $24,999: 28,142
$25,000 to $34,999: 29,596
$35,000 to $49,999: 43,784
$50,000 to $74,999: 58,297
$75,000 to $99,999: 39,969
$100,000 to $149,999: 43,534
$150,000 to $199,999: 17,613
$200,000 or more: 20,260

Percent of families below poverty level: 7.8% (32.2% of which were female householder families with related children under 5 years)

2002 FBI Crime Index Total: 42,671

Municipal Government

The governments of the city and county of San Francisco are consolidated into one unit. San Francisco adopted a mayor-council form of government in 1932, with eleven council members elected at large to four-year terms. The mayor is directly elected to a four-year term but is not a member of the council, which is known as the board of supervisors.

Head Official: Mayor Gavin Newsom (D) (since 2004; current term expires 2008)

Total Number of City Employees: 28,732 (2003)

City Information: City Hall, telephone (415)337-4701

Economy

Major Industries and Commercial Activity

Since the days of the Gold Rush, San Francisco has been an important financial center. Located halfway between London and Tokyo as well as between Seattle and San Diego, San Francisco is at the center of global business. Because of its natural, landlocked harbor, San Francisco has thrived on trade and shipping since its early days. Today, through its main port in Oakland, eight smaller ports, and three key airports, the Bay area handles nearly 30 percent of West Coast trade. The port system is augmented by San Francisco International Airport, the country's ninth largest and the world's fourteenth largest airport.

San Francisco's economic activity attracts and supports a range of industries. As the base for some of the country's largest banks, the Pacific Exchange, and over 30 international financial institutions, San Francisco is a center for world commerce. Most recently San Francisco is considered the birthplace of new media; its South Park neighborhood houses some of the most innovative new technology companies in the world. San Francisco's Mission Bay neighborhood is a model for collaborative innovation between the biotechnology industry and academic researchers.

World War II started a local boom in defense industries, resulting in subsequent high-technology development that hasn't ceased. Nearby Silicon Valley, along with Stanford University, are considered to be among the places where the worldwide technology boom began, and they remain on the leading edge today. More than 2,800 Bay Area companies produce computers, semiconductors and related components, scientific instruments, and various other electronic systems and equipment. Aerospace industries such as the National Aeronautic and Space Administration (NASA) and Lockheed also maintain major research facilities in the area.

Another important high-technology industry in the area is medical science; several hundred companies in the Bay Area are setting the pace in research and development of pharmaceutical products, medical electronics, and genetic engineering. Almost one third of the total worldwide biotechnology workforce is employed in San Francisco and the surrounding region. Other prominent industries are tourism, which generates $6.73 billion in tourist spending each year and is the largest industry in the region; fashion apparel, with the Bay Area home to the world's largest apparel maker, Levi Strauss & Co.; health care; education; and restaurants.

Items and goods produced: paper boxes, confectionery, paints, chemicals, glass, leather, lumber, textiles, steel, clothing, bags, furniture, auto parts, electric machinery, matches, clay, rubber products, tools, beverages

Incentive Programs—New and Existing Companies

Local programs— Businesses that create new permanent jobs in San Francisco receive a two-year credit against their city payroll tax liability for the new employees as part of the New Jobs Tax Credit. San Francisco's enterprise zone offers a variety of city and state economic benefits for businesses that locate within it. With the Mayor's Office of Community Development Loan Fund, companies that create jobs in the city and meet certain federal criteria are eligible for loans ranging from $1,000 to $250,000. San Francisco is a state-designated Recycling Market Development Zone, enabling businesses involved in recycling to utilize low-interest loans, technical assistance, siting and permitting assistance, and reduced permit application fees. SFWorks is a program that assists employers in hiring low-income individuals who are

transitioning to work or trying to advance their careers. Many businesses that participate may qualify for a number federal and state hiring tax credits, ranging from $2,400 to $8,500.

*State programs—*Companies that purchase manufacturing or R&D equipment for use anywhere in California are allowed a tax credit equal to 6 percent of the costs paid or incurred for acquiring the property as part of the Manufacturers' Investment Credit program. The California research and development tax credit allows companies to receive a credit of 8 percent for qualified research expenses (research done in-house), and 12 percent for basic research payments (payments made in cash to an outside company).

*Job training programs—*The San Francisco Private Industry Council (PIC), the organization responsible for administering the federal Workforce Investment Act (WIA) programs, funds offers significant benefits to employers who hire PIC trainees. Under the on-the-job training program, the PIC will reimburse employers 50 percent of wages paid to participants for as long as the first 6 months of employment. The California Employment Training Panel (ETP) assists businesses in training employees through a cost reimbursement program. The California State Enterprise Zone (EZ) Hiring Tax Credit is a state income tax credit for employers who hire job seekers from targeted groups. Employers can claim up to $31,605 in tax credits over a five-year period when they hire qualified employees.

Development Projects

Pacific Bell Park, the new home of the San Francisco Giants, was completed in April 2000. The $306 million project took more than 2,000 construction workers and more than 650,000 bricks to build the 42,000-seat stadium. San Francisco's premier convention facility, Moscone Center, added an additional 300,000 square feet of function space in 2003. With the completion of Moscone West, which opened in 2003, today's Moscone Center is a collection of facilities covering more than 20 acres on three adjacent blocks. It anchors the 87-acre Yerba Buena Center redevelopment district in a neighborhood of hotels, theaters, restaurants, museums, galleries, housing, parks, and urban recreation centers. The new Sony Metreon retail and entertainment complex and Children's Center are also located in the Yerba Buena Center. The Children's Center includes facilities for childcare, ice skating, and bowling, as well as an arts and technology center.

San Francisco continues to invest in improvements that fuel its world-class reputation. Located midway between London and Tokyo, America's closest major city to the Pacific Rim, it sits at the center of the global community. A multiyear, $2.4 billion program to bring San Francisco International Airport into the 21st century was nearly completed in 2005, and includes new parking garages, a consolidated rental car center, and other amenities. In 2003, a $1.5 billion new Bay

Area Rapid Transit (BART) station began connecting trains to the heart of San Francisco and the East Bay; an intra-airport rail system links airport terminals and facilities together. Revitalization of San Francisco's scenic waterfront, which runs 7.5 miles along its northern and southern perimeters, is an ongoing project to reconnect the city to this historic area and enliven the area for both residents and visitors; the project will include the addition of an expanded ferry terminal and new office space.

Economic Development Information: The San Francisco Partnership, 465 California Street, 9th Floor, San Francisco, CA 94104; telephone (415)352-8801; fax (415)956-3844; email info@sfp.org

Commercial Shipping

San Francisco International Airport is served by all of the major air freight companies; some 600,000 tons of cargo are handled each year. The port of San Francisco has terminals offering six berths, on-dock rail, acres of paved land for staging cargo, more than 550,000 square feet of covered storage for weather-sensitive cargo, cranes capable of working both breakbulk and containers, and 624 reefer outlets. Once a major West Coast cargo port that lost much of its business to Oakland, a resurgence has happened in recent years and strategic plans are underway to continue the volume increase of cargo shipping.

Labor Force and Employment Outlook

San Francisco has the highest concentration of new immigrants in the nation, providing a continuous supply of workers at all levels of expertise. The city also boasts some of the most well-trained professionals in the United States, with nearly 70 percent of San Franciscans having educational training beyond high school. Approximately 30 percent have a bachelor's degree, nearly twice the state level, and more than 16 percent of residents hold a graduate or professional degree, compared to 9.5 percent for the state.

The city's workforce is a magnet for business and employment. According to the U.S. Department of Labor, San Francisco's diverse and educated population results in one of the most productive workforces in the country and the world. Growth is expected to continue in the areas where San Francisco is already strong: high-technology industries, medical science and health-related fields, and finance. As the sixth largest metropolitan market in the United States, San Francisco offers future opportunities in areas such as retail trade, service industries, and restaurants.

Small businesses thrive in San Francisco; according to the city there are a multitude of small and medium sized businesses in the city, and 95 percent of all of the city's businesses employ 50 workers or less.

The following is a summary of data regarding the San Francisco metropolitan area labor force, 2004 annual averages.

Size of nonagricultural labor force: 938,400

Number of workers employed in . . .
   natural resources and mining: 200
   construction: 43,200
   manufacturing: 44,700
   trade, transportation, and utilities: 164,700
   information: 43,900
   finance: 88,200
   professional and business services: 175,000
   education and health services: 99,900
   leisure and hospitality: 113,500
   government: 128,000

Average hourly earnings of production workers employed in manufacturing: $19.93

Unemployment rate: 3.6% (December 2004)

Largest private companies (based on revenue)	*Number of employees*
New United Motor	4,800
Bechtel Group Inc.	2,150
Levi Strauss & Co.	1,900
FirstAmerica Automotive Inc.	1,300
Lucas Film Limited	1,300
DHL Worldwide Express	1,023
USS-POSCO Industries	979

Cost of Living

San Francisco's cost of living is one of the highest in the country, due in part to the tight labor market and the high cost of housing, food, and other consumer goods. It is reported that Bay Area residents possess the third-highest discretionary income in the United States. This is because of the high percentage of an educated workforce and the concentration of jobs in high-paying industries. Its housing market has experienced record-breaking appreciation, with the median home price increasing by nearly 96 percent since the early 1990s. Although the residential property tax is low, because property values are high, the absolute payment is relatively high.

The following is a summary of data regarding several key cost of living factors for the San Francisco area.

2004 (3rd Quarter) ACCRA Average House Price: $846,000

2004 (3rd Quarter) ACCRA Cost of Living Index: 182.4
   (U.S. average = 100.0)

State income tax rate: Ranges from 1.0% to 9.3%

State sales tax rate: 6% (public utilities and prescription drugs are exempt)

Local income tax rate: None

Local sales tax rate: 1.25%

Property tax rate: Real-estate (secured property) taxes are set for the 2003–2004 roll year at $1,117 per $100 of full value as determined by the last assessment or as re-assessed at the time of sale.

Economic Information: San Francisco Partnership, 465 California Street, 9th Floor, San Francisco, CA 94104; telephone (415)352-8801; fax (415)956-3844; email info@sfp .org

Education and Research

Elementary and Secondary Schools

Founded in 1851, the San Francisco Unified School District (SFUSD) was the first public school district established in California. The SFUSD is a multicultural, multilingual, major urban public school system in which ethnic and racial diversity is considered a strength. English is the second language of nearly one-third of SFUSD students. The student body is currently 10.3 percent white, 21.3 percent Latino/Latina, 15.2 percent African American, 30.5 percent Chinese, 1 percent Japanese, 0.9 percent Korean, .06 percent Native American, 6.7 percent Filipino, and 11.9 percent other non-white ethnicities. The SFUSD encompasses all of San Francisco County, making it one of the largest in the state of California. The school board consists of seven partisan members who appoint the superintendent. The San Francisco school system provides a rigorous curriculum that develops student curiosity and creativity while preparing them for success at college and in careers.

The following is a summary of data regarding San Francisco public schools as of the 2003–2004 school year.

Total enrollment: 58,566

Number of facilities
  elementary schools: 78
  middle schools: 17
  senior high schools: 21
  other: 39 children's centers

Student/teacher ratio: varies by school, subject, and grade level

Teacher salaries (2001-2002)
  minimum: $38,000
  maximum: $64,326

Funding per pupil: Figure available on a per-school basis only

A number of private and parochial schools provide alternative forms of education in the San Francisco area.

Public Schools Information: San Francisco Unified School District, 555 Franklin Street, San Francisco, CA 94102; telephone (415)241-6000

Colleges and Universities

San Francisco has many fully accredited colleges and universities, including San Francisco State University (enrollment 28,804); the University of California, San Francisco (enrollment 2,800); Golden Gate University (enrollment 3,092); the University of San Francisco (enrollment 6,415); City College of San Francisco (17,819); the Hastings College of the Law; and the Academy of Art College. These and other area institutions offer graduate and professional degrees in more than 100 fields of specialization. Nearby Stanford University and the University of California, Berkeley, two schools with international reputations, provide still more opportunities for educational pursuits.

Libraries and Research Centers

The San Francisco Public Library consists of the main library and 26 other branches throughout the city, providing a total of more than 2 million volumes, as well as films, videotapes, CDs, recordings, art reproductions, and extensive services for the hearing impaired. The library's special collections include material on calligraphy, the history of printing, Panama Canal manuscripts, science fiction and fantasy, San Francisco history, gay and lesbian history, and a document department featuring United Nations, federal, state, and local documents. By the year 2010, the Main's collection is projected to hold 1.3 million books, 6 million microfiche and microfilm items, and 340,000 bound periodicals. In November 2000, a $129 million bond measure passed that will provide the public with seismically safe, accessible, code compliant branch libraries in every neighborhood of San Francisco. Combined with other state and local, public and private fund sources, this program will allow the renovation of 19 branches, replace four leased facilities with city-owned branches, and construct a new branch in Mission Bay; in 2005 several projects were completed, with construction or preliminary assessments underway at other branches and new building sites. A variety of other professional, scholastic, and special interest libraries serve the metropolitan area.

The city's proximity to Silicon Valley produces a large amount of research activity. Stanford University and the University of California, Berkeley are world-class research institutions specializing in a variety of fields. Other important research centers include the University of California, San Francisco Medical Center, which conducts extensive bio-genetic research, and the Lawrence Livermore Laboratories, which works with high-energy lasers and weapons research. The California Pacific Medical Center Research Institute conducts clinical trials and research programs in a variety of medical subjects, including pain, cancer, AIDS, cardiovascular disease, hepatitis, and others.

Public Library Information: San Francisco Public Library, 100 Larkin Street, San Francisco, CA 94102; telephone (415)557-4400

Health Care

The major public facility is the San Francisco General Hospital, a 580-bed acute care center that also serves as a regional teaching hospital. It is the largest acute inpatient and rehabilitation hospital for psychiatric patients in the city. The 23-acre hospital complex contains an internationally-recognized emergency and trauma center, psychiatric services, the nation's first AIDS unit, the Alternative Birth Center, and the innovative Women's Health Center. In 2003 the Avon Comprehensive Breast Center was opened, which planned to increase the number of underserved women who receive mammograms by 5,000 annually. Because of legislation passed in 1996 requiring that all California acute care hospitals meet upgraded seismic safety standards by either retrofitting existing buildings or constructing new facilities, San Francisco General Hospital is currently exploring options for rebuilding and relocating patients to a new campus by 2013.

Recreation

Sightseeing

San Francisco contains so many interesting attractions in such a small area that visitors find something unique on almost any street. Most points of interest are within walking distance or a short ride away. The ride itself can be an attraction when taken on one of the city's famous cable cars, the nation's only moving historical landmarks, now restored and servicing a 10-mile route in the heart of the city.

Historic and scenic beauty is evident all over the city. The original mission and the Presidio, both built in 1776 out of simple adobe brick, can still be toured. Jackson Square, the former Barbary Coast, and Portsmouth Square, the original center of the early town, are both in renovated areas that highlight different periods of the city's history. Many of the residential sections that surround the downtown district were spared destruction in the earthquake and fire of 1906, and they offer examples of Victorian architecture. Displayed in hillside vistas, the colorful houses give the city a Mediterranean look. The downtown area also contains a number of striking modern structures like the pyramidal Transamerica Building, and the impressive Civic Center complex, including the domed City Hall.

Perhaps the most unique features of San Francisco are its clusters of distinct ethnic neighborhoods. The most famous is Chinatown, the largest Chinese district outside of Asia, a 24-block area of authentic bazaars, temples, restaurants, and distinctive Oriental architecture. Recent additions to the area include a two-level gateway to the district, ornately carved by Taiwanese craftsmen, and the Chinese Cultural Center. Next to Chinatown is the North Beach area, once home to the "beatnik" culture. Filled with Italian influences—cafes, gelato parlors, delicatessens, cappuccino houses, and restaurants—the area also contains a number of jazz clubs, art galleries, and theaters. The Mission District, a business and residential area of colorful Victorian buildings, is home to a predominantly Spanish-speaking population and the original Levi Strauss clothing factory, still in operation. A five-tiered pagoda welcomes visitors to Nihonmachi, a section of sushi bars, theaters, shops, restaurants, and hotels that reflect the Japanese culture.

Golden Gate Park, just west of the downtown area, is more than 1,000 acres of landscaped greenery that was once a barren area of windswept sand dunes. The park was created in 1846 and houses flowered meadows, an arboretum and botanical garden containing more than 6,000 plant species, and a 5-acre Japanese tea garden. Also located in the park are the Conservatory of Flowers, a children's playground with an antique carousel, and a small herd of bison, a tradition since 1890.

The city's waterfront offers a variety of entertainments. Several islands in the bay provide scenic picnic areas. Alcatraz Island, home of "The Rock," the former escape-proof federal prison, is now open for tours; advance reservations are suggested. Ocean Beach, on the Pacific side of the peninsula, provides a view of Seal Rocks, a small island occupied by a colony of sea lions. At the northern end of Ocean Beach is the San Francisco Zoo, one of the top ten in the nation. More than 1,000 animals inhabit the exhibits, including snow leopards, a rare white tiger, and a colony of koala bears. The zoo also features the computer-designed Primate Discovery Center, Gorilla World, the world's largest natural gorilla habitat, and a children's zoo.

Golden Gate National Recreation Area, one of the largest urban parks in the world and host to more than 16 million

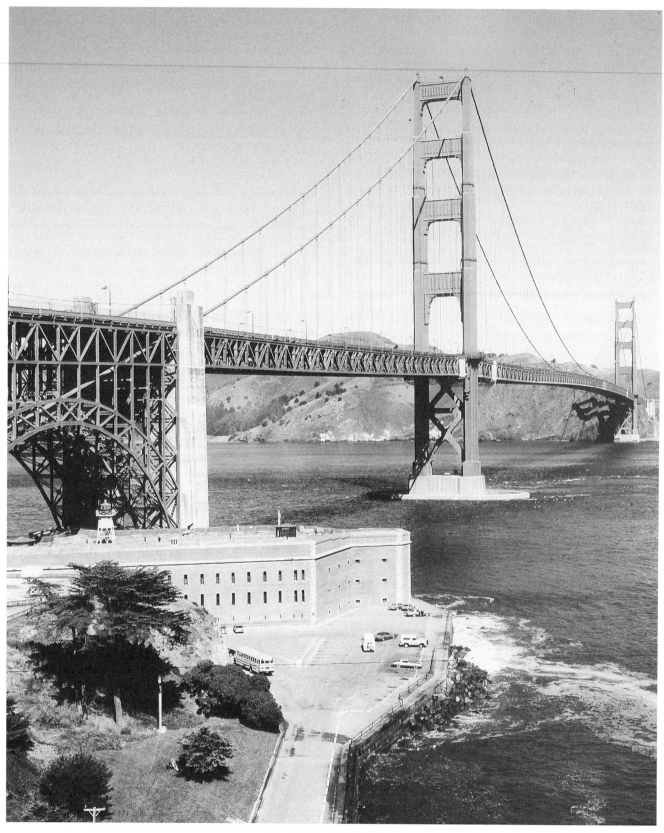

The Golden Gate Bridge.

visitors each year, is located on both sides of the Golden Gate, the entrance to San Francisco Bay. Its 75,398 acres contain stunning cliff-top views of the bay and the ocean, a network of hiking trails, valleys, and beaches, and the Fort Point National Historic Site, a brick fort built in 1861. The Golden Gate Bridge, with its pedestrian walkway, connects the two sides of the park.

Arts and Culture

San Francisco enjoys a cultural scene as varied as its population. Theater, music, and dance can be found in a multitude of outlets. The heart of the city's cultural life is located in the area around the Civic Center Plaza, where the San Francisco War Memorial and Performing Arts Center blends in with the neighboring civic buildings. The Center includes the Louise M. Davies Symphony Hall, home of the San Francisco Symphony, a world-class orchestra that is one of the oldest in the United States. The newly renovated War Memorial Opera House is home to the internationally acclaimed San Francisco Opera and the equally renowned San Francisco Ballet.

Visitors and residents enjoy Broadway shows, improvisational comedy, musical revues, and dramatic theater throughout the city. Situated on San Francisco's Union Square is TIX Bay Area, a half-price ticket booth that has day-of tickets to performances at many of the large and smaller houses. Within walking distance are American Conservatory Theater, Cable Car Theater, Curran Theater, Mason Street Theater, and Theater on the Square.

Museums in San Francisco are varied and plentiful. Located on the waterfront is the National Maritime Museum, a collection of ship models, relics, photographs, and paintings, as well as several restored vessels docked at the adjacent pier. The American Carousel Museum features a collection of hand-carved antique carousel figures. Other area museums include the San Francisco African American Historical and Cultural Society, the Museum of the California Historical Society, and the Wells Fargo History Museum.

The California Academy of Sciences, formerly in Golden Gate Park, is now in a new location downtown and consists of an aquarium, a planetarium, and a natural history museum. The Steinhart Aquarium houses more than 14,000 aquatic specimens including penguins, dolphins, seals, crocodiles, and rare Australian lungfish. The Morrison Planetarium will reopen with modern features in a brand new facility. The Natural History Museum houses many exhibits of natural science including the Earth and Space Hall with its simulated earthquake and the Gem and Mineral Hall.

The park also contains two art museums. The M. H. de Young Museum houses a diverse collection, including galleries tracing the history of art, as well as displays of American art, pre-Columbian gold work, and works by masters such as El Greco and Rembrandt. In October 2005, the museum will reopen in its brand new home, a state-of-the-art, 293,000 square foot facility. The nearby Asian Art Museum houses the Avery Brundage Collection, which contains more than 500 examples of Chinese art in addition to art of the Middle East, the Indian subcontinent, and Southeast Asia.

At the heart of San Francisco's Yerba Buena Gardens, situated south of Market Street near the Financial District, is a bustling center for arts and culture that includes the San Francisco Museum of Modern Art, which is the first museum on the West Coast devoted solely to twentieth-century art. The Jewish Museum and Mexican Museum are two of the many organizations in the process of building their new facilities nearby. Other area art museums include the San Francisco Crafts and Folk Art Museum, the Chinese Culture Center Museum, the Galeria de la Raza, the Mexican Museum of San Francisco, the Ansel Adams Center for Photography, Cartoon Art Museum, and the Museo Italo Americano.

Festivals and Holidays

San Francisco is known for its celebratory spirit, which is reflected in the calendar of festivals and special events. One of the biggest celebrations occurs in February with the week-long Chinese New Year festival, an exotic blend of parades, outdoor festivals, and other cultural programs in America's largest Chinese community. March brings the seven-day St. Patrick's Day Celebration. The attention shifts to the Japanese district for the annual Cherry Blossom Festival in April, consisting of cultural programs, exhibitions, and a parade of dancers and costumed performers.

For almost a century, thousands of runners have flocked to San Francisco in May for the annual Bay to Breakers, which is part fundraiser for a variety of charities and part celebration of the city's diversity. June brings the two-day San Francisco Lesbian, Gay, Bisexual and Transgender Parade, the world's largest gay pride event. The San Francisco Waterfront Festival is an Independence Day party that unfailingly delivers brilliant fireworks over the Bay. Also in July is the North Beach Jazz Festival, which underscores the rich history of the San Francisco jazz scene. This 5-day celebration of the Soul of San Francisco begins on Wednesday when more than 40 bars and clubs along Grant Street host local and national jazz talent. In September, people can sample the sinful fruits of chocolatiers at the Ghirardelli Square Chocolate Festival. The Holiday Festival of Lights in December takes place at Fisherman's Wharf and launches the Bay Area holiday season in style.

Sports for the Spectator

The Bay Area is home to two Major League Baseball franchises, the American League Oakland A's and the National

League San Francisco Giants, as well as to the National Basketball Association's Golden State Warriors, the National Hockey League's San Jose Sharks, and the pro-soccer league's San Jose Clash. The National Football Leagues' San Francisco 49ers was the first professional sports franchise on the West Coast, and have made several trips to the Super Bowl. During the past 16 seasons, San Francisco's football team has won more than 70 percent of its games and posted an NFL record of 13 straight seasons with 10 or more victories. Thoroughbred racing can be enjoyed at Golden Gate Fields or Bay Meadows, two of America's premier horse racing facilities. The Laguna Seca Raceway and the Infineon Raceway provide a variety of motor sports nearby. The city annually sponsors one of the largest marathons in the country, the San Francisco Marathon, as well as several other running events throughout the year. Area colleges and universities also field teams in most sports and maintain extensive spectator facilities.

Sports for the Participant

San Francisco offers a wide array of choices for those who are sports minded. Aquatic sports are especially popular because of the city's proximity to water. Yachting, boating, swimming, water skiing, boardsailing, surfing, fishing, and hang gliding from cliffs are among the favorite activities. The 75,398-acre Golden Gate Recreation Area is filled with hiking and bicycling trails, campgrounds, and wildlife preserves. The San Francisco Recreation and Parks Department administers and maintains more than 200 parks, playgrounds, and open spaces throughout the city, including two outside the city limits: Sharp Park in Pacifica and Camp Mather in the High Sierras. The system also includes 15 large, full-complex recreation centers; 9 swimming pools; 5 golf courses; and hundreds of tennis courts, ball diamonds, athletic fields, and basketball courts. The department is also responsible for the Marina Yacht Harbor, Candlestick Park, the San Francisco Zoo, and the Lake Merced Complex, which is operated for recreational purposes under the San Francisco Water Department.

Shopping and Dining

San Francisco offers some of the best shopping in the world, so it is no wonder that tourists and serious shopaholics alike want to spend some time and money in San Francisco's varied shopping centers, districts and malls. Union Square, Hayes Valley, upper Fillmore, the Mission, Sacramento Street, Chinatown and downtown's San Francisco Shopping Center offer a unique style with one-of-a-kind shops; each mall and neighborhood offers a distinctive feel suited to any shopper's mood. Other major shopping districts include Ghirardelli Square, which is a group of stores built around the Ghirardelli chocolate factory, and the Cannery, a lavishly remodeled former produce processing plant. Other popular shopping destinations are the Anchorage at Fisherman's Wharf, and downtown's Embarcadero Center. In addition, each ethnic neighborhood supports its own distinctive section of shops, open-air markets, and restaurants. San Francisco is famous for its vast and varied assortment of bookstores.

San Francisco has been called "the weight watcher's Waterloo" because of its tempting restaurants, many holding international reputations. Nearly 4,000 restaurants in the city are geographically concentrated at the rate of about 95 per square mile. Dining styles and venues include supper clubs, American grills, California-Asian hybrids, haute vegetarian, modest bistros, and fine-dining destinations.

Seafood fresh off the boat can be obtained at restaurants along Fisherman's Wharf; farmland, vineyards, and cattle ranches in the surrounding area provide an abundance of other fresh ingredients. Sourdough bread is a San Francisco specialty. Many international restaurants, serving dishes from around the world and prepared with exact authenticity, are scattered throughout the city's numerous ethnic neighborhoods.

Visitor Information: San Francisco Convention and Visitors Bureau, Convention Plaza, 201 Third Street, Suite 900, San Francisco, CA 94103; telephone (415)391-2000; fax (415)362-7323.

Convention Facilities

The city of San Francisco hosts more than a million meeting, convention, and trade show delegates annually. Convention planners come to San Francisco not only because of the attractions in the Bay Area, but also for the excellent facilities. The city's Civic Center, called "the grandest Civic Center in the country" by architectural critics, houses extensive meeting facilities. The Bill Graham Civic Auditorium seats 7,000 people, with two adjoining halls that seat another 900 people. Underneath the auditorium is the Brooks Exhibit Hall, a 90,000-square-foot open exhibition area. The Moscone Center offers 600,000 square feet; a 300,000-square-foot expansion was completed in 2003.

The city has nearly 32,719 hotel rooms available. All the rooms are within easy traveling distance of the main convention sites. Most of the major hotels in the area provide ample meeting space, ballrooms, registration lobbies, and exhibit areas.

Convention Information: San Francisco Convention & Visitors Bureau, Convention Plaza, 201 Third Street, Suite 900,

San Francisco, CA 94103; telephone (415)391-2000; fax (415)362-7323.

Transportation

Approaching the City

The San Francisco International Airport is the ninth busiest in the nation, handling more than 40 million passengers on more than 1,300 flights a day from more than 35 airlines. An efficient customs clearance, modern facilities, and computerized ground transportation information make the airport easy to use. A $2.4 billion expansion, including a new international terminal, centralized rental car center, and new AirTrain system is currently underway. Many of the downtown hotels offer free transportation to and from the airport.

The city is at the intersection of several major highways. U.S. 101 and S.R. 1, the Pacific Coastal Highway, converge on San Francisco from the north and south. From the east, Interstate 80 and U.S. 50 serve the city. Interstate Loops 580 and 680 provide access to Interstate 5, the major north-south route from Canada to Mexico.

Amtrak rail service is available, as is CalTrain, a commuter service that operates from San Francisco to San Jose. Bus service is offered via Greyhound Bus Lines.

Traveling in the City

Because of the city's compact size, walking is a favored means of transportation, but when the distance is too great, several public transportation options are available. The famous cable cars are not only a tourist attraction, but also a convenient way for commuters to travel in the downtown area. The city's Municipal Railway System (Muni) light-rail vehicles, descendants of the cable cars, travel underground in the inner city and above ground in the outlying areas; bearers of Muni Passports have access to Muni's entire 978-vehicle fleet of buses, trolleys, light-rail vehicles, and cable cars. Muni is the country's seventh largest transit system in terms of ridership. The Bay Area Rapid Transit (BART) is an ultra-modern train system linking the city with 43 stations in the East Bay Area. The year 2005 marks BART's seventh of a critical $1.2 billion program to renovate system infrastructure to provide optimum on-time performance, safe and comfortable station and train environments, and enhanced system accessibility. Four ferry services also connect the city with Oakland and Berkeley across the bay.

Communications

Newspapers and Magazines

San Francisco is prominent in the publishing industry on both the regional and national levels. The city is served by two major daily newspapers, the morning *San Francisco Chronicle* and the evening *San Francisco Examiner.* A number of weekly special interest, alternative, foreign-language, and neighborhood papers are also printed. Several nationally distributed magazines are based in the city, as are many trade, industry, and technical journals. Among the many local and national publications are *San Francisco, Mother Jones,* and *MacWorld.* A variety of scholarly, medical, and professional journals are published in San Francisco.

Television and Radio

Fifteen television stations provide viewing choices from the commercial networks, public television, and foreign-language stations. Additional channels are available through cable service. Thirty-one AM and FM radio stations broadcast in San Francisco, offering a range of music, news, and information programming.

Media Information: San Francisco Chronicle, 901 Mission Street, San Francisco, CA 94103-2988; telephone (415)777-1111. *San Francisco Examiner,* 110 Fifth Street, San Francisco, CA 94103; telephone (415)777-5700

San Francisco Online

California Historical Society. Available www.californiahistoricalsociety.org

City of San Francisco Home Page. Available www.ci.sf.ca.us

San Francisco Chamber of Commerce. Available www.sfchamber.com

San Francisco Chronicle. Available www.sfgate.com/chronicle

San Francisco Convention & Visitors Bureau (for information on events, activities, transportation, and lodging reservations). Available www.sfvisitor.org

San Francisco Examiner. Available www.examiner.com

San Francisco Partnership's. Available www.sfp.org

San Francisco Public Library. Available www.sfpl.lib.ca.us

San Francisco Unified School District. Available www.sfusd.k12.ca.us

Selected Bibliography

Caen, Herb, *Baghdad by the Bay* (Garden City, NY: Doubleday, 1949)

Gold, Herbert, *Bohemia: Where Art, Angst, Love, and Strong Coffee Meet* (New York: Simon & Schuster, 1993)

Lewis, Oscar, *San Francisco: Mission to Metropolis* (San Diego: Howell-North Books, 1980)

Twain, Mark, *Mark Twain's San Francisco* (New York: McGraw-Hill, 1963)

Twain, Mark, *Roughing it in California* (Kentfield, CA: L-D Allen Press, 1953)

Twain, Mark, *The Washoe Giant in San Francisco* (San Francisco: G. Fields, 1938)

Wheeler, Richard S., *Aftershocks* (New York: Forge, 1999)

San Jose

The City in Brief

Founded: 1777 (incorporated, 1850)

Head Official: City Manager Del Borgsdorf (since 1999)

City Population
  1980: 629,442
  1990: 782,224
  2000: 894,943
  2003 estimate: 898,349
  Percent change, 1990–2000: 13.6%
  U.S. rank in 1980: 17th
  U.S. rank in 1990: 11th
  U.S. rank in 2000: 11th

Metropolitan Area Population (CMSA)
  1990: 6,253,311
  2000: 7,039,361

Percent change, 1990–2000: 12.6%
U.S. rank in 1980: 4th
U.S. rank in 1990: 4th
U.S. rank in 2000: 5th

Area: 175 square miles (2000)
Elevation: 67 feet above sea level
Average Annual Temperature: 57.1° F
Average Annual Precipitation: 18.5 inches

Major Economic Sectors: Manufacturing, services, government
Unemployment Rate: 6.2% (January 2005)
Per Capita Income: $26,697 (1999)

2002 FBI Crime Index Total: 24,139

Major Colleges and Universities: San Jose State University, San Jose/Evergreen Community College District

Daily Newspaper: *San Jose Mercury News*

Introduction

Once a quiet, medium-sized city at the center of a thriving agricultural area, San Jose was transformed in less than 30 years into a huge metropolis and a phenomenon in U.S. economic history. As the result of the computer revolution, San Jose became the capital of the "Silicon Valley," a vast complex of electronics industries that stretches throughout California's Santa Clara County. From 1950 to 1980, a period of tremendous growth and prosperity, the population of San Jose increased fourfold. Like other major urban areas, however, the city has been forced to confront the problems that come with unbridled development: traffic congestion, air pollution, housing shortages, and a strained infrastructure. A 1985 recession in the Silicon Valley produced a stagnant economy, from which the city recovered by the twenty-first century. San Jose consistently ranks high in polls that rate cities for business climate, livability, and fun.

Geography and Climate

San Jose is located in the Santa Clara Valley at the southern tip of San Francisco Bay, 48 miles south of San Francisco and 40 miles south of Oakland. The area is known as the Southern Peninsula. San Jose is the seat of Santa Clara County and the center of a large and expanding metropolitan area bordered by the Santa Cruz Mountains on the west and the Diablo Mountain range on the east. The Coyote and Guadalupe rivers run through the city. San Jose's climate is mild and semi-arid, with humidity varying from 67 percent in January to 51 percent in July.

Area: 175 square miles (2000)

Elevation: 67 feet above sea level

Average Temperatures: January, 48.7° F; July, 62.7° F; annual average, 57.1° F

Average Annual Precipitation: 18.5 inches

History

San Jose Begins as Agricultural Center for State

San Jose was California's first civic settlement, founded in 1777 by Mexican colonists and named El Pueblo de San Jose de Guadalupe for St. Joseph and the Guadalupe River near the town site. The town was established in order to bring agricultural development to the Alta California territory; each settler was issued animals, farm implements, seeds, and a 10-dollar monthly stipend. These farmers joined Spanish missionaries who were already in the area. The Native American inhabitants of the region were the Olhone; the disruption of their culture by the missionaries and farmers and the spread of diseases eventually led to their virtual extermination.

As a supply station for prospectors during the gold rush, San Jose underwent a population explosion; upon incorporation in 1850 the city's inhabitants numbered 5,000 people. San Jose was the state capital from 1849 to 1851, and then became an important stage and boat link on the route to San Francisco until the advent of the railroad in 1864. Growth continued through the 1880s, reaching a culmination with the real estate boom and bust of 1887 when land sales totaled $2 million per day before the market collapsed. By the turn of the century San Jose was a major center for the cultivation of apricots, prunes, and grapes; with rail connections to other cities, it was also an important regional shipping hub.

High-Technology Revolution

Prior to World War II San Jose, with its 18 canneries and 13 packing houses, was the world's largest canning and dried-fruit packing center. The city also pioneered the manufacture of specialized mechanical farm equipment in California; among the products introduced by local inventors were the spray pump and the steam-powered stemmer-crusher for wine making. In the 1950s, however, San Jose was transformed from a farming community to a high-technology capital by another of its natural resources: silicon. This element is used in making semiconductors, a basic component in high-technology industries. Thus San Jose and Santa Clara County came to be known as "Silicon Valley." Originating at Stanford University in nearby Palo Alto, a vast military-industrial complex, which includes the Ames Research Facility of the National Aeronautics and Space Administration (NASA) at Moffett Field, ultimately spread throughout the Southern Peninsula.

San Jose's largest population boom was triggered by this high-technology revolution, and growth continued unabated from the 1950s through the early 1980s. Buoyed by the success of computer companies, a steady flow of venture capital poured into San Jose and Santa Clara County to finance new firms that sprang up almost overnight. Expansion began to moderate only with the 1985 recession in the computer industry. Unemployment remains relatively low in the San Jose metropolitan area, as more than 20 percent of the semiconductors and related devices made in the United States continue to be produced in the Silicon Valley. The city nevertheless has been faced with problems resulting from uncontrolled development. Steps have been taken toward a solution, in the form of a new light-rail system designed to alleviate traffic congestion and stricter controls on expansion and construction. By the end of the twentieth century, residents and city planners alike were looking ahead. At the start of the twenty-first century, San Jose boasted great economic opportunity, many jobs, and a high standard of living. The area frequently ranks near the top of quality of life studies sponsored by universities and national media.

Historical Information: History Museums of San Jose Archives, 1650 Senter Road, San Jose, CA 95112; telephone (408)287-2290

Population Profile

Metropolitan Area Residents (CMSA)
1990: 6,253,311
2000: 7,039,361
Percent change, 1990–2000: 12.6%
U.S. rank in 1980: 4th
U.S. rank in 1990: 4th
U.S. rank in 2000: 5th

City Residents
1980: 629,442
1990: 782,224
2000: 894,943
2003 estimate: 898,349
Percent change, 1990–2000: 13.6%
U.S. rank in 1980: 17th
U.S. rank in 1990: 11th
U.S. rank in 2000: 11th

Density: 5,117.9 people per square mile (2000)

Racial and ethnic characteristics (2000)
White: 425,017
Black or African American: 31,349
American Indian and Alaska Native: 6,865
Asian: 240,375
Native Hawaiian and Pacific Islander: 3,584
Hispanic or Latino (may be of any race): 269,989
Other: 167,353

Percent of residents born in state: 44.8% (2000)

Age characteristics (2000)
Population under 5 years old: 68,243
Population 5 to 9 years old: 68,484
Population 10 to 14 years old: 62,439
Population 15 to 19 years old: 61,487
Population 20 to 24 years old: 64,418

Population 25 to 34 years old: 160,945
Population 35 to 44 years old: 155,751
Population 45 to 54 years old: 111,383
Population 55 to 59 years old: 38,770
Population 60 to 64 years old: 29,163
Population 65 to 74 years old: 41,962
Population 75 to 84 years old: 24,085
Population 85 years and older: 7,813
Median age: 32.6 years

Births (2003)
Total number: 26,997

Deaths (2002)
Total number: 8,642 (of which, 138 were infants under the age of 1 year)

Money income (1999)
Per capita income: $26,697
Median household income: $70,243
Total households: 276,408

Number of households with income of . . .
less than $10,000: 13,166
$10,000 to $14,999: 8,364
$15,000 to $24,999: 17,854
$25,000 to $34,999: 20,285
$35,000 to $49,999: 32,824
$50,000 to $74,999: 55,453
$75,000 to $99,999: 43,337
$100,000 to $149,999: 51,374
$150,000 to $199,999: 19,818
$200,000 or more: 13,933

Percent of families below poverty level: 6.0% (28.8 % of which were female householder families with related children under 5 years)

2002 FBI Crime Index Total: 24,139

Municipal Government

San Jose operates under a council-manager form of government. The eleven council members include the mayor; all serve four-year terms. The city manager is appointed by the mayor and the council to an open-ended term. San Jose is the seat of Santa Clara County.

Head Official: City Manager Del Borgsdorf (since 1999)

Total Number of City Employees: 6,300 (2004)

City Information: Information Center, City Hall, 801 North First Street, San Jose, CA 95110; telephone (408)277-5800

Economy

Major Industries and Commercial Activity

The rapid expansion of high-technology industries triggered uninterrupted growth in the Silicon Valley—San Jose and Santa Clara County—from the 1950s through the early 1980s. The 1985 recession, however, left a stagnant economy, pointing to a need to diversify the economic base of the area. Studies indicated that high-technology companies had to move toward decreased reliance on the defense industry. By the early 1990s businesses in San Jose and Santa Clara County showed less than 20 percent of their budgets devoted to government contracts. The city was encouraged by a 1992 study that reported the nation's beleaguered semiconductor industry claimed 43.8 percent of the world market, up from a low of 36.9 percent in 1988.

By 1997 the nation was riding the wave of a booming New Economy—involving the creation of new companies that put the Internet to use to change the way business is done. High technology had become a major factor in the economic growth of U.S. cities, and San Jose was at the center of it all. By 2000 San Jose was a mecca for hot startup companies and venture capital dollars. San Jose, and in particular the Silicon Valley region, is a hotbed of technology and technological innovation. The area has received more patents than any other technology region in the United States. Technology businesses centered here continue to grow and expand in the twenty-first century, as does the growth of service and support businesses to the industry.

Incentive Programs—New and Existing Companies

Local programs—The city of San Jose adopted a Local Preference Policy in May 2004. The policy works to encourage local companies to work with other local companies and the city to promote further job growth for residents and to keep "more of the City of San Jose's spending within the regional economy." The Local Preference Policy goes hand in hand with the Small Business Opportunity Program, which works to smooth the process for small businesses of selling their products and services to the city.

A variety of loans, bonds, and special funds are available to local businesses in San Jose. Among them are the Development Enhancement Special Fund, which helps businesses secure loan funds for expansion, working capital, inventory, or other qualified business expenses; Industrial Development Bonds offer financing options for manufacturing firms that are job-generating; the Lenders for Community Development program provides access to small business loans and lines of credit; and the Revolving Loan Fund makes funds available to small businesses for a variety of uses.

The San Jose Silicon Valley Chamber of Commerce works to develop and maintain the metropolitan area economy. Their particular focus is on aiding small and medium-sized companies involved in international business. The chamber's international trade program includes seminars, networking events, and exhibitions. The San Jose Downtown Association also works to stimulate and improve business conditions. The SBA/CiscoSystems/San Jose Entrepreneur Center provides services to entrepreneurs and small businesses.

State programs—An 18-square mile state-designated Enterprise Zone offers businesses operating in the zone significant tax savings and other financial benefits. The zone consists of San Jose's downtown area and benefits retail, commercial, and high-tech businesses located there. Benefits of operating in the Enterprise Zone include Sales and Use Tax Credits; Hiring Tax Credits; Net Operating Loss Carryover and Net Interest Deduction for Lenders programs; and a Business Expense Deductions program. San Jose is also a designated Foreign Trade Zone, which allows companies to reduce, delay, or eliminate customs fees on imported goods. The Silicon Valley Export Assistance Center offers state and government programs that assist companies who wish to export goods.

Job training programs—The Silicon Valley Workforce Investment Network works with local businesses and residents. The network's one-stop system offers resources for job seekers, as well as services to businesses that include pre-employment screening, access to qualified applicants, training programs, and assistance with employee transitions.

Items and goods produced: missiles; rocket boosters; computers; atomic electrical equipment; fruit, vegetable, and fish cans; dairy products; chemicals; aluminum; paint; fiberglass; matches; medical equipment

Development Projects

In 2003 and 2004, more than 240,000 square feet of retail space was added in downtown San Jose. The Neighborhood Business Districts (NBD) program was established as part of an effort to boost retail business in San Jose's older neighborhoods; its efforts have resulted in 40 new restaurants and retail stores opening among the districts by early 2005. CIM Group's Central Place was approved in early 2005; construction on the downtown mixed-use highrise housing project will begin in fall 2005.

A massive plan for the redevelopment of North San Jose, or the Innovation Triangle, is on the ballot for city council to vote on in spring 2005. The North San Jose 2030 plan calls for a redevelopment of the approximately 42 million square feet of industrial space in the Innovation Triangle, which is currently home to more than 1,200 multinational companies. The plan cites that the space is currently "functionally obsolete," and calls for renovations as well as an additional

26.7 million square feet of new research and development space and office space, 32,000 new housing units, and 1.4 million square feet of retail space.

A $2.8 billion expansion of the San Jose International Airport was underway in 2005, with phased completion dates and expansions and improvements ranging from new concourses and parking garages, terminal and roadway improvements, and an Automated People Mover. When completed in 2015, the airport will serve 17.6 million passengers annually, up from 11.5 million.

Economic Development Information: San Jose Silicon Valley Chamber of Commerce, 310 South First Street, San Jose, CA 95113; telephone (408)291-5250

Commercial Shipping

Nearly half of the traffic at San Jose International Airport is business related, which makes the facility an important factor in the Silicon Valley economy. Revenues from freight shipments average more than $10 million annually; cargo handled at the airport in 2004 exceeded 5 million pounds. Four air cargo carriers and several air freight services maintain facilities at the airport. Two major rail freight lines and a number of motor freight carriers also operate in the metropolitan area.

Labor Force and Employment Outlook

According to San Jose's Office of Economic Development, more than 85 percent of the region's new jobs come from companies that are less than 10 years old. A well-educated and abundant work force coupled with the great quantity of high-level jobs created annually combine to create a shortage of qualified employees in the region. With more than 7,000 technology companies, the technology industry is responsible for employing more than 300,000 people.

The following is a summary of data regarding the San Jose metropolitan area labor force, 2004 annual averages.

Size of non-agricultural labor force: 859,900

Number of workers employed in . . .
   natural resources and mining: 100
   construction: 41,700
   manufacturing: 170,100
   trade, transportation and utilities: 130,000
   information: 32,700
   financial activities: 35,000
   professional and business services: 165,900
   educational and health services: 94,500
   leisure and hospitality: 69,800
   other services: 24,900
   government: 94,700

Average hourly earnings of production workers employed in manufacturing: $17.21

Unemployment rate: 6.2% (January 2005)

Largest employers	Number of employees
County of Santa Clara	14,800
Cisco Systems	13,400
City of San Jose	7,200
IBM Corporation	6,400
San Jose Unified School District	3,360
Hitachi	2,900
Agilent Technologies	2,880
Xilinx	2,600
Adobe Systems	2,000
Good Samaritan Health System	1,850
KLA Tencor Instruments	1,850
Novellus Systems	1,800
Cadence Design Systems, Inc.	1,760
Sanmina-SCI	1,750

Cost of Living

San Jose suffers from a severe shortage of affordable housing and is among the most expensive cities to live; conversely, San Jose residents also have the highest disposable income in the nation.

The following is a summary of data regarding key cost of living factors for the San Jose area.

2004 (3rd Quarter) ACCRA Average House Price: $766,310

2004 (3rd Quarter) ACCRA Cost of Living Index: 170.8 (U.S. average = 100.0)

State income tax rate: Ranges from 1.0% to 9.3%

State sales tax rate: 6%

Local income tax rate: None

Local sales tax rate: 1.25%

Property tax rate: Average 1.1% of full cash value

Economic Information: San Jose Silicon Valley Chamber of Commerce, 310 South First St., San Jose, CA 95113; telephone (408)291-5250; fax (408)286-5019; email info @sjchamber.com. State of California, Employment Development Department, 800 Capitol Mall, MIC 83, Sacramento, CA 95814

Education and Research

Elementary and Secondary Schools

Fourteen school districts serve the population of San Jose, including the largest, San Jose Unified School District.

News in 2005 was of the district's continuing budget difficulties, with the district facing a $9-11 million deficit for the 2005-2006 school year and a $11-13 million deficit for the following year. Cited as contributing to the crisis was a steadily declining enrollment, a decrease in state funding, and increases in operational expenses; of special concern are possible school closings.

The following is a summary of data regarding the San Jose Unified School District as of the 2002–2003 school year.

Total enrollment: 32,612

Number of facilities
    elementary schools: 27
    junior high/middle schools: 7
    senior high schools: 7
    other: 1 college preparatory

Student/teacher ratio: 21.5:1

Teacher salaries (2002-2003)
    Minimum: $33,128
    Maximum: $72,665

Funding per pupil: $8,546 (2001-2002)

More than 60 private and parochial schools serve San Jose.

Public Schools Information: San Jose Unified School District, 855 Lenzen Avenue, San Jose, CA 95126; telephone (408)535-6000

Colleges and Universities

Based in San Jose is San Jose State University, the oldest public institution of higher learning on the West Coast, as well as one of the largest universities in the 23-campus California State University system. San Jose State University educates nearly 30,000 students and offers 134 bachelor's and master's degrees in 110 concentrations; the university prides itself on being the top supplier of engineering, computer science, and business graduates to the Silicon Valley high-tech workforce. The San Jose/Evergreen Community College District is comprised of San Jose City College and Evergreen Valley College; both award associate of arts and science degrees, and occupational and technical training to their more than 30,000 students. The University of Phoenix-North California Campuses has a facility in San Jose, which awards bachelors and masters degrees. Also located in the San Jose area are technical and vocational schools, adult learning centers, and extension facilities. Several colleges and universities—some of them considered among the best in the nation—are within driving distance of San Jose. They include Stanford University, Santa Clara University, and the University of California campuses at Berkeley and Santa Cruz.

Libraries and Research Centers

The San Jose Public Library system operates a main facility, 21 branches, and a bookmobile. Library holdings consist of more than 1.9 million items. The newly-constructed $177.5 million Dr. Martin Luther King Junior Main Library opened in 2003. The new building, 7 years in planning, was a joint development effort between the city, San Jose State University, and the San Jose Redevelopment Agency. With 8 floors and more than 475,000 square feet, the library is among the largest in the country and serves more than one million visitors annually. The Main Library also houses a special collection in the California Room, featuring state and local history from 1849 to the present; the Cultural Heritage Center; and the Ira F. Brilliant Center for Beethoven Studies. In early 2005 three new neighborhood facilities had opened, adding square footage and replacing older library buildings; at the same time, four branches were closed and construction was beginning on new facilities.

The San Jose State University library, now part of the San Jose Public Library's Dr. Martin Luther King Junior Main Library, houses the Steinbeck Research Center, which contains the writings and memorabilia of novelist John Steinbeck, a San Jose area native, as well as the world's largest collection of the writer's first edition books.

San Jose institutions conduct research activities in such fields as gerontology, the environment, and telecommunications. IBM's Almaden Research Center conducts industrial research in computer science, software, computer storage technology, and physical and materials science and technology.

Public Library Information: Dr. Martin Luther King, Jr. Main Library, 150 E. San Fernando Street, San Jose, CA 95112; telephone (408)808-2000

Health Care

HCA Healthcare Corp. owns two major hospitals in San Jose: the Regional Medical Center of San Jose has 204 licensed beds and serves about 45,000 patients annually in its Emergency Department; Good Samaritan Hospital is a general acute-care hospital with a licensed bed capacity of 422. A source of contention at the end of 2004 was the closing of the city's only downtown hospital, the San Jose Medical Center. Citing major revenue losses, HCA closed the 324-bed hospital a full 3 years earlier than planned, leaving residents concerned about who would care for inner-city trauma victims.

Santa Clara Valley Medical Center, one of California's most high-tech public hospitals, is a 524-bed acute-care facility that houses a burn unit, a rehabilitation center for patients with spinal and head injuries, a trauma center, a high-risk maternity program, and a neonatal intensive-care unit. O'Connor hospital, sponsored by the Daughters of Charity, offer heart and cancer care, sports medicine, and a Wound Care Center. Stanford Hospital in nearby Palo Alto, is highly regarded for its work in a wide variety of specialties, notably cardiovascular treatment, and is the teaching facility for the Stanford University medical school. Only 20 minutes from San Jose, the hospital's 613 beds and more than 1,800 medical staff personnel serve more than 400,000 area residents annually. Stanford Clinics offer treatment in more than 100 specialties and subspecialties.

Recreation

Sightseeing

Most of the attractions in San Jose are related to the natural beauty of the area or to its historical past. Kelley Park is a popular site, offering a variety of diversions, including Happy Hollow Park and Zoo where visitors can enjoy family-oriented amusements and view wildlife in a 12-acre natural setting. The 16-acre San Jose Historical Museum on the park grounds features a recreated turn-of-the-century town with such exhibits as a working blacksmith shop, a Victorian home, and a doctor's office. Also located in Kelley Park is the Japanese Friendship Garden, featuring flowering trees and shrubs, waterfalls, and koi fish. Other botanical gardens in San Jose are Overfelt Botanical Gardens and the Municipal Rose Garden.

Alum Rock Park is a wildlife refuge containing mineral springs, trails, and picnic facilities; the Youth Science Institute based in the park offers educational programs and special events to acquaint children with nature. Ardenwood Historic Farm in neighboring Fremont is a working farm that demonstrates agrarian life from 1880 through the 1920s; among the exhibits are soap and candle making and the planting and harvesting of crops with horse-drawn equipment.

Especially popular with tourists is the Winchester Mystery House; according to legend, this "haunted" Victorian mansion, containing 160 rooms, was built by the wealthy but eccentric widow of the maker of the Winchester rifle to appease the spirits of the rifle's victims. Nationally known for its table wines, the San Jose area boasts dozens of wineries; many offer wine-tasting and tours of their facilities. Several theme parks operate in Santa Clara County, including Paramount's Raging Waters in San Jose's Lake Cunningham Regional Park and Paramount's Great America in nearby Santa Clara.

Arts and Culture

San Jose is becoming a regional center for the arts as local performing groups and organizations consistently draw larger audiences from throughout the Bay Area. A wide range of theatrical, musical, and dance performances is presented at the Center for the Performing Arts and the Montgomery Theater downtown.

The American Musical Theatre of San Jose entertains capacity crowds with three to four annual Broadway musicals. The San Jose Repertory Theatre produces classic and contemporary drama, and plays for children are staged by the San Jose Children's Musical Theater. The San Jose Symphony and Opera San Jose present full subscription seasons. The Ballet San Jose Silicon Valley is considered one of the country's most innovative ballet companies, with a repertoire of more than 120 modern and traditional classical ballets. HP Pavilion hosts varied performers such as U2 and Mormon Tabernacle Choir.

San Jose's museums and galleries specialize in a variety of fields. Attractions include the Children's Discovery Museum, offering hands-on exhibits, and The Tech Museum of Innovation, offering an IMAX theater and interactive experiences in new technologies. The Rosicrucian Egyptian Museum features the city's only planetarium as well as astronomical and scientific displays; a full-scale Egyptian tomb exhibit; and a collection of Egyptian artifacts.

The San Jose Museum of Art features changing exhibits of American art. The San Jose Museum of Quilts and Textiles, one of the few museums of its kind in the country, provides a showcase for the history of quilts and textiles. The work of local and Bay Area artists is shown at the Institute of Contemporary Art and at the Works Gallery.

Arts and Culture Information: San Jose Convention and Visitors Bureau, 408 Almaden Blvd., San Jose, CA 95110; telephone (408)295-9600; toll-free (800)726-5673

Festivals and Holidays

Special events and celebrations take place in the San Jose area throughout the year, many of them focusing on the cultural heritages of the region's diverse population. Winter events include January's San Jose International Auto Show; in February, the Vietnamese Spring Festival and Parade offers food, entertainment, games, and other fun highlighting Vietnamese culture in the city. Spring offerings include the San Jose Art Festival, a juried art show; and the Golden Circle Theatre Party, an annual black-tie benefit, both in March. April's annual Iris Show is a favorite of gardeners and iris aficionados; May brings cultural celebrations including the Nikkei Matsuri, Cinco de Mayo Parade and Festival, and the Zee Heritage India Festival. Summer events include the Comcast Jazz Festival and the weekend Downtown Farmers Market. Fall's offerings include dance and arts festivals, Halloween at Bonfante Gardens, and the Silicon Valley Marathon. San Jose's year winds down with a Holiday River Parade and Lighting Ceremony, and the Nuestra Navidad, an celebration of Christmas in the Mexican tradition.

Sports for the Spectator

San Jose is in an advantageous location for fans of professional sports. The National Hockey League's San Jose Sharks play at the HP Pavillion. The HP Pavillion also hosts the San Jose Stealth lacrosse and AFLs SaberCats football teams, as well as figure skating, boxing, and other sporting events. Major league soccer's San Jose Earthquakes play at San Jose State University's Spartan Stadium. The San Jose Giants, the farm club for the San Francisco Giants National League baseball team, play their home games at Municipal Stadium in San Jose. Horse racing is on view at Bay Meadows Racecourse in San Mateo and at the Santa Clara County Fairgrounds.

Several professional teams compete within driving distance of San Jose; among them are baseball's San Francisco Giants and Oakland Athletics, and Oakland's Golden State Warriors of the National Basketball Association (NBA).

Sports for the Participant

A variety of neighborhood and regional parks in the San Jose area provide facilities for a variety of activities such as water sports, baseball, tennis, golf, hiking, horseback riding, and wildlife study. San Jose's 144 large and small neighborhood parks and gardens, and another 9 regional parks, are maintained by the city; especially popular are Almaden Quicksilver Park, Alum Rock Park, and Lake Cunningham Regional Park. Numerous reservoirs and lakes are located throughout the region for sailing, waterskiing, and windsurfing. A number of golf courses exist in the area, including two Jack Nicklaus-designed golf courses, and the new Los Lagos Golf Course spanning Coyote Creek.

Shopping and Dining

With several major and outlet malls, regional shopping centers, and myriad neighborhood stores and specialty shops, San Jose can meet the needs of most consumers. San Jose's largest shopping center is Eastridge; a major renovation scheduled for completion in 2005 will offer shoppers one million square feet of shopping, dining, and entertainment options. The San Jose Flea Market is one of the nation's largest flea markets and attracts more than 2,000 sellers and more than 80,000 shoppers per week to its 8 miles of corridors and alleys. Shoppers will find anything from antiques and collectibles to freshly-made foods. The "Produce

Row" section of the market is touted as California's largest farmer's market.

Restaurants are plentiful in San Jose, offering American cuisine and ethnic specialties ranging from German and French to Mexican, Persian, Moroccan, and Thai dishes. Several authentic Japanese restaurants are clustered in historic Japantown. Santa Clara Valley wineries combine brunches, luncheons, and picnics with wine tastings; the area is noted for its Chardonnay, Zinfandel, and Johannisburg Riesling wines.

Visitor Information: San Jose Convention and Visitors Bureau, 408 Almaden Blvd., San Jose, CA 95110; telephone (408)295-9600; toll-free (800)726-5673

Convention Facilities

The principal convention and meeting place is the San Jose McEnery Convention Center. With a total of 425,000 square feet, the complex also contains the Center for the Performing Arts, Civic Auditorium, Parkside Hall, and Montgomery Theater.

There are more than 4,000 hotel and motel rooms in San Jose's downtown, and another 4,400 citywide. Hotels and motels in the San Jose metropolitan area, many of them new or recently renovated, provide accommodations for a variety of group functions. Among the unique meeting facilities are the Bay Meadows Racecourse, and the many museums and wineries in the area.

Convention Information: San Jose Convention and Visitors Bureau, 408 Almaden Blvd., San Jose, CA 95110; telephone (408)295-9600; toll-free (800)726-5673

Transportation

Approaching the City

The Norman Y. Mineta San Jose International Airport, located 10 minutes from downtown, is rated among the 31 busiest airports in the world, handling more than 11 million passengers annually; it is served by 12 airlines with more than 200 daily flights. In 2005 major construction was underway at the airport, with projects including new terminals, a people mover, more parking, runway extensions, and advanced security systems, all slated for completion in phases by 2015. Corporate and private aircraft are accommodated at San Jose Jet Center and Reid-Hillview Airport.

Three interstate highways serve San Jose: I-680 (north-south), which becomes I-280 (east-west); I-880 (north-south); and Highway101 (northeast-southwest).

Amtrak serves the San Jose train depot; rail commuter service to San Francisco is provided by Caltrain. Other intercity rail connections are made via the county bus system that links with BART (Bay Area Rapid Transit), an ultra-modern train system based in San Francisco; a $1 billion transit plan approved in 2000 will fund an eventual BART extension to San Jose. In early 2005, plans were still in the engineering stage for the project.

Traveling in the City

Santa Clara Valley Transportation Authority operates a 30-mile-long light rail system out of the downtown Transit Mall, which also provides antique trolleys and county transit buses connecting the city with Bay Area Rapid Transit to East Bay and San Francisco. The light rail system runs from Mountain View through downtown San Jose and ends in south San Jose residential and shopping areas.

Communications

Newspapers and Magazines

San Jose's daily newspaper is the *San Jose Mercury News.* The metropolitan area is also served by such publications as the weekly *The Business Journal* and the *San Jose Post-Record,* a daily legal newspaper. Among the bilingual newspapers published in San Jose are the *Vietnam Daily Newspaper, La Oferta Review,* a twice-weekly Spanish newspaper, and *El Observador,* a Latino weekly.

Television and Radio

Because of the proximity of communities in the Bay Area, San Jose shares a number of television and radio stations with other cities. Based in San Jose are four television stations—one public and three commercial—and ten AM and FM radio stations.

Media Information: *San Jose Mercury News,* 750 Ridder Park Drive, San Jose, CA 95190; telephone (408)920-5000

San Jose Online

City of San Jose home page. Available www.sanjoseca.gov

History San Jose (San José Historical Museum, Peralta Adobe & Fallon House). Available at www.historysanjose .org

San Jose Convention & Visitors Bureau. Available www .sanjose.org

San Jose Mercury News. Available www.mercurynews.com

San Jose Public Library. Available www.sjlibrary.org

San Jose Silicon Valley Chamber of Commerce. Available www.sjchamber.com

San Jose Unified School District. Available www.sjusd.org

Selected Bibliography

Beers, David, *Blue Sky Dream: A Memoir of America's Fall From Grace* (New York: Doubleday, 1996)

Branson, Po, *The First $20 Million Is Always the Hardest: A Silicon Valley Novel* (New York: Random House, 1997)

Farrell, Harry, *Swift Justice: Murder and Vengeance in a California Town* (New York: St. Martin's Press, 1992)

Kaplan, David A, *The Silicon Boys and Their Valley of Dreams* (William Morrow & Company, 1999)

Santa Ana

The City in Brief

Founded: 1869 (incorporated, 1886)

Head Official: Mayor Miguel A. Pulido (since 1986)

City Population
　1980: 203,713
　1990: 293,827
　2000: 337,977
　2003 estimate: 342,510
　Percent change, 1990–2000: 14.8%
　U.S. rank in 1980: 69th
　U.S. rank in 1990: 52nd
　U.S. rank in 2000: 51st

Metropolitan Area Population
　1980: 1,933,000
　1990: 2,410,668

　1990: 2,846,289
　Percent change, 1990–2000: 18.1%
　U.S. rank in 1980: 2nd (CMSA)
　U.S. rank in 1990: 2nd (CMSA)
　U.S. rank in 2000: 2nd (CMSA)

Area: 27.2 square miles (2000)
Elevation: 110 feet above sea level
Average Annual Temperature: 65.0° F
Average Annual Precipitation: 13.17 inches

Major Economic Sectors: Services, trade, manufacturing
Unemployment Rate: 5.8% (January 2005)
Per Capita Income: $12,152 (1999)

2002 FBI Crime Index Total: 12,038

Major Colleges and Universities: Rancho Santiago Community College

Daily Newspaper: *Orange County Register; Los Angeles Times Orange County*

Introduction

Santa Ana, the seat of California's Orange County, is the center of an area known as "the Golden Corridor." Surrounded by the rich farmland of the Santa Ana Valley, the city is part of a megalopolis that includes several incorporated cities; among them are Anaheim, Buena Park, and Fullerton. It is close to both the Los Angeles metropolitan area to the northwest and the San Diego metropolitan area to the southeast along the Pacific Coast. More than 76 percent of its residents are of Hispanic origin; thus, Santa Ana has retained its rich cultural heritage. Founded as a farming town, the city is now the financial and governmental center for Orange County.

Geography and Climate

Santa Ana is located in the Santa Ana Valley in southwestern California. Situated on the Santa Ana River, it is near the Santa Ana Mountains and about 12 miles from the coast of the Pacific Ocean. The sun shines approximately 300 days out of the year. Year-round humidity at noon is usually around 53 percent.

Area: 27.2 square miles (2000)

Elevation: 110 feet above sea level

Average Temperatures: January, 54.0° F; July, 72.0° F; annual average, 65.0° F

Average Annual Precipitation: 13.17 inches

History

Franciscans Settle Santa Ana Valley

The valley in which Santa Ana is located was discovered in July 1769, during a Franciscan expedition led by Don Gaspar Portola. The explorers christened the valley Santa Ana in honor of Saint Anne, also giving the name Santa Ana to the river flowing through the valley. One of the members of the Portola party, Father Junipero Serra, later founded a chain of Franciscan missions that still can be seen today. The El Camino Real, the King's Highway, which linked the missions, passes through the Santa Ana Valley.

Another member of the Portola group, a soldier named Antonio Yorba, and his nephew, Juan Peralta, received a Spanish grant for land extending from the foothills of the Santa Ana Canyon to the ocean. They used the land for grazing cattle and later developed irrigation systems fed by water from the Santa Ana River. The land was thus quite fertile, and the area soon became an agricultural center, with several ranches established in the valley.

City of Santa Ana Prospers

The 1849 California Gold Rush brought the region a population boom, which was followed by another major expansion during the Civil War. The valley's large ranches were subdivided and sold to the newcomers, many of whom later founded the cities of Santa Ana, Orange, and Tustin. Santa Ana's history began in 1869 when William H. Spurgeon purchased 70 acres from the Yorba heirs and drew up a town plan. Since the land had been part of the Santiago de Santa Ana ranch and since it was also near the Santa Ana River, the town was called Santa Ana.

Soon the new town became prosperous, boasting mail delivery twice a week and a number of stores and residences within its boundaries. Farms also were established throughout the valley; the rich soil and favorable climate permitted the cultivation of several crops. Santa Ana became a commercial center; because of its central location in the valley, it was a natural marketplace for crops produced in the surrounding region that is now Orange County. When rail transport arrived in the area in 1877, the town developed and population increased; in 1886 Santa Ana was incorporated. Three years later Orange County was separated from Los Angeles County and Santa Ana was named the county seat.

World War II brought further development as industry moved into the area. The population of Santa Ana increased from around 49,000 people in 1900 to nearly 210,000 residents in 1950. A city charter, providing for a council-manager form of government, was adopted in 1952. Since World War II, Santa Ana has become a financial and governmental center of Orange County.

Efforts began in the 1980s to restore and revitalize the city of Santa Ana, especially its downtown. As a result the city has become known for its historic downtown and Main Place shopping center, which created thousands of jobs in the heart of the city. Santa Ana residents of the twenty-first century enjoy cultural and ethnic diversity as well as continuing status as the financial and governmental center of Orange County.

Historical Information: Santa Ana Public Library, History Room, 26 Civic Center Plaza, Santa Ana, CA 92701; telephone (714)647-5267. Santa Ana Mountain Historical Society, 28192 Silverado Canyon Road (PO Box 301), Silverado, CA 92676; telephone (714)649-2216

Population Profile

Metropolitan Area Residents

1980: 1,933,000
1990: 2,410,668
2000: 2,846,289
Percent change, 1990–2000: 12.9%
U.S. rank in 1980: 2nd (CMSA)
U.S. rank in 1990: 2nd (CMSA)
U.S. rank in 2000: 2nd (CMSA)

City Residents

1980: 203,713
1990: 293,827
2000: 337,977
2003 estimate: 342,510
Percent change, 1990–2000: 14.8%
U.S. rank in 1980: 69th
U.S. rank in 1990: 52nd (State rank: 9th)
U.S. rank in 2000: 51st (State rank: 9th)

Density: 12,451 people per square mile (2000)

Racial and ethnic characteristics (2000)
   White: 144,425
   Black or African American: 5,749
   American Indian and Alaska Native: 4,013
   Asian: 29,778
   Native Hawaiian and other Pacific Islander: 1,160
   Hispanic or Latino (may be of any race): 257,097
   Other: 137,360

Percent of residents born in state: 38.6% (2000)

Age characteristics (2000)
   Population under 5 years old: 34,816
   Population 5 to 9 years old: 35,873
   Population 10 to 14 years old: 28,386
   Population 15 to 19 years old: 28,528
   Population 20 to 24 years old: 31,112
   Population 25 to 34 years old: 66,017
   Population 35 to 44 years old: 49,108
   Population 45 to 54 years old: 29,239
   Population 55 to 59 years old: 9,286
   Population 60 to 64 years old: 7,047
   Population 65 to 74 years old: 10,408
   Population 75 to 84 years old: 6,117
   Population 85 years and over: 2,040
   Median age: 26.5

Births (2002, Orange County)
   Total number: 44,796

Deaths (2002, Orange County)
   Total number: 16,789 (of which, 216 were infants under the age of 1 year)

Money income (1999)
   Per capita income: $12,152
   Median household income: $43,412
   Total households: 72,993
   Percentage of households with income of . . .
   less than $10,000: 4,581
   $10,000 to $14,999: 3,882
   $15,000 to $24,999: 8,941
   $25,000 to $34,999: 10,802
   $35,000 to $49,999: 13,448
   $50,000 to $74,999: 16,232
   $75,000 to $99,999: 7,755
   $100,000 to $149,000: 5,435
   $150,000 to $199,000: 974
   $200,000 and over: 943

Percent of families below poverty level: 16.1% (38.5% of which were female householder families with related children under 5 years)

2002 FBI Crime Index Total: 12,038

Municipal Government

In accordance with a charter adopted in 1952, Santa Ana operates under a council-manager form of government. The city is governed by a council consisting of six council members and an elected mayor. Council members are nominated from wards but are elected by voters from the entire city. Council members are elected to four-year terms and the mayor is elected every two years.

Head Official: Mayor Miguel A. Pulido (since 1986; current term expires November 2006)

Total Number of City Employees: 1,961 (2005)

City Information: City Hall, 20 Civic Center Plaza, Santa Ana, CA 92702; telephone (714)647-5400

Economy

Major Industries and Commercial Activity

Santa Ana boasts more than 13,000 in-city businesses; major industries include a mix of retail trade, service, and manufacturing firms.

Government is a major employer in Santa Ana; as the county seat, the city has offices at the county, state, and federal levels. Santa Ana is also a financial center, with 25 banks and 57 savings and loan associations. The aerospace and electronics industries, among the area's largest employers, figure significantly in the city's economy.

Santa Ana was the recipient of California's largest commercial loan program, which contributed to redevelopment of the downtown district. Part of the project were ten new banking and financial buildings and the Civic Center, which houses city, county, state, and federal government buildings. Several Fortune 500 companies, including Textron's Cherry Division, ITT Cannon, and Xerox, are located in Santa Ana.

Tourism is a major industry in Santa Ana and Orange County. Within a radius of 10 miles of the city are several of California's most popular tourist attractions, such as Disneyland, Knott's Berry Farm, and southern California beaches. Forty million people visit the Orange County area each year, spending more than $6.4 billion.

Items and goods produced: sugar; glass products; plumbing material; foam rubber products; dehydrating, electronic, and sporting equipment; concentrates; extracts; agricultural machinery; perfumes; feed; cement pipes; soft drinks; rivets; fasteners; canned and dried fruits and vegetables; packaged walnuts and oranges; poultry

Incentive Programs—New and Existing Companies

Local programs—The Orange County Business Council (OCBC) concentrates on attracting and retaining high-quality, high-paying and low-polluting jobs to Orange County. For business development, the OCBC is the single business point-of-contact for economic development and related business information in Orange County. As well, the OCBC leads the county in ensuring a quality workforce and advocating legislation to benefit businesses. Within the city of Santa Ana, 98 percent of commercial and industrial property is a designated Enterprise Zone that offers major tax breaks and other incentives to attract and retain business.

State programs—The State of California finances programs to help small and medium-sized businesses develop export markets and improve the quality of products and the skills of work forces. Parts of Santa Ana are designated part of a Federal Empowerment Zone. Santa Ana was the only town west of the Rockies to receive such a designation. As a Federal Urban Empowerment Zone, the city of Santa Ana will receive up to $100 million in performance grants to be used in the designated area. Up to $10 million will be paid out each year through 2008.

Job training programs—The Santa Ana Work/Opportunities/Resources/Knowledge (W/O/R/K/) Center is a non-profit organization comprised of a partnership between several agencies: The Santa Ana Workforce Investment Board, State Employment Development Department, Santa Ana College, and Orange County Social Services. The W/O/R/K Center is a one-stop shop designed to meet the job training and placement needs of the community. The center was awarded the largest grant ($867,000) given by the State of California for such programs in 2000.

Development Projects

Major recent commercial developments in Santa Ana include the Main Place regional shopping center, MacArthur Place mixed use area, and the Santa Ana Auto Mall. More than 5,000 acres of the city are within six focused redevelopment areas that include a variety of governmental, infrastructure, retail and residential projects.

Economic Development Information: Orange County Business Council, 2 Park Plaza, Suite 100, Irvine, CA, 92614-5904; telephone (949)476-2242; fax (949)476-9240.

Commercial Shipping

Air freight facilities for Santa Ana are available at John Wayne Airport. Rail freight service is provided by the Southern Pacific and Union Pacific railroads. More than 100 motor freight carriers link Santa Ana with markets throughout the country; overnight delivery service is available to several West Coast cities as well as to Tucson, Phoenix, Las Vegas, and Reno.

Labor Force and Employment Outlook

Santa Ana has a young, well-trained work force that comprises over 10 percent of Orange County's labor pool. Employment forecasts in the Orange County area are positive, with growth of 15 percent expected between 2001 and 2008. Unionization is prevalent in manufacturing, trucking, retailing, the hotel industry, warehousing, and some grocery and drugstore chains.

The following is a summary of data regarding the Santa Ana-Irvine-Anaheim metropolitan area nonagricultural labor force, 2004 annual averages.

Size of non-agricultural labor force: 1,460,000

Number of workers employed in . . .
   natural resources and mining: 600
   construction: 91,800
   manufacturing: 183,200
   trade, transportation and utilities: 264,300
   information: 33,500
   financial activities: 131,200
   professional and business services: 259,600
   educational and health systems: 130,400

government: 153,200
leisure and hospitality: 164,500
other services: 4,730

Average hourly earnings of production workers employed in manufacturing: $14.13

Unemployment rate: 5.8% (January 2005)

Largest private employers:	Number of employees
Ingram Micro Incorporated	3,000
Orange County Register	2,000
ITT Industries Cannon	1,500
Western Medical Centers	1,300
OneSource	1,100

Cost of Living

The following is a summary of data regarding key cost of living factors for the Santa Ana area.

2004 (3rd Quarter) ACCRA Average House Price: $674,000 (Orange County)

2004 (3rd Quarter) ACCRA Cost of Living Index: 151.5 (U.S. average = 100.0)

State income tax rate: Ranges from 1.0% to 9.3%

State sales tax rate: 6% plus .5% in Santa Ana (food and prescription drugs are exempt)

Local income tax rate: None

Local sales tax rate: 1.25% county and city, plus any district taxes imposed by the county (0.50% to 1.0%); comes into effect through general election

Property tax rate: limited to 1% of assessed value by state law. The local taxing body can add bonds approved by popular vote.

Economic Information: Santa Ana Chamber of Commerce, 2020 N. Broadway, 2nd Floor, Santa Ana, CA 92706; telephone (714)541-5353; fax (714)541-2238

Education and Research

Elementary and Secondary Schools

The Santa Ana Unified School District (SAUSD), the largest in Orange County and fifth (2005) largest in the state, is administered by a five-member, nonpartisan board of education that appoints a superintendent.

The district boasts distinctions such as two Nationally Distinguished Schools, several State Distinguished Schools, and numerous first or second place "Golden Bell" awards from the California School Boards Association for excellence in innovative programs. McFadden Intermediate received a GEARING Up federal grant in 2004 to create the McFadden Mathematics Institute; the Institute will offer advanced instruction and technology based materials for seventh and eighth grade students with proven math skills. Twenty-four elementary schools and four intermediate schools offer year-round programs. Ninety-one percent of the student body is Hispanic, and the district average of students who speak limited English was 71.4 percent in the 2003–2004 school year. Like many other California school districts, SAUSD faced tough budget prospects in 2005 as state funding shrank.

The following is a summary of data regarding Santa Ana's public schools as of the 2003–2004 school year.

Total enrollment: 62,874

Number of facilities
  elementary schools: 37
  intermediate schools: 9
  senior high schools: 7
  other: 5

Student/teacher ratio: 23:1

Teacher salaries
  average: $56,059 (2003–2004)

Funding per pupil: $4,682

A variety of private schools also operate in the city.

Public Schools Information: Santa Ana Unified School District, 1601 East Chestnut Avenue, Santa Ana, CA 92701; telephone (714)558-5501; email webmaster@sausd.k12.ca.us

Colleges and Universities

Rancho Santiago Community College District's 58 acre Santa Ana Campus is a two-year institution providing associate of arts degrees, vocational certificates, transfer programs to four year schools, and customized on-site employee training programs for local companies; the college is in the process of developing a Digital Media Center. Located within commuting distance of Santa Ana, other Orange County colleges include the University of California at Irvine, California State University at Fullerton, and Chapman College in Orange.

Libraries and Research Centers

The Santa Ana Public Library system operates a main facility, a Family Learning Center, a youth computer learning center, an adult computer lab, and a bookmobile. Holdings consist of more than 335,000 volumes and more than 400 periodicals, plus CDs, tapes, videos, and maps. Special collections include California and Santa Ana history, foreign language books and cassettes, and federal and state documents.

The Orange County Public Library, based in Santa Ana and operating 32 branches, holds more than 2.5 million volumes and 5,000 periodicals, and maintains a special collection of Law Library documents. Other libraries and research centers are affiliated with government agencies, colleges, hospitals, and private corporations. Research activities in botany are conducted at the Ranch Santa Ana Botanical Garden.

Public Library Information: City of Santa Ana Library, 26 Civic Center Plaza, Santa Ana, CA 92701; telephone (714)647-5250. Orange County Public Library, 1501 East St. Andrew's Place, Santa Ana, CA 92705; telephone (714)551-7159

Health Care

Three general hospitals are located in Santa Ana. They offer a range of specialties such as cardiac rehabilitation and hospice care. The largest medical facility is Western Medical Center with 280 beds, a Level II Trauma Center, and 800 primary care physicians. Nearby is the teaching hospital of the medical school at the University of California at Irvine; other medical schools in the area are the University of California at Los Angeles, the University of Southern California, and Loma Linda University.

Recreation

Sightseeing

A major tourist attraction in Orange County is the historical district in downtown Santa Ana. Placed on the National Register of Historic Places in 1984, the 21-block area is among the largest such districts in the state of California. It contains 100 buildings constructed between 1877 and 1934; among them are the Old County Courthouse (now a museum featuring changing exhibits related to local and regional history), the Fox West Coast Theatre, and Old City Hall. The district also features homes of prominent Santa Ana citizens. Tours of the Dr. Willella Howe-Waffle House, a restored Queen Anne Style home built in the 1880s, are available the first Saturday of each month.

Fairhaven Memorial Park is situated on 73 acres and features an arboretum harboring nearly 1,000 trees and numer-

ous plants from around the world. The park's historic mausoleum was built in 1916 of European marble and granite, with handcrafted stained-glass windows.

The Santa Ana Zoo is home to 260 animals and 84 species; among the rare and endangered species living at the zoo are the ring-tailed lemur, the margay cat, the white-handed gibbon, and the golden lion tamarin; the zoo welcomes 270,000 visitors each year. There are several other points of interest in Orange County, including world-famous Disneyland amusement park in Anaheim, and Knott's Berry Farm and the Movieland Wax Museum in Buena Park.

Within driving distance of Santa Ana are the Universal Studios tour, Magic Mountain, Raging Waters amusement park, Sea World, and the San Diego Zoo.

Arts and Culture

More than 1,000 cultural organizations are active in Orange County; among them are symphony orchestras, ballet companies, theater groups, and modern and folk dance troupes. Santa Ana is home to the Pacific Symphony Orchestra, which presents its summer season at Irvine Meadows Amphitheater and performs its regular season concerts at Segerstrom Hall in the Orange County Performing Arts Center. The center is one of three theater facilities in the nation to house all of the four performing arts—musical theater, symphony, opera, and ballet.

Among the other orchestras in the metropolitan area are the Orange County Youth Symphony and the American Youth Symphony. Theater groups include the South Coast Repertory Theatre; dance companies are the Gloria Newman Dance Theatre and the Penrod-Plastino Movement Theatre.

Artists Village is a thriving area of art galleries and studios. It includes the Santora Arts Complex, renowned for its flamboyant churrigueresque architecture, which offers the works of more than 38 artists in five galleries, including the Santa Ana College gallery; the Empire Market Building, which contains several galleries, artists' studios and a small theater; and the Cal State Fullerton Grand Central Art Center, which houses a student gallery and studios and the Alternative Repertory Theatre. The Orange County Center for Contemporary Art is also located in the village.

One of Orange County's most prominent museums is located in Santa Ana. The famous Bowers Museum of Cultural Art, a Spanish mission style building, houses collections pertinent to Orange County and California history; Native American, Pacific Rim, and African cultures; and natural history; it also features a hands-on "Kidseum," a five-star restaurant, and shops. The nearby Discovery Museum of Orange County has exhibits that chronicle the history of Orange County back to the nineteenth century. The Natural

The Bowers Museum of Cultural Art houses historical items from Orange County and California history.

History Museum in nearby Newport Beach displays fossils unique to Orange County and marine life such as whales and walrus. Art museums in the area include the Laguna Beach Art Museum Annex, the Muckenthaler Cultural Center, and the Newport Harbor Art Museum.

Sports for the Spectator

Santa Ana residents are within an easy drive of sporting events in Anaheim. The Major League Baseball Los Angeles Angels of Anaheim play home games in the 45,050 seat Angel Stadium. The Fullerton State Titans and the Anteaters of the University of California at Irvine field National Collegiate Athletic Association (NCAA) Division I teams. Los Alamitos Race Course features parimutuel thoroughbred and harness racing.

Sports for the Participant

Santa Ana's mild climate invites year-round athletic enjoyment. Some of Southern California's finest beaches are minutes away, and the city is located only 12 miles from the Pacific Ocean. Mountain ski resorts are within easy driving distance.

Shopping and Dining

South Coast Plaza Village in Santa Ana is a European-style marketplace. With 25 incorporated cities in Orange County, each with its own central shopping district and community shopping centers, the shopper has endless opportunities. More than 20 major regional shopping malls feature national department stores, specialty shops, and boutiques. Santa Ana is also within easy driving distance of Beverly Hills' famous Rodeo Drive, which is lined with luxury and designer shops.

Santa Ana has dozens of restaurants that offer a variety of cuisine, including traditional American, Continental, Italian, Asian, and Mexican dishes.

Visitor Information: Anaheim/Orange County Visitors Bureau, 800 W. Katella Ave., Anaheim, CA, 92802; telephone (714)765-8888

Convention Facilities

A number of Santa Ana's 43 hotels and motels—which offer more than 3,000 rooms—provide conference and convention facilities. Among the major hotels with meeting rooms are Saddleback Inn, Compri, the Grand Plaza Hotel, and Quality Inn Suites. The Hilton Anaheim and Towers houses a total of 100,000 square feet of flexible exhibit space and 60 meeting rooms; capacity ranges from 10 to 3,000 participants. The Doubletree Hotel Santa Ana offers 253 hotel rooms, two board rooms, a 7,000 square foot ballroom, reception space for more than 1,000 participants, and private dining. The Marriott Anaheim offers 35,000 square feet of exhibit space, three flexible ballrooms and eleven meeting rooms. Meeting space is also available at the Anaheim Convention Center.

Transportation

Approaching the City

Several airports are located in the Santa Ana metropolitan area. The John Wayne Airport, part of the Los Angeles hub, is 5 miles from downtown Santa Ana; it is served by 11 airlines and services 7.5 million passengers each year. The Los Angeles International Airport is 37 miles from downtown; other airports in the immediate area are Fullerton Municipal Airport, Long Beach Airport, and Ontario International Airport.

Four major highways lead into Santa Ana: I-5, the Santa Ana Freeway; S.R. 55, the Costa Mesa Freeway; S.R. 57, the Orange Freeway; and S.R. 22, the Garden Grove Freeway.

Traveling in the City

The Orange County Transit District operates 23 routes that interconnect with the Regional Transportation District (RTD), an intercity system. Special services are available for the handicapped and the hearing impaired. Centerline light rail currently offers 9.3 miles as part of a 90-mile Rail Master Plan adopted by Orange County; services include a direct line from The Depot at Santa Ana to the John Wayne Airport. The Regional Transportation Center is a hub for Amtrak, intercity buses, urban transit, a future rapid transit system, taxi cabs, an airport shuttle, and other transportation services.

Communications

Newspapers and Magazines

Published in Santa Ana is the morning *Orange County Register.* Santa Ana readers also have available to them the *Los Angeles Times Orange County.* Other newspapers and magazines published in Santa Ana are: *Azteca News,* a weekly Spanish community newspaper; *Dealernews, InfoText, The Psychiatric Times, Response TV,* and *Video Store.*

Television and Radio

Thirteen television stations, one of them based in Santa Ana, serve the city; cable is available. Santa Ana receives broadcasts from more than 60 AM and FM radio stations; two FM stations broadcast there.

Media Information: Orange County Register, Freedom Communications Inc., 625 N. Grand Ave., PO Box 11626, Santa Ana, CA 92701; telephone (714)835-1234

Santa Ana Online

City of Santa Ana Arts and Culture Information home page. Available www.aplaceforart.org

City of Santa Ana home page. Available www.ci.santa-ana.ca.us

Orange County Business Council home page. Available www.ocbc.org/index.asp

Orange County Department of Education home page. Available www.ocde.k12.ca.us

Orange County Register home page. Available www.ocregister.com

Santa Ana Chamber of Commerce home page. Available www.santaanacc.com

Santa Ana History home page (Historical Preservation Society). Available www.SantaAnaHistory.com

Santa Ana Public Library History Room home page. Available www.ci.santa-ana.ca.us/library/hr

Santa Ana Public Library home page. Available www.ci.santa-ana.ca.us/library

Santa Ana Unified School District home page. Available www.sausd.k12.ca.us

Selected Bibliography

Haas, Lisbeth, *Conquests and Historical Identities in California, 1769–1936.* (Berkeley: University of California Press, 1995)

COLORADO

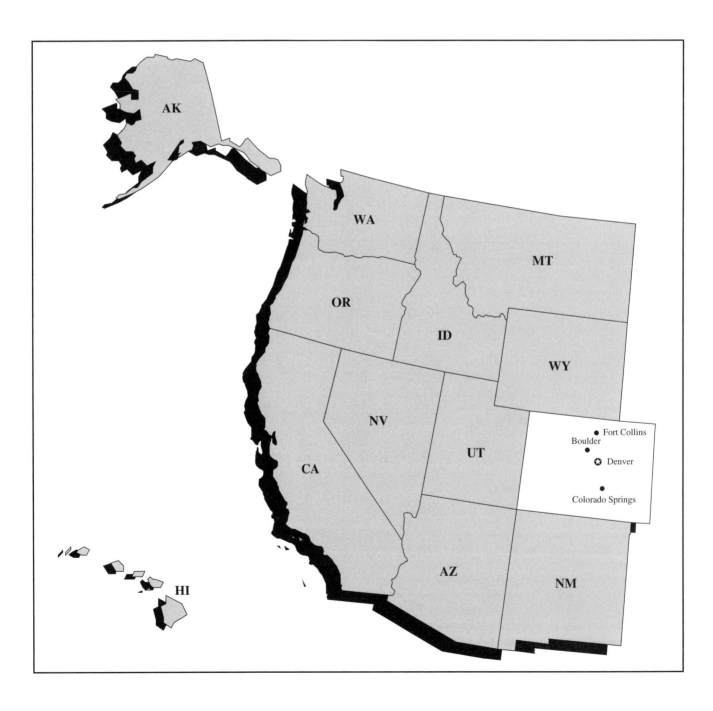

The State in Brief

Nickname: Centennial State
Motto: *Nil sine numine* (Nothing without providence)

Flower: Rocky Mountain columbine
Bird: Lark bunting

Area: 104,093 square miles (2000; U.S. rank: 8th)
Elevation: Ranges from 3,350 feet to 14,433 feet above sea level
Climate: Dry and sunny, with a wide daily and seasonal variation in temperature and with alpine conditions in the high mountains

Admitted to Union: August 1, 1876
Capital: Denver
Head Official: Governor Bill Owens (R) (until 2007)

Population
1980: 2,890,000
1990: 3,377,000
2000: 4,302,015
2004 estimate: 4,601,403
Percent change, 1990–2000: 30.6%
U.S. rank in 2004: 22nd
Percent of residents born in state: 41.1% (2000)
Density: 41.5 people per square mile (2000)
2002 FBI Crime Index Total: 195,936

Racial and Ethnic Characteristics (2000)
White: 3,560,005
Black or African American: 165,063
American Indian and Alaska Native: 44,241
Asian: 95,213
Native Hawaiian and Pacific Islander: 4,621
Hispanic or Latino (may be of any race): 735,601
Other: 309,931

Age Characteristics (2000)
Population under 5 years old: 297,505
Population 5 to 19 years old: 927,163
Percent of population 65 years and over: 9.7%
Median age: 34.3 years (2000)

Vital Statistics
Total number of births (2003): 69,341
Total number of deaths (2003): 29,462 (infant deaths, 416)
AIDS cases reported through 2003: 3,675

Economy
Major industries: Services, manufacturing, communications, transportation, agriculture
Unemployment rate: 4.8% (January 2005)
Per capita income: $34,510 (2003; U.S. rank: 8th)
Median household income: $50,224 (3-year average, 2001-2003)
Percentage of persons below poverty level: 9.4% (3-year average, 2001-2003)
Income tax rate: 4.63%
Sales tax rate: 2.9%

Boulder

The City in Brief

Founded: 1859 (incorporated 1871)
Head Officials: Mayor Mark Ruzzin (since 2001); City Manager Frank Bruno (since 2003)

City Population
    1980: 76,685
    1990: 85,127
    2000: 94,673
    2003 estimate: 93,051
    Percent change, 1990–2000: 11.2%
    U.S. rank in 1980: 250th
    U.S. rank in 1990: 257th
    U.S. rank in 2000: 283th (State rank: 9th)

Metropolitan Area Population (PMSA)
    1980: 189,625
    1990: 225,339
    2000: 291,288

    Percent change, 1990–2000: 29.3%
    U.S. rank in 1980: 21st (CMSA)
    U.S. rank in 1990: 22nd (CMSA)
    U.S. rank in 2000: 19th (CMSA)

Area: 25.37 square miles (2002)
Elevation: 5,340 feet above sea level
Average Annual Temperature: 51.8° F
Average Annual Precipitation: 102.13 inches total (83.1 inches of snow)

Major Economic Sectors: Services, trade, manufacturing, government
Unemployment Rate: 4.8% (January 2005)
Per Capita Income: $27,262 (1999)

2002 FBI Crime Index Total: 3,743

Major Colleges and Universities: University of Colorado at Boulder, Naropa University, Front Range Community College

Daily Newspaper: *Daily Camera*

Introduction

Boulder is sometimes called the ''Athens of the West'' in tribute to its dedication to education and the arts. The University of Colorado at Boulder and a host of private industries make the city one of America's leading science and research towns. Boulder also maintains a commitment to the arts, presenting a number of renowned music, theater, and arts festivals each year. The city's attractive setting near the Rocky Mountains and its abundant cultural and entertainment offerings make it a popular stop for business or recreation.

Geography and Climate

Boulder lies in a wide basin beneath Flagstaff Mountain just a few miles east of the continental divide and about 30 miles west of Denver. The large Arapahoe glacier provides water for a number of mountain streams that pass through Boulder, including Boulder Creek, which flows through the center of the city. The climate in Boulder is typically mild with dry, moderate summers and relatively comfortable winters. The city boasts more than 300 sunny days each year. Nearby mountains shield Boulder from the most severe winter storms. Most precipitation occurs during the winter and spring months, with snowfall averaging 83.1 inches.

Area: 25.37 square miles (2002)

Elevation: 5,340 feet above seal level

Average Temperatures: January, 32.8° F; July, 73.2° F; annual average, 51.8° F

Average Annual Precipitation: 102.13 inches (83.1 inches of snow)

History

A City Born of a Newspaper

For centuries before the coming of European explorers, the area surrounding what is now Boulder was a favorite winter campsite for a number of Native American groups, including the Arapaho, Ute, Kiowa, Comanche, Cheyenne, and Sioux. The area was rich in buffalo, elk, and antelope.

Economic depression in the East brought many pioneers and gold seekers to Colorado in the 1850s, and the first settlement in Boulder County was established at Red Rocks in 1858. An early settler, A. A. Brookfield, organized the Boulder City Town Company in 1859. The company laid out more than 4,000 lots, each with a price of $1,000. Few people could afford such a price, and by 1860 the population numbered only 364 residents.

Boulder City grew slowly through the 1860s, competing for prominence in the county with nearby Valmont, where the only newspaper in the area was printed. A group of Boulder citizens stole the printing press, and soon Boulder City was named the county seat, selected because it published the only newspaper in the area. In November 1871, Boulder was incorporated as a Colorado town, and ''City'' was dropped from the name.

A site for the University of Colorado was chosen in Boulder in 1872, and the Colorado state legislature appropriated funds for the institution in 1874, the same year that Boulder's first bank opened its doors. The city grew steadily through the turn of the century. In 1880 the population totaled 3,000 people, but modern conveniences like the installation of electricity in 1887 and a new railway depot in 1890 boosted the population to more than 6,000 people by 1900.

The twentieth century brought moderate growth for Boulder. In the late 1950s and early 1960s the development of high-technology industries had a great impact in the area. Companies like IBM and Rockwell and governmental agencies like the National Oceanic and Atmospheric Administration and the National Bureau of Standards moved into the area, resulting in an economic surge due to the creation of many new jobs. The development of the Boulder-Denver Turnpike further bolstered the area, driving Boulder's population from 20,000 in 1950 to 72,000 in 1972.

A Rocky Period for a Rocky Mountain Town

The convergence of the university environment with research centers and science and technology companies fueled continued growth in the 1990s. By the turn of the century, however, the economic scene had begun to change. A national and international recession contributed to a migration of residences and businesses from Boulder to neighboring communities, where real estate was often cheaper. Lower facility costs fostered a wide variety of businesses, and stores located outside the city began winning in competition for the retail spending of Boulder residents. Sales tax revenue in Boulder dropped by 20 percent between 2000 and 2003. Local businesses began to struggle, as did their employees, many of whom were forced to move from the city to less expensive locales.

Despite media attention in the 1990s and a rocky economical start to the new century, Boulder is an evolving and forward-looking city. Today, Boulder consistently ranks high in polls by magazines and organizations that rate cities based on livability.

Historical Information: Boulder Public Library, Carnegie Branch Library for Local History, 1125 Pine St., Boulder, CO 80302; telephone (303)441-3110

Population Profile

Metropolitan Area Residents (PMSA)
1980: 189,625
1990: 225,339
2000: 291,288
Percent change, 1990–2000: 29.3%
U.S. rank in 1980: 21st (CMSA)
U.S. rank in 1990: 22nd (CMSA)
U.S. rank in 2000: 19th (CMSA)

City Residents
1980: 76,685
1990: 85,127
2000: 94,673
2003 estimate: 93,051
Percent change, 1990–2000: 11.2%
U.S. rank in 1980: 250th
U.S. rank in 1990: 257th (State rank: 8th)
U.S. rank in 2000: 283th (State rank: 9th)

Density: 3,884.1 people per square mile (2000)

Racial and ethnic characteristics (2000)
White: 83,627
Black or African American: 1,154
American Indian and Alaska Native: 450
Asian: 3,806
Native Hawaiian and Pacific Islander: 48
Hispanic or Latino (may be of any race): 7,801
Other: 3,318

Percent of residents born in state: 24.2% (2000)

Age characteristics (2000)
Population under 5 years old: 3,888
Population 5 to 9 years old: 3,831
Population 10 to 14 years old: 3,947
Population 15 to 19 years old: 9,487
Population 20 to 24 years old: 17,413
Population 25 to 34 years old: 18,437
Population 35 to 44 years old: 12,840
Population 45 to 54 years old: 11,774
Population 55 to 59 years old: 3,331
Population 60 to 64 years old: 2,334

Population 65 to 74 years old: 3,474
Population 75 to 84 years old: 2,641
Population 85 years and older: 1,276
Median age: 29 years

Births (Boulder County, 2003)
Total number: 3,620

Deaths (Boulder County, 2003)
Total number: 1,472 (of which, 17 were infants under the age of 1 year)

Money income (1999)
Per capita income: $27,262
Median household income: $44,748
Total households: 39,610

Number of households with income of . . .
less than $10,000: 4,052
$10,000 to $14,999: 2,565
$15,000 to $24,999: 4,462
$25,000 to $34,999: 4,779
$35,000 to $49,999: 5,594
$50,000 to $74,999: 6,754
$75,000 to $99,999: 4,314
$100,000 to $149,999: 4,269
$150,000 to $199,999: 1,489
$200,000 or more: 1,332

Percent of families below poverty level: 6.4% (of which, 51.9% were female householder families with related children under 5 years)

2002 FBI Crime Index Total: 3,743

Municipal Government

Boulder has a council-manager form of government with a nine-member council elected to two- or four-year terms. The council elects the mayor from among its number for a two-year term and appoints a city manager.

Head Official: Mayor Mark Ruzzin (since 2001; current term expires November 2007); City Manager Frank Bruno (since 2003)

Total Number of City Employees: 1,212 (2005)

City Information: City of Boulder, 1777 Broadway, Boulder, CO 80302; telephone (303)441-3090; email ruzzinm @ci.boulder.co.us

Economy

Major Industries and Commercial Activity

The predominant industries in the Boulder are science and technology related. Helped out by the research activity at the University of Colorado at Boulder, a large high-technology, electronic, and aerospace industry has developed in and around the city. The phenomenal growth of these industries attracted the establishment of defense contractors, applied and pure research centers, and satellite and communications companies, which bring millions of dollars into the local economy each year.

The technology boom has filtered down into other Boulder industries, increasing the city's manufacturing and retail base. Education, health care, and government are also important sectors of the Boulder economy.

Items and goods produced: electronic devices, space hardware, recreational equipment, natural and organic food products

Incentive Programs—New and Existing Companies

Local programs—In an effort to reverse a downward economic trend early in the twenty-first century, the City of Boulder established an Economic Vitality Program in 2003. Guided by the Economic Vitality Advisory Board, the program's primary purpose is to attract new businesses and retain and expand existing businesses. Among the challenges it faces are Boulder's high facility costs, limited space for expansion, and poor condition of many older buildings. As a remedy, the program will apply industry-cluster initiatives—partnerships between businesses, government agencies, and research institutions involved in similar industries—to foster innovation and efficiency. The city's current clusters include software, bioscience, creative services, natural and organic food, and sustainable technologies.

The Economic Vitality Program also strives to make the local retail environment more attractive to Boulder's residents. The early 2000s brought the demise of the city's Crossroad Mall, due in large part to the opening of other shopping establishments in nearby communities. While retail sales for the larger region steadily increased, Boulder was losing $54 million each year in general merchandise sales from its residents, not to mention sales from shoppers visiting from other communities. To staunch the flow, the program intends to import the stores that are attracting Boulder's shoppers and to increase the number of unique shops that define the Boulder experience.

The program will also address other issues that hinder development in Boulder, including inconsistent, overly restrictive, and overly lengthy zoning and planning policies and procedures. A lack of available space is a barrier both for companies interested in establishing large complexes in the city as well as those seeking to expand their existing facilities, and may be remedied by a loosening of the city's restriction on building height. Transportation difficulties, particularly the limited parking availability, will also be considered.

Additionally, Boulder's Small Business Development Center provides valuable assistance to new and established small businesses. It offers three types of support: counseling, short- and long-term training, and access to such resources as market data, financing, and competitive information.

State programs—The Colorado Office of Economic Development & International Trade offers several types of incentives to attract and retain businesses. Its Infrastructure Assistance Program is designed to create new jobs, mainly in the low- and moderate-income ranges, in certain cities and counties within the state. Other business incentives include enterprise zone tax credits, local property tax incentives, and manufacturing revenue bonds.

Job training programs—The Small Business Development Center of Boulder provides both short- and long-term employee training to businesses seeking to expand or relocate to the area. Front Range Community College, through its Center for Workforce Development, offers a variety of training programs for both employer and employee. The Colorado Community College System has joined with the Colorado Office of Economic Development & International Trade to administer Colorado FIRST/Existing Industry Customized Training Programs. These programs, which received $2.7 million in funding in 2004, are designed to fund employee training for transferable job skills to benefit the company's competitive strength as well as the employee's long-term employment opportunities.

Development Projects

The Economic Vitality Program that was established in 2003 has several specific development initiatives. Among them is the development of the Boulder Transit Village, an 11.2-acre site that will combine transit service, including commuter rail, with residential and commercial space. The first phase of the project is scheduled to begin in 2006, and rail service is expected within 10 years. A second project is Twenty Ninth Street, an 850,000-square-foot shopping complex built on the site of the former Crossroads Mall. This mall, expected to open in 2006, will be an open-air shopping and entertainment venue anchored by Foley's, a 16-screen cinema, and The Home Depot.

Boulder has a number of other development projects in progress or recently completed. The first phase of the One Boulder Plaza project, a combination of residential, office, and retail space, began in 2001, and the final phase began in the summer of 2004. The Northwest Parkway, a toll road linking Boulder to the Denver International Airport, opened in November 2003 after a decade of planning and a total investment of $190 million. The St. Julien Hotel & Spa, featuring 200 guest rooms and a 10,000-square-foot spa and fitness center, opened its doors in February 2005. Restoration of the Sunrise Circle Amphitheater on Flagstaff Mountain, originally built in 1933, will be completed in the spring of 2005. A $2.1 million expansion to the Boulder County Jail is expected to be completed in April 2005, while the construction of a $1.9 million detoxification center is expected to break ground later that year.

Economic Development Information: Boulder Chamber of Commerce, 2440 Pearl St., Boulder, CO 80302; telephone (303)442-1044; fax (303)938-8837; email info@boulder chamber.com. Economic Vitality Program, City of Boulder, PO Box 79, Boulder, CO 80306; telephone (303)441-3090

Commercial Shipping

Commercial air shipping is available from a number of carriers at Denver International Airport (DIA). Approximately 400,000 tons of U.S. cargo pass through the airport each year. DIA is a hub for United Airlines, which handles 500,000 pounds of freight and mail each day. Commercial cargo carriers include FedEx, UPS, DHL, and Airborne, though nearly half of DIA's air cargo is handled by passenger carriers. In 2004 the airport's cargo facilities completed an expansion, adding 288,000 square feet of space. The airport is the site of Foreign Trade Zone #123, as well as areas for U.S. Customs and Department of Agriculture clearance. Approximately 50 freight forwarders and customs brokers also serve in the area. Freight rail service from two major transcontinental railways is also available; more than one dozen motor freight carriers maintain facilities in Boulder.

Labor Force and Employment Outlook

Boulder business managers and owners cite a high quality of life and a talented work base among the advantages of doing business in Boulder. The workforce is educated well above the national average, as 66.9 percent of Boulder residents had received a bachelor's degree or higher degree in 2000, compared with 24.4 percent in the U.S. as a whole. The university and the many technology- and research-oriented companies draw a large number of college graduates and professionals into the labor market.

The following is a summary of data regarding the Boulder metropolitan area labor force, 2004 annual averages.

Size of non-agricultural labor force: 157,600

Number of workers employed in . . .
construction and mining: 6,500

manufacturing: 18,900
trade, transportation and utilities: 22,400
information: 9,300
financial activities: 7,600
professional and business services: 27,000
educational and health services: 16,400
leisure and hospitality: 15,800
other services: 4,900
government: 28,700

Average hourly earnings of production workers employed in manufacturing: $16.46 (annual statewide average)

Unemployment rate: 4.8% (January 2005)

Largest county employers (2003)	*Number of employees*
University of Colorado at Boulder	7,500
IBM Corp.	4,800
Boulder Valley School District	4,200
Sun Microsystems Inc.	3,200
Storage Technology Corp.	2,735
St. Vrain School District	2,400
Ball Corp.	2,250
Boulder Community Hospital	2,102
Electronic Data Systems Corp.	2,000
Level 3 Communications Inc.	1,900

Cost of Living

Boulder's cost of living is higher than in neighboring communities. According to the Boulder Chamber of Commerce, in 2001 the average price for a single family home in the city of Boulder was $472,169, compared with $343,000 in Boulder County overall. That same year, the average cost for a condo or townhome was $214,148 in the city and $183,722 in the county.

The following is a summary of data regarding key cost of living factors for the Boulder area.

2004 (3rd Quarter) ACCRA Average House Price: $311,194 (Denver metro)

2004 (3rd Quarter) ACCRA Cost of Living Index: 104.8 (Denver metro) (U.S. average = 100.0)

State income tax rate: 4.75%

State sales tax rate: 2.9%

Local income tax rate: None

Local sales tax rate: 4.61%

Property tax rate: $10.005 per $1,000 of assessed value (2004)

Economic Information: Boulder Chamber of Commerce, 2440 Pearl St., Boulder, CO 80302; telephone (303)442-1044; fax (303)938-8837; email info@boulderchamber.com

Education and Research

Elementary and Secondary Schools

The Boulder Valley School District regulates the public schools in Boulder as well as the neighboring communities of Broomfield, Lafayette, Louisville, Mountain, Nederland, and Superior. The district's open enrollment policy enables students to enroll in a variety of schools, including focus or alternative schools. The board, comprised of seven members elected at-large to four-year terms, employs the superintendent.

The following is a summary of data regarding Boulder public schools as of the 2004–2005 school year.

Total enrollment: 27,947

Number of facilities
  elementary schools: 24
  middle schools: 8
  senior high schools: 5
  other: 15 (including 3 charter schools, 8 focus schools, and 4 combined-level schools)

Student/teacher ratio: 17:1

Teacher salaries
  minimum: $30,239
  maximum: $74,479

Funding per pupil: $6,021

A number of private and parochial schools also serve the Boulder area.

Public Schools Information: Boulder Valley School District, 6500 Arapahoe, Boulder, CO 80303; telephone (303)447-1010

Colleges and Universities

Boulder is the main campus of the University of Colorado (CU) university system, which also has campuses in Colorado Springs, downtown Denver, and the Health Sciences Center in Aurora and Denver. The Boulder campus is a major research and educational institution, with an enrollment of more than 32,000 students in 2003. It offers 3,400 courses in 150 areas of study, representing 85 majors for bachelor degrees, 70 for master's degrees, and 50 for doctoral degrees. Although the most popular undergraduate

programs in 2003 were psychology, pre-journalism and mass communications, and molecular, cellular, and development biology, CU has strong ties to the astronautics and astrophysics disciplines. The university is a primary research center in space sciences, and 16 of its alumni have become astronauts in the National Aeronautics and Space Administration (NASA) program.

Front Range Community College promotes academic and career advancement through associate degree and certificate programs in business, health, mathematics, advanced sciences, arts and humanities, world languages, computer information sciences, communication, and social sciences. The Naropa University is a Buddhist-inspired institution offering four-year degrees in an academic program that blends intellectual, artistic, and meditative disciplines. Accredited by the North Central Association of Colleges and Schools, Naropa enrolls more than 450 students in its three Boulder campuses; the school also features internship programs and study-abroad programs in Nepal and Bali, and is home to the Jack Kerouac School of Disembodied Poetics. The Boulder College of Massage Therapy offers a 1,000-hour certificate program in a variety of massage styles, as well as an Associate Degree of Occupational Studies in Massage Therapy.

Libraries and Research Centers

The Boulder Public Library consists of a main building and three branches with a total of more than 435,000 volumes and 1,100 periodical subscriptions. The library maintains special collections of children's literature, a Colorado Artists Registry, and municipal government; it also operates a Braille Computer Center. The Carnegie Branch Library for Local History contains a manuscript collection of more than 700,000 items, including some from before the area received the name Colorado, as well as historic photographs, newspapers, and oral histories. The University of Colorado library system, consisting of the central Norlin Library and five discipline-specific branch libraries, contains more than 11 million books, periodicals, and microforms, as well as special collections in juvenile literature, the history of silver, mountaineering, and Western history. The National Indian Law Library, which houses 4,000 items, is the only law library specializing in practice materials relating to federal and tribal Indian law. The Allen Ginsberg Library of the Naropa University houses books, journals, audio/visual media, and artwork, as well as special collections in university recordings, Tibetan volumes, and small press and chapbooks. A number of private and special interest libraries are also located in the city.

The University of Colorado at Boulder (CU) received more than $250 million in sponsored research monies in 2003; the two largest sponsors were the National Aeronautics and Space Administration (NASA) and the National Science

Foundation. Its nearly 100 research centers and institutes are involved in everything from music entrepreneurship to high energy physics. Some of the largest facilities are the Institute of Arctic and Alpine Research, the Institute for Behavioral Genetics, the Institute of Cognitive Science, the Colorado Center for Information Storage, the Joint Institute for Laboratory Astrophysics, and the Laboratory of Atmospheric and Space Physics. Three CU professors are recipients of a Nobel Prize, the most recent bestowed in 2001 for the discovery of a new form of matter.

Boulder is home to several research institutions of the federal government. The Cooperative Institute for Research in Environmental Sciences is a joint venture of CU and the National Office of Oceanic and Atmospheric Research. The National Weather Service maintains a weather forecast office in the city, which provides weather forecasts and data for 21 counties in Colorado. The National Center for Atmospheric Research offers free, guided tours of such exhibits as lightning, a tornado, a solar eclipse telescope, and aircraft models. Visitors can view the atomic clock and other science displays at the National Institute of Standards and Technology, which attracts 100 visiting researchers each year in addition to its 400 resident scientists, engineers, and other personnel.

Public Library Information: Boulder Public Library, 1000 Canyon Blvd., Boulder, CO 80302; telephone (303)441-3100

Health Care

Boulder Community Hospital is the largest health-care institution in the Boulder area. It is a full-service hospital with a 24-four-hour emergency room, an intensive care unit, a cardiac care unit, and a network of facilities that includes the Boulder Center for Sports Medicine, Boulder Community Foothills Hospital, Community Medical Center (an urgent care facility), and the Miriam R. Hart Regional Radiation Therapy Center. Boulder Community Hospital offered 265 beds in 2004, and 547 physicians in 48 medical specialties had privileges at the hospital.

Recreation

Sightseeing

A highlight of downtown Boulder is the 16-mile-long Boulder Creek Path, which runs along the creek through the center of the city. The banks of the creek have been restored to their natural state, parks and picnic areas have been formed—including the attractive Boulder Sculpture Park—and many small waterfalls along the way are perfect for kayaking and tubing. The Open Space & Mountain Parks division of the City of Boulder encompasses 12 free public nature hikes of varying difficulty, each offering some of the most scenic views in the region. Among them is Sawhill Ponds, featuring 18 ponds; Flagstaff Mountain, a 6,850-foot peak that is home to the Flagstaff Nature Center; Royal Arch, a sandstone arch through which the city of Boulder can be viewed from above; and Boulder Falls, a five-acre site known as the ''Yosemite of Boulder Canyon.''

Boulder also caters to those who prefer less strenuous sightseeing excursions. Free tours are offered by the Celestial Seasonings Tea Co., including a tea sampling bar and a walk through the Mint Room, and by the Redstone Meadery, brewer of a honey wine known as mead. Gateway Park Fun Center features go-karts, batting cages, and miniature golf.

Arts and Culture

The Boulder Philharmonic Orchestra has been performing since 1958, and holds the majority of its performances at the Macky Auditorium Concert Hall on the campus of the University of Colorado at Boulder. Also performing at the Macky is Boulder Ballet, the major dance company of Boulder County. The Boulder Concert Band, comprised of 70 community members, offers a concert series and summer concerts in the area parks. Other musical institutions include the Boulder Chorale, the Boulder Youth Choir and Youth Symphony, and the Boulder Chamber Orchestra, which was founded in 2004. The Nomad Theatre is Boulder's only professional resident theater. Upstart Crow is an ensemble acting company whose season runs from early fall to midsummer and offers five major works. Boulder's Dinner Theatre entertains 80,000 attendees each year with food, drink, and major Broadway musicals.

In 2003 the American Association of Museums bestowed accreditation to the University of Colorado at Boulder (CU) Museum of Natural History, the only university museum in Colorado ever to receive this honor. This museum houses nearly four million specimens of biology, anthropology, and geology, including fossils, local animals, and Southwestern cultural artifacts. The CU Heritage Center contains exhibits that chronicle the university's past, such as the baseball bat and glove used by alumnus Robert Redford in *The Natural,* as well as a moon rock on loan from the National Aeronautics and Space Administration (NASA) and space suits worn by former graduates who became astronauts. CU is also the site of the Sommers-Bausch Observatory and the Fiske Planetarium, the largest of its kind between Chicago and Los Angeles.

The city's many museums are not limited to the CU campus. The Boulder Museum of History houses nearly 30,000 ob-

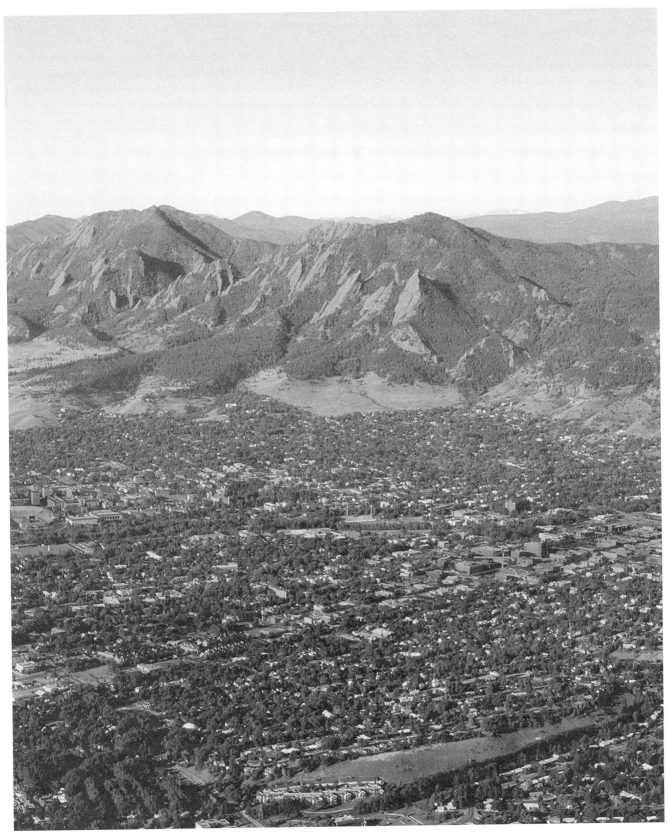

Boulder sits at the base of the scenic Rocky Mountains.

jects from Boulder's past, dating back to the 1800s. The Carnegie Branch Library for Local History, located in Boulder's original library building, contains thousands of books, diaries, photographs, oral history audiotapes, and genealogical papers. The Leanin' Tree Museum of Western Art houses one of the largest and best collections of contemporary Western art in America, featuring award-winning bronzes from the National Academy of Western Art, a series on Cowboy Artists of America, and other exhibits. Collage Children's Museum has 4,700 square feet of interactive exhibits for youngsters.

Boulder offers more than 30 art galleries, as well as several art museums. The Boulder Museum of Contemporary Art features regional, national, and international exhibitions and performances. The University of Colorado at Boulder Art Galleries contain the works of regional artists and students as well as major national and international artists, and houses the Colorado Collection, a state-owned collection of 5,000 pieces. The Charles A. Haertling Sculpture Park displays the work of such artists as Jerry Wingren, Dennis Yoshikawa Wright, Tom Miller, and Beth Juliar-Skodge.

Festivals and Holidays

Boulder's most famous festival is the Colorado Shakespeare Festival, regarded as one of the best in the nation. The festival is held each summer at the University of Colorado at Boulder's outdoor Mary Rippon Theatre and the indoor University Theatre. January brings the Boulder Bach Festival, a three-day event featuring an orchestra, chorus, and soloists performing the works of Johann Sebastian Bach. For more than a month during the summer, the Colorado Music Festival presents classical music performed by musicians from around the world. The Pearl Street Art Fair is held each July, and the Aerial Dance Festival, featuring demonstrations of dancing through the air, takes place the following month. Film festivals include the Boulder International Film Festival, held for four days in February, and the Moondance International Film Festival, a competition that takes place each May. A variety of aspects of adventure is presented at the Boulder Adventure Film Festival each April.

The city hosts a number of unique festivals and events. The annual Polar Bear Plunge attracts participants intrepid enough to jump into the Boulder Reservoir on New Year's Day. The International Mead Festival, held in February, features more than 80 meads from seven countries and is the world's largest competition for mead, a beverage made of wine fermented with honey. Another record-setting event is held the following month, as the world's shortest parade—Boulder's St. Patrick's Day Parade—takes place over a course covering less than one city block. The Kinetics Sculpture Challenge, preceded a week earlier by the Kinetics Parade, invites teams to race kinetically designed

sculptures over both land and water. The Boulder Creek Festival, which draws approximately 130,000 people over Memorial Day Weekend, features a rubber duck race, a children's fishing derby, and dog-agility demonstrations along with typical festival activities and fare. Several holiday events take place in November and December, including Switch on the Holidays, the Holiday Festival, and the Lights of December Parade.

Sports for the Spectator

The University of Colorado at Boulder provides the major sporting attractions in the city. The university's football team, the *Buffaloes,* is a member of the Big 12 Conference. The university also offers men's and women's basketball, cross country, golf, skiing, tennis, and track and field, and women's soccer and volleyball.

Sports for the Participant

Boulder was voted the ''Nation's Reigning Bike Friendly Community'' by the League of American Bicyclists in 2004. Residents love to bicycle, and Boulder boasts 35 miles of bike lanes, 48 miles of multiuse paths, and 50 miles of bike routes. On occasion, the city will even plow snow off important bike paths before plowing certain roads. Each year Boulder turns national Bike to Work Day in June into Bike to Work Week and offers free tune-ups, safety clinics, and ''Walk and Roll'' events.

Boulder offers a variety of outdoor activities the year round. Natural areas like the Boulder Creek Path and the city's large mountain park feature hiking, camping, and boating. The city operates more than 60 parks—800 acres of maintained park land and an additional 200 acres of natural land—offering recreational facilities of all kinds. There are 48 tennis courts, 22 ballfields, and 15 soccer fields, and as well as the public Flatirons Golf Course. Boulder is also a short distance away from several popular ski resorts and dozens of state and national parks.

Boulder, named ''America's Best Running City'' by *Runner's World* magazine in 2001, hosts several athletic competitions. The Bolder Boulder 10K race brings 50,000 runners from around the world to the city on Memorial Day. Three weeks later is the 5430 Sprint Triathlon, the first of three races making up the Boulder Triathlon Series; the second is the Boulder Peak Triathlon, held in July; followed in August by the 5430 Long Course Triathlon. Colorado's largest running event is the Nike ACG Boulder Backroads Marathon & Half Marathon, which takes place each September at the Boulder Reservoir.

Shopping and Dining

A major attraction in the downtown area is the Historic Pearl Street Mall district. Set up for pedestrian traffic, the mall is lined with shops, galleries, and restaurants. Along the way, street performers, gardens, and sculptures make the stroll enjoyable. Several large suburban malls add to countless smaller shops and specialty stores scattered throughout the area. Scheduled to open in the autumn of 2006 is Twenty Ninth Street, an 850,000-square-foot shopping center with an open-air environment that will be anchored by Foley's and a 16-theater cinema. More than 300 restaurants in Boulder offer a wide variety of foods, from traditional Western fare to exotic ethnic foods. Patrons won't find a smoking section in any of these establishments, as the city has adopted a no-smoking policy in its restaurants and taverns.

Visitor Information: Boulder Convention & Visitors Bureau, 2440 Pearl St., Boulder, CO 80302; telephone (303)442-2911; toll-free (800)444-0447; fax (303)938-2098; email visitor@bouldercvb.com

Convention Facilities

Although lacking a full-fledged convention center, Boulder has a number of facilities offering meeting space. The Millennium Harvest House Boulder can accommodate small functions as well as up to 500 people on its outdoor pavilion and up to 600 in its Grand Ballroom. The historic Hotel Boulderado, a national registered landmark, offers 8,000 square feet of space and accommodates meetings for up to 200 people and receptions up to 300. Several other hotels provide meeting space, as do facilities at the University of Colorado at Boulder, namely the 2,047-seat Macky Auditorium Concert Hall and the University Memorial Center, whose 9,418-square-foot Glenn Miller Ballroom can accommodate 700 attendants. The Boulder Theater can seat up to 860 conference delegates.

Convention Information: Boulder Convention & Visitors Bureau, 2440 Pearl St., Boulder, CO 80302; telephone (303)442-2911; toll-free (800)444-0447; fax (303)938-2098; email visitor@bouldercvb.com

Transportation

Approaching the City

The majority of air traffic comes through Denver International Airport, located 42 miles from Boulder and served by 23 passenger airlines. The new Northwest Parkway toll road connects the airport with Boulder, and costs $5.25 each way.

Hourly shuttle service and limousine service from the airport to Boulder is also available. Jefferson County Airport is located 11 miles from Boulder, and provides commuter air service, as does the Boulder Municipal Airport, located three miles northeast of the central business district.

Interstate 25, Colorado's major north-south highway, runs just to the east of Boulder. The Boulder-Denver Turnpike connects the two cities, and I-70 at Denver provides links east and west. Other major highways include U.S. Highways 36, 52, 93, and 287.

Traveling in the City

Major thoroughfares in the city include Broadway and Twenty-Eighth Street, running north and south, and Iris Avenue, Canyon Boulevard, Arapahoe Road, and Baseline Road, all running east and west. The Regional Transportation District (RTD) operates a fleet of buses serving the metropolitan area. The HOP line makes 40 stops in a loop throughout central Boulder, while the SKIP lines runs north and south along Broadway; other RTD bus lines in Boulder are the JUMP, DASH, BOUND, and STAMPEDE.

Bicycling is extremely important to travel in Boulder, as 10 percent of its resident ride bikes on a regular basis. Bicycle paths parallel all major traffic arteries, and total more than 200 miles. A fleet of 150 bright green bicycles, part of the Spokes for Folks ''Green Bikes Program,'' are provided free to residents as loaner vehicles to be shared by all residents of the city. The Annual Walk and Bike Week encourages commuters to get out of their cars and either pedal or walk to and from work. Local businesses, such as restaurants and bicycle mechanics, offer free incentives to participants.

Communications

Newspapers and Magazines

Boulder is served by two daily newspapers, the morning *Daily Camera* and the morning *Colorado Daily*. *Boulder Weekly* is a free, alternative newspaper, and the *Boulder County Business Report* focuses on economic, industrial, and business news every other week. The *Campus Press,* written by and for students of the University of Colorado at Boulder, is distributed each Thursday. Boulder's love of outdoor sports is reflected in some of the nationally distributed magazines published in the city, including *Inside Triathlon, Ski, Skiing,* and the competitive bicycling magazine *VeloNews.* Other publications include *Delicious Living!* and *Soldier of Fortune,* as well as a number of several scholarly journals and trade publications.

Television and Radio

Five television stations broadcast to Boulder audiences, three representing the major commercial networks and two independent stations; cable service is available. Two AM and two FM radio stations broadcast alternative/new music, public radio, and University of Colorado programming.

Media Information: *Daily Camera,* 1048 Pearl St., Boulder, CO 80302; telephone (303)442-1202

Boulder Online

Boulder Chamber of Commerce. Available www.boulder chamber.com

Boulder Community Hospital. Available www.bch.org

Boulder Convention & Visitors Bureau. Available www.bouldercoloradousa.com

Boulder Public Library System. Available www.boulder.lib.co.us

Boulder Valley School District. Available www.bvsd.k12.co.us

City of Boulder Home Page. Available www.ci.boulder.co.us

Daily Camera. Available www.thedailycamera.com

Economic Vitality Program. Available www.ci.boulder.co.us/economic_vitality

University of Colorado at Boulder. Available www.colorado.edu

Selected Bibliography

Pettem, Silvia, *Behind the Badge: 125 Years of the Boulder, Colorado, Police Department* (Boulder, CO: The Book Lode LLC, 2003)

Pettem, Silvia, and Liston Leyendecker, *Boulder: Evolution of a City* (Niwot, CO: University Press of Colorado, 1994)

Whitney, Gleaves, *Colorado Front Range: A Landscape Divided* (Boulder, CO: Johnson Books, 1983)

Colorado Springs

The City in Brief

Founded: 1871 (incorporated, 1872)

Head Official: Mayor Lionel Rivera (since 2003)

City Population
 1980: 215,150
 1990: 283,112
 2000: 360,890
 2003 estimate: 370,448
 Percent change, 1990–2000: 27.5%
 U.S. rank in 1980: 66th
 U.S. rank in 1990: 54th
 U.S. rank in 2000: 48th (State rank: 2nd)

Metropolitan Area Population
 1980: 309,000
 1990: 397,014
 2000: 516,929

Percent change, 1990–2000: 31.3%
U.S. rank in 1980: 105th
U.S. rank in 1990: 90th
U.S. rank in 2000: 80th

Area: 186 square miles (2000)
Elevation: 6,035 feet above sea level
Average Annual Temperature: 47.8° F
Average Annual Precipitation: 17.4 inches

Major Economic Sectors: Tourism, military, space technology, computers and electronics, healthcare, printing and publishing, manufacturing
Unemployment Rate: 5.4% (December 2004)
Per Capita Income: $22,496 (1999)

2002 FBI Crime Index Total: 20,247

Major Colleges and Universities: University of Colorado at Colorado Springs, United States Air Force Academy, Colorado Technical College, Colorado College

Daily Newspapers: *The Gazette*

Introduction

At the foot of Pikes Peak, the highest peak of the Rocky Mountains, Colorado Springs is a city surrounded by natural beauty that draws millions of visitors a year. Its municipal parks include the breathtaking Garden of the Gods, once sacred Native American tribal grounds. Upon ascending Pikes Peak in 1893, Katharine Lee Bates wrote the words to "America the Beautiful"; the lyrics "purple mountains' majesty" refer to the vistas around Colorado Springs. Now an important center of military installations, Colorado Springs is home to the United States Air Force Academy, the North American Air Defense Command (NORAD), U.S. Air Force and U.S. Space Commands, Consolidated Space Operations Center, and Fort Carson.

Geography and Climate

Colorado Springs is located on a high, flat plain at the foot of the Rocky Mountains, in eastern central Colorado. To the east of the city are rolling prairie lands and to the north is Monument Divide. The climate of Colorado Springs is relatively mild and dry, since the city is protected from harsh weather by the Rocky Mountains in the west. In the winter, Colorado Springs is warmed by the Chinook, a wind whose name means "snow eater."

Area: 186 square miles (2000)

Elevation: 6,035 feet above sea level

Average Temperatures: January, 28.1° F; July, 69.6° F; annual average: 47.8° F

Average Annual Precipitation: 17.4 inches

History

Rowdiness and Refinement Coexist in City's Early Days

The history of Colorado Springs is the history of two very different communities, one wild and rowdy, the other a model of controlled growth. The area was first discovered by settlers of European descent in 1806 when Zebulon Montgomery Pike came upon a mountain he named Pikes Peak and attempted to climb it. Later, several tribes of Native Americans, namely the Ute, Arapaho, and Cheyenne, lived and battled in the region. They declared what is now called the Garden of the Gods to be sacred ground where the tribes could meet in peace and bathe in the mineral springs.

Mountains rich in silver and gold brought miners into the area. A settlement developed and was called El Dorado City, because of its proximity to the gold mines. This became Colorado City, a rough town full of saloons where frequent brawls and gun fights raged. In 1871, the Denver & Rio Grande Western Railroad, the first narrow-gauge line in Colorado, came to the region. The railroad was directed by General William Jackson Palmer, who began to plan a community near Colorado City. Palmer envisioned the town as a playground for the rich, rivaling the elegant resorts on the East Coast. First called the Fountain Colony, the town was incorporated as Colorado Springs in 1872. According to what was called "The Palmer Pattern of Responsibility," Colorado Springs was planned with schools, libraries, churches, parks, and a college. Citizens of "good moral character and strict temperance habits" were purposely sought; intemperance and industry were relegated to Colorado City across the railroad tracks.

City Becomes Tourist and Military Center

Tourists from throughout the country flocked to Colorado Springs and to the spa at nearby Manitou Springs. By the turn of the century Colorado Springs was the wealthiest city per capita in the United States. At this time it earned the nickname Little London, reflecting the number of Tudor-style houses constructed in the area. During this age of the elegant hotel, the rich and the titled were drawn to the Rocky Mountains—especially Colorado Springs—to play polo and hunt foxes. Colorado City, after suffering great economic vicissitudes tied to the mining industry, was absorbed by Colorado Springs in 1971.

Since World War II, Colorado Springs has become an important focal point of the U.S. military. Fort Carson Army Base was established in the early 1940s; the United States Air Force Academy was completed in 1958. In 1966 the North American Air Defense Command (NORAD) was installed inside Cheyenne Mountain as the first warning system for North America against a nuclear missile strike. The United States Olympic Committee created an Olympic Training Grounds in Colorado Springs in 1978. Athletes come from throughout the world to train there, surrounded by the beauty of the Rocky Mountains. With a young, educated work force, beautiful weather, and an expanding military and high tech economy, Colorado Springs' future as a growth center in the West will continue for some time to come.

Historical Information: Colorado College, Charles Learning Tutt Library, 1021 North Cascade Avenue, Colorado Springs, CO 80903; telephone (719) 389-6184

Population Profile

Metropolitan Area Residents

1980: 309,000

1990: 397,014

2000: 516,929

Percent change, 1990–2000: 31.3%

U.S. rank in 1980: 105th

U.S. rank in 1990: 90th

U.S. rank in 2000: 80th

City Residents

1980: 215,150

1990: 283,112

2000: 360,890

2003 estimate: 370,448

Percent change, 1990–2000: 27.5%

U.S. rank in 1980: 66th

U.S. rank in 1990: 54th

U.S. rank in 2000: 48th (State rank: 2nd)

Density: 1,942.9 people per square mile (2000)

Racial and ethnic characteristics (2000)

White: 291,095

Black or African American: 23,677

American Indian and Alaska Native: 3,175

Asian: 10,179

Native Hawaiian and Pacific Islander: 764

Hispanic or Latino (may be of any race): 43,330

Other: 18,091

Percent of residents born in state: 29.6% (2000)

Age characteristics (2000)

Population under 5 years old: 26,920

Population 5 to 9 years old: 26,695

Population 10 to 14 years old: 26,489

Population 15 to 19 years old: 25,828

Population 20 to 24 years old: 26,686

Population 25 to 34 years old: 55,543

Population 35 to 44 years old: 62,744

Population 45 to 54 years old: 48,562

Population 55 to 59 years old: 15,310

Population 60 to 64 years old: 11,334

Population 65 to 74 years old: 18,505

Population 75 to 84 years old: 12,297

Population 85 years and over: 3,977

Median age: 33.6 years

Births (2002, El Paso County)

Total number: 8,530

Deaths (2002, El Paso County)

Total number: 3,408 (of which, 59 were infants under the age of 1 year)

Money income (1999)

Per capita income: $22,496

Median household income: $45,081

Total households: 141,757

Number of households with income of . . .

less than $10,000: 9,379

$10,000 to $14,999: 6,966

$15,000 to $24,999: 17,815

$25,000 to $34,999: 18,686

$35,000 to $49,999: 25,750

$50,000 to $74,999: 30,608

$75,000 to $99,999: 16,171

$100,000 to $149,999: 10,893

$150,000 to $199,999: 2,854

$200,000 or more: 2,635

Percent of families below poverty level: 6.1% (41.7% of which were female householder families with related children under 5 years)

2002 FBI Crime Index Total: 20,247

Municipal Government

Colorado Springs operates under a council-mayor form of government. Elections are held every four years for mayor, four council members-at-large, and four council members from the districts where they reside. Colorado Springs is the seat of El Paso County.

Head Official: Mayor Lionel Rivera (since 2003; current term expires 2007)

Total Number of City Employees: 2,500 (2004)

City Information: City Hall, PO Box 1575, Colorado Springs, CO 80901; telephone (719)385-CITY

Economy

Major Industries and Commercial Activity

The economy of Colorado Springs is based primarily on the military installations in the area as well as on the aerospace and electronics industries and tourism. The military employs one fifth of the work force in the city. Fort Carson, a U.S.

Army base, is the largest employer, maintaining more than 15,000 people on its payroll. The U.S. Air Force Academy, Fort Peterson Air Force Base (AFB), and the North American Air Defense Command (NORAD) are also major employers.

Colorado Springs is a center for space research. The city is the site of the Combined Services Space Center and the Consolidated Space Operations Center, which are involved in the Strategic Defense Initiative and handle military missions of the Space Shuttle. The U.S. Space Foundation (USSF) and the Space Commands at Peterson AFB also provide a conducive environment for developing future space-related projects. As a result of growth in the aerospace industry, several high-technology firms have been attracted to Colorado Springs. Hewlett-Packard and 17 other major electronics companies, combined, employ nearly 10,000 workers.

Since the turn of the century, when the city's grand hotels made it famous, Colorado Springs has been a major tourism center. Pikes Peak and the natural beauty of the surrounding area drew over 6.2 million visitors in 2003; the U.S. Air Force Academy is the main man-made attraction in the state. The city's average gross income from tourism is near $1 billion, providing a substantial boost to the construction industry.

Items and goods produced: advertising film, granite, concrete, dairy products, brooms, novelties, chemicals, pottery, bricks, airplane engine mounts, machine tools, shell fuses, electric motors, castings, electronics, plastics, steel culverts, printed and published works

Incentive Programs—New and Existing Companies

Local programs—At the local level, El Paso County contains an Urban Enterprise Zone offering state and local credits for new jobs, investment, and research and development expenditures. The Greater Colorado Springs Economic Development Council will package private and public incentives for relocating or expanding companies that are tailored to the specific needs of the company. The private sector and government in Colorado Springs cooperate to encourage new business and industry through such incentives as low corporate tax rates, a Foreign Trade Zone, and training programs. The Colorado Office of Business Development and International Trade offers services in bringing national and foreign investment to the state.

State programs—In 2004 *Forbes* magazine rated Colorado Springs the 24th Best Place for business in the entire country. There are numerous venture capital firms throughout the state, including the Colorado Quality Investment Capital Program.

Job training programs—The Colorado Flexible Industry Related Start-up Training program is available to assist companies; Pikes Peak Community College has its Corpo-

rate Workforce and Economic Development Center for delivery of training funded under this program. The Pikes Peak Workforce Center helps with placement, job matching, and training workers. The Colorado Office of Business Development and International Trade offers Colorado First grants for new businesses and Existing Industry grants for training and staff retention purposes.

Economic Development Information: The Greater Colorado Springs Economic Development Corporation, 90 S. Cascade Ave. Suite 1050 Colorado Springs, CO 80907; telephone (719)471-8183; fax (719)471-9733; email csedc @csedc.org

Development Projects

Development in the downtown area is booming due to the Colorado Springs Downtown Partnership. The Depot Arts District is planned to offer affordable housing, studio, and retail space. Palmer Village will be a new neighborhood in the Southwest Downtown Area, bringing urban renewal to an underused area. The Pikes Peak Outdoor Market, featuring dozens of vendors selling Colorado produce, free-range meat, fine art and crafts opened on 2004, with an indoor market opening in 2005.

Three business parks on the north side of Colorado Springs saw considerable activity in the late 1990s and early 2000, with commitments by several large ''new economy'' companies. Progressive Insurance will build a 150,000 square-foot data center near its recently completed call center in 2005. Intel Corp. opened a new manufacturing operation; software giant Oracle Corp. constructed a building to house its customer support center; financial investment firm T. Rowe Price built a 147,000-square-foot building for a customer service center and planned additional space in the area; and mountain bike equipment maker RockShox Inc. moved its San Jose, California, headquarters and manufacturing operation there. In 2004, Configuresoft relocated its corporate headquarters to fit its expansion. Also on the city's north side Focus on the Family, a media and publishing ministry, completed a $12.6 million expansion, and Compassion International planned a $23 million headquarters. Developers have been so impressed with the economic health of Colorado Springs and with the quality of the companies that have moved in, that more speculative space is planned.

Commercial Shipping

Established as a Foreign Trade Zone, Colorado Springs is a link in the country's import-export shipping network. Eight air cargo carriers operate from Colorado Springs Municipal Airport, and the metropolitan area is served by two major rail freight lines. About 20 motor freight carriers ship goods through terminals in the city.

Labor Force and Employment Outlook

Colorado Springs boasts a youthful, well educated, willing labor force. Sources of labor include former military personnel, military dependents, retirees, college students, and commuters from other Colorado cities. Labor/management relations are described as excellent; there is a low level of unionization throughout Colorado.

The population of Colorado Springs grew 27 percent between 1990 and 2000, and the number of high-tech jobs in the city has grown greatly in that time. These factors have spurred a shortage of affordable housing and a demand for skilled workers; rapid growth has also begun to strain the local infrastructure. This, in combination with other factors nationwide, is expected to slow local growth.

The following is a summary of data regarding the Colorado Springs metropolitan area labor force, 2004 annual averages.

Size of non-agricultural labor force: 247,900

Number of workers employed in . . .
   mining and construction: 15,900
   manufacturing: 20,100
   trade, transportation and utilities: 39,300
   information: 9,900
   financial activities: 17,200
   professional and business services: 35,500
   educational and health services: 23,600
   leisure and hospitality: 29,700
   other services: 14,200
   government: 42,600

Average minimum hourly wages of manufacturing workers: $ 16.13

Unemployment rate: 5.4% (December 2004)

Largest employers	Number of employees
Fort Carson	15,159
U.S. Air Force Academy	6,410
Peterson AFB/NORAD/Space Command	5,542
Colorado Springs School District #11	3,440
Memorial Hospital	3,100
Penrose-St. Francis Health Services	2,981
City of Colorado Springs	2,424
Hewlett-Packard	2,200
Schriever AFB	2,107
El Paso County	2,029
WorldCom	2,000
Amtel	1,850

Cost of Living

The following is a summary of data regarding key cost of living factors in the Colorado Springs area.

2004 (3rd Quarter) ACCRA Average House Price: $250,088

2004 (3rd Quarter) ACCRA Cost of Living Index: 96.0 (U.S. average = 100.0)

State income tax rate: 4.63%

State sales tax rate: 2.9%

Local income tax rate: None

Local sales tax rate: 2.5% city and 1% county

Property tax rate: ranges between 59 mills and 90 mills depending on school district and other special taxing districts; the average in 2003 was 67 mills. The 2003 residential assessment rate for taxes due in 2004 was 7.96 percent of market value

Economic Information: The Greater Colorado Springs Chamber of Commerce, 2 North Cascade Avenue, Suite 110, Colorado Springs, CO 80903; telephone (719)635-1551; fax (719)635-1571

Education and Research

Elementary and Secondary Schools

In Colorado, school district boundaries are independent of city or other political boundaries. There are 15 public school districts within El Paso County; six districts of varying size serve urban areas of Colorado Springs. Colorado Springs School District Eleven, the fourth largest system in the state and largest in the city, is administered by a seven-member, nonpartisan board of education that appoints a superintendent to a two-year contract. Composite SAT scores are consistently above the national average.

The following is a summary of data regarding Colorado Springs School District Eleven as of the 2002–2003 school year.

Total enrollment: 32,368

Number of facilities
   elementary schools: 39
   junior high/middle schools: 9
   senior high schools: 9
   other: 6

Student/teacher ratio: 16.9:1

Teacher salaries
   minimum: $27,217
   maximum: $63,668

Funding per pupil: $7,298 (2002-2003)

About 7,300 students attend 39 parochial and private schools in Colorado Springs, Pre-K through 12th grade. Pine Creek High School, a $16 million technology magnet school, opened in 1998; the school prepares students for college or employment in regional business and provides them with a sense of community.

Public Schools Information: Colorado Springs School District Eleven, 1115 North El Paso Street, Colorado Springs, CO 80903; telephone (719)520-2000; fax (719)577-4546

Colleges and Universities

The Colorado Springs area is home to 20 colleges and universities, including the United States Air Force Academy, the University of Colorado at Colorado Springs, and Colorado College. The University of Colorado is a state school offering both undergraduate and master's degrees in interdisciplinary programs such as geography, earth sciences, and environmental studies. Colorado College, opened in 1874, has grown with the city, and offers an unusual learning environment: the Block Plan has students take only one intensive course at a time. Thirty technical, professional, and business schools, including Colorado Technical College, are also located in Colorado Springs.

Libraries and Research Centers

The Pikes Peak Library District (PPLD) serves the residents of El Paso County except Manitou Springs and Widefield School District #3. Residents in those two areas can check out PPLD materials through the Colorado Library Card program. Library facilities include two main facilities—Penrose Public Library and the East Library and Information Center—9 branches, and two bookmobiles for the city and county. A new building for the Fountain Branch is scheduled for completion in the spring of 2006. The library district maintains several diverse and specialized collections. The circulating collection includes books, vertical file materials, audio and video cassettes, record albums, CDs, and DVDs. The library subscribes to hundreds of periodicals and newspapers. The Local History and Genealogy collections, housed in the 1905 Carnegie Library, include books, photographs, manuscripts, maps, blueprints, newspapers, city directories, oral histories, and other items spanning more than 125 years of local and regional history. About 30 other libraries and research centers are housed in the city; most are affiliated with educational institutions, government agencies, hospitals, and churches. The United States Air Force Academy Library, with more than 300,000 volumes, maintains a collection on aeronautics history before 1910; special interests also include falconry and military history. The Charles Leaming Tutt Library at Colorado College houses 435,000 volumes, plus 1,300 periodicals, a government

documents repository, the college's Special Collections & Archives, and the Crown Tapper Teaching & Learning Center devoted to exploring ways to improve teaching in the electronic age.

Public Library Information: Pikes Peak Library District, 5550 North Union Boulevard, PO Box 1579, Colorado Springs, CO 80918; telephone (719)531-6333

Health Care

The Colorado Springs metropolitan area is served by five major hospitals. Memorial Hospital, with 477 beds, was named in 2004 by ModernHealthcare as one of the nation's top 100 hospitals for cardiovascular care. It is also a regional center for high-risk pregnancies, with a Level III Neonatal Intensive Care Unit. Penrose-St. Francis Health Services runs Penrose Hospital, Penrose Community Hospital, and St. Francis Health Center. Penrose Hospital completed a $52 million expansion in 2005 with the opening of ''E Tower,'' containing critical care and cardiac units, a wellness center, a chapel, and a new main lobby. SemperCare Hospital is a long-term acute care hospital with 30 beds. There are a variety of rehabilitation centers, nursing homes and behavioral health centers in the city and surrounding county.

Recreation

Sightseeing

Colorado Springs is one of the premier vacation spots in the United States, the majestic natural beauty of Pikes Peak being a principal attraction. Visitors can venture up High Drive, a one-way road without guardrails, to see the spectacular vistas. North Cheyenne Canyon contains unusual rock formations and waterfalls that cascade down the mountains. In the Garden of the Gods, northwest of the city, visitors can hike or horseback ride through huge red sandstone rock formations; the Garden of the Gods is particularly lovely to visit at sunrise or sunset, when the sun's rays set off the natural splendor of the rocks. At High Point a camera obscura is provided for viewing the landscape that surrounds the point.

Cheyenne Mountain Zoo displays more than 600 wild animals from around the world in the U.S.'s only mountain zoo. The African Rift Valley area opened in 2003 and features Colobus monkeys, giraffes, other African animals and birds, and an interactive African Play Village for kids. The price of

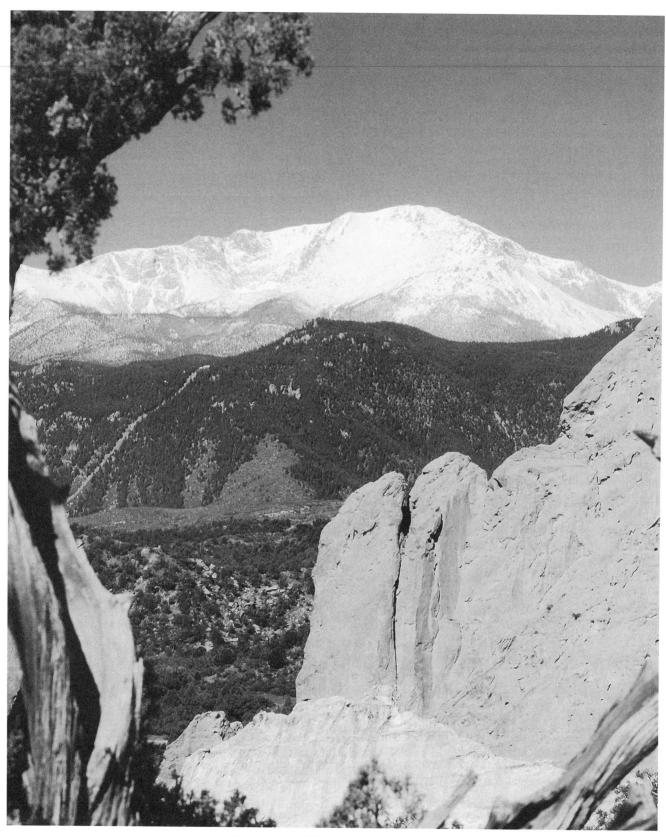

Pike's Peak and the Garden of the Gods.

admission includes a visit to the Will Rogers Shrine of the Sun, which exhibits mementos of this famous American humorist and an 80-foot high observation tower. The May Natural History Museum of the Tropics houses more than 7,000 exotic insects from jungles around the globe.

The U.S. Air Force Academy is one of Colorado Springs's most popular tourist attractions. Visitors can tour the unusual multi-spired chapel, Honor Court and visitor's center. The Pikes Peak Cog Railway takes visitors on a 3-hour round trip tour to the summit of the mountain, at 12,110 feet above sea level. At the U.S. ProRodeo Hall of Fame, rodeo memorabilia is on display.

Arts and Culture

The Colorado Springs Philharmonic presents classical, pops and jazz performances October through May at the Pikes Peak Center. The Chamber Orchestra of the Springs performs five programs a year of pieces meant for small orchestras. The DaVinci Quartet plays concerts in various venues in Colorado Springs and Denver and offers community outreach to local schools. The Colorado Springs Choral Society has been performing classical and modern pieces since 1956. Students from Colorado College perform during the school year and during the Summer Music Festival, Vocal Arts and New Music Symposia, and during Extraordinary Dance Festival. The famous Broadmoor Hotel resort complex features international performers and hosts concerts.

The Star Bar Players presents four plays per season in the Lon Chaney Theater at the Civic Auditorium. Theatreworks at the University of Colorado presents Shakespeare and contemporary and classic plays. The REP presents musicals at the Fine Arts Center of Colorado Springs. Drama and dance students at Colorado College perform regular seasons at the college. Colorado Springs Dance Theatre sponsors national and international companies to perform at the Pikes Peak Center.

Colorado Springs is home to 20 major museums and galleries, including the Museum of the American Numismatic Association, which houses one of the largest collections of coins and medals in the world. The Fine Arts Center of Colorado Springs is a regional center for all the arts, containing the Taylor Museum of Art, the Bemis School of Art, and a performing arts department, presenting plays, dance, music, and films. Also located in Colorado Springs are the World Figure Skating Hall of Fame and Museum and the Pioneer's Museum, which exhibits displays pertaining to the history of the region. Featuring demonstrations of gold-panning techniques, the Western Museum of Mining and Industry showcases machinery used in early gold and silver mining operations. The Peterson Air and Space Museum displays historic aircraft and a moon rock. The Taylor Collection of Native American and Hispanic Art is maintained at the Fine

Arts Center. The Rock Ledge Ranch Historic Site celebrates the history of Colorado Springs by recreating the settlements of Native Americans and the lives of the settlers of the frontier in the 1800s, with costumed interpreters and special programs.

Festivals and Holidays

Among the annual events in Colorado Springs is the impressive Easter Sunrise Service, celebrated at Gateway Rocks in the Garden of the Gods. Territory Days on Memorial Day weekend brings 100,000 visitors to Colorado Avenue for free entertainment, food, and crafts. On Independence Day is the International Chili Cook-Off in Memorial Park. One hundred cooks engage in an original recipe competition, sharing the day with a fireworks celebration and a performance by the Colorado Springs Philharmonic. At the end of July the Annual Broadmoor Ice Revue at the Broadmoor World Arena features Olympic skaters. The Pikes Peak or Bust Rodeo in Penrose Stadium, one of the top 10 outdoor rodeos in the country, takes place at the end of August. The celebration includes a parade through downtown Colorado Springs and a street breakfast. August also brings the national Little Britches Rodeo in which children from ages 8 to 18 compete for titles at the Penrose Stadium. Labor Day weekend features the Hot Air Balloon Classic, with the ascension of scores of colorful hot air balloons. The Southwestern Figure Skating Championship comes to the World Arena in October. December brings the Festival of Lights Christmas Parade and Gallery of Trees at the Fine Arts Center.

Sports for the Spectator

A number of sports events are available for viewing in Colorado Springs. The Sky Sox play professional Triple A baseball at Sky Sox Stadium as an affiliate of the Colorado Rockies in the Pacific Coast League. Football fans enjoy watching the U.S. Air Force Academy team compete against top college teams. Basketball, hockey and other college sports are played at University of Colorado and Colorado College. The Pikes Peak Auto Hill Climb, the Broadmoor Invitational Men's and Women's Golf Tournaments, and rodeo events also interest spectators in the Colorado Springs area. Greyhounds race at Rocky Mountain Greyhound Park from late August to late November. The U.S. Olympic Complex periodically hosts Olympic Sports Festivals. Pikes Peak International Raceway hosts NASCAR and Indy car races

Sports for the Participant

Outdoor activities abound in Colorado Springs, including climbing, white-water rafting, fishing, hiking, horseback riding, cave exploring, and gliding. The city maintains over 12,000 acres with 15 community and regional parks (including Garden of Gods and North Cheyenne Canon Parks) biking and hiking trails, 6 sports complexes, and 123 neighborhood parks. The El Pomar Youth Sports Complex includes 12 baseball fields of various sizes, 8 soccer/lacrosse fields, 6 volleyball courts, and a playground. The Broadmoor Hotel resort complex offers skeet and trap shooting as well as skiing and ice skating in the winter and golfing on three challenging courses during the warmer months. Echo Canyon River Adventures offers half- and multi-day rafting adventures on the Arkansas River. Pikes Peak Alpine School offers instruction for all levels in rock and ice climbing, mountaineering, and back country skiing.

Shopping and Dining

Colorado Springs is served by four major malls, including The Citadel and The Outlets at Castle Rock. Stores specializing in Western gear and Native American art can be found in many areas. In addition, the Old Colorado City Historic District contains many small shops, and the Garden of the Gods Trading Post stocks fine Indian jewelry and Colorado giftware.

Because Colorado Springs is at the center of a popular resort area, it enjoys cuisine from around the world, as well as local Western-style establishments offering barbecue and chuckwagon fare and Mexican foods. Rocky Mountain trout is a local delicacy. The Broadmoor Hotel maintains nine dining rooms with a range of prices and cuisines. Gourmet food is served at the historic Briarhurst Manor Inn. The Flying W Chuckwagon Supper and Western Show combines fine dining for the family with cowboy music.

Visitor Information: Colorado Springs Convention and Visitors Bureau, 515 South Cascade, Suite, Colorado Springs, CO 80903; telephone (719)635-7506; toll-free (877)745-3773; fax (719)635-4968

Convention Facilities

Since the turn of the century, Colorado Springs has drawn a steady flow of tourists; since the 1970s the city has made itself equally amenable to conventions and conferences, providing a number of meeting facilities. The Colorado Springs World Arena accommodates 8,000 people for general sessions and the exhibit floor offers 19,500 square feet of space or 180 booths. The Phil Long Expo Center has over 100,000 square feet of exhibition space and can accommodate up to 455 booths. There are many hotels that offer convention and meeting facilities. The 700-room Broadmoor has 114,000 square feet of meeting space and the 316-room Cheyenne Conference Mountain Resort offers 40,000 square feet. There is also the Wyndham Colorado Springs Hotel with 310 rooms and 13,000 square feet of meeting space; Sheraton Colorado Springs Hotel, with 500 rooms

and 42,000 square feet of meeting space; and the DoubleTree Hotel Colorado Springs World Arena with 299 rooms and 21,135 square feet of meeting space. There are more than 13,500 hotel rooms in the city.

Convention Information: Colorado Springs Convention and Visitors Bureau, 515 South Cascade, Colorado Springs, CO 80903; telephone (719)635-7506; toll-free (800)888-4748; fax (719)635-4968

Transportation

Approaching the City

The Colorado Springs Airport, located east of the city, is served by 8 major airlines, providing 110 daily flights to 13 cities. The airport sits on more than 7,200 acres with two parallel runways and one crosswind runway. It has one of the lowest rates of delays of major airports in the country.

Four major highways lead into Colorado Springs: I-25 (north-south), U.S. 85/87 (north-south), I-70 (east-west), and U.S. 50 (north-south). Commercial bus transportation into the city is available through interstate bus lines.

Traveling in the City

The main north-south thoroughfare in Colorado Springs is I-25, called Monument Valley Freeway within the city. Midland Expressway (U.S. 24) runs east and west, becoming Platte Avenue after it crosses I-25. Other important arteries are Garden of the Gods Road, Uintah Street, and Fillmore Street, all running east and west. Some of the mountain roads are not furnished with guardrails and are not accessible to such vehicles as recreational vans.

Springs Transit is the city's mass transportation system. Thirty-one bus routes run during the day with limited service at night. Many routes meet at the downtown Springs Transit terminal.

Communications

Newspapers and Magazines

The major daily newspaper in Colorado Springs is the morning *The Gazette*. Weekly publications include *The Colorado Springs Independent* and the *Colorado Springs Business Journal*. Local concerns publish sports and hobby oriented magazines of interest to fans of hockey, whitewater kayaking, rafting, canoeing, cycling, hang gliding, rodeo, skating, coin collecting, and table tennis.

Television and Radio

Three commercial television stations broadcast in Colorado Springs; one cable provider is based in the city. The city also receives broadcasts from television stations located in nearby Grand Junction and Pueblo. Fourteen AM and FM radio stations in Colorado Springs schedule a range of music, news, and information programming.

Media Information: The Gazette, 30 South Prospect, Colorado Springs, CO 80903; telephone (716)632-5511.

Colorado Springs Online

Charles Leaming Tutt Library. Available www.cc.colorado .edu/library/specialcollections/Walk/Tutt.html

City of Colorado Springs Home Page. Available www .springs.gov

Colorado Springs Convention & Visitors Bureau. Available www.experiencecoloradosprings.com

Colorado Springs Gazette Available www.gazette.com

Colorado Springs School District Eleven. Available www .cssd11k12.co.us

Greater Colorado Springs Chamber of Commerce. Available www.cscc.org

Greater Colorado Springs Economic Development Corporation. Available www.coloradosprings.org

Pikes Peak Library District. Available library.ppld.org

School Demographics. Available cde.state.co.us/cdedistrict/ dist1010.htm

Selected Bibliography

Finley, Judith Reid, *Time Capsule 1900: Colorado Springs A Century Ago* (Colorado Springs, Colo.: Pastword Publications, 1998)

Denver

The City in Brief

Founded: 1858 (incorporated, 1861)

Head Official: Mayor John W. Hickenlooper (D) (since 2003)

City Population
 1980: 493,000
 1990: 467,610
 2000: 554,636
 2003 estimate: 557,748
 Percent change, 1990–2000: 18.6%
 U.S. rank in 1980: 24th
 U.S. rank in 1990: 26th
 U.S. rank in 2000: 31st

Metropolitan Area Population (PMSA)
 1980: 1,429,000
 1990: 1,622,980
 2000: 2,109,282

Percent change, 1990–2000: 29.9%
U.S. rank in 1980: 21st (PMSA)
U.S. rank in 1990: 22nd (MSA)
U.S. rank in 2000: 19th (MSA)

Area: 153 square miles (2000)
Elevation: 5,332 feet above sea level
Average Annual Temperature: 50.0° F
Average Annual Precipitation: 15.81 inches

Major Economic Sectors: Communications, utilities, transportation
Unemployment Rate: 5.6% (January 2005)
Per Capita Income: $24,101 (1999)

2002 FBI Crime Index Total: 32,132

Major Colleges and Universities: University of Denver, Metropolitan State University, University of Colorado at Denver

Daily Newspapers: *The Denver Post; Rocky Mountain News*

UNION STATION

SAKURA SQUARE

N

WAZEE ST.

BLAKE ST.

MARKET ST.

LARIMER ST.

SKYLINE PARK

CHAMBER OF COMMERCE

LARIMER SQUARE

LAWRENCE ST.

ARAPAHOE ST.

CURTIS ST.

CHAMPA ST.

TO STAPLETON AIRPORT

TO BLACK AMERICAN WESTERN MUSEUM

20TH ST.

20TH AVE.

19TH ST.

18TH ST.

OR

ID

WY

NV

UT

Denver

CO

CA

AZ

NM

0 KILOMETERS 0.5 1

MILES 0.25 0.5

SPEER BLVD.

UNIV. OF COLORADO DENVER

DENVER PERFORMING ARTS COMPLEX

STOUT ST.

CALIFORNIA ST.

16TH ST.

17TH ST.

15TH ST.

WELTON

GLENARM PL.

TREMONT PL.

COURT PL.

CLEVELAND

19TH AVE.

TO MUSEUM OF NATURAL HISTORY

MUSEUM OF WESTERN ART

18TH AVE.

17TH AVE.

16TH AVE.

METRO STATE COLLEGE

14TH ST.

COLORADO CONVENTION CENTER

12TH ST.

13TH ST.

VISITORS CENTER

DENVER COMMUNITY COLLEGE

TO MILE HIGH STADIUM

40

U.S. MINT

CITY & COUNTY BLDG.

CIVIC CENTER PARK

COLFAX AVE.

40

TO CITY PARK AND ZOO

STATE CAPITOL

14TH AVE.

FOX ST.

DENVER ART MUSEUM

DENVER PUBLIC LIBRARY

COLORADO HISTORY MUSEUM

13TH AVE.

ELATI ST.

DELAWARE ST.

CHEROKEE ST.

BANNOCK ST.

ACOMA ST.

BROADWAY

LINCOLN

SHERMAN ST.

GRANT ST.

LOGAN ST.

PENNSYLVANIA ST.

PEARL ST.

WASHINGTON ST.

12TH AVE.

LIPAN ST.

KALAMATH ST.

SANTA FE DR.

INCA ST.

GALAPAGO ST.

SPEER BLVD.

11TH AVE.

CHERRY CREEK

10TH AVE.

SUNKEN GARDENS PARK

9TH AVE.

Introduction

Denver, dubbed the Mile High City, is the commercial, financial, and transportation capital of the Rocky Mountain region. A concentration of federal government offices makes it the administrative center of this area as well. Denver's history has included frequent boom periods, but redirection and economic diversification became necessary during the late 1960s through the early 1980s. The city is undergoing a renaissance, with downtown development paving the way for Denver's projected ascendance in high-technology industries as the nation's population shifts southwestward. Set in a verdant plain at the foot of the Rocky Mountains, Denver is noted for its quality of life and the blending of modern innovation and Western tradition; because of its high quality lifestyle Sperlings for MSN ranked the city as second of America's "Ten Best Places To Live" in 2003.

Geography and Climate

Denver is situated in the high plains at the eastern edge of the Rocky Mountains, which protect the city from severe winter weather. These mountains, reaching higher than 14,000 feet, are the dominant feature of the area. The South Platte River bisects the city, and many creeks, small lakes, and reservoirs grace the metropolitan area. Denver's climate is semiarid and relatively mild, with more sunny days than either Miami, Florida or San Diego, California. Although visitors must make some adjustment to the high altitude, they find that the area's low humidity makes even the highest and lowest temperatures seem less extreme.

Area: 153 square miles (2000)

Elevation: 5,332 feet above sea level

Average Temperatures: January, 30.1° F; August 72.0° F; annual average, 50.0° F

Average Annual Precipitation: 15.81 inches

History

Discovery of Gold Brings Settlers to Denver Area

For centuries, the mountains and plains of Colorado were used as hunting grounds by Native Americans, and eventually the more sophisticated, agricultural tribes like the Anasazi established villages. In the sixteenth century, the Spanish explored the region where Denver is now located, but no Europeans established permanent settlements until the mid-1800s, when gold was discovered at Pikes Peak. In 1858, a supply center for the mining towns was established on the site of a tribal village at the junction of the South Platte River and Cherry Creek. The town was called St. Charles; later it was renamed Denver City after James W. Denver, governor of the Kansas Territory, and was incorporated in 1861.

The gold boom soon ended, but some of the fortune hunters stayed on to settle in the new town. During the 1860s, much of the town was destroyed by fire; a ravaging flash flood killed 20 people; and the citizens repelled frequent attacks from the Plains tribes and even an assault by a Confederate Army. With the arrival of rail transportation in 1870 a steady influx of settlers insured the future of the thriving town, and when Colorado attained statehood in 1876, Denver was named the state capital. By 1879 it boasted a population of 35,000 people and the first telephone service in the West.

Silver Boom and Bust; Economy Diversifies

A silver boom in the 1880s ushered in another period of rapid growth, filling Denver with the Victorian mansions of silver barons and making it the most elegant city in the West. The collapse of the silver market in the panic of 1893 staggered the city's economy, so the city began to diversify. By the early 1900s, Denver had become the commercial and industrial center of the Rocky Mountain region, as well as a leader in livestock sales, agriculture, and tourism.

Denver sustained a period of relatively slow development until the 1930s. Prior to World War II, when such federal government agencies as the Geological Survey, the U.S. Mint, Lowry Air Force Base, the Bureau of Land Management, and the Air Force Accounting Center were established in the area, Denver experienced another population surge that continued through the 1950s. During the 1960s Denver lost population as residents moved to the suburbs to escape inner city deterioration. Growth slowed again in the mid-1970s as a result of the oil industry crisis. The effects of this downturn, however, were ultimately positive. As a result of efforts to diversify the economy, Denver became known as "the energy capital of the west," with a focus on alternative energy sources such as solar and wind power. In fact, by 1980 approximately 1,200 energy companies were located in Denver.

Growth slowed again in the mid-1980s when plans for oil shale development were curtailed; construction of high-rise office buildings downtown nevertheless continued unabated. A sleek, modern landscape has emerged in Denver where a Western frontier town once stood. As Denver entered the twenty-first century, it reflected the economic downturn due to the high-tech industry but has since stabilized and strengthened to remain the principal commercial, financial, and industrial hub of the Rocky Mountain region.

Historical Information: Colorado Historical Society, Stephen H. Hart Library, 1300 Broadway, Denver, CO 80203; telephone (303)866-2305; email research@chs.state.co.us

Population Profile

Metropolitan Area Residents (PMSA)
1980: 1,429,000
1990: 1,622,980
2000: 2,109,282
Percent change, 1990–2000: 29.9%
U.S. rank in 1980: 21st
U.S. rank in 1990: 22nd
U.S. rank in 2000: 19th

City Residents
1980: 493,000
1990: 467,610
2000: 554,636
2003 estimate: 557,478
Percent change, 1990–2000: −18.6%
U.S. rank in 1980: 24th
U.S. rank in 1990: 26th (State rank: 1st)
U.S. rank in 2000: 31st (State rank: 1st)

Density: 3,616.7 people per square mile (2000)

Racial and ethnic characteristics (2000)
White: 362,180
Black or African American: 61,149
American Indian and Alaska Native: 7,290
Asian: 15,611
Native Hawaiian and other Pacific Islander: 648
Hispanic or Latino (may be of any race): 175,704
Other: 86,464

Percent of residents born in state: 40.1%

Age characteristics (2000)
Population under 5 years old: 37,769
Population 5 to 9 years old: 34,473
Population 10 to 14 years old: 31,315
Population 15 to 19 years old: 32,259
Population 20 to 24 years old: 45,534
Population 25 to 34 years old: 113,676
Population 35 to 44 years old: 86,420
Population 45 to 54 years old: 71,000
Population 55 to 59 years old: 22,573
Population 60 to 64 years old: 17,191
Population 65 to 74 years old: 30,643
Population 75 to 84 years old: 23,369
Population 85 years and over: 8,414
Median age: 33.1 years

Births: (2003, Denver County)
Total number: 10,365

Deaths (2003, Denver County)
Total number: 4,321 (of which, 72 were infants under the age of 1 year)

Money income (1999)
Per capita income: $24,101
Median household income: $39,500
Total households: 239,235

Number of households with income of . . .
less than $10,000: 24,286
$10,000 to $14,999: 15,173
$15,000 to $24,999: 31,541
$25,000 to $34,999: 34,121
$35,000 to $49,999: 41,136
$50,000 to $74,999: 43,712
$75,000 to $99,999: 21,836
$100,000 to $149,999: 16,662
$150,000 to $199,999: 4,912
$200,000 or more: 6,036

Percent of families below poverty level: 10.6% (42.0% of which were female householder families with related children under 5 years)

2002 FBI Crime Index Total: 32,132

Municipal Government

The city and county of Denver share the same boundaries and operate under a government that performs both municipal and county functions. Denver's mayor council form of government invests its mayor, who is elected to a four-year term, with strong executive powers. The 13 council members also serve for 4 years.

Head Official: Mayor John W. Hickenlooper (D) (since 2003; current term expires 2007)

Total Number of City Employees: 12,485 (2005)

City Information: City of Denver, 945 S. Huron St., Denver, CO 80223; telephone (303)698-4900

Economy

Major Industries and Commercial Activity

Following record economic and population growth in the 1950s, Denver weathered reversals tied to the fluctuating petroleum market in the 1970s and 1980s. By the late 1980s the city had taken measures toward establishing a diversified economic base. Major companies in the Denver metropolitan area employ workers in a range of fields such as air transportation, telecommunications, aerospace, and manufacturing. The city is also a major energy research center and a regional headquarters for government agencies.

The financial and commercial capital of the Rocky Mountain region, Denver's downtown banking district—dubbed the "Wall Street of the Rockies"—consists of major national and international institutions. The city is the transportation hub for a large portion of the western United States; consumer and industrial goods are transported by air, rail, and truck through Denver to more than 30 million people annually. Denver is a Foreign Trade Zone, providing advantages to companies involved in international trade. To its advantage, the city's geographic position and location within the Mountain Time Zone make it the largest city in the United States to offer one-bounce satellite uplinks with real-time connections to 6 of 7 continents in one day.

Denver's central location—it is 346 miles west of the exact geographic center of the country—places it in an advantageous position for future economic development and growth. Analysts predict that the U.S. population is shifting south and west, with future concentration expected in the area from California to Utah and to the Gulf coast in Texas. Denver is at the center of this region; projections indicate that the city will become a high-technology research, development, and manufacturing hub for the entire Southwest.

Items and goods produced: computer storage and peripherals, beverages, mining and farming machinery, rubber goods, fabricated metals, chemicals and allied stone and clay products, western clothing, transportation equipment, scientific instruments, feed, flour, luggage

Incentive Programs—New and Existing Companies

Local programs—The Mayor's Office of Economic Development & International Trade (MOED/IT) works to retain and create quality jobs, assists organizations in expansion or relocation, and provides a multitude of business development services. It promotes the city as a business location particularly for foreign companies and promotes Denver companies entering international markets. MOED/IT assists with financing, economic incentives, regulatory requirement assistance, and other services as needed. MOED/IT also administers the Denver Urban Enterprise Zone, which assists business with state tax credits for job creation. Together with the Colorado International Trade office, MOED/IT supports the Colorado/Denver Representative Office in London.

State programs—A variety of state and federal programs are available to assist business in relocating and expanding in Denver. Enterprise Zone Tax Credits and Manufacturing Revenue Bonds are among them. The State of Colorado's Business Retention and Expansion program helps smooth the path for area businesses by removing local or statewide barriers.

Job training programs—The Mayor's Office of Workforce Development offers the Colorado FIRST program which connects employment, job readiness, education, and training services into a network of resources at the local and state level. This system links Colorado's employers to a variety of qualified applicants and provides job-seekers with access to employment and training opportunities at six workforce training centers throughout the city as well as additional resources across the country. The menu of core services includes: career counseling and assessment, employer and job-seeker access to automated job postings, information on job trends, assistance in filing Unemployment Insurance claims, and help in finding federal, state, and city dollars to cover some or all of the costs of training opportunities.

Development Projects

The $4.3 billion Denver International Airport is one of the largest airports in the world; it is known for its aesthetics, aviation safety, customer satisfaction and passenger convenience and is the fifth busiest airport in America. The airport continues to spur significant hotel development nearby. The city has spent hundreds of millions of dollars on Denver's downtown, and has plans for future expansion of several museums, theaters, hotels, and government buildings as well as transportation facilities and parks. Invesco Field at Mile High, a $364 million, 76,000-seat stadium replaced Mile High Stadium as the home of the Denver Broncos in 2001; and in 2004 an expansion of the Denver Convention Center was unveiled.

Economic Development Information: Mayor's Office of Economic Development and International Trade, 201 W. Colfax, Dep 208, Denver, CO 80202; John Huggins, Director; telephone (720)913-1999; email john.huggins@ci .denver.co.us. Denver One Stop Career Center, 1391 N. Speer Blvd., Denver, CO 80204; telephone (720)865-5700; email info@mowd.org

Commercial Shipping

Denver is the commercial transportation center for an eight-state area, providing a hub for two major rail freight companies, more than 160 motor freight carriers, and a number of air cargo services. With negotiated motor freight rates and the city's designation as a Free Trade Zone, Denver has created a competitive marketplace for the import and export of goods.

Labor Force and Employment Outlook

Employers in Denver choose from a highly educated labor pool. The city ranks second in the nation for the number of residents with bachelors degrees and 64 percent of residents age 24 and older have attended college. Local analysts predict a healthy economy, based on Denver's quality labor force, affordable cost of living, high quality of life, and low commercial lease rates. With a diverse employment base across many sectors, Denver is in a prime position for growth well into the twenty-first century.

The following is a summary of data regarding the Denver metropolitan area labor force, 2004 annual averages.

Size of non-agricultural labor force: 1,167,600

Number of workers employed in . . .
   construction and mining: 86,200
   manufacturing: 72,100
   trade, transportation and utilities: 233,000
   information: 51,500
   financial activities: 98,500
   professional services: 183,400
   educational and health services: 116,500
   leisure and hospitality: 118,100
   other services: 44,700
   government: 163,600

Average hourly earnings of production workers employed in manufacturing: $16.89

Unemployment rate: 5.6% (January 2005)

Largest private employers	Number of employees
Qwest Communications	13,200
HealthONE	8,600
King Soopers, Inc. (grocery stores)	7,800
United Airlines	6,600
Lockheed Martin (aerospace research/ production)	7,700
Centura Health	6,100

Cost of Living

The costs for housing and health care in Denver are somewhat above the national average, while the cost of utilities is substantially below the national average.

The following is a summary of data regarding key cost of living factors for the Denver area.

2004 (3rd Quarter) ACCRA Average House Price: $311,194

2004 (3rd Quarter) ACCRA Cost of Living Index: 104.8 (U.S. average = 100.0)

State income tax rate: 4.63%

State sales tax rate: 2.9%

Local income tax rate: (Occupational tax) $5.75 per month per employee for all workers who receive income greater than $500 a month

Local sales tax rate: ranges from 3.6% to 8.45% throughout the metro area

Property tax rate: In Colorado, the tax assessor first determines the actual value of a property, then applies the residential rate to get the assessed value. In 2004 the residential rate was 7.96%.

Economic Information: Metro Denver Chamber of Commerce, 1445 Market Street, Denver, CO 80202; telephone (303)620-8092; fax (303)534-3200

Education and Research

Elementary and Secondary Schools

The Denver Public School system is directed by a seven-member board of education that administers policy and establishes direction. The Denver public schools provide programs for slow and gifted learners, college preparation, and career training. The four goals of the system are literacy, school readiness, school-to-career, and neighborhood centers.

The following is a summary of data regarding Denver's public schools as of the 2003–2004 school year.

Total enrollment: 72,489

Number of facilities
   elementary schools: 90
   middle schools: 20
   senior high schools: 14

Student/teacher ratio: 25:1

Teacher salaries
   average: $52,271

Funding per pupil: $5,739 (2001-2002)

The metropolitan area is served by 19 other public school districts and numerous private and parochial institutions, including the Colorado Academy and St. Mary's Academy for Girls.

Public Schools Information: Denver Public Schools, 900 Grant Street, Denver, CO 80203; telephone (720)423-3411; email communications@dpsk12.org

Colleges and Universities

The metropolitan Denver area supports 10 four-year colleges and universities and 5 two-year and community colleges with a combined enrollment of more than 125,000 students. The University of Denver Daniels School of Business has been ranked 9th in the *Wall Street Journal* regional business school rankings (2004). A wide variety of undergraduate degrees and numerous graduate and professional degrees are offered along with the opportunity to study at several excellent research institutions. Non-traditional education is well represented by such institutions as the Colorado Free University, which has an open admissions policy. More than 60 vocational and technical schools serve the region.

Libraries and Research Centers

Denver's Central Library underwent expansion in the mid-1990s to its current square footage of 540,000. The addition houses the Children's Library, the Burnham Hoyt Room popular adult library, and Marietta Baron Teen Space. The Denver Public Library maintains 22 branches and a bookmobile and holds more than 2.5 million books, periodicals, subscriptions, microforms, and audiovisual materials, plus 2.2 million government publications.

The Denver area boasts almost 90 other public, special interest, and research libraries. Among them are the Colorado Talking Book Library, the Denver Medical Library, the University of Colorado Law Library, and many high-technology and university-related libraries.

Research activities in such fields as environmental sciences, allergy and immunology, biochemical genetics, health services, mass spectrometry, biochemical parasitology, alcohol, taste and smell, sports sciences, applied mechanics, public management, social science, mineral law, mass communications, family studies, the Holocaust, Islamic-Judaic studies, and international relations are conducted at centers in the Denver area.

Public Library Information: Denver Public Library, 10 West Fourteenth Avenue Parkway, Denver, CO 80204-2731; telephone (720)865-1111

Health Care

For years Denver has attracted those seeking to enjoy the respiratory benefits of the area's climate and mountain air. Today, Denver is the medical center of the Rocky Mountains, operating more than twenty-five major hospitals, many of which have earned national and international reputations as leading medical research and treatment facilities.

The city has a large number of physicians practicing in every specialty.

Among the city's most prominent hospitals are Children's Hospital, a state-of-the-art children's hospital serving a 10-state area. The National Jewish Medical and Research Center is a teaching and research center for respiratory, allergic, and immunological diseases; the center also houses the Environmental Lung Center. The Rose Medical Center offers a wide range of services and specializes in diabetes treatment, obstetrics, and videoscopic surgery and is the health care provider for the Colorado Avalanche, Denver Nuggets, and Colorado Rush.

Health care services continue to expand in Denver. Among recent developments is the $175 million Exempla Good Samaritan Medical Center opened in north Denver in 2003 offering adult critical care, cardiac and vascular, neonatal, radiology and imaging, rehabilitation, surgical, woman and family, pediatrics, and orthopedic services. Other major hospitals in the city include the University of Colorado Health Sciences Center, the AMC Cancer Research Center, Denver General Hospital, the Swedish Medical Center, the Colorado Psychiatric Hospital, the St. Anthony Central Hospital, and Fitzsimmons Army Medical Center.

Recreation

Sightseeing

Denver offers attractions ranging from historic Western landmarks to modern amusement parks. Downtown, the Colorado State Capitol features a 24-carat gold-plated dome; the 13th step of its stairway is set at the altitude of exactly one mile above sea level. A few blocks away is the United States Mint, where nearly a third of the nation's gold supply is stored. Larimer Square, Denver's first main street and a restored Victorian historical district, is an especially popular tourist site. Also downtown is Elitch Gardens, a year-round amusement park offering more than 26 thrill rides, formal gardens, restaurants, and shops. Across the river, Colorado's Ocean Journey, open and under renovation in 2005, combines the qualities of aquariums and sea life parks in an exciting interactive experience that is both fun and educational. The 80-acre Denver Zoo is a modern facility, housing more than 4,000 animals in natural environments; a highlight is a new exhibit featuring 14 African species and 50 animals in a natural and educational habitat called Predator Ridge. It has been listed as one of the 10 best zoos in the nation.

The area is filled with historic buildings, homes, and mansions that are open to the public. Many Denver neighborhoods retain a large part of their historical and architectural

The 1889 Navarre building was once Denver's classiest bordello and gambling hall. Today it is home to the Museum of Western Art.

integrity, offering excellent examples of Victorian, Georgian, and Italianate styles. Popular tour sites in the area include the Coors Brewery in nearby Golden, the Denver Botanic Gardens, and Washington Park, a replica of President Washington's gardens at Mount Vernon. Several bus and guided walking tours of Denver are also available.

Arts and Culture

The arts are well supported in Denver, both in recently constructed facilities and elegant historically preserved buildings. The Denver Performing Arts Complex (PLEX), covering a four-block area, is an $80 million, architecturally stunning complex, second largest in the country behind New York's Lincoln Center, which offers almost every facet of the cultural world from Shakespearean drama to popular music. Many small theaters, galleries, and open-air exhibits can also be found throughout the city.

Denver enjoys a thriving performance community comprised of a number of theater and dance companies, as well as music and opera groups. Germinal Stage Denver, an avant-garde theater, stages five or six productions a year, and each summer the University of Colorado at Boulder sponsors a Shakespeare Festival. Dance in all its forms, from folk to ballet to modern, is performed frequently throughout the area. The Boettcher Concert Hall, considered one of the great music halls in the country, was the first symphony hall in the round in the United States, and is the home of the renowned Colorado Symphony Orchestra. Opera is presented by Opera Colorado; in 2005 Opera Colorado will be moving into its new home, the Ellie Caulkins Opera House.

The Colorado History Museum displays exhibitions highlighting the history of Colorado and the West with changing and permanent exhibits on Native Americans, miners, and other settlers. The Museum of Outdoor Arts is a unique museum without walls that showcases a blend of architecture, fine art, and landscaping. Offering a versatile collection of activities for children of all ages, the Children's Museum of Denver includes live theater, playscapes for children of all ages, a market, assembly plant, and a fire station.

The Denver Art Museum is an impressive seven-story structure containing more than 30,000 art objects; a highlight is the world's leading collection of Native American art. The Colorado Railroad Museum, housed in a replica of an 1880s depot, is considered to be one of the best privately supported rail museums in the United States. Also of interest is a Museum of Miniatures, Dolls and Toys and the Denver Firefighters Museum.

Festivals and Holidays

Denver schedules an abundance of festivals and special events throughout the year. The National Livestock Show and Rodeo, which has been called the "Super Bowl of cattle shows," occurs each January. It features nearly a month of western music performances, prize-winning livestock exhibitions, and rodeo events with the country's top rodeo stars. The show culminates with the award for Livestock's Man of the Year. From May through September, outdoor shows and musical events are held at Red Rocks and Fiddlers Green amphitheaters and at LoDo.

Other special events in Denver include the nation's second largest St. Patrick's Day parade in March, followed by the Littleton River Festival in May. The Colorado Renaissance Festival, a recreation of medieval England, takes place each weekend during June and July. The Colorado Indian Market, featuring the art, dances, food, and culture of native Americans, is held in January. Larimer Square is the site of the annual Oktoberfest.

Sports for the Spectator

Denver fields a professional team in almost every major sport. The Denver Broncos of the National Football League won back-to-back Super Bowls in 1998 and 1999. The team moved to Invesco Field at Mile High Stadium in 2001. The National Basketball Association's Nuggets have had several playoff successes. The Colorado Rockies National League Baseball team play home games at Coors Field. The Colorado Avalanche, Denver's National Hockey League team won the Stanley Cup in 2001. Denver area colleges and universities compete in a variety of sporting events. In 2004 a Sports Business Research Network report described Denver as the most loyal and enthusiastic of America's top 41 sports cities.

Auto racing takes place at the Colorado National Speedway, and for those who enjoy parimutuel betting, the greyhound races at the Mile High Kennel Club in Commerce City provide plenty of excitement. Denver is also a major stop on the National Rodeo Circuit.

Sports for the Participant

The nearby Rocky Mountains provide abundant opportunities for sports-minded individuals year round. In the winter, skiers from the world over come to try their luck on the famous slopes. Rock and mountain climbing, fly fishing in the clear mountain streams, white-water canoeing and rafting, and hiking through the splendid mountain vistas are among the most popular recreations in spring, summer, and fall.

A $45 million, 24-year project to clean up the stretch of the South Platte River that runs through Denver has resulted in bike paths and a series of 11 beautiful parks; man-made boat chutes provide kayaking and rafting opportunities, and the banks of the river are lined with picnic areas and wetlands. Denver County maintains more than 205 parks, 29 recreation centers, 14,000 acres of Denver Mountain Parks, and 2,500 acres of natural areas along with numerous baseball fields, basketball courts, and other sports venues. There are more than 75 public and private golf courses in the metropolitan area and several area lakes offering water skiing, sailing, swimming, and fishing.

Shopping and Dining

Denver's newest shopping venue, Colorado Mills, opened in 2004 and offers 200 new stores. In downtown, Denver Pavilions retail and entertainment center covers two square blocks in the heart of downtown Denver and features 34 stores, 6 restaurants, a nightclub, and 15 movie theaters. Flatiron Crossing opened in 2000 and offers indoor/outdoor shopping in 200 stores and a 14-theater movie complex. A variety of other shopping experiences can be found in Denver, ranging from small, specialized shops to large national outlet malls. The Sixteenth Street Mall, a sculptured pedestrian walkway stretching for over a mile in the downtown district, is lined with shops and restaurants. The recently revitalized Cherry Creek Shopping Center features upscale department stores and more than 160 specialty shops in an enclosed mall. The adjacent Cherry Creek Shopping District is known for its aesthetically appealing shops and galleries. With the success of Larimer Square, a renovated historical area of specialty stores, the entire lower downtown area is rapidly attracting unique shops, galleries, and restaurants. Denver's Tattered Cover Book Store has been hailed by *The New York Times* as "one of the truly great independent book stores in America."

Other interesting areas include Sakura Square, a group of Asian markets and art galleries; and Tivoli, a converted brewery that houses many shops, movie theaters, and some of Denver's finest restaurants. Park Meadows is a 1.5 million square foot shopping center located 12 miles south of the city; it is designed to resemble a mountain ski resort and is anchored by Nordstrom, Foley's, and Dillard's.

Denver is well known for its fine beefsteak and traditional Western fare, but a much wider range of dining experiences is also available at more than 2,000 restaurants, from fast food to haute cuisine. Area specialties include spicy Mexican dishes, local fish and game delicacies such as buffalo, elk, venison, and Rocky Mountain trout, and native Southwestern food. A large number of international and ethnic restaurants complete the dining choices. A favorite nighttime gathering spot is LoDo, or Lower Downtown, which has been transformed since the opening of nearby Coors Field from an industrial warehouse district into a thriving area of elegant restaurants and sports bars.

Visitor Information: Denver Metro Convention and Visitors Bureau, 1555 California, Suite 300, Denver, CO 80202; telephone (303)892-1112

Convention Facilities

The Colorado Convention Center in downtown Denver is within walking distance of more than 5,000 hotel rooms, and within a 20-minute drive of nearly 12,000 others. The convention center, located along the river in the heart of downtown, contains more than 600,000 square feet of exhibit space, 100,000 square feet of meeting rooms, two ballrooms (including a 35,000 square foot ballroom and a 50,000 square foot ballroom), theater-style seating for 7,000 people, 1,000 covered parking spaces and state of the art multimedia facilities. The center underwent a massive $268 million expansion that nearly doubled its space, which was completed in 2003.

The National Western Complex, located at the northern end of the downtown area near I-70, contains a 6,600-seat stadium arena, a 40,000-square-foot exhibit hall, a multi-use events center, and the 120,000-square-foot Hall of Education.

Other meeting and exhibition facilities include the Denver Coliseum, McNichols Arena, Red Rocks Amphitheater, the Denver Merchandise Mart and Exposition Center, and the Adams County Regional Park Complex. Most of the major hotels in the city offer extensive meeting, banquet, and ballroom facilities, as do many of the larger mountain resorts.

Convention Information: Denver Metro Convention and Visitors Bureau, 1555 California, Suite 300, Denver, CO 80202; telephone (800)480-2010

Transportation

Approaching the City

Denver International Airport is served by all major airlines with non-stop daily flights to 40 states. Amtrak provides passenger rail service with westbound passengers treated to a scenic route through the Rocky Mountains.

Denver is at the crossroads of three major interstate highways. Colorado 470 tollway is the southwest quarter of a new beltway highway system that encircles the metro area and provide easy access to the airport. The first segment of the eastern half of the new beltway has been completed.

Traveling in the City

Orienting oneself in Denver is made considerably easier by the natural landmark of the Rocky Mountains, readily visible to the west. Denver's street numbers are divided north and south by Ellsworth Avenue and east and west by Broadway. In general, east-west roads are called ''avenues'' and north-south designated as ''streets.'' Above Ellsworth, the streets bear numbers; below Ellsworth the streets are named.

The Regional Transportation District (RTD) offers 170 bus routes, 14 miles of light rail and SkyRide transportation to and from Denver International Airport.

Communications

Newspapers and Magazines

Denver readers are served by two major daily morning newspapers, *The Denver Post* and the *Rocky Mountain News,* as well as by many smaller neighborhood weeklies and a business weekly—*The Denver Business Journal.* Local magazines include *Colorado Country Life, Colorado Legionnaire, Colorado Outdoors,* and *The Bloomsbury Review.* Many trade and collegiate publications are based in the city as well.

Television and Radio

The six major television stations in the Denver area represent commercial networks, public television, independent stations, and special interest channels; a number of channels are offered by area cable systems as well. More than 45 AM and FM radio stations provide listeners with a variety of musical and special programming.

Media Information: The Denver Post, 1560 Broadway, Denver, CO 80202; telephone (303)820-1010; toll-free (800)832-4609; *Rocky Mountain News,* 400 West Colfax Avenue, Boulder, CO 80204; telephone (303)892-5000; toll-free (800)933-1990

Denver Online

City of Denver. Available www.denvergov.org

Colorado Historical Society. Available www.colorado history.org

Denver Metro Convention & Visitors Bureau. Available www.denver.org

Denver Post. Available www.denverpost.com

Denver Public Library. Available www.denver.lib.co.us

Denver Public Schools. Available www.denver.k12.co.us

Mayor's Office of Employment and Training. Available www.moet.org

Metro Denver Chamber of Commerce. Available www.denverchamber.org

Rocky Mountain News. Available www.rockymountainnews.com

Selected Bibliography

Noel, Thomas J., *The City and the Saloon: Denver, 1858–1916* (Lincoln: University of Nebraska Press, 1982)

Whitford, David, *Playing Hardball: The High-Stakes Battle for Baseball's New Franchises* (Doubleday: 1992)

Fort Collins

The City in Brief

Founded: 1862 (incorporated 1869)

Head Official: Mayor Doug Hutchinson (R) (since 2005)

City Population
   1980: 64,092
   1990: 87,491
   2000: 118,652
   2003 estimate: 125,740
   Percent change, 1990–2000: 33.5%
   U.S. rank in 1990: 230th (State rank: 7th)
   U.S. rank in 2000: 206th (State rank: 5th)

Metropolitan Area Population
   1980: 149,184
   1990: 186,136 (MSA)
   2000: 251,494 (MSA)

   Percent change, 1990–2000: 35.1%
   U.S. rank in 1990: 166th
   U.S. rank in 2000: 142nd

Area: 47 square miles (2000)
Elevation: 5,003 feet above sea level
Average Annual Temperature: 47.9° F
Average Annual Precipitation: 15 inches of rain; 55 inches of snow

Major Economic Sectors: services, trade, government, manufacturing
Unemployment Rate: 5.0% (December 2004)
Per Capita Income: $22,133 (1999)

2002 FBI Crime Index Total: 5,371

Major Colleges and Universities: Colorado State University, Front Range Community College

Daily Newspaper: *Fort Collins Coloradoan*

Introduction

Fort Collins is located on the Cache la Poudre River at the foot of the Rocky Mountains. The city's clean water and clean air make for a healthy environment. Fort Collins boasts a very active cultural scene, which is enhanced by events offered at Colorado State University. The surrounding countryside has breathtaking cliffs, clear skies, and beautiful lakes and waterfalls—nature at its best. The city consistently appears on lists of the best places to live in the United States, and in May 2003 it was chosen as one of America's best places to live by *Men's Journal* magazine.

Geography and Climate

Located at the western base of the "Front Range" of the Rocky Mountains, Fort Collins is about 65 miles north of Denver and 45 miles south of Cheyenne, Wyoming. The city lies along the banks of the Cache La Poudre River, and the Great Plains lie to the east.

Fort Collins lies in a semi-arid region and experiences four seasons. The city has 300 days per year with sunshine, and the average summer high temperature is 85 degrees. Annual snowfall averages 55 inches, and the snow generally melts within a few days.

Area: 47 square miles (2000)

Elevation: 5,003 feet above sea level

Average Temperatures: January, 57.2° F; July, 71.2° F; average annual temperature, 47.9° F

Average Annual Precipitation: 15 inches of rain; 55 inches of snow

History

Travelers crossing the country on the Overland Trail often stopped at Camp Collins, which was established on the Cache La Poudre River in 1862. The camp was named for Colonel W. O. Collins, a commander of the eleventh Ohio Cavalry at Fort Laramie, Wyoming. The fort was built to protect the important trading post from attacks by native Americans. In 1864 a community grew around the fort and became a center of trading, shipping, and manufacturing. Fort Collins was incorporated in 1869.

As farmers settled in the outlying areas, other settlers began moving to the new town, where they opened stores, livery stables, and other businesses. The first buildings of the state agricultural college, located in Fort Collins by vote of the state legislature, were erected in the 1870s. By that time the town boasted a post office, a general store, a rooming house, a mill, and its first school house.

During the first half of the 1870s the town population began to dwindle due to the failure of the town's first bank, a grasshopper infiltration, and business problems. The economy was given a boost by the arrival of the Colorado Central Railroad later in the decade. Soon after, the development of irrigation canals brought water to the area, greatly expanding farming options. Barley, wheat, and oat growing were especially successful, as were the cultivation of sugar beets and alfalfa.

The 1880s saw the construction of a number of elegant homes and commercial buildings. Beet tops proved to be excellent and abundant food for local sheep, and by the early 1900s the area was being referred to as "Lamb feeding capital of the world." In 1903 the Great Western sugar processing plant was built in the city.

Fort Collins gained a reputation as a very conservative city in the twentieth century, with prohibition of alcoholic beverages being retained from the late 1890s until 1969. Although the city was affected by the Great Depression, it nevertheless experienced slow and steady growth throughout the early part of the twentieth century. During the middle of the century the population of the city doubled, and an era of economic prosperity occurred. Old buildings were razed to make way for new, modern structures. By the 1960s, though, citizens had formed a group to preserve and restore the older buildings that add such beauty and character to the city. The Fort Collins Historical Society was formed in 1974 to encourage the preservation of historic buildings and documents, and to provide educational opportunities for people to learn about the city's past.

Today's Fort Collins offers a rich mix of history with the cultural interest of a university town and an attractiveness to new, higher-tech businesses; add to that the plethora of outdoor activities and beauty offered in and around the city. When in 2003 *Men's Journal* magazine was choosing America's best places to live, it looked for cities with small town familiarity, outdoor activities, cultural amenities, and active lifestyle. Fort Collins fit the description admirably.

Historical Information: Fort Collins Public Library, Local History Collection, 201 Peterson Street, Fort Collins, CO 80524; telephone (970)221-6688

Population Profile

Metropolitan Area Residents
1980: 149,184
1990: 186,136
2000: 251,494
Percent change, 1990–2000: 35.1%
U.S. rank in 1990: 166th
U.S. rank in 2000: 142nd

City Residents
1980: 64,092
1990: 87,491
2000: 118,652
2003 estimate: 125,740
Percent change, 1990–2000: 33.5%
U.S. rank in 1980: 301st
U.S. rank in 1990: 240th (state rank: 7th)
U.S. rank in 2000: 206th (state rank: 5th)

Density: 2,549.3 people per square mile (in 2000)

Racial and ethnic characteristics (2000)
White: 106,347
Black or African American: 1,213
American Indian and Alaska Native: 715
Asian: 2,948
Native Hawaiian and other Pacific Islander: 143
Hispanic or Latino (may be of any race): 10,402
Other: 4,281

Percent of residents born in state: 36.2% (2000)

Age characteristics (2000)
Population under 5 years old: 7,001
Population 5 to 9 years old: 7,047
Population 10 to 14 years old: 7,317
Population 15 to 19 years old: 11,305
Population 20 to 24 years old: 19,036
Population 25 to 29 years old: 20,107
Population 35 to 44 years old: 17,285
Population 45 to 54 years old: 13,855
Population 55 to 59 years old: 3,783
Population 60 to 64 years old: 2,586
Population 65 to 74 years old: 4,544
Population 75 to 84 years old: 3,412
Population 85 years and over: 1,374
Median age: 28.2 years (2000)

Births (2003, Larimer County)
Total number: 3,500

Deaths (2003, Larimer County)
Total number: 1,545 (of which, 23 were infants under
the age of 1 year)

Money income (1999)
Per capita income: $22,133
Median household income: $44,459
Total households: 45,882

Number of households with income of . . .
less than $10,000: 3,903
$10,000 to $14,999: 2,814
$15,000 to $24,999: 5,877
$25,000 to $34,999: 5,438
$35,000 to $49,999: 7,409
$50,000 to $74,999: 9,031
$75,000 to $99,999: 5,614
$100,000 to $149,999: 3,826
$150,000 to $199,999: 997
$200,000 or more: 860

Percent of families below poverty level: 5.5% (46.1% of
which were female householder families with related
children under 5 years)

2002 FBI Crime Index Total: 5,371

Municipal Government

Fort Collins has a mayor-council form of government with
six council persons who serve four-year terms, and a mayor
who serves a two-year term.

Head Official: Mayor Doug Hutchinson (R) (since 2005)

Total Number of City Employees: 1,400 (2004)

City Information: City of Fort Collins, 300 LaPorte Avenue, PO Box 580, Fort Collins, CO 80522-0580; telephone
(970)221-6500

Economy

Major Industries and Commercial Activity

Fort Collins' economy has been described as well-balanced,
with a good mix of manufacturing and service-related businesses. Local business leaders claim that the city's economy is
insulated from some of the ups and downs in the regional and
the national economies by the "highly sophisticated and rapidly advancing technological progress" of the city's industries. Fort Collins has a strong manufacturing base; it is home
to such firms as Hewlett Packard, WaterPik, Woodward,
In-Situ, and Anheuser-Busch. The city has been experiencing
low unemployment rates and a steady increase in household

incomes, increasing purchasing power that can only further stimulate the local economy. A variety of high-tech companies have relocated to Fort Collins because of the resources of Colorado State University and its research facilities. New housing construction has added to the city's economic growth.

Items and goods produced: pharmaceuticals, electronic components and accessories, aircraft and parts, scientific instruments, measuring and controlling instruments, radio and TV equipment, industrial chemicals, engines, turbines, communications equipment

Incentive Programs—New and Existing Companies

Local programs—The city of Fort Collins has established an economic development policy that allows the rebate of use taxes paid by qualifying firms on qualifying equipment. On a case-by-case basis, the county will consider negotiating financial incentives, giving up to a 50 percent credit towards a company's personal property tax liability for up to four years. In 2004, the community created the Fort Collins Technology Incubator, acquiring 6,500 square feet of office space and transforming the 7 year old Fort Collins' ''Virtual Incubator'' into an incubator with walls. The technology incubator is a cluster of programs designed to nurture startup businesses. Incubator companies receive discounted business services from top-notch community resources, advisory groups, Colorado State University resources, and strategic planning counseling as well as idea sharing amongst other entrepreneurs.

The Northern Colorado Economic Development Corporation supports existing employers and recruits new employers to the region. It assists local companies to grow and expand and, in partnership with Colorado State University, encourages technology transfer to nurture local start-up companies. Fort Collins can negotiate with new business facilities an incentive payment equal to not more than the amount of the increase in property tax liability over pre-enterprise zone levels; and a refund of local sales taxes on purchases of equipment, machinery, machine tools, or supplies used in the taxpayer's business in the Enterprise Zone.

State programs—Colorado's Enterprise Zone tax benefits offer incentives for private enterprise to expand and for new businesses to locate in economically distressed areas of the state. They include a three percent investment tax credit for equipment investment, a $500 job tax credit for hiring new employees in an enterprise zone, double job tax credits for agricultural processing, a $200 job tax credit for employer health insurance, research and development tax credits, credits for the rehabilitation of vacant buildings, and exemptions from state sales and use tax on the purchase of manufacturing and mining equipment.

Job training programs—The Colorado FIRST customized job training program assists employers in training new or current workers in permanent, non-seasonal jobs and custom designs job-specific training programs. FIRST provides financial assistance to eligible businesses for direct training costs including instructor wages, travel, and per diem allowances; development of curriculum and instruction materials; cost of essential training supplies, equipment and space; and training at the employer's location or at local community college or vocational schools. Employers who carry out a qualified job training program for their enterprise zone employees, or who participate in a school-to-work program with a local school, may be able to claim an income tax credit of 10 percent of their eligible training ''investment.'' Front Range Community College and Colorado State University provide excellent employee training resources. Larimer County Employment and Training/Colorado Job Service offers comprehensive, coordinated employment and training services.

Development Projects

In 2004 In-Situ, Inc. a producer of environmental monitoring information and systems, chose Fort Collins as its headquarters and built a state-of-the-art office/manufacturing and multi-media training facility. In-Situ regularly introduces new water market innovations for patent and does business in more than 70 countries.

Economic Development Information: Northern Colorado Economic Development Corporation, 2725 Rocky Mountain Avenue #410, Loveland, CO 80538; telephone (970)667-0905; fax (970)669-4680; email mfoley@ncedc.com

Commercial Shipping

Parcel service for Fort Collins is provided by Federal Express, Airport Express, Airborne, Burlington Air Express, Emery, United Parcel Service, Pony Express, and Purolator. Fort Collins has two-day rail freight access to the west coast or the east coast and has eight motor freight carriers. Many local industrial sites have rail freight spur service. The city is served by the Union Pacific and Burlington Northern Santa Fe railroads.

Labor Force and Employment Outlook

Fort Collins' labor force has been described as young, well-educated, and energetic. Studies have indicated that many of the graduates of Colorado State University stay in the city.

Fort Collins exhibits outstanding economic stability. In a 2002 report on the economic strength of U.S. metropolitan statistical areas (MSA), POLICOM Corporation ranked Fort Collins-Loveland as the eighth strongest economy in the nation. Economic strength is a combination of both the rate and consistency of growth, and the information is obtained by examining 25 years of data in 18 different categories in the economy.

The following is a summary of data regarding the Fort Collins-Loveland labor force, 2004 annual averages.

Size of non-agricultural labor force: 128,500

Number of workers employed in . . .
  construction and mining: 9,800
  manufacturing: 14,700
  trade, transportation and utilities: 21,800
  information: 2,400
  financial activities: 5,500
  professional and business services: 14,200
  educational and health services: 13,400
  leisure and hospitality: 15,300
  other services: 4,300
  government: 27,000

Average hourly wage of production workers employed in manufacturing: $16.13

Unemployment rate: 5.0% (December 2004)

Largest county employers	Number of employees
Colorado State University	6,948
Poudre School District	3,732
Hewlett Packard	3,000
Poudre Valley Health System	2,814
Agilent Technologies	2,800
Thompson School District	2,000
City of Fort Collins	1,400
Larimer County	1,394
McKee Medical Center	950
Advanced Energy	800

Cost of Living

The following is a summary of data regarding several key cost of living factors for the Fort Collins metropolitan area.

2004 (3rd Quarter) ACCRA Average House Price: $213,900 (Greeley metro)

2004 (3rd Quarter) ACCRA Cost of Living Index: 91.7 (Greeley metro) (U.S. average = 100.0)

State income tax rate: 4.63%

State sales tax rate: 2.9%

Local income tax rate: None

Local sales tax rate: 3%

Property tax rate: The residential assessment rate for 2003-2004 is 7.96% of actual value based on market values as of June 30, 2002; reappraised every two years

Economic Information: Northern Colorado Economic Development Corporation, 2725 Rocky Mountain Avenue #410, Loveland, CO 80538; telephone (970)667-0905; fax (970)669-4680; email mfoley@ncedc.com.

Education and Research

Elementary and Secondary Schools

The Poudre School District is led by a seven-member Board of Education committed to actively recruiting administrators and teachers displaying high standards of excellence. The school district is the second largest employer in Fort Collins.

The following is a summary of data regarding Poudre School District #1 as of the 2003–2004 school year.

Total enrollment: 24,891

Number of facilities
  elementary schools: 27
  junior high/middle schools: 9
  senior high schools: 4
  other: 3 charter schools, 3 special program elementary schools, 1 alternative high school, 1 alternative junior high school, multiple early childhood and alternative secondary programs

Student/teacher ratio: 17:1

Teacher salaries
  minimum: $30,030
  maximum: $70,839

Funding per pupil: $7,299

Public Schools Information: Support Services, Poudre School District, 2407 La Porte Avenue, Fort Collins, CO 80521

Colleges and Universities

Colorado State University (CSU), with 24,700 students, is a land-grant institution that consists of 8 colleges and more than 150 programs of study. Founded in 1870, its campuses cover 5,612 acres in Larimer County, including the main campus, a foothills campus, an agricultural campus, and the Pingree Park mountain campus, which is the summer campus for natural resources education. CSU offers eight major degree programs including agricultural sciences, applied human sciences, liberal arts, business, engineering, natural resources, veterinary medicine and biomedical sciences, and natural sciences. CSU also offers a unique major called equine science in which prospective veterinarians or those pursing a career in equine production learn about the behavior, nutrition, management, reproductive management, disease management, and the training of horses. Front Range Community College (FRCC), the largest community college in Colorado with more than 23,000 students, grants associates degrees in arts, science, general studies, and applied science. The college offers 12 high school vocational programs, and more than 100 degree and certificate programs. The Larimer Campus of FRCC offers 175,000 square feet of space on 47 acres in Fort Collins as well as partnerships with Colorado State University, Poudre Valley Hospital, McKee Medical Center, Columbine Health Systems, Village Homes' Observatory Village, Microsoft, and Oracle.

Libraries and Research Centers

The Fort Collins Public Library was established in 1900, the sixth pubic library in the state. The library maintains the Gates Computer Learning Lab and, in partnership with Front Range Community College, the Harmony Library and Harmony Library Electronic Learning Center. The library also participates in innovative cooperative projects with the local school district and Colorado State University. The library holds nearly 400,000 items and has a special local history archive.

Wildlife is the focus of the special library at the Colorado Division of Wildlife, which has nearly 9,000 books. Special collections of the Colorado State University Library include agriculture, agricultural economics, biomedical science, engineering, hydrology, and natural resources.

Fort Collins has a great range of research institutes covering a myriad of subjects. Facilities are maintained by the Centers for Disease Control Division of Vector-Borne Infectious Diseases, the Colorado Cooperative Fish & Wildlife Research Unit, the Colorado Water Resource Research Institute, and the Cooper Institute for Research in the Atmosphere. The Rocky Mountain Research Station conducts research on experimental forests, ranges, and watersheds, and oversees research on more than 200 natural areas.

Colorado State University has a variety of research groups focusing on subjects such as animal reproduction, biotechnology, engineering, environmental toxicology, irrigation management, microscopy, nutrition, hydraulics, manufacturing, marrow transplantation, vehicle emissions, and solar energy.

Public Library Information: Fort Collins Public Library, 201 Peterson St., Fort Collins, CO 80524-2990; telephone (970)221-6742; fax (970)221-6687 (circulation)

Health Care

By virtue of the broad scope of medical services available, Fort Collins has become a regional health center. Poudre

Valley Hospital has 295 beds, 19 surgical suites, and 23 critical care patient rooms; it is home to a regional heart center, a regional neurosciences center that cares for victims of head and back injury, stroke, spinal cord and nervous system diseases, and a regional orthopedic program. The hospital also offers a surgery center, oncology unit, regional wound care center, a 24-hour emergency department, adult and adolescent psychiatric programs, and a breast diagnostic center. The hospital has a birthing center and Level II nursery, and offers an off-site comprehensive homecare program, home infusion therapy, and comprehensive rehabilitation programs. Poudre Valley Health System added a new ambulatory care center and medical office building (the Harmony Campus) and a mental health and substance abuse facility (Mountain Crest Behavioral Health Center) on the south side of Fort Collins in the spring of 2000 and broke ground on a cardiac and trauma care center (Medical Center of Rockies) in nearby Loveland in March 2004.

Recreation

Sightseeing

''Soapstone'' Natural Area was acquired by the city in 2004. Covering more than 16,000 square miles, the area is known as an important archaeological site and is admired for its varied terrain. ''Soapstone'' will receive an official name and be open to the public in 2009.

More than 40 historic sites can be visited in the Fort Collins Area, and 26 of them are listed in or eligible for the National Register of Historic Places. Tours of Avery House, a restored Victorian residence built by one of the city's prominent citizens, are offered year round. Visitors may also tour the two-story Strauss Cabin, which was built in 1864 by George Strauss and modeled after structures found in South Carolina. The Old Federal Building is a 1912 structure that housed the post office on its main floor for 60 years. The 1881 Spruce Hall on the campus of Colorado State University is the oldest complete building still standing on the campus. Ammons Hall, also on the campus, is a 1922 Italian Renaissance building that is still being used a women's physical education facility. Many other sites worth observing are on the Historic Buildings map available through the Fort Collins Convention and Visitors Bureau.

Beer enthusiasts and those merely curious will enjoy touring the Anheuser-Busch Brewery, which includes a visit with the famous Clydesdale horses and a trip to the sampling room. Several micro-breweries in town invite visitors to enjoy their variety of offerings. A metal menagerie of mythical and real creatures are on view at farmer/sculptor Bill

Swets' dairy farm, known as the Swetsville Zoo. The zoo also has a miniature live steam railroad train and a display of antique farming equipment. Young and old enjoy hopping a ride aboard the Fort Collins Municipal Railway streetcar, which runs May to September, weather permitting.

Arts and Culture

The premier facility for the performing arts in Fort Collins is Lincoln Center, with its 1,180-seat performance hall, two theaters, and four exhibit galleries. The center hosts nearly 1,750 events each year, among them an annual season of Broadway shows, dance, and musical events. OpenStage Theater Company, a regional professional theater group, stages its seasons in the facility's 220-seat Mini-Theater. Based on the tradition of eighteenth-century salons, the 48-seat Bas Bleu Theater provides an intimate setting for poetry, plays, and musical performances. Good food and theater can be combined at the Carousel Dinner Theater, which presents dramas, comedies, and popular musicals. Colorado State University presents six plays each year at the school's Johnson Hall. Other theater groups in the city include the Debut Theater Company, Fort Collins Children's Theater, the Front Range Chamber Players, and OpenStage Theater. A variety of dance performances is offered by the Canyon Concert Ballet and Dance Connection. Several performing halls are located at Colorado State University.

Musical experiences in the city come in many forms, featuring such groups as the Larimer Chorale, Opera Fort Collins, and the Fort Collins Symphony. The primary visual arts center of the city is the PowerPlant Visual Arts Center, located in a renovated power plant. The Fort Collins Museum highlights the area's past, including a display of pre-Columbian Folsom points discovered at a major archaeological site in northern Larimer County. Other displays range from those of the Plains Indians to Fort Collins' beginnings as a trade and agricultural center. Experiences with hands-on science are available to youngsters at the Discovery Center Museum, with its opportunities for experimenting and testing scientific theories. Visitors can visit pioneer cabins and a one-room school house.

Festivals and Holidays

Fort Collins' festival season begins with its annual St. Patrick's Day Celebration downtown. The city's Hispanic community is honored at the Cinco De Mayo celebration, which features dancing, entertainment, and food. Patrons are invited to tap kegs of beer at June's Colorado Brewers' Festival downtown. Fireworks light the sky at City Park's annual Fourth of July Celebration. On Skookum Day, also in July, Fort Collins' history is re-enacted with demonstrations of blacksmithing, milking, quilting, branding, and weaving. August is enlivened by the Larimer County Fair, and by the New West Fest, featuring more than 300 booths, events, performances, evening concerts, and children's activities.

The city celebrates the harvest during Oktoberfest, and the holiday season is launched with Lincoln Center's Great Christmas Hall, with its juried art exhibit, homemade crafts, and decorated trees. In December, festivities include carolers and Christmas celebrations in Old Town, and the New Year is welcomed in with a community-wide celebration for the whole family called First Night.

Sports for the Spectator

Colorado State University students engage in a variety of sports competitions throughout the year. The CSU Rams are represented by both male and female teams in a variety of sports, including football, basketball, cross country, golf, softball, swimming and diving, tennis, track and field, volleyball, and water polo.

Sports for the Participant

Fort Collins is home to a variety of walking, running, and bicycling events and tournaments. The Cache La Poudre River provides some of the finest fishing in the state. The city has more than 75 miles of designated bikeways through many natural areas in the city. Duffers may choose from six golf courses within the city limits. Lory State Park offers 2,400 acres for horseback riding, boating, hiking, and picnicking. The Edora Pool and Ice Center and Mulberry Pool feature swimming and exercise programs, as well as youth and adult hockey and public ice skating. The young or young at heart will enjoy skateboarding at Northside Azatlan Community Center, Edora Skateboard Park, and Fossil Creek Skateboard. In winter, Lory State Park's trails and rolling hills attract cross country skiers; tubing and sledding are also popular. Several renowned Colorado mountain ski resorts are within a few hours of Fort Collins. Rocky Mountain National Park offers scenic drives and hikes and is only one hour's drive away.

Shopping and Dining

Shopping in Fort Collins can involve browsing antique stores and flea markets or seeing the latest fashions at one of its major malls, such as Foothills Mall, The Square Shopping Center, or University Mall. At Historic Old Town, restored buildings filled with specialty shops, galleries, boutiques, and outdoor cafes beckon the visitor.

Visitor Information: Fort Collins Convention and Visitors Bureau, 3745 East Prospect Rd.#200, Fort Collins, CO 80525; toll-free (800)274-FORT; telephone (970)491-3388; fax (970)491-3389; email information@ftcollins.com

Convention Facilities

Fort Collins has nearly 2,000 hotel rooms, ranging from budget rooms to luxury suites. Colorado State University, in the heart of Fort Collins, has 50,000 square feet of convention facilities at its Lory Students Center. The center can accommodate meetings, receptions, and banquets for up to 1,100 people. Other convention facilities include 10 auditoriums with accommodations for up to 400 in the Clark Building, a total of 4,400 beds in the residence halls, dining facilities in each residence hall, and an arena that seats 6,000. Lory's main ballroom has 12,728 square feet of space. The Pingree Park Conference Center offers seven meeting rooms, two dorms and seven cabins on its 1,200 acre campus. Campus lodging is available late May through mid-August.

The Holiday Inn at University Park, with 259 rooms, offers nearly 20,000 square feet of convention space that can accommodate 1,300 people for a banquet. There are several facilities around the city that can handle small group meetings.

Convention Information: Fort Collins Convention and Visitors Bureau, 3745 East Prospect Rd. #200, Fort Collins, CO 80525; telephone 1-800-274-FORT, (970)491-3388; fax (970)491-3389; email information@fortcollins.com

Transportation

Approaching the City

Allegiant Air offers airplane service into Fort Collins/Loveland Airport. Denver International Airport, which is 25 miles to the south, is served by nearly 20 airlines. Fort Collins can be approached from Denver by car via Interstate 25. Greyhound offers bus service into the city.

Traveling in the City

Fort Collins' downtown streets form a grid with Interstate 25 running north and south on the east side of the city. U.S. Highway 287 runs east and west in the northwest sector of the city. Transfort, Fort Collins' local bus transportation system, provides 16 routes and operates daily. Alternative transportation is encouraged in the city; bicycle commuters benefit from city incentives and excellent bike paths through town. Maps for a walking tour of the historic downtown district can be obtained from the Downtown Business Association.

Communications

Newspapers and Magazines

The *Fort Collins Coloradoan,* which appears Monday through Sunday mornings, is the city's daily paper.

The *Fort Collins Weekly* serves Larimer and Weld Counties. The bimonthly *Northern Colorado Business Report,* reports on the growing business market in Northern Colorado with an increasing emphasis on high-tech and e-business.

Television and Radio

No television stations broadcast from Fort Collins, but service is available from surrounding communities. Two AM, six FM, and the CSU student-run radio stations serve the city with a variety of programming including public radio, news/talk, adult contemporary, and alternative music formats.

Media Information: The *Fort Collins Coloradoan,* PO Box 1577, Fort Collins, CO 80524; telephone (970)493-6397

Fort Collins Online

City of Fort Collins Home Page. Available fcgov.com

Colorado Department of Labor & Employment, Labor Market Information. Available www.coworkforce.com

Coloradoan Available www.coloradoan.com

Fort Collins Convention & Visitors Bureau. Available www.ftcollins.com

Fort Collins Public Library. Available fcgov.com/library

Larimer County. Available www.co.larimer.co.us

Northern Colorado Economic Development Corporation. Available www.ncedc.com

Selected Bibliography

Fleming, Barbara Allbrandt, *Fort Collins, A Pictorial History* (Virginia Beach, VA: Donning, 1992)

Fort Collins Friends of the Library, comp. *Talking About Fort Collins: Selections from Oral Histories* (Fort Collins: City of Fort Collins, 1992)

Horan, Bob, *Colorado Front Range Bouldering: Fort Collins* (Evergreen, Colo.: Chockstone Press, 1995)

Swanson, Evadine Burris, *Fort Collins Yesterdays* (Fort Collins: G & H Morgan, 1993)

HAWAII

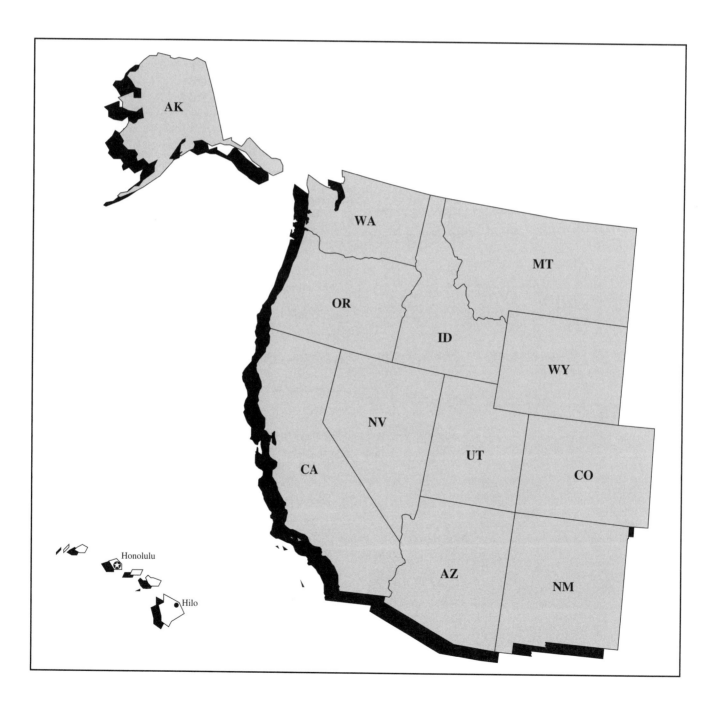

The State in Brief

Nickname: Aloha State
Motto: *Ua mau ke ea o ka aina i ka pono* (The life of the land is perpetuated in righteousness)

Flower: Hibiscus
Bird: Hawaiian goose

Area: 10,930 square miles (2000; U.S. rank: 43rd)
Elevation: Ranges from sea level to 13,796 feet above sea level
Climate: Mild, tropical

Admitted to Union: August 21, 1959
Capital: Honolulu
Head Official: Governor Linda Lingle (R) (until 2006)

Population
  1980: 965,000
  1990: 1,135,000
  2000: 1,211,537
  2004 estimate: 1,262,840
  Percent change, 1990–2000: 9.3%
  U.S. rank in 2004: 42nd
  Percent of residents born in state: 56.9% (2000)
  Density: 188.6 people per square mile (2000)
  2002 FBI Crime Index Total: 75,238

Racial and Ethnic Characteristics (2000)
  White: 294,102
  Black or African American: 22,003
  American Indian and Alaska Native: 3,535
  Asian: 503,868
  Native Hawaiian and Pacific Islander: 113,539
  Hispanic or Latino (may be of any race): 87,699
  Other: 15,147

Age Characteristics (2000)
  Population under 5 years old: 78,163
  Population 5 to 19 years old: 249,088
  Percent of population 65 years and over: 13.3%
  Median age: 36.2 years (2000)

Vital Statistics
  Total number of births (2003): 18,068
  Total number of deaths (2003): 8,955 (infant deaths, 139)
  AIDS cases reported through 2003: 1,318

Economy
  Major industries: Government; services; finance, insurance, and real estate; agriculture; tourism
  Unemployment rate: 2.9% (January 2005)
  Per capita income: $30,589 (2003; U.S. rank: 22nd)
  Median household income: $49,839 (3-year average, 2001-2003)
  Percentage of persons below poverty level: 10.7% (3-year average, 2001-2003)
  Income tax rate: Ranges from 1.4% to 8.25%
  Sales tax rate: 4.0%

Hilo

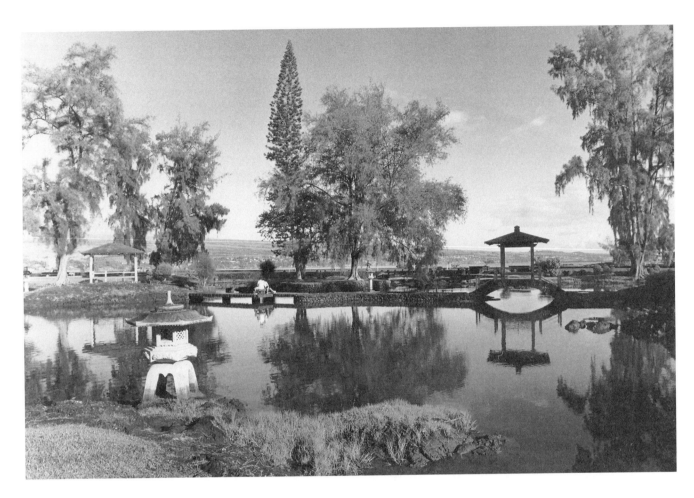

The City in Brief

Founded: 1822 (incorporated, 1911)

Head Official: Mayor Harry Kim (since 2000)

City Population
   1980: 35,269
   1990: 37,808
   2000: 40,759
   2003 estimate: Not reported
   Percent change, 1990–2000: 7.8%
   U.S. rank in 1980: Not reported
   U.S. rank in 1990: Not reported
   U.S. rank in 2000: Not reported

City and County Population
   1990: 120,317
   2000: 148,667
   2003 estimate: 158,423
   Percent change, 1990–2000: 23.6%

Area: 54 square miles (2000)
Elevation: 38 feet above sea level
Average Annual Temperature: 73.0° F
Average Annual Precipitation: 134 inches

Major Economic Sectors: Agriculture, trade, tourism, government
Unemployment rate: 3% (Hawaii, January 2005)
Per Capita Income: $18,220 (1999, Hilo CDP)
2002 Actual Crime Index Offenses: 6,936 (Hawaii County)

Major Colleges and Universities: University of Hawaii at Hilo, Hawaii Community College

Daily Newspaper: *Hawaii Tribune-Herald*

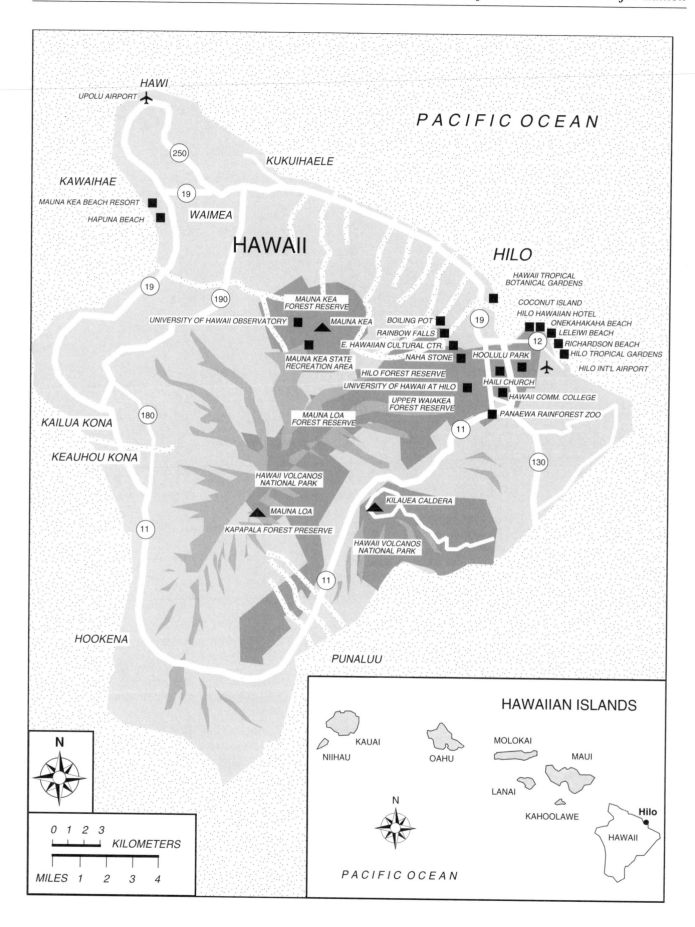

Introduction

The city of Hilo is the main port of the island of Hawaii, the largest island in the chain. It is the business and government center of the island, as well as the shipping and service center of the various industries in the vicinity. With more than 100 inches of rain annually, the city is the rainiest in the United States. The rainfall encourages the city's major industries—raising tropical flowers and fruit. Tourism is growing rapidly, spurred in part by the Hawaii Volcanoes National Park, which is 30 miles away. Hilo curves around a crescent bay where the lower foothills of Mauna Loa and Mauna Kea emerge. In recent years the city has attracted retirees and escapees from the faster-paced life on other islands. The city boasts a modern, convenient airport and a deep water harbor, and serves as the transportation hub for the island. The city, whose name means "new moon," is slowly transforming itself from a plantation town whose economy centered on sugar cane to a university town that is attracting a slew of new construction and research dollars.

Geography and Climate

Hilo is located on Hilo Bay on the eastern side of the island of Hawaii, 216 miles southeast of Honolulu (on the island of Oahu). The area's topography is mostly sloping, from the tops of the scenic Mauna Kea and Mauna Loa mountains to the sea. Hilo is located less than 30 miles from Kilauea, one of the most active volcanoes on earth, which has been emitting lava since 1983. Lava flows have been responsible for the destruction of nearly 200 homes since then, and they continue to menace the island. Much of the lava has reached the ocean, enlarging the island of Hawaii by about 500 acres.

The Hilo region has a warm semitropical climate and experiences abundant rainfall without the droughts and shortages that trouble other parts of the island. The rain, which generally falls during the night, keeps the area fresh and green. It also results in many waterfalls. Hilo's rich soil is conducive to the growth of a variety of diversified agricultural products. At the summit of Mauna Kea the temperature ranges from about 31 to 43 degrees. In winter there is frost above the 4,000-foot level and snow above the 10,000-foot level.

Area: 54 square miles (2000)

Elevation: 38 feet above sea level

Average Temperature: January, 71.3 80° F; July, 75.5° F; annual average, 73.0° F

Average Annual Precipitation: 134 inches

History

Popular Trading Post Attracts Missionaries, Scientists

The city of Hilo has been a trading place from the time Hawaiian tribes came up the Wailuku River, which separated Hilo from Hamakua, and shouted out what goods they had to offer. In the 1800s, although Honolulu reigned supreme as the principal whaling base of the Pacific, Hilo came in third behind Koloa as alternative anchorages. Foreign ships found anchorages between the coral heads of Hilo's wide bay, and thereafter the dredging of a channel permitted steamships to enter the area.

Missionaries settled Hilo in 1822. The region was first studied scientifically by Lord Byron and his men of the ship *Blonde* in 1825. Titus Cona, a missionary at Hilo, was the foremost volcanologist of his time and made frequent visits to the volcano.

The beginnings of Hilo's tourist industry date back to the 1870s when Hilo was one of a number of sites on a standard sightseeing route. Particularly popular were visits to the volcano of Kilauea east of Mauna Loa.

By the early 1900s, Hilo's sugar industry was booming and the city became the commercial center of the island. A railroad connected Hilo with other parts of the island. Hilo became the seat of Hawaii County in 1905 was incorporated as a city in 1911.

Hilo Beset by Volcanic Eruptions and Tidal Waves

In March 1868, a volcanic eruption resulted in formidable destruction. The city experienced close calls from the eruption of Mauna Loa in 1942 and in 1984. Two tsunamis have also caused major damage. In 1946 a tidal wave swept half the town inland and then dragged the remains out to sea. Hilo rebuilt and constructed a stone breakwater across the bay to protect the harbor. Another tidal wave destroyed a major part of the waterfront business district and the city's beachfront in 1960, sweeping 61 Hiloites out to sea. Civic leaders, vowing that such destruction would never recur, drained the lowland crescent and raised a new hill 26 feet above sea level and mounted a new government and commercial center. Today, however, the beach is still gone.

Hilo's cultural diversity adds to the city's charm. Japanese, Polynesian, Filipino, Chinese, Puerto Rican, Portuguese, and Russian residents make up the city's mixed-race culture of today. Since their arrival, Japanese people have had an important influence on the city, from serving on the city council to starting entrepreneurial businesses. Business people of all races join the Japanese Chamber of Commerce and

Industry and the Japanese newspaper, the *Hilo Times,* is published in the city.

Population Profile

City and County Residents
1990: 120,317
2000: 148,667
2003 estimate: 158,423
Percent change, 1990–2000: 23.6

City Residents
1980: 35,269
1990: 37,808
2000: 40,759
2003 estimate: Not reported
Percent change, 1990–2000: 7.8%
U.S. rank in 1980: Not reported
U.S. rank in 1990: Not reported
U.S. rank in 2000: Not reported

Density: 750.8 per square mile (2000)

Racial and ethnic characteristics (2000)
White: 15,764
Black or African American: 471
American Indian and Alaska Native: 1,078
Asian: 25,172
Native Hawaiian and other Pacific Islander: 13,922
Hispanic or Latino (may be of any race): 3,579
Other: 385

Percent of residents born in state: 78.7% (2000)

Age characteristics (2000)
Population under 5 years old: 2,301
Population 5 to 9 years old: 2,859
Population 10 to 14 years old: 2,965
Population 15 to 19 years old: 3,319
Population 20 to 24 years old: 2,806
Population 25 to 34 years old: 4,352
Population 35 to 44 years old: 5,576
Population 45 to 54 years old: 5,842
Population 55 to 59 years old: 2,215
Population 60 to 64 years old: 1,701
Population 65 to 74 years old: 3,473
Population 85 years and older: 2,471
Median age: 38.6 years

Births (North Hilo and South Hilo, 2003)
Total number: 613

Deaths (North Hilo and South Hilo, 2003)
Total number: 519

Money income (1999)
Per capita income: $18,220 (Hilo CDP)
Median household income: $39,139
Total households: 14,577

Number of households with income of . . .
less than $10,000: 1,876
$10,000 to $14,999: 919
$15,000 to $24,999: 1,977
$25,000 to $34,999: 1,824
$35,000 to $49,999: 2,253
$50,000 to $74,999: 2,655
$75,000 to $99,999: 1,650
$100,000 to $149,999: 1,061
$150,000 to $199,999: 196
$200,000 or more: 182

Percent of families below poverty level: 11.1% (51.1% of which were female householder families with related children under 5)

2002 Actual Crime Index Offenses: 6,936 (Hawaii County)

Municipal Government

The Island of Hawaii has one governmental unit, the County of Hawaii. There is no formal government at the city or municipal level, although Hilo serves as the headquarters for all government activities on the Island. The city is governed by the county of Hawaii, which has a mayor elected for up to two four-year terms and a nine-member council representing each of the county's nine districts during two-year terms. Mayor Harry Kim, first elected to office in 2000, is the first mayor of Korean descent in the United States.

Head Official: Mayor Harry Kim, County of Hawaii (since 2000; current term expires 2008)

Total Number of County Employees: 2,300 (2003)

County Information: Hawaii County, 25 Aupuni Street, Hilo, HI 96720; telephone (808)961-8521

Economy

Major Industries and Commercial Activity

Hilo has a diversified economy that includes agriculture, tourism, aquaculture, livestock, trade, education, and government.

The Big Island was a world center for the production of raw sugar from 1876 to 1994, when the last plantation closed. Today, the tremendous rainfall produces a genuine paradise of flowers, from exotic anthuriums and orchids to tropical blooms of all sorts. The city, which is the center for the world's largest tropical flower industry, exports fresh cut flowers, sprays, and potted plants from various farmer cooperatives and flower farms. About 1 million acres of the island's total 1.8 million acres are devoted to agriculture, a $500 million per-year industry.

Livestock is an economic mainstay, with sales of beef, hogs, dairy and poultry products, and honey totaling more than $25 million annually. Cattle ranches, including Parker Ranch, said to be the largest privately-owned ranch in the world, produce 70 percent of livestock marketed in the state of Hawaii. Nearly 115,000 cattle are raised on the Big Island and most are shipped to the U.S. mainland and Canada for processing. The Big Island is Hawaii's largest producer of honey, with its honey and queen bee industries producing more than 1 million pounds annually.

Aquaculture, another important industry on the island, has been a mainstay of economic life since the first Polynesian settlers came to the Big Island. Abalone, carp, catfish, clams, flounder, milkfish, moi, mullet, ornamental fish, oyster, prawns, sea cucumber, seaweed, shrimp, snails, sturgeon, tilapia, and rainbow trout are among the fish and seafood harvested. Several types of microalgae are also being cultivated for pharmaceutical and nutritional products. Aquafarms on the Big Island, totaling more than 170 acres, produce 11 million pounds of aquaproducts annually.

Despite serious agricultural problems ranging from drought to harmful bacteria, the Big Island produces more than four-fifths of the state's production of fruit (other than pineapples), including bananas, guavas, oranges, tangerines, and avocados; the bulk of the state's macadamia nuts and papaya; the vast majority of its coffee; crops such as ginger, Chinese cabbage, leaf lettuce, greenhouse tomatoes, and cucumbers; and orchids, anthuriums, and other nursery products for domestic and foreign markets. A recent problem for Hilo's agricultural industry has been the infestation of the coqui frog. The increasing population of this amphibian has threatened the island's ecosystem.

The tourism industry has all but bypassed the town of Hilo due to its lack of a decent beach and the 134 inches of rainfall annually. Since Hilo has never been a tourist destination, the town has retained its historic character and has not suffered from the infrastructure problems associated with high-rises and big-city development. However, it just may be that historic character that is attracting new visitors to the city. Leisure and hospitality services comprised the largest of the major industrial sectors in the area in 2003. According

to *Hawaii Business Magazine,* ''In 2003, the town received 219,262 cruise ship passengers from 116 foreign ship calls. By 2007, the city expects to receive 418,600 visitors from 219 domestic and foreign ship calls.'' Recent marketing efforts have focused on drawing Japanese visitors.

Hilo's Foreign Trade Zone (FTZ) is ideally situated adjacent to Hilo Harbor and the Hilo International Airport, less than a mile from downtown Hilo. This 31-acre site is the first such zone designated by the State of Hawaii to attract manufacturers to Hawaii. The FTZ allows companies locating there to import parts for assembly and export the finished product without paying import duties. It was given a boost when NIC Americas, Inc., became its first tenant. NIC Americas manufactures a device that uses electrical arcing to destroy used needles from health care facilities. The company represented Hilo's first significant new manufacturing facility in recent times; if successful it could lead to other FTZ tenants.

Television, film and commercial production also contributes to Hilo's economy. The County of Hawaii hosted 129 film productions from ten countries in 2003-2004, an increase from the prior year. Revenues were stable however, due to an increase in small films and a decrease in large revenue productions.

Items and goods produced: flowers, fruit, cattle, fish, macadamia nuts, coffee

Incentive Programs—New and Existing Companies

Local programs— Hawaii's Small Business Development Center Network is a partnership of the University of Hawaii at Hilo and the U.S. Small Business Administration. With the aim of helping small business become established or expand, the Network offers one-on-one counseling, seminars, workshops and conferences.

State programs—Most business incentives are offered at the state level. These include direct financial incentives such as Industrial Development Bonds, a Capital Loan Program, customized industrial training, and investment of public funds in return for equity or ownership positions in private businesses. Tax incentives are also offered along with Hawaii Urban Enterprise Zones Program. Other tax incentives for businesses on the Big Island include no personal property taxes; no taxes on inventory, equipment, furniture and machinery; no tax on goods manufactured for export; no unincorporated business tax; and banks and financial institutions pay only one business tax. High technology businesses can also take advantage of unparalleled tax breaks through legislative initiatives (ACT 221, SLH 2001) and the State Foreign Trade Zone program and Enterprise Zone Partnership.

Job training programs—The Workforce Development Division of Hawaii's Department of Labor and Industrial Relations oversees One-Stop Workforce Assistance Centers, a job placement and training system to help people find work and employers find suitable workers, and the Employment & Training Fund (ETF), a job skills upgrade program for current workers. Employers can receive customized training grants for their workplace or they can nominate a current worker for an established training course.

Job Training Information: Workforce Development Division, Hawaii Department of Labor and Industrial Relations, Kaikoo Mall, 777 Kilauea Ave., #121, Hilo, HI 96720; telephone (808)974-4126; fax (808)974-4125

Development Projects

Since the fall of the Big Island's sugar plantations in the mid-1990s, "Hilo has transformed itself from a plantation town to a university town," according to Richard West, executive director of the Hawaii Island Economic Development Board in a 2004 article in *Hawaii Business Magazine.* Hilo has seen the addition of several new science and technology developments in the early 2000s. One of the largest new projects is the Mauna Kea Astronomy Education Center (MKAEC), a $28 million facility showcasing the astronomy research conducted on the summit of the Mauna Kea volcano. Located in the University of Hawaii at Hilo's University Park of Science and Technology, the center is expected to attract 200,000 visitors annually when it opens in July 2005. The U.S. Department of Agriculture's Agricultural Research Service broke ground on a $60 million research lab in Fall 2004. In 5 stages, the Pacific Basin Agricultural Research Center (PBARC) will eventually encompass 120,000 square feet of laboratories, an administration building, greenhouse facilities, and insect rearing facilities. Additional research dollars will come to Hilo with the opening of the U.S. Forest Service Institute of Pacific Islands Forestry, a $12 million forest research laboratory.

Economic Development Information: County of Hawaii Department of Research and Development, 25 Aupuni Street, Hilo, HI 96720; telephone (808)961-8366. Hawaii Department of Labor and Industrial Relations, telephone (808)586-8842. Hilo Hamakua Community Development Corporation, County of Hawaii, 25 Aupuni Street, Hilo, HI 96720.

Commercial Shipping

Hilo Harbor has an entrance depth of 35 feet, and the harbor basin has a length of 2,300 feet and a width of 1,400 feet. There are 2,787 linear feet of piers, and storage area totals 122,000 square feet of shedded and 492,000 square feet of open space. Plans on the drawing board for the harbor include the separation of the commercial shipping and cruise ship activities to accommodate the increasing demand of cruise lines which would like to dock there.

Labor Force and Employment Outlook

Hilo's job outlook has been improving slowly and steadily. The city's economic recovery has mirrored the state's reviving economy. The County of Hawaii's unemployment rate has improved from 9.5 percent in 1995 to 5.1 percent in the last quarter of 2004. This is compared to 3 percent for the entire state. According to the FDIC, every major industry in the State of Hawaii posted employment gains in 2004, with the tourism sector benefiting the most. The leisure and hospitality sector and the retail trade sector together accounted for 40 percent of the job growth in the state. Solid job gains were also seen in the health services sector. The FDIC also reported at a 2004 Business Outlook Forum that "economists were upbeat about the state's economic future and respondents surveyed by the Bank of Hawaii expressed near record-high business confidence."

The following is a summary of data regarding the city of Hilo labor force as of 2000.

Size of civilian labor force: 19,902

Number of workers employed in. . .
  construction: 1,151
  manufacturing: 418
  retail trade: 2,224
  transportation, warehousing, and utilities: 1,159
  finance, insurance, real estate, rental and leasing: 818
  *arts, entertainment, recreation, accommodation and
    food services:* 1,895
  public administration: 1,565
  educational, health and social services: 4,505
  other services: 880

Average hourly earnings of workers employed in manufacturing: $13.13 (2003)

Unemployment rate: 3% (Hawaii, January 2005)

Largest employers	*Number of employees*
State of Hawaii	7,450
County of Hawaii	2,250
C. Brewer & Co. (holding company)	1,987
Hilton Waikoloa Village	1,200
U.S. Government	850
Mauna Lani Resort Inc.	800
KTA Superstores	776
Mauna Lani Bay Hotel	650

Cost of Living

Median single family home resale price in Hawaii County in 2002 was $194,500. The following is a summary of data regarding key cost of living factors for the Hilo area.

2004 (3rd Quarter) ACCRA Average House Price: Not reported

2004 (3rd Quarter) ACCRA Cost of Living Index: Not reported

State income tax rate: Ranges from 1.4% to 8.25%

State sales tax rate: 4.0%

Local income tax rate: None

Local sales tax rate: None

Property tax rate: $9.10 per $1,000 assessed valuation for improved land and buildings; $5.55 per $1,000 valuation for owner-occupied residences

Economic Information: County of Hawaii, Department of Economic Development and Tourism, 25 Aupuni Street Room 219, Hilo, HI 96720; telephone (808)961-8366; fax (808)935-1205. Hawaii Island Chamber of Commerce, 106 Kamehameha Ave, Hilo, HI 96720; telephone (808)935-7178; fax (808)961-4435; email hicc@interpac.net

Education and Research

Elementary and Secondary Schools

Hawaii is the only state with a single, unified statewide school system, comprised of seven districts, one of which is the Hawaii District, which covers the island of Hawaii. An elected board of education formulates educational policy and supervises the public school system. Ten members are elected from Oahu and a total of three from all other islands. One non-voting student member is appointed.

The following is a summary of data regarding Hilo's public schools as of the 2003–2004 school year.

Total enrollment: 26,221 (2002)

Number of facilities
  elementary schools: 8
  junior high/middle schools: 2
  senior high schools: 2
  other: 3 charter schools

Student/teacher ratio: elementary and secondary, 16.8:1 (statewide average)

Teacher salaries (statewide average)
  minimum: $29,000
  maximum: $58,000

Funding per pupil: $7,455 (statewide average 2002-2003)

There are seven private schools in Hilo. They are Emakaala School; Haili Christian School; Hale Aloha Nazarene School; Kamehamaha Schools; Mauna Loa School; and St. Joseph's Elementary and Junior/Senior high school.

Colleges and Universities

The city of Hilo is the home of three universities. University of Hawaii at Hilo offers two- and four-year programs in areas such as agriculture, arts and sciences, and vocational and technical training. It also currently offers five master's degrees and will offer two doctoral programs in the mid-2000s. Hawaii Community College has career, technical and academic programs. Akamai University is an alternative graduate school designed for mid-career adult students.

Libraries and Research Centers

The Hilo Public Library, part of the Hawaii State Public Library System, contains books, periodicals, videotapes, sound recordings, and provides internet access to its patrons. It is the largest public library on the island and the second busiest in circulation statewide. Other libraries in the city include the Hilo Hospital Medical Library, which features consumer health materials; the State Supreme Court Third Circuit Court Law Library; and the University of Hawaii at Hilo Libraries, whose sytem holds more than 250,000 volumes, 1,650 periodical subscriptions, and 225,000 microfiche titles.

University Park of Science and Technology on the campus of the University of Hawaii at Hilo (UH-Hilo) is home to six U.S. and international observing facilities. They include the British-Canada-Netherlands Joint Astronomy Centre, Gemini North Telescope, Caltech Submillimeter Observatory, Subaru National Astronomical Observatory of Japan, University of Hawaii Institute for Astronomy, and Smithsonian Submillimeter Array. The Mauna Kea Astronomy Education Center is a new state-of-the-art interpretive and research center and planetarium, located in University Park. The Beaumont Agricultural Research Center engages in research on agronomy, animal breeding and nutrition, horticulture, plant pathology, and soil chemistry with particular reference to island crops and plants. The U.S. Geological Survey's Hawaiian Volcano Observatory is located at the rim of Kilauea, 30 miles from Hilo; Kilauea is said to be the most studied volcano in the world.

Public Library Information: Hilo Public Library, 300 Waianuenue Avenue, PO Box 647, Hilo, HI 96720; telephone (808)933-4650

Health Care

Hilo Medical Center is the city's primary hospital with 225 beds offering general medical, surgical and obstetric care, as well as emergency services. Other east Hawaii medical facilities include the Hale Hoola Hamakua long-term care facility in Honokaa and the Kau Critical Access Hospital in Pahala. The North Hawaii Community Hospital in Kameula serves the 31,000 residents in the northern region of the Big Island. These facilities have led to growth in the island's medical profession and to an expectation that the region will become the health and medical center of the Pacific Rim; this in turn could make the island attractive as a retirement center. Federal funding of $18.4 million was approved in December 2003 to build a Veteran's hospital in Hilo. The hospital will be a 95-bed long-term care and adult day-care center, which will further stimulate the need for medical workers.

Recreation

Sightseeing

Hilo's quaint downtown contains wooden clapboard and stucco buildings with corrugated tin overhangs covering the sidewalks. A walk through town reveals flower and fruit stalls, fish markets, butcher shops, soda fountains, seed shops, and luncheonettes. Hilo has many magnificent gardens and parks.

At Hawaii Volcanoes National Park, a powerful active volcano can be glimpsed firsthand by car or helicopter at the fire pit crater of Kilauea. Rangers can provide maps and directions for optimum viewing of the volcano, if it is active, and for walks along the 11-mile trail. The Visitors Center offers a beginner's class on volcanology featuring films and pamphlets.

The center of the historic downtown is Kalakauna Park, a grassy square with a large banyan tree, a statue of the king, and a reflecting pool. On one side of the square is the 1919 Federal building, which combines Neo-Classical and Spanish Mission characteristics. Opposite the Federal Building is the East Hawaii Cultural Center. Other buildings of interest are the Zen Buddhist Temple, Taishoji Soto Mission, and the Haili Church, built in 1857 by missionaries from New England.

The Naha Stone, a gigantic stone sitting in front of the Hilo Public Library, is said to have been upended by King Kamehameha with his bare hands. Legend has it that only a chief of royal blood can budge it at all and anyone who can turn it over is a potential island king.

The Panaewa Rainforest Zoo is one of the few natural tropical rainforest zoos in the United States. Animals on display include pygmy hippopotamuses, rainforest monkeys, a tapir, jungle parrots, rainforest tigers, and endangered species of Hawaiian birds.

A drive down Banyan Drive offers views of tree-lined lanes with 50-year-old banyan trees first planted by President Franklin D. Roosevelt and other celebrities of the times. Old Mamalahoa Highway Scenic Drive, 5 miles north of the city, follows the Hamakua Coast through beautiful rainforest jungles with scenic views of the coast.

Rainbow Falls provides a view of cascading water surrounded by beautiful flowers. Nearby the Boiling Pots are turbulent rapids with deep, swirling pools and falls. Coconut Island, just offshore from Liliuokalani Park, contains picnic tables and shelters and is often used for local cultural events. Leleiwi Beach Park provides another ideal picnic spot and a good place for swimming, snorkeling, surfing, and netfishing since its seawall offers easy access to the ocean. The park's Richardson Ocean Center is a free marine life interpretive center.

The Suisan Fish Market Auction is a daily multilingual auction of tuna and other tropical fish and seafood delicacies. On Wednesdays and Saturdays the Hilo Farmers' Market features breadfruit, papaya, avocados, stalks of ginger and other tropical flowers, as well as craft and gift items from more than 100 area farmers and crafters.

The Hilo Tropical Gardens provide views of a miniature rain forest of waterfalls and tropical flowers surrounded by lily ponds and Oriental bridges. The Nani Mau Gardens feature 20 acres of flowers, fruit trees, walking paths, pools and waterfalls. A nature preserve on 17 acres, the Hawaii Tropical Botanical Garden boasts hundreds of waterfalls, and numerous varieties of flowers and native animals.

Arts and Culture

The East Hawaii Cultural Center features changing art exhibits and dance and musical performances. The University of Hawaii-Hilo Theatre is the primary center for performing arts in the area.

The Lyman Mission House and Museum, built in 1839, is the oldest structure in Hilo. The restored house is furnished with period antiques that reflect the time when early Christian missionaries lived on the island. An attached museum features exhibits of Stone Age implements, feather leis, a large house made of grass, and various artifacts from Japan, Portugal, Korea, and the Philippines. The museum's Earth Heritage Gallery showcases the island's natural history including specimens of volcanic minerals and Hawaiian land shells and the Island Heritage Gallery showcases native history and culture.

The Pacific Tsunami Museum in Downtown Hilo provides educational exhibits about tsunamis which have caused more damage in Hilo than anywhere on all the Hawaiian Islands.

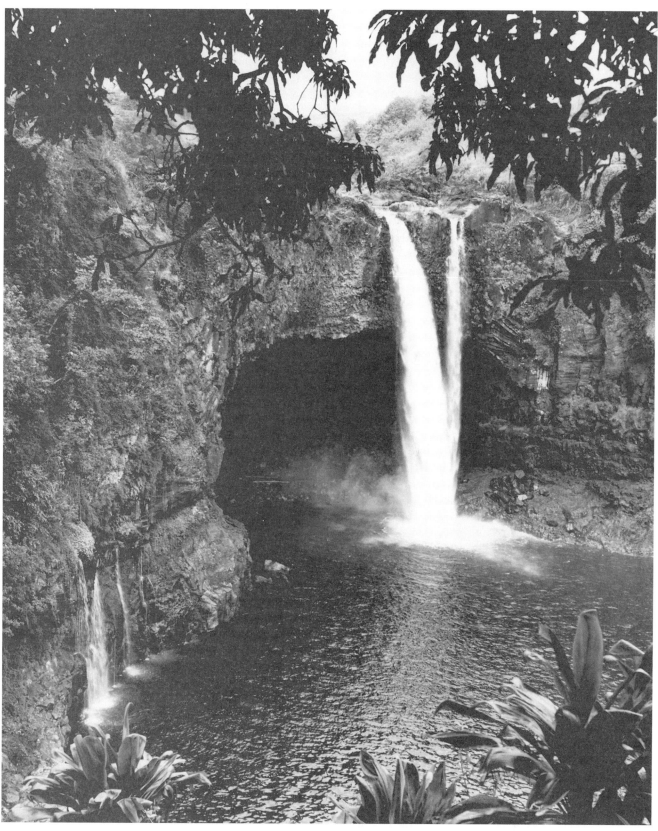

Rainbow Falls near Hilo.

Festivals and Holidays

Hilo welcomes the Chinese New Year in February with a festival in Kalakuau Park featuring food, crafts, art, exhibitions, demonstrations, fireworks, and traditional dancers. The Kona Brewers Festival in March showcases 60 types of beer and chefs from 25 local restaurants preparing tropical culinary creations. Bluegrass, Hawaiian, and rock music, a "trash fashion show," hula and fire dancers are also part of the festivities. The Merry Monarch Festival, held for a week each spring, is the state's biggest hula festival and draws the most publicity. Started in 1971, the festival offers parades and other attractions in addition to the three-night hula competition, which is the festival's claim to fame. The Ethnic Foods Festival is celebrated in May. October's Hilo Macadamia Nut Festival features a parade, arts and crafts fair, bake-off, music and dance exhibitions, and sports activities.

Sports for the Spectator

The University of Hawaii at Hilo Vulcans offer intercollegiate basketball, volleyball, baseball, and softball competitions. Minor league baseball's Hilo Stars participate in the Hawaii Winter Baseball League.

Sports for the Participant

Water sports reign supreme in Hilo and include fishing, skin diving, and sailing. Also popular are hunting, horseback riding, mountain biking, and other outdoor activities. The Big Island offers black, white, and green sand beaches; among them are Leleiwi Beach Park, a black sand beach that offers swimming, snorkeling and fishing, and Onekahakaha Beach Park, the city's only white sand beach with a safe inlet for swimming. The best surfing is found off Leleiwi and Richardson beaches.

Two golf courses are located in the town of Hilo— the Hilo Municipal Golf Course and the Naniloa Golf Club. Sixteen more public and semi-private courses are a short drive away. Skiing is occasionally possible atop Mauna Kea.

Shopping and Dining

Hilo offers a variety of shopping opportunities, ranging from national chain stores to bookstalls and specialty shops that carry such items as Hawaiian handicrafts, wooden bowls, jewelry, and native furniture. There are three major shopping centers in the city, including the multimillion-dollar Prince Kuhio Plaza Shopping Center, Hilo Shopping Center, and Kaiko'o Mall, as well as the revitalized "Main Street" of downtown Hilo. Hilo's Bayfront area along Kamehameha Avenue is home to shops in historic buildings featuring native Hawaiian art and authentic Hawaiian wear. The East Hawaii Cultural Center is a good spot to find authentic, locally made Hawaiian gifts and souvenirs such as books, cards, jewelry, sculptures, and wood objects.

Hilo's residents and visitors enjoy a variety of dining spots that feature Cajun, Mexican, Italian, Japanese, Thai, Filipino, Chinese, Hawaiian, and traditional American fare. The fresh catch of the day is forever popular with visitors, especially the aholehole, or Hawaiian flagtail, a reef fish raised in island ponds. Ahi (tuna), Mahi-Mahi and opakapaka (blue snapper) are also served in area restaurants. Suman, a Filipino sticky-rice sweet wrapped in a banana leaf and cooked in coconut milk, is a favorite dish sold by street vendors in Hilo. Other unique dining spots include an espresso bar featuring pure Kona coffee and various places with evening luaus.

Visitor Information: Big Island Visitors Bureau, 250 Keawe Street, Hilo, HI 96720; telephone (808)961-5797; fax (808)961-2126. Destination Hilo, PO Box 1391, Hilo, HI 96721; telephone (808)966-8331; fax (808)966-9886

Convention Facilities

The county of Hawaii's Hoolulu Park Complex provides the Afook-Chinen Civic Auditorium, with 11,342 square feet that can accommodate 3,550 people theater-style, 1,000 people classroom-style, and 500 people banquet-style. The Conference Center at the University of Hawaii at Hilo can host groups as small as 25 and as large as 600, with reception facilities for 1000 people. The Edith Kanakaole Multipurpose Pavilion, with 18,720 square feet of space, can seat 4,500 people theater-style, 2,000 people for a reception, and 750 people banquet-style. The Seven Seas Luau House's 5,000 square feet can seat 700 people theater- or classroom-style, and 500 people for banquets. The Hilo Hawaiian Hotel offers a 5,040-square-foot banquet room that can accommodate small and large groups. The Hawaii Naniloa Resort offers seating for up to 400 people.

Convention Information: Big Island Visitors Bureau, 250 Keawe Street, Hilo, HI 96720; telephone (808)961-5797; fax (808)961-2126

Transportation

Approaching the City

The county of Hawaii's airports are Hilo International and Kona International. There are frequent inter-island flights by Aloha Airlines, Island Air, Pacific Wings and Hawaiian

Airlines, as well as flights to major U.S. cities; daily direct flights from Tokyo are available. Four hotels are located within a five mile radius of the Hilo airport. A major highway system encircles the island of Hawaii, and driving time from the Kona International Airport to Hilo is about two hours and fifteen minutes. State Highway 19 approaches Hilo from the north and State Highway 11 approaches from the south. State Highway 200 runs west into the interior of the island.

Traveling in the City

The island of Hawaii has more than 1,450 miles of highways. Since the area surrounding the city of Hilo is large, a rental car may be preferable to depending on taxi service. Major streets in Hilo include Kinoole St. and Kilauea Avenue, which run northwest to southeast, and Waianuenue Avenue, which runs east and west. Bayfront Highway follows the coastline and scenic Banyan Drive curves around the major resort area. County bus service is provided by ''Hele-On.'' The Hawaii County Mass Transit Agency offers a Shared Ride Taxi program which provides inexpensive door to door transportation in the cities of Hilo and Kona.

Communications

Newspapers and Magazines

The *Hawaii Tribune-Herald* is Hilo's daily morning paper.

Television and Radio

No network television stations broadcast from Hilo, but all major networks are available for viewing from Hilo via programming from neighboring Oahu. Hawaiian Cable-vision system offers a wide selection of programming. The city is served by four AM and three FM radio stations.

Media Information: *Hawaii Tribune-Herald,* 355 Kinoole Street, Box 767, Hilo, HI 96721; telephone (808)935-6621; fax (808)969-9100

Hilo Online

Destination Hilo. Available www.destinationhilo.org

Downtown Improvement Association. Available www .down townhilo.com

Hawaii County Home Page. Available www.hawaii-county .com

Hawaii Department of Labor and Industrial Relations. Available dlir.state.hi.us

Hawaii Island Chamber of Commerce. Available www.hicc .biz

Hawaii Tribune-Herald. Available www.hawaiitribune-herald.com/index.html

Hawaii Visitors and Convention Bureau. Available www .gohawaii.com/bigisland

Hilo Public Library. Available www.librarieshawaii.org/locations/hawaii/hilo.htm

State Department of Education School Reports (individual schools). Available doe.k12.hi.us/reports.htm

State of Hawaii. Available www.hawaii.gov

Selected Bibliography

Ball, Pamela, *Lava: A Novel* (New York: Henry Holt, 1998)

Honolulu

The City in Brief

Founded: 1100 (by Hawaiians); 1795 (incorporated, 1907)

Head Official: Mayor Mufi Hannemann (since 2005)

City Population
   1980: 365,048
   1990: 377,059
   2000: 371,657
   2003 estimate: 380,149 (Honolulu CDP)
   Percent change, 1990–2000: −1.4%
   U.S. rank in 1980: 36th
   U.S. rank in 1990: 44th
   U.S. rank in 2000: 55th

City and County Population
   1980: 763,000
   1990: 836,231
   2000: 876,156

   Percent change, 1990–2000: 4.8%
   U.S. rank in 1980: 47th
   U.S. rank in 1990: 51st
   U.S. rank in 2000: 55th

Area: 86 square miles (2000)
Elevation: 15 feet above sea level
Average Annual Temperature: 77.2° F
Average Annual Precipitation: 22.02 inches

Major Economic Sectors: Services (especially tourism), military, agriculture, construction
Unemployment Rate: 2.8% (January 2005)
Per Capita Income: $24,191 (1999)

2002 FBI Crime Index Total: 57,271

Major Colleges and Universities: University of Hawaii at Manoa, Chaminade University of Honolulu, Hawaii Pacific University, Brigham Young University-Hawaii

Daily Newspapers: *The Honolulu Advertiser; Honolulu Star-Bulletin*

Introduction

Honolulu, the capital of Hawaii and the seat of Honolulu county, is a cosmopolitan city. Its name means "protected harbor," and it serves as the crossroads of the Pacific Ocean with ship and air connections to the U.S. mainland, Asia, Australia, and New Zealand. The city is the principal port for the Hawaiian Islands and an important center for military defense with several bases, including Pearl Harbor Naval Base, located in the area. Millions of visitors are drawn annually to Honolulu's mild, semitropical climate and to the beautiful beaches of Waikiki.

Geography and Climate

Honolulu as a city is defined by the U.S. Census Bureau as the area from Makapuu south of the Koolau Mountain range summit to the western edge of Halawa Valley. Located along the southern coast of Oahu, Honolulu is the third largest of the Hawaiian Islands, just south of the Tropic of Cancer in the Pacific Ocean. The city is situated on a narrow plain between the ocean and the Koolau mountain range; it climbs the Punchbowl, an extinct volcano. Although the climate is semi-tropical, the trade winds usually keep the city comfortable, until the "kona" or southerly winds blow for a few weeks in the summer. Honolulu's weather exhibits the least seasonal change of any city in the United States, with only a few degrees difference between winter and summer.

Area: 86 square miles (2000) (City and county area in 2000: 600 square miles)

Elevation: 15 feet above sea level

Average Temperatures: January, 72.9° F; August, 81.4° F; annual average, 77.2° F

Average Annual Precipitation: 22.02 inches

History

Native Hawaiians Meet Westerners, Begin Trading Goods

Historians estimate that the first settlers, Polynesians, came to the Hawaiian Islands fifteen hundred years ago, with the last migration occurring around 750 A.D. By the time Westerners came to the islands, the Hawaiian people had devel-

oped a highly structured society composed of chiefs, who claimed the right of divine rule, and commoners, who worked the land and the sea.

British Captain James Cook first sighted Oahu in 1778, when he named the islands the Sandwich Islands after the Earl of Sandwich. William Brown was the first to enter Honolulu's harbor, in 1794. In 1795, King Kamehameha I unified the Hawaiian Islands, conquering the king of Oahu. Kamehameha settled at Waikiki, turning the harbor at Honolulu into a center of trade with the West for such goods as fur, sandalwood, and whale products. While bringing the islands into the modern world, such trade also threatened the native Hawaiian culture.

Rise of Sugar Industry Erodes Traditional Way of Life

Honolulu was such a convenient center of trade between the Orient and the West that it became the seat of a series of European occupations: Russia in 1816, England in 1843, and France in 1849. New England missionaries began arriving in 1820; some of their buildings, preserved by the Mission Houses Museum, can be seen today. The missionaries established schools and also functioned as government advisors to the royal Hawaiians. During the mid-nineteenth century the whaling industry began to decline and the sugar industry grew. The cultivation of sugar cane brought in a great influx of immigrant labor from throughout the Pacific basin; the descendants of these peoples are partially responsible for modern Honolulu's cosmopolitanism. A 1876 treaty that admitted sugar duty-free into the United States strengthened the power of this industry.

King Kamehameha III proclaimed Honolulu as the capitol city in 1850. The territorial legislature created county level governments in 1905. Incorporated that year, the County of Oahu included that island plus all the small islands beyond Niihau to but not including Midway Island 2,000 miles away. In 1907 the county was renamed the City and County of Honolulu.

At the time Honolulu was named the capitol city, traditional Hawaiian life was breaking down. The islands were basically ruled by the sugar interests consisting of an oligarchy of plantation owners. Native customs were declining both through the breakdown of taboos and the introduction of guns and liquor. Furthermore, the Hawaiian people were not immune to diseases brought to them by the Westerners; within a hundred years of the islands' discovery by the West, 80 percent of the native population was dead. The language and history of the Hawaiians is nevertheless preserved, partly through native dance and folklore.

In 1893 Queen Liliuokalani, the last Hawaiian monarch, was deposed by a group of American businessmen and U.S.

Marines, and in 1898 the islands were annexed by the United States. In 1907 Honolulu was incorporated as a city and county. Through the efforts of Prince Jonah Kuhio Kalanianaole, a member of Congress from 1902 to 1922, Pearl Harbor was dredged, extending the sea power of the United States. On December 7, 1941, Pearl Harbor was bombed by the Japanese, but it survived to become the most important staging area for the United States in the Pacific during World War II. The area around Honolulu is still an important constellation of military bases.

Hawaii achieved statehood in 1959 and joined the Union as the 50th state with Honolulu as its capital. Today Honolulu is the Aloha state's center of business, culture, and politics. In recent years, Hawaiian sovereignty has become a contested political issue. In 1993 President Clinton signed an official apology acknowledging the U.S. role in the overthrow of the Hawaiian kingdom. A 2003 U.S. Supreme Court decision addressed the issue of sovereignty and the elections of government officials in Hawaii. In 2005, the Native Hawaiian Government Reorganization Act was reintroduced in the House and Senate. The legislation calls for the U.S. government to recognize Native Hawaiians as it does American Indians and Native Alaskans. The legislation would also provide a process by which the U.S. recognizes the Native Hawaiian governing entity.

Historical Information: Bernice P. Bishop Museum Library, 1525 Bernice Street, Honolulu, HI 96817; telephone (808)847-3511; fax (808)841-8968

Population Profile

Metropolitan Area Population
1980: 763,000
1990: 836,231
2000: 876,156
Percent change, 1990–2000: 4.8%
U.S. rank in 1980: 47th
U.S. rank in 1990: 51st (State rank: 1st)
U.S. rank in 2000: 55th

City Residents
1980: 365,048
1990: 377,059
2000: 371,657
2003 estimate: 380,149
Percent change, 1990–2000: − 1.4%
U.S. rank in 1980: 36th
U.S. rank in 1990: 44th (State rank: 1st)
U.S. rank in 2000: 55th

Density: 4,336.6 people per square mile (2000)

Racial and ethnic characteristics (2000)
White: 73,093
Black or African American: 6,038
American Indian and Alaska Native: 689
Asian: 207,588
Native Hawaiian and Pacific Islander: 25,457
Hispanic or Latino (may be of any race): 16,229
Other: 3,318

Percent of residents born in state: 52.5% (2000)

Age characteristics (2000)
Population under 5 years old: 18,896
Population 5 to 9 years old: 20,440
Population 10 to 14 years old: 19,915
Population 15 to 19 years old: 21,098
Population 20 to 24 years old: 24,346
Population 25 to 34 years old: 53,911
Population 35 to 44 years old: 57,175
Population 45 to 54 years old: 53,649
Population 55 to 59 years old: 20,128
Population 60 to 64 years old: 15,842
Population 65 to 74 years old: 32,445
Population 75 to 84 years old: 25,694
Population 85 years and over: 8,118
Median age: 39.7 years

Births (2002)
Total number: 13,166 (City and County of Honolulu)

Deaths (2002)
Total number: 6,557 (City and County of Honolulu)

Money Income (1999)
Per capita income: $24,191
Median household income: $45,112
Total number: 140,401

Number of households with income of . . .
less than $10,000: 13,795
$10,000 to $14,999: 7,218
$15,000 to $24,999: 15,912
$25,000 to $34,999: 17,065
$35,000 to $49,999: 22,545
$50,000 to $74,999: 24,824
$75,000 to $99,999: 15,188
$100,000 to $149,999: 14,321
$150,000 to $199,999: 5,014
$200,000 and over: 4,519

Percent of families below poverty level: 7.9% (36.3% of which were female householder families with related children under 5 years)

2002 FBI Crime Index Total: 57,271

Municipal Government

The city of Honolulu and the county of Honolulu are administered jointly by a mayor-council form of government. The mayor and nine council members serve a four-year term.

Head Official: Mayor Mufi Hanneman (since 2005; current term expires 2009)

Total Number of City and County Employees: 11,350 (2005)

City Information: Mayor's Office, 530 South King Street, Honolulu, HI 96813; telephone (808)523-4141; fax (808)527-5552

Economy

Major Industries and Commercial Activity

Honolulu began its economic life in the mid-nineteenth century as a port for whalers; it was also a trade center for nations bordering the Pacific, dealing in such goods as sandalwood, whale oil, and fur. While markets for sandalwood and whale oil decreased, sugar and pineapple markets increased dramatically. In fact, the powerful sugar industry, owned mainly by Americans, engineered the downfall of Hawaii's last monarch and the islands' annexation by the United States. Today, one-fifth of the land in Honolulu County is zoned for agriculture, but fields are now giving way to new homes and commercial development. With the closure of sugar plantations, challenges arise to find the most productive use for these lands. Diversified agriculture has been on a steady upward trend. Aquaculture, which includes cultivated species of shellfish, finfish and algae, has grown in recent years. In 2002, Honolulu county had 30 aquaculture operations which produced $4.2 million in sales.

In addition to serving as the business and trading hub of the Hawaiian Islands, Honolulu is the transportation crossroads of the Pacific, connecting East with West. The city's recently expanded harbor facilities handle cargo for several international steamship companies, and a Foreign Trade Zone is based there. Other important elements of Honolulu's economic base include tourism, military defense, research and development, and manufacturing. With millions of visitors coming each year to enjoy Honolulu's climate and beaches, tourism contributes $10 billion annually to the local economy. Pearl Harbor Naval Shipyard, Marine Base Kaneohe, and Schofield Barracks Army base provide revenues that are unaffected by the normal business cycle. As the

home of the University of Hawaii at Manoa, Honolulu is a center for research and development, especially in the areas of oceanography, astrophysics, geophysics, and biomedicine. The city and county of Honolulu also contains many commercial, industrial and retail properties.

Items and goods produced: jewelry, clothing, food and beverages, rubber products, construction materials, and electronics and computer equipment

Incentive Programs—New and Existing Companies

State programs—State programs available include direct financial incentives such as Industrial Development Bonds, a Capital Loan Program, the Urban Honolulu Enterprise Zone Program, customized industrial training, and investment of public funds in return for equity or ownership positions in private businesses. Also at the state level, tax incentives for technology-related companies are available through 2010 with the extension of Hawaii's Act 215 relating to capital investment.

Job training programs—The Hawaii Department of Labor and Industrial Relations oversees One-Stop Workforce Assistance Centers, a job placement and training system to help people find work and employers find suitable workers, and the Employment & Training Fund (ETF), a job skills upgrade program for current workers. Employers can receive customized training grants for their workplace or they can nominate a current worker for an established training course.

Development Projects

With available research centers at the University of Hawaii as well as the area's defense contracting industry, Honolulu is looking to diversify its economy in the following areas; alternate energies, astronomy and space sciences, defense-dual use technologies, diversified agriculture, information and communication technologies, life science-biotech, and marine sciences. The film and digital media industry is growing and is supported by the City and County Honolulu Film Office.

A private and local government-supported "Second City," Kapolei, is constructed in an area 20 miles from downtown Honolulu. The Kapolei region contains the state's largest industrial park and second busiest commercial harbor. New amenities to the area include shopping centers, golf courses, parks, and the Hawaiian Waters Adventures Park.

Hawaii is ranked first in investment money coming from Asia to finance real estate projects and other industries. In 2001, Hawaii received $9.95 billion in foreign investment from Asia.

A $300 million Waikiki Beach Walk redevelopment project will rejuvenate walkways, hotels, retail complexes and entertainment areas along one of the most visited beaches in Honolulu. A four-year $200 million renovation is planned for Honolulu International Airport.

Economic Development Information: The Office of Economic Development, 530 S. King Street, Honolulu, HI 96813; telephone (808)547-7878; fax (808)547-7808

Commercial Shipping

Honolulu's location in the mid-Pacific makes it a major stopover for trans-Pacific sea and air shipments. Honolulu Harbor has a highly successful Foreign Trade Zone and 10 major shipping companies serving the port. The harbor also has terminals for commercial fishing, cruise ships, and ferries.

Labor Force and Employment Outlook

Honolulu County's four major industry sectors are government; trade, transportation, and utilities; leisure and hospitality; and professional and business services. These four industries account for about two-thirds of the total employment in Honolulu County. Services and trade are considered the two largest growth industries for the County.

The following is a summary of data regarding the Honolulu metropolitan area labor force, 2004 annual averages.

Size of non-agricultural labor force: 428,800

Number of workers employed in . . .
  construction and mining: 20,400
  manufacturing: 12,000
  trade, transportation and utilities: 79,300
  information: 8,900
  financial activities: 22,100
  professional and business services: 57,200
  leisure and hospitality: 60,500
  educational and health services: 53,300
  other services: 19,000
  government: 95,700

Average hourly earnings of production workers employed in manufacturing: $13.66

Unemployment rate: 2.8% (January 2005)

Largest employers	Number of employees
U.S. Government	91,850
City and County of Honolulu	11,350
Queen's Medical Center	3,000
Bank of Hawaii	2,500

Cost of Living

Because land is scarce and tourist development has driven up the cost of living, Hawaii is one of the top ranking states in housing costs. About 65 percent of housing in Honolulu is condominiums. The median single family home resale price in 2002 was $335,000. Housing rentals, fuel, and food costs are among the highest in the country. These conditions force many Hawaiians to work two or three jobs to survive, ranking it second in the nation for multiple part-time employment.

The following is a summary of data regarding key cost of living factors for the Honolulu area.

2004 (3rd Quarter) ACCRA Average House Price: $673,932

2004 (3rd Quarter) ACCRA Cost of Living Index: 168.2 (U.S. average = 100.0)

State income tax rate: Ranges from 1.4% to 8.25%

State sales tax rate: 4.0%

Local income tax rate: None

Local sales tax rate: Levied by state

Property tax rate: $3.75–$5.72 per $1,000 valuation (residential)

Economic Information: Chamber of Commerce of Hawaii, 1132 Bishop St. Suite 402, Honolulu, HI 96813; telephone (808)545-4300; fax (808)545-4369

Education and Research

Elementary and Secondary Schools

Hawaii is the only state with a single, unified statewide school system, comprised of seven districts, four on the island of Oahu and three on the neighbor islands. The four districts on Oahu are in the city and county of Honolulu; metropolitan Honolulu falls in the Honolulu District. An elected board of education formulates educational policy and supervises the public school system. Seven members are elected according to geographic region and six are elected at-large. One non-voting student member is appointed.

The following is a summary of data regarding the Honolulu District public schools as of the 2004–2005 school year.

Total enrollment: 32,454

Number of facilities
  elementary schools: 39
  intermediate schools: 9
  senior high schools: 6
  other: 3

Student/teacher ratio: elementary and secondary, 16.8:1 (statewide average)

Teacher salaries (statewide average)
  minimum: $29,000
  maximum: $58,000

Funding per pupil: $7,455 (statewide average 2002-2003)

A variety of private and special education schools are licensed by the state and serve the school-age population.

Public and Private Schools Information: Department of Education, 1390 Miller St., PO Box 2360, Honolulu, HI 96804; telephone (808)586-3230

Colleges and Universities

More than 53,000 students are enrolled in area higher education institutions. The University of Hawaii at Manoa, with an enrollment of more than 22,300 students, offers both undergraduate and graduate programs. It is especially known for its programs in the marine sciences, tropical agriculture, geophysics, astronomy, and Asian and Pacific cultures. On the campus of the University of Hawaii at Manoa is the East-West Center, which is an institution of technical and cultural exchange with Asian and Pacific countries.

Chaminade University of Honolulu is a small, private institution affiliated with the Society of Mary of the Roman Catholic Church. Also located in Honolulu is Hawaii Pacific University, Hawaii's largest private university. There are four community colleges.

Libraries and Research Centers

The Hawaii State Public Library System is based in Honolulu and operates 50 libraries throughout the state. Holdings consist of more than two million volumes (more than 1.5 million housed on Oahu) as well as newspapers, magazines, tapes, films, and special collections including Hawaiian history and state and federal documents. The system also maintains the Library for the Blind and Physically Handicapped, located in Honolulu.

Specialized libraries are affiliated with local colleges and universities, government agencies, hospitals, and corporations. Research activities in such fields as agriculture, livestock, the environment, freshwater and marine ecology, marine biology, marine mammalogy, water resources, cancer, biomedicine, astronomy, geophysics, labor, and industrial relations are conducted primarily by the University of Hawaii and federal government agencies.

Public Library Information: Hawaii State Public Library System, 478 South King Street, Honolulu, HI 96813; telephone (808)586-3500

Health Care

The city and county of Honolulu is served by eight major hospitals. The Queen's Medical Center in downtown Honolulu is the largest private hospital in the state, with 505 acute care beds and 28 sub-acute care beds. Cardiac rehabilitation centers are maintained at Kaukini Medical Center and Tripler Army Medical Center. The University of Hawaii is constructing a Health and Wellness Center at the new Kaka'ako campus which will house the John A. Burns School of Medicine, the Cancer Research Center of Hawaii, and a biomedical technology research park. Gamma Knife technology has recently become available at the St. Francis Medical Center. More than 16,000 primary care physicians, specialty care physicians, nurses, and medical technicians serve the Honolulu area.

Recreation

Sightseeing

The beauty of Honolulu's natural surroundings, its fascinating mix of cultures, and its unique layering of history offer much for the visitor to see and do. Honolulu abounds in the exotic flora and fauna of a semitropical island. The Honolulu Zoo houses an excellent collection of tropical birds as well as animals from around the world. A highlight of the zoo is the Kubuni Reserve. In this 12-acre African savanna, animals roam free within 30 different habitats. The Waikiki Aquarium has exhibits which educate and promote conservation of marine life, including coral reef environments and endangered species such as the monk seal. In 2000, the Waikiki Aquarium was designated as a Coastal Ecosystem Learning Center. At Sea Life Park, visitors can watch dolphins, penguins, and sea lions perform as well as swim with stingrays and dolphins.

The University of Hawaii at Manoa maintains the 200 acre Lyon Arboretum which offers paths and trails throughout its beautifully landscaped gardens. The Foster Botanical Garden was established in 1855 by Queen Kalama, wife of King Kamehameha III, and features a prehistoric glen planted with grasses, ferns, and palms. Other botanical gardens include Ho'omaluhia, Koko Crater, Lili'uokalani, and Wahiawa. Exotic flowers can also be seen at the Queen Kapiolani Hibiscus Garden.

A number of historic buildings are located in Honolulu. The stately Iolani Palace is the only royal palace in the United States, although it was inhabited by Hawaiian royalty for only 11 years. Completed by King David Kalahaua in 1862,

Iolani Palace, official residence of the last monarchs of Hawaii.

it served as a prison for Queen Liliuokalani. Honolulu's first church, the Kawaiahoa Church, was built in 1841 from blocks of coral and was the place of worship for Hawaiian rulers. The State Capitol, resembling a volcano, is designed to reflect various facets of the state of Hawaii.

The exhibits at the Hawaii Maritime Center focus on Hawaii's whaling days, the history of the Honolulu Harbor and the *Falls of Clyde,* a four-masted sailing ship built in 1878, which carried passengers and cargo between Honolulu and San Francisco. An underwater park is located at Hanauma Bay Beach Park where novices at snorkeling and SCUBA diving can view a coral reef. Other historical sites include Diamond Head State Monument, the U.S.S. Arizona Memorial, the Battleship Missouri Memorial, and the National Cemetery of the Pacific.

Arts and Culture

With a symphony, opera, theater groups, and numerous museums, Honolulu is the cultural center of the state of Hawaii. The Honolulu Symphony presents a classical concert series as well as a pop series at the Blaisdell Center Concert Hall. Also housed at Blaisdell Center is the Hawaii Opera Theater, which provides a season of grand opera and operettas. The Waikiki Shell is also a part of the Blaisdell Center and is an open-air amphitheater which hosts a variety of concerts and events. Broadway performances and dramatic classics are presented at Diamond Head Theatre and Manoa Valley Theatre, while the Kennedy Theatre at the University of Hawaii at Manoa is the site of student productions. Adjacent to the Waikiki Shell is a Hula Show Area where performances take place several times a week.

Honolulu's museums offer a range of experiences. The Bishop Museum is known for its collection of Polynesian artifacts, considered to be among the best in the world. The museum also presents hands-on exhibits and a planetarium where the constellations may be viewed as they appear from the island of Hawaii. New to the Bishop museum will be a 16,000 square-foot Science Learning Center opening in the fall of 2005. The Honolulu Academy of Arts houses permanent exhibits of oriental and occidental art, including the Kress collection of Italian Renaissance paintings and the Asian collection, featuring art and artifacts from throughout the Orient. In 2001, the museum opened its new $28 million Luce Pavilion Complex which added two 4,000-square-foot galleries. The Mission Houses Museum is comprised of the three oldest American buildings in Hawaii; the Frame house, the oldest, was built in 1821 and is furnished with period pieces that help show how the missionaries lived.

Festivals and Holidays

A number of holidays and festivals celebrating Honolulu's unique mix of cultures are held throughout the year. The Narcissus Festival, in January or early February, marks the Chinese New Year with lion dances and pageants. The Cherry Blossom Festival runs from January to March and is the largest running ethnic celebration in the state. A highlight of the event is the selection of a Cherry Blossom Queen and Court. Prince Kuhio Day on March 26, a state holiday, is held in honor of the prince who served in the U.S. Congress for 20 years. The Honolulu Festival takes place in March and celebrates ethnic harmony. The Hawaii Invitational International Music Festival occurs in April with high school, junior high, and college band participants. Lei Day on May 1st is one of Honolulu's most popular unofficial holidays; festivities include hula dances, contests for the best lei, and the crowning of the Lei Queen. The Hawaii State Fair occurs on weekends from mid-May through mid-June at the Aloha Stadium. The Pan Pacific-Matsuri Festival held in June promotes cultural exchange between Hawaiian and Japanese cultures. In addition to dance, art, and music, the Festival includes a golf open and a half marathon run. The King Kamehameha Celebration, a state holiday observed on June 11, honors the king who united the Hawaiian Islands. The Hawaii International Jazz Festival held in late July celebrates Jazz with international artist. The Ukulele Festival held annually in July presents a variety of ukulele players during free concerts. The Japan Festival is celebrated in July; nearly one-third of Honolulu's population is Japanese. The Prince Lot Hula Festival in July showcases ancient and modern versions of the dance at Queen Kapiolani Bandstand. The Aloha Festival, observed for one week between the beginning of September through mid-October, celebrates *Makahiki,* the traditional harvest time when taxes were paid, with pageants and street parties known as *Ho'olaule'a.* The Annual Orchid Show in late October shows thousands of varieties of plants and flowers, especially the exotic orchids which grow in the area. The Hawaii International Film Festival in late November and early December brings together award-winning film directors from the nations which border the Pacific Ocean.

Sports for the Spectator

Honolulu sports fans enjoy a variety of college sports, which include baseball, softball, basketball, soccer, golf, tennis, and track and field. The NFL Pro Bowl is held in February each year at the Aloha Stadium. The American Basketball Association is opening a new franchise in Honolulu for the 2005-2006 season. Spectators can also enjoy car racing at Hawaii Raceway Park.

Sports for the Participant

Honolulu's Waikiki beach draws more visitors than any other beach on the island, offering a host of water sports such as swimming, sailing, snorkeling, surfing, scuba diving, kayaking, or outrigger canoeing. Scuba equipment, surfboard and windsurf boards can be rented; lessons are also available. Charter boats for deep-sea fishing can be rented; during spring and summer there are particularly rich runs of game fish such as marlin and tuna.

Honolulu is also popular for hang gliding and parasailing. Visitors can take helicopter tours or go whale watching. Other activities include hiking, jogging, biking, horseback riding, tennis, and golf. Thousands of runners convene in Honolulu in December for the 26.2 mile Honolulu Marathon. The Honolulu Triathlon takes place every year in April.

Shopping and Dining

Shopping is a pleasurable pastime in Honolulu. Located in the city is Ala Moana, one of the largest open-air shopping centers in the world with more than 240 stores and dining and entertainment venues. Hotels along the beach in Waikiki are full of shops, and downtown Fort Street has been converted into a pedestrian mall. Also located within the city are the Royal Hawaiian and the Kahala Mall Shopping Centers. The Cultural Plaza in Chinatown Historic District features a variety of ethnic shops and stores. Temari, a center for Asian and Pacific arts that is not actually a store, offers two- to three-hour workshops to visitors. The former Dole Pineapple Cannery now houses retail shops oriented toward tourists. The newly developed Aloha Tower Market Place next to the Hawaii Maritime Center offers many shops and restaurants catering to tourists.

Honolulu cuisine is truly international. Hawaiian specialties include *mahimahi* (dolphin fish), *poi* (rounded taro root), and *puaa kalua* (a whole pig slow-roasted in a pit). Local restaurants offer a range of Oriental foods—Chinese, Japanese, Thai, and Korean—as well as European fare such as French, German, and Italian. Restaurants also serve popular Cajun and Creole dishes.

Visitor Information: Hawaii Visitors & Convention Bureau, 2270 Kalakaua Avenue, Suite 801, Honolulu, HI 96815; telephone (808)923-1811; toll-free (800)GO HAWAII (464-2924); fax (808)923-0293.

Convention Facilities

Honolulu's principal meeting facility is the beautiful four-story Hawaii Convention Center, which offers a 200,000-square-foot ground floor exhibition hall; a second floor exclusively for parking with 700 parking stalls; a third floor with 107,426 square feet of meeting room space that can be configured into 47 meeting rooms; and a grand ballroom and rooftop garden on the fourth floor. Inside, a $2 million Hawaiian art collection with paintings of volcanoes, moun-

tains, ocean, waterfalls, taro, and fishponds are displayed alongside images of Hawaiian royalty, gods, and myths; above, soaring rooftop canopies recall images of Polynesian sailing canoes. The building is open to the outdoors and sits on landscaped grounds featuring terraces, lanais, and courtyards that occupy more than six acres of the 10-acre site.

Convention Information: Hawaii Visitors & Convention Bureau, 2270 Kalakaua Avenue, Suite 801, Honolulu, HI 96815; telephone (808)923-1811; fax (808)923-0293

Transportation

Approaching the City

Isolated from the mainland, Honolulu is reached primarily by plane. Honolulu International Airport, a major center for Pacific air travel, is served by 31 domestic and foreign airlines as well as inter-island carriers. Hawaii's Department of Transportation is arranging for the airport to undergo a terminal modernization project. Honolulu may also be reached by ship; cruise lines sail regularly between Honolulu and SanFrancisco.

Traveling in the City

Because of the irregular shape of the city, Honolulu residents define directions according to landmarks such as the mountains and the sea rather than standard compass orientations.

TheBus, owned by the City and County of Honolulu but operated separately, provides public transportation to the entire island on a fleet on 525 buses. Oahu Transit Service also has a fleet of 100 buses equipped to transport people with disabilities. The Waikiki Trolley Service, with a fleet of 50 trolleys, provides transportation to shopping centers, museums, and other points of interest.

Communications

Newspapers and Magazines

Honolulu's daily newspapers are *The Honolulu Advertiser* and the *Honolulu Star-Bulletin*. There are also several non-English papers serving Honolulu. *Honolulu Magazine* features topics and events of local interest. Among the nearly 50 periodicals published in Honolulu are *Bamboo Ridge, The Hawaii Writers' Quarterly,* a literary magazine;*Biography,* a journal acting as a forum for learned articles dealing with life-writing; *Building Management Hawaii* and *China Review International.* Business publications include*Hawaii Business*and *Pacific Business News.*

Television and Radio

Eleven commercial television stations and one public station broadcast from Honolulu; cable service is also available. Thirty-five FM and AM radio stations broadcast in Honolulu; several offer multilingual programming.

Media Information: The Honolulu Advertiser, telephone (808)525-8090; fax (808)525-8037. *Honolulu Star-Bulletin,* telephone (808)529-4747; fax (808)529-4750

Honolulu Online

Chamber of Commerce of Hawaii. Available www.coc hawaii.com

City and County of Honolulu. Available www.co.honolulu .hi.us

Hawaii Department of Education. Available www.doe.k12 .hi.us

Hawaii Department of Labor and Industrial Relations. Available www.hawaii.gov/labor

Hawaii Visitors and Convention Bureau. Available www .gohawaii.com

Honolulu Advertiser. Available www.honoluluadvertiser .com

Honolulu Star-Bulletin. Available www.starbulletin.com

Oahu Visitors Bureau. Available www.visit-oahu.com

Social and economic trends. Available www.Hawaii.gov/ dbedt

State of Hawaii. Available www.hawaii.gov

Selected Bibliography

Cowing, Sue, ed., *Fire in the Sea: An Anthology of Poetry and Art* (Honolulu: University of Hawaii Press in association with the Honolulu Academy of Arts, 1996)

Penisten, John, *Honolulu* (Minneapolis, MN: Dillon Press, 1989)

Twain, Mark, *Letters from Honolulu* (Honolulu: T. Nickerson, 1939)

Tyau, Kathleen, *A Little Too Much Is Enough* (New York: Norton, 1995)

IDAHO

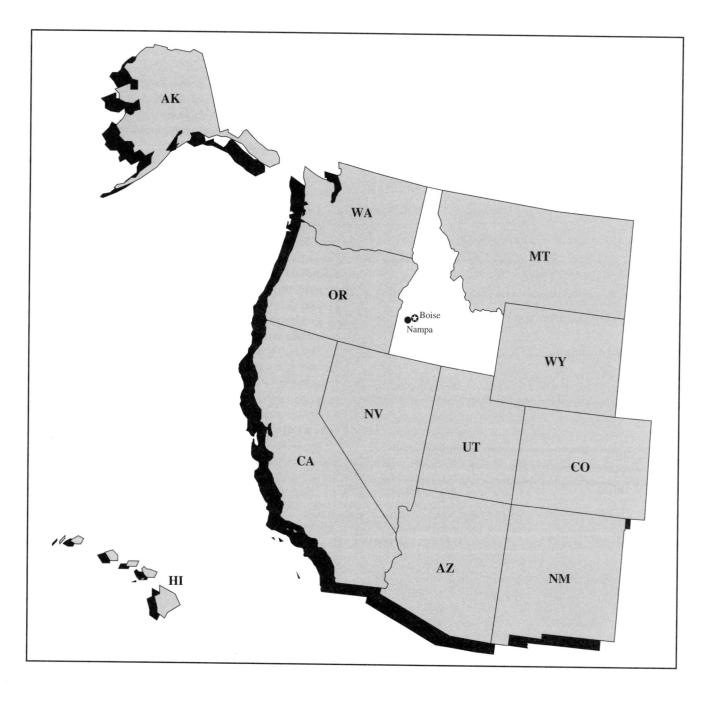

The State in Brief

Nickname: Gem State
Motto: *Esto perpetua* (Let it be perpetual)

Flower: Syringa
Bird: Mountain bluebird

Area: 83,570 square miles (2000; U.S. rank: 14th)
Elevation: Ranges from 710 feet to 12,662 feet above sea level
Climate: Tempered by Pacific westerly winds, varying by altitude; hot summers in the arid south, cold snowy winters in the central and northern mountains

Admitted to Union: July 3, 1890
Capital: Boise
Head Official: Governor Dirk Kempthorne (R) (until 2007)

Population
    1980: 944,000
    1990: 1,006,749
    2000: 1,293,953
    2004 estimate: 1,393,262
    Percent change, 1990–2000: 28.5%
    U.S. rank in 2004: 39th
    Percent of residents born in state: 47.2% (2000)
    Density: 15.6 people per square mile (2000)
    2002 FBI Crime Index Total: 42,547

Racial and Ethnic Characteristics (2000)
    White: 1,177,304
    Black or African American: 5,456
    American Indian and Alaska Native: 17,645
    Asian: 11,889
    Native Hawaiian and Pacific Islander: 1,308
    Hispanic or Latino (may be of any race): 101,690
    Other: 54,742

Age Characteristics (2000)
    Population under 5 years old: 97,643
    Population 5 to 19 years old: 316,222
    Percent of population 65 years and over: 11.3%
    Median age: 33.2 years (2000)

Vital Statistics
    Total number of births (2003): 21,823
    Total number of deaths (2003): 10,466 (infant deaths, 158)
    AIDS cases reported through 2003: 274

Economy
    Major industries: Mining, lumbering, agriculture, high technology, tourism
    Unemployment rate: 4.1% (February 2005)
    Per capita income: $25,583 (2003; U.S. rank: 46th)
    Median household income: $40,230 (3-year average, 2001-2003)
    Percentage of persons below poverty level: 11.8% (1999)
    Income tax rate: Ranges from 1.6% to 7.8%
    Sales tax rate: 6.0%

Boise

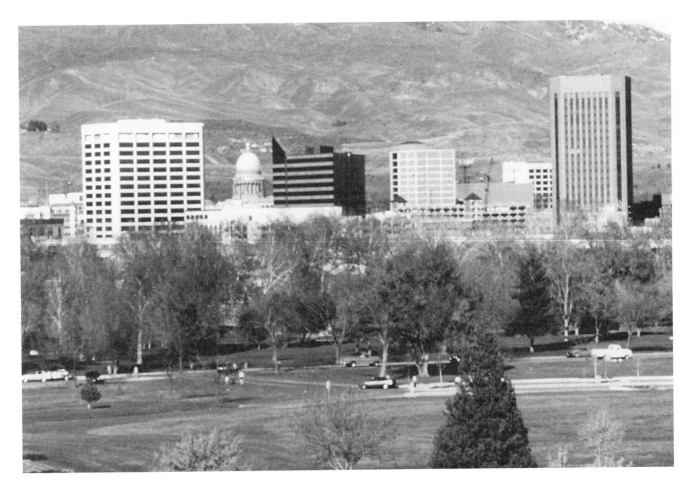

The City in Brief

Founded: 1834 (incorporated, 1864)

Head Official: Mayor David H. Bieter (D) (since 2004)

City Population
　1980: 102,451
　1990: 126,685
　2000: 185,787
　2003 estimate: 190,117
　Percent change, 1990–2000: 37.5%
　U.S. rank in 1980: 162nd
　U.S. rank in 1990: 145th
　U.S. rank in 2000: 105th

Metropolitan Area Population
　1980: 256,881
　1990: 295,851
　2000: 464,840
　Percent change, 1990–2000: 45.4%
　U.S. rank in 1980: Not reported
　U.S. rank in 2000: 97th

Area: 63.8 square miles (2000)
Elevation: 2,842 feet above sea level
Average Annual Precipitation: 12.11 inches of rain, 20.9 inches of snow

Major Economic Sectors: Services, agriculture, government, manufacturing, high-technology
Unemployment Rate: 4.4% (February 2005)
Per Capita Income: $22,696 (1999)

2002 FBI Crime Index Total: 8,748

Major Colleges and Universities: Boise State University, University of Idaho-Boise Center

Daily Newspaper: *The Idaho Statesman*

Introduction

Boise, the capital of Idaho and the largest city in the state, is the commercial, financial, and cultural center of the northern Rockies region. Known as the ''City of Trees,'' Boise is among the fastest-growing metropolitan areas in the nation. At the same time, the city has maintained a high quality of life through cooperation between business, government, and citizens. An easy blending of historic structures and modern buildings in the downtown district attests to the fact that Boise remains close to its Western heritage while moving with the times. Noted for its mild climate, clean environment, and friendly people, Boise is set in a fertile agricultural area called ''Treasure Valley.''

Geography and Climate

Boise is situated in a wide river valley at the foot of the Rocky Mountains. The Boise River runs out of a canyon to the south and through the center of the city, joining the Snake River about 40 miles to the north. The climate is tempered year-round by air from the Pacific Ocean. Summers are dry with hot periods that rarely last more than a few days; autumn weather is usually ideal. Winter storms produce much of the yearly precipitation; cold spells are common, but warm Chinook winds (moist air from the Pacific) bring periods of mild weather. Low humidity is raised slightly by agricultural irrigation.

Area: 63.8 square miles (2000)

Elevation: 2,842 feet above sea level

Average Temperatures: January, 29.9° F; August, 72.2° F; annual average (mean): 50.9° F

Average Annual Precipitation: 12.11 inches of rain, 20.9 inches of snow

History

Gold Brings Prospectors, Settlers

In 1834 the Hudson's Bay Company founded a trading post for wagon trains along the Oregon Trail on the Snake River northwest of Boise's present site. The region that is now Boise was originally a small forested area along the Boise River, an oasis in the arid northwestern mountains. The spot was called ''Les Bois,'' which means ''wooded'' in French, and thou-sands of emigrants passed through on their way to settle in Oregon. Gold was discovered in the area in 1862, bringing a number of prospectors, and the site became a convenient supply point for the mining camps in the mountains.

The U.S. Army constructed Fort Boise in 1863, and the town became the territorial capital in 1864, when it was also incorporated as a city. Several more gold strikes occurred in the next few years, and by1868 the town had more than four hundred permanent structures, more than half of which were residential. The Idaho Penitentiary was built in the town in 1870 and at one time or another housed many legendary western desperadoes.

Gold Dries Up; Irrigation Systems Bring Farms

After the gold boom ended, the population declined, and Boise faced an uphill battle for survival. The town was in an isolated location, far off the major lines of transportation, and the climate was too dry to support farming. A determined core of citizens set out to make the area livable by developing irrigation systems, planting crops, and mapping out a town with shady streets running along the river.

Boise approached the twentieth century as a remote place, reachable only by the difficult wagon trails. The city became the state capital when Idaho entered the Union, and the Capitol building was erected in 1920. A long struggle to obtain railway service finally succeeded when the elegant Union Pacific Depot (now the Boise Depot) was built in 1925. A number of dams and reservoirs were constructed in the years before World War II to improve the agricultural outlook and provide a water supply and hydroelectric power for the growing city.

During World War II the military became a strong presence in the Boise area when a flying and training base was established at Gowen Field. In the 1960s, a new city charter was drawn up, allowing the city to annex many of the suburban areas and doubling the population. The 21st century has brought continuing population growth due to Boise's desirable climate, urban renewal, job opportunities, quality of life, and favorable climate.

Historical Information: Idaho State Historical Society Library, Library and Archives Building, 450 North Fourth Street, Boise, ID 83702; telephone (208)334-3356; fax (208)334- 3198; email archivist rhouse@ishs.state.id.us

Population Profile

Metropolitan Area Residents
1980: 256,881

1990: 295,851
2000: 464,840
Percent change, 1990–2000: 45.4%
U.S. rank in 1980: Not reported
U.S. rank in 1990: Not reported
U.S. rank in 2000: 97th

City Residents

1980: 102,451
1990: 125,685
2000: 185,787
2003 estimate: 190,117
Percent change, 1990–2000: 37.5%
U.S. rank in 1980: 162nd
U.S. rank in 1990: 145th (State rank: 1st)
U.S. rank in 2000: 105th (State rank: 1st)

Density: 2,913.1 people per square mile (2000)

Racial and ethnic characteristics (2000)
  White: 171,204
  Black or African American: 1,437
  American Indian and Alaska Native: 1,300
  Asian: 3,870
  Native Hawaiian or other Pacific Islander: 302
  Hispanic origin (may be of any race): 8,410
  Other: 3,241

Percent of residents born in state: 43.2% (2000)

Age characteristics (2000)
  Population under 5 years old: 13,116
  Population 5 to 9 years old: 12,933
  Population 10 to 14 years old: 13,029
  Population 15 to 19 years old: 13,860
  Population 20 to 24 years old: 15,920
  Population 25 to 34 years old: 30,194
  Population 35 to 44 years old: 29,837
  Population 45 to 54 years old: 25,321
  Population 55 to 59 years old: 7,618
  Population 60 to 64 years old: 5,347
  Population 65 to 74 years old: 8,830
  Population 75 to 84 years old: 7,085
  Population 85 years and over: 2,697
  Median age: 32.8 years

Births (2002, Ada County)
  Total number: 4,939

Deaths (2002, Ada County)
  Total number: 1,881 (of which 32 were infants under
    the age of 1 year)

Money income (1999)
  Per capita income: $22,696
  Median household income: $42,432
  Total households: 74,609

Number of households with income of . . .
  less than $10,000: 4,934
  $10,000 to $14,999: 4,072
  $15,000 to $24,999: 10,405
  $25,000 to $34,999: 10,351
  $35,000 to $49,999: 13,439
  $50,000 to $74,999: 15,537
  $75,000 to $99,999: 7,759
  $100,000 to $149,999: 5,313
  $150,000 to $199,999: 1,328
  $200,000 or more: 1,471

Percent of families below poverty level: 5.9% (41.8% of
  which were female householder families with related
  children under 5)

2002 FBI Crime Index Total: 8,748

Municipal Government

Boise has been led by a mayor-council form of government
since the adoption of a new city charter in 1961. The council
is comprised of six part-time members, elected to four-year
terms. A full-time mayor is elected every four years.

Head Official: Mayor David H. Bieter (D) (since 2004;
  current term expires 2008)

Total Number of City Employees: 1,507 (2005)

City Information: City of Boise, PO Box 500, Boise, ID
83701; telephone (208)384-4422; fax (208)384-4420; email
mayor&council@cityofboise.org

Economy

Major Industries and Commercial Activity

Boise began as a supply and service center for the mining
camps in the nearby mountains. It continues today as an
important commercial hub for smaller towns and agricultural establishments in the northern Rockies. In addition to
mining, farming and timber have played important roles in
the development of the Boise economy.

The present economy has shifted away from its traditional
sources towards a more diversified base. State government
is one of the city's main employers, since Boise is the capital
of Idaho. Boise ranks sixth in the nation for the number of
corporate headquarters located in the city (in relation to its
population base); corporate headquarters in the city include

Albertson's, a supermarket chain; Boise Cascade wood and paper products; Morrison Knudsen, an engineering and construction firm; the J.R. Simplot Company with frozen foods, phosphates, and cattle; Micron Technology, which manufactures semiconductors; TJ International, with specialty building products; and Washington Group International. Several other major companies are headquartered or have major facilities in the area. Tourism is another large source of revenue for the Boise area. High technology industries are becoming an increasingly important sector, and the Army National Guard's Gowen Field also has an economic impact.

Incentive Programs—New and Existing Companies

Local programs—Boise State University provides various services for the business community through its Idaho Business and Economic Development Center, Boise Future Foundation, Center for Management Development, Simplot/Micron Instructional Technology Center, Small Business Development Center, and the College of Technology.

State programs—The state of Idaho encourages business development through low taxes, reasonable rates, and tax incentives such as job creation and investment credits and tax exemptions.

Job training programs—Several training schools are located in the Boise area.

Development Projects

Boise is working on three major ongoing urban renewal projects. The oldest project, called the Central renewal project, is focused on downtown Boise's core and has resulted in the vibrant downtown Boise visitors and residents see today. Ongoing funding of the Central project is planned for use in additional infrastructure, beautification and public arts projects. The River/Myrtle renewal project, also underway, is located south of downtown Boise. With a focus on attracting high-tech tenants, this urban renewal project is developing a technical infrastructure. The Westside renewal project encompasses 47 acres of downtown Boise. Renewal plans encompass a 25-year span with completion of all projects in 2025. The Westside project will bring multi-use development to downtown, including office, residential, retail, restaurants, entertainment venues, and hotels.

Economic Development Information: Boise Metro Area Economic Development Council (Shirl Boyce), 250 S. 5th St., Suite 800, Boise, ID 83702; telephone (208)472-5230, email sboyce@boisechamber.org

Commercial Shipping

A Grant Thornton *General Manufacturing Climates* study ranked Idaho the best state in the nation for transportation because of its infrastructure and strategic location in the

Pacific Northwest. Rail freight carriers serve the Boise metropolitan area via the Union Pacific Railroad. A variety of motor freight lines, air freight, package express companies, and air courier services are also part of Boise's commercial transportation industry.

Labor Force and Employment.

Boise's skilled work force is educated above the national average and it remains diverse because of a high percentage of immigration. Thirty-three percent of residents have a bachelor's degree or higher; the Boise metro area was ranked the seventh best place to do business in the nation by *Forbes* magazine in 2004.

The following is a summary of data regarding the Boise-Nampa metropolitan area labor force, 2004 annual averages.

Size of non-agricultural labor force: 241,600

Number of workers employed in . . .
  construction and mining: 17,100
  manufacturing: 29,500
  trade, transportation and utilities: 45,800
  financial services: 12,900
  information: 4,200
  professional and business services: 34,700
  educational and health services: 29,700
  leisure and hospitality: 21,500
  other services: 6,900
  government: 38,800

Average hourly earnings of production workers employed in manufacturing (statewide): $13.72

Unemployment rate: 4.4% (February 2005)

Largest private employers	*Number of employees*
Micron Technology, Inc.	9,500
St. Luke's Medical Center	4,250
Hewlett-Packard Company	4,000
Albertson's, Inc. (retail food chain)	3,800
J.R. Simplot	3,800

Cost of Living

Boise boasts rates for residential, commercial, and industrial electricity and natural gas that are among the lowest in the country.

The following is a summary of data regarding key cost of living factors for the Boise area.

2004 (4th Quarter) ACCRA Average House Price: Not reported

2004 (4th Quarter) ACCRA Cost of Living Index: Not reported (U.S. average = 100.0)

State income tax rate: Ranges from 2.0% to 8.2%

State sales tax rate: 5.0%

Local income tax rate: None

Local sales tax rate: 5%

Property tax rate: average 1.7% in 2004; ranges from 1 to 2.7%

Economic Information: Idaho Department of Commerce, 700 West State Street, PO Box 83720, Boise, ID 83720-0093; telephone (208)334-2470; toll-free (800)842-5858; fax (208)334-2631. Boise Metro Chamber of Commerce, 250 South 5th Street, Boise, ID 83702; telephone (208)472-5200; fax (208)472-5201; email info@boisechamber.org

Education and Research

Elementary and Secondary Schools

The Independent School District of Boise City #1 is the city's public elementary and secondary school system. The largest district in the state, it is administered by a seven-member, nonpartisan board of trustees that appoints a superintendent. In 2004 the Boise School District received the Gold Medal Award presented by *Expansion Management Magazine*. Factors weighed included graduation rates and college board scores; the community's financial commitment to its children's education; student-teacher ratios, per-pupil expenditures and teachers salaries; and level of affluence and adult education in the district. The ranking places the Boise School District in the upper 16 percent of all districts nationwide; Boise is the only district with this award in the state of Idaho. The Boise School District boasts highly educated teachers, fifty percent of whom have masters—more than double the state average.

The following is a summary of data regarding the Independent School District of Boise City #1 as of the 2001-2002 school year.

Total enrollment: 25,883

Number of facilities
  elementary schools: 34
  junior high schools: 8
  senior high schools: 5
  other: 2

Student/teacher ratio: elementary: 23.25:1; middle: 22.13:1; senior: 22.1:1

Teacher salaries
  minimum: $27,501
  maximum: $60,744

Funding per pupil: Not available

There are 22 private and parochial schools with a total enrollment of nearly about 3,100 students in the Boise area.

Public Schools Information: Boise School District Public Information Specialist, 8169 W. Victory Rd., Boise ID 83709; telephone (208)338-3400; fax (208)338-3487

Colleges and Universities

Boise State University is the largest institution of higher learning in the state, with an enrollment of about 18,500 students. The university offers more than 190 programs, including an accredited Master's degree program in business administration, a construction management program, and an engineering program. The Simplot/Micron Technology Center, located on the university campus, has formed a partnership with the public and private sectors, designed to develop and present effective training programs. The facility contains state-of-the-art computer systems and video and audio production studios. Students in Boise may earn bachelors', masters', and doctoral degrees in civil, electrical, and mechanical engineering from the University of Idaho while attending classes on the Boise State campus, where the College of Technology has been in operation since 1990. Boise State University and the Boise community began planning for a community college in 2004; the campus will be dispersed through the city and serve diverse populations. The metropolitan area is also served by three private colleges: Albertson College of Idaho in Caldwell, Northwest Nazarene University in Nampa, and Boise Bible College.

Libraries and Research Centers

The Boise Public Library serves the greater Boise area with a collection of more than 355,000 volumes, as well as newspapers and magazines, government documents, videos, CDs, cassette tapes, Kidpacks, books on tape, computer software, CD-ROM indexes, and microfilm. A branch is located at Boise Towne Square Mall and a bookmobile and personal delivery of materials to the homebound are available. The Idaho State Library contains more than 36,000 volumes; it also operates an extensive blind and physically handicapped service, providing more than 58,000 talking books as well as more than 5,000 large-print books. Boise State University's library holds more than 530,000 books and more than 6,000 newspaper and serial subscriptions. A number of smaller private, corporate, and special interest libraries are also located in the Boise metropolitan area. Research activities in such fields as technology, audio and video production, computers, and data processing are conducted at centers in the Boise area.

Public Library Information: Boise Public Library, 715 South Capitol Boulevard, Boise, ID 83702-7115; telephone (208)384-4076

Health Care

The Boise medical community offers 6 hospitals, 750 licensed physicians, and more than 1,200 hospital beds. The major hospitals in Boise are Saint Alphonsus Regional Medical Center, an acute-care facility featuring a regional trauma center; and Saint Luke's Regional Medical Center. St Luke's was the recipient of the Consumer Chose Award for excellence, designating it as Idaho's preferred hospital; the hospital provides general treatment, specialty care, and surgical services, as well as neonatal and pediatric intensive care. The newest facility is the 29 million dollar Idaho Elks Rehabilitation Hospital (opened in 2001), which specializes in rehabilitation services in the areas of audiology, brain injury, cardiopulmonary, orthopedics, pediatrics and stroke/neurology. The Veterans Administration Medical Center, a teaching hospital affiliated with the University of Washington School of Medicine, offers general care, and outpatient, mental health, and substance abuse clinics. Also located in Boise are Treasure Valley Hospital for patients needing surgery, Mountain States Tumor Institute, and 11 nursing homes.

Recreation

Sightseeing

The best way to see Boise is on the popular Tour Train, a replica of an 1890s steam-powered locomotive that originates in Julia Davis Park and takes an hour-long trip through the city's historic neighborhoods and the central business district. Other attractions in the park include Zoo Boise, the Memorial Rose Garden, and an outdoor bandshell where summer concerts are performed.

The downtown area contains several historic points of interest. The Idaho State Capitol, erected in 1920, is a smaller version of the Capitol building in Washington, D.C., and is the only statehouse in America heated by natural geothermal energy. At the other end of Capitol Boulevard is the Boise Depot, constructed in 1925 and modeled after a Spanish mission. The station is surrounded by the beautiful Platt Gardens. Other historic sites in Boise include the Old Boise district and the Eighth Street Marketplace, two restored neighborhoods. The O'Farrell Cabin, the first structure built in Boise, is located in Military Reserve Park. The area surrounding Boise offers many attractions, including restored wild west towns like Idaho City and the Snake River Birds of Prey area. Other pleasurable activities are scenic mountain and canyon drives and tours of the local vineyards in Idaho's wine country.

Arts and Culture

The Morrison Center for the Performing Arts, a 2,030-seat facility located on the Boise State University campus, is the site of much of the city's cultural activity. The center hosts performances by the Boise Philharmonic Orchestra and Ballet Idaho as well as special events that range from rock concerts to touring Broadway productions. The city holds an annual Shakespearean festival, and several area theatrical groups perform throughout the year. Among them are the Boise Little Theater, the Idaho Theater for Youth, and the Stage Coach Theater.

The city is home to a number of museums and art galleries. The Idaho Historical Museum, located in Julia Davis Park, is a unique open-air museum that features an Old West saloon, a blacksmith's shop, and western and native American artifacts. The restored Idaho State Penitentiary (called the "Old Pen") now houses several museums, including the Idaho Transportation Museum and the Electricity Museum. The Idaho Black History Museum recently relocated from the former penitentiary to St. Paul Baptist Church in Julia Davis park; exhibits relate the importance of the African American culture to the heritage of Idaho and the nation. The Boise Art Museum, also in Julia Davis Park, contains a permanent collection of regional and national art; it also hosts a number of traveling exhibits each year. The Idaho Botanical Garden, featuring a variety of themed gardens, is adjacent to the "Old Pen." Other art galleries in the city include the Art Attack Gallery, Brown's Galleries, Gallery 601, and the Art Source Gallery.

Festivals and Holidays

A number of special events are scheduled in the Boise area throughout the year. Spring is celebrated with the Apple Blossom Festival; seven days of festivities include a rodeo, parade, carnival, festival, and crowning of the Apple Blossom Queen. The National Old Time Fiddlers' Contest takes place for seven days each June in nearby Weiser, Idaho, one hour northwest of Boise. The Boise River Festival, held the last full Thursday through Sunday in June, is a popular event. Summer also brings the Spirit of Boise Balloon Classic in late June; the Idaho Shakespeare Festival, featuring Shakespeare under the Stars; and the Western Idaho Fair, an old fashioned country fair that lasts for 10 days in August. Boise's Basque population, the largest concentration in North America, presents three days of cultural activities every July, including performances by the famous Oinkari Basque Dancers. Oktoberfest at the Idaho Botanical Garden includes music, dance, food and beverage.

Sports for the Spectator

The Boise Hawks, members of the Northwest League and affiliated with the Chicago Cubs, play baseball from mid-June through early September at Memorial Stadium. The

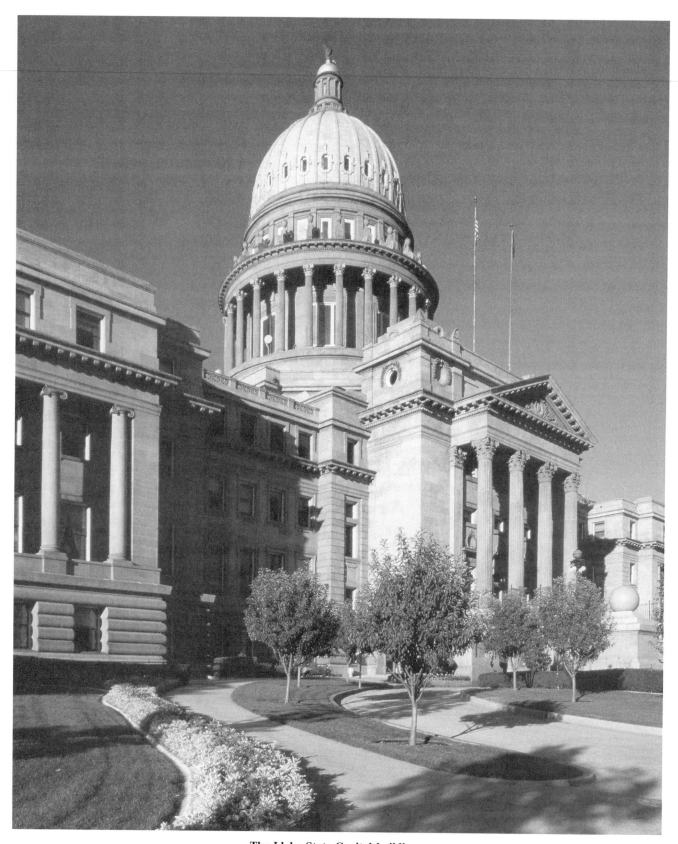

The Idaho State Capitol building.

Hawks won their sixth Northwest League Championship in 2004. The Idaho Sneakers, the state's only major league franchise, offer World TeamTennis action at Bank of America Centre, also the site for hockey action from the Idaho Steelheads of the East Coast Hockey League. In the community of Nampa, about 20 miles from Boise, basketball fans flock to watch the Idaho Stampede of the Continental Basketball Association.

A complete program of collegiate sports is offered at Boise State University, featuring a championship football team and a nationally recognized basketball team. Thoroughbred and harness racing, along with parimutuel wagering, are featured at Les Bois Race Track. Championship drag racing is held at Firebird Raceway. Fans of rodeo enjoy the famous Snake River Stampede in Nampa and the Caldwell Night Rodeo in Caldwell. Meridian Speedway offers drag racing and stock car racing. In women's sports action, there is the annual St. Luke's Women's Fitness Celebration, a run/walk event that ranks among the largest of its kind in the nation. The Nike Boise Open golf tournament is part of the PGA Tour.

Sports for the Participant

Boise offers an abundance of outdoor activities. The area's 91 parks feature facilities for boating, tennis, golf, swimming, jogging, cycling, and other recreational activities. The Boise River, which runs through downtown Boise, is a popular spot for tubing, canoeing, and fishing; 16 acres on both sides of the river form the Boise River Greenbelt offering 25 miles of paved and graveled paths. Many area reservoirs offer a full range of water activities. Both day and night skiing can be enjoyed at Bogus Basin, a 45-minute drive from downtown Boise; five other ski areas are within a three-hour drive. The nearby mountains are favorite hiking, fishing, and camping locations, while the nearby Payette and Salmon Rivers are known worldwide by kayakers and rafters for their exciting white water.

Shopping and Dining

Old Boise and the Eighth Street Marketplace, two distinctive historical districts in Boise, have been converted into unique shopping areas. The Hyde Park district features a number of antique shops, and State Street marketplace is a group of specialty shops in a modern complex. Several shopping malls are open in the area, including Boise Towne Square, which offers more than 175 stores, and the Boise Factory Outlet Mall.

Dining opportunities in Boise are diverse and usually inexpensive. Cuisines range from simple yet filling Western fare to exotic international specialties such as Basque, Mexican, Chinese, Indian, Egyptian, and Vietnamese. Several elegant dining places feature French, Continental, and New American dishes.

Visitor Information: Boise Convention and Visitors Bureau, PO Box 2106, Boise, ID 83701; telephone (208)344-7777; toll-free (800)635-5240; fax (208)344-6236; email info@boisechamber.org

Convention Facilities

The Boise Center on the Grove offers a total of 50,000 square feet of meeting space, and features a glass-fronted 8,500-square-foot lobby; a 7,000-square-foot auditorium that will seat more than 300 people; and a 25,000-square-foot central meeting space. About 1,000 hotel rooms are within walking distance of the Boise Center. Other facilities include Boise State University's Taco Bell Arena, which seats up to 13,000 spectators and has 17,472 square feet of open floor space. The Morrison Center for the Performing Arts, also on the Boise State campus, has a 2,000 seat main hall and two teaching/studying halls. The Nampa Civic Center in nearby Nampa offers banquet seating for up to 1,200 people, a 648-seat auditorium and more than 42,000 square feet of convention space. There are more than 4,600 hotel rooms in Boise; most of the major hotels provide meeting, banquet, and ballroom facilities.

Convention Information: Boise Convention and Visitors Bureau, PO Box 2106, Boise, ID 83701; telephone (208)344-7777; toll-free (800)635-5240; fax (208)344-6236; email info@boisechamber.org

Transportation

Approaching the City

The Boise Air Terminal, located a few miles south of downtown, is served by 12 major national and regional airlines with 90 daily departures and 88 arrivals.

Two major highways lead into Boise. I-84 runs east and west, connecting the metropolitan area with the West Coast and the midwestern states. U.S. 20/26 runs diagonally west to southeast through the center of the city.

Traveling in the City

Streets south of the Boise River tend to form a grid pattern; north of the river, streets follow the contours of the foothills of the Rocky Mountains and the streams that flow through town.

ValleyRide provides bus service on fixed routes as well as Access services for people with disabilities.

Communications

Newspapers and Magazines

Boise is served by one daily newspaper, *The Idaho Statesman,* and two weekly papers. Locally-published magazines focus on religion, families, wildlife, farming, and sheep and cattle growing.

Television and Radio

Two commercial television stations and one cable network broadcast from Boise. Nineteen AM and FM radio stations serve the Boise area with a diverse blend of music, news, and information.

Media Information: *The Idaho Statesman,* 1200 North Curtis Road, PO Box 40, Boise, ID 83706; email pcarson @boise.gannett.com

Boise Online

Boise Area Chamber home page. Available www.boise.org

Boise Convention & Visitors Bureau home page. Available www.boise.org

Boise Public Library home page. Available www.ci.boise.id .us./library

Boise School District home page. Available www.sd01.k12 .id.us

City of Boise home page. Available www.ci.boise.id.us

Idaho Data Center home page. Available www.cl.idaho.gov/ portal

Idaho State Library home page. Availablwww.lili.org

The Idaho Statesman home page. Available www.idaho statesman.com

Nampa

The City in Brief

Founded: 1891

Head Official: Mayor Tom Dale (since 2002)

City Population
  1990: 28,365
  2000: 51,867
  2003 estimate: 64,269
  Percent change, 1990–2000: 73.5%
  U.S. rank in 2000: 688th (State rank: 2nd)

Metropolitan Area Population
  1990: 295,851
  2000: 432,345
  Percent change, 1990–2000: 46.1%
  U.S. rank in 2000: 96th

Area: 20 square miles (2000)
Elevation: Average 2,492 feet above sea level
Average Annual Temperature: 64.4° F
Average Annual Precipitation: 11.7 inches of rain; 21.4 inches of snow

Major Economic Sectors: agriculture, manufacturing, education, health care
Unemployment Rate: 4.4% (February 2005)
Per Capita Income: $14,491 (1999)
2004 ACCRA Average House Price: Not reported
2004 ACCRA Cost of Living Index: Not reported

2002 FBI Crime Index Total: 2,871

Major Colleges and Universities: Northwest Nazarene University, Boise State University, Albertson College of Idaho

Daily Newspaper: *Idaho Press Tribune*

Introduction

Nampa, the second-largest city in Idaho, was established in the late 1800s as a result of the completion of the Oregon Short Line railroad. Although the origins of the name Nampa are unknown, it is believed to be a Shoshoni Indian word meaning "moccasin," or "footprint." Once highly dependent on agricultural production, the city's economy has become more diverse and now also relies on manufacturing. Nampa boasts a mild climate, excellent parks and recreation, and proximity to Idaho's state capital, Boise. Northwest Nazarene University is located in Nampa, and the Snake River Stampede, one of the nation's top ten rodeos, is held every year in July. With nearly 50 percent population growth between 1990 and 2000, Nampa continues to thrive as it grows and diversifies.

Geography and Climate

Located in the heart of Idaho's Treasure Valley, or "Banana Belt," Nampa enjoys a mild climate year-round. Its high desert location is bordered to the north by the Front Range of the Rocky Mountains and to the south by the Owyhee Mountains. Nampa enjoys warm summers with an average temperature of 92° F, but the low humidity makes for a pleasant environment. Winter lows average 20.2° F. Nampa's winters are mild, with minimal snowfall. Blizzards are rare, and snow that does fall rarely stays on the ground for more than a few days. Nampa's climate is ideal for the production of agricultural goods, which make up a substantial part of the region's economy. Nampa is located just 16 miles from Boise, Idaho's state capital.

Area: 20 square miles (2000)

Elevation: 2,492 feet above sea level

Average Temperatures: January, 20.2° F; July, 92.0° F; annual average, 64.4° F

Average Annual Precipitation: 11.7 inches of rain; 21.4 inches of snow

History

Nampa's Early Years

Although Native American tribes had settled in Idaho for hundreds of years, little human settlement occurred in the area that is now Nampa until the late 1800s. Settlement in

Nampa began in 1883, a direct result of the completion of the Oregon Short Line Railroad. At that time, Caldwell resident James A. McGee and businessman Alexander Duffes decided to invest in the development of this new town. Duffes filed a claim under the Idaho Homestead Act, and in 1886 McGee and Duffes formed the Nampa Land and Improvement Company and filed the town's articles of incorporation. Initially, the Short Line bypassed Nampa, but due to increased traffic it soon became necessary to provide a connecting line between the Oregon Short Line and Boise. The Idaho Central Railway was built to make that connection, and Nampa was a stop along the way.

Nampa was incorporated in 1891. Population and business development continued to grow into the 1890s, mainly a result of irrigation made possible by the Phyllis Canal, but in 1894 Duffes mortgaged Nampa's unsold lots in an attempt to boost the slowing economy. The loan source defaulted and the town spiraled into debt. In 1896, Colonel W.H. Dewey paid the debt and received 2,000 deeds to town lots. He was crucial to the continued development of Nampa, as he began a survey of a route for the Boise, Nampa, Owyhee Railway that eventually linked Boise with the mining towns of the Owyhee Valley.

A Modern City Emerges

As the 20th century began, the Western Idaho Sugar Company and the Crescent Brewing Company were both established in Nampa. These companies utilized local farmers and created jobs at their processing plants. But a business decline was followed by a fire in 1909, which caused the destruction of more than 60 stores in downtown Nampa. By the 1920s, however, Nampa had once again established itself as a stable community. The Northwest Nazarene School, now Northwest Nazarene University, was established in 1913 by Eugene Emerson. During World War I, Nampa's farming community benefited from high crop prices. However, when the bottom of the market fell out after the war was over, many farmers were bankrupted. The economy was revived in 1942, when the Amalgamated Sugar Company opened a sugar beet plant in Nampa, which spurred farm productivity.

In 1949, the Nampa Industrial Corporation (NIC) was formed to encourage other economic development beyond farming. By the 1970s the NIC's investment in land and facility improvements had resulted in a more diverse economy, having encouraged new businesses and industries to locate in Nampa.

Today, Nampa has grown to become Idaho's second-largest city, boasting a thriving economy and excellent quality of life.

Historical Information: Canyon County Historical Museum, 1200 Front Street, Nampa, ID 83653; telephone (208)467-7611

Population Profile

Metropolitan Area Residents
1990: 295,851
2000: 432,345
Percent change, 1990–2000: 46.1%
U.S. rank in 2000: 96th

City Residents
1990: 28,365
2000: 51,876
2003 estimate: 64,269
Percent change, 1990–2000: 73.5%
U.S. rank in 2000: 688th

Density: 2,612 people per square mile (2000)

Racial and ethnic characteristics (2000)
  White: 43,281
  Black or African American: 206
  American Indian and Alaska Native: 490
  Asian: 484
  Native Hawaiian and Pacific Islander: 92
  Hispanic or Latino (may be of any race): 9,282
  Other: 5,833

Percent of residents born in state: 46.1% (2000)

Age characteristics (2000)
  Population under 5 years old: 5,465
  Population 5 to 9 years old: 4,651
  Population 10 to 14 years old: 3,800
  Population 15 to 19 years old: 3,849
  Population 20 to 24 years old: 4,797
  Population 25 to 34 years old: 9,112
  Population 35 to 44 years old: 6,606
  Population 45 to 54 years old: 4,747
  Population 55 to 59 years old: 1,723
  Population 60 to 64 years old: 1,324
  Population 65 to 74 years old: 2,574
  Population 75 to 84 years old: 12,282
  Population 85 years and older: 937
  Median age: 28.5 years

Births (2002, Canyon County)
  Total number: 2,901

Deaths (2002, Canyon County)
  Total number: 971 (of which, 18 were infants under
    the age of 1 year)

Money income (1999)
  Per capita income: $14,491
  Median household income: $34,758
  Total households: 18,270

Number of households with income of . . .
  less than $10,000: 1,713
  $10,000 to $14,999: 1,327
  $15,000 to $24,999: 3,015
  $25,000 to $34,999: 3,141
  $35,000 to $49,999: 4,022
  $50,000 to $74,999: 3,333
  $75,000 to $99,999: 1,123
  $100,000 to $149,999: 435
  $150,000 to $199,999: 86
  $200,000 or more: 75

Percent of families below poverty level: 8.7% (33.2% of
  which were female householder families with related
  children under 5 years)

2002 FBI Crime Index Total: 2,871

Municipal Government

Nampa operates under a mayor-council form of government. The mayor is elected at large every four years; the four council members serve staggered four year terms.

Head Official: Tom Dale (since 2002; current term expires 2006)

Total Number of City Employees: 635 (2005)

City Information: City Hall, 411 3rd Street South, Nampa, ID 83651; telephone (208)465-2200

Economy

Major Industries and Commercial Activity

Historically, Nampa has been known as a strong agricultural base. Canyon County produces more than 90 percent of the world's sweet corn seed, and is also a leader in the production of livestock, dairy, and alfalfa. Located in the heart of Idaho's wine country, Nampa also produces its share of grapes. Vineyards in Nampa and surrounding areas grow Cabernet Sauvignon, Cabernet Franc, Roussanne, Pinot Gris, Merlot, and Syrah varietals. The climate, geography, and location along the Snake River make for ideal growing conditions. Nampa also has a strong manufacturing base, with furniture, boxes, wood products, and computer chips as some of the goods produced. Nampa has benefited from the technology boom: computer equipment manufacturer MCMS is headquartered in Nampa. It is among the city's top employers. Education continues to be a major source of employment in Nampa, with Nampa School District 131 and higher education institutes Northwest Nazarene University and Boise State University's Canyon County Center providing jobs for more than 1,200 people.

Items and goods produced: sweet corn, livestock, alfalfa, dairy products, grapes, computer equipment, cardboard boxes, and furniture

Incentive Programs—New and Existing Companies

Local programs—In recent years, Nampa has experienced rapid economic growth and development. Several companies make their headquarters in Nampa, and many national retailers have opened outlets in Nampa, attracted by Nampa's explosive population growth and pro-business environment. Several entities have been established to encourage business growth and development. The Nampa Industrial Corporation was formed in 1949 to create business opportunities in Nampa through the investment in and development of industrial property. The NIC also assists with community initiatives. The Chamber of Commerce supports local businesses by providing services such as monthly luncheons, small business consultations, networking opportunities, marketing ideas, and sponsorship opportunities for its members. The Boise Metro Economic Development Council (BMEDC) serves the Boise-Nampa area with the goals of creating long-term jobs and encouraging economic development in the community. The BMEDC provides free, customized services to businesses relocating, expanding, or establishing themselves in the Boise Metro Area.

State programs—Idaho is an aggressive pro-business state. The Idaho Department of Commerce and Labor provides services to business owners to assist them in starting, relocating, running, and closing a business. The state offers several incentives to business owners, including a three percent income tax credit to qualifying new investments. A five percent research and development tax credit is offered for qualified research performed in Idaho. The state also offers 100 percent tax exemptions on property tax, and 100 percent sales tax exemption on goods in transit, pollution control equipment, industrial fuels and raw materials, and production equipment and materials used to produce goods. Reimbursements and credits are available for employee training and the creation of new jobs.

Job training programs—The Boise State University Selland College of Applied Technology provides apprenticeship and job training programs to students who are enrolled in the college's Apprenticeship Programs offered by the Center for Workforce Training. Students receive on-the-job training while working as full-time, paid employees. Students also receive classroom training related to their chosen profession. The Center for Workforce Training offers career training programs for adults as well as programs to help businesses increase their productivity. In addition to training in the classroom, the Center offers online training programs and courses.

Development Projects

As Idaho's second-largest city, Nampa continues to attract new business development. In 2004 home improvement retailer Home Depot opened a 102,000 square-foot store in Nampa. In early 2004 Costco announced plans to build a retail center adjacent to the new Karcher Interchange off of Interstate 84. The warehouse club will be one of two anchors of a new, 600,000 square-foot retail development, which will be the only retail center on the I-84 interchange.

In early 2005 the Nampa Industrial Corporation gave a $1,132,000 gift to Boise State University to help construct the Center for Construction and Transportation Technology on the BSU West campus in Nampa. The technical building will train students for careers and spur workforce development in fields such as automotive repair, welding, plumbing, and automotive and diesel technology.

Economic Development Information: Idaho Commerce and Labor, 317 West Main Street, Boise, ID 83735; telephone (208)332-3570; fax (208)334-6300. Center for Workforce Training, Selland College of Applied Technology, Boise State University, 1464 University Drive, Technical Services Building, Boise, ID 83706; toll-free (800)632-6586; fax (208)426-4487.

Commercial Shipping

Nampa is served by the Union Pacific Railroad and 14 commercial truck lines that transport goods produced in Nampa throughout the country. Air freight is handled at Nampa Municipal Airport.

Labor Force and Employment Outlook

Nampa's economy has become less dependent on agriculture as it has become a center for business and manufacturing. However, Nampa has recently suffered a loss of jobs in the manufacturing sector due to the closing of several local plants.

The following is a summary of data regarding the Boise-Nampa metropolitan area labor force, 2004 annual averages.

Size of nonagricultural labor force: 241,600

Number of workers employed in . . .
   construction and mining: 17,100
   manufacturing: 29,500
   trade, transportation and utilities: 45,800
   information: 4,200
   financial activities: 12,900
   professional and business services: 34,700

educational and health services: 29,700
leisure and hospitality: 21,500
other services: 6,900
government: 38,800

Average hourly earnings of production workers employed in manufacturing (statewide): $13.72

Unemployment rate: 4.4% (February 2005)

Largest employers	Number of employees
Nampa School District 131	1,300
MCMS	1,000
Mercy Medical Center	650
Amalgamated Sugar	500
Nestle's Brand Food Service Co.	350
Woodgrain Millwork, Inc.	340
Pacific Press Publishing	280
Home Style Industries	275
Northwest Nazarene College	210

Cost of Living

Nampa's cost of living, as well as its housing prices, are slightly below the national average.

The following is a summary of data regarding several key cost of living factors for the Nampa area.

2004 ACCRA Average House Price: Not reported

2004 ACCRA Cost of Living Index: Not reported

State income tax rate: 1.6% to 7.8%

State sales tax rate: 6.0%

Local income tax rate: 1.00% (occupational)

Local sales tax rate: none

Property tax rate: 2.209% (2004)

Economic Information: Nampa Chamber of Commerce, 1305 3rd Street South, Nampa, ID 83651; telephone (208)466-4641. Boise Metro Economic Development Council, 250 South 5th Street, Boise, ID 83702; telephone (208)472-5230.

Education and Research

Elementary and Secondary Schools

Nampa School District 131 (NSD) is the third largest school district in the state of Idaho. More than 13,000 students attend the district's elementary, middle, and high schools, as well as two alternative high schools. A growing district, NSD has a

new elementary school under construction with a fall 2005 opening date, and a new high school scheduled to open in 2006. Nampa School District offers special education and gifted programs to help meet the needs of its student population.

The following is a summary of data regarding Nampa School District 131 2004–2005 school year.

Total enrollment: 13,183

Number of facilities
elementary schools: 12
middle schools: 3
senior high schools: 2
alternative high schools: 2

Student/teacher ratio: 19.02:1 (2003-2004)

Teacher salaries (2004-2005)
minimum: $25,000
maximum: $47,688

Funding per pupil (2002): $5,820

Nampa Christian Schools and St. Paul's Catholic School are private schools that offer religious-based educations.

Public Schools Information: Nampa School District 131, 619 S. Canyon, Nampa, ID 83686; telephone (208)468-4600; fax (208)468-4638

Colleges and Universities

Four institutions of higher learning serve the Nampa area, including Northwest Nazarene College and Boise State University Selland College of Applied Technology, both located in Nampa. Boise State University is located in Boise, and Albertson College is in nearby Caldwell. Northwest Nazarene University is a four-year, private Christian liberal arts university offering undergraduate and graduate degrees in such fields as arts, humanities, science, theology, and education. Boise State University is a public university that offers undergraduate, graduate, and technical programs. Courses are offered in eight colleges: applied technology, arts and sciences, business and economics, education, engineering, graduate studies, health sciences, and social sciences and public affairs. In 2004 the University conferred 2,850 degrees. On campus Residential Colleges, based on the Oxford system, is the University's housing program; residential students are assigned to residence halls and dormitories based on common interests or fields of study. The Boise State University Selland College of Applied Technology, one of Boise State University's eight colleges, operates a campus at the Canyon County Center in Nampa. The college offers degree and certificate programs; it is the only public technical college in southwest Idaho. The University is currently planning to expand its community college program, which will include a Nampa campus. Albertson College, in Caldwell, is another private liberal arts university with a total of 26 majors.

Libraries and Research Centers

The Nampa Public Library serves the Nampa community; non-residents may obtain a library card and utilize the library's resources for an annual fee. Nampa Public Library card holders are allowed to borrow materials from six other area consortium libraries, including the Boise Public Library. The consortium has a collection of more than 500,000 books, videos, sound recordings, and other materials. In addition to a wide selection of current books, magazines, and media materials, the library has computer terminals with Internet access available for patron use. Patrons may also access the library's database via its Internet website. The Northwest Nazarene University Riley Library is open to students and faculty, as well as members of the Nampa community. Materials at Albertsons Library at Boise State University are available to students, faculty, and staff, as well as "special borrowers" who meet certain criteria.

A variety of research centers, particularly associated with the universities, exist in Nampa and conduct research in the fields of biology and agriculture, among others.

Public Library Information: Nampa Public Library, 101 Eleventh Avenue South, Nampa, ID 83651; telephone (208)468-5800

Health Care

Mercy Medical Center, the only hospital within Nampa city limits, is a private hospital affiliated with the Catholic church. Founded in 1917 by the Sisters of Mercy, the hospital has grown to include two medical campuses in Nampa. The hospital provides emergency services and a 14-bed emergency room, as well as outpatient and hospice services; cancer care, maternity care, surgery, and interventional cardiology services are among the hospital's specialties. In recent years, Mercy Medical has invested in state of the art technology and equipment, including the Galileo computerized system for orthopedic surgery.

Recreation

Sightseeing

Visitors to Nampa enjoy a wealth of activities and recreational opportunities. Museums that celebrate Nampa's heritage, year-round outdoor activities, and a variety of shopping and dining experiences help make Nampa a great place to work and live.

Nampa museums celebrate the history of Nampa, Canyon County, and the United States. One of Nampa's newest museums is the Warhawk Air Museum, a 20,000 square foot facility dedicated to preserving the country's World War II history from the home front to the war front, as well as to trace the history of flight from the advent of aviation through the space age. Its collection includes two of the few remaining Curtiss P-40 World War II fighter airplanes and a rare World War II P-510 razorback Mustang fighter plane. The museum also hosts traveling NASA space exhibits, and often hosts special events and ceremonies to honor veterans and commemorate World War II events.

The Canyon County Historical Museum, located in Canyon County's original train depot, displays both Canyon County and Union Pacific Railroad memorabilia. An authentic 1940s era caboose and model railroad are among the exhibits in the building that has been called "Idaho's finest example of Baroque architecture." A farmer's market is held outside the museum on Saturdays during the months of May through October.

At the Swiss Village Cheese Factory, visitors can watch cheese being made. The Van Slyke Agricultural Museum, located in Caldwell Memorial Park, is an open-air museum that features log cabin replicas and antique farm equipment. Visitors to the Deer Flat National Wildlife Refuge at Lake Lowell enjoy swimming, fishing, hunting, boating, and bird watching on more than 11,000 acres of land.

Arts and Culture

With several state of the art exhibit and performance facilities, Nampa is becoming known for its arts scene. The Brandt Center at Northwest Nazarene University is a performing arts center that attracts musical and dramatic performances attended by both students and the community at large. Its Samuel Swayne theatre can accommodate up to 1,500 people, and two guest suites accommodate up to 15 guests each for private viewings and receptions. The Brandt Center's Friesen Art Galleries provide gallery space for Northwest Nazarene University's art students to exhibit their work.

The Caldwell-Nampa Alliance of Community Theatre (CAN-ACT) was established in 1981 and is the Nampa area's only community theatre group outside of Boise. The not-for-profit troupe performs comedies, dramas, and musicals in the CAN-ACT Theater located in the Karcher Mall. Auditions for CAN-ACT's four yearly plays are open to community members.

In 2003 the Majestic Entertainment Foundation, Inc. was formed to refurbish downtown Nampa's historic Pix

Theatre, which was closed in 2002. Upon completion the theatre will be used for the viewing of films and lectures, religious services, educational programs, and community events.

Festivals and Holidays

Parade America, Idaho's largest patriotic parade, is held in May. Each July, the Snake River Dayz Festival is held in conjunction with the Snake River Stampede rodeo. The week-long festival features concerts, a fun run, a golf tournament, the Taste of Canyon County, a fun zone for children, and the Chamber of Commerce Griddles and Fiddles pancake breakfast. At the same time, Downtown Nampa Stampede Dayz features live music, pony rides, and craft and food booths. Nampa Community Fun Night is held in late August or early September and includes games for children, music, and food. America's Most Apeelin' Spud Fest is held in October. The event includes music, food, games, and fun runs.

Sports for the Spectator

Although Nampa has no professional sports teams, Boise State University's indoor track team competes at Nampa's Idaho Center. The state-of-the-art track facility has also been used for other prestigious events such as the USA Masters Indoor Track and Field Championships and the Western Athletic Conference Indoor Championships. Sports fans can also take in collegiate-level sports played by Northwest Nazarene University's teams, including baseball and softball, basketball, cross county, track and field, men's golf, and women's volleyball.

The Snake River Stampede, held annually in July, is ranked among the country's top 10 professional rodeos. The arena at the Idaho Center seats up to 10,000 people who take in bull riding, barrel racing, mutton busting (for children), bareback riding, steer wrestling, and roping events.

Sports for the Participant

Nampa residents enjoy a wealth of outdoor activities year-round. Seven city parks cover more than 127 acres. Available facilities include play areas, covered picnic shelters, baseball and softball fields, tennis courts, archery ranges, Little League fields, swimming pools, basketball courts, and a BMX track. A 140,000 square foot recreation center provides residents with a climbing wall, basketball courts, an indoor track, five swimming pools, activity rooms, and a senior center.

Nampa has two public golf courses and one private golf course. Ridgecrest Golf Course, Nampa's newest public course, has received a four-star rating from *Golf Digest* magazine. Runners can participate in 5K and 10K fun runs during July's Snake River Dayz festivities.

Shopping and Dining

Nampa retailers range from national chains to locally owned specialty stores, ensuring something for everyone. Karcher Mall's tenants include Bon-Macy's, Radio Shack, Sam Goody, and Big 5 Sporting Goods. Mass retailers such as ShopKo, Old Navy, and Wal-Mart can be found in the Meridian Crossroads development. Downtown Nampa is home to many unique retailers, including antique, book, jewelry, and flower stores. The Boise Factory Outlet is just a short drive away, and includes outlet stores for companies such as Reebok and Eddie Bauer.

Nampa diners enjoy a variety of restaurants, from national chains to local establishments. The family-owned Generations restaurant offers steak and seafood, with their French dip sandwich among the more popular menu items. Copper Canyon is an upscale eatery known for its elegant presentation and extensive wine list. Asian restaurant House of Kim, located in downtown Nampa, serves Chinese, Thai, and Malaysian cuisine. The Dutch Inn, known for its salad bar, also serves breakfast, lunch, and dinner entrees. The Mona Lisa is a fondue restaurant that has found its niche as a special occasion restaurant. Cheese fondue appetizers and chocolate dessert fondues are part of a meal package that allows diners to cook their own main courses at pots on their table. Other area eateries include chains such as Applebee's, Denny's, Sizzler, and various fast food establishments.

Visitor Information: Nampa Chamber of Commerce, 1305 Third Street South, Nampa, ID 83651; telephone (208)466-4641.

Convention Facilities

The Nampa Civic Center is Idaho's second largest full-service convention and performing arts center. With 42,500 square feet of space, the Civic Center hosts more than 750 events each year. Meetings, conventions, banquets, receptions, trade shows, and performing arts programs are among the events hosted there. Up to 14 separate meeting spaces can accommodate groups of up to 1,000. In addition to the 30,000 square feet of meeting space, the Civic Center boasts a 12,200 square foot exhibit area and a 640 seat theatre.

The Idaho Center Complex is comprised of four venues: an amphitheatre, an arena, the Idaho Horse Park, and the Idaho Sports Center. The arena can accommodate up to 6,000 people, and the amphitheatre seats 11,000 people. Events such as concerts, basketball games, and ice shows, as well as trade shows and conventions, are held at the Idaho Center. The Idaho Horse Park, opened in 2002, consists of indoor and outdoor arenas, an English riding facility, warm-up pens, stalls, and stock pens. The Idaho Sports Center Complex is the newest addition to the Idaho Center. The 100,000 square foot multi-purpose building is the indoor track facility for Boise State University and is home to the only Mondo 200-meter banked track west of Nebraska.

Convention Information: Nampa Civic Center, 311 Third Street South, Nampa, ID 83651; telephone (208)468-5500. Idaho Center, 16200 Can-Ada Road, Nampa, ID 83687; telephone (208)468-1000.

Transportation

Approaching the City

The nearby Boise City Airport provides air service to 23 U.S. cities. Twelve commercial airlines operate daily flights out of the airport. By car, Nampa is accessible via Interstate 84. Greyhound provides bus service to Nampa.

Traveling in the City

Nampa is accessible from Interstate 84 via three interchanges and is relatively easy to navigate. Highway 45 extends through downtown Nampa toward the Snake River and Owyhee County. Roads in downtown Nampa are numbered, with avenues running north-south and streets running east-west. ValleyRide provides public transportation services for the Treasure Valley. Although ValleyRide provides transit service throughout Boise, they also provide fixed-line and door-to-door bus service in Nampa and Caldwell. The Ada County Highway District offers a commuters bus from Caldwell to Boise that stops in Nampa. The Treasure Valley Metro provides commuter service between Nampa, Meridian, and Boise during peak commute times.

Communications

Newspapers and Magazines

The Idaho Press-Tribune is published in Nampa and serves the Canyon County market. Published daily in the morning, the paper also maintains an Internet presence on its website.

Television and Radio

Nampa has two commercial television stations and one radio station broadcasting within city limits; the city also receives programming from nearby Boise.

Media Information: Idaho Press-Tribune, 1618 North Midland Boulevard, Nampa, ID 83651; telephone (205)967-9241.

Nampa Online

Boise Metro Economic Development Council. Available www.boisechamber.org/ec_dev/bmedc.htm

Boise State University Canyon County Center. Available www.boisestate.edu/extendedstudies/othersites/canyon countyctr.html

City of Nampa Home Page. Available www.ci.nampa.id.us

Idaho Center. Available www.idahocenter.com

Idaho Commerce and Labor. Available www.cl.idaho.gov

Idaho Department of Commerce. Available www.idaho works.com

Idaho Press-Tribune. Available www.idahopress.com

Nampa Chamber of Commerce. Available www.nampa.com

Nampa Public Library. Available www.lili.org/nampa

Nampa Public Schools. Available www.sd131.k12.id.us

Northwest Nazarene University. Available www.nnu.edu

MONTANA

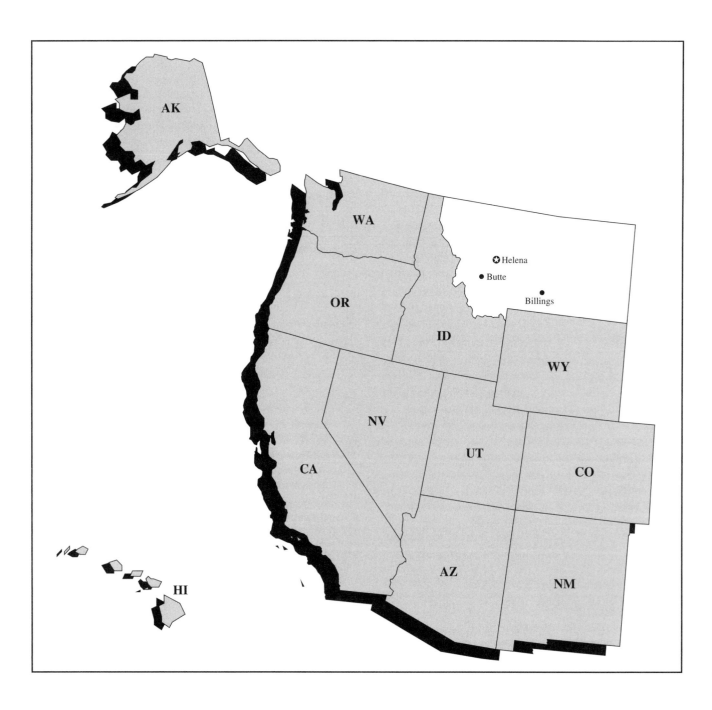

The State in Brief

Nickname: Treasure State
Motto: *Oro y plata* (Gold and silver)

Flower: Bitterroot
Bird: Western meadowlark

Area: 147,042 square miles (2000; U.S. rank: 4th)
Elevation: Ranges from 1,800 feet to 12,799 feet above sea level
Climate: Continental; heavy snows in the west, hot dry summers in the east

Admitted to Union: November 8, 1889
Capital: Helena
Head Official: Governor Brian Schweitzer (D) (until 2009)

Population
    1980: 786,690
    1990: 799,065
    2000: 902,195
    2004 estimate: 926,865
    Percent change, 1990–2000: 12.9%
    U.S. rank in 2004: 44th
    Percent of residents born in state: 56.1% (2000)
    Density: 6.2 people per square mile (2000)
    2002 FBI Crime Index Total: 31,948

Racial and Ethnic Characteristics (2000)
    White: 817,229
    Black or African American: 2,692
    American Indian and Alaska Native: 56,068
    Asian: 4,691
    Native Hawaiian and Pacific Islander: 470
    Hispanic or Latino (may be of any race): 18,081
    Other: 5,315

Age Characteristics (2000)
    Population under 5 years old: 54,869
    Population 5 to 19 years old: 202,571
    Percent of population 65 years and over: 13.4%
    Median age: 37.5 years (2000)

Vital Statistics
    Total number of births (2003): 11,421
    Total number of deaths (2003): 8,280 (infant deaths, 79)
    AIDS cases reported through 2003: 175

Economy
    Major industries: Services, trade, government, agriculture
    Unemployment rate: 4.5% (February 2005)
    Per capita income: $25,775 (2003; U.S. rank: 45th)
    Median household income: $34,375 (3-year average, 2001-2003)
    Percentage of persons below poverty level: 14.6% (1999)
    Income tax rate: Ranges from 2.0% to 11.0%
    Sales tax rate: None

Billings

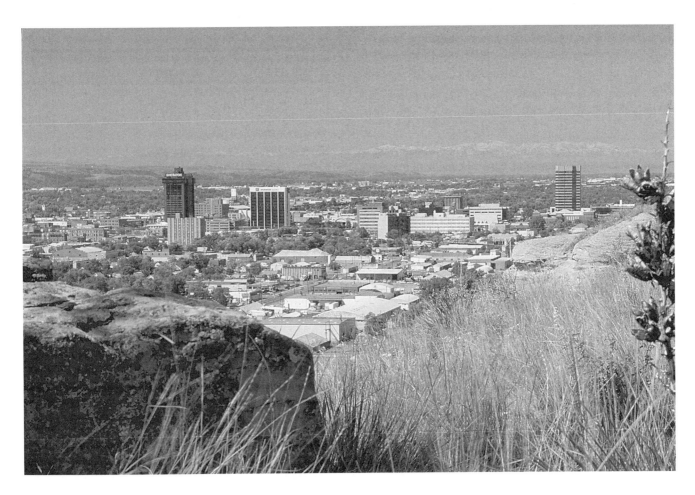

The City in Brief

Founded: 1882 (incorporated, 1885)

Head Official: Mayor Charles F. Tooley (D) (since 1995)

City Population
  1980: 66,798
  1990: 81,125
  2000: 89,847
  2003 estimate: 95,220
  Percent change, 1990–2000: 10.7%
  U.S. rank in 1980: 294th
  U.S. rank in 1990: 263rd
  U.S. rank in 2000: 307th

Metropolitan Area Population
  1980: 108,035
  1990: 113,419
  2000: 129,352
  Percent change, 1990–2000: 14.0%
  U.S. rank in 2000: 221st

Area: 33.82 square miles (2000)
Elevation: 3,126 feet above sea level
Average Annual Temperature: 49.2° F
Average Annual Precipitation: 13.65 inches

Major Economic Sectors: Agriculture, services, government, finance, oil and gas
Unemployment Rate: 4.1% (February 2005)
Per Capita Income: $19,207 (1999)

2002 FBI Crime Index Total: 4,486

Major Colleges and Universities: Montana State University-Billings, Rocky Mountain College

Daily Newspaper: *The Billings Gazette*

TO CUSTER BATTLEFIED

YELLOWSTONE

Billings

MT

WY

CO

ID

UT

WA

OR

NV

CA

BITTEROOT

METRAPARK

HISTORIC DEPOT

WESTERN HERITAGE CENTER

RIVERSIDE

LAKE ELMO

CHIEF BLACK OTTER TRAIL

1ST AVE. S.

1ST AVE. N.

JACKSON

L A K E   E L M O

WICKS

MONTANA STATE UNIVERSITY–BILLINGS

6TH AVE. N.

COURTHOUSE

33RD ST.

JACKSON

KING

STATE

ORCHARD

GOVERNORS

27TH ST.

ST. VINCENT HOSPITAL

DEACONESS BILLINGS CLINIC

DIVISION

S. BILLINGS

YELLOWSTONE COUNTY HISTORICAL MUSEUM

5TH ST. W.

CALHOUN

LOGAN INT'L AIRPORT

6TH ST. W.

MOORE

ROCKY MOUNTAIN COLLEGE

RIMROCK

POLY

GRAND

15TH ST. W.

CENTRAL

MONAD

MONTANA

17TH ST. W.

24TH ST. W.

RIMROCK MALL

ZOO MONTANA

SHILOH

KILOMETERS

MILES

N

TO BOZEMAN, YELLOWSTONE NATIONAL PARK

Introduction

Billings is the largest city in Montana and the commercial, cultural, and industrial center of a large region of the northern Rocky Mountains. Known as the "Magic City," Billings has grown phenomenally since its founding in 1882, until 1970 doubling in size every 30 years. The city is also the processing and distribution hub for a rich agricultural area that encompasses more than 125,000 miles. Excellent road, rail, and air transportation networks helped the region's retail trade to reach $1.9 billion in 2000. Many scenic attractions such as Yellowstone National Park are nearby, and the wide variety of available recreation activities make the Billings area a popular vacation spot.

Geography and Climate

Billings is located in southern Montana in the fertile Yellowstone River valley, with mountains on three sides. The Yellowstone River flows along the eastern boundary of the city. The mountains shelter the city from the most severe winter weather, but blizzard conditions are not uncommon in the spring and fall. Moist air from the Pacific Ocean, called "Chinook winds," often brings surprisingly warm weather in the winter and cooler temperatures in the summer. Spring features the most unpredictable weather, and summers are typically dry with cool nights.

Area: 33.82 square miles (2000)

Elevation: 3,126 feet above sea level

Average Temperatures: January, 22.8° F; August, 72.5° F; annual average, 49.2° F

Average Annual Precipitation: 13.65 inches

History

Native Americans Resist Settlement

For thousands of years before the coming of European settlers, the site of present-day Billings was hunted by migratory peoples. Traces of their camps and elaborate cave drawings have been discovered and preserved at many sites in the region. By the time of America's westward expansion, the predominant tribes in the area included the Crow, Sioux, and Cheyenne.

The Lewis and Clark Expedition of 1806 passed through the present site of Billings, and just 30 miles away William Clark climbed Pompey's Pillar, a 200-foot-high natural rock formation, which he named after the son of his female Indian guide. Although many Europeans explored the area, fierce resistance from the natives prevented any settlement. This led to the so-called "Sioux War," one of the more intense struggles between the U.S. Army and the native people. The infamous Battle of the Little Bighorn, where a large group of Sioux and Cheyenne warriors killed General George Custer and his entire 7th cavalry, took place 65 miles to the southeast of the future site of Billings.

Railroad Brings Ranchers, Farmers

Billings was founded in 1882 by the Northern Pacific Railroad as a rail head for the company's western line and named for the president of the railroad, Frederick Billings. Over the next six months more than 2,000 people settled in the town, which was incorporated as a city in 1885. The wide-open prairie lands were ideal for cattle grazing, and a number of large ranches grew up around the town. During the early twentieth century, families of settlers known as "homesteaders" arrived in the area, taking advantage of the offer of free land. Typically, a family and all its possessions would arrive in one freight car and receive a 40-acre plot of land. Conditions were difficult, but many families struggled through their first years and eventually developed successful farms.

Irrigation had been introduced in the Yellowstone Valley in 1879. Sugar beet growing was thus made possible, and a sugar refinery was built in 1906. Immigrant laborers came to work the fields—first Japanese, then Russo-Germans, and finally Mexicans. The Russo-German workers were unusually industrious; soon they bought their own land at the Huntley Irrigation project outside Billings, where they constituted a third of the population by 1940.

Abundant Natural Resources Contribute to Growth

Billings grew steadily during the 1900s, spurred on by the development of vast natural resources such as minerals, coal, natural gas, and oil. At one time Billings was the largest inland wool shipping point in the United States. In 1933 pulp-drying equipment was installed at the sugar refinery; a thriving livestock industry developed around animals fed on beet pulp. By 1938 more than 600,000 acres of land around Billings was irrigated.

A true hub city and gateway to the West, Billings has become the commercial, health care, and cultural capital of the "Midland Empire," a vast area of agricultural, mountainous, wilderness, and sometimes forbidding terrain that includes eastern Montana, the western Dakotas, and Northern Wyoming. It is also an important refining and shipping center for agricultural and energy products.

Historical Information: Montana State University-Billings Library, 1500 North Thirtieth Street, Billings, MT 59101-0298; telephone (406)657-1662

Population Profile

Metropolitan Area Residents

1980: 108,035
1990: 113,419
2000: 129,352
Percent change, 1990–2000: 14.0%
U.S. rank in 2000: 221st

City Residents

1980: 66,798
1990: 81,125
2000: 89,847
2003 estimate: 95,220
Percent change, 1990–2000: 10.7%
U.S. rank in 1980: 294th
U.S. rank in 1990: 263rd
U.S. rank in 2000: 307th

Density: 2,656 people per square mile (2000)

Racial and ethnic characteristics (2000)
  White: 82,539
  Black or African American: 495
  American Indian and Alaska Native: 3,088
  Asian: 533
  Native Hawaiian and Other Pacific Islander: 38
  Hispanic or Latino (may be of any race): 3,758
  Other: 1,300

Percent of residents born in state: 57.2% (2000)

Age characteristics (2000)
  Population under 5 years old: 5,882
  Population 5 to 9 years old: 5,985
  Population 10 to 14 years old: 6,063
  Population 15 to 19 years old: 6,290
  Population 20 to 24 years old: 6,483
  Population 25 to 34 years old: 11,869
  Population 35 to 44 years old: 13,882
  Population 45 to 54 years old: 12,284
  Population 55 to 59 years old: 4,330
  Population 60 to 64 years old: 3,440
  Population 65 to 74 years old: 6,464
  Population 75 to 84 years old: 4,969
  Population 85 years and over: 1,906
  Median age: 36.8 years

Births (2002, Yellowstone County)
  Total number: 1,790

Deaths (2002, Yellowstone County)
  Total number: 1,167 (of which 7 were infants under the age of one year)

Money income (1999)
  Per capita income: $19,207
  Median household income: $35,147
  Total households: 37,470

Number of households with income of . . .
  less than $10,000: 3,686
  $10,000 to $14,999: 3,642
  $15,000 to $24,999: 5,823
  $25,000 to $34,999: 5,512
  $35,000 to $49,999: 6,677
  $50,000 to $74,999: 7,029
  $75,000 to $99,999: 2,641
  $100,000 to $149,999: 1,518
  $150,000 to $199,999: 437
  $200,000 or more: 505

Percent of families below poverty level: 9.2% (57.4% of which were female householder families with related children under 5 years)

2002 FBI Crime Index Total: 4,486

Municipal Government

Billings has a mayor-council form of government with ten council members elected to a four-year term. Until the 1995 election the mayor was elected to a two-year term; the mayor now serves a four-year term. The mayor and city council are the city's only policy-making bodies. A city administrator is hired by the mayor and city council and may be removed by a simple majority vote of the mayor and council. Billings is also the seat of Yellowstone County.

Head Official: Mayor Charles F. Tooley (D) (since 1995; current term expires 2007)

Total Number of City Employees: 750 (2005)

City Information: City of Billings, 210 North 27th Street, PO Box 1178, Billings, MT 59103; telephone (406)657-8200; email ctooley@magiccity.org

Economy

Major Industries and Commercial Activity

Agriculture has been one of the leading economic forces in Billings since its founding, and it continues to play a major role today. Because of extensive irrigation, the Yellowstone Valley and the northern Great Plains are some of the nation's most fertile agricultural regions. The city is the transportation, processing, and packaging center for this large, productive area. The main agricultural products include sugar beets, grain, and livestock such as cattle and sheep.

The energy industry (oil, natural gas, and coal) is also an important part of the economic picture in Billings. The mountains around the city and throughout eastern Montana are a rich source of coal, oil, and natural gas. A number of refineries and purification plants are located in the Billings area to process the raw materials into usable energy resources.

Billings is the retail and wholesale trade center for a vast area of land in the northern Rocky Mountain states and a primary and secondary market population of almost half a million people, reaching from Denver, Colorado, to Calgary, Alberta, and from Minneapolis, Minnesota, to Seattle, Washington. Billings is also the medical and educational capital of the region. The city's medical community, including two major hospitals and more than 40 clinics, provides the most advanced health care in the four-state area. Three major colleges and a highly-rated public school system provide jobs and a well-trained workforce. It is also difficult to underestimate the impact of tourism and recreational diversity on the area's economy. The proximity of nearby Yellowstone National Park, as well as a wide array of other wilderness territories, mountain trails, rivers, and streams in the area bring much-needed tourist dollars and act as a magnet to companies and workers looking to relocate.

Items and goods produced: raw and refined energy products, sugar, flour, farm machinery, electric signs, furniture, paint, metal ornaments, cereal, creamery and meat products, canned vegetables, concrete, sugar beets, wheat, beans, livestock

Incentive Programs—New and Existing Companies

Local programs—The Billings Small Business Development Center (SBDC) is part of a statewide network of resource and technical service providers that assist start-up and existing businesses. The SBDC staff provides confidential business counseling, training and information to small business leaders and entrepreneurs. Services are provided at no charge and are funded by the Small Business Administration, Montana Department of Commerce, Yellowstone County, and local organizations. Areas of assistance include technical assistance in writing business plans for new and existing businesses, financial analysis, planning and state and private capital sources; assistance with marketing research, analysis and strategy as well as advertising, packaging and promotion; business plan review and critique; preBusiness workshops; and one-on-one counseling for existing and start-up business management. Additionally, the Business Development Council of the Chamber of Commerce maintains a comprehensive inventory of local and state programs. It also helps identify location alternatives, provides technical assistance, and maintains current information on Billings and its trade area.

State programs—State of Montana tax incentives include property tax reduction; no inventory, use, or sales tax; new industry income tax credits; small business investment tax credit; and tax reduction on pollution control equipment.

Development Projects

In 2004 renovations were completed on the historic Acme Hotel on North Broadway. Built in 1911 and rich with local history, the hotel was converted to residential homes, lofts, and commercial space in an area that included several more loft developments from refurbished buildings such as the Securities Building, Montana Avenue Lofts, and a proposed development at One South Broadway. Recent additions to the city's cultural and commercial growth include the $6 million Skyfest Amphitheatre, which presents outdoor concerts alongside the Yellowstone River, a $6.2 Yellowstone Art Museum expansion, and the conversion of several former hotels that were once stops on the Northern Pacific Railroad into coffee shops, antique stores, and restaurants.

Economic Development Information: Billings Area Chamber of Commerce, 815 South 27th Street, PO Box 31177, Billings, MT 59107-1177; telephone (406)245-4111; toll-free (800)711-2630; fax (406)245-7333; email blgscvb @visitmt.com

Commercial Shipping

Via Billings Logan International Airport a number of carriers provide air freight and express mail service to the city. Burlington Northern Railroad and Montana Rail Link operate rail lines from the Billings area. Burlington Northern also operates an intermodal (surface, sea, and air transportation) hub in Billings.

Labor Force and Employment Outlook

The Billings-area work force is educated above the national average, and a 2004 study found that one in four workers was overqualified for the jobs they were performing, creating an excellent climate for technical and higher-wage businesses looking to relocate to the area. The Billings area economy is service-based which includes specialized manufacturing, processing, and professional services to support the region's rural agricultural and energy economies. Billings serves as the regional hub for medical services, higher education, professional business services, retail and distribution, and travel and lodging.

The following is a summary of data regarding the Billings metropolitan area labor force, 2004 annual averages.

Size of non-agricultural labor force: 73,300

Number of workers employed in . . .
   trade, transportation, and utilities: 19,400
   professional and business services: 8,500
   educational and health services: 11,200
   leisure and hospitality: 9,700
   government: 9,800

Average hourly earnings of production workers employed in manufacturing: $14.87 (Montana average, 2004)

Unemployment rate: 4.1% (February 2005)

Largest county employers (2000)	*Number of employees*
Federal Government	2,480
Deaconess Billings Clinic	2,250
Billings School District #2	2,030
St. Vincent Hospital and Health Center	1,740
State of Montana	1,490
City of Billings	850
Better Business Systems	675
Yellowstone County	660
Wells Fargo Bank	615
First Interstate Bank	480

Cost of Living

The following is a summary of data regarding key cost of living factors for the Billings area.

2004 (3rd Quarter) ACCRA Average House Price: $227,500

2004 (3rd Quarter) ACCRA Cost of Living Index: 98.3 (U.S. average = 100.0)

State income tax rate: Ranges from 2.0% to 11.0%

State sales tax rate: None

Local income tax rate: None

Local sales tax rate: None

Property tax rate: 3.22% per $150,000 of assessed value

Economic Information: Billings Area Chamber of Commerce, 815 South 27th Street, PO Box 31177, Billings, MT

59107-1177; telephone (406)245-4111; fax (406)245-7333. Office of Research & Analysis, Montana Department of Labor & Industry, PO Box 1728, Helena, MT 59624; telephone (406)444-2430; fax (406)444-2638 or (800)633-0229 (within Montana) or (800)541-3904 (outside Montana); email questions4RAD@state.mt.us

Education and Research

Elementary and Secondary Schools

The Billings Public Schools District is governed by a nine-member School Board, which appoints a superintendent. With more than 15,000 students, it is the largest district in Montana. The district oversees 21 elementary schools, four middle schools, three high schools, two ninth-grade academies, an alternative high school, a Career Center, and an Adult Education program that offers GED accreditation, basic math, English, science, and other pre-collegiate coursework. Special education, enrichment programs, education for disadvantaged children, adult education, and extracurricular activities are offered by the district.

The following is a summary of data regarding the Billings Public Schools District as of the 2002–2003 school year.

Total enrollment: 15,778

Number of facilities
   elementary schools: 21
   middle schools: 4
   senior high schools: 5 (including a career center and alternative school)

Student/teacher ratio: K-8, 16.3:1; 9-12, 17.8:1

Teacher salaries (2002)
   minimum: $24,990
   maximum: $54,205

Funding per pupil: $5,947 (K-8); $7,538 (9-12)

A number of private and parochial schools also serve the metropolitan area.

Public Schools Information: Billings Public Schools, 415 North 30th St., Billings, MT 59101-1298; telephone (406)247-3777; fax (406)496-2070; email sbond@in-tch.com

Colleges and Universities

There are two four-year institutions of higher education in Billings. Montana State University-Billings is a public, state-supported school with a 2005 enrollment of 4,600 students. A satellite campus of 12,000 student Montana State University-Bozeman, the college offers two-year associate and four-year bachelor's degrees in more than 100 programs of study on a 112 acre-campus in Montana's largest city. The University is strongest in areas of Arts and Sciences, Allied Health, Education, Business, and Technology (including nursing); students can earn master's degrees in education and business administration. Rocky Mountain College is affiliated with the United Church of Christ, the United Methodist Church, and the United Presbyterian Church. It offers undergraduate degrees in more than 40 liberal arts and professionally-oriented majors and has an enrollment of about 1,000 students on a 60-acre Billings campus.

Libraries and Research Centers

The Parmly Billings Library contains more than 300,000 items, including 250,000 books (of these, more than 9,000 are large-print editions). There are also 190 magazine subscriptions, 7,000 music CDs, approximately 8,000 books on tape or CD, 11,000 videos, and 1,400 interactive CDs (games and other software). There are also 5 word processing centers and 18 Internet stations. Key collections include a full-text database research center, an Auto Repair Reference Center, Heritage Quest Online Genealogy Resources, and the NoveList Fiction Guide. There is an Outreach program and Infomobile for senior citizens. Other major libraries in the community are those of Montana State University-Billings and Rocky Mountain College.

Public Library Information: Parmly Billings Library, 510 North Broadway, Billings, MT 59101; telephone (406)657-8257; email refdesk@billings.lib.mt.us

Health Care

Billings provides the main medical services for a four-state area, with state-of-the-art equipment and highly skilled personnel. The community is served by nearly 500 physicians and dentists. Most of the health care facilities are concentrated in a 114-acre medical corridor that encompasses both of the city's major hospitals and 20 other health-related facilities.

Billings Deaconess Hospital, part of the Deaconess-Billings Clinic Health System, is a 272-bed Level II trauma center with general care and specialized services that include a cardiac care center, cancer services, an intensive care unit, the Kidney Center, a psychiatric center, pulmonary services, Women's Resource Center, occupational health and wellness, orthopedics and sports medicine, and a Research Insti-

tute. In 2004 ground was broken on a $27 million expansion to the hospital's Regional Emergency and Trauma Center.

A 302-bed Level II trauma center, the St. Vincent Hospital and Health Center is operated by the Sisters of Charity of Leavenworth and provides comprehensive inpatient and outpatient services, special services for women and seniors, and expertise in cardiology, orthopedics, general internal medicine, pediatrics, emergency and trauma, neurosciences, rehabilitation, neonatology, and oncology.

Other medical facilities in Billings are the Northern Rockies Cancer Center, Rimrock Foundation, which provides treatment for addictive disorders such as chemical dependency, co-dependency, compulsive gambling, and eating disorders, and several mental health facilities.

Recreation

Sightseeing

Downtown Billings contains the Billings Historical District, a renovated area that consists of most of the original business district. The Castle Corner is a replica of the Potter Palmer Mansion in Chicago, an interesting structure modeled after English castles. The railroad brought prosperity to Billings, and prosperity brought Preston B. Moss. In 1901, architect H.J. Hardenbergh (designer of the Waldorf-Astoria and Plaza Hotels in New York City) created the elegant Moss estate. The three-story Moss Mansion remains authentically furnished and open year-round at 914 Division Street. The Black Otter Trail, beginning at the edge of the city, is a winding highway that follows the "rimrocks," natural sandstone cliffs that border the city on the north and east. Boothill Cemetery, burial ground for residents of the frontier town of Colson, and the Range Rider of Yellowstone, a life-sized bronze statue by artist Charles Christadora, are both located along the Black Otter Trail, as are Sacrifice Cliff and Yellowstone Kelly's gravesite. Pictograph Cave State Park, southeast of Billings, has cave paintings made by Indians who lived and hunted for wooly mammoth in the region some 4,500 years ago.

A number of national monuments, parks, and recreation areas are located near Billings, most within a two-hour drive. Little Bighorn Battlefield National Monument, site of Custer's Last Stand, is 65 miles southeast of the city, and Pompey's Pillar, a spectacular natural rock formation, is 28 miles east of Billings.

The Little Bighorn Battlefield National Monument lets visitors relive the clash between General George Custer's 7th Cavalry and more than 3,000 warriors led by Crazy Horse.

Yellowstone National Park is the world's first such park; President Theodore Roosevelt proclaimed it so during his presidential tenure, and visitors today can see its famous geysers, painted canyons, and wildlife much as the way Roosevelt saw it. On the way from Billings to Yellowstone, Montana's highest peak is on view from Highway 212 over the Beartooth Mountain Pass.

Arts and Culture

The only major performing arts center in the region, the Alberta Bair Theater for the Performing Arts is the site of most of the cultural activity in Billings. The Fox Committee for the Performing Arts and the Billings Community Concert Association are both responsible for bringing a wide range of cultural events to the city each year, including jazz, opera, ballet, and popular music concerts. The Billings Symphony Orchestra and Chorale performs approximately ten concerts each season, including an annual free concert in the park.

The Western Heritage Center features changing exhibits pertaining to the region's history, and the Yellowstone County Museum contains historical relics and dioramas depicting scenes from Billings's past. The Yellowstone Art Museum museum holds one of the region's best collections of contemporary and historic art, including an impressive collection of Western art particularly strong in the works of Montana artists Russell Chatham and Deborah Butterfield; it also sponsors lectures and concerts.

MetraPark fairground holds concerts, rodeos, and the annual MontanaFair. Canyon Creek and a nature trail wind through ZooMontana's 70 acres of exotic animal exhibits.

Festivals and Holidays

Annual events in and around Billings include ArtWalk and the MSU-Billings Wine and Food Festival in May, the Moss Mansion County Fair and Strawberry Festival in June, July's Crazy Days downtown and the Skyfest Parade and Balloon Rally; on Labor Day weekend the Heritage of the Yellowstone Folklife Festival is held at Eastern Montana College. Western traditions are observed with Native American craft demonstrations, cowboy cooking and games, calf roping, and a concert featuring cowboy music and poetry. Ethnic roots are preserved in the serving of foods of various nationalities, including Native American, Dutch, Norwegian, Yugoslavian, Hispanic, Hutterite, Chinese, Scottish, Laotian, German, and Welsh. On the fourth weekend in September the traditional German harvest festival, Herbstfest, is held in nearby Laurel. German foods, dancing, and music are featured. Downtown Billings is the site of Harvest Fest each October. Late November has the Holiday Parade and Christmas stroll occurs each December downtown.

Sports for the Spectator

Billings supports four professional sports teams. The Billings Mustangs, a baseball farm team of the Cincinnati Reds, play at Cobb Field; the Billings Mavericks of the National Indoor Football League play home games at 8,700 seat MetraPark arena; the Billings Bulls, who play junior hockey, and the new Billings Rims, set to begin play in 2005, are also at the MetraPark. Thoroughbred racing and parimutuel betting are offered at Yellowstone Exhibition, and the city features several rodeo events each year, including the Northern Rodeo Association finals, which have been held in Billings for 30 years. Auto racing takes place at Magic City Speedway, five miles east of town on Hwy 10.

Sports for the Participant

The mountains near Billings offer a complete range of year-round outdoor activity in some of America's most spectacular terrain: skiing (at nearby Red Lodge Mountain, and further away Big Sky and the new Moonlight Basin resort), hiking, hunting, fishing (some of the world's legendary trout streams are nearby, such as Rock Creek and the Stillwater, Boulder, Musselshell, Big Horn, and Yellowstone Rivers), camping, and a wide variety of water recreation. At a number of lakes and reservoirs, swimming, boating, sailing, and water skiing can be enjoyed. The city of Billings operates more than 40 parks that feature swimming pools, tennis courts, athletic fields, jogging and biking paths, and other recreational facilities. There are several public and private golf courses in the city.

Shopping and Dining

Rimrock Mall downtown is the largest shopping area, with more than 100 shops, including Dillard's, JCPenney, Eddie Bauer, Gap, and Bath and Body Works. West Park Plaza is another large enclosed shopping center. There are at least a dozen smaller shopping areas in Billings. Western boutiques to specialty shops serve up quality merchandise and great bargains, all with no sales tax, in the historic downtown shopping district or the Billings Heights area on Main Street.

Restaurants in Billings feature traditional Western fare as well as exotic ethnic cuisine in settings ranging from casual and inexpensive to elegant and intimate. Most restaurants are clustered around the main shopping and commercial areas of downtown on Montana Avenue (Eleven Café, McCormick's, Q, The Rex, and Sweet Ginger) and North Broadway (Travel Café, Creoles, Gunsmoke Barbecue, Montana Brewing Company, and Papa Eddie's Grill).

Visitor Information: Billings Area Chamber of Commerce, PO Box 31177, Billings, MT 59107-1177; telephone (406)245-4111; toll-free (800)735-2635

Convention Facilities

The primary meeting facility in Billings is MetraPark, a multipurpose major event center located on the Rimrocks overlooking downtown. MetraPark features a 30,000-square-foot arena in addition to an exhibition space totaling more than 200,000 square feet with 10 break-out rooms. Total seating capacity is 12,000 people. The complex contains an art pavilion and a covered grandstand for outdoor events, a half-mile track used for both horse racing and auto racing, and is surrounded by nearly 90 acres of parking. The facility is diverse enough to hold large trade shows, professional sporting events for three local franchises, national touring shows and musical acts, and Gold Wing Road Riders Wing Ding gatherings.

The Holiday Inn Grand Montana Hotel & Convention Center is the largest facility in the four-state region to be built in conjunction with a hotel; recently renovated, it contains 50,000 square feet of meeting space in 15 rooms that accommodate groups from 10 to 4,600. Located downtown is the Alberta Bair Theater, which serves as the site of business meetings and conventions as well as performances, with a theater capacity of 1,400 people.

Conference and convention facilities for large and small groups are available in several hotels, motels, and bed-and-breakfast establishments throughout the Billings metropolitan area, including the Historic Northern Hotel, Sheraton Billings Hotel, and the Billings Hotel and Convention Center. Billings offers more than 3,400 hotel rooms and nearly 350 million square feet of meeting space. Alternatives to city hotel accommodations can be found outside Billings at the Double Spear Ranch in Pryor, Montana.

Convention Information: Billings Area Chamber of Commerce, 815 South 27th Street, PO Box 31177, Billings, MT 59107-1177; telephone (406)245-4111; toll-free (800)711-2630

Transportation

Approaching the City

Billings Logan International Airport is only 2 miles from the downtown district and serves most of eastern Montana and northern Wyoming with more than 50 flights daily from major airlines and regional carriers. America West, Big Sky, Delta, Horizon, Northwest, Skywest, Frontier, and United all service Billings with planes as large as 757s.

Billings is at the junction of two interstate highways: I-90, connecting the city with the Pacific Northwest and the southern Rocky Mountain states; and I-94, providing a link with the midwestern states. U.S. 87, 310, and 212 also meet in Billings.

Billings is served by regional and interstate bus lines. As of 2005 there was no regular passenger rail service in or out of Billings.

Traveling in the City

Billings Metropolitan Transit operates 17 routes within the city. In 2004 Federal funds were authorized for the purchase of 16 new buses over a 3-year period. Auto traffic on major thoroughfares is light compared to most metropolitan areas. The downtown area is laid out in a grid pattern with numbered streets.

Communications

Newspapers and Magazines

Billings has one major daily newspaper, *The Billings Gazette* (morning). Weekly papers focusing on business, agriculture, and general news include *Agri-News, Montana Farmer,* and *Western Livestock Reporter. Montana Land Magazine* is published quarterly.

Television and Radio

Bresnan Communications provides cable television and high-speed internet service in Billings. All four major television networks (ABC, CBS, NBC, Fox) broadcast to the Billings area. 13 AM and 19 FM radio stations can be picked up in the Billings area.

Media Information: The Billings Gazette, PO Box 36300, Billings, MT 59107; telephone (406)657-1200; toll-free (800)543-2505; email gbruce@billingsgazette.com

Billings Online

Big Sky Development Authority. Available www.bigskyedc .org

Billings Area Chamber of Commerce. Available www .billingschamber.com

Billings Convention and Visitors Bureau. Available billingscvb.visitmt.com

Billings Cultural Partners. Available www.downtown billings.org

The Billings Gazette. Available www.billingsgazette.com

Billings Public Schools. Available www.billings.k12.mt.us

City of Billings home page. Available ci.billings.mt.us

Montana Labor Market Information. Available jsd.dli.mt .gov/lmi/lmi.htm

Parmly Billings Library. Available www.billings.lib.mt.us

Selected Bibliography

Raban, Jonathan, *Bad Land: An American Romance* (New York: Pantheon, 1996)

Van West, Carroll, *Capitalism on the Frontier: Billings and the Yellowstone Valley in the Nineteenth Century* (Lincoln: University of Nebraska Press, 1993)

Butte

The City in Brief

Founded: 1864 (incorporated, 1879)

Head Official: Chief Executive Paul Babb (since 2005)

City Population (Butte/Silver-Bow balance)
  1980: 37,205
  1990: 33,336
  2000: 33,892
  2003 estimate: 32,519
  Percent change, 1990–2000: 1.6%
  U.S. rank in 1980: 605th
  U.S. rank in 1990: 806th
  U.S. rank in 2000: 887th

Metropolitan Area Population (Silver Bow County)
  1980: 38,092
  1990: 33,941
  2000: 34,606

Percent change, 1990–2000: 1.9%
U.S. rank in 2000: 1,262

Area: 716.2 square miles (2000)
Elevation: ranges from 5,484 to 6,463 feet above sea level
Average Annual Temperature: 53.2° F (maximum), 27.1° F (minimum)
Average Annual Precipitation: 12.75 inches

Major Economic Sectors: Transportation, energy research, medicine, tourism
Unemployment rate: 6.0% (January 2005, Silver Bow County)
Per Capita Income: $17,068 (2000)
2004 ACCRA Average House Price: Not reported
2004 ACCRA Cost of Living Index: Not reported

2002 FBI Crime Index Total: Not reported

Major Colleges and Universities: Montana College of Mineral Science and Technology

Daily Newspaper: *Montana Standard*

WOOLMAN

THE ORIGINAL MINE

BUTTE - SILVERBOW JAIL

FEDERAL BLDG.

OLD BUTTE FIRE HALL

COPPER KING MANSION

COURTHOUSE

ANACONDA PAY OFFICE

BERKELEY PIT

HENNESSY BLDG.

ARTS CHATEAU

SILVER
BOW CLUB

OLD CITY HALL

CONTINENTAL PIT

MONTANA TECH

WORLD MUSEUM
OF MINING

COPPER

GRANITE

BROADWAY

PARK

MERCURY

PLATINUM

STEEL

WESTERN

EMMET

EXCELSIOR

WASHINGTON

IDAHO

MONTANA

MAIN

IRON

CIVIC CENTER

GRAND

TEXAS

HARRISON

SHERIDAN

FRONT

CHAMBER OF COMMERCE

KAW

BLACKTAIL CREEK

COBBAN

OTTAWA

CONTINENTAL

HARRISON

ROWE

LEXINGTON

HILL

SAMSON

OUR LADY OF
THE ROCKIES

HOLMES

BUTTE - SILVER
BOW AIRPORT

DALY

EMPIRE

WAUKESHA

0   1   2

KILOMETERS

MILES   0.5   1   1.5   2

N

115

15 90

WA

ID

MT

Butte

OR

WY

CA

NV

UT

CO

Introduction

Once dependent almost solely on the mining industry—in the early 1900s it was called "the richest hill on earth" because of the valuable ores that lay beneath it—Butte, like many older American cities, is in the midst of a transition toward a more diversified economy. With easy access to western and midwestern markets, Butte is one of the west's major transportation hubs; the city is also moving into enterprises related to energy research and high-altitude sports training. Despite the changes underway, Butte retains its multiethnic heritage and its connection to the breathtaking natural beauty of the surrounding Rocky Mountains. For statistical and other purposes, Butte is traditionally linked with Silver Bow County.

Geography and Climate

Butte is located in Summit Valley in the heart of the Rocky Mountains on the west slope of the Continental Divide in southwestern Montana. Silver Bow Creek, part of the Columbia River system—and called Clark Fork outside the city—runs through Butte. The climate is semi-arid, with a growing season of 81 days.

Area: 716.2 square miles (2000)

Elevation: ranges from 5,484 to 6,463 feet above sea level

Average Temperatures: January, 15.4° F; July, 62.9° F; annual average: 53.2° F (maximum); 27.1° F (minimum)

Average Annual Precipitation: 12.75 inches

History

Discovery of Gold and Silver Brings Settlers to Region

The area surrounding Butte's present location remained uninhabited before gold was discovered in 1864 in Silver Bow Creek. Native Americans and explorers passed through the region, but found no attractions for permanent settlement until two prospectors detected placer deposits in the creek; they named the site the Missoula lode. Other prospectors came, and by 1867 the population of the mining settlement reached 500 people. Water was scarce, however, and the town began to decline; the 1870 census recorded only about 200 people.

One of the region's first prospectors, William Farlin, returned in 1874 to claim several outcrops of quartz that he had discovered previously. Before long a silver boom began, bringing a chaos of claim staking and claim jumping as prospectors overran the site. Investors William Clark and Andrew Davis constructed mills for extracting gold and silver, and by 1876, when a townsite patent was issued, the prosperous camp numbered 1,000 residents. Marcus Daly, representing Salt Lake City mining entrepreneurs, arrived that same year and bought the Alice Mine, naming it Walkerville for his employers. In 1879 Butte, which had been named for Big Butte, a volcanic cone to the northwest, was incorporated as a city.

Copper Discovered; Butte Thrives; Unions Formed

In 1880 Daly sold his interest in the Walker mining operations and bought the Anaconda Mine. As he was digging for silver, Daly struck copper, thus initiating the industry that eventually made him one of the country's wealthiest and most powerful men. Daly attracted investors from as far away as Boston and New York, and within a year the town had several mines and mining companies. In a lifelong rivalry with William Clark for control of Butte, Daly finally won out as the "boss" of a one-industry town. The arrival of the Union Pacific Railroad in 1881 ensured Butte's success as the leading producer of copper in the United States.

With a population of 14,000 people in 1885, Butte supported banks, schools, a hospital, a fire department, churches, and a water company. Copper production and the development of mining companies continued until the turn of the century, when Daly joined with the Rockefeller family to form the Amalgamated Copper Mining Company, one of the early twentieth-century trusts. By the first decade of the twentieth century Butte was a major rail hub, with four railroads connecting in the city. Amalgamated, having bought out other mining companies in Butte, changed its name back to the Anaconda Copper Mining Company in 1915.

The labor movement was important to Butte's history. The Butte Miner's Union was formed in 1878 to protect miners from the dangers of working underground. The Butte delegation was the largest at the 1906 founding convention of the International Workers of the World (IWW) in Chicago. During the early twentieth century the union's power began to decline when mining companies were consolidated and management became indifferent to worker demands. The dynamiting of the union hall in 1914 and the lynching of an IWW organizer in 1917 led to seven years of martial law in Butte. The worst hardrock mining disaster in American history, the Spectacular Mine Fire, also took place in 1917, killing 168 miners.

Present-day Butte neighborhoods such as Dublin Gulch, Finntown, Chinatown, and Corktown attest to the city's diverse ethnic roots. Since the community's earliest days immigrants from all over the world settled in Butte to work the mines. When the placer camp was started in 1864, Chinese miners were the first to arrive. Later came Cornish, Irish, and Welsh laborers, and for a time Irish workers formed the dominant group. Then Serbs, Croats, French Canadians, Finns, Scandinavians, Jews, Lebanese, Mexicans, Austrians, Germans, and African Americans added to the ranks of miners.

Mining Declines; Economy Diversifies

Throughout the first half of the twentieth century, the mining industry continued to dominate the Butte economy. Changes began to take place, however; underground mining gave way to pit mining in the 1950s when high-grade copper-ore deposits were exhausted and above-ground exploration for low-grade ore began. In 1976 Anaconda was bought by Atlantic Richfield Company; in 1983 the mines were completely closed. Unemployment rose to more than 17 percent and Butte's survival seemed threatened. That same year a task force composed of government and business leaders was formed to ensure a future for Butte through a concerted effort to diversify the city's economy. Since then, mines have reopened, a transportation hub was built at the Port of Montana, the U.S. High Altitude Sports Center was located in the city, and several high-technology firms have established facilities in the area. These efforts at economic stability, diversification, and growth have been recognized by the Montana Ambassadors, the Pacific Institute, the U.S. Corporation for Economic Development, and *Newsweek* magazine, which commented in an article about the area's steady decline and stagnant economy, that "in Montana, Butte has engineered the most dramatic turnaround."

Historical Information: Butte Silver-Bow Public Archives, PO Box 81, Butte, MT 59703; telephone (406)497-6226

Population Profile

Metropolitan Area Residents (Silver Bow County)
1980: 38,092
1990: 33,941
2000: 34,606
Percent change, 1990–2000: 1.9%
U.S. rank in 2000: 1,262

City Residents (Butte/Silver Bow balanced)
1980: 37,205
1990: 33,336
2000: 33,892
2003 estimate: 32,519

Percent change, 1990–2000: 1.6%
U.S. rank in 1980: 605th
U.S. rank in 1990: 806th
U.S. rank in 2000: 887th

Density: 47.3 people per square mile (2000)

Racial and ethnic characteristics (2000)
White: 32,325
Black or African American: 53
American Indian and Alaska Native: 675
Asian: 147
Hawaiian or Other Pacific Islander: 21
Hispanic or Latino (may be of any race): 927
Other: 200

Percent of residents born in state: 73.3% (2000)

Age characteristics (2000)
Population under 5 years old: 1,947
Population 5 to 9 years old: 2,250
Population 10 to 14 years old: 2,407
Population 15 to 19 years old: 2,451
Population 20 to 24 years old: 2,231
Population 25 to 34 years old: 3,796
Population 35 to 44 years old: 5,246
Population 45 to 54 years old: 4,801
Population 55 to 59 years old: 1,820
Population 60 to 64 years old: 1,491
Population 65 to 74 years old: 2,628
Population 75 to 84 years old: 2,057
Population 85 years and over: 767
Median age: 38.9 years

Births (2003)
Total number: 398

Deaths (2003)
Total number: 402

Money income (1999)
Per capita income: $17,068
Median household income: $30,516
Total households: 14,176

Number of households with income of . . .
less than $10,000: 1,720
$10,000 to $14,999: 1,558
$15,000 to $24,999: 2,577
$25,000 to $34,999: 2,175
$35,000 to $49,999: 2,251
$50,000 to $74,999: 2,427
$75,000 to $99,999: 758
$100,000 to $149,999: 463
$150,000 to $199,999: 108
$200,000 or more: 139

Percent of families below poverty level: 10.7% (57.9% of which were female householder families with related children under 5 years)

2002 FBI Crime Index Total: Not reported

Municipal Government

The governments of the city of Butte and Silver Bow County are combined and are administered by a Chief Executive and council. The twelve council members and the Chief Executive all serve four-year terms.

Head Official: Chief Executive Paul Babb (since 2005; current term expires 2009)

Total Number of City Employees: 480 (2000)

City Information: Butte/Silver Bow Government Courthouse, 155 West Granite, Butte, MT 59701; telephone (406)497-6260

Economy

Major Industries and Commercial Activity

Since Butte's founding during a gold boom, its principal industry has been mining. From the mid-1880s to the 1980s, Butte produced an estimated $22 billion in minerals mined. More than 8 percent of the nation's copper continues to be produced in Butte, joining other important minerals such as lead, zinc, and magnesium. In the 1970s, when underground mines were closed, the copper industry began to decline; it reached its lowest point in 1983 when mining operations in the Butte area completely ceased for a time.

This recession began to ease in 1986 when copper mines were reopened, creating more than 300 jobs. This upsurge brought development in other areas such as transportation, tourism and recreation, small businesses, technology, energy research, medicine, and communications. Accolades have poured in during recent years, lauding Butte's economic resurgence, even earning the town a four-minute spot on the Paul Harvey radio program. Lou Tice of the Pacific Institute in Seattle hailed Butte as a "city on the move." Citing the economic rebirth of Butte, Tice attributed the successes to ". . . its people—their tenacity, their hard work and the remarkable goals they set."

Items and goods produced: motors, dairy and food products, compressed and liquefied gases, beverages, optical goods, chemicals, steel fabrications, phosphate products

Incentive Programs—New and Existing Companies

Local programs—The Butte/Silver Bow Tax Increment Financing Industrial District (Butte has two, comprising 1,300 acres) directs new tax dollars accrued from new development within the district to assist further development within the boundaries of the district. There are four other tax incentive programs available to local businesses that qualify. The Butte Local Development Corporation (BLDC), a principal catalyst in the region's economic turnaround, is considered one of the best economic development organizations for its size in the country. Its mission is to create jobs through industrial development. BLDC accomplishes these goals through capital acquisition, land and infrastructure development, development and maintenance of informational tools, economic analysis and planning, and numerous other activities. The BLDC also administers five loan programs.

State programs—State of Montana tax incentives include property tax reduction; no inventory, use, or sales tax; new industry income tax credits; small business investment tax credit; and tax reduction on pollution control equipment.

Development Projects

Government and industry leaders have organized to encourage expansion of Butte's economic base by capitalizing on the area's natural resources: agriculture, forest products, and mining. Steps have been made to reopen mines or help existing mines stay in business. The Montana Copper mine was reopened in 2003, creating 330 jobs and $11 million in annual payroll for local workers. The BDLC in 2004 announced renewed efforts to keep the Golden Sunlight and Luzenac America mines in operation, as well as provide assistance to the Northwestern Energy Corporation as it went through bankruptcy proceedings. The recently completed Port of Montana Hub, intended to facilitate the loading and transporting of minerals and forest products by rail and motor freight carriers, is expected to contribute significantly to the area's economic development. Other steps toward economic stabilization include the opening of a small business incubator, the establishment of Butte's Cyber Village and Silicon Mountain Technology Park where several science and technology firms have started up or relocated, and the development of the U.S. High Altitude Sports Center. Other efforts either completed or underway by 2005 included development of an East Side Urban Renewal Area, a music and entertainment district downtown, a new community ice center and jail, and improvements to the Civic Center.

Once called an "environmental wasteland" because of the damage done to it by mining and smelting, Butte is gradually recovering. The Atlantic Richfield Corporation (ARCO) had spent more than $400 million on reclamation work to repair damage in the area by capping mine tailings with clean dirt, landscaping, and re-vegetating damaged land. In 2004 ARCO agreed to contribute an additional $50 million to the Montana Superfund in efforts to clean up the Clark Fork Basin.

Economic Development Information: Butte Local Development Corporation, PO Box 507, Butte, MT 59703; telephone (406)723-4349; fax (406)723-4672

Commercial Shipping

Butte is a major inland port from which imported cargo is shipped via rail and motor carrier to points throughout the Midwest. Butte is located at the only rail interline in the state of the Union Pacific and Burlington Northern railroads. Piggyback service is provided, and trains run up to twelve times weekly from Butte. Several motor freight carriers regularly transport goods through facilities in Butte, with overnight and second-day delivery to major cities in the West and Midwest; in addition, well over 1,000 motor freight carriers serving the state have access to Butte.

Labor Force and Employment Outlook

When the Butte Job Service surveyed 10 major employers in the Butte area, they reported rates of absenteeism from 1 to 2 percent, and turnover rates that average 3 percent. Butte's labor force in 2005 included many potential employees and other well-trained workers with skills and experience beyond their present employment. Silver Bow County has experienced ups and downs in employment levels as it has made the difficult transition to a more diversified economy. Growth in the 1990s was driven in a large part by construction of the American Silicon Minerals corporate headquarters in Butte. Following the loss of construction jobs in 1999, employment losses were once again experienced with the shutdown of Montana Resources in mid 2000. Between December 1999 and December 2002, growth increased an average of 0.1% per year, and that pace has held to the mid-2000s. A particular bright spot has been the city's success in luring international firms to the Silicon Mountain Technology Park and Cyber Village.

The following is a summary of data regarding the Silver Bow County labor force as of 2001.

Size of labor force: 15,816

Average hourly earnings of production workers employed in manufacturing: $14.87 (Montana average, 2004)

Unemployment rate: 6.0% (January 2005, Silver Bow County)

Largest employers	Number of employees
Montana Tech	676
Butte School District No. 1	658
St. James Community Hospital	535
Northwestern Energy	511
Wal-Mart	430
Butte-Silver Bow Local Government	412
Community Counseling and Correctional	275
Advanced Silicon Materials	232
M.S.E. Inc.	200

Cost of Living

The following is a summary of data regarding key cost of living factors for the Butte area.

2004 ACCRA Average House Price: Not reported

2004 ACCRA Cost of Living Index: Not reported

State income tax rate: Ranges from 2.0% to 11.0%

State sales tax rate: None

Local income tax rate: None

Local sales tax rate: None

Property tax rate: $669.24 per $1,000 of taxable value. Assessed at 1.82% to 1.54% of the actual market value (2005)

Economic Information: Butte/Silver Bow Chamber of Commerce, 1000 George St, Butte MT 59701; telephone (406)723-3177; toll-free (800)735-6814; email chamber @buttecvb.com. Research & Analysis Bureau, Montana Department of Labor & Industry, PO Box 1728, Helena, MT 59624; telephone (406)444-2430

Education and Research

Elementary and Secondary Schools

The public elementary and secondary school system in Butte is Butte School District #1. The district is overseen by an eight-member elected school board and is administered by a superintendent appointed by the board. In 2005 the district was comprised of seven elementary schools, one middle school, and one high school. The district considers itself one of the most technologically advanced in Montana, with 100 percent internet access for all students. The district offers a full range of after-school latchkey and enrichment programs, adult education, and a unique Retired Seniors Volunteer

Program (R.S.V.P.) that brings local retirees together with students to form tutoring and mentoring relationships.

The following is a summary of data regarding Butte's public schools as of the 2002–2003 school year.

Total enrollment: 4,936

Number of facilities
elementary schools: 7
middle schools: 1
senior high schools: 1
other: 1

Student/teacher ratio: 16.8:1 (elementary and middle school); 15.8: 1 (high school)

Teacher salaries (state figure, 2002-2003)
average: $35,754

Funding per pupil: $5,863 elementary; $8,298 high school

Several religious and secular parochial elementary and high schools provide alternatives to public education in the Butte metropolitan area.

Public Schools Information: Butte School District #1, 111 North Montana, Butte, MT 59701; telephone (406)496-2000

Colleges and Universities

Montana Tech of the University of Montana, originally chartered as the Montana State School of Mines, comprises three colleges, one school, and the Montana Bureau of Mines and Geology. Montana Tech offers 6 certificate, 9 associates, 19 bachelors, and 11 masters programs. With a 2005 enrollment of 2100 students, the school conducts basic and applied research and provides graduates with degrees in such fields as geophysical engineering, mineral processing, and petroleum engineering. Butte Vo Tech, formerly independent but now under the umbrella of Montana Tech and the University of Montana, offers career training in a number of vocations, including data processing, practical nursing, and automotive mechanics technology. Both Montana State University-Bozeman and the University of Montana in Missoula are within a two-hour drive of Butte.

Libraries and Research Centers

The Butte-Silver Bow Library is located in Butte. Holdings consist of 75,000 volumes and nearly 200 periodical subscriptions, with special collections relating to Montana architecture, historic preservation, and fishing. The library is the headquarters for the Montana Public Library Film Service. The Butte-Silver Bow Public Archives holds information on local families and history, plus more than 30 labor history and 70 personal collections. The Historic Hearst Free Library in Anaconda offers more than 43,000 volumes, 66 periodicals, 16 newspapers, and a repository of historic memorabilia.

The Montana College of Mineral Science and Technology Library houses nearly 50,000 volumes, 78,446 maps, and 425,636 documents including paper, microform, and electronic media. The library is a depository for federal and state government documents. In addition, the Montana College of Mineral Science and Technology conducts research activities in such fields as water resources, earthquakes, mines, and geology. Butte is home to the National Center for Appropriate Technology Research Library. Most of the other libraries and research centers in the city also specialize in energy and technology.

Public Library Information: Butte-Silver Bow Library, 226 West Broadway Street, Butte, MT 59701; telephone (406)723-3361

Health Care

The chief medical provider for the Butte-Silver Bow area is the St. James Healthcare system, part of the Montana region of the Sisters of Charity of Leavenworth Health System, which also has operations in Billings and Miles City. The Butte facility employs more than 600 people, including 75 doctors, and has more than 100 beds. St. James provides medical services in the fields of cardiology, neurosciences, oncology, orthopedics, women's and children's services, emergency services, MRI, pain management, renal dialysis, and others. A number of other institutions provide mental health services, dental care, hospice care, chiropractic care, chemical dependency rehabilitation, and more.

Recreation

Sightseeing

In 2002 Butte was one of only 12 towns in America to be named a distinctive destination by the National Trust for Historic Preservation. A popular Trolley Tour takes visitors to all the key sights—Old No. 1, a replica of the city's original electric trolley car system, operates four times daily from the first of June through Labor Day. Both St. Lawrence Church and the Serbian Orthodox Church have stunning frescoes that are open to public viewing. Butte's historic district also showcases several homes built during the days of the mining barons. The Copper King Mansion, built in 1888, was the Elizabethan-Victorian-style home of William

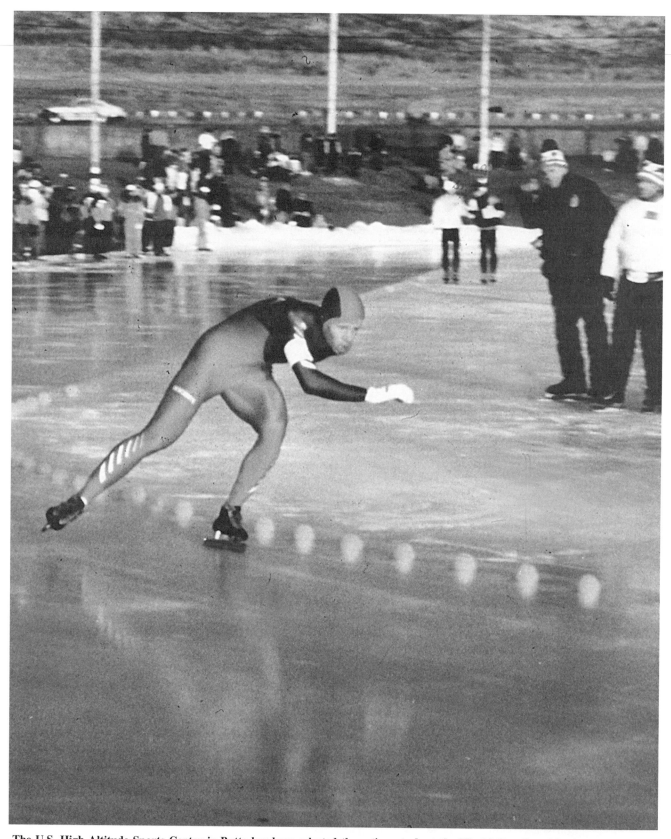

The U.S. High Altitude Sports Center in Butte has been selected three times to host the World Cup Speedskating competition.

S. Clark, whose battle with Marcus Daly for control in Butte has become a local legend; the mansion is now a bed and breakfast inn. Another impressive structure is the Charles Clark Mansion, also called the Arts Chateau, home of William A. Clark's son and a replica of a French chateau; completely restored and housing an arts center and gallery, it has been designated as a National Historic Structure. On the west side of the city are other fashionable, late-nineteenth-century homes.

Overlooking Butte from Montana Tech Hill is a statue of Marcus Daly by Augustus Saint-Gaudens. North of the downtown district stands the "gallows frame" of the Original Mine, which was used to raise and lower miners and ores from the underground mine. To the east of the city is the Berkeley Pit, started in 1955, and once the largest truck-operated open pit copper mine in the United States; it is an example of the process that replaced underground vein mining. The Granite Mountain Memorial commemorates the 168 miners who died during a 1917 fire at the Granite Mountain and Speculator mines. Also east of Butte, atop the Continental Divide, is Our Lady of the Rockies, a statue of the Christian religion's Virgin Mary. Standing 90 feet high and floodlighted at night, the statue is a nondenominational monument to motherhood that was built with donated materials and labor and completed in 1985.

Among the points of interest within driving distance of Butte are ghost towns such as Alder Gulch, Cable, Granite, and Philipsburg, where legends were formed and fortunes made during the gold and silver booms.

Arts and Culture

A culturally active city, Butte supports a symphony, a community arts center, and a theater company. The Mother Lode, completed in 1923 as a Masonic Temple but never occupied by Masons, has been rehabilitated and serves as southwest Montana's premier performing arts center. The Butte Symphony Orchestra programs a four-concert season featuring a choral group and soloists. Theater is presented by Orphan Girl Theater and the Mother Lode Theater. Opera productions and appearances by national touring groups and speakers are also scheduled in the city.

Butte's principal museums are related to the mining industry. The World Museum of Mining and Hell Roarin' Gulch, a popular attraction in the area, features indoor and outdoor exhibits that replicate an early mining environment. Among the indoor displays are models of mines, minerals, fire fighting equipment, a Stanley steam engine, and an electric hoist. Outdoor exhibits include a reconstructed 1900 mining camp, with a print shop, Chinese laundry, bank, drug store, millinery shop, and other authentic structures. Also featured at the museum is a tour on the Neversweat and Washoe Railroad aboard a train drawn by an M-10 locomotive; the tour starts at the museum, traveling past mines and head frames, to nearby Kelly mine. Commentary on mine history is presented. The Dumas Brothel was the longest-running establishment of its kind in America; Butte once had as many as 2,400 ladies of the evening working in town. The Mineral Museum at Montana Tech exhibits 1,500 items from its collection of more than 15,000 mineral specimens gathered from throughout the world; a highlight is a display of fluorescent minerals. The Mai Wah preserves the history of Butte's Chinese miners.

The Picadilly Museum of Transportation houses a fascinating array of exhibits about transportation in America, from antique cars to gas pumps to road signs. The Mother Bottego House honors Celestine Mary Bottego, who spent 15 years in Butte and has been nominated for beatification. At the Butte-Silver Bow Arts Chateau a professional art gallery mounts changing exhibits of works by local and national artists. Several private art galleries are also located in the city.

Festivals and Holidays

The Arts Chateau holds a Wine Tasting Festival in February. The Winternational Sports Festival, a multisport event, begins in February and continues into March, when St. Patrick's Day festivities such as a parade and the Friendly Sons of St. Patrick Banquet also take place. On March 16 the Finnish-American community gives thanks to St. Urho for chasing the grasshoppers out of Finland. Ghost Walks takes place in April at the Mining Museum. July is an event-filled month; included among the activities are the Arts Chateau Summer Display, Evel Knievel Days, and the Freedom Festival parade and community picnic. An Ri Ra—the Montana Gaelic Cultural Festival—takes place each August. Mining Heritage Day happens in September. The year ends with the annual Christmas Stroll, Ice-Sculpting Contest, and Festival of Trees.

Sports for the Spectator

Butte's U.S. High Altitude Sports Center has three times been chosen as the site of the World Cup Speedskating competition. Other sporting events include state wrestling tournaments and rodeos.

Sports for the Participant

Butte has some 30 parks ranging from mini parks on lots to major parks such as Stodden and the recently built Copper Mountain Sports and Recreation Complex north of Timber Butte. Municipal parks located in Butte provide such facilities as a swimming pool, basketball courts, baseball and football fields, tennis courts, golf courses, an Olympic-sized skating rink, and running/walking tracks. Recreational areas outside the city include the Blacktail Creek and Alice Pit Walking Trails, the Red Mountain Highlands (a 10,000 foot peak), Humburg Spires rock climbing site, kayaking on Big Hole and Madison rivers, downhill skiing at Maverick Mountain and Discovery Basin, and a number of golf layouts that offer spectacular scenery in the Butte foothills. Golfers may particularly wish to visit town of Anaconda, 26 miles from Butte, where an $11 million, 200-acre golf course designed by Jack Nicklaus has been built atop the ruins of a smelting plant. Butte is surrounded by lakes, streams, and reservoirs where trout fishing, boating, and waterskiing are popular pastimes.

Shopping and Dining

Historic Uptown has several unique stores that deal in antiques, toys, and tools, and art galleries that specialize in Western art. In addition to the Butte Plaza Mall, a shopping plaza that features a major department store, Butte's Harrison Avenue has small shops and stores with specialties ranging from locally made crafts and gifts to sporting equipment.

More than 80 restaurants in Butte provide a variety of choices that include fast food and family dining, as well as the more formal atmosphere of supper clubs. Among the cuisines offered are Chinese, Greek, Italian, and traditional American. Local favorites include The Acoma on Broadway, Gamer's Café on Park, the Gold Rush Casino and Restaurant on Galena, and Pork Chop John's (three locations). A local specialty is pasties, which are meat pies that were originally brought to Butte by Cornish miners in the 1870s.

Visitor Information: Butte/Silver Bow Chamber of Commerce, 1000 George St, Butte MT 59701; telephone (406)723-3177; toll-free (800)735-6814; email chamber @buttecvb.com

Convention Facilities

The Butte Civic Center, accessible to about 1,300 hotel and motel rooms and bed and breakfast inns in the metropolitan area, is a prime meeting facility both in the city and in the Northwest. Located in close proximity to major population centers, the complex offers a range of facilities for large and small group functions and sporting and recreational events. Total seating capacity is approximately 6,000 people, with parking for up to 1,200 vehicles on site or in the immediate area.

Meeting and convention accommodations are also available at the city's two major hotels. The Copper King Park Hotel features ten multipurpose meeting rooms, including a recreation area with more than 7,000 square feet of space, a convention center providing more than 5,000 square feet,

smaller rooms with seating for small groups, and a ballroom accommodating up to 1,200 participants. The Best Western features large and small meeting rooms, indoor pool, spa, and fitness center, and the Hops Bar and Casino. The Fairmont Chalets and Fairmont Hot Springs Resort offer a more relaxed, country setting outside of Butte.

Convention Information: Butte/Silver Bow Chamber of Commerce, 1000 George St, Butte MT 59701; telephone (406)723-3177; toll-free (800)735-6814; email chamber @buttecvb.com

Transportation

Approaching the City

The Bert Mooney Airport is served by Alaska Airlines, Sky West, Horizon Air, and Delta Airlines. Most flights connect in Salt Lake City or through Bozeman/Seattle. Greyhound and Rimrock lines provide bus transportation.

The principal highways into Butte are Interstate-15, running north and south, and Interstate-90, approaching from the northwest, which intersect in the city. A network of seven state highways also serves Butte.

Traveling in the City

Butte is laid out on a grid pattern, although some streets run diagonally to follow railroad or freeway routes. Harrison Avenue is the main north-south thoroughfare. Butte Transit System provides bus service.

Communications

Newspapers

Butte's daily morning newspaper is the *Montana Standard.* Students at Montana Tech publish the *Technocrat.*

Television and Radio

In 2003 Bresnan Communications bought the rights to Butte cable television and invested several million dollars to upgrade the number of channels available and to bring high-speed internet to Butte citizens. Viewers have access to ABC, CBS, and NBC television broadcasts. 93.1 FM is the city's Public Radio outlet. Seven other FM radio stations and two AM stations originate their signals from Butte. A number of other radio stations can be picked up from neighboring communities.

Media Information: The *Montana Standard,* 25 W. Granite St., Butte, MT 59701; telephone (406)496-5500; email editor@mtstandard.com

Butte Online

Butte Chamber of Commerce. Available www.butteinfo.org

Butte Local Development Corporation. Available www .buttemontana.org

Butte Public School District #1. Available www.butte.k12 .mt.us

Butte-Silver Bow Local Government. Available www.co .silverbow.mt.us

Montana Standard. Available www.mtstandard.com

Only in Butte. History stories about Butte's past. Available www.butteamerica.com/hist.htm

Selected Bibliography

Ciabattari, Mark, "The Fall and Rise of Butte, MT" *The New York Times Magazine,* March 1, 1992, pp. 48+

Hammett, Dashiell, *Red Harvest* (South Yarmouth, MA: J. Curley, 1983)

Morris, Patrick F. *Anaconda Montana: Copper Smelting Boomtown on the Western Frontier.* (Bethesda, Md.: Swann Pub., 1997)

Writers Program, Montana, *Copper Camp: Stories of the World's Greatest Mining Town, Butte, Mont.* (New York: AMS Press, 1976)

Writers Project of Montana, *Copper Camp: The Lusty Story of Butte, Montana, the Richest Hill on Earth* (Riverbend Publishing, 2001)

Helena

The City in Brief

Founded: 1864 (chartered, 1881)

Head Official: Mayor James E. Smith (I) (since 2001)

City Population
  1980: 23,938
  1990: 24,699
  2000: 25,780
  2003 estimate: 26,718
  Percent change, 1990–2000: 2.8%
  U.S. rank in 2000: Not reported

Lewis & Clark County Population
  1980: 43,039
  1990: 47,495
  2000: 55,716
  2003 estimate: 57,137
  Percent change, 1990–2000: 17.3%
  U.S. rank in 2000: 847th (among counties; state rank 6th)

Area: 14 square miles (2000)
Elevation: 4,090 feet above sea level
Average Annual Temperature: 44.0° F
Average Annual Precipitation: 11.32 inches

Major Economic Sectors: Government, services, finance
Unemployment Rate: 5.5% (January 2005)
Per Capita Income: $20,020 (1999)

2002 FBI Crime Index Total: Not reported

Major Colleges and Universities: Carroll College, Helena College of Technology

Daily Newspaper: *Helena Independent Record*

361

Introduction

Helena, known as the "City of Gold," lies at the heart of the Rocky Mountains in a fertile region with rolling hills. On the outskirts of the city lies the giant Helena National Forest, which provides spectacular scenery and many opportunities for outdoor activities. Once a mining boom town, Helena is now a major social and governmental center of the American west, offering amenities not usually found in a city of its size.

Geography and Climate

Helena is located in west-central Montana in the foothills of the Big Belt Mountains on the eastern slope of the Continental Divide, 48 miles north-northeast of Butte, Montana. Helena is located midway between Glacier and Yellowstone national parks and fertile valleys lie to the north and east. The Missouri River flows northward nearly 10 miles east of the city.

Helena has a modified continental climate with warm, dry summers and moderately cold winters. Mountains located to the north and east of the city sometimes deflect shallow masses of arctic air to the east, but at times cold air can be trapped in the valley for days. During the coldest period, from November through February, temperatures sometimes drop to 0° F or below. Summer temperatures are usually under 90° F and the mountains account for marked changes in temperature from day to night. April through July is the rainy season, while late summer, fall, and winter are quite dry.

Area: 14 square miles (2000)

Elevation: 4,090 feet above sea level

Average Temperatures: January, 20.2° F; July, 67.8° F; annual average, 44.0° F

Average Annual Precipitation: 11.32 inches

History

Land of the Prickly Pear

Archaeological evidence shows that native Americans inhabited the valley in which greater Helena is situated more than 12,000 years ago. Although never serving as the permanent home of any particular tribe, the valley was a crossover area for Salish, Crow, Bannock, and Blackfeet tribal members.

In 1805, members of the Lewis and Clark expedition were the first white men to visit the valley. While investigating the area on foot, William Clark stepped on and had to remove 17 cactus spines from his feet. This caused him to name the nearby creek and valley Prickly Pear. In the early nineteenth century trappers came to the area, later to be pushed aside by groups of white settlers.

In 1862 a group of immigrants in a wagon train decided to build houses for the winter in Prickly Pear Valley, but this settlement proved temporary. In 1864, four ex-Confederate soldiers from Georgia discovered placer gold in Last Chance Gulch, the heart of Helena's present-day downtown. The gold strike attracted hundreds of miners eager to find riches. Over the next 20 years 3.5 billion dollars worth of gold was discovered in the gulch. By 1888 Helena was home to more millionaires per capita than anywhere else in the world.

Early settlers considered naming their new boom town "Pumpkinville" or "Squashtown," but instead settled on the suggestion of John Somerville, who named the place after his hometown of Helena in Minnesota. The inhabitants chose to pronounce it HELL-uh-nuh, with the accent on the first syllable. Its original residents were mainly of English, Scottish, Irish, and German descent.

Becomes Territorial, Then State Capital

By 1870, Helena, with a population of 3,106 people, had become the most important town in the Montana Territory. Other nearby settlements turned into ghost towns after gold supplies were exhausted. But Helena's geographical location helped it become a business hub for other mining communities such as Marysville to the west and Rimini to the southwest. It became a vital bank, trade and farming town.

In the late 1870s the discovery of rich silver and lead deposits in nearby Wickes, Corbin, and Elkhorn further stimulated development in the area and helped Helena grow and prosper. The fact that Helena was on an important stagecoach route also spurred its growth as a hub city.

In 1875 Helena was made the capital of the Montana Territory. When Montana became a state in 1889, citizens disputed whether the capital should be Helena or Anaconda, another popular mining town. Copper rivals Marcus Daly, who supported Anaconda, and William A. Clark, who supported Helena, spent more than $3 million as each fought to have his city chosen for the honor. Helena finally won the vote in 1894. The city soon saw a tremendous amount of new construction. In time, Helena became the center of Montana political, social, and economic life. Between 1880 and 1890, the population grew from 3,624 to 13,834 people.

City Experiences Booms and Busts

By the late 1880s, wealthy Helena citizens had erected pretentious mansions and constructed a streetcar to transport them to the outskirts of town where they lived. They also drove about town, first in coaches driven by top-hatted drivers, and later in electric cars that stalled on the hills. Their Italianate, Romanesque, baroque, and Gothic-style houses featured cupolas, turrets, and hand-carved trim. The inhabitants of the mansions were served by a small army of maids and butlers.

The good times for many of the city's more than 13,000 residents continued until 1893, when the price of silver fell and many of the nouveau riche moved away. The spacious mansions were then taken over by members of the middle class who sometimes had problems paying to heat them. Many of the Mansion District homes can still be viewed today.

Like other Montana towns, Helena experienced boom-or-bust cycles. Prosperity returned once again between 1900 and 1910 when gold mining activity geared up at nearby Marysville and with the construction of the Canyon Ferry, Hauser, and Holter dams on the Missouri River, which employed a number of Helena residents. Then came a slump that lasted until the war years of 1914-1918, when once again the mines worked to meet the demand for metals during World War I. But another slump followed.

Helena in the Twentieth Century and Beyond

In the first part of the twentieth century, Helena's population showed modest growth, rising from 12,515 people in 1910 to 15,056 by 1940. This growth occurred despite several major fires and a 1935 earthquake that caused four deaths and $4 million in damages. Shocks of lesser intensity occurred in 1936 and 1937 but did no further harm.

During the mid-1930s, at the time of the Great Depression, the federal government employed hundreds of Helena citizens to repair the State Capitol and the county courthouse and to landscape a city park. New federal monetary policies increased the price of gold and silver and stimulated mining, which once again regained its importance in the life of the city.

The city's population stood at 17,581 people in 1950. During the 1960s, urban renewal changed the face of downtown Helena, and a pedestrian mall was built to attract tourists. Preservation fervor and urban renewal programs in the 1970s resulted in further downtown development. In recent decades, Montana residents have begun to truly appreciate and make efforts to preserve the beautiful terrain of their state. In 1992, the Montana House of Representatives voted to protect 1.5 million acres of Montana from development,

including some local Helena area sites. In 2005, the National Trust for Historic Preservation named Helena one of America's Dozen Distinctive Destinations, recognizing the city as "unique and lovingly preserved".

Today, Helena is an attractive place that retains vintage residential and commercial structures while providing modern shops, distinctive restaurants, and modern entertainment centers for residents and visitors alike.

Historical Information: Montana Historical Society, PO Box 201201, 225 N. Roberts, Helena, MT, 59620-1201; telephone (406)444-2694; email mhslibrary@mt.gov

Population Profile

Lewis & Clark County Residents

1980: 43,039
1990: 47,495
2000: 55,716
2003 estimate: 57,137
Percent change, 1990–2000: 17.3%
U.S. rank in 2000: 847th (for counties; state rank 6th)

City Residents

1980: 23,938
1990: 24,699
2000: 25,780
2003 estimate: 26,718
Percent change, 1990–2000: 2.8%
U.S. rank in 2000: Not reported

Density: 1,840.7 people per square mile (2000)

Racial and ethnic characteristics (2000)
   White: 24,434
   Black or African American: 59
   American Indian and Alaska Native: 541
   Asian: 201
   Native Hawaiian and Pacific Islander: 18
   Hispanic or Latino (may be of any race): 430
   Other: 98

Percent of residents born in state: 55.5% (2000)

Age characteristics (2000)
   Population under 5 years old: 1,501
   Population 5 to 9 years old: 1,558
   Population 10 to 14 years old: 1,628
   Population 15 to 19 years old: 1,962
   Population 20 to 24 years old: 1,999
   Population 25 to 34 years old: 2,931
   Population 35 to 44 years old: 3,919

Population 45 to 54 years old: 4,309
Population 55 to 59 years old: 1,414
Population 60 to 64 years old: 975
Population 65 to 74 years old: 1,640
Population 75 to 84 years old: 1,403
Population 85 years and older: 541
Median age: 38.8 years

Births (2002)
Five year average: 12.1 per 1000 population (county)

Deaths (2002)
Five year average: 7.9 per 1000 population (county)

Money income (2000)
Per capita income: $20,020
Median household income: $34,416
Total households: 11,476

Number of households with income of . . .
less than $10,000: 1,438
$10,000 to $14,999: 908
$15,000 to $24,999: 1,725
$25,000 to $34,999: 1,767
$35,000 to $49,999: 1,809
$50,000 to $74,999: 2,228
$75,000 to $99,999: 911
$100,000 to $149,999: 464
$150,000 to $199,999: 130
$200,000 or more: 96

Percent of families below poverty level: 9.3% (58.3% of which were female householder families in poverty)

2002 FBI Crime Index Total: Not reported

Municipal Government

Helena, the capital of Montana and the seat of Lewis & Clark County, has a city charter form of government. The mayor and four commissioners are elected to the city commission, each serving four-year terms. The daily affairs of the city are administered by a city manager, who is appointed by the commission.

Head Official: Mayor James E. Smith (since November 2001; current term expires 2005)

Total Number of City Employees: 275 (2005)

City Information: Mayor's Office, City of Helena, 316 N. Park Avenue, Helena, MT 59623; telephone (406)447-8410

Economy

Major Industries and Commercial Activity

For many years Helena has enjoyed a record of economic stability. It serves as a major governmental center for the county, state, and federal government. It is also a trading and transportation center for nearby livestock, mining, and farming enterprises. In an area rich in silver and lead deposits, Helena maintains an interest in mineral production and processing, and the nearby city of East Helena is the site of smelters, quartz crushers, and zinc reduction works. The Helena area is also a telephone communications center, and industries such as sand and gravel and ranching remain important. Statewide, Montana's fastest-growing industries include education and instruction, waste management, and construction. Specific occupations showing significant growth include textile machinery operation, septic and sewer maintenance, and computer software engineering.

Government positions account for 31 percent of Helena's workforce, while private sector jobs comprise 62 percent. Many of the private businesses rely on the government and its employees as their customers.

Items and goods produced: refined and smelted metals, paints, ceramics, concrete, machine parts, baking products, sheet metal, prefabricated houses, bottled beverages

Incentive Programs—New and Existing Companies

Local programs—The Montana Business Information Center (BIC) in Helena is a one-stop center that provides a multitude of planning tools as well as free onsite counseling provided by the Service Corps of Retired Executives (SCORE), Small Business Development Center (SBDC), and other Small Business Administration resources. The Montana BIC's resources include a reference library, a video center, and a computer lab designed specifically for small business research. The Small Business Administration offers a variety of financing options for small businesses, including long-term loans for machinery and equipment, general working capital loans, revolving lines of credit, and microloans. Similarly, Gateway Economic Development Corp. offers loans and tax rebates to new or expanding businesses in Lewis and Clark County and the surrounding area. The Downtown Helena Business Improvement District offers grants up to $2000 for retailers opening or expanding in the downtown area.

State programs—The state of Montana offers general incentives including net operating loss carry backs and carry forwards, depreciation, and dependent care assistance. New and expanding incentives include license tax credit for new or expanded jobs and reduced property assessments for research and development. Various tax exemptions are available for qualified businesses in research and development, domestic international sales corporations, free port merchandise, and business inventories.

Job training programs—The Small Business Development Center provides training, counseling, research, and other specialized assistance through its Helena office. NxLevel Entrepreneurial Training Programs, available through the Montana Department of Commerce, are in-depth training courses for entrepreneurs and business owners. NxLevel for Entrepreneurs is a 12-session course designed to help existing business owners improve growth and profits. NxLevel for Agricultural Entrepreneurs and NxLevel for Microentrepreneurs are similar programs aimed at new ventures and the self-employed.

Development Projects

Projects currently planned for Helena focus on business development, transportation, and branding. An ongoing downtown revitalization planning process has resulted in suggestions for an outdoor market, building restoration, and increased residential space. The City Commission voted to construct a new traffic lane on the Downtown Walking Mall, and to rename the road leading from the I-90 to downtown Last Chance Gulch (currently the name of the main downtown street only) to improve accessibility for tourists. Other plans call for new or upgraded freeway interchanges and improvements in water quality and availability.

Recently completed projects include the full restoration of the State Capitol building and construction of the Great Northern Town Center, a main street business and shopping district.

Economic Development Information: Small Business Administration-Montana District Office, 10 West 15th Street, Suite 1100, Helena, Montana, 59626; telephone (406)441-1081; fax (406)441-1090. Montana Finance Information Center, 301 S. Park, Helena, MT 59601; telephone (406)841-2732; fax (406)841-2771. Downtown Helena, Inc., 225 Cruse Ave., Suite B, Helena, MT 59601; telephone (406)447-1535. Montana Department of Commerce, PO Box 200501, Helena, MT 59620-0501; telephone (406)841-2700; fax (406)841-2701

Commercial Shipping

Air freight service is provided by FedEx, Airborne Express, and UPS. Freight service is also provided by Montana Rail Link, which provides national coverage in connection with Burlington Northern & Santa Fe Railway.

Labor Force and Employment Outlook

The Helena area labor force includes a high percentage of young, educated workers. The percentage of adults in the community who have received high school and college diplomas is considerably higher than the state and national average. Helena's stable economy is based primarily on a range of government agencies and small businesses. Skills in demand include textile machinery operation, septic and sewer maintenance, and computer software engineering. In recent years, growth has been observed in the fields of education and instruction, waste management, and construction.

The following is a summary of data regarding the Montana labor force, 2004 annual averages (Helena figures not available).

Size of nonagricultural labor force: 411,575

Number of workers employed in . . .
　　natural resources and mining: 7,242
　　construction: 24,717
　　manufacturing: 19,100
　　trade, transportation and utilities: 86,067
　　information: 7,800
　　financial activities: 21,058
　　professional and business services: 33,050
　　educational and health services: 54,225
　　leisure and hospitality: 54,458
　　other services: 17,000
　　government: 86,917

Average hourly earnings of production workers employed in manufacturing: $14.87

Unemployment rate: 5.5% (January 2005)

Largest private employers	Number of employees
St. Peter's Community Hospital	565
Blue Cross/Blue Shield	470
Veterans Administration Hospital	375
Shodair Children's Hospital	220
Qwest	210
Dick Anderson Construction	198
Carroll College	189

Cost of Living

The cost of living for Helena residents is comparable to the national average. According to the Helena Chamber of Commerce, housing, utilities, and goods and services all have lower than average cost. The cost of health care in Helena is slightly higher than the national rate.

The following is a summary of data regarding several key cost of living factors for the Helena area.

2004 (3rd Quarter) ACCRA Average House Price: $218,169

2004 (3rd Quarter) ACCRA Cost of Living Index: 96.3 (U.S. average = 100.0)

State income tax rate: 2% to 11% (corporate business tax rate: 6.75%)

State sales tax rate: None

Local income tax rate: None

Local sales tax rate: None

Property tax rate: 647.74 mills minimum, applies to taxable value as set by the state of Montana

Economic Information: Montana Department of Commerce, Census and Economic Information Center, 301 S. Park Ave., PO Box 200505, Helena, MT 59620-0505; telephone (406)841-2740

Education and Research

Elementary and Secondary Schools

Helena Public Schools states that its mission is to challenge and empower each student to become a competent, productive, responsible, caring citizen. Nearly half of the teachers have a master's degree or beyond, while 42 percent have one to three years of education beyond a bachelor's degree. Students consistently score above average in national standardized testing in all academic areas.

The Helena school district enjoys one of the lowest teacher-to-pupil ratios in the state. The curriculum includes many accelerated and advanced placement courses. Nearly 60 percent of the district's graduating seniors attend four-year colleges or universities, earning over $3 million annually in scholarships. Another 25 percent of high school graduates move on to trade school, two-year colleges or the military.

The following is a summary of data regarding the Helena public school system as of the 2003–2004 school year.

Total enrollment: 8,090

Number of facilities
elementary schools: 11
junior high/middle schools: 2
senior high schools: 2
other: 1

Student/teacher ratio: 15:1

Teacher salaries
Average: $45,789

Funding per pupil: Not available

Public Schools Information: Helena Public Schools, 55 South Rodney, Helena, MT 59601; telephone (406)324-2000; fax (406)324-2022

Colleges and Universities

Helena's Carroll College, established in 1909, is a Catholic liberal arts college with an enrollment of about 1,500. Students enjoy small classes and easy access to faculty members, and half of the students go on to graduate school. In 2005 *U.S. News & World Report* ranked Carroll among the Western region's best colleges for the 11th year in a row. Carroll College offers bachelor of arts degrees in a variety of fields, as well as eight pre-professional programs and a variety of research and internship opportunities in the capital city.

Helena College of Technology is a two-year college that is part of the University of Montana. More than 700 students receive technical education in accounting, computer science, aviation, construction, nursing, machine tooling, and other fields. The college also offers associate of science and arts degrees in general studies. Montana University also provides graduate programs and continuing education classes in Helena.

Libraries and Research Centers

The Lewis & Clark County Library's main facility is in downtown Helena and the system has three branches in nearby towns. The library contains 115,000 items, including books, periodicals, vertical files, and audio-visual tapes. Built in 1976, the library serves 50,000 patrons annually.

The Research Center of the Montana Historical Society, also in Helena, contains more than 40,000 books and pamphlets relating to Montana, 2,000 bound volumes of Montana newspapers, more than 8,000 maps, as well as initial township plots, topographical maps, music scores, and other items. Its special collections focus on the Lewis & Clark expedition, fur trading, and General Custer and the Battle of the Little Big Horn. It also has an extensive photograph collection featuring approximately 400,000 images.

The Montana State Library is the primary facility for state government as well as for the blind, physically handicapped, and learning disabled. Its focus is on Montana's natural resources. Every Montanan is entitled to borrow from the State Library, although local libraries often borrow titles on behalf of their patrons.

Other local libraries include the college libraries of Carroll College and the Helena College of Technology, and those of St. Peter's Community and Shodair hospitals, as well as libraries of the Montana state legislature, the Montana Department of Commerce, the Montana Natural Heritage Program, the Montana Department of Special Resources, the State Law Library, and the U.S. Geological Survey Water Resources Division Library.

Research institutions include the Montana Science Institute, which explores natural history and ecology of the Missouri River and conservation of native species, and the Nature Conservancy-Montana Chapter, which identifies rare plants and animals and works to protect rare species.

Public Library Information: Lewis & Clark County Library, 120 S. Last Chance Gulch, Helena, MT 59601; telephone (406)447-1690; fax (406)447-1687

Health Care

Helena citizens have the service of two local hospitals. St. Peter's Community Hospital offers comprehensive inpatient, outpatient, and home care service. The facility, founded in 1883, provides obstetrics, surgery, emergency care, a cancer treatment center, and a full range of diagnostic services. In 2004 St. Peter's began an expansion project to meet the anticipated needs of Helena's growing population. Shodair Children's Hospital provides inpatient and outpatient psychiatric services, and treatment of genetic disorders. Located just outside Helena is Fort Harrison Veterans Hospital.

Health Care Information: St. Peter's Community Hospital, 2475 Broadway, Helena, MT 59601; telephone (406)442-2480. Shodair Hospital, 2755 Colonial Drive, PO Box 5539, Helena, MT 59604; telephone (406)444-7500

Recreation

Sightseeing

The focal point of sightseeing in Helena is the 17-block Historic Downtown District. In this part of town is found a mix of retail stores, galleries, lodging, restaurants, historic buildings, and entertainment centers. The imposing State Capital Building is constructed of Montana granite and boasts a classic dome made of radiant copper. It now serves as the symbol of Montana. The interior is decorated with murals by artists E.S. Paxon, Charles M. Russell, and others. The meeting of Lewis and Clark with a group of native Americans is depicted in a large mural by Russell.

Tours are offered of several impressive local structures. The original governor's mansion, which was built in 1888 in the Queen Anne style, contains furnishings popular during the early twentieth century. Helena Civic Center, built in 1921, is a Moorish-style edifice with a 175-foot minaret, an onion

dome, and intricate exterior brickwork. Just outside Helena to the north is another impressive facility, Fort Harrison, which was once an army garrison and is now a veterans' hospital.

The Montana Historical Society Museum features the C.M. Russell painting collections, as well as temporary exhibits of western art. The Montana Homeland Exhibit portrays Montana history throughout the eras.

The imposing St. Helena Cathedral, with its white marble altar, stained-glass windows, and 230-foot spires, is modeled after famous churches in Austria and Germany. Gold nuggets, gold wire, gold coins, and gold dust are on display at the Gold collection at downtown's Norwest Bank and the Federal Reserve Bank on Neill Avenue. The Guardian of the Gulch is a landmark fire tower built in 1876 and one of just five similar towers remaining in the United States.

Dotting the hillsides on Helena's west side are dozens of stately private homes, built by rich merchants and miners a century ago. The Last Chance Tour Train provides hour-long tours of the city. A guided Missouri riverboat tour follows the path taken by Lewis and Clark nearly two centuries ago. Northeast of Helena, Canyon Ferry Dam offers information and interactive displays of the region's wildlife as well as the Lewis and Clark expedition.

Arts and Culture

A major cultural facility in Helena is the Myrna Loy Center, named after the beloved Montana-born actress. It is housed in the city's 1880s-era former jailhouse, and features performing arts activities, literary events, films, and art shows. The Carroll College Theatre presents live performances throughout the year. The Toadstone Theatre Company offers professional and community childrens' theater and Grandsteet Theatre offers live performances of Broadway shows using community-based volunteers. The Montana Shakespeare Company presents Shakespeare's classics in Performance Park Square, an outdoor venue.

Helena's Holster Museum of Art displays various works of art from historical to contemporary times. It also offers workshops, readings, and discussions. The Archie Bray Foundation for Ceramic Arts, which offers beautiful display pieces for sale, has attained a national reputation for training potters. The Ghost Art Gallery in Helena's old mining district features architecture and themes from nearby ghost towns, as well as western and wildlife art by fine local artists.

Music lovers attend performances of the Helena Symphony; in addition to a regular season of performances by its own chorale of 150 members, it offers community concerts. Four-part harmony is the focus of the Sweet Adelines Performing Chorus.

Festivals and Holidays

Downtown Helena is the site of many special events, including festivals, street dances, theater productions, sled dog races, car rallies, art exhibits, and street fairs. The annual Western Rendezvous of Art takes place in August, featuring art shows, seminars, an auction and a fixed price sale, and a gala awards banquet. Music fills the air in September during the Last Chance Bluegrass Festival, while October is enlivened by Bullfest and Oktoberfest celebrations. November brings the Bald Eagle Migration and Downtown Helena Fall Art Walk, while December hails the holidays with the Festival of Trees and Winter Fair.

The excitement of the Race to the Sky Sled Dog Race warms hearts in February, and children of all ages enjoy April's Railroad Fair and Kite Festival. The Governor's Cup Marathon and the Sleeping Giant Swing 'n Jazz Jubilee draw crowds in June while July brings the excitement of the Last Chance Stampede & Rodeo and the Mt. Helena Music Festival.

Sports for the Spectator

Helena is the home of the Helena Brewers minor league baseball team of the Pioneer League; the Helena Bighorns hockey club, which plays NAHL hockey at the Helena Ice Arena; the Carroll College Fighting Saints; and high school teams that compete in tennis, baseball, football, soccer, hockey, golf, rugby, and basketball.

Sports for the Participant

Within easy access to Helena residents and visitors are millions of acres of public lands, top rated fisheries, and many lakes, rivers, and reservoirs that are used for boating, sailing, wind surfing, and other water sports. Also available are hunting, backpacking, biking, skiing, and snowmobiling. There are more than 25 area parks. Mount Helena City Park and Helena National Forest each have miles of hiking and biking trails. The local recreation department offers facilities for running, racquetball, weight training, and horseback riding. Centennial Waterslide Park is a family-focused indoor facility with slides and swimming pools. Helena Skate Park offers ledges, quarter pipes, and banks with free access for skateboarders and in-line skaters. There are two public golf courses and one private, numerous tennis courts, and several health clubs. Hikers on the Blackfoot Meadows or the Continental Divide trails may spot such wildlife as elk, moose, mountain goats, bighorn sheep, black bears, otters, beavers, and mink.

Shopping and Dining

Helena's largest shopping center is Capital Hill Mall, which is located near the Capital complex and contains 40 specialty shops and two major department stores. What was once the Last Chance Gulch mine is now Helena's main street and a pedestrian mall. Downtown Helena is dotted with specialty shops and galleries, especially throughout the Walking Mall and Reeders' Alley, a complex of red brick buildings from the 1870s that once served as miners' shanties. Principal shopping centers include Northgate Plaza and Lundy Center. Discount shopping can be found at WalMart, Shopko, Target, Big-K and Gibson's.

For a small city, Helena has a varied selection of ethnic dining spots that feature Mexican, Thai, Chinese, Mediterranean, French, German, Italian, and classic American cuisines. Beer lovers can sample local micro brews from the Sleeping Giant Brewery, Kessler Brewery, or Blackfoot River Brewing Company.

Visitor Information: Helena Convention & Visitor Bureau, 225 Cruse Ave., Helena, MT 59601; telephone (406)447-1530 or (800)743-5362

Convention Facilities

Most conferences in Helena are held at one of the following three facilities. The Best Western Helena Great Northern Hotel offers sleeping accommodations in 101 rooms and a convention capacity of 600 people. The Holiday Inn Helena Downtown has 71 sleeping rooms and can host up to 200 people in its newly remodeled meeting and banquet facilities. Jorgenson's Inn and Suites has 115 sleeping rooms and can accommodate up to 250 people for banquets or conventions.

Convention Information: Helena Convention & Visitors Bureau, 225 Cruse Ave., Suite A, Helena, MT 59601; telephone (406)447-1530 or (800)743-5362

Transportation

Approaching the City

Interstate 15 runs along the east side of Helena, northward toward Great Falls and southward toward Butte. It intersects with U.S. Highways 12/287 that run east and west and extend toward East Helena. Helena Airport is located 2.5 miles from the center of the city. SkyWest, Comair, Horizon, Northwest, and Big Sky Airlines provide 14 daily flights to the city. Bus service is provided by Rimrock Trailways, which connects with Greyhound.

Traveling in the City

The major north-south routes are U.S. 12, which is known as Montana Avenue, and North Last Chance Gulch, also known as Main Street. Neill Avenue, 6th, 9th and Lyndale are major east-west streets. Transportation is provided by door-to-door bus service and a city taxi service.

Communications

Newspapers and Magazines

Helena's local newspapers include the *Independent- Record,* a daily, and the *Adit,* a shopping weekly. Magazines published locally include *Montana Magazine,* a regional interest magazine, *The Montana Catholic,* and the *Montana* historical magazine, as well as the *Montana Stockgrower,* the *Montana Food Distributor, Trial Trends* and *U.S. Toy Collector Magazine.*

Television and Radio

One private television station broadcasts from Helena, and there is one local cable company. The city has four local FM radio stations and three AM stations. They feature adult contemporary, easy listening, country, classic rock, and news and talk formats.

Media Information: Independent-Record, PO Box 4249, Helena, MT 59604; telephone (406)447-4000

Helena Online

City of Helena. Available www.ci.helena.mt.us

Helena Chamber of Commerce. Available www.helena chamber.com/index.html

Helena Convention & Visitors Bureau. Available helenacvb .visitmt.com

Helena Public Schools. Available www.helena.k12.mt.us

Independent-Record. Available www.helenair.com

Lewis & Clark County Library. Available www .lewisandclark library.org

Montana Business Information Center. Available www.sba online.sba.gov/regions/states/mt/mtbics.html

Selected Bibliography

Evans, Nicholas, *The Horse Whisperer* (New York: Delacourte Press, 1995

Petrick, Paula Evans, *No Step Backward: Women and Family on the Rocky Mountain Mining Frontier, Helena, MT: 1865-1900,* (Helena, MT: Helena Montana Historical Society Press, 1987)

Rodgers, Joni, *Crazy for Trying* (Denver: MacMurray & Beck, 1999)

NEVADA

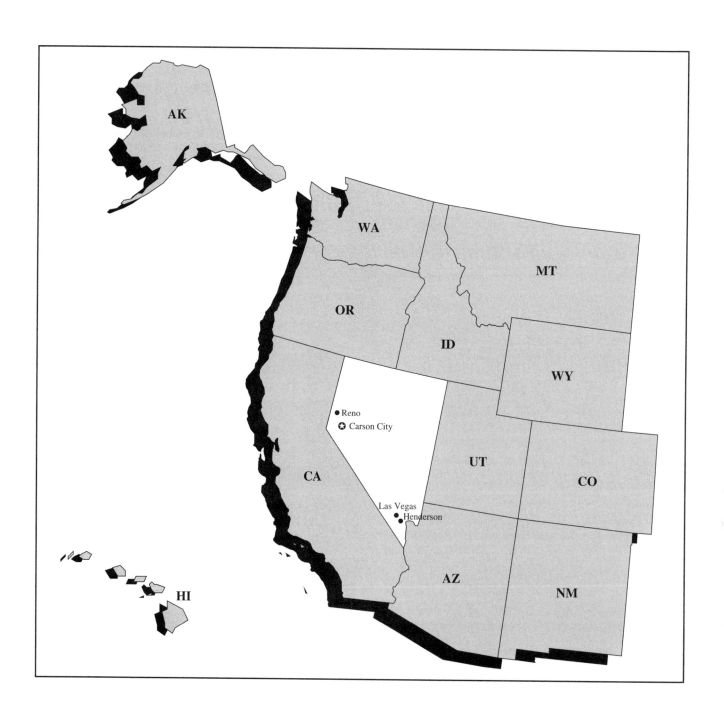

The State in Brief

Nickname: Silver State
Motto: All for our country

Flower: Sagebrush
Bird: Mountain bluebird

Area: 110,560 square miles (2000; U.S. rank: 7th)
Elevation: 479 feet to 13,140 feet above sea level
Climate: Semi arid, with temperatures that vary with altitude as well as season; extremely cold winters in the north and west, ovenlike summer heat in parts of the south

Admitted to Union: October 31, 1864
Capital: Carson City
Head Official: Governor Kenny Guinn (R) (until 2007)

Population
   1980: 800,493
   1990: 1,201,833
   2000: 1,998,257
   2004 estimate: 2,334,771
   Percent change, 1990–2000: 66.3%
   U.S. rank in 2004: 35th
   Percent of residents born in state: 21.3% (2000)
   Density: 18.2 people per square mile (2000)
   2002 FBI Crime Index Total: 97,752

Racial and Ethnic Characteristics (2000)
   White: 1,501,886
   Black or African American: 135,477
   American Indian and Alaska Native: 26,420
   Asian: 90,266
   Native Hawaiian and Pacific Islander: 8,426
   Hispanic or Latino (may be of any race): 393,970
   Other: 159,354

Age Characteristics (2000)
   Population under 5 years old: 145,817
   Population 5 to 19 years old: 415,684
   Percent of population 65 years and over: 11.0%
   Median age: 35.0 years (2000)

Vital Statistics
   Total number of births (2003): 33,585
   Total number of deaths (2003): 17,759 (infant deaths, 203)
   AIDS cases reported through 2003: 2,654

Economy
   Major industries: Services; finance, insurance, and real estate; trade; government
   Unemployment rate: 3.9% (February 2005)
   Per capita income: $31,487 (2003; U.S. rank: 19th)
   Median household income: $46,118 (3-year average, 2001-2003)
   Percentage of persons below poverty level: 10.5% (1999)
   Income tax rate: None
   Sales tax rate: 5.0% to 9.0%

Carson City

The City in Brief

Founded: 1858 (incorporated, 1875)

Head Official: Mayor Marv Teixeira (R) (since 2005)

City Population
    1980: 32,022
    1990: 40,443
    2000: 52,457
    2003 estimate: 55,311
    Percent change, 1990–2000: 29.7%
    U.S. rank in 2000: 680th (State rank: 9th)

Area: 155.66 square miles (2000)
Elevation: 4,600 feet above sea level

Average Annual Temperatures: January, 33.6° F; July, 69.9° F

Average Annual Precipitation: 11.8 inches of rain, 22 inches of snow

Major Economic Sectors: Government, services, trade, manufacturing
Unemployment Rate: 5.8% (January 2005)
Per Capita Income: $20,943 (1999)

2002 FBI Crime Index Total: Not reported

Major Colleges and Universities: Western Nevada Community College

Daily Newspaper: *The Nevada Appeal*–Carson City Edition

To Railroad Museum

Introduction

Carson City, Nevada's state capital, is also a year-round vacation destination offering a wide variety of recreational activities. Long called the ''hub of the Sierras,'' the city's distinct character was molded by the industries that dominated the area in the late 1800s—logging, mining, and the railroad. Carson City is now mainly a center of government, but entertainment, shopping, skiing, golf, and fishing keep the thriving capital alive with a sense of its own unique culture, charm, and Wild West adventure. In recent times, the city has seen a migration of people seeking an improved quality of life, many of them from California. Today, the city boasts a beautiful historic district amid an actively growing business environment that provides ample opportunities for companies and workers alike. Lively casinos continue to flourish and complement the small-town feel of the community.

Geography and Climate

Carson City is located in northwestern Nevada in the foothills of the Sierra Nevada range. It lies 30 miles south of Reno, Nevada in the Carson River Valley near Lake Tahoe, which is 14 miles to the west. Carson City includes an area that stretches across the Carson Range of the Sierra Mountains to Eagle Valley and the Pine Nut Mountains. It is bordered on the north by Washoe and Storey counties, and on the west by the state of California.

Carson City has a pleasant, semi-desert climate, and boasts an average of 265 sunny days annually. Summers are warm and dry with peak temperatures reaching into the 90° F range, while temperatures can drop into the 50° F range during the evenings. Winters are cold and dry with snow, but not in the amounts of nearby areas that are at a much higher elevation. The temperatures range from the high teens to the 40° F range. Annual snowfall in the city averages about 22 inches.

Area: 155.66 square miles (2000)

Elevation: 4,600 feet above sea level

Average Temperatures: January, 33.6° F; July, 69.9° F

Average Annual Precipitation: 11.8 inches of rain, 22 inches of snow

History

Gold Leads the Way

For nearly 4,000 years before the coming of white settlers, the Washoe Indians occupied the land along the Sierra Nevada Mountain Range that borders Nevada and California. In 1851 a group of prospectors decided to look for gold in the area that is now Carson City. Unsuccessful in that attempt, they opened up a trading post called Eagle Station on the Overland Stagecoach route. It was used by wagon trains of people moving westward. The surrounding area came to be called Eagle Ranch, and the surrounding meadows as Eagle Valley. In time, a number of scattered settlements grew up in the area and the Eagle Ranch became its social center.

As a growing number of white settlers came to the area and began to develop the valleys and mountains of the Sierra Nevada, the Washoe people who for so long had occupied the area were overwhelmed. Although lands were allotted to individual Indians by the federal government starting in the 1880s, they did not offer sufficient water. As a result, the Washoe tended to set up camp at the edges of white settlements and ranches in order to work for food. It would not be until the twentieth century that parcels of reservation land were established for them.

Many of the earliest settlers in the Carson City area were Mormons led to Eagle Valley by Colonel John Reese. When the Mormons were summoned to Salt Lake City, Utah, by their leader, Brigham Young, many sold their land for a small amount to area resident John Mankin, who later laid claim to the entire Eagle Valley. In time he subdivided the land and sold tracts of it.

Birth of Carson City

In 1858, an ambitious New Yorker named Abraham Curry, along with three partners, bought most of Eagle Valley, including the ranch and trading post. Curry was correct in his prophecy that the western part of Utah Territory was soon to become a state, and he had the present-day site of Carson City surveyed. He promoted Eagle Valley, a fertile though rather deserted place, as the site of the future state capital.

Soon Major William M. Ormsby also became an enthusiastic promoter of a town that did not yet exist. He named it in honor of legendary mountain man Kit Carson, whose name was also borne by a nearby river. The town was laid out with wide streets and had a four-square city area that he named Capitol Square, but that later came to be called the Plaza.

In 1859 the rich (chiefly silver), was discovered mere miles from the site of Carson City, setting off a rush to the area.

Curry sold his claim to the Comstock for a few thousand dollars, but those who bought it became millionaires. Still, Curry is remembered in the name of the mine, the Gould and Curry.

By 1860 the town's population stood at 500 people. Soon Abe Curry took steps to have Carson City named territorial capital. He argued that it was close to the main lines of travel in the region. On November 25, 1861, Carson City was named the permanent capital of Nevada Territory and the Ormsby County seat. A plaza was established at the site for future public buildings.

Carson Named Capital of New State

Just one year later, the population of the town had nearly doubled. The year 1862 saw Carson become a station on the Pony Express and the eastern end of a telegraph line from San Francisco. Soon the town became a freighting and supply point for many mining and ranching communities in the central and southern part of Nevada.

About this time, both Carson and the entire surrounding area were having problems with cattle rustlers, claim jumpers, and other outlaws. As a result, the legislature passed laws designed to establish order. When the new legislature could not find a site large enough to accommodate its numbers, Abe Curry offered it the use of his Warm Springs Hotel, a rather primitive building located near the Carson River. In the early days a canvas curtain was used to divide the Nevada senate from the state assembly.

In October 1864, Nevada became a state, and Carson City was chosen to serve as the state capital. By then, Curry owned a sandstone quarry, a brickyard, a saloon, and the Great Basin Hotel. When a courthouse was needed, Curry again came to the rescue. He sold his Great Basin Hotel to the State of Nevada and it was used as a courthouse and legislature building into the 1870s. Because it was two miles out of town, Curry transported the legislators in Carson's first horse-drawn streetcar.

The Early Years of a Capital City

A few years later the Warm Springs building was converted into a territorial prison and Curry became its first warden. Prison labor used local sandstone to construct many of Carson City's early buildings. In 1870, a branch of the U.S. Mint was built in Carson and Curry was appointed its first superintendent. The mint processed the rich ore found in nearby mines. In rapid succession, Curry resigned that position, lost a bid to become Nevada's lieutenant governor, and built the huge stone roundhouse and shops for the Virginia & Truckee Railroad. This became America's richest short-line railroad, connecting the Comstock mines with mills on the Carson River. In 1873 Curry died of a stroke.

During those early years, Nevada's legislative business was punctuated by fistfights, vote-buying, and other acts of political corruption. In 1872, a State Capitol building, a large square stone structure with rafters made of hewn logs, was completed. That same year saw the completion of a 52-mile railroad linking Carson City to Virginia City, and other lines were to follow. In 1880, the population stood at about 8,000 people.

As a New Century Dawned

During the last decades of the nineteenth century, Carson City experienced boom and bust cycles common to the area. With the decline of the nearby mines, the population too began to decline. Railroad traffic through Carson City came to a halt when the Southern Pacific Railroad built a branch rail line that bypassed the city. That, and the departure of the rootless, restless miners, resulted in Carson City's settling down into a quiet community. In the late 1800s Carson City became home to the Stewart Indian School, which educated thousands of native American children between 1890 and 1980, teaching them English and the ways of the white people.

In 1897, Carson City became the focus of worldwide attention when it became the site of a world heavyweight championship fight in which Britain Bob Fitzsimmons won over "Gentleman Jim" Corbett. A motion picture of the fight, the first of its kind, thrilled audiences, despite its bluish tint and flickering images. But soon after, between 1890 and 1900, the population of Carson City dropped from nearly 4,000 to just over 2,000 people.

Carson City in the Twentieth Century

Carson City's fortunes gradually declined through World War I and with the coming of the worldwide economic downturn known as the Great Depression. By 1930, the population had declined to only about 1,500 citizens, a quarter of what it had been 50 years earlier. Then in 1931 state legislation was enacted that permitted gambling in the area and provided for speedy divorce and simple marriage procedures. These moves brought more tourists into the area.

Soon the population began to grow again, reaching 2,478 in 1940, doubling to 5,163 by 1960, then tripling that figure by 1970, when the population stood at 15,468 people. In 1969, Ormsby County was merged with Carson City, and government services were consolidated. The population doubled again in 1980 to 32,022 then jumped by 20,000 more in 2000.

Today, as the site of a state prison, the Nevada Gaming Commission, and a variety of state department headquarters and federal agencies, the small city is economically thriving and serves as the power center of Nevada. The city's planners are set to complete a comprehensive 20-year "master plan" by the end of 2005 that will address a variety of needs—growth, housing, economic factors, and environmental issues among them—and propose action steps and long-range strategies for success. The business climate is diverse and expansive and is driven by a highly educated workforce and prime open land for future development. Pleasant weather conditions throughout the year draw visitors to outdoor activities in addition to the wide array of entertainment options. A new freeway scheduled to open in 2006 will support an increase in travel throughout the city and to nearby vacation destinations.

Historical Information: Nevada State Library and Archives, 100 N. Stewart St., Carson City, NV 89701-4285; telephone (775)684-3310 or (775)684-3360; fax (775)684-3330; email nslref@clan.lib.nv.us. State of Nevada, Department of Cultural Affairs, Division of Museums and History Office, 708 N. Curry St., Carson City, NV 89703; telephone (775)687-4340; fax (775)687-4333

Population Profile

Metropolitan Area Residents
Carson City is an independent municipality, thus not part of any county or Metropolitan Statistical Area.

City Residents
1980: 32,022
1990: 40,443
2000: 52,457 (of which, 27,102 were males and 25,355 were females)
2003 estimate: 55,311
Percent change, 1990–2000: 29.7%
U.S. rank in 2000: 680th (State rank: 9th)

Density: 365.9 people per square mile (2000)

Racial and ethnic characteristics (2000)
   White: 44,744
   Black or African American: 946
   American Indian and Alaska Native: 1,259
   Asian: 930
   Native Hawaiian and Other Pacific Islander: 76
   Hispanic or Latino (may be of any race): 7,466
   Other: 3,391

Percent of residents born in state: 23.8% (2000)

Age characteristics (2000)
   Population under 5 years old: 3,289
   Population 5 to 9 years old: 3,495
   Population 10 to 14 years old: 3,473
   Population 15 to 19 years old: 3,196
   Population 20 to 24 years old: 2,946
   Population 25 to 34 years old: 6,766

   Population 35 to 44 years old: 8,370
   Population 45 to 54 years old: 7,724
   Population 55 to 59 years old: 2,949
   Population 60 to 64 years old: 2,412
   Population 70 to 74 years old: 4,096
   Population 75 to 84 years old: 2,950
   Population 85 years and over: 791
   Median age: 38.7 years

Births (2003)
   Total number: 721

Deaths (2003)
   Total number: 656 (of which, 1 was an infant under the age of 1 year)

Money income (1999)
   Per capita income: $20,943
   Median household income: $41,809
   Total households: 20,237

Number of households with income of . . .
   less than $10,000: 554
   $10,000 to $14,999: 499
   $15,000 to $24,999: 1,473
   $25,000 to $34,999: 1,689
   $35,000 to $49,999: 2,560
   $50,000 to $74,999: 3,299
   $75,000 to $99,999: 1,728
   $100,000 to $149,999: 1,129
   $150,000 to $199,999: 257
   $200,000 or more: 245

Percent of families below poverty level: 6.9% (34.4% of which were female householder families with related children under 5 years)

2002 FBI Crime Index Total: Not reported

Municipal Government

The city and county of Carson, Nevada, have been coextensive since 1969, when the city merged with what was formerly Ormsby County to form a consolidated municipality. The city is governed by a mayor and a four-member board of supervisors, all elected to serve overlapping four-year terms. An appointed city manager performs administrative functions for the city's board of supervisors and oversees city staff and departments.

Head Official: Mayor Marv Teixeira (R) (since 2005; current term expires 2008)

Total Number of City Employees: 700–799 (2004)

City Information: City Hall, Carson City, 201 N. Carson St., Suite 1, Carson City, NV 89701; telephone (775)887-2100; fax (775)887-2286

Economy

Major Industries and Commercial Activity

Carson City has a growing and diverse economy, with a population that increased by 64 percent between 1980 and 2000. It is the regional retail and commercial center for northwestern Nevada, which is devoted to irrigated farming, livestock raising, and mining of silver and other minerals. It draws from a trade area of about a quarter of a million people with 14 percent of the city's employees working in the manufacturing industry, making it the state's leading city in that category. The city's retail and commercial growth are also expected to continue at a healthy rate.

Since gambling was legalized in 1931, tourism has also been important to the Carson City economy, and the resort city is drawing increasingly more visitors. The service industry is by far the largest in the city representing 30 percent of the local workforce, which includes hotel, gaming, and tourism workers.

As the seat of state government, which meets in the city for two months every two years, and a center for federal government, the government sector employs about one out of four city residents and is the second largest industry.

Taxable sales totaled over $860 million in 2003 with nearly half of that from car and other retail sales. The cost of doing business is about 10 percent less than in Nevada's metropolitan areas, and land and labor costs are also lower. Carson City serves as one of the health care hubs for the region, providing hospitals and multispecialty clinics.

Items and goods produced: calculators and computers, refurbished aircraft turbines, retail display furniture, plastic moldings, plumbing supplies, fiberglass light poles, aerospace components, and welding accessories

Incentive Programs—New and Existing Companies

Local programs—Carson City is able to save employers time and money through the major project review process, and a local one-stop shop that issues building permits. According to the Northern Nevada Development Authority, Nevada does not offer short-term incentives to attract business. It relies instead on having no corporate taxes and no personal income taxes or inventory taxes to make its cities very competitive. In addition, accessible government, a thriving business climate, and sensible regulations also draw business.

State programs—The State of Nevada administers Small Business Administration loans. The Nevada Development Capital Corporation (NDCC) provides more than $3 million from Nevada banks, utilities, and mining companies and other firms to help finance growth opportunities for new and existing businesses. It provides flexible financing to small Nevada businesses that do not qualify for more conventional financing.

The Nevada Revolving Loan Fund (NRLF) offers loans of up to $100,000 to for-profit businesses in need of gap financing to complete business projects. The Nevada Industrial Development Revenue Bond Program makes loans available to qualified manufacturers who are buying land, building new facilities, and purchasing new equipment. The Micro Enterprise Loan Fund works with the Community Business Resource Center (CBRC) to help provide economic self-sufficiency for entrepreneurs through training, technical assistance, and access to credit.

Job training programs—Western Nevada Community College works closely with area businesses in providing specialized training courses for employees. Nevada's "Train Employees Now" program has customized industrial training programs to assist new and expanding businesses in training new or potential employees. Eligible businesses contribute 25 percent of the total training costs. Working to ensure that companies have an adequate workforce is the Job Opportunities in Nevada (JOIN) that offers training and educational opportunities for job seekers; Nevadaworks assists employers in developing employees' skills.

Development Projects

In 2003 the city held a groundbreaking for the new Carson City Freeway that will provide another north-south option for local travelers. The challenging and long-discussed project is estimated to cost nearly $70 million; the 4.8-mile northern half is scheduled to open in 2006. The Carson City Senior Center more than doubled in size to 33,000 square feet with its July 2004 expansion. In the summer of 2004 the Comstock Casino debuted its 9,500-square-foot 100-slot facility and 2002 saw the Ormsby House Hotel & Casino's revival with $20 million in renovations. With a growing population comes an increased need for medical facilities, which will be addressed with the opening of the $132 million Carson-Tahoe Regional Medical Center in late 2005.

Economic Development Information: Carson City Community Development Dept., 2621 Northgate Ln., Ste. 62, Carson City, NV 89706; telephone (775)887-2180; fax (775)887-2287

Commercial Shipping

With a strategic location on two major highway corridors, more than 60 local, regional, and national carriers provide trucking services in Reno. Shipments from Carson City are able to reach nine western states on a next-day basis. The Burlington Northern Santa Fe and Union Pacific Railroads provide regional freight service.

Labor Force and Employment Outlook

Nevada and Carson City's abundant availability of skilled workers and the area's moderate salaries have made the area attractive to new businesses. Training programs supported by the state and pro-business policies have helped make Nevada the fastest growing state in the nation with an anticipated 15 percent increase in the workforce by 2010. Local wages are reasonable because the cost of living remains reasonable in Carson City. Nineteen percent of the local residents hold college degrees, and 82 percent have earned high school diplomas.

The following is a summary of data regarding the Carson City area labor force, 2004 annual averages.

Size of nonagricultural labor force: 31,800

Number of workers employed in . . .
   manufacturing: 3,100
   trade, transportation, and utilities: 4,300
   professional and business services: 2,300
   leisure and hospitality: 3,900
   government: 10,500

Average hourly earnings of production workers employed in manufacturing: $14.60 (Nevada average)

Unemployment rate: 5.8% (January 2005)

Largest employers	*Number of employees*
State of Nevada	5,000–5,499
Carson City School District	1,000–1,499
Carson-Tahoe Hospital	800–899
City of Carson City	700–799
Nevada Department of Transportation	700–799
Western Nevada Community College	500–599
Carson City Nugget	500–599
Casino Fandango	400–499
Chromalloy Nevada	300–399
Legislative Counsel Bureau	300–399

Cost of Living

The following is a summary of data regarding several key cost of living factors for the Carson City area.

2004 ACCRA (3rd Quarter) Average House Price: $329,876

2004 ACCRA (3rd Quarter) Cost of Living Index: 110.2 (U.S. average = 100.0)

State income tax rate: None; no corporate income tax

State sales tax rate: 6.5% (food and prescription drugs are exempt)

Local income tax rate: None

Local sales tax rate: None

Property tax rate: $2.63 per $100 assessed value

Economic Information: Carson City Area Chamber of Commerce, 1900 S. Carson St., Carson City, NV 89701; telephone (775)882-1565; fax (775)882-4179; email ccchamber@carsoncitychamber.com. Nevada Department of Business & Industry, Office of the Labor Commissioner, 675 Fairview Dr., Ste. 226, Carson City, NV, 89701; telephone (775)687-4850; fax (775)687-6409

Education and Research

Elementary and Secondary Schools

Carson High School is one of the top-rated schools in Nevada. Since 1999 it has shared in a $5 million joint-use project with Western Nevada Community College named the Jim Randolph High-Tech Center. Providing about 230 computers, it assists students in preparing for careers in electronics, automated technology, drafting, business, and allied health.

The following is a summary of data regarding the Carson City public school system as of the 2003–2004 school year.

Total enrollment: 8,798

Number of facilities
   elementary schools: 6
   junior high/middle schools: 2
   senior high schools: 2
   other: 1

Student/teacher ratio: K, 21:1; 1-2, 15:1; 3, 17:1; 4-5, 24:1; 6-8, 25:1

Teacher salaries (2000–2001)
   minimum: $26,220
   maximum: $51,242

Funding per pupil: $6,669

Five schools provide private, religion-based education in the city and enroll approximately 600 students.

Public Schools Information: Carson City Schools, 1402 W. King St., Carson City, NV 89703; telephone (775)283-2110; fax (775)283-2092

Colleges and Universities

Western Nevada Community College is a two-year public institution that offers about 50 associate degree programs, as well as basic education and job development skills programs. It enrolls more than 6,000 students at its campuses in Carson City, and in Fallon and Douglas counties. The college offers diverse degree and certificate programs, schedules evening and weekend as well as daytime classes, and provides small class sizes and one-on-one counseling opportunities for students.

Libraries and Research Centers

Carson City Library, built in 1966, offers over 116,000 volumes, 200 periodical subscriptions, and 3,200 audio tapes. The library has a collection on Nevada history and a large print section.

Western Nevada Community College opened the 34,000-square-foot New Library & Student Center on its Carson City campus in January 2004. Other libraries in the city include the Nevada State Library & Archives, the library of the Nevada State Museum, and the Nevada Supreme Court Library.

Public Library Information: Carson City Library, 900 N. Roop St., Carson City, NV 89701; telephone (775)887-2244

Health Care

The 128-bed Carson-Tahoe Hospital is the city's not-for-profit community hospital that employs over 185 physicians in 25 different specialties. The facility includes a Life Stress Center featuring in- and out-patient psychiatric and addiction services, a 24-hour emergency room that is northern Nevada's designated trauma center, state-of-the-art diagnostic facilities, nutritional counseling, wellness programs, and a cardiac care center along with a separate rehabilitation and physical therapy facility. In late 2005 the hospital anticipates the grand opening of its new Carson-Tahoe Regional Medical Center with 146 beds on 300,000 square feet with a construction cost of about $132 million.

Health Care Information: Carson City Government, Environmental Health Department, 3303 Butti Way, Bldg. #1, Carson City, NV 89701; telephone (775)887-2190; email cceh@ci.carson-city.nv.us

Recreation

Sightseeing

The Carson City Chamber of Commerce provides an illustrated map with details about various local historic sites.

Tours in a horse-drawn surrey are available. The Governor's Mansion, a 1909 example of classic southern Colonial design, is on the 2.5-mile Kit Carson Trail, a blue line painted on the sidewalk that takes visitors past a variety of historic sites. The route passes 60 historical homes, churches, and buildings featuring Victorian architecture. Also along the route are several museums. Visitors to the State Library and Archives Building can peruse its rich collection on Nevada history and view the original Nevada Constitution.

Historical homes that highlight the tour include the Bliss Mansion, an 1879 15-room mansion with seven marble fireplaces; the 1859 Roberts House, a Gothic revival structure that was moved to the city from its first site in Washoe City; and the 1876 Chartz House.

The silver-domed State Capitol, rebuilt during the 1970s, features portraits of Nevada governors, Nevada artifacts, and Old (Nevada) Supreme Court and legislative chambers that are open to the public when not in use. The Federal Building, once the federal courthouse, a post office, and a state library, and now the Paul Laxalt Building in honor of a popular Nevada politician, houses the state Tourism Commission.

The Nevada State Museum, inside the old Carson City U.S. mint, has displays on the history of the area, an exhibit that illustrates the process of making coins, a realistic mock underground mine, and an exhibit showing bears, bobcats, and other animals native to the area. The Fire Museum displays a century's worth of fire-related memorabilia, including goggles, helmets, hose carts, and Currier & Ives prints of New York fires. The Children's Museum offers displays and activities for the younger set such as 25 hands-on exhibits and a walk-in kaleidoscope.

The Stewart Indian Cultural Center houses the Cassinelli arrowhead collection, traditional basketry, grinding rocks, Great Basin artifacts, and the Indian School collection, as well as a gift shop. The Dat-So-La-Lee Museum features memorabilia of the famed Nevada basket weaver of the same name. Her original baskets, worth up to $250,000 each, remain on display at the Nevada State Museum and in other museums throughout the country.

Focusing on Nevada's rich railroad heritage, the Nevada State Railroad Museum's collection contains more than 60 pieces of rolling stock, including 6 steam locomotives, and more than 50 passenger and freight cars, many of which once operated on the famous Virginia and Truckee line. The museum also contains an assortment of exhibits relating to railroading in Nevada. At the Great Basin Wildlife Center, opened in 1992, visitors can observe coyotes, foxes, eagles, raccoons, a mountain lion, and a black bear, as well as geology and botany displays.

A short drive from Carson City is Virginia City, site of the legendary Comstock Lode mining operation, which pro-

The Nevada State Library.

duced both gold and silver. Virginia City provides a glimpse into the days of the Old West. The booming mines there spurred the construction of quartz reduction mills along the Carson River and helped Carson City become a thriving commercial center beginning in the 1860s. Today's shops, saloons, museums, and rides on the Virginia & Truckee Railroad are fun for visitors old or young. Major sites in Virginia City include the Nevada State Fire Museum, with memorabilia from the Comstock Era; the mining and silver artifacts displayed at the MacKay Mansion; the antiques on display at the ornate 1886 home known as the Castle; and the Territorial Enterprise, a newspaper office that gave famous writer Mark Twain his start in journalism.

Carson City draws visitors with its 11 major gambling casinos, Best Western Carson Station Hotel-Casino, Best Western Pinon Plaza Hotel Resort, Cactus Jack's, Carson City Nugget, the Carson Horseshoe Club, Casino Fandango, Comstock Casino, Ormsby House Hotel & Casino, Silver Dollar Casino, Slotworld, and Slotworld's Cabaret.

Arts and Culture

The King Street Gallery, a showcase of the Nevada Artists Association, displays the works of over 75 local artists. Western Nevada Community College Art Gallery features works by local and regional artists. The Great Basin Gallery features fine contemporary art from Nevada and the region.

The Proscenium Players, Nevada's second-oldest year-round theater company, present dramas and comedies at the Brewery Arts Center, which also features other performing groups. The Renaissance Projects theater company also presents productions throughout the year. Affiliated with Western Nevada Community College, the Western Nevada Musical Theatre Company stages plays and musicals on campus.

The Carson City Symphony, renamed in 1998 from Carson City Chamber Orchestra, presents five annual classical concerts. Residents also enjoy the music of the Carson Chamber Singers who perform occasional concerts.

Festivals and Holidays

September calls for a trip to nearby Virginia City for the annual International Camel and Ostrich Races. Begun as a hoax, the event is now one of the most popular in the state. Since 1997 September has also been the time for the three-day *Salsa y Salsas* family celebration with food, entertainment, and dancing. October's special events in Carson City include the Nevada Day Parade and four-day celebration, the La Ka Le'l Be Nevada Day Pow Wow, filled with arts, crafts, dancing, the Chili Cook-Off, the High Desert Sierra Jazz Festival, and the Ghost Walk tour of homes decorated for Halloween. The December holidays are ushered in by the

Silver & Snowflake Tree Lighting ceremony with caroling, and the Victorian Christmas Tour of houses on the Kit Carson Trail.

March is the month for the Mother Earth Pow Wow and the Cowboy Jubilee & Poetry Evening, which features cowboy poets and barbecues. March also features a traditional St. Patrick's Day parade. April brings the Eagle Valley Muzzle Loaders Spring Rendezvous. June's big events are the Downtown A-Fair, and the Stewart Indian Museum Pow Wow, as well as A Taste of Downtown, which features a food tasting from the city's restaurants along with live music and dancing. The Kit Carson Rendezvous and Wagon Train event, also in June, features a mountain man encampment, trader's row, an Indian pow wow, and mock gunfights, all in celebration of Nevada's history. Independence Day in July is hailed by a four-day celebration with the traditional fireworks and Silver Dollar Car Classics, a street dance, and music concerts.

Sports for the Participant

Included within about 600 acres of city parks is Mills Park, which offers tennis courts, indoor and outdoor pools, a mini-golf course, and a children's one-mile train ride. The park is also the home of the Carson City Skateboard Park that provides a skateboard area with platforms, ramps, and spectator seating. Centennial Park has several soccer and softball fields, tennis courts, a public golf course, and shady picnic sites. Residents and visitors can make use of the "Divine Nine" golf courses within the city limits. Horseback riding is also popular in the area, especially on the Mount Rose Wilderness trails. At the edge of town is an old hot springs where bathers can soak in a 100° F spring water pool, and make use of hot tubs, massage facilities, and an adjoining restaurant and motel.

Sports enthusiasts enjoy hunting for birds and big game such as elk, deer, antelope, and bighorn sheep. In addition, the city is only 45 minutes from several prime skiing areas at nearby Lake Tahoe.

Shopping and Dining

The once shabby block that houses the landmark St. Charles Hotel has been transformed into a delightful collection of shops and restaurants. Other major shopping areas include various downtown blocks, as well as Eagle Station Shopping Center, Southgate Shopping Center, and Silver City.

Diners in Carson City can choose from among 40 restaurants with American and ethnic cuisines, including Basque, Asian, Southwestern, and Italian. The Carlson House is a popular modern restaurant set in the wonderfully restored 1876 Rinckel Mansion, the city's second-oldest residence, with service offered in the garden during the summer months. Adele's French restaurant is set in a lovely Victorian house near the town center, while nearby Silvana's features Italian dishes. Breakfast lovers enjoy the hot cakes at Scott's and the hearty omelets at the Cracker Box or Heidi's Dutch Mill Restaurant.

Visitor Information: Carson City Convention & Visitors Bureau, 1900 S. Carson St., Ste. 100, Carson City, NV 89701; telephone (775)687-7410 or (800)NEVADA-1; fax (775)687-7416

Convention Facilities

Carson City has a variety of meeting and convention facilities. The 31,020-square-foot Pony Express Pavilion can accommodate up to 3,000 people and offers table, theater, or bleacher-style seating. The Carson City Community Center can seat 700 people theater-style, and the Carson City Nugget has facilities for about 500 people on 8,600 square feet. The Best Western Pinon Plaza Resort can handle groups of 30 to 250 people in its 3,000-square-foot facilities. The 120-seat meeting room at the Plaza Hotel offers an outstanding panoramic view of the city. Historic Brewery Arts Center offers their art gallery for smaller groups while its restored 2,200-square-foot meeting room has space for up to 200 guests.

Convention Information: Carson City Convention & Visitors Bureau, 1900 S. Carson St., Ste. 100, Carson City, NV 89701; telephone (775)687-7410; toll-free (800)NEVADA-1; fax (775)687-7416

Transportation

Approaching the City

The Carson City Airport does not provide commercial services, but Reno-Cannon International Airport, just 30 miles to the north of Carson City, is served by many major airlines. Carson City is located at the intersection of U.S. Highway 395, which links cities from Canada to Mexico, and U.S. Highway 50, a direct route from west to east. Amtrak provides rail service to the Reno/Sparks area, 30 miles north of Carson City. Greyhound bus lines offer daily service to Los Angeles, Sacramento, Las Vegas, Reno, and other destinations.

Traveling in the City

Because the city has no freeway off-ramps, U.S. 395 and U.S. 50 serve as the main north-south and east-west highways, as well as the main streets in the city. However, the 9.7-mile Carson City Freeway project that began in 2003 is expected to wrap up sometime in 2006 and will provide an alternate north-south route. The city has six buses for local service that were acquired in 2004, and a dial-a-ride service is available to residents.

Communications

Newspapers and Magazines

The *Nevada Appeal–Carson City Edition* is the daily newspaper. *Nevada Magazine*, a bimonthly which carries feature stories on events and people in the state, is also published in Carson City. Other locally published magazines include *The Wine Trader,* and *Range Magazine,* a consumer magazine covering cowboys and people who work the land in the western United States.

Television and Radio

Carson City receives its television coverage from nearby Reno's network and public stations, but has its own cable company. The city has one AM and one FM radio stations broadcasting religious and oldies formats.

Media Information: *Nevada Appeal,* PO Box 2288, Carson City, NV 89702; telephone (775)882-2111 or (800)221-8013

Carson City Online

Carson City Area Chamber of Commerce. Available www .carsoncitychamber.com

Carson City Convention & Visitors Bureau. Available www .carson-city.org or www.visitcarsoncity.com

Carson City Economic Development. Available www .carson cityecondev.com

Carson City Library. Available www.carson-city.nv.us/ library

Carson City School District. Available www.carsoncity schools.com

City of Carson City home page. Available www.carson-city .nv.us

Nevada State Library and Archives. Available dmla.clan.lib
.nv.us/docs/NSLA

State of Nevada, Department of Cultural Affairs, Division of
Museums and History. Available dmla.clan.lib.nv.us/docs/
museums

Selected Bibliography

McLaughlin, Mark. *Sierra Stories: True Tales of Tahoe.* (Carnelian
Bay, CA: Mic Mac Publishers, 1997)

Twain, Mark. *Roughing It.* (Berkeley, CA: University of California
Press, 1996)

Henderson

The City in Brief

Founded: 1941 (incorporated April 16, 1953)

Head Official: Mayor Jim Gibson (D) (since 1997)

City Population
    1980: 24,363
    1990: 62,942
    2000: 175,381
    2003 estimate: 214,852
    Percent change, 1990–2000: 169.4%
    U.S. rank in 2000: 118th (State rank: 2nd)

Metropolitan Area Population (part of Las Vegas MSA)
    1980: 528,000
    1990: 852,737
    2000: 1,563,282
    Percent change, 1990–2000: 83.3%

U.S. rank in 1980: 72nd
U.S. rank in 1990: 53rd
U.S. rank in 2000: 32nd

Area: 80 square miles (2000)
Elevation: 1,940 feet above sea level
Average Annual Temperature: 68.0° F
Average Annual Precipitation: 4.5 inches of rain

Major Economic Sectors: services, hospitality, retail, goods, government, construction
Unemployment Rate: 4.2% (Las Vegas-Paradise; January 2005)
Per Capita Income: $26,815 (1999)

2002 FBI Crime Index Total: 81,627 (Las Vegas MSA)

Major Colleges and Universities: Nevada State College; University of Nevada, Las Vegas; Community College of Southern Nevada

Daily Newspaper: *Las Vegas Review Journal*

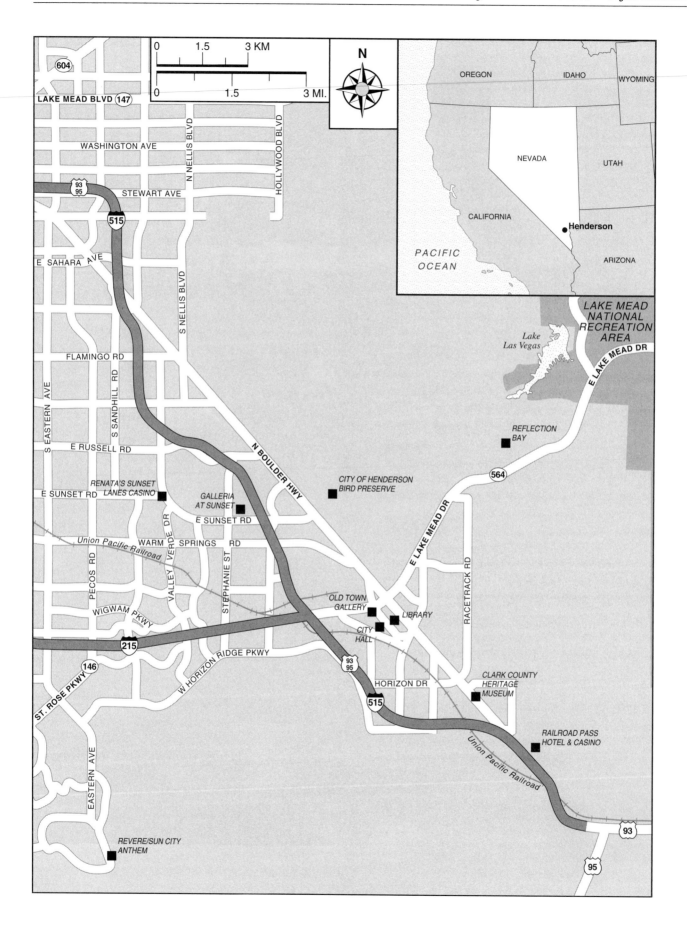

Introduction

Henderson, Nevada was pronounced a "city of destiny" by then-president John F. Kennedy while on a visit to Southern Nevada during his brief time in office. Incorporated during World War II, Henderson became known only 10 years prior when it sprung up from the desert floor as the home of the Basic Magnesium Plant, which supplied the U.S. forces with magnesium for munitions and airplane parts during the war. Post-war, Henderson quieted as the plant closed and out-of-work residents sought greener pastures. Quick thinking and creativity by city leaders and developers brought money and new residents back to Henderson, saving it from "ghost town" status. Now a bustling metropolis making its own name in the shadow of a glittering Las Vegas, Henderson is the second largest city in Nevada.

Geography and Climate

Henderson sits at the southern rim of the Las Vegas Valley. At an elevation of 1,940 feet above sea level, the city is only 7 miles southeast of Las Vegas and about midway between Las Vegas and Boulder City (home of the Hoover Dam). Residents and visitors enjoy warm weather, with an average temperature of just under 70 degrees most months of the year, low humidity, and very little rain. Winter snows are visible in the mountains, but snow is rare in the city.

Area: 80 square miles (2000)

Elevation: Averages 1,940 feet above sea level

Average Temperatures: January, 44.0° F; July, 88.0° F; annual average, 68.0° F

Average Annual Precipitation: 4.5 inches of rain

History

Spanish Move Through Area

Spanish explorers moved through Southern Nevada in the early 1800s, discovering and naming Las Vegas as a stop on their way to California. Mormon missionaries established a settlement and built a fort in 1855 in Las Vegas but didn't stay long. In the latter half of the century, Las Vegas, and with it the area that is now Henderson, was detached from Arizona territory to become part of Nevada. Small farming communities developed, but things were quiet in the area

until construction on the Boulder Dam was begun in 1931, bringing thousands to the area for work.

A City Born Overnight

Southern Nevada had but a handful of residents in the early decades of the twentieth century. Henderson, quite literally, was created almost overnight in 1941, as building began on a plant that was, at the time, a massive undertaking in the middle of desert land. Magnesium and its importance in munitions and to the brewing war were the key to the city's beginning.

In 1941 a Cleveland, Ohio manufacturer named Howard Eells and his newly formed Basic Magnesium Inc. (BMI) company signed a contract with the U.S. Defense Plant Corp. to build the Basic Magnesium Plant. Only days after signing, the government asked Eells to expand the planned site to 10 times its original size, making it 1.75 miles long and .75 miles wide, the largest such magnesium plant in the world. More than 13,000 workers—which was 10 percent of the entire state's population at the time— lived in ramshackle housing or "tent cities" until construction began on a company town in 1942. Under scrutiny for attempting to profit from the war, Eells sold BMI to Anaconda Copper Mining Co. that year. Anaconda was charged with finishing the plant, and the burgeoning city was named not after Eells, but for former senator Charles P. Henderson for his role in helping to get the plant financed and built.

For the next few years, BMI exceeded its planned production rates and employees numbered 14,000 at peak production. However, by 1947 magnesium was no longer needed for defense, the plant closed, and more than half of the employees left. Almost as quickly as the city was built, it all but disappeared. Henderson stood in danger of becoming a ghost town, and in 1947 the U.S. War Asset Administration offered the entire city for sale as war surplus property. In a brochure created to help sell the city, a description was provided that outlined the housing, streets, alleys, sanitary systems, schools, general buildings, shops, churches, and other city amenities.

Last Ditch Effort Saves City

In an effort to save Henderson, the Chamber of Commerce convinced the Las Vegas Chamber of Commerce to issue an invitation to the entire Nevada Legislature to come visit Boulder Dam (now Hoover Dam). They were asked to evaluate the Basic Magnesium site and explore the possibility of construction of a power generator at the dam, which would bring new workers and provide work for those Henderson residents that remained. The plan worked—a bill was unanimously approved, giving the Colorado River Commission of Nevada authority to purchase the plant. By 1953 signs of improvement were well underway and the city was officially incorporated, with a population of 7,410 residents.

Modern Henderson Emerges

Throughout the 1960s and 1970s, Henderson remained a relatively small factory town. In the early 1980s, the first master planned community, Green Valley, was plotted. Henderson's population in 1980 was 24,363; by 1990 it had more than doubled, and by the end of the twentieth century Henderson had reached 175,381. Local estimates project the 2010 population will reach 310,000 as a steady stream of new residents and businesses continue to be attracted to the area. By 1999 Henderson overtook Reno as Nevada's second largest city.

The city celebrated its 50 year birthday in 2003. Henderson's unparalleled growth in the past two decades shows little signs of slowing. It's no wonder that Nevada's second largest city, with a thriving economy, master-planned communities, world-class recreation, and proximity to several of the country's national and man-made treasures, is one of the fastest-growing cities in the nation.

Historical Information: City of Henderson, City Hall, 240 Water Street, Henderson, NV 89009. Nevada State Museum & Historical Society, 700 Twin Lakes Drive, Las Vegas, NV 89107; telephone (702)486-5205

Population Profile

Metropolitan Area Residents
1980: 528,000
1990: 852,737
2000: 1,563,282
Percent change, 1990–2000: 83.3%
U.S. rank in 1980: 72nd
U.S. rank in 1990: 53rd
U.S. rank in 2000: 32nd

City Residents
1980: 24,363
1990: 62,942
2000: 175,381
2003 estimate: 214,852
Percent change, 1990–2000: 169.4%
U.S. rank in 2000: 118th (State rank: 2nd)

Density: 2,200.8 people per square mile (2000)

Racial and ethnic characteristics (2000)
    White: 148,181
    Black or African American: 6,590
    American Indian and Alaska Native: 1,236
    Asian: 6,983
    Native Hawaiian and Pacific Islander: 728

Hispanic or Latino (may be of any race): 18,785
    Other: 5,549

Percent of residents born in state: 18.7% (2000)

Age characteristics (2000)
    Population under 5 years old: 11,939
    Population 5 to 9 years old: 12,727
    Population 10 to 14 years old: 12,491
    Population 15 to 19 years old: 10,788
    Population 20 to 24 years old: 9,884
    Population 25 to 34 years old: 27,065
    Population 35 to 44 years old: 29,937
    Population 45 to 54 years old: 25,272
    Population 55 to 59 years old: 9,868
    Population 60 to 64 years old: 7,632
    Population 65 to 74 years old: 11,222
    Population 75 to 84 years old: 5,408
    Population 85 years and older: 1,148
    Median age: 35.9 years

Births (2002, Clark County)
    Total number: 23,756

Deaths (2003, Clark County)
    Total number: 12,751

Money income (1999)
    Per capita income: $26,815
    Median household income: $55,949
    Total households: 66,555

Number of households with income of . . .
    less than $10,000: 2,698
    $10,000 to $14,999: 2,265
    $15,000 to $24,999: 5,453
    $25,000 to $34,999: 7,003
    $35,000 to $49,999: 10,996
    $50,000 to $74,999: 16,734
    $75,000 to $99,999: 9,817
    $100,000 to $149,999: 7,322
    $150,000 to $199,999: 2,026
    $200,000 or more: 2,241

Percent of families below poverty level: 3.9% (27.1% of which were female householder families with related children under 5 years)

2002 FBI Crime Index Total: 81,627 (Las Vegas MSA)

Municipal Government

The city of Henderson received its charter only relatively recently, in 1965. The mayor and city council have legislative power of the city through the charter; the city manager is charged with executive duties and general administration of the city. The mayor and four city councilmen are elected at large on a nonpartisan basis, and councilmen must be from different wards of the city's four wards. Majority vote by the mayor and city council decides on all issues, including land use, business licensing, city ordinances, and city fund expenditures.

Head Official: Mayor Jim Gibson (D) (since 1997; current term expires 2009)

Total Number of City Employees: 2,781 (2005)

City Information: City Hall, 240 Water St., Henderson, NV 89009; telephone (mayor and council) (702)267-2085

Economy

Major Industries and Commercial Activity

For most of Henderson's short history, the city has been a manufacturing center. Though its beginnings were fast and furious as a magnesium producer for World War II efforts, Henderson's economy today has diversified. The city is still a manufacturing center and a producer of metals and industrial chemicals, but its diversification includes a competitive marketplace for communications technology.

In the past two decades, city leaders, businesses, and the community have been working together to diversify the city's economy with aggressive programs to attract modern industries. The top industries showing growth in Henderson are education services, medical and biomedical technology, the supplier industry, and computer and electronic transfer. In addition, businesses that service senior citizens are sprouting up in the area as more seniors relocate there.

A modern ''boom town,'' Henderson's growth shows no signs of slowing, as city estimates count nearly 6,000 people moving to the region each month. Major corporations with large offices or headquarters in Henderson include Levi Strauss & Company, Ocean Spray Cranberries, Ford Credit, and Good Humor-Breyers. Henderson's growing community and highly favorable business climate continues to attract businesses to the area.

Due only in part to Henderson's proximity to Las Vegas, it goes without saying that a large portion of economic gain stems from the tourism and services industry.

Items and goods produced: baked goods, clothing, food products

Incentive Programs—New and Existing Companies

Several city and state programs are available to assist new, current, or expanding businesses in the City of Henderson.

Local programs—The City of Henderson can offer partial exemption from public utilities license or franchise fees for gas or electricity; businesses must meet stringent requirements to take advantage of this program. The city's department of economic development staff, along with community resource partners, work together to provide relocating or expanding businesses with needed resources. The city's Redevelopment Agency, as part of the Downtown Investment Strategy plan, offers development incentives via grants, low-interest loans, and other financing to businesses for building improvements, equipment, start-up capital, and other expenses; two of the most successful programs are the Facade Improvement Program and the Revolving Loan Fund.

State programs—A variety of state programs exist for new, expanding, or established businesses in Henderson. The Sales Use and Tax Abatement Program offers tax breaks on eligible machinery and equipment for businesses with operations that are consistent with the state's economic diversification and development plans. The Sales and Use Tax Deferral Program defers taxes on qualifying equipment purchases of more than $100,000. Personal Property Tax Abatements are available for qualified new businesses.

Job training programs—The Nevada Department of Employment, Training, and Rehabilitation offers a variety of job training services to both employers and job seekers, including applicant recruitment and screening, tax credit benefits, training programs and career enhancement programs, and labor market information. The Train Employees Now (TEN) program, administered by the State of Nevada Commission on Economic Development, helps new and expanding firms by providing intensive skills-based training programs tailored to the company's needs. The TEN program utilizes training providers such as local businesses and community colleges. The Family Support Center at Nellis Air Force Base offers job information and employer connections to spouses and family members of base personnel. A variety of programs exist through the area's educational institutions.

Development Projects

According to the city's office of economic development, 18 companies either expanded their existing facilities or established new ones—each developing or adding square footage of 5,000 feet or more—in Henderson in 2003. Of those 18 companies, seven were manufacturing operations; the others are made up of services, software, educational, and office or headquarter space.

The Henderson Redevelopment Agency was created in 1995 and utilizes tax increment financing funds for projects in three designated areas of Henderson: downtown, Tuscany, and Cornerstone. In 2005 a variety of projects had set construction start dates or were already underway as part of the city's redevelopment plans, among those are projects totaling more than 230,000 square feet of residential, retail, and office space. A new amphitheater was under construction in the Water Street District, the city's arts and culture center. Other Water Street improvements include sidewalk expansions and beautification of pedestrian areas.

The Ritz-Carlton Lake Las Vegas opened in 2003 in the new resort development area of Lake Las Vegas in Henderson. A spectacular, European villa-style hotel and spa, the hotel offers beautiful views from its 8 floors and 349 rooms. The hotel's $500 million price tag includes a 25,000 square foot full-service spa; two championship golf courses; a pool; 33,000 square feet of banquet, meeting, and ballroom space; and a 40,000 square foot casino.

In January 2005 ground broke on The Pinnacle, a $2 million, mixed-use structure on Water Street in downtown. The Pinnacle is expected to be finished in summer of the same year, and will offer a coffeehouse and bakery on the ground floor, with offices on the second and third floors. Parkline Lofts, under development in early 2005, is a loft-style, 65-unit condominium development in a targeted downtown redevelopment area. Water Street South, expected to be finished by the end of 2005, will consist of 30,400 square feet of retail and office space.

Economic Development Information: City of Henderson Economic Development, 240 Water Street, Henderson, NV 89009; telephone (702)267-1650.

Commercial Shipping

Southern Clark County is the hub of an extensive transportation network serviced by three highway corridors: Interstate 15, U.S. Highway 95, and U.S. Highway 93. More than 50 motor freight carriers serve the area. In addition, a variety of warehousing and support services are available in Clark County, including foreign trade zone accommodations, packaging support, and U.S. customs service. McCarran International Airport handles in excess of 600,000 pounds of arriving and departing cargo. McCarran International Air Cargo Center offers cargo storage and handling and operates in a designated Foreign Trade Zone (FTZ). Union Pacific Railroad runs northeast/southwest through Clark County, linking the area to markets in most states.

Labor Force and Employment Outlook

Henderson's rapid population expansion in the last several decades especially means that local businesses experience no shortages of labor supply. Area businesses draw from a southern Nevada workforce of more than 800,000 people. Additionally, the array of vocational and technical trade schools, higher education institutions, and opportunities for customized training programs enhance both business and employment prospects.

The following is a summary of data regarding the Henderson (including Las Vegas-Paradise) metropolitan area labor force, 2004 annual averages.

Size of nonagricultural labor force: 811,700

Number of workers employed in ...
  natural resources and mining: 400
  construction: 88,100
  manufacturing: 23,200
  trade, transportation and utilities: 140,000
  information: 10,200
  financial activities: 46,000
  professional and business services: 95,400
  educational and health services: 53,900
  leisure and hospitality: 247,600
  other services: 23,500
  government: 83,100

Average hourly earnings of production workers employed in manufacturing: $14.60 (Nevada average)

Unemployment rate: 4.2% (Las Vegas-Paradise; January 2005)

Largest county employers	Number of employees
Clark County School District	20,000 +
Clark County	9,000-9,999
Bellagio Hotel & Casino	8,000-8,999
MGM Grand Hotel & Casino	7,000-7,999
Mandalay Bay Resort & Casino	7,000-7,999
Mirage Hotel & Casino	5,000-5,999
State of Nevada	5,000-5,999
Caesars Palace Hotel & Casino	4,000-4,999
Las Vegas Metropolitan Police	4,000-4,999
University of Nevada, Las Vegas	4,000-4,999

Cost of Living

Henderson's cost of living, as well as its housing prices, are somewhat above the national average.

The following is a summary of data regarding several key cost of living factors for the Henderson area.

2004 (3rd Quarter) ACCRA Cost of Living Index: 113.3 (U.S. average = 100.0)

2004 (3rd Quarter) ACCRA Average House Price: $353,798

State income tax rate: None

State sales tax rate: 7.5%

Local income tax rate: None

Local sales tax rate: 7.5%

Property tax rate: 2.9027-2.9468 (depending on tax district) per $100 assessed value (2005)

Economic Information: Sierra Pacific Power Company Economic Development; Grant Sims, Economic Development Manager; phone (775)834-3716; fax (775)834-3384; email gsims@sppc.com. City of Henderson Economic Development, 240 Water Street, Henderson, NV 89009; telephone (702)267-1650

Education and Research

Elementary and Secondary Schools

The Clark County School District serves about 250,000 students in all of Clark County—a 7,927 square mile section of Nevada—which includes the city of Henderson. Schools in the entire district total 186 elementary, 51 middle, 38 high schools, 28 alternative schools, and 8 special schools or programs. The large system is divided into five regions; the population of Henderson is served by the Southeast Region. Several grants were recently awarded the school system: the Local Plan grant provides $40 million for expansion and improvements to programs serving students with disabilities; the Gear Up program will provide $845,000 towards efforts to decrease dropout rates, raise academic achievement in the high schools, and develop college preparatory coursework; and the Library Books grant will provide $253,000 for library purchases in the elementary and secondary schools. A variety of magnet schools exist throughout the district, in addition to English as a second language programs, vocational training, language immersion, and fine arts specialties. The school district is constantly expanding; in 2002 the district reported a "typical year" as including 14,000 new students, 12-14 new schools, and 1,300 new employees.

The following is a summary of data regarding the Southeast Region of the Clark County School District public schools.

Total enrollment: 58,268 (2003-2004)

Number of facilities
  elementary schools: 39
  junior high/middle schools: 12
  senior high schools: 9
  other: 1 vocational trade center

Student/teacher ratio: 18:1 elementary; 30:1 secondary

Teacher salaries (2004-2005)
  minimum: $37,354
  maximum: $57,480

Funding per pupil: $5,501

Public Schools Information: Clark County School District, 2832 East Flamingo Road, Las Vegas, NV 89121; telephone (702)799-5011

Colleges and Universities

Henderson offers residents several major institutions of higher learning. The Community College of Southern Nevada (CCSN) system, with a campus in Henderson, educates more than 30,000 students in occupational training, university transfer preparation, continuing education, developmental education, and counseling and guidance programs. CCSN's top disciplines include dental hygiene, culinary arts, computing and information technologies, resorts and gaming, nursing and other health professions, automotive technology, air conditioning, and criminal justice. The University of Nevada Las Vegas (UNLV) in nearby Las Vegas enrolls more than 20,000 area residents and confers undergrad, graduate, and doctoral degrees. UNLV also has a School of Dental Medicine and a School of Medicine; both educate students as well as provide low-cost health care to residents. Also in Las Vegas, the International Academy of Design & Technology offers two- and four-year programs in Fashion Design, Interior Design, and Visual Communications.

Libraries and Research Centers

The Henderson District Public Libraries operates four branches throughout the city and served nearly 700,000 visitors in 2004 with holdings of about 289,000 items in all branches. The newest of the branches, the Paseo Verde Library, was constructed in 2002 and houses a Genealogy Collection, a Government Documents Collection, library administrative offices, and a Friends of Henderson Libraries Bookstore and Coffee Shop.

The Las Vegas-Clark County Library District serves more than 850,000 area residents in all of Clark County with 24 branches and a comprehensive resource of informational materials. The district's Green Valley branch resides in Henderson. The Community Colleges of Southern Nevada library system, as well as the University of Nevada Las Vegas libraries, are available for public use as well.

The Desert Research Institute's (DRI) main research campus in Las Vegas carries out about 300 scientific research projects at any given time. Environmental research programs focus on three core divisions of atmospheric sciences, earth and ecosystems sciences, and hydrologic sciences.

DRI maintains a library that is available to researchers and scholars. A variety of other specialized libraries and research centers are located in the area.

Public Library Information: Henderson District Public Libraries, 280 S. Green Valley, Henderson, NV 89012; telephone (702)492-7252

Health Care

St. Rose Dominican Hospitals operates three medical campuses, with the Rose de Lima Campus and the Siena Campus both in Henderson. The third facility, the San Martín Campus in Warm Springs, is slated to open in 2006. Rose de Lima, with 138 beds, offers emergency and surgical services, rehabilitation, obstetrical services, community outreach, and kidney stone treatment services, among others. Siena opened in 2000 and is a 214-bed acute care facility with pediatrics services, neurosurgery, an open-heart surgery center, emergency department, obstetrics and surgical services, diagnostic imaging, and others. A variety of hospitals and clinics exist in nearby Las Vegas.

Recreation

Sightseeing

Less than 20 miles southeast of Henderson is the Hoover Dam. A National Historic Landmark, and recognized as one of America's Seven Modern Civil Engineering Wonders by the American Society of Civil Engineers, the dam entertains more than a million visitors and tour-goers annually. Lake Mead National Recreation Area in nearby Boulder City offers opportunities for a leisurely afternoon outdoors or multi-day, multi-activity trips, and dinner or dinner-and-dance cruises are available on a Mississippi-style paddlewheeler.

Ghost towns of the Old West are popular tourist destinations; several exist within an hour's drive of the city. Ethel M. Chocolates, a mainstay in Henderson though originating in Tacoma, Washington, offers tours of the chocolate factory (samples included) and the botanical cactus gardens on its grounds.

Arts and Culture

Henderson's Veterans Memorial Wall on Water Street honors not only those who have fought for their country, but those who played a part in Henderson's heritage. The wall

was dedicated in 2004 and is inscribed with more than 1,000 names.

The Clark County Museum tells the story of southern Nevada in a variety of exhibits, including prehistoric dioramas, Native American collections, a walk-in mine, and a pueblo. Heritage Street, an outdoor exhibit of the museum, offers a look at the structures and homes of the early 1900s, including a replicated newspaper print shop, historic homes, and the 1932 Boulder City Depot. The Howard W. Cannon Aviation Museum at the airport tells of the history of aviation in the region.

The Nevada Chamber Symphony, founded in 1985, presents four concerts and a holiday pops series each season. Many performances are free at a variety of venues, some outdoors, throughout the city.

The Arts Council of Henderson, a nonprofit group, works to bring arts programming to Henderson residents. One of the Council's ventures is the annual Nevada Shakespeare in the Park, presented in cooperation with the city of Henderson, American Nevada Corporation, and the Clark County School District. Shakespeare in the Park presents one play per season over one October weekend, with a performance each day. An Elizabethan Festival precedes each daily performance. Theatre in the Valley presents community theater in a season of four to five shows per year.

Festivals and Holidays

The St. Patrick's Day Parade and Block Party, celebrating 39 years in 2005, is celebrated in March in downtown Henderson. For nearly a week in April the FLW Outdoors EverStart Series offers fishing competition action at Lake Mead. In late April at the Lake Las Vegas Resort, crews compete in the Dragon Boat Race and Festival. ArtFest happens over Mother's Day weekend in May in downtown Henderson's Water Street district, featuring more than 200 artists, music, food, and fun kids' events. Also in May, *Bon Appetit* magazine spends the weekend at several area hotels and resorts, offering culinary demonstrations, wine tastings, brunches, and dinners during the Annual Bon Appetit Wine & Spirits Focus. Fourth of July events and fireworks happen citywide. September features the Super Run Car Show, with car cruises and drag racing, concerts, and food at Water Street and various locations throughout the city. The Nevada Silverman, an iron-distance triathlon event in November, offers spectators and participants views of the Lake Mead National Recreation Area.

Sports for the Spectator

While no sports teams reside in the city of Henderson, nearby Las Vegas offers enthusiasts many opportunities to cheer for their favorite sports. The Las Vegas 51s, triple A affiliate of the Los Angeles Dodgers, play minor league baseball at Cashman Field in Las Vegas. The AFL's Las Vegas Gladiators play professional indoor football at the Thomas & Mack Center. The Las Vegas Wranglers, members of the ECHL Division, also play at the Thomas & Mack Center. The new Las Vegas Strikers of the National Premier Soccer League play at the Bettye Wilson Soccer Complex. The University of Las Vegas offers collegiate sporting events in baseball, soccer, football, and basketball. The Las Vegas Moter Speedway offers NASCAR and other motor sports events. High-profile boxing matches are often scheduled in Las Vegas.

Sports for the Participant

Henderson and nearby areas are an outdoor lover's paradise. The city of Henderson offers visitors 621 acres of outdoor opportunities in 40 parks—Henderson's parks and recreation system is nationally recognized. Among Henderson's outdoor amenities in the park system and beyond are 42 ballfields, 50 tennis courts, more than 11 miles of trails, and 10 golf courses. The city of Henderson's bird viewing preserve is a 147-acre migratory bird and wetland area featuring basins, ponds, and lagoons; signs, kiosks and nature trails guide visitors.

The Lake Mead National Recreation Area consists of a manmade lake in a massive crater created during the building of the Hoover Dam, offering opportunities for boating, swimming, kayaking, hiking, horseback riding, and fishing. Bootleg Canyon, also in Boulder city, is heralded as one of the best mountain biking spots in the U.S. and offers more than 20 miles of challenging terrain. Red Rock Canyon, a 197,000-acre National Conservation Area, presents a variety of outdoor opportunities, including hiking and biking trails, rock climbing, a visitor's center with interpretive programs, and Spring Mountain State Park. Ten area golf courses beckon year-round.

Shopping and Dining

The Galleria at Sunset mall is anchored by Dillard's, Robinsons May, JCPenney, and Mervyn's, and offers 140 stores and restaurants on two levels with fountains, skylights, and desert flowers in its indoor landscaping. The District at Green Valley Ranch, part residential development and part stylish shopping mecca, offers a ''main street'' shopping experience for its loft residents and visitors alike, with 40 upscale shops and restaurants on the development's street level. Shoppers looking for bargains can head to the Las Vegas Outlet Center, featuring 135 outlet shops. Shoppers in Henderson's Water Street District area will find a variety of unique shops, boutiques, galleries, and restaurants. The Country Fresh Farmers Market operates throughout the spring and summer on Fridays in the Water Street District. Henderson's variety of restaurants satisfy urges for area

favorites like steak and Mexican food; other tastes tempted include French, Chinese, Italian, Japanese, Greek, and Thai.

Visitor Information: Henderson Convention and Visitors Bureau, 200 Water Street, Henderson, NV 89009; telephone (702)267-2171; toll-free (877)775-5252; fax (702)267-2177; email info@visithenderson.com

Convention Facilities

The Henderson Convention Center offers 10,080 square feet of column-free exhibition space, 3,765 square feet of meeting rooms, and a 500 square foot pre-function area. The center accommodates 1,000 people theater-style, 600 banquet-style, and 450 classroom-style. The Ritz-Carlton Lake Las Vegas opened in 2003 in the new resort development area of Lake Las Vegas in Henderson, offering 33,000 square feet of flexible meeting space. Other hotels with convention facilities in Henderson include The Fiesta-Henderson Hotel Casino, Green Valley Ranch Resort, Hyatt Regency Lake Las Vegas Resort, and Sunset Station Hotel Casino. Citywide, there is more than 100,000 square feet of space available for meetings, conventions, or events; in total, there are 11 hotels in Henderson proper and more than 130 hotels within 15 miles of downtown Henderson.

Convention Information: Henderson Convention and Visitors Bureau, 200 Water Street, Henderson, NV 89009; telephone (702)267-2171; toll-free (877)775-5252; fax (702)267-2177; email info@visithenderson.com

Transportation

Approaching the City

McCarran International Airport serves Henderson, Las Vegas, and all of Clark County and southern Nevada. In April 2005 the airport debuted its $125 million expansion, consisting of an 11-gate wing that will allow the airport to handle an additional 3.1 million passengers annually. The 6th busiest airport in the nation, McCarran is served by 44 airlines. The Henderson Executive Airport accommodates private and general aviation aircraft.

Four major highways bring travelers into and out of Henderson: I-15, US 93/95, Highway 146, and the Southern Nevada Beltway (I-215). North-south I-15 links travelers to west to California and east to the East Coast via I-80, I-70, and I-40.

Traveling in the City

Amtrak Thruway provides bus service between Los Angeles, California, and Las Vegas. Greyhound provides bus service to and from nearby Las Vegas with connections throughout the west. The Citizens Area Transit (CAT) provides local bus service throughout Clark County; 305 buses cover 49 routes, providing transportation to nearly 150,000 riders each day.

Communications

Newspapers and Magazines

Henderson's only newspaper is the *Henderson Home News,* published weekly. The *Showbiz Weekly* is published in Henderson and covers local entertainment in Las Vegas. Henderson residents are also served by the daily *Las Vegas Review-Journal,* as well as by a variety of other publications coming from Las Vegas.

Television and Radio

Henderson's one commercial television station is a Fox network; the area is served by Las Vegas' five television stations and one cable station. No radio stations broadcast from Henderson, although residents enjoy programming from Las Vegas' 16 AM and FM channels.

Media Information: Henderson Home News, 2300 Corporate Circle, Suite 150, Henderson, NV; telephone (702)435-7700; fax (702)434-3527. *Las Vegas Review-Journal,* PO Box 70, Las Vegas, NV 89125; telephone (702)383-0211

Henderson Online

Center for Business and Economic Research at the University of Nevada, Las Vegas. Available www.unlv.edu/Research_Centers/cber

City of Henderson. Available www.cityofhenderson.com

Clark County School District. Available ccsd.net

Henderson Chamber of Commerce. Available www.hendersonchamber.com

Las Vegas-Clark County Library District. Available www.lvccld.org

Las Vegas Review-Journal. Available www.reviewjournal.com

Las Vegas Sun. Available www.lasvegassun.com

Nevada State Museum and Historical Society. Available dmla.clan.lib.nv.us/docs/museums/lv/vegas.htm

This Was Nevada (internet column on Nevada History from the State of Nevada Department of Culture, originally printed in the Henderson Home News). Available dmla.clan.lib.nv.us/docs/dca/thiswas/thiswas.htm

Selected Bibliography

Armstrong-Ingram, Jackson R., *Henderson, Nevada: Images of America* (South Carolina: Arcadia Publishing, 2002)

Bowers, Michael W., *The Sagebrush State: Nevada's history, government, and politics* (Reno: University of Nevada Press, 2002)

City of Henderson, ed., *An American Journey: Henderson, 50 Years* (Henderson, NV: City of Henderson, 2004)

Hulse, James W., *The Silver State: Nevada's heritage reinterpreted* (Reno: University of Nevada Press, 2004)

Toll, David W., *The complete Nevada traveler: the affectionate and intimately detailed guidebook to the most interesting state in America* (Virginia City, NV: Gold Hill Pub., 2002)

Las Vegas

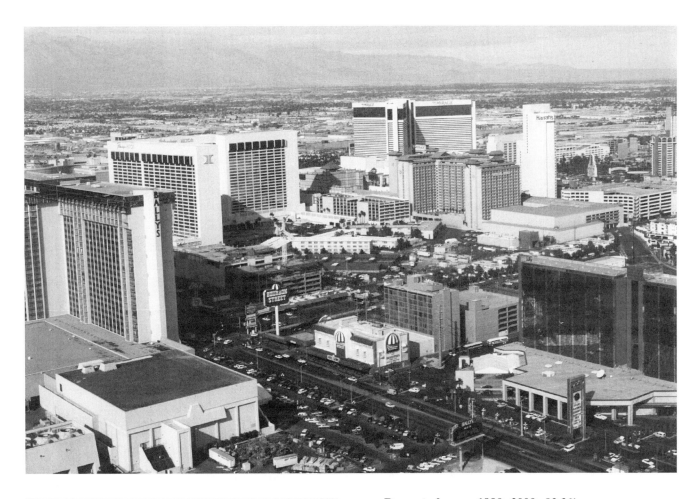

The City in Brief

Founded: 1905 (incorporated, 1911)

Head Official: Mayor Oscar B. Goodman (since 1999)

City Population
  1980: 164,674
  1990: 258,877
  2000: 478,434
  2003 estimate: 517,017
  Percent change, 1990–2000: 84.1%
  U.S. rank in 1980: 89th
  U.S. rank in 1990: 63rd
  U.S. rank in 2000: 39th (State rank: 1st)

Metropolitan Area Population
  1980: 528,000
  1990: 852,737
  2000: 1,563,282

Percent change, 1990–2000: 83.3%
U.S. rank in 1980: 72nd
U.S. rank in 1990: 53rd
U.S. rank in 2000: 32nd

Area: 113 square miles (2000)
Elevation: 2,180 feet above sea level
Average Annual Temperature: 67.1° F
Average Annual Precipitation: 4.16 inches
Major Industries: Gaming, tourism, mining, retailing, warehousing
Unemployment Rate: 4.0% (February 2005)
Per Capita Income: $22,060 (1999)

2002 FBI Crime Index Total: 81,627

Major Colleges and Universities: Nevada State College, University of Nevada at Las Vegas, Community College of Southern Nevada

Daily Newspapers: *Las Vegas Review Journal*

TO LAKE MEAD

CRAIG
CHEYENNE
CAREY
E. LAKE MEAD
E. OWENS
WASHINGTON
E. BONANZA
STEWART
E. CHARLESTON
E. OAKEY
E. SAHARA
TROPICANA
SILVER BOWL STADIUM

NELLIS AIR FORCE BASE

NELLIS

BOULDER HIGHWAY

LAMB

SPECTRUM VILLAGE

PECOS

MOJAVE

CASHMAN FIELD

EASTERN

LIED DISCOVERY CHILDREN'S MUSEUM

CIVIC CENTER

FREMONT

MARYLAND PARKWAY

NORTH LAS VEGAS

THE STRIP

DESERT INN

BOULEVARD MALL

TWAIN

FLAMINGO

UNIVERSITY OF NEVADA, LAS VEGAS

MCCARRAN INTL. AIRPORT

CITY HALL

CONVENTION CTR.

MARTIN LUTHER KING

W. OWENS

LAS VEGAS BUSINESS CTR.

COMMUNITY COLLEGE OF SOUTHERN NEVADA

DOWNTOWN TRANSPORTATION CTR.

VALLEY MEDICAL CTR.

UNIVERSITY MEDICAL CENTER

RANCHO

FASHION SHOW MALL

LAS VEGAS

CAESARS PALACE

MGM GRAND THEME PARK SITE

NORTH LAS VEGAS AIR TERMINAL

VALLEY VIEW

LAS VEGAS

N

KILOMETERS

W. BONANZA

LAS VEGAS EXPRESSWAY

W. CHARLESTON

W. OAKEY

W. SAHARA

ARVILLE

MILES

TONOPAH HIGHWAY

DECATUR

DESERT INN

W. SPRING MOUNTAIN

FLAMINGO

TROPICANA

JONES

LAS VEGAS TECHNOLOGY CTR.

SMOKE RANCH

W. LAKE MEAD

VEGAS

WASHINGTON

TORREY PINES

ALTA

TENAYA

ROCK SPRINGS

RAINBOW

CRAIG
ALEXANDER
CHEYENNE
WEST CLIFF

BUFFALO

DURANGO

WY

ID

UT

AZ

OR

NV

Las Vegas

CA

MEXICO

Introduction

Las Vegas is unique among U.S. cities. Famous for luxury casinos and show palaces offering non-stop recreation on the "Strip" and in downtown Casino Center, the city has over the years become synonymous with glitter and glamour. Las Vegas since the late 1980s has acquired another identity as a center for business, finance, transportation, and services; still the "Entertainment Capital of the World," it has actively and successfully cultivated a diversified economy. The Las Vegas resident can enjoy legalized gaming, yet more often will take advantage of the diverse range of cultural and recreational opportunities offered in the city and in the surrounding area.

Geography and Climate

Las Vegas is located in the center of Vegas Valley, a desert region of about 600 square miles, which is surrounded by the Sierra Nevada Mountains and the Spring Mountains. The seasons are hot, windy, and dry, with desert conditions and maximum temperatures of 100 degrees F during the summer; because of the mountains, however, summer nights are cool. Winters are mild. The mountains around Las Vegas reach elevations of over 10,000 feet, acting as barriers to moisture from the Pacific Ocean. Rainfall is minimal and there are about 216 clear days during the year. Snowfall is rare.

Area: 113 square miles (2000)

Elevation: 2,180 feet above sea level

Average Temperatures: January, 45.5° F; July, 91.1° F; annual average, 67.1° F

Average Annual Precipitation: 4.16 inches

History

Forts Built; Farmers Settle; Hoover Dam Built

Las Vegas was discovered by Spanish explorers, who gave the site its name—meaning "meadows"—because of the verdant grassland fed by natural aquifers. Las Vegas served as a watering place on the Spanish trail to California. In 1855 Mormon missionaries established a settlement, cultivating the land and building a fort to provide protection to travelers on the Salt Lake—Los Angeles Trail. They abandoned the place two years later when the enterprise became unprofitable, but their fort is still standing and is the oldest historical site in Las Vegas. In 1864 Fort Baker, a U.S. Army post, was built nearby; in 1867 Las Vegas was detached from the Arizona territory and became part of the Nevada territory.

Around that time Las Vegas began to expand as a series of farmers cultivated the land. The area encompassed 1,800 acres when it was sold to William Clark, a Montana senator. In 1905 Clark auctioned off parcels of land for the building of the Union Pacific Railroad link between Salt Lake City and Los Angeles. The town was incorporated in 1911. Construction on the Hoover Dam—originally the Boulder Dam—on the Colorado River was begun in 1931, bringing to the area thousands of men seeking employment. The seventy-story-high dam, which is regarded as one of the wonders of the modern world, still supplies affordable power to parts of California, Arizona, and Nevada.

Gaming, Lenient Laws, Climate Attract Visitors, Settlers

Another significant event occurred in 1931: the legalization of casino gambling in Nevada. The gaming and entertainment industries boomed in Las Vegas after World War II. A street lined with large, glittering casino hotels came to be known as the "Strip"; downtown, in Casino Center, lavish palaces featured the country's top entertainers. By the 1950s Las Vegas, dubbed the "Entertainment Capital of the World," had become synonymous with the unique form of recreation it had created. Because of lenient state laws, Las Vegas also became popular as a wedding site; eventually wedding chapels were operating around the clock, and each year thousands of couples were coming to the city to be married.

Since the 1930s Las Vegas's population has steadily increased, jumping from slightly under 8,500 people in 1940 to nearly 25,000 people in 1950. By 1960 almost 65,000 people lived in Las Vegas, and in 1980 the census figure was 164,674 people. Between 1980 and 1990 there was a more than 60 percent increase, or a total of 278,000 people. Newcomers, primarily from California, are attracted by the favorable climate, the high standard of living, low tax rate, and jobs produced by a boom in business and the entertainment and gaming industries. In the 1990s an average of 6,000 to 7,000 people moved into Clark County each month; that figure remains in the mid-2000s.

Las Vegas' population continues to grow by leaps and bounds, nearly doubling between 1990 and 2000, with no real signs of slowing. On May 15, 2005, Las Vegas celebrated its centennial birthday with citywide parties and events on the day and throughout the year— one such celebration included a 130,000 pound cake registered with the Guinness Book of World Records.

Historical Information: Nevada State Museum & Historical Society, 700 Twin Lakes Drive, Las Vegas, NV 89107; telephone (702)486-5205

Population Profile

Metropolitan Area Residents

1980: 528,000
1990: 852,737
2000: 1,563,282
Percent change, 1990–2000: 83.3%
U.S. rank in 1980: 72nd
U.S. rank in 1990: 53rd
U.S. rank in 2000: 32nd

City Residents

1980: 164,674
1990: 258,877
2000: 478,434
2003 estimate: 517,017
Percent change, 1990–2000: 84.1%
U.S. rank in 1980: 89th
U.S. rank in 1990: 63rd
U.S. rank in 2000: 39th (State rank: 1st)

Density: 4,222.5 people per square mile (2000)

Racial and ethnic characteristics (2000)
  White: 334,230
  Black or African American: 49,570
  American Indian and Alaska Native: 3,570
  Asian: 22,879
  Native Hawaiian and Pacific Islander: 2,145
  Hispanic or Latino (may be of any race): 112,962
  Other: 46,643

Percent of residents born in state: 19.7% (2000)

Age characteristics (2000)
  Population under 5 years old: 36,900
  Population 5 to 9 years old: 37,034
  Population 10 to 14 years old: 32,467
  Population 15 to 19 years old: 29,033
  Population 20 to 24 years old: 30,616
  Population 25 to 34 years old: 77,156
  Population 35 to 44 years old: 76,139
  Population 45 to 54 years old: 59,610
  Population 55 to 59 years old: 23,896
  Population 60 to 64 years old: 20,286
  Population 65 to 74 years old: 33,985
  Population 75 to 84 years old: 17,411
  Population 85 years and older: 3,901
  Median age: 34.5 years

Births (2002, Clark County)
  Total number: 23,756

Deaths (2003, Clark County)
  Total number: 12,751

Money income (1999)
  Per capita income: $22,060
  Median household income: $44,069
  Total households: 177,223

Number of households with income of . . .
  less than $10,000: 13,766
  $10,000 to $14,999: 9,523
  $15,000 to $24,999: 22,283
  $25,000 to $34,999: 23,115
  $35,000 to $49,999: 30,839
  $50,000 to $74,999: 36,385
  $75,000 to $99,999: 19,940
  $100,000 to $149,999: 13,665
  $150,000 to $199,999: 3,415
  $200,000 or more: 4,292

Percent of families below poverty level: 8.6% (34.3% of which were female householder families with related children under 5 years)

2002 FBI Crime Index Total: 81,627

Municipal Government

Las Vegas has a council-manager form of government. The five council members and the mayor are elected to four-year terms. The city's foremost spending priority is public safety.

Head Official: Mayor Oscar B. Goodman (since 1999; current term expires 2007)

Total Number of City Employees: 2,800 (2005)

City Information: City of Las Vegas, 400 East Stewart Avenue, Las Vegas, NV 89101; telephone (702)229-6241; fax (702)385-7960

Economy

Major Industries and Commercial Activity

Tourism drives the economy in Las Vegas, with 37 million people visiting the city each year. According to the University of Nevada's Center for Business and Economic Research Center, the figure for visitor spending in 2004 was a staggering $33.7 billion. In 2004, 20 percent of all jobs were gaming-related.

Though many miles away, the terrorist attacks of September 11, 2001, had a devastating effect on the Las Vegas economy, costing thousands who worked in the entertainment and service industries their jobs in the weeks following. While the city had mostly recovered by 2003, other problems had set in, namely difficulties in drawing tourists to the other aspects of the city, in particular the downtown area. Developments in 2004 and 2005 are helping to revitalize the downtown economy.

Constant population growth means that the housing construction industry is vitally important. In 2000 more than 21,000 new homes and 26,000 resale homes were purchased; more than one third of Las Vegas homes are only five years old or less. In early 2005 there were 20 residential development projects of more than 300 acres each currently underway.

While the entertainment and service industries are, collectively, the largest employers in Las Vegas, the major single employer is the Clark County School District.

Incentive Programs—New and Existing Companies

Local programs—To encourage industrial development, the Las Vegas business community works in cooperation with the state of Nevada to provide various incentives through minimal taxation, vocational training programs, no-cost site location services, special loan plans, and limited liability protection. The city is a foreign trade zone, making it an attractive foreign business destination.

State programs—In addition to Nevada's lenient tax structure, the state offers several programs to entice new business. Several tax abatement and tax deferral programs exist, as well as renewable energy abatements, industrial development bonds, global trade program, community development block grants, and others.

Job training programs—The Nevada Department of Employment, Training, and Rehabilitation offers job training programs to both employers and job seekers, including applicant recruitment and screening, tax credit benefits, training programs and career enhancement programs, and labor market information. The Train Employees Now (TEN) program, administered by the State of Nevada Commission on Economic Development, helps new and expanding firms by providing intensive skills-based training programs tailored to the company's needs. The TEN program utilizes training providers such as local businesses and community colleges. Other programs exist through the area's educational institutions.

Development Projects

The 1990s saw major developments in the casino/resort area, with 18 new venues alone built in the last two years of the century, many themed after famous cities throughout the world. The race to build the most outrageous casino/resort in Las Vegas may be never-ending, but the area's more estab-

lished resorts are quick to follow suit with expansions to match. When finished in late 2005, a $376 million expansion at Caesars Palace will include a 949-room, 26-story tower, which will bring the resort's number of hotel rooms to more than 3,300. Part of the expansion includes an addition to the resort's convention and meeting facilities, and upgrades to existing rooms and facilities.

Off "the Strip," the new Renaissance Las Vegas Hotel opened in December 2004 on Paradise Road adjacent to the Las Vegas Convention Center. It offers 548 rooms on 14 floors, a variety of amenities, and more than 20,000 square feet of meeting space.

Wynn Las Vegas opened in spring 2005, topping out at the world's most expensive casino resort with a price tag of $2.7 billion. On 217 acres and with 2,716 rooms—each at a minimum of 630 square feet and built at a price tag of one million per room— the hotel is extravagantly appointed. Wynn Las Vegas features an 18-hole golf course; its own Ferrari-Maserati dealership; an art gallery featuring the likes of Picasso, Vermeer, Cezanne, Gauguin, and Rembrandt; and 18 restaurants.

At any given time in Las Vegas, planned community developments are in various construction phases. Summerlin, one such community along the western rim of the Las Vegas Valley, is the fastest growing master planned community in the country. At 22,500 acres and with 16 separate villages each with its own major park, golf course, and schools, Summerlin will continue to grow with new homes and residents until approximately 2020.

As part of efforts to revitalize the downtown area, in 2005 the Internal Revenue Service moved into its new home in a 61-acre former railroad yard west of the casino district—an area targeted by city officials for development.

Economic Development Information: Office of Business Development, City of Las Vegas, 400 Las Vegas Boulevard South, Las Vegas, NV 89101; telephone (702)229-6551; fax (702)385-3128. City of Las Vegas Economic Development Division, telephone (702)229-6551. Las Vegas Chamber of Commerce, 3720 Howard Hughes Pkwy., Las Vegas, NV, 89109-0320; telephone (702)735-1616; fax (702) 735-2011; email info@lvchamber.com

Commercial Shipping

McCarran International Airport handles more than 600,000 pounds of arriving and departing cargo annually; the airport's Air Cargo Center offers cargo storage and handling services in a designated Foreign Trade Zone (FTZ). Other warehousing and support services are available, including package support and U.S. customs service. More than 50 motor freight carriers serve Southern Clark County, which is the hub of an extensive transportation network serviced by three highway corridors consisting of Interstate 15, U.S. Highway 95, and U.S. Highway 93. Union Pacific Railroad runs northeast/southwest through the county.

Labor Force and Employment Outlook

The labor force in Las Vegas continues to expand as people move into the region in record numbers (approximately 6,000 each month). Las Vegas boasts the highest rate of new job growth in the country. The Las Vegas job base continues to expand at record rates; by December 2005 that rate was 8 percent, the fastest pace in the nation. The gaming and hospitality industries in Las Vegas are expected to continue to improve.

The following is a summary of data regarding the Las Vegas metropolitan area labor force, 2004 annual averages.

Size of nonagricultural labor force: 811,700

Number of workers employed in . . .
  natural resources and mining: 400
  construction: 88,100
  manufacturing: 23,200
  trade, transportation and utilities: 140,000
  information: 10,200
  financial activities: 46,000
  professional and business services: 95,400
  educational and health services: 53,900
  leisure and hospitality: 247,600
  other services: 23,500
  government: 83,100

Average hourly earnings of production workers employed in manufacturing: $14.60 (Nevada average)

Unemployment rate: 4.0% (February 2005)

Largest county employers	Number of employees
Clark County School District	20,000+
Clark County	9,000-9,999
Bellagio Hotel & Casino	8,000-8,999
MGM Grand Hotel & Casino	7,000-7,999
Mandalay Bay Resort & Casino	7,000-7,999
Mirage Hotel & Casino	5,000-5,999
State of Nevada	5,000-5,999
Caesars Palace Hotel & Casino	4,000-4,999
Las Vegas Metropolitan Police	4,000-4,999
University of Nevada, Las Vegas	4,000-4,999

Cost of Living

Nevada's low taxes make everything else cheaper: wages, rents, and energy costs. The average rent of a two bedroom apartment at the end of 2004 was $752 per month.

The following is a summary of data regarding key cost of living factors for the Las Vegas area.

2004 (3rd Quarter) ACCRA Cost of Living Index: 113.3 (U.S. average = 100.0)

2004 (3rd Quarter) ACCRA Average House Price: $353,798

State income tax rate: None

State sales tax rate: 7.5%

Local income tax rate: None

Local sales tax rate: 7.5% (9% hotel room tax)

Property tax rate: 3.0815% of assessed value

Economic Information: Las Vegas Chamber of Commerce, 3720 Howard Hughes Pkwy., Las Vegas, NV, 89109-0320; telephone (702) 735-1616; fax (702)735-2011; email info @lvchamber.com. Nevada Department of Employment, Training and Rehabilitation, Information Development and Processing, Research and Analysis Bureau, 500 E. Third St., Carson City, NV 89713- 0001; telephone (775)684-0450; email lmi@govmail.state.nv.us.

Education and Research

Elementary and Secondary Schools

The Clark County School District is divided into five regions and educates about 250,000 students in the entirety of Clark County with a total of 186 elementary, 51 middle, 38 high schools, 28 alternative schools, and 8 special schools or programs. Las Vegas proper is served by the district's Southeast Region. Several grants were recently awarded the school system: the Local Plan grant provides $40 million for expansion and improvements to programs serving students with disabilities; the Gear Up program will provide $845,000 towards efforts to decrease dropout rates, raise academic achievement in the high schools, and development of college preparatory coursework; the Library Books grant will provide $253,000 for library purchases in the elementary and secondary schools. The school district is constantly expanding; in 2002 the district reported a ''typical year'' as including 14,000 new students, 12-14 new schools, and 1,300 new employees.

The following is a summary of data regarding the Southeast Region of the Clark County School District public schools.

Total enrollment: 58,268 (2003-2004)

Number of facilities
  elementary schools: 39
  junior high/middle schools: 12
  senior high schools:
  other: 1 vocational trade center

Student/teacher ratio: 18:1 elementary; 30:1 secondary

Teacher salaries (2004-2005)
  minimum: $37,354
  maximum: $57,480

Funding per pupil: $5,501

Twenty-eight private and parochial elementary and secondary schools serve the Las Vegas metropolitan area. There are also more than 90 pre-schools and day care centers.

Public Schools Information: Clark County School District, 2832 East Flamingo Road, Las Vegas, NV 89121; telephone (702)799-5011

Colleges and Universities

Officially opened in 1957 and occupying 337 acres in the metropolitan area, the University of Nevada at Las Vegas enrolled 27,000 students in 2004 and offers them more than 200 undergraduate and graduate programs; engineering, computer science, business, economics, and hotel management are especially strong fields. The university also has a School of Medicine that is affiliated with the University Medical Center, and a School of Dental Medicine. Located in the Las Vegas area are the three campuses of the Community College of Southern Nevada (CCSN), the largest institution in the University of Nevada System, enrolling more than 30,000 students including those taking online courses. Among the top disciplines at CCSN are dental hygiene, culinary arts, computing and information technologies, resorts and gaming, nursing and other health professions, automotive technology, air conditioning, and criminal justice. The International Academy of Design & Technology offers two- and four-year programs in Fashion Design, Interior Design, and Visual Communications.

Libraries and Research Centers

Located in one of the fastest growing metropolitan areas in the United States, the Las Vegas-Clark County Library District supports more than 850,000 area residents with 24 branches and a comprehensive resource of informational materials. Serving an area larger than the state of Connecticut, the system's collection exceeds 2.3 million items and includes special collections focusing on fine art, the Southwestern region, the building and construction industry and trades, grants and foundations, health sciences, business and finance, aviation, Nevada history, and the hotel and gaming industry. The library is a depository for federal and state government documents.

A variety of specialized or research libraries are also located in Las Vegas; most are affiliated with local corporations, government agencies, and educational institutions. The Church of Jesus Christ of Latter-Day Saints maintains a branch of its genealogical library in Las Vegas. Desert Research Institute's research centers carry out about 300 projects focusing on the environment each year. Other research activities in the region focus on the natural history, exercise physiology, computer science, information sciences, and business and economics.

Public Library Information: Las Vegas-Clark County Library District, 833 Las Vegas Boulevard North, Las Vegas, NV 89101; telephone (702)382-3493

Health Care

Among the 11 major hospitals serving the area is the Sunrise Hospital and Medical Center. With about 700 beds and 1,400 physicians, it maintains a 145-bed children's hospital along with centers for renal transplants, sleep disorders, and epilepsy. Affiliated with the University of Nevada School of Medicine, the University Medical Center (UMC) was named in 2004 among the top 50 hospitals by *U.S. News & World Report* for neurosurgery and neurology along with being the state's sole hospital on the annual ''America's Best Hospitals'' list. UMC's Lions Burn Care Center, the only such facility in Nevada, has gained national recognition; the center also maintains a free-standing trauma center and the state's first pediatric emergency department. Mountain View Hospital features 235 beds and 1,200 physicians while the Desert Springs Hospital Medical Center has 286 beds and is the only diabetes treatment center in the area accredited by the American Diabetes Association. In addition to its 409 beds and more than 2,800 staff members, Valley Hospital Medical Center also operates ''Flight for Life,'' an emergency helicopter service for a wide area surrounding Las Vegas. The University of Nevada School of Medicine's Genetics Program, based in Las Vegas, offers counseling to prospective parents about inherited diseases and provides clinical care to children with birth defects.

Recreation

Sightseeing

Most people visit Las Vegas to see shows featuring world-famous entertainers and to try their luck at the gaming tables. But the city offers much more to see and do. The

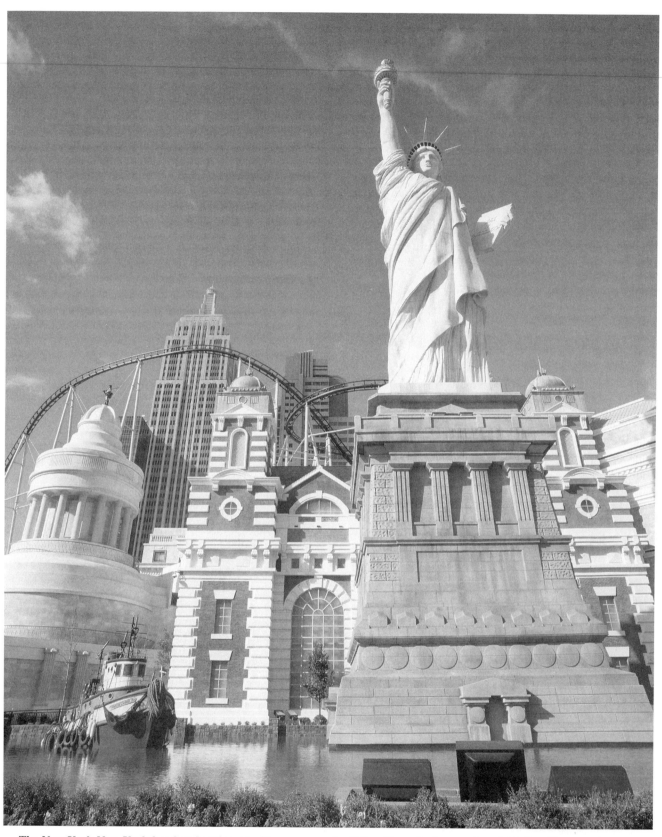

The New York-New York hotel and casino provides an example of the glitz and glamour for which Las Vegas casinos are famous.

streets of Las Vegas, with neon and glittering lights, are themselves a popular attraction. Also within the city limits is the Old Mormon Fort; built in 1855, it is the oldest structure in the area and tours are offered daily.

East of the city, Lake Mead National Recreation area boasts 500 miles of scenic shoreline created when the Hoover Dam was constructed. Located 30 miles southeast of the city is Hoover Dam, the tallest concrete dam in the Western Hemisphere. The popular site draws about one million visitors annually to its tourist center while millions more drive over it. Only 15 miles west of Las Vegas is Red Rock Canyon, where a 13-mile scenic route winds through a natural landscape inhabited by wild burros and bighorn sheep; hikers and bicyclists can also enjoy 30 miles of trails. Some 40 miles north, the Valley of Fire State Park contains beautiful desert land, rock formations, and rock drawings surviving from ancient civilizations. Tour buses travel from Las Vegas to Grand Canyon National Park in northern Arizona, where visitors can choose from hiking, camping, biking, fishing, and boating. Several ghost towns are within an hour's drive of Las Vegas; Bonnie Springs Old Nevada, southwest of the city, is a recreated town that evokes the lawless days of the Old West.

Arts and Culture

World famous for entertainment, Las Vegas is a city where nightlife lasts 24 hours a day and spectacular casino resorts and venues feature international stars. There is also an active and acclaimed arts community in Las Vegas; theater, dance, and concert performances as well as lectures are staged at the Reed Whipple Cultural Arts Center. The center is home to the Las Vegas All-Star High School Jazz Band, the Las Vegas Youth Orchestra, and the Rainbow Company Youth Theatre. The Charleston Heights Arts Center presents theater and musical performances as well as exhibits by local and regional artists. The Community College of Southern Nevada offers dance, theater, and musical performances.

The University of Nevada at Las Vegas, with three performing arts venues, is the heart of the cultural community. The university hosts performances by Nevada Ballet Theatre, Symphony Orchestra, Sierra Wind Quintet, Chamber Music Southwest, and the Charles Vanda Master Series.

The Las Vegas Clark County Library District kicked off a partnership with the Nevada Chamber Symphony for the 2004-2005 season, with concerts scheduled in the Clark County Library on Flamingo Road. The Library District also hosts theatrical, dance, and other musical performances.

Several museums are located in the city. The Liberace Museum exhibits a collection of rare pianos, including pianos owned by Frederic Chopin and George Gershwin. The Nevada State Museum and Historical Society specializes in the

natural history of Southern Nevada, while the Las Vegas Natural History Museum focuses on the region's wildlife and natural environment, both past and present. The Lied Discovery Children's Museum offers 100 hands-on exhibits that let children explore science, arts, and humanities in a fun and educational way.

The Bellagio Gallery of Fine Art in the Bellagio Resort features two to three exhibitions annually, with works from top art museums and private collections. The Las Vegas Art Museum offers more than 170 works from a variety of mediums. The University of Nevada at Las Vegas maintains an art gallery in the Ham Fine Arts Building on campus, featuring the work of faculty members, touring artists, and students. Las Vegas area commercial galleries show the work of local and nationally known artists.

Festivals and Holidays

Las Vegas hosted a year of celebratory events throughout 2005, including festivals, concerts, exhibits, theater, and events honoring the city's history and unique style.

Las Vegas hosts the Antiquarian and Used Book Fair in January. The entire month of May is designated Jazz Month, showcasing local and national artists. Helldorado Days in May celebrate the Old West era with rodeos and parades. The Greek Festival in October features authentic food and dancing. National Finals Rodeo is held in December.

Sports for the Spectator

Las Vegas hosts a number of national sports competitions, including the Michelin Championship golf tournament of the PGA Tour, Seniors Golf, and the National Finals Rodeo. The city also has a baseball team, the Las Vegas 51s, the Triple A farm club of professional baseball's Los Angeles Dodgers, who play at Cashmen Field. The AFL's Las Vegas Gladiators play professional indoor football at the Thomas & Mack Center. The Las Vegas Wranglers, members of the ECHL Division, also play at the Thomas & Mack Center. Collegiate sports are represented by the UNLV Rebels basketball team plus teams who play golf, baseball, soccer, football, and women's basketball. Championship boxing events are scheduled year-round in Las Vegas.

Sports for the Participant

Although Las Vegas is in the desert, there are facilities for a number of water sports, including fishing, boating, waterskiing, and canoeing at nearby Lake Mead and on the Colorado River. Las Vegas City parks and Clark County parks continue to be developed to meet the needs of an expanding population; both provide a variety of athletic programming, tennis courts and ballfields, swimming pools, golf courses, community centers, activities, classes, and workshops. Wet 'n' Wild, located on the Strip, is a 26-acre water park that contains water slides, a wave pool, and swimming area. More than 30 golf courses exist in the area.

Shopping and Dining

Shopping center construction is constantly taking place in the city. A major attraction is the $100 million Forum Shops at Caesars Palace, which opened in 1992 and expanded to 675,000 square feet (an increase of 175,000 square feet) in 2004 that brought its entrance to a prominent position on Las Vegas Boulevard. Described as combining the opulence of Rodeo Drive with the glitter of the Las Vegas Strip, the Roman-inspired complex houses about 160 upscale shops, art galleries, and a $5 million animated fountain. The Galleria at Sunset Mall in nearby Henderson features one million square feet of enclosed mall space anchored by four department stores and housing more than 140 specialty shops. Boulevard Mall is Nevada's largest indoor shopping mall with 150 shops. The Fashion Show has seven anchor stores and features ''The Cloud,'' a canopy that is suspended 20 stories over the mall and serves the dual purpose of sunshade during the day and movie projection screen at night. Unusual shopping experiences can be found at the medieval-themed Shopping Courtyard with live jousting between stores and all that is French at the Rue de la Paix center.

More than 750 restaurants with choices ranging from haute cuisine to inexpensive fare, are located in Las Vegas. One such place is Spago, run by internationally-known chef Wolfgang Puck, who uses French cooking techniques to create an eclectic menu. Puck also features a more casual bar and grill within the city bearing his name. In 2004 Bobby Flay, successful chef and star of a popular television show on the Food Network, opened the Mesa Grill at Caesars Palace. Major resort hotels all feature gourmet menus; most hotels on ''the Strip'' and downtown offer buffet dining. Some examples of the culinary variety available include: AJ's Steakhouse, located in the Hard Rock Hotel; Hard Rock Cafe, residing just outside of the hotel; Planet Hollywood, at Caesars Palace; and the Eiffel Tower Restaurant, inside the Paris Las Vegas Hotel that is shaped to resemble the famous French structure.

Visitor Information: Las Vegas Visitor Information Center, 3150 Paradise Rd., Las Vegas, NV 89109-9096; telephone (702)892-7575; toll-free (877)VISITLV

Convention Facilities

Las Vegas is among the nation's foremost meeting destinations, with convention trade being one of the city's major industries. Las Vegas hosted more than 5.7 million conven-

tion and meeting participants in 2004, which had an economic impact of more than $6.8 billion. More than 131,000 hotel rooms are available throughout Las Vegas. Along with entertainment and recreation, well-appointed meeting facilities and luxury hotels and resorts are the attractions that consistently draw large and small groups to the city. Las Vegas boasts more than 130,000 hotel and motel rooms citywide; 17 of the 20 largest hotels in the nation are located in Las Vegas.

The Las Vegas Convention Center, after expansions in the late 1990s and then further expansion in the early 2000s, encompasses 3.2 million square feet. Nearly 2 million square feet are available for exhibit space in 16 exhibit halls, while 144 meeting rooms (more than 243,000 square feet) handle seating capacities ranging from 20 to 5,500 people. A grand lobby and concourse area of 109,515 square feet, catering services, state-of-the-art technological service, and ample parking round out the offerings.

Cashman Center in downtown Las Vegas contains more than 100,000 square feet of meeting and exhibit space, 12 meeting rooms, a 1,900-seat theater, and an outdoor stadium that seats 10,000 people. Many of the hotels and motels in the city provide facilities for large and small group functions.

Convention Information: LVCVA Meetings Division, 3150 Paradise Road, Las Vegas, NV 89109; telephone (702)892-0711; fax (702)892-2824 (ask for the Meetings Division)

Transportation

Approaching the City

Seemingly isolated in the middle of the desert, Las Vegas is, in fact, easily accessible. McCarran International Airport, located 5 miles south of the business district, is the 6th busiest airport in the United States; in 2005 the airport unveiled its new, $125 million expansion, an 11-gate wing that is expected to allow the airport to handle an addition 3.1 million passengers annually. Forty-four air carriers operate out of McCarran.

The city is served by three major highways. I-15 connects Las Vegas with Los Angeles and Salt Lake City. U.S. 95 leads into the city from the northwest and U.S. 93/95 enters from the southeast.

Amtrak Thruway provides bus service between Los Angeles, California, and Las Vegas. Greyhound provide bus service to and from nearby Las Vegas with connections throughout the west.

Traveling in the City

The streets of Las Vegas are laid out in a grid system. The primary north-south routes are Main Street and Las Vegas Boulevard—locally known as the "Strip"—which runs parallel to I-15. Main east-west thoroughfares are Flamingo Road, Tropicana Avenue, and Sahara Avenue. Within the city U.S. 95 is known as the Las Vegas Expressway.

Citizens Area Transit (CAT) operates 49 routes to points throughout the city and metropolitan area, with buses and trolleys serving the "Strip" every fifteen minutes. CAT services extend throughout Clark County, providing service to 150,000 riders each day with 305 buses that cover 49 routes. The Las Vegas Monorail runs along a four mile route along "the Strip," linking major resorts, hotels, attractions, and the convention center. Plans to extend the route to downtown were being discussed in 2005.

Communications

Newspapers and Magazines

The major daily newspaper is the *Las Vegas Review-Journal,* a morning paper. *Las Vegas Sentinel-Voice* is a weekly African American community newspaper, and the *Sun* is a general weekly community newspaper. *Nevada Senior World* is a monthly newspaper focusing on active seniors. Several small, special interest journals and magazines are also published in the city; among them are *Nevada Business Journal,* which focuses on the Nevada business climate, and *What's On In Las Vegas Magazine,* published every other week. Other publications include scholarly journals, and Jewish publications, and those focused on art, foodservice, and business.

Television and Radio

Four commercial and one public television stations broadcast in Las Vegas. Cable television service is available by subscription.

Sixteen AM and FM radio stations broadcast from Las Vegas, featuring diverse programming, including news, information, and music ranging from jazz to classical. Additional stations are received from surrounding communities.

Media Information: Las Vegas Review-Journal, PO Box 70, Las Vegas, NV 89125; telephone (702)383-0211

Las Vegas Online

Center for Business and Economic Research at the University of Nevada, Las Vegas. Available www.unlv.edu/Research_Centers/cber

City of Las Vegas home page. Available www.lasvegas nevada.gov

Clark County home page. Available www.co.clark.nv.us

Clark County School District. Available ccsd.net

Las Vegas Chamber of Commerce. Available www.lv chamber.com

Las Vegas-Clark County Library District. Available www .lvccld.lib.nv.us

Las Vegas Convention and Visitors Authority. Available www.lasvegas24hours.com

Las Vegas Review-Journal. Available www.reviewjournal .com

Las Vegas Sun. Available www.lasvegassun.com

Nevada State Museum and Historical Society. Available dmla.clan.lib.nv.us/docs/museums/lv/vegas.htm

"One City One Site." Available www.lasvegas.com

Vegas.com (entertainment, dining, attractions, book a room, travel tips). Available www.vegas.com

Selected Bibliography

Hopkins, A.D., and K.J. Evans, eds., *The First 100: Portraits of the Men and Women Who Shapes Las Vegas* (Las Vegas, Nev.: Huntington Press, 2000)

Kranes, David, *Low Tide in the Desert: Nevada Stories* (Las Vegas: University of Nevada, 1996)

Moehring, Eugene P., *Resort City in the Sunbelt, Las Vegas 1930–1970* (U. of Nevada Press, 1989)

Vinson, Barney, *Las Vegas Behind the Tables* (Grand Rapids, Mich.: Gollehon, 1986)

Reno

The City in Brief

Founded: 1868 (incorporated, 1903)

Head Official: Mayor Robert Cashell (since 2002)

City Population
- 1980: 100,756
- 1990: 133,850
- 2000: 180,480
- 2003 estimate: 193,882
- Percent change, 1990–2000: 34.5%
- U.S. rank in 1980: 169th
- U.S. rank in 1990: 132nd
- U.S. rank in 2000: 130th

Metropolitan Area Population
- 1980: 193,623
- 1990: 254,667
- 2000: 339,486

Percent change, 1990–2000: 33.3%
U.S. rank in 1990: 132nd
U.S. rank in 2000: 119th

Area: 69.34 square miles (2000)
Elevation: 4,400 feet above sea level
Average Annual Temperature: 51.1° F
Average Annual Precipitation: 7.29 inches of rain, 23.1 inches of snow

Major Economic Sectors: Tourism, gaming, manufacturing, transportation
Unemployment Rate: 10.5% (January 2005)
Per Capita Income: $22,520 (1999)

2002 FBI Crime Index Total: 11,626

Major Colleges and Universities: University of Nevada, Reno, Truckee Meadows Community College, Morrison University, Sierra Nevada College

Daily Newspaper: *Reno Gazette-Journal*

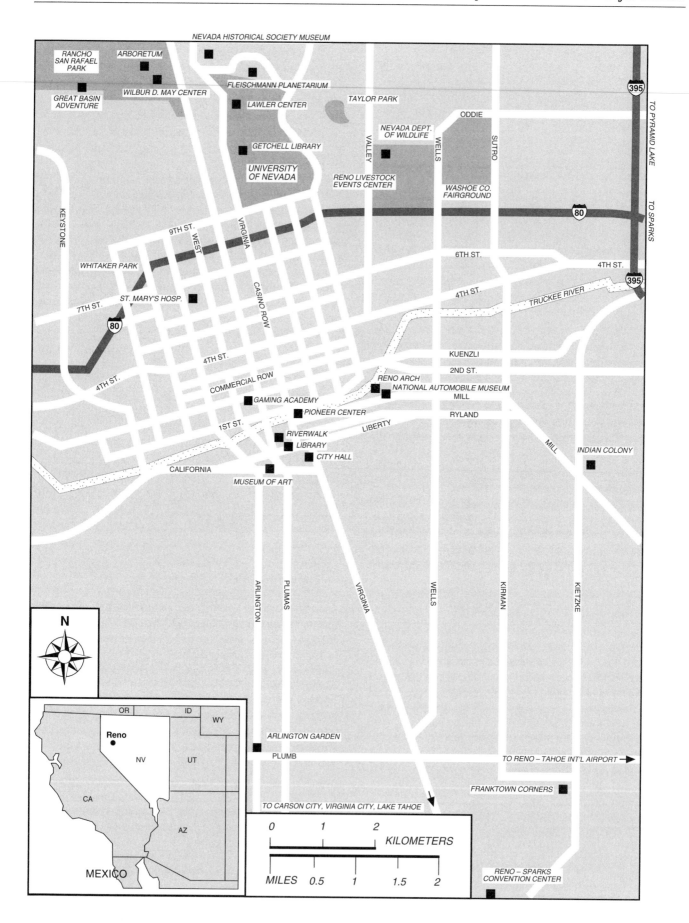

Introduction

Reno is known as "The Biggest Little City in the World" because of its outstanding western hospitality, fine dining, entertaining stage shows, top-name performers, history, culture, and 24-hour gaming excitement. The region also offers a wide variety of outdoor recreation including golf and skiing. Golfers can choose from courses in lake, high desert, and mountain settings. Lake Tahoe, located less than an hour's drive from downtown Reno, boasts the largest concentration of ski resorts in North America. Nevada's liberal tax structures, along with Reno's free port status and central location in the West, also make the area an important regional warehouse and distribution center. Reno's abundance of desirable features resulted in *Time* magazine naming it among the top cities for "quality of life and business friendly atmosphere" in November 2003.

Geography and Climate

Reno is located at the western border of Nevada—in a valley known as the Truckee Meadows—about 20 miles east of the Sierra Nevada mountains and Lake Tahoe, the second largest alpine lake in the world. The Truckee River passes between Reno and its sister city, Sparks. Temperatures in the region are mild, but can fluctuate as much as 45 degrees between day and night. The temperature at night during the summer rarely rises above 60 degrees. More than half the annual precipitation falls from December to March, in the form of mixed snow and rain, with snow accumulation seldom lasting longer than three or four days. Low humidity and sunny skies are prevalent throughout the year.

Area: 69.34 square miles (2000)

Elevation: 4,400 feet above sea level

Average Temperatures: January, 33.3° F; August, 69.8° F; annual average: 51.1° F

Average Annual Precipitation: 7.29 inches of rain, 23.1 inches of snow

History

Reno's Beginnings

Reno's history began when Charles William Fuller arrived in the Truckee Meadows in 1859 and occupied a piece of land on the south bank of the Truckee River. By early 1860, he had constructed a bridge and small hotel, and the place was known as Fuller's Crossing. In the following year, Fuller sold his bridge and hotel to Myron C. Lake, who renamed the spot Lake's Crossing and soon was charging a toll on the bridge. The Crossing became an important station on one of the main routes between northern California and the silver mines of Virginia City and the Comstock Lode.

Lake was the crossing's only property owner until the Central Pacific Railroad (later renamed Union Railroad) crossed the Sierra Nevada in 1868 and pushed its tracks into the Truckee Meadows. Under terms of an agreement between Myron Lake and Central Pacific, a new town was laid out at the crossing; ownership was divided between Lake and the railroad. Almost overnight, buildings began to appear on the town site and the new settlement was named Reno in honor of General Jesse Lee Reno (1823–1862), a Union army officer who was killed during the Civil War.

In 1871, the Nevada State Legislature moved the Washoe County seat to Reno, where one year later the Virginia & Truckee Railroad extended its line. The town soon became an important commercial center on the transcontinental railroad and a transfer point for the immense wealth coming out of the Comstock Lode. The University of Nevada was moved from Elko to Reno in 1885.

Gaming Gains Prominence, Modern Times

At the beginning of the twentieth century, Reno gained national notoriety after a number of famous people obtained divorces in the city under Nevada's lenient laws. Newspapers sensationalized the incidents, dubbing Reno the "divorce capital." Reno's sister city, Sparks, was established in 1904 as a division point on the Southern Pacific Railroad. After the legalization of casino gambling by the state legislature in 1931, Reno filled with gambling establishments–marking the start of a tourist industry that flourishes today.

In the shadow of the casinos, Reno has quietly grown into an important transportation hub for the western United States and has developed a diverse economic base. The city leaders have recognized this and responded by creating aggressive expansion plans including a railroad system that will eventually bolster travel in the area along with the boom the construction brings. Modern Reno boasts a thriving cultural scene, a refurbished downtown area, and an expanding tourist industry fueled not by the casinos, but by the many year-round resorts in the nearby mountains. The area's mix of recreational opportunities—from outdoor activities to gambling to plush accommodations—coupled with a warm climate that features more than 300 sunny days every year has been the backbone to the success of the city. The effects are evident in its population and business growth, and many have taken notice such as the authors of "Cities Ranked & Rated" that listed Reno in 2004 among the top 10 best places to live. With 30 *Fortune* 500 companies in the region that magazine also named Reno as one of three "top booming towns" in March 2004.

Historical Information: Nevada Historical Society-Research Library, 1650 N. Virginia St., Reno, NV 89503; telephone (775)688-1190; fax (775)688-2917

Population Profile

Metropolitan Area Residents
1980: 193,623
1990: 254,667
2000: 339,486
Percent change, 1990–2000: 33.3%
U.S. rank in 1990: 132nd
U.S. rank in 2000: 119th

City Residents
1980: 100,756
1990: 133,850
2000: 180,480
2003 estimate: 193,882
Percent change, 1990–2000: 34.5%
U.S. rank in 1980: 169th
U.S. rank in 1990: 132nd
U.S. rank in 2000: 130th (State rank: 3rd)

Density: 2,611.4 people per square mile (2000)

Racial and ethnic characteristics (2000)
White: 139,793
Black or African American: 4,651
American Indian and Alaska Native: 2,271
Asian: 9,555
Native Hawaiian and Pacific Islander: 1,004
Hispanic or Latino (may be of any race): 34,616
Other: 16,712

Percent of residents born in state: 24.1%

Age characteristics (2000)
Population under 5 years old: 12,626
Population 5 to 9 years old: 11,976
Population 10 to 14 years old: 10,937
Population 15 to 19 years old: 12,102
Population 20 to 24 years old: 15,434
Population 25 to 34 years old: 28,638
Population 35 to 44 years old: 28,164
Population 45 to 54 years old: 24,591
Population 55 to 59 years old: 8,628

Population 60 to 64 years old: 6,781
Population 65 to 74 years old: 10,962
Population 75 to 84 years old: 7,382
Population 85 years and over: 2,259
Median age: 34.5 years

Births (2003, Washoe County)
Total number: 5,398

Deaths (2003, Washoe County)
Total number: 2,953 (of which, 31 were infants under the age of 1 year)

Money income (1999)
Per capita income: $22,520 (1999)
Median household income: $40,530 (1999)
Total households: 73,859

Number of households with income of . . .
less than $10,000: 6,374
$10,000 to $14,999: 4,633
$15,000 to $24,999: 10,398
$25,000 to $34,999: 10,202
$35,000 to $49,999: 13,100
$50,000 to $74,999: 14,492
$75,000 to $99,999: 7,015
$100,000 to $149,999: 4,884
$150,000 to $199,999: 1,275
$200,000 or more: 1,486

Percent of families below poverty level: 8.3% (48.1% of which were female householder families with related children under 5 years)

2002 FBI Crime Index Total: 11,626

Municipal Government

Reno operates under a mayor-city council-city manager form of government. The seven council members and the mayor, who appoint a city manager, all serve a four-year term.

Head Official: Mayor Robert Cashell (since 2002; current term expires 2006)

Total Number of City Employees: 1,500–1,999 (2004)

City Information: City of Reno, PO Box 1900, Reno, NV 89505; telephone (702)334-2099; fax (702)334-3110; email renodirect@cityofreno.com

Economy

Major Industries and Commercial Activity

Tourism is the major industry in the Reno area. The hotel and casino industry attracts more than five million visitors annually and adds over $4 billion to the local economy each year. The business climate also has a strong presence in manufacturing and logistics in industries such as computers, electronics, financial services, and communications. This diversity supports the thriving local economy and includes a wide range of restaurants and retail options. The nearby mountains draw many tourists to the highest concentration of ski resorts in America, and contribute to the unlimited year-round recreational opportunities

Items and goods produced: cement, labeling devices, suntan lotion, valves, dairy and food products, pet food, microwaves, electronic equipment, livestock, agricultural produce

Incentive Programs—New and Existing Companies

Because a majority of tax revenues in Nevada are generated from the tourism and gaming industries, Nevada's tax burden is one of the lightest in the nation. Nevada is one of only seven states without a personal income tax and one of only three without a corporate income tax. New and expanding companies can benefit from several different programs including sales and use tax abatements and deferrals, personal property tax abatements, business tax abatements, and the Train Employees Now program that assists in defraying the cost of training new employees. All programs have conditions and criteria that a company must meet in order to qualify; for example, minimum capital investment, minimum number of jobs created, minimum wage requirements, and a health plan available to employees and dependants. Application for all incentives must be made to the Nevada State Commission on Economic Development.

Job training programs—The Nevada Department of Employment, Training, and Rehabilitation offers job training services to both employers and job seekers, including applicant recruitment and screening, tax credit benefits, training programs and career enhancement programs, and labor market information. The Train Employees Now (TEN) program, administered by the State of Nevada Commission on Economic Development, helps new and expanding firms by providing intensive skills-based training programs tailored to the company's needs. The TEN program utilizes training providers such as local businesses and community colleges. Job Opportunities in Nevada (JOIN) works to ensure that companies have an adequate workforce while offering training and educational opportunities for job seekers; Nevadaworks assists employers in developing employees' skills. The public school district's Glenn Hare Occupational Center provides training in areas identified by local employers. Training, recruiting, and continuing education resources in Reno also include Truckee Meadows Community College and the University of Nevada, Reno. Several other educational programs are geared toward meeting the needs of employers such as the Nevada Prepaid Tuition Program, the Millennium Scholarship Plan, and the Technology Center programs.

Development Projects

The city of Reno is rolling with economic development in the downtown area and the local government actively creates plans to ensure progress continues. One example is the $65 million, 118,000-square-foot Reno Events Center whose debut in late 2005 will broaden Reno's already prosperous appeal as a convention draw. Also critical to the success of the area is a long-anticipated plan to build depressed railroad tracks, named ReTRAC, to facilitate travel. Discussed for many decades, the construction, scheduled for completion in early 2006, is estimated to have an overall $360 million economic impact.

The Washoe Medical Center expanded in 2004 with the acute care facility South Meadows, which represented the first community hospital to open in the area in about two decades. In spring 2005 the Washoe County Library system added the new $6.3 million, 30,000-square-foot Spanish Springs branch library.

Economic Development Information: Economic Development Authority of Western Nevada (EDAWN), 5190 Neil Rd., Ste. 111, Reno, NV 89502; telephone (702)829-3700; fax (702)829-3710; email info@edawn.org

Commercial Shipping

Reno/Sparks is situated at the hub of an extensive transportation network. Nevada borders five western states and provides overnight ground service to most of the West Coast major markets.

The area is also located on two major highway corridors: Interstate 80 and US 395. Currently, over 60 local, regional and national carriers provide trucking service in the Reno/Sparks area including the 167,000-square-foot United Parcel Service (UPS) regional package-sorting hub in Sparks. Rail freight service is provided by Burlington Northern Santa Fe and Union Pacific Railroads.

The Reno/Tahoe International Airport is among the nation's busiest airports with 90 daily departures to about two dozen nonstop U.S. destinations. Air Cargo in the Reno/Sparks area handles approximately 291,000 pounds daily with a total of more than 106 million pounds in 2004.

The Reno/Sparks foreign trade zones are popular to business, as they provide economically favorable conditions and operational flexibility. Currently, Reno/Sparks has eight sites with more than 7,500 acres of building space.

Labor Force and Employment Outlook

The availability of skilled workers and competitive compensation levels makes the Reno/Sparks area especially attractive to new businesses. More than 20,000 students attend the five colleges in the area. State-supported training programs and pro-business policies have helped make Nevada the fastest growing state in the nation. As a right-to-work state, Nevada's law states that no person shall be denied the opportunity to obtain or retain employment because of non-membership in a labor organization.

The following is a summary of data regarding the Reno metropolitan area labor force, 2004 annual averages.

Size of non-agricultural labor force: 208,500

Number of workers employed in . . .
  natural resources and mining: 400
  construction: 19,800
  manufacturing: 14,000
  trade, transportation, and utilities: 43,600
  information: 3,100
  financial activities: 10,700
  professional and business services: 23,600
  educational and health services: 19,300
  leisure and hospitality: 39,000
  other services: 7,500
  government: 27,200

Average hourly earnings of production workers employed in manufacturing: $14.60 (Nevada average)

Unemployment rate: 10.5% (January 2005)

Largest county employers	Number of employees
Washoe County School District	7,500–7,999
University of Nevada, Reno	4,000–4,499
Washoe County Government	2,500–2,999
International Game Technology	2,500–2,599
Washoe Medical Center, Inc.	2,000–2,499
Silver Legacy Resort Casino	2,000–2,499
Reno Hilton (casino)	1,500–1,999
Eldorado Hotel & Casino	1,500–1,999
Peppermill Hotel Casino-Reno	1,500–1,999

Cost of Living

The following is a summary of data regarding key cost of living factors for the Reno area.

2004 (3rd Quarter) ACCRA Average House Price: $290,000

2004 (3rd Quarter) ACCRA Cost of Living Index: 106.1 (U.S. average = 100.0)

State income tax rate: None

State sales tax rate: 6.5% (food and prescription drugs are exempt)

Local income tax rate: None

Local sales tax rate: 0.875%

Property tax rate: $3.64 per $100 assessed value

Economic Information: Economic Development Authority of Western Nevada (EDAWN), 5190 Neil Rd., Ste. 111, Reno, NV 89502; telephone (702)829-3700; fax (702)829-3710; email info@edawn.org. Nevada Department of Employment, Training & Rehabilitation, Information Development and Processing, Research and Analysis Bureau, 500 E. Third St., Carson City, NV 89713; telephone (775)684-3849; fax (775)684-3850; email detradmn@nvdetr.org

Education and Research

Elementary and Secondary Schools

Reno is part of the Washoe County School District. The district is governed by a board of trustees that consists of seven nonpartisan members. The superintendent is appointed by the board.

Reno public school students consistently score above state and national averages on standardized tests, including the Iowa Test of Basic Skills/Iowa Test of Educational Development (ITBS/ITED) and, for high school students, the ACT and SAT college entrance exams. Five Reno public high schools have been named by *Newsweek* as among the best in the country. The district also was awarded SchoolMatch's "What Parents Want" honor in 2003.

The following is a summary of data regarding Reno public schools as of the 2003–2004 school year.

Total enrollment: 62,098

Number of facilities
  elementary schools: 61
  middle schools: 15
  senior high schools: 14
  other: 1

Student/teacher ratio: 1-2, 16:1; 3, 19:1; 4-6, 26:1; 7-8, 26.5:1; 9-12, 27:1

Teacher salaries
  minimum: $27,907
  maximum: $57,292

Funding per pupil: $6,025

Public Schools Information: Washoe County School District, 425 E. Ninth St., PO Box 30425, Reno, NV 89520-3425; telephone (775)348-0200

Colleges and Universities

The University of Nevada, Reno, founded in 1864, enrolled more than 15,000 degree-seeking students in fall 2004 at both the undergraduate and postgraduate levels. The university includes schools of medicine, journalism, and education; a college for training judges (National Judicial College); and the only program in Basque studies in the country (many Nevadans trace their ancestry to Basque sheepherders from Spain). The Truckee Meadows Community College offers two-year associate's degrees as well as adult education programs. A number of business, vocational, and professional schools are also located in the Reno area. Morrison University focuses on business degrees while the Sierra Nevada College in Lake Tahoe takes advantage of its location by presenting many science and environmental programs.

Libraries and Research Centers

The Washoe County Library System consists of 14 library branches strategically placed around the county with a new branch, Spanish Springs, that opened in early 2005. Six of the branches are "Partnership Libraries," which are housed in public school libraries but serve the entire public in their neighborhoods. One branch is a virtual branch on the Internet. The library has more than 943,000 items including books, videos, audios, and materials in microformat, CD-ROMs, database access, and several hundred periodical subscriptions. Special collections focus on gambling, Nevada history, and U.S. and Nevada documents.

The University of Nevada, Reno Libraries offer resources in paper and electronic formats, including over one million texts and journals available in-house, as well as electronic access to the full-text articles of over 8,000 journals. Films, audio and video tapes, maps, and government documents are also available. Special collections include Basque materials (50,000 volumes and 1,500 journals), Nevada and the Great Basin collection, rare books and prints, and a collection of contemporary arts books.

The Desert Research Institute (DRI), Nevada's primary research institution of the University and Community College System of Nevada (UCCSN), maintains facilities in Reno (the 470-acre Dandini Research Park) and oversees about 300 separate projects throughout the state, conducting studies in areas such as air quality and climatic changes in the western United States over the last two million years. The University of Nevada is a hotbed for research activities as represented by its surpassing $100 million in financial support received in the 2000–2001 academic year.

Public Library Information: Washoe County Library, 301 S. Center St., Reno, NV 89501; telephone (775)327-8349; fax (775)327-8393; email internet@washoe.lib.nv.us

Health Care

Three major hospitals serve Reno, including Washoe Medical Center, recipient of the 2002 American Alliance of Healthcare Providers "Facility of Choice" that features a cardiac rehabilitation center, a trauma center, and has more than 500 beds; the 380-bed St. Mary's Regional Medical Center; and Northern Nevada Medical Center. The hospitals provide 24-hour emergency room facilities and various specialized treatment programs. The medical community consists of about 800 physicians and approximately 3,000 registered and licensed practical nurses. Other health-related facilities include the University of Nevada School of Medicine.

Recreation

Sightseeing

Downtown Reno glitters with brightly-lit casinos and 24-hour entertainment. In the middle of it all stands the city's best-known symbol, the Reno Arch. The arch welcomes visitors with its slogan, "The Biggest Little City In The World." There have been four arches since the original was erected in 1929. The arch which welcomed visitors from 1934 to 1963 can now be seen on Lake Street, in front of the National Automobile Museum.

One of the country's finest and most extensive collections of antique cars is on display at the National Automobile Museum (The Harrah Collection). Opened in 1989, more than 220 vehicles are featured, including horseless carriages, cars owned by celebrities, and experimental cars of the future.

Described by the *Los Angeles Times* as the "Taj Mahal of Tenpins," the National Bowling Stadium is the only facility of its kind in the world. The stadium features 78-championship lanes, Paul Revere's Kick's Diner & Dance Club, and an IWERKS theater where giant screen movies are shown daily.

The Wilbur D. May Center features a museum, an indoor arboretum, and a botanical garden surrounded by a beautiful park. During summer months, the center's Great Basin Adventure provides children with a full day of activities including pony rides, a "hands-on" discovery room, a log flume

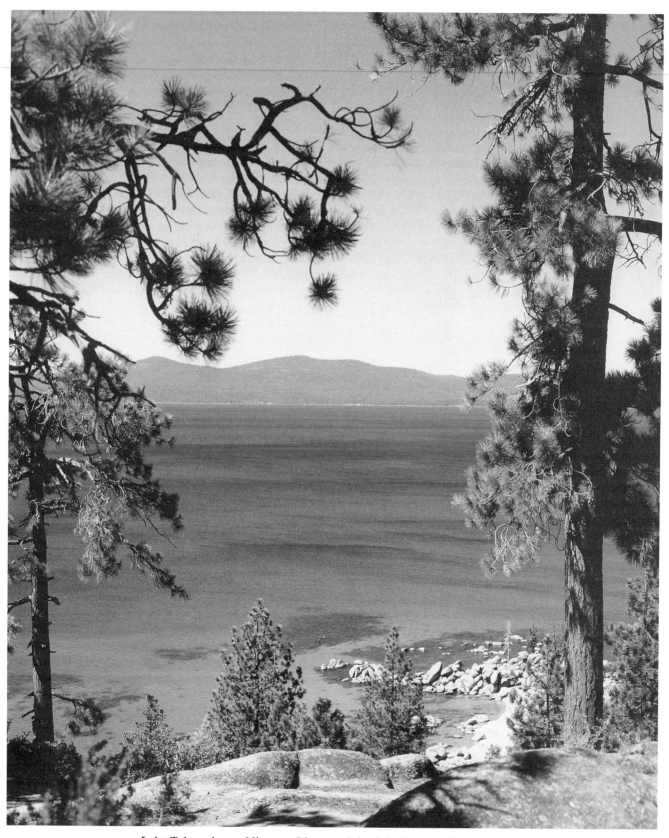

Lake Tahoe, the world's second largest alpine lake, is a popular attraction.

ride, a petting zoo, and a playground complete with dinosaurs. In 2005 a new visitor educational center was being developed costing about $4 million that will include an information area, greenhouse, classrooms, library, bookstore, and master gardener area.

Daytrip excursions also provide visitors with a number of sightseeing options. Reno serves as a base camp to some of the most unique attractions on the West Coast. Pyramid Lake, just east of Reno, is shrouded in the mysteries of Indian legend and prehistoric past; Virginia City, still the liveliest ghost town in the West, is only a 35-mile drive from Reno; Carson City, Nevada's State Capital, is only 30 miles from Reno; and nearby Lake Tahoe was described by Mark Twain as "surely the fairest picture the whole earth affords."

Arts and Culture

Reno offers a flourishing and diverse community of artistic talent. The 1,500-seat Pioneer Center for the Performing Arts is the home of the Reno Philharmonic, the Sierra Nevada Master Chorale, the Reno Dance Company, and a Best of Broadway series that gives scheduled performances throughout the year. A chamber orchestra, opera company, and two ballet troupes round out the Reno experience. The University of Nevada, Reno, presents a variety of art galleries, music, and performing arts.

The Nevada Museum of Art, originally called the Nevada Art Gallery in 1931, debuted its new four-level, 55,000 square foot location in May 2003 and features a permanent collection along with video and experimental exhibitions. A library, cafe, sculpture garden, and store are among the other modern amenities offered.

Reno's own summer arts festival, Uptown Downtown ARTown, was named one of the top 100 Events in North America by the American Bus Association. The festival takes place every July, when more than 150 events at three dozen locations are featured throughout the month.

Festivals and Holidays

Special events are plentiful and varied in Reno. In April, snowmobilers flock to SledFest with rides on the trails and a tradeshow. The Reno Rodeo, the "wildest, richest rodeo in the west," takes place over nine days in June and infuses nearly $35 million into the local economy. In August, the Reno area celebrates America's love affair with cars and rock 'n' roll during the five-day Hot August Nights. The celebration features more than 5,000 classic cars from 36 states, vintage music, parades, and drag racing. September is full of celebrations that include the Great Reno Balloon Race, the National Championship Air Races and Air Show, and Street Vibrations (for motorcycle enthusiasts). October brings the Eldorado's Great Italian Festival and the Celtic Festival.

Sports for the Spectator

Reno is making a name for itself as the mountain golf capital of the world. Since 1999 the PGA Tour's Greens.com Open at Reno-Tahoe (formerly Reno-Tahoe Open) has taken place at Montreux Golf and Country Club in August, where some of the world's best professional golfers compete. A celebrity-packed golfing event, the American Century Celebrity Championship, is also held annually at Edgewood-Tahoe in July.

Two of the country's largest bowling organizations, the American Bowling Congress (ABC) and the Women's International Bowling Congress (WIBC), hold tournaments at the National Bowling Stadium. Dubbed "Pin Palace" by *USA Today*, thousands of bowlers are drawn to the city's high-technology facility on a regular basis.

Sports for the Participant

Reno offers a seemingly limitless variety of indoor and outdoor activities. Snow-packed mountains, less than an hour from Reno, feature the largest concentration of world-class ski/snowboard resorts in North America. In the summer months, the same mountains, as well as the valley below, offer hiking and mountain biking. Since 1994 the three-day annual Mighty Tour De Nez Classic has featured different levels of regional bicyclers. Lake Tahoe, "the Jewel of the Sierra," is the perfect place for a day of canoeing, water skiing, swimming, and more.

High desert, rolling hills and mountainous alpine terrain make for some of the greatest golf courses found anywhere. The Reno-Tahoe area boasts more than 40 courses, 4,000 feet above sea level so golfers can watch their balls fly further through the thin air. The Reno area also offers great fishing in a variety of streams, rivers, and lakes. Non-resident fishing licenses are available at most sporting goods stores.

Shopping and Dining

More than 90 area shopping centers sell items ranging from the usual designer apparel to Native American handicrafts and Western art and clothing. Popular centers in Reno include Arlington Gardens Mall, Franktown Corners, Southwest Pavilion, Meadowood Mall, Park Lane Mall, and Indian Colony Corners. Sparks is home to Victorian Square Plaza.

Restaurants in Reno range from simple to extravagant. A local specialty is family-style Basque dinners.

Visitor Information: Reno's downtown Visitors Center is located in the lobby of the National Bowling Stadium, on the corner of Center and 4th Street; telephone (775)334-2600; Meadowood Mall Visitors Center is at 500 Meadowood Mall Circle, on the corner of S. McCarran Blvd. and S. Virginia Street; telephone (775)827-8450. The mailing address for both centers is Reno-Sparks Convention & Visitors Authority, PO Box 837, Reno, NV 89504-0837; general information number telephone (800)FOR-RENO; email info @visitrenotahoe.com

Convention Facilities

In the heart of downtown the two-floor Reno Events Center, estimated at $65 million, is slated to open in December 2005 with an overall size of 118,000 square feet—56,000 of it being floor space. In July 2002 the Reno-Sparks Convention Center completed an extensive expansion costing more than $100 million that provides convention and meeting planners with a modern, high-tech facility. The convention center's space increased to nearly 500,000 square feet and includes 53 meeting rooms and exhibit space totaling 381,000 square feet.

Meeting attendees can visit the National Bowling Stadium in Reno, where customized tournaments on its 78 championship lanes can be arranged for groups of anywhere between 50 and 2,000 people.

The Motel 6 Reno Livestock Events Center provides space for livestock and equestrian events, as well as meetings. It includes 35,000 square feet of exhibit space, a climate-controlled indoor arena seating 6,200 and a lighted, 9,000-seat outdoor arena.

Theater-style seating for more than 1,500 people is available at the Pioneer Center for the Performing Arts in downtown Reno. The Lawlor Events Center, a large multipurpose arena on the campus of the University of Nevada, Reno is also available for conventions and can seat up to 12,400.

Reno has more than 20,000 first-class guestrooms all within minutes of the Reno-Sparks Convention Center and Reno-Tahoe International Airport. More than 12 hotels have their own convention facilities and the largest hotel offers more than 2,000 rooms and 200,000 square feet of convention space.

Convention Information: Reno-Sparks Convention & Visitors Authority, PO Box 837, Reno, NV 89405-0837; telephone (800)FOR-RENO; email info@visitrenotahoe.com

Transportation

Approaching the City

The Reno/Tahoe International Airport (RTIA) is located three miles south of downtown Reno. The airport handles

about 14,000 arriving and departing passengers on about 90 commercial flights per day from 11 major airlines, and is an international Port of Entry. Passenger rail service is available from Amtrak via the "California Zephyr," described as the most scenic train ride in the United States, with daily service from San Francisco and Chicago. The city is also served by commercial bus lines.

Interstate highway 80 runs through Reno's downtown region, west to San Francisco, and east to Salt Lake city. The US 395 freeway passes just to the east of the city, connecting Reno with Portland and Seattle to the north and Los Angeles to the south.

Traveling in the City

Washoe County's Regional Transportation Commission (RTC) runs the Reno Citifare that operates 65 buses providing continuous travel throughout the metropolitan area, most with wheelchair accessibility. RTC's CitiLift offers bus service to those with special transportation needs. The Sierra Spirit bus line gives free rides to passengers in the downtown area. Major thoroughfares in the city include Virginia Street, Plumb Lane, Kietzke Lane, and Mill Street.

Communications

Newspapers and Magazines

The *Reno Gazette-Journal* is the city's daily and Sunday newspaper, published in the morning. The *Daily Sparks Tribune* is a daily newspaper published in neighboring Sparks since 1910. *Ahora Spanish News* is a semi-monthly Hispanic community newspaper. Also published in Reno are *Sagebrush* (a collegiate newspaper), *Reno News and Review*, and *Showtime Magazine*.

Television and Radio

Five commercial television stations are based in Reno; a variety of channels are available from the local cable system. Twenty-three radio stations broadcast from the Reno/Tahoe area.

Media Information: *Reno Gazette Journal,* PO Box 22000, Reno, NV 89520; telephone (775)788-6200

Reno Online

City of Reno. Available www.cityofreno.com

Economic Development Authority of Western Nevada. Available www.edawn.org

Nevada Department of Employment, Training & Rehabilitation. Available detr.state.nv.us

Reno Gazette Journal. Available www.rgj.com

Reno-Sparks Chamber of Commerce. Available www.reno-sparkschamber.org

Reno-Sparks Convention & Visitors Authority. Available www.visitrenotahoe.com

Reno Visitor's Center. Available www.visitrenotahoe.com

Truckee Meadows Community College. Available www.tmcc.edu

Washoe County Library. Available www.washoe.lib.nv.us

Washoe County School District. Available www.washoe.k12.nv.us

Selected Bibliography

Betts, Doris, *The Sharp Teeth of Love: A Novel* (New York: Scribner, 1998)

Land, Barbara and Myrick Land, *A Short History of Reno* (Reno: University of Nevada Press, 1995)

Twain, Mark, *Mark Twain of the Enterprise; Newspaper Articles and Other Documents, 1862–1864* (Berkeley: U. of California Press, 1957)

NEW MEXICO

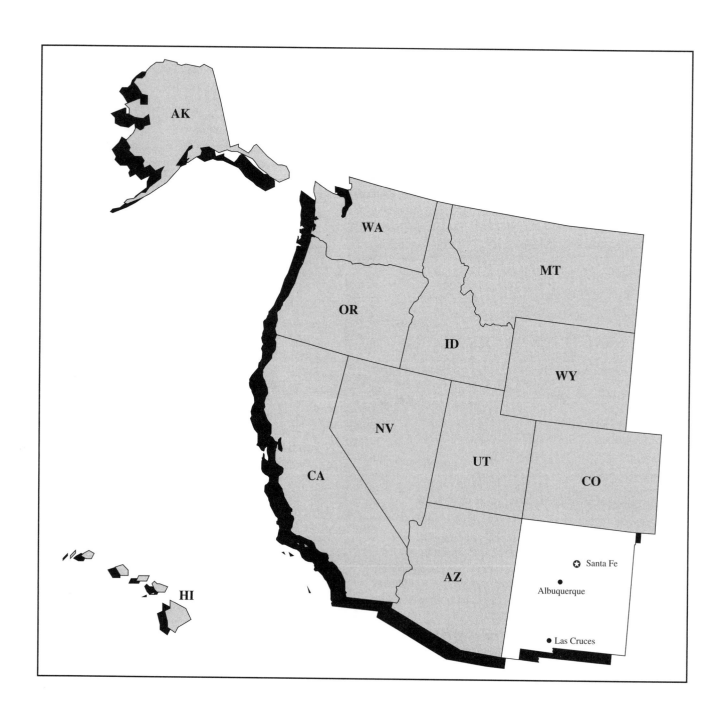

The State in Brief

Nickname: Land of Enchantment
Motto: *Crescit eundo* (It grows as it goes)

Flower: Yucca
Bird: Roadrunner

Area: 121,589 square miles (2000; U.S. rank: 5th)
Elevation: Ranges from 2,842 feet to 13,161 feet above sea level
Climate: Semi arid and sunny, with temperatures varying according to elevation

Admitted to Union: January 6, 1912
Capital: Santa Fe
Head Official: Governor Bill Richardson (D) (until 2007)

Population
    1980: 1,302,894
    1990: 1,515,069
    2000: 1,819,046
    2004 estimate: 1,903,289
    Percent change, 1990–2000: 20.1%
    U.S. rank in 2004: 36th
    Percent of residents born in state: 51.5% (2000)
    Density: 15.0 people per square mile (2000)
    2002 FBI Crime Index Total: 94,196

Racial and Ethnic Characteristics (2000)
    White: 1,214,253

Black or African American: 34,343
American Indian and Alaska Native: 173,483
Asian: 19,255
Native Hawaiian and Pacific Islander: 1,503
Hispanic or Latino (may be of any race): 765,386
Other: 309,882

Age Characteristics (2000)
    Population under 5 years old: 130,628
    Population 5 to 19 years old: 434,231
    Percent of population 65 years and over: 11.7%
    Median age: 34.6 years (2000)

Vital Statistics
    Total number of births (2003): 27,672
    Total number of deaths (2003): 14,636 (infant deaths, 157)
    AIDS cases reported through 2003: 1,182

Economy
    Major industries: Government; manufacturing; services; finance, insurance, and real estate; trade
    Unemployment rate: 5.6% (February 2005)
    Per capita income: $25,502 (2003; U.S. rank: 47th)
    Median household income: $35,265 (3-year average, 2001-2003)
    Percentage of persons below poverty level: 18.4% (1999)
    Income tax rate: Ranges from 1.7% to 6.8%
    Sales tax rate: 5.0%

Albuquerque

The City in Brief

Founded: 1706 (incorporated, 1891)

Head Official: Mayor Martin Chavez (since 2001)

City Population
   1980: 332,920
   1990: 384,915
   2000: 448,607
   2003 estimate: 471,856
   Percent change, 1990–2000: 15.9%
   U.S. rank in 1980: 44th
   U.S. rank in 1990: 38th (State rank: 1st)
   U.S. rank in 2000: 42nd (State rank: 1st)

Metropolitan Area Population
   1980: 485,430
   1990: 589,131
   2000: 712,738

Percent change, 1990–2000: 21.0%
U.S. rank in 1980: 80th
U.S. rank in 1990: 77th
U.S. rank in 2000: 62nd

Area: 180.64 square miles (2000)
Elevation: 5,311 feet above sea level
Average Annual Temperature: 56.0° F
Average Annual Precipitation: 8.12 inches

Major Economic Sectors: Trade, government, manufacturing
Unemployment Rate: 4.9% (January 2005)
Per Capita Income: $20,884 (1999)

2002 FBI Crime Index Total: 35,762

Major Colleges and Universities: University of New Mexico, University of Phoenix, Albuquerque Technical-Vocational Institute, College of Santa Fe at Albuquerque

Daily Newspapers: *Albuquerque Journal; The Albuquerque Tribune*

Introduction

Surrounded by natural beauty, Albuquerque is at the center of Native American pueblo country in New Mexico, the "Land of Enchantment." The state's largest city, Albuquerque retains deep roots in the past and simultaneously stands on the cutting edge of the future. The original Spanish town was built on the site of the oldest farming civilization in North America; modern Albuquerque is the focal point of the "Rio Grande Research Corridor," one of the nation's primary space-research complexes. The city's residents have maintained ethnic traditions and preserved a high quality of life while at the same time fostering modern growth and economic development.

Geography and Climate

Albuquerque is situated in the middle of the Rio Grande valley. To the east of the city are the Sandia and Manzano mountains; to the west are five volcanic cones that mark the beginning of high plateau country. The climate in Albuquerque, termed "arid-continental," is sunny and dry with very low humidity. Half of the annual precipitation falls between July and September in heavy afternoon thundershowers. During the winter one can ski on Sandia Peak and play a round of golf on the same day.

Area: 180.64 square miles (2000)

Elevation: 5,311 feet above sea level

Average Temperatures: January, 36.0° F; August, 76.5° F; annual average, 56.0° F

Average Annual Precipitation: 8.12 inches

History

Early Native American and Spanish Influences

The region surrounding present-day Albuquerque was home to several groups of Native American peoples, including "Sandia Man," who lived there and hunted mastodon during the ice age 25,000 years ago. Albuquerque was later inhabited by the ancient Anasazi Indians. Their huge apartment-like buildings, constructed 3,000 years ago of stone and adobe, are still standing. The city continues to be a center of Native American culture: most of New Mexico's 19 pueblos—including the thousand-year-old, still-inhabited Acoma Pueblo—are within an hour's drive. To the north is Sandia Pueblo Indian Reservation. Albuquerque's modern architecture, particularly buildings on the University of New Mexico campus, combines modern design elements with native American and Hispanic motifs.

Albuquerque was founded as a villa in 1706 by Spanish colonists, who were attracted to the banks of the Rio Grande by the green pastures they needed to graze their sheep. The city is named for a Spanish Duke, the tenth Duke of Alburquerque (over time the first "r" in his name was dropped). The first structure built in Albuquerque was a church named for the city's patron saint, San Felipe de Neri. The original adobe walls remain standing in the part of the city known as Old Town.

City Becomes Distribution Center

Although the topography of the land—the mountains to the east and the Rio Grande to the west—afforded the settlement natural protection, Albuquerque was regularly threatened during the nineteenth century by hostile attacks, particularly from the Navajo and Apache. In the meantime, the town assumed a role as purveyor of goods to the West and served as a link in trade with Mexico. Situated on the Old Chihuahua trail, an extension of the Santa Fe Trail, Albuquerque's stores and warehouses were perfectly positioned to supply forts that were established in the Southwest to protect westward-moving settlers. Albuquerque became a U.S. Army post in 1846 and was occupied by the Confederacy for two months during the Civil War.

In 1880 rail travel arrived in Albuquerque. The town's strength as a transportation and trade center grew as manufactured goods were shipped in from the East and raw materials and livestock were transported from the West. A bustling new town quickly sprang up around the railroad, then grew to take in historic Old Town. In 1883 Albuquerque became the seat of Bernalillo County, and in 1891 it was incorporated as a city. Already an established oasis of civilization, Albuquerque, unlike other southwestern towns, never suffered from the boisterousness of the Old West.

Development of Atomic Bomb Brings High Technology

Until World War II, Albuquerque remained a small, quiet city. Then the development of the atomic bomb at nearby Los Alamos brought the town into the nuclear age. Now an important part of the Rio Grande Research Corridor, Albuquerque has undergone record population growth. It is a center of large high-technology industries that have evolved around the research and development of atomic energy and space exploration, drawing as well hundreds of smaller research firms. The city's celebration of its 2006 tricentennial is underway, with events and exhibits honoring Albuquerque's art, history, and culture. Culturally and economically diverse, Albuquerque remains historically aware and looks forward to a prosperous future.

Population Profile

Metropolitan Area Residents

1980: 485,430
1990: 589,131
2000: 712,738
Percent change, 1990–2000: 21.0%
U.S. rank in 1980: 80th
U.S. rank in 1990: 77th
U.S. rank in 2000: 62nd

City Residents

1980: 332,920
1990: 384,915
2000: 448,607
2003 estimate: 471,856
Percent change, 1990–2000: 15.9%
U.S. rank in 1980: 44th
U.S. rank in 1990: 38th (State rank: 1st)
U.S. rank in 2000: 42nd (State rank: 1st)

Density: 2,483.4 people per square mile (2000)

Racial and ethnic characteristics (2000)
White: 321,179
Black or African American: 13,854
American Indian and Alaska Native: 17,444
Asian: 10,068
Native Hawaiian and Pacific Islander: 452
Hispanic or Latino (may be of any race): 179,075
Other: 85,610

Percent of residents born in state: 46.7% (2000)

Age characteristics (2000)
Population under 5 years old: 30,883
Population 5 to 9 years old: 30,577
Population 10 to 14 years old: 30,248
Population 15 to 19 years old: 31,988
Population 20 to 24 years old: 34,115
Population 25 to 34 years old: 67,150
Population 35 to 44 years old: 71,632
Population 45 to 54 years old: 61,732
Population 55 to 59 years old: 20,694
Population 60 to 64 years old: 15,918
Population 65 to 74 years old: 27,512
Population 75 to 84 years old: 19,542
Population 85 years and older: 6,616
Median age: 34.9 years

Births (2002)
Total number: 8,741

Deaths (2002)
Total number: 4,405

Money income (1999)
Per capita income: $20,884
Median household income: $38,272
Total households: 183,625

Number of households with income of . . .
less than $10,000: 18,109
$10,000 to $14,999: 12,706
$15,000 to $24,999: 26,597
$25,000 to $34,999: 26,293
$35,000 to $49,999: 31,682
$50,000 to $74,999: 33,373
$75,000 to $99,999: 17,097
$100,000 to $149,999: 12,205
$150,000 to $199,999: 2,947
$200,000 or more: 2,616

Percent of families below poverty level: 10.0% (53.1% of which were female householder families with related children under 5 years)

2002 FBI Crime Index Total: 35,762

Municipal Government

Albuquerque operates under a mayor-council form of government, with a full-time mayor, nine council members—all of whom serve four-year terms—and a chief administrative officer, who is appointed by the mayor. The city is the seat of Bernalillo County.

Head Official: Mayor Martin Chavez (since 2001; current term expires 2005)

Total Number of City Employees: 6,940 (2003)

City Information: City of Albuquerque, PO Box 1293, Albuquerque, NM 87103; telephone (505)768-3000

Economy

Major Industries and Commercial Activity

The largest city in New Mexico, Albuquerque is also its economic center; it accounts for nearly half of the state's economic activity. Part of its success can be attributed to a diverse economic base consisting of government, services, trade, agriculture, tourism, manufacturing, and research and development. In 2004 *Forbes* magazine ranked Albuquerque the 12th best city in the nation for doing business.

The Rio Grande River valley contains rich farm and pasture lands that support a sizable food industry, based mainly on fruit and produce, in the Albuquerque area. Since its early years as a stop on the Santa Fe Trail, the city has been a transportation and service center. Albuquerque is also home to more than 700 manufacturing firms—many of them located in well-planned industrial parks—that produce such goods as trailers, food products, electronic components, neon and electric signs, hardware, and machine tools. Among the major manufacturing firms that call Albuquerque home are Intel, GE, and General Mills.

The Rio Grande Research Corridor, a constellation of high-technology industries, sprang up in the wake of the development of nuclear research during and after World War II. Each year, more than $4 billion is spent on research and development in the region. The area's major employers are part of this complex. Sandia National Laboratories, a government research and development lab, is involved in laser technology and solar energy. Kirtland U.S. Air Force Base, the area's largest employer and the sixth-largest military base in the world, is a weapons research center. In 2004, the value of the base's economic impact to Albuquerque was $3.3 billion.

For nearly a century people have valued Albuquerque for its dry air, which is especially beneficial to those with respiratory problems. Today the city's medical services and facilities are a vital part of the local economy. The year-round sunny weather attracts pleasure seekers as well; more than four million tourists visit Albuquerque each year, to ski the Sandia Mountains and to absorb the city's rich ethnic heritage.

Items and goods produced: machine tools, fabricated structural steel, furniture, hardware, textiles, paints, varnishes, fertilizers, scientific instruments, electronic equipment, neon and electric signs, native American jewelry and curios

Incentive Programs—New and Existing Companies

Among the factors that draw businesses to Albuquerque are the city's extraordinarily low cost of living (based on cost of labor, energy, taxes, and office space), which in 2004 was ranked the lowest of all U.S. cities; and its highly-educated workforce.

Local programs—The Albuquerque Economic Development group (AED), is a private, nonprofit organization that recruits companies to the Albuquerque area. AED provides site-selection assistance, labor market analysis, business incentive

analysis, workforce recruitment and job-training assistance, and coordination of state and local assistance, among other services. Many high technology activities are carried out in Albuquerque; Technology Ventures Corporation, a non-profit organization, serves as a bridge between the public and private sectors for the commercialization of technologies developed at the national labs and research universities there, and assists in the expansion of existing businesses.

State programs—New Mexico offers a variety of incentives to all new and expanding businesses. Its Build to Suit program facilitates building construction, and ePort New Mexico is a one-stop information source offering permitting and licensing. The state's financial incentives include: no inventory taxes; tax credits for high-wage jobs, technology jobs, and childcare; a tax deduction for research and development services; a job training incentive program (the cornerstone of the state's incentives, allowing New Mexico to pay half the salary for new hires for up to half a year); exemptions for qualified businesses from property taxes on land, buildings, and equipment, and from personal property tax on equipment; and laboratory partnerships with small businesses. Further incentives are available for manufacturers, customer support centers, aerospace and aircraft industries, producers of agriculture or energy, and filmmakers. In addition, the state enacted a major personal income tax reduction in 2003, and New Mexico's property taxes are second lowest in the nation.

Economic Development Information: Albuquerque Economic Development, University Center Research Park, 851 University Boulevard SE, Suite 203, Albuquerque, NM 87106; telephone (505)246-6200

Development Projects

Among the many businesses that have located or expanded in Albuquerque in the early 2000s are: Gap, Inc., which opened a corporate shared services center in 2001; Victoria's Secret Catalog, which expanded its support center in 2001, adding 380 jobs; Blue Cross/Blue Shield, which expanded in 2002, adding 500 jobs; ClientLogic, a customer service and technical support center for high-technology companies, which expanded in 2002-2003, adding 500 jobs; Tempur-Pedic Mattress, which broke ground on a $56 million manufacturing plant in 2004; and Eclipse Aviation, a personal jet manufacturer undergoing an expansion slated for completion in 2007, expected to add 300 jobs. The $73 million Alvarado Transportation Center Project is partially completed and operational as of 2005; by 2006 it will be an intermodal transportation center linking commercial and city/state bus and rail services.

Commercial Shipping

Since the days of the Santa Fe Trail, Albuquerque has been an important center for the transportation of goods. The city's economy benefits from the Santa Fe Railway and the 46 motor freight carriers, 29 of which have local terminals, that link Albuquerque with major markets throughout the country.

New Mexico is a Freeport State, meaning that business inventories for resale, raw materials, and interstate commerce products stored there temporarily are not subject to state or local property taxes. Albuquerque offers an international airport, Albuquerque International Sunport, with a port of entry from Mexico; the airport moves approximately 146 million tons of freight cargo annually. Foreign trade zones operate in Albuquerque and nearby Rio Rancho.

Labor Force and Employment Outlook

Employment growth in Albuquerque in 2004 was 2.4 percent. Growth of around 1.5 percent is anticipated for 2005 and 2006. The city's labor force is relatively young, skilled, and educated: Albuquerque is notable for its high percentage of advanced degree holders. Albuquerque's work force is routinely cited for its productivity, and *Area Development Magazine* recently ranked the city number one in the nation, for manufacturing productivity in terms of dollars of output per worker.

The following is a summary of data regarding the Albuquerque metropolitan area labor force, 2004 annual averages.

Size of non-agricultural labor force: 370,800

Number of workers employed in . . .
construction and mining: 25,800
manufacturing: 22,600
trade, transportation and utilities: 66,200
information: 9,400
financial activities: 19,200
professional and business services: 59,200
educational and health services: 45,200
leisure and hospitality: 36,300
other services: 11,900
government: 74,900

Average hourly earnings of production workers employed in manufacturing: $14.64

Unemployment rate: 4.9% (January 2005)

Largest employers	*Number of employees*
Kirtland AFB (Civilian)	17,125
University of New Mexico	15,835
Albuquerque Public Schools	11,700
Sandia National Laboratories	7,700
City of Albuquerque	6,940
Presbyterian	5,800
State of New Mexico	5,660
Lovelace Sandia Health System	5,400
Kirtland AFB (Military)	5,240
Intel Corporation	5,200

Cost of Living

The following is a summary of data regarding key cost of living factors for the Albuquerque area.

2004 (3rd Quarter) ACCRA Average House Price: $256,100

2004 (3rd Quarter) ACCRA Cost of Living Index: 100.8 (U.S. average = 100.0)

State income tax rate: Ranges from 1.7% to 6.8%

State sales tax rate: 5.0%

Local income tax rate: None

Local sales tax rate: 0.5625% (city); 1.1875% (county)

Property tax rate: Residential, 27.027 to 43.860 mills; non-residential 32.857 to 51.724 mills (2004)

Economic Information: Greater Albuquerque Chamber of Commerce, PO Box 25100, Albuquerque, NM 87125; telephone (505)764-3700; fax (505)764-3714. New Mexico Department of Labor, Economic Research and Analysis, 401 Broadway NE, Albuquerque NM 87102

Education and Research

Elementary and Secondary Schools

The Albuquerque Public Schools (APS) system, 34th largest in the nation as of the 2001–2002 school year, is administered by a nonpartisan, seven-member school board and a superintendency team.

The following is a summary of data regarding Albuquerque's public schools.

Total enrollment: 86,557

Number of facilities
elementary schools: 80
middle schools: 26
senior high schools: 11
other: 10

Student/teacher ratio: ranges from 17:1 in kindergarten to 27:1 in high school

Teacher salaries
average: $36,038 (2002-2003)

Funding per pupil: $5,695 (2000–2001)

About 13 percent of the city's children attend the more than 70 private or parochial schools in the Albuquerque area.

Among these schools, Albuquerque Academy is regarded as one of the top private schools in the nation.

Public Schools Information: Albuquerque Public Schools, 725 University Boulevard SE, Albuquerque, NM 87106; telephone (505)842-8211

Colleges and Universities

The University of New Mexico (UNM), the state's largest institution of higher learning and part of the Rio Grande Research Corridor complex, is based in Albuquerque, with branch campuses in Gallup, Los Alamos, Taos, Los Lunas, and west Albuquerque. The main campus has an annual enrollment of more than 24,000 students. UNM is particularly strong in Latin American studies, flamenco dance, anthropology, and medicine—its rural medicine, primary care, and family medicine programs rank among the top 10 in the U.S. Other four-year institutions in Albuquerque include the New Mexico campus of the University of Phoenix, offering bachelor's and advanced degrees in business and nursing; the Metropolitan College of Court Reporting; a campus of ITT Technical Institute, which offers degrees in information technology, electronics technology, drafting and design, business, and criminal justice; and National American University, which offers degrees in accounting, business administration and management, and computer and information sciences. The city is also home to Albuquerque Technical-Vocational Institute (TVI), the largest community college in New Mexico. TVI offers associate's degrees in occupational fields as well as liberal arts.

Libraries and Research Centers

The Rio Grande Valley Library System, the largest public library system in New Mexico, is a Consortium of the City of Albuquerque, Bernalillo County and the City of Rio Rancho. Public library service is available through a large Main Library and 16 branches throughout the Albuquerque area (including a Special Collections Library specializing in genealogy and regional history, and the Erne Pyle Branch, former home of the famed World War II correspondent, displaying a collection of his memorabilia), and the nearby Rio Rancho Public Library. The library system has a collection of more than 1.4 million items, including periodicals and audio-visual materials.

The University of New Mexico General Libraries maintains more than 2 million volumes and nearly 11,000 periodical subscriptions. Its collection includes that of the Center for Southwest Research, UNM's resource center for the study of New Mexico and the Southwest. Branch libraries on campus provide subject collections in business, fine arts, and science and engineering. Collection strengths include Latin American history, regional photography, music and architecture, American Indian affairs, and maps. The Health Sciences Library serves the Medical School and the health professions statewide. The Law School Library is the primary legal library in the state and has special collections in American Indian and Latin American Law.

Research activities in such fields as water resources, Southwestern biology, power systems, alternative energy, artificial intelligence, robotics, anthropology, satellite data analysis, business and economics, Native American law, aging and health policy issues, Latin America, and Hispanic and Chicano studies are conducted at centers in the Albuquerque area. The University of New Mexico is the state's primary research university. Among its research units are the Center for Advanced Studies (quantum optics, laser physics, etc.), the Center of Biomedical Research Excellence, the New Mexico Engineering Research Institute, the Center for High Technology Materials, the High Performance Computing Education & Research Center, the Center for Micro-Engineered Materials, and the Latin American Institute. Other research centers based in Albuquerque include the Behavioral Health Research Center of the Southwest, which conducts research on substance abuse and other behavioral health issues, and the Air Force Research Lab at Kirtland Air Force Base, where space- and missile-related research is performed. Sandia National Laboratories, based in nearby Sandia, performs national security research.

Public Library Information: Main Library, 501 Copper Avenue NW, Albuquerque, NM 87102; telephone (505)768-5141

Health Care

In the 1920s Albuquerque, like many other cities in the Southwest, became a mecca for people suffering from respiratory diseases and allergies who seek relief in the warm, dry climate. Today, advanced medical care is available at the University of New Mexico Health Sciences Center, which encompasses the following patient facilities: UNM Hospital, New Mexico's only Level 1 Trauma Center; Carrie Tingley Hospital for pediatric rehabilitation and orthopaedics; UNM Children's Hospital, currently undergoing a $239 million, 476,555-square-foot expansion scheduled for completion in 2007; UNM Cancer Research & Treatment Center, New Mexico's only academic center for cancer treatment; UNM Psychiatric Center; and UNM Children's Psychiatric Hospital.

Albuquerque's other major hospitals are the 453-bed Presbyterian Hospital, New Mexico's largest acute care hospital; Albuquerque Regional Medical Center, which specializes in orthopedics, ophthalmology, neurology and neurosurgery, oncology, and cardiology; and Lovelace Medical Center, where the first astronauts were tested and which has been ranked as one of America's best hospitals.

Recreation

Sightseeing

Albuquerque's unique mixture of Native American, Hispanic, and Anglo heritages provides visitors with a variety of activities. Albuquerque's spiritual heart is Old Town, dating to the city's founding in 1706, where an arts community flourishes. Old Town is an atmospheric area of quaint adobe-style buildings with flat roofs and rounded edges, with windows frequently decorated with strings of dried chili peppers for good luck, and winding cobblestone or brick walkways leading to tucked-away patios and gardens. Old Town's Plaza features an outdoor Native American market offering traditional arts and crafts such as textiles, jewelry, and pottery. Also located in Old Town is San Felipe de Neri church, the city's oldest building, enclosing the adobe walls of the original presidio (fort).

The landscape surrounding the city is particularly scenic and provides some of the area's principal attractions. To the west is a high mesa and five extinct volcanos; to the east are the magnificent Sandia and Manzano mountains. Sandia Crest in the Cibola National Forest, 30 miles from Albuquerque, offers a breathtaking view that encompasses 11,000 square miles. A skylift operates there throughout the year, carrying skiers and hikers up the mountain. The Aerial Tramway, 2.7 miles in length and the longest tramway in the world, runs to the top of 10,378-foot Sandia Peak.

Evidence of Albuquerque's Native American roots can be found in the numerous pueblos around the city, many of them at least a thousand years old and some still inhabited. Active pueblos within an hour's drive of Albuquerque include Acoma, Cochiti, Isleta, Jemez, Laguna, Sandia, San Felipe, Santa Ana, Santo Domingo, and Zia. Acoma is perhaps the most spectacular; a walled adobe village atop a sheer rock mesa, the community dates to the eleventh century or earlier and is thought to be the longest continuously-occupied community in the country. Reminders of the ancient native civilization also exist in dozens of ruins and archaeological sites, among them Petroglyph State Monument, where some 25,000 prehistoric images, some as much as 3,000 years old, can be found in the rocks.

The Rio Grande Nature Center State Park, located a few miles north of Old Town, offers 2 miles of nature trails through the Southwest *bosque,* the grove of cottonwood growing along the Rio Grande. The Albuquerque Biological Park consists of three separate facilities: Rio Grande Zoological Park, Albuquerque Aquarium, and Rio Grande Botanic Garden. The zoo sits on 64 acres and is an oasis for both exotic and native species, such as seals and sea lions, gorillas, orangutans, elephants, polar bears, giraffes, camels, tamarins, koalas, Mexican wolves, mountain lions, monkeys, jaguars, zebras, and rhinoceros; one of the missions of the zoo is the breeding of endangered species. The zoo's Africa wing, opened in 2004, has 17 separate exhibits and 23 species of mammals and birds, including chimpanzees, warthogs, red river hogs, cheetahs, hippopotamus, DeBrazza's monkeys, spotted hyenas, African wild dogs, Marabou storks, Cape griffon vultures, lappet-faced vultures, wattled cranes, white-faced whistling ducks, Lady Ross's turacos, and golden-breasted starlings. At the Albuquerque Aquarium visitors can follow the story of a drop of water as it enters the upper Rio Grande high in the San Juan Mountains of Colorado and flows past canyons, deserts, and valleys in New Mexico, Texas, and Mexico, before reaching the Gulf of Mexico. The aquarium features exhibits of Gulf of Mexico saltwater species; a highlight is the 285,000 gallon tank housing brown, sandtiger, blacktip, and nurse sharks; brightly-colored reef fish; eels; and sea turtles. The Botanic Garden is 20 acres of developed land that includes a 10,000-square-foot conservatory divided into a Desert Pavilion and a Mediterranean Pavilion. New at the botanic garden in 2004 is Rio Grande Heritage Farm, a 1920s-style farm with an adobe farmhouse, barn, farm animals, orchard, grape vineyard, flowers, and vegetable crops.

Glancing skyward in Albuquerque, spectators frequently see the colorful spectacle of hang-gliders and hot-air balloons drifting slowly past. A combination of sunshine and topography produces steady geothermal winds, making the area ideal for wind sports and earning for the city the nickname of "Hot Air Balloon Capital of the World."

Albuquerque's Central Avenue, which runs east-west through the city, is considered one of the best-preserved sections of historic Route 66 in the state. Along the avenue are more than 100 classic structures, including diners, motor courts, and theaters, in architectural styles ranging from Streamline Moderne to Pueblo Deco.

Arts and Culture

Albuquerque actively promotes its rich cultural community. In 1979 City Council created an ordinance that assigns 1 percent of monies generated by revenue bonds and general obligation bonds to public construction and public art. Consequently, Albuquerque abounds with sculptures and murals attesting to the city's artistic energies. Along Central Avenue, from historic Old Town on the east through downtown and the university area to Nob Hill on the west, is Albuquerque's "cultural corridor." In the numerous theaters, museums, galleries, and cafes, and at other sites along this

The Pueblo Cultural Center specializes in preserving the history and culture of the Pueblo peoples.

route, the stimulating and diverse cultural life of Albuquerque is on view.

Albuquerque has more than 30 performing arts centers and groups. The KiMo Theater, an ornate 1927 Pueblo Deco-style landmark downtown, is on the National Register of Historic Places; it serves as a performing arts theater, hosting a number of groups, with seating for 700. The Albuquerque Little Theatre presents comedies, mysteries, and light classics in its own playhouse near Old Town. La Compañía de Teatro de Albuquerque—one of the few major Hispanic companies in the United States and Puerto Rico—stages a series of bilingual productions including comedies, dramas, and musicals. Vortex Theatre offers off-Broadway original and classic plays.

Albuquerque is home to the New Mexico Ballet Company, founded in 1972, which performs classic dances in the KiMo Theatre and in Popejoy Hall on the University of New Mexico campus. Dance performances by visiting artists and groups can also be seen at KiMo Theatre. Popejoy Hall, the primary facility in the city for the performance of orchestral music and opera, is home to the Ovation Series—which offers a variety of events including drama and comedy, and ballet and modern dance—and the New Mexico Symphony. Based in the city and one of the southwest's most prestigious orchestras, the symphony presents classical, baroque, and pops, as well as Symphony Under the Stars and other special concerts. Musical Theatre Southwest, formerly the Civic Light Opera, performs classical and new musicals and is one of the largest producers of community theater in the country. Chamber Music Albuquerque, established in 1942, brings chamber ensembles from around the world to Albuquerque.

Many of Albuquerque's museums concentrate on area history and culture. The New Mexico Museum of Natural History and Science features exhibits exploring the geological and anthropological history of New Mexico, through Paleozoic-era fossils, full-scale dinosaur models, a walkthrough volcano, and a replica of an ice-age cave. The Indian Pueblo Cultural Center specializes in the authentic history and culture of the Pueblo peoples; the center includes exhibits tracing the history, artifacts, and contemporary art of New Mexico's 19 pueblos, the Pueblo House Children's Museum, a restaurant serving Native American foods, and an outdoor arena where Native American dancers perform on weekends. The National Hispanic Cultural Center, opened in 2000, explores Hispanic history and literature as well as visual, performing, media, and culinary arts. Located on the University of New Mexico campus, the Maxwell Museum of Anthropology displays ethnic, anthropological, and archaeological artifacts. Some date back 10,000 years, with especially strong collections from Southwestern cultures. The National Atomic Museum exhibits the history of atomic energy, including the Manhattan Project that pro-

duced the first atomic bomb, as well as non-military applications of nuclear energy.

The Albuquerque Museum of Art and History displays southwest art and explores 400 years of Albuquerque history. The museum features works by New Mexican artists from the early 20th century to the present, and numerous artifacts from the area's Spanish-American period, such as swords, helmets, and horse armor. A 40,000 square-foot expansion, completed in 2005, allows the museum to display more of its permanent collection. With an emphasis on the early modernist period, the University of New Mexico Art Museum houses a collection of nineteenth- and twentieth-century American and European art, including one of the largest university-owned photography collections in the nation. The Jonson Gallery, located on the University of New Mexico campus, is the home of the late New Mexico modernist painter Raymond Jonson and exhibits more than 2,000 of his works. The National Hispanic Cultural Center's 11,000 square-foot gallery space displays contemporary and traditional Hispanic art. The KiMo Gallery at KiMo Theatre presents the work of local artists. The South Broadway Cultural Center Gallery mounts exhibitions by local and regional artists; workshops are available for emerging artists of all ages.

Festivals and Holidays

In 2006 Albuquerque will be 300 years old. The city is celebrating its tricentennial for 18 months, from April 2005 to October 2006, with events and exhibits honoring Albuquerque's art, history, and culture. Many of Albuquerque's yearly events celebrate the city's ethnic heritage. At the National Fiery Foods/Barbeque Show, held in early March, attendees can sample spicy sauces, salsas, candies, and more. The Rio Grande Arts and Crafts Festival, held in mid-March, features some 200 artists and crafters from across the country. Native American dancing and feast-day observances take place at numerous pueblos located within an hour's drive of the city. In April, the Gathering of Nations Pow Wow, held on the University of New Mexico campus, features more than 3,000 Native American dancers and singers representing some 500 tribes; more than 800 artists, crafters, and traders at its Indian Traders Market; and a Miss Indian World pageant. The New Mexico Arts and Crafts Fair, in June, showcases the works of some 200 New Mexican artisans. Each Saturday during the summer, Summerfest at Civic Plaza celebrates the food and culture of the city's various ethnic groups, and presents live music and entertainment. In September, the New Mexico Wine Festival in nearby Bernillo offers wine tastings, an art show, and entertainment. Also in September, the 17-day New Mexico State Fair, regarded as one of the top fairs in the United States, presents a professional rodeo, concerts, livestock shows, and other events. Feria Artistica, held in October, is a juried Spanish Market observing Albuquerque's

Spanish roots, reaching back more than 400 years. The annual Albuquerque International Balloon Fiesta is one of the most-photographed events in the world. A 9-day festival in October, it features the mass ascension of some 800 balloons; at night, balloons filled with luminous gas light the sky. The Weems Artfest, in November, is billed as New Mexico's number one arts and crafts festival; a three-day event, the Artfest shows the works of approximately 260 artisans from around the world. Albuquerque is known as the "City of Little Lights," during the annual Luminaria festival in December. Tours are available.

Sports for the Spectator

The Albuquerque Isotopes, part of the Pacific Coast League, bring minor league baseball to Albuquerque at the new Isotopes Park (a $25 million renovation of Albuquerque Sports Stadium), which has seating for 12,215. The New Mexico Slam is a basketball team in the World Basketball League; they play at the Albuquerque Convention Center. The city is famous for the University of New Mexico Lobos, especially the football and basketball teams; the football team plays a September-to-November season at the university's 30,000 seat Stadium, and the basketball team plays from November to March at "The Pit," the university's 17,121-seat Arena. The New Mexico Scorpions, part of the Western Professional Hockey League, play at Tingley Coliseum. Rodeos and horse racing are other popular spectator sports in Albuquerque.

Sports for the Participant

With 800 neighborhood parks, 12 public swimming pools, 4 public and 7 private golf courses, 220 outdoor tennis courts, 23 ball fields, 43 miles of bikeways, and 20 community centers, Albuquerque has much to offer the outdoor enthusiast. Los Altos Park, the city's largest park, offers baseball and softball diamonds, an enclosed heated pool, tennis courts, a lighted golf course, and a children's recreational area. The Los Altos Skate Park, designed for BMX bikers, skateboarders, and in-line skaters, is the largest park of its kind in the southwest. Biking trails can be found at Sandia Peak and the Rio Grande Nature Center. Fishing is available in irrigation and drainage ditches, stocked with trout by the state, and in nearby mountain streams. Among other favorite outdoor adventures are hiking the trails in Cibola National Forest, camping, horseback riding, and downhill and cross-country skiing at Sandia Peak Ski area. Albuquerque's calm, steady winds also provide perfect conditions for hang gliding and hot-air ballooning.

Shopping and Dining

Albuquerque is a shopper's paradise. Numerous shops and galleries in Old Town specialize in art items and crafts produced by local artisans, such as textiles and the turquoise and silver jewelry for which the region is famous. Authentic pre-

historic, historic, and contemporary Native American pottery, paintings, photography, and furniture are also for sale in Albuquerque. Sandia Pueblo, just north of Albuquerque, runs its own crafts market, Bien Mur Indian Market Center.

Other shopping needs can be met at Coronado Center, Winrock Center, and Cottonwood Mall, three of New Mexico's largest shopping centers; the historic Nob Hill district, offering some 130 shops, galleries, and restaurants; the underground First Plaza Galleria in the historic downtown district; and the Flea Market held every weekend at the New Mexico State Fairgrounds.

For dining pleasure Albuquerque offers a diverse range of restaurants, from family to fancy. Many feature regional specialties, including authentic Native American food, Hispanic and Mexican cuisine, and western barbecue. The core ingredients of what is known as Northern New Mexican Cuisine—a blending of Hispanic and Pueblo cuisines—are beans, corn, and chili. Several restaurants in Old Town are housed in picturesque adobe buildings.

Visitor Information: Albuquerque Convention and Visitors Bureau, 20 First Plaza Center NW, Albuquerque, NM 87102; telephone (505)842-9918; toll-free (800)284-2282

Convention Facilities

As the economic and industrial heart of New Mexico, and as a city known for its commitment to the past and to the future, Albuquerque is an ideal meeting place for conferences and conventions. Albuquerque's unique ethnic heritage and spectacular setting, plus its generous meeting facilities and hotels providing 14,000 guest rooms, promote the mixing of business with pleasure.

The city's primary meeting place is the Albuquerque Convention Center, located in the heart of downtown. The 600,000 square-foot complex offers 167,562 square feet of exhibition space, a 31,000 square-foot ballroom, and a 2,350-seat auditorium. It can accommodate more than 9,000 attendees and has banquet space for up to 6,000 people. The convention center is within walking distance of more than 900 guest rooms, as well as restaurants and clubs offering a variety of entertainment. Facilities for large groups are also available at Expo New Mexico at the State Fairgrounds; which offers flexible indoor and outdoor space, with an indoor capacity of 12,000 and outdoor capacity of 20,000 people.

Convention Information: Albuquerque Convention and Visitors Bureau, 20 First Plaza Center NW, Albuquerque, NM 87102; telephone (505)842-9918; toll-free (800)284-2282

Transportation

Approaching the City

Albuquerque is a designated Port of Entry into the United States. When arriving in Albuquerque by plane, visitors are greeted by the Albuquerque International Sunport terminal, which introduces them to local art and pueblo architecture. Located within the city limits, the airport is served by 8 major commercial airlines and 5 commuter airlines. The airport offers nonstop service to 27 cities across the country, plus nonstop service to 7 in-state cities.

Albuquerque is at the crossroads of two major highway routes: Interstate 25, running from Canada to Mexico, and Interstate 40—formerly Route 66—intersecting the city from east to west.

Passenger bus transportation into Albuquerque is available through commercial bus companies. Train service is provided by Amtrak; Albuquerque is a stop along its Southwest Chief route, a daily line between Los Angeles and Chicago.

Traveling in the City

The landscape surrounding Albuquerque—the Sandia Mountains to the east and mesas to the west—provides convenient landmarks for finding direction in the city. Dividing Albuquerque into quadrants are Interstate 40, which runs east to west, and Interstate 25, known as the Pan American Freeway, which runs north to south. The streets form a grid accommodating this intersection. Central Avenue (old Route 66), called the "spine" of the city, is parallel to Interstate 40.

Albuquerque's mass transit service is provided by ABQ Ride. During the major festivals held in the city, such as the International Balloon Fiesta, the State Fair, and Luminaria, ABQ Ride supplies special service to and from the event venues. A trolley serves shoppers and tourists, running between Old Town, the zoo, and downtown. A light rail system is expected to be completed and running in 2006.

The city also maintains a number of well-lit and well-paved paths for bicycle travel, including 70 miles of on-street bike lanes.

Communications

Newspapers and Magazines

Albuquerque is served by two daily newspapers, the morning *Albuquerque Journal* and the evening *Albuquerque Tri-*bune, and by the weekly newspapers *New Mexico Business Weekly,* which covers business media, and *El Hispano News,* a Spanish-language newspaper. Magazines published there include *abqARTS, New Mexico Business Journal,* and *New Mexico Woman.*

Television and Radio

Ten television stations, including affiliates for the major commercial networks and public television, serve metropolitan Albuquerque. Cable television is available by subscription. Approximately 40 AM and FM radio stations broadcast to Albuquerque-area listeners, offering a wide variety of programming, including Spanish- and Navajo-language features. Albuquerque Public Schools operates an instructional radio station that features educational programming as well as jazz and Latin music.

Media Information: Albuquerque Journal, 7777 Jefferson Street NE, Albuquerque, NM, 87109; Newsroom telephone (505)823-3800. *Albuquerque Tribune,* PO Drawer T, Albuquerque, NM, 87103; telephone (505)823-7777

Albuquerque Online

Albuquerque Convention & Visitors Bureau. Available www.abqcvb.org

Albuquerque Journal. Available www.abqjournal.com

Albuquerque Public Schools. Available www.aps.edu/aps

Albuquerque Tribune. Available www.abqtrib.com

Bernalillo County home page. Available www.bernco.gov

City of Albuquerque home page. Available www.cabq.gov

Greater Albuquerque Chamber of Commerce. Available www.gacc.org

New Mexico Department of Labor. Available www.dol.state.nm.us

Rio Grande Valley Library System. Available www.cabq.gov/rgvls

Selected Bibliography

Anaya, Rudolfo A., *Alburquerque* (Albuquerque: U. of New Mexico Press, 1992)

Chilton, Lance, et al., *A New Guide to the Colorful State* (University of New Mexico Press, 1984)

Simmons, Mark, *Albuquerque: A Narrative History* (University of New Mexico Press, 1982)

Las Cruces

The City in Brief

Founded: 1848; incorporated 1907

Head Official: William Michael Mattiace (since 2003)

City Population
  1980: 45,086
  1990: 62,648
  2000: 74,267
  2003 estimate: 76,990
  Percent change, 1990–2000: 19.5%
  U.S. rank in 1980: 475th
  U.S. rank in 1990: 396th (State rank: 2nd)
  U.S. rank in 2000: 408th (State rank: 2nd)

Metropolitan Area Population
  1980: 96,340
  1990: 135,510

  2000: 174,682
  Percent change, 1990–2000: 29.0%
  U.S. rank in 1990: 208th
  U.S. rank in 2000: 181st

Area: 52.22 square miles (2000)
Elevation: 3,909 feet above sea level
Average Annual Temperature: 64.0° F
Average Annual Precipitation: 8.5 inches rain, 3.2 inches snow

Major Economic Sectors: government/military, services, trade, education, agriculture
Unemployment Rate: 6.3% (January 2005)
Per Capita Income: $15,704 (1999)

2002 FBI Crime Index Total: Not reported

Major Colleges and Universities: New Mexico State University, La Dona Branch Community College

Daily Newspaper: *Las Cruces Sun-News*

Introduction

Las Cruces, Spanish for "city of crosses," is located in the Mesilla Valley, a wonderfully varied area of forests, river valley, and vast desert. The seat of Dona Ana County, the city is near White Sands Missile Range, where the first atomic bomb was tested. The city's spectacular setting boasts the Organ Mountains to the east and the surrounding Chihuahua Desert, with the Rio Grande running through the middle. Since the end of the nineteenth century, the city has been the political, social, and business hub for southern New Mexico. The Forbes/Milken Institute named Las Cruces among the top three small metro areas for business and careers in 2002, 2003, and 2004, and *Money* magazine placed it in the top eight places to retire, based on factors such as weather, crime, and economy.

Geography and Climate

Las Cruces is located 45 miles from the Mexican border and 40 miles northwest of El Paso, Texas. Bordered by the Organ Mountains in the east and the legendary Rio Grande on the west, Las Cruces is located in the heart of the fertile Mesilla Valley.

Las Cruces enjoys 350 days of sunshine annually, with less than 9 inches of average annual rainfall, which happens mostly at night, and only 3.2 inches of snowfall. Because it is situated over a natural underground aquifer, it does not suffer the water problems of a number of southwestern cities. Also, unlike many desert cities, Las Cruces experiences four mildly distinct seasons, with the harder part of the winter occurring during December and January, when the average daytime temperature is 57 degrees. Light snow does fall in the winter but seldom lasts longer than one day. June is generally the hottest month, with an average temperature of 94 degrees. The monsoon season, when heavy thunderstorms can occur daily, takes place in July and August.

Area: 52.22 square miles (2000)

Elevation: 3,909 feet above sea level

Average Temperatures: January, 41.5° F; June, 77.4° F; annual average, 64.0° F

Average Annual Precipitation: 8.5 inches of rain, 3.2 inches of snow

History

Long Before Humans

Before the first human inhabitants, the area around Las Cruces was populated by a teeming variety of reptiles and amphibians, who left many fossils when the great inland sea that once covered southern New Mexico retreated 600 million years ago. The Smithsonian has stated that the area holds "the world's best-fossilized footprints from the Permian Period."

Early Paleolithic Indians traversed the area about 20,000 years ago, and Anasazi tribes built cliff dwellings over most of New Mexico 10,000 years ago. The Mogollon tribe thrived in the Las Cruces region until they mysteriously disappeared around 1450 A.D. They left many petroglyphs, or rock drawings, scattered around the vicinity for scientists to gain a glimpse into their way of life.

Blazing A Trail

The first European visitors came to the Las Cruces area in 1535 when Spanish explorers, led by Cabeza de Vaca, passed through. In 1589, the first colonists arrived, led by Don Juan Onate, motivated by legends of seven ancient cities of gold. The group's livestock were driven in front of them, blazing a trail called El Camino Real, which led from Chihuahua, Mexico, to Santa Fe. Another trail blazed by this same group was dubbed Jornado del Meurto, or Journey of Death. As they attempted to forge a path more direct than the one which followed the meandering Rio Grande, the brutal desert conditions claimed the lives of many men and the Apaches claimed more.

Control of the region changed hands often from the 1600s to about 1850. The Pueblo Indians rebelled against their Spanish conquerors in the late seventeenth century and enjoyed self-rule for a time. In 1821 the Mexican Revolution overthrew the Spanish and created the Republic of Mexico. Soon after that, U.S. westward expansion caused friction and an eventual war with Mexico. This was resolved with the 1848 Treaty of Guadalupe Hidalgo, followed by the 1854 Gadsden Purchase, which claimed much of northern Mexico's land as U.S. territory. The region was even briefly under Confederate rule when Texas troops marched on it in 1862. They were later defeated by Union soldiers near Santa Fe.

After the Civil War ended, the Army installed Fort Seldon to help guard travelers against attacks by the Apache. The Buffalo Soldiers of the 125th Infantry, African Americans, were among the first to men the fort. With the coming of the railroad and more and more new immigrants, the Apache threat abated and the fort officially closed in 1891.

The small town of Mesilla is intertwined with the history of Las Cruces. Mesilla was founded by residents who were not happy with the Treaty of Guadalupe Hidalgo and wished to remain Mexican citizens, hence moving across the Rio Grande. Ironically, the Gadsden Purchase a few years later placed them back under U.S. rule.

A Glimpse of Modern Las Cruces

In 1849 the first blocks of the city were laid out with rawhide ropes and stakes. Plots were quickly claimed by settlers and gold miners hoping to find their fortune in the Organ Mountains. The coming of the railroad increased growth of the town quickly. The Santa Fe Railroad had planned to lay track through Mesilla, which had been a depot of the Butterfield Stage Coach, but someone in Las Cruces offered them free land. From then on, Las Cruces grew rapidly while Mesilla remained a sleepy little border town.

Las Cruces continued to grow quickly yet rather quietly into the 1900s as New Mexico became the 47th state in 1912. The quiet was suddenly disturbed when the first atomic bomb was tested north of Las Cruces on July 16, 1945. The area used for the test site, fittingly, was the Jornado del Muerto area. The following year World War II ended and Las Cruces was officially incorporated as a city.

Today, Las Cruces remains one of the fastest growing metro areas in the nation, and the second largest city in New Mexico. In addition to thriving business in trade, government, and agriculture, the unique and stunning scenery of the region has made it an attractive place to film movies and music videos. Las Cruces celebrated its 150th birthday in 1998 with festivities that carried on into the millennium. It remains a true crossroads, not only of highways but of cultures and customs, which blend together amiably to become a very pleasant place to live.

Historical Information: Rio Grande Historical Collections, New Mexico State University Library, PO Box 30006 Las Cruces, NM 88003-3006; telephone (505)646-3839; fax (505)646-7477; email archives@lib.nmsu.edu

Population Profile

Metropolitan Area Residents
1980: 96,340
1990: 135,510
2000: 174,682
Percent change, 1990–2000: 28.9%
U.S. rank in 1990: 208th
U.S. rank in 2000: 181st

City Residents
1980: 45,086
1990: 62,648
2000: 74,267
2003 estimate: 76,990
Percent change, 1990–2000: 19.5%
U.S. rank in 1980: 475th
U.S. rank in 1990: 396th (State rank: 2nd)
U.S. rank in 2000: 408th (State rank: 2nd)

Density: 1,425.7 people per square mile

Racial and ethnic characteristics (2000)
   White: 51,248
   Black or African American: 1,738
   American Indian and Alaska Native: 1,289
   Asian: 863
   Native Hawaiian and Pacific Islander: 55
   Hispanic or Latino (may be of any race): 38,421
   Other: 16,031

Percent of residents born in state: 46.7% (2000)

Age characteristics (2000)
   Population under 5 years old: 5,195
   Population 5 to 9 years old: 5,251
   Population 10 to 14 years old: 5,054
   Population 15 to 19 years old: 6,244
   Population 20 to 24 years old: 8,771
   Population 25 to 34 years old: 9,981
   Population 35 to 44 years old: 9,976
   Population 45 to 54 years old: 8,265
   Population 55 to 59 years old: 2,972
   Population 60 to 64 years old: 2,837
   Population 65 to 74 years old: 5,280
   Population 75 to 84 years old: 3,306
   Population 85 years and over: 1,135
   Median age: 31.2 years (2000)

Births (2002)
   Total number: 3,081

Deaths (2002)
   Total number: 1,129

Money Income (1999)
   Per capita income: $15,704
   Median household income: $30,375
   Total households: 29,184

Number of households with income of . . .
   less than $10,000: 4,666
   $10,000 to $14,999: 3,247
   $15,000 to $24,999: 4,287
   $25,000 to $34,999: 4,030
   $35,000 to $49,999: 4,939
   $50,000 to $74,999: 4,483

$75,000 to $99,999: 2,085
$100,000 to $149,999: 957
$150,000 to $199,999: 189
$200,000 or more: 218

Percent of families below poverty level: 17.2% (41.4% of which were female householder families with related children under 5 years)

2002 FBI Crime Index Total: Not reported

Municipal Government

Las Cruces has a council-manager form of government with six council members elected by district serving staggered terms. Both the mayor and the council members serve four year terms.

Head Official: William Michael Mattiace (since March 2003; current term expires 2007)

Total Number of City Employees: 1,251 (2004)

City Information: City of Las Cruces, PO Box 20000, Las Cruces, NM 88004, telephone (505)541-2000

Economy

Major Industries and Commercial Activity

Like many other sunbelt communities, Las Cruces' economy is booming. The city is the fastest-growing metro area in New Mexico and among the top 10 in the United States. The median age is younger than the state or national average, providing a prime, mostly bilingual, labor source. Private and public sectors continue to fuel the economy, whereas the conditions in other parts of the country, such as climate, cost of living, and quality of life, are less attractive to people and companies looking to relocate.

The four mainstays of the local economy are agriculture, commerce, education, and defense/aerospace. Since World War II, federal, state, and local government have become the main source of jobs in the area, due to the proximity of New Mexico State University (NMSU) and White Sands Missile Range. NMSU is the city's largest employer, and it also provides training and education for research facilities at White Sands. White Sands Missile Range is the Army's largest installation, and the largest military installation in the Western Hemisphere covering more than 2.2 million acres, and is used by the Navy, Air Force, and NASA. Other

government agencies, universities, private industries, and even foreign militaries conduct research there as well.

Although Las Cruces was never primarily an industrial town, manufacturing and commerce has been growing in importance. The North American Free Trade Agreement, or NAFTA, passed in 1994, has influenced this trend, as has the opening in 1991 of the border crossing at Santa Teresa, just 40 miles south of Las Cruces. Many companies are finding it advantageous to relocate in the Mesilla Valley area in order to do business with maquilladoras, (factories) in Mexico. NAFTA and the Mexican government's maquilladora program enacted in the 1960s encourage this type of trade by lowering or completely eliminating tariffs. For example, a U.S. company may send automobile parts to be assembled in Mexico; when the assembled car is shipped back, duties are paid only on the value added in Mexico. Molded plastics and electronic components are the top materials purchased by the maquilladoras.

On the U.S. side of the border, there are nine industrial and research parks in Dona Ana County. Reports from 2000 indicate the sale price of land in these developed lots ranged from only $.50 to $2.50 per square foot. Some are municipally owned and some private, but most have rail and interstate access and utilities included.

Las Cruces is definitely a land of peppers. Chile, cayenne, jalepeno, and bell peppers in every color imaginable are all raised locally. The pungent aroma of roasting peppers and the sight of strings of red peppers drying on rooftops enliven the local scene. Stahmann Farms on Highway 28, which originally focused on cotton and tomatoes, is now the world's largest producer of pecans. Other agricultural products include cotton, onions and various other vegetables, and dairy products. Research into developing new plant strains, particularly of peppers, takes place at New Mexico State University.

An enormous influx of retirees, students, and tourists has boosted the economy and has led to a building boom, including many senior citizen residences. A total of 796 new building permits for single-family units were issued in 2003, at an average cost of $144,900.

Items and goods produced: peppers, pecans, cotton and other agricultural products, electronics parts and molded plastics, repair parts for machines, packaging materials, chemicals.

Incentive Programs—New and Existing Companies

Local Programs—The city may issue Industrial Revenue Bonds (IRBs) for new businesses and industries, and will work with private bond counsel of the company and the State Investment Council to have the bonds purchased by the State Investment Pool or through a private placement. These

IRBs can be used for construction, site costs, equipment, and training. The City Special Projects Office assists in expediting all permit applications. Dona Ana County also has the Investment Credit Act which encourages employers to locate in the area. The act requires companies to hire new workers and gives tax credits for machinery and other expenses. Las Cruces' 220 acre foreign trade zone exists in three sub-areas adjacent to the Las Cruces airport and West Mesa Industrial Park.

State programs—The city of Las Cruces participates in all New Mexico incentives for new businesses. These programs feature a 100 percent property tax abatement for up to 30 years; state income tax abatement or exemption; real property related business loans; 800/WATS phone line tax exemption; research and development tax reduction (both state and local); corporate child care tax credit; cultural preservation tax credit for businesses that restore a property listed in the New Mexico Register of Cultural Properties; and Community Development Block Grant (CDBG) loans for acquiring property, working capital, equipment, and construction. The Severance Tax Loan Program and the Community Development Revolving Loan Fund both provide money for establishing and expanding businesses in the area. New Mexico's 27J exemption helps small business ventures raise capital. State of New Mexico Investment Council Venture Capital Investment is a program that gives funds to experienced partnerships that have demonstrated successful investment performance. Still other state-wide programs include Enchantment Land Certified Development Company, which administers low interest, fixed rate, low down payment loans; and the New Mexico Community Development Loan program which is geared toward helping low income people. Funding for the latter, for example, can be used to build housing developments as well as business.

Job Training Programs—On-site and classroom job training is available at NMSU through the State of New Mexico Industrial Development Training Program. Some features of the program include training customized to individual companies' needs, and freedom of the employers to select training candidates. It is not limited to economically disadvantaged people.

Development Projects

Housing needs are on the minds of developers and planners in Las Cruces and any fast growing city. Las Cruces issued over 1,200 permits in 2004 for construction of all types of commercial and residential buildings. The Community Development Department has cooperated with 16 agencies to obtain over $1.1 billion for services for low income families, including helping 25 families though its Home Rehabilitation Program. This city department has also helped rewrite zoning codes according to citizen's requests, and has de-

signed the future Mesquite Historic District community garden.

A major accomplishment was to facilitate commercial airline service at Las Cruces International Airport as of November 2004. Before this, the nearest full service airport was 40 miles away in El Paso, Texas. In the mid-2000s, a $3 million construction project dubbed ''Community of Hope'' is ongoing, renovation of the downtown Rio Grande Theatre was completed, playground equipment was replaced in 25 parks, and there were many other renovations of various city facilities, such as flood drains, street signs, and traffic signals. The importance of water and wastewater management to the region was not overlooked. A two million gallon capacity Telshor water tank was restored and nearly $1 million was spent for various upkeep projects on Las Cruces' more than 390 miles of water lines and 50 wells.

Economic Development Information: Mesilla Valley Economic Development Alliance, 2345 East Nevada, Las Cruces, NM 88001; telephone (505)525-2852; fax (505)523-5707. Las Cruces-Dona Ana County Economic Development Council; telephone (505)524-1745

Commercial Shipping

Overnight shipping is available to most major western cities, including Dallas, Houston, San Antonio, Phoenix, San Diego, Los Angeles, and Denver. Two Railroads provide direct rail services: Burlington Northern-Santa Fe and Union Pacific-Southern Pacific, and the newer border crossing at Santa Teresa is to be a future rail port of entry. Air freight service is provided by all major companies. Six major commercial trucking firms offer freight service for the area.

Labor Force and Employment Outlook

The city's labor force has been described as capable, technically skilled, dependable, and cost effective. Job growth continues to increase by roughly two percent per year.

The following is a summary of data regarding the Las Cruces labor force, 2004 annual averages.

Size of nonagricultural labor force: 61,700

Number of workers employed in . . .
   construction and mining: 3,900
   manufacturing: 8,800
   trade, transportation, and utilities: 9,500
   information: 1,100
   financial activities: 2,400
   professional and business services: 4,900
   educational and health services: 9,000
   leisure and hospitality: 6,100
   other services: 1,500
   government: 20,300

Average hourly earnings of production workers employed in manufacturing: $12.86

Unemployment rate: 6.8% (February 2005)

Largest county employers	Number of employees
New Mexico State University	6,980
White Sands Missile Range	4,357
Las Cruces Public Schools	3,316
NASA	1,500
City of Las Cruces	1,251
Memorial Medical Center	1,198
Walmart	700
Allied Signal Aerospace	667
Excel Agent Services	300

Cost of Living

The following is a summary of data regarding several key cost of living factors for the Las Cruces metropolitan area.

2004 (3rd Quarter) ACCRA Average House Price: $275,188

2004 (3rd Quarter) ACCRA Cost of Living Index: 99.5 (U.S. average = 100.0)

State income tax rate: Ranges from 1.7% to 8.2%

State sales tax rate: 5.0% (prescription drugs and certain food and medical expenses exempt)

Local income tax rate: None

Local sales tax rate: 7.0%

Property tax rate: $27.53 per $1,000 of 33.3% of assessed value

Economic Information: Greater Las Cruces Chamber of Commerce, 760 W. Picacho, Las Cruces, NM 88005; telephone (505)524-1968. Mesilla Valley Economic Development Alliance, 2345 E. Nevada, Las Cruces, NM 88001; telephone (505)525-2852. New Mexico Department of Labor, Las Cruces Area Office, 200 E. Griggs Avenue, Las Cruces, NM 88001; telephone (505)526-9622.

Education and Research

Elementary and Secondary Schools

Las Cruces Public Schools is the state's second largest school district and the third-largest employer in Dona Ana County. Specialized programs include a Bilingual Education Program geared to English proficiency and academic and ultimately career success. There is also a preschool program for toddlers younger than kindergarten age, an in-school program for pregnant teens, and a drug abuse prevention program. A new "Drop Back In" Mentorship program matches at-risk student with adult mentors. There are also special vocational/technical programs featuring nontraditional, nonacademic training for fields such as construction. Programs for special education students and for the gifted or talented are strong.

The following is a summary of data regarding the Las Cruces Public School District as of the 2003–2004 school year.

Total Enrollment: 23,100

Number of facilities
  elementary schools: 22
  middle schools: 7
  high schools: 4

Student/teacher ratio: 16:1

Teacher salaries
  minimum: $32,120
  maximum: $54,587

Funding per pupil: $6,414

Public Schools Information: Las Cruces Public Schools, 505 S. Main, Suite 249, Las Cruces, NM 88001; telephone (505)527-5800

Colleges and Universities

New Mexico State University (NMSU), with 16,428 students, is home to six colleges: Agriculture and Home Economics, Business Administration, Education, Engineering, Arts and Sciences, and Health and Social Service. NMSU offers 77 baccalaureate, 50 masters, and 20 doctoral programs, plus a specialist in education in four study areas. With 780 faculty members, the student teacher ratio is about 19 to one; about 81 percent of the faculty has earned doctoral degrees. NMSU offers Ph.D. degrees in engineering, business, agricultural science, and arts and sciences. NMSU is regarded among the top ten colleges and universities in the United States in research and development.

Dona Ana Branch Community College (DABCC), actually a branch of new Mexico State University and located on NMSU's campus, was instituted in 1973 to meet the needs of students who wish to achieve one year certificates and two year associates degrees in medical, technical, and business fields. The college's Adult Basic Education Outreach Program and Community Education Program have been noted by the U.S. Department of Education for promoting literacy and preparing individuals for high school equivalency exams. DABCC also has programs for high school students in Dona Ana County. Enrollment is around 5,000 and is expected to reach 7,000 by 2010.

Libraries and Research Centers

The Las Cruces public library, called Thomas Branigan Memorial Library, has more than 165,000 items which include audio, video, and microform media as well as print items. The library provides free internet access seven days a week, a Bookmobile, a Spanish Collection, almost 500 subscriptions to newspapers and periodicals, and a genealogy collection. The New Mexico State University Library holds over a million volumes housed in two buildings on the Las Cruces main campus. The Branson Library houses items pertaining to the Arts, Humanities, and Social Services, while the Zuhl Library contains government documents, special collections, and categories of Sciences, Engineering, and Business

Major research centers at New Mexico State University include the Engineering Research Center, which coordinates research functions in many engineering disciplines; the Physical Science Laboratory, which performs research, development, testing, and evaluation for NASA; The Rio Grande Corrido, which includes the NMSU computing research laboratory, focusing on artificial intelligence and genetic engineering; and Arrowhead Research Park and Genesis Center, specializing in research and development and providing affordable incubator space for small technology based start-up companies. The Carnegie Foundation ranked New Mexico State as a Level One research facility; it receives more than $300 million in total research contracts. Waste Management Education and Research Consortium helps develop environmental management resources; New Mexico Water Resource Research Institute explores water issues; New Mexico Border Research Institute plays an integral role in promoting international trade and cultural exchange; and the Advanced Manufacturing Center has a mission to enhance education, research, and business in the manufacturing industry. There are also the Arts and Sciences Research Center and an agricultural experiment station, and the university interacts with outside military and industrial research facilities in the area.

Public Library Information: Branigan Memorial Library, 200 E. Picacho, Las Cruces, NM 88001; telephone (505)528-4000

Health Care

Las Cruces has three medical facilities serving its health care needs. Memorial Medical Center (MMC) recently signed a 40-year, $150 million dollar agreement with Province Healthcare, which will enable it to add 99 private rooms to its 286-bed acute care facility. MMC offers emergency and urgent care, comprehensive cancer care at Ikard Cancer Treatment Center, imaging services, maternal/infant care, lab services, Memorial Heart Center for Heart and Vascular Care, outpatient surgery, Women's Health and Wellness, pediatrics, a neonatal care center, behavioral services, and various rehabilitation services among others. Additional services are offered at its new freestanding annex, Memorial HealthPlex, an outpatient surgery center with diagnostic imaging, lab services, and endoscopy. The Mesilla Valley Hospital, with 86 beds, offers adult and child psychiatric care, and chemical dependency treatment. The newest choice in health care in Las Cruces is Mountain View Regional Medical Center, which opened in 2002. It boasts a state of the art, full service emergency room and all private inpatient rooms. Among other key services at Mountain View are the Comprehensive Women's Center, cardiology services, surgery services, diagnostic imaging, inpatient rehabilitation, a pain management center, and an ADA certified diabetes program.

Recreation

Sightseeing

A popular attraction is the monument and white crosses which mark the graves of the travelers from Taos who were ambushed and killed by Apaches in 1830, and for which the city is purported to be named. White Sands Missile Range displays missiles and weapons at its visitor's center. Its museum traces the origins of space and nuclear research. Separate and distinct from the missile range is White Sands National Monument, an area of over 275 square miles of pure gypsum. Nature tours, including Lake Lucero, are given. Visitors can explore the world's largest pecan farms at Stahmann Farms, about 7 miles south of the city. History buffs of the Old West will enjoy San Albino Church in old Mesilla, one of the oldest missions in the region; the Fort Seldon State Monument on the site of the former cavalry fort; and the Historical Museum of Lawmen, located at the Dona Ana County Sheriff's Department, which displays law enforcement memorabilia. The only federally funded monument to the Bataan Death March heroes can be found in Veterans Park in Las Cruces along Roadrunner Parkway. It was dedicated in 2001 and sculpted by local artist Kelly Hester.

Arts and Culture

Founded by Tony-award-winning playwright Mark Medoff, The American Southwest Theatre Company performs five or six regular season productions a year plus a children's show at New Mexico State University. Professional actors from the London Stage Company produce Shakespearean

Las Cruces celebrates its Hispanic culture through events such as the Cinco de Mayo Festival and Folklorico de la Tierra del Encanto.

plays with the group once a year. The Las Cruces Community Theatre group produces five shows annually and holds a one-act festival of experimental plays in the winter. Opportunities for Creative Theater Students offers student performances at the NMSU Attic Theater.

Las Cruces boasts a number of interesting museums. Five are run by the city itself: the Las Cruces Historical Museum (formerly the Branigan Cultural Center), the Museum of Natural History, The Museum of Fine Art and Culture, The Railroad Museum, and the Bicentennial Log Cabin. The log cabin was originally in the Black Mountain range in Grant, New Mexico, until the mining industry ended and Grant became a ghost town. The log cabin was transported and completely rebuilt by Las Cruces Association of Home Builders, and features original furnishings and artifacts from the 1880s. The Las Cruces Historical Museum displays both historical and fine arts items in a turn-of-the-century parlor. The Museum of Fine Art and Culture was completed in spring of 1999. The Las Cruces Railroad and Transportation Museum holds artifacts from New Mexico's railroading past. The museum of Natural History displays plants and animals from the Chihuahuan Desert region and has programs running the gamut from dinosaurs to astronomy. The New Mexico Farm and Ranch Heritage Museum is the largest of its kind in the world and educates the public on everything in the 3,000-year history of agriculture in New Mexico. New Mexico State University has its own University Museum in Kent Hall on the main campus, which holds mostly anthropological artifacts including historic and prehistoric art objects. Space Murals, Inc. is a combination giant water tower mural and museum honoring space exploration and astronauts. Visitors to the Gadsden Museum get a taste of life and times of the Albert Jennings Fountain family, who played a crucial role in Las Cruces history. The museum exhibits Indian artifacts and objects from the Civil War, paintings and china, and outlines the history of the Gadsden Purchase.

Festivals and Holidays

Las Cruces hosts holidays and fiestas year round, many of them celebrating the city's Hispanic culture. Starting in mid-January is the Mesilla Valley Balloon Rally, when 90 or more colorful balloons fill the sky. April offers four happenings: the La Vina Blues and Jazz Thing features cool music sponsored by New Mexico's oldest winery; the Trinity Site Tour in White Sands Missile Range where the first atomic explosion was set off; the Border Book Festival, featuring renowned visiting authors, food, fun, and live acts; and the annual Frontier Days at Fort Seldon. Cinco de Mayo festivities take place in May, with Mexican food, dancing, and music in old Mesilla. Also in May, the Fiesta de San Ysidro celebrates agriculture and Hispanic traditions, and ends with a Blessing of the Fields and the hot GLASS Fly-In, showcasing the latest

in flight technology. Another wine festival dubbed The Vintner's Splash is held at the end of May.

Fourth of July is celebrated with the Electric Light Parade and fireworks. In September and October, kids and grown ups alike enjoy the Mesilla Valley Maze, which includes hay rides to a pumpkin patch and finding one's way through twists and turns cut into a corn field. In early September is the Hatch Chile Festival, honoring the Mesilla Valley as the chile capital of the world with food, crafts, an auction, and more. An hour north of Las Cruces, Hillsboro holds its apple festival the first week of September. Diez y Seis de Septiembre commemorates Mexican Independence day with folk dances, mariachi music, and traditional Mexican foods. The world's largest enchilada is constructed each year at the Whole Enchilada Fiesta, with an accompanying parade and other festivities. The end of September and the beginning of October bring the Southern New Mexico State Fair, with food, music, an auction, livestock shows, and a rodeo. La Vina, New Mexico's oldest winery, holds its namesake festival in October. The Annual Mesilla Jazz Happening holds court in two places, the old Historic Plaza and the new Mercado Plaza, with horse drawn shuttles giving free rides between the two plazas. Then in mid October "Cowboy Days" unfolds, with roping and riding demonstrations, food and music, and cowboy poetry.

While the Anglo world celebrates Halloween, in Las Cruces there is Dia de los Muertos, or Day of the Dead, with candlelit processions, homemade altars in the streets, and a giant piñata. November brings the Annual Renaissance Craftfaire where artisans present their works in a juried art show and exhibition. In mid-November the International Mariachi Conference and Concert arrives to New Mexico State University and Young Park. Finally, in December, Christmas Carols and Luminarias set historic old Mesilla aglow.

Sports for the Spectator

New Mexico State University offers Division I NCAA college sports with 6 men's and 10 women's teams. Many games are held at Aggie Memorial Football Stadium with a capacity of more than 30,000 people.

Sports for the Participant

Las Cruces is home to more than 60 parks, many of which have playgrounds, picnic tables, and special events throughout the year. The city's four recreation centers have weight rooms and racquetball and basketball courts. Therapeutic recreation is offered at Mesilla Park Recreation Center. Summer programs include swimming, tennis, track and field, and computer camp. Other city recreation department offerings are soccer, football, softball, basketball, BMX, track and field, swimming lessons, volleyball, and boxing.

Shopping and Dining

Shopping in Las Cruces can be a delightfully varied experience. Mesilla Valley Mall houses 74 stores, including both national chain stores and small boutiques. Rated one of the top 10 open-air markets in the country, the Las Cruces Farmers & Crafts Market presents more than 200 local artisans and farmers twice a week, year round. Visitors to Las Cruces are drawn to Old Mesilla, a picturesque village of galleries, unique stores and restaurants built around the town plaza, with buildings dating back to the 1850s. Mesilla is only five minutes from downtown Las Cruces. Visitors to Rancho Mesilla may sample a variety of chile pepper products while kids of all ages are entertained by llamas that roam the property. Also in Mesilla, Lowry Farms offers fresh or frozen berries, pecans, corn, flowers and ornamentals, and jams and jellies made on site.

Besides the wonderful Southwestern cuisine featuring dishes of local peppers and other produce, Las Cruces has more than 70 restaurants running the gamut from fast food and deli fare to Chinese, Japanese, continental, Italian, and, of course, Mexican fare.

Visitor Information: Las Cruces Convention and Visitors Bureau, 211 N. Water St., Las Cruces, NM 88001; telephone (505)524-8521; toll-free (800)FIESTAS

Convention Facilities

The Las Cruces Hilton has 203 rooms and nearly 6,500 square feet of convention and meeting facilities, including a 5,000 square foot Grand Ballroom and smaller executive conference rooms. The Best Western Mesilla Valley Inn is the second largest hotel with 170 rooms, and six conference rooms that can accommodate from 16 to 400 people.

Convention Information: Las Cruces Convention and Visitors Bureau, 211 N. Water St., Las Cruces, NM 88001; telephone (505)521-2144 or (800)FIESTAS

Transportation

Approaching the City

Interstate 10, which is a direct route to Phoenix, Los Angeles, Houston, and Dallas, and Interstate 25, which is the direct route to Albuquerque and Denver, traverse the city's south end. U.S. Highway 70 presents a direct route to Interstate Highway 40 at Amarillo. The Las Cruces Interna-

tional Airport, eight miles west of the city, offers commercial service to Albuquerque by Mesa Airlines, and more recently to various cities in the Southwest by Westward Airways. Negotiations are ongoing for increased commercial air service out of Las Cruces, but more air travel takes place at the El Paso International Airport in Texas, about 52 miles to the south of Las Cruces. American, Continental, America West, Delta, United, Frontier, AeroLitoral, and Southwest airlines fly to over 70 cities from El Paso.

Bus and shuttle service is offered by Greyhound-Trailways, Enchanted Southwest Tours, and the Las Cruces Shuttle Service.

Traveling in the City

Local bus service is offered by Roadrunner Transit, and taxis are available from the Checker/Yellow Cab Company.

Communications

Newspapers and Magazines

Las Cruces is served by the *Sun-News,* which is published every morning, and the *Las Cruces Bulletin,* a community newspaper that comes out each Thursday. Locally published magazines include *New Mexico Farm and Ranch,* a monthly covering equipment, techniques, and laws affecting the farming industry in New Mexico. The scholarly journal *Tamara,* covers organization science and is published out of New Mexico State University's Department of Management.

Television and Radio

Las Cruces has two AM and five FM radio stations that broadcast a variety of formats including country, Hispanic news/talk, adult contemporary, and public radio programming. The city has one public television station and one cable station.

Media Information: *Sun-News,* 256 West Las Cruces Avenue, Las Cruces, NM 88005; telephone (505)541-5400; fax (505)541-5498. *Las Cruces Bulletin,* 1210 East Madrid, Las Cruces, NM 88001; telephone (505)524-8061, fax (505)526-4621

Las Cruces Online

City of Las Cruces home page. Available www.las-cruces.org

Greater Las Cruces Chamber of Commerce. Available www.lascruces.org/chamber

Las Cruces Convention and Visitors Bureau. Available www.lascrucescvb.org

Las Cruces Public Schools. Available lcps.k12.nm.us/LCPS

Las Cruces Sun-News. Available www.lcsun-news.com

Mesilla Valley Economic Development Alliance. Available www.mveda.com

New Mexico Department of Education school fact sheets. Available sde.state.nm.us/divisions/ais/datacollection/dcr factsheets.html

New Mexico Department of Labor. Available www3state .nm.us/dol

New Mexico State University Library. Available lib.nmsu .edu/siteindex.html

Southwest New Mexico Online Magazine. Available www .gilanet.com/swnmonline

Selected Bibliography

Harris, Linda G., *Las Cruces: An Illustrated History* (Las Cruces, New Mexico: Arroyo Press, 1993)

Santa Fe

The City in Brief

Founded: 1607 (incorporated, 1846)

Head Official: Mayor Larry Delgado (since 1998)

City Population
    1980: 48,953
    1990: 56,537
    2000: 62,203
    2003 estimate: 66,476
    Percent change, 1990–2000: 8.0%
    U.S. rank in 1980: 431st
    U.S. rank in 1990: 428th
    U.S. rank in 2000: 508th (State rank: 3rd)

Metropolitan Area Population
    1980: 93,118
    1990: 117,043
    2000: 147,635

Percent change, 1990–2000: 26.1%
U.S. rank in 1980: Not reported
U.S. rank in 1990: Not reported
U.S. rank in 2000: 205th (MSA)

Area: 37.33 square miles (2000)
Elevation: 7,000 feet above sea level
Average Annual Temperature: 49.3° F
Average Annual Precipitation: 14 inches, 32 inches of snow

Major Economic Sectors: Government, tourism, services, trade
Unemployment Rate: 4.2% (January 2005)
Per Capita Income: $25,454 (1999)

2002 FBI Crime Index Total: 4,929

Major Colleges and Universities: The College of Santa Fe, St. John's College, Santa Fe Community College

Daily Newspaper: *The Santa Fe New Mexican*

Introduction

Founded before Massachusetts's Plymouth Colony and the second oldest city in the United States, Santa Fe is a cultural center for the Southwest. The Santa Fe Opera is known throughout the world, and the city is a gathering place for writers and artists. The capital of the state of New Mexico, Santa Fe is a blend of Native American, Spanish, New Mexican, and Anglo (English) cultures. The architectural integrity of the city's high-walled adobe structures and narrow, winding streets has been preserved through careful planning. At the same time, Santa Fe is a center for commerce, light industry, and science and technology.

Geography and Climate

Santa Fe is located in the northern Rio Grande Valley at the southern end of the Rocky Mountains. Situated in the foothills of the Sangre de Cristo mountain range, the city has a nearby pine forest. Because of the mountain setting, Santa Fe enjoys a semi-arid continental climate, with moderate summers and winters. Humidity is low and the sun shines approximately 300 days per year. Snowfall averages 32 inches annually in the city; deep snow does remain at higher altitudes during the winter.

Area: 37.33 square miles (2000)

Elevation: 7,000 feet above sea level

Average temperatures: January, 40.0° F; July, 91.0° F; annual average, 49.3° F

Average Annual Precipitation: 14 inches, 32 inches of snow

History

Native American and Spanish Influences

During prehistoric times a village built by the Tano tribe stood on the site now occupied by Santa Fe. Evidence from the Tano culture, uncovered in the few ruins left by Spanish settlers, indicates that civilization existed on the site as far back as 1050 to 1150 A.D. The settlement was abandoned around 200 years before the arrival of the Spanish. The spot was called Kuapoga—"place of the shell beads near the water"—by the Pueblos. Santa Fe was founded in either 1607 or 1609 (there is some confusion about the year) by

Don Pedre de Peralta, the third governor of the Province of New Mexico, who built the Palace of Governors and the Plaza and planned a walled city. The palace was occupied by a succession of sixty Spanish governors for more than 200 years, and Santa Fe has been a seat of government since its founding.

Throughout Spanish rule of the territory Santa Fe was a center for exploration and mission work. Franciscan friars built eleven churches and by 1617 had converted more than 14,000 Native Americans to their form of Christianity. Conflict arose, however, when the Native Americans continued to practice their own religion. In 1680 a number of the Spanish settlers were killed in a conflict with natives; the survivors fled to El Paso del Norte, abandoning the town. The Native Americans established their own community in Santa Fe; occupying the palace and appointing a governor, they held the town for twelve years until the arrival of De Vargas, Spanish governor of the province. He made peace and returned the following year with a statue of the Christian New Testament's Virgin Mary. Making his entry on the site of present day Rosario Chapel, he vowed to pay yearly homage to "Our Lady of Victory." Since that time, in fulfillment of this vow the De Vargas Procession has been held in Santa Fe.

Mexico and United States Claim Santa Fe

When Mexico won independence from Spain in 1821, Santa Fe came under the control of Mexico. Trade was then opened between Santa Fe and the United States over a route that came to be known as the Santa Fe Trail. In 1846 the United States claimed Santa Fe; the city has been under U.S. jurisdiction ever since, except for two weeks during the Civil War when the Confederates seized control after the battle of Valverde. The Santa Fe Trail eventually fell into disuse when rail travel advanced to the region. Santa Fe flourished, however, benefiting from the new trade connections that were made possible by the railroad.

City Becomes Art Colony, Capital of State

Around the turn of the century, artists, attracted by the climate and the beauty of the area, moved to Santa Fe, and the city soon became popular as an art colony. When New Mexico attained statehood in 1912, Santa Fe, as the capital, entered a period of prosperity; government workers arrived to live in the city and federal and state buildings were constructed around the Plaza. By 1920 the population had grown from 5,000 to more than 7,000 people, and by the 1940s it was over 20,000 people.

In 1957 the city established zoning codes designed to maintain a uniform architectural style. Two types of architecture are permitted: Pueblo, characterized by rounded parapets and rough-hewn woodwork, and Territorial, featuring brick coping and milled, often decorative woodworking.

Santa Fe's populace reflects the city's Native American, Spanish, and Anglo heritage, and the cultural traditions of these groups have been retained. However, after an influx of new residents in the 1980s, the 1990 census reported that for the first time since the city's founding, Hispanic residents were a minority. During the 1990s the city experienced some tensions between locals—many of them poor—and newcomers, who are driving up the cost of housing and otherwise altering the landscape. Economic frustrations continue into the early 2000s, as wages linger at almost 20 percent below the national average, while the cost of living has remained well above the national average. The city has taken steps to remedy the issue; a "living wage" city ordinance was passed in 2003 to raise minimum wages.

Historical Information: Fra Angelico Chavez Memorial History Library and Photographic Archive, 110 Washington Ave., Santa Fe, NM 87504; telephone (508)476-5090. Special Collections, Santa Fe Community College Library, telephone (505)428-1352

Population Profile

Metropolitan Area Residents
1980: 93,118
1990: 117,043
2000: 147,635
Percent change, 1990–2000: 26.1%
U.S. rank in 1980: Not reported
U.S. rank in 1990: Not reported
U.S. rank in 2000: 205th (MSA)

City Residents
1980: 48,953
1990: 56,537
2000: 62,203
2003 estimate: 66,476
Percent change, 1990–2000: 8.0%
U.S. rank in 1980: 431st
U.S. rank in 1990: 428th (State rank: 3rd)
U.S. rank in 2000: 508th (State rank: 3rd)

Density: 1,666.1 people per square mile (2000)

Racial and ethnic characteristics (2000)
  White: 47,459
  Black or African American: 409
  American Indian and Alaska Native: 1,373
  Asian: 791
  Native Hawaiian and Pacific Islander: 49
  Hispanic or Latino (may be of any race): 29,744
  Other: 12,122

Percent of residents born in state: 44.8% (2000)

Age characteristics (2000)
  Population under 5 years old: 3,348
  Population 5 to 9 years old: 3,374
  Population 10 to 14 years old: 3,565
  Population 15 to 19 years old: 3,925
  Population 20 to 24 years old: 3,910
  Population 25 to 34 years old: 8,497
  Population 35 to 44 years old: 9,512
  Population 45 to 54 years old: 10,741
  Population 55 to 59 years old: 3,821
  Population 60 to 64 years old: 2,862
  Population 65 to 74 years old: 4,542
  Population 75 to 84 years old: 2,959
  Population 85 years and older: 1,147
  Median age: 39.8 years

Births (2002)
  Total number: 1,662

Deaths (2002)
  Total number: 792

Money income (1999)
  Per capita income: $25,454
  Median household income: $40,392
  Total households: 27,493

Number of households with income of . . .
  less than $10,000: 2,606
  $10,000 to $14,999: 1,615
  $15,000 to $24,999: 3,672
  $25,000 to $34,999: 3,793
  $35,000 to $49,999: 4,615
  $50,000 to $74,999: 5,123
  $75,000 to $99,999: 2,839
  $100,000 to $149,999: 1,787
  $150,000 to $199,999: 708
  $200,000 or more: 735

Percent of families below poverty level: 9.5% (22.2% of which were female householder families with related children under 5 years)

2002 FBI Crime Index Total: 4,929

Municipal Government

Santa Fe operates under a council-mayor, city-manager form of government, administered by an eight-member council and a mayor who are elected to four-year terms. Santa Fe is the seat of Santa Fe County and, as the state capital, the site of meetings of the State Legislature.

Head Official: Mayor Larry Delgado (since 1998; current term expires 2006)

Total Number of City Employees: 1,719 (2005)

City Information: City of Santa Fe, PO Box 909, 200 Lincoln Avenue, Santa Fe, NM 87504-0909; telephone (505)955-6590

Economy

Major Industries and Commercial Activity

Santa Fe's economy has been based largely on tourism and state government. As capitol of New Mexico, the government is the largest employer in the area. Santa Fe receives an average of 1.6 million visitors annually; in 2004, readers of *Condé Nast Traveler* magazine ranked Santa Fe second only to San Francisco as the best travel destination in the country. Tourism boosts the city's retail industry, which brings in more than $1 billion annually.

Because of the city's proximity to Los Alamos National Laboratory (LANL), 45 miles away, scientific research has also become a factor. Operated by the University of California for the U.S. Department of Energy, LANL is one of the largest research laboratories in the nation. It is an important center for work on defense-related projects, conducting research on technology associated with nuclear weapons and deterrence, as well as energy production and health, safety, and environmental concerns, among other areas. Over one third of LANL's employees live in Santa Fe, and several new research-related firms and high-technology spinoff companies have located in Santa Fe.

Health care and light manufacturing are other significant economic sectors. Santa Fe has emerged as a regional medical center; St. Vincent Regional Medical Center is one of the city's largest employers and serves seven counties. Products manufactured by local companies include electronic instruments and textiles.

Items and goods produced: art, pumice products, weavings, Native American arts and crafts, textiles, electronic instruments, aluminum ware

Incentive Programs—New and Existing Companies

Local programs—The Santa Fe Business Incubator, considered one of the best of its kind in the nation, assists new businesses with all aspects of start-up. The Small Business Development Center provides one-on-one business advising, encourages and instructs entrepreneurs, and is a strong advocate for local business growth and development.

SCORE (Service Corps of Retired Executives) provides business counseling and support. Santa Fe Economic Development, Inc. supports entrepreneurs and works with businesses interested in relocating to the area.

State programs—New Mexico offers a variety of incentives to all new and expanding businesses. Its Build to Suit program facilitates building construction, and ePort New Mexico is a "one-stop" information source offering permitting and licensing. The state's financial incentives include: no inventory taxes; tax credits for high-wage jobs, technology jobs, and childcare; a tax deduction for research and development services; a job training incentive program (the cornerstone of the state's incentives: New Mexico can pay half the salary for new hires for up to half a year); exemptions for qualified businesses from property taxes on land, buildings, and equipment, and from personal property tax on equipment; and laboratory partnerships with small businesses. Further incentives are available for manufacturers, customer support centers, aerospace and aircraft industries, producers of agriculture or energy, and filmmakers. In addition, the state enacted a major personal income tax reduction in 2003, and New Mexico's property taxes are second lowest in the nation.

Development Projects

To attract businesses that rely on high-speed technology, Santa Fe is constructing a "Santa Fe Light Trail" system of digital microwave and fiber facilities; it will be a hybrid network available to the business community as well as educational facilities and local and state government agencies. A new civic center for the city is scheduled for completion in 2007.

Commercial Shipping

Santa Fe is linked with major western and midwestern markets via rail freight service provided by the Santa Fe Southern Railroad, which maintains a main line through nearby Lamy. Several rail sidings are conveniently located in the city's industrial areas. Several interstate motor freight carriers connect Santa Fe with markets on both the East and West Coasts; major parcel express lines also serve the city. Air cargo service is available at Santa Fe Municipal Airport.

Labor Force and Employment Outlook

Santa Fe's economy is lead by government and tourism, and as of 2005, two out of three jobs in the city are in either the government or service sector. Corporations of substantial size are absent from the economy, and recruitment efforts encourage entrepreneurship and small business development. Unemployment is relatively low. Wages, especially in the service industry, have remained low (nearly 20 percent less than the national average) while the cost of living index is high (up to 20 percent higher than the national average).

A "living wage" ordinance, passed in 2003, attempts to raise minimum wages to remedy this problem.

The following is a summary of data regarding the Santa Fe metropolitan area labor force, 2004 annual averages.

Size of non-agricultural labor force: 60,600

Number of workers employed in . . .
  construction and mining: 4,500
  manufacturing: 1,200
  trade, transportation and utilities: 10,200
  information: 900
  financial activities: 2,900
  professional and business services: 5,100
  educational and health services: 8,300
  leisure and hospitality: 8,900
  other services: 3,000
  government: 15,500

Average hourly earnings of production workers employed in manufacturing: $14.64

Unemployment rate: 4.2% (January 2005)

Largest employers	Number of employees
State of New Mexico	9,443
Santa Fe School District	1,850
U.S. Government	1,750
City of Santa Fe	1,719
St. Vincent Hospital	1,450
Santa Fe Community College	717
Santa Fe Opera	650
College of Santa Fe	564

Cost of Living

The following is a summary of data regarding key cost of living factors for the Santa Fe area.

2004 (3rd Quarter) ACCRA Average House Price: $315,950

2004 (3rd Quarter) ACCRA Cost of Living Index: 109.0 (U.S. average = 100.0)

State income tax rate: Ranges from 1.7% to 6.8%

State sales tax rate: 5.0%

Local income tax rate: None

Local sales tax rate: 1.0625% (city); 1.25% (county)

Property tax rate: 0.017494 multiplied by one-third of full market value (2004)

Economic Information: Santa Fe County Chamber of Commerce, PO Box 1928, Santa Fe, NM 87504; telephone (505)988-3279; email trish@santafechamber.com. New

Mexico Department of Labor, Economic Research and Analysis, 401 Broadway NE, Albuquerque NM 87102. Bureau of Business and Economic Research, 1 University of New Mexico, Albuquerque, NM 87131; telephone (505)277-2216; fax (505)277-7066

Education and Research

Elementary and Secondary Schools

The Santa Fe Public Schools system is the third largest district in the state of New Mexico. It is administered by a five-member, nonpartisan board of education that establishes educational policies and appoints a superintendent.

The following is a summary of data regarding Santa Fe's public schools.

Total enrollment: approximately 13,000

Number of facilities
  elementary schools: 20
  junior high school: 4
  senior high schools: 3
  other: 3 charter schools

Student/teacher ratio: 15.9:1 (2002-2003)

Teacher salaries (2002-2003)
  average: $34,356

Funding per pupil: $5,924 (2001-2002)

Additionally, Santa Fe has a large network of private schools, consisting of 32 schools ranging from pre-Kindergarten through 12th grade, one of which—the Santa Fe Indian School—is a federally funded boarding school for Native Americans, run by the All Indian Pueblo Council.

Public Schools Information: Santa Fe Public Schools, 610 Alta Vista Street, Santa Fe, NM 87505; telephone (505)467-2000; fax (505)995-3302

Colleges and Universities

Santa Fe has several institutes of higher learning, all of which have an enrollment of less than 2,000. The College of Santa Fe is a private college offering associate and baccalaureate degrees; it is particularly known for its programs in the performing, visual, moving image, and creative writing arts, and also has strong programs in the humanities, education, business, conservation science, and social science. St. John's College, which has a campus in Annapolis, Maryland as well as in Santa Fe, offers baccalaureate and advanced degrees. St. John's is distinctive for its "great books" curriculum; learning is based upon the study of books and no textbooks are used. The Institute of American Indian Arts, a fine arts college, offers associate and baccalaureate degrees in creative writing, studio arts, visual communications, and museum studies. Southwestern College, devoted to the study of mental health, offers master's degrees in counseling, counseling with a concentration in grief and loss, and art therapy. Southwest Acupuncture College offers a Master of Science in Oriental Medicine. Santa Fe Community College serves area residents with two-year college preparatory and technical and vocational curricula.

Libraries and Research Centers

The Santa Fe Public Library operates two branches in addition to its main facility downtown. Holdings include nearly 300,000 volumes, as well as periodical subscriptions, records, films, maps, and special collections on the Southwest and New Mexico. The New Mexico State Library, with more than 300,000 volumes and 700 periodical subscriptions, is a federal and state documents depository. Research libraries located in Santa Fe house special collections pertaining to such diverse topics as Southwestern culture, comparative religion, and Sherlock Holmes; other libraries are affiliated with local colleges and government agencies. The Santa Fe Institute conducts research activities in the physical, biological, computational, and social sciences, in areas such as cognitive neuroscience, computation in physical and biological systems, economic and social interactions, evolutionary dynamics, network dynamics, and robustness. The National Center for Genome Resources examines the influence of genetic variability on infectious disease progression.

Public Library Information: Santa Fe Public Library, 145 Washington Avenue, Santa Fe, NM 87501; telephone (505)955-6780; fax (505)955-6676

Health Care

Santa Fe's St. Vincent Regional Medical Center is the largest medical center in Northern New Mexico, and has the region's only Level III Trauma Center. It is the major regional medical center for a 19,000-square-mile area covering seven counties. St. Vincent has 268 licensed beds, and employs some 250 physicians representing 22 medical specialties. Non-profit and non-affiliated, it was established in 1865 and is the oldest hospital in the state. The medical center is known for its heart and vascular center, which has the first rural EKG network in the nation; it allows rural EMS personnel to transmit an electrocardiogram directly to the medical center.

Recreation

Sightseeing

Santa Fe's historic downtown plaza, once the terminus of the Santa Fe Trail, has been a center of activity in Santa Fe since the city's founding. The plaza area is full of restaurants, shops, art galleries, and museums. Also here is St. Francis Cathedral, a grand structure built in the French Romanesque style, unusual in this city of Spanish-Pueblo architecture. Santa Fe's first Roman Catholic archbishop, Jean Baptiste Lamy, started the cathedral; both the bishop and the building were the inspiration for Willa Cather's novel, *Death Comes to the Archbishop.* A wooden icon in the cathedral's north chapel is the oldest representation of the Madonna in the United States.

Other historical buildings include Santuario de Guadalupe, the nation's oldest shrine dedicated to Our Lady of Guadalupe; built in the late 1700s, its adobe walls are three feet thick. Our Lady of Light Chapel, also known as Loretto Chapel, was built between 1873 and 1878 and is the oldest stone masonry building in the city; it is known for its spiral wooden Miraculous Staircase, apparently made without nails or a support beam. San Miguel Mission, one of the oldest mission churches in the nation, was built in 1610 by the Tlaxcala natives, who were servants of Spanish soldiers and missionaries; on display is a bell that was cast in Spain in 1356 and brought to Santa Fe in the early 19th century. The New Mexico State Capitol building, the only round capitol building in the United States, was built in the shape of a Southwestern Indian *zia,* which represents the circle of life. The Palace of the Governors has been home to 60 Spanish, Mexican, and American governors, among them Lew Wallace, who wrote the novel *Ben Hur* there during his 1877-1881 tenure. Built in 1610, it became a history museum in 1909.

Canyon Road, just north of the capitol building, was once a Native American trail and defines one of the oldest districts in the city. Just west of Canyon Road is Barrio de Analco, now called East de Vargas Street, among the oldest continuously inhabited streets in the nation; many historic homes are located here. The Cross of the Martyrs, overlooking the city, is a large white cross built in 1920 to commemorate the Franciscans killed by native Pueblos in 1680. The Commemorative Walkway leading to the monument has been the route for various religious processions, particularly in September during Fiesta, the celebration of the return of the Spanish to Santa Fe in 1692.

Santa Fe is surrounded by twelve Pueblo villages, each of which retains its own distinct culture and holds special events relating to its unique traditions; all are located within an hour's drive of the city.

The Palace of the Governors was originally built as Spain's seat of government in the early seventeenth century.

Arts and Culture

Home of more than 20 music groups, theater companies, and dance groups, Santa Fe supports one of the best and most active arts communities in the country. The famous Santa Fe Opera, which attracts audiences from throughout the world, presents its performances in a partially open-air amphitheater located on a wooded hill north of the city. It is known for its performances of the classics, obscure works by classical composers, and American premiers of modern works. Its eight-week season runs from June to August. The Santa Fe Symphony Orchestra and Chorus performs classical and popular works at the Lensic Performing Arts Center; the center's lavish Lensic Theater, built in 1931 as a film and vaudeville house, received an $8.2 million restoration, which was completed in 2001. The Desert Chorale choral group performs at venues throughout the city and is known for blending Renaissance melodies and avant-garde compositions.

Students at the College of Santa Fe stage their productions in the Greer Garson Theatre. Their season, which runs from October to May, consists of several presentations of four plays. Santa Fe Playhouse, established in the 1920s, performs dramas, avant-garde works, and musical comedy in a historic adobe theater.

The María Benitez Teatro Flamenco performs flamenco music and dance in a summer season at the María Benitez Theatre at the Radisson Hotel. The company is comprised of Benitez, who has been named the best flamenco dancer of her generation by *Dance* magazine, and flamenco dancers and musicians from throughout the United States and Spain.

Santa Fe is home to several museums specializing in a variety of fields. The Museum of New Mexico, described as the most important modern cultural institution in the state, houses the Palace of Governors, Museum of Indian Arts and Culture, Museum of Fine Arts, and Museum of International Folk Art. The Palace of the Governors, the nation's oldest continually used building, houses exhibits relating to Native American, Spanish, Mexican, and American frontier history. Its governor offices have been restored and preserved. The Museum of Indian Arts and Culture showcases exhibits pertaining to the history and contemporary culture of the Pueblo, Navajo, and Apache peoples, including pottery, basketry, woven fabrics, jewelry, and contemporary crafts. Opened in 1987, its massive collection has been built over the course of nearly 80 years of research and acquisition by the Laboratory of Anthropology. The Museum of Fine Arts, built in 1917, is the oldest art museum in the state; it was built in the style of the mission church at nearby Acoma Pueblo. The museum maintains a collection of more than 20,000 works, with a specialty in regional art from throughout the 20th century to the present. The Museum of Interna-

tional Folk Art, the largest of its kind in the world, has more than 130,000 items of folk art from around the world, including dolls and puppets, masks, textiles, ceramics, furniture, clothing, and Spanish colonial artworks.

The Georgia O'Keeffe Museum houses the largest collection of the artist's work in the world. The museum features revolving exhibits of O'Keeffe's paintings, watercolors, pastels, charcoals, and sculptures, and also hosts exhibitions of works by some of O'Keeffe's contemporaries. The Wheelwright Museum of the American Indian, housed in a building shaped like a Navajo hogan, features rotating single-subject displays of jewelry, tapestry, pottery, baskets, and paintings crafted by Native Americans throughout the Southwest. The Institute of American Indian Arts Museum focuses on works by students and faculty members; with more than 7,000 works, it is the largest collection of contemporary American Indian art in the world. The Santa Fe Children's Museum was developed to offer hands-on exhibits for the whole family. Santa Fe's newest museum is the Museum of Spanish Colonial Art, which presents a variety of Hispanic media—including santos (painted and sculpted images of saints), textiles, tinwork, silverwork, goldwork, ironwork, straw appliqué, ceramics, furniture, and books—dating from the Middle Ages through the present.

Festivals and Holidays

Many of Santa Fe's events reflect the cultural diversity of the city. During the Chimayo Pilgrimage, on Good Friday, thousands walk on foot to the Santuario de Chimayo, a small church believed to aid in miracles. The Rodeo de Santa Fe, a popular regional competition, is held in June; the four-night rodeo features entrants from several states competing in such events as bareback bronco riding, calf roping, steer wrestling, and barrel racing. The annual Traditional Spanish Market is held in July; it is the oldest and largest market in the country for Spanish Colonial artists. More than 300 Hispanic artisans offer traditional artforms including santos, textiles, tinwork, furniture, straw appliqué, and metalwork. The market also presents live music, art demonstrations, and regional foods. The Indian Market, held in August, is the country's largest and most prestigious Native American art show. More than 1,000 artisans offer basketry, blankets, jewelry, pottery, woodcarvings, rugs, sandpaintings, and sculptures. Tribal dancing and craft demonstrations are also presented. La Fiesta de Santa Fe in September, which dates to 1712, is the oldest community celebration in the country. Highlights include Spanish dancing, mariachi music, food and craft booths, and parades and ceremonies including a pet parade, a historical/hysterical parade, and a fiesta mass of thanksgiving held at St. Francis Cathedral, followed by a candle-lit procession from the cathedral to the Cross of the Martyrs. The Santa Fe Wine and Chile Fiesta, a five-day event, is also held in September. The Winter Spanish Market, in December, is a smaller version of July's market; some 150 artisans offer their wares.

Drawing on the traditions of three cultures—Native American, Spanish, and Anglo—Christmas celebrations in Santa Fe take on a special flair. As part of the festivities, *farolitos*—luminaries made of paper bags, sand, and candles—set the town aglow on Christmas Eve. Indian pueblos schedule winter dances, bonfires, and processions in late December and January.

Sports for the Spectator

Polo teams sponsored by local merchants compete in Sunday games from June through Labor Day at the Santa Fe Polo Club.

Sports for the Participant

Outdoor activities can be pursued throughout most of the year in Santa Fe. Outdoor enthusiasts can mountain-bike through the area's high-desert terrain, hike in the area's 1,000 miles of national forest trails, golf at one of Santa Fe's three golf courses, or play tennis at one of 48 tennis courts. Within the Santa Fe National Forest are wilderness areas—Pecos, Dome, and San Pedro parks—that are ideal for hiking, camping, fishing, and hunting. Resorts at Ojo Caliente and Jemez Springs furnish bath houses for the enjoyment of the natural hot springs for which northern New Mexico is famous. Skiing is a flourishing sport in Santa Fe. Seven ski areas within a two-hour drive provide facilities for every level of skiing expertise. Ski Santa Fe, a 30-minute drive through the Sangre De Cristo Mountains from Santa Fe, is an especially popular spot. Cross-country skiing areas are also nearby.

Shopping and Dining

Santa Fe has been described as a shopper's "Shangri-La." With hundreds of stores in the downtown area alone, the city offers boutiques and specialty shops, 200 art galleries, and several large shopping centers. Locally designed and crafted items such as clothing, jewelry, pottery, and furniture are featured.

Prime shopping areas include the historic Canyon Road area, home to a large, eclectic mix of small shops and galleries; and the plaza area, which features the greatest concentration of Native American crafts, as well as the Santa Fe Arcade, a three-story shopping center that opened in 2004. The Guadelupe district, a recently redeveloped area close to the rail-yard, features numerous specialty stores and cafes. Located in this area is the Sanbusco Market Center, a remodeled warehouse occupied by unique shops and restaurants. Other Santa Fe shopping highlights include the local treats at the Santa Fe Farmer's Market, and the variety of wares at the Tesuque Flea Market.

A specialty of Santa Fe is northern New Mexico cuisine, which is a mixture of Pueblo Indian, Spanish Colonial, and Anglo frontier cooking. It differs from "Tex-Mex" food in that northern New Mexican cooks use heavy meats for such dishes as *carne adovada,* or marinated pork. Green chiles, pinto beans, and blue corn tortillas are also used in local dishes. *Sopaipillas,* deep-fried puff pastries drizzled with honey, are especially popular. Among other dining options are Western-style steak and barbeque, vegetarian cuisine, and Italian, Chinese, Sushi, Thai, Indian, Korean, Mediterranean, French, and Native American restaurants.

Visitor Information: Santa Fe Convention and Visitors Bureau, 201 West Marcy, PO Box 909, Santa Fe, NM 87504; telephone (505)955-6200; toll-free (800)777-CITY

Convention Facilities

The principal meeting facility in Santa Fe is Sweeney Convention Center, located downtown within easy access of the historical district, cultural attractions, shopping, restaurants, and more than 1,500 hotel and motel rooms. Sweeney Convention Center has 22,000 square feet of space for exhibitions, banquets, and meetings. The center features flexible seating and exhibition arrangements in its 10,000-square-foot main floor area; up to 80 booths, banquets for 700 people, and theater-style seating for 1,200 people can be accommodated in this space. Six additional meeting rooms each provide 1,300 square feet with a seating capacity of approximately 200 people. Plans are underway to replace the Sweeney Convention Center with a 68,950-square-foot, $42 million center by 2007.

Convention Information: Santa Fe Convention and Visitors Bureau, 201 West Marcy, PO Box 909, Santa Fe, NM 87504; telephone (505)955-6200; toll-free (800)777-CITY

Transportation

Approaching the City

The major airport closest to Santa Fe is Albuquerque International Sunport, 65 minutes away. Shuttle companies offer transportation between the airport and Santa Fe. Santa Fe Municipal Airport, located nine miles southwest of the city's central business district, accommodates commuter flights and private aircraft. The Roadrunner Shuttle meets every flight to transport travelers to any Santa Fe location.

The principal highway routes into Santa Fe are I-25, running east and west along the southern perimeter of the city, and I-84/285, which bisects the city from north to south.

Amtrak's Southwest Chief, a line running between Chicago and Los Angeles, schedules twice-daily arrivals and departures at Lamy, 20 miles south of Santa Fe; regular shuttle service is provided from the village to Santa Fe.

Intercity commercial bus transportation is available through two buslines.

Traveling in the City

Santa Fe Trails Bus System provides affordable public transportation on seven routes throughout the city.

Communications

Newspapers and Magazines

Santa Fe's major daily newspaper is *The Santa Fe New Mexican,* the oldest newspaper in the West. The weekly *Santa Fe Reporter* is published on Wednesdays. Magazines published in Santa Fe include the *Santa Fean,* featuring articles on New Mexico history and travel, restaurants, events, and attractions; and *New Mexico Magazine,* founded in 1923, which covers such topics as the state's multicultural heritage, arts, climate, environment and diverse people.

Television and Radio

Two television stations broadcast from Santa Fe; several others, including network affiliates, are broadcast from nearby Albuquerque. Cable service is available by subscription. Eight AM and FM radio stations broadcasting in Santa Fe, one of which plays Spanish music. Santa Fe also receives programming from Albuquerque.

Media Information: *The Santa Fe New Mexican,* 202 E Marcy Street, Santa Fe, NM 87501; telephone (505)983-3303; email info@sfnewmexican.com

Santa Fe Online

Bureau of Business and Economic Research, University of New Mexico. Available at www.unm.edu/~bber

City of Santa Fe home page. Available www.santafenm.gov

New Mexico Department of Labor. Available www.dol.state.nm.us

Santa Fe Economic Development, Inc. Available www.sfedi.org

The Santa Fe New Mexican. Available www.sfnewmexican.com

Santa Fe Public Library. Available www.santafelibrary.org

Santa Fe Public Schools. Available www.sfps.k12.nm.us

Selected Bibliography

Dennis, Lisl, and Landt Dennis, *Behind Adobe Walls: The Hidden Homes and Gardens of Santa Fe and Taos* (San Francisco, Calif.: Chronicle Books, 1997)

OREGON

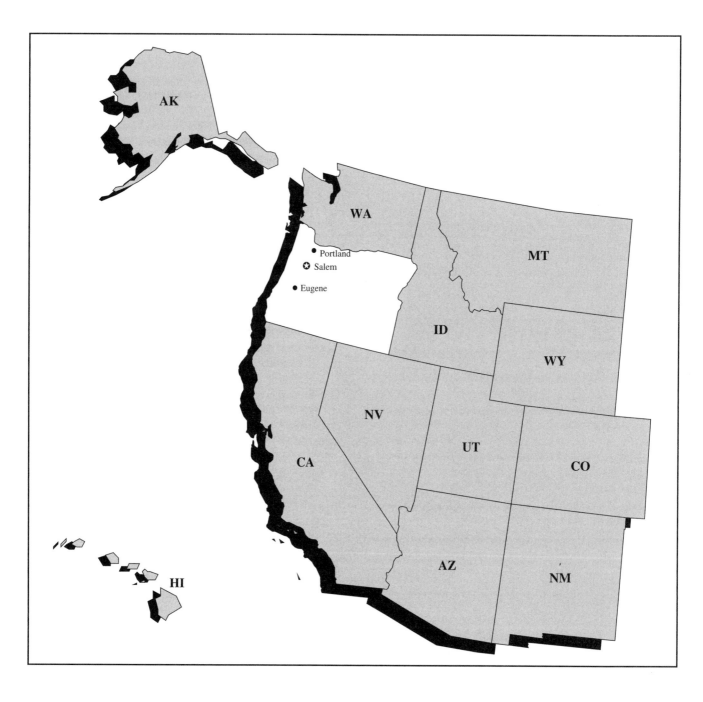

The State in Brief

Nickname: Beaver State
Motto: Alis Volat Propriis (She flies with her own wings)

Flower: Oregon grape
Bird: Western meadowlark

Area: 98,380 square miles (2000; U.S. rank: 9th)
Elevation: Ranges from sea level to 11,239 feet above sea level
Climate: Mild and humid with frequent rainfall in western third; dry with extremes of temperature in the interior two-thirds

Admitted to Union: February 14, 1859
Capital: Salem
Head Official: Governor Ted Kulongoski (D) (until 2007)

Population
  1980: 2,633,105
  1990: 2,842,321
  2000: 3,421,399
  2004 estimate: 3,594,586
  Percent change, 1990–2000: 20.4%
  U.S. rank in 2004: 27th
  Percent of residents born in state: 45.3% (2000)
  Density: 35.6 people per square mile (2000)
  2002 FBI Crime Index Total: 171,443

Racial and Ethnic Characteristics (2000)
  White: 2,961,623
  Black or African American: 55,662
  American Indian and Alaska Native: 45,211
  Asian: 101,350
  Native Hawaiian and Pacific Islander: 7,976
  Hispanic or Latino (may be of any race): 275,314
  Other: 144,832

Age Characteristics (2000)
  Population under 5 years old: 223,005
  Population 5 to 19 years old: 720,999
  Percent of population 65 years and over: 12.8%
  Median age: 36.3 years (2000)

Vital Statistics
  Total number of births (2003): 45,911
  Total number of deaths (2003): 30,973 (infant deaths, 270)
  AIDS cases reported through 2003: 2,586

Economy
  Major industries: Manufacturing; finance, insurance, and real estate; trade
  Unemployment rate: 6.6% (February 2005)
  Per capita income: $28,806 (2003; U.S. rank: 32nd)
  Median household income: $42,429 (3-year average, 2001-2003)
  Percentage of persons below poverty level: 11.6% (1999)
  Income tax rate: Ranges from 5.0% to 9.0%
  Sales tax rate: None

Eugene

The City in Brief

Founded: 1846 (incorporated, 1862)

Head Official: Mayor Kitty Piercy (D) (since 2005)

City Population
   1980: 105,624
   1990: 112,733
   2000: 137,893
   2003 estimate: 142,185
   Percent change, 1990–2000: 21.1%
   U.S. rank in 1980: 151st
   U.S. rank in 1990: 159th (2nd in State)
   U.S. rank in 2000: 160th (2nd in State)

Metropolitan Area Population
   1980: 275,000
   1990: 282,912
   2000: 322,959
   Percent change, 1990–2000: 14.2%

   U.S. rank in 1980: 115th
   U.S. rank in 1990: 119th
   U.S. rank in 2000: 123rd

Area: 41.0 square miles (2000)
Elevation: 369 feet above sea level
Average Annual Temperature: 52.1° F
Average Annual Precipitation: 50.90 inches

Major Economic Sectors: Services, trade, government, agriculture
Unemployment Rate: 6.5% (February 2005)
Per Capita Income: $21,315 (1999)
2004 ACCRA Average House Price: Not reported
2004 ACCRA Cost of Living Index: Not reported

2002 FBI Crime Index Total: 9,382

Major Colleges and Universities: University of Oregon, Lane Community College, Northwest Christian College, Gutenberg College, Eugene Bible College

Daily Newspaper: *The Register-Guard*

SPRINGFIELD

PIONEER PARKWAY EAST

PIONEER PARKWAY WEST

TO MCKENZIE - WILLAMETTE HOSPITAL

G ST.

E ST.

SPRINGFIELD CITY HALL & MUSEUM

MAIN

PUBLIC LIBRARY

A ST.

5

5

CENTENNIAL

AUTZEN STADIUM

ALTON BAKER PARK

ISLAND PARK

WALNUT

HENDRICKS PARK

AGATE

LAURELWOOD GOLF COURSE

UNIVERSITY

NW CHRISTIAN COLLEGE

SACRED HEART HOSPITAL

UNIVERSITY OF OREGON

HILYARD

PATTERSON

FERRY

MILL

HIGH

PEARL

AMAZON PARK

19TH AVE.

TO LANE COMM. COLLEGE

EUGENE

HARLOW

COBURG

CAL YOUNG

OAKWAY

BELTLINE

OAKWAY GOLF COURSE

105

WILLAMETTE RIVER

COUNTRY CLUB

CHESHIRE

SKINNER BUTTE PARK

5TH ST. SHOPS

CITY HALL

HULT CTR. FOR THE PERFORMING ARTS

LANE CO. COURT HOUSE

SATURDAY MARKET

DOWNTOWN MALL

CHAMBER OF COMMERCE

PUBLIC LIBRARY

WILLAMETTE

OLIVE

CHARNELTON

LINCOLN

LAWRENCE

WASHINGTON

JEFFERSON

CONVENTION & VISITORS BUREAU

6TH AVE.

7TH AVE.

8TH AVE.

BROADWAY

10TH AVE.

11TH AVE.

12TH AVE.

13TH AVE.

18TH AVE.

105

OWEN MEMORIAL ROSE GARDENS

1ST AVE.

RIVER

TO EUGENE AIRPORT

BLAIR

99

LANE CO. FAIRGROUNDS & CONVENTION CTR.

N

MT

WY

CO

ID

UT

NV

WA

OR

CA

●Eugene

MILES   0   0.25   0.5   1

KILOMETERS   0   0.5   1

Introduction

Eugene is Oregon's second largest city and the seat of Lane County. Together with Springfield it is also the second largest metropolitan area in the state. It is the commercial and cultural center for a large agricultural and timber region, as well as an important retail trade and transportation hub in the state of Oregon. Situated halfway between the ocean and the mountains, Eugene offers many recreational possibilities year round.

Geography and Climate

Eugene is located in the center of western Oregon, about 100 miles south of Portland and halfway between the Pacific Ocean and the Cascade Mountains in the broad Willamette River valley. Temperatures are usually moderate throughout the year, with most rainfall occurring from October to May. Winters are warmed by prevailing winds from the southwest, and summers are kept mild and dry by cooling northwestern winds.

Area: 41.0 square miles (2000)

Elevation: 369 feet above sea level

Average Temperatures: January, 39.8° F; August, 66.4° F; annual average, 52.1° F

Average Annual Precipitation: 50.90 inches

History

A site near present-day Eugene was settled in 1846 by Eugene F. Skinner at the base of a mountain peak called Ya-po-ah by the Calapooya tribe. The settlement was named Skinner's, and in 1852 a townsite was laid out by Skinner and Judge D. M. Risdon, who erected the first house within the corporate limits. Attempts to establish the town were foiled by heavy rains, however, and it was given the nickname "Skinner's Mudhole." The settlers moved to higher ground, construction succeeded, and in 1853 the town, taking its founder's given name, was chosen as the seat of newly created Lane County. The first post office in the region was built there the same year; Eugene was incorporated in 1864. The University of Oregon was established in Eugene in 1876.

Agriculture, milling, and transportation were the principal industries during Eugene's early years. A steady steamship trade was conducted between the town and Portland from the late 1850s until 1871, when construction of the Oregon & California Railroad brought an end to water transportation. By the end of the Civil War Eugene's population had reached 1,200 residents and the city was becoming highly industrialized. With lumbering as a principal industry, the city was the site of sawmills, shingle mills, planing mills, and box factories. Cottonwood and balm trees indigenous to the area were used to produce excelsior. Mining was also an important part of the economy. Agriculture continued to expand; wheat had been the major crop, and many farmers soon turned to fruit growing and dairy farming as well. Creameries, canneries, and flour mills were built for the processing of agricultural products. A major influence on the city as a cultural and education center began in 1872, when the University of Oregon was founded.

Along with industrial development, however, Eugene maintained a livable environment for its residents. By the 1940s the city was noted for its parklike appearance: comfortable, well-kept homes were set in landscaped lawns and shade trees lined the streets. Business districts occupied impressive brick and concrete buildings. With a major university, the city had also become the cultural center for the region. Eugene's population expanded steadily throughout the first half of the twentieth century, reaching nearly 51,000 people in 1967. By 1980, the population had nearly doubled. A slowdown in the timber industry during the early 1980s halted expansion.

Eugene is thriving in the mid 2000s. The city continues to be a lumber and wood-products center, where a high percentage of the nation's plywood is produced. A growing vineyard and wine industry is flourishing. It is also an increasingly important hub for Oregon high tech businesses and industries. With retail, industrial, educational, and professional institutions and enterprises serving a metropolitan population of more than 300,000 people, Eugene is the fourth largest market in the Pacific Northwest.

Historical Information: Lane County Museum Library Archives, 740 West Thirteenth Avenue, Eugene, OR 97402; telephone (541)687-4239

Population Profile

Metropolitan Area Residents
1980: 275,000
1990: 282,912
2000: 322,959

Percent change, 1990–2000: 14.2%
U.S. rank in 1980: 115th
U.S. rank in 1990: 119th
U.S. rank in 2000: 123rd

City Residents

1980: 105,624
1990: 112,733
2000: 137,893
2003 estimate: 142,185
Percent change, 1990–2000: 21.1%
U.S. rank in 1980: 151st
U.S. rank in 1990: 159th (State rank: 2nd)
U.S. rank in 2000: 160th (State rank: 2nd)

Density: 3,403.2 people per square mile (2000)

Racial and ethnic characteristics (2000)
  White: 121,546
  Black or African American: 1,729
  American Indian and Alaskan Native: 1,281
  Asian: 4,916
  Native Hawaiian and Other Pacific Islander: 294
  Hispanic or Latino (may be of any race): 6,843
  Other: 3,003

Percent of residents born in state: 40.8% (2000)

Age characteristics (2000)
  Population under 5 years old: 7,367
  Population 5 to 9 years old: 7,550
  Population 10 to 14 years old: 8,029
  Population 15 to 19 years old: 11,585
  Population 20 to 24 years old: 17,390
  Population 25 to 34 years old: 20,591
  Population 35 to 44 years old: 18,656
  Population 45 to 54 years old: 20,184
  Population 55 to 59 years old: 5,864
  Population 60 to 64 years old: 4,020
  Population 65 to 74 years old: 7,252
  Population 75 to 84 years old: 6,677
  Population 85 years and over: 2,728
  Median age: 33.0 years

Births (2003)
  Total number: 3,754

Deaths (2003)
  Total number: 2,715 (of which, 30 were infants under
    the age of 1 year)

Money income (1999)
  Per capita income: $21,315
  Median household income: $35,850
  Total households: 57,996

Number of households with income of . . .

less than $10,000: 7,952
$10,000 to $14,999: 4,257
$15,000 to $24,999: 8,267
$25,000 to $34,999: 7,882
$35,000 to $49,999: 9,681
$50,000 to $74,999: 9,698
$75,000 to $99,999: 4,673
$100,000 to $149,999: 3,423
$150,000 to $199,999: 961
$200,000 or more: 1,202

Percent of families below poverty level: 8.7% (25.5% of
  which were female householder families with related
  children under 5 years)

2002 FBI Crime Index Total: 9,382

Municipal Government

Eugene operates under a council-manager form of government with a mayor and eight council members elected in
non-partisan elections for four years. Half the council is
elected every two years. The council hires the city manager.

Head Official: Mayor Kitty Piercy (D) (since 2005; current
  term expires January 2009)

Total Number of City Employees: 1,465 (2003)

City Information: Eugene City Hall, 777 Pearl Street,
Eugene, OR 97401; telephone (541)682-5010; email
webweaver@ci.eugene.or.us

Economy

Major Industries and Commercial Activity

Lumber is the largest industry in the Eugene area, where a
number of manufacturing concerns produce lumber and
wood products. The region is the nation's largest producer of
softwood lumber and plywood products, although weak
prices in the early 2000s have hurt the industry somewhat.
Agriculture ranks second to the wood industry in the local
economy, with a wide variety of crops grown. The Willamette Valley wine industry is a growing sector of the
economy. A sizable food processing industry has grown up
around the agricultural activity, and the area has seen recent
growth in the RV manufacturing industry, such as the arrival
of Legacy Coach to produce high-end luxury motor coaches.

Eugene serves central and southern Oregon as a retail and wholesale trade center. Services, government, and tourism are also contributors to the overall economy.

Items and goods produced: lumber, recreational vehicles, canned fruits and vegetables, dairy and meat products, chickens and chicken fryers, sheep, grass seed, metals, machinery, compact discs, computer software, plastics, electronic instruments, computer memory disks, sport and pleasure boats.

Incentive Programs—New and Existing Companies

In recent years the emphasis in the Willamette Valley has switched from business recruitment to business retention and expansion programs designed to help resident companies "stay put and stay healthy." Among the many incentives available to businesses in Eugene are financial programs offered at the local level, such as the Eugene Business Development Funds; and at the state level, such as the Oregon Research & Technology Development Accounts and the Brownfields Redevelopment Fund. Other incentives include enterprise zones, new construction exemptions, and tax credits. Workforce incentive programs include employee recruiting, screening, and evaluating; customized training at Lane Community College; on-the-job training reimbursement; and certification services.

Job training programs—The state of Oregon's education program consists of a statewide apprenticeship program and has students choose between job training or a college preparatory program after the tenth grade. The program is to be installed in stages in schools through the year 2010. The Employer Workforce Training Fund is an Oregon grant program for employers wanting to upgrade the skills of their employees to the trade or healthcare sectors. The Lane Workforce Partnership oversees programs based on those grants, and also runs the JOBS Welfare-to-Work program. WorkSource Oregon centers not only help match employees and their skills's with employers, but also help bring workers to training programs, such as those at Lane Community College.

Development Projects

Aggressive efforts to diversify the local economy have resulted in several industrial expansions in the area; software development, RV manufacturing, and environmental technology-related fields are especially high-growth businesses. Royal Caribbean Cruise Lines will build a 200,000-square-foot national customer service center in the Eugene-Springfield area starting in 2005. Construction is planned to begin in 2006 on the new research center for the Oregon Nanoscience and Microtechnologies Institute by the University of Oregon campus. The city of Eugene has been upgrading its emergency services with the new down-

town Fire Station 1 at a cost of $5.1 million, and a $2.8 million Firehouse 11, both of which opened in 2005. Also in 2005 construction began on the Lane County Armed Forces Reserve Center in Springfield, the total cost of which is $32 million. The University of Oregon is restoring Reser Stadium, home of the Beavers football team, for $80 million, adding amenities and expanding seating to 55,000.

Economic Development Information: Eugene Area Chamber of Commerce, 1401 Willamette Street, Eugene, OR 97401; telephone (541)484-1314; fax (541)484-4942. Lane Metro Partnership, PO Box 10398, Eugene, OR 97440; telephone (541)686-2741; fax (541)686-2325; email business@lanemetro.com. Oregon Employment Department, 875 Union Street N.E., Salem, OR 97301; telephone (503)378-4824; toll-free (800)237-3710; email info@emp.state.or.us

Commercial Shipping

A number of air-freight services operate out of Eugene Airport, notably Alaska/Horizon. More than 50 interstate truck carriers serve metropolitan Eugene and the West Coast via Interstate 5. Eugene is close to three deep-water ports, including the Port of Portland and the International Port of Coos Bay, for shipping to Asia. The Union Pacific and Burlington Northern railroads run through the area for shipping goods throughout North America.

Labor Force and Employment Outlook

Eugene boasts a skilled labor force with a good work ethic and low turnover rates. One third of the adult population has had four or more years of college. The city is the hub of one of the country's top 100 industrial areas. Continued growth is forecast in non-lumber manufacturing sectors, such as electronic and biotech technologies.

The following is a summary of data regarding the Eugene-Springfield metropolitan area labor force, 2004 annual averages.

Size of non-agricultural labor force: 143,500

Number of workers employed in . . .
   natural resources and mining: 1,000
   construction: 6,700
   manufacturing: 19,300
   trade, transportation and utilities: 26,700
   information: 3,300
   financial activities: 7,700
   professional and business services: 15,500
   educational and health services: 18,600
   leisure and hospitality: 13,600
   other services: 4,900
   government: 26,200

Average hourly earnings of production workers employed in manufacturing: $14.89

Unemployment rate: 6.5% (February 2005)

Largest county employers	Number of employees
PeaceHealth Oregon	4,125
University of Oregon	3,760
Monaco Coach Corp.	2,200
U.S. Government	2,000
Lane Community College	2,000
Lane County	1,786
Eugene School District 4J	1,651
Springfield School District	1,500
City of Eugene	1,465
McKenzie-Willamette Medical Center	1,200

Cost of Living

The Chamber of Commerce describes Eugene housing as "plentiful, varied and built to last." Eugene is the center of many environmentally friendly housing construction projects and developments. The Chamber reported that the average home sale price in 2003 was almost $169,000. The average rental price of a 3-bedroom home was $900-$1200 per month and the average 2-bedroom apartment/duplex rented for $575-760 per month in 2003.

The following is a summary of data regarding key cost of living factors for the Eugene area.

2004 ACCRA Average House Price: Not reported

2004 ACCRA Cost of Living Index: Not reported

State income tax rate: Ranges from 5.0% to 9.0%

State sales tax rate: None

Local income tax rate: None

Local sales tax rate: None

Property tax rate: Real Property tax rate for the city of Eugene is $5 to $10 per $1,000 assessed valuation (2005)

Economic Information: Eugene Area Chamber of Commerce, 1401 Willamette Street, Eugene, OR 97401; telephone (541)484-1314; fax (541)484-4942. Lane Metro Partnership, PO Box 10398, Eugene, OR 97440; telephone (541) 686-2741; fax 686-2325; email business@lanemetro.com. Oregon Employment Department, 875 Union Street N.E., Salem, OR 97301; telephone (503)378-4824 or (800) 237-3710; email info@emp.state.or.us

Education and Research

Elementary and Secondary Schools

Oregon Schools were rated fifth best in the nation by the Midwestern Research Institute. Eugene is home to three school districts, with the largest being Eugene School District 4J, which is the fourth largest in Oregon. A seven-member board, elected at large, governs the district. The board employs the superintendent.

Alternative public schools include International High School, three foreign language immersion schools (French, Spanish and Japanese), and an arts magnet school. Eugene's public school students consistently score higher on standardized tests than the state and national averages.

The following is a summary of data regarding Eugene public schools.

Total enrollment: 18,735

Number of facilities
  elementary schools: 26
  middle schools: 8
  senior high schools: 4
  other: 18 alternative schools

Student/teacher ratio: 22.7:1

Teacher salaries (2004–2005)
  minimum: $37,097
  maximum: $86,075

Funding per pupil: $7,100 (2002–2003)

Eugene is also served by three private high schools and 15 other private schools from Pre-K to grade 8, including religious and special education centers for all students, the gifted, and the physically and mentally challenged.

Public Schools Information: School District 4J, Eugene Public Schools, 200 North Monroe, Eugene, OR 97402-4295; telephone (541)687-3321

Colleges and Universities

The University of Oregon, a major research and educational institution with an enrollment of about 20,000 students, is located in Eugene. The university has schools in the arts and sciences, architecture, business, music, education, journalism and law. Lane Community College offers two-year associate and vocational degrees, serving almost 35,000 students in both credit and non-credit course study. Gutenberg College offers liberal arts education from a Protestant Christian base. Other educational institutions in Eugene are Northwest Christian College, Eugene Bible College, Oregon Business College, and the National Academy of Artistic Gymnastics.

Libraries and Research Centers

The Eugene Public Library consists of three locations: the Downtown Library, the Bethel Branch, and the Sheldon Branch. The system contains more than 360,000 items including books, periodical subscriptions, CDs, DVDs, audio and video tapes, and art reproductions. The library's special collections include fine children's literature and a state documents department. The University of Oregon's Knight Library holds 2.1 million volumes, more than 21,000 periodical subscriptions, and special collections on the American West, American missions and missionaries, Esperanto, Oriental literature and art, politics, and zeppelins. Other libraries at the university specialize in law, architecture, science, and mathematics. Northwest Christian College's library holds 65,000 volumes and Lane Community College holds 60,000 volumes.

Research activities in such fields as the environment, botany of the Pacific Northwest, molecular biology, marine biology, cellular biology, neuroscience, materials science, solar energy, chemical physics, applied materials, forest industries, labor, industrial relations, work organizations, ocean and coastal law, women and gender roles, human development, communication, recreation, mental retardation, and mass communications are conducted at centers in the Eugene area primarily through the University of Oregon. Technicians at Eugene's Riverfront Research Park engage in industrial research and development, data processing, and computer software development. The Southern Willamette Research Corridor, also in Eugene, is a 40-mile research, development, and specialized manufacturing site that facilitates cooperative ventures between area colleges and universities, industry, and local government.

Public Library Information: Eugene Public Library, 100 West 10th Avenue, Eugene, OR 97401; telephone (541)682-5450

Health Care

Two major hospitals serve Eugene. The largest is Sacred Heart General Hospital, with 432 beds and 57 intensive care units. The largest hospital between Portland and San Francisco, it is a general-care facility that features an intensive-care newborn unit, a cancer care unit, a state-of-the-art heart center, and orthopedics and rehabilitation services. The McKenzie-Willamette Medical Center is a full-care hospital and Level III Trauma Center containing 114 beds and 13 mother/newborn units; it offers short-stay surgery and home care services. Nearly 500 physicians and surgeons serve the

area, representing 46 fields and 12 surgical specialties. Traditional and alternative physical and mental health care services are offered at area clinics.

Health Care Information: Sacred Heart Medical Center, 1255 Hilyard St., Eugene, OR 97401-3718; telephone (541) 686-7300. McKenzie-Willamette Medical Center, 1460 G Street, Springfield, OR 97477; telephone (541) 726-4400

Recreation

Sightseeing

Eugene's Willamette River banks are lined with miles of paths and a number of picnic areas and scenic parks, including the 5-acre Owen Memorial Rose Garden. The Hendricks Park Rhododendron Garden features more than 6,000 rhododendrons and azaleas. Culminating at Spencer Butte, the city's highest point, the South Hills Ridgeline Trail showcases a variety of plants and wildlife. The Mount Pisgah Arboretum has trails throughout its 209 acres and multiple habitats. Tours of many historic homes and buildings, such as the Shelton McMurphey Johnson House from 1888, are also available in Eugene.

The surrounding area offers a number of attractions, such as scenic drives, a national park, wildlife and natural areas, mine and winery tours, and historic sites.

Arts and Culture

Eugene has a large and varied arts community. Companies that perform music include the Eugene Symphony, the Eugene Opera Company, the Oregon Mozart Players, the Oregon Festival of American Music, and the Eugene Youth Symphony; all these groups call the Hult Center for the Performing Arts home. The Shedd Institute is home to the Oregon Festival of American Music, which runs year round and features an eclectic variety of performers. Summer music concerts are held at the Cuthbert Amphitheatre in Alton Baker Park. The McDonald Theater, a historic restored movie house, presents touring and local musicians and performers.

The Eugene Ballet performs several times during the year at the Hult Center. The Actor's Cabaret of Eugene has been presenting plays and musicals since 1979. The Very Little Theatre is a volunteer community theater group that dates back to 1929. The Lord Leebrick Theatre Company presents five plays a year. The Hult Center is also home to the Wilamette Repertory Theatre.

The University of Oregon Natural History Museum contains exhibits in archeology, paleontology, and zoology. The Science Factory Children's Museum and Planetarium, formerly

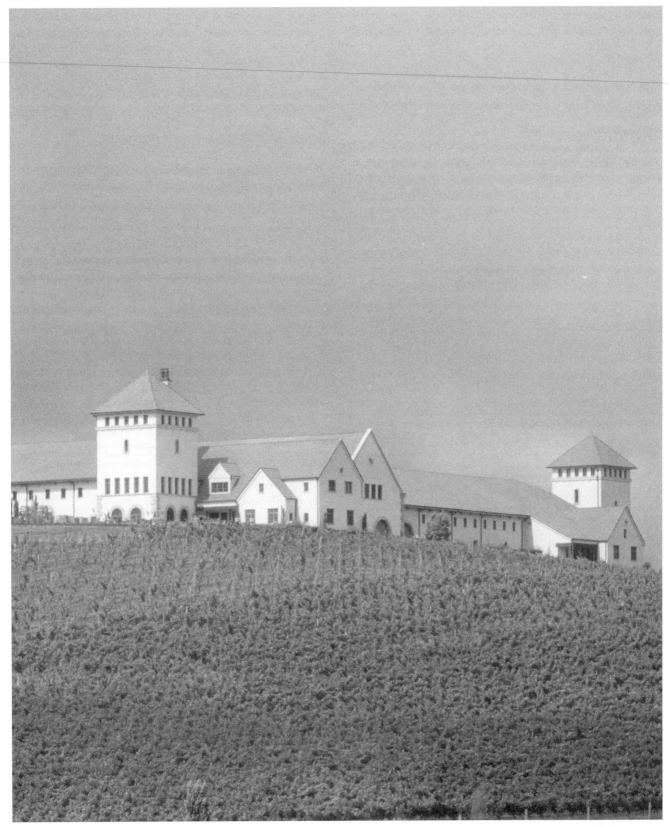

Many wineries around Eugene are open to the public.

the Willamette Science and Technology Center, re-opened in 2002 and has 50 interactive exhibits and planetarium shows. Relics and memorabilia pertaining to the history of the Eugene area can be viewed at the Lane County Historical Museum. The Maude Kerns Art Center displays a number of works by local artists as well as traveling exhibits. The University of Oregon's Jordan Schnitzer Museum of Art reopened in 2005 with a new addition that doubled the size of the museum. It houses a famous collection of Asian Art and hosts numerous special exhibits each year.

Festivals and Holidays

The Oregon Bach Festival is an annual highlight of Eugene's special events calendar. Held for two weeks in late June and early July, the festival is hosted on the University of Oregon campus and at the Hult Center. It features performances by internationally acclaimed soloists and orchestral, choral, and chamber music groups interpreting the compositions of eighteenth-century German composer Johann Sebastian Bach. Eugene also celebrates with a Folk Festival in May, a Country Fair in July, and Eugene Celebration, taking place for three days beginning in late September.

Sports for the Spectator

Professional baseball is represented in Eugene by the minor league Eugene Emeralds, a Class A farm club for the Chicago Cubs, who play at Civic Stadium. The University of Oregon fields teams in every major sport, competing at the National Collegiate Athletic Association (NCAA) Division I level; games are played at the 10,000-seat MacArthur Court and at the 42,000-seat Autzen Stadium, while track and field events take place at Hayward Field. Eugene is also a major center of track and field events, hosting the National Track and Field Championships on a regular basis.

Sports for the Participant

A wide range of outdoor recreation activities are available in and around Eugene, located only 60 miles away from either the mountains or the ocean. The Cascade Mountains offer opportunities for winter skiing and summer hiking, camping, and rafting. The glacier-fed McKenzie and Willamette rivers offer water sports such as fishing, boating, and kayaking. The city maintains nearly 2,000 acres of park land, with jogging trails, bike paths, pools, 24 athletic fields, 23 tennis courts, bowling alleys, a roller rink, an outdoor skateboard facility, and a major lighted softball complex. Emerald KIDSPORTS provides nearly 24,000 young people with organized sports programs such as soccer, baseball, softball, football, basketball, and volleyball.

Shopping and Dining

Valley River Center is an enclosed mall with 145 retail, food, and specialty businesses. The Fifth Street Public Market is a collection of specialty and craft shops and restaurants, and hosts musicians, artists, and special events. Boutiques can be found in Eugene Downtown. Saturday Market, an open-air market featuring fresh produce, handcrafted goods, and ethnic foods, is open from April to Christmas. Gateway Mall, in nearby Springfield, has 80 stores and a 29-screen movie theater. Hundreds of area restaurants present fresh Oregon salmon, lamb, wines, apples, pears, and berries among their offerings. Coffee shops and cafes abound.

Visitor Information: Convention and Visitors Association of Lane County Oregon, 754 Olive St., Eugene OR 97401; telephone (541)484-5307; toll-free (800)547- 5445; fax (541)343-6335; email info@cvalco.org

Convention Facilities

The Lane County Convention Center/Fairgrounds in Eugene offers a convention center, an equestrian and livestock pavilion, a state-of-the-art ice arena, 2,500 parking spaces, and full catering service. Other Eugene venues include the City Conference Center, the Hult Center for the Performing Arts, the Florence Events Center in Florence, Oregon, the Valley River Inn and Convention Center, and the McKenzie River Conference Center. In addition, there are numerous hotels, motels, resorts, lodges, and conference facilities throughout Lane County, including the Hilton Eugene & Conference Center, one of the largest convention centers between San Francisco and Portland. It offers 30,000 square feet of meeting and exhibit space ranging from intimate boardrooms to convention halls and ballrooms. The Eugene/Springfield metropolitan area offers approximately 3,500 sleeping rooms.

Convention Information: Convention and Visitors Association of Lane County Oregon, 754 Olive St., Eugene OR 97401; telephone (541)484-5307; toll-free (800)547- 5445; fax (541)343-6335; email info@cvalco.org

Transportation

Approaching the City

Eugene Airport is located 9 miles north of Eugene by Interstate 5, and is served by 4 major air carriers on 30 flights daily. Amtrak provides passenger rail service north to Vancouver on the Amtrak Cascades Line, and south to Los Angeles on the Coast Starlight.

The major north-south route from Canada to Mexico along the West Coast, I-5, runs through Eugene. U.S. 126 connects the city with the Pacific coast and eastern Oregon.

Traveling in the City

Public transportation is provided by Lane Transit District buses to all parts of the city and to some rural areas. The system provides convenient stops at schools and downtown, and is 100 percent wheelchair accessible. The city maintains miles of off-street bike paths and on-street bike lanes.

Communications

Newspaper and Magazines

Eugene is served by one daily morning newspaper, *The Register-Guard* (Oregon's second-largest daily), *Eugene Weekly,* a Thursday paper presenting arts and entertainment information along with news, and by several smaller neighborhood and special-interest weekly newspapers. The University of Oregon publishes the *Oregon Daily Emerald.* Magazines published in Eugene include *Skipping Stones,* an international, multicultural magazine for children; *Alternatives*, an environmental and political quarterly, *Oregon Voice,* a general interest magazine by students from the University of Oregon, and several scholarly journals.

Television and Radio

Three television stations broadcasting from Eugene offer ABC and CBS, and commercial/religious programming. Five AM and eight FM radio stations broadcast music, information, Christian and sports programs from Eugene, and many other stations are received from other communities in the metropolitan area.

Media Information: The Register-Guard, 3500 Chad Drive, PO Box 10188, Eugene, OR 97440-2188; telephone (541)485-1234

Eugene Online

City of Eugene home page. Available www.ci.eugene.or.us

Convention & Visitors Association of Lane County Oregon. Available www.cvalco.org

Eugene Area Chamber of Commerce. Available www .eugenechamber.com

Eugene Public Library. Available www.ci.eugene.or.us/ Library/index.html

Eugene School District 4J. Available www.4j.lane.edu

Lane Metro Partnership. Available www.lanemetro.com

Oregon Economic Development Department. Available www.econ.state.or.us

The Register-Guard. Available www.registerguard.com

Portland

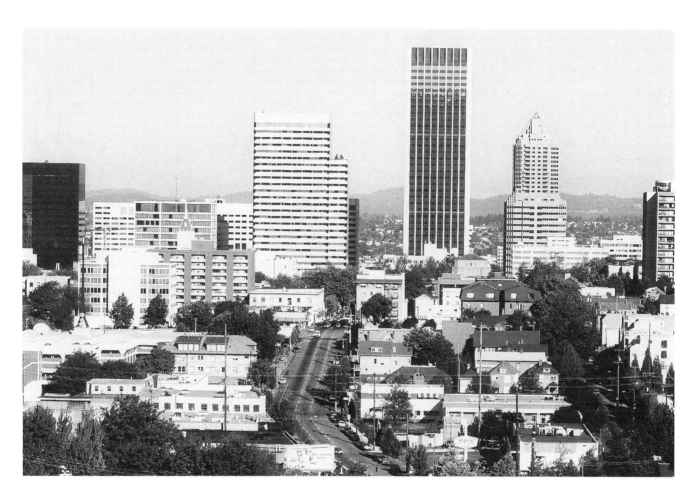

The City in Brief

Founded: 1845 (incorporated 1851)

Head Official: Mayor Tom Potter (D) (since 2005)

City Population
1980: 366,383
1990: 485,975
2000: 529,121
2003 estimate: 538,544
Percent change, 1990–2000: 8.9%
U.S. rank in 1980: 35th
U.S. rank in 1990: 30th
U.S. rank in 2000: 35th

Metropolitan Area Population (PMSA)
1980: 1,106,000
1990: 1,515,452
2000: 1,874,449
Percent change, 1990–2000: 12.1%
U.S. rank in 1980: 26th (CMSA)
U.S. rank in 1990: 27th (CMSA)
U.S. rank in 2000: 23rd (CMSA)

Area: 130 square miles (2000)
Elevation: Averages 173 feet above sea level
Average Annual Temperature: 53.4° F
Average Annual Precipitation: 40.5 inches

Major Economic Sectors: Services, trade, manufacturing, government
Unemployment Rate: 6.6% (January 2005)
Per Capita Income: $22,643 (2000)

2002 FBI Crime Index Total: 43,327

Major Colleges and Universities: Portland State University, Oregon Health Sciences University, Reed College, Lewis & Clark College, University of Portland, Marylhurst University

Daily Newspaper: *The Oregonian*

KILOMETERS

MILES

N

VANCOUVER, WA.

FORT VANCOUVER NAT'L HISTORIC SITE

MILL PLAIN

HAYDEN ISLAND

COLUMBIA RIVER

SMITH LAKE

MARINE

GOVERNMENT ISLAND

FOREST PARK

PORTLAND ROAD

BY PASS

WILLAMETTE

PORTLAND INTERNATIONAL AIRPORT

COLUMBIA

LOMBARD

UNIVERSITY OF PORTLAND

WILLAMETTE

SWAN ISLAND

PORTLAND BLVD.

PENINSULA PARK ROSE GARDEN

KILLINGSWORTH

WILLAMETTE RIVER

PORTLAND

INTERSTATE AVE.

VANCOUVER

MARTIN LUTHER KING

FREMONT

12TH AVE.

33RD AVE.

42ND AVE.

82ND AVE.

ALAMEDA

SANDY

U.S. CUSTOM HOUSE

BURNSIDE

MARITIME CTR.

WASHINGTON

ADLER

PARK

BROADWAY

S.W. 11TH AVE.

S.W. 10TH AVE.

S.W. 6TH AVE.

S.W. 5TH AVE.

S.W. 3RD AVE.

S.W. 2ND AVE.

S.W. 1ST AVE.

FRONT

MORRISON BRIDGE

N

COURT HOUSE

LIBRARY

MAIN

ART MUSEUM

MADISON

JEFFERSON

OREGON HISTORY CENTER

COLUMBIA

HAWTHORNE BRIDGE

CLAY

PORTLAND STATE UNIV.

MARKET

DOWNTOWN PORTLAND

ROSE QUARTER

MEMORIAL COLISEUM

ROSE GARDEN ARENA

BROADWAY

COLUMBIA CHRISTIAN COLLEGE

MARSHALL

LOVEJOY

UNION STA.

GRAND

BURNSIDE

STARK

STARK

CIVIC STADIUM

BURNSIDE

MORRISON

BELMONT

MT. TABOR PARK

HOYT ARBORETUM

WASHINGTON PARK

DOWNTOWN

BROADWAY

6TH AVE.

HAWTHORNE

39TH AVE.

WARNER PACIFIC COLLEGE

JAPANESE GARDEN

MUSEUM OF SCIENCE & IND.

INT'L ROSE TEST GARDEN

METRO WASHINGTON PARK ZOO

CHILDREN'S MUSEUM 2ND GENERATION

BROADWAY DR.

PORTLAND COMMUNITY COLLEGE

DIVISION

POWELL

BEAVERTON

CANYON

PATTON

SHATTUCK

OREGON HEALTH SCIENCES UNIV.

V.A. HOSP.

TERWILLIGER

ROSS ISLAND

17TH AVE.

26TH AVE.

28TH AVE.

52ND AVE.

82ND AVE.

HOLGATE

REED COLLEGE

CRYSTAL SPRINGS RHODODENDRON GARDENS

HAROLD

DUKE

VERMONT

OAKS AMUSEMENT PARK

TACOMA

MULTNOMAH

LEWIS & CLARK COLLEGE

MILWAUKIE

WA

ID

MT

Portland

OR

WY

LAKE OSWEGO

BOONES FERRY

COUNTRY CLUB

MCLOUGHLIN

RIVERSIDE

CA

NV

UT

CO

LAKE OSWEGO

Introduction

Portland, known as the ''City of Roses,'' is the result of both chance and planning. Having obtained its name by the flip of a coin, the city is today the model of a metropolitan area that has been effectively integrated with its environment through controlled growth and development. Set in the natural beauty of northwest Oregon and lacking such big-city problems as traffic congestion, pollution, and litter, Portland is laced with parks, gardens, and fountains. A deep-water port, international airport, and a diverse economy make Portland a thriving commercial center, but the primary commitment is to preserving the city's individuality, its healthful environment, and its friendly atmosphere.

Geography and Climate

Located 110 miles from the Pacific Ocean, Portland lies between two mountain ranges, the Cascade Range to the east and the lower Coast Range to the west, in the Willamette River valley, one of the world's most fertile river valleys. The city is divided by the Willamette River, which flows into the Columbia River just to the north. Winters are rainy in Portland, with 55 percent of the annual rainfall occurring between the months of November and February, but the marine air keeps temperatures moderate, and the summers are mild, with temperatures rarely over 90 degrees.

Area: 130 square miles (2000)

Elevation: Averages 173 feet above sea level

Average Temperatures: January, 39.4° F; August, 67.3° F; annual average, 53.4° F

Average Annual Precipitation: 40.5 inches

History

The area surrounding present-day Portland was originally inhabited by the Multnomah and Clackamas tribes, who had established several villages by the 1830s. Most of these people died from smallpox epidemics and other diseases. Meriwether Lewis and William Clark were the first settlers of European descent to travel through the Portland area during their 1806 expedition. Clark named the Willamette River after the Multnomah village he found on Sauvie Island.

The future site of Portland was originally a clearing in the woods, appropriately known as ''The Clearing,'' where Native Americans and traders stopped to rest on trips between Oregon City and Fort Vancouver. The land underwent a series of ownerships until Amos Lovejoy and Francis Pettygrove bought it and mapped out a town called ''Stumptown'' in 1845. Four years later the two men, Lovejoy from Boston and Pettygrove from Portland, Maine, decided to flip a coin to determine the town's new name. Pettygrove won and the town became Portland.

Portland grew steadily through the California gold rush, reporting a population of 821 residents, a post office, and a newspaper—the *Weekly Oregonian*—in the 1850 census. Portland was incorporated in 1851 and became the seat of newly created Washington County (later renamed Multnomah County) in 1854. That same year the town advanced toward becoming a major trade center when its harbor was selected as the West Coast terminal for *The Petonia,* the U.S. mail steamer. Prior to the Civil War the salmon industry began to grow, enhancing Portland's economic status. The city experienced catastrophe when, in 1872 and 1873, the downtown area was heavily damaged by fire; civic leaders subsequently decided to rebuild only with cast iron, brick, and stone. The construction of the first transcontinental railroad in 1883, linking Portland with the East Coast, brought renewed prosperity. By the turn of the century the population had grown to 90,000 people.

Portland continued to expand steadily through the early decades of the twentieth century; the Alaska gold rush, the 1905 Lewis and Clark Centennial Exposition, and the construction of the Bonneville Dam in the 1930s were important factors in its growth. During World War II the city was a ship-building and manufacturing center.

In the 1960s and 1970s Portland's city leaders were able to avoid problems experienced by other large metropolitan areas through economic diversification, controlled growth, and environmental planning. A precedent had already been set by early planners who had integrated parks and green spaces into the city's lay-out; later, city planners instituted an ordinance to protect scenic views. Local government continues to work on the Region 2040 growth plan to manage all aspects of growth in the metropolitan area to the year 2040. In 2005, Mayor Tom Potter took office with the goal of continuing to move Portland forward.

Historical Information: Oregon Historical Society Regional Research Library, 1200 SW Park Avenue, Portland, OR 97204; telephone (503)222-1741

Population Profile

Metropolitan Area Residents (PMSA)

1980: 1,106,000
1990: 1,515,452
2000: 1,874,449
Percent change, 1990–2000: 23.7%
U.S. rank in 1980: 26th (CMSA)
U.S. rank in 1990: 27th (CMSA)
U.S. rank in 2000: 23rd (CMSA)

City Residents

1980: 366,383
1990: 485,975
2000: 529,121
2003 estimate: 538,544
Percent change, 1990–2000: 8.9%
U.S. rank in 1980: 35th
U.S. rank in 1990: 30th (State rank: 1st)
U.S. rank in 2000: 35th

Density: 3,932.2 people per square mile (2000)

Racial and ethnic characteristics (2000)
White: 412,241
Black or African American: 35,115
American Indian and Alaska Native: 5,587
Asian: 33,470
Native Hawaiian and other Pacific Islander: 1,993
Hispanic or Latino (may be of any race): 36,058
Other: 18,760

Percent of residents born in state: 44.0% (2000)

Age characteristics (2000)
Population under 5 years old: 32,300
Population 5 to 9 years old: 31,184
Population 10 to 14 years old: 30,031
Population 15 to 19 years old: 32,046
Population 20 to 24 years old: 40,454
Population 25 to 34 years old: 97,000
Population 35 to 44 years old: 86,604
Population 45 to 54 years old: 78,367
Population 55 to 59 years old: 23,195
Population 60 to 64 years old: 16,777
Population 65 to 74 years old: 28,215
Population 75 to 84 years old: 23,829
Population 85 years and over: 9,119
Median age: 35.2 years

Births (2003)
Total number: 9,340

Deaths (2003)
Total number: 6,859 (of which, 42 were infants under the age of 1 year)

Money income (1999)
Per capita income: $22,643
Median household income: $40,146
Total households: 223,987

Number of households with income of . . .
less than $10,000: 22,245
$10,000 to $14,999: 14,023
$15,000 to $24,999: 29,823
$25,000 to $34,999: 31,186
$35,000 to $49,999: 38,638
$50,000 to $74,999: 44,516
$75,000 to $99,999: 20,667
$100,000 to $149,999: 14,735
$150,000 to $199,999: 3,761
$200,000 or more: 4,393

Percent of families below poverty level: 8.5% (43.6% of which were female householder families with related children under 5 years)

2002 FBI Crime Index Total: 43,327

Municipal Government

Portland is the last large city in the United States to operate under a commission form of government, with five council members, including the mayor, elected to staggered four-year terms. Each member casts an equal vote in council and each undertakes administrative responsibilities for a group of city bureaus. The mayor receives the authority to make budget assignments and traditionally proposes the annual budget for council approval; otherwise, governing power is invested in the council as a whole.

Portland is also home to the nation's only directly elected regional government. The body, known as Metro, controls growth by wielding authority over land use, transportation, and environment.

Head Official: Mayor Tom Potter (D) (since 2005, current term expires 2009)

Total Number of City Employees: 7,659 (2005)

City Information: Portland City Hall, 1221 SW 4th Avenue, Room 110, Portland, Oregon 97204; telephone (503)823-6868; email cityinfo@ci.portland.or.us

Economy

Major Industries and Commercial Activity

Early in its history, Portland's economy was based on the Columbia and Willamette rivers and their access to the Pacific Ocean. The town was a supply hub for area farming communities and a regional shipping center. The deep, fresh-water port helped the city grow into an important part of the growing lumber industry, and a number of manufacturing concerns settled there because of the ease of transportation.

Today, Portland is the third largest export tonnage port on the West Coast, with import and export shipments of $11.8 billion in 2003. Easy access to the north/south and east/west interstate freeway system, international air service, and both west coast intercontinental railroads make Portland an important distribution center.

Portland enjoys a long history of association with high-technology industries, beginning with Tektronix in 1946. There are now more than 1,200 technology companies currently operating in Portland. In 2004, Portland's largest employer was microcomputer components manufacturer Intel Corporation. Well-established support industries and far-sighted commercial planning continue to draw electronics, computer, and other high-technology companies to the area.

Items and goods produced: electronics, machinery, food products, transportation equipment

Incentive Programs—New and Existing Companies

Local programs—World Trade Center Portland assists businesses involved in international trade. Business in Portland allows area businesses to access valuable information to help them succeed, including site location assistance, store-front improvement grants, contract opportunities, and economic and demographic data. The Port of Portland, working with other local and state departments, offers a variety of businesses development and incentive programs, including a Small Business Development Program, a Disadvantaged Business Enterprise Program, and a Mentor Program. The Portland Development Commission administers a variety of programs to assist new, existing, and expanding businesses, such as the new Economic Opportunity Fund and the Enterprise Zone, E-Commerce Zone, Storefront Improvement Program, Quality Jobs Program, Employee Investment Program, and other assistance programs.

State programs—Among the incentives available to businesses in Portland are several financial programs offered at the state level, together with tax incentives, new construction exemptions, and tax credits. These include the Brownfield Redevelopment Fund, Business Development Fund, Capital Access Program, Entrepreneurial Development Loan Fund, and several others. The State's Department of Energy administers a Small Scale Energy Loan, which offers low-interest loans to businesses that save energy or produce energy from renewable resources.

Job training programs—The state of Oregon administers an educational program, the first in the nation, that establishes a statewide apprenticeship program and allows students to choose between job training or a college preparatory program after the tenth grade. The state's JOBS Plus program allows employers who hire a JOBS Plus-eligible worker to receive benefits that include reimbursements, the opportunity to train and evaluate the worker during the contract period, and the opportunity to treat the employee as a temporary employee.

Worksystems, Inc., funds providers of career placement and training services. A network of One Stop Centers offers job-seekers assistance with their career planning and job search activities. Due to an increase in the non-native English speaking population, services are also provided in Spanish, Russian, Vietnamese, and Chinese.

Development Projects

In 1999 the North Macadam Urban Renewal Plan was adopted by the City Council. The plan seeks to develop vacant and underdeveloped land in the North Macadam area. Technical, environmental, and transportation difficulties had prevented previous efforts to develop the land. Redevelopment efforts have focused on providing transportation connections, space for housing and businesses, and greenway and open space connections. In 2005, development efforts were still ongoing.

In 2004 the Portland Development Commission, Metropolitan Exposition Recreation Commission, and Portland Oregon Visitors Association began to solicit proposals from vendors to construct a Headquarters Hotel adjacent to the Oregon Convention Center. It is hoped that the hotel, when completed in 2008, will attract larger conventions and trade shows to the Convention Center, add jobs to the Portland workforce, and increase tax revenues.

In 2005 construction began to make improvements on NW Third and Fourth Avenues between Burnside and Glisan Streets, which encompasses the Old Town/Chinatown area. The project is a partnership between the Portland Development Commission and the Portland Office of Transportation. The $5.35 million project will include improvements to streets and sidewalks, installation of trees and streetlights, and public art.

Economic Development Information: Portland Business Alliance, 520 SW Yamhill Street, Portland, OR 97204; telephone (503)224-8684; fax (503)323-9186; email info @portlandalliance.com

Commercial Shipping

Portland's comprehensive transportation system comprises ocean shipping, transcontinental railways and highways, river barging, and a major international airport. The shipping industry is keyed to a lifeline of ship, rail, air, and truck service. Both West Coast transcontinental railroads and 110 trucking lines provide shippers with options for moving cargo. At the Port of Portland's five marine terminals, container ships, grain ships, bulk and breakbulk carriers, and auto carriers work around the clock. The Port of Portland leads the nation in wheat exports and is ranked fourth in the nation for auto imports. In addition, barges ply the Columbia/Snake river system, the second largest waterway in the nation, feeding the Port's Terminal 6 from as far upriver as Lewiston, Idaho, more than 300 river miles away. Foreign Trade Zone #45, administered by the Port of Portland, provides an additional incentive for international trade activity.

Labor Force and Employment Outlook

The work force in Portland is well-educated and very stable. The job turnover rate is low and productivity is high, compared to other metropolitan areas. The unemployment rate has remained below the national average for several years.

The following is a summary of data regarding the Portland-Vancouver metropolitan area labor force, 2004 annual averages.

Size of non-agricultural labor force: 946,100

Number of workers employed in . . .
  construction and mining: 55,000
  manufacturing: 119,900
  trade, transportation and utilities: 193,500
  information: 22,500
  financial activities: 65,600
  professional and business services: 121,200
  educational and health services: 115,300
  leisure and hospitality: 87,599
  other services: 34,600
  government: 130,900

Average hourly earnings of production workers employed in manufacturing: $15.84

Unemployment rate: 6.6% (January 2005)

Largest employers	*Number of employees*
Intel Corporation	14,890
Providence Health System	13,496
Oregon Health and Science University	11,400

Largest employers	*Number of employees*
Fred Meyer Stores	10,500
Legacy Health System	7,972
Kaiser Foundation	6,731
Safeway Inc.	6,000
NIKE Inc.	5,742
Albertson's Food Centers	5,600
U.S. Bank	4,138

Cost of Living

The following is a summary of data regarding key cost of living factors for the Portland area.

2004 (3rd Quarter) ACCRA Average House Price: $292,952

2004 (3rd Quarter) ACCRA Cost of Living Index: 113.2 (U.S. average = 100.0)

State income tax rate: Ranges from 5.0% to 9.0%

State sales tax rate: None

Local income tax rate: None

Local sales tax rate: None

Property tax rate: ranges from $14.00 to $20.30 per $1,000 assessed value (Multnomah County, 2004–2005)

Economic Information: Portland Business Alliance, 520 S.W. Yamhill Street, Portland, OR 97204; telephone (503)224-8604; fax (503)323-9186. Oregon Employment Department, 875 Union Street N.E., Salem, OR 97301; telephone (800)237-3710; email info@emp.state.or.us

Education and Research

Elementary and Secondary Schools

Portland is served by five school districts. The Portland Public School District, the largest in the state of Oregon, is governed by a nonpartisan, seven-member board that appoints a superintendent. Special programs offered by the district include a gifted and talented program, summer school remedial and enrichment classes, special education, and career education. Magnet schools in the district offer dual language immersion programs in Spanish, Japanese, and Chinese; a living history curriculum; schools for the performing arts; and early intervention programs.

The following is a summary of data regarding Portland's public schools as of the 2004–2005 school year.

Total enrollment: 53,000

Number of facilities
   elementary schools: 60
   middle schools: 18
   senior high schools: 16
   other: 4 (plus many contract education programs)

Student/staff ratio: 30:1

Teacher salaries
   minimum: $29,013
   maximum: $60,976

Funding per pupil: $7,242 (2002-2003, state of Oregon)

A variety of private education options exist in the Portland metro area, including the well-known Oregon Episcopal School and The Catlin Gabel School. Three Catholic high schools, several Montessori and Waldorf schools, and arts-centered schools serve the area's students.

Public Schools Information: Portland Public Schools, 501 North Dixon, Portland, OR 97227; telephone (503)916-2000; email pubinfo@pps.k12.or.us

Colleges and Universities

Portland is home to several accredited institutions of higher education. Concordia College is a private four-year college affiliated with the Lutheran Church-Missouri Synod offering bachelor's degrees in business administration, education, health and social sciences, liberal arts, theological studies, and environmental remediation. Lewis & Clark College, founded by Presbyterian pioneers, offers 26 majors and 23 minor programs. Marylhurst University is a private institution offering coursework leading to master's and bachelor's degrees to students of all ages. Oregon Health Sciences University houses schools of medicine, nursing, and dentistry, and is Oregon's only academic health center.

Portland State University offers strong liberal arts and sciences programs to augment its concentration on engineering, computer science, international trade, and business. Reed College is an independent liberal arts and sciences college. The University of Portland, a Catholic university, offers 60 majors and 12 graduate degrees in its College of Arts and Sciences and four professional schools (Business, Education, Engineering, and Nursing). Based in the Portland metropolitan area is the Oregon Graduate Institute of Science and Technology.

Libraries and Research Centers

The Multnomah County Library, the oldest public library west of the Mississippi, maintains a Central Library and 16 other branches throughout the metropolitan area. Total holdings include more than 2 million items including books, periodicals, videos, audio cassettes, compact discs, films, rec-

ords, and maps. The County Library and its branches together host more than 450 computer work stations. The Multnomah County Library is Oregon's largest public library system.

Area universities also offer extensive library services, and there are a number of special interest and research libraries in the area, serving science, industry, and business interests. Oregon Health Sciences University is where both the artificial heart valve and cardiac angioplasty were developed; research there continues to be the catalyst for clinical and educational advancements in heart treatment. Cancer research in the areas of cancer biology, hematologic malignancies, solid tumors, and cancer prevention and control is also performed at Oregon Health Sciences University. The Vollum Institute for Advanced Biomedical Research studies brain function at the molecular level. At Oregon Medical Laser Center, researchers study the use of lasers in medicine. Other areas of medical research include cancer research at the Robert W. Franz Cancer Research Center and multidisciplinary research at the Earl A. Chiles Research Institute. Research activities in such fields as public health, computing and information systems, nuclear science, urban studies, population and census, sociology, psychology, aging, human services, and the Middle East are conducted at other centers in the Portland area.

Public Library Information: Multnomah County Library, 801 SW Tenth Avenue, Portland, OR 97205; telephone (503)988-5123

Health Care

Portland is the center for health care in the state of Oregon, with major hospitals collaborating to offer quality care at a moderate cost. Playing a prominent role is the Oregon Health & Science University (OHSU), which includes the University Hospital and Doernbecher Children's Hospital as well as the Casey Eye Institute, the Child Development and Rehabilitation Center, 9 primary care clinics, more than 150 specialty clinics, and dental clinics. OHSU also operates four interdisciplinary centers that focus on aging, women's health, cancer, and interventional therapy. OHSU shares technology, personnel, and training with the Portland Veterans Affairs Medical Center to help keep health care costs down. Residents who seek nontraditional medical treatment have access to licensed acupuncturists and to practitioners trained at a local naturopathic college. Senior services are coordinated by the Multnomah County Aging Services Division to help senior citizens remain active in the community. Providence Health Services operates seven hospitals and medical centers in the Portland metro area. In 2003, Providence Newberg Hospital, Providence Milwaukie Hospital, and Providence St. Vincent

Medical Center were named among the top 100 hospitals in the nation—and the only hospitals in Oregon—by research company Solucient. One of the Portland area's top employers, Providence hospitals specialize in cancer care, rehabilitation, cardiac care, children's emergency care, surgical services, sports medicine, and maternity care.

Recreation

Sightseeing

Portland offers sightseeing attractions both in the city itself and in the surrounding area. A walking tour of downtown encompasses two separate national historical districts, including the largest preserved example of nineteenth-century cast iron architecture in the West, and a number of other nineteenth-century landmarks intermixed with distinctive modern buildings. The controversial Portland Building is the first major post-modern architectural structure in the country. The award-winning Pioneer Courthouse Square bustles with activity from outdoor art exhibits, concerts, and sidewalk vendors.

Portland is proud of its outdoor public art and fountains, including Portlandia, a 35-foot tall hammered copper sculpture of a kneeling woman, and Ira's Fountain, a cascading water sculpture dotted with islands and terraces across from the Civic Auditorium. Other attractions include The Grotto, a 60-acre shrine; the Japanese Garden, the most authentic example of Japanese gardens outside of Japan; the International Rose Test Garden; and the Classical Chinese Garden in the Old Town/Chinatown district.

Many other attractions can be found just outside of the city. Vineyards in the Willamette Valley are open to the public for tours and wine tastings. Some of the nation's most beautiful natural scenery can be found around nearby Mount Hood and the Columbia Gorge. Portland is 110 miles away from the Pacific Ocean.

Arts and Culture

The Portland Center for the Performing Arts is the center of art activity in the city presenting more than 900 annual events and featuring the Arlene Schnitzer Concert Hall, Newmark Theatre, Dolores Winningstad Theatre, and Keller Auditorium. Portland's performing arts groups include Oregon Symphony, Portland Opera, Oregon Ballet Theatre, Portland Center State, Portland Youth Philharmonic, Portland Gay Men's Chorus, and Chamber Music Northwest.

The Oregon Historical Society's History Center houses exhibits tracing the history of the Pacific Northwest from prehistoric times to the present. The Oregon Maritime Center and Museum features ship models, navigational instruments, hardware, and historical exhibits. The Oregon Museum of Science and Industry (OMSI), one of the nation's largest, offers hands-on displays pertaining to science, including a walk-in replica of a space station, a planetarium, and a computer center.

Displaying exhibits of commercial memorabilia, the American Advertising Museum specializes in the history of American marketing since 1683. The World Forestry Center has recreational and educational exhibits relating to the forestry industry; a special attraction is a 70-foot talking tree.

The Portland Art Museum, one of the 25 largest museums in the country, houses collections of 35 centuries of world art, including European works from the Renaissance to the present, nineteenth- and twentieth-century American art, and Native American, Asian, and West African art. In 2000 the museum unveiled three new centers in its Millennium Project expansion: the Center for Native American Art, Center for Northwest Art, and the outdoor public sculpture gardens. The most recent project in the expansion program began in February 2004 as renovation and restoration started on the museum's ''North Building,'' a former Masonic Temple acquired in 1991.

The Northwest Film and Video Center features traditional, historical, and experimental exhibits in the media of film and video. One of the oldest nonprofit art galleries in the nation, the Contemporary Crafts Gallery displays artworks in clay, fiber, glass, wood, and metal.

Washington Park is home to many children's attractions, including the Portland Children's Museum. It features hands-on exhibits for children through 10 years of age. The Oregon Zoo, which opened in 1887, houses animals from around the world. The zoo's latest project is a Great Northwest exhibit, which features animals and ecosystems of the Pacific Northwest region. Also of interest to children and book-lovers alike is the Beverly Cleary Sculpture Garden in Grant Park, which showcases bronze statues of Ramona Quimby and Henry Huggins and his dog Ribsy—characters made famous in the Portland author's classic children's books.

Festivals and Holidays

The centerpiece of Portland's special events schedule is the annual Portland Rose Festival, which lasts for 25 days each June. The festival features more than 70 events, including the Grand Floral Parade (second largest all-floral parade in the nation), a waterfront carnival, a juried fine arts festival, and an Indycar race.

Spring and summer bring several area jazz festivals, including the Mt. Hood Jazz Festival in August, which brings

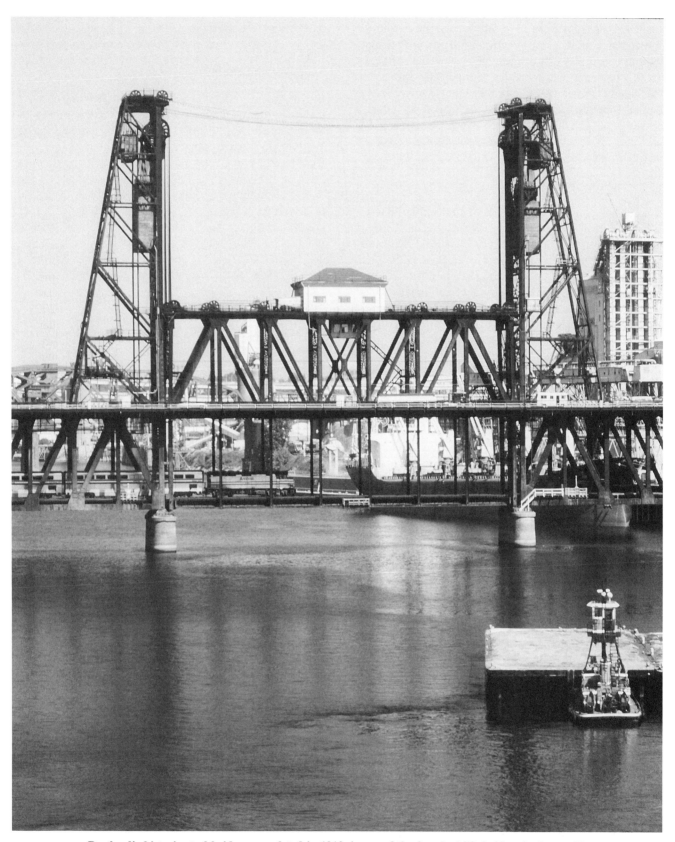

Portland's historic steel bridge, completed in 1912, is one of the few dual-life bridges in the world.

renowned jazz musicians from all over the country to the Portland area. In August, "The Bite: A Taste of Portland" presents a three-day extravaganza of music while Portland's finest restaurants and cafes demonstrate their specialties. The Portland Arts Festival is held in June, followed by the Oregon Brewers Festival in July. The Christmas holidays are highlighted by the spectacular Holiday Parade of Christmas Ships. A variety of festivals and events throughout the year celebrate the region's microbreweries and wineries.

Sports for the Spectator

Professional sports in Portland are led by the National Basketball Association's Portland Trail Blazers, frequent playoff contenders, who play at the Rose Garden arena. Professional minor league baseball is represented by the Portland Beavers, a Triple-A affiliate of the San Diego Padres. The Portland Timbers are Portland's professional soccer franchise and members of the First Division of United Soccer Leagues. Both the Beavers, and the Timbers play their home games at Portland's PGE Park. Hockey action is brought to fans by the Portland Winter Hawks of the Western Hockey League, which is a major source of talent for the National Hockey League. A wide range of other sports activities can be viewed at several of the area's universities.

Portland Meadows features quarterhorse and thoroughbred racing from October through April, and nearby Multnomah Kennel Club provides greyhound racing in an enclosed facility. Stock and Indycar racing take place at the Portland International Raceway. Portland also hosts the Wrangler Rodeo Classic.

Sports for the Participant

Portland offers a variety of ways to satisfy the sporting urge. The mountains provide opportunities for outdoor sports such as rock climbing and hiking. Timberline Lodge, a National Historic Landmark, serves one of Mt. Hood's five ski areas and offers the only lift-serviced summer skiing in the country. Local rivers feature all water sports; the Portland area is a fishing paradise, offering everything from fly fishing for trout in mountain streams and salmon-fishing in the rivers to all-day deep-sea excursions on charter boats. Hood River, Oregon, is a windsurfing mecca on the Columbia Gorge. The Portland Marathon, held in early October, has been ranked as one of the premier marathon events in the country; its 26.2-mile course is open to walkers as well as runners.

The Portland Parks & Recreation department maintains 10,510 acres which include 102 neighborhood parks; more than 160 urban, regional, community and habitat parks and gardens; 4 golf courses; and 50 recreation facilities. Parks range in size from the 4,700-acre Forest Park to Mill Ends Park, the world's smallest park at 36 inches by 36 inches in diameter. Facilities include two amphitheaters; a skateboard park; tennis courts; sports fields; playgrounds; arts, music, and dance centers; and sports, fitness, and arts programming.

Shopping and Dining

Lloyd Center, Portland's first and largest shopping center, is located in the downtown core in the city's northeast section. Here, more than 200 stores surround an indoor ice rink. Washington Square, Jantzen Beach Super Center, and Clackamas Town Center are all located within a 20-minute drive of downtown. The Galleria includes several floors of unique urban shopping and dining. Pioneer Place in the heart of downtown features four city blocks of dining, shopping, entertainment, and the first-ever Sundance Film Center for Independent Film. Powell's City of Books, the world's largest new and used independent bookstore, is located in downtown Portland and stocks more than a million books.

The Skidmore/Old Town National Historic District at the north end of downtown offers many shopping possibilities. The New Market Theatre also houses shops and restaurants. Saturday Market, the largest open-air crafts market in continuous operation in the country, is open Saturday and Sunday, March through December, and features more than 300 vendors. The Water Tower at John's Landing is the home of a unique blend of shops and restaurants. The Sellwood and Hawthorne Boulevard Districts in southeast Portland and the Multnomah District in southwest Portland are favorites of antique hunters.

Portland features a number of restaurants specializing in fresh, grown-in-Oregon foods, as well as spots to sample famous Pacific seafood. The Chinatown district offers regional Chinese cuisine; a large number of other restaurants specialize in many ethnic foods. More than a dozen nationally ranked restaurants emphasize elegance and formal dining, and there are many informal bistros and other places to mix dining with nightlife.

Visitor Information: Portland Oregon Visitors Association, 1000 SW Broadway, Suite 2300, Portland, OR 97205; telephone (503)275-9750; toll-free (800)962-3700; email info @pova.com

Convention Facilities

The Oregon Convention Center, located in the center of downtown along the Willamette River, contains a total of nearly one million square feet of enclosed space, with 255,000 square feet of exhibit space, 50 meeting rooms, two grand ballrooms, and an 800-space parking garage. In 2003, the Oregon Convention Center completed a major expansion that doubled the center's size. Offering greater flexibility and more options than ever before, the Oregon Convention Center is the largest meeting facility in the Pacific Northwest.

The Portland Memorial Coliseum Complex, adjacent to the Convention Center, features 108,000 square feet of exhibit space; 15 meeting rooms, the largest of which is a 25,200 square-foot area; and arena-style seating for 13,000 people.

Portland offers several convention complexes that are all within a few minutes of more than 11,000 hotel rooms. Montgomery Park is a unique trade center located five minutes northwest of downtown Portland. It contains 19,000 square feet of exhibition and meeting space complemented by a 135-foot high glass atrium.

The Portland Center for the Performing Arts's Brunish Hall offers space for 200 people for meetings, conferences, or other events. Other meeting and exhibition facilities include Expo Center and the Washington County FairPlex. Most major hotels in the city offer extensive meeting, banquet, and ballroom facilities.

Convention Information: Portland Oregon Visitors Association, 1000 SW Broadway, Suite 2300, Portland, OR 97205; telephone (503)275-9750 or (800)962-3700, fax (503)275-9284.

Transportation

Approaching the City

Portland's airport, Portland International Airport (PDX), is one of the fastest-growing major airports on the West Coast, with more 17 commercial carriers offering daily nonstop flights from Portland to various destinations; the airport served more than 13 million passengers in 2004. The airport is 9 miles east of the central city, a 15-minute car ride. The Portland International Airport is owned and operated by the Port of Portland.

Two major interstate highways intersect in Portland, I-5, running north-south from southern California into Canada, and I-84, running east-west. U.S. highways 26 and 30 are other east-west routes. Portland is bypassed by I-405, on the western edge of the downtown area, and I-205, running through the eastern suburbs.

Amtrak serves the Portland area with daily train service; commercial bus service is also available.

Traveling in the City

Portland is divided into five areas—southwest, southeast, north, northeast and northwest—with the Willamette River bisecting the city. Street addresses match the location of these areas. A total of eleven bridges cross the river. The major streets are Grand Avenue, Martin Luther King Jr. Blvd., Sandy Boulevard, and SE Eighty-second Street. Downtown, streets are mostly one way, with adjacent streets flowing in opposite directions.

TriMet, Portland's mass transit system, is ultra-modern and efficient, highlighted by MAX, a light-rail system that connects the downtown area with three counties. Westside MAX serves commuters in suburbs west of town as far west as Hillsboro. This line boasts the deepest subterranean transit station in North America, and public artwork decorates all 20 Westside MAX stations. A 300-block area in the heart of downtown has been designated as the Fareless Square, where trips beginning and ending within the area do not require the usual fare. TriMet also has 93 bus lines that serve Multnomah, Clackamas, and Washington counties.

Communications

Newspapers and Magazines

Portland's major daily newspaper, *The Oregonian*, has been in publication since the 1850s. The paper's affiliated website provides news and local coverage online as well as archives to past stories. In 2001, *The Oregonian*, received two Pulitzer Prize medals, for public service and feature writing. *Willamette Week* and many smaller neighborhood weeklies, as well as *The Skanner* and *Portland Observer*, both serving the African American community, are among the other Portland area newspapers. *Retirement Life News* serves active senior citizens. *The Portland Business Journal* provides news pertaining to the Portland business community. Local magazines include *Oregon Business Magazine* and a quarterly publication of the Oregon Historical Society.

Television and Radio

Four television stations in the area represent the commercial networks and public television; other channels are available on cable and from neighboring communities. Twenty-three AM and FM radio stations serve the Portland area with a variety of musical and other programming.

Media Information: *The Oregonian*, 1320 SW Broadway, Portland, OR 97201; telephone (503)221-8327

Portland Online

Business in Portland. Available www.businessinportland .org

City of Portland home page. Available www.portlandonline .com

Multnomah County Library. Available www.multcolib.org

Oregon Economic Development Department. Available www.econ.state.or.us

The Oregonian. Available www.oregonlive.com

Portland Art Museum. Available www.portlandartmuseum .org

Portland Business Alliance. Available www.portland alliance.com

Portland Oregon Visitors Association. Available www .travel portland.com or www.pova.org

Portland Public Schools. Available www.pps.k12.or.us

Selected Bibliography

Hawkins, William John, and William F. Willingham, *Classic Houses of Portland, Oregon: 1850–1950* (Portland, Oregon: Timber Press, 1999)

Will, Robin, *Beauty of Portland* (Portland, OR: LTA Publishing, 1989)

Salem

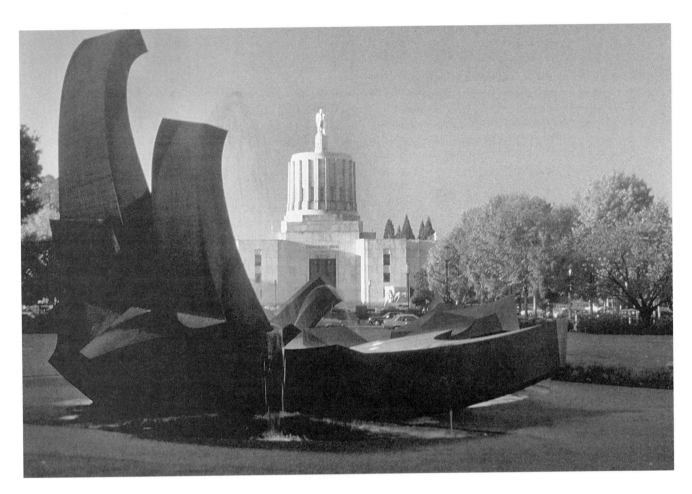

The City in Brief

Founded: 1848 (incorporated, 1860)

Head Officials: Mayor Janet Taylor (since 2003); City Manager Robert Wells

City Population
  1980: 89,091
  1990: 107,793
  2000: 136,924
  2003 estimate: 142,914
  Percent change, 1990–2000: 25.8%
  U.S. rank in 1980: 195th
  U.S. rank in 1990: 178th
  U.S. rank in 2000: 162nd

Metropolitan Area Population
  1980: 250,000
  1990: 278,024
  2000: 347,214
  Percent change, 1990–2000: 24.9%

U.S. rank in 1980: 126th
U.S. rank in 1990: 122nd
U.S. rank in 2000: 129th

Area: 46.37 square miles (2000)
Elevation: 171 feet above sea level at State Capitol
Average Annual Temperature: 52.6° F
Average Annual Precipitation: 39.2 inches of rain, 6.4 inches of snow

Major Economic Sectors: Agriculture, lumber, government, services, trade, high technology
Unemployment Rate: 7.7% (February 2005)
Per Capita Income: $19,141 (1999)
2004 ACCRA Average House Price: Not reported
2004 ACCRA Cost of Living Index: Not reported

1999 FBI Crime Index Total: 12,077

Major Colleges and Universities: Willamette University, Chemeketa Community College, Western Baptist Bible College; Tokyo International University (branch)

Daily Newspaper: *Statesman Journal*

TO CHAMPOEG STATE PARK   TO CHEMEKETA COMMUNITY COLLEGE, MT. ANGEL

WA

ID   MT

• **Salem**

OR

WY

CA

NV   UT   CO

STATE FAIRGROUNDS
& EXPO CENTER

MADISON

JEFFERSON

NORWAY

SHIPPING

HOOD

GAINES

MARKET

BELMONT

E ST.

D ST.

WILLAMETTE RIVER

WATER

DIVISION

UNION

MARION

A.C. GILBERT'S DISCOVERY VILLAGE

CENTER

WATER

CHEMEKETA

COURT

STATE

MID-VALLEY ARTS COUNCIL

FERRY

TRADE

CITY HALL

SALEM PEACE PLAZA

MISSION

BUSH HOUSE

PASTURE PARK

99E

COMMERCIAL

LIBERTY

HIGH

CHURCH

COTTAGE

WINTER

SUMMER

CAPITOL

FRONT

W. SUMMER

E. SUMMER

STATE LIBRARY

STATE CAPITOL

WILLAMETTE UNIVERSITY

TRADE

MILL

BELLEVIEW

OAK

LESLIE

12TH ST.

13TH ST.

14TH ST.

MARION COUNTY
HISTORICAL SOCIETY

VISITOR CENTER   MISSION MILL VILLAGE

AMTRAK

15TH ST.

16TH ST.

STRAND

17TH ST.

18TH ST.

19TH ST.

22   TO AIRPORT, SILVER FALLS STATE PARK →

HISTORIC DEEPWOOD ESTATE

N

0 KILOMETERS 0.5   1

MILES   0.25   0.5

99E TO ENCHANTED FOREST

Introduction

Salem is the capital of Oregon and the third largest city in the state. Situated in the middle of a large, fertile agricultural region, host to a booming wine industry in the Willamette Valley, and known as the ''Cherry City,'' Salem is the processing and transportation center for the surrounding area. A clean environment, the natural scenic beauty of its location, and the recreational activities afforded by the nearby mountains contribute to the high quality of life for which Salem is noted. In addition, careful planning and intelligent zoning have made the city attractive to new business and industry.

Geography and Climate

Salem is located about 60 miles inland from the Pacific Ocean in the Willamette Valley and about halfway between Portland and Eugene. The Willamette River flows on the western edge of the central city. The city is bounded by the Coast Range of mountains on the west and the Cascade Range on the east. Moist Pacific air is the dominant weather feature, moderating temperatures year round. The city and especially the nearby mountains receive a large amount of rainfall; more than 70 percent occurs between November and March and only about 6 percent during the summer. Severe storms and extreme temperatures are uncommon.

Area: 46.37 square miles (2000)

Elevation: 171 feet above sea level at State Capitol

Average Temperatures: January, 40.3° F; August, 67.0° F; annual average, 52.6° F

Average Annual Precipitation: 39.2 inches of rain, 6.4 inches of snow

History

The site of present-day Salem was called ''Chemeketa'' by the Calapooya tribe. The word means ''meeting'' or ''resting place,'' and the tribe used the region for many years in that capacity. In 1840, Jason Lee, a Methodist-Episcopal missionary, moved his mission to the area and called it ''Chemeketa,'' but most settlers referred to it as ''The Mill,'' because of its proximity to Mill Creek. Two years later, the mission established the Oregon Institute, a training school for the local Native Americans that eventually became Willamette University.

The mission was closed in 1844, but in 1848, a town was laid out on the site and called Salem. Some controversy remains over who actually named the town Salem, but historians agree that it was either David Leslie or W. H. Wilson. A fierce battle over where to locate the capital of the Oregon Territory began when the capital was moved from Oregon City to Salem in 1851. In 1853 the Oregon State Legislature began debate on whether to change the town's name to Thurston, Valena, or Corvallis, but a vote in 1855 retained the town's original name. The capital was moved again in 1855, but it returned to Salem later that same year. A suspicious fire that destroyed the Capitol building in late 1855 added to the controversy. When Oregon became a state in 1859, Salem was named the tentative capital, but it was not until 1864 that the city was officially chosen as the capital by election. Salem was incorporated as a city in 1860, and the present Capitol building was built in 1938, after the previous building was destroyed by fine in 1935.

Beginning as a wool processing center, Salem has grown to be an important center for the processing of agricultural products and lumber, as well as a hothouse for technology and information companies. The city's historic buildings, surrounding natural beauty, and modern amenities make it a draw for new residents and businesses alike.

Historical Information: Marion County Historical Society Museum, 260 Twelfth St., SE, Salem, Oregon 97301-4101; telephone (503)364-2128; Fax (503)391-5356; email mchs @open.org

Population Profile

Metropolitan Area Residents
1980: 250,000
1990: 278,024
2000: 347,214
2003 estimate: 363,000
Percent change, 1990–1998: 24.9%
U.S. rank in 1980: 126th
U.S. rank in 1990: 122nd
U.S. rank in 2000: 129th (CMSA)

City Residents
1980: 89,091
1990: 107,793
2000: 136,924
2003 estimate: 142,914
Percent change, 1990–2000: 25.8%

U.S. rank in 1980: 195th

U.S. rank in 1990: 178th (State rank: 3rd)

U.S. rank in 2000: 162nd (State rank: 3rd)

Density: 2,994.0 people per square mile (2000)

Racial and ethnic characteristics (2000)
White: 132,327
Black or African American: 1,750
American Indian and Alaskan Native: 2,064
Asian: 3,304
Native Hawaiian and other Pacific Islander: 643
Hispanic or Latino (may be of any race): 19,973
Other: 10,820

Percent of residents born in state: 45.0% (2000)

Age characteristics (2000)
Population under 5 years old: 10,190
Population 5 to 9 years old: 9,620
Population 10 to 14 years old: 9,244
Population 15 to 19 years old: 10,159
Population 20 to 24 years old: 11,252
Population 25 to 34 years old: 20,659
Population 35 to 44 years old: 20,539
Population 45 to 54 years old: 18,252
Population 55 to 59 years old: 5,679
Population 60 to 64 years old: 4,291
Population 65 to 74 years old: 7,541
Population 75 to 84 years old: 6,653
Population 85 years and over: 2,845
Median age: 33.6 years

Births, Marion County (2003)
Total number: 5,094

Deaths (2003)
Total number: 2,622 (of which, 4 were infants under the age of 1 year)

Money income (1999)
Per capita income: $19,141
Median household income: $38,881
Total households: 50,585

Number of households with income of . . .
less than $10,000: 4,497
$10,000 to $14,999: 3,490
$15,000 to $24,999: 6,903
$25,000 to $34,999: 7,530
$35,000 to $49,999: 9,309
$50,000 to $74,999: 10,231
$75,000 to $99,999: 4,580
$100,000 to $149,999: 2,771
$150,000 to $199,999: 595
$200,000 or more: 679

Percent of families below poverty level: 10.5% (27.6% of which were female householder families with related children under 5 years)

2002 FBI Crime Index Total: 12,077

Municipal Government

Salem operates under a council-manager form of government with eight council members elected to four-year terms by wards; the mayor serves for two years and is elected at-large. The council hires the city manager. Salem is the seat of Marion County.

Head Officials: Mayor Janet Taylor (since 2003; current term expires 2007); City Manager Robert Wells

Total Number of City Employees: 1,190 (2000)

City Information: City of Salem, 555 Liberty Street SE, Salem, OR 97301; telephone (503)588-6255; email Manager@open.org

Economy

Major Industries and Commercial Activity

The major industry in Salem, as the state's capital and county seat of Marion County, is government, where state, local, and federal governments employ 28 percent of Salem's workers. Trade, transportation and utilities comprise 16 percent; education and health services make up 13 percent; and professional and business services make up a further 10 percent of jobs in the metropolitan area (in 2003).

Agriculture and livestock, which is highly diversified in the Salem area, was valued in 2002 at more than $556 million in Marion and Polk counties. Vegetables and fruits, nursery and greenhouse crops, grass seed, and dairy products led with more than 50 percent of the total agricultural value. During the peak of food processing time in August and September, some 10,000 workers are employed in the industry. Contributing to this growth is the Willamette Valley wine industry, which is gaining a strong national reputation for its wine varieties.

Manufacturing in the Salem area has become increasingly diverse. Major manufacturing employers include the traditional food processors, fabricated metal products, high-tech equipment such as cell phones, snow boards, and area newspapers. Most employment classified as lumber and wood products is actually in the manufactured building industry making pre-fabricated structures.

Items and goods produced: high-tech components, vegetable and fruit products, wood and paper products, grass seed, ornamental plants, dairy products, manufactured homes, and metal products

Incentive Programs—New and Existing Companies

In recent years the emphasis in the Willamette Valley has switched from business recruitment to business retention and expansion programs designed to help resident companies "stay put and stay healthy." Most incentive programs are state loan, worker-training, and tax credit packages provided by the Oregon Economic Development Department and arranged through the Mid-Willamette Valley Council of Governments or the Salem Economic Development Corp. (SEDCOR). The Salem area has three enterprise zones for qualified manufacturing and wholesale distribution firms that allow a three- to five-year property tax exemption on improvements.

Job training programs—The state of Oregon has approved an education program, the first in the nation, that establishes a statewide apprenticeship program and has students choose between job training or a college preparatory program after the tenth grade. The program is to be installed in stages in schools through the year 2010. The state's JOBS Plus program allows employers who hire a JOBS Plus-eligible worker to receive benefits that include reimbursements, the opportunity to train and evaluate the worker during the contract period, and the opportunity to treat the employee as a temporary employee. Chemeketa Community College's Training & Economic Development Center in downtown Salem has a variety of programs to help small businesses develop and to assist existing businesses to expand. SEDCOR has partnered with Chemeketa and the Oregon Manufacturers Extension Partnership (OMEP) to run the Oregon Gateway Project to train business and workers in state-of-the-art manufacturing processes at the Advanced Manufacturing and Technology Institute (AMTI) at the college.

Development Projects

In 2001 Courthouse Square Transit Mall was completed. It consists of a bus transfer area, office and retail space, and a parking garage. In 2005 the new Salem Conference Center and attached Phoenix Grand Hotel opened in the heart of downtown Salem, just a few blocks from the state capitol building. The Meridian, a 130,000 square foot mixed-use development of luxury condominiums and medical offices will begin construction in 2005 near Salem Hospital. The largest development project to be started in the mid-2000s is the development of the Mill Creek area labeled as "Salem

Regional Employment Center." This 646 acre parcel will be developed as an industrial area with business and industry parks, with 100 acres set aside as open space and wildlife habitat.

Economic Development Information: SEDCOR, 350 Commercial St. N.E., Salem, OR 97301; telephone (503)588-6225; fax (503)588-6240; email sedcor@sedcor.org. Salem Area Chamber of Commerce, 1110 Commerical Street NE, Salem, OR 97301; telephone (503)581-1466; fax (503)581-0972; email info@salemchamber.org. Employment percentages from the Oregon Employment Department at www .qualityinfo.org.

Commercial Shipping

Salem is located on the main lines of the Union Pacific and Burlington Northern Santa Fe railroads. Located in Salem are 28 long haul truck lines with seven terminals. Interstate 5, the primary north-south highway of the West Coast, passes through the east side of Salem, and Interstate 84 connects to states in the east. Nearby Portland has marine terminals and deep water ports, ranking third on the West Coast in cargo shipped. The Salem Municipal Airport at McNary Field is a 750-acre facility with a 5,800-foot ILS, precision runway that has full facilities for corporate and general aviation aircraft.

Labor Force and Employment Outlook

The Salem area labor force is diversified, with skilled and semi-skilled components including metal workers, assemblers, electrical/electronic technicians, machine operators, computer operators, and programmers.

The Salem area economy in the mid-2000s is very healthy. Employment is expected to continue to grow, although at a slightly slower pace than that of the 1990s. The high percentage of government workers has shown to have a stabilizing effect on the area's economy. There are projections that population growth will slow, but as baby boomers retire, more job openings will become available.

The following is a summary of data regarding the Salem metropolitan area labor force, 2004 annual averages.

Size of non-agricultural labor force: 141,300

Number of workers employed in . . .
 natural resources and mining: 1,400
 construction: 7,200
 manufacturing: 14,600
 trade, transportation and utilities: 23,500
 information: 1,600
 financial activities: 7,100
 professional and business services: 12,200
 educational and health services: 18,300

leisure and hospitality: 12,100

other services: 5,100

government: 38,300

Average hourly earnings of production workers employed in manufacturing: $13.90

Unemployment rate: 7.7% (February 2005)

Largest private employers	*Number of employees*
Salem Hospital	3,300
Spirit Mountain Hotel/Casino	1,500
T-Mobile	1,000
Norpac Foods (food processing)	700
Fred Meyer	700
Kaiser Permanente	700
Willamette University	650
SUMCO Oregon	600
Roth's	500
State Farm Insurance	474

Cost of Living

The following is a summary of data regarding several key cost of living factors for the Salem area.

2004 ACCRA Average House Price: Not reported

2004 ACCRA Cost of Living Index: Not reported

State income tax rate: Ranges from 5.0% to 9.0%

State sales tax rate: None

Local income tax rate: None

Local sales tax rate: None

Property tax rate: $19.32 per $1,000 assessed valuation

Economic Information: SEDCOR, 745 Commercial St. N.E., Salem, OR 97301; telephone (503)588-6225; fax (503)588-6240. Oregon Employment Department, 875 Union Street, Salem, OR 97311; telephone (800)237-3710

Education and Research

Elementary and Secondary Schools

The Salem-Keizer Public Schools is the second largest school district in the state. It is governed by a seven-member, nonpartisan school board that appoints the superintendent. Like many districts, in the 2004-2005 school year Salem-Keizer faced budget cuts, but pledged to keep the focus of their programs on academic achievement and overall student success.

The following is a summary of data regarding Salem public schools as of the 2004–2005 school year.

Total enrollment: 38,236

Number of facilities
  elementary schools: 45
  middle schools: 10
  senior high schools: 6
  other: 4 charter schools

Student/teacher ratio: K-2, 26:1; 3-5, 28:1; 6-8, 29.5:1; 9-12, 30:1

Teacher salaries
  minimum: $30,443
  maximum: $58,784

Funding per pupil: $6,941 (2002-2003)

Salem is also served by 26 parochial and private schools spanning pre-K to 12th grade.

Public Schools Information: Salem-Keizer Public Schools, 2450 Lancaster Dr. NE, Salem, OR 97305; telephone (503)399-3000

Colleges and Universities

Salem is home to Willamette University, a private school affiliated with the Methodist Church that traces its roots back to 1842. With an enrollment of more than 1,500, the university offers a wide range of undergraduate degrees in many fields and a number of postgraduate programs, including law, teaching, and management. Recent additions to the campus include the F.W. Olin Science Center, the Hallie Ford Museum of Art, and the Mary Stuart Rogers Music Center. Chemeketa Community College serves more than 48,000 students annually, and offers one- and two-year associates degrees. A branch of Tokyo International University opened in Salem in 1989 to meet Japanese corporations' increased demand for a culturally adapted workforce. Other area colleges and universities are Western Baptist College, George Fox University, and Western Oregon State College in Monmouth.

Libraries and Research Centers

The Oregon State Library provides quality information service to Oregon state government, provides reading materials to blind and print-disabled Oregonians, and provides leadership, grants, and other assistance to improve local library service for all Oregonians. Among its more than one million items are in-depth collections in business, history, political and social sciences, federal and state government publications, genealogy, and a comprehensive collection of materials about Oregon. In addition, its Library for the Blind and Physically Handicapped collection consists of more than 50,000 cassette, large print, Braille, and talking book titles.

The Salem Public Library maintains a main library, one branch, and a bookmobile with a total of more than 300,000 items, including more than 800 periodical titles. The library features a special photographic history collection. At Willamette University the Mark O. Hatfield Library houses more than 300,000 volumes and about 1,400 periodical subscriptions; and the J.W. Long Law Library houses collections of Oregon, national, and international law titles.

Public Library Information: Salem Public Library, 585 Liberty Street SE, Salem, OR 97301 telephone (503)588-6315

Health Care

Salem Hospital, with 454 beds, is the major health-care facility in the city, providing a wide range of services in several locations. Salem Hospital's service area includes Marion, Polk, and portions of Yamhill counties. Salem Hospital is one of the largest of Oregon's 63 acute care hospitals. The hospital's Center for Outpatient Medicine, just east of the hospital, houses outpatient programs, outpatient surgery, imaging, a Sleep Disorders Center, and other programs. In 2003, a $50 million Family Birth Center facility was added; in 2005 plans were underway for a $330 million construction program that will eventually replace the existing hospital. The Salem Hospital Regional Rehabilitation Center, at 2561 Center Street NE, provides comprehensive inpatient and outpatient rehabilitation services as well as home care. Other Salem Hospital facilities include a Psychiatric Medicine Center, an Outpatient Mammography and MRI Center, and an Urgent Care Center

Additional community health care providers are the Mid-Willamette Valley Hospice, Northbank Surgical Center, skilled nursing and adult foster care providers, and a number of physician clinics also furnishing care to Salem residents. Kaiser Permanente runs two medical office buildings in the city.

Health Care Information: Salem Hospital, Community Relations Office, 665 Winter St. SE, Salem, OR 97301-3919; telephone (503)370-5269; toll-free (800)876-1718

Recreation

Sightseeing

The State Capitol building in downtown Salem is constructed of white marble and features a 22-foot bronze and gold leaf statue, "The Oregon Pioneer." Willson Park, next to the Capitol, contains the Waite Fountain, a replica of the Liberty Bell, and a gazebo for open-air concerts. Bush's Pasture Park is a large park near the Willamette River and downtown Salem that features the Bush House, a Victorian mansion; historic Deepwood House and Gardens, a 5.5-acre estate built in the Queen Anne style; Bush Barn Art Center; and Bush Conservatory. The Salem Municipal Rose Garden is also located in the park. Riverfront Park on the Willamette River has an amphitheatre, a playground and picnic areas, is home to Salem's Riverfront Carousel, featuring hand-carved horses. The A.C. Gilbert Discovery Village, a children's museum, is also in Riverfront Park. Salem Saturday Market brings local farmers and artisans to the corner of Marion and Summers Streets May through October. The Reed Opera House, built in 1869, has been renovated and now contains a number of shops and restaurants.

Attractions at Enchanted Forest, a family-run amusement park, include Storybook Lane in a woodland setting, a Western mining town, summer comedy theater, a haunted house, the Ice Mountain roller coaster, and bobsled and log flume rides. The Salem area features more than 20 wineries within an hour's drive.

Arts and Culture

Theatrical performances are held year-round by the Pentacle Theatre, a community theater group. The Elsinore Theatre presents international and national tours of musicians and theatrical performances, hosts a children's play series, and presents films on Wednesdays. The Willamette Playhouse is where theatre majors from the Willamette University perform, along with the university's Distinguished Artists Series that brings speakers, concerts, and plays to the venue. Musical performances by local groups include classical and pops concerts backed by the Oregon Symphony Association of Salem. The Willamette Falls Symphony presents three concerts a year. Salem is also home to concert and jazz bands, a chamber music group, and men's and women's barbershop choirs. The Hallie Ford Museum of Art, the state's largest art museum, opened in 1998. It houses Willamette University's collection of Indian baskets, Northwest paintings, prints, photographs, sculpture, and European, Asian, and American art. The A.C. Gilbert Discovery Village is the largest children's museum in the Northwest and includes the National Toy Hall of Fame. Half of the museum is housed in a Victorian home once occupied by Gilbert's

The Bush House.

uncle and the other half is in a Victorian building separated from the first by a charming outdoor activity center.

Mission Mill Museum is a 5-acre site that is home to the Thomas Kay Woolen Mill, the historic buildings of the Jason Lee House, the Parsonage, the John D. Boon House, and Pleasant Grove Church. The modern PGE Waterpower Interpretive Center showcases the importance of waterpower to Salem's textile industry.

Arts and Culture Information: Mid-Valley Arts Council, 189 Liberty Street NE, Ste 208, PO Box 149, Salem OR 97308-0149; telephone (503)364-7474

Festivals and Holidays

The Oregon Wine and Food Festival, billed as "The first taste of the wine season" is held at the Oregon State Fairgrounds in February. In April, the Oregon Ag Fest at the State Fairgrounds brings over 20,000 visitors a year to enjoy the Trade, Garden and Craft Show, live entertainment, food, and petting zoo. In June, Riverfront Park hosts the Salem World Beat Festival, with music, dance, crafts, and food from around the world. The Salem Art Fair and Festival occurs annually in the third weekend in July and exhibits the works of artists from throughout the Northwest. Also in July is Salem Hoopla, an all-ages 3-on-3 basketball tournament held right on Court Street, and the Marion County Fair takes place at the State Fairgrounds. The Oregon State Fair is a 12-day celebration each August that features floral and art exhibits, agricultural displays, a midway, and live entertainment. The nearby Bavarian-style community of Mt. Angel holds a popular Oktoberfest each fall. The Festival of Lights Parade in December features floats and marching bands on a route through downtown at night.

Sports for the Participant

More than 1,800 acres, 29 miles of trails, 42 developed parks, and 26 undeveloped parks in Salem offer a variety of outdoor recreational activities. Water sports include fishing, swimming, and boating. Twenty-eight parks maintain ball fields, and there are also 23 public tennis courts and 7 public golf courses; some provide accommodations for the handicapped. Minto Brown Island Park, the largest park at 900 acres, is located along the river about a mile from Salem's center city and contains picnic grounds, jogging and bike paths, and a wildlife refuge. Within 50 miles of Salem are coastal beaches and state and federal recreational areas and parks.

Shopping and Dining

The downtown Salem Center Mall, Lancaster Mall, and Woodburn Company Stores Outlet Mall are the three main shopping areas in Salem. A system of skywalks connects the four major department stores downtown. A number of other specialty stores and smaller shops, such as Mission Mill Village, featuring antiques and crafts in a historic village setting, are scattered throughout the area.

Salem restaurants specialize in fresh, grown-in-Oregon foods and famous Pacific seafood along with cuisine from around the world. The Willamette Valley's vineyards produce a variety of fine wines that area restaurants proudly feature.

Visitor Information: Salem Convention and Visitors Association, 1313 Mill Street SE, Salem, OR 97301; telephone (503)581-4325; toll-free (800)874-7012; fax (503)581-4540

Convention Facilities

There are numerous options when pondering where to meet and stay in Oregon's capital city. The new Salem Convention Center, which opened in 2005, has 29,000 square feet of meeting and exhibition space in 14 rooms, and is attached to the all-suite Phoenix Grand Hotel. The Pavilion at the Oregon State Fair & Exhibition Center offers more than 110,000 square feet of meeting and exhibit space for groups of 30 to 4,000 persons. There are eight other buildings available at the Fairgrounds, including a horse barn, a livestock building, and an amphitheater, all available for events or meetings. The historic Reed Opera House in downtown Salem has two ballrooms with catering facilities for elegant receptions for up to 300 people, and the Elsinore Theatre can be rented for events. From historic settings to great exhibit halls, Salem is an easy choice for convention groups.

Convention Information: Salem Convention and Visitors Association, 1313 Mill Street SE, Salem, OR 97301; telephone (503)581-4325; toll-free (800)874-7012; fax (503)581-4540

Transportation

Approaching the City

Airport shuttles make round trips from Portland International Airport, 61 miles from Salem. Interstate 5, the major West Coast interstate highway, and Interstate 84, for destinations to the east, run through Salem. Passenger rail service is available from Amtrak with two trains daily. The city is also served by Greyhound bus line.

Traveling in the City

The downtown area and much of the rest of Salem is laid out in a grid pattern. Major thoroughfares include State Street, Center Street, Commercial Street, and River Road. Salem-Keizer Transit, also known as Cherriots, operates 25 bus lines with a fleet of more than 50 buses throughout the metropolitan area.

Communications

Newspaper and Magazines

Salem readers support one major daily morning newspaper, the *Statesman Journal,* and a number of weekly papers that provide business, agricultural, government, and general news, including Willamette University's Collegian. Among the magazines published in Salem are *Dialogue*, a magazine for the visually impaired, *The Capital Press*, a farming newspaper for the Pacific Northwest, *Oregon Beef Producer,* and *Oregon Food Journal.*

Television and Radio

Two television stations broadcast from Salem: PAX and WB affiliates. Salem is also served by a number of stations broadcasting from Portland, Oregon, as well as cable television. Five FM and AM radio stations are located in Salem, and along with broadcasters from the surrounding communities, serve the area with an assortment of music, news, and informational programming.

Media Information: Statesman Journal, 280 Church St. NE, Salem, OR 97309; telephone (503)399-6611; toll-free (800)874-7012

Salem Online

City of Salem home page. Available www.cityofsalem.net

Oregon Economic Development Department. Available www.econ.state.or.us

Salem Area Chamber of Commerce. Available www.salem chamber.org

Salem Convention & Visitors Association. Available www .travelsalem.com

Salem Economic Development Corporation. Available www.sedcor.org

Salem-Keizer Public Schools. Available www.salkeiz.k12 .or.us

Salem Public Library. Available www.salemlibrary.org

Statesman Journal. Available www.statesmanjournal.com

UTAH

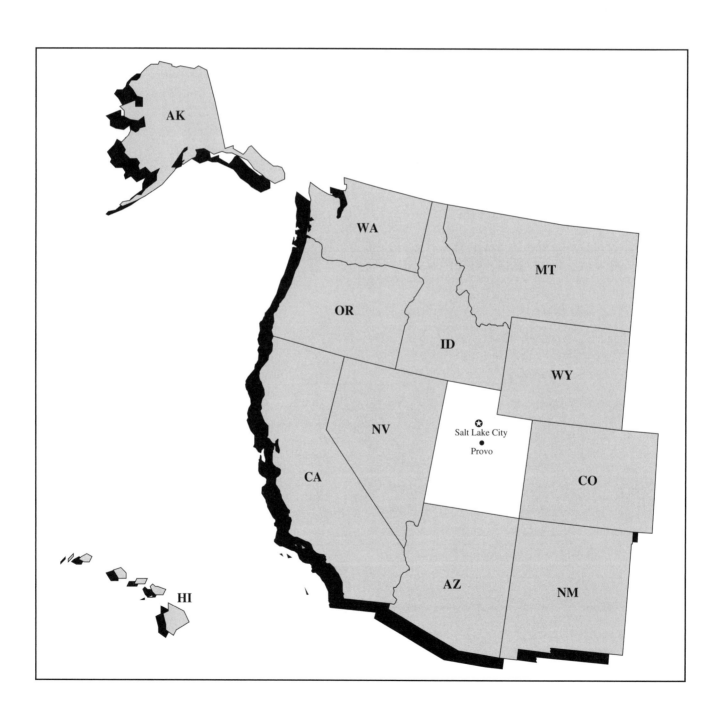

The State in Brief

Nickname: Beehive State
Motto: Industry

Flower: Sego lily
Bird: California gull

Area: 84,898 square miles (2000; U.S. rank: 13th)
Elevation: Ranges from 2,000 feet to 13,528 feet above sea level
Climate: Generally arid with abundant sunshine, higher temperatures in the southwestern desert, cooler weather and lower temperatures in high plateaus and mountains

Admitted to Union: January 4, 1896
Capital: Salt Lake City
Head Official: Governor John Huntsman (R) (until 2009)

Population
   1980: 1,461,000
   1990: 1,722,850
   2000: 2,233,169
   2004 estimate: 2,389,039
   Percent change, 1990–2000: 29.6%
   U.S. rank in 2004: 34th
   Percent of residents born in state: 62.9% (2000)
   Density: 27.2 people per square mile (2000)
   2002 FBI Crime Index Total: 103,129

Racial and Ethnic Characteristics (2000)
   White: 1,992,975
   Black or African American: 17,657
   American Indian and Alaska Native: 29,684
   Asian: 37,108
   Native Hawaiian and Pacific Islander: 15,145
   Hispanic or Latino (may be of any race): 201,559
   Other: 93,405

Age Characteristics (2000)
   Population under 5 years old: 209,378
   Population 5 to 19 years old: 601,599
   Percent of population 65 years and over: 8.5%
   Median age: 27.1 years (2000)

Vital Statistics
   Total number of births (2003): 49,949
   Total number of deaths (2003): 13,426 (infant deaths, 252)
   AIDS cases reported through 2003: 1,098

Economy
   Major industries: Manufacturing; trade; government; finance, insurance, and real estate; services; mining; agriculture; tourism
   Unemployment rate: 4.8% (February 2005)
   Per capita income: $25,230 (2003; U.S. rank: 48th)
   Median household income: $49,143 (3-year average, 2001-2003)
   Percentage of persons below poverty level: 9.4% (1999)
   Income tax rate: Ranges from 2.30% to 7.0%
   Sales tax rate: 4.75%

Provo

The City in Brief

Founded: 1849 (incorporated, 1851)

Head Official: Mayor Lewis K. Billings (R) (since 1998)

City Population
1980: 74,111
1990: 86,835
2000: 105,166
2003 estimate: 105,410
Percent change, 1990–2000: 20.7%
U.S. rank in 1980: Not reported
U.S. rank in 1990: 239th
U.S. rank in 2000: 244th (State rank: 3rd)

Metropolitan Area Population
1980: 218,000
1990: 263,590

2000: 368,536
Percent change, 1990–2000: 39.8%
U.S. rank in 1980: Not available
U.S. rank in 1990: 129th
U.S. rank in 2000: 111th

Area: 41.79 square miles (2000)
Elevation: 4,540 feet above sea level
Average Annual Temperature: 53.3° F
Average Annual Precipitation: 20.13 inches of rain; 60.40 inches of snow

Major Economic Sectors: Services, construction, trade
Unemployment Rate: 4.9% (February 2005)
Per Capita Income: $13,207 (1999, Utah County)

2002 FBI Crime Index Total: 3,657

Major Colleges and Universities: Brigham Young University, Utah Valley State College

Daily Newspaper: *The Daily Herald*

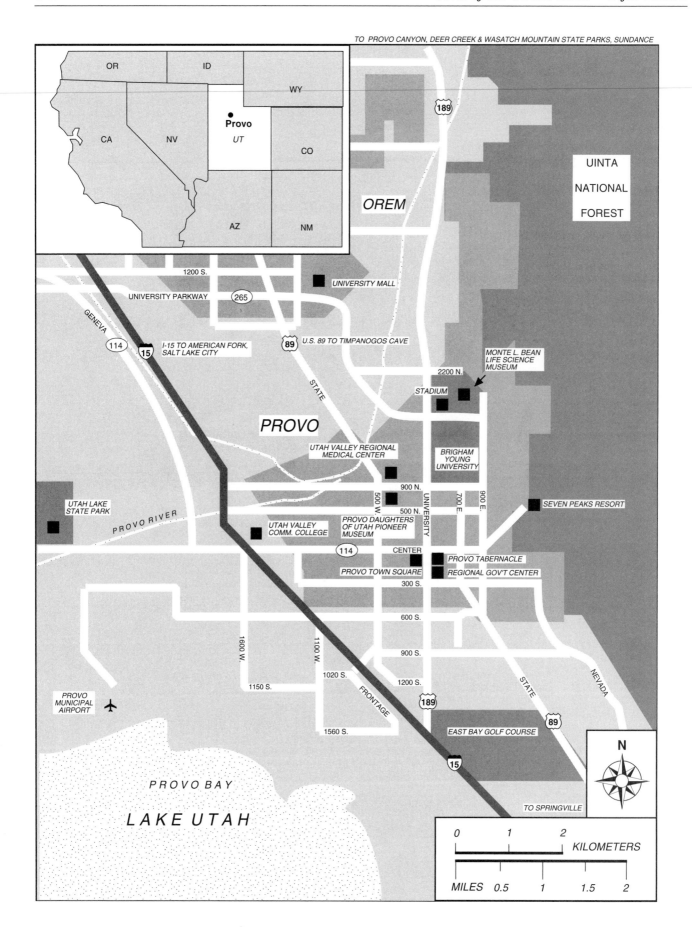

TO PROVO CANYON, DEER CREEK & WASATCH MOUNTAIN STATE PARKS, SUNDANCE

OR

ID

WY

CA

NV

● **Provo**

UT

CO

AZ

NM

UINTA

NATIONAL

FOREST

OREM

189

1200 S.

UNIVERSITY MALL

UNIVERSITY PARKWAY

265

GENEVA

114

15

I-15 TO AMERICAN FORK,
SALT LAKE CITY

89

U.S. 89 TO TIMPANOGOS CAVE

STATE

MONTE L. BEAN
LIFE SCIENCE
MUSEUM

2200 N.

STADIUM

PROVO

UTAH VALLEY REGIONAL
MEDICAL CENTER

BRIGHAM
YOUNG
UNIVERSITY

900 N.

500 W.

500 N.

UNIVERSITY

700 E.

900 E.

SEVEN PEAKS RESORT

UTAH LAKE
STATE PARK

PROVO RIVER

UTAH VALLEY
COMM. COLLEGE

PROVO DAUGHTERS
OF UTAH PIONEER
MUSEUM

114

CENTER

PROVO TABERNACLE

PROVO TOWN SQUARE

REGIONAL GOV'T CENTER

300 S.

600 S.

900 S.

1600 W.

1100 W.

1020 S.

1200 S.

NEVADA

STATE

1150 S.

FRONTAGE

189

PROVO
MUNICIPAL
AIRPORT

89

1560 S.

EAST BAY GOLF COURSE

15

N

TO SPRINGVILLE

PROVO BAY

LAKE UTAH

0		1		2	
				KILOMETERS	

MILES   0.5   1   1.5   2

Introduction

Provo is the commercial center and county seat of Utah County, and one of the fastest growing areas in the nation. A high-technology mecca, the Provo area is home to one of the largest concentrations of computer software companies in the nation after California's Silicon Valley. The city is one of the top iron and steel producers in the West, as well as an agricultural center producing berries and orchard fruit. Many ski areas, campgrounds, state parks, lakes, and rivers are located within Utah County. Fishing, camping, hiking, and hunting facilities are nearby. Brigham Young University is the center for many local activities in the city, which is the headquarters of the Uinta National Forest with its many scenic drives through the Wasatch Mountains and Provo Canyon. The city has a very well-educated population—more than 90 percent of its residents have graduated from high school. Housing is affordable and the crime rate is two to three times lower than in most comparable cities. In 2004 Provo was ranked sixth in the ''Best Places for Business and Careers'' survey by *Forbes* magazine, which considered job and income growth, cost of doing business, and workforce qualification in its rankings.

Geography and Climate

Provo is located in Utah Valley, 38 miles south of Salt Lake City, 263 miles northeast of St. George, and 80 miles south of Ogden. It is situated on the Provo River between Utah Lake to the west and the Wasatch Mountain Range to the east. It sits on a shelf along the famous shoreline of prehistoric Lake Bonneville and is nurtured by the Provo River.

The area experiences four seasons with low humidity that makes the air cool rapidly after sunset, resulting in comfortably cool evenings. The temperature dips below zero on only three days per year on average. Generally 57 days of the year are above 90 degrees and 15 days are below freezing. The wettest month of the year is usually May while June is the driest month.

Area: 41.79 square miles (2000)

Elevation: 4,540 feet above sea level

Mean Temperatures: January, 30.7° F; July, 76.4° F; annual average, 53.3° F

Average Annual Precipitation: 20.13 inches of rain; 60.40 inches of snow

History

Two Franciscan friars, Francisco Dominguez and Silvestre de Escalante, were the first Spaniards to visit the area that makes up present-day Utah County. They arrived in the area from Santa Fe, New Mexico, in search of a direct route to Monterey, California. Arriving in 1776, Father Escalente described the Provo/Orem Valley as having comfortable weather both day and night. ''This place is the most pleasant, beautiful, and fertile land in all New Spain,'' he wrote. The two priests instructed the native Americans in Christian teachings, and though they promised to return, no further record of them remains.

Etienne Provost, a French Canadian trapper, was the next recorded European visitor. He arrived in the area in 1825 with a band of men in search of fur-bearing animals. The trappers were visited by 20 or 30 natives, whose leader told them that they could not smoke peace pipes together because there was iron in the vicinity. Provost and his men moved their knives and guns further away, and subsequently the natives attacked them with hidden knives and tomahawks, killing 17 of the 22 men. Provost and four other men escaped and made their way to the mountains.

The Mormon pioneers, fleeing religious persecution in Illinois, were the next European visitors to the area. Brigham Young led his followers to Salt Lake Valley in 1847, where they immediately began planting crops and constructing houses. In 1849 a permanent settlement in Provo was established by Mormon pioneers.

Provo was founded in 1850 as Fort Utah, named after the Ute tribe that inhabited the region. Later, the name was changed to Fort Provo in honor of Provost, the French trapper.

A war between the settlers and the native tribes took place in 1850, and the Walker War followed in 1853. The Mormons built a fort that they called Fort Utah as a protection against their native enemies. Shortly after, settlers began building houses around the fort. By 1852 hotels and businesses had been established.

By 1861 all of the Utah Valley was being settled. Even though lack of water remained a problem, many of the earlier settlers from nearby valleys began living on the lands that now comprise the city of Orem. When railroad connections were built from Salt Lake City (1873) and Scofield (1878), Provo became a shipping point for the region's mines. Provo is the seat of Brigham Young University (founded in 1875) and Utah Valley State College. Nearby are the Uinta National Forest, with headquarters in Provo; a state fish hatchery; a wild bird refuge; and Provo Peak.

Today, Provo is one of the fastest growing metropolitan areas in the nation, with population gains of nearly 40 percent in the 1990s and into the new millennium. The area boasts a high quality of life due in part to its proximity to an abundance of recreational and leisure options in the nearby Wasatch Mountains and Utah Lake. Provo is also ranked as one of the Country's most "stress-free" cities.

Historical Information: Department of History, Brigham Young University, 2130 JFSB, Provo, UT 84602; telephone (801)422-4335

Population Profile

Metropolitan Area Residents

1980: 218,000
1990: 263,590
2000: 368,536
Percent change, 1990–2000: 39.8%
U.S. rank in 1980: Not reported
U.S. rank in 1990: 129th
U.S. rank in 2000: 111th

City Residents

1980: 74,111
1990: 86,835
2000: 105,166
Percent change, 1990–2000: 20.7%
U.S. rank in 1980: Not reported
U.S. rank in 1990: 239th
U.S. rank in 2000: 244th (State rank: 3rd)

Density: 2,653.2 people per square mile (2000)

Racial and ethnic characteristics (2000)
   White: 93,094
   Black or African American: 486
   American Indian and Alaska Native: 846
   Asian: 1,924
   Native Hawaiian and other Pacific Islander: 882
   Hispanic or Latino (may be of any race): 11,013
   Other: 5,368

Percent of residents born in state: 46.3% (2000)

Age characteristics (2000)
   Population under 5 years old: 9,139
   Population 5 to 9 years old: 5,636
   Population 10 to 14 years old: 5,092
   Population 15 to 19 years old: 15,278
   Population 20 to 24 years old: 30,510
   Population 25 to 34 years old: 17,345
   Population 35 to 44 years old: 7,090
   Population 45 to 54 years old: 5,384
   Population 55 to 59 years old: 2,061
   Population 60 to 64 years old: 1,611
   Population 65 to 74 years old: 2,950
   Population 75 to 84 years old: 2,248
   Population 85 years and older: 822
   Median age: 22.9 years

Births (Utah County, 2003)
   Total number: 10,972

Deaths (Utah County, 2003)
   Total number: 1,736 (of which, 58 were infants under the age of 1 year)

Money income (1999)
   Per capita income: $13,207
   Median household income: $36,393
   Total households: $29,266

Number of households with income of . . .
   less than $10,000: 2,424
   $10,000 to $14,999: 2,361
   $15,000 to $24,999: 5,395
   $25,000 to $34,999: 4,726
   $35,000 to $49,999: 5,487
   $50,000 to $74,999: 4,594
   $75,000 to $99,999: 2,141
   $100,000 to $149,999: 1,436
   $150,000 to $199,999: 330
   $200,000 or more: 372

Percent of families below poverty level: 12.5% (42.0% of which were female householder families with related children under 5 years)

2002 FBI Crime Index Total: 3,657

Municipal Government

Provo has a council-mayor form of government with a mandatory chief administrative officer. Seven members make up the Provo Municipal Council; five representing municipal districts and two city-wide representatives.

Head Official: Mayor Lewis K. Billings (R) (since 1998; current term expires 2006)

Total Number of City Employees: 740 (2004)

City Information: City of Provo, 351 West Center Street PO Box 1849, Provo, UT 84603; telephone (801)852-6100; fax (801)852-6107

Economy

Major Industries and Commercial Activity

The Provo-Orem area has a diverse economy with every employment sector well represented. The area is home to the second largest concentration of software technologies companies in the United States and has the third largest concentration of high-technology companies. There is also a large concentration of biotech companies located in the area.

Some of the world's major software companies are located in the area, including Novell, Inc., Symantec and Corel, creating opportunities for more than 400 small to mid-range high-technology companies. Provo is also home to such giants as Nestle Frozen Foods and Nu Skin Enterprises Inc. High-technology companies in the Provo/Orem area include Micron Technology, Ameritech Library Services, Convergys, Folio Corporation, Viewsoft, and Nimbus Manufacturing, among others.

The notable work ethic of local employees and the appeal of a serene mountain community have made Provo ideal for a wide variety of manufacturers, communications firms, and marketing and retail organizations, including Banta Press, Nature's Sunshine, Sears Telecatalog, PowerQuest Corp., and Powder River Manufacturing. Many industrial parks offer a variety of settings for light to heavy industry with abundant, low-cost utilities.

As other sectors of the economy have prospered in recent years, retailers have seen dramatic increases as well. Provo is a magnet for many of the surrounding counties and the major shopping areas are easily accessible from I-15 and other main routes.

Items and goods produced: iron, steel, software, fruit, electronics, apparel

Incentive Programs—New and Existing Companies

Local programs—Most incentive programs are at the state level. Provo City's Redevelopment Agency provides support for starting a new business by offering assistance in preparing a business plan and demographic information necessary for decision making.

State programs—The Utah Small Business Development Center (USBDC) helps established and start-up companies prepare business plans, set sales goals, identify customers and the competition, analyze the market, find property, and research financing sources. The USBDC is part of a network that operates in all 50 states and is supported by the federal government. It offers a five-week business planning class and other classes including management, risk management, accounting, computerizing one's business, budgeting, cash management, and running a home-based business. The State of Utah makes available a Revolving Loan Fund, which provides up to $100,000 to qualified applicants for working capital, equipment, and lease improvements, etc. The Utah Microenterprise Loan Fund provides financing to owners, particularly those who are socially or economically disadvantaged, of both new and existing companies who don't have access to traditional funding sources. Job tax credits and investment tax credits are available to manufacturing, recycling, information technology, and warehousing businesses that relocate or establish themselves in designated rural areas. Companies can receive tax credits for getting involved in recycling activities in recycling zones, for example. The State of Utah's Office of Technology Development offers assistance in creating and developing technology-oriented businesses through its Centers of Excellence Program. The State helps companies commercialize leading edge technologies which have been developed in selected research programs at universities in Utah.

Job training programs—The Small Business Development Center in Orem/Provo provides free personal consulting services and low-cost skill-based training to owners and managers of small businesses and to prospective entrepreneurs.

Development Projects

One of the largest redevelopment projects Provo City has undertaken has been the Ironton Redevelopment Project. Potential plans for the 338-acre former Ironton Steel mill abandoned since 1962 include a commercial/industrial business park. Environmental clean-up to remove contaminants from the coke and iron-making operations are underway and the city has started construction of South Mountain Vista Parkway at Ironton.

Completed in March 2005, the new Wells Fargo Center is a 100,000 square foot, seven-story mixed use building in Provo. The building is home to Wells Fargo Bank, as well as MultiLing Corp., a translation and language services company, plus other professional offices and residential condominiums on the top three floors.

Construction of a new convention center and hotel for downtown Provo and a new cultural arts facility at the former Provo City Library were in the planning stages in 2005.

Economic Development Information: Provo City Economic Development, 425 West Center St., Provo, UT 84603; telephone (801)852-6160

Commercial Shipping

Provo is served by the Denver & Rio Grand Western and the Union Pacific railroads, which offer second-morning service to 90 percent of the Western markets. The Provo area is served by 40 major trucking lines. The expanding Provo Municipal Airport can serve and handle most aircraft and is equipped with an instrument-landing system and a weather-reporting capability.

Labor Force and Employment Outlook

The Provo-Orem area boasts low unemployment; favorable taxes; a young, educated, "internationally skilled" work force; and a growing population. Utah's labor market is made up of a large percentage of young people. The Provo work force not only has a high education level, among its other qualities are foreign language ability, foreign service experience, and a strong work ethic. The state of Utah ranks among the nation's leaders in job growth, with nonfarm employment continuing to grow in 2004-2005. All sectors posted job growth in 2004, and the largest gains could be seen in the professional and business services sector; the trade, transportation and utilities sector; and the construction sector. Utah Valley remains one of the hottest high-tech areas in the nation, which continues to bring in entrepreneurs, big business, and new and higher-paying jobs.

The following is a summary of data regarding the Provo-Orem metropolitan area labor force, 2004 annual averages.

Size of non-agricultural labor force: 162,900

Number of workers employed in . . .
  construction and mining: 11,900
  manufacturing: 17,500
  trade, transportation and utilities: 26,300
  information: 7,100
  financial activities: 6,100
  professional and business services: 19,600
  educational and health services: 33,900
  leisure and hospitality: 12,800
  other services: 4,000
  government: 23,700

Average hourly earnings of production workers employed in manufacturing: $13.80 (Provo-Orem MSA)

Unemployment rate: 4.9% (February 2005)

Largest employers (2002)	Number of employees
Brigham Young University	14,500
Alpine School District	6,213
IHC Health Care Services	3,650
Utah Valley State College	3,165
Nebo School District	2,371
Convergys	2,000
Provo School District	1,900
Nestle USA Food Group Inc.	1,899
Novell, Inc. (manufacturing)	1,800
Modus Media International	1,200

Cost of Living

Overall cost of living in Provo/Orem ranks close to the national average.

The following is a summary of data regarding key cost of living factors for the Provo area.

2004 (3rd Quarter) ACCRA Average House Price: $239,650 (Salt Lake City metro)

2004 (3rd Quarter) ACCRA Cost of Living Index: 97.3 (Salt Lake City metro) (U.S. average = 100.0)

State income tax rate: Ranges from 2.30% to 7.0%

State sales tax rate: 4.75%

Local income tax rate: None

Local sales tax rate: 6.25%

Property tax assessment rate: .002787 applied to 55% of assessed value for residential property and 100% of assessed value for commercial property (2005)

Economic Information: The Provo Orem Chamber of Commerce, 51 South University Avenue, Suite 215, Provo, UT 84601; telephone (801)851-2555.

Education and Research

Elementary and Secondary Schools

In addition to educating students from kindergarten to grade twelve, the Provo School District assists students in preschool and latch-key programs, as well as through programs for the physically challenged. In addition to the traditional schools, Provo has one school for children with physical and emotional challenges too severe for mainstreaming. For 18 percent of Provo students, English is their second language; Provo students speak 43 different languages. Scores on college entrance exams are above state and national averages. Provo School District was named one of the top 100 school districts in the nation in 2000 by *Offspring* magazine, a *Wall Street Journal* publication. The District has seen declining enrollment between 1996 and 2003 of two percent.

The following is a summary of data regarding the Provo School District as of the 2003–2004 school year.

Total enrollment: 13,227

Number of facilities
  elementary schools: 13
  middle schools: 3
  senior high schools: 2

other: 1 alternative high school, 1 special needs school, 1 adult high school, 1 single-track year-round school

Student/teacher ratio: 19.3:1

Teacher salaries
    average: $35,800

Funding per pupil: $5,103 (2001-2002)

Because public education in the Utah Valley is highly regarded, there are few private schools. Among the private schools are Challenger School, a K-12 school based on a structured learning environment; Provo Canyon School, an alternative school; and several Montessori Schools.

Public Schools Information: Provo City School District, 280 West 940 North, Provo, UT 84604-3394; telephone (801)374-4800. Utah State Office of Education, 250 East 500 South, Salt Lake City, UT 84111-4200; telephone (801)538-7500

Colleges and Universities

Brigham Young University (BYU) is located in the city at the base of the Wasatch Mountains. Founded in 1875 by Brigham Young, BYU is the largest private university in the United States. Owned by the Mormon Church, the university has more than 32,000 full-time, part-time and evening students and offers a wide variety of academic programs. Particularly notable are its business administration programs, broadcast journalism program, and law and engineering schools. Utah Valley State College enrolls more than 26,000 students and awards bachelor's degrees in accounting, behavioral science, biology, business management, business/ marketing education, chemistry, computer science, early childhood and elementary education, environmental tech, criminal justice, integrated and paralegal studies, fire science, history, hospitality management, mathematics, nursing, information technology, and technology management. Other Provo institutions of higher learning include Provo College and Stevens Henager College of Business, which train students in special and entry-level skills.

Libraries and Research Centers

The Provo City Library at Academy Square, opened in 2001, holds 176,496 volumes, 350 periodicals, and more than 10,000 records and audio tapes, video tapes, and compact discs. Its special collections center on Utah and Utah County history. Other libraries in the city include the Utah State Hospital's Patients Library and Brigham Young University Library, which houses more than two million volumes and features special collections on linguistics, poetry, children's literature, Victorian literature, and oral history.

Provo has many research centers affiliated with Brigham Young University. They encompass such areas as engineering, computers, cancer, sociology, literature, thermodynamics, Western studies, communications, international studies, earth science, agriculture, psychology, religion, life science, anthropology, business, religion, and women's studies. BYU was recognized in 2002 by *The Chronicle of Higher Education* as the country's best university at turning research dollars into inventions and new companies. The U.S. Forest Service has a Shrub Sciences Laboratory maintained in cooperation with Brigham Young University. Utah State University supports 25 research projects. The University houses the Ross A. Smart Veterinary Diagnostic Laboratory engaging in animal disease diagnosis.

Public Library Information: Provo City Library at Academy Square, 550 North University Ave., Provo, UT 84601; telephone (801)852-6650

Health Care

The Provo/Orem area is served by three major hospitals—Utah Valley Regional Medical Center (UVRMC) in Provo, Orem Community Hospital in Orem, and Timpanogos Regional Hospital in Orem. UVRMC is a 330-bed tertiary and acute care facility. Special features at UVRMC include magnetic resonance imaging and computerized tomographic scanning capabilities, laser technology, intensive care and coronary care units, the Newborn ICU and Cancer Services, Emergency and Trauma Services, Critical Care, Women's and Children's Services, and Behavioral Health. The majority of health care facilities in the area are run by Intermountain Health Care (IHC), the regional health care provider which operates UVRMC and Orem community Hospital. MountainStar Health Care operates Timpanogos Regional Hospital. Special services provided by IHC include free seminars, many free or low-cost medical screenings and tests, and information "hot lines." Other IHC facilities in Provo are the Utah Valley Heart Center and the Utah Valley Rehabilitation Center. Surgical facilities in Provo are Healthsouth Provo Surgical Center and Central Utah Surgical Center.

Mental health care services are available at Utah State Hospital, Charter Canyon Hospital and Counseling Center and at Wasatch Mental Health Center.

Recreation

Sightseeing

The Provo/Orem area is one of the most scenic in the country. Visitors can view the breathtaking Bridal Veil Falls

America's Freedom Festival in Provo is held on July 4.

from the Provo Canyon floor. The falls can be seen from Highway 189, which curves alongside the Provo River up the beautiful Provo Canyon Scenic Byway. A turn onto the Alpine Loop Scenic Backway (Highway 92) goes past the Sundance Resort and the Timpanogos Cave National Monument. Located in American Fork Canyon, the cave is actually three highly decorated limestone caverns that can be observed on a 1.5-mile hike.

Built in 1972, Provo Latter Day Saints Temple is located on a hillside above the Brigham Young University campus. It is an architecturally striking building faced with white cast stone and topped with a segmented spire. The Provo Latter Day Saints Tabernacle is a historic structure built in 1898 that is still in active use, hosting many religious and cultural events.

The award-winning McCurdy Historical Doll Museum has more than 4,000 dolls, 47 miniature rooms, toys, and a toy shop. The Monte L. Bean Life Science Museum on the Brigham Young University campus contains a large collection of trophy animals and displays of animal habitats. The Brigham Young University Earth Science Museum features animals large and small from dinosaurs to ancient forms of sea life.

The Sundance Resort, 15 miles northeast of Provo, provides fine dining, a spa, plays, art workshops, and nature experiences throughout the summer in addition to excellent skiing in winter.

The Trafalga Family Fun Center in Orem contains a 400-foot waterslide, indoor and outdoor miniature golf courses, and a game room. Thanksgiving Point in nearby Lehi is a 700-acre oasis featuring restaurants, a visitor center and giftshop, a professional golf course, academy driving range, clubhouse, tennis ranch, animal farm, equestrian center, shopping village, North American Museum of Ancient Life, and acres and acres of awe-inspiring gardens. Recent additions to Thanksgiving Point are a dinner theater seating more than 1,000 and Electric Park for parties, reunions, and fairs, both slated for a 2005 opening.

Arts and Culture

Hundreds of cultural events are sponsored annually in Provo, including concerts, symposiums, plays, lectures, classes, art exhibits, and museum displays. The Museum of Art at Brigham Young University (BYU) is one of the largest of its kind in the intermountain West and houses an impressive permanent collection of fine art. The B. F. Larson Gallery at BYU exhibits works by contemporary artists. Fine art is on display at the Brownstone Gallery. The Springville Museum of Art in nearby Springville houses an extensive collection of the works of Utah artists, highlighted by the month-long National Art Exhibit in April.

The Sundance Institute, an arts community near Provo, fosters creativity in film, and visual and performing arts, and presents arts events throughout the year, including its internationally-recognized Film Festival.

The historic Latter Day Saints Tabernacle hosts a roster of internationally known performers as well as the Utah Valley Symphony, a 90-member community orchestra. Brigham Young University is a major source of music, dance, and drama events at its Harris Fine Arts Center. Utah Regional Ballet is the resident ballet company at Utah Valley State College in Orem. The Center Street Musical Theater presents dinner theater in downtown Provo. The Provo Theatre Company stages five to six musical, comedy, and dramatic productions from September through July.

Festivals and Holidays

Provo kicks off the New Year with its First Night community celebration of the arts in an alcohol-free setting, followed by the annual Sundance Film Festival held near the end of January each year. Utah Pioneer Days in May features the Miss Orem Pageant. America's Freedom Festival in Provo on July 4 is the largest Independence Day celebration in the country. This grand three-week event begins with balloon festivals; gala balls; clogging competitions; 10K, 5K, and one mile runs; and explodes with an enormous parade. More than 700 folkdancers from many countries gather at the Springville World Folkfest in July for the largest event of its kind in the country. From May through September, many cities in Utah County hold individual city festivals. WinterFest in downtown Provo during the month of December celebrates the holiday season with concerts, a parade, living nativity, decorated storefronts and a ''Lights On'' celebration.

Sports for the Spectator

Brigham Young University's (BYU) basketball team plays its games throughout the winter at the 23,000-seat Marriott Center arena. The BYU Cougars hold home football games at their 65,000-seat stadium on campus. The Utah Valley State Wolverines play basketball at the McKay Center in Orem. Some of the other sports presented at BYU and Utah Valley State College are basketball, baseball, track, volleyball, gymnastics, rugby, wrestling, and swimming.

Sports for the Participant

The city of Provo has 28 parks, 2 ice rinks, 4 swimming pools, 10 golf courses, more than 35 tennis courts, 1 soccer field, and 7 baseball and softball diamonds. The city maintains a rifle and pistol shooting range year-round for public use. Within an hour's drive from Provo are 7 downhill ski resorts, including Park City and Snowbird. Robert Redford's Sundance Resort, which offers mountain biking trails as well as skiing, is 20 minutes from the city of Provo Canyon. In and surrounding

Provo/Orem are 10 public golf courses and 2 private country clubs. Nearby Utah Lake State Park and Deer Creek Reservoir in Heber Valley provide water skiing, fishing, boating, camping, canoeing, and other water sports. Fly-fishing in the Provo River is popular, and hunting of elk, deer, moose, and bighorn sheep is also possible. Maps and trail guides to the area can be obtained at the U.S. Forest Service's main office in Provo. Climbers have access to both indoor and outdoor ropes courses at the CLAS Ropes Course facility.

Seven Peaks Resort, located at the foot of Maple Mountain in Provo, is a waterpark with a variety of water amusements including the world's tallest water slides, wave pool, and children's activity areas. The park's acres of lush lawns and pavilions make it a favorite site for picnics and parties. Thanksgiving Point in nearby Lehi is a 700-acre oasis featuring a variety of outdoor activities.

Shopping and Dining

Provo boasts two newer malls: the modern Provo Towne Center and The Shops at Riverwoods. Provo Town Center Mall is anchored by Dillard's, JCPenney, and Sears department stores. The Shops at Riverwoods features modern, upscale shops in a nostalgic Main Street USA setting. Provo Town Square is a specialty theme mall in the heart of the city. All the buildings are restored historic structures housing restaurants, shops, and entertainment facilities. Provo University Parkway has recently developed into a major shopping area with large department stores and small specialty shops. University Mall in the University Parkway corridor in Orem contains 185 stores and restaurants.

The city of Provo has more than 200 eating places. The Provo/Orem area hosts a variety of ethnic restaurants including American, Chinese, Japanese, Indian, Italian, and Mexican. Vegetarian fare, bars/nightclubs, and fast foods of all kinds are also popular. Allie's American Grill at the Provo Marriott, Carvers, Los Hermanos, and Magelby's are local favorites for dining. At Sundance Resort, The Tree Room offers elegant dining by candlelight; the Foundry Grill Room features lighter, bistro-style dining; and the Owl Bar offers spirits, local brews, and a bistro-style menu for the benefit of private club members (temporary memberships are available); all rooms are known for their exceptional fare.

Visitor Information: The Utah County Convention & Visitors Bureau, 111 S. University Ave., Provo, UT 84601; telephone (801)851-2100

Convention Facilities

The cities of Provo and Orem have two major conference facilities and one special events center. The Provo Marriott Hotel and Conference Center has 21 meeting rooms for a total of more than 28,000 square feet, and 330 sleeping rooms, including more than 100 suites. The Brigham Young University Conference Center is a full-service facility featuring 34 conference rooms. It can be scheduled for programs that are consistent with BYU's educational mission and is a smoke- and alcohol-free facility.

Provo hotels with conference facilities are: Best Western CottonTree Inn, Courtyard by Marriott, Hampton Inn, and Holiday Inn. Other nearby hotel conference facilities are located in Orem, American Fork, and Payson.

In addition to the conference centers, the Provo area offers many options for hosting large groups including the Provo City Library at Academy Square, Historic County Courthouse, Springville Museum of Art, Thanksgiving Point, Alpine Art Center, and Scera Theater in Orem, among others.

The David O. McKay Events Center at Utah Valley State College features an 8,500-seat arena, four multipurpose athletic courts of 5,000 square feet each, two 2,500-square-foot meeting spaces, four concession stands, six locker rooms, in-house catering, full equipment rental, and ticketing services. Sundance Resort's facilities include more than 11,000 square feet of meeting space and 102 sleeping units in a rustic, alpine atmosphere. The fairground facilities at Spanish Fork include a 7,000 seat main arena, plus two additional arenas totaling more than 60,000 square feet.

Convention Information: The Utah County Convention & Visitors Bureau, 111 S. University Ave., Provo, UT 84601; telephone (801)851-2100

Transportation

Approaching the City

Provo/Orem is intersected by U.S. Highways 50, 89, 91, and 189, as well as by Interstate 15. Provo is located within an hour's drive of Salt Lake International Airport, which is ranked among the world's busiest. The airport schedules 972 flights daily, serving 85 cities with non-stop flights. Bus service to the city is also available.

Traveling in the City

The Utah Transit Authority provides daily mass transit service to both the Provo/Orem and Salt Lake City metropolitan areas. It offers complete routes serving all of the major business areas in Provo. The metropolitan area is served by one taxi company.

Communications

Newspapers and Magazines

The Daily Herald is Provo's daily newspaper. The *Daily Universe* newspaper is published by the students at Brigham Young University. Magazines published in Provo include *BYU Studies, BYU Magazine, Prelude, Provo/Orem Metroguide, Al-Arabiyya* (a scholarly journal for Arabic language teachers), *The Western North American Naturalist,* and *Scandinavian Studies.*

Television and Radio

Provo has three AM and one FM radio station that encompass religion, music, talk, and public broadcasting, and a television station on the campus of Brigham Young University.

Media Information: *The Daily Herald,* 1555 North Freedom Blvd., PO Box 717, Provo, UT 84603; telephone (801)375-5103; toll-free (800)880-8075.

Provo Online

City of Provo home page. Available www.provo.org

The Daily Herald. Available www.harktheherald.com

Provo City Economic Development. Available www.provo.org/econdev.econdev_main.html

Provo City Library. Available www.provo.lib.ut.us

Provo City School District. Available www.provo.edu/index1.html

Provo Orem Chamber of Commerce. Available www.thechamber.org

Utah County Convention & Visitors Bureau. Available www.utahvalley.org/p_home.asp

Utah State Office of Education. Available www.usoe.k12.ut.us

Salt Lake City

The City in Brief

Founded: 1847 (incorporated, 1851)

Head Official: Mayor Ross C. "Rocky" Anderson (NP) (since 2000)

City Population
1980: 163,033
1990: 159,928
2000: 181,743
2003 estimate: 179,894
Percent change, 1990–2000: 13.6%
U.S. rank in 1980: 90th
U.S. rank in 1990: 108th
U.S. rank in 2000: 129th

Metropolitan Area Population
1980: 910,000
1990: 1,072,227
2000: 1,333,914

Percent change, 1990–2000: 24.4%
U.S. rank in 1980: 41st
U.S. rank in 1990: 38th
U.S. rank in 2000: 35th

Area: 109 square miles (2000)
Elevation: 4,330 feet above sea level
Average Annual Temperature: 51.8° F
Average Annual Precipitation: 15.7 inches

Major Economic Sectors: Construction, transportation, trade, utilities, finance, information, education and health services
Unemployment Rate: 5.2% (January 2005)
Per Capita Income: $20,752 (1999)

2002 FBI Crime Index Total: 19,059

Major Colleges and Universities: University of Utah, Westminster College, Salt Lake Community College-South City Campus, LDS Business College

Daily Newspapers: *The Salt Lake Tribune; Deseret News*

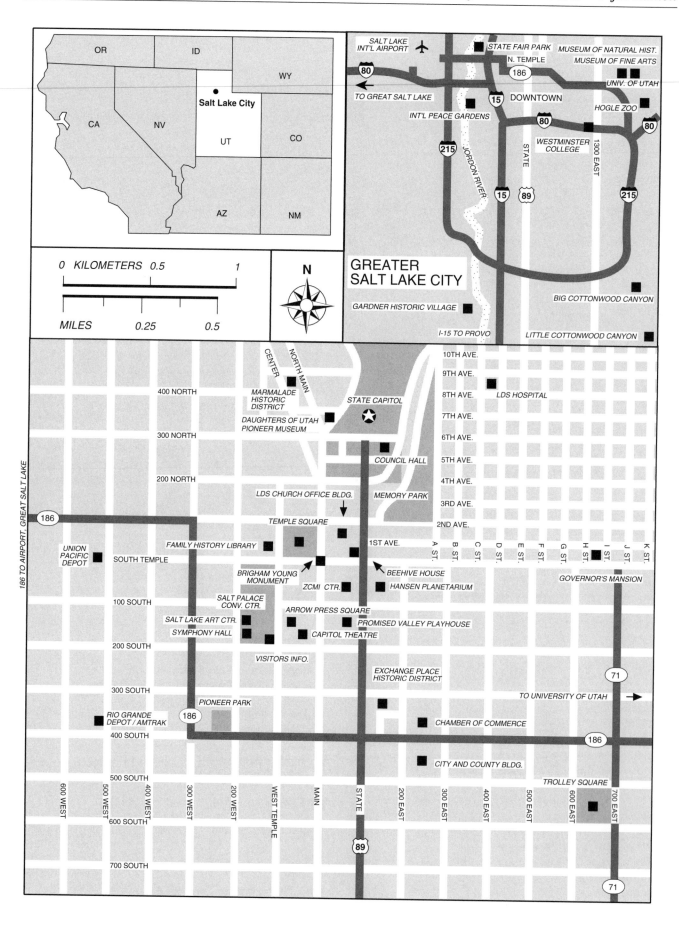

Introduction

Salt Lake City is the state capital and largest city in Utah. Founded in 1847 by religious leader Brigham Young, the city is the world headquarters of the Church of Jesus Christ of Latter-day Saints (Mormons). From its early days as a mining and railroad town, Salt Lake City has emerged as the commercial and cultural hub for a large area of the western mountain region. The city recently played host to the 2002 Winter Olympics. The nearby mountains, historical and religious landmarks, and the uniqueness of the Great Salt Lake also make the city a prominent tourist attraction.

Geography and Climate

Salt Lake City is bounded on three sides by mountain ranges and on the northwest by the Great Salt Lake. The Jordan River flows just to the west of the downtown district. Mountains shield the city from much of the severe winter weather common to the area, and the lake also serves to moderate the temperatures. Summer days are typically hot and dry, with cool nights and little precipitation. The winters are cold but not severe, with snow remaining on the ground through most of the season. Spring, especially in March, is the season of heavy rain and high winds from Pacific storms.

Area: 109 square miles (2000)

Elevation: 4,330 feet above sea level

Average Temperatures: January, 36.4° F; July, 92.2° F; annual average, 51.8° F.

Annual Average Precipitation: 15.7 inches

History

European Explorers Replace Native Americans

For thousands of years, the inhabitants of the northern Utah region were hunter-gatherers. Artifacts dating as far back as 12,000 years have been found in caves near the Great Salt Lake. About 500 B.C. the Fremont tribe, a less nomadic, agricultural society, settled in the area, building impressive cliff dwellings and drawing elaborate rock paintings, many of which can still be viewed today. Changing environmental conditions eventually made primitive farm-

ing impossible, and by the twelfth century, the area was populated mainly by the Ute, Paiute, and Shoshone tribes of nomadic hunters.

The first Europeans to travel through the area were the Spanish, coming from New Mexico in search of a direct route to Monterey, California, in 1776. In the early 1800s, fur trappers and ''mountain men'' explored the region, discovering the Great Salt Lake and mapping the mountain passes. A number of government expeditions explored the area, and a steady stream of settlers bound for California began to pass through.

Mormons Settle, Lay Out Town; Religious Beliefs Questioned

A group of Mormon pioneers led by Brigham Young settled in the Salt Lake Valley in 1847, laying out a town they called Great Salt Lake City. From the beginning the city was well planned, with a grid of ten-acre plots separated by streets 132 feet wide. The industrious settlers began planting crops and developing intricate irrigation systems, eventually forming more than 500 settlements in the Utah area. Disaster was averted in 1848 when, as drought and plagues of insects threatened the crops, flocks of seagulls arrived to consume the insects, thereby saving the harvest.

In 1848 the settlers organized the State of Deseret and applied for statehood with a government headed by the Mormon Church. Congress denied the petition and instead created Utah Territory in 1850. Salt Lake City was incorporated in 1851, and in 1856 it replaced Fillmore as the territorial capital. Misunderstandings about Mormon religious beliefs and political outrage at the Mormon practice of polygamy led to the so-called ''Utah War'' in 1857 between the Mormon settlers and the U.S. Government. Although the dispute was settled peacefully in 1858, relations between the church and the territorial government were strained for many years.

City Becomes State Capital; Regional Mines, Industry Thrive

The two ends of the transcontinental railroad met just 40 miles north of Salt Lake City in 1869, tying Utah with the outside world. Over the next twenty years, hundreds of copper, silver, and lead mines were developed in the region, bringing a large number of non-Mormon settlers. Under continued pressure, the practice of polygamy was officially stopped by the church in 1890. This paved the way for women's suffrage in Utah, which had been a political lever in the national polygamy debate. The majestic Mormon Temple, begun in 1853, was completed in 1892, and Utah entered the Union in 1896 as the third suffrage state with Salt Lake City as the capital.

During the early twentieth century Salt Lake City assumed the look of a modern city. The State Capitol building and a number of other impressive structures were built, electric trolley cars began service on the city's streets, and large residential sections developed around the city. Like most cities, Salt Lake City suffered during the Great Depression, but prosperity returned during World War II amidst a construction boom and increased demand for metals. Industrial expansion continued postwar with downtown development and beautification projects becoming a focus in the 1970s and 1980s.

In 2002 Salt Lake City hosted the "best attended" Olympic Winter Games in history, with 1.6 billion tickets sold and another 4 billion television viewers. The city continues to reap the benefits of improved infrastructure and a significant increase in tourism.

In recent years Salt Lake City has been consistently recognized for its prosperity and quality of life. In 2003 *Fortune* magazine ranked the city third-best in America for business. *Yahoo!* magazine listed it among the nation's top 25 "Wired Cities"; and the sixth edition of *Places Rated Almanac* ranked the Salt Lake City/Ogden area as the best place to live in North America.

Historical Information: Utah State Historical Society Library, 300 South Rio Grande Street, Salt Lake City, UT 84101; telephone (801)533-3500; fax (801)533-3503

Population Profile

Metropolitan Area Residents
1980: 910,000
1990: 1,072,227
2000: 1,333,914
Percent change, 1990–2000: 24.4%
U.S. rank in 1980: 41st
U.S. rank in 1990: 38th
U.S. rank in 2000: 35th

City Residents
1980: 163,033
1990: 159,928
2000: 181,743
2003 estimate: 179,894
Percent change, 1990–2000: 13.6%
U.S. rank in 1980: 90th
U.S. rank in 1990: 108th (State rank: 1st)
U.S. rank in 2000: 129th (State rank: 1st)

Density: 1,666.1 people per square mile (2000)

Racial and ethnic characteristics (2000)
White: 143,933
Black or African American: 3,433
American Indian and Alaska Native: 2,442
Asian: 6,579
Native Hawaiian and Pacific Islander: 3,437
Hispanic or Latino (may be of any race): 34,254
Other: 15,482

Percent of residents born in state: 49.1% (2000)

Age characteristics (2000)
Population under 5 years old: 14,432
Population 5 to 9 years old: 11,507
Population 10 to 14 years old: 10,488
Population 15 to 19 years old: 12,835
Population 20 to 24 years old: 21,381
Population 25 to 34 years old: 35,731
Population 35 to 44 years old: 25,021
Population 45 to 54 years old: 19,630
Population 55 to 59 years old: 6,058
Population 60 to 64 years old: 4,739
Population 65 to 74 years old: 8,852
Population 75 to 84 years old: 7,914
Population 85 years and older: 3,155
Median age: 30.0 years

Births (2003)
Total number: 18,223 (Salt Lake County)

Deaths (2003)
Total number: 5,312 (Salt Lake County)

Money income (1999)
Per capita income: $20,752
Median household income: $36,944
Total households: 71,492

Number of households with income of . . .
less than $10,000: 7,660
$10,000 to $14,999: 5,193
$15,000 to $24,999: 11,087
$25,000 to $34,999: 9,920
$35,000 to $49,999: 11,801
$50,000 to $74,999: 12,733
$75,000 to $99,999: 5,810
$100,000 to $149,999: 4,304
$150,000 to $199,999: 1,326
$200,000 or more: 1,658

Percent of families below poverty level: 10.4% (38.4% of which were female householder families with related children under 5 years)

2002 FBI Crime Index Total: 19,059

Municipal Government

Salt Lake City has a council-mayor form of government with the mayor elected at large. The mayor and seven council members serve a four-year term. The city is also the seat of Salt Lake County and the capital of Utah.

Head Official: Mayor Ross C. "Rocky" Anderson (NP) (since 2000; current term expires 2007)

Total Number of City Employees: 2,687 (2004)

City Information: Salt Lake City Corporation, 451 South State Street, Salt Lake City, UT 84111; telephone (801)535-6333

Economy

Major Industries and Commercial Activity

Salt Lake City was originally a farming community; it also depended on mining until the early 1980s when foreign competition began to erode profits from that industry. Today it has grown into a diverse economic region. As the state capital, county seat of Salt Lake County, and the largest city in the four-county Wasatch Front metropolitan area, the city is a government, commercial, and industrial center for Utah and much of the Intermountain West.

The service sector produces the most jobs in the city, especially computer and health care services. Government employment is considerable, with the State of Utah, University of Utah, and Salt Lake County among the city's top employers. A number of national financial institutions have established branch offices in Salt Lake City, making it the center of banking and finance for the region. Salt Lake City is the largest retail and wholesale market in Utah, and the city supports a thriving tourism industry. The construction industry remains significant. Salt Lake City is the international headquarters of the Church of Jesus Christ of Latter-day Saints.

Items and goods produced: petroleum products, electronics, missiles

Incentive Programs—New and Existing Companies

Local programs—The Salt Lake County Office of Business Economic Development offers incentives to new and existing companies in the form of loans, grants, and on-the-job training. It also provides no-cost monthly workshops. The Salt Lake City Department of Economic Development of-fers similar incentives as well as assistance with site selection, financial planning, and permit applications.

State programs—Utah's Centers of Excellence Program funds viable research at the college and university level, bridging the gap between technological innovation and marketplace success. Since its creation in 1986 the program has resulted in thousands of new high-tech jobs and significant growth for many of the state's tech companies. The Economic Development Corporation of Utah plays a dual role in the state's commercial success, promoting expansion of local companies as well as relocation for out-of-state firms. EDCUTAH offers a considerable network of public- and private-sector contacts, as well as support with site selection, media relations, and industry research. The Utah Small Business Development Center (USBDC) helps established and start-up companies prepare business plans, set sales goals, identify customers and the competition, analyze the market, and research financing sources. The USBDC operates in partnership with the U.S. Small Business Administration, the Utah Department of Community and Economic Development, and Salt Lake Community College. It offers training and resources in the areas of entrepreneurship, business development, the law, international business, financial management, e-commerce, and computer technology. The Salt Lake Chamber of Commerce represents 1,900 businesses across the state, lobbying the government and providing networking opportunities to benefit its member companies.

Job training programs—Custom Fit is an employee training program offered through the Utah College of Applied Technology, state colleges, and the local business community. It provides training in specific technologies, computer skills, safety certification, leadership, management and team-building. The Utah State Legislature allocates annual funding to Custom Fit, covering a substantial portion of the cost to employers.

State funding is also provided for Short Term Intensive Training programs across Utah. Training is offered at the state college level at a 66 percent discount to potential employers or employees. The program is customized to match full-time job seekers with the needs of specific companies.

Development Projects

Construction in Salt Lake City has declined somewhat since a boom leading up to the 2002 Winter Olympics. The Gateway, a multi-use development on Salt Lake City's west side, was completed in 2001. Covering nearly 30 acres, Gateway offers shopping, dining, and entertainment in an open-air setting, as well as office and residential housing space.

A recently completed $1.59 billion reconstruction of Interstate 15 will address traffic concerns in the Salt Lake area for the next 20 years. A commuter railway from Weber County to downtown Salt Lake City is expected to open in 2007. A $20 million Intermodal Transportation Center is under construction in the Gateway area, and will accommodate bus, automobile, bicycle, Amtrak, and Greyhound passengers.

Intermountain Health Care is planning a $362 million flagship hospital in the Salt Lake Valley with a projected completion date of 2006. The Salt Palace Convention Center will also complete its latest expansion in 2006.

Other projects in the planning phase or construction include a $45 million renovation of the Utah Theatre, restoration of the historic Frank Moss Courthouse, expansion of the Utah Children's Museum in a new Gateway location, and increased meeting space and accommodations at several major hotels.

Economic Development Information: Economic Development Corporation of Utah, 201 South Main Street, Suite 2010, Salt Lake City, UT 84111; telephone (801)328-8824; fax (801)531-1460

Commercial Shipping

Utah's free port law makes it an ideal location for the import and export of goods. Salt Lake City is a full-service customs port city with a foreign trade zone. The Salt Lake International Airport handles more than 550 million pounds of air cargo and express mail each year.

Southern Pacific and Union Pacific railways offer freight service throughout Utah. The state's railroad lines all converge in the Salt Lake-Ogden area, making it a convenient interline switching route for destinations across the country. About 2,000 interstate and intrastate motor freight carriers operate in Utah.

Labor Force and Employment Outlook

The services sector is Salt Lake City's largest employment division, with approximately 1,100 new jobs added in the last year. Health care and computer technology are two dominant subsections. Construction remains important to the local economy, despite declining employment since the 2002 Olympic Winter Games. Trade employment also remains high. Salt Lake City's unemployment rate is declining, and the Salt Lake Chamber of Commerce expects continued job growth in the years to come.

The following is a summary of data regarding the Salt Lake City metropolitan area labor force, 2004 annual averages.

Size of nonagricultural labor force: 565,000

Number of workers employed in ...
  construction and mining: 34,800
  manufacturing: 52,100
  trade, transportation and utilities: 118,600

information: 17,700
financial activities: 44,700
professional and business services: 84,900
educational and health services: 53,000
leisure and hospitality: 51,600
other services: 18,200
government: 89,300

Average hourly earnings of production workers employed in manufacturing: $15.34

Unemployment rate: 5.2% (January 2005)

Largest employers	Number of employees
State of Utah	22,000
Intermountain Health Care	22,000
University of Utah	17,000
Salt Lake County	6,000
Smith's Food & Drug Centers	6,000
U.S. Postal Service	5,500
Delta Air Lines	5,000
Novus Credit Services	5,000
Salt Lake City School District	4,000
Cordant Technologies	3,500
Qwest Communications	3,000
Zions First International Bank	3,000
Salt Lake City Corporation	3,000
PacifiCorp	2,500
Wells Fargo	2,000
Sears Roebuck and Company	2,000
Fred Meyer Stores	2,000

Cost of Living

The following is a summary of data regarding several key cost of living factors for the Salt Lake City area.

2004 (3rd Quarter) ACCRA Average House Price: $239,650

2004 (3rd Quarter) ACCRA Cost of Living Index: 97.3 (U.S. average = 100.0)

State income tax rate: Up to 7.0% on taxable income exceeding $7,500

State sales tax rate: Ranges from 5.75% to 7.0% (depending on municipality)

Local income tax rate: none

Local sales tax rate: 6.6% (Salt Lake City)

Property tax rate: Levied at the state and local level, based on assessed valuation; rate in 2005, .015288%

Economic Information: Economic Development Corporation of Utah, 201 South Main Street, Suite 2010, Salt Lake City, UT 84111; telephone (801)328-8824; fax (801)531-

1460. Governor's Office of Planning and Budget, Demographic and Economic Analysis, 116 State Capitol, Salt Lake City, UT 84114; telephone (801)538-1036;fax (801) 538-1547. Utah Department of Workforce Services, PO Box 45249, Salt Lake City, UT 84145-0249; telephone (801)526-9675; fax (801)526-9211; email dwscontactus @utah.gov. Bureau of Economic and Business Research, University of Utah, David Eccles School of Business, 1645 E Campus Center Dr., Rm 401, Salt Lake City, UT 84112-9302; telephone (801)581-6333; fax (801)581-3354; email bureau@business.utah.edu

Education and Research

Elementary and Secondary Schools

The Salt Lake City School District is sixth-largest in Utah. It's mission is to advocate for all students, provide education of the highest quality, and prepare students for opportunities in the future. Many district schools are currently in the midst of a 10-year reconstruction and renovation program.

The following is a summary of data regarding Salt Lake City public schools as of the 2002–2003 school year.

Total enrollment: 24,850

Number of facilities
  elementary schools: 27
  intermediate schools: 5
  senior high schools: 4

Student/teacher ratio: 20.02:1

Teacher salaries
  average: $38,268 (State of Utah)

Funding per pupil: $7,284

Public Schools Information: Salt Lake City School District, 440 East 100 South, Salt Lake City, Utah 84111-1891; telephone (801)578-8599; fax (801)578-8248. Utah State Office of Education, 250 East 500 South, PO Box 144200, Salt Lake City, UT 84114-4200; telephone (801)538-7500

Colleges and Universities

Salt Lake City is home to the University of Utah, the oldest university in the West. Founded in 1850, the university covers more than 1,000 acres and includes the Red Butte Garden and Arboretum. One of the country's top 30 public research universities, the University of Utah is known for its technology transfer program to move research into practical applications in the business world; it also has a medical school.

Salt Lake City is also home to prestigious Westminster College, a private non-denominational institution offering 24 undergraduate majors and a range of post-graduate degree and certificate programs. Other local colleges include the Salt Lake Community College and LDS Business College. Adult education is available through the Salt Lake City campus of the University of Phoenix.

Libraries and Research Centers

The Salt Lake City Public Library System consists of a main library and 5 branch locations, with a total of more than 750,000 volumes and 600 periodical subscriptions, as well as films, audio tapes, maps, and art reproductions. The library also contains special collections of old and rare material from the region's past. A new Main Library was unveiled in 2003, featuring a six-story curving, climbable wall, spiraling fireplaces, a multi-level reading area and a rooftop garden. The 240,000-square-foot space is double the size of the previous library. Several other branches were also remodeled or expanded in 2003.

The Salt Lake County Library System consists of a main library and 18 branches offering a variety of exhibits, events and collections. Salt Lake City is also home to the Utah State Library Program for the Blind and Disabled, which serves visually impaired, physically disabled, and reading disabled patrons across the western states. The library has more than 14,000 Braille books, 53,000 books on cassette, and 14,000 large-print books. The University of Utah maintains a large library system. A number of private, research, and special interest libraries also serve the city.

The Church of Jesus Christ of Latter-Day Saints Library houses a genealogical library, considered to be the largest of its kind in the world. Open to the public free of charge, the collection contains family history, local history, and vital records. The library is visited by approximately 1,900 patrons each day.

Centers in the Salt Lake City area conduct research activities in such fields as the environment, entomology, engineering design, biomedical engineering, toxicology, lasers, radiobiology, occupational and environmental health, astrophysics, astronomy, communications, nuclear engineering, physical electronics, remote sensing and cartography, mineral technology, isotope geology, seismology, mining, business and economics, finance, public affairs, politics, energy law, gerontology, the American West, the Middle East, and archaeology.

Public Library Information: Salt Lake City Public Library, 210 East 400 South, Salt Lake City, UT 84111; telephone (801)524-8200. Salt Lake County Library System, 2197 Fort Union Blvd, Salt Lake City, UT 84121-3139; telephone (801)943-4636; fax (801)942-6323

Health Care

Utah boasts some of the healthiest people in the country. In 2003 the state was ranked third-healthiest in the U.S. by the United Health Foundation. Utah has the lowest smoking rate in the nation, and also records some of the lowest cancer, heart disease, and infant mortality rates.

A major focus for health care in Salt Lake City is the University Health Services Center, the teaching and research hospital for the University of Utah Medical School. The system consists of 850 physicians and health-care professionals, inpatient and outpatient services, same-day surgery, a 90-bed psychiatric hospital, and 24-hour assessment and referral services. Intermountain Health Care is a non-profit organization based in Salt Lake City. It includes 21 hospitals and has a mandate to provide quality care regardless of a patients' abilities to pay. Primary Children's Medical Center was ranked one of the top 10 children's hospitals in the country in 2003. The Intermountain Shriners Hospital for Children provides no-cost care and services for children with disorders of the bones, muscles and joints.

Recreation

Sightseeing

Downtown Salt Lake City boasts a number of popular attractions. The State Capitol with its spectacular copper-clad dome is located on Capitol Hill, which offers a view of the city and surrounding area. At Temple Square, the headquarters of the Mormon Church, the Salt Lake Temple displays six spires, fifteen-foot-thick granite walls, and a golden statue of the Angel Moroni. Also on the square are the famous Mormon Tabernacle, built in 1867 with no interior supports, and the Seagull Monument, honoring the birds that saved the settlers' first crops.

Other sights in the city include Beehive House, the restored residence of Brigham Young, who gave it the name because he wanted his followers to be as industrious as bees. Fort Douglas, a 9,000-acre historical fort, is filled with interesting military architecture dating from 1862. Utah's Hogle Zoo contains a collection of exotic birds and animals in a natural setting, including a new elephant habitat planned for 2005. This Is The Place Heritage Park contains an operational pioneer community as it was in 1847, as well as "This Is The Place" Monument, marking the spot where Brigham Young chose the area as a home for the Mormons.

The Great Salt Lake, over 90 miles long and 48 miles wide, is the second most salty body of water in the world. The high salinity makes it a unique swimming experience: it is almost impossible for a person to sink in the water. A different type of aquatic entertainment is found at Raging Waters, a family-oriented theme park with more than 30 different water rides and a picnic area. Clark Planetarium presents daily star shows and images from the Hubble Telescope. Olympic Cauldron Park is a new and stunning addition to the city, featuring the 72-foot Olympic Cauldron, which housed the Olympic Flame; the Hoberman Arch, where athletes stood to receive their medals; a visitor center; and a theatre dedicated to the memory of the 2002 Olympic Winter Games.

Arts and Culture

Salt Lake City is home to a number of acclaimed cultural organizations. The world-famous Mormon Tabernacle Choir, an American institution for many years, is based in Salt Lake City. The Utah Symphony performs 260 concerts nationally and internationally each year; the orchestra performs locally in Maurice Abravanel Hall, a world-class acoustic space. The historic Capitol Theatre is home to the Utah Opera and Ballet West, one of the nation's leading companies. The Rose Wagner Performing Arts Center includes an art gallery and several performance spaces for new and established artists.

Theatrical performances are scheduled at Desert Star Playhouse, featuring live musical comedy melodrama, honky-tonk piano, and audience participation; Hale Center Theater, offering comedies and musicals for the whole family to enjoy; Off Broadway Theatre, staging comedy and improvisation; Promised Valley Playhouse, presenting theater in a restored turn-of-the-century showplace; and Salt Lake Community College Grand Theatre, featuring Broadway musicals.

Several interesting museums are located in Salt Lake City. The Daughters of the Utah Pioneers Museum houses a collection of dolls, textiles, and frontier furniture in a replica of the famous Salt Palace. Located in a restored nineteenth century railroad station, the Utah Historical Society features exhibits on the history of Utah's various ethnic groups. The Fort Douglas Military Museum inside the restored fort displays items relating to the military history of the state. Hill Air Force Base Aerospace Museum maintains a collection of military aircraft, missiles, vehicles and uniforms. The Utah Museum of Natural History contains a large collection of dinosaur skeletons excavated from many local sites, as well as exhibits on animals and minerals of the region.

The Salt Lake Art Center houses traveling art exhibits from around the world as well as a permanent collection and a sculpture garden. On the campus of the University of Utah, the Utah Museum of Fine Arts contains paintings by artists such as Rubens, antique tapestries, and Louis XIV furniture.

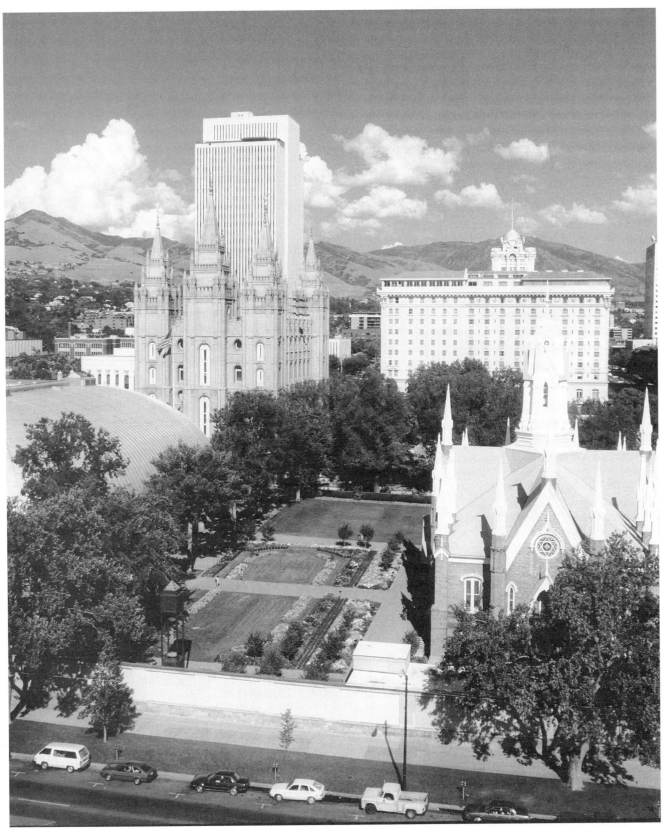

The Mormon Temple, the Mormon Tabernacle, and the Seagull Monument can all be found at Temple Square.

The Museum of Church History and Art chronicles the early development of the Church of Jesus Christ of Latter-day Saints. The Chase Home Museum of Utah Folk Arts is dedicated to the work of Utah's ethnic, native, and rural artists.

Festivals and Holidays

The Utah Arts Festival, the nation's first statewide arts festival, takes place in June and provides exciting performance and visual art, crafts, and ethnic foods. June is also the time for the prestigious Gina Bachauer International Piano Foundation Festival and Competition. The Festival of the American West, held on the Utah State University campus in Logan, occurs annually during the last week of July/early August. Pioneer Harvest Days happens every September in Pioneer Trail State Park, featuring authentic examples of historic craftwork, including butter making, weaving, blacksmithing, adobe brick making, and pioneer games. September is a busy month in Salt Lake City, with the Salt Lake City Jazz Festival and the Utah State Fair, which features midway rides, livestock and art exhibits, and special entertainment nightly. The Christmas season begins the day after Thanksgiving when more than 300,000 lights are turned on in Temple Square. The Sundance Film Festival takes place in the Salt Lake area every January. The Madeleine Festival takes place at the Cathedral of the Madeleine each spring, offering free cultural performances to the community. The annual Great Salt Lake Bird Festival takes place in May, as well as Living Traditions, a three-day festival honoring folk artists of the Salt Lake Valley.

Sports for the Spectator

Salt Lake City is home to two professional basketball teams: the NBA's Utah Jazz and the WNBA's Utah Starzz. Both teams play in the $90 million, state-of-the-art Delta Center. Hockey is represented by the American Hockey League's Utah Grizzlies, who also play at Delta Center. The Salt Lake Stingers, a Triple A affiliate of the Anaheim Angels, play baseball at Franklin Covey Field from April through mid-September. The University of Utah fields competitive teams in most major collegiate sports. Salt Lake City is also host to two professional soccer teams, an indoor football team, and a number of rodeo events on the national rodeo circuit. The nearby Bonneville Salt Flats is the site of numerous auto races and frequent attempts to set the land speed record.

Sports for the Participant

The Salt Lake City area offers an abundance of outdoor activities. The nearby mountains provide year-round recreation: hiking, fishing, camping, and winter skiing. Some of the nation's most popular ski resorts such as Snowbird, Park City, Deer Valley, Sundance, Alta, and Solitude are within a 40-minute drive of the city. Non-traditional sports such as ski-jumping and luge are offered at new facilities constructed for the 2002 Olympic Winter Games. The area's rivers offer white-water rafting, canoeing, and innertubing. Many area lakes are ideal spots for all forms of water activity—boating, sailing, water skiing, and swimming.

Gallivan Utah Center Plaza has a skating rink. Salt Lake City operates a number of parks that feature swimming pools, jogging trails, playing fields, tennis courts, and other recreational facilities. Several championship-grade golf courses are located in the city as well.

Shopping and Dining

America's first department store, the Zions Cooperative Mercantile Institution, opened in Salt Lake City in 1868 and continues to operate today in ZCMI Center Mall. A number of major shopping centers are located in the city, including Crossroads Plaza and Trolley Square, a theme mall located in a group of restored trolley barns. The Gateway, Salt Lake's only open-air entertainment, dining, and shopping venue, was completed in 2001. It features 90 shops and restaurants, a restored 1908 Union Pacific Depot and the Olympic Legacy Plaza. Many small shops and boutiques are scattered throughout the metropolitan area.

Because of its diverse ethnic population, Salt Lake City features a variety of international restaurants; many are prominent nationally. Everything from inexpensive fast food to elegant, intimate dining can be found in the more than 300 restaurants located in the valley.

Visitor Information: Salt Lake City Convention & Visitors Bureau, 90 South West Temple, Salt Lake City, Utah 84101; telephone (801)521-2822; fax (801)534-4927

Convention Facilities

The Salt Palace Convention Center, located in the center of the downtown district, is the city's major convention facility. It features 365,000 square feet of exhibit space, a 45,000-square-foot ballroom, and 53 meeting rooms. When the expansion of the center is complete in 2006, the capacity of the Salt Palace will have increased by 40 percent.

There are more than 4,200 hotel rooms and 90 restaurants within walking distance of the Salt Palace Convention Center and another 7,000 hotel rooms in the city. Several of the major hotels also contain extensive meeting, banquet, and ballroom accommodations. The Delta Center offers meeting rooms ranging in size from 400 to 10,000 square feet.

Convention Information: Salt Lake City Convention & Visitors Bureau, 90 South West Temple, Salt Lake City, Utah 84101; telephone (801)521-2822; fax (801)534-4927

Transportation

Approaching the City

The Salt Lake International Airport offers 972 daily flights on 16 airlines, and is located just minutes from downtown Salt Lake City. In 2004 the airport served 18.3 million customers. The Utah Transit Authority provides transportation to and from the airport; taxis are available, and many area hotels provide complimentary shuttle service.

Salt Lake City is at the junction of two major interstate highways, Interstate 15 running north-south and Interstate 80 running east-west. Interstate 215 forms a commuter loop and by-pass around the inner city.

Amtrak provides national passenger rail service from Salt Lake City's Gateway area. The TRAX light rail system serves Salt Lake County.

Traveling in the City

Walking is perhaps the best way to see the city's sights. Salt Lake City was laid out in a grid pattern by the early Mormon pioneers with exceptionally wide streets, which makes automobile travel easy and pleasurable compared to most larger metropolitan areas. Streets are named according to their distance and relationship to Temple Square. Salt Lake City recently implemented an intelligent CommuterLink system to decrease traffic congestion.

The Utah Transit Authority (UTA) operates more than 100 different routes throughout a 1,400-square-mile area. Free fare zones operate downtown. UTA also provides service to ski resorts in winter, and door-to-door transportation for the disabled.

Communications

Newspapers and Magazines

Salt Lake City is served by two major daily newspapers, *The Salt Lake Tribune* and *Deseret News.* The Latter-Day Saints publish three titles: *Church News,* a weekly newspaper; *The Friend,* a magazine for children aged three to eleven; and *New Era,* a magazine for teens. Magazines published in the city include *Salt Lake Magazine* and several scholarly, medical, and industry magazines.

Television and Radio

Salt Lake City's 10 television stations represent the commercial networks and independent and instructional channels. The city is also served by a variety of cable channels. Nearly two dozen AM and FM radio stations broadcast from the Salt Lake City area, providing a wide range of music, news, and informational programming.

Media Information: *The Salt Lake Tribune,* 143 S. Main Street, Salt Lake City, UT 84111; telephone (801) 257-8742. *Deseret News,* 30 E 100 South, PO Box 1257, Salt Lake City, UT 84110; telephone (801)237-2100

Salt Lake City Online

City of Salt Lake City home page. Available www.ci.slc.ut.us

Deseret News. Available www.deseretnews.com/dn

Discover Southern Utah! Available www.infowest.com/Utah

Salt Lake City Public Library. Available www.slcpl.lib.ut.us

Salt Lake City Public Schools. Available www.slc.k12.ut.us

Salt Lake Convention and Visitors Bureau. Available www.saltlake.org

The Salt Lake Tribune. Available www.sltrib.com

Utah State Office of Education. Available www.usoe.k12.ut.us

Selected Bibliography

Ayres, Becky, *Salt Lake City* (Minneapolis, MN: Dillon Press, 1990)

Miller, Marjorie, *Salt Lake City: Jewel of the Wasatch* (Yellow Cat Flats, Utah: Yellow Cat Publishing, 2000)

Naifeh, Steven W., *The Mormon Murders: A True Story of Greed, Deceit, and Death* (New York: Weidenfeld and Nicolson, 1988)

WASHINGTON

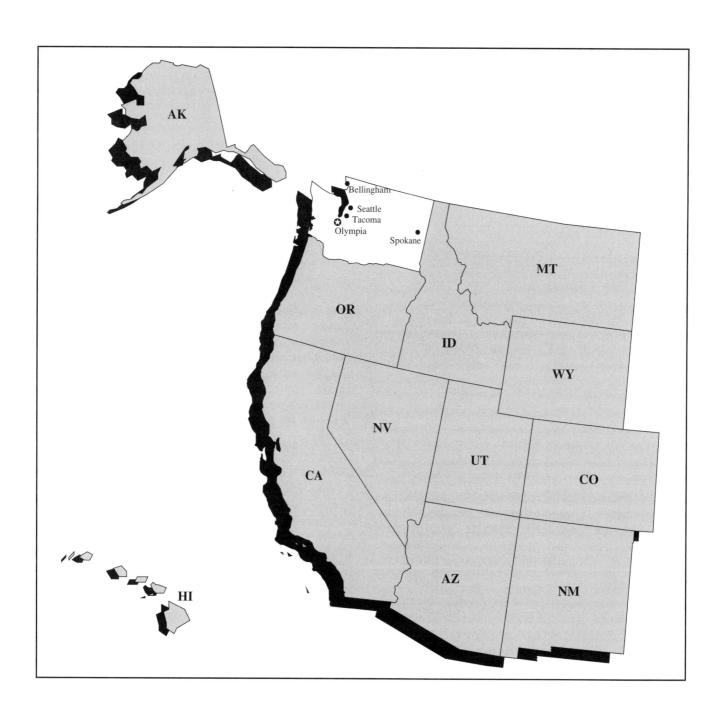

The State in Brief

Nickname: Evergreen State
Motto: *Al-Ki* (By and by)

Flower: Coast rhododendron
Bird: Willow goldfinch

Area: 71,299 square miles (2000; U.S. rank: 18th)
Elevation: Ranges from sea level to 14,410 feet above sea level
Climate: Generally mild and humid in the western region dominated by the Pacific Ocean; semi arid in the eastern region; heavy snows in higher elevation

Admitted to Union: November 11, 1889
Capital: Olympia
Head Official: Governor Christine Gregoire (D) (until 2009)

Population
  1980: 4,132,000
  1990: 4,866,692
  2000: 5,894,121
  2004 estimate: 6,203,788
  Percent change, 1990–2000: 21.1%
  U.S. rank in 2004: 15th
  Percent of residents born in state: 47.2% (2000)
  Density: 88.6 people per square mile (2000)
  2002 FBI Crime Index Total: 309,931

Racial and Ethnic Characteristics (2000)
  White: 4,821,823
  Black or African American: 190,267
  American Indian and Alaska Native: 93,301
  Asian: 322,335
  Native Hawaiian and Pacific Islander: 23,953
  Hispanic or Latino (may be of any race): 441,509
  Other: 228,923

Age Characteristics (2000)
  Population under 5 years old: 394,306
  Population 5 to 19 years old: 1,288,713
  Percent of population 65 years and over: 11.2%
  Median age: 35.3 years (2000)

Vital Statistics
  Total number of births (2003): 80,091
  Total number of deaths (2003): 44,736 (infant deaths, 416)
  AIDS cases reported through 2003: 5,108

Economy
  Major industries: Trade; manufacturing; finance, insurance, and real estate; government; services; agriculture
  Unemployment rate: 5.5% (February 2005)
  Per capita income: $33,264 (2003; U.S. rank: 13th)
  Median household income: $45,960 (3-year average, 2001-2003)
  Percentage of persons below poverty level: 10.6% (1999)
  Income tax rate: None
  Sales tax rate: 6.5% (food and prescription drugs are exempt)

Bellingham

The City in Brief

Founded: as Whatcom (1852); renamed Bellingham (1903)

Head Official: Mayor Mark Asmundson (NP) (since 1996)

City Population
 1980: 45,794
 1990: 52,179
 2000: 67,171
 2003 estimate: 71,289
 Percent change, 1990–2000: 28.7%
 U.S. rank in 1980: 466th
 U.S. rank in 1990: 477th (State rank: 9th)
 U.S. rank in 2000: 461st (State rank: 10th)

Metropolitan Area Population
 1980: 107,000
 1990: 127,780
 2000: 166,814
 Percent change, 1990–2000: 30.5%
 U.S. rank in 1980: Not reported
 U.S. rank in 2000: 185th

Area: 31.74 square miles (2000)
Elevation: 68 feet above sea level
Average Annual Temperature: 51.5° F
Average Annual Precipitation: 38 inches of rain, 20 inches of snow

Major Economic Sectors: trade, services, government
Unemployment Rate: 6.0% (January 2005)
Per Capita Income: $19,483 (1999)

2002 FBI Crime Index Total: 5,108

Major Colleges and Universities: Western Washington University, Whatcom Community College, Northwest Indian College

Daily Newspaper: *The Bellingham Herald*

0   1   2
KILOMETERS

MILES   0.5   1   1.5   2

N

Bellingham
WA   MT

OR   ID

WY

CA   NV   UT   CO

TO LUMMI

BELLINGHAM INTERNATIONAL AIRPORT

5

AIRPORT

MARINE

BENNETT

MAPLEWOOD

NORTHWEST

BAKERVIEW

WHATCOM COMMUNITY COLLEGE

MERIDIAN

JAMES

WOBURN

MT. BAKER HWY.

BARKLEY

SUNSET

ORLEANS

BIRCHWOOD

ST. JOSEPH HOSPITAL

BELLINGHAM TECHNICAL COLLEGE

ILLINOIS

MERIDIAN

5

ALABAMA

ELM

GIRARD

CORNWALL

JAMES

DUPONT

CHESTNUT

OHIO

IOWA

WOBURN

YEW

CIVIC FIELD

ELECTRIC

LAKE WHATCOM

DOWNTOWN

BELLINGHAM BAY

STATE

FOREST

GARDEN

VISITOR AND CONVENTION CENTER

LAKEVIEW

YEW

WESTERN WASHINGTON UNIVERSITY

BILL MACDONALD PKWY

S. COLLEGE

TAYLOR

HARRIS

24TH

32ND

OLD FAIRHAVEN PKWY

5

SAMISH WAY

CHUCKANUT

5

TO LARRABEE STATE PARK

FARRAGUT

ELLSWORTH

DUPONT

GIRARD

GRANT

HALLECK

YOUNG

NEW

CORNWALL

CITY HALL

OHIO

MUSEUM OF ART AND HISTORY

LOTTIE

CENTRAL

LIBRARY

CHILDREN'S MUSEUM

PROSPECT

FLORA

CHAMPION

COMMERCIAL

MT. BAKER THEATRE

CHAMPION

MAGNOLIA

CORNWALL

BAY

COMMERCIAL

HOLLY

RAILROAD

STATE

FOREST

GARDEN

CHESTNUT

DOWNTOWN

Introduction

Bellingham, a coastal city built around the deep water harbor of Bellingham Bay, is set against the backdrop of the Cascade Mountains. Bellingham is the last major city before the coast of Washington state meets the border of Canada. It was named in honor of Sir William Bellingham, who was director of stores for the British Admiralty. The renovated old, historic buildings, views of the water and the mountain, and gorgeous sunsets make for a picture-postcard setting.

Geography and Climate

Bellingham is the seat of Whatcom County, the most northwestern county in the United States. The city is located 90 miles north of Seattle, 50 miles south of Vancouver, British Columbia, and 20 miles from the Canadian border at Baline. Bellingham, situated at the foot of 10,788-foot Mount Baker, is set on several hills overlooking the 172 San Juan Islands.

Bellingham has a mild, maritime climate with temperatures ranging from 45 to 60 degrees in spring and fall, 30 to 50 degrees in winter, and 60 to 80 degrees in summer. Most days have at least partial sunshine and snow; sleet and hail occur only about 15 days per year.

Area: 31.74 square miles (2000)

Elevation: 68 feet above sea level

Average Temperatures: January, 40.5° F; July, 63.5° F; annual average, 51.5° F

Average Annual Precipitation: 38 inches of rain, 20 inches of snow

History

European Contact with Natives Minimal at First

Long before the coming of Europeans, ancestors of local Bellingham tribes—the Lummi, the Nooksack, and the Semiahmoo—established camps along the bay as part of the great migration over the land bridge that once extended from Asia to North America. Salmon from the surrounding waters was their dietary mainstay, supplemented by roots, berries, and shellfish. The tribes engaged in both warfare and trade at various times. Some historians contend that Spanish explorers were the first white men to visit the area; if so, little evidence of them remains. The Lummi and Semiahmoo still live in the area and salmon remains their chief source of sustenance.

British Captain George Vancouver weighed anchor in nearby Birch Bay during his explorations of the Puget Sound in 1792, and Lt. Joseph Widbey charted Vancouver Bay. Widbey and his men may have seen a community of more than 3,000 natives living near the bay. Vancouver is said to have named the site of present-day Bellingham after the British admiralty controller who outfitted his ships.

As a result of reports carried back to Europe about the bounty of the region, traders began to arrive and a fur industry burgeoned in the early 1800s. From 1825 to 1846 the Hudson's Bay Company held domain over the region, but in the latter year the United States and Great Britain established a boundary at the 49th Parallel, and the Hudson's Bay Company relocated to Vancouver.

Industries Emerge; A Rush for Gold

In 1852, assisted by Lummi tribesmen, Henry Roeder built a sawmill on what is now Whatcom Creek. This initiated a period of coal mining and milling that continued for many decades. Whatcom County was established in 1854. Although the area of Bellingham remained untouched during the Indian War of 1855–1856, an infantry group was sent to Bellingham Bay in 1856 to establish Fort Bellingham.

More than 10,000 people were drawn to Bellingham during the Fraser River Gold Rush of 1858. A tent city mushroomed, until would-be prospectors were advised by Canadian officials that before starting digging they had to report to Victoria, British Columbia. Eventually, fire and fatalities brought difficult times to the mining industry, and Roeder's mill site was sold to a company from Kansas City. Soon after, a boom was initiated by the building of a railroad that connected Bellingham to the trans-Canada railroad line. Other major segments of the economy at that time were farming, fishing, and canning. In the late 1880s the town of Fairhaven, now part of Bellingham, was promoted as the "next Chicago" by entrepreneur Nelson Bennett, and hundreds of workers were hired to build hotels, homes, and office buildings. People began arriving at the rate of 300 per month, among them gamblers and prostitutes. A vigilante group tried to keep the peace until a police force was finally formed in 1890. In 1902 a brewery was founded in Bellingham that at its height produced more than 100,000 barrels of beer annually. However, the Bellingham Bay Brewery disappeared forever with the beginning of prohibition in 1917.

Bellingham was formed in 1903 with the consolidation of four towns—Whatcom, New Whatcom, Fairhaven, and Bellingham—into one town with the name Bellingham. During the late 1800s tall ships could be seen loading coal, salmon, and timber for transport to cities around the globe. Prosperous businessmen began building impressive homes in the Sehome Hill section of the city, many of which are now used for student housing. The Whatcom Normal School opened in 1899, later to become Western Washington College of Education in 1937, Western Washington Sate College in 1961, and finally Western Washington University within the following decade.

In June 1999 a fuel pipeline exploded along Whatcom Creek, killing three people along with thousands of fish and other wildlife. The tragedy resulted in major changes to federal pipeline laws and the creation of a Washington State Office of Pipeline Safety. After a rocky economical start to the twenty-first century, today's Bellingham is a growing and vibrant community set to the scenic backdrop of majestic Mt. Baker.

Historical Information: Center for Pacific Northwest Studies, Goltz-Murray Archives Building, Western Washington University, Bellingham, WA 98225-9123; telephone (360)650-7747; fax (360)650-3323; email cpnws@wwu.edu

Population Profile

Metropolitan Area Residents
1980: 107,000
1990: 127,780
2000: 166,814
Percent change, 1990–2000: 30.5%
U.S. rank in 1980: Not reported
U.S. rank in 1990: Not reported
U.S. rank in 2000: 185th

City Residents
1980: 45,794
1990: 52,179
2000: 67,171
2003 estimate: 71,289
Percent change, 1990–2000: 28.7%
U.S. rank in 1980: 466th
U.S. rank in 1990: 477th (State rank: 9th)
U.S. rank in 2000: 461st (State rank: 10th)

Density: 2,619.3 people per square mile (2000)

Racial and ethnic characteristics (2000)
White: 59,031

Black or African American: 655
American Indian and Alaska Native: 997
Asian: 2,853
Native Hawaiian and Pacific Islander: 116
Hispanic or Latino (may be of any race): 3,111
Other: 1,450

Percent of residents born in state: 49.4% (2000)

Age characteristics (2000)
Population under 5 years old: 3,502
Population 5 to 9 years old: 3,228
Population 10 to 14 years old: 3,151
Population 15 to 19 years old: 6,373
Population 20 to 24 years old: 11,603
Population 25 to 34 years old: 9,616
Population 35 to 44 years old: 8,186
Population 45 to 54 years old: 8,690
Population 55 to 59 years old: 2,584
Population 60 to 64 years old: 1,881
Population 65 to 74 years old: 3,537
Population 75 to 84 years old: 3,292
Population 85 years and older: 1,528
Median age: 30.4 years

Births (2003)
Total number: 876

Deaths (2003)
Total number: 988 (of which, 2 were infants under the age of 1 year)

Money income (1999)
Per capita income: $19,483
Median household income: $32,530
Total households: 28,012

Number of households with income of . . .
less than $10,000: 3,925
$10,000 to $14,999: 2,389
$15,000 to $24,999: 4,476
$25,000 to $34,999: 3,962
$35,000 to $49,999: 4,530
$50,000 to $74,999: 4,654
$75,000 to $99,999: 1,847
$100,000 to $149,999: 1,450
$150,000 to $199,999: 450
$200,000 or more: 329

Percent of families below poverty level: 14.9% (of which, 61.9% were female householder families with related children under 5 years)

2002 FBI Crime Index Total: 5,108

Municipal Government

Bellingham has a mayor-council form of government. Six council members serve four-year terms and a seventh council member serves a two-year term as a council person-at-large. The mayor serves a four-year term.

Head Official: Mayor Mark Asmundson (NP) (since 1996; current term expires 2007)

Total Number of City Employees: 892 (2003)

City Information: City of Bellingham, Bellingham City Hall, 210 Lottie St., Bellingham, WA 98225; telephone (360)676-6900; email mayorsoffice@cob.org

Economy

Major Industries and Commercial activity

The year 2001 delivered a number of blows to Bellingham's economy. Georgia-Pacific Corp. closed its pulp and paper mill, resulting in the loss of 420 high-paying jobs and nearly $1 million to the local economy each year. Alcoa's Intalco Works aluminum plant also shut down part of its Bellingham operations, further trimming the local workforce. Heightened border security after the September 11th terrorist strikes significantly reduced the number of visitors from Canada that spent their retail and entertainment dollar in Whatcom County.

Local officials realized that the area's dependence on resource-based industries made it particularly susceptible to such events, and that diversification was necessary to ensure future stability and growth. The downfall of diversification is that tourism- and other service-related jobs tend to pay far less than manufacturing jobs. While hospitality jobs paid an average of $26,000 per year in Whatcom County, the jobs lost at Georgia-Pacific paid about $52,000 a year, according to Jim Vleming, a state economist, in the July 31, 2002, issue of *The Seattle Times.*

Still, jobs in service industries are increasingly important, not just to Bellingham's economy but to that of the nation as a whole. This is due in large part to the emergence of technology-driven sectors in the 1990s. Whatcom County employment in services increased from 18.9 percent in 1981 to 25.6 percent in 2000, while manufacturing employment shrunk from 20.8 percent to 14.3 percent over the same period.

Bellingham's economy has been traditionally based on agriculture, fishing, and timber. Today, these segments are still vital components of the local economy, though of less importance than they once had been. The bulk of Whatcom County's agricultural activity involves berry and dairy farming. Although the number and size of farms has been steadily declining, production has been climbing. In 2001 the county's 201 dairy farms produced milk valued at $185 million, compared to the 480 farms and $130 million in production in 1985. During 2000, workers in Whatcom County's berry farms produced more blueberries and raspberries than any other county in the state, and ranked second in strawberries. Seed potatoes and apples are also important crops.

Commercial fishing, one of the area's oldest industries, has taken a drastic downturn due to overfishing, shortened seasons, and falling prices. Once home to one of the largest commercial fishing fleets, Whatcom County had 740 commercial vessels in 1985; by 2002 the Port of Bellingham reported only 177 such vessels. The forestry industry tends to be more stabile, as loggers in Whatcom County rely more on private lands than on public timberlands, making them more impervious to federal environmental restrictions on public resources.

Despite the losses in paper and aluminum segments, manufacturing remains an important industry in Whatcom County. Manufacturing of wood products and transportation equipment has seen gains in recent years. Boatbuilding is a crucial segment of the transportation equipment sector, as its focus has shifted from fishing vessels to the production of luxury yachts and military boats.

Healthcare is becoming increasingly vital to the local economy. Comprised of such areas as hospitals, nursing and residential care, ambulatory clinics, and social assistance, the healthcare field employed nearly 7,600 residents of Whatcom County in 2003. Across the nation, healthcare is a booming industry, driven by an aging and increasingly obese population. The Bureau of Labor Statistics estimates that certain segments of this industry will experience a growth of up to 4.5 percent in wages between 2002 and 2012.

Items and goods produced: boats, lumber and wood products, tissue paper, refined oil and petroleum products, blueberries, strawberries, raspberries, seed potatoes, apples, processed frozen foods, baked goods

Incentive Programs—New and Existing Companies

Local programs—The Bellingham Whatcom Economic Development Council promotes local businesses, products, and services, and helps firms in interfacing with regional, national, and international markets. It assists businesses by providing information on expansion and investment decisions, and by providing liaison with government officials and community leaders. It also offers a revolving loan program and a public infrastructure program. Additionally, the Port of Bellingham, a municipal corporation, offers an industrial revenue bond program and a foreign trade zone program to benefit local businesses.

State programs—The state of Washington offers a number of incentive programs to attract new and expanding businesses to the state. Among them are B & O tax credits; sales/ use tax deferrals for technology and manufacturing companies as well as for firms relocating or expanding in distressed areas; and loan programs that apply to rural areas and the redevelopment of brownfields.

Job training programs—Job training programs are offered by the state of Washington, and the Bellingham Whatcom Economic Development Council facilitates the implementation of workforce development programs. Training programs for a variety of industries, including healthcare and manufacturing, are offered by such institutions of higher learning as Bellingham Technical College, Northwest Indian College, Western Washington University, and Whatcom Community College.

Development Projects

Funding for the Depot Market Square was secured in 2004. When completed, this development will serve not only as the permanent home of the Bellingham Farmers Market, but also as a community gathering place for public and private events. Elsewhere in Bellingham, the first phase of construction of the Bellwether on the Bay was completed in the early 2000s, with the second phase underway in 2005. Bellwether on the Bay is a mixed-use complex occupying 15 acres of waterfront property. Phase I developments include two office buildings, the four-star Hotel Bellwether, a fitness center and spa, and a variety of restaurants and shops.

Aside from commercial developments, Bellingham has devoted considerable resources to improve culture, recreation, and the general quality of life. The Taylor Avenue Dock and Boardwalk was completed in 2004; this $2.9 million project restored and improved the historic dock and built a new boardwalk connecting the dock to Boulevard Park. September 2004 hailed the grand opening of the Studio Theatre, a 3,000-square-foot room within the historic Mt. Baker Theatre to host small-scale musical and theatrical productions. Also in 2004, a clean-up and restoration project was initiated at the Holly Street Landfill. Reconstruction of portions of the Civic Field Complex, including its grandstands, football field and track, stadium, and skate park, will be completed in stages from 2005 through 2006 at the cost of over $9.9 million.

Economic Development Information: Bellingham/Whatcom Chamber of Commerce & Industry, 1201 Cornwall Ave., Ste. 100, PO Box 958, Bellingham, WA 98227; telephone

(360)734-1330; fax (360)734-1332; email chamber @bellingham.com. Bellingham Whatcom Economic Development Council, 105 E Holly St., PO Box 2803, Bellingham, WA 98227; telephone (360)676-4255; toll-free (800)810-4255; fax (360)647-9413; email info@bwedc.org. Greater Whatcom Partnership for a Sustainable Economy, c/o Port of Bellingham, 1801 Roeder Ave., PO Box 1677, Bellingham, WA 98227; telephone (360)676-2500

Commercial Shipping

Whatcom County has four major locations for U.S.-Canada border crossings: two in Blaine, one in Lynden, and one in Sumas. Freight rail service is offered in Bellingham by the Burlington Northern Santa Fe, Canadian Rail, and Canadian Pacific railroads. Among its motor freight companies are Puget Sound Truck Lines, Roadway Express, and Yellow Transportation. The area is also home to 10 local freight brokers. Bellingham International Airport (BIA) serves as a base for charter airlines and is a port of entry for general aviation aircraft. The airport is home to Foreign Trade Zone #129, an area where foreign goods bound for international destinations can be temporarily stored without incurring an import duty. BIA also offers customs brokerage and air cargo services, and as of 2002 houses a U.S. Customs office.

The Port of Bellingham, a municipal corporation dedicated to fulfilling the essential transportation needs of the region, operates a cargo terminal with three ship berths, backed up by two warehouses. Among its exports are wood pulp and aluminum ingots from local factories; its primary import is cottonseed pulp for cattle feed. The port administers five federally designated foreign trade zones to promote manufacturing, warehousing, and trade in the region.

Labor Force and Employment Outlook

The following is a summary of data regarding the Bellingham metropolitan area labor force, 2004 annual averages.

Size of nonagricultural labor force: 76,900

Number of workers employed in . . .
  construction and mining: 7,000
  manufacturing: 8,200
  trade, transportation and utilities: 14,700
  financial activities: 3,000
  professional and business services: 6,100
  leisure and hospitality: 8,800
  government: 15,500

Average hourly earnings of production workers employed in manufacturing: $18.27 (2004 annual statewide average)

Unemployment rate: 6.0% (January 2005)

Largest employers	Number of employees
Western Washington University	2,235
St. Joseph Hospital	1,757
Bellingham School District	1,651
Whatcom County	930
City of Bellingham	892
Haggen Inc.	843
Sodexho Services	648
Brown & Cole	634
T-Mobile	525
Fred Meyer Inc.	441

Cost of Living

According to the U.S. Bureau of Economic Analysis, the per capita personal income for Whatcom County was $23,133 in 2002. This figure was not only below the national average of $29,469, it trailed behind Washington state overall, at $31,230. Explanations include increased competition from Canada, a decline in high-paying manufacturing jobs combined with an increase in low-paying service jobs, and an increase in the number of part-time employees.

The following is a summary of data regarding several key cost of living factors for the Bellingham metropolitan area.

1999 (4th Quarter) ACCRA Average House Price: $179,000

1999 (4th Quarter) ACCRA Cost of Living Index: 107.8 (U.S. average = 100.0)

State income tax rate: None

State sales tax rate: 6.5% (food and prescription drugs are exempt)

Local income tax rate: None

Local sales tax rate: 1.7%

Property tax rate: $11.40 per $1,000 of assessed value (2005)

Economic Information: Bellingham/Whatcom Chamber of Commerce & Industry, 1201 Cornwall Ave., Ste. 100, PO Box 958, Bellingham, WA 98227; telephone (360)734-1330; fax (360)734-1332; email chamber@bellingham.com

Education and Research

Elementary and Secondary Schools

The Bellingham School District offers special programs for disabled students, those with learning disabilities, and exceptionally capable students. The schools have computers and related technology in every classroom. An early childhood preschool program and Head Start classes are offered. In 2000 the Bellingham School District was one of only 10 districts in the state to be recognized as a "model of achievement" and receive a five-year, $4.49 million Bill & Melinda Gates Foundation Grant.

The following is a summary of data regarding the Bellingham School District as of the 2003–2004 school year.

Total enrollment: 10,440

Number of facilities
  elementary schools: 13
  junior high/middle schools: 4
  senior high schools: 3 comprehensive; 1 alternative

Student/teacher ratio: 16:1

Teacher salaries
  minimum: $30,023
  maximum: $56,557

Funding per pupil: $7,365

Bellingham has one Montessori preschool, seven religious and private schools for pre-kindergarten through eighth grade, one religious school for first through twelfth grade, and one religious high school.

Public Schools Information: Bellingham Public Schools, 1306 Dupont St., Bellingham, WA 98225; telephone (360)676-6400; fax (360)676-2793; email trowe@bham.wednet.edu

Colleges and Universities

Western Washington University, with nearly 12,500 students, overlooks the city on Sehome Hill. Founded in 1893, the school became a regional university in 1977. College programs include business and economics, fine and performing arts, humanities and social sciences, science and technology, the Huxley College of Environmental Studies, the Woodring College of Education, and Fairhaven College, an interdisciplinary liberal arts college. Western Washington University's graduate school offers master's degrees in art, business administration, education, music, science, and teaching.

More than 7,000 students are enrolled in Whatcom Community College, which offers a variety of two-year programs in such areas as accounting, computer information sciences, education, English, graphic design, library and information science, massage, paralegal studies, and visual and performing arts; a program in nursing was added in the fall of 2005. Northwest Indian College, one of the fastest-growing Native American colleges in the country, offers its 942 students associate degrees in Native American Studies, Oksale Native Education, Chemical Dependency Studies, and Life Sciences, as well as a certificate program in Native American Studies; additional programs in a variety of areas of professional development and vocational training are offered through the Training Institute. Degree and certificate programs in more than 50 fields, from culinary arts to radiologic technology, are offered at Bellingham Technical College. Washington State University, based in Pullman, has a Whatcom County Extension that offers non-credit education and degree programs in the fields of gardening and agriculture, family living, and environment and natural resources.

Libraries and Research Centers

The Bellingham Public Library's main building was built in 1949, and was remodeled and expanded in 1985. Its Fairhaven branch, which celebrated its centennial in December 2004, occupies an original 1912 Carnegie building on the south side of the city. The library system has a collection of more than 400,000 items that range from original manuscripts to the latest CDs, videos, and books on tape. The library offers free Internet access to patrons, quality programs for children, reference service for adults, and an online local newspaper index and catalogue, as well as a complete database of community resources. The library has a special collection on local history and is a U.S. and state documents depository.

Bellingham's colleges and universities maintain a number of libraries, many of which are open to the public. Western Washington University has a number of research institutes and libraries, including those focusing on such areas as Canadian-American studies, Pacific Northwest studies, demographics, watershed studies, economic education and research, environmental toxicology, and vehicle research. Its special collections include the Ford Fly Fishing Collection, Northwest Collection, Rare Books Collection, and the Western Collection. The Whatcom County Law Library houses more than 15,000 books and CDs covering Washington laws and practice guides, federal laws, U.S. Supreme Court reports, case law from 49 states, and legal reference materials. Bellingham Technical College maintains an Information Technology Resource Center.

Public Library Information: Bellingham Public Library, 210 Central Ave., Bellingham, WA 98225; telephone (360)676-6860

Health Care

The people of Bellingham are served by St. Joseph's Hospital, which has 253 beds across two campuses. The hospital has a staff of 270 physicians, a medical surgical intensive care unit, a trauma center, and emergency, obstetrics, and oncology departments. Services offered include open heart surgery, outpatient surgery, psychiatric and addiction care for children and adults, and geriatric services. The city is also home to more than 80 dentists, 14 naturopathic physicians, and 80 chiropractors.

Recreation

Sightseeing

Bellingham's museums are devoted to an array of topics. The Whatcom Museum of History & Art, located in downtown Bellingham, is comprised of four buildings, each with its own theme: the 1892 Old City Hall, Whatcom Children's Museum, Syre Education Center, and Arco Exhibits Building. The American Museum of Radio and Electricity is the only one of its kind in North America. This museum, which completed an expansion in 2001, houses artifacts and interactive exhibits spanning from the onset of the scientific exploration of electricity in the 17th century to the evolution of broadcast radio and its impact on American culture. The Bellingham Railway Museum chronicles the heritage and operation of railroads in Whatcom and Skagit counties. Mindport Exhibits is a collection of interactive and fine arts exhibits designed to encourage exploration, discovery, and thought. Nearby, the Lynden Pioneer Museum focuses on the heritage of Whatcom County prior to World War II with exhibits covering Front Street, agriculture, rural Victorian lifestyles, transportation, natural resources, veterans, and the military.

The International Peace Arch, located about 20 miles north of Bellingham, is one of the world's few landmarks to be listed on the national historic registries of two countries. The 67-foot-tall arch has one foot in Canada and the other in the United States, and represents the longest undefended boundary—3,000 miles—in the world. It commemorates the signing of the Treaty of the Ghent, which ended the war between Britain and the United States. A number of celebrations take place there each year. From May to September is a sculpture exhibition of both Canadian and American artists that includes festivities each weekend. The Peace Arch Celebration, also known as Hands Across the Border, is held in June. September brings the annual Peace Arch Dedication Days, or ''Sam Hill Days,'' that reenact the anniversary of the arch.

Arts and Culture

The Mt. Baker Theatre has been offering theatrical entertainment since 1927. The Moorish-Spanish style former vaudeville movie palace, which is on the National Historic Register, seats 1,500 people. The theater boasts a 100-foot

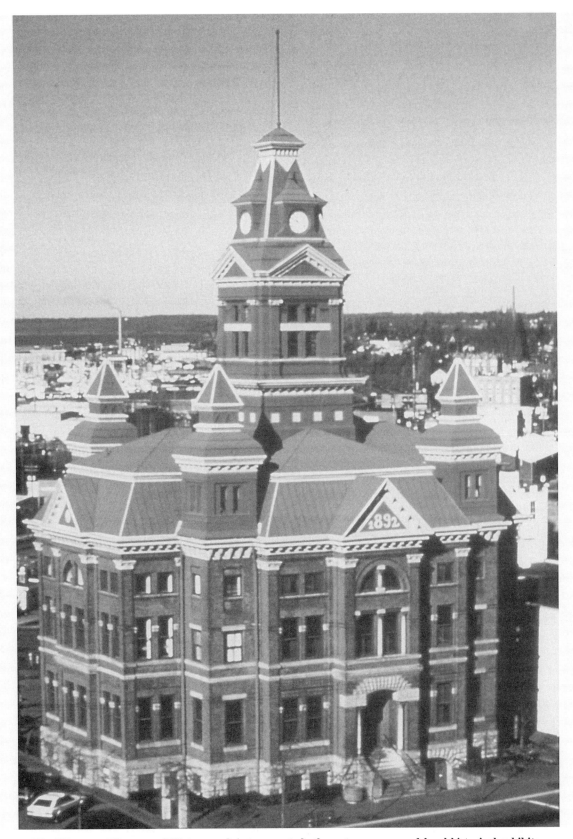

The Whatcom Museum of History and Art presents both contemporary and local historical exhibits.

Moorish tower, open-beamed lobby, 80-foot interior dome, an original 215-pipe organ, state-of-the-art staging capabilities, and, some speculate, a resident ghost. The theater hosts more than 100 live events annually, including touring Broadway shows. The Studio Theatre, a 2004 addition to the Mt. Baker Theatre, stages performances in an intimate setting. Mt. Baker Theatre is also the site for performances by the Whatcom Symphony Orchestra, Mt. Baker Youth Symphony, and Mt. Baker Organ Society.

The oldest community theater company in the Northwest, the Bellingham Theatre Guild, presents a year-round venue of comedies, dramas, and musicals. Western Washington University offers a wide range of performances including their summer stock season, a theatre arts series of dramas and comedies, and a performing arts series featuring world-renowned musicians and dance companies. Cutting-edge and classic jazz are the focus of the Pacific Northwest Jazz Alliance, which performs at various spots around the city.

Arts and Culture Information: Bellingham/Whatcom County Convention & Visitors Bureau, 904 Potter St., Bellingham, WA 98229; telephone (360)671-3990; fax (360)647-7873; email tourism@bellingham.org

Festivals and Holidays

The highlight of Memorial Day weekend is Bellingham's annual Sea to Ski Race, an athletic contest dating from the 1800s that is accompanied by parades, carnivals, art and garden shows, house tours, and street fairs. The Bellingham Scottish Highland Games take place in early June. Later that month in nearby Fairhaven is the annual Bowler Hat Bocce Ball Tournament, in which teams are encouraged to dress in 1890s period attire. Aerial acrobatics and fireworks turn the eyes toward the skies above the Port of Bellingham in June for AIRFEST. The Fourth of July is celebrated with the Viewing of the Blast Over Bellingham Bay. Later that month brings the Raspberry Festival at the Bellingham Farmers Market, and cowboys turn out for the International Bull-A-Rama. The Mount Baker Blues Festival in July has been voted the Best Blues Event in the state. The Bellingham Festival of Music, held for two weeks each August, features classical, chamber, jazz, and world music. Families flock to downtown's Chalk Art Festival later in the month.

For hundreds if not thousands of years, Native Americans in the Pacific Northwest have held ceremonies in honor of the salmon. This tradition is carried on at the Salmon and Corn Festival/Oktoberfest. Also in autumn is the Eldridge Area Historical Home Tour. Mount Baker is the site for the Mount Baker Country Christmas and the Western Washington University Department of Music's *Messiah* production. In December, the Lights of Love is celebrated at Bellingham Public Library.

Sports for the Spectator

The Bellingham Bells, with a season that runs from June through August, is a part of the West Coast Collegiate Baseball League. The Western Washington University Vikings compete in cross country, football, softball, track and field, volleyball, rowing, golf, soccer and men's and women's basketball. Students of Whatcom Community College participate in men's and women's basketball and soccer, and women's volleyball.

Sports for the Participant

In 2001 *Outside* magazine named Bellingham one of its top 10 "Dream Towns" for outdoor recreation. The city has an extensive network of hiking and biking trails, swimming pools and beaches, picnic grounds, fishing sites, softball and soccer fields, and beautiful gardens. At 10,788 feet, Mt. Baker is the highest peak in the North Cascade mountain range. It not only offers some spectacular views, it has the longest ski season in the state, with runs that curve below Mt. Shuksan. Bellingham ranked number seven of the "Best Golf Cities" by *Golf Digest* in 2002, and with 14 courses, Whatcom County boasts the largest concentration of public golf courses in the Pacific Northwest. Water sports abound, with sailing, kayaking, rafting, and whale watching among the favorites. Charter trips are available to the San Juan Islands or Victoria, B.C.

More than 110,000 athletes from around the world participate in the annual Sea to Ski Race, an 82.5-mile relay for teams of eight. The race begins with cross-country skiing at Mount Baker, followed by downhill skiing, running, road cycling, canoeing, mountain biking, and kayaking to the finish at Bellingham Bay. The Human Race, held each June, is a 5K/10K walk-run event in which participants raise money for their favorite charities. The course of the Baker's Healthy Start Foundation Triathlon, held each August, begins from the banks of Lake Whatcom and ends at Bloedel Donovan Park. September brings the Bellingham Traverse, a team event involving running, mountain and road biking, and canoeing/kayaking around downtown Bellingham, as well as the Discover Bellingham VolksFest, a three-day event comprised of a variety of walks.

Shopping and Dining

Shopping opportunities in Bellingham encompass both large regional malls and charming boutiques. Downtown Bellingham boasts two million square feet of businesses and shops. The Victorian buildings in the city's Fairhaven District hold a variety of specialty shops and eateries. Bellis Fair, the regional shopping mall, has 150 stores and more than 900,000 square feet of retail space, and is anchored by four major department stores. Outlet centers just a few miles from the town center draw bargain hunters. The Sunset

Square Shopping Center houses more than 40 stores and restaurants, as well as a movie theater.

Beer-lovers enjoy the fare at the Boundary Bay Brewery Company, where hand-crafted ales and lagers are served in a historic warehouse, and at the Orchard Street Brewery, which serves gourmet cuisine with its homemade brew. Local eateries range from casual cafes and burger joints to restaurants offering Italian, Mexican, and Chinese cuisine, to an upscale steak house with scenic views. The Silver Reef Casino, located in Ferndale, offers food and drink, live entertainment, and gaming, as does the Skagit Valley Casino Resort.

Visitor Information: Bellingham/Whatcom County Convention & Visitors Bureau, 904 Potter St., Bellingham, WA 98229; telephone (360)671-3990; fax (360)647-7873; email tourism@bellingham.org

Convention Facilities

Northwest Washington Fairgrounds, located in nearby Lynden, offers more than 70,000 square feet of meeting space in eight rooms, the largest of which can seat 5,000 people. Within the city of Bellingham, the Mt. Baker Theatre offers three meetings rooms that can accommodate 120-1,500 people. The Bellingham unit of the Boys & Girls Clubs of Whatcom County provides more than 13,000 square feet of meeting space, and Western Washington University offers 24 separate rooms that can each seat up to 750 attendees.

A number of area facilities provide both meeting space and lodging. Semiahmoo Resort offers 7,200 square feet in the largest of its 17 meeting rooms. The Best Western Lakeway Inn & Conference Center has 12 meeting rooms that can seat from 504 to 700 people. The Homestead Farms Golf Resort & Convention Center, located 20 miles north of Bellingham in Lynden, has 6 meeting rooms, the largest of which is 2,400 square feet in size.

Convention Information: Bellingham/Whatcom County Convention & Visitors Bureau, 904 Potter St., Bellingham, WA 98229; telephone (360)671-3990; fax (360)647-7873; email tourism@bellingham.org

Transportation

Approaching the City

Bellingham is located along western America's Interstate-5 corridor, nearly equidistant from Seattle and Vancouver,

British Columbia. State Routes 11, 539, 542, and 544 form a highway grid that covers most of the interior of western Whatcom County, linking with I-5 near Bellingham. Bellingham International Airport provides service to more than 250,000 passengers annually. Horizon Airlines flies passengers to the Seattle-Tacoma International Airport, Allegiant Air provides direct service four times each week to Las Vegas, NV, and San Juan Airlines runs daily to Friday Harbor and San Juan Island. The Airporter Shuttle delivers passengers to local points. At the Port of Bellingham, the Bellingham Cruise Terminal and Fairhaven Station launch cruises by ferry to Alaska, the San Juan Islands, and Victoria, British Columbia. Amtrak provides passenger rail service to Seattle and Vancouver, B.C., and Canadian Pacific and Canadian Rail travel east through Canada. Regional bus service is offered by Greyhound Bus Lines.

Traveling in the City

Interstate 5 runs north and south through the center of Bellingham. State Highway 11 runs north and south down the coast of Bellingham Bay at the south end of town. The Whatcom Transportation Authority provides local bus service around Bellingham and to Blaine, Ferndale, and Lynden.

Communications

Newspapers and Magazines

Bellingham's daily paper is *The Bellingham Herald,* which appears every morning. *The Western Front* is published twice-weekly from fall to spring by students of Western Washington University. The *Bellingham Business Journal* and the *Northwest Business Monthly* focus on local business news and features each month.

Television and Radio

One independent television station broadcasts out of Bellingham, which has two cable TV stations. Bellingham has two AM and four FM radio stations, covering classical music, jazz, rock, news, talk, and public radio.

Media Information: *The Bellingham Herald,* 1155 N. State St., Bellingham, WA 98225; telephone (360)676-2600

Bellingham Online

The Bellingham Herald. Available www.bellinghamherald.com

Bellingham Public Library. Available www.bellingham publiclibrary.org

Bellingham Public Schools. Available www.bham.wednet .edu

Bellingham/Whatcom Chamber of Commerce and Industry. Available www.bellingham.com

Bellingham/Whatcom County Convention & Visitors Bureau. Available www.bellingham.org

Bellingham Whatcom Economic Development Council. Available www.www.bwedc.org

City of Bellingham home page. Available www.cob.org

Greater Whatcom Partnership for a Sustainable Economy. Available www.whatcompartnership.org

Selected Bibliography

Dillard, Annie, *The Living* (New York: HarperCollins Publishers, 1992)

Gilliland, Miki, *Entering Bellingham* (Bellingham: Bayside Press, 1989)

Manning, Harvey, *Walking the Beach to Bellingham* (Corvallis, OR: Oregon State University Press, Reprint Edition, 2002)

Roth, Lottie Roeder, *The History of Whatcom County* (Seattle: Pioneer Historical Publishing Co., 1926)

Olympia

The City in Brief

Founded: 1846 (incorporated, 1859)
Head Officials: Mayor Mark Foutch (NP) (since 2004);
   City Manager Steve Hall (since 2003)

City Population
   1980: 27,447
   1990: 33,729
   2000: 42,514
   2003 estimate: 43,963
   Percent change, 1990–2000: 26.0%
   U.S. rank in 1990: Not reported
   U.S. rank in 2000: Not reported (State rank: 17th)

Metropolitan Statistical Area Population
   1980: 124,264
   1990: 161,238
   2000: 207,355
   Percent change, 1990–2000: 28.6%
   U.S. rank in 1990: 12th (CMSA)
   U.S. rank in 2000: 13th (CMSA)

Area: 18.52 square miles (2000)
Elevation: 221 feet above sea level
Average Annual Temperature: 49.9° F
Average Annual Precipitation: 50.59 inches

Major Economic Sectors: Government, services, trade
Unemployment Rate: 5.7% (January 2005)
Per Capita Income: $22,590 (1999)

2002 FBI Crime Index Total: 2,791

Major Colleges and Universities: The Evergreen State
   College, South Puget Sound Community College, Saint
   Martin's University

Daily Newspaper: *The Olympian*

Introduction

Olympia, Washington's capital, is a city rich in history and natural beauty. Known for its spectacular view of the Olympic Mountains, the city serves as the gateway to Olympic National Park and headquarters for the Olympic National Forest. Local residents enjoy quiet neighborhoods with lovely tree-lined streets, an abundance of parks, good schools, and a high overall quality of life.

Geography and Climate

Olympia sits on a low flat at the southern end of Puget Sound on the shores of Budd Inlet's two bays, between Seattle and the Olympic Mountains to the north, Mt. Rainier to the northeast, and Mt. Saint Helens to the south. The city is further divided by Capitol Lake.

The city and the surrounding area experience fair-weather summers and the grey, wet overcast winters of the Pacific Northwest. Tempered by the Japanese trade current, the mild northwest climate favors lushly forested landscapes replete with ferns and mosses. Rainfall tends to be spread out over a large number of days. With about 52 clear days out of every 365, Thurston County residents live under some form of cloud cover 86 percent of the year, with more than a trace of rain falling on almost half of the days of the year.

Area: 18.52 square miles (2000)

Elevation: 221 feet above sea level

Average Temperatures: January, 37.9° F; July, 63.2° F; annual average, 49.9° F

Average Annual Precipitation: 50.59 inches

History

Territorial Days

Before British Captain George Vancouver sailed into Puget Sound Bay in 1791 and made the first known European contact with the native tribes, the Nisqually, Duwamish, Suquamish, and Puyallup Indians hunted, gathered, and fished in the region where Olympia now stands. The United States and Great Britain jointly controlled the region until the boundary between U.S. territory and Canada was established in 1846. The Pacific Northwest Region was then called Oregon Territory.

White settlement of what later became Olympia began in 1846 with a joint claim filed under a homestead law by partners Edmund Sylvester, a Maine fisherman, and Levi Lathrop Smith, an easterner who wanted to be a minister but was prevented by epilepsy from pursuing that career. Smith called his portion of the claim Smithfield. For two years, Smith and Sylvester were the only white residents in Smithfield (then Oregon Territory); the area was covered with virgin forest. When Smith drowned in Puget Sound in 1848, Sylvester took over his partner's claim. By the end of 1848, a trail had been cleared between Smithfield and New Market to the south (now Tumwater), and four families, about fifteen single men, and Father Pascal Ricard and his small band of Oblate missionaries had settled in Smithfield. In 1850 a city was laid out and Smithfield was renamed Olympia after the Olympic Mountains that can be seen in the distance. In 1853 Washington Territory became separate from Oregon Territory. Olympia (population 150), the largest settlement in Washington Territory, was named its capital and Isaac Stevens arrived to serve as Washington's first territorial governor.

Governor Stevens predicted a golden future for Washington Territory. He moved quickly to open up the area to white settlement, promising to survey a route for a transcontinental railway and to convince the natives to cede their land and move to reservations. By 1854 most of the tribes had done so, but intermittent outbreaks of hostility throughout the 1850s deterred extensive settlement. Delays in constructing a transcontinental railroad and the 1849 discovery of gold in California drew prospective settlers from the Northwest. The outbreak of the Civil War in 1861 nearly halted the westward migration of settlers.

City's Desire for Prominence Thwarted

Blessed with abundant natural resources, Olympia remained small but prospered. The year 1852 marked many firsts for the town. Coal was discovered, saw mills were built, a fledgling trade industry was started with California, road and school districts were established, and Washington's first newspaper, the weekly *Columbian,* published its first issue. In 1853 a Methodist minister took up residence and began to build a church, classes began at the Olympia Public School, and the city's first theatrical performance was held. Olympia's population grew from fewer than 1,000 people in 1860 to 1,203 residents in 1870. By 1872 Olympia seemed on its way to becoming Washington's great city; that year, however, a severe earthquake shook Olympia, as did the decision by the Northern Pacific railroad not to end the line at Olympia. Instead, the railway went to Tacoma, taking with it much of Olympia's trade and industry.

Meanwhile, people began moving to Seattle instead of Olympia. Still, with its strategic location near virgin forest land and the waterfalls at Tumwater, Olympia flourished as a saw mill town. Furniture, shingles, timber, pilings, and coal were loaded aboard ships bound from Olympia Harbor to California. Olympia served as a social center for isolated settlers throughout Washington, who traveled by steamboat to attend picnics and fairs there. By 1890 Olympia's population stood at 4,698 inhabitants. A year earlier, in 1889, Washington had become a state; Olympia fought bids by several other cities for the right to remain state capital and won in a statewide vote. At the time, state government was housed in a single frame building.

The decade of the 1890s was marked by progress and disappointments. The Olympia Brewing Company, which would become one of Olympia's greatest claims to fame, was founded in 1896 in Tumwater. Telephone lines and electric light poles were erected, dredging began for a modern port, a street railway system was built, and the elegant Olympia Hotel was completed (but destroyed by fire in 1904); however, an economic depression left citizens complaining that their diet consisted of nothing but clams, and Olympia's population fell to 3,863 residents by 1900. By this time, Seattle and Tacoma had surpassed Olympia as the big cities of the Puget Sound area.

Twentieth-Century Advances

In 1901 the state bought Olympia's Thurston County Court House to serve as the Capitol building, but Olympians could not rest easy with their title of state capital until the present Capitol complex was finally completed in 1935 after delays due to the 1890 and 1930 depressions.

Olympia had escaped the worst of the Indian wars of the 1850s, and in the twentieth century managed to escape the labor troubles and various upheavals that beset other Washington cities. The city benefited when World War I brought a huge demand for Olympic peninsula spruce to make airplanes. Waterborne trade lost by 1920 to other Puget Sound ports picked up after a 1925 revitalization of the Port of Olympia, and ships once again began loading lumber bound for the Orient.

Olympia suffered a severe earthquake in 1949. A year later the city celebrated its centennial, 100 years from the date Olympia was laid out. By then Olympia ranked twelfth among Washington's cities in population and boasted one high school, one radio station, a "video" station, and two newspapers. With a population in 1953 of 16,800 people, Olympia was a typical small town where the sidewalks were "rolled up" each evening. One by one, state government offices were moving from Olympia to Seattle, and the city feared it would lose its capital status. Finally, four local businessmen filed a lawsuit against the state to stop the

exodus; the eighteen state agencies were ordered back to Olympia in a decision that opined: "it was not the intention of the framers of the constitution that the state capital should be composed of empty buildings to collect cobwebs and stand in disuse."

Then began a flurry of construction of government buildings on what had once been residential streets. Despite decades of effort, Olympia was less successful in luring industry, thus managing to escape the attendant smog and pollution. In the 1960s and 1970s Olympia lost many of its downtown retail businesses to shopping malls in the then-rural towns of Lacey and Tumwater.

Efforts to preserve the downtown emphasized people-friendly projects while discouraging skyscrapers. Olympia served as a west coast port of entry and exit from which agricultural products and oysters were shipped. However, government had become the leading source of local employment and has a strong influence on most aspects of life in the city.

Challenges in the New Century

The turn of the century brought several challenges to Olympia. Some, like a national recession and the terrorist attacks of 2001, affected the entire United States and beyond. Others were more specific to the region. On February 28, 2001, the 6.8-magnitude Nisqually Earthquake occurred, with an epicenter only 10 miles from Olympia. A gradual yet significant loss of manufacturing jobs spurred the goal of diversification, particularly into technology—a segment in which Olympia was lagging behind the state's other regions. The question of the new resident of Olympia's Executive Mansion hung in the balance for two months. The gubernatorial race between Democrat Christine O. Gregoire and Republican Dino Rossi was finally settled, after several recounts, in Gregoire's favor in January 2005.

Historical Information: Washington State Capital Museum, 211 W. 21st Ave., Olympia, WA 98501; telephone (360)753-2580

Population Profile

Metropolitan Area Residents (PMSA)
1980: 124,264
1990: 161,238
2000: 207,355
Percent change, 1990–2000: 28.6%
U.S. rank in 1990: 12th (CMSA)
U.S. rank in 2000: 13th (CMSA)

City Residents

1980: 27,447

1990: 33,729

2000: 42,514

2003 estimate: 43,963

Percent change, 1990–2000: 26.0%

U.S. rank in 1990: Not reported

U.S. rank in 2000: Not reported (State rank: 17th)

Density: 2,544.4 people per square mile (2000)

Racial and ethnic characteristics (2000)

   White: 36,246

   Black or African American: 805

   American Indian and Alaska Native: 553

   Asian: 2,473

   Native Hawaiian and Pacific Islander: 125

   Hispanic or Latino (may be of any race): 1,863

   Other: 713

Percent of residents born in state: 45.3% (2000)

Age characteristics (2000)

   Population under 5 years old: 2,307

   Population 5 to 9 years old: 2,449

   Population 10 to 14 years old: 2,664

   Population 15 to 19 years old: 2,859

   Population 20 to 24 years old: 3,914

   Population 25 to 34 years old: 6,471

   Population 35 to 44 years old: 6,436

   Population 45 to 54 years old: 6,434

   Population 55 to 59 years old: 2,029

   Population 60 to 64 years old: 1,279

   Population 65 to 74 years old: 2,449

   Population 75 to 84 years old: 2,261

   Population 85 years and older: 962

   Median age: 36 years

Births (2003)

   Total number: 959

Deaths (2003)

   Total number: 1,281 (of which, 6 were infants under the age of 1 year)

Money income (1999)

   Per capita income: $22,590

   Median household income: $40,846

   Total households: 18,673

Number of households with income of . . .

   less than $10,000: 1,923

   $10,000 to $14,999: 1,340

   $15,000 to $24,999: 2,511

   $25,000 to $34,999: 2,519

   $35,000 to $49,999: 2,931

   $50,000 to $74,999: 3,826

   $75,000 to $99,999: 1,835

   $100,000 to $149,999: 1,370

   $150,000 to $199,999: 226

   $200,000 or more: 192

Percent of families below poverty level: 6.9% (of which, 39.4% were female householder families with related children under 5 years)

2002 FBI Crime Index Total: 2,791

Municipal Government

Olympia has a council-manager form of government. Power lies with the council, which sets policy and makes budgetary decisions. Seven elected, non-partisan council members representing the community at-large, not individual districts, serve staggered four-year terms, with Position 1 designated as the Mayor's position. A city manager is hired by the council to advise and administer all city affairs.

Head Officials: Mayor Mark Foutch (NP) (since 2004; current term expires 2008); City Manager Steve Hall (since 2003)

Total Number of City Employees: 530 (2005)

City Information: City of Olympia, 900 Plum St. SE, PO Box 1967, Olympia, WA 98507-1967; telephone (360)753-8447; email cityhall@ci.olympia.wa.us

Economy

Major Industries and Commercial Activity

The city's early development was based on its port facilities and lumber-based industries, and later oyster farming and dairying. Following World War II, Olympia served as a major service center for lumber communities west of Thurston County, while the Port of Olympia remained a major transportation center for shipping logs and finished lumber. But during the mid- twentieth century, the decline of the local timber industry resulted in the loss of many of the local associated milling and secondary operations.

During the 1970s, Olympia expanded as a center of offices and homes for state employees, military personnel, and their respective families. This further diminished Thurston County's already modest farm sector as housing development pushed into the remaining fertile prairies. Dairy and truck (mostly berry) farming continued in the south county, interspersed with small hobby farms.

In the late 1960s and early 1970s, the state legislature approved and financed construction of the Evergreen State College. The four-year public institution became an economic and cultural fixture in Thurston County with faculty, staff, and students contributing to the local housing and retail sectors. On a smaller scale, South Puget Sound Community College and Saint Martin's University in nearby Lacey also drove the housing demand. In the late 1980s the Olympia waterfront and downtown were revitalized, and an effort began to draw new businesses to the area.

Manufacturing continued to be a major economic segment in the early 2000s, though a set-back was experienced with the closure of the Miller Brewing plant in June 2003. Wood and food processing segments were stagnating, while plastics, industrial supplies, and machinery were experiencing growth. Area companies in these growth segments include Dart Containers Inc., Albany International Corp., Big Toys Inc., and Amtech Corp. Overall, though, the number of manufacturing jobs is projected to decrease slightly until the late 2000s, when it is expected to regain the employment level it had in 1990.

Agriculture, another industry traditional to Olympia, also waned, although production is still higher than in nearby counties. In 2002 Thurston County produced crops valued at $49 million, and its livestock, poultry, and related products were valued at $65 million. Although the size of farms continues to decrease, the number of farms actually increased, with 1,155 farms operating in 2002. As with agriculture, the timber industry is dominated by smaller, family-owned operations.

As the capital of the state of Washington, Olympia relies on the state government to be a stabilizing factor for the local economy. According to the Thurston Regional Planning Council, state government was the county's second-largest industry behind services in 2000, employing 22,750 people. In addition to the jobs it supports directly, state government also supports the economy by attracting tourists, as does the region's gambling industry. *The Olympian* reported in 2005 that tourism spending in the area jumped from $153.4 million in 1998 to $209.7 million in 2003. The annual sessions of the state legislature in the winter and spring mark the first tourist season of the year, with summertime recreation and attractions, including tours of state buildings, following.

Compared to other regions in the state, Olympia and Thurston County are home to a relatively small number of technology companies. To attract them, economic development officials promoted the area's telecommunication infrastructure, low property price, and educated workforce. In 2004 Univera Inc., a biotechnology firm, relocated to Thurston County from Colorado. Other recent additions to the area are Reach One, an Internet service provider, and Fast Transact, a processor of credit card transactions.

Items and goods produced: wood products, processed foods, metal and paper containers

Incentive Programs—New and Existing Companies

Local programs—Olympia has no corporate or personal income tax, and no inventory tax. Thurston County offers exemptions on sales and use tax for manufacturing equipment, repair and replacement parts, and labor; for manufacturing machinery and equipment used for research and development; and for warehouse/distribution facilities and equipment. A tax credit of up to $2 million is available for research and development in the high technology industry. Tax exempt revenue bonds for manufacturing, ranging from $1 million to $10 million, are also available.

State programs—The state of Washington offers a number of incentive programs to attract new and expanding businesses to the state. Among them are B & O tax credits; sales/use tax deferrals for technology and manufacturing companies as well as for firms relocating or expanding in distressed areas; and loan programs that apply to rural areas and the redevelopment of brownfields.

Job training programs—South Puget Sound Community College provides specialized job training for public and private employees, contracts with businesses to provide specialized job training, and operates a comprehensive Cooperative Work Experience program. The Washington state Job Skills Training Program offers employers a 50 percent match for training costs. The federal Workforce Investment Act (WIA), formerly Job Training Partnership Act (JTPA), may match up to 50 percent of wages for on-the-job training of dislocated workers.

Development Projects

Faced with a higher cost of living, residents of such large cities as Seattle were migrating to Thurston County by the beginning of the twenty-first century. According to the Thurston Regional Planning Council, 77 percent of the county's increase in population between 1990 and 2000 was attributed to in-migration. This influx, combined with relatively low interest rates, drove development projects. In 2004 the Red Wind Casino completed a $31 million expansion, and the area's other tribal casinos completed similar upgrades. The Westfield Shoppingtown Capital mall expanded and renovated, and was pursuing the construction of a 16-screen movie complex in 2005. Elsewhere in Thurston County, construction of new office buildings for the state government were in progress, including the 160,000-square-foot, $35-million Cherry Street Plaza in Tumwater.

Economic Development Information: Economic Development Council of Thurston County, 665 Woodland Square Loop SE, Ste. 201, Lacey, WA 98503; telephone (360)754-

6320; fax (360)407-3980; email busdev@thurstonedc.com. Thurston Regional Planning Council, 2404 Heritage Ct. SW, Ste. B, Olympia, WA 98502; telephone (360)786-5480; fax (360)754-4413; email info@trpc.org

Commercial Shipping

After years of struggling with an identity as a failing bastion of log exporting, the Port of Olympia reported its first profitable year in nearly a decade with a surplus of $400,000 in 2004. The turnaround was primarily due to diversification into such bulk commodities as metals and limestone, and the controversial move into military shipments to support the war in Iraq. The 60-acre, deepwater port offers three berths, a U.S. Customs bonded warehouse, and a cargo yard for breakbulk, bulk, rolling stock, and containerized cargoes. The Port of Olympia is also the site of Foreign Trade Zone #216, an area where foreign goods bound for international destinations can be temporarily stored without incurring an import duty.

The Port of Olympia owns and operates Olympia Regional Airport, a general aviation-transport facility for corporate, commercial, and recreational users. The airport is 20 minutes by air to the Seattle-Tacoma International Airport and 50 minutes away from Vancouver, B.C. Nearly 90 miles of active rail lines lie in Thurston County. Burlington Northern Santa Fe, Union Pacific, and the Puget Sound & Pacific Railroad serve the area, with the Tri-City & Olympia Railroad also serving the Port of Olympia.

Labor Force and Employment Outlook

Olympia's workforce surpasses much of the nation in educational attainment. Of adults aged 25 years or older in 2000, 91.6 percent of Olympians had obtained a high school diploma, compared to the national average of 80.4 percent. That discrepancy is even greater in terms of college education, with 40.3 percent of Olympia's residents earning a bachelor's degree or higher, while only 24.4 percent did so across the United States as a whole.

The following is a summary of data regarding the Olympia metropolitan area labor force, 2004 annual averages.

Size of nonagricultural labor force: 93,000

Number of workers employed in . . .
   construction and mining: 5,100
   manufacturing: 3,300
   trade, transportation and utilities: 14,600
   financial activities: 3,800
   professional and business services: 7,100
   leisure and hospitality: 7,400
   government: 35,600

Average hourly earnings of production workers employed in manufacturing: $18.27 (2004 annual statewide average)

Unemployment rate: 5.7% (January 2005)

Largest Thurston County employers (2004)	*Number of employees*
State of Washington	20,000-25,000
Local Government	10,000-15,000
Providence St. Peter Hospital	1,000-5,000
Tribal Government	1,000-5,000
Federal Government	500-1,000
Group Health Cooperative	500-1,000
Columbia Capital Medical Center	100-500
Wal-Mart Stores Inc.	100-500
St. Martin's University	100-500
Costco Wholesale Corp.	100-500

Cost of Living

Thurston County set a new record for housing prices in January 2005, when the average price for a home was $224,104, up from the previous record of $223,884 that was set in November. These figures demonstrate a rapid increase in housing costs, driven by people migrating from more crowded and costly counties to the north, as well as those taking advantage of low interest rates to purchase larger homes.

The following is a summary of data regarding several key cost of living factors for the Olympia area.

2004 (3rd Quarter) ACCRA Cost of Living Index: 102.2

2004 (3rd Quarter) ACCRA Average House Price: $244,960

State income tax rate: None

State sales tax rate: 6.5%

Local income tax rate: None

Local sales tax rate: 1.9%

Property tax rate: 13.119 per $1,000 of assessed value (2005)

Economic Information: Thurston County Chamber, 1600 E. 4th Ave., Olympia, WA 98507; telephone (360)357-3362, fax (360)357-3376, email info@thurstonchamber.com

Education and Research

Elementary and Secondary Schools

One of the oldest districts in the state of Washington, the Olympia School District was founded in 1852, nearly 40 years before Washington statehood. The district offers five alternative programs for students in elementary, middle, or high school grades. It also offers an Early Childhood Program for children under five years with developmental disabilities and the Program for Academically Talented Students serving students in grades two through five.

Olympia High School, one of the oldest public secondary schools in Washington, was built in 1906. The building was completely renovated in the late 1990s, and rededicated in October 2000. Taxpayers in February 2004 approved additional funds to renovate and update the district's other facilities.

Beginning with the graduating class of 2008, all students enrolled in the Olympia School District must meet new graduation requirements that include 22 credits, completion of the "High School and Beyond" plan, a Certificate of Academic Achievement, and a culminating project.

The following is a summary of data regarding the Olympia school district as of the 2003–2004 school year.

Total enrollment: 9,234

Number of facilities
 elementary schools: 11
 junior high/middle schools: 4
 senior high schools: 2
 other: 1

Student/teacher ratio: 16:1

Teacher salaries
 minimum: Not available
 maximum: Not available

Funding per pupil: $7,213 (2002–2003)

Olympia is home to seven private and religious schools.

Public Schools Information: Olympia School District, 1113 Legion Way SE, Olympia, WA 98501; telephone (360)596-6100; fax (360)596-6111

Colleges and Universities

The Evergreen State College, a public liberal arts and sciences institution founded in 1969, enrolled more than 4,400 students in 2004. The Olympia campus accounted for 93 percent of enrollment, with Grays Harbor, Tacoma, and Tribal Reservations sharing the remainder. Emphasizing interdisciplinary studies rather than traditional majors, Evergreen offers a Bachelor's of Arts and a Bachelor's of Science in Liberal Arts, with the opportunity to concentrate in biology, communications, computer science, energy systems, environmental studies, health and human services, humanities, language, management and business, marine studies, mathematics, Native American studies, performing arts, physical science, politics and economics, pre-law, pre-medicine, and visual arts. Master's degree programs are offered in environmental studies, public administration, and teaching.

South Puget Sound Community College is a two-year, public institution that serves all adults regardless of their previous education. Approximately 6,000 students each semester pursue associates degrees in arts, general studies, technical arts, and nursing. The college also offers non-credit community education classes, adult literacy, and high school completion programs.

U.S. News & World Report ranked Saint Martin's University 44th among the best Western universities for Master's programs in its "America's Best Colleges 2005." St. Martin's, located in nearby Lacey, is a four-year, co-educational college with a strong liberal arts foundation that also encompasses business, education, and engineering. Known as Saint Martin's College until changing its name in August 2005, the school offers 22 undergraduate programs, six graduate programs, and numerous pre-professional and certification programs. St. Martin's, one of 18 U.S. Benedictine Catholic colleges, has more than 1,700 full- and part-time students enrolled at its main campus in Olympia and its extension campuses at the Fort Lewis Army Post, McChord Air Force Base, and Olympic College at Bremerton.

Libraries and Research Centers

The Timberland Regional Library system has 27 community libraries, including the Olympia branch, and four cooperative library centers across the counties of Grays Harbor, Lewis, Mason, Pacific, and Thurston. The system encompassed 1.49 million items in 2003, including more than one million books, 152 electronic books, more than 220,000 magazines, 36 online reference databases, and numerous videos, CDs/records/cassettes, audio books, pamphlets, CD-ROMs, and DVDs. The Olympia Timberland Library was founded in 1909 with a collection of 900 books. The McCleary Timberland Library, located in Grays Harbor County, opened in June 2003. That same year the Timberland Regional Library system became the state's first public library system to join with the Library of Congress as a partner in the national Veterans History Project.

Other local libraries include the college libraries at the Evergreen State College, whose special collections include a Rare Books room and the Chicano/Latino Archive, South Puget Sound Community College, Providence St. Peter Hospital, and the Washington State Capital Museum.

The Washington State Library has more than half a million volumes and periodicals, with special collections on Washington newspapers, Washington authors, and Washington state documents. It is a U.S. government and Washington State depository library.

State of Washington governmental libraries include those of the Attorney General's Office, the Department of Information Services, the Department of Natural Resources, the

Office of the Secretary of State, the State Superintendent of Public Instruction, and the Washington State Law Library.

Local research institutes include the Cascadia Research Collective, the Evergreen Freedom Foundation, The Evergreen State College Labor Education and Research Center, the Washington State Institute for Public Policy, and the Washington Department of Fish and Wildlife Fish Program.

Public Library Information: Olympia Timberland Library, 313 8th Ave. SE, Olympia, WA 98501; telephone (360)352-0595. Washington State Library, PO Box 42460, Olympia, WA; telephone (360)753-5590

Health Care

Olympia has two hospitals and functions as the regional medical center for five surrounding counties. The Providence Health System operates the 390-bed Providence St. Peter Hospital and the 191-bed Providence Centralia Hospital, each of which have served the community's health care needs for a century. Providence St. Peter is the largest hospital in the region, offering a full spectrum of acute care, specialty and outpatient services, including cardiac surgery, obstetrics, medical rehabilitation, emergency care, and outpatient surgery. In 2003 Providence St. Peter Hospital opened a $27.5 million emergency center and clinical laboratory.

Capital Medical Center, established in 1985, has 119 beds and 238 physicians. The full-service hospital includes emergency care, private birthing suites, a same-day private-room surgery center, pain management services, a lymphedema program, senior programs, and a sleep disorder center.

Health Care Information: Providence St. Peter Hospital, 413 Lilly Rd NE, Olympia, WA 98506; telephone (360)491-9480; toll-free (800)956-2574. Capital Medical Center, 3900 Capital Mall Dr. SW, Olympia, WA 98502; telephone (360)754-5858; fax (360)956-2574

Recreation

Sightseeing

Located on the Olympic Peninsula, nearby Olympic National Park encompasses the Olympic Mountains and Pacific Ocean beaches. Beautiful Olympic National Forest, which surrounds the park, is the site of three rain forests.

Capitol Lake Park provides a spectacular view of the state capitol buildings, the lake, and surrounding wooded bluffs.

The Capitol grounds feature the Executive Mansion, the campus gardens, war memorials, and a conservatory. The Capitol group of buildings, completed in 1935, consists of six white sandstone structures located on a hill in the city's southern section. The marble interior Legislative Building at the center of the cluster has a 287-foot high dome, similar to that of the U.S. Capitol, and one of the highest of its kind in the world.

Heritage Fountain invites children and adults to don a swimsuit and splash among its 47 water spouts. The fountain is part of the Heritage Park, a scenic pedestrian district stretching from the Capitol Grounds to Percival Landing. Percival Landing, on the city's waterfront, has a 1.5 mile boardwalk featuring works of art and interpretive displays outlining the history of the harbor. A walk along the Port Plaza provides mountain views from the working waterfront and a visit to the nationally recognized Batdorf and Bronson Coffee roasters shop.

Yashiro Japanese Garden, a traditional Asian garden designed in the ancient hill and pond style, honors Olympia's sister city of Yashiro, Japan. The walled garden features classic gates built without nails. The City of Yashiro presented two cutstone lanterns and a 13-tier pagoda as gifts to the garden.

Chief William Shelton's Story Pole, located on the Washington State Capital Campus, was dedicated in 1940 to commemorate the relationship between Northwest Native tribal governments and the State of Washington. The American Revolution is remembered in downtown Sylvester Park with a monument to the End of the Oregon Trail, a leg of a pioneer trail that ran to the shores of Puget Sound.

The Nisqually Wildlife Refuge has 3,000 acres of land and waters to provide refuge and nesting places for migratory waterfowl, songbirds, raptors, and wading birds. The Woodard Bay Natural Resource Conservation Area is a wildlife sanctuary for bald eagles, seals, otters, and bats, and is one of the most important heron rookeries in Washington.

Four tribal casinos operate in Thurston County. Located in Olympia, the Red Wind Casino is open daily from 9 a.m. to 5 a.m., and features slot machines, table games, dining, and live entertainment. The area's other casinos are Hawk's Prairie, Little Creek, and Lucky Eagle.

Arts and Culture

Olympia residents enjoy a variety of arts and cultural facilities and events. Each year, the Capitol Campus draws more than half a million visitors who tour the Legislature as well as the stately buildings, grounds, gardens, and artwork. The State Capital Museum, adjacent to the Capitol Campus, houses exhibits that document the story and political and cultural life of the city and state. Built in the 1850s, the

Washington State War Memorial.

Bigelow House Museum, one of the oldest homes in the Pacific Northwest, offers tours of the house's original furnishings. The exhibits at the Hands-On Children's Museum, across from the Capitol Campus, allow children to enjoy a first-hand experience of science and art. At the east side of the Olympia Airport, the Olympic Flight Museum features historic aircraft from around the world.

The Washington Center for the Performing Arts presents a full season of performances by resident and touring groups, offering music, dance, theater, and family entertainment. Groups in residence at the center include Ballet Northwest, Youth Symphonies, the Olympia Symphony Orchestra, and the Washington Shakespeare Festival. The Masterworks Choral Ensemble is a southwest Washington chorus based in Olympia. The Capital Playhouse, a semi-professional theater company, presents five musical performances in its season. The State Theater is the venue for Harlequin Productions, whose eclectic performances include both new works and innovative treatments of classics. The Olympia Film Society shows independent, international, and classic film year-round at the Capital Theater, offers special live performances, and annually produces a nationally recognized film festival.

The city's popular Music in the Park program takes place at noon each Friday from mid-July through August; its sister program, Music in the Dark, offers evening concerts on Wednesdays. The largest Art Walk in the state occurs in Olympia each April and October, with businesses featuring visual arts, performances, and poetry of local artists.

Olympia's downtown art galleries include the Childhood's End Gallery, Cornerstone Pottery, and State of the Arts Gallery. The Evergreen Galleries on that college's campus feature changing exhibits.

Olympia is known as a center for independent rock and punk music produced and performed locally. Cover charges are generally low or non-existent, venues are often no-frills, and shows are frequently all-ages events. Folk, jazz, and bluegrass are traditionally strong draws as well. The Capitol Theater Backstage offers all-ages shows and the Piper's Lady club offers weekly jam sessions; bluegrass, Irish, and open-mike nights are also offered.

Festivals and Holidays

Olympia's first celebration of the year is April's Procession of the Species, a celebration of arts and the natural world that culminates in a procession of residents in masks and costumes. Percival Landing is the site of May's annual Wooden Boat Fair, which features wooden boats, international foods, and craft booths. Also in May is the annual Swantown Boatswap & Chowder Challenge, a day dedicated to boats, marine equipment, and clam chowder. Nearby that same month are the annual Harbor Shorebird Festival at the Grays Harbor

National Wildlife Refuge, and the Lacey Grand Prix Electric Car Race & Alternative Fuel Fair.

Summer begins with Duck Dash & Bite of Olympia, a June event featuring entertainment, children's activities, and a rubber duck race. Evergreen State College sponsors Super Saturday, a free festival for all ages, that same month. Also in June is the annual Olympic Air Show, held at the Olympic Flight Museum. July brings the Dixieland Jazz Festival, a four-day event, and Capital Lakefair, one of the largest community festivals in the state. The Thurston County Fair is held over the first weekend of August. For more than 60 years, the Pet Parade has invited the children of the city to parade the downtown streets with their favorite pets or toys, costumes, or creations of their own. Sand in the City, Washington's largest sand sculpting competition, takes place at the Olympia Waterfront Port Plaza each August.

Olympia Harbor Days is held over Labor Day weekend, and features the Tugboat Races & Festival. In September the Percival Play Day features activities and attractions for families. Octoberfest at the Farmers Market highlights the month, which also includes the ArtsWalk and the Children's Halloween Party at Olympia Center. In December, the spotlight is on the Parade of Lighted Boats at the city's waterfront.

Sports for the Spectator

The Geoducks, the sports teams of Evergreen State College, compete in cross country, track and field, volleyball, and men's and women's basketball and soccer. St. Martin's University teams, nicknamed the Saints, participate in baseball and softball, cross country, track and field, volleyball, and men's and women's basketball and golf. Nearby Tacoma is home to the Tacoma Rainiers baseball team, a Triple-A affiliate of the Seattle Mariners.

Sports for the Participant

Olympia's location on the Puget Sound and nearby mountains make outdoor recreation very popular, especially hiking, kayaking, skiing, and sailboating. Thurston County boasts 11 golf courses, including Vicwood, one of Washington's newest championship-rated courses. An abundance of parks and forests nearby and in the city include the very popular Tolmie State Park and Millersylvania State Park. Burfoot Park, which covers 50 acres of property with 1,100 feet of saltwater beach frontage on Budd Inlet, offers nature trails and beach access that feature beautiful views of the State Capitol and the Olympic Mountains.

The Capital City Marathon winds through various parts of town each May. Nearby Rochester is the site for June's Swede Day 5K Fun Run/Walk. The following month the Washington State Senior Games take place throughout Thurston County, with a series of athletic competitions in 20 sports for men and women aged 50 and higher.

Shopping and Dining

The Westfield Shoppingtown Capital mall encompasses more than 100 stores and restaurants, and is anchored by JCPenney, Macy's, and Mervyn's. Olympia's Farmers Market, the second largest in the state, offers the finest in handicrafts, baked goods, and fresh produce. It is located on Budd Inlet, the southernmost reach of the Puget Sound.

Naturally, the star of Olympia's cuisine is the wonderful fish and seafood that have made the area famous. In addition to Northwest fare, diners may choose from ethnic cuisine, oven fired pizza, or family dining spots. The Olympia Brewery, one of the area's most recognizable landmarks, has been producing brew for more than a century. At its site in nearby Tumwater, visitors can enjoy a tour and the hospitality tasting room.

Visitor Information: State Capital Visitor Center, 14th & Capitol Way, Olympia, WA 98504; telephone (360)586-33460; fax (360)586-4636. Olympia-Thurston County Visitor & Convention Bureau, PO Box 7338, Olympia, WA 98507; telephone (360)704-7544; toll-free (877)704-7500; fax (360)704-7533; email info@visitolympia.com

Convention Facilities

Thurston County offers more than 1,650 hotel rooms and over 100,000 square feet of meeting space. The Thurston County Fairgrounds, located in Olympia, features three buildings including the Thurston Expo Center, which was completed in July 2002. The Olympia Center and the Washington Center for the Performing Arts each offer facilities for a variety of meeting and exhibition events. The Washington State Capital Museum houses several venues for conferences, among them the Coach House and the Conference Room. The Norman Worthington Conference Center on the St. Martin's University campus in nearby Lacey has 4,752 square feet of open area that can be partitioned into four smaller rooms of approximately 1,100 square feet each.

Convention Information: Olympia-Thurston County Visitor & Convention Bureau, PO Box 7338, Olympia, WA 98507; telephone (360)704-7544; toll-free (877)704-7500; fax (360)704-7533; email info@visitolympia.com

Transportation

Approaching the City

Olympia can be approached from the east by Interstate 5. In the center of the city, Interstate 5 turns southward. State highway 12 runs westward beginning at the center of the city. State highway 101 runs northward from the west side of Olympia.

Olympia is served by Seattle-Tacoma International Airport. Located 45 miles northwest of downtown Olympia, "Sea-Tac Airport" handled nearly 29 million passengers in 2004. The Olympia Regional Airport, situated in Tumwater, is home to aircraft service operations, hangars, corporate offices, and a modern public terminal. The airport provides tower-controlled and full-instrument approach access for a variety of recreational, commercial, and corporate users.

Traveling in the City

Olympia's downtown streets are arranged in a grid to the east of Budd Inlet. Local bus transportation is available on the free Capitol Shuttle. The Intercity Transit has routes to nearby cities. Amtrak provides rail transportation, and bus service is provided by Greyhound.

Communications

Newspapers and Magazines

The Olympian is the city's daily newspaper. Three monthly newspapers published locally are *The Thurston-Mason Senior News, Washington State Grange News,* an agricultural paper, and *Works in Progress,* a community newspaper.

Television and Radio

Olympia has one cable television station, as well as two FM and one AM radio station with nostalgia, country music, classical, soft rock, and eclectic programming.

Media Information: *The Olympian,* 111 Bethel St. NE, PO Box 407, Olympia, WA; 98507; telephone (360)754-5400; fax (360)754-5408; email service@theolympian.com

Olympia Online

City of Olympia. Available www.ci.olympia.wa.us

Economic Development Council of Thurston County. Available www.thurstonedc.com

Olympia School District. Available kids.osd.wednet.edu

Olympia-Thurston County Visitor & Convention Bureau. Available www.visitolympia.com

The Olympian. Available www.theolympian.com

Thurston County Chamber. Available www.thurston chamber.com

Thurston Regional Planning Council. Available www.trpc .org

Timberland Regional Library. Available www.timberland .lib.wa.us

Selected Bibliography

Christie, Rebecca A., *Workingman's Hill: A History of an Olympia Neighborhood* (Olympia, WA: Bigelow House Preservation Association, 2001)

Newell, Gordon, *So Fair a Dwelling Place: A History of Olympia and Thurston County, Washington* (Olympia, WA: Gordon Newell and F. George Warren, 1984)

Seattle

The City in Brief

Founded: 1851 (incorporated, 1869)

Head Official: Mayor Greg Nickels (D) (since 2001)

City Population
   1980: 493,846
   1990: 516,259
   2000: 563,374
   2003 estimate: 569,101
   Percent change, 1990–2000: 9.1%
   U.S. rank in 1980: 23rd
   U.S. rank in 1990: 21st
   U.S. rank in 2000: 30th

Metropolitan Area Population (PMSA)
   1980: 1,607,000
   1990: 2,033,128
   2000: 2,414,616

Percent change, 1990–2000: 23%
U.S. rank in 1980: 18th (CMSA)
U.S. rank in 1990: 14th (CMSA)
U.S. rank in 2000: 13th (CMSA)

Area: 83.9 square miles (2000)
Elevation: Ranges from sea level to 450 feet above sea level
Average Annual Temperature: 52.4° F
Average Annual Precipitation: 36.6 inches

Major Economic Sectors: Services, trade, manufacturing, government
Unemployment Rate: 4.7% (January 2005)
Per Capita Income: $30,306 (1999)

2002 FBI Crime Index Total: 46,432

Major Colleges and Universities: University of Washington, Seattle Pacific University, Seattle University

Daily Newspapers: *The Seattle Times; Seattle Post-Intelligencer*

Introduction

Little more than a century ago, Seattle—nicknamed "The Emerald City"—was a pioneer outpost and a quiet lumbering town. Transformed by the Yukon gold rush into a thriving metropolis, Seattle has become the transportation, manufacturing, commercial, and services hub for the Pacific Northwest as well as the largest urban area north of San Francisco, California. The city's arts community has gained an international reputation, annually drawing audiences from throughout the United States and abroad. Nestled between two magnificent mountain ranges, with a breathtaking view of a lake and bay, Seattle enjoys a climate one observer has likened to "an airborne ocean bath."

Geography and Climate

Seattle is situated on a series of hills in a lowland area on Puget Sound's eastern shore between the Olympic Mountains to the west and the Cascade Mountains to the east. Westerly air currents from the ocean and the shielding effects of the Cascade range produce a mild and moderately moist climate, with warm winters and cool summers. Extremes in temperature are rare and of short duration, and the daily fluctuation is slight. While Seattle is known for its pronounced rainy season and frequent cloudy weather, the average annual rainfall is actually less than that of many other cities in the United States, including New York and Atlanta.

Area: 83.9 square miles (2000)

Elevation: Sea level to 450 feet above sea level

Average Temperatures: January, 40.8° F; August, 66.1° F; annual average, 52.4° F

Average Annual Precipitation: 36.6 inches

History

Illinois Farmers Build Sawmills in Seattle

The original inhabitants of the region surrounding the site of present-day Seattle were the Suquamish tribe. Their chief, Sealth, befriended a group of Illinois farmers who settled in the area in 1851. These settlers, the first people of European descent to arrive north of the Columbia River, had established a town at Alki Point on Elliott Bay then moved to the location of present-day Pioneer Square. They named their new town Seattle in gratitude to Chief Sealth.

Finding an abundant lumber resource in the rich forests, the settlers set up sawmills for the preparation of logs for export to San Francisco, where the 1849 gold rush had generated a building boom. By 1853 the lumber industry was thriving in the area, and for several years it provided the sole economic base of Seattle, which was incorporated in 1869.

City Rebuilds After Fire; Becomes Commercial Center

In 1889 a great fire, ignited by a flaming glue pot in a print shop, destroyed the entire business district, consuming sixty blocks. Damaged wood-frame buildings were replaced by masonry structures on a higher elevation than the original storefronts, resulting in the creation of an underground city that is a popular tourist attraction in modern Seattle. The city recovered fairly quickly from the setback caused by the fire.

During the last decade of the nineteenth century Seattle became a rail and maritime commercial center when the Great Northern Railroad reached town and the city was selected by a major shipping line as the port of entry for trade with the Orient. The Alaska gold rush brought further growth and development, and Seattle, dubbed the "gateway to the Klondike," increased in population from 56,842 people in 1897 to 80,600 people in 1900. Prosperity continued and within the next decade the population grew to 240,000 residents.

Rise of Aerospace Industry; World's Fair Brings Tourists

Seattle's aerospace industry began when a small local firm that became the Boeing Company—now the world's foremost manufacturer of jet aircraft and spacecraft—started making two-seater biplanes in 1916. The shipping and aircraft industries continued to play an important role in the city's economy during both world wars and into the 1960s.

The Seattle World's Fair in 1962 brought new economic dimensions to the region, establishing Seattle as a tourist and entertainment center. As a result of the reduction of federal support for aerospace projects in the 1970s, the city's reliance on the aircraft industry shifted to development of its position as a transportation hub in the international market. Since 1975 Seattle has undergone renewed economic expansion to become the financial, industrial, and trade center for the Pacific Northwest.

Seattle made international headlines in 1999 when the city played host to the World Trade Organization meeting. Forty thousand demonstrators gathered to protest globalization; city leaders had hoped that the summit would showcase Seattle as a world-class friend to free trade. The event highlighted the tension between those who liked the new high-tech, high-wealth Seattle and those who believed that Seattle is losing its small-town charm.

Today, Seattle is a hotbed of activity in the Pacific Northwest. Located just two hours south of Vancouver, Canada, the city of Seattle is an international port that boasts several professional sports teams, hundreds of restaurants, a myriad of cultural venues, and a lifestyle that is unique to the Pacific Northwest.

Population Profile

Metropolitan Area Residents (PMSA)
1980: 1,607,000
1990: 2,033,108
2000: 2,414,616
Percent change, 1990–2000: 23%
U.S. rank in 1980: 18th (CMSA)
U.S. rank in 1990: 14th (CMSA)
U.S. rank in 1998: 13th (CMSA)

City Residents
1980: 493,846
1990: 516,259
2000: 563,374
2003 estimate: 569,101
Percent change, 1990–2000: 9.1%
U.S. rank in 1980: 23rd
U.S. rank in 1990: 21st (State rank: 1st)
U.S. rank in 2000: 30th

Density: 6,717.0 people per square mile (2000)

Racial and ethnic characteristics (2000)
White: 394,889
Black or African American: 47,541
American Indian and Alaskan Native: 5,659
Asian: 73,910
Native Hawaiian and Other Pacific Islander: 2,804
Hispanic or Latino (may be of any race): 29,719
Other: 13,423

Percent of residents born in state: 38.8% (2000)

Age characteristics (2000)
Population under 5 years old: 26,215
Population 5 to 9 years old: 24,459
Population 10 to 14 years old: 23,425
Population 15 to 19 years old: 29,648
Population 20 to 24 years old: 51,014
Population 25 to 34 years old: 122,282
Population 35 to 44 years old: 95,077

Population 45 to 54 years old: 81,453
Population 55 to 59 years old: 24,839
Population 60 to 64 years old: 17,164
Population 65 to 74 years old: 29,463
Population 75 to 84 years old: 27,273
Population 85 years and over: 11,071
Median age: 35.4 years

Births (2003)
Total number: 7,245

Deaths (2003)
Total number: 4,592

Money income (1999)
Per capita income: $30,306
Median household income: $45,736
Total households: 258,635

Number of households with income of . . .
less than $10,000: 5,192
$10,000 to $14,999: 3,524
$15,000 to $24,999: 8,594
$25,000 to $34,999: 10,558
$35,000 to $49,999: 16,344
$50,000 to $74,999: 25,631
$75,000 to $99,999: 17,952
$100,000 to $149,999: 15,790
$150,000 to $199,999: 5,444
$200,000 or more: 6,469

Percent of families below poverty level: 6.9% (37.9% of which were female householder families with related children under 5 years)

2002 FBI Crime Index Total: 46,432

Municipal Government

Seattle operates under a mayor-council form of government. The mayor is elected to a four-year term; the nine council members, elected at large, serve staggered four-year terms. Seattle is the seat of King County.

Head Official: Mayor Greg Nickels (D) (since 2001; current term expires December 31, 2005)

Total Number of City Employees: 3,220 (2003)

City Information: City Hall, 600 4th Avenue Floor 1, PO Box 94726, Seattle, WA 98124; telephone (206)684-2489

Economy

Major Industries and Commercial Activity

While Seattle has in the past been largely dependent on the aerospace industry (it is the headquarters of the Boeing Company, the world's largest aerospace firm), the city's diverse economy is also based on the manufacture of transportation equipment and forest products as well as food processing and advanced technology in computer software, biotechnology, electronics, medical equipment, and environmental engineering. In 2003 Corbis, one of the world's leading providers of digital images, moved its headquarters to downtown Seattle. Nonmanufacturing activities, however, comprise more than 85 percent of the Seattle economy; international trade, for instance, is a leading industry, accounting for a large portion of jobs statewide.

The Port of Seattle, the second largest handler of container cargo in the country, provides a direct connection to the Orient and serves as a major link in trade with markets in Alaska, on the Gulf of Mexico, and on the Atlantic Coast. With its multifaceted transportation network of freeways, railroads, an airport, a ferry system, and port facilities, Seattle is the principal trade, distribution, financial, and services center for the Northwest. Tourism continues to be a vital part of the city's economy.

Items and goods produced: food products, textiles, aluminum, iron and steel products, lumber, flour, clothing, airplanes, canned fish and fruit

Incentive Programs—New and Existing Companies

Among the incentives available to businesses in Seattle/ King County are customized employee training, low interest loans, and tax deferrals. In addition to federal government assistance, state and local governments in the area have offered a package of incentives to meet the unique needs of business and industry.

Development Projects

With Seattle mired in a recession in the aftermath of the September 11, 2001, terrorist attacks on the United States, Mayor Greg Nickels created the Economic Opportunity Task Force to revitalize distressed neighborhood business districts and work on policies that benefit the University of Washington. Also at the top of the mayor's economic development agenda were transportation issues, including replacement of the Alaskan Way Viaduct, the expansion of the Seattle monorail, and the improvement of Sound Transit's light rail line.

Perhaps one of the area's most ambitious projects, the replacement of the Alaskan Way Viaduct with a tunnel, has been announced. Because the adjacent seawall is deteriorating and the viaduct itself was severely damaged in the 2001 Nisqually earthquake, both structures need to be rebuilt in order to remove a threat to public safety and the economy. The viaduct is one of the state's most important transportation corridors, carrying 110,000 vehicles a day. Since 2001, millions of dollars have been spent to secure it. The next steps for the project will be to complete a Final Environmental Impact Statement in 2006 and pursue funding for the project. Construction to replace the viaduct and seawall will begin in 2009, pending available funding.

Numerous apartment, condominium, hotels, retail, and other spaces are under construction or renovation in the downtown area. The new 362,987-square-foot Downtown Central Library opened in May 2004. The first phase of construction to transform eight acres of waterfront property adjoining Myrtle Edwards Park into an open space began in June 2004. The park will have a two-story pavilion, parking for 54 vehicles, and pedestrian walkways as well as a pedestrian overpass.

In addition to a massive, $300 million expansion of Terminal 18, the Port of Seattle has been carrying out other projects as a part of the Seattle Seaport Terminal Project. The plan consists of numerous smaller projects that are expected to improve the port's terminals for businesses, tourists, and passengers. In past decades, the Port has invested $2.1 billion in facilities improvements and plans to invest an additional $2.9 billion over the next decade. Dredging the east waterway of the Duwamish River is expected to cost $7.5 million and will help make several more of the Port's container berths deep enough to accommodate the next generation of container ships. This will also create jobs both on the waterfront and throughout the region. The first phase of a $12.7 million cruise terminal began in 2000; Norwegian Cruise Line and Royal Caribbean International will use the port for new cruise services.

Economic Development Information: City of Seattle Office of Economic Development, telephone (206)684-8090; fax (206)684-0379. State of Washington, Department of Community, Trade and Economic Development, telephone (206)464-6282. Trade Development Alliance of Greater Seattle, telephone (206)389-7301

Commercial Shipping

Seattle's economy benefits from Seattle-Tacoma International Airport, which is served by 16 cargo carriers. The city's most important commercial asset is Elliott Bay, one of the finest deep-water ports in the world. The Port of Seattle is the fifth largest container port in the United States and the twentieth largest in the world. It can accommodate ships up to 1,400 feet in length and provides generous warehouse space. Two transcontinental railroads and more than 170 motor freight carriers transport goods to and from Seattle.

Labor Force and Employment Outlook

Seattle offers an educated, skilled, productive, and stable work force, who are attracted to the area by the quality of life. Although experts proclaim that the post-September 11, 2001, recession has ended, it will not be until beyond 2005 that the area will surpass employment levels seen at the peak of the economic boom in December 2000.

In spite of recent setbacks, local analysts expect continued growth in the Seattle area, especially in manufacturing industries (mainly aircraft and biotechnology) and services.

The following is a summary of data regarding the Seattle-Bellevue-Everett metropolitan area labor force, 2004 annual averages.

Size of nonagricultural labor force: 1,335,500

Number of workers employed in . . .
   natural resources and mining: 1,300
   construction: 76,400
   manufacturing: 145,300
   trade, transportation, and utilities: 260,100
   information: 72,200
   financial activities: 89,700
   professional and business services: 181,800
   educational and health services: 138,700
   leisure and hospitality: 122,600
   other services: 49,100
   government: 198,400

Average hourly earnings of production workers employed in manufacturing: $18.27 (2004 annual statewide average)

Unemployment rate: 4.7% (January 2005)

Largest county employers	*Number of employees*
The Boeing Company	64,000
Port of Seattle	11,225
Alaska Air Group Inc.	11,150
Microsoft Corporation	11,000
University of Washington	10,000

Cost of Living

The cost of living in Seattle is not inexpensive, given the relatively high price of housing. The average monthly rental cost for a two-bedroom, two-bathroom, unfurnished apartment is $913. The estimated purchase price for a new home (three bedrooms and two full baths) with approximately 1,800 square feet of living space in the Seattle area is $313,983.

The following is a summary of data regarding several key cost of living factors for the Seattle area.

2004 (3rd Quarter) ACCRA Average House Price: $354,843

2004 (3rd Quarter) ACCRA Cost of Living Index: 122.7 (U.S. average = 100.0)

State income tax rate: None

State sales tax rate: 6.5% (food and prescription drugs are exempt)

Local income tax rate: None

Local sales tax rate: 1.0%

Property tax rate: $10.21-12.18 per $1,000 assessed value (2004)

Economic Information: *The Greater Seattle Datasheet,* City of Seattle, Office of Intergovernmental Relations, telephone (206)684-8055; fax (206)684-8267

Education and Research

Elementary and Secondary Schools

Seattle Public Schools is the largest district in the state. The system is administered by a nonpartisan, seven-member school board that appoints a superintendent.

The following is a summary of data regarding Seattle's public schools as of the 2003–2004 school year.

Total enrollment: 46,730

Number of facilities
   elementary schools: 61
   middle schools: 12
   senior high schools: 10
   other: 16 alternative schools

Student/teacher ratio: 24.3:1

Teacher salaries
   minimum: $30,826
   maximum: $56,217

Funding per pupil: $6,229

More than 300 private and parochial schools, preschools, and special schools also operate in the Seattle metropolitan area.

Public Schools Information: Seattle Public Schools, 815 Fourth Avenue North, PO Box 19116, Seattle, WA 98109; telephone (206)298-7000

Colleges and Universities

The University of Washington (which enrolls nearly 40,000 students), Seattle Pacific University (which enrolls 3,800), and Seattle University (which enrolls 3,900) are the major four-year accredited institutions of higher learning in Seattle. They offer baccalaureate degrees in a wide range of disciplines and graduate degrees in such fields as education, law, software engineering, and medicine. A number of community colleges, vocational schools, and adult-education centers serve Seattle residents.

Libraries and Research Centers

In addition to its main branch downtown, the Seattle Public Library system operates 23 branches throughout the city. Its collection consists of more than 2.5 million items. Special collections focus on aeronautics, African Americans, and Northwest history. In 1998 Seattle voters approved a $196.4 million bond measure to upgrade the Seattle Public Library system with new facilities, technology, and books. The new, 362,987-square-foot facility, which opened May 2004, includes a 275-seat auditorium and parking for 143 vehicles.

The University of Washington's library, said to be the largest and most comprehensive in the Northwest, holds more than 6 million volumes. Special libraries there are affiliated with universities, government agencies, hospitals, and local corporations, which concentrate on such fields as medicine, business, banking, law, and science.

The University of Washington is the heart of research study in Seattle, including the areas of microcomputer architecture, digital systems theory, speech and image processing, artificial intelligence, and metallurgical and ceramic engineering. Other major research facilities are the Fred Hutchinson Cancer Research Center and the Battelle Memorial Institute.

Public Library Information: Seattle Public Library, 1000 Fourth Avenue, Seattle, WA 98104-1193; telephone (206)386-4636

Health Care

With a national reputation for its diagnostic and treatment facilities, which include more free clinics than in any other West Coast city, Seattle-King County is the health care center for the Pacific Northwest. The metropolitan area offers 26 general acute-care and five special purpose centers providing thousands of beds and physicians. University of Washington Hospital is the teaching hospital for the University of Washington. Among its other leading health care institutions are Children's Hospital and Regional Medical Center, the Fred Hutchinson Cancer Research Center, Virginia Mason Medical Center, and Swedish Medical Center. Bailey-Boushay House, a residence where people with HIV

can be treated less expensively than at traditional centers, has provided over a decade of life-changing care. The Seattle Cancer Treatment and Wellness Center is the only cancer center in the Pacific Northwest where medical oncologists work side by side with practitioners of alternative medicine.

Recreation

Sightseeing

Seattle is consistently ranked among the top U.S. tourist destinations. Many attractions are located in the pedestrian-scale downtown area or within easy access by bus and monorail. Tourists can choose from several diversions, including historical sites, internationally acclaimed cultural events, and outdoor activities in the spectacular mountains, forests, and waters surrounding the city.

A popular Seattle landmark is the Space Needle, focal point of the Seattle Center, the 74-acre park and building complex constructed for the 1962 World's Fair. The 605-foot Space Needle features an observation deck for viewing the city, Puget Sound, and adjacent Cascade and Olympic mountains. At its base is the $100 million Experience Music Project, a nonprofit interactive museum tracing the history of American music, which was funded entirely by Microsoft co-founder Paul Allen. The Seattle Center, linked to the central business district by free bus service and the high-speed Monorail, contains an amusement park and sponsors outdoor concerts as well as other events.

Pioneer Square, near the waterfront downtown, is the city's historic district. This area offers a trip back to late-1800s Seattle via cobblestone streets, the original Skid Road (an expression that later evolved into Skid Row), and restored brick and sandstone buildings, many of them housing shops and restaurants. A unique point of interest beneath Pioneer Square is the ''underground city,'' five blocks of sidewalks and storefronts that were left standing after the 1889 fire, when the street levels were raised.

Seattle offers an abundance of attractions related to the maritime industry. Harbor traffic on Elliott Bay can be observed from Waterfront Park, located in the pier area just off Alaskan Way. South of the park at Pier 53, the Seattle Fire Department boats, *Alki* and *Chief Seattle,* are berthed; a favorite local event is practice day, when the fireboats shoot high water arcs into the bay. At Fishermen's Terminal, a working commercial fishing port, residents and visitors enjoy watching fishermen mend nets and tend their boats. Hiram M. Chittenden Locks, among the busiest locks in the world, furnish diversion for navigation enthusiasts as scores of large and small vessels are transferred daily between salt

The Seattle Art Museum, designed by architect Robert Venturi, opened in 1991.

and fresh water. The Seattle Aquarium on the downtown waterfront links the waterfront to First Avenue, which lies just above. For those wanting to go out onto the water, ferries provide rides along the coast and across the sound; tour boats offer longer cruises and excursions to points of interest in the area.

Seattle is known for the Woodland Park Zoo, which contains about 1,000 animals in their natural habitats with minimal fencing and barriers; special features are 50 endangered species and the world's largest group of liontail macaques. Washington Park on the University of Washington campus is the setting for the Arboretum, 200 acres of public gardens, including a Japanese tea garden, with especially striking displays of blossoms and foliage during spring and fall.

Arts and Culture

Seattle is the cultural and entertainment hub of the Pacific Northwest as well as one of the nation's leading cities for theater and opera. Rivaled only by New York in the number of equity theaters based in the area and considered one of the leading U.S. cities for opera performances, Seattle is the only place in the Western Hemisphere where Richard Wagner's *Ring* cycle is performed annually. Attaining wide recognition has in fact become a Seattle tradition, yet cultural events also emphasize regional artists and performers.

The arts scene includes the Seattle Symphony, located in the world-class Benaroya Hall; Seattle Opera; the Pacific Northwest Ballet; numerous art galleries; the Seattle Art Museum; the Seattle Asian Art Museum; and the Experience Music Project rock and roll museum. The 2003–2004 season marked the Seattle Symphony's Centennial Season.

The city is rich in theater arts with 80 companies, 13 of which are professional. The Seattle Opera, recognized internationally for its compelling and accomplished performances, moved into its new state-of-the-art home, Marion Oliver McCaw Hall, in August 2003. The Seattle Repertory Theatre Company, the city's principal and nationally-acclaimed professional theater company, stages its annual productions at the Bagley Wright Theater at Seattle Center. Downtown's Paramount Theatre houses both the Fifth Avenue Theatre and visiting Broadway shows. Live theater is presented by area companies, including a Contemporary Theater (ACT), now housed at the renovated Eagle's Auditorium; Empty Space; and Intiman. Several small theaters are also active in the Seattle metropolitan area. Dramatic and musical performances are regularly scheduled at the University of Washington. Seattle hosts large-scale musical concerts and has gained international attention as the place of origin of many trend-setting rock and pop groups.

Seattle supports a number of museums and galleries specializing in a wide range of areas. The Seattle Art Museum displays a large collection of Oriental, Asian, African, and modern art; of special interest is a collection of paintings by the Northwest Mystics school. The Charles and Emma Frye Art Museum downtown features exhibits of eighteenth- and nineteenth-century and contemporary paintings. The Bellevue Art Museum in Bellevue Square specializes in works by regional artists. The Henry Art Gallery at the University of Washington is one of the oldest art museums in the state. Commercial galleries, most of them clustered around Pioneer Square, regularly schedule shows.

The Museum of Flight traces the history of flight from Leonardo da Vinci to the present with such exhibits as ''Apollo,'' which chronicles manned space exploration, and more than forty aircraft. The Suquamish Museum is devoted to the preservation of Puget Sound native culture; artifacts, photographs, and oral histories are featured. Daybreak Star Arts and Cultural Center in Discovery Park pays homage to Northwest Coast tribes through indoor and outdoor displays of paintings and carvings. The Burke Museum displays artifacts and geological materials relating to Northwest Coast native and Pacific Rim cultures; dinosaur exhibits are a highlight. The Museum of History and Industry concentrates on the heritage of Seattle, King County, and the Pacific Northwest. The Pacific Science Center, located at Seattle Center, presents exhibits pertaining to science; laser shows and films are shown at the Eames/IMAX Theater; the Science Center also is home to the Boeing 3D IMAX Theatre. The Seattle Children's Museum, also at Seattle Center, offers such hands-on activities as a child-size neighborhood for both adults and children.

Festivals and Holidays

Seattle and its environs, a major attraction for the television and film industry, support an annual, world-famous international film festival. Other festival celebrations include the International Children's Theater Festival and the Bite of Seattle food festival. The Northwest Folklife Festival is held at Seattle Center on Memorial Day weekend in May; this annual event features traditional folk music, folk dances, and the culture of the people of the Pacific Northwest. Held annually for 23 days in mid-July to early August, the Seattle SEAFAIR includes boat races and exhibitions, parades, a queen coronation and pageant, fishing derbies, food, and entertainment. Also in July and August is the famous Pacific Northwest Wagner Festival, presenting performances of the composer's complete *Ring* cycle, staged at Seattle Center Opera House. Seattle Center is the site on Labor Day weekend of the Seattle Arts Festival, popularly known as ''Bumbershoot;'' rated as one of the five top festivals in the nation, it is a celebration of the city's arts community with more than 400 performances ranging from grunge bands to Russian tightrope walkers. The year closes with the Harvest Festival in November and the Christmas Cruise in December.

Sports for the Spectator

Seattle is the only city in the Northwest to support professional teams in all three major sports. The Seattle Seahawks of the American Football Conference play at Qwest Field, a 72,000-seat, open-air stadium built in 2002. The Seattle Mariners play American League baseball at Safeco Field, which has a retractable roof. The SuperSonics, a National Basketball Association team, hold their games in the Key Arena in the Seattle Center, which is also the scene of hockey action from the Seattle Thunderbirds of the Western Hockey League. Soccer fans enjoy matches featuring the Seattle Sounders at Qwest Field. WNBA women's basketball is played by the Seattle Storm. Area colleges and universities field teams in all primary sports. There is also horse racing at Emerald Downs, minor league baseball with the Everett Aquasox and Tacoma Rainiers, PRCA Rodeo, and numerous other spectator and participatory sports.

Sports for the Participant

Considered one of the best recreational cities in the United States, Seattle offers a variety of outdoor activities. Especially popular are water sports such as fresh- and salt-water fishing, boating, swimming, scuba diving, and whitewater rafting on lakes and waterways within an hour of downtown. Hiking and horseback riding can be enjoyed on miles of forest trails maintained in area parks and mountains; skiing and mountain climbing, including guided climbs to the top of Mount Rainier, can be pursued at several locations in the mountains surrounding Seattle. Five golf courses, 151 tennis courts, 12 beaches, 10 swimming pools, and 33 play fields can be found in the area's 397 parks and open spaces.

Shopping and Dining

Shopping can be a unique experience in Seattle, where high-fashion merchandise and recreational gear coexist on shop counters. Major department stores and designer boutiques are located downtown within walking distance of hotels and in suburban shopping centers throughout the area. Seattle is the nation's primary manufacturing and retail center for recreational and outdoor equipment. Northwest Native American handicrafts and art items are available at local artisan centers, specialty shops, and galleries and museums; goods imported from the Orient are featured at shops in Seattle's International District, where Chinatown is located. Historic Pike Place Market near Pioneer Square is one of the few remaining authentic farmer's markets in the nation. A terraced walkway leads from the market to Alaskan Way, a colorful waterfront streetcar route lined with piers, marine equipment shops, and seafood restaurants.

Seafood is a Seattle specialty, and seafood stands and restaurants featuring dishes prepared from daily catches abound. The city has also gained a national reputation as the center for "Northwest cuisine:" Olympia oysters, geoduck clams, wild mushrooms, fresh produce, whole-grain breads, and local cheeses and wines. Many restaurants feature scenic locations that enhance dining pleasure, and opportunities for alfresco dining are plentiful. Asian food is found on many local menus, and citizens have gone wild for coffee—coffee shops and espresso carts can be found in the usual locations and even in gas stations and hardware stores.

Visitor Information: Seattle/King County Convention & Visitors Bureau, 701 Pike Street, Suite 800, Seattle, WA 98101; telephone (206)461-5800; fax (206)461-5855; email visinfo@seeseattle.org.

Convention Facilities

The Washington State Convention and Trade Center is the city's major meeting and conference facility. The facility currently offers 54 meeting rooms and ballrooms totaling approximately 105,000 square feet of space, and exhibit space totaling 205,700 square feet. The Convention Center expansion, which was completed in July 2001, includes a magnificent new arch spanning Pike Street, along with an office tower at the northeast corner of 7th and Pike. The center sits on top of Interstate 5, within walking distance of more than 9,000 hotel rooms. Just north of downtown, the 831,000-square-foot Seattle Center also hosts conventions and meetings. Lynnwood Convention Center, Meydenbaur Center, and Bell Harbor International Conference Center are among other locations used for trade shows and meetings. Hotels and motels throughout the metropolitan area provide a total of nearly 25,000 rooms as well as additional convention and meeting accommodations.

Convention Information: Seattle/King County Convention & Visitors Bureau, 701 Pike Street, Suite 800, Seattle, WA 98101; telephone (206)461-5800; fax (206)461-5855; email conventions@seeseattle.org

Transportation

Approaching the City

Air travelers to Seattle are served by the Seattle-Tacoma International Airport (Sea-Tac), the sixteenth busiest commercial airport in the United States. The airport is currently being upgraded with a new runway that will enable aircraft to land in any weather conditions. A new South Terminal and new Central Terminal and Pacific Marketplace were completed in 2004. Plans are also underway for a multi-year capital improvement project slated for completion by 2010 that will add needed capacity.

Two interstate highways serve Seattle: I-5 (north-south) and I-90 (east-west). Passenger rail service is available from Amtrak's four daily trains. Seattle is the southern terminus of the Alaska Marine Highway System; ferries transporting passengers and motor vehicles operate year round from points in southeast Alaska. Passenger rail service to major U.S. destinations is provided by Amtrak, and buses connect Seattle with U.S. and Canadian cities and with Tijuana, Mexico.

Traveling in the City

Avenues in Seattle run north and south and streets run east and west. The city center is perhaps best explored on foot. Seattle's bus- and trolley-based mass transit system, Metro Transit, operates routes throughout the Seattle-King County area, with service in downtown Seattle provided free of charge from 6 a.m. to 7 p.m. A five-year plan to upgrade facilities, equipment, systems, and services is scheduled for completion in 2007.

Communications

Newspapers and Magazines

Seattle's major daily newspapers are the evening *The Seattle Times* and the morning *Seattle Post-Intelligencer.* Seattle is also the headquarters for several weekly, biweekly, or monthly publications appealing to ethnic groups, such as *Northwest Asian Weekly,* and *Korea Central Daily. Slate,* an online publication developed by Microsoft, is based in Seattle.

Television and Radio

All major television networks have affiliates in Seattle, and cable service is available. More than 30 AM and FM radio stations are based in Seattle, providing music, news, and features; other stations broadcast from neighboring communities.

Media Information: *The Seattle Times,* 1120 John St., Seattle, WA 98109; telephone (206)264-2111; *Seattle Post-Intelligencer,* 101 Elliott Ave. W., Seattle WA 98119; telephone (206)464-2111

Seattle Online

City of Seattle home page. Available www.pan.ci.seattle.wa.us

enterpriseSeattle. Available www.edc-sea.org

Greater Seattle Chamber of Commerce. Available www.seattlechamber.com

Seattle Daily Journal of Commerce. Available www.djc.com

Seattle-King County Convention & Visitors Bureau. Available www.seeseattle.org

Seattle Post-Intelligencer. Available seattlep-i.com

Seattle Public Library. Available www.spl.org

Seattle Public Schools. Available www.seattleschools.org

Seattle Times. Available seattletimes.nwsource.com

Washington State Tourism home page. Available www.tourism.wa.gov

Selected Bibliography

Dillard, Annie, *The Living* (New York: HarperCollins, 1992)

Ochsner, Jeffrey Karl, *Shaping Seattle Architecture: A Historical Guide to the Architects* (Seattle: University of Washington Press, 1994)

Rex-Johnson, Braiden, and Paul Souders, *Inside the Pike Place Market: Exploring America's Favorite Farmer's Market* (Seattle, Wa.: Sasquatch Books, 1999)

Spokane

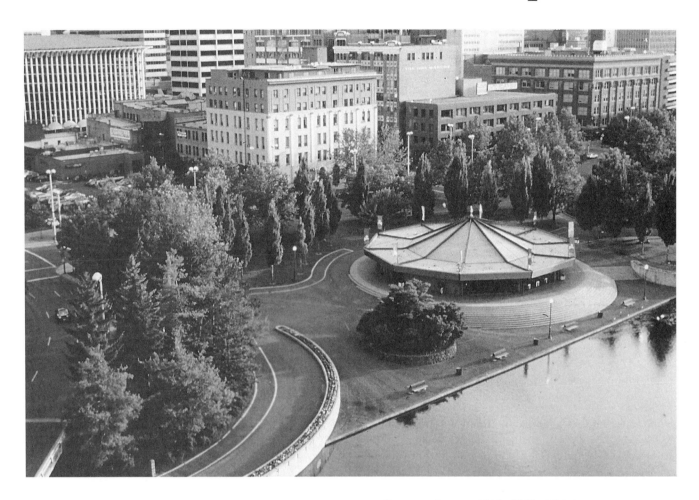

The City in Brief

Founded: 1878 (incorporated, 1881)

Head Official: Mayor James West (since 2003)

City Population
 1980: 171,300
 1990: 177,165
 2000: 195,629
 2003 estimate: 196,624
 Percent change, 1990–2000: 9.8%
 U.S. rank in 1990: 94th
 U.S. rank in 2000: 110th

Metropolitan Area Population
 1980: 341,835
 1990: 361,333
 2000: 417,939

Percent change, 1990–2000: 15.7%
U.S. rank in 1990: 101st
U.S. rank in 2000: 98th

Area: 58 square miles (2000)
Elevation: Ranges from 1,898 to 2,356 feet above sea level
Average Annual Temperature: 47.3° F
Average Annual Precipitation: 16.5 inches

Major Economic Sectors: Services, manufacturing, health care, retail trade
Unemployment Rate: 7.1% (February 2005)
Per Capita Income: $21,587 (1999)

2002 FBI Crime Index Total: 15,895

Major Colleges and Universities: Eastern Washington University, Gonzaga University, Whitworth College, Washington State University-Spokane, Spokane Community Colleges, City University

Daily Newspapers: *The Spokesman-Review*

Introduction

Spokane is the commercial and cultural hub of a large area known as the "Inland Empire" or the "Inland Northwest," a rich agricultural region. The picturesque beauty of its surroundings makes the city an attractive vacation spot, and population and economic growth have brought many metropolitan amenities to the once quiet, out-of-the-way town. Although the city suffered some decline during the late 1980s and early 1990s, Spokane has undergone an impressive $1 billion urban renaissance and, through its many development projects, has ensured its status as a hub of economic, recreation, and culture in the Pacific Northwest.

Geography and Climate

Spokane is located near the eastern border of Washington, about 20 miles from Idaho and 110 miles south of the Canadian border. The city lies on the eastern edge of the Columbia Basin, a wide sloping plain that rises sharply to the east towards the Rocky Mountains. The Spokane River and its waterfalls bisect the city. Summers are typically dry and mild, and winters can bring periods of cold, wet weather. Snowfall rarely accumulates to depths greater than one foot.

Area: 58 square miles (2000)

Elevation: Ranges from 1,898 to 2,356 feet above sea level

Average Temperatures: January, 27.1° F; July, 68.8° F; annual average, 47.3° F

Average Annual Precipitation: 16.5 inches

History

Spokane Area Popular with Traders

For years before the coming of European explorers, the land around the present-day city was settled by the Spokane tribe. Explorers and trappers passed through the area, but no settlements were built until 1810, when Finan McDonald and Joco Finlay built a trading post called Spokane House at the junction of the Spokane and Little Spokane rivers. In 1812, John Clarke of the Pacific Fur Company built Fort Spokane not far from the trading post. The house and fort soon became a popular meeting place for traders, trappers, and Native Americans, and the buildings were sold to the North West Company in 1813.

The Hudson's Bay Company bought the North West Company in 1821 and dismantled Spokane House. The area was once again left to local tribes. Chief Garry, the leader of the Middle and Upper Spokane tribes, had been educated at the Red River Mission school and converted to Presbyterianism. He built a school for his people and taught them English and religion, as well as modern agricultural methods. At about the same time, the first missionaries arrived in the area, establishing a mission on Walker's Prairie, 25 miles north of Spokane Falls.

The great westward expansion of the 1840s attracted a number of settlers to the area, but a clash with local tribes, culminating in the Whitman Massacre, led to the closing of eastern Oregon (the Spokane area was then part of the Oregon Territory) to settlement in the 1850s. In 1871 J. J. Downing and his family located a claim on the banks of the Spokane River. Within a year, the small settlement included a sawmill, a post office, and a general store. In 1873, James N. Glover, who is called the "father of Spokane," rode through the area on horseback. He was, he wrote, "enchanted . . . overwhelmed . . . with the beauty and grandeur of everything." Glover bought the rights to Downing's land and sawmill and opened a store and stable. His early trade was with the Spokane and Coeur d'Alene Indians who lived in the region. The town was registered as Spokane Falls in 1878. By 1880, the town had a population of 75 people, a weekly newspaper, and several baseball teams. In 1881 it was incorporated.

Rapid Population Growth Builds Sophisticated City

Spokane Falls grew steadily throughout the ensuing decades, changing from a rough frontier community into a solid city, complete with all the trappings of Eastern culture: a college, a library, and a number of theaters. The transcontinental railroad reached Spokane Falls in 1883, ensuring the town's success. Fire destroyed much of the town in 1889, but residents quickly rebuilt. By 1890, the city had a population of 30,000 people and changed its name to Spokane when Oregon entered the Union. By 1910, the population had jumped to over 100,000 people.

In 1974 the city was host to the World's Fair, Expo '74, which focused the world's attention on Spokane. Development of Expo '74 buildings and other improvements at the fair site in downtown Spokane created a modern city center with an extensive system of enclosed skywalks. Expansion and development continued through the 1990s and into the new century. Faced with the possibility of losing important downtown retailers, Spokane embarked upon an ambitious and large-scale effort at renewing the city center. These efforts have been enormously successful, as Spokane has continued to attract new retailers and businesses as well as residents who are fleeing high prices in California and in Seattle.

Historical Information: Eastern Washington State Historical Society, Research Library and Archives, 2316 W. First Avenue, Spokane, WA 99204; telephone (509)456-3931; fax (509)456-2770

Population Profile

Metropolitan Area Residents

1980: 341,835
1990: 361,333
2000: 417,939
Percent change, 1990–2000: 15.7%
U.S. rank in 1980: 96th
U.S. rank in 1990: 101st
U.S. rank in 2000: 98th

City Residents

1980: 171,300
1990: 177,196
2000: 195,629
Percent change, 1990–2000: 9.8%
U.S. rank in 1990: 94th
U.S. rank in 2000: 110th (State rank: 2nd)

Density: 3,343.36 people per square mile (2000)

Racial and ethnic characteristics (2000)
   White: 175,081
   Black or African American: 4,052
   American Indian and Alaska Native: 3,444
   Asian: 4,399
   Native Hawaiian and Other Pacific Islander: 372
   Hispanic or Latino (may be of any race): 5,857
   Other: 1,727

Percent of residents born in state: 52.7% (2000)

Age characteristics (2000)
   Population under 5 years old: 13,676
   Population 5 to 9 years old: 13,571
   Population 10 to 14 years old: 13,196
   Population 15 to 19 years old: 14,315
   Population 20 to 24 years old: 15,574
   Population 25 to 34 years old: 28,401
   Population 35 to 44 years old: 29,472
   Population 45 to 54 years old: 25,631
   Population 55 to 59 years old: 8,163
   Population 60 to 64 years old: 6,329
   Population 65 to 74 years old: 12,073

Population 74 to 84 years old: 10,737
Population 85 years and over: 4,491
Median age: 34.7 years

Births (2003)
   Total number: 6,333

Deaths (2003)
   Total number: 2,394 (of which, 33 were infants under the age of 1 year)

Money income (1999)
   Per capita income: $21,587
   Median household income: $32,273
   Total households: 81,762

Number of households with income of . . .
   less than $10,000: 10,395
   $10,000 to $14,999: 7,071
   $15,000 to $24,999: 13,359
   $25,000 to $34,999: 12,988
   $35,000 to $49,999: 13,594
   $50,000 to $74,999: 13,661
   $75,000 to $99,999: 5,415
   $100,000 to $149,999: 3,546
   $150,000 to $199,999: 761
   $200,000 or more: 972

Percent of families below poverty level: 11.1% (52.5% of which were female householder families with related children under 5 years)

2002 FBI Crime Index Total: 15,895

Municipal Government

Spokane's mayor-council form of government formerly elected a mayor and six other council members to four-year terms; the council employed a city manager for the day-to-day operation of the city. In 1999 Spokane voters adopted a strong-mayor form of government, eliminating the city manager position. The city council still has seven members; a council president now presides over meetings instead of the mayor, so there are eight elected city officials instead of seven.

Head Official: Mayor James West (since 2003; current term expires December 2007)

Total Number of City Employees: 2,082 (2005)

City Information: City Hall, West 808 Spokane Falls Boulevard, Spokane, WA 99201; telephone (509)625-6250; e-mail jwest@spokanecity.org

Economy

Major Industries and Commercial Activity

Natural resources have traditionally provided much of the economic activity for the Spokane area, a major center for the timber, agriculture, and mining industries in the region. A number of manufacturing companies have located in Spokane, drawn by the easy access to raw materials. Finished wood products, metal refinery and fabrication, and food processing are among the leaders in manufacturing. The outlying areas are part of an abundant agricultural system, providing a large amount of the nation's apples, peas, hops, pears, asparagus, lentils, soft wheat, and sweet cherries. A number of wineries and breweries also operate in the area. These industries continue to be important elements in the local economy, but in recent years the economy has diversified to encompass high-technology and service companies. Health-related industries employ more people than any other industry in Spokane. The city provides specialized care to many patients from the surrounding areas, as far north as the Canadian border. The city is also the wholesale and retail trade and service center of the 80,000-square-mile Inland Northwest region. In addition, the educational services industry employed the most workers in 2002 with more than 17,000 jobs.

All branches of the U.S. armed forces are represented in Spokane County. The largest military facility is Fairchild Air Force Base, which employs 3,359 military and 863 civilian personnel. The military units and their personnel combine to have an economic impact on the regional economy of $411 million annually. Tourism is the fourth largest industry in the state, and Spokane is a center for tourist activity. Health care accounts for approximately 13.5 percent of the local employment base. Spokane has also seen the recent development of economic activity in the lucrative high-tech and biotech sectors. The city is the site of a 100-block wireless network- the largest of its kind in the country- which is seen as symbolic of its dedication to the development of technological opportunities and resources.

In 2002 Kaiser Aluminum, a major employer with a 60-year presence in the region, filed for bankruptcy. Despite the loss of jobs and revenue, Spokane has rebounded by working to make the city attractive to retail and small businesses.

Items and goods produced: silver, lead, zinc, timber, poultry, dairy, vegetable, fruit, and meat products, aluminum, magnesium, clay and cement products, machinery and metal products, flour, feed, cereal, petroleum products, paper, electrical fixtures

Incentive Programs—New and Existing Businesses

Local programs—The Spokane Area Economic Development Council works with businesses to locate and utilize local and state business incentives. The Spokane Neighborhood Economic Development Alliance offers two revolving loans to businesses and nonprofits expanding or creating new jobs in Spokane.

State programs—A wide variety of tax incentives exist at the state level for businesses operating, expanding, or relocating to Spokane. Industry- and area-specific tax incentives are available, as well as loans, bonds, credits, and grants.

Job training programs—Spokane businesses are assisted largely by working with the higher education community, including such organizations as Applied Technology Center, part of the Community Colleges of Spokane; ITT Technical Institute, which focuses on preparing graduates for careers in technology, and the Spokane Intercollegiate Research and Technology Institute, which uses the collective resources of local colleges to accelerate the development of technology companies. The Spokane Area Workforce Development Council administers employment and training programs for local economically disadvantaged youths and adults through the Spokane City-County Employment and Training Consortium. The Council also supports local economic growth by working to improve the workforce development system.

Development Projects

In 2000, the Spokane Symphony purchased the 1931 Art Deco Fox Theater and is conducting a $28.4 renovation and restoration of the building. Development is also ongoing in the Davenport Arts District, a 10-block area adjacent to the Davenport Hotel (which was reopened in 2002 after renovations), which is filled with new and proposed galleries, restaurants, performance venues, and a jazz club. Spokane's River Park Square, a downtown redevelopment project that is considered one of the city's most ambitious in decades, has continued to expand. The 400,000-square-foot property includes two full-service restaurants; each fills 8,000 square feet and has its own entrance. The $110 million River Park Square mall is anchored by a 137,000-square-foot Nordstrom store and a 90,000-square-foot AMC Theatres multiscreen cinema.

In 2003, ground was broken for the new CenterPlace facility at the 77-acre, multi-use development Mirabeau Point in the Spokane Valley. Mirabeau Point already includes a 45,000-square-foot YMCA complex, a 37,000-square-foot cultural/senior center, a central plaza, hiking trails, an ice skating pond, and multiple park areas. Also begun in 2003 and slated for completion in 2007 is a major expansion of the Spokane Convention Center. Budgeted at $80 million total and working in phases, the renovation and construction consists of new amenities in the existing areas, and a new 100,000 square foot exhibition hall. Developers are committed to employing environmentally-friendly building techniques throughout the project, including non-toxic materials and utilizing energy efficiency, natural light, and water conservation.

Expected to begin in June 2005 the city of Spokane has set aside $117 million for street improvements over a 10-year period. The project will repair about 110 miles of residential streets and arterials throughout Spokane.

Economic Development Information: Economic Development Council, 801 West Riverside, Suite 302, Spokane, WA 99201; telephone (800)SPOKANE; email edc@EDC .Spokane.net.

Commercial Shipping

More than 30 air freight companies operate facilities at Spokane International Airport, and the Burlington Northern and Union Pacific railroads also serve the city. Many motor freight concerns operate regularly scheduled trucks in and out of Spokane.

Labor Force and Employment Outlook

A large, experienced work force is available in Spokane; about 80 percent of workers are native Washingtonians. The health and service industries enjoy strong employment outlooks, as does manufacturing. Seasonal employment at harvest time is always available.

The following is a summary of data regarding the Spokane metropolitan area labor force, 2004 annual averages.

Size of non-agricultural labor force: 199,700

Number of workers employed in . . .
  mining and construction: 11,600
  manufacturing: 17,200
  transportation, trade, and public utilities: 41,000
  information: 3,000
  financial activities: 12,600
  professional and business services: 20,800
  education and health services: 33,000
  leisure and hospitality: 18,200
  other services: 8,900
  government: 33,600

Average hourly earnings of production workers employed in manufacturing: $18.27 (2004 annual statewide average)

Unemployment rate: 7.1% (February 2005)

Largest employers	Number of employees
Fairchild Air Force Base	5,616
Sacred Heart Medical Center	3,232
U.S. Federal Government	3,174
Spokane School District 81	3,126
State of Washington	2,878

Cost of Living

The following is a summary of data regarding key cost of living factors for the Spokane area.

2004 (3rd Quarter) ACCRA Average House Price: $255,323

2004 (3rd Quarter) ACCRA Cost of Living Index: 102.8 (U.S. average = 100.0)

State income tax rate: None

State sales tax rate: 6.5% (food and prescription drugs are exempt)

Local income tax rate: None

Local sales tax rate: 2%

Property tax rate: Averages $14.94 in city, $14.21 in county, per $1,000 of assessed value (2005)

Economic Information: Economic Development Council, 801 West Riverside, Suite 302, Spokane, WA 99201; telephone (800)SPOKANE; email edc@EDC.Spokane.net. Department of Revenue, Taxpayer Information and Education Section, PO Box 47478, Olympia, WA 98504-7478; telephone (800)829-1040; email Communications@dor.wa.gov. Spokane Area Chamber of Commerce, 801 West Riverside Avenue, Spokane, WA 99201; telephone (509)624-1393; fax (509)747-0077; email info@chamber.spokane.net

Education and Research

Elementary and Secondary Schools

Spokane School District Number 81, representing all city schools, is the second largest in the state. Students' test scores are consistently above the national average, and over 70 percent of teachers hold master's degrees. In 2003 a facility and technology improvement bond was passed in the district which is allowing for various school updates as well as construction of new schools.

The following is a summary of data regarding Spokane public schools as of the 2002–2003 school year.

Total enrollment: 31,362

Number of facilities
  elementary schools: 35
  middle schools: 6
  senior high schools: 6
  other: 3

Student/teacher ratio: average 18:1

Teacher salaries
average: $46,110

Funding per pupil: $8,069

A variety of state-approved private elementary and secondary schools augment the public school system, including parochial schools, special schools such as the Lilac Blind Foundation, Montessori programs, and the Spokane Guild's School and Neuromuscular Center. The Spokane Art School offers classes, workshops, and master classes.

Public Schools Information: Spokane Public Schools, Community Relations Division, 200 North Bernard, Spokane, WA 99201; telephone (509)354-7297

Colleges and Universities

Eastern Washington University (EWU), a state-operated school located about 15 miles from Spokane in Cheney, Washington, offers four-year undergraduate degrees in more than 100 academic majors, 10 masters degrees, and 55 graduate programs of study. The university operates a branch in downtown Spokane and enrolls about 9,700 students.

Gonzaga University and Law School, founded by the Jesuits in 1887, offers 50 undergraduate degree programs, 27 masters' degree programs, a doctoral program in educational leadership, and a J.D. (law degree). Washington State University at Spokane, a multi-campus research university, enrolls more than 16,000 students throughout the university system, 739 of whom study at the Spokane campus. These three institutions, together with Whitworth College and the Spokane Community Colleges, operate as a collaborative project the Spokane Intercollegiate Research and Technology Institute, which uses the collective resources of the institutions to improve the economic vitality of the region. Community Colleges of Spokane serve more than 23,000 students in a six-county region, awarding more than 4,400 two-year degrees each year in 120 professional and technical programs.

Libraries and Research Centers

Founded in 1904, the Spokane Public Library system comprises a Downtown Library overlooking Spokane Falls and five branch libraries. Total holdings include nearly 600,000 volumes; more than 35,000 video, music, and audiotapes and CDs; and a periodicals collection numbering more than 700 titles. Special collections include Northwest history, history of the book, genealogy, oral history, African American, and U.S., Washington state, and Spokane County government documents. The library system also sponsors community programs for residents of all ages.

Special libraries in Spokane include the Crosby Library at Gonzaga University, which contains a collection of Bing Crosby records and other memorabilia. Research at the new

Spokane Intercollegiate Research and Technology Institute at Riverpoint focuses on technology transfer for commercial uses. The Health Research and Education Center at Washington State University Spokane develops clinical and applied research in biomedical and social health areas. The Washington Institute for Mental Illness Research and Training recruits and retrains qualified professionals at state hospital to use modern treatments.

Public Library Information: Spokane Public Library, 906 West Main Avenue, Spokane, WA 99201; telephone (509)444-5300

Health Care

Six major hospitals are located in Spokane, four of which are full service facilities. The city is the center of specialized care for the entire Inland Northwest area, offering an expert team of cardiac surgeons and more than 18,500 health care professionals, including more than 900 physicians. Sacred Heart Medical Center, a 623-bed facility, is a leader in heart, lung, and kidney transplant services. In 2003, the hospital opened the region's first full-service children's hospital; a Women's Health Center was added in 2004. The Shriners Hospital for Crippled Children is also based in Spokane. The Community Mental Health Center, which provides mental health services to children, adults, and the elderly, is nationally recognized and the largest and most comprehensive community mental health center in Washington.

Recreation

Sightseeing

Riverfront Park, the site of Expo '74, is a 100-acre urban park that has been developed into a collection of cultural and recreational attractions including a theater, art gallery, a skating rink, an antique carousel composed of 54 hand-carved horses, a train, and an exciting gondola ride over Spokane Falls. The park also features a historic 1909 carousel. Historic Fort George Wright, a 1,500-acre complex, was established in 1894 on a plateau overlooking the river. Other points of interest in the city include Manito Park, with its beautiful Rose Hill and Japanese garden, and Cliff Park, site of Review Rock, a large formation with steps cut into the sides that offers a beautiful view of the city.

The area around Spokane offers a number of attractions, including several ghost towns, the Spokane Plains Battlefield,

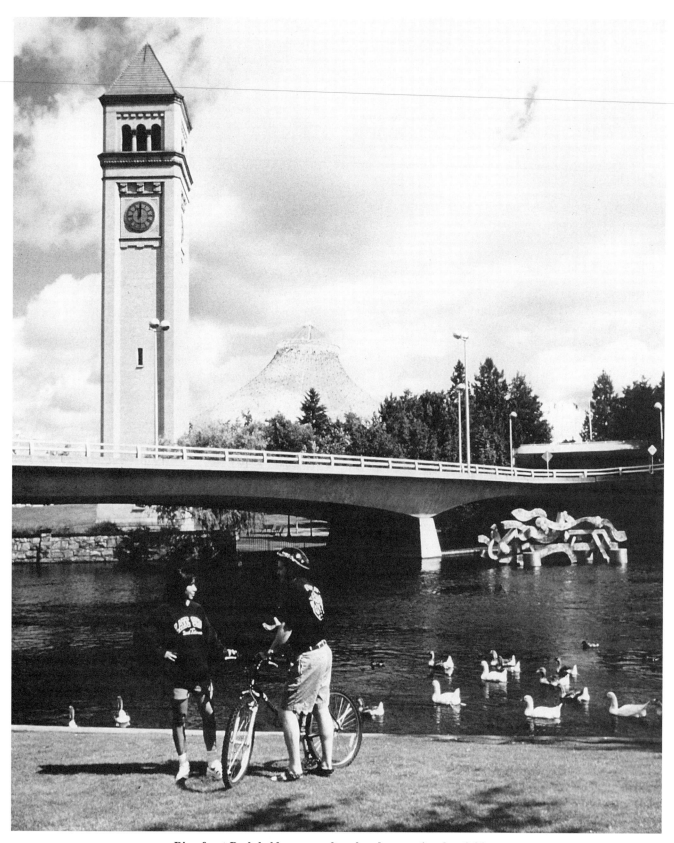

Riverfront Park holds many cultural and recreational activities.

and the Turnbull National Wildlife Refuge. A variety of historic homes, churches, and architecture are available for touring in the Spokane area. Spokane's local wineries have won prestigious awards and offer tours, tastings, and sales.

Arts and Culture

Spokane's 12,500-seat Veteran's Memorial Arena is a focal point for special events. In addition, the newly expanded 2,700-seat Opera House and the more intimate The Met Performing Arts Center host national and international touring companies and entertainers. Music is provided by the Spokane Symphony Orchestra, housed in the Opera House, which presents a full season of classical music, including special children's performances and Super Pops! by the Spokane Jazz Orchestra, which presents up to a dozen concerts a year; and by Allegro-Baroque and Beyond, Connoisseur Concerts, the Spokane Chamber Music Association, and Uptown Opera. Theater is represented by the region's only resident professional company, Interplayer's Ensemble, whose seven-play season runs from September to June; by Spokane Civic Theatre; and by several amateur community theaters and smaller groups. The Big Easy Concert House, home to a concert hall and dance club, has opened in a renovated office block adjacent to the arts district. Area colleges and universities also contribute to the cultural scene.

The new Northwest Museum of Arts and Culture (formerly the Cheney Cowles Museum) reopened after a major $26 million expansion. The museum houses permanent collections of regional history and American Indian artifacts, as well as five art galleries and educational facilities. The historic Campbell House, a museum since 1925, is now a part of the Northwest Museum complex, with tours of the home available by reservation. A proposed science center is likely to be the next development at the growing museum. Additionally, the Jundt Art Museum on the campus of Gonzaga University includes two large gallery spaces and an exhibition lounge.

Festivals and Holidays

The Northwest Bach Festival celebrates the music of J.S. Bach in venues throughout the city for one week at the end of January or early February. The annual Spokane Music and Arts Festival in April draws artists and musicians from all over the Pacific Northwest. Bloomsday, the country's largest timed road race, is held on the first Sunday in May. Later that month, the Spokane Lilac Festival runs for 10 days and features such activities as a flower show, parades, concerts, games, entertainment. Begun in 1938, the festival also showcases local foods and crowns a lilac queen. In June, Spokane plays host to Hoopfest, the world's largest three-on-three basketball tournament. The Spokane County Fair, a tradition since the late 1800s, happens in September.

Sports for the Spectator

The newly-remodeled Spokane Arena hosts the Spokane Chiefs of the Western Hockey Association. The Spokane Indians, a minor league farm team of professional baseball's Texas Rangers, play at Avista Stadium. The Spokane Shadow, a USL Premier League, plays soccer at Joe A. Albi Stadium. The Gonzaga Bulldogs athletic teams, members of the National Collegiate Athletic Association (NCAA) Division I, engage in intercollegiate competition at Gonzaga University. Spokane Raceway Park offers stock car and drag racing, while Playfair offers thoroughbred horse races during the summer and fall.

Sports for the Participant

Seventy-six lakes and four major rivers within a 50-mile radius of Spokane offer a wide variety of water activity. For hikers and nature lovers, a 70-mile pathway called Centennial Trail begins near the old Spokane House fur trading post and winds through Riverside State Park, Riverfront Park in downtown Spokane, and eastward past Coeur d'Alene, Idaho. The Trail was recently expanded to include 37 paved miles on the Spokane River. The city and county maintain more than 75 parks, many of which feature athletic fields, tennis courts, swimming pools, skating rinks, recreational programming, and other facilities. More than 30 public and private golf courses exist in the county. The nearby mountains offer year-round recreation: skiing in the winter and fishing, hunting, camping, canoeing, hiking, and other outdoor activities in the warmer months. In the summer months, floating excursions are available on the Spokane River, while several nearby rivers provide whitewater rafting opportunities. Rock climbing is available just outside of Spokane, and seven ski areas are within a two hour drive.

Shopping and Dining

Spokane shoppers are served by seven major shopping centers in the city and a number of smaller plazas and specialty shopping districts. Retail establishments in downtown Spokane are connected by a 16-block system of enclosed skywalks. The shopping opportunities at River Park Square and in the retail district are unmatched in the Inland Northwest. Spokane's restaurants offer fine international and traditional American dishes. Specialties include fresh salmon and locally-produced wines. More than 500 dining establishments can be found in the Spokane area.

Visitor Information: Spokane Area Visitor Information Center, 201 W. Main, Spokane, WA 99201; telephone (509)747-3230; toll-free (888)SPOKANE. Travel Development Division, Department of Commerce and Economic Development, General Administration Building, Olympia, WA 98504; telephone (360)586-2088; toll-free (800)544-1800

Convention Facilities

The Spokane Convention Center is located on the banks of the Spokane River in the downtown district. The facility consists of 58,000 square feet of convention and banquet space along with 20,000 square feet of storage space. Renovation of the Convention Center is ongoing, with a projected completion date of 2007. At that time, the Center will have grown to over 100,000 square feet and will have expanded convention facilities, as well as new exhibition and display space. The adjoining 28,000-square-foot Washington State International Agricultural Trade Center, with a 300-seat theater expands the capacity, offering space to more than 8,000 people. The 2,700-seat Spokane Opera House is located within the Convention Center. The Spokane Veterans Memorial Arena provides 173,100 square feet of exhibit space and festival seating for 12,500 people. The Joe A. Albi Stadium is a large outdoor arena that seats 28,500 people.

More than 2,000 hotel rooms are available within walking distance of the major convention sites in Spokane; about 6,800 hotel rooms total exist in the surrounding area. Most of the larger hotels maintain ample facilities for conventions such as banquet space, conference rooms, and ballrooms.

Convention Information: Spokane Convention and Visitors Bureau, 801 W. Riverside, Spokane, WA 99201; telephone (509)624-1341

Transportation

Approaching the City

The Spokane International Airport is a multimillion-dollar complex located a few minutes from the downtown area and served by ten major airlines and three air cargo carriers. The city is also served by three commercial bus lines and by Amtrak.

Interstate 90 passes through Spokane, connecting the city with Seattle to the west and with points east. U.S. Highway 2 also runs east and west through the city. U.S. 395 continues north out of Spokane into Canada, and U.S. 195 leads south from the city.

Traveling in the City

Generally in Spokane, the east-west roads are designated as avenues, and the north-south roads are referred to as streets. Major east-west thoroughfares in the city include Francis,

Wellesley, Mission, Sprague, and 29th avenues. North-south arteries include Maple, Monroe, Division, Hamilton, Greene-Market, Argonne, and Sullivan streets.

Communications

Newspaper and Magazines

Spokane readers are served by one daily newspaper, *The Spokesman-Review,* which presents a special entertainment section on Friday. *Journal of Business* is among the biweekly business journals published in the city. *The Pacific Northwest Inlander,* a weekly newspaper, has an extensive arts and entertainment section. Other newspapers focus on senior living, the outdoors, and collegiate interests.

Television and Radio

Spokane has six television stations representing the major commercial networks and public television. The area is also served by a cable system that provides a wide variety of viewing options. Twenty-eight AM and FM radio stations broadcast in Spokane, which also receives programming from neighboring communities.

Media Information: The Spokesman-Review, West 999 Riverside Avenue, PO Box 2160, Spokane, WA 99210; telephone 509(459-5068); toll-free (800)338-880; email danc@spokesman.com

Spokane Online

City of Spokane home page. Available www.spokanecity.org

Spokane Area Chamber of Commerce. Available www.spokanechamber.org

Spokane Area Convention & Visitors Bureau. Available www.visitspokane.com

Spokane Public Library. Available splnet.spokpl.lib.wa.us

Spokane Public Schools. Available www.sd81.k12.wa.us.

Spokane Veterans Memorial Arena events. Available www.spokanearena.com

The Spokesman-Review. Available www.spokane.net

Selected Bibliography

Alexie, Sherman, *Reservation Blues* (Warner, 1995)

Tacoma

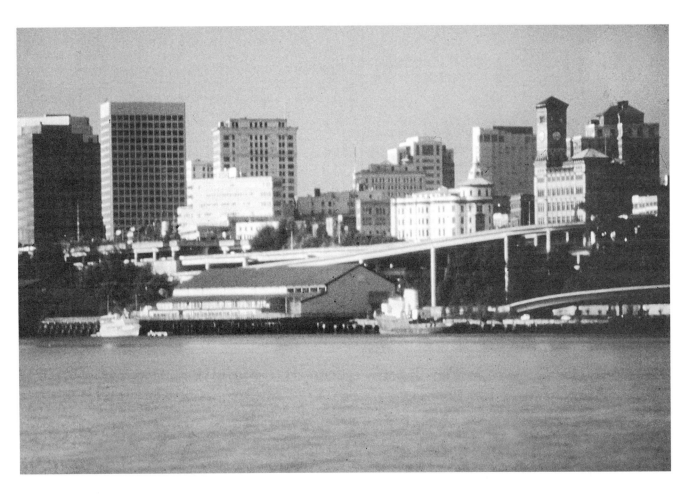

The City in Brief

Founded: 1852 (incorporated, 1884)

Head Official: City Manager James L. Walton (since 2003)

City Population
  1980: 158,501
  1990: 176,664
  2000: 193,556
  2003 estimate: 196,790
  Percent change, 1990–2000: 9.1%
  U.S. rank in 1980: 97th
  U.S. rank in 1990: 95th
  U.S. rank in 2000: 114th

Metropolitan Area Population (PMSA)
  1980: 486,000
  1990: 586,203
  2000: 700,820

Percent change, 1990–2000: 19.5%
U.S. rank in 1980: 18th (CMSA; includes Seattle)
U.S. rank in 1990: 14th (CMSA; includes Seattle)
U.S. rank in 2000: 13th (CMSA; includes Seattle)

Area: 50 square miles (2000)
Elevation: 380 feet above sea level
Average Annual Temperature: 53.1° F
Average Annual Precipitation: 39.2 inches

Major Economic Sectors: Services, international trade, government, military, high technology
Unemployment Rate: 6.6% (January 2005)
Per Capita Income: $19,130 (2000)

2002 FBI Crime Index Total: 20,182

Major Colleges and Universities: Pacific Lutheran University, University of Puget Sound, University of Washington in Tacoma

Daily Newspaper: *The News Tribune*

Introduction

Tacoma's name is derived from the Native American word "Tahoma," meaning "Mother of the Waters," referring to the shadow of Mt. Rainier that looms over the city. Tacoma's beautiful natural setting affords views of the nearby Cascade Range and the more distant Olympic Mountains. Tacoma is home to a deep-water harbor, among the busiest in the United States, that has played an important role in the city's economic development. Nationally recognized for careful municipal planning, Tacoma has been nicknamed the "City of Destiny." In 2004 Partners for Livable Communities named the Tacoma and Pierce County area one of "America's Most Livable Communities."

Geography and Climate

Situated on Commencement Bay, an inlet of Puget Sound, Tacoma lies at the foot of Mt. Rainier in the Puyallup River valley, bordered by mountains. It is about 36 miles south of Seattle. The climate is quite mild throughout the year. Although the area has the reputation of being rainy, Tacoma actually receives less rain than New York City. Most of the precipitation falls in the winter, when snow blankets the mountains.

Area: 50 square miles (2000)

Elevation: 380 feet above sea level

Average Temperatures: January, 40.8° F; July, 65.4° F; annual average: 53.1°

Average Annual Precipitation: 39.2 inches

History

Slow Rise of Lumber Industry; Arrival of Settlers

The first people to live in the Puyallup Valley on the shore of Commencement Bay were the Nisqually and Puyallup Native American tribes. Captain George Vancouver was the first person of European descent to explore the area when, in 1792, he sailed his ship up Puget Sound and named Mt. Rainier for Peter Rainier, an officer in the British Navy. Commencement Bay was charted and named in 1841 by a member of the Charles Wilkes Expedition. Permanent European settlement was achieved in the region in 1852 when a Swedish immigrant, Nicholas De Lin, built a sawmill at the

junction of two creeks and soon conducted a thriving lumber business.

Settlers fled the area in 1855 after hearing rumors of native hostilities; they returned when the Commencement Bay tribe was relocated to a nearby reservation, leaving the area free for other settlers. General Morton Matthew McCarver, who named the settlement Tacoma, was responsible for promoting extensive development by buying tracts of land and bringing in other settlers.

When the Hanson & Ackerman Mill was built in 1869 by a group of San Francisco investors, Tacoma became established in the lumber industry. The mill started a boom, as laborers, artisans, and shopkeepers arrived with their families to settle in Tacoma; with a population of two hundred people, the town soon boasted mail service, electric lights, and a telegraph. In 1873 Tacoma was selected as the terminus for the Northern Pacific Railroad; construction was stopped 20 miles short of Tacoma, however, when an economic crash forced the railroad's investors to pull out of the project. The government recalled the workers, who insisted upon being paid thousands of dollars in back wages before they completed the line.

Railroad Assists Industrial Development

The railroad increased Tacoma's industrial development. Coal mines were opened and Tacoma became the major coaling station on the Pacific Coast. The lumber industry expanded while new industries included a flour mill, a salmon cannery, and machine shops. The town continued to grow, and with a population of 4,400 residents, Tacoma was incorporated in 1884. During the following year a group of residents, who blamed Chinese workers for an employment recession that came with the completion of the railroad, formed the Law and Order League and forcibly deported the Chinese. The insurgents were tried in court but were later acquitted.

Transcontinental rail service to Tacoma was completed in 1887, bringing further development; the completion of the Stamford Pass Tunnel and the establishment of the Northern Pacific Railroad general offices in Tacoma gave an even greater boost to the lumber and coal industries. Record numbers of settlers arrived and the town flourished. Since Tacoma's economy was closely tied to the railroad industry, however, more than half of the city's banks closed when the Reading Railroad went bankrupt. The economy recovered to some degree with the creation of the Weyerhaeuser Timber Company in 1900. During World War I the shipping industry boomed, and the city profited from its proximity to Camp Lewis (later renamed Fort Lewis). Commencement Bay was declared an official U.S. Port of Entry in 1918.

Although the Great Depression of the 1930s brought hard times to Tacoma, World War II stimulated industrial growth and prosperity because of the city's location near Fort Lewis and McChord U.S. Air Force Base. Since then Tacoma has maintained its economic stability. During the 1950s Tacoma underwent extensive city planning. Voters adopted a progressive council-manager form of government, and massive renovation of the city's infrastructure was implemented. As the new century gets underway and the city's population increases, Tacoma continues to attract new industries while balancing environmental and quality-of-life concerns.

Historical Information: Washington State History Museum, 1911 Pacific Avenue, Tacoma, WA 98402; telephone (253)272-3500; email web@wshs.wa.gov

Population Profile

Metropolitan Area Residents (PMSA)

1980: 486,000
1990: 586,203
2000: 700,820
Percent change, 1990–2000: 19.5%
U.S. rank in 1980: 18th (CMSA; includes Seattle)
U.S. rank in 1990: 14th (CMSA; includes Seattle)
U.S. rank in 2000: 13th (CMSA; includes Seattle)

City Residents

1980: 158,501
1990: 176,664
2000: 193,556
2003 estimate: 196,790
Percent change, 1990–2000: 9.1%
U.S. rank in 1980: 97th
U.S. rank in 1990: 95th
U.S. rank in 2000: 114th

Density: 3,864.9 people per square mile (2000)

Racial and ethnic characteristics (2000)
White: 133,704
Black or African American: 21,757
American Indian or Alaskan Native: 3,794
Asian: 14,656
Native Hawaiian and Other Pacific Islander: 1,798
Hispanic origin (may be of any race): 13,262
Other: 5,695

Percent of residents born in state: 48.6% (2000)

Age characteristics (2000)
Population under 5 years old: 13,593
Population 5 to 9 years old: 14,026
Population 10 to 14 years old: 14,160
Population 15 to 19 years old: 14,075

Population 20 to 24 years old: 14,212
Population 25 to 34 years old: 29,891
Population 35 to 44 years old: 31,261
Population 45 to 54 years old: 24,971
Population 55 to 59 years old: 8,214
Population 60 to 64 years old: 6,159
Population 65 to 74 years old: 10,428
Population 75 to 84 years old: 8,800
Population 85 years and over: 3,766
Median age: 33.9 years

Births (2002, Pierce County)
Total number: 10,001

Deaths (2002, Pierce County)
Total number: 5,430 (of which, 63 were infants under the age of 1 year)

Money income (1999)
Per capita income: $19,130
Median household income: $37,879
Total households: 76,127

Number of households with income of . . .
less than $10,000: 8,354
$10,000 to $14,999: 5,488
$15,000 to $24,999: 10,167
$25,000 to $34,999: 10,901
$35,000 to $49,999: 13,937
$50,000 to $74,999: 14,766
$75,000 to $99,999: 6,804
$100,000 to $149,999: 4,047
$150,000 to 199,999: 829
$200,000 or more: 834

Percent of families below poverty level: 11.4% (49.3% of which were female householder families with related children under 5 years)

2002 FBI Crime Index Total: 20,182

Municipal Government

Tacoma's council-manager form of government provides for the election of nine city council members—a mayor, five members serving districts, and three at-large members. All serve four-year terms. The council hires a city manager.

Head Official: City Manager James L. Walton (since 2003)

Total Number of City Employees: 3505 (2005)

City Information: City Hall, 747 Market Street, Tacoma, WA 98402; telephone (253)591-5000

Economy

Major Industries and Commercial Activity

Named one of ''America's Most Livable Communities'' in 2004 by national nonprofit organization Partners for Livable Communities, Tacoma has attracted companies of all sizes. In recent years, more than a hundred high-technology businesses have relocated, opened, or expanded in the area. It is home to the seventh busiest container handling port in the United States; these containers handle imports ranging from sporting goods to VCRs, and exports ranging from lumber to apples. Other major cargoes handled by the port include forest products, grain, and automobiles. A major gateway port for international trade, the Port of Tacoma covers more than 2,400 acres of land. Port activities generate more than 28,000 jobs and $477 million in wages in Pierce County.

The rapidly growing high-technology sector adds to a diverse economy strong in agricultural and forest products, manufacturing, health care, financial and professional services, and the military, with McChord U.S. Air Force Base and Fort Lewis Army Post located in Pierce County. Significant work in satellite imaging, automated fingerprint and radio frequency identification systems, and Internet and computer services continues because of multiple broadband telecommunications systems, including the city's fiber-optic Click! Network, launched in November 1998. Over the past several years, the City of Tacoma, along with investors from the private sector, have spent $300 million on the city's telecommunications infrastructure through Click! Network, which continues expansion with new construction and additional services for customers.

Tacoma is an important center for agricultural and forest products. The first business established in Tacoma was a saw mill; Tacoma's economy is still heavily involved with timber. Regional enterprises produce more flower bulbs than the Netherlands, as well as crops, such as berries and rhubarb, which require heavy seasonal employment. Tourism is also important to Tacoma's economy. Visitors are attracted to the waters of Commencement Bay and the state and national parks surrounding Tacoma.

Items and goods produced: lumber products, pulp, paper, clothing, chemicals, furniture, flour, furnaces, railroad car wheels, candy, food products, meat and fish

Incentive Programs—New and Existing Companies

Local programs—The City of Tacoma offers a variety of business loan programs, tax credits for new job creation, industrial revenue bonds, sales and use tax exemption on machinery and equipment, a variety of housing-related programs, financial incentives for historic properties, and others.

State programs—Part of Tacoma is a designated state Empowerment Zone; employers locating within this area and who meet certain hiring requirements are eligible for tax credits, special financing, and contracting programs. Other state programs available to businesses in Tacoma include tax deferral programs and business and occupation tax credits to businesses operating in distressed areas, high technology businesses, international services businesses, and manufacturers meeting program requirements.

Job training programs—In addition to job training programs at the area educational institutions, several other training programs exist, including the City of Tacoma Local Apprenticeship and Training Programs (LEAP), which offers apprenticeship programs, training, and opportunities to work on city public works projects. Pierce County WorkSource offers training programs and workshops for residents seeking jobs.

Development Projects

As the 21st century gets underway, new and renewal projects abound in Tacoma. A new pedestrian bridge connects the new $63 million Museum of Glass to the esteemed Washington State Historical Museum. Next door is the new Tacoma Art Museum, which opened in 2003 in a space twice the size as it previously inhabited. Its old location was bought and renovated by the Asia Pacific Cultural Center. Across the Thea Foss Waterway, a $15 million Pioneer Museum of Motorcycles recently opened. The $89.7 million convention center, anchored in the heart of downtown Tacoma opened in 2004. Also in 2004 ground was broken on a much-needed new police headquarters. Newly operational light rail lines now stretch all the way to Seattle. Plans are currently underway for the new Harold E. LeMay Classic Car Museum, to be located on 9 acres next to the Tacoma Dome and slated for opening in 2008.

In 2002 the state legislature approved funding for the construction of a second bridge span across the Tacoma Narrows. The new bridge, which will be built parallel to the existing bridge, is expected to be completed in March 2007. Team Tacoma, a local development group, is planning a $25 million project along the waterway that includes condominiums, parking areas, and a mix of commercial and retail spaces. The Tacoma campus of the University of Washington recently dedicated two new buildings, while students at the University of Puget Sound are getting a new, 184-resident dormitory.

Economic Development Information: Tacoma Pierce County, 1001 Pacific Avenue, Suite 400, Tacoma, WA 98402; telephone (253)627-2836; fax (253)627-8783. Tacoma Economic Development Department, 747 Market Street, 9th Floor, Tacoma, WA 98402; telephone (253)591-5364; fax (253)591-5232; email director ryan.petty@ci.tacoma.wa.us

Commercial Shipping

The Port of Tacoma is the sixth largest container port in North America, and one of the country's primary gateways for trade with Japan, China, Taiwan, and Thailand. Tacoma is also strongly tied to Alaska's economy, with the port handling more than 75 percent of all waterborne commerce going from the Lower 48 to Alaska. A new 171-acre mega-container terminal opened in January 2005, part of a $34.1 million plan to meet the needs of the Port's existing customers and to attract additional customers.

The city is also an important rail shipping hub and is served by two major transcontinental railroads: Burlington Northern–Santa Fe and Union Pacific. These two railroads link Tacoma to major markets in the Midwest and East Coast. Rail is also used to move a variety of export commodities through Tacoma—everything from Midwest corn to John Deere tractors. More than 200 trucking companies work to move goods through the city, and major air freight carriers serve Seattle-Tacoma International Airport, located about 30 minutes from Tacoma.

Labor Force and Employment Outlook

Tacoma draws from a stable work force of skilled and unskilled workers that has steadily attracted new business and industry. Local firms can rely on more than one million workers who live within an hour's commute of the city. Tacoma-Pierce County has experienced an extensive history of mature labor relations. Employment opportunities are said by local analysts to be on the increase. Civic and business leaders continue to predict a prosperous future for the city, based on its economic diversity and availability of abundant natural resources.

The following is a summary of data regarding the Tacoma labor force, 2004 annual averages.

Size of nonagricultural labor force: 254,500

Number of workers employed in . . .
   mining: 400
   construction: 8,500
   manufacturing: 19,500
   trade, transportation, and utilities: 49,100
   information: 3,100
   financial activities: 13,800
   professional and business services: 22,100
   education and health services: 37,700
   leisure and hospitality: 24,900
   other services: 1,700
   government: 53,400

Average hourly earnings of production workers employed in manufacturing: $18.27 (2004 annual statewide average)

Unemployment rate: 6.6% (January 2005)

Largest employers	Number of employees
Fort Lewis Army Post	31,450
McChord Air Force Base	8,368
Washington State	7,857
Multicare Health System	3,748
Tacoma Public Schools	3,590
Franciscan Health System	3,521
Pierce County Government	3,173

Cost of Living

The following is a summary of data regarding several key cost of living factors in the Tacoma area.

2004 (3rd Quarter) ACCRA Average House Price: $255,772

2004 (3rd Quarter) ACCRA Cost of Living Index: 106.2 (U.S. average = 100.0)

State income tax rate: None

State sales tax rate: 6.5% (food and prescription drugs are exempt)

Local income tax rate: None

Local sales tax rate: 8.4 to 8.8%

Property tax rate: $3.23 per $1,000 assessed value (2004; assessed yearly)

Economic Information: Tacoma-Pierce County Chamber of Commerce, 950 Pacific Avenue, Suite 300, PO Box 1933, Tacoma, WA 98401; telephone (253)627-2175; fax (206)597-7305

Education and Research

Elementary and Secondary Schools

Tacoma School District #10, the third largest system in the state, is administered by a five-member, nonpartisan school board that selects the superintendent.

The following is a summary of data regarding the Tacoma public schools as of the 2003–2004 school year.

Total enrollment: 32,258

Number of facilities
   elementary schools: 36
   middle schools: 11
   senior high schools: 7

Student/teacher ratio: 22.7:1

Teacher salaries
  minimum: $32,154
  maximum: $64,258

Many private and parochial schools in Tacoma offer alternative and religious curricula.

Public Schools Information: Tacoma Public Schools, Central Administration, 601 S. 8th St., PO Box 1357, Tacoma, WA 98401-1357; telephone (253)571-1000

Colleges and Universities

Tacoma is home to numerous universities and colleges. Pacific Lutheran University and the University of Puget Sound, both private, grant baccalaureate and advanced degrees in such fields as business, music, and law. University of Puget Sound is considered integral to the area's economy. Tacoma Community College and Pierce College provide occupational training and college preparatory curricula. Also located in the area is the University of Washington-Tacoma, where enrollment is expected to reach 6,000 students by 2007. Private technical institutes include Clover Park, Bates, and Business Computer Training Institute.

Libraries and Research Centers

Tacoma is served by two public library systems. The Tacoma Public Library, with a downtown facility housed in a renovated 1903 Carnegie Library building plus nine branches, maintains holdings of more than 1.18 million items including books, 2,210 periodical subscriptions, plus records, slides, tapes, films, maps, and art reproductions. Special collections include city archives and World War I books and posters; the library is a depository for federal and state government documents. The Pierce County Library System operates 17 branches in addition to its downtown location; holdings consist of more than 1.1 million volumes. Several specialized libraries in the city are affiliated with government agencies, universities, corporations, churches, and a local newspaper.

Research activities in such fields as invertebrate zoology, herpetology, and ornithology are conducted at the University of Puget Sound's James R. Slater Museum of Natural History in Tacoma.

Public Library Information: Tacoma Public Library, 1102 Tacoma Avenue South, Tacoma, WA 98402-2098; telephone (253)591-5666. Pierce County Library System, 3005 112th Street East, Tacoma, WA 98446; telephone (253)536-6500

Health Care

Tacoma's health care community has been nationally recognized in specialized areas, including cancer treatment, kidney dialysis, and burn care, as well as in cardiac care and pediatrics. The 320-bed St. Joseph Medical Center and 106-bed St. Clare Hospital are ranked among the nation's top hospitals. Among the ten hospitals located in Tacoma are two facilities for children, the Mary Bridge Children's Health Center and the Child Study and Treatment Center. Governmental agencies provide a number of programs that assist in substance abuse care, mental health, preventive medicine, and family planning.

Recreation

Sightseeing

Tacoma offers the sightseer a variety of diversions. The city is bordered by miles of waterfront parks and beaches. One of several parks located in the city is the 702-acre Point Defiance Park, which includes miles of walking trails through the wilderness and along the waterfront. In 2005 the park celebrates its 100-year anniversary, highlighted by special events throughout the year. Its zoo includes animals native to the Puget Sound area; it is also known for its excellent aquarium. Other attractions within Point Defiance Park include Fort Nisqually, a restored trading post; Camp Six, a re-creation of a logging camp; and Never Never Land, a forested area that once was populated with fairy tale scenes but since 2004 has been refurbished for parties and other gatherings. The city's first off-leash dog park is located at Rogers Park. The Narrows Bridge, spanning the Sound between Tacoma and the Gig Harbor Peninsula, is the fifth longest suspension bridge in the United States.

Wright Park downtown offers lawn bowling and horseshoe pitching; it is also the site of the Seymour Botanical Conservatory. In 2004 park officials decided to enhance park facilities, including expansion of the Conservatory. Other points of interest are Union Station and the Old City Hall, built in the style of the Italian Renaissance; both are National Historic Landmarks.

A little more than an hour from Tacoma is Mt. Rainier National Park, which provides a closer view of the mountain that dominates the city's landscape. More than 300 miles of trails in the park provide plenty of opportunity for hiking and exploring. Climbing courses and skiing instruction are available. Plans are currently underway at the park to prepare an Intelligent Transportation System to enhance visitors' experience there, including web cameras showing traffic conditions, interactive websites, and toll-free numbers to obtain road, weather, and traffic conditions. Kopachuck State Park and Penrose Point State Park are also in the vicinity.

Arts and Culture

Tacoma has a vibrant arts community with excellent museums and professional theater and opera companies. Downtown Tacoma, which in recent years has been attempting to re-establish the theater district as the "heart of the city," has revitalized its Broadway Center for the Performing Arts. The Broadway Center, which includes the historic Pantages and Rialto theaters, as well as the Theatre on the Square, is home to many performances year-round. In addition, the University of Puget Sound and Pacific Lutheran University offer ongoing performances from September through June.

In 2002 Tacoma became home to the new International Museum of Glass, featuring works of glass artists from throughout the world. Recognized glass artist Dale Chihuly is a Tacoma native. His work can be viewed in the historic Union Station on Pacific Avenue. The Tacoma Art Museum has a rich collection of American, European, and Asian art and offers stimulating rotating exhibits on an ongoing schedule. Its new facility opened in May 2003 and is twice the size of its previous location. The Antoine Predock–designed building features a unique flexible exhibition area that wraps around an indoor, open-air stone garden.

The Washington State History Museum has the largest collection of Northwest artifacts in the state. Its interactive exhibits chronicle the natural, social, and industrial history of the Pacific Northwest. The Washington State Capitol Museum features exhibits that reflect regional Native American history.

Tacoma's anchor arts groups include the Northwest Sinfonietta, Tacoma Philharmonic, Tacoma Symphony Orchestra, Tacoma Actors Guild, Tacoma Art Museum, Tacoma Little Theatre, Children's Museum of Tacoma, and Tacoma Youth Symphony. The Broadway Center offers touring productions September through June for families and general audiences. Often programs at the Broadway Center feature companion education activities for school children. Visitors to Tacoma can also enjoy a variety of public art. Highlights not to be missed include displayed public art projects on the Ruston Way waterfront and the literary, visual, and sound art forms at the walkway at Point Defiance. The University of Washington Tacoma campus is located in the middle of downtown Tacoma. A stroll through the campus takes the visitor past a variety of contemporary art created by some of Washington state's finest artists, including Buster Simpson, Dan Senn, and Dale Chihuly.

Festivals and Holidays

Tacoma's special events calendar is filled throughout the year. The Home and Garden Show, the Palmer/Wirfs Antique Show, and the Northwest Bridal Expo are held in January. The Wintergrass Bluegrass Festival takes place in February, followed by the Northwest Antique Show in March. The Annual Daffodil Festival and the Annual Spring Barrel Wine Tasting Tour are fun April events. The Sound to Narrows Race draws crowds annually in June. July in Tacoma is especially festive, with the Fourth of July Celebration in Old Town, the Tacoma Freedom Fair and Fireworks Display, and the Taste of Tacoma. Summer festivals continue with the Pierce County Fair, Downtown Farmers Market, and the Tall Ships Festival, which includes world-class sailing ships at the waterfront.

Fall brings the Western Washington Fair, Oktoberfest, the Puyallup Canine Fest, and the Holiday Food and Gift Festival. The year closes with the Victorian Country Christmas in December, followed by the Downtown Tacoma Tree Lighting Ceremony, and First Night Celebrations on New Year's Eve.

Sports for the Spectator

The Tacoma Rainiers, the Triple A farm team for professional baseball's American League Seattle Mariners, play baseball at Cheney Stadium. Both Pacific Lutheran University and the University of Puget Sound field teams in major sports.

Sports for the Participant

In addition to the recreational opportunities provided by the Cascade Mountains and the 361 freshwater lakes in Pierce County, Tacoma operates four public golf courses and tennis courts are located in the public parks. The city also maintains a number of public beaches and piers for swimming and fishing.

Shopping and Dining

Boutiques and antique shops can be found at Tacoma's Old Town Historic District, the city's original business district. The downtown business district has shops, boutiques, and galleries. Freighthouse Square is a public market with restaurants, specialty shops, and special events. The Tacoma Mall, one of the largest in the Northwest, is considered "Pierce County's Premier Mall."

Tacoma is salmon country and the city is home to numerous seafood restaurants. Ruston Way, along the western side of the peninsula, is dotted with restaurants and is referred to as "Restaurant Row."

Visitor Information: Tacoma Economic Development Department, 747 Market Street, 9th Floor, Tacoma, WA 98402; telephone (253)591-5364; fax (253)591-5232. Tacoma Regional Convention and Visitor Bureau, 1119 Pacific Avenue, 5th Floor, Tacoma, WA 98402; telephone (253)627-2836; toll-free (800)272-2662; fax (253)627-8783; email info@traveltacoma.com

Convention Facilities

November 2004 marked the completion of a new downtown convention center. The 200,000-square-foot facility is adjacent to the 319-room Sheraton and the new 162-room Marriott Courtyard, which is scheduled for completion in 2005. The facility connects the Broadway Theater District with the rapidly developing cultural area anchored by the Washington State History Museum and the University of Washington Tacoma campus.

Meeting facilities are available at the 6.1-acre Tacoma Dome Entertainment Complex. The Dome, located near Commencement Bay in downtown Tacoma, contains a 30,000-square-foot Convention Hall with a seating capacity for 2,000 participants. The hall can be divided into six soundproof rooms, providing seminar space. The dome's arena can provide additional seating space for 3,000 persons. The Shanaman Sports Museum, which aims to preserve the area's sports heritage, is also located inside the Dome. Along with the arena, the Convention Hall offers 150,000 square feet of space. Banquet and meeting space are available at Saint Helens Convention Center, a historic landmark. Several other hotels and motels providing additional meeting space are located in the Tacoma area.

Convention Information: Tacoma Regional Convention and Visitor Bureau, 1119 Pacific Avenue, 5th Floor, Tacoma, WA 98402; telephone (253)627-2836; toll-free (800)272-2662; fax (253) 627-8783; email info@travel tacoma.com

Transportation

Approaching the City

Seattle-Tacoma International Airport (Sea-Tac) is a modern facility with an underground monorail. The airport is located 18 miles north of the city. The airport is currently being upgraded with a new runway that will enable aircraft to land in any weather condition.

The primary north-south motor route to Tacoma is Interstate 5, which runs between Canada and Mexico. East-west access is provided by S.R. 16.

Amtrak furnishes rail service into Tacoma with several trains each day. An extensive ferry system serves Puget Sound.

Traveling in the City

Tacoma occupies an irregular peninsula with its street pattern conforming roughly to a grid within those constraints. The principle north-south arteries are Pacific Avenue, North Pearl, and Ruston Way, which runs along the eastern coast of the peninsula. The major east-west thoroughfares are Sixth Avenue and S.R. 16, which enters Tacoma across the Narrows Bridge. Interstate 5 bisects the city on a southwest to northeast axis.

Sound Transit offers its 37,000 daily riders several ways of getting around. ST Express buses run from Tacoma, Gig Harbor, and Lakewood to downtown Seattle and back. ST Express buses also run from Lakewood and Tacoma to Seattle-Tacoma International Airport. Sounder commuter trains run some 80 miles on weekdays, connecting from Everett and Tacoma into Seattle and back. The Tacoma Link light rail trains began operating in August 2003 and have become a primary factor in the renaissance of downtown Tacoma. Construction is currently underway on a 14-mile Central Link light rail line, to begin carrying passengers in 2009. Future Sound Transit plans include adding more bus transit facilities and increasing the hours of operation for all services.

Communications

Newspaper and Magazines

The major daily newspaper in Tacoma is *The News Tribune.* Other publications serving Tacoma include *Tacoma Reporter* and *The Northwest Dispatch*, serving the African American community, and *The Ranger,* for military personnel. Among other periodicals originating in Tacoma are *Senior Scene, Northwest Guardian*, and *Pierce County Business Examiner.*

Television and Radio

Four television stations are based in Tacoma; because of the city's proximity to Seattle, broadcasts from Seattle television stations are also received in the metropolitan area. More than 30 AM and FM radio stations serve Tacoma with music, news, and special interest programming.

Media Information: *The News Tribune,* 1950 South State Street, Tacoma, WA 98411; telephone (253)597-8742

Tacoma Online

City of Tacoma home page. Available www.cityoftacoma .org

The News Tribune. Available www.thenewstribune.com

Pierce County Library System. Available www.pcl.lib.wa.us

Tacoma-Pierce County Chamber of Commerce. Available www.tacomachamber.org

Tacoma-Pierce County Visitors and Convention Bureau. Available www.traveltacoma.org

Tacoma Public Library. Available www.tpl.lib.wa.us

Tacoma School District #10. Available www.tacoma.k12.wa.us

Selected Bibliography

Alexie, Sherman, *Reservation Blues* (New York: Warner Books, 1995)

WYOMING

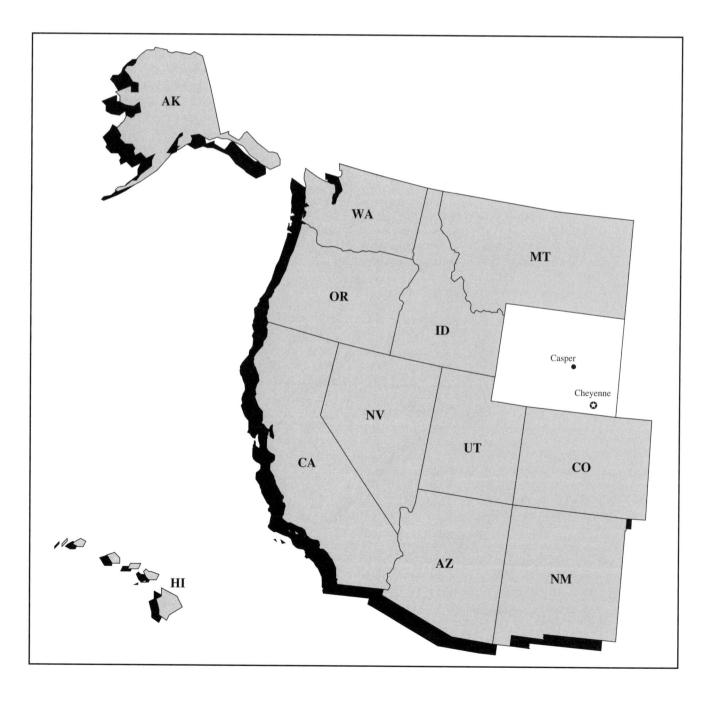

The State in Brief

Nickname: Equality State, Cowboy State
Motto: Equal rights

Flower: Indian paintbrush
Bird: Meadowlark

Area: 97,813 square miles (2000; U.S. rank: 10th)
Elevation: Ranges from 3,100 feet to 13,084 feet above sea level
Climate: Continental; semi arid and cool, with mild summers and severe winters; temperature varies with elevation

Admitted to Union: July 10, 1890
Capital: Cheyenne
Head Official: Governor Dave Freudenthal (D) (until 2007)

Population

1980: 470,000
1990: 453,588
2000: 493,782
2004 estimate: 506,529
Percent change, 1990–2000: 8.9%
U.S. rank in 2004: 51st
Percent of residents born in state: 42.5% (2000)
Density: 5.1 people per square mile (2000)
2002 FBI Crime Index Total: 17,858

Racial and Ethnic Characteristics (2000)

White: 454,670
Black or African American: 3,722
American Indian and Alaska Native: 11,133
Asian: 2,771
Native Hawaiian and Pacific Islander: 302
Hispanic or Latino (may be of any race): 31,669
Other: 12,301

Age Characteristics (2000)

Population under 5 years old: 30,940
Population 5 to 19 years old: 114,406
Percent of population 65 years and over: 11.7%
Median age: 36.2 years (2000)

Vital Statistics

Total number of births (2003): 6,615
Total number of deaths (2003): 4,173 (infant deaths, 46)
AIDS cases reported through 2003: 96

Economy

Major industries: Mining; finance, insurance, and real estate; government; construction
Unemployment rate: 2.9% (February 2005)
Per capita income: $32,235 (2003; U.S. rank: 16th)
Median household income: $41,501 (3-year average, 2001-2003)
Percentage of persons below poverty level: 11.4% (1999)
Income tax rate: None
Sales tax rate: 4.0%

Casper

The City in Brief

Founded: 1888 (incorporated in 1889)

Head Official: Guy V. Padgett, III (since 2005)

City Population
    1980: 51,016
    1990: 46,742
    2000: 49,644
    2003 estimate: 50,632
    Percent change, 1990-2000: 6.2%
    U.S. rank in 1990: 559th (2nd in state)
    U.S. rank in 2000: Not reported (2nd in state)

Metropolitan Area Population (PMSA)
    1980: 71,856
    1990: 61,226
    2000: 66,533

Percent change, 1990-2000: 8.6%
U.S. rank in 2000: 275th

Area: 23.9 square miles (2000)
Elevation: 5,140 feet above sea level
Average Annual Temperature: 45.2° F
Average Annual Precipitation: 14.75 inches rainfall; 77 inches snowfall

Major Economic Sectors: mining, education, health services, social services, retail trade, tourism
Unemployment Rate: 4.2% (January 2005)
Per Capita Income: $19,409 (1999)
2004 ACCRA Average House Price: Not reported
2004 ACCRA Cost of Living Index: Not reported

2002 FBI Crime Index Total: 2,725

Major Colleges and Universities: Casper College, University of Wyoming outreach program

Daily Newspaper: *Casper Star Tribune*

Introduction

In the days of the Wild West and Manifest Destiny, all roads led to Casper—the city was sited at the nexus of a number of important trails of the time, including the Oregon Trail, the Pony Express route, the Mormon Trail, the Bozeman Trail, the California Trail, and the Bridger Trail. Today the nexus is more that of the past as represented by traditional agriculture coupled with the future of energy and conservation. Casper is the geographic heart of Wyoming and keeps the economy pulsing with oil and gas exploration, thriving livestock ranches, and a burgeoning tourist industry.

Geography and Climate

At almost a mile above sea level, Casper rests at the foot of Casper Mountain and follows the contours of the North Platte River. With the Laramie Mountain Range of the Rocky Mountains to the west and the Wyoming plains to the east, Casper has been uniquely situated between natural resources for energy and outdoor adventure exploration on the one hand and agricultural endeavors on the other.

Casper sits within the area characterized by the National Weather Service as the ''comfort zone,'' with year-round low humidity moderating the cold of winter and the heat of summer. Casper averages 275 days of sunshine every year and experiences an average wind speed of 12.9 miles per hour. The city's location and climate make it a jumping-off point for outdoor adventures.

Area: 23.9 square miles (2000)

Elevation: 5,140 feet above sea level

Average Temperatures: January, 22.4° F; July, 70.8° F; annual average, 45.2° F

Average Annual Precipitation: 14.75 inches rainfall; 77 inches snowfall

History

Back to the Source

Before there were people, there was the river—the North Platte River begins its meandering journey in the mountains near Casper, running east across the Great Plains to merge with its sister river, the South Platte, to become simply the Platte River. Water, mountains, and plains were a lure from the beginning; evidence of human occupation dates back more than 12,000 years with the Clovis peoples, followed by the Folsom and the Eden Valley peoples. A mix of hunting and gathering tribes occupied the area until approximately 500 A.D., eventually morphing into Native American tribes more familiar in today's world.

The original residents of Wyoming were nomadic Plains Indians, including tribes as disparate as the Arapaho, Sioux, Cheyenne, Crow, Lakota, Blackfeet, Kiowa, Nez Perce, and Shoshone. The tribes relied on the land and the roaming buffalo herds for sustenance; when European explorers and hunters began a wholesale slaughter of the buffalo, coinciding with an interest in herding native peoples to a containment area in Oklahoma, armed conflicts escalated in the clash of cultures and interests. In 1812, fur trappers had followed beaver and buffalo populations to the northern Rockies. The Oregon Trail had been scouted out in 1823, and its ever-deepening ruts reflected the entrenched U.S. belief in its manifest destiny to expand westward.

The Western Civil War

By 1847, a network of travel routes converged at a spot just west of present-day Casper; here the Emigrant Trail crossed from the south side to the north side of the North Platte River. When the first Mormon wagon train passed through this area on its way to what would become Utah, Brigham Young arranged for a ferry to be set up for the use of future travelers. The Mormon Ferry soon faced competition as more emigrants passed that way and decided to cash in on a good idea. One entrepreneurial French-Canadian trader named John Baptiste Richard decided to build a bridge across the North Platte and charge a toll for crossing it. The area was now not just a way-station but an encampment.

Local residents established a trading post along the Emigrant Trail in 1859, taking advantage of the growing stream of wagon trains. As the local population grew along with the number of emigrants, friction developed with local tribes of Lakota, Arapaho, and Cheyenne Indians. As a result, the trading post was transformed into a fort by the military, and two pitched battles between the army and the native tribes took place in 1865. In the first conflict, Lieutenant Caspar Collins was killed while attempting to rescue another soldier. Lt. Collins' father already had a fort named after him in Colorado, so the military named the Wyoming fort ''Casper'' in his honor, inadvertently using a misspelling that had been transmitted by telegraph. The seeds of present-day Casper had been planted.

Black Gold, Texas Tea

Casper in 1888 was a true Wild West town; a railroad had been built through the town in an effort to ease travel to riches of gold in California and fertile land in Oregon. Isolation and lawlessness attracted a rough crowd of renegades and outlaws, and the original township developed a main street lined with saloons on one side. By necessity, the first public building in Casper was a jail. Lynchings were not an uncommon occurrence.

Oil was struck in nearby Salt Creek Field in 1889, an event that has come to define Casper as the "oil capital of the Rockies." The city was flooded with an influx of claim jumpers looking to capitalize on the promised wealth. In 1895, the first oil refinery was constructed. Oil workers known as "roughnecks" followed, along with gamblers, prostitutes and corrupt businessmen. Cattlemen went to war against the sheepmen. The local law struggled to keep up with the shenanigans of the populace, passing laws to prevent women from walking on the saloon side of Main Street and to make illegal the discharge of firearms within city limits.

Local municipal leaders were set on Casper becoming the state capital and a centerpiece of the West. As the economy continued to thrive, construction was begun on some of the tallest buildings in Wyoming during the early 20th century. But, a city that lives on oil can die on oil.

Nearly a Ghost Town

Few communities escaped the repercussions of the Great Depression, and Casper was not an exception. In 1929, the city's population diminished by 50 percent; the struggle continued until World War II spurred renewed demand for oil and gas supplies.

The city has experienced cycles of boom and bust beginning in the 1960s, riding the wave of oil and gas prices. Today, Casper is profiting from U.S. conflicts with oil-producing nations and has additionally seen the growth of more consistent industries in the areas of health care, social services and tourism. Figurative fisticuffs have taken the place of literal gunfights as the oil industry negotiates its place in a city that is increasingly conscious of its finite and infinitely beautiful natural resources.

Historical Information: Wyoming State Historical Society, 1829 North Piney Creek Road, Casper, WY 82604-1721

Population Profile

Metropolitan Area Residents (CMSA)
1980: 71,856
1990: 61,226
2000: 66,533
Percent change, 1990–2000: 8.6%

U.S. rank in 2000: 275th

City Residents
1980: 51,016
1990: 46,742
2000: 49,644
2003 estimate: 50,632
Percent change, 1990–2000: 6.2%
U.S. rank in 1990: 559th (2nd in state)
U.S. rank in 2000: Not reported (2nd in state)

Density: 2,073.2 people per square mile

Racial and ethnic characteristics (2000)
    White: 46,680
    Black or African American: 428
    American Indian and Alaskan Native: 495
    Asian: 425
    Native Hawaiian and Pacific Islander: 10
    Hispanic or Latino (may be of any race): 2,656
    Other: 1,011

Percent of residents born in state: 46.4% (2000)

Age characteristics (2000)
    Population under 5 years old: 3,264
    Population 5 to 9 years old: 3,458
    Population 10 to 14 years old: 3,758
    Population 15 to 19 years old: 4,122
    Population 20 to 24 years old: 3,455
    Population 25 to 34 years old: 6,125
    Population 35 to 44 years old: 7,649
    Population 45 to 54 years old: 7,016
    Population 55 to 59 years old: 2,211
    Population 60 to 64 years old: 1,852
    Population 65 to 74 years old: 3,606
    Population 75 to 84 years old: 2,402
    Population 85 years and over: 746
    Median age: 36.1

Births
    Total number: 897 (2002; Natrona County)

Deaths
    Total number: 616 (2002; Natrona County)

Money income (1999)
    Per capita income: $19,409
    Median household income: $36,567
    Total households: 20,343

Number of households with income of . . .
    less than $10,000: 1,761
    $10,000 to $14,999: 1,689
    $15,000 to $24,999: 3,101
    $25,000 to $34,999: 3,185
    $35,000 to $49,999: 3,680

$50,000 to $74,999: 3,948
$75,000 to $99,999: 1,772
$100,000 to $149,999: 866
$150,000 to $199,999: 196
$200,000 or more: 238

Percent of families below poverty level: 8.5% (53.5% of which were female householder families with children under 5 years)

2002 FBI Crime Index Total: 2,725

Municipal Government

The City of Casper operates under a Council-Manager form of government; in staggered elections, the city's three wards each elect three representatives from the citizenry residing in that ward. All legislative authority resides within the nine-member council. The council in turn appoints a mayor and a vice president from among its own ranks; each of these officials serves for one year. A manager is hired by the city to coordinate municipal business and respond to citizen concerns.

Head Official: Guy V. Padgett, III (since 2005; current term expires December 2006)

Total Number of City Employees: 505 (2005)

City Information: City of Casper, 200 N. David, Casper, WY 82601; telephone (307)235-8400

Economy

Major Industries and Commercial Activity

In 2004, *Forbes* magazine named Casper one of the nation's ''Top 25 Best Small Places for Business'' based on the comparatively low costs of operating in the Casper area. The city's central location and proximity to a wealth of natural resources has attracted mining and petroleum exploration industries to the area.

Casper also grew up as a cattle and sheep ranching town, and remains as such today. Businesses related to the care and feeding of livestock have maintained a hold on the economy in Casper and the surrounding Natrona County area.

The medical industry is healthy, as Casper serves as the site for a Department of Veterans Affairs Clinic in addition to the Wyoming Medical Center. The tourism trade is growing as well, grounded in local Wild West history, rodeos, and proximity to natural wonders such as Grand Teton National Park and Yellowstone.

Items and goods produced: oil, natural gas, coal, gravel, fire equipment, agricultural products

Incentive Programs—New and Existing Companies

Local programs—The lack of a local income tax and a low municipal sales tax rate are the main business incentives employed by the City of Casper. The Foreign Trade Zone at Natrona County International Airport provides further encouragement for importers to frequent Casper, as international goods can be warehoused at the airport without undergoing full U.S. Customs scrutiny.

State programs—Wyoming's primary business incentive is a non-existent corporate income tax rate, coupled with relatively minimal sales tax rates. The state also does not tax intangibles or inventory and has kept property taxes low.

Job training programs—The Casper Workforce Center is part of a statewide network of workforce development resources, including services for businesses, job seekers and employment data researchers. Expanding businesses can tap into the Business Training Grant program for new positions, which subsidizes tuition, registration, travel, continuing education and wages associated with newly-created positions in growing companies. Large and small business owners can take advantage of the Wyoming Job Network to search online for prospective employees; the Workforce Center additionally operates an Alien Labor Certification program, which allows employers to utilize immigrant labor for positions that are difficult to fill with U.S. citizens. On the other side of immigrant labor issues, the Workforce Center offers a Migrant and Seasonal Farmworker program, with bilingual staffers encouraging economic self-sufficiency among migrant workers through job training and employment matching services.

Job seekers can avail themselves of several programs organized under the Workforce Investment Act passed in 1998. The intent of the act was to create a seamless continuum of employment, education, and training programs to support business with a skilled workforce. Programs supported by the act include Title II Adult Basic Education, Title IV Vocational Rehabilitation programs, dislocated worker programs, youth tutoring, alternative secondary school services, youth summer employment programs, youth internships, and job shadowing. The Workforce Center offers specialized programs for older workers and workers who identify themselves as having disabilities.

Development Projects

The proposed McMurry Business Park planned along the extension of 2nd Street in Casper is likely to be a $25 million investment property zoned for commercial use. Covering 500 acres, the project will involve access road improvements and major utility installations.

Not to be outdone, the Natrona County International Airport Business Park has undergone a sizable expansion during the last few years, including up to 18,000 square feet of available office space, approximately 135 buildings that can accommodate businesses that range from manufacturing to retail to aviation, and an adjacent acreage that has been designated for future development.

The Downtown Casper Reconstruction and Improvement Project is designed to revitalize an aged and deteriorating area in an effort to make it more inviting to tourists and businesses. A one-cent sales tax is providing the funding, with construction beginning in spring 2005 and expected to end in fall 2006.

Commercial Shipping

The largest airport in Wyoming, the Natrona County International Airport, is located in Casper and encompasses Foreign Trade Zone #157, which allows imported goods to remain onsite without undergoing full U.S. Customs processing. Four regional carriers offer business class travel; both Sky West and Northwest Airlines also offer cargo transportation services. The airport is additionally home to the air cargo facilities of UPS, FedEx and DHL package delivery services.

Burlington Northern Santa Fe (BNSF) Railway passes through Casper, with routes to the West Coast, the Southwest, the Midwest, and other points west of the Mississippi River. Freight services offered include agricultural, mineral, industrial, and consumer goods. Freight forwarding and direct connections with dock spurs are available to shippers.

Casper's central location makes it a highway hub, with Interstate 25, U.S. Highways 20 and 87, and state highways 220, 254 and 20 all meeting within its city limits. Casper is served by approximately 48 over-the-road trucking companies and has access to package delivery services such as UPS, FedEx and DH.

Labor Force and Employment Outlook

While it's expected that Wyoming will remain identified with production of natural gas and coal, a slight decline in total mining jobs is anticipated. Most employment growth is expected to occur in non-goods producing sectors, including service and retail trade. The State of Wyoming predicts that the aging of the baby boomer generation will result in possible labor shortages as that group retires. An aging population will also increase demand for health care and social services, creating a potential spike in those professions.

The following is a summary of data regarding the Casper metropolitan statistical area labor force, 2004 annual averages.

Size of nonagricultural labor force: 35,800

Number of workers employed in . . .
   natural resources and mining: 3,000
   construction: 2,400
   manufacturing: 1,500
   trade, transportation and utilities: 8,200
   information: 500
   financial activities: 1,800
   professional and business services: 2,800
   educational and health services: 4,500
   leisure and hospitality: 3,400
   other services: 1,700
   government: 5,500

Average hourly earnings of production workers employed in manufacturing: $16.88

Unemployment rate: 4.2 (January 2005)

Largest employers	*Number of employees (2004)*
Natrona County School District #1	1,427
Wyoming Medical Center	921
The Industrial Company	600
Key Energy	558
City of Casper	505
Casper College	343
OfficeMax	339
Wyoming Machinery Company	315
Natrona County Government	278
McMurry Ready Mix	225
True Companies	201

Cost of Living

The following is a summary of data regarding key cost of living factors for the Casper area.

2004 ACCRA Cost of Living Index: Not reported

2004 ACCRA Average House Price: Not reported

State income tax rate: None

State sales tax rate: 4%

Local income tax rate: None

Local sales tax rate: 1%

Property tax rate: assessed at 9.5% of market value

Economic Information: Casper Area Economic Development Alliance, 300 South Wolcott Suite 300, Casper, WY 82601; telephone (307)577-7011; toll-free (800)634-5012

Education and Research

Elementary and Secondary Schools

The Natrona County School District serves students not just in Casper but also the communities of Midwest, Edgerton, Mills, Evansville, Bar Nunn, Alcova, Mountain View, and Powder River. The school district emphasizes site-based decision making in schools of choice, a system that allows parents to enroll students in any school without regard to location. Ideally, this encourages a cooperative approach between school administration, parents, and students in targeting an educational environment that best fits the needs of the individual.

The district operates a K-12 substance abuse program that has been recognized at the national level, along with specialized services for English language learners. Since 2001, the school district has offered an after-school program and community learning center at two elementary schools, with stated goals of retention, improved academic performance, life-long learning, and a safe drug-free environment. Outreach is also conducted for students who are homebound and those who are homeless.

The Natrona County School District created a planetarium in 1966, which over the years has brought the stars and planets to more than 500,000 students. The Casper Planetarium also presents programs for the public throughout the year, including the This Month's Sky series.

The following is a summary of data regarding Natrona County School District as of the 2004–2005 school year.

Total enrollment: 11,532

Number of facilities
  elementary schools: 27
  junior high schools: 7
  high schools: 4
  rural schools: 4

Student teacher ratio: junior high, 16.3:1; high school, 17.6:1

Teacher salaries
  average: $42,286

Funding per pupil: $6,911

Public Schools Information: Natrona County School District, 970 N. Glenn Rd., Casper, WY 82601; telephone (307)577-0200

Colleges and Universities

Perched in the foothills of Casper Mountain, higher education takes on a literal meaning at Casper College. One of the largest community colleges, Casper College offers students a choice of 50 academic majors and more than 30 technical and career programs. The college enrolls a total of 3,800 students in small, personal classes in Business, Health Sciences, Trades and Technology, and Life Sciences programs, among others. The college also provides free Adult Basic Education and General Educational Development (GED) assistance in the Werner Technical Center.

The University of Wyoming in nearby Laramie maintains an outreach school in conjunction with the Casper College; the University of Wyoming/Casper College Center offers 14 baccalaureate degrees, 13 master's programs and a variety of certification programs. Coursework is completed onsite, via teleconferencing or through web-based instruction, with internships and educational travel experiences offered in various degree programs.

At the Natrona County International Airport, the Aircraft Rescue Firefighting training program offers classroom and hands-on experience with firefighting techniques unique to aeronautical equipment. Small classes ensure individual attention as students learn to deal with hazardous materials, ventilation issues, fire behavior, and search and rescue procedures.

Libraries and Research Centers

The Natrona County Library's main branch is located in the heart of Casper with branch libraries maintained in the communities of Edgerton and Mills. The library offers access to 204,922 books, 4,312 audio materials and 4,264 video materials, supplemented by 352 serial subscriptions and online research resources. Children's programs include a Reader's Advisory program that recommends books tailored to particular ages and interests; outreach programs to schools and community groups; educational games and reference programs; Storytime; a summer reading program; and Dial-a-Story with a new story available by phone every week.

The Goodstein Foundation Library at Casper College contains a collection of 118,000 volumes catering to the needs of faculty and students at the college. The library subscribes to more than 500 periodicals, with access to more than 20,000 full-text periodicals available online. The library is also home to a Western history collection, with materials focused on Casper and Natrona County.

Public Library Information: Natrona County Public Library (Main Branch), 307 East Second Street, Casper, WY 82601; telephone (307)237-4935

Health Care

The Wyoming Medical Center in Casper serves the Natrona County area and also draws patients from rural communities of greater distances. The state's largest medical facility is licensed for 206 beds after undergoing a significant expansion in 2001, which added a new emergency department and trauma center. The facility houses two Centers of Excellence, the Heart Center of Wyoming and the Wyoming Neuroscience and Spine Center. In addition to those specialties, the Wyoming Medical Center provides a range of services such as urology, magnetic resonance imaging, inpatient rehabilitation, Flight for Life, urology, cancer treatment, and pediatrics.

The main campus of the Wyoming Behavioral Institute is located in Casper, with substance abuse and mental health services for adults, adolescents, and children. The facility offers initial assessment, intensive inpatient treatment, detoxification programs, and outpatient therapy.

The Department of Veterans Affairs Casper Clinic serves as an outreach center connecting military veterans to health care and counseling services, including making arrangements for bus travel to V.A. hospitals in Cheyenne or Sheridan. A number of other specialty clinics operate in Casper, addressing medical concerns around dermatology, allergies, and women's health care.

Recreation

Sightseeing

A sightseeing tour of Casper would start where the town started—at the convergence of the multiple travel routes to the West. The National Historic Trails Interpretive Center accurately portrays the experiences of emigrants who traversed the Oregon, California, Mormon, Bridger, Bozeman, and Pony Express Trails. The museum has incorporated the history of Wyoming's native peoples in displays that include a simulated crossing of the North Platte River in a replica Conestoga wagon. An award-winning audiovisual feature recreates the days of early Casper in a way that brings pioneer existence alive for modern visitors.

The natural segue is to next visit the Fort Caspar Museum and Historical Site, located along the historical trail system. The buildings of the original fort have been reconstructed, with structures including the 1859 Guinard bridge and the 1847 Mormon ferry utilized in crossings of the North Platte. Exhibits range from prehistoric natural history items to recent regional development in central Wyoming.

While in the vicinity, visitors can enjoy a leisurely ramble along the Platte River Parkway, an 11-mile paved path that connects residential neighborhoods to natural areas. The Platte River Commons in downtown Casper continues along the riverbank; within the downtown area, the Art for the Streets program has sprinkled the historic area with 31

sculptures. "Painted Past" Living History Tours through the downtown area highlight myths, legends and true stories of Casper's checkered past.

The Mormon Handcart Visitors' Center commemorates the hardships and survival of members of the Church of Jesus Christ of Latter-Day Saints traveling as part of the Martin and Willie Handcart Companies in 1856. As the group traveled westward, it encountered a raging blizzard that forced the company to hole up in a local cove for four days. During the ensuing wait for rescuers, many members of the group died from starvation or exposure. Visitors to the site today can pull a handcart to the cove or can participate in guided camping treks.

Arts and Culture

The Nicolaysen Art Museum and Discovery Center contains one large and six small galleries exhibiting art from or about the Rocky Mountain Region. Exhibitors at "the Nic" often include contemporary living artists from the area. The Discovery Center allows visitors to create their own art in a self-guided studio containing interactive exhibits, and the Wyoming Science Adventure Center generates interest in sciences through fun, interactive displays. Workshops and educational programs are offered throughout the year as well, with a special emphasis on quilting.

The West Wind Gallery is operated by the Casper Artists' Guild, the members of which show and sell their works under the gallery's roof. The gallery occasionally hosts artists from out of state and also offers classes.

The Tate Geological Museum is located on the grounds of Casper College and is home to a collection of more than 3,000 fossil and mineral specimens. The museum offers a Saturday Club experience for local youth in which they study local geology and animal fossils. Adults can take part in paleontology and geology fieldwork expeditions coordinated through the museum, with visits to Wind River Reservation, and the Morrison and Lance Formation sites. Casper College also houses the Werner Wildlife Museum featuring more than 285 birds and 100 other various species.

The formative history of Casper is further represented at the Salt Creek Museum in the city of Midwest, where books, memorabilia and reminiscences reflect on more than 100 years of oil field action in the area. The Wyoming Veteran's Memorial Museum at the airport is located in the building where bombing crews trained during World War II.

The Wyoming Symphony Orchestra performs "The Nutcracker" seasonally in conjunction with the Western Ballet Theater, which involves local dancers for that event. Five more performances per season round out the orchestra's schedule at the John F. Welsh Auditorium.

Young musicians from 4th graders to 21 year olds participate in The Troopers Drum and Bugle Corps, regardless of musical experience. The Troopers travel around the U.S. throughout the summer, performing and competing in drum and bugle corps contests. Further musical offerings are provided through the Casper Chamber Music Society, the Casper Children's Chorale, Casper Civic Chorale, Casper Fiddle Club, Casper Municipal Band, Choral Arts Ensemble, Metropolitan Brass Quintet, Oil City Slickers, and ARTCORE.

Productions ranging from the classical to the contemporary are performed by the players of Stage III, an all-volunteer community theater located in historic downtown Casper. The theater department at Casper College presents similarly varied fare to audiences in the Gertrude Krampert Theatre. A musical and three plays are presented each academic year, while the summer season offerings are often musicals or comedies.

Arts and Culture Information: Casper Area Convention & Visitors Bureau, 330 South Center Street, Suite 420, Casper, WY 82601; telephone (307)234-5362; toll free (800)852-1889; email visitors@casperwyoming.info

Festivals and Holidays

The year kicks off in January with the Windy City Quilt Festival. Casper residents fire up for the Cowboy State Games in February, an Olympic-style event composed of a mix of indoor and outdoor competitive sports. The Games run for five weekends during the month. Casper sees a local version of March Madness with the 1A and 2A State Basketball Tournament being held at the Casper Events Center early in the month. March is also time for the Super Flea Market at the Fairgrounds. The spring winds of April support the Central Wyoming Kite Flyers Fun Fly at the Soccer Complex, and Casper College hosts its rodeo. Temperate May weather ushers in a flock of activities such as the high school rodeo, the Kid's Fishing Derby, a dog show, and a car exhibition. The festivities continue in June with the Casper Antique Show early in the month and the Governor's Cup Sailboat Regatta at Alcova Lake a few weeks later.

The Fourth of July blasts off with a Fireworks Festival and a Cavalry baseball game, followed by the Rocky Mountain Regional Dance Festival, the Whitewater kayak rodeo, and the Beartrap Music Festival at the end of July. The Kiwanis Club hosts a golf tournament at the end of August, and cooler fall temperatures in September are perfect for the Platte River Fall Festival and Great Duck Derby. In mid-October, Casper hosts the local Special Olympics events. The holiday months of November and December respectively see the advent of the Meals on Wheels Craft Fair and the Tate Museum Holiday Open House.

Sports for the Spectator

Casper grew up around the livestock industry, so it's no surprise that rodeo is the major spectator sport. Casper hosts two large rodeo events: the College National Finals Rodeo and the Central Wyoming Fair and Rodeo. The College National Finals Rodeo takes place in mid-June each year and features the top rodeo event qualifiers from colleges and universities from across the U.S. Events include barrel racing, calf roping, and bull riding to just name a few. The Central Wyoming Fair and Rodeo is held in mid-July, with Pro Rodeo Cowboys Association competitions in roping, bareback riding, saddle bronc and bull riding events among others.

During the summer months, baseball fans can see tomorrow's stars playing for the Casper Rockies, the minor league affiliate of the Colorado Rockies. The team plays at Mike Lansing Field. In the spring, sports are still staying indoors with the Wyoming Cavalry football team, a member of the National Indoor Football League. Formed in 2001, the Cavalry finished the inaugural season second in the nation and have a rowdy, faithful following. The Wyoming Golden Eagles round out the spectating season with All American Professional Basketball League competition.

Sports for the Participant

Afficionados of the Wild West will relish the opportunity to participate in historic wagon train trips arranged through local companies. A similar desire to experience pioneer Casper could spur a visit to a working cattle and guest ranch located about 65 miles southwest of the city.

For folks who prefer to provide their own locomotion, the Casper Marathon takes place in early June, with marathon, half-marathon, and marathon relay options. The course is described as flat with few hills, and runners are invited to "come run with the herd."

A slightly less strenuous workout can be found at the Casper Municipal Golf Course, an 18-hole course with a practice range, putting and chipping greens, and a 19th Hole Restaurant and Lounge. The course is open from April 1st to November 1st each year.

The North Platte River offers ample outdoor recreation opportunities, such as kayaking through the Parkway Whitewater Park. This man-made whitewater facility runs for half a mile over structures that create turbulent water for kayak maneuvers. Canoes and rafts can also navigate through the Whitewater Park or pursue a more relaxed pace on other stretches of the North Platte. Fly fishing along the river can yield large brown and rainbow trout.

Birding excursions at the Audubon Center, Edness Kimball Wilkins State Park, and Jackson Canyon may produce sightings of bald and golden eagles, hummingbirds, bluebirds, hawks, sandpipers, wild turkeys, and grosbeaks. Birding field trips are offered almost every weekend of the year through the Murie Audubon Society.

Casper Mountain is the scene of outdoor adventure year-round, with alpine skiing, Nordic skiing and snowshoeing in the winter and hiking during the spring, summer and fall seasons. Casper is within an easy day's drive of Yellowstone National Park, Grand Teton National Park, and Devil's Tower Monument, all of which offer a range of trails in addition to campsites. Serious rock climbers can head east a few hours to Vedauwoo in southeast Wyoming; this startling and impressive collection of rock formations has something for everyone, from the scrambler to the multi-pitch climber.

Shopping and Dining

Casper's historic downtown area contains a mix of antique shops and other retailers, including the largest western merchandise store in Wyoming. The Eastridge Mall is the site of a number of national franchise stores combined with shops owned locally. Fast food outlets, grocery stores, and home supply stores are located nearby. Based near the foothills of Casper Mountain, the Sunrise Shopping Center is anchored by a restaurant and a bowling alley at one end and a gym at the other. The Hilltop Shopping Center focuses on local businesses, while the Beverly Plaza Shopping Center is home to national franchises. Other shopping areas include Plaza East, Millview Center, and CY Avenue/Highway 220 Shopping Strip.

Traditional American cuisine rules in Casper, with at least 36 restaurants offering downhome and family-style cooking. Approximately eight Mexican eateries meet the needs of spice-craving palates, while another eight establishments serve up varieties of Asian fare. As might be expected in cattle country, steakhouses are popular as well. A handful of fine dining, Italian, seafood, and barbecue restaurants flesh out the dining options in Casper. Basic and gourmet coffees are available at the six java houses in town.

Visitor Information: Casper Area Convention & Visitors Bureau, 992 N. Poplar St., Casper, WY 82601; telephone (307)234-5362; toll-free (800)852-1889; fax (307)261-9928; email visitors@casperwyoming.info

Convention Facilities

The Casper Events Center was constructed on a hill at the north end of the city and its massive maroon roof is visible from practically all points in Casper. The arena is shaped like a horseshoe, with a 28,200 square foot main floor that can hold up to 154 exhibition booths. Concourse exhibit space encompasses 7,900 square feet, while meeting rooms add another 6,204 square feet of usable space. Sound and lighting systems can be configured for sporting events, concerts, trade shows and banquets.

The Central Wyoming Fairgrounds can accommodate trade shows, conferences, receptions, rodeos, and RV parking. A multi-purpose sports facility opened in 2000 and covers 76,875 square feet, while the Grandstand and Arena have seating capacity for 5,200.

Several local hotels offer meeting, convention, and conference space, including the Holiday Inn on the River, the Parkway Plaza Hotel & Convention Centre, and the Ramkota Hotel Casper.

Convention Information: Casper Area Convention & Visitors Bureau, 992 N. Poplar St., Casper, WY 82601; telephone (307)234-5362; toll-free (800)852-1889; fax (307)261-9928; email visitors@casperwyoming.info

Transportation

Approaching the City

Natrona County International Airport (NCIA) is Wyoming's largest airport and is located at the geographic center of the state. Four regional carriers provide service through NCIA, including Delta, Sky West, United, and Northwest Airlines.

Casper's central location makes it a highway hub, with Interstate 25, U.S. Highways 20 and 87, and state highways 220, 254, and 20 all meeting within its city limits. Casper is served by the Greyhound bus company, which maintains a station in the Parkway Plaza Hotel.

Traveling in the City

While Casper is fitted to the meandering contours of the North Platte River, the streets are laid out on a straightforward north-south, east-west grid pattern. Numbered streets run east and west, while name streets run north and south for the most part, making navigation simpler.

In April of 2005, Casper inaugurated its new fixed route transit system, known as '' The Bus.'' With 4 routes and 65 stops, The Bus will offer reduced fares to elderly and disabled patrons.

The 11-mile Platte River Parkway provides a safe and fast route for bike commuters to ride into downtown Casper.

Communications

Newspapers and Magazines

Casper's daily paper is the *Casper Star Tribune,* delivered mornings and providing comprehensive coverage of international, national, regional, and local news stories. A special insert on Saturdays conveys community events and special features. Billed as "Casper's community newspaper," the *Casper Journal* is focused on local news, sports, and community events. The *Wyoming Business Report* is an affiliate of two similar periodicals published along the Front Range in Colorado. The bi-monthly paper is circulated to 10,000 readers, providing coverage of banking, technology, energy, investing, and agribusiness issues.

Television and Radio

Two network television affiliates are located in Casper—CBS and ABC—but the community has relays for transmissions of public television and other network stations. Casper's FM radio selection runs the gamut from classic rock to country to top 40 formats. Talk radio, news, oldies and Christian music are available on AM radio.

Casper Online

Casper Area Chamber of Commerce. Available www.casperwyoming.org/index.html

Casper Star Tribune. Available www.casperstartribune.net

Casper Wyoming Convention & Visitors Bureau. Available www.casperwyoming.info

City of Casper. Available www.casperwy.gov

Natrona County Government. Available www.newedc.net/natrona/index.htm

Natrona County School District. Available www.ncsdweb.ncsd.k12.wy.us/index.html

Wyoming State Historical Society. Available wyshs.org

Selected Bibliography

Casper Chronicles Casper, WY: Casper Zonta Club (1964)

Cheyenne

The City in Brief

Founded: 1867 (incorporated, 1867)

Head Official: Mayor Jack R. Spiker (since 2001)

City Population
    1980: 47,283
    1990: 50,008
    2000: 53,011
    2003 estimate: 54,374
    Percent change, 1990–2000: 6%
    U.S. rank in 1980: 451st
    U.S. rank in 1990: 504th
    U.S. rank in 2000: 520th

Metropolitan Area Population (Laramie County)
    1980: 68,600
    1990: 73,142
    2000: 81,607
    Percent change, 1990–2000: 11.6%
    U.S. rank in 2000: 637th

Area: 21.19 square miles (2000)
Elevation: 6,062 feet above sea level
Average Annual Temperature: 45.6° F
Average Annual Precipitation: 14.1 inches of rain; 51.3 inches of snow

Major Economic Sectors: Public administration, wholesale and retail trade, services
Unemployment Rate: 4.3% (February 2005)
Per Capita Income: $19,809 (1999)

2002 FBI Crime Index Total: 2,476

Major Colleges and Universities: Laramie County Community College, University of Wyoming-Laramie

Daily Newspaper: *The Wyoming Tribune Eagle*

TO CASPER

25
87
85

124

211

IRON MOUNTAIN

F. E. WARREN
AIR FORCE BASE

LAUGHLIN

FOUR MILE

WESTERN HILLS

YELLOWSTONE

POWDERHOUSE

RIDGE

COLLEGE

LAKE TERRY

KIWANIS LAKE

FRONTIER DAYS OLD WESTERN MUSEUM

LAKE ABSSARRACA

85

FRONTIER PARK

SLOANS LAKE

25

8TH AVE.

6TH AVE.

WINDMILL

O'NEIL

PIONEER

CAPITOL

2ND AVE.

EVANS

CHEYENNE MUNICIPAL AIRPORT

V.A. HOSP.

BRIMMER PARK

30

RANDALL

LAKEVIEW CEMETERY

CONVERSE

PERSHING

PLANT

26TH ST.

22ND ST.

UNICOVER CORP. FIRST
DAY COVER MUSEUM

STATE MUSEUM

GOVERNORS' MASION

19TH ST.

UNITED MEDICAL CENTER

LITTLE THEATRE

AMES

MEMORIAL HOSP.

HAPPY JACK

STATE CAPITOL

SUPREME COURT

MERCI TRAIN

STATE LIBRARY

CIVIC CTR.

NATIONWAY

CHEYENNE PLAZA

WYOMING PLAZA

CAMPSTOOL

MARTIN LUTHER
KING PARK

ATLAS THEATRE

OLDTOWN MALL

TIVOLI BLDG - CHAMBER OF COMMERCE

30

5TH ST.

80

TO WYOMING HEREFORD RANCH

PARSLEY

CLEAR CREEK PARK

80

LARAMIE COMM. COLLEGE

N

25

COLLEGE

87

WYOMING INFORMATION CTR.

TO VEDAUWOO, SNOWY RANGE, UNIV. OF WY.

85

0   1   2
KILOMETERS

MILES   0.5   1   1.5   2

WA

ID

MT

OR

WY

Cheyenne

CA

NV

UT

CO

Introduction

Cheyenne, the capital of Wyoming, began as a railroad town and, during the height of the colorful cattle days, became the wealthiest city in the world. Cheyenne has retained its Western frontier traditions while keeping pace with the twenty-first century. The seat of Laramie County, Cheyenne continues to be a railroad and livestock center; the city is also a primary industrial area in the state as well as the site of a major military base. Cheyenne is known for its quality of life and for high clean air ratings.

Geography and Climate

Surrounded by rolling prairie, Cheyenne is located between the North and South Platte rivers. The Laramie Mountains 30 miles west of the city form a ridge that is part of the Rocky Mountain range and that significantly influences local temperature and weather. Winds passing over the ridge from the northwest through the west to southwest produce a Chinook effect, particularly during the winter. (Chinooks are warm, moist winds from the sea.) Because of the terrain and wind patterns, Cheyenne experiences wide daily temperature fluctuations of 30 degrees in the summer and about 23 degrees in the winter. Snow falls during late winter and early spring, with yearly snowfall averaging 51.3 inches.

Area: 21.19 square miles (2000)

Elevation: 6,062 feet above sea level

Average Temperatures: January, 26.1° F; August, 66.8° F; annual average, 45.6° F.

Average Annual Precipitation: 14.1 inches of rain; 51.3 inches of snow

History

Rough-and-Tumble Beginnings of Railroad Terminus

The region where present-day Cheyenne stands was originally occupied by a Native American Plains tribe in the Algonquian linguistic family. The townsite was initially a campsite for the U.S. Army's Major General Grenville M. Dodge and his troops, who were charged in 1865 with finding a railroad route over the Laramie Mountains. In 1867, when Dodge became chief engineer for the Union Pacific Railroad, he established a terminal town there; he named it Cheyenne for the local tribe. Dodge received some

criticism in the local press for his mispronunciation of the word, which was actually ''shai-en-na;'' but his two-syllable version was accepted through usage.

Fort D. A. Russell was built in 1867 to protect railroad construction crews. Soon real estate speculators, merchants, gamblers, and tradesmen converged on Cheyenne in hopes of profiting from the construction project. Violent disputes arose over ownership of the land, since the railroad had already claimed it and citizens questioned the company's right to do so. Eventually troops from Fort Russell were called in; land jumpers were run out of town and could not return until they promised to acknowledge the railroad's claim.

A town charter was accepted by the Dakota Territorial Legislature in 1867 and Cheyenne was thereupon incorporated. By the end of that year the population had risen to 4,000 people, and lots were selling for $2,500. Makeshift buildings gave the town a raffish appearance, but even before railroad construction began, Cheyenne enjoyed the elements of a stable community; churches had been built and the first school, with 114 pupils, was opened in 1867. Within a year Cheyenne was thriving. More than 300 businesses were in operation, and the diverse citizenry included engineers, lawyers, artists, Native Americans, trappers, hunters, laborers, gamblers, and gunslingers. The town, however, was soon overrun by lawlessness.

The early Cheyenne closely resembled the Wild West towns depicted in novels and films. Dodge named it the gambling center of the world and some dubbed it ''Hell on Wheels.'' Mayhem and violence were a way of life, with the saloon and the cemetery being the most important places in town. In an attempt to impose order, the churches backed an ordinance that closed saloons for four hours on Sundays; another ruling required visitors to check their guns. But laws were virtually unenforceable, so the vigilante ''committee'' became a substitute for the courts. Although the city government had been given powers by the Dakota Legislature upon incorporation, civic leaders found the vigilante approach to be more effective. When the jail became full, for instance, prisoners were driven from town with a whip or a six-shooter; frequently the committee executed perpetrators of severe crimes.

Riches Flow from Cattle, Sheep, Gold

A degree of peacefulness returned when railroad construction moved on toward Sherman Pass and transients followed. But then the first Sioux War broke out north of the Platte River, and Fort Russell became the supply depot for the Rocky Mountain region. In 1868 Cheyenne was made the seat of Laramie County; the following year it was named the capital of the new Wyoming territory. By the 1870s Cheyenne was the center of a prosperous ranching area where cattle were bred for a European beef market. Visiting Englishmen, who spent summers in Cheyenne and winters in Europe, joined wealthy cattle owners to found the Cheyenne Club, where they dined in luxury and struck deals that affected the cattle industry throughout the West. Furnished in the English style and serving the finest liquors in the world, the club employed a foreign chef whose cuisine was known nationwide.

With the opening of the Black Hills gold fields in 1875, the town profited from a new industry as Cheyenne merchants supplied miners and prospectors with provisions and equipment. The Cheyenne and Black Hills Stage Company was formed to transport passengers and cargo between the railroad and the mines. When electric lights were installed in 1882, Cheyenne was the wealthiest city per capita in the world. Cheyenne was named the capital of the new state of Wyoming in 1890, and the Capitol building was erected in the city. By 1890 the population had reached 10,000 people.

Before the turn of the century many ranchers had begun raising sheep, which adapted well to the climate and the native grasses; sheep raising continues to be an important industry in the area. During the twentieth century Cheyenne became an industrial and manufacturing center, and the Francis E. Warren U.S. Air Force Base was established at Fort Russell. In spite of extensive development as one of the state's largest cities (one out of five Wyoming residents lives in Cheyenne) and as a commercial, industrial, and transportation hub, Cheyenne has maintained a high quality of life and a pollution-free environment.

Historical Information: Wyoming State Archives, Barrett Building, 2301 Central Avenue, Cheyenne, WY 82002; telephone (307)777-7826; fax (307)777-7044; email wyarchive@state.wy.us

Population Profile

Metropolitan Area Residents (Laramie County)
1980: 68,600
1990: 73,142
2000: 81,607
2003 estimate: 84,083
Percent change, 1990–2000: 3%
U.S. rank in 2000: 637th

City Residents
1980: 47,283
1990: 50,008
2000: 53,011
2003 estimate: 54,374
Percent change, 1990–2000: 5.6%
U.S. rank in 1980: 451st
U.S. rank in 1990: 504th (State rank: 1st)

U.S. rank in 2000: 520th (State rank: 1st)

Density: 2,511.4 people per square mile (2000)

Racial and ethnic characteristics (2000)
White: 46,707
Black or African American: 1,472
American Indian and Alaskan Native: 430
Asian: 561
Native Hawaiian and Pacific Islander: 59
Hispanic or Latino (may be of any race): 6,646
Other: 2,356

Percent of residents born in state: 36.9% (2000)

Age characteristics (2000)
Population under 5 years old: 3,422
Population 5 to 9 years old: 3,677
Population 10 to 14 years old: 3,755
Population 15 to 19 years old: 3,683
Population 20 to 24 years old: 3,337
Population 25 to 34 years old: 7,362
Population 35 to 44 years old: 8,387
Population 45 to 54 years old: 7,423
Population 55 to 59 years old: 2,562
Population 60 to 64 years old: 2,090
Population 65 to 74 years old: 3,723
Population 75 to 84 years old: 2,638
Population 85 years and older: 952
Median age: 36.6 years

Births (2001, Laramie County)
Total number: 1,116

Deaths (2001, Laramie County)
Total number: 681

Money income (1999)
Per capita income: $19,809
Median household income: $38,856
Total households: 22,346

Number of households with income of . . .
less than $10,000: 1,744
$10,000 to $14,999: 1,587
$15,000 to $24,999: 3,245
$25,000 to $34,999: 3,435
$35,000 to $49,999: 4,502
$50,000 to $74,999: 4,456
$75,000 to $99,999: 2,076
$100,000 to $149,999: 935
$150,000 to $199,999: 154
$200,000 or more: 933

Percent of families below poverty level: 6.3 (37.3% of which were female householder families with related children under 5 years)

2002 FBI Crime Index Total: 2,476

Municipal Government

Cheyenne operates under a mayor-council form of government; the nine council members and the mayor serve four-year terms. The nine council members represent three city wards and serve staggered four-year terms. A council president and vice-president elected from among the council members each serve one-year terms. The mayor and council members serve as Cheyenne's legislative body, which is responsible for regulating city growth and development, enacting ordinances, appropriating city funds, and establishing city rules and regulations.

Head Official: Mayor Jack R. Spiker (since 2001; current term expires 2005)

Total Number of City Employees: 564 (2005)

City Information: City of Cheyenne, 2101 O'Neil Avenue, Cheyenne, WY 82001; telephone (307)637-6300

Economy

Major Industries and Commercial Activity

Cheyenne's economy is based mainly on light manufacturing, agriculture, the military and government, tourism, services, and transportation. Cattle- and sheep-raising continue to be important in the region, yet the economy of Cheyenne has become diversified with the development of industries such as fertilizer processing plants. Other manufacturing includes electronic products and precision instruments as well as restaurant equipment. F. E. Warren U.S. Air Force Base, site of a major installation of the Strategic Air Command, is the city's largest employer; federal, state, and county government offices are located in Cheyenne. Major private sector employers include United Medical Center, Union Pacific Railroad, Lowe's Companies, Inc., Sierra Trading Post, Echo Star Communications, Frontier Refining, WalMart, Little America, Hitching Post Inn, and Life Care Cheyenne. With access to two railroads, to interstate freeways, and to commercial air service, the city is a vital transportation center for the state of Wyoming.

Items and goods produced: ski wear, oil, fertilizer, flight instruments and testing equipment

Incentive Programs—New and Existing Companies

Local programs—At the local level, Cheyenne LEADS, a private, not-for-profit economic development organization, assists non-retail businesses through such services as site location, employee training, and demographic and financial assistance. The Wyoming Business Council's regional office in Cheyenne offers expansion assistance for current businesses, and relocation assistance for businesses looking to expand into the area.

State programs—Wyoming's history of minimal involvement in its citizens' lives is reflected in its low taxes on businesses and individuals. There is no corporate or personal state income tax and no sales and use tax on fuel, power, or raw materials used in the manufacturing process. Goods in transit or manufactured or assembled and sold outside the state are exempt from tax, and the tax on gasoline and diesel fuel is among the lowest in the country. The state offers a variety of loan, grant, and bond programs available to new, expanding, and relocating businesses.

Job training programs—Laramie County School District provides education programs at the secondary level in areas such as agricultural science, industrial technology, business and marketing education, health occupations, and core employability skills. Cheyenne colleges work with both businesses and the community to develop training programs for businesses and potential employees. Our Families Our Future in Cheyenne provides assistance to populations living below poverty through training programs and job search help. Our Families Our Future works with Wyoming agencies, community colleges, and employers; the organization began the CLIMB program in 2004 to train eligible single mothers in the field of medical transcription.

Development Projects

In 2001, city leaders, the chamber of commerce, and other individuals and organizations got together to finalize the Greater Cheyenne Vision 2020 plan. The plan calls for a variety of projects to revitalize the city's downtown, as well as create economic development, quality jobs, new entertainment and recreation opportunities, and transportation options.

Recently, United Medical Center of Cheyenne completed a $31 million renovation of one of Wyoming's largest hospitals. The 198-bed hospital, a public facility owned by Laramie County, spent $15 million to build a new patient tower and reconstruct its front entrance. Completed in 2002, the project received the Wyoming Engineering Society Presidential Project Award. In 2002, home-improvement retailer Lowe's Companies, Inc. opened a 1,000,000-square-foot regional distribution center. In 2004 Cheyenne LEADS purchased 612 acres on which the West I-80 Business Park will be built. This second of two business parks owned by LEADS will have its own interchange onto I-80.

Economic Development Information: Cheyenne LEADS, 1720 Carey, Suite 401, PO Box 1045, Cheyenne, WY 82003; telephone (307)638-6000; toll-free (800)255-0742; email info@cheyenneleads.org

Commercial Shipping

A major transportation center in the state, Cheyenne routes air cargo service through Cheyenne Regional Airport. Two railroads provide daily freight transportation, and a variety of motor freight carriers move goods through facilities in Cheyenne and onto interstates 80 and 25.

Labor Force and Employment Outlook

Cheyenne's labor force is described as available, educated, and productive. Although the local unemployment rate is low, a 2001 study conducted by PathFinders Resources found there are about 12,300 underemployed workers in Laramie and Goshen counties in Wyoming and portions of nearby Larimer and Weld counties in Colorado.

In July 2004 *Kiplinger's Personal Finance* ranked Cheyenne the top tax-friendly city in the country. Wyoming residents gain from the state's lenient tax structure, including no personal income tax, capital gains tax, and corporate income taxes. The state does not levy estate tax beyond the federal pick-up level, nor does it levy an electric utilities tax. Low health insurance rates are also in effect.

The following is a summary of data regarding the Cheyenne labor force, 2004 annual averages.

Size of non-agricultural labor force: 40,700

Number of workers employed in . . .
 construction and mining: 2,600
 manufacturing: 1,500
 trade, transportation and utilities: 8,600
 information: 1,000
 financial activities: 2,000
 professional and business services: 3,200
 educational and health services: 3,100
 leisure and hospitality: 4,400
 other services: 1,600
 government: 12,400

Average hourly earnings of production workers employed in manufacturing (State of Wyoming): $16.74

Unemployment rate: 4.3% (February 2005)

Largest employers	Number of employees
F.E. Warren U.S. Air Force Base	4,190
State of Wyoming	3,574
U.S. Government	1,811
Laramie County School District #1	1,794
United Medical Center	992
Union Pacific Railroad	700

Cost of Living

The following is a summary of data regarding key cost of living factors for the Cheyenne area.

2004 (3rd Quarter) ACCRA Average House Price: $340,193

2004 (3rd Quarter) ACCRA Cost of Living Index: 111.0 (U.S. average = 100.0)

State income tax rate: None

State sales tax rate: 4.0%

Local income tax rate: None

Local sales tax rate: 1.0%

Property tax rate: 77.31 mills on 9.5% of residential market value (2004)

Economic Information: Greater Cheyenne Chamber of Commerce, 301 West 16 Street, PO Box 1147, Cheyenne, WY 82003-1147; telephone (307)638-3388; fax (307)778-1450. Laramie County Community College, Center for Economic and Business Data, 1400 E. College Drive, Cheyenne, WY 82007; telephone (307)778-1325; fax (307)778-4309

Education and Research

Elementary and Secondary Schools

Public elementary and secondary schools in Cheyenne are part of Laramie County School District #1 (LCSD1). The district, the largest in the state, is administered by a seven-member Board of Trustees and a superintendent. The Cheyenne Schools Foundation works "to engage community interest and support for enhanced academic, personal, and vocational opportunities for LCSD1 students beyond the capacity of the local school district budget." The Foundation also provides grants to benefit district and school-wide projects as well as teachers for classroom projects that address student needs.

Among the special programs offered by the school district is a magnet school for high-potential elementary students. Eighty percent of elementary and secondary students are involved in one or more extracurricular activities, which include music, sports, clubs, and after-school projects. The Community Based Occupational Education (CBOE) High School is an alternative education program that helps students meet the academic standards for the State of Wyoming and LCSD1 as well as gain employable business skills for the future.

The following is a summary of data regarding Laramie County School District #1 as of the 2003–2004 school year.

Total enrollment: 13,065

Number of facilities
    elementary schools: 26
    junior high schools: 3
    senior high schools: 4

Student/teacher ratio: 15:1

Teacher salaries
    minimum: $26,450
    average: $40,455

Funding per pupil: $8,179

Four private elementary and middle schools and one private senior high school are located in Cheyenne.

Public Schools Information: Laramie County School District #1, 2810 House Avenue, Cheyenne, WY 82001; telephone (307)771-2100

Colleges and Universities

Laramie County Community College, which provides a two-year curriculum, is based in Cheyenne. Also located in the county are Embry-Riddle Aeronautical University, Preston University, Kennedy-Western University, and Park College. The University of Wyoming-Laramie, the state's only public university, is less than 45 miles west of Cheyenne. Popular majors there are elementary and secondary education and social work.

Libraries and Research Centers

The Laramie County Library System, established in 1886, is the oldest continually operating county library system in the country. In addition to its main library in Cheyenne, the Laramie County Library System operates two branches and a bookmobile serving the rural eastern portion of the county. Its holdings include about 258,000 volumes as well as periodical titles, microfiche, maps, CDs, videos, DVDs, and music CDs; the library also offers Internet connectivity, books-on-tape, video games, and art reproductions. Special collections are the Carpenter Collection of Western Americana and material on the elk of North America. The library's genealogy collection includes extensive materials from the Wyoming State Library and the Family History Library of the Church of Jesus Christ of Latter Day Saints.

The Wyoming State Library is also located in Cheyenne. It contains more than 130,000 volumes and is a federal, state, and regional document depository. The Wyoming Center for the Book, established in 1995, operates as a program within the Wyoming State Library. A state affiliate of the Library

of Congress Center for the Book, it "promotes the values of a literate and learned society through a variety of programs including a database of Wyoming writers and literary guide." The Laramie County Community College Instructional Resources Center is also located in Cheyenne. Other specialized libraries in the city are affiliated with hospitals, fraternal organizations, colleges, and government agencies.

The University of Wyoming-Laramie conducts research activities in dozens of disciplines, such as education; biological, physical, and social sciences; business and economics; mathematics; and politics and government in Wyoming. At the university's Archaeological Dig Site in Pine Bluffs, researchers extract relics and prehistoric artifacts dating back 8,000 years.

Public Library Information: Laramie County Library System, 2800 Central Avenue, Cheyenne, WY 82001; telephone (307)634-3561

Health Care

Cheyenne is a regional healthcare center. Major facilities are United Medical Center (UMC) East and West, with a combined total of 198 beds. Specialized services offered include cancer treatment, cardiovascular care and surgery, acute care and chemical-dependency services. The hospital recently opened a new tower that includes five floors of private patient rooms and connects to the existing building. UMC is designated as a regional trauma center by the Wyoming Department of Health Office of Emergency Medical Services. The Cheyenne Veteran's Administration Hospital provides medical care to military personnel and their families and to veterans. Facilities at the F.E. Warren U.S. Air Force Base provide medical and dental care for military personnel and their families.

Recreation

Sightseeing

Cheyenne features several sites that recall the city's past. The Tivoli Building, which houses the Chamber of Commerce, was completed in 1892. It is among the best examples of Victorian architecture in the Rocky Mountain region. The former Union Pacific Depot is an equally fine example of Romanesque architecture. Located on Capitol Avenue, the Wyoming State Capitol building contains historic photographs and a display of native wildlife; near the Capitol is a

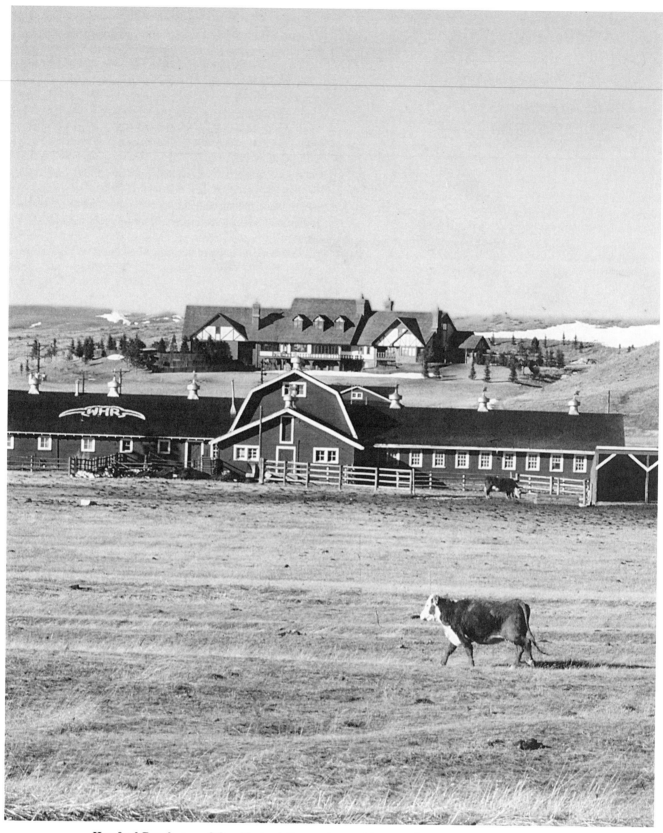

Hereford Ranch, one of the oldest existing western cattle operations, was established in 1883.

statue of Esther Hobart Morris, a pioneer in the women's suffrage movement. A guided walking tour of historic Cheyenne is available.

The French Merci Train was sent to the American people by French citizens in 1946 as a ''thank-you'' for the Friendship Train that carried food from America to France during World War II. The Big Boy steam engine—''Old Number 4004''—is the world's largest steam locomotive and was retired from the Union Pacific Railroad in 1956. F. E. Warren U.S. Air Force Base houses intercontinental ballistic missiles; free tours are conducted.

Recalling the days of cattle barons, the Wyoming Hereford Ranch east of Cheyenne was established in 1883; still in operation and producing Hereford cattle, it is the oldest continuous registered livestock operation in the county. The ranch hosts visitors and community events. Terry Bison Ranch is a working guest ranch that offers chuckwagon dinners, trout fishing, and horse-drawn wagon tours into a bison herd.

The Cheyenne Botanic Gardens in Lions Park, open 365 days a year, is a public botanical garden as well as a municipal nursery and community garden. Their conservatory is entirely solar heated; 50 percent of the garden's electricity is also solar-generated. Displays include rose, cacti, and herbs, and plants native to the area.

Other points of interest are historic Lakeview Cemetery, and the Wyoming Game & Fish Visitors Center, featuring wildlife exhibits ranging from grizzly bears to big horn sheep.

Arts and Culture

Cheyenne supports an active cultural community. The Civic Center is the site of performances by Broadway touring companies, major symphony orchestras, and popular entertainers. Residents also enjoy concerts by the Cheyenne Symphony Orchestra from September through May and occasionally in the summer. The Cheyenne Little Theatre stages plays with local directors and actors at its own playhouse; in the summer it stages melodramas at the historic Atlas Theatre.

Several museums are located in Cheyenne. The Wyoming State Museum displays western memorabilia and chronicles the history of Wyoming. The Wyoming Arts Council Gallery displays the works of Wyoming artists. The Nelson Museum of the West houses cowboy and Indian collectibles and wildlife trophies from around the world. The Governors' Mansion, a state historic site and an example of colonial-revival architecture, was home to the state's governors from 1905 to 1976; guided tours are available. At the Cheyenne Frontier Days Old West Museum, highlights include Oglala Sioux artifacts, a Union Pacific railroad exhibit, and a collection of horse-drawn vehicles.

Festivals and Holidays

The foremost event in the Cheyenne area is Cheyenne Frontier Days. Taking place during the last full week in July, it is billed as the world's largest outdoor rodeo. Frontier Days features daily rodeos, concerts, parades, pancake breakfasts, Native American dances, shootouts, and a carnival. The festivities attract hundreds of thousands of people. Running concurrently is the annual Western Art Show at the Old West Museum in Frontier Park. In June and July Cheyenne Gunslinger Gunfights are enacted. In August Cheyenne hosts the Laramie County Fair. Oktoberfest is held in the fall. Highlights of the Christmas season are the Christmas parade, craft show, and concert, held at the end of November.

Sports for the Spectator

There are no major league professional sports teams in Wyoming. Cheyenne is home of the oldest rodeo event in the world; other rodeos are presented in the city throughout the year. The Wyoming State Open Golf Tournament is held at the Airport Golf Club, and Holiday Park in Cheyenne is host to the Wyoming Governor's Cup Tennis Tournament. The city is also the site of state youth baseball and softball tournaments.

Sports for the Participant

Cheyenne maintains 24 city parks which cover more than 600 acres, plus 15 miles of the Cheyenne Greenway Trail. The city has 14 baseball fields, nine softball fields, 12 tennis courts, 5 golf courses, and 2 public swimming pools. Curt Gowdy State Park is located 25 miles outside of the city, while the Vedauwoo and Happy Jack recreational areas are approximately 30 miles away. Facilities for such sports as hunting, fishing, boating, camping, trap-shooting, snowmobiling, polo, tennis, and waterskiing are available.

Shopping and Dining

Shopping in downtown Cheyenne is enhanced by a sense of tradition; among the wide selection of stores, shops, and boutiques are several that have been in the city for many years. Nine shopping areas are located throughout the city. Frontier Mall features national retailers such as JCPenney, Bath and Body Works, American Eagle, and Dillard's. Cheyenne Farmer's Market, open half-days from August to October, sells fresh fruits, vegetables, and more.

Cheyenne offers a range of dining experience from traditional Southwestern specialties to Continental and ethnic cuisine such as Mexican, Italian, Greek, and Japanese. Numerous fast-food restaurants are also located in Cheyenne.

Visitor Information: Cheyenne Area Convention and Visitors Bureau, One Depot Square, 121 W. 15th Street, Suite 202, Cheyenne WY 82001; telephone (307)778-3133; toll-free (800)426-5009; fax (307)778-3190; email info @cheyenne.org. Wyoming Travel Information Center, I-25 and College Drive, Cheyenne, WY 82002; telephone (307)777-7777

town and historic districts and to the air force base from mid-May through mid-September. Occasionally the governor will greet riders as they pass his residence.

Convention Facilities

Cheyenne offers four convention facilities accommodating a combined total of 3,110 persons. More than 2,000 hotel and motel rooms are located in the Cheyenne area. Several hotels and motels also provide meeting accommodations.

Convention Information: Cheyenne Area Convention and Visitors Bureau, One Depot Square, 121 W. 15th Street, Suite 202, Cheyenne WY 82001; telephone (307)778-3133; toll-free (800)426-5009; fax (307)778-3190; email info @cheyenne.org

Transportation

Approaching the City

The major routes into Cheyenne are Interstate 25, which runs north and south contiguous with U.S. 85 and 87; east-west I-80; and U.S. 30, which bisects the city southwest to east. Highway 85 provides access from the north- and southeast.

Great Lakes Airlines, operated out of Cheyenne Regional Airport, operates daily shuttle flights to Denver International Airport. From there travelers may connect to flights around the world. Shuttle service from the Denver Airport is available. Casino Express operates monthly gambling excursion flights to Elko, Nevada. Rail transportation is provided by Amtrak, and commercial bus service is available from points throughout Wyoming.

Traveling in the City

The Cheyenne Transit Program is Cheyenne's city-operated bus system. It serves Cheyenne and surrounding areas. The Cheyenne Street Railway takes visitors through the down-

Communications

Newspapers and Magazines

Cheyenne's daily newspaper is the *Wyoming Tribune Eagle*; in addition to the print edition, an online edition of the paper can be accessed via the Internet. *Warren Sentinel* is a weekly paper published by Wyoming Newspapers for F.E. Warren Air Force Base. Also published in Cheyenne are *Wyoming Wildlife,* a Wyoming Fish and Game Department magazine on hunting, fishing, and environmental issues, and *Wyoming Stockman-Farmer.*

Television and Radio

One television station affiliated with a major network broadcasts from Cheyenne. The city also receives four stations from Denver and Casper; cable is available. The area is served by seven AM and FM radio stations that feature news and information, music, and special programming.

Media Information: Wyoming Newspaper Group, 702 West Lincolnway, Cheyenne, WY 82001; telephone (307)634-3361

Cheyenne Online

Cheyenne Area Convention and Visitors Bureau. Available www.cheyenne.org

Greater Cheyenne Chamber of Commerce. Available www .cheyennechamber.org

Laramie County School District. Available www.laramie1 .k12.wy.us

Wyoming Tribune-Eagle. Available www.wyomingnews .com

Cumulative Index

The one hundred eighty-nine cities featured in *Cities of the United States,* Volume 1: *The South,* Volume 2: *The West,* Volume 3: *The Midwest,* and Volume 4: *The Northeast,* along with names of individuals, organizations, historical events, etc., are designated in this Cumulative Index by name of the appropriate regional volume, or volumes, followed by the page number(s) on which the term appears in that volume.